International Human Rights

International Human Rights
Problems of Law, Policy, and Practice

Fourth Edition

Late Richard B. Lillich
of the University of Virginia

Hurst Hannum
Professor of International Law
The Fletcher School of Law and Diplomacy, Tufts University
Sir Y.K. Pao Professor of Public Law, University of Hong Kong

S. James Anaya
The University of Arizona

Dinah L. Shelton
The George Washington University

ASPEN
PUBLISHERS

76 Ninth Avenue, New York, NY 10011
http://lawschool.aspenpublishers.com

a Wolters Kluwer business
http://lawschool.aspenpublishers.com

Printed in the United States of America.

1 2 3 4 5 6 7 8 9 0

ISBN 0-7355-5557-5

Library of Congress Cataloging-in-Publication Data

International human rights : problems of law, policy, and practice / [edited by]
Richard B. Lillich ... [et al.]. — 4th ed.
p. cm.
ISBN 0-7355-5557-5
1. Human rights. I. Lillich, Richard B.

K3240.I5783 2006
341.4′8 — dc22

2006005709

About Aspen Publishers

Aspen Publishers, headquartered in New York City, is a leading information provider for attorneys, business professionals, and law students. Written by preeminent authorities, our products consist of analytical and practical information covering both U.S. and international topics. We publish in the full range of formats, including updated manuals, books, periodicals, CDs, and online products.

Our proprietary content is complemented by 2,500 legal databases, containing over 11 million documents, available through our Loislaw division. Aspen Publishers also offers a wide range of topical legal and business databases linked to Loislaw's primary material. Our mission is to provide accurate, timely, and authoritative content in easily accessible formats, supported by unmatched customer care.

To order any Aspen Publishers title, go to *http://lawschool.aspenpublishers.com* or call 1-800-638-8437.

To reinstate your manual update service, call 1-800-638-8437.

For more information on Loislaw products, go to *www.loislaw.com* or call 1-800-364-2512.

For Customer Care issues, e-mail *CustomerCare@aspenpublishers.com*; call 1-800-234-1660; or fax 1-800-901-9075.

Aspen Publishers
a Wolters Kluwer business

Summary of Contents

Table of Contents

Chapter 2 55

Guaranteeing Human Rights by Treaty

Is There a Right to a Safe and Healthy Environment?

Chapter 3 135

The Development of Human Rights Norms Through Non-Binding Instruments

How and Why Do New International Human Rights Norms Emerge other than by Treaty?

Chapter 4 209

Human Rights in Extremis

How Can Human Rights Be Protected in Civil Strife and Armed Conflict?

Chapter 5 323

Who is Obligated to Promote and Protect Human rights?

Oil Exploration and Exploitation in the Niger River Delta

Chapter 7 533

UN Mechanisms for Addressing Violations of Human Rights

What Petition and Other Procedures Are Available for Implementing Human Rights Standards?

Chapter 8 617

The European System for the Protection of Human Rights

Can Regional Systems to Protect Human Rights Be More Effective than UN Mechanisms?

Chapter 10 787

Coercing Compliance with Human Rights Norms: Sanctions and Armed Intervention

Can the International Community Prevent Human Rights Violations by Threatening or Using Force?

Chapter 12 979

The Problem of Fact-Finding and Evidence

How Are Human Rights Violations Investigated?

Chapter 13 1063

Human Rights and Foreign Policy

The United States–China Relationship

Preface

This coursebook is intended to introduce the student to the established and developing international law governing the protection of human rights. There is now a substantial body of this law, which encompasses substantive norms, procedural rules, and national, regional, and global institutions whose mandate it is to promote, monitor, and supervise international human rights. In this increasingly interdependent world, in which human rights issues are a concern of nearly every country's foreign ministry, human rights law has become an integral part of international law per se, and no one with pretensions of being an international lawyer can ignore its content entirely.

At the same time, international human rights law — as it is generally understood — does not encompass every social good or even every international norm whose purpose is to improve the human condition. Among the issues that are extremely relevant to the lives of millions of people but that are not addressed in depth in this coursebook are theories of economic development, trade and employment, refugees, and migration. And, of course, many moral, social, and philosophical issues appropriately lie beyond the reach of international law of any kind.

The materials in this book are organized around a number of problems, selected to illustrate the real issues that face human rights lawyers and to demonstrate how and why human rights law has developed in the way that it has. Most of the 13 chapters are organized around a specific factual situation, and each is accompanied by selected readings, comments, and questions designed to raise the most significant contemporary human rights issues. The situations presented are intended to serve as points of departure for the exploration of the relevant principles, procedures, and policies for protecting human rights through the international legal process. They are not intended to provide a comprehensive survey of the subject, and the goal is simply to concentrate the student's attention on how international law can be invoked to protect human rights in concrete cases. The coursebook is thus a teaching tool, not an encyclopedia or bibliography.

The first five chapters consider the substantive content of international human rights law today. The first three chapters examine the development of human rights law historically and its gradual definition through treaties, customary law, and so-called "soft law" instruments. Chapter 4 introduces the student to the related norms of international humanitarian law (or the law of war), in the context of the "war on terror" proclaimed in the aftermath of September 11, 2001. Chapter 5 examines the scope of a state's obligations under international human rights law, as well as the obligations that might be imposed on other actors, including international organizations, transnational and national corporations, and even individuals.

The next section of six chapters deals with various aspects of the implementation of human rights norms. Chapter 6 considers the crucial element of domestic enforcement, focusing on developments in U.S. jurisprudence over the past 30 years. The next three chapters deal with supervisory mechanisms created by the United Nations and two of the three regional human rights regimes; the third regional system of protection (Africa) is considered by way of example in Chapter 5. Chapters 10 and 11 examine the most extreme forms of enforcement: coercion against governments, through the imposition of sanctions and even the use of military force, and holding individuals criminally accountable for human rights violations that also constitute international or domestic crimes.

The final two chapters address particular issues of human rights implementation that combine law and politics. Chapter 12 analyzes issues associated with fact-finding by both nongovernmental organizations and international bodies. Chapter 13 surveys the complex issue of how human rights concerns have been (or should be) integrated into a country's relations with other states.

This coursebook is designed primarily for use in a one-semester, three-hour course or seminar at the law school or university level. With some omissions, it also could be used in a shorter seminar, although balancing depth and breadth of coverage is always difficult. While a background in international law would certainly be helpful to both students and teachers, it is not required for an adequate understanding of most of the materials. Some of the particularly technical legal issues, such as domestic implementation, might be omitted if the book is used in a school or department of international relations, as opposed to a law school or faculty.

The problem-oriented nature of the materials is designed to engage the student in concrete issues and the application of human rights law to the "real world." Philosophical issues are addressed at various points in the book, but our primary purpose is to explore the *practice* of human rights in depth, rather than the theory. Many of the problems lend themselves to student role-playing, and the materials present different perspectives and positions on many of the more hotly contested issues in human rights. For all of its sophistication, human rights law — indeed, international law in general — is in constant movement, and many of the materials present the student with alternatives that are actively under discussion rather than offering the "correct" answer to every question.

Finally, this casebook attempts primarily to present a picture of international human rights law as it is, not as we might wish it to be, while understanding it is constantly evolving. Human rights advocates can justifiably claim a great deal of success over the past 50 years, and the shield of sovereignty that protected states from external criticism over how they treated their own citizens is gone forever. At the same time, however, merely adopting new declarations or citing the progressive opinions of independent experts does not automatically create binding, effective international law. International law is under challenge today from many quarters, and human rights law is not immune from that challenge. Only with a full understanding of the constraints on international law can students (and activists) move forward in the most effective manner possible. There is no dichotomy between realism and idealism, since both are necessary; however, neither cynicism disguised as realpolitik nor willfully exaggerated claims for the power of law are useful.

The first edition of this book was published in 1979, when issues such as domestic enforcement of human rights norms, international criminal accountability, and the use of force against human rights violators were little more than theories. It is a tribute to the prescience of the authors of that first edition, Richard Lillich and Frank Newman, that the subjects addressed 25 years later have largely remained the same. Of course, those who have used previous editions will notice that the great majority of material in this edition is different from that in the third edition, as the past decade has brought significant changes and challenges to the field of human rights.

Hurst Hannum
S. James Anaya
Dinah L. Shelton

April 2006

Acknowledgments

This edition of the casebook was greatly facilitated by the support its three authors, Hurst Hannum, S. James Anaya, and Dinah L. Shelton, have had from their respective universities and from many colleagues, friends, and loved ones. In particular, Hurst Hannum would like to thank Bridget Kimball for her excellent research assistance and extensive documentation on chapters 4, 10, and 11; Caroline Nolan for sorting through innumerable permission requests; Lupita Ervin for her work on permissions and many other tasks related to the book over the years; and Ann Hannum for putting up with too many long hours in the midst of a major household move. Thanks are also due to The Fletcher School for a summer research grant in 2005.

S. James Anaya is likewise grateful to the University of Arizona Rogers College of Law for grant monies and research support, and to the University of Sevilla Faculty of Law for its hospitality and the use of its library in the summer of 2005. Furthermore, he thanks Moira Gracey, Maia Campbell, and Leonardo Alvarado for assisting with the research for chapters 1, 3, 6, 7, and 12; Luis Rodriguez-Piñero, Bartolomé Clavero, Robert Williams, Jr., and Marina Hadjioannou for their useful insights and other support; and Jana Happel, Andrea Anaya Happel, and Emilio Anaya Happel for tolerating the many absences from home life, soccer games, and Mariachi performances required to complete work on this book.

For her part, Dinah L. Shelton gratefully acknowledges the assistance of Daniel Nadel (JD, George Washington University Law School, 2006) in preparing the documentary supplement.

Countless colleagues at other universities, in government, at international organizations, and in private practice and non-governmental organizations have shared their experiences with us and helped us to understand (and, we hope, explain) the complexities of several areas of the ever expanding and changing body of international human rights law. We thank them all.

The editors also wish to express their appreciation to the following authors, periodicals, and publishers for their permission to reproduce materials from their publications.

Acheson, Dean, The Arrogance of International Lawyers, 2 International Law 591, 591-599 (1968). Reprinted by permission.

Alston, Philip, The Commission on Human Rights in The United Nations and Human Rights 139, 145-153, 155, 158-161, 165, 167-168, 171-173, 175-177, 180-181 (Philip Alston ed. 1992). Reprinted by permission of Oxford University Press.

Anaya, James, Indigenous Peoples in International Law 16-19 (2d ed. 2004). Reprinted by permission of Oxford University Press.

———, The Maya Petition to the Inter-American Commission on Human Rights: Indigenous Land and Resource Rights, and the Conflict over Logging and Oil in Southern Belize in Giving Meaning to Economic, Social, and Cultural Rights 180-211 (Isfahan Merali and Valerie Oosterveld eds. 2001). Reprinted by permission of the University of Pennsylvania Press.

Anstey, Roger, The Atlantic Slave Trade and British Abolition 1760-1810 94-97, 126-127, 212-217 (1975). Reprinted by permission.

Asiimwe, Arthur, Rwanda Estimates 1 Million Face Genocide Charges, Reuters, January 14, 2005. Reprinted by permission.

Association of the Bar of the City of New York, Committee on International Human Rights, The Inter-American Commission: A Promise Unfulfilled, 48 The Record 589, 598-602, 603-604, 606-608, 611-613 (1993).

Bassiouni, Cherif, Appraising UN Justice-Related Fact-Finding Missions, 5 Washington University Journal of Law & Policy 35 (2001). Reprinted by permission.

Baxter, Modernizing the Law of War, 78 Military Law Review 165, 168-173 (1978). This article is reprinted from the Military Law Review, Department of the Army Pamphlet 27-100 Series: The opinions and conclusions expressed therein are those of the individual author, and do not necessarily represent the views of the Judge Advocate General's School, the United States Army, or any other governmental agency.

Belgrade Minimal Rules of Procedure for International Human Rights Fact-Finding Missions. Reproduced with permission from 75 American Journal of International Law 163, 163-165 (1981), © The American Society of International Law.

Benatar, Pat and Roger Capps, "My Clone Sleeps Alone." Reprinted with permission.

Bilder, Richard, Human Rights and U.S. Foreign Policy: Short-Term Prospects, 14 Virginia Journal of International Law 597, 597-609 passim (1974). Reprinted by permission.

———, Rethinking International Human Rights: Some Basic Questions, 1969 Wisconsin Law Review 171, 205-207. Copyright 1969 by the Board of Regents of the University of Wisconsin System. Reprinted by permission of the Wisconsin Law Review.

Bolivar, Simon, Message to the Congress of Bolivia (May 25, 1826) in Selected Writings of Bolivar, 1810-1830 (Vicente Lecuna and Harold A. Bierck eds. 1951). Reprinted by permission.

Borelli, Silvia, Casting Light on the Legal Black Hole: International Law and Detentions Abroad in the "War on Terror," 87 International Review of the Red Cross 39, 45, 48-49, 52-53, 65, 68 (No. 857, March 2005). Reprinted by permission.

Bowden, Mark, Black Hawk Down, A Story of Modern War 63, 106, 125, 217 (1999). Copyright © 1999. Used by permission of Grove/Atlantic, Inc.

Bradley, Curtis, The Juvenile Death Penalty and International Law, 52 Duke Law Journal 485, 541-544, 557 (2002). Reprinted by permission.

Buchwald, Art, Moderate Repression, International Herald-Tribune, December 20-21, 1980, at 16. Reprinted by permission.

Buergenthal, R. Norris, The Inter-American System for the Protection of Human Rights in 2 Human Rights in International Law 482-484 (Theodor Meron ed. 1984). Reprinted by permission.

Buergenthal, R. Norris and Dinah Shelton, Protecting Human Rights in the Americas, Selected Problems 299-301 (3d ed. 1990). Reprinted by permission.

Buergenthal, Thomas and John Bolton. An Exchange. Reproduced with permission from 1993 American Society of International Law, Proceedings 241-242, © The American Society of International Law.

Carey, John, UN Protection of Civil and Political Rights 63-69 (1970). Reprinted by permission.

Carothers, Thomas, Democracy and Human Rights: Policy Allies or Rivals? 17 Washington Quarterly 109, 110-111 (1994).

———, The Democracy Nostrum, 11 World Policy Journal 47, 47-48 (No. 3, 1994).

Cassese, Antonio, International Criminal Law 37-38, 40, 41 (2003). Reprinted by permission of Oxford University Press.

Charlesworth, Hilary, Feminist Methods in International Law. Reproduced with permission from 93 American Journal of International Law 379, 382-383, 387-388 (1999), © The American Society of International Law.

Cmiel, Kenneth, The Emergence of Human Rights Politics in the United States, 86 Journal of American History 1231-1250 (December 1999). Copyright © Organization of American Historians. All Rights Reserved. Used with permission of the copyright holder.

Conetta, Carl, Disappearing the Dead: Iraq, Afghanistan, and the Idea of a "New Warfare," Project on Defense Alternatives Research Monograph #9, sec. 7 (2004). Reprinted by permission.

Currah et al., Doing the Rights Thing? The World Bank and the Human Rights of People Living in Poverty, World Vision Briefing Paper 7-8, 12-13, 15, 17-19 (2003). Reprinted by permission.

Davis, David, The Problem of Slavery in the Age of Revolution: 1770-1823 41-44 (1975). Reprinted by permission.

Douglass, Frederick, The Meaning of July Fourth for the Negro, Rochester, NY (July 5, 1852) in 2 The Life and Writings of Frederick Douglass: The Pre-Civil War Decade, 1850-1860 188-192 (Philip S. Foner ed. 1950). Reprinted by permission.

Draper, Gerald, Human Rights and the Law of War, 12 Virginia Journal of International Law 326, 326-333 (1972). Reprinted by permission.

Editorial, Speak Louder on Rights in China, The New York Times, August 29, 1994, at A14. Reprinted by permission.

Feder, Don, Human Rights Not a Foreign Policy Concern, Boston Globe, March 11, 2002.

Fisch, Audrey, American Slaves in Victorian England: Abolitionist Politics in Popular Literature and Culture 52-54, 70-71 (2000). Reprinted with permission of Cambridge University Press.

Fitzpatrick, Joan, Human Rights in Crisis: The International System for Protecting Rights During States of Emergency 36-38, 52-66 (1994). Reprinted by permission of the University of Pennsylvania Press.

———, Rendition and Transfer in the War Against Terrorism: Guantánamo and Beyond, 25 Loyola of Los Angeles International & Comparative Law Review 457, 471, 480-481, 490-492 (2003). Reprinted by permission.

———, The Role of Domestic Courts in Enforcing International Human Rights Law in Guide to International Human Rights Practice 247, 253-254 (Hurst Hannum ed., 3d ed. 1999). Reprinted by permission.

Franck, Thomas M., Editorial Comment, Criminals, Combatants, or What? An Examination of the Role of Law in Responding to the Threat of Terror. Reproduced with permission from 98 American Journal of International Law 686 (2004), © The American Society of International Law.

Glennon, Michael J., Limits of Law, Prerogatives of Power: Interventionism after Kosovo 177-178, 203 (2001). Reprinted with permission.

Goldsmith, Jack, The Self-Defeating International Criminal Court, 70 University of Chicago Law Review 89, 89-92, 95-99, 101-102 (2003). Reprinted by permission.

Graling, A. C. and David Rieff, Global Rights? A Debate Between Graling and Rieff, 38 Prospect Magazine, London (February 1999). Reprinted with permission.

Hannum, Hurst, Fact-Finding by Non-Governmental Human Rights Organizations in Fact-Finding Before International Tribunals 293, 301-303 (Richard B. Lillich ed. 1992). Reprinted with permission.

———, The Rights of Persons Belonging to Minorities in Human Rights: Concepts and Standards 277-294 passim (Janusz Symonides ed. 2000). Reprinted with permission.

Heijder, Alfred, Codes of Professional Ethics Against Torture in Amnesty International USA, Code of Professional Ethics 3, 5-7 (ACT 07/01/84, 1984). Reprinted with permission.

Henkin, Louis, Editorial Comment, NATO's Kosovo Intervention: Kosovo and the Law of "Humanitarian Intervention." Reproduced with permission from 93 American Journal of International Law 824, 824-825 (1999), © The American Society of International Law.

———, The International Bill of Rights 9-11 (Louis Henkin ed. 1981). Reprinted with permission.

Heyns, Christof, The African Regional Human Rights System: The African Charter, 108 Penn State Law Review 679, 680, 681-682, 686, 687, 688-689, 691-692, 693-694, 695-696, 697-698, 700-701 (2004). Reprinted with permission.

Howard-Hassman, Rhonda E., The Second Great Transformation: Human Rights Leapfrogging in the Era of Globalization, 27 Human Rights Quarterly 1, 4, 5-6, 13, 31, 32, 33, 36-37, 38-40 (2005). © The Johns Hopkins University Press. Reprinted with permission of The Johns Hopkins University Press.

Howland, Todd, Op-Ed: In Haiti, Rhetoric Trumps Human Rights, Boston Globe, August 16, 2005, at A15. Reprinted with permission.

Howse, Robert and Makau Mutua, Protecting Human Rights in a Global Economy: Challenges for the World Trade Organization, Rights and Democracy (2000). Reprinted with permission.

Humphrey, John, The International Bill of Rights: Scope and Implementation, 17 William & Mary Law Review 529, 577 (1976).

———, The International Law of Human Rights in the Middle Twentieth Century in The Present State of International Law and Other Essays 75 (1973). Reprinted by permission of Aspen Publishers, a division of Wolters Kluwer.

———, The Universal Declaration of Human Rights: Its History, Impact and Juridical Character in Human Rights: Thirty Years After the Universal Declaration 21-37 (B.G. Ramcharan ed. 1979). Reprinted with permission.

IBRD/World Bank, Development and Human Rights: The Role of the World Bank 2-4, 5-6, 8, 11, 12, 30 (1998).

Ignatieff, Michael, Is the Human Rights Era Ending? The New York Times, February 5, 2002, at A25. Reprinted with permission.

Independent International Commission on Kosovo, Kosovo Report 41-42, 43, 44, 50, 67, 71, 72, 74, 76-78, 82-83, 88, 97 (2000). Reprinted by permission of Oxford University Press.

Inter-American Court of Human Rights, Case of the Mayagna (Sumo) Community of Awas Tingni: Transcript of the public hearing on the merits, November 16, 17, and 18, 2000, at the seat of the Court (unofficial translation), published in 19 Arizona Journal of International and Comparative Law 129, 132-156 (2002). Reprinted by permission.

International Commission of Jurists, Disappointing Start to New U.N. Procedure on Human Rights, 9 International Commission of Jurists Review 5, 5-7 (1972). Reprinted with permission.

———, Human Rights and U.S. Foreign Policy 32-38 (1984). Reprinted with permission.

———, Human Rights Report on Greece, 7 International Commission of Jurists Review 9, 10 (1971). Reprinted with permission.

———, Note, Greece: Justice in Blinkers, 1 International Commission of Jurists Review 6, 6-7 (1969). Reprinted with permission.

International Law Association, Committee on the Enforcement of Human Rights Law, Final Report on the Status of the Universal Declaration of Human Rights in National and International Law, Report of the Sixty-Sixth Conference 525, 544-549 (Buenos Aires 1995). Reprinted with permission.

———, Report of the Seventieth Conference 797 (New Delhi 2002).

Interview with Guy Womack, "Hardball with Chris Matthews," MSNBC, January 5, 2005.

Kamminga, Menno, T., Lessons Learned from the Exercise of Universal Jurisdiction in Respect of Gross Human Rights Offenses, 23 Human Rights Quarterly 940, 941-942, 943-944, 951-953, 954, 955, 956-958, 959, 960, 963, 964-965 (2001). © The Johns Hopkins University Press. Reprinted with permission of The Johns Hopkins University Press.

Kirsch, Philippe and Valerie Oosterveld, Negotiating an Institution for the Twenty-First Century: Multilateral Diplomacy and the International Criminal Court, 46 McGill Law Journal 1141, 1143, 1145-1153, 1155-1158 (2001). Reprinted with permission of the McGill Law Journal.

Kiss, Alexandre, Permissible Limitations on Rights in The International Bill of Rights: The Covenant on Civil and Political Rights 290 (L. Henkin ed. 1981).

Kissinger, Henry, Continuity and Change in American Foreign Policy, 15 Society 97, 99-102 (1977). Reprinted with permission.

———, The Pitfalls of Universal Jurisdiction, 80 Foreign Affairs (2001). Reprinted with permission.

Koh, Harold Hongju, Review Essay: Why Do Nations Obey International Law? Reprinted by permission of the Yale Law Journal Company and William S. Hein Company from the Yale Law Journal, Vol. 106, pages 2599-2659.

Kourous, George and Tom Barry, U.S. China Policy: Trade, Aid, and Human Rights, 1(5) Foreign Policy in Focus (November 1996). Reprinted with permission.

Levesque, Christian A., The International Covenant on Civil and Political Rights: A Primer for Raising a Defense Against the Juvenile Death Penalty in Federal Courts, 50 American University Law Review 755, 784-785 (2001). Reprinted with permission.

Lieutenant Duffy's Statement in Crimes of War: A Legal, Political-Documentary, and Psychological Inquiry into the Responsibility of Leaders, Citizens, and Soldiers for Criminal Acts in Ways 248, 249-254 (Richard A. Falk, Gabriel Kolko, and Robert Lifton eds. 1971). Reprinted with permission.

Lillich, Robert, Invoking International Human Rights Law in Domestic Courts, 54 University of Cincinnati Law Review 367, 394-395 (1985).

———, U.S. Foreign Policy, Human Rights, and Foreign Trade and Investment in Private Investors Abroad–Problems and Solutions in International Business in 1979 281, 288-291 (1979). Reprinted with permission.

Lynch, Colum, U.N. Sexual Abuse Alleged in Congo, Peacekeepers Accused in Draft Report, The Washington Post, December 16, 2004, at A26. © 2004, The Washington Post. Reprinted with permission.

Marks, Stephen, Emerging Human Rights: A New Generation for the 1980s? 33 Rutgers Law Review 435, 451-452 (1981). Reprinted by permission.

McDougal, Myers S. and W. Michael Reisman, Rhodesia and the United Nations: The Lawfulness of International Concern. Reproduced with permission from 62 American Journal of International Law 1, 1-19 (1968), © The American Society of International Law.

McGrory, Mary, Human Rights Retreat, The Washington Post, July 7, 1994, at Al. Reprinted with permission.

Medina, Cecilia, The Inter-American Commission on Human Rights and the Inter-American Court of Human Rights: Reflections on a Joint Venture, 12 Human Rights Quarterly 439-447 (1990). © The Johns Hopkins University Press. Reprinted with permission of The Johns Hopkins University Press.

Meron, The Case for War Crimes Trials in Yugoslavia, 72 Foreign Affairs 122 (1993).

Miers, Suzanne, Slavery and the Slave Trade as International Issues 1890-1939, 19(2) Slavery and Abolition 16-37 (1998). Reprinted with permission.

Murphy, Sean, Humanitarian Intervention: The United Nations in an Evolving World Order 217-243 (1996). Reprinted by permission of the University of Pennsylvania Press.

Orentlicher, Diane, Bearing Witness: The Art and Science of Human Rights Fact-Finding, 3 Harvard Human Rights Journal 83, 85, 92-108, 135 (1990). © 1990 by the President and Fellows of Harvard College and the Harvard Human Rights Journal.

———, Settling Accounts: The Duty to Prosecute Human Rights Violations of a Prior Regime. Reprinted by permission of the Yale Law Journal Company and William S. Hein Company from the Yale Law Journal, Vol. 100, pages 2537-2615.

———, Whose Justice? Reconciling Universal Jurisdiction with Democratic Principles, 92 Georgetown Law Journal 1057, 1059-1060, 1133-1134 (2004). Reprinted with permission.

———, Yugoslavia War Crimes Tribunal. Reproduced with permission from ASIL Focus 1-4 (No. 1, 1993), © The American Society of International Law.

Overholt, William H., Be Tougher on Burma Than China, Asian Wall Street Journal, July 4, 2003. Reprinted with permission.

Priest, Dana and Barton Gellman, U.S. Decries Abuse but Defends Interrogations: "Stress and Duress" Tactics Used on Terrorism Suspects Held in Secret Overseas Facilities, The Washington Post, December 26, 2002, at A1. © 2002, The Washington Post. Reprinted with permission.

Ramcharan, Bertrand, Evidence in International Law and Fact-Finding in the Field of Human Rights 64, 77-80 (Bertrand Ramcharan ed. 1982). Reprinted with permission.

Ratner, Steven, Editorial Comment, Belgium's War Crimes Statute: A Postmortem. Reproduced with permission from 97 American Journal of International Law 888, 888-889, 891-892, 893, 896 (2003), © The American Society of International Law.

Ratner, Steven and Jason Abrams, Accountability for Human Rights Atrocities in International Law 8-9, 10-11, 155, 156-157 (2001). Reprinted by permission of Oxford University Press.

Reinisch, August, Developing Human Rights and Humanitarian Law Accountability of the Security Council for the Imposition of Economic Sanctions. Reproduced with permission from 95 American Journal of International Law 851, 851-852 (2001), © The American Society of International Law.

Restatement (Third) of the Foreign Relations Law of the United States sec. 702 (1987). © 1987 by the American Law Institute. Reprinted with permission of the American Law Institute.

Robertson, A. H., Human Rights in the World 255-259 (J. G. Merrills ed., 3d ed. 1989). Reprinted with permission.

Rodley, Nigel S., The Treatment of Prisoners Under International Law, 279 (1987). Reprinted by permission of Oxford University Press.

Rodley, Nigel S. and Davis Weissbrodt, United Nations Nontreaty Procedures for Dealing with Human Rights Violations in Guide to International Human Rights Practice 45, 69-71 (Hurst Hannum ed., 4th ed. 2004). Reprinted with permission.

Schachter, Oscar, The Charter and the Constitution: The Human Rights Provisions in American Law, 4 Vanderbilt Law Review 643, 646-653 (1951). Reprinted with permission.

Scheffer, David, Original Intent at the Global Criminal Court, Wall Street Journal Europe, September, 20, 2002. Reprinted with permission.

Schell, Orville H., Carter on Rights — A Re-Evaluation, The New York Times, October 25, 1984, at A27. Reprinted with permission.

Schwelb, Egon, The Influence of the Universal Declaration of Human Rights on International and National Law. Reproduced with permission from 1959 American Society of International Law Proceedings 217, © The American Society of International Law.

———, The International Court of Justice and the Human Rights Clauses of the Charter. Reproduced with permission from 66 American Journal of International Law 337, 338, 341-350 (1972), © The American Society of International Law.

Sen, Amartya, Human Rights and Asian Values, The New Republic, July 14-July 21, 1997. Reprinted with permission.

Shelton, Dinah, The Boundaries of Human Rights Jurisdiction in Europe, 13 Duke Journal of International & Comparative Law 95, 96-102 (2003). Reprinted with permission.

———, Commentary and Conclusions in Compliance and Commitment: The Role of Non-Binding Instruments in the International Legal System 449-463 (2000). Reprinted by permission of Oxford University Press.

———, Compliance Mechanisms [Periodic Reports] in United States Ratification of the International Covenants on Human Rights 151, 153-155 (H. Hannum and D. Fischer eds. 1993). © The American Society of International Law. Reprinted with permission.

———, Human Rights, Environmental Rights, and the Right to Environment, 28 Stanford Journal of International Law 103, 105, 106-109, 121-122 (1991). Reprinted by permission.

———, Human Rights in Managing Global Issues 424, 438-442 (P.J. Simmons & C. de Jonge Oudraat eds. 2001). Reprinted by permission of the Carnegie Endowment for International Peace.

———, The Inter-American Human Rights System in Guide to International Human Rights Practice 130-138 (4th ed., Hurst Hannum ed. 2004). Reprinted with permission.

———, The Promise of Regional Human Rights Systems in The Future of International Human Rights 365-366, 369-370, 373, 377, 390-391, 393, 396 (B.H. Weston and S.P. Marks eds. 2000). Reprinted with permission.

———, Protecting Human Rights in a Globalized World, 25 Boston College International & Comparative Law Review 273, 275-276, 278-280 (2002). Copyright © 2002 by Boston College Law School. Reprinted with permission.

Shestack, Jerome J., An Unsteady Focus: The Vulnerabilities of the Reagan Administration's Human Rights Policy, 2 Harvard Human Rights Year Book 25, 36-39 (1989). © 1989 by the President and Fellows of Harvard College and the Harvard Human Rights Journal.

Smith, Andrew, International Conflict and the Media, A Curriculum Guide: Incubator Baby Incident. At http://www.globaled.org/curriculum/cm18a.html and http://www.globaled.org/curriculum/ cm18h.html. Reprinted by permission.

Smith, Daniel, New Protections for Victims of International Armed Conflicts: The Proposed Ratification of Protocol II by the United States, 120 Military Law Review 59, 63-65 (1988). This article is reprinted from the Military Law Review, Department of the Army Pamphlet 27-100 Series: The opinions and conclusions expressed therein are those of the individual author, and do not necessarily represent the views of the Judge Advocate General's School, the United States Army, or any other governmental agency.

Solf, Waldemar A., Problems with the Application of Norms Governing Interstate Armed Conflict to Non-International Armed Conflict, 13 Georgia Journal of International & Comparative Law 291, 295-296 (1983). Reprinted with permission.

Steinhardt, Ralph, Laying One Bankrupt Critique to Rest: Sosa v. Alvarez Machain and the Future of International Human Rights Litigation in U.S. Courts, 57 Vanderbilt Law Review 2241, 2283-2287 (2004). Reprinted by permission.

———, in *Sustainability*, The Changing Landscape of Liability: A Director's Guide to Trends in Corporate Environmental, Social and Economic Liability 1, 6, 8-9, 20-21, 30 (2004). Reprinted with permission.

Temperley, Howard, The Ideology of Antislavery in The Abolition of the Atlantic Slave Trade: Origins and Effects in Europe, Africa and the Americas 26-29 (D. Eltis and J. Walvin eds. 1981). Reprinted by permission of the University of Wisconsin Press.

Thoolen, Hans and Berth Verstappen, Human Rights Missions: A Study of the Fact-Finding Practice of Non-Governmental Organizations 24-26, 31-32 (1986). United Nations Environment Program, Geo Yearbook: An Overview of Our Changing Environment 2004-2005 2, 3, 52, 72-80 (2005). Reprinted with permission.

U.S. Institute for Peace, U.S. Human Rights Policy: A 20 Year Assessment, United States Institute of Peace Special Report (June 16, 1999). Reprinted with permission.

Walvin, James, The Public Campaign in England Against Slavery, 1787-1834 in The Abolition of the Atlantic Slave Trade: Origins and Effects in Europe, Africa and the Americas 69-76 (D. Eltis and J. Walvin eds. 1981). Reprinted by permission of the University of Wisconsin Press.

Weiss, Thomas G., Sanctions as a Foreign Policy Tool: Weighing Humanitarian Impulses, 36 Journal of Peace Research 499 (No. 5, 1999). Reprinted by permission of Sage Publications Ltd. Copyright © International Peace Research Institute (Oslo) PRIO, 1999.

Yokota, Yozo and Chiyuki Aoi, Japan's Foreign Policy Towards Human Rights: Uncertain Changes in Human Rights and Comparative Foreign Policy (D. Forsythe ed. 2000). Reprinted with permission.

International Human Rights

Chapter 1

The Concept of Human Rights

From Morality To Law: The Abolition of Slavery

I. The Concept of Human Rights

What do we mean by "human rights"? There is no simple answer, despite the widespread usage of the term or its equivalent in diverse languages. At its core, however, the concept of human rights embraces a certain universe of values having to do with human dignity. These values, and the claims to which they give rise, are understood to apply across national boundaries and cultural divides. Although deemed universal in some sense, human rights draw their content from diverse sources — for some, fundamental moral or ethical precepts discerned through rational thought; for others, religious ideals handed down over time; and, for still others, an understanding of social consensus at some level. Whatever the source or content of human rights, the widespread perception is that they necessarily belong to everyone *inherently*; human rights are not granted by temporal authority, rather they are to be recognized and upheld by it to maintain legitimacy.

The concept of human rights can be seen at work in the Declaration of Independence of the thirteen colonies that became the original United States, through which its drafters defied the British sovereignty asserted over them on the grounds of "truths" held "self-evident, that all men are created equal, that they are endowed by their Creator with certain inalienable Rights, that among these are Life, Liberty and the pursuit of Happiness." The Western liberal tradition of the eighteenth century that inspired these words, and similar words that heralded the French Revolution, is often regarded as the intellectual wellspring of what we know today as human rights. Yet non-Western philosophical and intellectual traditions also lay claim to precepts of universal and inherent human rights, giving the concept of human rights a multicultural foundation for its common postulates of human dignity.

In his concurring opinion in the Namibia case before the International Court of Justice, Judge Ammoun linked the idea of human equality with "[t]wo streams of thought "established on the two opposite shores of the Mediterranean, a Graeco-Roman stream represented by Epictetus, Lucan, Cicero and Marcus Aurelius; and an Asian and African stream, comprising the monks of Sinai and Saint John Climac, Alexandria with Plotinus and Philo the Jew, Carthage to which Saint Augustine gave new lustre." *Legal Consequences for States of the Continued Presence of South Africa in Namibia (South West Africa) notwithstanding Security Council Resolution 276 (1970)*, Advisory Opinion, 1971 I.C.J. 16, 77-78. Equality and other human rights precepts can also be found in expressions of thinking developed among peoples indigenous to the the Americas and Asia.

For the Navajo of North America, for example, "the idea of being superior to a fellow Navajo or nature is discouraged. There is an innate knowledge in each on of us that we are to treat with respect all persons and nature with whom we share this world." Judicial Branch of the Navajo Nation, Annual Report, The Navajo Concept of Justice, at 1 (1988). Based on this tradition, Navajo customary law continues to be invoked in Navajo courts to protect human rights such as freedom of expression and political participation. See *Navajo Nation v. Crockett*, 24 Indian L. Rep. 6027 (Navajo 1996); *Bennett v. Navajo Board of Election Supervisors*, 17 Indian L. Rep. 6099 (1990).

Asian authors expressed the idea of human rights from at least the fifth century B.C. Chinese philosopher Hsün-tzu wrote "In order to relieve anxiety and eradicate strife, nothing is as effective as the institution of corporate life based on a clear recognition of individual rights." UNESCO, Birthright of Man 39 (1969). The Code of Hammurabi (1795-1750 B.C.), the oldest written legal code known today, represented a codification and development of the customary law of the region and was probably based upon earlier codes that are now lost. In the Preamble to the Code, Hammurabi expressed the fundamental purposes of government: "to bring about the rule of righteousness in the land, to destroy the wicked and the evil-doers, so that the strong should not harm the weak . . . and enlighten the land, to further the well-being of mankind."

However much there may be broad convergence around basic conceptions of human rights, abuses of human rights have abounded over time and space. In part, this is because of shifting ideas about what is right and wrong; in many cases, what is today considered an affront to human rights was once considered acceptable behavior, at least by a sizable or powerful group. In part, human rights abuses occur simply because of the persistent and often widespread tendency of persons in positions of power to fall short of expectations or worse. Throughout the world there have been powerful opponents of human rights who have sought to retain privilege, hierarchy, hereditary rule, and property. In eighteenth-century Europe, human rights proponents challenged and in turn were challenged by vested interests: Thomas Paine was hung in effigy in English cities; Voltaire's writings were banned. Reactionary authors referred to the "monstrous fiction" of human equality. Jeremy Bentham rejected the idea of natural or inherent rights, labeling it "nonsense on stilts." In his strongly held view, people should know "their proper place."

Individuals and groups have joined to assert basic rights against perceived wrongs through actions that transcend national boundaries and that have eventually influenced official law, policy, and behavior. Today, there is a substantial body of human rights norms recognized in various written international written instruments, accompanied by procedures to promote their implementation. Human rights have become part of international law and transnational relations out of efforts to shape perceptions about the essence of human dignity and to bring behavior in line with those perceptions and the values they represent.

II. The Movement to Abolish Slavery and the Slave Trade

A. *Introduction*

The process by which the concept of human rights is harnessed to generate legal obligation and change is illustrated by the attack against and eventual official demise of slavery. Notwithstanding the American Declaration of Independence and its proclamation of equality for all (at least men), slavery was legal in much of the United States for nearly a century after the country's birth, just as it was in much of the world. Slavery had existed throughout history and across the globe, but it changed fundamentally in the sixteenth century with the onset of the trans-Atlantic slave trade from Africa. The numbers alone exceeded any past practice. Between 1519 and 1866, some nine and a half million Africans were imported as slaves into North America, while a further million died on the voyage. The trade reached its peak in the 1780s, when an average of 100,000 people were imported to the Americas annually to be sold as slaves. See James A. Rawley, *The Transatlantic Slave Trade: A History* (rev. ed. 2005). Of course, countless other slaves were carried to Europe, the Caribbean, and Central and South America. Slavery was reinforced by ideologies of racism, apartheid, and segregation. From the sixteenth to the nineteenth centuries, the international slave trade flourished, and slavery was legal in most countries of the world.

Yet, almost from the beginning, a small but vocal minority in the slave trading countries expressed its determined opposition to slavery, joining the mostly unheard voices of slaves themselves. These individuals began to organize the world's first human rights nongovernmental organizations in the modern genre. They published articles and pamphlets; they preached against slavery; and they organized active campaigns of protest. Slaves themselves engaged in uprisings in Saint-Dominique, Haiti, and elsewhere. Many of those most outspoken against the abuse were themselves former and reformed slave traders or slave owners. Unlike many, they saw a gap between the proclamations of rights — especially in England, the United States, and France — and the practice of slavery; and they invoked the high ideals of religion and philosophy to mount opposition. They were thus able to draw intellectual and moral strength from the general proclamations of human rights. As economic factors evolved to allow for the rapid accumulation of wealth without dependence on slavery, the abolitionist movement gained strength.

Public pressure grew throughout the first part of the nineteenth century on both sides of the Atlantic. In Britain, public agitation forced members of Parliament to confront the issue. Following a slave revolt, Haiti became independent in 1804. As early as 1807, public opinion forced votes in the U.S. Congress and British Parliament to end the participation of both countries in international slave trading. The U.S. Act to Prohibit the Importation of Slaves was matched by the British Act for the Abolition of the Slave Trade. Both made it illegal to trade in, purchase, sell, barter, or transport any human cargo for the purpose of slavery, although ownership of slaves was not proscribed.

Neither law could be effective without international cooperation and the agreement of other nations. The focus turned to the Congress of Vienna in 1814-1815, where anti-slavery activists pressed for action, including the outright eradication of slavery. About this time, Thomas Clarkson's highly influential tract, Evidence on the Subject of the Slave Trade, was translated from English into French, German, Spanish, and Italian. The British delegate at the Congress of Vienna complained about the public pressure being mounted, but its force could not be denied. The Congress of Vienna established a special committee on the international slave trade and finally agreed to sign the Eight Power Declaration, which acknowledged that the international slave trade was "repugnant to the principles of humanity and universal morality" and that "the public voice in all civilized countries calls aloud for its prompt suppression." Yet the declaration did not make slave trading a crime, call for the arrest of slavers, or provide machinery for enforcement.

A legally binding treaty soon followed, however. During the Congress itself, a treaty signed November 20, 1815 among Britain, Russia, Austria, Prussia, and France included a pledge to consider measures "for the entire and definitive abolition of a Commerce so odious and so strongly condemned by the laws of religion and nature." The Treaty of Ghent, signed by the United States and Britain that same year, declared that traffic in slaves was "irreconcilable with the principles of humanity and justice." Treaty of Peace and Amity, Feb. 18, 1815, 12 T.I.A.S. 47.

Anti-slavery societies continued their pressure, led by Lord Wilberforce in the United Kingdom. In addition, the Pope instructed all Catholics to abstain from the slave trade. In 1840, the first World Anti-Slavery Conference was organized. Eventually governments responded. By 1882, a network of more than 50 bilateral agreements permitted the search of suspected slave ships on the high seas, without regard to flag. Domestically, states slowly emancipated their slaves in response to public pressure. Britain did so in 1833, France in 1848, and most Latin American countries did so as they became independent. The issue of slavery was a major factor in the U.S. Civil War, and President Lincoln issued the Emancipation Proclamation in 1863. In the late 1880s, Cuba and Brazil became the last countries in the Western Hemisphere to abolish slavery.

By 1890, the governments of several countries were prepared to take effective international action. They negotiated the 1890 General Act for the Repression of the African Slave Trade, which referred to the "crimes and devastations engendered" by trafficking in humans. The convention required that actions be taken to suppress the slave trade at sea and along inland caravan routes, to prosecute and punish slave traders, and to liberate captured slaves. (Ironically and tragically, this humanitarian impulse also served to provide a pretext for colonial occupation throughout Africa.) The agreement reflected the principle of shared international responsibility to respond to gross human rights violations and marked the first general agreement on a common standard of behavior for all states. Further agreements on abolition of slavery and repression of the slave trade were concluded in 1919, 1926, and 1956.

The extracts below show the evolution in moral understanding about slavery, the coincidence of political and economic factors that made it easier to oppose it, and the rhetorical assault on maintaining slavery as a legal institution. These materials are followed by the celebrated Sommersett case of 1772, in which a British court gave legal expression to the mounting opposition to slavery wherever it existed, and by a description of subsequent international legal developments against slavery.

B. The Moral and Philosophical Evolution

David Brion Davis, The Problem of Slavery in the Age of Revolution 1770-1823

42-44 (1975) (footnotes omitted)

The emergence of an international antislavery opinion represented a momentous turning point in the evolution of man's moral perception, and thus in man's image of himself. The continuing "evolution" did not spring from transcendent sources: as a historical artifact, it reflected the ideological needs of various groups and classes. The explanation must begin, however, with the heritage of religious, legal, and philosophical tensions associated with slavery — or in other words, with the ways in which Western culture had organized man's experience with lordship and bondage.

From antiquity slavery has embodied symbolic meanings connected with the condition and destiny of man. For the Greeks (as for Saint Augustine and other early Christian theologians) physical bondage was part of the cosmic hierarchy, of the divine scheme for ordering and governing the forces of evil and rebellion. For the ancient Hebrews, slavery could be a divine punishment; a time of trial and self-purification prior to deliverance; and the starting point for a historical mission. The literature of Hellenistic and early Christian times is saturated with the paradoxes of human bondage: man was a slave to sin or to his own passions; his incapacity for virtuous self-government justified his external bondage; yet he might escape his internal slavery by becoming the servant of universal reason — or of the Lord. Emancipation from one form of slavery depended on the acceptance of a higher and more righteous bondage....

... The early Christian view of slavery was of central importance in reconciling the masses to the existing social order. It constituted the core of an ideology that encouraged hope, patience, endurance, and submission, while reminding the powerful of their own fallibility.... Thus Saint Thomas Aquinas could affirm that slavery was contrary to the first and highest intent of nature, and yet insist that it conformed to the second intent of nature, which was adjusted to man's limited capacities. He could therefore suggest that slavery was a necessary part of the governing pattern of the universe, speak of the slave as the physical instrument of his owner, and find scholastic justifications for the Roman rule that the child of a free man and a bondwoman should be a slave. Neither Luther nor Calvin, one may note, had any notion that Christian liberty could alter the fact that some men are born free and others slaves. Indeed, as a result of the verdict of many centuries, one could not begin to assert the universal sinfulness of slavery without questioning the doctrine of original sin and challenging the entire network of rationalization for every form of subordination.

Roger Anstey, The Atlantic Slave Trade and British Abolition 1760-1810

94-97 (1975) (footnotes omitted)

The world of the late eighteenth century was quite different. The French Revolution manifested the most radical change in values and institutions that

Christendom had yet known. Traditional authority was dethroned; Christianity was dismissed with a scorn which demonstrated the Jacobins' belief that the dismissal was final, whilst the whole life of the revolutionary state attested the belief that society could be given a different direction. In England, after an initial heady exaltation, there were few who wanted change to go so far and so fast: but the very force of Burke's condemnation of the 'presumption' of men in supposing they have made discoveries in the realm of morality, government and in ideas of liberty, and his scorn of their 'pert loquacity' in giving voice to their claim, testifies to the existence of a different attitude to change than that professed by Newton and Pope.

Included in the change of values was a clear shift in attitudes towards subject peoples. Even people generally opposed to radical change in the state — Burke is a striking example — believed British policy towards the Americans to be immoral and thus called into question the whole nature of imperial power....

Nowhere is the change of view more marked than in attitudes towards slavery and the slave trade.... Nearly every school of thought which dealt with ethical problems had, from about the middle of the century, come up with specific condemnations of slavery sometimes persuasively encapsulated in a corpus of moral or legal philosophy. And very varied were these schools. Gisborne wrote his widely read *Principles of Moral Philosophy* (1789) not least to counter the doctrine of expediency propounded by Paley in *The Principles of Moral and Political Philosophy* (1785); but both condemned slavery and the slave trade. A major segment of French Enlightenment opinion and especially the Abbé Raynal, whose work was very influential in England, was hostile to slavery; so, opposed in almost everything else, was John Wesley. Dr Johnson strongly opposed slavery; so did Rousseau whom Johnson detested.

This change must be explored a little further, and it may be as well to spell out the mode of exploration, and its limits. It is *not* our purpose [here] to argue that a change in moral and intellectual attitudes to slavery is a sufficient explanation of abolition — that first great triumph of the anti-slavery cause. The aim is the much more limited one of arguing that the content of received wisdom had so altered by the 1780s that educated men and the political nation, provided they had no direct interest in the slave system, would be likely to regard slavery and the slave trade as morally condemned, as no longer philosophically defensible. They might, it can reasonably be inferred, even be prepared to support abolition, provided that they had no direct interest in the slave system, provided that they could be assured that the national interest would not thereby be significantly harmed, and to the extent that anything so novel as a positive measure of institutional reform could command support. The role which is to be credited to a change in ideas is therefore noteworthy but limited.... A more dramatic role was the achievement of the two religious groups in the abolition movement, Quakers and Evangelicals. Though influenced by the currents of thought of their age, their inspiration was essentially religious. That inspiration will be investigated in some depth because it produced a new, four-square, theologically based condemnation of slavery and a dynamic of faith and action which largely created and sustained the abolition campaign....

C. *Economic and Political Factors*

Howard Temperley, The Ideology of Antislavery

In The Abolition of the Atlantic Slave Trade: Origins and Effects in Europe, Africa and the Americas 26-29 (David Eltis and James Walvin eds., 1981) (footnotes omitted)

[Britain and the northern United States] both had experienced remarkable rates of economic growth in the course of the eighteenth century. Probably nowhere else in the world was the relative increase in wealth and population more striking than in the thirteen colonies. This, as we all know, was one of the factors which persuaded the British government to attempt to tighten its hold on the colonists, and so helped to precipitate the break with the mother country. Yet Britain's own rate of growth during these years, although less marked in relative terms, was also impressive, whether we compare it with what had happened in previous centuries or with the experiences of her political rivals. This was, as economic historians continually remind us, a period of crucial importance for the previous millennium, the gains of the eighteenth century represented the departure point from which began the sustained growth that has characterized the modern world. Britain and her ex-colonies were in the forefront of this development. Materially speaking, they had reason to feel proud of their achievement.

A second characteristic that Britain and the northern states (as opposed to the South) shared was the fact that they had achieved this prosperity without direct recourse to slave labor, at least on any significant scale. To be sure, there was slavery in Britain right up to the end of the eighteenth century (the Sommersett decision [infra, at 14] notwithstanding), and it lingered on in the northern states even longer. As late as 1820 there were still eighteen thousand slaves in the northeastern United States, and at the time of the first census in 1790 the figure was more than double that; but compared with the situation south of the Mason-Dixon line this represented a relatively modest stake in the institution. It must also be remembered that both Britain and the northern states had profited, and were continuing to profit on an ever-increasing scale, from the employment of slaves elsewhere. Nevertheless, the fact remains that, so far as their domestic arrangements were concerned, both were committed to an essentially free-labor system.

These points are too obvious to dwell on. Yet they are worth emphasizing if only because they help to explain why men in these two societies were so ready to accept ideas of progress, and in particular ideas of progress which linked individual freedom to material prosperity. The two, needless to say, are not necessarily connected. More often that not, they have been seen as opposing principles, the assumption being that the pursuit of the one must necessarily entail the sacrifice of the other. Implicit in the whole idea of government is the belief that individual freedom must be given up to secure the benefits of an ordered society, among which must be included a measure of material satisfactions. How much freedom needs to be sacrificed is a matter of opinion, but history is not wanting in examples of societies welcoming tyrants because the alternatives of anarchy and lawlessness were regarded as even less acceptable. So the commonly expressed eighteenth-century view that freedom and prosperity were not only reconcilable but mutually supportive, and that the more you had of the one the more you could expect of the other, is something that needs explaining. The explanation, I suggest, is to be found not in the ideas of the philosophers, still less in theories about the general progress of the human mind, but in the immediate lives of people of the period.

This, then is one way of relating material and intellectual developments, and one that throws a good deal of light on the thinking of such figures as Adam Smith and the exponents of the secular anti-slavery argument generally. For what is striking about the secular case against slavery is the *assumption* that slavery was an economic anachronism. Smith's own attitudes are particularly revealing, because of all eighteenth century commentators he was probably the one best qualified to argue the case against it on strictly economic grounds. Yet . . . the case he actually presents is not based on economics at all, at least not in any cost-accounting sense, but on the general proposition that greater freedom would lead to greater prosperity. Like other eighteenth century thinkers he expresses himself in terms of universal principles, but at bottom it is a historical argument, derived from his own beliefs about the nature of the historical process. Whatever the objective truths of Smith's arguments, the fact remains that they are very much the product of one kind of society, and indeed of one particular class within that society.

. . . But until the eighteenth century . . . slavery was accepted with that fatalism which men commonly reserve for aspects of nature which, whether they are to be celebrated or deplored, have to be borne. To argue against slavery was to argue against the "facts of life." Before slavery could become a political issue — or even, in the proper sense, a moral issue — what needed to be shown was that the world could get along without it. And what better demonstration could there be than the development, within the heartland of Western civilization, of societies which not only did without slavery but which did very well without it, and which furthermore appeared to owe their quite remarkable dynamism to the acceptance of principles which represented the direct negation of the assumptions upon which slavery was founded.

James Walvin, The Public Campaign in England against Slavery, 1787-1834

In The Abolition of the Atlantic Slave Trade: Origins and Effects in Europe, Africa and the Americas 69-73 (David Eltis and James Walvin, eds. 1981) (most footnotes omitted)

In the years after the war, as in 1791-92, the abolitionist cause was helped by being carried along by the wider political debate about rights [in Great Britain]. These were, after all, the years when the politics of Catholic emancipation, electoral reform, poor relief, unionization, and industrial legislation were at their height. Yet slavery was seen to subsume many of the other political arguments about rights; it was, in fact, the most extreme form of a denial of rights. Throughout these years there was a growing awareness of the facts of slavery . . . at every level black slavery formed a stark contrast to the very rights demanded by so many groups in Britain. And, in a nation which was itself permeated by the advance of large nonconformist communities (particularly in working-class areas) and by evangelicalism within the established church, slavery seemed to ever more people to be morally offensive.... By the mid-1820s support for slavery had clearly become an electoral liability for parliamentary candidates. Conversely, it was assumed that right-thinking candidates would favour gradual emancipation.

By that time abolitionism had also taken on a new perspective, and one which was to gain in stridency in subsequent years. The question of the economics of slavery became ever more prominent in political argument. Early in 1822 Cropper had privately raised the question of East Indian sugar and the artificial protection which kept West Indian sugar viable and costly to the British consumer. By October 1822 [the economic] issue had broken into print. Within four years, open support for freely imported East Indian sugar had become a major political objection to slave-grown sugar, as one parliamentary candidate noted: "the difference in the duty on East and West India sugars operates as a bounty on slavery, and as a tax on the people of England, which they may reasonably require to be removed."[33] Elsewhere it was argued that slavery was "supported by an annual donation from this county, of *nearly four million sterling*, given in the way of exclusions, bounties, and prohibitory duties...."[34] The message was clear; the British consumer of sugar was maintaining the slave system. As the 1820s advanced, this argument, so consonant with growing contemporary economic ideology, could be found with growing frequency and stridency in abolitionist meetings and literature and in Parliament. Indeed, the economic critique of slavery soon became a plea for free trade, and by April 1827 "the Chambers of Commerce of Manchester and Birmingham and the merchants and manufacturers of Leeds and other places" were demanding both free trade and an end to the sugar duties. The new industrial nation had come to see that slavery was inimical to its wider economic interests....

It was in the slaveholders' interests to undermine the credibility of antislavery and to denounce abolitionist tactics; they belittled the petitions, suggesting that they were rigged, copied, or the result of intemperate excitement. Yet abolitionists never doubted that all the evidence pointed to genuine and a massive popular support. And from June 1825 we are able to trace this support in greater detail through the columns of the *Anti-Slavery Monthly Reporter*, which ran until 1836. Founded by Macaulay, the *Reporter* provided a superb mirror of the world of abolitionism, particularly in the provinces. Indeed, this publication itself became a main focus for activity, for, widely distributed throughout the country, it gave information, guidance, and direction to the national cause.

The most striking contribution of the *Reporter* was the prodigious volume of information about slave society that it fed to the reading public. One issue after another regaled its swelling readership with the minutiae of slave life; the nature of slave work, leisure, housing, family patterns, punishments, and religions – any and all facets of slave society passed through the pages of the *Reporter*. Moreover, this journal provided the invaluable service of distinguishing *between* the slave

33. Speeches and Addresses of the Candidates for the Representation of the County of York in the Year 1826 (Leeds, 1826), p. 26.

34. Address to the Public on the Present State of the Question Relative to Negro Slavery in the British Colonies (York, 1828), p. 14.

societies of the different islands. The result was that a much more sophisticated analysis of Caribbean slavery began to emerge in the political debate. Perhaps it is this feature which makes the later phase of the abolitionist struggle so appealing to a modern historian. One finds, for example, exemplary analyses of slave populations (from registration returns), with telling comparisons with slavery in the United States. Any plantocratic claim was immediately followed by a detailed and documented abolitionist answer. Equally important was the *Reporter*'s regular resumé of official government evidence. Government pronouncements, publications, colonial laws, and ministerial missives were reported, analysed, and challenged. The *Reporter* made accessible to the public information which would otherwise have been embalmed in official publications. This was particularly true of correspondence between ministers and the colonies. The sum total of these efforts was to make public what had previously been a private and secretive world of politics. This inevitably made life difficult for the men concerned – but it made for excellent pressure group politics, and it illustrated, to anyone interested, just what could be achieved through such pressures. In the process, the role of the minister began to change, for he was now subjected to pressures from without as well as from within.

The abolitionist argument about rights shows how far the wider political debate had advanced since the 1790s. At that earlier period belief in the "rights of man" had tended to be the preserve of the popular radicals, but by the 1820s this term – given an even wider meaning – had become a central abolitionist belief. Emancipationists in Norwich in 1825 thought slavery "to be utterly inconsistent with the inalienable natural rights of men."[35] Of course, the arguments about slavery were inevitably about the slaves' "Civil and Religious Liberties,"[36] Methodists in Yorkshire considered slavery "directly contrary to the natural Rights of Man,"[37] and it is striking that the abolitionist petitions which flooded Parliament – upward of 3,500 by 1832 – were steeped in a political vocabulary which, in the 1790s, had been the preserve of artisan radicals. Indeed, in the 1790s men were jailed and transported for seeking such rights for themselves; thirty years later, many thousands of Englishmen demanded these same rights – for black slaves. Some spoke of the slaves' "inalienable Rights of liberty of which they have been barbarously robbed," others of the need to restore their "Constitutional Freedom."[38]

D. The Rhetoric of Abolition

Simon Bolivar, Message to the Congress of Bolivia (May 25, 1826)

In Selected Writings of Bolivar, 1810-1830, pp.596 (Vicente Lecuna and Harold A. Bierck eds., 1951)

Slavery is the negation of all law and a sacrilege. . . . Examine this crime from every aspect and tell me if there is a single Bolivian so depraved as to wish to sanctify by law this shameless violation of human dignity. . . . No one can violate

35. Anti-Slavery Monthly Reporter, no. 6 (November, 1825), p. 57.
36. Journal of the House of Lords, 63: 53.
37. Ibid. p. 101.
38. Journal of the House of Lords, 63:22.

the sacred doctrine of equality. . . . God has willed freedom to man, who protects it in order to exercise the divine faculty of free will.

Audrey A. Fisch, American Slaves in Victorian England: Abolitionist Politics in Popular Literature and Culture

52-54, 70-71 (2000) (some text references converted to footnotes; others omitted)

. . . [B]y 1853, tales of slavery were indeed a "staple" in the Victorian literary marketplace: at least twenty American slave narratives appeared in English editions by mid-century, and it is likely that other narratives circulated in American editions. . . . Slave narratives, R.J.M. Blackett writes, "sold faster than they could be printed . . ." C. Peter Ripley concurs with Blackett's findings and adds that in England the narratives sold "well, probably better than in America, as a rule. . . ." The slave narratives offered African-American men and women an opportunity to speak their minds, if only through the medium of words on a page . . . "[P]ictures of slavery by the slave" were calculated to, and did, exert "a very wide influence on public opinion" because they are "a vivid exhibition of the force and working of the native love of freedom in the individual mind." . . . Under the politically acceptable mantle of abolitionism, then, the slave narrative offered Victorian readers the excitement for which they were eager: graphic scenes of torture, murder, sexual violence, and the thrill of escape. . . . The titillating entertainment of the narratives was also clothed in the morally acceptable fabric of the Christian odyssey tradition. . . .

. . . Through lecture tours that varied along a continuum of pomp and politics, African-American abolitionists brought information about American slavery to people from all walks of life throughout the British Isles. . . . African-Americans spoke to groups ranging from a few to several thousand people. They spoke often; as Blackett records, the [African-American abolitionist Frederick] "Douglass delivered fifty lectures in the first four months of his visit, the number rising by the end of his nineteen-month tour to three hundred." An appearance often involved more than just a lecture; while speaking about their personal life experiences and about the experiences of other black men and women in American slavery, the lecturer might present enormous panoramas depicting scenes of American slavery (none of which are known to have survived), reveal personal scars (Houston A. Baker has called these public displays of the physical markings of slavery the "Negro exhibit"), or display the instruments of torture used in slavery. Even in traditional anti-slavery circles, African-American abolitionists were, as C. Peter Ripley writes, "essential to the cause": the "attraction of rubbing shoulders with the black American abolitions . . . had no substitute."

. . . [T]ensions run deep between the "mother-country" and its rebellious child over this "fashion" for Others. . . . England, casting itself as the land of freedom, sloganeering that each visitor is a "man and [a] brother," competes with the United States, the land of surpassing democratic freedoms, the newly born "model republic." And even though American national security is not literally threatened by the "utter depopulation" of slave plantations, the popularity of visitors like Frederick Douglass in England represents a threat to America's national identity as the "model republic."

Frederick Douglass, The Meaning of July Fourth for the Negro, Rochester, NY (July 5, 1852)

In The Life and Writings of Frederick Douglass, Vol.II, Pre-civil War Decade, 1850-1860, at 188-201 (Philip S. Foner ed., 1950)

Fellow citizens, pardon me, allow me to ask, why am I called upon to speak here today? What have I, or those I represent, to do with national independence? Are the great principles of political freedom, and of natural justice, embodied in that Declaration of Independence, extended to us? And am I, therefore, called upon to bring our humble offering to the national altar, and to confess the benefits and express devout gratitude for the blessings resulting from your independence to us?

Would to God, both for your sakes and ours, that an affirmative answer could be truthfully returned to these questions! . . .

But such is not the state of the case. I say it with a sad sense of the disparity between us. I am not included within the pale of this glorious anniversary! Your high independence only reveals the immeasurable distance between us. The blessings in which you, this day, rejoice, are not enjoyed in common — the rich inheritance of justice, liberty, prosperity and independence, bequeathed by your fathers, is shared by you, not by me. The sunlight that brought light and healing to you, has brought stripes and death to me. This Fourth of July is *yours*, not *mine*. *You* may rejoice, *I* must mourn. To drag a man in fetters into the grand illuminated temple of liberty, and call him to join you in joyous anthems, were inhuman mockery and sacrilegious irony. Do you mean, citizens, to mock me, by asking me to speak today? . . .

Fellow citizens, above your national, tumultuous joy, I hear the mournful wail of millions! Whose chains, heavy and grievous yesterday, are, to-day, rendered more intolerable by the jubilee shouts that reach them. . . .

What, to the American Slave, is your 4th of July? I answer; a day that reveals to him, more than all other days in the year, the gross injustice and cruelty to which he is the constant victim. To him, your celebration is a sham; your boasted liberty, and unholy license; your national greatness, swelling vanity; your sounds of rejoicing are empty and heartless; your denunciation of tyrants, brass fronted impudence; your shouts of liberty and equality, hollow mockery; your prayers and hymns, your sermons and thanksgivings, which all your religious parade and solemnity, are, to Him, mere bombast, fraud, deception, impiety, and hypocrisy — a thin veil to cover up crimes which would disgrace a nation of savages. There is not a nation on the earth guilty of practices more shocking and bloody than are the people of the United States, at this very hour. . . .

Fellow citizens, I will not enlarge further on your national inconsistencies. The existence of slavery in this country brands your republicanism as sham, your humanity as a base pretence, and your Christianity as a lie. It destroys your moral power abroad; it corrupts your politicians at home. It saps the foundation of religion; it makes your name and hissing and bye-word to a mocking earth. It is the antagonistic force in your government, the only thing that seriously disturbs and endangers your Union. It fetters your progress; it is the enemy of improvement; the deadly foe of education; it fosters pride; it breeds insolence; it promotes vice; it shelters crime; it is a curse to the earth that supports it; and yet you cling to it as if it were the sheet anchor of all your hopes. Oh! Be warned! Be warned! A horrible reptile is coiled up in your nation's bosom; the venomous creature is nursing at the tender breast of your youthful republic; for the love of God, tear away, and fling from you the hideous monster, and let the weight of twenty millions crush and destroy it forever!

E. The Legal Evolution

One of the most celebrated cases in all of Anglo-American jurisprudence is the Case of James Sommersett, in which a British court ordered a ship commander to release a black slave whom the commander held at the behest of the slave's American owner for transport to Jamaica to be sold. The decision itself did not clearly render slave-holding illegal in all circumstances, but it certainly resonated as a statement that the tide was decidedly turning against slavery, not just as a matter of moral conviction but as a matter of law, at least in Great Britain.

The Case of James Sommersett

12 George III A.D. 1771-72, Lofft 1-18, 98 Eng. Rep. 499-510 (King's Bench, June 22, 1772)

On the 3d of December 1771, affidavits were made by Thomas Walklin, Elizabeth Cade, and John Marlow, that James Sommersett, a negro, was confined in irons on board a ship called the *Ann and Mary*, John Knowles commander, lying in the Thames, and bound for Jamaica; and Lord Mansfield, on an application supported by these affidavits, allowed a writ of Habeas Corpus, directed to Mr. Knowles, and requiring him to return the body of Sommersett before his lordship, with the cause of detainer.

Mr. Knowles on the 9th of December produced the body of Sommersett before Lord Mansfield, and returned for cause of detainer, that Sommersett was the negro slave of Charles Stewart, esq. who had delivered Sommersett into Mr. Knowles's custody, in order to carry him to Jamaica, and there sell him as a slave. Affidavits were also made by Mr. Stewart and two other gentlemen, to prove that Mr. Stewart had purchased Sommersett as a slave in Virginia, and had afterwards brought him into England, where he left his master's service; and that his refusing to return, was the occasion of his being carried on board Mr. Knowles's ship.

Lord Mansfield chusing to refer the matter to the determination of the court of King's bench, Sommersett with sureties was bound in recognizance for his appearance there on the second day of the next Hilary term; and his lordship allowed till that day for settling the form of the return [Ed. Note, Defendant's Answer] to the Habeas Corpus. . . .

The determination of the Court was suspended till the following Trinity term; and then the Court was unanimously of opinion against the return, and ordered that Sommersett should be discharged [freed]. . . .

ARGUMENT OF MR. FRANCIS HARGRAVE [1741-1821] FOR THE NEGRO.

The questions arising on this case, do not merely concern the unfortunate person, who is the subject of it, and such as are or may be under like unhappy circumstances. They are highly interesting to the whole community, and cannot be decided, without having the most general and important consequences; without extensive influence on private happiness and public security. The right claimed by Mr. Stewart in the detention of the negro, is founded on the condition of slavery, in which he was before his master brought him into England; and if that right is here recognized, domestic slavery, with its horrid train of evils, may be lawfully imported into this country, at the discretion of every individual, foreign and native. It will come not only from our own colonies, and those of other European nations; but from Poland, Russia, Spain, and Turkey, from the coast of Barbary, from the western and eastern coasts of Africa, from every part of the world, where it still continues to torment and dishonour the human species. It will be transmitted to us in all its various forms, in all the gradations of inventive cruelty: and by an universal reception of slavery, this country, so famous for public liberty, will become the chief seat of private tyranny. . . .

PROPERTIES USUALLY INCIDENT TO SLAVERY.

- Slavery always imports an obligation of perpetual service; an obligation, which only the consent of the master can dissolve.
- It generally gives to the master, an arbitrary power of administering every sort of correction, however inhuman, not immediately affecting the life or limb of the slave: sometimes even these are left exposed to the arbitrary will of the master; or they are protected by fines, and other slight punishments, too inconsiderable to restrain the master's inhumanity.
- It creates an incapacity of acquiring, except for the master's benefit.
- It allows the master to alienate the person of the slave, in the same manner as other property.
- Lastly, it descends from parent to child, with all its severe appendages.

BAD EFFECTS OF SLAVERY.

From this view of the condition of slavery, it will be easy to derive its destructive consequences.

- It corrupts the morals of the master, by freeing him from those restraints with respect to his slave, so necessary for control of the human passions, so beneficial in promoting the practice and confirming the habit of virtue.
- It is dangerous to the master; because his oppression excites implacable resentment and hatred in the slave, and the extreme misery of his condition

continually prompts him to risk the gratification of them, and his situation daily furnishes the opportunity.

- To the slave it communicates all the afflictions of life, without leaving for him scarce any of its pleasures; and it depresses the excellence of his nature, by denying the ordinary means and motives of improvement.
- It is dangerous to the state, by its corruption of those citizens on whom its prosperity depends; and by admitting within it a multitude of persons, who being excluded from the common benefits of the constitution, are interested in scheming its destruction.
- Hence it is, that slavery, in whatever light we view it, may be deemed a most pernicious situation: immediately so, to the unhappy person who suffers under it; finally so, to the master who triumphs in it, and
- to the state which allows it.

Origin of Slavery, and Its General Lawfulness Considered.

The great origin of slavery is captivity in war, though sometimes it has commenced by contract. It has been a question much agitated, whether either of these foundations of slavery is consistent with natural justice. It would be engaging in too large a field of enquiry, to attempt reasoning on the general lawfulness of slavery. I trust too, that the liberty, for which I am contending, does not require such a disquisition; and am impatient to reach that part of my argument, in which I hope to prove slavery reprobated by the law of England as an inconvenient thing.

Here therefore I shall only refer to some of the most eminent writers, who have examined, how far slavery founded on captivity or contract is conformable to the law of nature, and shall just hint at the reasons, which influence their several opinions. The ancient writers suppose the right of killing an enemy vanquished in a just war; and thence infer the right of enslaving him. In this opinion, founded, as I presume, on the idea of punishing the enemy for his injustice, they are followed by

- Albericus Gentilis,
- [Hugo] Grotius,
- [Samuel] Puffendorf,
- [Cornelius van] Bynkershoek [1673-1743], and
- many others.

But a very great writer of our own country, who is now living, controverts the sufficiency of such a consideration. Mr. [John] Locke [1632-1704] has framed another kind of argument against slavery by contract; and the substance of it is, that a right of preserving life is unalienable; that freedom from arbitrary power is essential to the exercise of that right; and therefore, that no man can by compact enslave himself.

Dr. Rutherforth endeavours to answer Mr. Locke's objection, by insisting on various limitations to the despotism of the master; particularly, that he has no right to dispel of the slave's life at pleasure. But the misfortune of this reasoning is, that though the contract cannot justly convey an arbitrary power over the slave's life, yet it generally leaves him without a security against the exercise of that or any other power.

I shall say nothing of slavery by birth; except that the slavery of the child must be unlawful, if that of the parent cannot be justified; and that when slavery is extended to the issue, as it usually is, it may be unlawful as to them, even though it is not so as to their parents. . . .

Decline of Slavery in Europe

At length however it fell into decline in most parts of Europe; and amongst the various causes, which contributed to this alteration, none were probably more effectual, than experience of the disadvantages of slavery; the difficulty of maintaining it; and a persuasion that the cruelty and oppression almost necessarily incident to it were irreconcilable with the pure morality of the Christian dispensation. . . .

It is sufficient here to say, that this great change began in Spain, according to Bodin, about the end of the eighth century [799 A.D.], and was become general before the middle of the fourteenth century [1350 A.D.].

Bartolus, the most famed commentator on the civil law in that period, represents slavery as in disuse, and the succeeding commentators hold much the same language. However, they must be understood with many restrictions and exceptions; and not to mean, that slavery was completely aud universally abolished in Europe. Some modern civilians [laymen], not sufficiently attending to this circumstance rather too hastily reprehend their predecessors for representing slavery as disused in Europe.

The truth is, that the ancient species of slavery by frequent emancipations became greatly diminished in extent; the remnant of it was considerably abated in severity; the disuse of the practice of enslaving captives taken in the wars between Christian powers assisted in preventing the future increase of domestic slavery; and in some countries of Europe, particularly England, a still more effectual method, which I shall explain hereafter, was thought of to perfect the suppression of it.

Revival of Domestic Slavery in America

Such was the expiring state of domestic slavery in Europe at the commencement of the sixteenth century, when the discovery of America and of the western and eastern coasts of Africa gave occasion to the introduction of a new species of slavery. It took its rise from the Portuguese, who, in order to supply the Spaniards with persons able to sustain the fatigue of cultivating their new possessions in America, particularly the islands, opened a trade between Africa and America for the sale of negro slaves. This disgraceful commerce in the human species is said to have begun in the year 1508, when the first importation of negro slaves was made into Hispaniola from the Portuguese settlements on the western coasts of Africa.

In 1540 the emperor Charles the fifth [1519-1556] endeavoured to stop the progress of the negro slavery, by orders that all slaves in the American isles should be made free; and they were accordingly manumitted by Lagasca the governor of the country, on condition of continuing to labour for their masters. But this attempt proved unsuccessful, and on Lagasca's return to Spain domestic slavery revived and flourished as before.

The expedient of having slaves for labour in America was not long peculiar to the Spaniards; being afterwards adopted by the other Europeans, as they acquired possessions there. In consequence of this general practice, negroes are become a very considerable article in the commerce between Africa and America; and domestic slavery has taken so deep a root in most of our own American colonies, as well as in those of other nations, that there is little probability of ever seeing it generally suppressed.

THE ATTEMPT TO INTRODUCE THE SLAVERY OF NEGROES INTO ENGLAND EXAMINED

I shall endeavour to shew, that the law of England never recognized any species of domestic slavery, except the ancient one of villenage* now expired, and has sufficiently provided against the introduction of a new slavery under the name of villenage or any other denomination whatever....

I shall not attempt to follow villenage in the several stages of its decline; it being sufficient here to mention the time of its extinction, which, as all agree, happened about the latter end of Elizabeth's reign or soon after the [1603] accession of James....

...If the law of England would permit the introduction of a slavery commencing out of England, the rules it prescribes for trying the title to a slave would be applicable to such a slavery, but they are not so; and from thence it is evident that the introduction of such a slavery is not permitted by the law of England. — The law of England then excludes every slavery not commencing in England, every slavery though commencing there not being ancient and immemorial....

I insist, that the unlawfulness of introducing a new slavery into England, from our American colonies or from any other country, is deducible from the rules of the English law concerning contracts of service. The law of England will not permit any man to enslave himself by contract. The utmost, which our law allows, is a contract to serve for life; and some perhaps may even doubt the validity of such a contract, there being no determined cases [precedents] directly affirming its lawfulness.

In the reign of Henry the 4th [1399-1413], there is [a precedent] a case of debt, brought by a servant against the master's executors, on a retainer to serve for term of life in peace and war for 100 shillings a year; but it was held, that debt did not lie for want [lack] of a speciality; which, as was agreed, would not have been necessary in the case of a common labourer's salary, because, as the case is explained by Brooke in abridging [reporting] it, the latter is bound to serve by statute....

...It may be asked, why it is that the law should permit the ancient slavery of the villein, and yet disallow a slavery of modern commencement?

* Villanege is a condition in English common law akin to serfdom. A villein, though technically free, was considered to 'belong' to his lord; he was bound to render any service demanded of him by his lord, was not permitted to assert rights against his lord in court, and was unable to dispose of property — Eds.

To this I answer, that villenage sprung up amongst our ancestors in the early and barbarous state of society; that afterwards more humane customs and wiser opinions prevailed, and by their influence rules were established for checking [limiting] the progress of slavery; and that it was thought most prudent to effect this great object, not instantaneously by declaring every slavery unlawful, but gradually by excluding a new race of slaves, and encouraging the voluntary emancipation of the ancient race.

... [I]f the arguments against a new slavery in England are well founded, they reach the king as well as his subjects. If it has been at all times the policy of the law of England not to recognize any slavery but the ancient one of the villein, which is now expired; we cannot consistently attribute to the executive power a prerogative of rendering that policy ineffectual.

It is true, that the law of nations may give a right of retaliating, on an enemy, who enslaves his captives in war; but then the exercise of this right may be prevented or limited by the law of any particular country. A writer of eminence on the law of nations, has a passage very applicable to this subject. His words are, "If the civil law of any nation does not allow of slavery, prisoners of war who are taken by that nation cannot be made slaves." He is justified in his observation not only by the reason of the thing, but by the practice of some nations, where slavery is as unlawful as it is in England.

The Dutch when at war with the Algerines, Tunisians, or Tripolitans, make no scruple of retaliating on their enemies; but slavery not being lawful in their European dominions, they have usually sold their prisoners of war as slaves in Spain, where slavery is still permitted.

To this example I have only to add, that I do not know an instance, in which a prerogative of having captive slaves in England has ever been assumed by the crown; and it being also the policy of our law not to admit a new slavery, there appears neither reason nor fact to suppose the existence of a royal prerogative to introduce it....

It must be agreed, that where the *lex loci* cannot have effect without introducing the thing prohibited in a degree either as great, or nearly as great, as if there was no prohibition, there the greatest inconvenience would ensue from regarding the *lex loc*, and consequently it ought not to prevail. Indeed, by receiving it under such circumstances, the end [purpose] of a prohibition would be frustrated, either entirely or in a very great degree; and so the prohibition of things the most pernicious in their tendency would become vain and fruitless.

And what greater inconveniences can we imagine, than those, which would necessarily result from such an unlimited sacrifice of the municipal law to the law of a foreign country?

I will now apply this general doctrine to the particular case of our own law concerning slavery. Our law prohibits the commencement of domestic slavery in England; because it disapproves of slavery and considers its operation as dangerous and destructive to the whole community.

But would not this prohibition be wholly ineffectual, if slavery could be introduced from a foreign country? In the course of time, though perhaps in a progress less rapid, would not domestic slavery become as general, and be as completely revived in England by introduction from our colonies and from foreign countries, as if it was permitted to revive by commencement here; and would not the same inconveniences follow?

To prevent the revival of domestic slavery effectually, its introduction must be resisted universally, without regard to the place of its commencement; and therefore in the instance of slavery, the *lex loci* must yield to the municipal law....

HARGRAVE'S CONCLUSION.

Upon the whole, the return to the *Habeas Corpus* in the present case, in whatever way it is considered, whether by inquiry into the foundation of Mr. Stewart's right to the person and service of the negro, or by reference to the violent manner in which it has been attempted to enforce that right, will appear equally unworthy of this court's approbation. By condemning the return, the revival of domestic slavery will be rendered as impracticable by introduction from our colonies and from other countries, as it is by commencement here. Such a judgment will be no less conducive to the public advantage, than it will be conformable to natural justice, and to principles and authorities of law; and this court, by effectively obstructing the admission of the new slavery of negroes into England, will in these times reflect as much honour on themselves, as the great judges, their predecessors, formerly acquired, by contributing so uniformly and successfully to the suppression of the old slavery of villenage.

ARGUMENTS OF THE OTHER COUNSEL....

MR. WALLACE'S STATEMENT

Mr. Wallace. The question has been stated, whether the right [to own slaves] can be supported here; or, if it can, whether a course of proceedings at law be not necessary to give effect to the right? It is found in three quarters of the globe, and in part of the fourth. In Asia the whole people; in Africa and America far the greater part; in Europe great numbers of the Russians and Polanders.

As to captivity in war, the Christian princes have been used to give life to the prisoners; and it took rise probably in the Crusades, when they gave them life, and sometimes franchised them, to enlist under the standard of the Cross, against the Mahometans. The right of a conqueror was absolute in Europe, and is in Africa.

The natives are brought from Africa to the West Indies; purchase is made there, not because of positive law, but there being no law against it. It cannot be in consideration by this or any other Court, to see, whether the West India regulations are the best possible; such as they are, while they continue in force as laws, they must be adhered to.

As to England, not permitting slavery, there is no law against it; nor do I find any attempt has been made to prove the existence of one. Villenage itself has all but the name.

DUNNING'S ARGUMENT FOR SHIP CAPTAIN KNOWLES

Mr. Dunning. It is incumbent on me to justify captain Knowles's detainer of the negro; this will be effected, by proving a right in Mr. Stewart; even a supposed one: for till that matter was determined, it were somewhat unaccountable that a negro should depart his service, and put the means out of his power of trying that right to effect, by a flight out of the kingdom.

I will explain what appears to me the foundation of Mr. Stewart's claim. Before the writ of Habeas Corpus issued in the present case, there was, and there still is, a great number of slaves in Africa, (from whence the American plantations are supplied) who are saleable, and in fact sold.

Under all these descriptions is James Sommersett. Mr. Stewart brought him over to England; purposing to return to Jamaica, the negro chose to depart the service, and was stopt and detained by captain Knowles, until his master should set sail and take him away to be sold in Jamaica. . . .

Freedom has been asserted as a natural right, and therefore unalienable and unrestrainable; there is perhaps no branch of this right, but in some at all times, and all places at different times, has been restrained: nor could society otherwise be conceived to exist. For the great benefit of the public and individuals, natural liberty, which consists in doing what one likes, is altered to the doing what one ought.

The gentlemen who have spoke with so much zeal have supposed different ways by which slavery commences; but have omitted one, and rightly, for it would have given a more favourable idea of the nature of that power against which they combat. We are apt (and great authorities support this way of speaking) to call those nations universally, whose internal policies we are ignorant of, barbarians; (thus the Greeks, particularly, styled many nations, whose customs, generally considered, were far more justifiable and commendable than their own:) unfortunately, from calling them barbarians, we are apt to think them so, and draw conclusions accordingly.

There are slaves in Africa by captivity in war, but the number far from great, the country is divided into many small, some great territories, who do, in their wars with one another, use this custom.

There are of these people, men who have a sense of the right and value of freedom, but who imagine that offences against society are punishable justly by the severe law of servitude. For crimes against property, a considerable addition is made to the number of slaves. They have a process by which the quantity of the debt is ascertained, and if all the property of the debtor in goods and chattels is insufficient, he who has thus dissipated all he has besides, is deemed property himself; the proper officer (sheriff we may call him) seizes the insolvent, and disposes of him as a slave. We don't contend under which of these the unfortunate man in question is, but his condition was that of servitude in Africa; the law of the land of that country disposed of him as property, with all the consequences of transmission and alienation; the statutes of the British Legislature confirm this condition, and thus he was a slave both in law and fact.

I do not aim at proving these points; not because they want evidence, but because they have not been controverted, to my recollection, and are, I think, incapable of denial. . . .

Let me take notice, neither the air of England is too pure for a slave to breathe in, nor the laws of England have rejected servitude. Villenage in this country is said to be worn out; the propriety of the expression strikes me a little. Are the laws not existing by which it was created? A matter of more curiosity than use, it is, to enquire when that set of people ceased. The Statute of Tenures did not however abolish villenage in gross; it left persons of that condition in the same state as before; if their descendants are all dead, the gentlemen are right to say the subject of those laws is gone, but not the law; if the subject revives, the law will lead the subject. If the Statute of Charles the 2d ever be repealed, the law of villenage revives in its full force....

It would be a great surprize, and some inconvenience, if a foreigner bringing over a servant, as soon as he got hither, must take care of his carriage, his horse, and himself, in whatever method he might have the luck to invent. He must find his way to London on foot. He tells his servant, Do this; the servant replies, Before I do it, I think fit to inform you, sir, the first step on this happy land sets all men on a perfect level; you are just as much obliged to obey my commands.

Thus neither superior, or inferior, both go without their dinner.

We should find singular comfort, on entering the limits of a foreign country, to be thus at once devested of all attendance and all accommodation. The gentlemen have collected more reading than I have leisure to collect, or industry (I must own) if I had leisure: very laudable pains have been taken, and very ingenious, in collecting the sentiments of other countries, which I shall not much regard, as affecting the point or jurisdiction of this Court....

LORD MANSFIELD [for the court]. The question is, if the owner had a right to detain the slave, for the sending of him over to be sold in Jamaica. In five or six cases of this nature, I have known it to be accommodated by agreement between the parties: on its first coming before me, I strongly recommended it here.

But if the parties will have it decided, we must give our opinion. Compassion will not, on the one hand, nor inconvenience on the other, be to decide; but the law: in which the difficulty will be principally from the inconvenience on both sides. Contract for sale of a slave is good here; the sale is a matter to which the law properly and readily attaches, and will maintain the price according to the agreement.

But here the person of the slave himself is immediately the object of enquiry; which makes a very material difference. The now question is, Whether any dominion, authority or coercion can be exercised in this country, on a slave according to the American laws? The difficulty of adopting the relation, without adopting it in all its consequences, is indeed extreme; and yet, many of those consequences are absolutely contrary to the municipal law of England.

We have no authority to regulate the conditions in which law shall operate. On the other hand, should we think the coercive power cannot be exercised: it is now about 50 years since the opinion given by two of the greatest men of their own or any times, (since which no contract has been brought to trial, between the masters and slaves;) the service performed by the slaves without wages, is a clear indication they did not think themselves free by coming hither....

Mr. Stewart advances no claims on contract; he rests his whole demand on a right to the negro as slave, and mentions the purpose of detainure to be the sending of him over to be sold in Jamaica.

If the parties will have judgment, *'fiat justitia, ruat cœlum;'* let justice be done whatever the consequence....

The Court is greatly obliged to the gentlemen of the Bar who have spoke on the subject; and by whose care and abilities so much has been effected, that the rule of decision will be reduced to a very easy compass. I can not omit to express particular happiness in seeing young men, just called to the Bar, have been able so much to profit by their reading.

I think it right the matter should stand over [be postponed]; and if we are called on for a decision, proper notice shall be given.

Trinity Term, [Monday], June 22, 1772, 98 ER 510.

LORD MANSFIELD. On the part of Sommerset, the case which we gave notice should be decided this day, the Court now proceeds to give its opinion. . . .

. . . The only question before us is, whether the cause on the return is sufficient. If it is, the negro must be remanded; if it is not, he must be discharged.

Accordingly, the return states, that the slave departed and refused to serve; whereupon he was kept, to be sold abroad.

So high an act of dominion must be recognized by the law of the country where it is used. The power of a master over his slave has been exceedingly different, in different countries.

The state of slavery is of such a nature, that it is incapable of being introduced on any reasons, moral or political, but only by positive law, which preserves its force long after the reasons, occasion, and time itself from whence it was created, is erased from memory.

It is so odious, that nothing can be suffered to support it, but positive law.

Whatever inconveniences, therefore, may follow from the decision, I cannot say this case is allowed or approved by the law of England; and therefore the black must be discharged.

Suzanne Miers, Slavery and the Slave Trade as International Issues 1890-1939

19(2) Slavery and Abolition 16-37 (1998) (footnotes omitted)

HUMANITARIANISM AND DIPLOMACY 1890-1919

Slavery became a major international concern from the day in 1807 when the British outlawed their own slave trade [with the Abolition of the Slave Trade Act adopted subsequent to *Sommersetts* case]. Once this step was taken it was clearly in Britain's interest to get rival colonial and maritime powers to follow suit in order to prevent this lucrative trade from passing into foreign hands and providing foreign colonies with needed manpower. In 1815 the British tried to get other powers to outlaw it and even to establish a permanent committee to monitor progress. However, their rivals saw this as an attack on their commerce and on their colonies. They would only agree to append a declaration to the Treaty of Vienna [ending the Napoleonic wars] proclaiming that the slave trade was "repugnant to the principles of humanity and universal morality."* This was an important step in the direction of the present human rights movement, but it had no practical value. There followed a long and bitter campaign, during which, by bribery and cajolery, the British secured a network of treaties giving the Royal Navy unique powers to search and seize suspected slavers flying the flags of other nations. As the result of this campaign, the British came to view themselves as the leaders of an international 'crusade' against slavery, the burden of which they had

* Declaration Relative to the Universal Abolition of the Slave Trade, Feb. 8, 1815, 63 Consol. T.S. 473 (Treaty of Vienna, Annex XV), para. 1. — Eds.

borne almost alone. British statesmen recognized that the cause was popular with the electorate and that Parliament would sanction expenditure and high handed action against foreign countries if these were presented as anti-slavery measures. Thus, the 'crusade' could often be used to further other interests – a fact not lost on rival powers....

By the 1870s the Atlantic slave traffic was a thing of the past. The trade, however, still flourished in Africa and there was an active export traffic to the Muslim world. Attention was forcefully drawn to this by European traders and missionaries penetrating ever further into the interior as the European colonial powers began to partition the coast in the 1880s. Africans took up arms against the intruders and by 1888 the French Cardinal Lavigerie found his missions on the Great Lakes under attack. In response, he launched an anti-slavery 'crusade' of his own, with papal blessing, calling for volunteers to combat this scourge in the heart of Africa.

The British, anxious to retain their leadership of the anti-slavery movement and worried at the prospect of unofficial crusaders rampaging around Africa, persuaded Leopold II of Belgium, ruler of the Congo Independent State, to invite the leading maritime and colonial powers, together with the Ottoman Empire, Persia and Zanzibar, to Brussels to discuss concerted action against the export of slaves from Africa. The colonial powers, led by the wily king, proceeded to negotiate a treaty against the African slave trade on land, as well as at sea, and carefully designed it to serve their territorial and commercial ambitions.

The Brussels Act of 1890[†] was a humanitarian instrument in so far as it reaffirmed that 'native welfare' was an international responsibility; and bound signatories to prevent slave raiding and trading, to repatriate or resettle freed and fugitive slaves, and to cut off the free flow of arms to the slaving areas. But it had important practical advantages for the colonial rulers. By binding them to end the trade in slaves and arms, it not only dealt a blow to African resistance, but was an attempt to prevent unscrupulous colonial administrations from attracting trade to their territories by allowing commerce in these lucrative products. By stating that the best means of attacking the traffic was to establish colonial administrations in the interior of Africa, to protect missionaries and trading companies, and even to initiate Africans into agricultural and industrial labour, it put an anti-slavery guise on the colonial occupation and exploitation of Africa.... Finally, the Act broke new ground by establishing the first international supervisory machinery — bureaux in Brussels and Zanzibar — for the exchange of information on the slave traffic and on the antislavery legislation of signatory powers.

It was the first comprehensive international treaty against the slave trade, but it dealt only with the African traffic....

The League of Nations and Slavery

By 1919 the occupation of the African coast by European powers had reduced the export of slaves to a small smuggling traffic to Arabia and the Persian Gulf. Slave raiding had been eradicated in all but the remotest areas of Africa. Slave

† General Act for the Repression of African Slave Trade, signed at Brussels on July 2, 1890, T.S. 383. — Eds.

dealing had been outlawed and in most colonial possessions slavery no longer had a legal status. The Brussels Act had lapsed during the first World War and in 1919 the colonial powers had no desire to renew it. They wished to be free of its commercial clauses and believed that the slave traffic was now so small that it was no longer needed. To the regret of the humanitarians, they abrogated it. Instead a single clause was inserted into one of the treaties signed at St. Germain-en-Laye in 1919 binding signatories to try to secure "the complete suppression of *slavery in all its forms*"‡ as well as to end the slave trade. Moreover, article 23 of the Covenant of the newly established League of Nations bound members to 'secure and maintain fair and humane conditions of labour and the just treatment of the native inhabitants under their control'. This enlarged the scope of the international obligation to include the suppression of slavery and other abuses of 'native labour' and extended it beyond Africa. Significantly, however, no time limit for action was laid down and no definition of 'fair and humane conditions of labour' was attempted. The major African colonial powers wanted no international supervision of their colonial policies. They could not avoid it in the case of the former German colonies, which were now divided between Britain, France and Belgium to be administered as League Mandates, supervised by the Permanent Mandates Commission. But they were determined not to accept any scrutiny of their policies in other territories. They doubtless hoped that the slavery clauses in the treaty of St. Germain and the League Covenant were a sufficient sop to allay whatever remained of European and American interest in slavery.

. . . Finding the British government unwilling to take [further action within the League, the Anti-Slavery Society] persuaded the New Zealand delegate to the League, Sir Arthur Steel-Maitland — a British member of parliament — to raise the question of slavery at the League Assembly in September 1922. As a result, in an entirely new departure, the League launched an investigation into slavery everywhere and asked all members for reports on their own territories. This widening of its scope was a vain attempt to disarm Portuguese suspicions that the inquiry was really directed against their oppressive labour policy, which [the Anti-Slavery Society] had long attacked. To [the Society's] consternation Britain, the only power with eye-witness accounts from southwest Ethiopia as well as the Hijaz, ducked the whole issue by simply reporting that there was no slavery in the British Empire. When pressed in Parliament, the government published a White Book to show that the slave trade in Ethiopia was declining. [The Society] marshaled [its] cohorts for a debate in the House of Lords, and, in July 1923, the Foreign Secretary was forced to promise to send for up-to-date information for the League. Both the peers and the press reminded him of Britain's traditional role as leader of the anti-slavery movement. The message was clear — the cause was still popular. . . .

THE TEMPORARY SLAVERY COMMISSION (TSC) 1924-25

Meanwhile, the League, set in motion by the resolution of 1922 and finding little response to its appeal for information, appointed the Temporary Slavery

‡ Convention revising the General Act of Berlin, February 26, 1885, and the General Act and Declaration of Brussels, July 2, 1890, signed at Saint-Germain-en-Laye, September 10, 1919, 8 L.N.T.S 27, art.11. — Eds.

Commission in 1924 to inquire into slavery worldwide. This body, carefully designed by the colonial powers to have no bite and very little bark, set the pattern for those that followed.... [I]t was limited to eight experts on slavery — private individuals appointed by the League, not by their governments, hence theoretically 'independent'. But six were nationals of the leading colonial powers — Britain, France, Portugal, Italy, Belgium and Holland... all of these but the Italian were either serving or retired colonial officials....

...The colonial governments, fearful of damaging revelations, and determined not to allow any supervision of their colonial administrations, insisted that the TSC be both temporary and purely advisory. It had no power to launch investigations and could only take evidence from nongovernmental organizations (NGOs) approved by their own governments. States had to be able to reply to accusations against them before these could be considered. Finally, to limit its only real weapon — publicity — it met in private and the League decided whether or not to publish its reports which, of course, were carefully vetted by the imperial governments.

Circumscribed as it was, the TSC went much further than the colonial powers, including the British, wanted. Led by [the British and International Labour Organization experts], under the rubric 'slavery in all its forms', it condemned serfdom, the sale of children for domestic service, concubinage, and slave dealing under guise of adoption or marriage. In the case of pawning (the pledging of a person for credit) and peonage or debt-slavery, it recommended restricting the amount of labour that could be demanded for the debt, and that the debt be extinguished on the death of the debtor. It discussed child betrothal, inheritance of widows, dowry payments and even polygyny, but shied off condemning them outright. As for slavery, it merely recommended abolition of its legal status so that those slaves who wished to remain with their owners could do so, but it urged that slaves be told that they could leave.

To the surprise of the Foreign Office it also dealt with forced labour. Claiming that this often deteriorated into slavery, it recommended that it be limited to essential public works and be adequately paid, that administrators should not be allowed to recruit labour for private enterprises, and chiefs should not be allowed to use it for themselves. Finally it suggested that the protection of indigenous labour should be taken on by the [International Labour Organization. The British and ILO experts] had hoped to draw up a 'charter' of rights for native labour but objections from the colonial governments killed the idea....

Its most fruitful recommendation was that the League negotiate a convention against the slave trade, slavery and forced labour. This unwelcome proposal might have died had [the British expert] not forced the hand of the British government by sending them a draft treaty. He opened up a veritable Pandora's box. The Foreign Office was sympathetic — only a few weeks before the House of Lords had again complained that Britain was not playing its traditional role — but his proposals sent alarm signals through other departments.... It was decided, however, that some action was needed to placate the humanitarians and to ensure that no other power stole Britain's thunder as leader of the anti-slavery movement. An interdepartmental committee, therefore, hammered out a watered down version of the treaty, which was presented to the League. The anti-slavery lobby...demanded more, and other colonial powers demanded less than the British asked for, but finally the Slavery Convention of 1926 was signed.

The Slavery Convention of 1926**

This treaty, which is still in force, was the first international instrument specifically directed against slavery. . . .

Slavery, vaguely defined as 'the status of a person over whom all or any of the rights attaching to ownership are exercised', was to be suppressed 'in all its forms'. But the forms were not spelt out and suppression was to be undertaken only 'progressively and as soon as possible'. Thus even Ethiopia, where slavery was still legal, could sign the Convention. New ground, however, was broken by a clause which declared that forced labour was only to be used for public purposes and had to be adequately remunerated and performed from home. Again much of the force was lost because its use for private enterprises was to be phased out 'progressively and as soon as possible'. Significantly, the Convention contained no machinery for enforcement. France and Italy would not even accept a commitment to send reports to the League. All that could be agreed was that each member should keep the League informed of its anti-slavery regulations.

Nevertheless, the Convention had important repercussions. The League invited the ILO to take action against forced labour resulting in the Forced Labour Convention of 1930†† — the first in a series of agreements for the protection of indigenous labour. As for slavery, publicity surrounding the meetings of the TSC and the discussion of the Convention kept the question before the public for several years. In the British empire this had an impact at the grassroots level. Colonial administrations were ordered to review their laws to ensure that slavery no longer had any legal status. Hence the spate of new ordinances issued at this time in Sierra Leone, where slaves were now told of their rights, and in the Gold Coast and a number of other territories. In Sudan more vigorous action was taken to end slavery and to resettle fugitive slaves from Ethiopia. In many cases these new laws simply reaffirmed existing ones, while in others results were meager. In Bechuanaland, for instance, administrators had refused to admit that there was any servitude. Now they had to agree that by the League definition the domination of hunters and gatherers by pastoral groups was indeed a form of slavery. But only minimal action was taken. . . . In most of Britain's African possessions, however, more uniform and stronger laws were now on the statute books, even if they were not always enforced.

[After pointing out that practices in slavery continued in much of the world despite the Convention, the author goes on to discuss the mechanisms developed by the League to promote compliance with the Convention through information gathering and review of state reports. These include the Committee of Experts on Slavery and its successor, the Advisory Committee on Slavery, which met periodically and issued recommendations until 1938, when the League itself was about to expire under the pressures of the impending war.]

** Slavery Convention, September 25, 1926, entered into force March 9, 1927. 60 L.N.T.S. 253. The Convention was subsequently amended to refer to the United Nations rather than the League of Nations through the Protocol amending the Slavery Convention, approved by U.N. General Assembly resolution 794 (VIII) of October 23, 1953, entered into force December 7, 1953, 182 U.N.T.S. 51. — Eds.

†† Convention (No. 29) Concerning Forced or Compulsory Labour, International Labour Conference, June 28, 1930, entered into force May 1, 1932. — Eds.

The Impact of the League Committees

In the realm of human rights the League of Nations committees have an important place. They gave notice that slavery was under attack and helped to get the question of forced labour and the protection of native labour taken up by the ILO. In practical terms the TSC resulted in the negotiation of the Slavery Convention of 1926 — the first international instrument specifically directed against slavery. Because of the insistence of the committee, this convention also condemned practices 'analogous to slavery'. Although these were not spelt out in the treaty, the TSC report described them. These now, therefore, became international questions. In 1956 the United Nations negotiated a Supplementary Convention on slavery[‡‡] and related institutions which identified them. As chattel slavery gradually died out — outlawed everywhere by 1970, although not completely ended — so these became the main focus of international attention. Today they are discussed annually at the United Nations Working Group on Contemporary Forms of Slavery which has met every year since 1975.

Comments and Questions

1. The prohibition of slavery and the international slave trade through a series of treaties beginning in the late nineteenth century eventually developed into an international norm that is now widely identified to be one of jus cogens, that is, a norm binding on all states — whether or not they have subscribed to a particular treaty or custom — and from which states cannot derogate. See *Restatement (Third) of the Foreign Relations Law of the United States* §702 cmt. n (1987) (slavery is a jus cogens violation of international law whether committed by a state or a private party under color of law). For a discussion of jus cogens norms in international law generally, see Mark W. Janis, *An Introduction to International Law* 61, 62-67 (4th ed. 2003).

2. Well before the anti-slavery treaties, the Articles of the Treaties of Peace, signed at Munster and Osnabruck in Westphalia on October 24, 1648, ended the Thirty Years War between Protestant and Catholic areas of Europe. While the Treaty of Westphalia is often cited as the beginning of the nation-state system and modern international law, the treaty is also significant for various human rights provisions. First, the treaty declared an amnesty for all offenses committed during the "troubles" (Article II) and provided for restitution of property and ecclesiastical or lay status (Articles VI-XXXIV). Second, freedom of contract was supported by annulling those contracts procured under duress and threats. Freedom of movement and commerce and the right to legal protection also were included. Most importantly, Article XXVIII protected religious freedom, providing:

> That those of the Confession of Augsburg, and particularly the Inhabitants of Oppenheim, shall be put in possession again of their Churches, and Ecclesiastical Estates, as they were in the Year 1624. As also that all others of the said Confession of Augsburg,

‡‡ Supplementary Convention on the Abolition of Slavery, the Slavery Trade, and Institutions and Practices Similar to Slavery, adopted by a Conference of plenipotentiaries convened by Economic and Social Council resolution 608 (XXI) of April 30, 1956 at Geneva, September 7, 1956, entered into force April 30, 1957, 266 U.N.T.S. 3. — Eds.

> who shall demand it, shall have the free Exercise of their Religion, as well in public Churches at the appointed Hours, as in private in their own Houses, or in others chosen for this purpose by their Ministers, or by those of their Neighbours, preaching the Word of God.

The Westphalian Treaty of Osnabruch with Sweden contained a similar provision. Pope Innocent X promptly declared null and void the articles in the treaties of Westphalia relating to religious matters, but a limited principle of religious liberty was established, as was the link between peace and respect for human rights.

3. Many states abolished slavery through domestic legislation or jurisprudence in the years after the English precedent in the Sommersett case, but the last state in the Western Hemisphere to legally ban slavery, Brazil, did not do so until 1898. Taking into account state practice and the progressive adoption of international instruments, at what point could it be said that the slave trade and then slavery became a violation of customary international law? Note that Japan has refused to give an official apology or make reparations to the so-called comfort women, who were forced into brothels during World War II, arguing that there was no customary law against slavery and rejecting the assertion that the women were de facto slaves. See Comm. H.R., Report of Special Rapporteur Gay McDougall, UN Doc. E/CN.4/Sub.2/1998/13, para. 4 (1998). Japan had ratified in 1925 the International Convention for the Suppression of the Traffic in Women and Children (1921); the International Agreement for the Suppression of the White Slave Traffic (1904); and the International Convention for the Suppression of the White Slave Traffic of 1910 as reaffirmed in 1921. But Japan was not a party to the 1926 Convention to Suppress the Slave Trade and Slavery, 46 Stat. 2183, 60 L.N.T.S. 253.

Basing its claims on ILO agreements, the Federation of Korean Trade Unions requested the International Labor Organization to rule that "comfort women" were forced laborers. The ILO Committee of Experts agreed, despite Japanese contentions that the agreements did not apply to "colonial territories" such as occupied Korea. See ILO, Report of the Committee of Experts on the Application of Conventions and Recommendations, Forced Labour Convention, 1930 (No. 29), Observations (2000). Does it matter whether a practice is denominated forced labor or slavery? How would you distinguish one from the other?

4. The materials above identify philosophical and religious precepts, as well as economic and political considerations, that converged to generate and provide traction to the anti-slavery movement. It is apparent that the dominant white populations of both Great Britain and the northern American states eventually came to agree on an essentially moral objection to slavery, whether from secular philosophical or religious notions of justice, an objection that was obviously shared by blacks who were slaves or descended from slaves. This moral position coincided with conditions that diminished the appeal of slavery to the economic or political self-interest of the dominant elites. Do you think that moral objection to slavery would have succeeded in shifting dominant opinion without the economic and political factors that cut against or were at least neutral toward slavery? Did moral objections offset competing economic and political factors to encourage the shift in dominant opinion? In examining the end of segregation in the southern United States in the mid-twentieth century, Derrick Bell advances an "interest convergence theory," which holds that non-dominant groups are only likely to be

successful in achieving major social change when that change also directly or indirectly serves elite self-perceived material interests. See Derrick A. Bell, Jr., *Race, Racism, and American Law* 212-214 (3d ed. 1992). How, if at all, does this notion illuminate the process of abolition?

5. At the height of the abolitionist movement, leading moral and political philosophers of the time, religious leaders, community organizations, the media, and black activists all articulated the moral objection to slavery in one way or another. As Suzanne Miers' piece shows, the efforts of such nongovernmental actors in Great Britain, in particular, had a political impact that was felt internationally and that influenced British foreign policy against slavery to be implemented with more resolve than it otherwise would likely have been. What was the source of the power or influence of these nongovernmental actors? What lessons about the role of nongovernmental actors can be drawn from this example of international human rights norm-building, an issue to which the present book will return frequently?

6. Slavery in the United States was not abolished until after a bloody civil war. The economic and political factors that had made slavery undesirable in the northern American states and Great Britain did not simultaneously have the same impact in the southern American states, where slavery remained legal. See Robert William Fogel, *Without Consent or Contract: The Rise and Fall of American Slavery* 34-40 (1989). The prevailing thinking in the South, including that based on theology, continued to defend slavery as moral. See Drew Gilpin Faust, *The Creation of Confederate Nationalism: Ideology and Identity in the Civil War South* (1988); Larry E. Tise, *Proslavery: A History Of The Defense Of Slavery In America, 1701-1840* (1987). The major southern religious denominations outwardly defended slavery, including, for example, the Southern Baptists, who in 1995 recognized their historical role in perpetuating slavery and discrimination and issued a request for "forgiveness." See Southern Baptist Convention, Resolution on Racial Reconciliation on the 150th Anniversary of the Southern Baptist Convention (June 1995). It was not until after the Civil War and the effective domestic prohibition of slavery throughout the United States and most other countries that slavery became illegal under international treaties. What does this say about the ability of international law to impose human rights standards where those standards are not already part of a social consensus or are not already part of domestic law?

7. Reparations for slavery in the United States have been claimed and offered since well before emancipation in 1865. In 1774, Thomas Paine proposed reparations for the injuries caused by "the wickedness of the slave trade," Archive of Thomas Paine, Thomas Paine: African Slavery in America, *http://www.mediapro.net/cdadesign/paine/afri.html*. For more recent proposals, see Bruno Bittker, *The Case for Black Reparations* (1973) and Randall Robinson, *The Debt: What America Owes to Blacks* (2000). Between 1890 and 1917, over 600,000 of the 4 million emancipated slaves in the United States applied for pensions from the government on the basis that their labor subsidized the wealth of the nation. They formed the Ex-slave Mutual Relief, Bounty and Pension Association and lobbied without success for 26 years. See Christopher Hitchens, "Debt of Honor," in *Should America Pay? Slavery and the Raging Debate on Reparations* 171 n.12 (Raymond A. Winbush ed., 2003). At the end of the U.S. Civil War there were about 4.5 million slaves of African origin in the United States who were promised 40 acres of land and a mule (the phrase and the promise come from General William Tecumseh Sherman's Special Field Order No. 15 of January 16, 1865),

but instead were subjected to disenfranchisement and de jure discrimination during the following century. Issues of race continue to divide people in the United States, where the descendents of slaves today number about 35 million persons. Many among these descendants continue to seek redress, e.g., by filing claims against individuals and companies for an accounting of their profits and assets acquired with slave labor. See Vern E. Smith, *Debating the Wages of Slavery*, Newsweek, Aug. 27, 2001, at 20. U.S. Congressman John Conyers first introduced a Reparations Study Bill (H.R. 40) in 1989 and has renewed the proposal in each subsequent session of Congress. Are reparations required or appropriate? See Chapters 5 and 9, pages *infra*.

8. Despite treaty and customary international law against slavery, the practice continues in some regions of the world and has taken on new forms. On contemporary forms of slavery, including human trafficking, see David Weissbrodt and Anti-Slavery International, Abolishing Slavery and Its Contemporary Forms, UN Doc. HR/PUB/02/4 (2002). Ethical, strategic, and legal issues arise for human rights activists and nongovernmental organizations when confronted with modern incidents of slavery. One group in Sudan has been severely criticized for buying the freedom of slaves. Is this a legitimate means to emancipate the oppressed, or does it constitute complicity in maintaining the market for human beings?

III. The Philosophical Underpinnings of Human Rights

A. *Natural Law*

The right of every human being not to be enslaved is now firmly entrenched in international law. But, as we have seen, this human right was asserted well before it became proscribed by treaties, international custom, or generally accepted international legal principles. Characteristic of human rights discourse, this assertion was grounded in theories of justice or religious conviction that did not depend at their inception on legal authority emanating from the acts of states but that rather served to challenge that legal authority.

Appeals of this type to theories or notions of justice as "higher authority" are a core element of contemporary human rights discourse. Such appeals also are central to the natural law tradition, which had strong roots in international law even before the anti-slavery movement. Natural law theory and methodology was at the foundation of the work of early theorists associated with the beginnings of modern international law. These same theorists are often credited with introducing human rights in international law through their examination long ago of the rights of indigenous peoples.

S. James Anaya, Indigenous Peoples in International Law

16-19 (2d ed. 2004) (endnotes omitted)

The advent of European exploration and conquest in the Western Hemisphere following the arrival of Christopher Columbus brought on questions of the first order regarding the relationship between Europeans and the indigenous peoples they encountered. Within a frame of thinking traditionally linked to the rise of modern international law, prominent European theorists questioned the legality and morality of claims to the "New World" and of the ensuing, often brutal, settlement patterns. Enduring figures in this discussion were the Dominican clerics Bartolome de las Casas (1474-1566) and Francisco de Vitoria (1486-1547). De las Casas gained notoriety as an ardent defender of the people indigenous to the Western Hemisphere who became known to the world as (the other) Indians. De las Casas, having spent several years as a Roman Catholic missionary among the Indians, gave a contemporaneous account of the Spanish colonization and settlement, vividly describing the enslavement and massacre of indigenous people in the early sixteenth century in his *History of the Indies*. De las Casas was particularly critical of the Spanish *encomienda* system, which granted Spanish conquerors and colonists parcels of lands and the right to the labor of the Indians living on them.

Francisco de Vitoria, primary professor of theology at the University of Salamanca, joined de las Casas in confirming the essential humanity of the Indians of the Western Hemisphere. Never having traveled across the Atlantic, however, Vitoria was less concerned with bringing to light Spanish abuses against the Indians than with establishing the governing normative and legal parameters. Vitoria held that the Indians possessed certain original autonomous powers and entitlements to land, which the Europeans were bound to respect. At the same time, he methodically set forth the grounds on which Europeans could be said validly to acquire Indian lands or assert authority over them. Vitoria's lectures on the Indians established him among the often cited founders of international law. His prescriptions for European encounters with indigenous peoples of the Western Hemisphere contributed to the development of a system of principles and rules governing encounters among all peoples of the world. Vitoria's influence on later theorists is evident in the seventeenth-century work of Hugo Grotius, the most prominent of the "fathers" of international law.

The early European jurisprudence concerned with indigenous peoples and associated with the early development of international law was the legacy of medieval European ecclesiastical humanism. This jurisprudence perceived a normative order independent of and higher than the positive law or decisions of temporal authority. Conceptions about the source of higher authority, characterized as natural or divine law, varied. For Vitoria and other Spanish school theorists, God figured prominently as the source of legal authority, and law merged with theology. Grotius moved toward a secular characterization of the law of nature, defining it as a "dictate of right reason" in conformity with the social nature of human beings. This perceived higher authority, whatever its source, provided the jurisprudential grounds for theorists to conceive of and examine norms from a fundamentally humanist, moral perspective, and to withhold the imprimatur of law from acts of earthly sovereigns found to violate the moral code. Thus the early international law theorists were prepared to confront official practices and declare unlawful even the acts of monarchs when these acts were at odds with the perceived natural law. Further, the naturalist theorists viewed the law applying to sovereigns as part of an integrated normative order encompassing all levels of human interaction....

Within this historical jurisprudential frame, the threshold question for determining the rights and status of the American Indians was whether they were rational human beings. In his published lectures, *On the Indians Lately Discovered* (1532), Vitoria answered this question in the affirmative. He surmised that

> the Indians are not of unsound mind, but have, according to their kind, the use of reason. This is clear, because there is a certain method in their affairs, for they have polities which are orderly arranged and they have definite marriage and magistrates, overlords, laws, and workshops and a system of exchange, all of which call for the use of reason; they also have a kind of religion.

From this premise, Vitoria rejected the view that papal donation to the Spanish monarchs provided a sufficient and legitimate basis for Spanish rule over Indian lands in the Western Hemisphere. Pope Alexander VI had purported to grant the Spanish monarchs all territories discovered by their envoys that were not already under the jurisdiction of Christian rulers. And the Spanish monarchy had viewed this donation as establishing legal title to New World lands, in addition to entrusting the Spanish crown with the mission of converting Indians to Christianity. Invoking precepts informed by "Holy Scripture," Vitoria held that the Indians of the Americas were the true owners of their lands, with "dominion in both public and private matters." Neither emperor nor pope, he said, possessed lordship over the whole world. Further, Vitoria maintained that discovery of the Indians' lands alone could not confer title in the Spaniards "anymore than if it had been they who had discovered us."

While unambiguously rejecting title by discovery or papal grant, Vitoria found more palatable the argument that the Spaniards could legitimately assume authority over Indian lands for the Indians' own benefit. Although Vitoria found the Indians sufficiently rational to possess original rights and dominion over lands, he entertained the view that they

> are unfit to found or administer a lawful State up to the standard required by human and civil claims. Accordingly they have no proper laws nor magistrates, and are not even capable of controlling their family affairs; they are without any literature or arts, not only the liberal arts, but the mechanical arts also; they have no careful agriculture and no artisans; and they lack many other conveniences, yea necessaries, of human life. It might, therefore, be maintained that in their own interests the sovereigns of Spain might undertake the administration of their country, providing them with prefects and governors for their towns, and might even give them new lords, so long as this was clearly for their benefit.

Vitoria pondered this view with ambivalence. He said, "I dare not affirm it at all, nor do I entirely condemn it." Nonetheless, the argument articulated but not adopted by Vitoria to justify Spanish administration over Indian lands was a precursor to the trusteeship doctrine later adopted and acted upon by nineteenth-century states. Of more generally foreboding significance, implicit in Vitoria's pejorative characterization of American Indians, was the measurement of cultural expression and social organization by the European standard: Although they met some standard of rationality sufficient to possess rights, the Indians could be characterized as "unfit" because they failed to conform to the European forms of civilization with which Vitoria was familiar.

Against the backdrop of this Eurocentric bias, Vitoria ultimately constructed a theory of just war to justify Spanish claims to Indian lands in the absence of Indian consent. Within the early naturalist frame, Indians not only had rights but obligations as well. Accordingly to Vitoria, under the Roman *jus gentium*, which he viewed as either "natural law or . . . derived from natural law," Indians were bound to allow foreigners to travel to their lands, trade among them, and proselytize in favor of Christianity. In his lecture, *On the Indians, or On the Law of War Made by the Spaniards on the Barbarians*, Vitoria concluded that the Indians' persistent interference in Spanish efforts to carry out these activities could lead to "just" war and conquest. Vitoria counseled, however, against sham assertions of "imaginary causes of war."

Thus Vitoria articulated a duality in the normative construct deemed applicable to European contact with non-European indigenous peoples. On the one hand, the American Indians were held to have rights by virtue of their essential humanity. On the other hand, the Indians could lose their rights through conquest following a "just" war, and the criteria for determining whether a war was "just" were grounded in a European value system. The essential elements of this normative duality were advanced by other important European theorists of the period associated with the beginnings of international law, including Francisco Suarez (1548-1617), Domingo de Soto (1494-1560), Balthasar Ayala (1548-1584), and Alberico Gentilis (1552-1608).

Writing a century after Vitoria, Grotius continued in this vein, although without specifically addressing the rights of American Indians. In his famous treatise, *On the Law of War and Peace* (1625), Grotius, like Vitoria, rejected title by discovery as to all lands inhabited by humans, "even though the occupant may be wicked, may hold wrong views about God, or may be dull of wit. For discovery applies to those things which belong to no one." Further, Grotius affirmed that the ability to enter into treaty relationships is a necessary consequence of the natural rights of *all* peoples, including "strangers to the true religion": "According to the law of nature this is no degree a matter of doubt. For the right to enter treaties is so common to all men that it does not admit of a distinction arising from religion." Grotius likewise endorsed the concept of just war, but in keeping with his secularized conception of the law of nature, he discarded the Christian mission as alone constituting grounds for war or conquest. Grotius identified three broad "justifiable causes" for war: "defence, recovery of property, and punishment."

As illustrated by de las Casas, Vitoria, and Grotius, in its classic form the "natural law approach begins with the assumption that there are natural laws, both theological and metaphysical, which confer certain particular rights upon individual human beings. These rights find their authority either in divine will or in specified metaphysical absolutes." Myers S. McDougal et al., *Human Rights and World Public Order* 68 (1980). Especially in its classical form, the natural law tradition is often criticized for its propensity to being captured by a particular religious or cultural perspective, as appears to be the case in Vitoria's assessment of the rights and status of American Indians. Vitoria was able to perceive in the indigenous people of "newly discovered" lands certain inherent rights based on their prior occupancy of those lands, but the same body of natural law that gave rise to those rights was deemed to limit and condition them within a religious and cultural perspective that, according to Professor Anaya, ultimately favored the non-indigenous discoverers. Assuming that Vitoria's ultimate conclusions about the rights and status of indigenous peoples in the Americas were flawed under today's standards of justice, did Vitoria's reasoning and analysis on this subject nonetheless contribute to international human rights? In what way was Vitoria's method of reasoning similar to that invoked by many who challenged the validity of slavery?

B. *Legal Postivism*

The natural law tradition, as well as the analytical method by which human rights proponents of diverse backgrounds converge on common fundamental demands, contrasts with legal positivism. Positivism focuses attention on the state as the relevant source of authority and thus sees norms only or mainly as the positive enactments of states. Legal positivism came to dominate international legal theory in the late nineteenth and early twentieth centuries, as reflected in, e.g., John Westlake, *Chapters on the Principles of International Law* (1894); William E. Hall, A *Treatise on International Law* (Alexander P. Higgins ed., 8th ed. 1924); and Charles C. Hyde, *International Law Chiefly as Applied and Interpreted by the United States* (1922).

An extensive body of human rights norms can now be found in numerous treaties adopted by states or can be deemed to have been consented to by states through custom, as this book demonstrates (see especially Chapters 2 and 3). Hence, it is now possible to embrace human rights from even a purely legal positivist perspective; for example, the rights of children as articluated in the Convention on the Rights of Child have now been accepted as legally binding by the 192 parties to that treaty.

Nonetheless, as we shall see throughout this coursebook, the modern scope of human rights engages not just states but also international institutions, nongovernmental organizations, individual claimants, and other actors; human rights practice involves much more than the straightforward application of existing legal texts or readily discernible custom. Human rights activists continue to propose new human rights norms, and the line between what the law *is* and what the law *ought* to be is often blurred. As a result, human rights discourse inevitably draws heavily on pre-positive notions of justice, very much in the natural law tradition.

C. *Critical Legal Studies*

Another relevant perspective on international law is the body of legal theory commonly known as "critical legal studies" (CLS), which involves inquiry into political context, power structures, and paradigms of thinking related to the articulation of legal norms and to the processes within which they function. See generally David Trubek, *Where the Action Is: Critical Legal Studies and Empiricism*, 36 Stan. L. Rev. 575 (1984); Phillip Trimble, *International Law, World Order, and Critical Legal Studies*, 42 Stan. L. Rev. 811 (1990); Nigel Purvis, *Critical Legal Studies in Public International Law*, 32 Harv. Int'l L. J. 81 (1991). While advancing widely disparate avenues of criticism, the CLS movement includes as one of its central contentions that law is indeterminate and ultimately subject to political choice, rather than politically neutral in its conception and application. CLS scholars tend to see international human rights law in particular as limited by or even favoring power structures grounded in the primacy of states within the construct of an international legal order that is perpetuated by the world's political elites, so that the ability of international human rights law to act as a force against oppression in many contexts is hamstrung or nonexistent. For example, David Kennedy, one of the principal proponents of this criticism, has written:

> Although the human rights vocabulary expresses relentless suspicion of the state, by structuring emancipation as a relationship between an individual right holder and the state, human rights places the state at the center of the emancipatory promise. However much one may insist on the priority or pre-existence of rights, in the end rights are enforced, granted, recognized, implemented, their violations remedied, by the state. By consolidating human experience into the exercise of legal entitlements, human rights strengthens the national governmental structure and equates the structure of the state with the structure of freedom. To be free is... to have an appropriately organized state. We might say that the right-holder imagines and experiences freedom only as a *citizen*. This encourages autochthonous political tendencies and alienates the "citizen" from both his or her own experience as a person and from the possibility of alternative communal forms.

David Kennedy, *The International Human Rights Movement: Part of the Problem?*, 15 Harv. Hum. Rts. J. 101, 113 (2002). How is Kennedy's criticism different from the observation that international treaty regimes for implementing human rights are inherently weak because states cannot be forced to accept them? How do the anti-slavery movement and its outcome support or detract from Kennedy's criticism? What alternative might there be to the protection of human rights by the state? For a rejoinder to Kennedy, see Hillary Charlesworth, *Author! Author!: A Response to David Kennedy*, 15 Harv. Hum. Rts. J. 127 (2002).

D. *Feminist Perspectives*

Feminist legal scholars offer additional criticisms of international human rights law, as exemplified by the following extract.

Hilary Charlesworth, Feminist Methods in International Law

93 Am. J. Int'l L. 379, 382-83, 387-88 (1999) (footnotes omitted)

... Feminist methods emphasize conversations and dialogue rather than the production of a single, triumphant truth. They will not lead to neat "legal" answers because they are challenging the very categories of "law" and "nonlaw." Feminist methods seek to expose and question the limited bases of international law's claim to objectivity and impartiality and insist on the importance of gender relations as a category of analysis. The term "gender" here refers to the social construction of differences between women and men and ideas of "femininity" and "masculinity" — the excess cultural baggage associated with biological sex....

One technique for identifying and decoding the silences in international law is paying attention to the way that various dichotomies are used in its structure. International legal discourse rests on a series of distinctions; for example, objective/subjective, legal/political, logic/emotion, order/anarchy, mind/body, culture/nature, action/passivity, public/private, protector/protected, independence/dependence. . . .

The operation of public/private distinctions in international law provides an example of the way that the discipline can factor out the realities of women's lives and build its objectivity on a limited base. One such distinction is the line drawn between the "public" world of politics, government and the state and the "private" world of home, hearth and family. Thus, the definition of torture in the Convention against Torture requires the involvement of a public (governmental) official. On this account, sexual violence against women constitutes an abuse of human rights only if it can be connected with the public realm; for example, if a woman is raped by a person holding a public position for some type of public end. The Declaration on the Elimination of Violence against Women, adopted by the General Assembly in 1993, makes violence against women an issue of international concern but refrains from categorizing violence against women as a human rights issue in its operative provisions. The failure to create a nexus between violence against women and human rights was due to a fear that this might dilute the traditional notion of human rights. It was said that the idea of human rights abuses required direct state involvement and that extending the concept to cover private behavior would reduce the status of the human rights canon as a whole.

This type of public/private distinction in international human rights law is not a neutral or objective qualification. Its consequences are gendered because in all societies men dominate the public sphere of politics and government and women are associated with the private sphere of home and family. Its effect is to blot out the experiences of many women and to silence their voices in international law. . . .

Another public/private distinction incorporated (albeit unevenly) in international criminal law — via human rights law — is that between the acts of state and nonstate actors. Such a dichotomy has gendered aspects when mapped onto the reality of violence against women. Significantly, the ICC statute defines torture more broadly than the Convention against Torture, omitting any reference to the involvement of public officials. Steven Ratner has suggested, however, that some sort of distinction based on "official" involvement is useful as a criterion to sort out those actions against human dignity that should engender state and individual international criminal responsibility and those (such as common assault) that should not. The problem, from a feminist perspective, is not the drawing of public/private, or regulated/nonregulated, distinctions as such, but rather the reinforcement of gender inequality through the use of such distinctions. We need, then, to pay attention to the actual operation of boundary drawing in international law and whether it ends up affecting women's and men's lives differently. For example, the consequence of defining certain rapes as public in international law is to make private rapes seem somehow less serious. The distinction is made, not by reference to women's experiences, but by the implications for the male-dominated public sphere.

For additional reading on feminist perspectives, see Hillary Charlesworth, Christine Chinkin and Shelly Wright, *Feminist Approaches to International Law*, 85 Am J. Int'l L. 613 (1991); Hilary Charlesworth and Christine Chinkin, *The Boundaries of International Law: A Feminist Analysis* (2000); *Human Rights of Women: National and International Perspectives* (Rebecca Cook ed., 1994);

Barbara Stark, *Nurturing Rights: An Essay on Women, Peace, and International Human Rights*, 13 U. Mich. J. Int'l L. 144 (1991); but cf. Catherine Harries, *Daughters of our Peoples: International Feminism Meets Ugandan Law and Custom*, 25 Colum. Hum. Rts. Rev. 493 (1994) (criticizing the standard feminist perspective for its Western orientation at the expense of the problems of women in underdeveloped countries).

E. *Cultural Relativism*

Finally, the very idea of universal human rights norms has been criticized on the grounds that it is necessarily linked to a particular cultural perspective to the exclusion or at the expense of others. In essence, critics assert that the moral assessments implicit in identifying and asserting human rights, like the assessments for discerning natural law, are inevitably driven by cultural conditioning. The diversity of cultures in the world is said to give rise to diverse moral assessments, the existence of which undermine the concept of human rights as universal and inherent.

This point is often illustrated by comparing the human rights norms articulated in contemporary international documents to entrenched cultural practices that on their face seem to violate those norms, such as the practice of female circumcision. In many parts of Africa, girls or young women have their clitoris or other genitalia painfully cut and removed as part of a ritualistic right of passage with deep historical and cultural roots. See Katherine Brennan, *The Influence of Cultural Relativism on International Human Rights Law: Female Circumcision as a Case Study*, 7 Law & Ineq. 367 (1991). For an overview of and response to criticisms based on cultural relativism, see Fernando Teson, *International Human Rights and Cultural Relativism*, 25 Va. J. Int'l L. 869 (1985); Rhoda E. Howard, *Cultural Absolutism and the Nostalgia for Community*, 15 Human Rts. Q. 315 (1993).

Today's international human rights movement, as pointed out earlier, draws on the natural law tradition and its embarce of a universal normative order. In contemporary human rights discourse, moral and ethical standards are articulated across national and cultural boundaries, by reference to values and normative assessments beyond the rules adopted by states. See David Sidorsky, "Contemporary Reinterpretation of the Concept of Human Rights," *in Essays on Human Rights* 88, 89 (D. Sidorsky ed., 1979). Human rights discourse, like natural law theory, is dynamic, admitting new truths or notions of justice within ever evolving patterns of thought. What may distinguish the modern human rights movement from the natural law tradition is its aspiration to universality not just in the application of norms across cultural divides but also in its attempts to ground those norms in the value systems of diverse cultures. While thus drawing on the natural law tradition, modern human rights discourse is less dogmatic or absolutist in the assessment of the source, nature, and content of norms than classical natural law theory. It professes to be open to different cultural perspectives and to reason from first principles, without necessarily ascribing to them unchanging divine or metaphysical roots. Effectively answering the critique of cultural relativism, Professors McDougal, Laswell, and Chen have written of "fundamental demands" associated with a "world public order of human dignity" that are now common across the globe:

> Different peoples located in different parts of the world, conditioned by varying cultural traditions and employing divergent modes of social organization, may of course assert these fundamental demands in many different modalities and nuances of international practice. There would appear, however, to be an overriding insistence, transcending all cultures and climes, upon the greater production and wider distribution of basic values, accompanied by increasing recognition that a world public order of human dignity can tolerate wide differences in specific practices by which values are shaped and shared, so long as all demands and practices are effectively appraised and accommodated in terms of common interest.

McDougal et al., supra, at 5-6.

In recent years, many of the arguments asserting that specific regional or cultural values differ from human rights norms have come from Asia. Compare, e.g., Bilahari Kausikan, *Asia's Different Standard*, 92 Foreign Pol'y 24 (Fall 1993), with Aryeh Neier, *Asia's Unacceptable Standard*, 92 Foreign Pol'y. 42 (Fall 1993); for similar relativist views from an African perspective, see, e.g., Josiah A.M. Cobbah, *African Values and the Human Rights Debate: An African Perspective*, 9 Hum. Rts. Q. 309 (1987); Makau Mutua, *Savages, Victims, and Saviors: The Metaphor of Human Rights*, 42 Harv. Int'l L.J. 201 (2001).

Nobel laureate Amartya Sen responds to some of these critiques in the following extract.

Amartya Sen, Human Rights and Asian Values

The New Republic, July 14-July 21, 1997

I want to examine the thesis that Asian values are less supportive of freedom and more concerned with order and discipline, and that the claims of human rights in the areas of political and civil liberties, therefore, are less relevant and less appropriate in Asia than in the West. The defense of authoritarianism in Asia on the grounds of the special nature of Asian values calls for historical scrutiny. . . .

II. . . .

The size of Asia is itself a problem. Asia is where about 60 percent of the world's population lives. What can we take to be the values of so vast a region, with so much diversity? It is important to state at the outset that there are no quintessential values that separate the Asians as a group from people in the rest of the world and which fit all parts of this immensely large and heterogeneous population. The temptation to see Asia as a single unit reveals a distinctly Eurocentric perspective. Indeed, the term "the Orient," which was widely used for a long time to mean essentially what Asia means today, referred to the positional vision of Europe, as it contemplated the direction of the rising sun. . . .

Still, the recognition of heterogeneity in the traditions of Asia does not settle the issue of the presence or the absence of a commitment to individual freedom and political liberty in Asian culture. The traditions extant in Asia differ among themselves, but they may share some common characteristics. It has been asserted, for example, that the treatment of elderly members of the family (say, aged parents) is more supportive in Asian countries than in the West. It is possible to argue about this claim, but there would be nothing very peculiar if some similarities of this kind or other kinds were to obtain across the diverse cultures of Asia. Diversities need not apply to every field. The question that has to be asked, rather, is whether Asian countries share the common feature of being skeptical of freedom and liberty, while emphasizing order and discipline. The advocates of Asian particularism allow internal heterogeneity within Asia, but in the context of a shared mistrust of the claims of political liberalism. Authoritarian lines of reasoning often receive indirect backing from certain strains of thought in the West itself. There is clearly a tendency in America and Europe to assume, if only implicitly, the primacy of political freedom and democracy as a fundamental and ancient feature of Western culture, one not to be easily found in Asia. There is a contrast, it is alleged, between the authoritarianism implicit in, say, Confucianism and the respect for liberty and autonomy allegedly deeply rooted in Western liberal culture. Western promoters of personal and political freedom in the non-Western world often see such an analysis as a necessary preliminary to bringing Western values to Asia and Africa.

In all this, there is a substantial tendency to extrapolate backwards from the present. Values that the European enlightenment and other relatively recent developments have made widespread cannot really be seen as part of the Western heritage as it was experienced over millennia. In answer to the question, "at what date, in what circumstances, the notion of individual liberty . . . first became explicit in the West," Isaiah Berlin has noted: "I have found no convincing evidence of any clear formulation of it in the ancient world." This view has been disputed by Orlando Patterson, among others. He points to particular features in Western culture, particularly in Greece and Rome, and in the tradition of Christianity, which indicate the presence of selective championing of individual liberty.

The question that does not get adequately answered — it is scarcely even asked — is whether similar elements are absent in other cultures. Berlin's thesis concerns the notion of individual freedom as we now understand it, and the absence of "any clear formulation" of this can certainly co-exist with the advocacy of selected components of the comprehensive notion that makes up the contemporary idea of individual liberty. Such components are found in the Greco-Roman world and in the world of Jewish and Christian thought. But such an acknowledgment has to be followed up by examining whether these components are absent elsewhere — that is, in non-Western cultures. We have to search for the parts rather than the whole, in the West and in Asia and elsewhere. . . .

In the terms of such an analysis, the question has to be asked whether these constitutive components can be found in Asian writings in the way they can be found in Western thought. The presence of these components must not be confused with the absence of the opposite, that is, with the presence of ideas and doctrines that clearly do not emphasize freedom and tolerance. The championing of order and discipline can be found in Western classics as well. Indeed, it is by no means clear to me that Confucius is more authoritarian than, say, Plato or Augustine. The real issue is not whether these non-freedom perspectives are present in Asian traditions, but whether the freedom-oriented perspectives are absent from them.

This is where the diversity of Asian value systems becomes quite central. An obvious example is the role of Buddhism as a form of thought. In Buddhist tradition, great importance is attached to freedom, and the traditions of earlier Indian thinking to which Buddhist thoughts relate allow much room for volition and free choice. Nobility of conduct has to be achieved in freedom, and even the ideas of liberation (such as moksha) include this feature. The presence of these elements in Buddhist thought does not obliterate the importance of the discipline emphasized by Confucianism, but it would be a mistake to take Confucianism to be the only tradition in Asia — or in China. Since so much of the contemporary authoritarian interpretation of Asian values concentrates on Confucianism, this diversity is particularly worth emphasizing.

Indeed, the reading of Confucianism that is now standard among authoritarian champions of Asian values does less than justice to Confucius's own teachings, to which Simon Leys has recently drawn attention. Confucius did not recommend blind allegiance to the state. When Zilu asks him "how to serve a prince," Confucius replies: "Tell him the truth even if it offends him." The censors in Singapore or Beijing would take a very different view. Confucius is not averse to practical caution and tact, but he does not forgo the recommendation to oppose a bad government. "When the [good] way prevails in the state, speak boldly and act boldly. When the state has lost the way, act boldly and speak softly." . . .

IV.

It is important to recognize that many of these historical leaders in Asia not only emphasized the importance of freedom and tolerance, they also had clear theories as to why this is the appropriate thing to do. . . .

The point of discussing all this now is to demonstrate the presence of conscious theorizing about tolerance and freedom in substantial and important parts of the Asian traditions. We could consider many more illustrations of this phenomenon from writings in early Arabic, Chinese, Indian and other cultures. Again, the championing of democracy and political freedom in the modern sense cannot be found in the pre-enlightenment tradition in any part of the world, West or East. What we have to investigate, instead, are the constituents, the components, of this compound idea. It is the powerful presence of some of these elements — in non-Western as well as Western societies — that I have been emphasizing. It is hard to make sense of the view that the basic ideas underlying freedom and rights in a tolerant society are "Western" notions, and somehow alien to Asia, though that view has been championed by Asian authoritarians and Western chauvinists.

V.

I would like to conclude with a rather different issue, which is sometimes linked to the debate about the nature and the reach of Asian values. The championing of Asian values is often associated with the need to resist Western hegemony. The linkage of the two issues, which has increasingly occurred in recent years, uses the political force of anticolonialism to buttress the assault on civil and political rights in post-colonial Asia.

This linkage, though quite artificial, can be rhetorically quite effective. Thus Lee Kuan Yew has emphasized the special nature of Asian values, and has made powerful use of the general case for resisting Western hegemony to bolster the argument for Asian particularism. The rhetoric has extended to the apparently defiant declaration that Singapore is "not a client state of America." This fact is certainly undeniable, and it is an excellent reason for cheer, but the question that has to be asked is what this has to do with the issue of human rights and political liberties in Singapore, or any other country in Asia.

The people whose political and other rights are involved in this debate are not citizens of the West, but of Asian countries. The fact that individual liberty may have been championed in Western writings, and even by some Western political leaders, can scarcely compromise the claim to liberty that people in Asia may otherwise possess. As a matter of fact, one may grumble, with reason, that the political leaders of Western countries take far too little interest in issues of freedom in the rest of the world. There is plenty of evidence that the Western governments have tended to give priority to the interests of their own citizens engaged in commerce with the Asian countries and to the pressures generated by business groups to be on good terms with the ruling governments in Asia. It is not that there has been more bark than bite; there has been very little bark, too. What Mao once described as a "paper tiger" looks increasingly like a paper mouse.

But even if this were not the case, and even if it were true that Western governments try to promote political and civil rights in Asia, how can that possibly compromise the status of the rights of Asians? In this context, the idea of "human rights" has to be properly understood. In the most general form, the notion of human rights builds on our shared humanity. These rights are not derived from citizenship in any country, or membership in any nation. They are taken as entitlements of every human being. These rights differ, therefore, from constitutionally created rights guaranteed for specified people (such as American citizens or French nationals). The human right of a person not to be tortured is affirmed independently of the country of which this person is a citizen, and also irrespective of what the government of that country — or any other country — wants to do. Of course, a government can dispute a person's legal right not to be tortured, but that will not amount to disputing what must be seen as the person's human right not to be tortured.

Since the conception of human rights transcends local legislation and the citizenship of the individual, the support for human rights can come from anyone — whether or not she is a citizen of the same country as the individual whose rights are threatened. A foreigner does not need the permission of a repressive government to try to help a person whose liberties are being violated. Indeed, insofar as human rights are seen as rights that any person has as a human being (and not as a citizen of any particular country), the reach of the corresponding duties can also include any human being (irrespective of citizenship). . . .

To conclude, the so-called Asian values that are invoked to justify authoritarianism are not especially Asian in any significant sense. Nor is it easy to see how they could be made, by the mere force of rhetoric, into an Asian cause against the West.

The people whose rights are being disputed are Asians, and, no matter what the West's guilt may be (there are many skeletons in many closets throughout the world), the rights of Asians can scarcely be compromised on those grounds. The case for liberty and political rights turns ultimately on their basic importance and on their instrumental role. And this case is as strong in Asia as it is elsewhere.

There is a great deal that we can learn from studies of values in Asia and Europe, but they do not support or sustain the thesis of a grand dichotomy (or a "clash of civilizations"). Our ideas of political and personal rights have taken their particular form relatively recently, and it is hard to see them as "traditional" commitments of Western cultures. There are important antecedents of those commitments, but those antecedents can be found plentifully in Asian cultures as well as Western cultures.

The recognition of diversity within different cultures is extremely important in the contemporary world, since we are constantly bombarded by oversimple generalizations about "Western civilization," "Asian values," "African cultures," and so on. These unfounded readings of history and civilization are not only intellectually shallow, they also add to the divisiveness of the world in which we live. The authoritarian readings of Asian values that are increasingly championed in some quarters do not survive scrutiny. And the grand dichotomy between Asian values and European values adds little to our understanding, and much to the confounding of the normative basis of freedom and democracy.

Comments and Questions

1. Recall that Lord Mansfield surmised, as a predicate to ordering Sommersett's release, that the "state of slavery is of such a nature, that it is incapable of being introduced on any reasons, moral or political, but only by positive law, which preserves its force long after the reasons, occasion, and time itself from whence it was created, is erased from memory." Contrast this with Chief Justice John Marshall's opinion for the U.S. Supreme Court several years later in *The Antelope*, 23 U.S. 10 (Wheat.) 66 (1825), a case that arose from the seizure in international waters off the coast of Florida of The Antelope by a U.S. revenue cutter for suspected violations of federal statutes prohibiting the international slave trade. Spain and Portugal claimed the Africans on board the ship as property of citizens of their countries, arguing that U.S. law could not apply to infringe upon the trade in that property because the slaves were being transported on the high seas for delivery to Brazil, where the slave trade remained legal. The Court agreed that the United States must recognize the claims of Spain and Portugal to the return of the slaves on the basis of the applicable rules of admiralty and international law. Distinguishing between natural and positive law, Justice Marshall opted for the latter in justifying the Court's decision:

> That [the slave trade] is contrary to the law of nature will scarcely be denied. That every man has a natural right to the fruits of his own labour, is generally admitted; and that no other person can rightfully deprive him of those fruits, and appropriate them against his will, seems to be the necessary result of this admission. . . .

> Throughout Christendom . . . war is no longer considered as giving a right to enslave captives. But this triumph of humanity has not been universal. The parties to the modern law of nations do not propagate their principles by force; and Africa has not yet adopted them. Throughout the whole extent of that immense continent, so far as we know its history, it is still the law of nations that prisoners are slaves. Can those who have themselves renounced this law, be permitted to participate in its effects by purchasing the beings who are its victims?
>
> Whatever might be the answer of a moralist to this question, a jurist must search for its legal solution, in those principles of action which are sanctioned by the usages, the national acts, and the general assent, of that portion of the world of which he considers himself as a part, and to whose law the appeal is made. If we resort to this standard as the test of international law, the question, as has already been observed, is decided in favour of the legality of the trade. Both Europe and America embarked in it; and for nearly two centuries, it was carried on without opposition, and without censure. A jurist could not say, that a practice thus supported was illegal, and that those engaged in it might be punished, either personally, or by deprivation of property.
>
> It follows that a foreign vessel engaged in the African slave trade, captured on the high seas in time of peace, by an American Cruiser, and brought in for adjudication, would be restored.

Id. at 120-123. In contrast to Justice Marshall in *The Antelope*, was Lord Mansfield in Sommersett's case exercising judicial authority inappropriately by giving primacy to precepts of natural law? Or was it Justice Marshall's reasoning that was flawed? Did it matter that Sommersett was being held in British territory, while The Antelope was seized on the high seas? See the discussion of the territorial scope of human rights treaties in Chapter 8, pages 626-647.

2. During the drafting of the Universal Declaration of Human Rights, the French Jesuit philosopher Teilhard de Chardin opined that the process could reach agreement on a catalogue of human rights provided it did not have to agree on why humans had them. What are the advantages and disadvantages of the various theories discussed above with respect to the actual or desirable sources of international human rights law? Would it be a persuasive answer that, in light of the plethora of norms discussed in this book, it just doesn't matter any more? For an excellent overview of positivist, natural law, and other philosophical approaches to human rights, also see Jerome J. Shestack, *The Philosophic Foundations of Human Rights*, 20 Hum. Rts. Q. 201 (1998).

3. Is the cultural basis of the practice of female circumcision a proper defense against the charge that it is a violation of human rights? See generally UN Committee on the Elimination of Discrimination Against Women, General Recommendation No. 14, UN Doc. A/45/38 (1990) (recommending that states "[t]ake appropriate and effective measures with a view to eradicating the practice of female circumcision"). Could the practice of slavery be defended on cultural grounds, given its grounding in cultural and religious perspectives and lifestyles of earlier periods?

4. Do you agree or disagree with the proposition that there are certain basic values that are common to all or most cultures of the world? Is the concept of "human dignity" advanced by Professor McDougal and his colleagues, supra p. 38-39, an advance over natural law in attempting to capture the source of these values? Assuming that human rights proponents of diverse cultural backgrounds do in fact converge on common "fundamental demands," what explains this?

5. The issue of relativism versus universality was debated thoroughly at the UN's 1993 World Conference on Human Rights, held in Vienna. The conference adopted the following statement by consensus:

> All human rights are universal, indivisible and interdependent and interrelated. The international community must treat human rights globally in a fair and equal manner, on the same footing, and with the same emphasis. While the significance of national and regional particularities and various historical, cultural and religious backgrounds must be borne in mind, it is the duty of States, regardless of their political, economic and cultural systems, to promote and protect all human rights and fundamental freedoms.

World Conference on Human Rights, Final Declaration and Programme of Action, UN Doc. A/CONF.157/23 (July 12, 1993), sec. I, para. 5.

Contrast this with Article 4 of the Universal Declaration on Cultural Diversity, proclaimed by the UN Educational, Scientific, and Cultural Organization on Nov. 2, 2001:

> The defence of cultural diversity is an ethical imperative, inseparable from respect for human dignity. It implies a commitment to human rights and fundamental freedoms, in particular the rights of persons belonging to minorities and those of indigenous peoples. No one may invoke cultural diversity to infringe upon human rights guaranteed by international law, nor to limit their scope.

Are the two declarations consistent? To what extent can respect for cultural diversity coexist with the application of universal human rights?

6. Is it possible to distinguish between the human rights obligations imposed on states and cultural practices that individuals may choose to follow? Which does international human rights law address? See generally the discussion in Chapter 5.

7. Do you agree with Charlesworth's criticism of the public/private distinction? If the distinction is abolished, does any difference remain between international human rights law and national criminal law?

8. Many works raise various aspects of cultural relativism. See, e.g., Abdullah Ahmend An-Na'im, *Human Rights in the Muslim World*, 3 Harv. Hum. Rts. J. 13 (1990); Mashood A. Baderin, *International Human Rights and Islamic Law* (2003); Edna Boyle-Lewicki, *Need Worlds Collide: The Crimes of Islamic Law and International Human Rights*, 13 N.Y. Int'l L. Rev. 43 (2000); Eva Brems, *Enemies or Allies? Feminism and Cultural Relativism as Dissident Voices in Human Rights Discourse*, 19 Hum. Rts. Q. 136 (1997); Chris Brown, *Universal Human Rights: A Critique*, 1 Int'l J. Hum. Rts. 41 (no. 2, 1997); *Confucianism and Human Rights* (Wm. Theodore de Bary and Tu Weiming eds., 1998); Jack Donnelly, *Cultural Relativism and Universal Human Rights*, 6 Hum. Rts. Q. 400 (1984); *The East Asian Challenge for Human Rights* (Joanne R. Bauer and Daniel A. Bell eds., 1999); Ann Elizabeth Mayer, *Islam and Human Rights: Traditions and Politics* (3rd ed. 1999); Chandra Muzzafar, "Human Rights and Hypocrisy in the International Order," in *Dominance of the West over the Rest* (Chandra Muzzafar ed., 1995); Ann-Belinda S. Preis, *Human Rights as Cultural Practice: An Anthropological Critique*, 18 Hum. Rts. Q. 286 (1996); Alison Dundes Renteln, *The Cultural Defense* (2004).

IV. A Brief History of Human Rights in International Law and Institutions

John P. Humphrey,* The International Law of Human Rights in the Middle Twentieth Century

In *The Present State of International Law and Other Essays* 75 (Bos, Maarten ed. 1973)

[Professor Humphrey's essay was a contribution to the centenary celebration of the International Law Association, a nongovernmental association comprised of academic scholars, practitioners, and government lawyers.]

I. Traditional Doctrine and Practice

When, a hundred years from now, the International Law Association celebrates its bicentenary, legal historians will surely be saying that one of the chief characteristics of midtwentieth century international law was its sudden interest in and concern with human rights. The founding fathers of the Association had no such special interest. Since human rights were — and indeed still are — essentially a relationship between the State and individuals — usually its own citizens — residing in its territory, they were, in traditional theory and practice, considered to fall within domestic jurisdiction and hence beyond the reach of international law, the norms of which governed the relations of States only. But there were some exceptions or at least it could be argued that there were. . . .

[The author proceeds to discuss the customary rules of international law governing the treatment of aliens and the doctrine of humanitarian intervention, discussed in Chapter 10.]

But if customary international law was only minimally and indirectly concerned with human rights, in the nineteenth and early twentieth centuries an increasing number of treaties were entered into the purpose of which was to protect, if only indirectly, the rights of certain classes of people. The most important of these were the treaties aimed at slavery and the slave trade. . . . Steps were also taken in the nineteenth century for the relief of sick and wounded soldiers and prisoners of war. By the Geneva Convention of 22 August, 1864, twelve States undertook to respect the immunity of military hospitals and their staffs, to care for wounded and sick soldiers and to respect the emblem of the Red Cross. The Convention was revised in 1929 and has been widely ratified.

In 1966, the second Berne Conference opened two conventions for signature which were forerunners of the many labour conventions which, after the first World War, would be adopted by the International Labour Organization: the International Convention respecting the Prohibition of Night Work for Women in Industrial Employment and the International Convention respecting the Prohibition of the Use of White (Yellow) Phosphorus in the Manufacture of Matches.

* John P. Humphrey served as Director of the Division of Human Rights of the United Nations, 1946-1966. — Eds.

II. The League of Nations

The peace settlement at the end of the First World War brought still more important developments. Attempts were made to enshrine human rights in the Covenant of the League of Nations. President Wilson sponsored an article on religious freedom; but when the Japanese suggested that mention also be made of the equality of nations and the just treatment of their nationals (which frightened some countries the laws of which restricted Asiatic immigration) both suggestions were withdrawn. Wilson put into his second draft an article under which the League would have required all new States to bind themselves, as a condition precedent to their recognition, to accord all racial and national minorities "exactly the same treatment and security, both in law and in fact, that is accorded the racial and national majority of their people." But the Peace Conference decided that the protection of minorities — though only in certain countries — would be dealt with not in the Covenant but by other treaty provisions and by declarations which certain States were required to make on their admission to the League.

Two articles dealing with human rights did find their way into the Covenant. One of these, Article 22, enunciated the principle that colonies and territories which as a consequence of the war had ceased to be under the sovereignty of the States which formerly governed them and which were inhabited by "peoples not yet able to stand by themselves under the strenuous conditions of the modern world," were to be put under the tutelage of advanced nations, who, as mandatories on behalf of the League, would be responsible for their administration under conditions which would guarantee amongst other things freedom of conscience and religion and the prohibition of abuses such as the slave trade. Provision was made for the creation of a permanent mandates commission to receive and examine the reports which the mandatories undertook to make.

The League's mandates system was taken over by the United Nations under a different name and subject to different rules. The [UN] Charter expressly says [in Article 76(c)] that one of the purposes of the Trusteeship system is to "encourage respect for human rights and fundamental freedoms for all without distinction as to race, sex, language or religion." The language used in Articles 73 and 74 relating to non-self-governing territories is not so forthright, but at a very early date, the General Assembly invited the administering powers to include, in the information to be transmitted under Article 73(e), a summary of the extent to which the Universal Declaration of Human Rights was being implemented in the non-self-governing territories under their administration. The work of the committee set up to receive reports on the administration of non-self-governing territories has now been taken over by the Special Committee on the Situation with regard to the Implementation of the Declaration on the Granting of Independence to Colonial Countries and Peoples. . . .

Human rights were also expressly dealt with in Article 23 of the Covenant. Members of the League, it said, would "endeavour to secure and maintain" fair and humane labour conditions, undertake to secure just treatment for the native inhabitants of territories under their control, and entrust the League with the supervision of agreements relating to the traffic in women and children.

Although President Wilson's suggestion that the Covenant contain a provision protecting minorities was not pursued, the Allied and Associated Powers did require certain newly created States, the territory of which had been increased by reason of the war, to grant the enjoyment of certain human rights to all inhabitants of their territories and to protect the rights of their racial, religious and linguistic minorities. These obligations were imposed by treaty and by the declarations which certain States were required to make on their admission to the League — provisions relating to minorities being put under the guarantee of the League Council.

[Professor Humphrey explains how the United Nations system at the time of his writing had not established an elaborate system for the protection of minorities such as that developed by the League.] The exception was the adoption in 1948 of the widely ratified Convention on the Prevention and Punishment of the Crime of Genocide, which is aimed at the worst kind of treatment that can be meted out to minorities, namely, "acts committed with intent to destroy, in whole or in part, a national, ethnical, racial or religious group as such." There is also a United Nations Sub-Commission on the Prevention of Discrimination and the Protection of Minorities [subsequently the Sub-Commission on the Promotion and Protection of Human Rights], the members of which are elected to act in their personal capacity. . . . [The mechanisms later developed by the UN to address issues concerning minorities and indigenous peoples are discussed in Chapter 3.]

The League of Nations also did important work on slavery. It created a special committee to study the question, was responsible for the drafting of the Slavery Convention of 1926, and, when Ethiopia applied for admission to the League, it required from her an undertaking to make special efforts to abolish slavery and the slave trade, Ethiopia recognizing that this was not a purely internal matter but one on which the League had a right to intervene.

The work of the League [against slavery] was continued by the United Nations. . . .

Like the League of Nations the International Labour Organization was created by the peace treaties after the First World War. This Specialized Agency, which now has a history of over half a century of achievement, has adopted well over a hundred conventions which fix international standards many of which deal with human rights and some of which were inspired by the United Nations. It also possesses elaborate systems for the implementation of these standards. Some of them, particularly those relating to reporting, could be well emulated by the United Nations. Other Specialized Agencies, including UNESCO and the World Health Organization have also done important work for the promotion of human rights.

To sum up, international law recognized, by the beginning of the Second World War, a whole series of rules and institutions, as well as some procedures for their implementation, the effect of which was to protect the rights of individuals and groups, even though, in the dominant theory, the individual was neither a subject of international law nor directly protected by it. International law protected the rights of aliens through their States. There may have been a right of humanitarian intervention. Slavery and the slave trade were outlawed. The League of Nations had developed a system for the protection of certain racial, religious and linguistic minorities. There were provisions in the Covenant of the League of Nations for the protection of the rights of the natives of colonial [territories], and the inhabitants of mandated territories and of women and children. And the International Labour Organization had adopted an impressive number of labour conventions, for the enforcement of which it possessed elaborate procedures.

III. The Impact of the Second World War and the United Nations

The Second World War and the events leading up to it was the catalyst that produced the revolutionary developments in the international law of human rights that characterize the middle twentieth century. So potent was this catalyst that it produced not only an unprecedented growth in human rights law, but the very theory of international law had to be adapted to the new circumstances. The individual now becomes a subject of international law which henceforth would more properly be known as "world law," He is directly protected by this law and can even in some cases seek his own remedy. And States can no longer rely on the plea of domestic jurisdiction. It was not only a matter of new norms being added within the confines of an existing order, but the very nature of that order had changed. What had happened was revolutionary. The Second World War was, as no other war has ever been, a war to vindicate human rights. This was recognized by the leaders of the Grand Alliance and perhaps best expressed by President Roosevelt when, in January 1941, before the United States entered the war, he defined four freedoms: freedom of speech, freedom of worship, freedom from want, freedom from fear — "everywhere in the world." These he said, were the "necessary conditions of peace and no distant millennium." Yet, when the Dumbarton Oaks Proposals were published in the fall of 1944 they contained only a general reference to human rights. The United Nations would, the Proposals said in a chapter on arrangements for international economic and social cooperation, "promote respect for human rights and fundamental freedoms" — something which considering its context and the generality of the language used hardly met the expectations of a public opinion shocked by the atrocities of the war.

The relatively strong human rights provisions in the Charter through which they run, as someone has said, like a golden thread, were largely, and appropriately, the result of determined lobbying by non-governmental organizations at the San Francisco Conference. Some of the countries represented at San Francisco would have accepted even stronger human rights provisions than found their way into the Charter. There was even an attempt, which failed, to incorporate in the Charter an International Bill of Rights. But the Charter did provide for the creation of a Commission on Human Rights which, as President Truman said in the speech by which he closed the Conference, would, it was generally understood, draft the bill.

This is not the place to analyse the human rights provisions of the Charter. But it should be said that Article One puts the promotion of respect for human rights on the same level as the maintenance of international peace and security as a purpose of the United Nations. And by Articles 55 and 56 member states pledge themselves to take joint and separate action "in cooperation with the Organization" for the promotion and universal respect of human rights, an undertaking which, according to a recent advisory opinion of the International Court of Justice (Advisory Opinion on the Continued Presence of South Africa in Namibia, [1977] I.C.J. 16), binds member states to observe and respect human rights. Reference has already been made to Article 68 which provided for the creation of a Commission on Human Rights.

The Commission on Human Rights held its first regular session in February, 1947 and, later in the same year, decided that the International Bill of Human

what ↓ *how ↓ why

→ but not to enforce ↓ is non-enforcement dis-respect

Rights would have three parts: a declaration, a convention or conventions (later called the Covenants) and measures of implementation. Under the chairmanship of the late Eleanor Roosevelt, it worked so efficiently that the first part of the bill was ready for consideration by the General Assembly at its third session and was adopted by it without dissenting vote, on 10 December 1948, as the Universal Declaration of Human Rights.

The Declaration was not meant to be a legally binding instrument. This is apparent from the form in which it was adopted (resolutions of the General Assembly ordinarily have the force of recommendations only), the decision to include substantially the same norms in a convention which would be binding on the states which ratified it, and the many explanations of votes which delegations made when the Declaration was adopted. That was a quarter of a century ago. Many international lawyers now say that, whatever the intentions of its authors may have been, the Declaration is now binding as part of customary law. The point has yet to come squarely before the International Court of Justice although the separate opinion of Judge Fuad Ammoun in the Advisory Opinion mentioned above is indicative. [Judge Ammon stated that "[a]lthough the affirmations of the Declaration are not binding qua international convention . . . , they can bind States on the basis of custom . . . , whether because they constituted a codification of customary law . . . , or because they have acquired the force of custom through a general practice accepted as law. . . . "] But whether the Declaration is now legally binding or not, it has great moral and political authority and its impact on the theory and practice of both international and national law has been profound. [The issue of the legal character of the Declaration is taken up in Chapter 3.]

In 1952, the General Assembly decided that there would be not one but two multilateral conventions or covenants on human rights, one on civil and political rights and the other on economic, social and cultural rights — a decision motivated chiefly by ideological considerations which split the United Nations down the middle. The Human Rights Commission completed its work on the two instruments in 1954, but it was only in 1966 that they were approved by the General Assembly and opened for signature. The long delay is partly explained by the fact that the debates on the drafts in the Third Committee were used for the ventilation of political controversies. [The Covenants came into force in 1976.] Apart from the fact that they . . . undoubtedly bind the states which ratify them, the Covenants are distinguished from the Declaration by the procedures which they contemplate for their implementation. If the Universal Declaration of Human Rights is now part of customary law, the chief raison d'être of the Covenants . . . is now the presence in them of these enforcement procedures. . . .

[The author proceeds to survey the implementation mechanisms contained in the two Covenants, which he believes are inadequate, matters that are considered in Chapter 7.]

It is vastly more difficult to obtain international agreement on procedures for implementation than on substantive norms. For, while states with disparate social systems may agree without too much difficulty on objectives, they have radically different methods for translating these objectives into reality. Implementation involves basic philosophical approaches and ultimate social goals. It was, therefore, to be expected that there would be fundamental disagreement in the United Nations on the establishment of international machinery for the enforcement of norms agreed on as expressions of immediate goals. . . .

V. A New Catalogue of Rights

This essay has been chiefly concerned with structural or institutional arrangements for the promotion and protection of human rights. In a sense, we have been discussing Hamlet without the Prince of Denmark. There are two reasons for this. In the first place, there is now relative agreement on the definition of human rights, something which appears most clearly, perhaps, from the fact that the Universal Declaration of Human Rights, which covers the whole gamut of rights, was adopted without dissenting vote. Something must be said, however, about the catalogue and nature of the human rights now recognized by international law.

The principal characteristic of the twentieth century approach to human rights has been its unambiguous recognition of the fact that all human beings are entitled to the enjoyment not only of the traditional civil and political rights but also of the economic, social and cultural rights without which, for most people, the traditional rights have little meaning. One of the chief claims of the Universal Declaration of Human Rights to a place in history is its recognition of this simple truth. The United Nations, however, has always recognized that there is a difference between what can be expected from States in the implementation of economic and social rights and in the enforcement of civil and political rights. The former are looked upon as programme rights, the implementation of which is to be progressive. This is particularly true of economically underdeveloped countries with large populations to feed, which can hardly be expected to guarantee the immediate implementation of all economic and social rights. Even highly industrialized States will hesitate before guaranteeing the right, for example, to work – on any literal interpretation of the meaning of that right. The decision of the General Assembly in 1952 to have two covenants instead of one was rationalized by such considerations; but it is probable that there were also other influences at work, including the fear, in some countries, of socialism. It would have been technically possible to include both categories of rights in the same instrument with different systems for their implementation, and thus to retain the essential unity of the two categories of rights recognized by the Universal Declaration of Human Rights.

Although the two kinds of rights complement each other, they often come into conflict. The dichotomy is closely related to the one between individual and collective rights. In the United Nations, when the Universal Declaration of Human Rights was adopted, first importance was still given to the rights of the individual as such. The present tendency is to give more importance to the rights of groups and of the collectivity, sometimes to the disadvantage of the individual. There have been times, indeed, when it has seemed that member states in their preoccupation with collective rights have had little concern for the traditional civil and political rights of individuals. But the conflict is not often expressed as clearly as an African delegate did when she explained the abstention of her country in the voting on the Optional Protocol to the Covenant on Civil and Political Rights. "Our abstention from the Optional Protocol," she said, "is our manifestation of our apprehension about the utilization of these rights (i.e. civil and political rights) for political ends or propaganda.... The young states must guarantee human rights. They also know better than anyone else that there can be no human rights where there is no state. That is why our countries are particularly concerned with the security of the state — in other words the collectivity at the expense of the individual." . . .

[Somewhat depressingly, such arguments continue to be raised today; one might query whether states or individuals are more secure than they were in 1973, when this article was written.]

VI. Conclusion

[One comes finally] to the question of the increasing politicization of human rights in the United Nations. Human rights cannot, nor is it desirable that they should, be divorced from politics. To do so would be to divorce them from reality. And as a matter of fact there has always been a good deal of political controversy in the debates on human rights in organs like the Third Committee of the General Assembly, the Human Rights Commission and, regrettably, even in a body of experts acting ostensibly in their individual capacity like the Sub-Commission on the [Promotion and Protection of Human Rights]. . . .

But there are also some encouraging developments. One of these is the expansion of the concept of human rights to cover new values . . . and new threats to human dignity. The Universal Declaration of Human Rights speaks, for example, of the right to privacy. But privacy was not threatened in 1948 as it now is by new developments in science and technology, including the computer. These and other contemporary challenges to human dignity are aggravated by their increasing transnational character and national measures will not be able to cope with them. It may be safely predicted, therefore, that, if the international community has a future, the United Nations will have to adjust itself to new circumstances and that the body of international human rights law will continue to grow.

. . . [I]t is still possible, notwithstanding temporary reverses in the United Nations, to speak of an ever growing interest of lawyers in international human rights law. But that interest no longer has as its chief source [World War II] and the events which led up to it, which are already beyond the experience of many international lawyers and other actors. The need to strengthen greatly the guarantees which international law can provide for the rights of individuals and groups is still paramount. More and more the individual stands alone in the face of an all-pervading State. Majorities are still intolerant. People are still discriminated against because of their race, sex, language, religion and other attributes. The great majority of people do not enjoy the economic, social and cultural rights without which there can be little human dignity. And . . . men and women are faced with new threats to their human dignity, including some unexpected byproducts of an advancing and otherwise beneficial technology. One thing is certain. The increasing contemporary interest in, and concern for, human rights does not necessarily mean that the men and women of the middle twentieth century, are more enlightened than their ancestors were or their descendants may turn out to be. Concern for the rights of the individual is more likely to be, as it has usually been in history, a sign that his rights are in special jeopardy and of a deep social malaise.

V. Final Comments and Questions

1. In his historical overview, Professor Humphrey predicts that international human rights law will continue to grow as additional challenges are taken on or arise. That prediction has held true, as numerous new human rights instruments and specialized procedures have been promulgated by the United Nations and other international institutions since Humphrey's piece was published in 1973. These new instruments and procedures cover an array of categories, including the rights of women, children, indigenous peoples, minorities, migrant workers, and human rights defenders, as well as a number of specific issues, such as torture, forced disappearances, religious intolerance, the environment, and the responsibilities of non-state actors. For a succinct overview of the contemporary UN human rights regime, see Office of the High Commissioner for Human Rights, *Human Rights: A Basic Handbook for UN Staff*, *www.ohchr.org/english/about/publications/docs/handbook.pdf*.

2. What does it mean to say that human rights are "inherent" and why are they so? Consider that elephants mourn their dead, bonobos transmit learning (i.e., cultural practices) to their young, chimpanzees use tools and can communicate in sign language, and dolphins as well as primates have exhibited altruistic behavior. See *Minding Animals: Awareness, Emotions, and Heart* (Marc Bekoff ed., 2002); Jeffery Moussaieff Masson and Susan McCarthy, *When Elephants Weep: The Emotional Lives of Animals* (1995). We share 98 percent of our genome with higher primates. At the end of the film *Blade Runner*, the dying replicant (i.e., robot) reaches out to save the life of the person who has been hunting him in order to kill him. What defines human? Cf. Stephen P. Marks, *Tying Prometheus Down: The International Law of Human Genetic Manipulation*, 3 Chicago J. Transnat'l L. 115 (2002).

3. Humphrey mentions the human rights challenges that may be faced in the future by advances in science and technology. Consider the quickly developing technology and research that, if continued, could lead to the capacity to clone humans. There appears to be general agreement worldwide that human reproductive cloning should be banned, although governments are deeply divided on the validity of research cloning of human embryos, which scientists claim could yield important medical advances. See generally National Research Council, *Scientific and Medical Aspects of Human Reproductive Cloning* (2002).

In 2005, the UN General Assembly adopted, by a vote of 84 to 34 with 37 abstentions, a Declaration on Human Cloning, GA Res. 59/280 (Mar. 8, 2005). The Declaration calls upon states to "prohibit all forms of human cloning inasmuch as they are incompatible with human dignity and the protection of human life." *Id.*, para. (b). Because of the non-binding character of the declaration and the fact that it does not reflect a consensus of states, it is not likely to impede the progress of research on embryonic cloning in many countries. Given that this ongoing research is likely to result in advances in embryonic cloning that would make reproductive cloning medically safe, many speculate that it is only a matter of time before human reproductive cloning will occur. See Kerry Lynn Mcintosh, *Illegal Beings: Human Clones and the Law* (2005); Stephen P. Marks, *Human Rights Assumptions of Restrictive and Permissive Approaches to Human Reproductive Cloning*, 6 J. Health & Hum. Rts. 81 (2002).

Contrary to popular belief, human clones would not be exact replicas of existing or dead persons; the identity in DNA would yield similarities fewer than those that exist between identical twins. Mcintosh, supra, at 53. Nonetheless, if human clones are produced, they may be stigmatized by a continuing aversion to reproductive cloning. Do current efforts to ban research contribute to stigmatizing potential human clones? Assuming that human clones may one day exist, how should the international human rights movement respond to any such stigmatization of clones or other difficulties they may encounter? Would extending human rights protections to clones in some way validate human cloning? Consider the clone army in the *Star Wars* movies and the following lyrics from the Pat Benatar song, "My Clone Sleeps Alone," which reflect likely stereotypes:

You know and I know my clone sleeps alone
She's out on her own — forever
She's programmed to work hard, she's never profane
She won't go insane, not ever. . . .

Your clone loves my clone, but yours cannot see
That's no way to be, in heaven
No sorrow, no heartache, just clone harmony
So, obviously, it's heaven.

No naughty clone ladies allowed in the eighties
No bed names, no sex games, just clone names and clone games
And you know and I know my clone sleeps alone. . . .

But they won't remember or ever be tender
No loving, no caring, no program for pairing
No VD, no cancer, on TV's the answer
No father, no mother, she's just like the other. . . .
And you know and I know my clone sleeps alone. . . .

Chapter 2

Guaranteeing Human Rights by Treaty

Is There a Right to a Safe and Healthy Environment?

As Chapter 1 has shown, efforts to protect human rights initially addressed only specific issues that affected more than one state, such as the slave trade and international armed conflict. It was the cataclysm of World War II that finally demonstrated to a large community of persons inside and outside government the need to undertake more general international efforts to promote and protect human rights. In law, the most obvious means to do so was through concluding binding agreements setting forth guaranteed rights and imposing obligations on states to secure them. Until the twentieth century most treaties were bilateral and contractual, but the proliferation of international organizations that began prior to World War I has given rise to a growing number of multilateral agreements that govern many aspects of international relations today.

The adoption of human rights treaties, is not free from controversy. It requires convincing governments, whose powers are limited by such treaties, to negotiate, conclude, and bind their states to the agreements. In addition, successful negotiations require achieving consensus on the catalogue and content of human rights, which is by no means easy in a heterogeneous international society. The duties of states that correspond to the rights must be articulated and agreement reached on establishing monitoring institutions and mechanisms. In many instances, positive results are achieved only due to the strong lobbying efforts of nongovernmental organizations and the leadership role of key states.

After human rights treaties are concluded and enter into force, other legal issues arise: How should the agreements be interpreted and gaps in their provisions be filled? To what extent can states opt out of provisions through reservations, limitations, and derogations? Do the monitoring bodies have implied as well as express powers? More generally, are human rights treaties different from other international agreements and do they thus require special rules to govern them?

This chapter looks at all of these issues through the prism of efforts to add a new human right, relating to the quality of the environment, to the catalogue of existing treaty protections. While environmental deterioration is recognized as a matter of international concern, the question of whether a rights-based approach is necessary or appropriate remains subject to debate, part of broader concerns about whether there are or should be criteria for determining when a widespread need or desire should be transformed into a right. The chapter first describes some of the current environmental issues and the link between human rights and the environment. It then reviews existing human rights treaties, starting with the general obligations imposed on members of the United Nations pursuant to the Charter. How treaties are developed, who sets the agenda, and whether or how a right to environment belongs on this agenda are matters taken up in the remainder of the chapter.

I. The State of the Global Environment and Human Well-Being

United Nations Environment Program, Geo Yearbook: An Overview of Our Changing Environment 2004-2005

2, 3, 52, 65-67, 72-80 (citations omitted)

The year 2004 strengthened the evidence of global warming and underlined the impacts of climate change on economies and the environment, as well as on human health and well-being. Four severe hurricanes in sequence brought havoc, tragedy and huge economic losses to the Caribbean and southern United States. While not all extreme weather events can be attributed directly to climate change, the intensity of such events is likely to increase as a result of global warming. . . . The European Environment Agency found clear trends of climate change impacts on glaciers, snow and ice, marine systems, terrestrial ecosystems and biodiversity, water, agriculture, human health and economy.

A number of other reports on the impacts of global warming found significant increases in the rate of melting of land and sea ice from the Arctic to

Mount Everest to the Antarctic, with major implications for humans and biodiversity. Meanwhile, evidence for the dominant human role in climate change continued to accumulate. Some scientists suggested that recent variations in solar activity have only had a minor influence in global warming. A further investigation concluded that emissions during the past century doubled the chances of the heat wave that hit Europe [in 2003], and predicted that by the 2040s, more than half of Europe's summers will be warmer than that of 2003....

Lack of access to clean potable water has been recognized as a factor increasing women's work burdens in those parts of the world where they are responsible for collecting water for basic needs like cooking, cleaning and hygiene. In some cases water collection can take up to 60 per cent of their working time. In rural Africa, women and girls spend as much as three hours a day fetching water, using up more than one-third of their daily caloric energy intake. This limits the time available for them to engage in wage-earning economic and social activities and development projects. Lack of clean water is also responsible for waterborne diseases among children — one of the major causes of child disease and mortality. This further adds to women's childcare responsibilities. The lack of easily accessible water has health implications for women as well.

Carrying heavy water jars over long distances during pregnancy can result in premature births, prolapsed uterus, or back injuries. Constant exposure to water while collecting, washing clothes, cleaning, and cooking puts women at greater risk of contracting water-related diseases. For instance, in eastern Tanzania, urinary schistosomiasis, a water-related disease, was most common among boys, and also among girls and women between the ages of 10 and 40. The incidence among boys was associated with swimming. Among women and girls, it was associated with the local practice of washing clothes while standing in schistosomiasis-infested water.

...The global trend towards privatization of public services may make matters worse, if increased water and energy prices result in decreased access to clean water for poor women. Women have been central in struggles against the privatization of public water services....

The link between health and the environment has been widely recognized, if not fully acted upon, in recent years. Unclean water and untreated sewage are responsible for the spread of water-borne diseases such as cholera and intestinal parasites. Limited access to water may be responsible for the spread of germs. Pollutants in the environment (including air pollutants from transport and industry, chemical toxins and heavy metals from industrial processes, and dioxins from waste incineration) pose a constant threat to the human body. Climate change is expected to increase the burden of disease considerably by allowing vectors to breed in latitudes or altitudes where current temperatures prevent them....

Scientists now regard certain chemicals such as PCBs, dioxins, DDT and at least 80 other pesticides as endocrine disrupters (which may interfere with normal hormone function, undermining disease resistance and reproduction. Some of them may cause declining sperm counts among men, infertility among women, miscarriages, and early puberty in girls....

Infectious diseases remain the leading cause of death in the world, accounting for about 15 million deaths per year — approximately 25 per cent of total global mortality. The impact is greatest in the developing world. In Africa and South Asia, infectious diseases are the underlying cause of two thirds of all deaths, killing mostly children and young adults. Infectious diseases are also a major cause of permanent disability and poor health and well-being for tens of millions of people, hindering economic development and sustainability in many parts of the world. The economic and social burden of diseases such as malaria is enormous. In addition to the long-term effects, short-term epidemics of emerging or re-emerging infectious diseases, such as SARS in Hong Kong, Taiwan, and Toronto and plague in India, have each cost billions of dollars. These recent epidemics underscore the fact that we live in a worldwide community that is tightly linked, and that all of us are susceptible to the burden of infectious diseases.

Decisions about land use can have direct and indirect impacts on infectious disease. Demand for land for agriculture and settlement has led to widespread deforestation and land cover change affecting wildlife habitat.... Opportunities for mosquito breeding in standing water are often increased by habitat and land-use change, by changes in natural water flows, by environmental degradation caused by human activities, and even by human-made containers such as discarded automobile tyres and non-biodegradable plastic....

Road building to open up wilderness for agriculture, mining, forestry, or other purposes can alter vector habitat, promoting the spread of vectors that favour more open areas. New roads can also lead to the migration of susceptible human populations to areas in which infectious disease pathogens and their vectors are present.

Humans are susceptible to many of the same diseases that plague the great apes (chimpanzees, bonobos, gorillas and orangutans). Historically there has been little contact between people and apes, so little opportunity for diseases to transfer. But in Central Africa, the growing migration of human populations and increased access to forest habitats have allowed the trade in wild meat (bushmeat) to flourish. Recent analyses have linked the first human cases in Ebola outbreaks to the handling of meat from infected apes.... Retroviruses including HIV and simian foamy virus (SFV) have also been contracted this way. HIV/AIDS is suspected to have originated from the fusion of two Simian Immunodeficiency Viruses, possibly acquired by humans through direct exposure to animal blood and secretions through hunting, butchering, or consumption of uncooked contaminated meat....

Intact ecosystems can help control diseases by providing a balance of species potentially involved in the life cycle of infectious diseases, along with predators and other agents that control or limit the animal reservoirs, vectors and pathogens. Disease agents that live much of their life cycle outside the human host, such as those responsible for water- and vectorborne diseases, are highly susceptible to environmental conditions. It is these diseases for which the greatest linkages to surrounding ecology have been found.

Anopheline mosquito species occupy a variety of ecological niches that can be altered by environmental changes. For example, partial deforestation, with subsequent changes in land use and human settlement patterns, has coincided with an upsurge of malaria and its Anopheline mosquito vectors in Africa, Asia, and Latin America. In eastern and southern Africa, the proportion of under-five deaths due to malaria doubled between 1982-89 and 1990-98....

Traditionally, concern about water and human health has focused on the diseases that result from inadequate or unsafe water supplies or sanitation. For example, the presence of human and animal wastes in surface waters has resulted in devastating outbreaks of cryptosporidiosis in North America and in cholera in many parts of the world. However, there are many other ways in which environment-related changes in human use and management of, and contacts with, water can affect disease incidence and transmission, at every scale from the puddle in the yard to a major irrigation system. Dam construction is a driving force in infectious disease because it alters the nature of aquatic habitats and affects species survival. The construction of large dams has caused an increased incidence of schistosomiasis. By providing habitats for infectious disease vectors, irrigation has resulted in dramatic increases in morbidity and mortality due to malaria in Africa and to Japanese encephalitis in Asia.

Emissions of carbon dioxide, methane, and other greenhouse gases from land use change and industrial activities are contributing to climate change, and thus may be indirectly involved in emerging and reemerging infectious diseases. Changes in climate inevitably lead to changes in habitat and a resultant change in the location of vectors. While the net effect globally remains uncertain and somewhat controversial, local changes in the risk of vector-borne infectious disease are virtually certain. Certain microbial organisms, such as *Neisseria meningitidis*, a common cause of meningitis, can be borne many miles on the wind in dusty conditions following exacerbated droughts in the Sahel. Cholera outbreaks are also influenced by climate events such as El Niño. . . .

In some parts of the world, illness and death from infectious diseases affect such a high proportion of the population that they severely threaten sustainable development. The current toll of human death and disability, as well as the social and economic disruptions caused by emerging and re-emerging infectious diseases, warrant a high priority for developing effective prevention and control measures. Because environmental change, in many cases, plays a major role in the emergence and re-emergence of infectious diseases, environmental policy can have a significant impact on the incidence and cost of these diseases.

Areas of potential action are very wide-ranging, covering many fields and potentially impacting the incidence of many diseases. They include protection of land, air, water, and natural habitats, and regulation of industrial chemicals and pesticide use. Effective disease prevention requires an intersectoral effort: environment, public health, industrial, agricultural, and urban policies need to be developed and implemented in concert. These efforts should occur in the context of existing national and international activities including those focused on global climate change and biodiversity. Environmental ministries and agencies may have a crucial role to play in human health. Emerging and re-emerging infectious disease should be a new area of policy concern, alongside more traditional concerns of pollution, quality of the environment and nature conservation. In some countries, governments may wish to consider adding routine infectious disease considerations, including the impact of habitat changes on hosts and vectors, to environmental impact assessments and to health impact assessments. . . .

Local measures such as reduction of unnecessary standing water to prevent malaria together with worldwide efforts to ensure safe water and improved sanitation could lead to public health triumphs. But they can only be achieved by giving a high priority to preventable health problems caused by environmental conditions. As the global SARS epidemic demonstrated, even a small number of cases of an emerging infection can cause major international social and economic disruption. In a globalizing world undergoing rapid environmental change, local actions must be combined with enhanced cooperation at global and regional levels.

The links between human rights and environmental protection seemed apparent at the first UN conference on the human environment, held in Stockholm in 1972. In the Stockholm Declaration on the Human Environment, the states participating in the conference established a foundation for linking human rights, health, and environmental protection, declaring in Principle 1: "Man has the fundamental right to freedom, equality and adequate conditions of life, in an environment of a quality that permits a life of dignity and well-being." UN Doc. A/CONF.48/14/Rev. 1, reprinted in 11 Int'l Legal Mat.1416 (1972). In 1990, the UN General Assembly recalled the Stockholm language, stating that all individuals are entitled to live in an environment adequate for their health and well-being. The resolution called for enhanced efforts to ensure a better and healthier environment. G.A. Res. 45/94, Need to Ensure a Healthy Environment for the Well-Being of Individuals (Dec. 14, 1990).

In the three decades since the Stockholm conference, international legal instruments and the decisions of human rights bodies have reformulated and elaborated the links that were established by these first declaratory statements. One approach posits environmental protection as a pre-condition to the enjoyment of internationally-guaranteed human rights, especially the rights to life and health. Environmental protection is thus an essential instrument in the effort to secure the effective universal enjoyment of human rights. Klaus Toepfer, Executive Director of the United Nations Environment Programme, reflected this approach in his statement to the 57th Session of the Commission on Human Rights in 2001:

> Human rights cannot be secured in a degraded or polluted environment. The fundamental right to life is threatened by soil degradation and deforestation and by exposures to toxic chemicals, hazardous wastes and contaminated drinking water.... Environmental conditions clearly help to determine the extent to which people enjoy their basic rights to life, health, adequate food and housing, and traditional livelihood and culture. It is time to recognize that those who pollute or destroy the natural environment are not just committing a crime against nature, but are violating human rights as well.

Another approach claims the right to a safe and healthy environment as an independent and new substantive human right. As you read the remainder of this chapter, ask yourself whether it is necessary to fill a gap in current human rights law with a new environmental treaty or whether it would weaken existing guarantees by "devaluing the currency"? How would a treaty creating a right to a safe and healthy environment help environmental protection or contribute to the enjoyment of other human rights?

II. The Protection of Human Rights through Treaties

A. *Why Rights and Why Treaties?*

In considering whether it is useful or appropriate to advocate adopting yet another declaration or treaty proclaiming a new human right, such as the right to a safe and healthy environment, it is worth questioning the conventional wisdom that the treaty (and even the declaration) approach to human rights problems warrants the extensive efforts the United Nations and other international organizations expend on it. The following brief readings introduce the themes of this chapter: what is the value of calling something a human right, what is the importance of including rights in legal instruments, and who sets the agenda and makes the decisions?

Dinah Shelton, *Human Rights, Environmental Rights, and the Right to Environment*

28 Stan. J. Int'l L. 103, 105, 106-09, 121-22 (1991) (citations omitted)

[C]urrent law and policy . . . see human rights and environmental protection as each representing different, but overlapping, societal values. The two fields share a core of common interests and objectives, although obviously not all human rights violations are necessarily linked to environmental degradation. Likewise, environmental issues cannot always be addressed effectively within the human rights framework, and any attempt to force all issues into a human rights rubric may fundamentally distort the concept of human rights. . . .

In order to contribute to environmental protection using a human rights approach — or vice versa — . . . several alternatives [exist]. First, environmental problems may be combated through the assertion of existing human rights, such as the rights to life, personal security, health, and food. In this regard, a safe and healthy environment may be viewed either as a pre-condition to the exercise of existing rights or as inextricably intertwined with the enjoyment of these rights. A second, intermediate position proposes a set of "environmental rights" (rights of the environment as well as rights to the environment?) based upon existing rights to information and the right to participate in political decision-making processes. Third and most ambitiously, a specific "right to environment" could be formulated and added to the current catalogue of human rights. . . .

Laws often respond to perceived social problems by restraining the exercise of power and establishing agreed norms of public conduct. Viewed from this perspective, laws protecting human rights respond to threats to human dignity and existence by upholding the fundamental, immutable foundations of human rights as recognized in international instruments. In addition, formulations of rights reflect emerging social values. For example, although slavery was once widespread, nations now universally repudiate it, and international law recognizes freedom from slavery as a non-derogable human right. More recently, a right to privacy has been recognized in response to technological advances spawning increased intrusion into home and family.

The goal of international human rights law, as expressed in the Universal Declaration of Human Rights and the International Covenants, is "freedom, justice and peace in the world." The means of achieving this goal begin with legal recognition of the equal and inalienable rights of all members of the human family and of the inherent dignity possessed by each individual. An immediate, practical objective of international human rights law is to gain international recognition of specific human rights. Successfully placing personal entitlements within the category of individual human rights preserves them from the ordinary political process. Individual rights may thus significantly limit the political will of a democratic majority, as well as a dictatorial minority. For example, in attempting to attain a widely accepted policy goal, even a representative democracy may not produce legislation that limits or abolishes the individual right to be free from cruel, inhuman, or degrading treatment or punishment. This limitation on domestic political decisions is potentially an important consequence of elaborating a right to environment, particularly given the high short-term costs involved in many environmental protection measures and the resulting political disfavor.

[S]ome environmentalists fear that a human-centered, utilitarian view of environmental law ultimately reduces all non-human aspects of the ecosystem to consideration of their short-term economic value to humanity, exacerbating resource over-exploitation and environmental deterioration. The result becomes particularly troublesome in countries where poverty and disease make economic development a priority and where long-term sustainability may be sacrificed to immediate gain. Of course, industrialized societies also have shown great unwillingness to sacrifice current lifestyles, including reliance on personal automobiles, in order to achieve environmental goals. One commentator, therefore, argues for acceptance of an independent basis for environmental protection, rather than linking environmental integrity to human needs. Reflecting the latter view to some extent, international instruments increasingly have recognized the intrinsic value of nature. For example, the World Charter for Nature proclaims that "every form of life is unique, warranting respect regardless of its worth to man. . . ." . . .

Not every social problem must result in a claim which can be expressed as a human right. Indeed, the criteria for considering a claim as a human right generate extensive debates, leading to a lack of consensus as to existing human rights. For example, despite United Nations proclamations of the indivisibility of civil and political rights from economic, social, and cultural rights, the United States government has . . . refused to give equal status to the latter. [T]he Reagan Administration Deputy Assistant Secretary of State for Human Rights and Humanitarian Affairs called the idea that economic and social rights constitute human rights a "myth." . . .

The volume of the debate increases when further claims are formally proposed for addition to the human rights catalogue. There are legitimate fears that the addition of numerous claims will devalue existing human rights. On the other hand, necessity may lead articulated claims to evolve into recognized rights where satisfaction of needs basic to human dignity is threatened beyond the ability of individual self-help. Some authors have proposed criteria which a claim must meet before it is included as a human right, while others have concluded that establishing substantive criteria for determining human rights is unworkable. In this regard, Richard Bilder has concluded that "in practice, a claim is an international human right if the General Assembly says it is."

Okechukwu Ibeanu, *Adverse effects of the illicit movement and dumping of toxic and dangerous products and wastes on the enjoyment of human rights*

Report of the Special Rapporteur, UN Doc. E/CN.4/2005/45 (2004)

18. Several mechanisms and bodies are in place at the international and regional levels to regulate the transboundary movement of hazardous wastes and products. In particular several environmental agreements . . . have among their overall objectives to reduce the negative effects that the movement of these dangerous products may have on human health and the natural environment. Existing multilateral environmental agreements (MEAs) most relevant to the mandate of the Special Rapporteur have been analyzed in previous reports by the Special Rapporteur. . . .

19. Although several of the existing MEAs aim to protect human health, the scope of their respective mandates — focusing largely on the technical and procedural aspects of movements of hazardous products and wastes — does not extend to consideration of the adverse effect on the full range of existing human rights of illicit movements. Furthermore, with the exception of the newly established Compliance Committee of the Aarhus Convention [on the Right to Environmental Information, to Public Participation in Environmental Decision-Making and to Redress for Environmental Harm], the MEAs do not allow for consideration of individual communications concerning alleged non-compliance resulting in human rights violations.

20. Thus, the value-added of the Special Rapporteur's mandate arises from its human rights focus, i.e. from the attention devoted to the link between the movement and dumping of dangerous products and wastes and their potential or real negative effects on the enjoyment of human rights, and how a human rights approach can ensure effective redress for any harm occurring as a result of such movements. In other words, the unique character of the Special Rapporteur's mandate derives from the fact that it poses human being and their rights at the core of his mission.

Richard B. Bilder, *Rethinking International Human Rights: Some Basic Questions*

1969 Wis. L. Rev. 171, 205-207 (1969)

Arguments favoring reliance on declarations and conventions emphasize that they define the content of human rights concepts and establish clearer standards of governmental conduct. They educate both officials and the general public in these norms, place governments failing to respect human rights on the defensive, and help create and legitimate internal and external pressures for human rights improvement. Conventions lift general standards to the level of concrete binding rules. Perhaps most important, declarations may stimulate, and conventions require, enactment of internal legislation to implement applicable human rights standards. For example, the provisions of the Universal Declaration have been drawn on by over a score of new nations in drafting their constitutions. In some cases they may help a government to legitimate reforms it itself wishes to undertake. Even where such legislation is initially pro forma, it tends over time to have a growing normative impact.

However there are limitations to such documents.... [T]hey may foster a harmful illusion of accomplishment and serve as an excuse for failure to pursue more practical, if more difficult, courses of action.

International human rights declarations, some argue, are of little real significance, Since they are only recommendations without binding legal effect, few governments may take them seriously.... Moreover, norms spelled out in declarations are frequently later reflected in conventions; where these conventions subsequently gain only limited acceptance, any informative value the declaration might have may be further diluted.

Conventions similarly may have many weaknesses. First, they are legally binding only on states which accept them, and governments with human rights problems within the scope of the convention may simply not become parties....

Second, the provisions of such conventions often reflect agreement only at the lowest common level. Even at this level, a basic lack of agreement or willingness to be committed may be reflected in deliberately vague standards, crippling exceptions, and numerous escape hatches.

Third, even ratification of conventions may have little relation to their observance. Outside (and some would say even within) the small circle of Western countries, the sense of obligation to international legal commitments may be weak, particularly with instruments such as human rights conventions where expectations of compliance are small. Absent effective procedures for authoritative interpretation and implementation, all governments know that the likelihood of being held to such promises is remote; lip-service can be paid and propaganda gains achieved at little risk.

Finally, the implicit faith that such international instruments place in internal law as a way of attaining human rights objectives may itself be over-optimistic. Even where governments do ratify and enact internal implementing legislation, the practical effect of such measures may be slight. Law on the books, without vigorous enforcement, may have little relation to actual conduct. In many cases social problems underlying human rights denials may be hard for law to reach in any case. Unfortunately, we still know very little about the relation between legal norms and structural and cultural factors in a society, of the ways law can be used to effect social change, or about how declared law actually penetrates into the attitudes, propensities and actions of officials and ordinary people. In less developed societies, the general population — and even officials — may not know or care about the written law. Law may even be regarded with hostility as traditionally an instrument of oppression. In other cases enforcement may require economic or political resources beyond a government's means. Thus, internal legislation protecting human rights may often prove only a beginning step in achieving solutions to human rights problems.

Of course, the truth may lie in between. Despite evident weaknesses, international instruments seem in fact to accomplish more than we might expect. Inevitably they legitimate human rights objectives and create some pressures for observance. That governments create obstacles in their drafting, refuse to ratify them, and constantly invoke their provisions in international debate show that they are regarded as of at least some significance. Over time their normative impact may grow as the standards they set are incorporated in their national constitutions and legislation and gradually permeate various societies. Even governments ratifying what they believe are innocuous conventions with which they were already in full compliance may discover that they have more human rights problems than they thought. Thus, the parties to the European Convention [have] becom[e] aware of hitherto unrecognized deficiencies in their criminal procedures and guarantees of due process.

Moreover, any doubts we may feel as to the effectiveness of conventions as an instrument of change should not blind us to their important role as an obstacle to retrogression. Conditions change and seemingly unimportant ratifications today may become significant tomorrow. For example, African governments may endorse the Race Convention as a weapon against anti-black racism, believing they incur no real commitments; but the problem of the future may be anti-white racism. The European Human Rights Convention proved an embarrassment to the Greek military junta and constitutes a continuing obstacle to any resurgent Nazism.

The problem may be less that international declarations and conventions accomplish too little than that we expect too much. If we recognize that they are only limited tools, we may see their contributions in better perspective. Most important, the dynamics of international organization make such instruments relatively easy to obtain, and we must do what we can. . . .

Comments and Questions

1. How do preferences emerge as claims and become translated into rights? Who sets the agenda? Are there lessons to be learned from the outlawing of slavery discussed in Chapter 1?

2. Some of the readings in the next section address the issue of whether there should be criteria for deciding when a claim should be included in the list of internationally-guaranteed human rights. Even with such criteria, is it true that the process is ultimately a political one and that human rights are whatever the General Assembly decides they are? Recall that the General Assembly has no law-making power and that its resolutions do not directly bind states. Thus, while the General Assembly may "create" rights, they are political rather than legal. Only treaties, discussed in this chapter and customary international law, discussed in Chapter 3, can create legally binding obligations on states.

B. *Human Rights Provisions in the UN Charter*

1. The Content of the Charter

The United Nations and Human Rights

Eighteenth Report of the Commission to Study the Organization of Peace 1-4 (1968)

I. The Development of the Concept of International Protection of Human Rights

It was during one of the darkest hours of the war, when the Axis powers achieved almost complete control of the European continent that President Roosevelt provided in his "Four Freedoms" — freedom of speech, freedom of religion, freedom from want and freedom from fear — a rallying cry for all those suffering from the ravages of war and totalitarianism. After another disaster, the Pearl Harbor attack, the Allied Governments agreed in Washington on the "Declaration by United Nations" which named as the basic goal of victory the preservation of "human rights and justice in their own lands as well as in other lands." Encouraged by this statement, various official and unofficial groups, both in the United States and other countries, started immediately to work on an International Bill of Rights which would be proclaimed by the United Nations after their victory and which would become one of the cornerstones of the new world order to be built after the war. While the official enthusiasm for a codification of the basic principles for the protection of human rights later cooled down, active pressure of non-governmental organizations led to the inclusion in the Charter of the United Nations of several provisions on human rights.

II. The Charter of the United Nations

In the preamble to the Charter, the peoples of the United Nations have reaffirmed their "faith in fundamental human rights, in the dignity and worth of the human person, in the equal rights of men and women and of nations large and small," and their determination "to promote social progress and better standards of life in larger freedom." Article 1 of the Charter lists among the main purposes of the United Nations the achievement of international cooperation "in promoting and encouraging respect for human rights and for fundamental freedoms for all without distinction as to race, sex, language, or religion." Similarly, in accordance with Article 55 of the Charter, the United Nations has the duty to promote "universal respect for, and observance of human rights and fundamental freedoms for all without distinction as to race, sex, language, or religion." In Article 56, all Members of the United Nations "pledge themselves to take joint and separate action in cooperation with the Organization for the achievement of the purposes set forth in Article 55."

The Charter of the United Nations contains also significant grants of power to various organs of the United Nations. Thus, under Article 13, the General Assembly has the duty to initiate studies and make recommendations for the purpose of "assisting in the realization of human rights and fundamental freedoms for all without distinction as to race, sex, language, or religion." Responsibility for the discharge of the functions set forth in Chapter IX of the Charter (which includes Articles 55 and 56 mentioned above) is vested by Article 60 in the General Assembly and, under the authority of the General Assembly, in the Economic and Social Council. In discharging this responsibility the Economic and Social Council may, according to Article 62, "make recommendations for the purpose of promoting respect for, and observance of, human rights and fundamental freedoms for all"; under Article 68, it has an obligation to set up a commission "for the promotion of human rights," which is the only functional commission expressly provided for by the Charter itself; and, under Article 64, it may make arrangements with the Members of the United Nations to obtain reports on steps taken by them to give effect to the recommendations of the General Assembly and of the Council. . . .

These provisions define clearly the obligations of all Members and the powers of the Organization in the field of human rights. While the provisions are general, nevertheless they have the force of positive international law and create basic duties which all Members must fulfill in good faith. They must cooperate with the United Nations in promoting both universal respect for and observance of human rights and fundamental freedoms for all without distinction as to race, sex, language, or religion. For this purpose, they have pledged themselves to take such joint and separate action as may be necessary. The General Assembly and, under the Assembly's authority, the Economic and Social Council are responsible, under Article 60 of the Charter, for the discharge of the functions of the United Nations in this area, and for this purpose may initiate such studies and make such recommendations as they may deem necessary. Any refusal to participate in the United Nations program to promote the observance of human rights constitutes a violation of the Charter. The General Assembly may recommend, under Article 14 of the Charter, "measures for the peaceful adjustment of any situation, regardless of origin, which it deems likely to impair the general welfare or friendly relations among nations, including situations resulting from a violation of the provisions of the present Charter setting forth the Purposes and Principles of the United Nations." As the obligation to promote and encourage respect for human rights is set forth in the statement of Purposes in Article 1 of the Charter, the broad powers of the General Assembly under Article 14 clearly apply in case of a violation of the duty to cooperate with the United Nations in this area.

As far as the United States is concerned, the Charter of the United Nations . . . has been ratified by the United States. . . . Being embodied in a treaty, the obligations under the Charter form part of the law of the United States. They impose directly an obligation upon the federal government to promote the observance of human rights by all means at its disposal.

2. Invocation of the Human Rights Clauses on the International Level

On the international level, the human rights clauses of the UN Charter have been invoked frequently. In drafting texts, the "obligations" of member states pursuant to Articles 55 and 56 are explicitly referred to in the preambles of nearly all UN human rights treaties. In inter-state relations generally, they are raised in the course of UN debates or other diplomatic exchanges. Occasionally, states have been known to argue before international tribunals that the Charter imposes legal obligations upon states that, in the particular case, the respondent state has violated. Thus, in the *Hostages Case,* 1980 I.C.J. 3 (Judgment of May 24, 1980), the United States urged the International Court of Justice (I.C.J.) to condemn Iran's seizure of 52 U.S. hostages as a violation of fundamental human rights recognized by the international community. "The existence of such fundamental rights for all human beings," the United States contended, "with the existence of a corresponding duty on the part of every State to respect and observe them, are now reflected, inter alia, in the Charter of the United Nations. . . ." Memorial of the United States (*U.S. v. Iran*), 1980 I.C.J, Pleadings (Case Concerning United States Diplomatic and Consular Staff in Tehran) 182 (Jan. 12, 1980), citing Articles 1, 55, and 56 of the UN Charter.

An earlier Advisory Opinion of the ICJ held that the policy of apartheid, as applied by South Africa in Namibia (South West Africa), constituted a violation of the legal obligations South Africa had assumed under the UN Charter. Consider the two relevant paragraphs of the Court's Advisory Opinion and the late Professor Schwelb's exegesis that follows.

Legal Consequences for States of the Continued Presence of South Africa in Namibia (South West Africa)

1971 I.C.J. 16, 37 (Advisory Opinion of June 21, 1971)

130. It is undisputed, and is amply supported by documents annexed to South Africa's written statement in these proceedings, that the official governmental policy pursued by South Africa in Namibia is to achieve a complete physical separation of races and ethnic groups in separate areas within the Territory. The application of this policy has required, as has been conceded by South Africa, restrictive measures of control officially adopted and enforced in the Territory by the coercive power of the former Mandatory [South Africa]. These measures establish limitations, exclusions or restrictions for the members of the indigenous population groups in respect of their participation in certain types of activities, fields of study or of training, labour or employment and also submit them to restrictions or exclusions of residence and movement in large parts of the territory.

131. Under the Charter of the United Nations, the former Mandatory had pledged itself to observe and respect, in a territory having an international status, human rights and fundamental freedoms for all without distinction as to race. To establish instead, and to enforce, distinctions, exclusions, restrictions and limitations exclusively based on grounds of race, colour, descent or national or ethnic origin which constitute a denial of fundamental human rights is a flagrant violation of the purposes and principles of the Charter.

[Both the Security Council and the General Assembly subsequently adopted resolutions commending the Court's Advisory Opinion. The Security Council noted it "with appreciation" (S.C. Res. 301 (1971), while the General Assembly took similar notice "with satisfaction" (G.A. Res. 2871 (1971).]

Egon Schwelb, *The International Court of Justice and the Human Rights Clauses of the Charter*

66 Am. J. Int'l L. 337, 338, 341-350 (1972)

[O]ne particular aspect of the Advisory Opinion [is] the interpretation by the Court of the human rights clauses of this Charter and Court's answer to the question whether States Members of the United Nations, by becoming parties to the Charter, have undertaken legal obligations in the matter of human rights. . . .

III. The Practice of the United Nations and of Member States

In the actual practice of the various organs of the United Nations over the past 25 years the obstacles to taking action based on the human rights provisions of the Charter have proved to be far less formidable than the cleavage of theoretical opinions of scholars and of abstract statements by governments would lead one to assume. In the practice of the United Nations and of its Members neither the vagueness and generality of the human rights clauses of the Charter nor the domestic jurisdiction clause have prevented the United Nations from considering, investigating, and judging concrete human rights situations, provided there was a majority strong enough and wishing strongly enough to attempt to influence the particular development. The cases of action of this type are too well known to require, and too numerous to permit of, listing in the present context. . . .

The question of human rights and discrimination in South Africa has occupied the United Nations since 1946. . . . The concern of the Organization was originally limited to the question of the treatment of Indians . . . in South Africa. Its scope was extended to cover the whole question of race conflict resulting from the policies of apartheid in 1952. In 1953 the General Assembly found that the racial policies of the Government of South Africa and their consequences are contrary to the Charter, a finding that was to be repeated on later occasions with increasing emphasis. In 1962 the General Assembly established a permanent organ, the Special Committee on the policies of apartheid of the Government of South Africa with the mandate to keep the racial policies of South Africa under review when the Assembly is not in session. . . .

[The author discusses in detail the activities of the Security Council and the Commission on Human Rights with regard to South Africa's violation of the human rights clauses in the Charter.]

IV. The View of the Court

When rendering its opinion on "the legal consequences for States of the continued presence of South Africa in Namibia, notwithstanding Security Council resolution 276 (1970)," the Court divided its reply into three parts dealing with the legal consequences of South Africa's continued presence respectively (1) for South Africa, (2) for other States Members of the United Nations, and (3) for states which are not Members of the United Nations. For the purposes of the present investigation it is necessary to deal only with the first part of the Court's conclusions. In regard to the consequences for South Africa, the Court found, by 13 votes to 2, that "the continued presence of South Africa in Namibia being illegal, South Africa is under obligation to withdraw its administration from Namibia immediately and thus put an end to its occupation of the Territory."

In Resolution 2145 (XXI) of October 27, 1966, the General Assembly, "convinced that the administration of the Mandated Territory [of South West Africa] by South Africa has been conducted in a manner contrary to the Mandate, the Charter of the United Nations and the Universal Declaration of Human Rights," had inter alia declared "that South Africa has failed to fulfill its obligations in respect of the administration of the Mandated Territory and to ensure the moral and material wellbeing and security of the indigenous inhabitants of South West Africa and has, in fact, disavowed the Mandate." The General Assembly had further decided that the Mandate conferred upon South Africa "is therefore terminated" and "that South Africa has no other right to administer the Territory."

In examining this action of the General Assembly which had been alleged to be ultra vires, the Court found that a material breach of its obligations had been committed by South Africa, that the supervisory powers of the Council of the League of Nations had passed to the General Assembly and that the latter in terminating the Mandate had acted within the framework of its competence. Among very many other objections against Resolution 2145 (XXI) of the General Assembly it was argued on behalf of South Africa that the consideration set forth in the resolution, "relating to the failure of South Africa to fulfill its obligations in respect of the administration of the mandated territory, called for a detailed factual investigation before the General Assembly could adopt resolution 2145 (XXI) or the Court pronounce upon its validity." In its oral statement and in written communications to the Court, the Government of South Africa expressed the desire to supply the Court with further factual information concerning the purposes and objectives of South Africa's policy of separate development or apartheid, contending that to establish a breach of South Africa's substantive international obligations under the Mandate it would be necessary to prove that a particular exercise of South Africa's legislative or administrative powers was not directed in good faith towards the purpose of promoting to the utmost the well-being and progress of the inhabitants. It is claimed by the Government of South Africa that no act or omission on its part would constitute a violation of its international obligations unless it is shown that such act or emission was actuated by a motive, or directed towards a purpose other than one to promote the interests of the inhabitants of the Territory.

In regard to this request made by South Africa, the Court found that

> . . . no factual evidence is needed for the purpose of determining whether the policy of apartheid as applied by South Africa in Namibia is in conformity with the international obligations assumed by South Africa under the Charter of the United Nations. In order to determine whether the laws and decrees applied by South Africa in Namibia, which are a matter of public record, constitute a violation of the purposes and principles of the Charter of the United Nations, the question of intent or governmental discretion is not relevant; nor is it necessary to investigate or determine the effects of those measures upon the welfare of the inhabitants. . . . [Here the Court cites paragraphs 130 and 131, quoted supra.]

When the Court speaks of "conformity with the international obligations assumed . . . under the Charter," of "a violation of the purposes and principles of the Charter," of the pledge to observe and respect human rights and fundamental freedoms for all, when it finds that certain actions "constitute a denial of fundamental human rights," and classifies them as "a flagrant violation of the purposes and principles of the Charter," it leaves no doubt that, in its view, the Charter does impose on the Members of the United Nations legal obligations in the human rights field.

The Court says that the former Mandatory had pledged itself to observe and respect, *in a territory having an international status*, human rights and fundamental freedoms for all without distinction as to race. The words indicate that the Court was dealing with a territory having an international status, a fact which was instrumental in the matter's having been brought before the General Assembly and the Security Council. If Namibia (South West Africa) had not been a territory having an international status, the question would not have been submitted to the Court. Moreover, the location of the acts constituting a violation of the Charter in such a territory might, the Court could be understood to say, be an aggravating circumstance, as it were. The inclusion of the words "in a territory having an international status" cannot be interpreted to mean that, in the view of the Court, to establish and to enforce distinctions, exclusions, restrictions and limitations exclusively based on grounds of race, color, descent or national or ethnic origin which constitute a denial of fundamental human rights is not a flagrant violation of the purposes and principles of the Charter, if committed elsewhere than in an international territory. The pledge (Articles 55 and 56) which the Court invokes, [however,] is not a pledge to promote universal respect for, and observance of, human rights and fundamental freedoms in international territories only, but "for all without distinction as to race, sex, language, or religion." What is a flagrant violation of the purposes and principles of the Charter when committed in Namibia, is also such a violation when committed in South Africa proper or, for that matter, in any other sovereign Member State or in a non-self-governing or Trust Territory. . . .

The statement in paragraphs 130 and 131 of the Advisory Opinion is not, if it is permissible to use a common law term in an international law context and in regard to an Advisory Opinion, an obiter dictum. It is an essential part of the ratio decidendi. The qualification as a flagrant violation of the purposes and principles of the Charter of the restrictive measures of control officially adopted and enforced in the Territory by the coercive power of South Africa was the justification for the Court's rejection of South Africa's desire to supply further factual information. It was the basis for the Court's decision that no factual evidence, additional to the documents annexed to South Africa's written statements, was needed for determining that the policy of separate development or apartheid in Namibia was not in conformity with the international obligations of South Africa. . . .

3. The Domestic Status of the Charter's Human Rights Clauses

Oscar Schachter, *The Charter and the Constitution: The Human Rights Provisions in American Law*

4 Vand. L. Rev. 643, 646-653 (1951) (footnotes omitted)

DO THE HUMAN RIGHTS PROVISIONS INVOLVE LEGAL OBLIGATIONS ON THE PART OF MEMBER STATES?

As we have seen, unless this question is answered in the affirmative, the human rights provisions cannot be considered as rules of law by American courts. But the question has of course wider significance than its implications for American law; for whether or not the Charter provisions on human rights prescribe legal duties is a matter of considerable importance to all of the Members of the United Nations. . . .

The principal provisions of the Charter involved are Articles 55(c) and 56. . . . It has been maintained by some authorities that in spite of the "pledge" expressly taken in Article 56, these provisions do not impose upon Members of the United Nations the legal obligation to respect and observe human rights and fundamental freedoms. The provisions of the Charter are characterized as statements of "guiding principles" or "general purposes," or indeed, as "legally meaningless and redundant." In support of this conclusion, the essential argument is that the United Nations has no compulsory powers in regard to human rights; this is an argument based first on the fact that the organs concerned with human rights (i.e. the General Assembly and the Economic and Social Council) may make only recommendations which have no obligatory effect and secondly on Article 2(7), forbidding United Nations intervention in matters of domestic jurisdiction. Kelsen also supports this position with special reference to the language of Article 56. He points out that the pledge is "to take joint and separate action operation with the Organization"; he then states that the only effective way to cooperate with the Organization is by compliance with the recommendations of the appropriate organs; but the Charter does not make such recommendations obligation; hence (he infers) it is left solely to the Members to decide what kind of action they think appropriate to achieve the cooperation sought by the Organization. Consequently, Kelsen concludes, the pledge does not express a "true obligation." [See H. Kelsen, *The Law of the United Nations* (1950).]

This brings us to the crux of the problem: Is the pledge to take action in cooperation with the Organization negated by the fact that the Organization admittedly cannot make mandatory decisions in regard to human rights? Or, stated in another way, if it is admitted (as it must be) that an organ may not "order" a

Member to take action regarding human rights, does that mean that the Member may act as it deems appropriate, entirely free from legal limitations under Article 56? Is it possible to have [a] legal obligation to act "in co-operation" which does not require full compliance with the recommendations of the Organization. In considering these questions it is necessary to review briefly the language and history of the human rights provisions. It may be useful to begin with the word "pledge" as used in Article 56. A pledge in its ordinary English meaning is a solemn promise or an undertaking; as used in a legal instrument, the word itself connotes a legal obligation. In the French version "les Membres s'engagent... à agir"; this too is the language of legal obligation. The discussions at San Francisco show that this was not accidental; it was stated that "pledge" has been used as a term at least as "strong" as the word "undertake" and that the Technical Committee which drafted the provision attached particular importance to this point. It is therefore difficult to avoid at least a prima facie conclusion that the pledge in Article 56 was intended to constitute a legal commitment on the part of Members.

Now, it is also true that in the course of formulating Article 56 many of the delegations insisted that this provision would not mean that the Organization would have the right to interfere with the internal affairs of Members. It was the understanding that Article 2(7), the "domestic jurisdiction" clause, applied to Articles 55 and 56 and consequently that "intervention" (or enforcement) of human rights by the United Nations was prohibited. But whatever may be the precise meaning of this clause it in no way implies that the pledge in Article 56 is without legal force. It is after all a common-place in international law that States assume duties of a legal character which are not enforceable by international organs. The Charter itself has many other articles imposing obligations with no provision for enforcement or implementation. Of course, some jurists consider that these are not true legal obligations since they do not involve sanctions for contrary conduct; but this is a specific use of the term obligation which is not generally accepted in international law or in the interpretation of the Charter. Throughout the Charter it is evident that obligations are imposed upon Members, even though in most cases these obligations do not have sanctions. Indeed, it may even be persuasively argued that the concern of the draftsmen in connection with Article 56 with the prohibition against intervention was based on their understanding and intention that this Article should constitute a legal undertaking, for if it were only a statement of purpose, there would have been little reason to stress noninterference by the Organization.

It is also of considerable significance that in the actual application of the Charter, the Members of the United Nations have found no incompatibility between the principle of nonintervention in Article 2(7) and the position that Members have a definite legal responsibility with respect to human rights by virtue of Article 56. In more than one resolution adopted by the General Assembly, it is clearly stated that Members have made a legal commitment to respect and observe human rights; and in the course of UN discussions, numerous representatives including several of legal eminence, have consistently maintained the position that the Charter imposes obligations of a legal character on Member States in regard to the observance of human rights.

This brings us to a further point of controversy; even if it is conceded that there is a legal commitment in Article 56, is it not merely a general duty to cooperate which can be construed by each State as it sees fit, and does this not in effect nullify the notion of a legal obligation? Here again, the travaux préparatoires afford some illumination. It appears from the San Francisco records that, at one stage, the pledge in Article 56 was threefold: it called for joint action, for separate action, and for co-operation with the Organization. The U.S. delegation then expressed doubt concerning the pledge to take separate action; it preferred simply a pledge to co-operate. But the Australian delegation, the original sponsor of this provision, continued to urge inclusion of a pledge to take separate action as distinguished from co-operation; this position was supported by the Belgian and British delegations. The final text represented a compromise: the pledge to take separate action was qualified by the phrase "in co-operation with the organization." This compromise text does not seem to have received further clarification in the San Francisco discussions; and no opinions were expressed specifically on what was meant by "co-operation with the Organization." It appears that the U.S. delegation favoured this qualification in order to eliminate the possibility of an interpretation under which the obligation would extend to "internal economic matters . . . and therefore the Organization would be permitted to intervene in them."

The foregoing history seems to bring out several points of significance in connection with this problem. First, it reveals that the draftsmen in San Francisco rejected a text which provided merely for a pledge to co-operate with the Organization and that they attached importance to the words "separate action," although such action was to be "in co-operation with the Organization." Secondly, it indicates that this latter expression was mainly intended to avoid the implication that "separate action" would open the door to intervention by the United Nations in domestic affairs. Thirdly, there is no indication that the phrase "co-operation" was intended to confer unlimited discretion on the Member States — a result which would be almost the direct opposite of the normal meaning of co-operation and of the committee's intentions. Admittedly, the record also indicates that the obligation is far from precise and leaves considerable latitude to each Member State to carry it out in its own way. But does this mean that it cannot be considered a legal obligation? In view of both the history and the language of this Article, this would certainly be an extreme conclusion; it would, in effect, make a mockery of the efforts of the draftsmen at San Francisco to formulate a pledge which would have legal significance and effectiveness. There is certainly no overriding reason to arrive at this result.

It must be borne in mind, in this respect, that the degree of precision required in a treaty is not the same as that demanded of a criminal statute. Treaty obligations are often expressed in general terms and leave broad discretion to the States which are Parties. But the fact that a State is free to carry out those obligations by its own methods and its own way does not destroy the legal character of this obligation. In the case of Article 56 there is no compelling reason to define a priori and in detail all the implications of the obligation; it is evident that there are large areas where the purposes under Article 55 are as yet so undefined that it is impossible to say what kind of action would be required if a State is to co-operate with the Organization.

However, it is equally evident that in other respects the broad language of Article 55 has specific meaning and effect; this is particularly true of clause (c) relating to human rights and fundamental freedoms. The clause itself contains the significant prohibition against discrimination because of race, sex, language or religion, a theme which is recurrent throughout the Charter and which in itself furnishes considerable content to the notion of human rights. Moreover, it must not be forgotten that the concept of human rights is not an abstract notion introduced for the first time in the Charter; it has had (under various names) a long and rich history in constitutional law, in the practice of states and in the development of the law of nations. Nor is it irrelevant in this connection to consider the wide measure of agreement regarding most specific rights and freedoms which was revealed during the preparation of the Declaration on Human Rights and by the specific resolutions adopted by the General Assembly and other principal organs. Though the outer boundaries of "human rights" remain undefined (perhaps undefinable) it can hardly be denied that the concept has a special core of meaning which is widely recognized and accepted. Certainly an American lawyer familiar with the due process and equal protection clauses and the other broad phrases of the U.S. Constitution is not likely take the position that a concept such as human rights must be denied legal effect because of its breadth and generality.

There is therefore no sufficient reason to characterize Article 56 as a mere statement of purpose, devoid of legal effect. To do so, as we have seen, would be contrary to both the language and the ascertainable intentions of the framers of the Charter. And even if it be granted that there is some obscurity in the text or the intent of the drafters, the choice between alternative interpretations should legitimately be resolved in favour of that construction which best effectuates the major purposes of the provision. In this case, obviously the major purpose is the promotion of human rights; if a "pledge" to take action to achieve that purpose is interpreted as having no obligatory effect, the whole point of the pledge is lost and it becomes entirely superfluous. A construction which renders an article virtually meaningless is certainly contrary to the principle of effectiveness in the interpretation of treaties. Undoubtedly, there are occasions when the rule of effectiveness may run counter to the manifest intention of the parties; in this case, however, effectiveness — at least to the extent of a legal commitment — is precisely what most of the drafters desired.

Thus, both major rules of interpretation — that based on intent and that on effectiveness — reinforce each other and, taken together, practically make inescapable the conclusion that the pledge in Article 56 constitutes a legal commitment on the part of Members to take action in co-operation with the Organization to achieve "respect for and observance of human rights and fundamental freedoms for all. . . ."

Note: U.S. Recognition of the Legal Status of the Human Rights Clauses

The United States upon numerous occasions has adopted Professor Schachter's reasoning sub silentio and argued that the human rights clauses of the UN Charter give rise to international legal obligations on the part of member states. Thus, when the revolutionary government of Iraq in early 1969 summary tried, convicted, and hung in public 14 of its nationals (9 of them Jews) on the ground that the were Israeli spies — their bodies displayed in a grisly carnival atmosphere — the U.S. Ambassador to the United Nations, Charles Yost, raised the matter with the Security Council in a letter (24 UN SCOR Supp. (Jan.-Mar. 1969) at 65, UN Doc. S/8987 (1969)), which said in part:

> The Government of the United States recognizes the legal right of any government to bring to trial and administer justice to any of its citizens. However, the manner in which these executions and the trials that preceded them were conducted scarcely conforms to normally accepted standards of respect for human rights and human dignity or to the obligations in this regard that the United Nations Charter imposes upon all Members. . . . The United States hopes that the worldwide revulsion aroused by the reports of these trials and executions will induce those responsible to carry out their solemn Charter obligations to promote "universal respect for and observance of human rights and fundamental freedoms for all without distinction as to race, sex, language or religion."

If you had been a Department of State lawyer assigned to the U.S. Mission to the United Nations, to which articles would you have referred had Security Council President Max Jakobson's office telephoned for further explanation of "the obligations in this regard that the United Nations Charter imposes upon all Members"? In response to an inquiry by one of our colleagues two years later, the Office of the Legal Adviser of the Department of State, in a letter dated March 18, 1971, explained that "it is the view of the United States Government that the right to a fair trial before an impartial tribunal is a 'fundamental freedom' and that the specific facts in the situation described in [the above letter] justified the statement by Ambassador Yost that the obligations of the Charter had not been met." Is this explanation satisfactory? Does it provide much guidance in identifying other international human rights obligations of states under the UN Charter? Could an argument be made that a safe and healthy environment is today included among the Charter guarantees?

The right to a fair trial is specifically guaranteed by Article 10 of the Universal Declaration of Human Rights and Article 14 of the International Covenant on Civil and Political Rights. See generally David Weissbrodt, *The Right to a Fair Trial under the Universal Declaration of Human Rights and the International Covenant on Civil and Political Rights* (2001). Why did Ambassador Yost not mention these instruments explicitly? Would not his argument have been strengthened by their invocation? Assuming for present purposes that the fair trial norms in these instruments have not achieved the status of customary international law, can they be read back into the UN Charter, as Professor Schachter suggests, to bind states as treaty law? Cf. Louis Henkin, *The Constitution at Sea*, 36 Me. L. Rev. 20I, 209 n. 31 (1984) ("The United States . . . is a party to the UN Charter which includes general human rights obligations, and it may be bound by, some of the provisions of the Universal Declaration of Human Rights, either as elaborations of the Charter obligation or under customary international law.").

Since the Yost letter, the United States repeatedly has taken the position that the human rights clauses of the UN Charter have legal effect and thus must be observed by all countries, including the United States. Thus, the Acting Legal Adviser of the Department of State, George Aldrich, observed in 1974 that "members of the United Nations have a legal duty to promote respect for and protection of human rights around the world. . . . The Charter of the United Nations and the Universal Declaration of Human Rights are the basic texts in this field. I would point, in particular, to articles 55 and 56 of the United Nations Charter. . . . The United States recognizes these obligations and is determined to live up to them." 1971 Dig. U.S. Prac. in Intl. L. 125 (1975). President Jimmy Carter reaffirmed this position in his March 1977 UN address, declaring that "[t]he solemn commitments of the United Nations Charter, of the United Nations Universal Declaration for Human Rights, of the Helsinki Accords, and of many other international instruments must be taken just as seriously as commercial or security agreements." 1977 Pub. Papers 444, 450-451. Moreover, as is set out above, the United States has invoked the human rights clauses before the International Court of Justice.

Comments and Questions

1. The human rights clauses in the UN Charter must be read against Article 2(7) thereof, which provides: "Nothing contained in the present Charter shall authorize the United Nations to intervene in matters which are essentially within the domestic jurisdiction of any state or shall require the Members to submit such matters to settlement under the present Charter; but this principle shall not prejudice the application of enforcement measures under Chapter VII." Note that each of the principal victorious powers in World War II had troublesome human rights problems of its own. The Soviet Union had its Gulag, the United States its de jure racial discrimination, France and Great Britain their colonial empires. Given their own vulnerability as far as human rights were concerned, it was not in the political interest of these countries to draft a Charter that established an effective international system for the protection of human rights, which is what some smaller democratic nations advocated.

Article 2(7) was intended to ensure that none of the human rights clauses of the Charter should "be construed as giving authority to the Organization to intervene in the domestic affairs of members states." 10 U.N.C.I.O. Docs. 83 (1945) (United States). A vast body of literature exists concerning this "domestic jurisdiction" clause and just what "intervention" by the United Nations it was intended to prohibit. See, e.g., Felix Ermacora, *Human Rights and Domestic Jurisdiction* (Article 2(7) of the Charter), 124 Recueil des Cours (Hague Academy of International Law 371 (1968-II)). Suffice it to say that, over the years, human rights questions — from their placement on the agenda through their investigation and debate to the actual adoption of specific recommendations — have come to be regarded by the United Nations as no longer "essentially within the domestic jurisdiction" of states. Would an argument against discussing human rights violations be given serious consideration today? Why would a state raise it in any event? For the practice of the United Nations, see Rosalyn Higgins, *The Development of International Law through the Political Organs of the United Nations* 58 (1963); Louis B. Sohn & Thomas Buergenthal, *International Protection of Human Rights* 556 (1973); Louis B. Sohn, *Rights in Conflict: The United Nations and South Africa* 48, 63 (1994). See also Cassese, "The General Assembly: Historical Perspective 1945-1989," in *The United Nations and Human Rights: A Critical Appraisal* 25 (Philip Alston ed., 1992). How important is subsequent practice in interpreting the constituting documents of international organizations? See Vienna Convention on the law of Treaties Art. 31.

2. In those cases where the Security Council determines that a state's human rights violations constitute either a "breach of the peace" or a "threat to the peace" under Article 39 of the Charter, Article 2(7) itself renders the "domestic jurisdiction" clause inoperable by specifically authorizing the adoption of economic sanctions or even the use of armed force against the offending state pursuant to Articles 41 and 42 of Chapter VII of the Charter. This issue is considered extensively in Chapter 10.

3. Although the I.C.J. in the South West Africa case clearly holds that the human rights clauses of the UN Charter create legal obligations for states "in a territory having an international status," do you agree with Schwelb's conclusion that these obligations also extend to state actions taken elsewhere than in an international territory? Note that the late Judge Dillard in his Separate Opinion cautioned that the Court was dealing with "a very specific and unique situation concerning a territory with international status, the administration of which engaged the supervisory authority of the United Nations." 1971 I.C.J, at 138. Should the Court's holding be so limited?

4. The Court in South West Africa also specifically held that South Africa's imposition of the policy of apartheid in Namibia constituted a "flagrant violation" of the human rights clauses of the UN Charter. How important to this conclusion is the fact that most Charter references to human rights are accompanied by the phrase "without distinction as to race, sex, language or religion?" Would segregation of women from public life similarly constitute a "flagrant violation?" Are "non-flagrant" human rights violations within the Court's rationale? If so, why? If not, how can one justify the U.S. assertion (see page 77 supra) that the UN Charter imposed a legal obligation on Iraq to accord criminal defendants a fair trial?

5. Since the Charter nowhere defines the scope or content of the "human rights and fundamental freedoms" that the United Nations shall promote and that member states shall help achieve, just what are the obligations assumed by states under the Charter? Does it matter when a state became a member of the United Nations? Whether and to what extent human rights norms developed after 1945 can be read back into the Charter to create legal obligations binding upon states was a hotly debated question in the years before the Court rendered its Advisory Opinion on South West Africa. Since 1971, however, the incorporation argument has gathered numerous adherents, and it has been raised in several U.S. domestic court cases. Among many commentators, see Richard B. Lillich, *Invoking International Human Rights Law in Domestic Courts,* 54 U. Cinn. L. Rev. 367, 378 n.54 (1981); Ralph Steinhardt, *Laying One Bankrupt Critique to Rest:* Sosa v. Alvarez-Machain *and the Future of International Human Rights Litigation in U.S. Courts*, 57 Vand. L. Rev. 2241 (2004).

C. *UN Human Rights Law-Making*

The previous section examined the meaning and effect of the human rights clauses of the UN Charter, a treaty binding the organization's member states. The present section analyzes what traditionally has been regarded as the UN's principal means of achieving universal respect for human rights — the sponsoring of multilateral treaties for the protection of specifically enumerated human rights.

The use of treaties for such a purpose is not new. As Chapter 1 describes, coordinated multi-state action was taken in the nineteenth century to combat the problem of slavery and the slave trade and to limit the means and methods of warfare. Since World War I, multilateral action for the protection of human rights increasingly has been channeled through international organizations. The International Labor Organization (ILO), for example, has adopted nearly 200 conventions and recommendations that seek to promote and protect the human rights of individuals and workers' associations.

The UN treaties have gone much further than most of their predecessors, however, in that they have obligated signatory states to make changes — sometimes drastic changes — in their own domestic legal regimes to bring them into conformity with international law norms. It is one thing for a state to agree to eradicate a practice that takes place on faraway continents or on the high seas; it is quite another to agree to take affirmative steps for the protection of oppressed individuals at home. In this respect, to the extent that states have ratified them, UN treaties represent a great advance in international human rights law.

Before examining specific human rights treaties of the UN, consider the diversity of human rights problems encompassed in Table 2-1, which lists the UN human rights treaties in force as of mid-2005. Table 2-1 demonstrates that the United Nations, in addition to promulgating general human rights treaties containing numerous articles covering a wide variety of individual rights (e.g., the International Covenant on Civil and Political Rights), has used treaties to combat specific human rights problems (e.g., the International Convention against Apartheid in Sports). Obviously this chapter — or even this coursebook — cannot begin to survey all the substantive provisions of the listed treaties. Much like a course in administrative law, which covers the administrative process rather than substantive administrative law, such as the Agricultural Adjustment Act, an introductory human rights course focuses primarily on the process of adopting and implementing substantive international human rights law, whether found in the UN Charter or UN (or other) international human rights instruments, and on the legal issues common to the various treaties. The reading immediately following the table describes some of the process of agenda-setting and norm creation in the field of human rights.

TABLE 2-1 UN Conventions in the Field of Human Rights as of June 29, 2005

		Date of signing/ adoption	*Entry into force*
1.	Convention on the Prevention and Punishment of the Crime of Genocide, 78 U.N.T.S. 277 (137 states parties)	Dec. 9, 1948	Jan. 12, 1951
2.	Convention for the Suppression of the Traffic in Persons and of the Exploitation of the Prostitution of Others, 46 U.N.T.S. 271 (78 states parties)	Mar. 21, 1950	July 25, 1951

3.	Convention relating to the Status of Refugees, 189 U.N.T.S. 137 (142 states parties)	July 28, 1951	Apr. 22, 1954
4.	Convention on the Political Rights of Women, 193 U.N.T.S. 135 (119 states parties)	Mar. 31, 1953	July 7, 1954
5.	Convention on the International Right of Correction, 435 U.N.T.S 191 (15 states parties)	Mar. 31, 1953	Aug. 24, 1962
6.	Protocol amending Slavery Convention, 182 U.N.T.S. 51 (59 states parties)	Oct. 23, 1953	Dec. 7, 1953
7.	Slavery Convention, as amended, 112 U.N.T.S. 51 (96 states parties)	Dec. 7, 1953	July 7, 1955
8.	Convention relating to the Status of Stateless Persons, 360 U.N.T.S. 117 (57 states parties)	Sept. 28, 1954	June 6, 1960
9.	Supplementary Convention on the Abolition of Slavery, the Slave Trade, and Institutions and Practices Similar to Slavery, 266 U.N.T.S. 3 (119 states parties)	Sept. 7, 1956	Apr. 30, 1957
10.	Convention on the Nationality of Married Women, 309 U.N.T.S. 65 (72 states parties)	Feb. 20, 1957	Aug. 11, 1958
11.	Convention on the Reduction of Statelessness, 989 U.N.T.S. 175 (29 states parties)	Aug. 30, 1961	Dec. 13, 1975
12.	Convention on Consent to Marriage, Minimum Age for Marriage, and Registration of Marriages, 521 U.N.T.S. 231 (51 states parties)	Dec. 10, 1962	Dec. 9, 1964
13.	International Convention on the Elimination of All Forms of Racial Discrimination, 660 U.N.T.S. 195 (170 states parties)	Mar. 7, 1965	Jan. 4, 1969
14.	International Covenant on Economic, Social and Cultural Rights, 993 U.N.T.S. (151 states parties)	Dec. 16, 1966	Jan. 3, 1976
15.	International Covenant on Civil and Political Rights, 999 U.N.T.S. 171 (154 states parties)	Dec. 16, 1966	Mar. 23, 1976

TABLE II-1 UN Conventions in the Field of Human Rights as of June 29, 2005

		Date of signing/ adoption	*Entry into force*
16.	Optional Protocol to the International Covenant on Civil and Political Rights, 999 U.N.T.S. 171 (105 states parties)	Dec. 16, 1966	Mar. 23, 1976
17.	Protocol relating to the Status of Refugees, 606 U.N.T.S. 267 (142 States parties)	Jan. 31, 1967	Oct. 4, 1967
18.	Convention on the Non-Applicability of Statutory Limitations to War Crimes and Crimes Against Humanity, 754 U.N.T.S. 73 (48 states parties)	Nov. 26, 1968	Nov. 11, 1970
19.	International Convention on the Suppression and Punishment of the Crime of Apartheid, 1015 U.N.T.S. 243 (103 states parties)	Nov. 30, 1973	July 18, 1976
20.	Convention on the Elimination of Discrimination against Women, 1249 U.N.T.S. 13 (180 states parties)	Dec. 18, 1979	Sept. 3, 1981
21.	Convention against Torture and Other Cruel, Inhuman, or Degrading Treatment or Punishment, 1465 U.N.T.S. 85 (139 states parties)	Dec. 10, 1984	June 26, 1987
22.	International Convention against Apartheid in Sports, 1500 U.N.T.S. 161 (59 states parties)	Dec. 10, 1985	Apr. 3, 1988
23.	Convention on the Rights of the Child, 1577 U.N.T.S. 3 (192 states parties)	Nov. 20, 1989	Sept. 2, 1990
24.	Second Optional Protocol to the International Covenant on Civil and Political Rights Aiming at the Abolition of the Death Penalty, 1642 U.N.T.S. 414 (54 states parties)	Dec. 15, 1989	July 11,1991
25.	International Convention for the Protection of All Migrant Workers and Members of Their Family, G.A. Res 45/158 (1990) (30 states parties)	Dec. 18, 1990	July 1, 2003

26.	Optional Protocol to CEDAW establishing an Individual Communications Procedure, GA Res. 54/4 of 6 Oct. 1999 (71 states parties)	Oct. 6, 1999	Feb. 22, 2000
27.	Optional Protocol to the CRC on the Involvement of Children in Armed Conflicts, GA Res. 54/263 (98 states parties)	May 25, 2000	Feb. 12, 2002
28.	Optional Protocol to the CRC on the Sale of Children, Child Prostitution and Child Pornography, GA Res. 54/263 (95 states parties)	May 25, 2000	Jan. 18, 2002
29.	Optional Protocol to the Convention against Torture, GA Res. 57/199 (10 states parties)	Dec. 18, 2002	not in force

Dinah Shelton, "Human Rights"

***In Managing Global Issues* 424, 438-42 (P.J. Simmons & Chantal de Jonge Oudraat eds., 2001)**

Human rights governance started with a revolutionary concept — that a government's treatment of those within its power is a matter of international concern — but it began with a modest objective, declaring and defining a set of fundamental rights, leaving to states the choice of means and policies to implement the norms. Over time, as the norms became more detailed, it became clear that international supervision of compliance with human rights obligations was required as part of the normative framework. International human rights law now usually progresses through similar stages: issue identification, debate, adoption of nonbinding declarations, negotiation of binding agreements (treaties), establishment of supervisory institutions and procedures, and further elaboration of the rights through decisions and judgments of the supervisory institutions. At all of these stages, a multiplicity of actors is involved because the issues touch individuals, governments, businesses, religious institutions, indeed, all parts of society. Success on any human rights issue usually involves coalition building. Coalitions are possible because personal relationships develop among people who work in the field, leading to agreement on issues, especially in intergovernmental and nongovernmental organizations, within networks and through informal links. . . .

As with other legal regimes, the agenda is set in reaction to perceived problems. The media plays an important role in identifying human rights issues that need resolution by documenting abuses and often creating an emotional response. For example, the famine in the early 1980s in Ethiopia had been in existence for two years before the international media drew attention to it and produced a movement for humanitarian aid. The outrage factor is very important in mobilizing public opinion and creating coalitions of NGOs and others;

compelling media imagery thus can be a significant factor in bringing an issue forward. For this reason, NGOs, victims, and their families use the media to expose human rights abuses and raise consciousness about particular issues, helping to shape the global agenda. . . .

States do raise human rights issues on their own, usually motivated by strategic and political considerations or historic rivalries. . . . This can be useful because political motivation does not minimize real human rights problems. Indeed, during the Cold War, U.S. emphasis on the right to leave and the misuse of psychiatric institutions in the Soviet Union, and Soviet accusations of U.S. racism, usefully pointed to abuses that required response. At the same time, the political motivation may undermine any effort to change state behavior by creating suspicion about the veracity of the complaints. It also may make the target state more intransigent when hostile states or traditional enemies raise issues.

NGOs and international civil servants working exclusively on human rights issues are clearly a major factor in agenda setting. [Felice Gaer] has called human rights NGOs the engine for virtually every advance made by the United Nations in the field of human rights since its founding. States often lag in pressing for human rights, which is only one of many matters of international concern for them. In addition, governments resent being criticized and do not want to promote consideration of human rights issues where they know they have problems. The topic of indigenous rights, for example, was placed on the agenda by indigenous groups working primarily with countries that had no indigenous peoples . . .

Some states do take a crucial leadership role. . . . Other states may step forward when national reforms have been instituted to address particular problems. The impartiality, credibility, and moral leadership of states on human rights impart more than traditional measures of state power; in many cases the United States has alone voted against measures (for example, the Declaration against Torture and the Convention on the Rights of the Child) that it has later come to approve (the United States is now a party to the Torture Convention). . . .

NGOs have been effective at getting issues on the international agenda. For example, Amnesty International's campaign on the death penalty led to three treaties being drafted: the Second Protocol to the ICCPR, the Sixth Protocol to the European Convention on Human Rights, and the Inter-American Protocol on the Abolition of the Death Penalty. Amnesty works through a grassroots, membership-based system that is global and well funded, which enables it to have considerable impact. . . .

Successful negotiations on human rights issues involve coalition building among states and nonstate actors because of the multiplicity of actors with divergent interests who participate in any negotiations for new human rights norms. For example, indigenous groups and supporting NGOs recently proposed the creation of intellectual property rights for traditional indigenous knowledge. States, indigenous groups, pharmaceutical companies, the World Intellectual Property Organization, environmental associations, the International Labor Organization, the World Health Organization, interested scholars, and the UN High Commissioner for Human Rights have participated in meetings on the topic. Trade-offs are made between the ideal and the possible; often the form as well as the content of the negotiated instrument reflect compromise and efforts to achieve consensus. It has proved easier to negotiate consensus on a new normative instrument if it is made legally nonbinding; nearly all human rights treaties today are preceded by a nonbinding declaration. . . .

On many issues, this global coalition of NGOs and medium and small powers achieved considerable success. For example, several groups representing torture survivors and other victims of abuse succeeded in obtaining provisions on victim compensation in the Statute of the International Criminal Court through alliance with key states, such as France, that saw the provisions as furthering continental legal approaches over common-law legal systems. . . . In subsequent human rights negotiations, the strategy of coalition building has been enhanced by the leadership exercised by "repeat players," those known to have expertise and an impartial commitment to human rights. In addition, an effective negotiating strategy to bring forward the human rights agenda has been to link it to other subjects, including economic assistance (U.S. Foreign Assistance Act, World Bank funding) and security arrangements (OSCE), to import elements of reciprocity and strengthen the leverage of those concerned with human rights.

1. Completing the International Bill of Rights

The International Bill of Human Rights consists of the Universal Declaration of Human Rights, the two International Covenants on Human Rights, and the two optional protocols to the Covenant on Civil and Political Rights. Proposals that a "Bill of Rights" or "Declaration of the Essential Rights of Man" be appended to the Charter were made but not acted upon at the San Francisco Conference. These efforts were revived at the very first meeting of the United Nations. Shortly thereafter, the newly created UN Commission on Human Rights was charged with drafting "an international bill of human rights." The Commission soon recognized that it would be relatively easy to adopt the text of a hortatory declaration, but that it would prove much more difficult to reach agreement on the wording of a legally binding treaty. The Commission decided, therefore, to work first on a declaration and to take up immediately afterwards the preparation of one or more draft treaties. This approach produced the Universal Declaration of Human Rights, which was adopted by the UN General Assembly in 1948. UN G.A. Res. 217A (III) (Dec. 10, 1948) (see Chapter 3). It took 18 more years before the treaties — the two Covenants and the Optional Protocol — were adopted by the Assembly and opened for signature. For the drafting history of these documents, see Louis B. Sohn, "A Short History of United Nations Documents on Human Rights," in *The United Nations and Human Rights* 101 (18th Report of the Commission to Study the Organization of Peace, 1968).

The Universal Declaration was "only" a UN resolution, supposedly having no binding effect on member states. The Declaration contains no enforcement provisions, thus rendering important the drafting of binding conventions committing signatory states to concrete enforcement procedures. At first, it was envisioned that the Universal Declaration would be followed immediately by a universal convention; political developments, however, dictated otherwise. A draft convention (labeled a covenant by its drafters) was prepared simultaneously with the Universal Declaration and submitted to the General Assembly at its 1948 session. The draft covenant underwent some revisions over the next two years before being submitted again for "basic policy decisions." One of these decisions concerned whether the covenant would provide for economic, social, and cultural rights, in addition to the civil and political rights already contained in it. Some states, however, were reluctant to commit themselves to undertaking economic, social, and cultural obligations on the ground that assuring such rights was more a function of a state's economic health than of its juridical norms.

The General Assembly accepted the force of this position and requested that two covenants — one on economic, social, and cultural rights and another on civil and political rights — be drafted simultaneously. It ultimately required another 14 years of painstaking effort for the Third Committee (the General Assembly's committee on economic and social issues, including human rights) to consider and pass upon all of the various articles of the two covenants. In 1966, the two documents, along with an Optional Protocol to the Civil and Political Covenant allowing states to permit petitions to be lodged against them by their victims, finally were ready for submission to the General Assembly for its approval. They were duly approved and opened for signature, and both covenants entered into force in 1976.

For an extensive discussion of the history of the International Bill of Rights, see *The United Nations and Human Rights*, Eighteenth *Report of the Commission to Study the Organization of Peace* 59-169 (1968); Johannes Morsink, *The Universal Declaration of Human Rights: Origins, Drafting, and Intent* (2000). A briefer treatment of the problems that arose during the drafting of the two covenants is found in the following extract.

Louis Henkin, "Introduction"

In *The International Bill of Rights* 9-11 (Louis Henkin ed., 1981)

The Universal Declaration was not generally conceived as law but as "a common standard of achievement" for all to aspire to; hence its approval without dissent. Some thought that the United Nations should rest on the Declaration and concentrate on encouraging states to raise their national norms and confront their national behavior to its standards. Instead, governments moved to convert the Declaration into binding legal norms.

The process was very, very long. In some part this was due to the ever-increasing number of states, all of which joined in the process and slowed the negotiations. In part, delay was due to the differences between a declaration and a binding covenant. Some states that had been prepared to declare a general principle wished it carefully defined and circumscribed if it were to be clearly a legal obligation with legal consequences, for though no state was compelled to adhere to any draft covenant that might emerge, most states wanted something they might be able to adopt if it became desirable; they were reluctant, moreover, to have a covenant adopted as the international norm in whose light their behavior would appear to be wanting. The process was also extended because there were strong pressures on the other hand to develop and elaborate the generalities of the Declaration and give them more specific content so that they would afford greater protection.

The Declaration, moreover, had not provided for its implementation, while many sessions were spent debating and elaborating means to enforce the new emerging legal undertakings. In substantial part, it took eighteen years to convert the Declaration into convention because it was necessary to accommodate, bridge, submerge, and conceal deep divisions and differences, especially between democratic-libertarian and socialist-revolutionary states — differences in fundamental conceptions about the relation of society to the individual, about his rights and duties, about priorities and preferences among them.

Western states fought for, and obtained, a division into two covenants, the Covenant on Civil and Political Rights and the Covenant on Economic, Social, and Cultural Rights. The two covenants recognize the difference in the character of rights in various subtle ways. For example, the Covenant on Civil and Political Rights is drafted in terms of the individual's rights: e.g., "Every human being has the inherent right to life"; "No one shall be held in slavery"; "All persons shall be equal before the courts and tribunals:" The Covenant on Economic, Social, and Cultural Rights, on the other hand, speaks only to the states, not the individual: "The States Parties to the present Covenant recognize the right to work"; "The States Parties . . . undertake to ensure . . . the right of everyone to form trade unions"; "The States Parties . . . recognize the right of everyone to education." There was wide agreement and clear recognition that the means required to induce compliance with social-economic undertakings were different from those required for civil-political rights. But the Covenant on Economic, Social and Cultural Rights is law, not merely exhortation and aspiration. . . .

Other delays resulted from sharp differences over the inclusion or scope of particular rights. Most of the states were concerned, or were more concerned, with values reflecting their struggle against colonialism, but not included in the Universal Declaration and not previously part of the accepted human rights ideology. They insisted that both Covenants include the right of all peoples to self-determination as well as to "economic self-determination," to "sovereignty" over their resources. Western states resisted, arguing that both are at best rights of a "people," not of any individual, and surely not — like human rights generally — rights of individuals against their own society. They argued, too, that the content of these norms was highly uncertain and controversial. The argument did not prevail, and identical provisions on self-determination now head both covenants. Also included in the Covenant on Civil and Political Rights were other, less controversial, rights not mentioned in the Declaration — freedom from imprisonment for debt, rights of children, and rights of minorities (Articles 11, 24, 27). That Covenant also prohibits propaganda for war and incitement to national, racial or religious hatred (Article 20). Some rights included in the Declaration were substantially elaborated. On the other hand, the right to enjoy private property, included in the Declaration, was finally omitted from the covenants. Much time was also spent in the attempt to bridge the demand of some states for effective means to enforce the covenants and the insistence of others on the "sovereignty" of states and resistance to international scrutiny and "intrusion."

2. Issue-Specific Human Rights Treaties

Concurrent with its effort to promulgate general human rights norms and necessary enforcement procedures through an International Bill of Rights, the UN began to use the treaty approach to combat human rights problems in specific subject areas, usually pressed by non-governmental human rights organizations. The first such treaty was the Convention on the Prevention and Punishment of the Crime of Genocide (the Genocide Convention). Drafted in 1948, the same year as the Universal Declaration, it came into force in 1951. Since the concept of advancing human rights by binding treaty was still relatively new, it was deemed advisable to forestall potential state opposition by choosing for attack at the outset the most odious violation of all. A second aspect of the Genocide Convention thought to make it particularly acceptable to states was the delegation of enforcement power and duty to each state party individually; no international supervisory mechanism was created. The United States ratified the Genocide Convention after 40 years. The Convention does declare that genocide, whether committed in time of peace or time of war, is a crime under international law, a concept discussed extensively in Chapter 11. See generally *Encyclopedia of Genocide and Crimes against Humanity* (Dinah Shelton ed., 2004); Rafael Lemkin, *Genocide as a Crime under International Law*, 41 Am. J. Int'l L. 145 (1947); William Schabas, *Genocide in International Law* (2000).

The International Convention on the Elimination of All Forms of Racial Discrimination (CERD) marked a significant advance over the Genocide Convention, in that it contains enforcement provisions similar to those adopted a year later for the Covenant on Civil and Political Rights and which would ultimately become standard practice. The CERD has been described as "the most comprehensive and unambiguous codification in treaty form of the idea of the equality of races." Egon Schwelb, *The International Convention on the Elimination of Racial Discrimination*, 15 Int'l & Comp. L.Q. 996, 1057 (1966). The Convention was largely an international response to outbursts of neo-Nazi activities around the world in 1959-1960. The General Assembly first adopted a Declaration on the Elimination of All Forms of Racial Discrimination (G.A. Res. 1904 (XVIII) (Nov. 20, 1963)), followed by the convention. The convention came into force in 1969, and the United States ratified it in 1994.

Sex discrimination, like racial discrimination, is prohibited by the human rights provisions of the United Nations Charter and by Article 2 of the Universal Declaration. The prohibition is repeated in Article 2(1) of the Civil and Political Covenant, Article 3 of which obligates states parties "to ensure the equal rights of men and women to the enjoyment of all civil and political rights set forth in the present Covenant." The UN General Assembly adopted a rather minimalist treaty on the political rights of women in 1953 and a more comprehensive treaty in 1979, on the elimination of all forms of discrimination against women (CEDAW); it entered into force in 1981. The CEDAW seeks to do away with discrimination against women, which it defines as "any distinction, exclusion, or restriction made on the basis of sex" that impairs the enjoyment by women of "human rights and fundamental freedoms in the political, economic, social, cultural, civil or any other field." (Article 1). In addition to the obligation to condemn discrimination against women, states undertake, inter alia, "to embody the principle of equality of men and women in their national constitutions or other appropriate legislation" and to adopt laws or other measures "including sanctions where appropriate, prohibiting all discrimination against women." (Article 2). The Convention also requires that states take a series of measures in the political, social, economic, and cultural realm to advance the enjoyment of equal rights by women in all walks of life. In one of its more far-reaching provisions, Article 5(a) requires states to take "all appropriate measures . . . [t]o modify the social and cultural patterns of conduct of men and women, with a view to achieving the elimination of prejudices and customary and all other practices which are based on the idea of the inferiority or superiority of either of the sexes or on stereotyped roles for men and women."

Torture is condemned by Article 5 of the Universal Declaration and also prohibited by Article 7 of the Civil and Political Covenant. Children not only are covered by the all-inclusive language of the Universal Declaration and the Civil and Political Covenant (e.g., "everyone") but also "are entitled to special care and assistance" under Article 25(2) of the former and are singled out for special protection by Articles 23(3) and 24 of the latter. While the question was raised whether specific human rights treaties dealing with these two areas really were needed, separate conventions (on torture in 1984 and children in 1989) were adopted and have been widely ratified.

Adoption of a convention on migrant workers in 1990 (which entered into force in 2003) and current work on treaties concerned with, inter alia, forced disappearances and persons with disabilities, indicate that human rights treaty-making by the United Nations is an open-ended process. Additional optional protocols to CEDAW, the Torture Convention, and the Child Convention were adopted between 1999 and 2002, and there is continuing discussion of a draft optional protocol which would create a petition procedure for the Covenant on Economic, Social and Cultural Rights.

Note: Specialized Agencies

The United Nations specialized agencies are legally independent organizations created by their own constitutions or charters, through which they establish their own organs and subsidiary bodies to fulfill their particular mandates. States must apply for membership and ratify the respective constituting treaties. Specialized agencies having responsibility for economic, social, cultural, educational, health, and related fields have beem brought into relationship with the United Nations through special agreements, concluded in accordance with article 63 of the UN Charter. An Inter-Agency Standing Committee helps to harmonize the activities of organizations that are part of the UN system.

Agencies such as the ILO, UNESCO, FAO, and WHO are directly involved in a number of specific human rights activities. Others, such as the World Bank Group, the International Monetary Fund, and the World Trade Organization, indirectly may have significant impact on human rights (see Chapter 5). The interaction of specialized agencies with the UN in the promotion of human rights is described in considerable detail in UN Centre for Human Rights, *United Nations Action in the Field of Human Rights* (1994); see also Stephen P. Marks, "Human Rights, Activities of Universal Organizations," in 2 *Encyclopedia of Public International Law* 893 (1995).

The International Labor Organization (ILO) was founded in 1919 and is the oldest organization concerned with human rights. The ILO focuses on those human rights related to the right to work and to working conditions, including the right to form trade unions, the right to strike, the right to be free from slavery and forced labor, equal employment and training opportunities, the right to safe and healthy working conditions, and the right to social security. The ILO also provides protections for vulnerable groups and has adopted standards on child labor, employment of women, migrant workers, and indigenous and tribal peoples. It seeks to guarantee these rights through the adoption of conventions (now more than 180) and recommendations containing core minimum standards, and additional flexible provisions that enhance the likelihood of ratification by states. These latter provisions are of particular importance because the ILO does not allow reservations to its conventions.

The ILO has also developed monitoring procedures that have influenced the work of the United Nations and regional organizations. Its tripartite system of governance, whereby each member state delegation is composed of government representatives along with representatives from employers' and workers' associations, ensures that the views of non-state actors are heard. The most important ILO conventions include the conventions on Forced Labor (No. 29) of 1930, Freedom of Association and Protection of the Right to Organize (No. 98) of 1949, Equal Remuneration (No. 100) of 1957, Abolition of Forced Labor (No. 1957), Discrimination (Employment and Occupation) (No. 111) of 1958, Indigenous and Tribal Peoples (No. 169) of 1989, and the Worst Forms of Child Labor (No. 182) of 1999. In 1998, the ILO responded to increasing concerns about the impact of globalization on worker rights by adopting on a Declaration of Fundamental Rights and Principles at Work, together with a follow-up procedure. The Declaration insists that all ILO Member States, by virtue of joining the organization, have an obligation to ensure the protection of four areas of human rights or core labor standards: freedom of association and the right to collectively bargain; freedom from child labor; freedom from forced or compulsory labor; and non-discrimination in employment. All member states must report annually if they have not ratified the relevant ILO conventions on these subjects, indicating the obstacles to ratification.

The ILO supervisory system requires that states report not only on ratified but on unratified conventions. Monitoring is carried out in the first place by a Committee of Experts, composed of twenty independent experts. The Committee meets annually to examine reports and may follow up with "Direct Requests" to governments and to organizations of workers and employers in the state concerned. If the Committee discovers more serious or persistent problems, it may make "Observations" to the government, which are published in the Committee's annual report to the Conference. The second supervisory body is the Committee on the Application of Conventions and Recommendations, established each year by the Conference with representatives of government, employers, and workers. On the basis of the Committee of Experts' Report, the Conference Committee selects specific important or persistent cases and asks the government to appear to discuss the situation. The Conference Committee then reports to the full Conference. In addition, the ILO has individual and collective complaints procedures. See Lee Swepston, "The International Labour Organization," in *Guide to International Human Rights Practice* (Hurst Hannum ed., 4th ed. 2004).

The UN Educational, Scientific and Cultural Organization (UNESCO), founded in 1945 and headquartered in Paris, is the primary agency responsible for cultural rights, including the right to education and rights to cultural property. Among its primary conventions are the 1962 Convention against Discrimination in Education and the 1954 Convention for the Protection of Cultural Property in the Event of Armed Conflict. It also adopted in 1997 a Universal Declaration on the Human Genome and Human Rights, the first international instrument to address human rights and modern biotechnology and to reject the cloning of human beings. UNESCO has a non-judicial communications procedure that was established in 1978, which allows a victim or anyone with reliable knowledge about a human rights violation concerned with education, science, or culture to submit a petition to UNESCO. See Stephen P. Marks, "The UN Educational, Scientific and Cultural Organization", in *Guide to International Human Rights Practice* (Hurst Hannum ed., 4th ed. 2004).

The constitution of the World Health Organization refers to the right to health, meaning the right of access to facilities, goods, services, and conditions necessary to enjoy the highest attainable standard of health. The constitution defines health as a state of complete physical, mental and social well-being and not merely as the absence of disease or infirmity. WHO has established a global program on HIV/AIDS which has been involved in standard-setting.

Finally, the Food and Agriculture Organization, one of the UN's largest specialized agencies, aims to ensure food security and alleviate hunger. In 2004, the FAO's Committee on World Food Security endorsed a set of voluntary guidelines to support the progressive realization of the right to adequate food in the context of national food security. The text was approved by the FAO Council in November 2004. (FAO doc. CL 127/REP, appendix D). The Guidelines are intended to demonstrate how to integrate a human rights approach in the operational activities of states, UN bodies, and civil society to ensure national food security. At the same time, the Guidelines indicate measures that states should adopt to implement the Covenant on Economic, Social and Cultural Rights.

Although not technically a UN specialized agency, the UN High Commissioner for Refugees also is involved with human rights and refugee protection activities in a wide range of countries. See generally Maryellen Fullerton, "The International Protection of Refugees," in *Guide to International Human Rights Practice* (Hurst Hannum ed., 4th ed. 2004); Guy Goodwin-Gill, *The Refugee in International Law* (2d ed. 1996); *Human Rights Protection for Refugees, Asylum-Seekers, and Internally Displaced Persons: A Guide to International Mechanisms and Procedures* (Joan Fitzpatrick ed. 2002).

3. Quality Control

Some observers have analyzed legal developments in terms of "generations" of rights, although the present authors find that approach less than helpful not the least because of its inaccuracy when applied to the evolution of international human rights law. The so-called first generation includes civil and political rights; the second generation is economic, social, and cultural rights; and the third generation includes such "solidarity" rights as peace, development, self-determination, and the environment. The following readings touch on aspects of this question in the context of the right to a healthy environment.

Stephen P. Marks, "Emerging Human Rights: A New Generation for the 1980s?"

33 *Rutgers L. Rev*. 435, 451-452 (1981)

Much hostility has been voiced against the idea of a new generation of human rights. Not only is proliferation of rights considered to be dangerous, but also the use of the term "generation" implies, the detractors say, that the rights belonging to earlier generations are outdated. It is also frequently said that the rights of the new generation are too vague to be justiciable and are no more than slogans, at best useful for advancing laudable goals of the UN, at worst useful for the propaganda of certain countries.

Indeed, it would weaken the idea of human rights in general if numerous claims or values were indiscriminately proclaimed as human rights. It is also true that the essential normative task in the field of human rights was accomplished during the first three decade after the founding of the UN, and that the more urgent task now is implementation. Nonetheless, I have tried to stress the dynamic nature of the process by which these rights are recognized and the consequent emergence of new human rights....

...[T]he human rights specialist is, to a certain extent, faced with the choice of resisting the rights which, whether he likes it or not, are emerging, or understanding and contributing to the process by which a limited number of new rights will succeed in attaining international recognition because (a) the need for them is sufficiently great and (b) the international community is ready to recognize them as human rights. He should seek to apply rigorous standards to the definition of new rights, and in particular, as Professor Rivero of France has insisted, see that they have a clearly defined object and an identifiable subject and can be reasonably expected to be enforced. Many human rights already recognized for several decades fall short of these standards. The proclamation of these rights nevertheless increased the likelihood that they would be translated into law and practice. As long as emerging rights are not so unrealistic or trivial as to be treated with mockery, their recognition does serve the advancement of the cause of human rights without endangering the rights of earlier generations. John Humphrey, Director of the U.N. Division of Human Rights for its first two decades, has written that "there are encouraging developments. One of these is the expansion of the concept of human rights to cover new values... and new threats to human rights." Although he was referring to the right to privacy, the statement is valid for the new generation of human rights.... If we are vigilant and require that proposed new rights be relevant to basic concerns of mankind, do not impinge upon existing rights, and may be followed up through an appropriate implementation machinery, there should be no reason to resist a new generation of human rights.

A.H. Robertson, *Human Rights in the World*

255-259 (J. G. Merrills ed., 3d ed. 1989)

In recent years a good deal of thought has been given to the question of extending the scope of human rights beyond those to be found in the Universal Declaration and the two international Covenants. An early indication of this tendency was the proclamation of a 'right to development,' The thinking here is that, quite apart from moral considerations, the economic development of the poorer countries of the world is essential to their social well being and political stability and that without it they are in no position to guarantee the civil, political, economic, social and cultural rights prescribed in the major international texts. As a consequence, the 'right to development' is asserted as a human right.

In a similar way, the concern felt in many countries and international organizations about the need for the protection of the environment, particularly against the pollution generated by modern industrial societies, has led some to the conclusion that there is a human right to a clean and healthy environment.

Then there are those who go further and consider that there is a human right to peace and a human right to share in the 'common heritage of mankind', that is the natural resources of the deep sea bed and other areas not subject to territorial sovereignty. . . .

A distinct but related question, which has been much discussed in the United Nations in recent years, is the establishment of a new international economic order. [The author devotes four paragraphs to describing the rise (but not the fall) of the new international economic order (NIEO).]

This brings us back to the so-called 'new rights': the right to development, the right to the environment, the right to share in the common heritage of mankind, the right to peace, and so on. Are these concepts human rights in any meaningful sense of that term? In trying to answer this question, there are several factors to be borne in mind.

In the first place, the word 'human' in the expression 'human rights' has a specific meaning. It indicates that the rights under consideration are rights pertaining to human beings by virtue of their humanity. As stated in both the UN Covenants, 'these rights derive from the inherent dignity of the human person'. In our view this means that the rights which can properly be called 'human rights' are rights of individual human beings stemming from their nature as human beings, and not rights of groups, associations, or other collectivities. This is borne out of the wording repeatedly used in the Universal Declaration and in the Covenant on Civil and Political Rights, 'Everyone has the right . . .'; while the Covenant on Economic, Social and Cultural Rights repeatedly stipulates that 'the States Parties . . . recognize the right of everyone to . . . the different rights protected'. It is quite clear from this language that what the Universal Declaration and the Covenants are concerned with is the rights of individual human beings. True, there is an exception in Article 1 of both Covenants, which states, 'All peoples have the right of self-determination.' But it is clear from the travaux that this was regarded as a special provision, and its exceptional character is underlined by the fact that [it] is placed in a distinct chapter of each Covenant, and separated from the articles relating to individual human rights.

This being so, is it accurate to designate as 'human-rights' so-called rights which pertain not to individuals but to groups or collectivities? Usage, of course, is a matter of convention and there is room for more than one view as to what is appropriate here. In our view, however, language and thinking will be clearer if we use the expression 'human rights' to designate individual rights and 'collective rights' to designate the rights of groups and collectivities, a distinction which also has the advantage of being consistent with much generally accepted practice.

The second consideration relates to the use of the word 'rights' in the expression 'new human rights.' Economic development, the protection of the environment, the common heritage of mankind and peace: are these concepts 'rights' in any meaningful sense? They can, and should, be objectives of social policy. They may be items in a political programme. However, they are certainly not legally enforceable claims. Most people no doubt prefer peace. But if one's country is at war, it is certain that there is no legally enforceable 'right to peace.' Naturally, it would be possible to define 'rights' in such a way as to include all desirable objectives of social policy, and in that event, the 'new human rights' would become 'rights' by virtue of the definition. But this would be to distort the ordinary meaning given to the term 'human rights' and, more seriously, would run together goals which enlightened humanity ought to pursue with claims which are already protected by international law. The trouble arises, then, because advocates of the 'new human rights' are confusing objectives of social policy with rights in the lawyers' sense. If one wishes to see some objective achieved — a clean and healthy environment, for example — it is tempting to say that this is a right to which we are all entitled. But it is not a good idea to take wishes for reality.

The last point to be borne in mind is that there is a crucial distinction between legal rights and moral rights. We may consider that we have a moral right to something — consideration from others, perhaps — when we have no legal right to it at all. Countless examples could be given. If advocates of the 'new human rights' assert that we have a moral right to peace, to the environment, and so on, then many will be inclined to agree. But there is all the difference in the world between these and other moral rights, on the one hand, and, on the other, rights, whether civil and political or economic and social, which have been incorporated in international treaties. While it is true that moral ideas provide both an incentive to create new law and a yardstick for its interpretation, until the process of law-making has taken place, 'new human rights' must remain in the realm of speculation.

Note: UN Action

In 1986, responding in part to scholarly criticism by Professors Alston (Philip Alston, *Conjuring Up New Human Rights: A Proposal for Quality Control*, 78 Am. J. Intl. L. 607 (1984)) and Meron (Theodor Meron, *Human Rights Law-Making in the United Nations* (1986)), plus the growing realization of many of its member states that its human rights "legislative" agenda was in chaos, the United Nations took an important initial step toward systematizing its development of new international human rights standards. The General Assembly responded to widespread concerns that proliferating claims for the recognition of additional specific human rights could threaten the integrity of the existing body of international human rights law by adopting Resolution 41/120 on "Setting International Standards in the Field of Human Rights." Read that resolution and the commentary on it by the International League for Human Rights that follows. Does this suggest a resistance to claims for the elaboration of new human rights, such as a right to a clean/healthy environment?

UN General Assembly Res. 41/120

Dec. 4, 1986

The General Assembly,

Recalling the extensive network of international standards in the field of human rights, which it, other United Nations bodies and the specialized agencies, have established,

Emphasizing the primacy of the Universal Declaration of Human Rights, the International Covenant on Civil and Political Rights and the International Covenant on Economic, Social and Cultural Rights in this network,

Reaffirming that effective implementation of these international standards is of fundamental importance,

Recognizing the value of continuing efforts to identify specific areas where further international action is required to develop the existing international legal framework in the field of human rights pursuant to Article 13, paragraph 1a, of the Charter of the United Nations.

Recognizing also that standard setting should proceed with adequate preparation,

Emphasizing that the standard setting activities of the United Nations should be as effective and efficient as possible,

1. *Calls upon* Member States and United Nations bodies to accord priority to the implementation of existing international standards in the field of human rights and urges broad ratification of, or accession to, existing treaties in this field;

2. *Urges* Member States and United Nations bodies engaged in developing new international human rights standards to give due consideration in this work to the established international legal framework;

3. *Reaffirms* the important role of the Commission on Human Rights, among other appropriate United Nations bodies, in the development of international instruments in the field of human rights;

4. *Invites* Member States and United Nations bodies to bear in mind the following guidelines in developing international instruments in the field of human rights; such instruments should, inter alia:

(a) Be consistent with the existing body of international human rights law;

(b) Be of fundamental character and derive from the inherent dignity and worth of the human person;

(c) Be sufficiently precise to give rise to identifiable and practicable rights arid obligations;

(d) Provide, where appropriate, realistic and effective implementation machinery, including reporting systems;

(e) Attract broad international support;

5. *Requests* the Secretary-General to provide appropriate specialized support to United Nations bodies working on standard setting in the field of human rights.

International League for Human Rights, *Human Rights at the United Nations: New Standard Setting*

Brief No. 10, at 2 (Oct. 1988) (emphasis in original)

[After summarizing the Resolution, the article states that it articulates several principles with significant implications for future UN human rights standard setting.]

First, the GA emphasized the "primacy" of the Universal Declaration and the two Covenants. At a minimum, this insistence on the primacy of the Universal Declaration and the Covenants requires that standards stated in new declarations or conventions not conflict with norms contained in those instruments.

Second, resolution 41/120 recognizes the value of additional standard setting in human rights, but calls for the UN and member states to give priority to the implementation of existing standards. Although the resolution highlights guidelines for standard setting, it advocates restraint in, if not abstention from, further law-making efforts until established norms have been transformed into practice. This emphasis on realization of existing human rights guarantees is reflected in the GA's reaffirmation of the "fundamental importance" of effective implementation of the Declaration and the Covenants and its reference to the "extensive network" of established human rights standards. In addition, the GA urged that the established legal framework be given "due regard" in developing new standards.

Third, law-making processes should be "as effective and efficient as possible." In this connection, the GA recognized the need for "adequate preparation" in the standard setting activities. Resolution 41/120 reaffirms the "important role" of the Commission on Human Rights . . . that process but does not elaborate on the nature of that role. The Secretary-General is requested to assist in the process by providing "appropriate specialized support" to bodies engaged in standard setting.

4. The Evolution of a Claimed Right to Environmental Quality

Dinah Shelton, Human Rights, Environmental Rights, and the Right to Environment

28 *Stan. J. Int'l L.* 103, 133-137 (1991) (citations omitted)

Issues Posed by the Right to Environment as a Human Right

In positive international law, a right to environment is not clearly or frequently stated. However, future human rights and humanitarian instruments will probably contain additional expressions of this emerging legal norm because the environmental movement continues to gather force as more global environmental problems are identified and because the link between human rights and the environment increasingly is recognized. In addition, the growing number of national constitutions which include a right to environment may lead governments to accept the norm on an international level as they recognize the interdependence of all states in regard to environmental protection. Even if the foundation of environmental protection suggests broader interests than human rights, the recognition that human survival depends upon a safe and healthy environment places the claim of a right to environment fully on the human rights agenda. Moreover, a right to environment could add elements of aesthetic [e.g., landscape] protection, a substantive area not protected under current human rights law or existing environmental rights.

However, if the goal of establishing a right to environment were accepted, the issue would be complicated by both temporal and geographic elements absent from consideration in regard to other human rights. . . . [T]he environmental rights of future generations are implicated. A depleted environment harms not only present generations, but future generations of humanity as well. First, an extinct species and whatever benefits it would have brought to the environment are lost forever. Second, economic, social, and cultural rights cannot be enjoyed in a world where resources are inadequate due to the waste of irresponsible prior generations. Third, the very survival of future generations may be jeopardized by sufficiently serious environmental problems. A right to environment thus implies significant, constant duties toward persons not yet born.

Another unusual aspect of a right to environment would be the potentially vast expansion of the territorial scope of state obligations. Present human rights instruments generally require each state to respect and ensure guaranteed rights "to all individuals within its territory and subject to its jurisdiction." This geographic limitation reflects the reality that a state normally will have the power to protect or the possibility to violate human rights only of those within its territory and jurisdiction. However, nature recognizes no political boundaries. A state polluting its coastal waters or atmosphere may cause significant harm to foreign individuals thousands of miles away. States that permit or encourage depletion of the tropical rain forest can contribute to global warming which may threaten the world environment.

Any elaboration of a right to an environment of a high quality must consider the temporal elements inherent in the protection of future generations, as well as the geographic extent of state responsibility for environmental harm. The required broad extension of state liability may prove to be the biggest single hurdle to establishing a right to environment. This problem seems to exist only within a human rights framework due to the structural differences between enforcement in human rights law and in an environmental regime. Most environmental protection treaties are not implemented through liability regimes or state responsibility, but rather through various incentive or trade-off mechanisms. In contrast, human rights treaties rely upon state reporting procedures, inter-state complaints, and individual petitions or complaints, all of which directly or indirectly permit attack or criticism of non-complying states.

Moreover, the term "environment" is neutral in itself, implying no measure of environmental quality. As a result, texts that speak of the right to environment generally add qualifying terms. The Stockholm Declaration utilizes the phrase "environment of a quality that permits a life of dignity and well-being." Constitutional texts that proclaim a right to environment or state duties to protect the environment add standards of varying specificity. For example, the Spanish Constitution speaks of "the right to enjoy an environment suitable for the development of the person." The 1979 Peruvian Constitution recognizes "the right to live in a healthy environment, ecologically balanced and adequate for the development of life and the preservation of the countryside and nature." These elaborations remain fairly nebulous; likewise, human rights treaties will not be able and should not try to define all the elements of environmental quality. It should be recognized that the same problem arises when interpreting and applying many other human rights, where equally conceptually difficult and vague terms such as "due process," "ordre public," "national security," "social security," and "self-determination" must be implemented.

These classic terms, long familiar to democratic societies, have attained precision through both legislative action and judicial interpretation. Public consciousness can take abstract terms in law and give them meaning in a concrete social and historical context, rendering them sufficiently precise to allow judicial decisions. There is no reason why such developments could not occur in the area of the environment. In many societies, the basic concept that the environment should be preserved and that each person should benefit from it already exists. Tribunals which have customarily dealt with human rights issues are capable of bringing content to a right to environment and particularly to the procedural duties corresponding to that right. Moreover, the increasingly effective supervisory technique of state reporting on implementation of human rights obligations seems well designed as a mechanism for enforcing an international right to environment.

Ultimately, the definition of a right to environment must include substantive environmental standards that quantitatively regulate harmful air pollution and other types of emissions. Although establishing quality standards requires extensive international regulation of environmental sectors based upon impact studies, such regulation is by no means impossible. While adoption of quality standards demands extensive research and debate involving public participation, substantive minima are a necessary complement to the procedural rights leading to informed consent. Otherwise, a right to environment would be ineffective in preventing serious environmental harm.

Establishing the content of a right through reference to independent and variable standards is used in human rights, especially with regard to economic entitlements. Rights to an adequate standard of living and to social security are implemented in varying measures by individual states based on general treaty provisions, according to changing economic indicators, needs, and resources. No precise standard exists, nor can such a standard be established in human rights treaties. Instead, the conventions state rights to "adequate" living conditions for health and well-being and to social security without defining the term further. The "framework" treaty allows national and local regulations to elaborate on these rights, since norms are easier to define and amend on the local level and are more responsive to the needs of the community.

A similar approach should be utilized to give meaning to a right to environment. Both the threats to humanity and the resulting necessary measures are subject to constant change based on advances in scientific knowledge and models of the environment. Thus, it is impossible for a human rights instrument to specify precisely the products which should not be used or the chemical composition of air which must be maintained. These matters will vary in the same way that the economic situations of communities change. The necessary measures to implement the right to environment will thus be determined by reference to independent environmental findings and regulations capable of rapid amendment. For this reason, international environmental instruments commonly regulate through the use of framework treaties of general obligation, supplemented by annexes or more easily amended protocols. The fact that the right to environment will be implemented in varying ways in response to different threats over time and place does not undermine the concept of the right, but merely takes into consideration its dynamic character.

In a . . . proposal to the Commission on Human Rights, the Ukrainian delegation called for the elaboration of ecological human rights in both substantive and procedural terms. The delegation's suggestions included: (1) the right to ecologically clean foodstuffs; (2) the right to ecologically harmless consumer goods; (3) the right to engage in productive activities in ecologically harmless conditions; (4) the right to live in ecologically clean natural surroundings; (5) the right to obtain and disseminate reliable information on the quality of foodstuffs, consumer goods, working conditions, and the state of the environment; (6) the right to participate in the solution of problems connected with the siting of industrial enterprises and the use of technology that might place the lives and health of people at risk; and (7) the right to compensation for the impairment of health due to the pollution of the environment and to other harmful influences acting on the environment or the irrational use of natural resources. The Ukrainian proposal, while demonstrating the feasible, though innovative, aspects of a right to environment, also indicates the limitations inherent in the right. In fact, the proposals are aimed at the elimination of pollution and environmental degradation immediately harmful to humans but give almost no direction to protection of nature on a broader basis. This approach may be correct from the human rights perspective, but it reinforces the need for environmental protection apart from human rights because it excludes endangered species, habitats, and other aspects of the environment.

In a human rights approach, the ultimate problem becomes one of balancing competing rights. For example, the right to environment may at times conflict with the right to property or the right to culture. In particular, environmental protection might in some cases require limits or restrictions on current uses of resources and property, or perhaps even a denial of property rights. However, the need to balance is not unique to the subject of environmental protection and human rights and has been effectively accommodated in other contexts.

Note: On the Evolution of Global, Regional, and National Standards

Most UN human rights treaties were drafted and adopted before environmental protection became a matter of international concern. There are thus few references to environmental issues in most human rights instruments, although the formulation of the right to health sometimes includes environmental matters. The International Covenant on Economic, Social and Cultural Rights, for example, guarantees the right to safe and healthy working conditions (Article 7(b)) and the right of children and young persons to be free from work harmful to their health (Article 10(3)). The right to health (Article 12) expressly calls on states to take steps for "the improvement of all aspects of environmental and industrial hygiene" and "the prevention, treatment and control of epidemic, endemic, occupational, and other diseases." The Convention on the Rights of the Child refers to aspects of environmental protection in respect to the child's right to health. Article 24 requires parties to take appropriate measures to combat disease and malnutrition "through the provision of adequate nutritious foods and clean drinking water, taking into consideration the dangers and risks of environmental pollution." The same article also requires that states parties provide information and education on hygiene and environmental sanitation to all segments of society.

ILO Convention No. 169 concerning Indigenous and Tribal Peoples in Independent Countries (1989) contains numerous references to the lands, resources, and environment of indigenous peoples (e.g., Articles 2, 6, 7, 15). Part II of the Convention addresses land issues, including the rights of the peoples concerned to the natural resources pertaining to their lands. Further, governments are to ensure adequate health services are available or provide resources to indigenous groups "so that they may enjoy the highest attainable standard of physical and mental health." (Article 25(1)). Article 30 requires that governments make known to the peoples concerned their rights and duties.

At present, formulations of a right to a certain level of environmental quality are found mainly in national law, regional human rights treaties, and environmental treaties. Some 56 constitutions throughout the world guarantee a right to an environment of a specified quality. Examples include Angola (Article 24(1): "all citizens shall have the right to live in a healthy and unpolluted environment"), Argentina (Article 41: "all residents enjoy the right to a healthy, balanced environment which is fit for human development . . ."), and Brazil (Article 225: "everyone has the right to an ecologically balanced environment, which is a public good for the people's use and is essential for a healthy life").

South African, Colombian, and Argentine courts, among others, have deemed justiciable their constitutional right to environment. In Costa Rica, a court stated that the rights to health and to the environment are necessary to ensure that the right to life is fully enjoyed. *Presidente de la sociedad Marlene S.A. v. Municipalidad de Tibas, Sala Constitucional de la corte Supreme de justicia*, Decision No. 6918/94 of Nov. 25, 1994.

At the regional level, the African Charter on Human and Peoples' Rights (discussed in Chapter 5, pages 327-333) was the first human rights treaty to expressly recognize the right of "[a]ll peoples" to a generally "satisfactory environment favorable to their development." Within Europe, the Organization of Economic Cooperation and Development (OECD) has stated that a "decent" environment should be recognized as one of the fundamental human rights. In an effort to specify environmental rights and obligations, the United Nations Economic Commission for Europe drafted the Aarhus Convention on Access to Information, Public Participation and Access to Justice in Environmental Matters, 2161 U.N.T.S. 447 (June 25, 1998), which affirms the fundamental principle that everyone has the right to an environment adequate for general health and well-being. The convention formulates this right primarily by developing the procedural rights of access to information, due process, and participation in decision-making.

The Organization of American States included a right to environment in its Additional Protocol to the American Convention on Human Rights in the Area of Economic, Social and Cultural Rights ("Protocol of San Salvador"), adopted Nov. 17, 1988, O.A.S.T.S. No. 69. Article 11, entitled "Right to a healthy environment," provides:

1. Everyone shall have the right to live in a healthy environment and to have access to basic public services.
2. The States Parties shall promote the protection, preservation and improvement of the environment.

The operative parts of the Protocol of San Salvador affirm the progressive nature of the obligations. Article 1 requires states to cooperate on an international level and to adopt all necessary measures "to the extent allowed by their available resources, and taking into account their degree of development" to protect the guaranteed rights. In addition, the parties must adopt domestic legislation or take other measures as necessary to make those rights a reality.

The regional human rights bodies have heard numerous cases involving environmental conditions linked to human rights violations. In the European system, in addition to the *Oneryildiz* case found in Chapter 5, see *Lopez Ostra v. Spain*, 303C Eur. Ct. H.R. (Dec. 9, 1994); *Guerra et al. v. Italy*, 1998-I Eur. Ct. H.R. (Grand Chamber) (Feb. 13, 1998); *Hatton and Others v. U.K.*, 2003-VIII Eur. Ct. H.R. 2003-VIII (July 8, 2003). In the Inter-American system, see *Awas Tigni (Sumo) Indigenous Community v. Nicaragua*, 66 Inter-Am. Ct. H.R. (ser. C) (2000), and Report No.40/04, Case 12.053 (Merits), *Maya Indigenous Communities of The Toledo District v. Belize* (Oct. 12, 2004). The Inter-American Commission's Report on the Situation of Human Rights in Ecuador, OAS Doc. OEA/Ser.L/V/II.96, doc. 10, rev 1 (1997) also contains a significant discussion of the legal obligations of states regarding the interrelationship of human rights, economic development, and environmental protection.

International legal instruments concerned with humanitarian norms during armed conflict also contain provisions to protect the environment. A long-standing principle holds that "the right of belligerents to adopt means of injuring the enemy is not unlimited" (Hague Convention (IV) Respecting the Laws and Customs of War on Land, Art. 22 Annex, sec. 2, ch. I). Among the relevant historical norms are those which prohibit the destruction of or damage to forests, orchards, fruit trees, or vines, and forbid the poisoning of wells, springs, and rivers. See e.g., Deut. 20:19-20. Several recent agreements contain general prohibitions against intentional environmental damage during armed conflict. For example, Article 35(3) of the 1977 Protocol I to the 1949 Geneva Conventions bans "methods or means of warfare which are intended, or may be expected, to cause widespread, long-term and severe damage to the natural environment." Similarly, Article I.1 of the 1977 Convention on the Prohibition of Military or Any Other Hostile Use of Environmental Modification Techniques, 1108 U.N.T.S. 151 (Dec. 10, 1976), provides that each state "undertakes not to engage in military or any other hostile use of environmental modification techniques having widespread, long-lasting or severe effects as the means of destruction, damage or injury to any other State Party." Article II of the convention defines an environmental modification technique as "any technique for changing — through the deliberate manipulation of natural processes — the dynamics, composition or structure of the earth, including its biota, lithosphere, hydrosphere and atmosphere, or of outer space." Finally, the 1981 Convention on Prohibitions or Restrictions on the Use of Certain Conventional Weapons Which May be Deemed to be Excessively Injurious or to Have Indiscriminate Effects (the Inhumane Weapons Convention), 1342 U.N.T.S. 137 (Oct. 10, 1980), prohibits incendiary attack on forests or other kinds of plant cover, except when the military uses such natural elements to cover, conceal, or camouflage combatants or other military objectives, or when the forests themselves become military objectives. See Jean-Marie Henckaerts and Louise Doswald-Beck, *1 Customary International Humanitarian Law* 143-58 (2005).

United Nations human rights organs began annually considering environmental issues in the late 1980s, when African countries expressed concern about transboundary movements of hazardous and toxic wastes. In 1988, the

UN Sub-Commission on Prevention of Discrimination and Protection of Minorities considered this question and adopted resolution 1988/26 (Sept. 1, 1988), drafted and co-sponsored primarily by its African members. The resolution refers to the right of all peoples to life and the right of future generations to enjoy their environmental heritage. It notes that the movement and dumping of toxic and dangerous products endangers basic human rights, such as the right to life, the right to live in a sound and healthy environment, and consequently the right to health. To help remedy these problems, the resolution called for a ban on the export of toxic and dangerous wastes and a global convention on that subject. In 1989, the Commission approved the Sub-Commission text. Res. 1989/42 (Mar. 6, 1989). Two months later, the Basel Convention on the Control of Transboundary Movements of Hazardous Wastes and Their Disposal was adopted, 1673 U.N.T.S. 57 (Mar. 22, 1989), although African states expressed disappointment at what they viewed as a weak agreement. The issue remained on the human rights agenda and gradually expanded to include dangerous products as well as wastes.

During its 1989 session, the Sub-Commission added the topic of human rights and the environment to its agenda and recommended appointment of a special rapporteur on human rights and the environment. Fatma Zohra Ksentini, the Special Rapporteur, subsequently presented a number of reports, including a final one that contained a draft declaration on human rights and the environment. UN Doc. E/CN.4/Sub.2/1999/9 (July 6, 1994). The Commission showed only lukewarm enthusiasm for the draft declaration and has decided each year since 1994 to ask for further comment by states and others stakeholders.

In 1995, a divided Commission appointed a special rapporteur to study the adverse effects of the illicit movement and dumping of toxic and dangerous products and wastes on the enjoyment of human rights. Res. 1995/81 (Mar. 8, 1981), adopted by a vote of 32 to 15, with six abstentions. The division was geographic, with all developing countries of the South voting in favor of the proposal and all Northern states expressing opposition. France, on behalf of the European Union, argued that the question could be dealt with much more effectively through instruments such as the Basel Convention, supra, and that the study "would lead to needless duplication of international mechanisms and to dissipation or wastage of resources." See 6 Y.B. Int'l Envtl. L. 178 (1995).

As part of a broad mandate, the Special Rapporteur was given explicit authority to receive and examine communications, engage in fact-finding on illicit traffic and dumping, and develop a complaint procedure on the subject. The rapporteur may recommend measures to states parties and provides an annual list of the countries and transnational corporations engaged in illicit dumping, as well as a census of persons killed, maimed, or otherwise injured due to the practice. In contrast to other international human rights procedures, this one produced a relatively large proportion of complaints or communications from states between 1995 and 2000. In the 1998 report, for example, the government of Paraguay informed the Special Rapporteur that it was investigating a serious case of illicit movement and dumping of toxic wastes that may have occurred in its territory and asked the Special Rapporteur for assistance in the investigation. In the 2000 report, three state-initiated cases were discussed: Cambodia against Taiwan; Panama against the United States; and Paraguay against a private company, Delta Pine. See UN Doc. E/CN.4/2000/50 and Add.1 (Mar. 20, 2000).

By 2005, nearly all global and regional human rights bodies had considered the link between environmental degradation and internationally-guaranteed human rights, including the right to health. A number of individual complaints have been brought, generally based upon rights to life, property, health, information, family, and/or private life. Underlying the complaints, however, are pollution, deforestation, and other types of environmental harm. These cases demonstrate several benefits of using one or more of the rights-based approaches to environmental and health problems. First, the emphasis on rights of information, participation, and access to justice encourages democratic values and promotes the rule of law in broad-based structures of governance. Experience demonstrates better decision-making and implementation of measures when those affected are informed and participate in the process; the legitimacy of the process exercises a pull toward compliance with the measures adopted. Another benefit of a rights-based approach is the ability to invoke international petition procedures to bring pressure to bear if governments lack the will to prevent or halt severe pollution that threatens human health and well-being (see, e.g. discussion of the Niger River delta case in Chapter 5, page 325-327, 355-364). In many instances, complainants have been afforded redress, and governments have taken measures to remedy the violation. Sometimes the problem is the result of a combination of governmental lack of capacity and lack of political will. Pollution may be caused by powerful enterprises whose business and investment are important to the state or the state may have inadequate monitoring systems to ensure air or water quality. Even in these instances, petition procedures can help to identify problems and encourage a dialogue to resolve them, including through the provision of technical assistance.

Given the existing human rights treaty provisions and developing case law, it may be asked whether recognizing an explicit right to a healthy, safe, and environmentally-sound environment would add to existing protections and further the international values represented by environmental law and human rights. The primary argument in favor of such a right is that it elevates the entire spectrum of environmental issues to the level of a fundamental value of society, equal to other rights and superior to ordinary legislation.

A decade ago, an international group of experts on human rights and environmental protection convened at the United Nations in Geneva and drafted a declaration of principles on human rights and the environment. The draft declaration was annexed to the final report of the Sub-Commission's special rapporteur on human rights and the environment in 1994 and has been under consideration by the Human Rights Commission since that time. See Draft Principles on Human Rights and the Environment, UN Doc. E/CN.4/Sub.2/1994/9, Annex I (July 6, 1994).

Comments and Questions

1. Some scholars have attempted to articulate criteria for defining human rights. See, e.g., Bertrand G. Ramcharan, *The Concept of Human Rights in Contemporary International Law*, 1983 Can. Hum. Rts. Y.B. 267, 280 ("Human rights are legal rights which possess one or more of certain qualitative characteristics, such as: appurtenance to the human person or group[;] universality[;] essentiality

to human life, security, survival, dignity, liberty, equality[;] essentiality for international order[;] essentiality in the conscience of mankind[;] essentiality for the protection of vulnerable groups."); Francis G. Jacobs, *The Extension of the European Convention on Human Rights to Include Economic, Social and Cultural Rights,* 3 Hum. Rts. Rev. 166, 170, 172 (1978) (arguing that a human right must be: 1) fundamental, 2) universal in the sense both that it is universally or very widely recognized and that it is guaranteed to everyone, and 3) capable of sufficiently precise formulation to give rise to legal obligations on the part of the state rather than merely setting a standard). Are these criteria convincing or useful? Recall Bilder's statement at the beginning of the chapter that human rights are what the General Assembly says they are. Is quality control needed?

2. There is a substantial body of literature, much of it polemical in nature, concerning so-called "third generation" human rights. Only the right to development has received substantial support within the UN system, among states, and from writers. The right to development was reaffirmed by the Vienna World Conference on Human Rights "as a universal and inalienable right and an integral part of fundamental human rights." Vienna Declaration and Programme of Action, UN Doc. A/CONF.157/23, at 5 (1993). Moreover, in its resolution establishing a UN High Commissioner for Human Rights, the General Assembly emphasized the need to observe not only the International Bill of Rights and other human rights instruments, but also its Declaration on the Right to Development, specifically instructing the High Commissioner to "recognize the importance of promoting a balanced and sustainable development for all people and of ensuring realization of the right to development...." G.A. Res. 48/141 (Dec. 20, 1993). In 1994, the Commission created an open-working group on the right to development, whose mandate is to "monitor and review progress made in the promotion and implementation of the right to development as elaborated in the Declaration on the Right to Development, at the national and international levels...." Comm. H.R. Res. 1998/72 (Apr. 22, 1998), para. 10(a)(i). One of the best attempts to articulate the meaning of the right to development is Arjun Sengupta, *On the Theory and Practice of the Right to Development,* 24 Hum. Rts. Q. 837 (2002), which is drawn from some of his work as the Commission's special rapporteur on the right to development from 1998 to 2004. Compare Jack Donnelly, *In Search of the Unicorn: The Jurisprudence and Politics of the Right to Development,* 15 Cal. West. Intl. L.J. 473, 508 (1985), who calls the right to development "not just a charming delusion, but a threat to human rights, and a particularly insidious threat because it plays upon our fondest hopes and best desires, and diverts attention from more productive ways of linking human rights and development."

3. For other perspectives on environmental rights, see Gudmundur Alfredson and Alexandre Ovsiouk, *Human Rights and the Environment,* 60 Nordic J. Int'l L. 19 (1991); S. James Anaya, *Indigenous Rights Norms in Contemporary International Law,* 8 Ariz. J. Int'l & U Comp. L.1 (1991); Philippe Cullet, *Definition of an Environmental Right in a Human Rights Context,* 13 Neth. Q. Hum. Rts. 25 (1995); Maguelonne Dejeant-Pons, "The Right to Environment in Regional Human Rights Systems," in *Human Rights in the Twenty-First Century* 595 (Paul Mahoney & Kathleen Mahoney eds., 1993); Maguelonne Dejeant-Pons and Marc Pallemaerts, *Droits de l'Homme et Environnement* (2002); Richard Desgagne, *Integrating Environmental Values into the European Convention on*

Human Rights, 89 Am. J. Int'l L.263 (1995); Joshua Eaton, *The Nigerian Tragedy, Environmental Regulation of Transnational Corporations and the Human Right to a Healthy Environment*, 15 B.U.I.L.J. 261 (1997); Gunther Handl, "Human Rights and Protection of the Environment: A Mildly 'Revisionist' View," in *Human Rights and Environmental Protection* (Antonio A. Cancado Trindade ed., 1992); Robert K. Hitchcock, *International Human Rights, the Environment, and Indigenous Peoples*, 1 Colo. J. Int'l Envtl. L. & Pol'y 1 (1994); *Human Rights Approaches to Environmental Protection* (Alan Boyle & Michael Anderson eds., 1996); Michael J. Kane, *Promoting Political Rights to Protect the Environment*, 18 Yale J. Int'l L. 389; Alexandre Kiss, *Le Droit á la Conservation de l'environnement*, 1 Rev. Universelle des Droits de l'Homme 445 (1990); James T. McClymonds, *The Human Right to a Healthy Environment: An International Legal Perspective*, 37 N.Y.L.S. L. Rev. 583 (1992); Neil Popovic, *In Pursuit of Environmental Human Rights: Commentary on the Draft Declaration of Principles on Human Rights and the Environment*, 27 Col. Hum. Rts. Rev. 487 (1996); Dinah Shelton, *What Happened in Rio to Human Rights?* 4 Y.B. Int'l Envtl. L. 75 (1994); id., "Environmental Rights", in *Peoples Rights* (Philip Alston ed., 2001); id., *Fair Play, Fair Pay: Protecting the Traditional Knowledge and Resources of Indigenous Peoples*, 1993 Y.B. Int'l Envtl. L. (1994); William Andrew Shutkin, *International Human Rights Law and the Earth: The Protection of Indigenous Peoples and the Environment*, 31 Va. J. Int'l L. 479 (1991); Lee Swepston, *A New Step in the International Law on Indigenous and Tribal Peoples: ILO Convention 169 of 1989*, 15 Okla. City U. L. Rev. 677 (1990); Janusz Symonides, "The Human Right to a Clean, Balanced and Protected Environment," in *Diritti Dell'uomo*; Melissa Thorme, *Establishing Environment as a Human Right*, 19 Den J. Int'l L. & Pol'y 302 (1991); Jon van Dyke, *A Proposal to Introduce the Right to a Healthy Environment into the European Convention Regime*, 13 Va. Envtl. L. J. 323 (1993).

III. Are Human Rights Treaties Different from Other International Legal Norms?

Until the second half of the nineteenth century, most treaties were bilateral and contained equal and reciprocal benefits and burdens for each of the two parties. Multilateral treaty-making emerged as a source of legal obligation with the advent of international conferences like the Congress of Vienna (1815) but only became prevalent with the creation of permanent international organizations. Such treaties may adopt uniform technical standards or "rules of the road," such as the treaties and regulations adopted in the framework of the International Civil Aviation Organization or the World Trade Organization. Alternatively, treaties may express agreement on fundamental international values, such as respect for human rights or protection of the environment. Treaties of this second type typically do not grant direct reciprocal benefits to the parties, in the same way that trade or extradition treaties do, but instead impose obligations often referred to as "unilateral" because the primary beneficiaries of the obligations are within the ratifying or acceding state itself. Given this characteristic, in addition to the moral foundations of human rights law and views about the proper role of government, some scholars and human rights bodies have questioned whether human rights treaties constitute a "special regime" in which the customary rules of treaty law are modified in key respects. Four issues in particular have arisen: interpretation, reservations, termination, and supremacy. Each of these is discussed briefly in the materials that follow. Consideration of the four issues almost inevitably gives rise to questions about the role of the supervisory bodies created by human rights treaties. These bodies, usually composed of independent experts, are discussed in more detail in Chapter 7. They generally have express powers to review state reports, issue views and observations, and, under optional clauses, consider interstate and individual petitions. Whether any implied powers may be derived from their mandates remains a matter of controversy.

A. *Interpretation*

Vienna Convention on the Law of Treaties

Adopted May 23, 1969, entered into force Jan. 27, 1980, 1155 U.N.T.S. 331

Article 31 Interpretation of Treaties

1. A treaty shall be interpreted in good faith in accordance with the ordinary meaning to be given to the terms of the treaty in their context and in the light of its object and purpose.

2. The context for the purpose of the interpretation of a treaty shall comprise, in addition to the text, including its preamble and annexes:

(a) any agreement relating to the treaty which was made between all the parties in connection with the conclusion of the treaty;

(b) any instrument which was made by one or more parties in connection with the conclusion of the treaty and accepted by the other parties as an instrument related to the treaty.

3. There shall be taken into account, together with the context:

(a) any subsequent agreement between the parties regarding the interpretation of the treaty or the application of its provisions;

(b) any subsequent practice in the application of the treaty which establishes the agreement of the parties regarding its interpretation;

(c) any relevant rules of international law applicable in the relations between the parties.

4. A special meaning shall be given to a term if it is established that the parties so intended.

Article 32 Supplementary Means of Interpretation

Recourse may be had to supplementary means of interpretation, including the preparatory work of the treaty and the circumstances of its conclusion, in order to confirm the meaning resulting from the application of article 31, or to determine the meaning when the interpretation according to article 31:

(a) leaves the meaning ambiguous or obscure; or

(b) leads to a result which is manifestly absurd or unreasonable.

Soering v. United Kingdom

Eur. Ct. H.R. (ser. A), No. 161, 11 Eur. Hum. Rts. Rep. 439 (July 7, 1989) (references omitted)

[The applicant in this case asserted that his extradition from the United Kingdom to the United States for prosecution in a capital case would violate the prohibition on torture and cruel, inhuman, degrading treatment, contained in Art. 3 of the European Convention on Human Rights, because it was reasonably foreseeable that he would be subjected to a "death row" phenomenon once in the US. The Court sets forth the principles it utilizes to interpret the Convention in the following extract.]

87. In interpreting the Convention regard must be had to its special character as a treaty for the collective enforcement of human rights and fundamental freedoms. Thus, the object and purpose of the Convention as an instrument for the protection of individual human beings require that its provisions be interpreted and applied so as to make its safeguards practical and effective. In addition, any interpretation of the rights and freedoms guaranteed has to be consistent with "the general spirit of the Convention, an instrument designed to maintain and promote the ideals and values of a democratic society."

88. Article 3 makes no provision for exceptions and no derogation from it is permissible under Article 15 in time of war or other national emergency. This absolute prohibition of torture and of inhuman or degrading treatment or punishment under the terms of the Convention shows that Article 3 enshrines one of the fundamental values of the democratic societies making up the Council of Europe. It is also to be found in similar terms in other international instruments such as the 1966 International Covenant on Civil and Political Rights and the 1969 American Convention on Human Rights and is generally recognised as an internationally accepted standard. The question remains whether the extradition of a fugitive to another State where he would be subjected or be likely to be subjected to torture or to inhuman or degrading treatment or punishment would itself engage the responsibility of a Contracting State under Article 3. That the abhorrence of torture has such implications is recognised in Article 3 of the United Nations Convention Against Torture and Other Cruel, Inhuman or Degrading Treatment or Punishment, which provides that "no State Party shall . . . extradite a person where there are substantial grounds for believing that he would be in danger of being subjected to torture." The fact that a specialised treaty should spell out in detail a specific obligation attaching to the prohibition of torture does not mean that an essentially similar obligation is not already inherent in the general terms of Article 3 of the European Convention. It would hardly be compatible with the underlying values of the Convention, that "common heritage of political traditions, ideals, freedom and the rule of law" to which the Preamble refers, were a Contracting State knowingly to surrender a fugitive to another State where there were substantial grounds for believing that he would be in danger of being subjected to torture, however heinous the crime allegedly committed. Extradition in such circumstances, while not explicitly referred to in the brief and general wording of Article 3, would plainly be contrary to the spirit and intendment of the Article, and in the Court's view this inherent obligation not to extradite also extends to cases in which the fugitive would be faced in the

receiving State by a real risk of exposure to inhuman or degrading treatment or punishment proscribed by that Article.

89. What amounts to "inhuman or degrading treatment or punishment" depends on all the circumstances of the case. Furthermore, inherent in the whole of the Convention is a search for a fair balance between the demands of the general interest of the community and the requirements of the protection of the individual's fundamental rights. As movement about the world becomes easier and crime takes on a larger international dimension, it is increasingly in the interest of all nations that suspected offenders who flee abroad should be brought to justice. Conversely, the establishment of safe havens for fugitives would not only result in danger for the State obliged to harbour the protected person but also tend to undermine the foundations of extradition. These considerations must also be included among the factors to be taken into account in the interpretation and application of the notions of inhuman and degrading treatment or punishment in extradition cases.

90. It is not normally for the Convention institutions to pronounce on the existence or otherwise of potential violations of the Convention. However, where an applicant claims that a decision to extradite him would, if implemented, be contrary to Article 3 by reason of its foreseeable consequences in the requesting country, a departure from this principle is necessary, in view of the serious and irreparable nature of the alleged suffering risked, in order to ensure the effectiveness of the safeguard provided by that Article. [The Court held that the United Kingdom would violate its obligations under the Convention should it proceed with the extradition.]

Selmouni v. France

1999-V Eur. Ct. H.R. (Grand Chamber) (July 28, 1999)

[The applicant complained of physical abuse at the hands of French police after he was arrested as a suspect in drug trafficking. He claimed his treatment violated Article 3 and his right to a hearing was denied under Article 6(1). The Court interpreted Article 3 as follows.]

91. The applicant submitted that the threshold of severity required for the application of Article 3 had been attained in the present case. He considered that the motive for the police officers' actions had been to obtain a confession, as he had been informed against and the police officers had been convinced that he was guilty even though the body search and the search of his hotel room at the time of his arrest had not yielded any evidence. He asserted that, aged 49, he had never been convicted or even arrested and that he stood by his refusal to admit any involvement in the drug trafficking being investigated by the police. He contended that the police officers had deliberately ill-treated him, given their constant questioning by day and, above all, by night. The applicant submitted that he had been subjected to both physical and mental ill-treatment. In his view, it was well known that such police practices existed, and that they required preparation, training and deliberate intent and were designed to obtain a confession or information. He argued that, in the light of the facts of the case, the severity and cruelty of the suffering inflicted on him justified classifying the acts as torture within the meaning of Article 3 of the Convention. . . .

95. The Court reiterates that Article 3 enshrines one of the most fundamental values of democratic societies. Even in the most difficult circumstances, such as the fight against terrorism and organised crime, the Convention prohibits in absolute terms torture and inhuman or degrading treatment or punishment. Unlike most of the substantive clauses of the Convention and of Protocols Nos. 1 and 4, Article 3 makes no provision for exceptions and no derogation from it is permissible under Article 15 §2 even in the event of a public emergency threatening the life of the nation.

96. In order to determine whether a particular form of ill-treatment should be qualified as torture, the Court must have regard to the distinction, embodied in Article 3, between this notion and that of inhuman or degrading treatment. As the European Court has previously found, it appears that it was the intention that the Convention should, by means of this distinction, attach a special stigma to deliberate inhuman treatment causing very serious and cruel suffering.

97. The United Nations Convention against Torture and Other Cruel, Inhuman or Degrading Treatment or Punishment, which came into force on 26 June 1987, also makes such a distinction, as can be seen from Articles 1 and 16. . . . [These articles are quoted in Chapter 4, page 274.]

99. The acts complained of were such as to arouse in the applicant feelings of fear, anguish and inferiority capable of humiliating and debasing him and possibly breaking his physical and moral resistance. The Court therefore finds elements which are sufficiently serious to render such treatment inhuman and degrading. . . . In any event, the Court reiterates that, in respect of a person deprived of his liberty, recourse to physical force which has not been made strictly necessary by his own conduct diminishes human dignity and is in principle an infringement of the right set forth in Article 3. . . .

100. In other words, it remains to be established in the instant case whether the "pain or suffering" inflicted on Mr Selmouni can be defined as "severe" within the meaning of Article 1 of the United Nations Convention. The Court considers that this "severity" is, like the "minimum severity" required for the application of Article 3, in the nature of things, relative; it depends on all the circumstances of the case, such as the duration of the treatment, its physical or mental effects and, in some cases, the sex, age and state of health of the victim, etc.

101. The Court has previously examined cases in which it concluded that there had been treatment which could only be described as torture. . . . However, having regard to the fact that the Convention is a "living instrument which must be interpreted in the light of present-day conditions," the Court considers that certain acts which were classified in the past as "inhuman and degrading treatment" as opposed to "torture" could be classified differently in future. It takes the view that the increasingly high standard being required in the area of the protection of human rights and fundamental liberties correspondingly and inevitably requires greater firmness in assessing breaches of the fundamental values of democratic societies.

102. The Court is satisfied that a large number of blows were inflicted on Mr Selmouni. Whatever a person's state of health, it can be presumed that such intensity of blows will cause substantial pain. Moreover, a blow does not automatically leave a visible mark on the body. However, it can be seen from Dr Garnier's medical report of 7 December 1991 (. . .) that the marks of the violence Mr Selmouni had endured covered almost all of his body.

103. The Court also notes that the applicant was dragged along by his hair; that he was made to run along a corridor with police officers positioned on either side to trip him up; that he was made to kneel down in front of a young woman to whom someone said "Look, you're going to hear somebody sing"; that one police officer then showed him his penis, saying "Here, suck this," before urinating over him; and that he was threatened with a blowlamp and then a syringe (see paragraph 24 above). Besides the violent nature of the above acts, the Court is bound to observe that they would be heinous and humiliating for anyone, irrespective of their condition.

104. The Court notes, lastly, that the above events were not confined to any one period of police custody during which — without this in any way justifying them — heightened tension and emotions might have led to such excesses. It has been clearly established that Mr Selmouni endured repeated and sustained assaults over a number of days of questioning.

105. Under these circumstances, the Court is satisfied that the physical and mental violence, considered as a whole, committed against the applicant's person caused "severe" pain and suffering and was particularly serious and cruel. Such conduct must be regarded as acts of torture for the purposes of Article 3 of the Convention.

106. There has therefore been a violation of Article 3.

Juan Humberto Sanchez Case, Interpretation of the Judgment on Preliminary Objections, Merits and Reparations

Inter-Am. Ct. H.R. (ser. A), No. 102 (Nov. 26, 2003), para. 56.

. . . [A]s this Court has indicated on repeated occasions, including in the instant case, part of the transcendental function of an international court is to carry out a dynamic interpretation of the treaties within its competence. As this Court indicated in Advisory Opinion No. 16, The Right to Information on Consular Assistance in the Framework of the Guarantees of the Due Process of Law [OC-16/99 of Oct. 1, 1999, Ser. A No. 16, para. 114]:

> This guidance is particularly relevant in the case of international human rights law, which has made great headway thanks to an evolutive interpretation of international instruments of protection. That evolutive interpretation is consistent with the general rules of treaty interpretation established in the 1969 Vienna Convention. . . . [T]his Court, in the Advisory Opinion on the Interpretation of the American Declaration of the Rights and Duties of Man (1989), . . . among others, ha[s] held that human rights treaties are living instruments whose interpretation must consider the changes over time and present-day conditions.

B. *Reservations*

Most human rights treaties do not include any provision on reservations, but potential parties may believe that certain reservations are an essential part of their acceptance of the treaty's provisions. The following extract from the Vienna Convention on the Law of Treaties, which on this point is generally considered to restate customary international law, provides the context for the subsequent discussion.

Vienna Convention on the Law of Treaties

Adopted May 23, 1969, entered into force Jan. 27, 1980, 1155 U.N.T.S. 331

ARTICLE 19 FORMULATION OF RESERVATIONS

A State may, when signing, ratifying, accepting, approving or acceding to a treaty, formulate a reservation unless:

(a) the reservation is prohibited by the treaty;

(b) the treaty provides that only specified reservations, which do not include the reservation in question, may be made; or

(c) in cases not falling under sub-paragraphs (a) and (b), the reservation is incompatible with the object and purpose of the treaty.

ARTICLE 20 ACCEPTANCE OF AND OBJECTION TO RESERVATIONS

1. A reservation expressly authorized by a treaty does not require any subsequent acceptance by the other contracting States unless the treaty so provides.

2. When it appears from the limited number of the negotiating States and the object and purpose of a treaty that the application of the treaty in its entirety between all the parties is an essential condition of the consent of each one to be bound by the treaty, a reservation requires acceptance by all the parties.

3. When a treaty is a constituent instrument of an international organization and unless it otherwise provides, a reservation requires the acceptance of the competent organ of that organization.

4. In cases not falling under the preceding paragraphs and unless the treaty otherwise provides:

(a) acceptance by another contracting State of a reservation constitutes the reserving State a party to the treaty in relation to that other State if or when the treaty is in force for those States;

(b) an objection by another contracting State to a reservation does not preclude the entry into force of the treaty as between the objecting and reserving States unless a contrary intention is definitely expressed by the objecting State;

(c) an act expressing a State's consent to be bound by the treaty and containing a reservation is effective as soon as at least one other contracting State has accepted the reservation.

5. For the purposes of paragraphs 2 and 4 and unless the treaty otherwise provides, a reservation is considered to have been accepted by a State if it shall have raised no objection to the reservation by the end of a period of twelve months after it was notified of the reservation or by the date on which it expressed its consent to be bound by the treaty, whichever is later.

ARTICLE 21 LEGAL EFFECTS OF RESERVATIONS AND OF OBJECTIONS TO RESERVATIONS

1. A reservation established with regard to another party in accordance with articles 19, 20 and 23:

(a) modifies for the reserving State in its relations with that other party the provisions of the treaty to which the reservation relates to the extent of the reservation; and

(b) modifies those provisions to the same extent for that other party in its relations with the reserving State.

2. The reservation does not modify the provisions of the treaty for the other parties to the treaty *inter se*.

3. When a State objecting to a reservation has not opposed the entry into force of the treaty between itself and the reserving State, the provisions to which the reservation relates do not apply as between the two States to the extent of the reservation.

Thus, reservations are permitted unless a treaty prohibits them. States have filed numerous reservations both to substantive and procedural provisions of human rights treaties. Roughly one-half the states parties to the Covenant on Civil and Political Rights (CCPR) have submitted one or more reservations. Very few objections have been filed, although examples include the objections of France, Germany, and the Netherlands to a statement by India that the right of self-determination applies only to peoples under foreign domination. Belgium and the Netherlands have declared that no reservation to a non-derogable right is permissible.

The ratification record and the number of reservations varies with the particular treaty. The effectiveness of the CEDAW in promoting the protection of the rights it guarantees has been particularly weakened by the many reservations made by states in ratifying this treaty. For an analysis of some of these reservations, see Katarina Tomaševski, *Women's Rights*, in *Human Rights: Concepts and Standards* 231, 235-38 (Janusz Symonides ed. 2000). These reservations seek to preserve various national or religious institutions that are in conflict with the Convention, which would seem to be precisely the purpose that reservations are designed to serve. However, some of the reservations raise serious questions about their legality, because Article 28(2) of the Vienna Convention declares that "a reservation incompatible with the object and purpose of the present Convention shall not be permitted." See Belinda Clerk, *The Vienna Convention Reservations Regime and the Convention on Discrimination Against Women*, 85 Am. J. Int'l L. 281 (1991). The effort to get states to withdraw their reservations received a boost from the 1993 Vienna World Conference on Human Rights, which called on the CEDAW Committee to "continue its review of reservations to the Convention" and urged states "to withdraw reservations that are contrary to the object and purpose of the Convention or which are otherwise incompatible with international treaty law." Vienna Declaration and Programme of Action, UN Doc. A/CONF.157/23, Sec. II, para. 39 (1993). See Donna Sullivan, *Women's Human Rights and the 1993 World Conference on Human Rights*, 88 Am. J. Int'l L. 152 (1994). More than two dozen states subsequently withdrew reservations that they had made at the time of ratification or accession.

Note: U.S. Reservations, Understandings, and Declarations to the Covenant on Civil and Political Rights

Despite the similarity of the Covenant on Civil and Political Rights to the U.S. Constitution and laws, one of President Carter's legacies to the ratification process was the precedent he created of recommending a reservation or other qualifying proviso not only in cases where the Covenant actually might conflict with the Constitution's guarantees (e.g., Article 20's restrictions on incitement to war and "hate speech" that might run afoul of the First Amendment), but also in any case where the Covenant, by setting a more humane standard than the Constitution, would require a modification of U.S. law (e.g. Article 7's prohibition of cruel, inhuman or degrading "treatment" as well as punishment.)

President Carter finally recommended the adoption of four reservations, one understanding, one statement, and two declarations. President Bush, following President Carter's path, went several steps further; his promised "few essential reservations and understandings" turned out to include a "package" of five reservations, five understandings, and four declarations. They are set out and then assessed in the following extracts.

International Covenant on Civil and Political Rights: The Administration's Proposed Reservations, Understandings and Declarations to the International Covenant on Civil and Political Rights

Hearing Before the Senate Comm. on Foreign Relations, 102d Cong., lst Sess. 8-9 (1991)

A. RESERVATIONS

1. FREE SPEECH

Article 20 does not authorize or require legislation or other action by the United States that would restrict the right of free speech and association protected by the Constitution and laws of the United States.

2. CAPITAL PUNISHMENT

The United States reserves the right, subject to its Constitutional constraints, to impose capital punishment on any person (other than a pregnant woman) duly convicted under existing or future laws permitting the imposition of capital punishment, including such punishment for crimes committed by persons below, eighteen years of age.*

* In *Roper v. Simmons*, 125 S.Ct. 1183 (2004), the Supreme court held that imposition of capital punishment on minors viloates the U.S. Constitution. The majority opinion referred to international opinion, the practice of other states, and human rights treaties, including the CCPR. Id. at 1198-99.

3. CRUEL, INHUMAN OR DEGRADING TREATMENT OR PUNISHMENT

The United States considers itself bound by Article 7 to the extent that "cruel, inhuman or degrading treatment or punishment" means the cruel and unusual treatment or punishment prohibited by the Fifth, Eighth and/or Fourteenth Amendments to the Constitution of the United States.

4. CRIMINAL PENALTIES

Because U.S. law generally applies to an offender the penalty in force at the time the offense was committed, the United States does not adhere to the third clause of paragraph 1 of Article 15.

5. JUVENILES

The policy and practice of the United States are generally in compliance with and supportive of the Covenant's provisions regarding treatment of juveniles in the criminal justice system. Nevertheless, the United States reserves the right, in exceptional circumstances, to treat juveniles as adults, notwithstanding paragraphs 2(b) and 3 of Article 10 and paragraph 9 of Article 14. The United States further reserves to these provisions with respect to individuals who volunteer for military service prior to age 18.

B. UNDERSTANDINGS

1. NON-DISCRIMINATION AND EQUAL PROTECTION

The Constitution and laws of the United States guarantee all persons equal protection of the law and provide extensive protections against discrimination. The United States understands distinctions based upon race, colour, sex, language, religion, political or other opinion, national or social origin, property, birth or any other status — as those terms are used in Article 2, paragraph 1 and Article 26 — to be permitted when such distinctions are, at minimum, rationally related to a legitimate governmental objective. The United States further understands the prohibition in paragraph of Article 4 upon discrimination, in time of public emergency, based "solely" on the status of race, colour, sex, language, religion or social origin not to bar distinctions that may have a disproportionate effect upon persons of a particular status.

2. RIGHT TO COMPENSATION FOR ILLEGAL ARREST AND MISCARRIAGE OF JUSTICE

The United States understands the right to compensation referred to in Articles 9(5) and 14(6) to require the provision of effective and enforceable mechanisms by which a victim of an unlawful arrest or detention or a miscarriage of justice may seek and, where justified, obtain compensation from either the responsible individual or the appropriate governmental entity. Entitlement to compensation may be subject to the reasonable requirements of domestic law.

3. SEPARATE TREATMENT OF THE ACCUSED AND JUVENILES

The United States understands the reference to "exceptional circumstances" in paragraph 2(a) of Article 10 to permit the imprisonment of an accused person with convicted persons where appropriate in light of an individual's overall dangerousness, and to permit accused persons to waive their right to segregation from convicted persons. The United States further understands that paragraph 3 of Article 10 does not diminish the goals of punishment, deterrence, and incapacitation as additional legitimate purposes for a penitentiary system.

4. RIGHT TO COUNSEL, COMPELLED WITNESSES, DOUBLE JEOPARDY

The United States understands that subparagraphs 3(b) and (d) do not require the provision of a criminal defendant's counsel of choice when the defendant is provided with court-appointed counsel on grounds of indigence, when the defendant is financially able to retain alternative counsel, or when imprisonment is not imposed. The United States further understands that paragraph 3(e) does not prohibit a requirement that the defendant make a showing that any witness whose attendance he seeks to compel is necessary for his defense. The United States understands the prohibition upon double jeopardy in paragraph 7 to apply only when the judgment of acquittal has been rendered by a court of the same governmental unit, whether the Federal Government or a constituent unit, as is seeking a new trial for the same cause.

5. FEDERALISM

The United States understands that this Convention shall be implemented by the Federal Government to the extent that it exercises legislative and judicial jurisdiction over the matters covered therein, and otherwise by the state and local governments; to the extent that state and local governments exercise jurisdiction over such matters, the Federal Government shall take measures appropriate to the Federal system to the end that the competent authorities of the state or local governments may take appropriate measures for the fulfillment of the Convention.

C. DECLARATIONS

1. NON-SELF-EXECUTING

The United States declares that the provisions of Articles 1 through 27 of the Covenant are not self-executing.

2. LIMITATIONS ON RIGHTS

It is the view of the United States that States Party to the Covenant should wherever possible refrain from imposing any restrictions or limitations on the exercise of the rights recognized and protected by the Covenant, even when such restrictions and limitations are permissible under the terms of the Covenant.

For the United States, Article 5, paragraph 2, which provides that fundamental human rights existing in any State Party may not be diminished on the pretext that the Covenant recognizes them to a lesser extent, has particular relevance to Article 19, paragraph 3, which would permit certain restrictions on the freedom of expression. The United States declares that it will continue to adhere to the requirements and constraints of its Constitution in respect of all such restrictions and limitations.

3. COMPETENCE OF THE HUMAN RIGHTS COMMITTEE

The United States declares that it accepts the competence of the Human Rights Committee to receive and consider communications under Article 41 in which a State Party claims that another State Party is not fulfilling its obligations under the Covenant.

4. NATURAL WEALTH AND RESOURCES

The United States declares that the right referred to in Article 47 may be exercised only in accordance with international law.

As discussed in Chapter 7, pages 600-601, most of the bodies that oversee human rights treaties have the possibility of adopting "General Comments," which are referred to briefly in Article 40(4) of the Covenant on Civil and Political Rights, in the context of the state reporting procedure. Such comments are addressed to all of the parties to a treaty and are designed to provide guidance to them in discharging their reporting obligations and interpreting the substantive provisions of the treaty. General Comments are relied upon by the committees in evaluating compliance by states with their obligations, be it in examining state reports or in expressing a committee's "views" on individual communications. Concerned about the numerous reservations made by states to the Covenant, the Human Rights Committee adopted the following General Comment in 1994.

Human Rights Committee, Issues relating to reservations made upon ratification or accession to the Covenant or the Optional Protocols thereto, or in relation to declarations under Article 41 of the Covenant

General Comment No. 24, UN Doc. CCPR/C/21/Rev.1/Add.6 (Nov. 4, 1994)

1. As of 1 November 1994, 46 of the 127 States parties to the International Covenant on Civil and Political Rights had, between them, entered 150 reservations of varying significance to their acceptance of the obligations of the Covenant. Some of these reservations exclude the duty to provide and guarantee particular rights in the Covenant. Others are couched in more general terms, often directed to ensuring the continued paramountcy of certain domestic legal provisions. Still others are directed at the competence of the Committee. The number of reservations, their content and their scope may undermine the

effective implementation of the Covenant and tend to weaken respect for the obligations of States parties. It is important for States parties to know exactly what obligations they, and other States parties, have in fact undertaken. And the Committee, in the performance of its duties under either article 40 of the Covenant or under the Optional Protocols, must know whether a State is bound by a particular obligation or to what extent. This will require a determination as to whether a unilateral statement is a reservation or an interpretative declaration and a determination of its acceptability and effects.

2. For these reasons the Committee has deemed it useful to address in a General Comment the issues of international law and human rights policy that arise. The General Comment identifies the principles of international law that apply to the making of reservations and by reference to which their acceptability is to be tested and their purport to be interpreted. It addresses the role of States parties in relation to the reservations of others. It further addresses the role of the Committee itself in relation to reservations. And it makes certain recommendations to present States parties for a reviewing of reservations and to those States that are not yet parties about legal and human rights policy considerations to be borne in mind should they consider ratifying or acceding with particular reservations.

3. It is not always easy to distinguish a reservation from a declaration as to a State's understanding of the interpretation of a provision, or from a statement of policy. Regard will be had to the intention of the State, rather than the form of the instrument. If a statement, irrespective of its name or title, purports to exclude or modify the legal effect of a treaty in its application to the State, it constitutes a reservation. Conversely, if a so-called reservation merely offers a State's understanding of a provision but does not exclude or modify that provision in its application to that State, it is, in reality, not a reservation.

4. The possibility of entering reservations may encourage States which consider that they have difficulties in guaranteeing all the rights in the Covenant none the less to accept the generality of obligations in that instrument. Reservations may serve a useful function to enable States to adapt specific elements in their laws to the inherent rights of each person as articulated in the Covenant. However, it is desirable in principle that States accept the full range of obligations, because the human rights norms are the legal expression of the essential rights that every person is entitled to as a human being. . .

6. The absence of a prohibition on reservations does not mean that any reservation is permitted. The matter of reservations under the Covenant and the first Optional Protocol is governed by international law. Article 19 (3) of the Vienna Convention on the Law of Treaties provides relevant guidance. . . . Even though, unlike some other human rights treaties, the Covenant does not incorporate a specific reference to the object and purpose test, that test governs the matter of interpretation and acceptability of reservations.

7. In an instrument which articulates very many civil and political rights, each of the many articles, and indeed their interplay, secures the objectives of the Covenant. The object and purpose of the Covenant is to create legally binding standards for human rights by defining certain civil and political rights and placing them in a framework of obligations which are legally binding for those States which ratify; and to provide an efficacious supervisory machinery for the obligations undertaken.

8. . . . Although treaties that are mere exchanges of obligations between States allow them to reserve *inter se* application of rules of general international law, it is otherwise in human rights treaties, which are for the benefit of persons within their jurisdiction. Accordingly, provisions in the Covenant that represent customary international law (and *a fortiori* when they have the character of peremptory norms) may not be the subject of reservations. Accordingly, a State may not reserve the right to engage in slavery, to torture, to subject persons to cruel, inhuman or degrading treatment or punishment, to arbitrarily deprive persons of their lives, to arbitrarily arrest and detain persons, to deny freedom of thought, conscience and religion, to presume a person guilty unless he proves his innocence, to execute pregnant women or children, to permit the advocacy of national, racial or religious hatred, to deny to persons of marriageable age the right to marry, or to deny to minorities the right to enjoy their own culture, profess their own religion, or use their own language. And while reservations to particular clauses of article 14 may be acceptable, a general reservation to the right to a fair trial would not be.

9. Applying more generally the object and purpose test to the Covenant, the Committee notes that, for example, reservation [sic] to article 1 denying peoples the right to determine their own political status and to pursue their economic, social and cultural development, would be incompatible with the object and purpose of the Covenant. Equally, a reservation to the obligation to respect and ensure the rights, and to do so on a non-discriminatory basis (article 2 (1)) would not be acceptable. Nor may a State reserve an entitlement not to take the necessary steps at the domestic level to give effect to the rights of the Covenant (article 2 (2)).

10. The Committee has further examined whether categories of reservations may offend the "object and purpose" test. In particular, it falls for consideration as to whether reservations to the non-derogable provisions of the Covenant are compatible with its object and purpose. While there is no hierarchy of importance of rights under the Covenant, the operation of certain rights may not be suspended, even in times of national emergency. This underlines the great importance of non-derogable rights. But not all rights of profound importance, such as articles 9 and 27 of the Covenant, have in fact been made non-derogable. One reason for certain rights being made non-derogable is because their suspension is irrelevant to the legitimate control of the state of national emergency (for example, no imprisonment for debt, in article 11). Another reason is that derogation may indeed be impossible (as, for example, freedom of conscience). At the same time, some provisions are non-derogable exactly because without them there would be no rule of law. A reservation to the provisions of article 4 itself, which precisely stipulates the balance to be struck between the interests of the State and the rights of the individual in times of emergency, would fall in this category. And some non-derogable rights, which in any event cannot be reserved because of their status as peremptory norms, are also of this character — the prohibition of torture and arbitrary deprivation of life are examples. While there is no automatic correlation between reservations to non-derogable provisions, and reservations which offend against the object and purpose of the Covenant, a State has a heavy onus to justify such a reservation.

11. The Covenant consists not just of the specified rights, but of important supportive guarantees. These guarantees provide the necessary framework for securing the rights in the Covenant and are thus essential to its object and

purpose. Some operate at the national level and some at the international level. Reservations designed to remove these guarantees are thus not acceptable. Thus, a State could not make a reservation to article 2, paragraph 3, of the Covenant, indicating that it intends to provide no remedies for human rights violations. Guarantees such as these are an integral part of the structure of the Covenant and underpin its efficacy. The Covenant also envisages, for the better attainment of its stated objectives, a monitoring role for the Committee. Reservations that purport to evade that essential element in the design of the Covenant, which is also directed to securing the enjoyment of the rights, are also incompatible with its object and purpose. A State may not reserve the right not to present a report and have it considered by the Committee. The Committee's role under the Covenant, whether under article 40 or under the Optional Protocols, necessarily entails interpreting the provisions of the Covenant and the development of a jurisprudence. Accordingly, a reservation that rejects the Committee's competence to interpret the requirements of any provisions of the Covenant would also be contrary to the object and purpose of that treaty.

12. The intention of the Covenant is that the rights contained therein should be ensured to all those under a State party's jurisdiction. To this end certain attendant requirements are likely to be necessary. Domestic laws may need to be altered properly to reflect the requirements of the Covenant; and mechanisms at the domestic level will be needed to allow the Covenant rights to be enforceable at the local level. Reservations often reveal a tendency of States not to want to change a particular law. And sometimes that tendency is elevated to a general policy. Of particular concern are widely formulated reservations which essentially render ineffective all Covenant rights which would require any change in national law to ensure compliance with Covenant obligations. No real international rights or obligations have thus been accepted. And when there is an absence of provisions to ensure that Covenant rights may be sued on in domestic courts, and, further, a failure to allow individual complaints to be brought to the Committee under the first Optional Protocol, all the essential elements of the Covenant guarantees have been removed. . . .

16. The Committee finds it important to address which body has the legal authority to make determinations as to whether specific reservations are compatible with the object and purpose of the Covenant. As for international treaties in general, the International Court of Justice has indicated in the *Reservations to the Genocide Convention Case* (1951) that a State which objected to a reservation on the grounds of incompatibility with the object and purpose of a treaty could, through objecting, regard the treaty as not in effect as between itself and the reserving State. Article 20, paragraph 4, of the Vienna Convention on the Law of Treaties 1969 contains provisions most relevant to the present case on acceptance of and objection to reservations. This provides for the possibility of a State to object to a reservation made by another State. Article 21 deals with the legal effects of objections by States to reservations made by other States. Essentially, a reservation precludes the operation, as between the reserving and other States, of the provision reserved; and an objection thereto leads to the reservation being in operation as between the reserving and objecting State only to the extent that it has not been objected to.

17. As indicated above, it is the Vienna Convention on the Law of Treaties that provides the definition of reservations and also the application of the object and purpose test in the absence of other specific provisions. But the Committee

believes that its provisions on the role of State objections in relation to reservations are inappropriate to address the problem of reservations to human rights treaties. Such treaties, and the Covenant specifically, are not a web of inter-State exchanges of mutual obligations. They concern the endowment of individuals with rights. The principle of inter-State reciprocity has no place, save perhaps in the limited context of reservations to declarations on the Committee's competence under article 41. And because the operation of the classic rules on reservations is so inadequate for the Covenant, States have often not seen any legal interest in or need to object to reservations. The absence of protest by States cannot imply that a reservation is either compatible or incompatible with the object and purpose of the Covenant. Objections have been occasional, made by some States but not others, and on grounds not always specified; when an objection is made, it often does not specify a legal consequence, or sometimes even indicates that the objecting party none the less does not regard the Covenant as not in effect as between the parties concerned. In short, the pattern is so unclear that it is not safe to assume that a non-objecting State thinks that a particular reservation is acceptable. In the view of the Committee, because of the special characteristics of the Covenant as a human rights treaty, it is open to question what effect objections have between States *inter se*. However, an objection to a reservation made by States may provide some guidance to the Committee in its interpretation as to its compatibility with the object and purpose of the Covenant.

18. It necessarily falls to the Committee to determine whether a specific reservation is compatible with the object and purpose of the Covenant. This is in part because, as indicated above, it is an inappropriate task for States parties in relation to human rights treaties, and in part because it is a task that the Committee cannot avoid in the performance of its functions. In order to know the scope of its duty to examine a State's compliance under article 40 or a communication under the first Optional Protocol, the Committee has necessarily to take a view on the compatibility of a reservation with the object and purpose of the Covenant and with general international law. Because of the special character of a human rights treaty, the compatibility of a reservation with the object and purpose of the Covenant must be established objectively, by reference to legal principles, and the Committee is particularly well placed to perform this task. The normal consequence of an unacceptable reservation is not that the Covenant will not be in effect at all for a reserving party. Rather, such a reservation will generally be severable, in the sense that the Covenant will be operative for the reserving party without benefit of the reservation.

19. Reservations must be specific and transparent, so that the Committee, those under the jurisdiction of the reserving State and other States parties may be clear as to what obligations of human rights compliance have or have not been undertaken. Reservations may thus not be general, but must refer to a particular provision of the Covenant and indicate in precise terms its scope in relation thereto. When considering the compatibility of possible reservations with the object and purpose of the Covenant, States should also take into consideration the overall effect of a group of reservations, as well as the effect of each reservation on the integrity of the Covenant, which remains an essential consideration. States should not enter so many reservations that they are in effect accepting a limited number of human rights obligations, and not the Covenant as such. So that reservations do not lead to a perpetual non-attainment of international human rights standards, reservations should not systematically reduce the obligations

undertaken only to those presently existing in less demanding standards of domestic law. Nor should interpretative declarations or reservations seek to remove an autonomous meaning to Covenant obligations, by pronouncing them to be identical, or to be accepted only in so far as they are identical, with existing provisions of domestic law. States should not seek through reservations or interpretative declarations to determine that the meaning of a provision of the Covenant is the same as that given by an organ of any other international treaty body.

20. States should institute procedures to ensure that each and every proposed reservation is compatible with the object and purpose of the Covenant. It is desirable for a State entering a reservation to indicate in precise terms the domestic legislation or practices which it believes to be incompatible with the Covenant obligation reserved; and to explain the time period it requires to render its own laws and practices compatible with the Covenant, or why it is unable to render its own laws and practices compatible with the Covenant. States should also ensure that the necessity for maintaining reservations is periodically reviewed, taking into account any observations and recommendations made by the Committee during examination of their reports. Reservations should be withdrawn at the earliest possible moment. Reports to the Committee should contain information on what action has been taken to review, reconsider or withdraw reservations.

Human Rights Committee, Consideration of Reports Submitted by States Parties under Article 40 of the Covenant, Comments of the Committee on the Report of the United States of America

UN Doc. CCPR/C/79/Add.50 (Apr. 7, 1995), paras. 267-304

267. The Committee expresses its appreciation at the high quality of the report submitted by the State party, which was detailed, informative and drafted in accordance with the guidelines. The Committee regrets, however, that, while containing comprehensive information on the laws and regulations giving effect to the rights provided in the Covenant at the federal level, the report contained few references to the implementation of Covenant rights at the state level.

268. The Committee appreciates the participation of a high-level delegation which included a substantial number of experts in various fields relating to the protection of human rights in the country. The detailed information provided by the delegation in its introduction of the report, as well as the comprehensive and well-structured replies provided to questions raised by members, contributed to making the dialogue extremely constructive and fruitful.

269. The Committee notes with appreciation that the Government gave publicity to its report, thus enabling non-governmental organizations to become aware of its contents and to make known their particular concerns. In addition, a number of representatives of these organizations were present during the Committee's consideration of the report. . . .

4. Principal Subjects of Concern

278. The Committee has taken note of the concerns addressed by the delegation in writing to its Chairman about the Committee's General Comment No. 24

(52) on issues relating to reservations made upon ratification or accession to the Covenant or the Optional Protocols thereto (CCPR/C/21/Rev.1/Add.6). Attention is drawn to the observations made by the Chairman of the Committee at the 1406th meeting, on 31 March 1995 (CCPR/C/SR.1406).

279. The Committee regrets the extent of the State party's reservations, declarations and understandings to the Covenant. It believes that, taken together, they intended to ensure that the United States has accepted only what is already the law of the United States. The Committee is also particularly concerned at reservations to article 6, paragraph 5, and article 7 of the Covenant, which it believes to be incompatible with the object and purpose of the Covenant. . . .

5. Suggestions and Recommendations

292. The Committee recommends that the State party review its reservations, declarations and understandings with a view to withdrawing them, in particular reservations to article 6, paragraph 5, and article 7 of the Covenant.

The reaction to the Committee's General Comment on reservations was divided. While many human rights activists welcomed it, states were far less positive. At the next election of members to the Committee, Mr. Mavrommatis, who had chaired the Committee since its beginning, was not re-elected. Another response to the controversy came in the UN's International Law Commission (ILC), a body of experts designated to "codify" and "progressively develop" international law. The ILC was responsible for the original draft of the Vienna Convention on the Law of Treaties. It thus proposed to take up the issue of reservations to treaties, with a clear focus on the practice of human rights bodies in general and the Committee in particular. The General Assembly approved the ILC's proposal, following which the ILC appointed its French member, Professor Alain Pellet, as rapporteur on the topic.

Prof. Pellet submitted ten reports between 1994 and 2005 (for the 2005 report, see UN Doc. A/CN.4/558 and Add.1 (June 1 and 14, 2005)). Following consideration of his first report by the ILC, Prof. Pellet summarized the conclusions he drew from the Commission's discussion, including what he perceived as a consensus that there should be no change in the relevant provisions of the Vienna Conventions. The following year, the ILC had before it the Special Rapporteur's second report on the topic, UN Doc. A/CN.4/477 and Add 1 (May 21 and June 13, 1996). The Special Rapporteur included in this report a draft resolution of the International Law Commission on reservations to multilateral normative treaties, including human rights treaties, which was addressed to the General Assembly for the purpose of drawing attention to clarifying the legal aspects of the matter. In 1997, the ILC adopted preliminary conclusions on reservations to normative multilateral treaties, including human rights treaties. In 2003, it send a letter to human rights bodies requesting their cooperation, attaching copies of its preliminary conclusions, and expressing an intention to conclude the matter in the coming years. The following extract from the 1997 ILC report indicates its rejection of a special regime for human rights treaties.

International Law Commission, Annual Report

UN Doc. A/CN.4/SER.A/1997/Add.1(Part 2), Ch. V, paras. 65-87, pp.46-49 (citations omitted)

(e) *The question of the unity or diversity of the legal regime for reservations to treaties, more particularly in relation to human rights treaties*

65. Chapter II of the report dealt with two substantive matters which were nonetheless closely linked, namely, the question of the unity or diversity of the legal regime for reservations to treaties, and second, the specific question of reservations to human rights treaties. In the context of the latter, the question also arose of consideration of the powers of human rights treaty monitoring bodies. In that regard, the Special Rapporteur was of the view that the Commission should draw firm and clear conclusions. The reactions of States in the course of the debate in the Sixth Committee at the fifty-first session of the General Assembly tended to favour the conclusions set out in his second report. Furthermore, the extreme importance and topicality of the subject, as well as the fact that a number of human rights treaty monitoring bodies had deferred any decision on the matter pending the outcome of the Commission's work, militated in favour of a stance on the part of the Commission. The Special Rapporteur also said that some new elements in the debate, although they had in the main backed up his positions, had nonetheless induced him to qualify them to some extent.

66. Taking up first the question of the unity or diversity of the reservations regime, the Special Rapporteur discussed the necessity of modifying the reservations regime to take account of the object and/or nature of the treaty. He pointed out that the basis for the reservations regime consisted of the relevant provisions of the 1969 Vienna Convention on the Law of Treaties, provisions that were later reproduced in the 1986 Convention (arts. 19-23). He also noted that the Convention provided that special rules were applicable to certain categories of treaties. Consequently, the problem of the unity or the diversity of the rules applicable to reservations had not escaped the authors of the Vienna Convention, who had not failed to differentiate them where they had deemed it necessary. Furthermore, where the authors of the Vienna Convention had wanted to reserve special treatment for a specific category of treaty, they had expressly done so. Those authors, mindful of the fact that a general rule could not ideally apply to all treaties, had devised them with the idea that they would apply to *all* multilateral treaties, with the exception of expressly named categories of treaties.

67. The Special Rapporteur nonetheless pointed out that no exception had seemed worthwhile with regard to the applicability of the regime in the case of normative treaties such as codification conventions or human rights treaties, although the latter had their own characteristics of a most striking non-synallagmatic nature.

68. He pointed out that the problem had resurfaced in the meanwhile and that a number of writers had argued that the Vienna regime was not applicable to reservations to normative treaties and more particularly to human rights treaties. That idea had spread, even to human rights bodies, and deserved to be considered in turn by the Commission, one of the "international law bodies."

69. In that regard, the Special Rapporteur emphasized that the so-called "normative" treaties, which corresponded to an earlier concept, that of "law-making" treaties, was a very diverse category, consisting of conventions codifying

private international law, ILO conventions, treaties on the law of armed conflict, trade, and so on. Furthermore, a treaty was rarely entirely normative or entirely synallagmatic: in most cases, including human rights, a treaty contained both contractual clauses recognizing reciprocal rights and obligations and "normative" clauses. From that standpoint, a normative treaty was simply a treaty in which the normative provisions predominated in quantitative terms.

70. The Special Rapporteur pointed out that the problem therefore was to determine whether the Vienna reservations regime was suited to the "normative provisions" of treaties, and section II of his report endeavoured to provide an answer, both *de lege lata* and *de lege ferenda*.

71. He also mentioned the Commission's reports of 1962 and 1966, in which the Commission had recognized the value of formulating rules applying to the greatest possible number of cases. The Vienna Conference had also endorsed those views, influenced by Latin American practice, because of their flexibility and adaptability, which were also characteristic of the whole of the Vienna regime.

72. Three mechanisms, the Special Rapporteur stated, ensured such flexibility and adaptability, namely (a) the prohibition (article 19 (c) of the Convention) on formulating a reservation *incompatible with the object and purpose of the treaty*, a general rule that precluded any rigidity by referring to the very essence of the treaty; (b) the system of *freedom* instituted under article 20 (4) and (5) and articles 21 and 22 enabling States parties not to be affected by the reservation, since they could decide to object to it, and lastly; (c) the *residual* character of the system, a fundamental feature which enabled the Vienna regime to operate not as a yoke but as a safety net. This feature meant that the system could be set aside if States so wished.

73. The Special Rapporteur drew two major conclusions from his analysis:

(a) The endless debate on whether or not reservations to treaties should be allowed was futile. Reservations to treaties were a fact of life; the Vienna rules, by their very flexibility, precluded any basic "deformation" of the treaty yet at the same time allowed for the broadest possible participation. It was better for a State to accept part of a treaty than simply decide not to become a party;

(b) There was no reason to rule out the application of the Vienna regime to so-called "normative" treaties.

74. The Special Rapporteur, summing up his analysis in paragraphs 136 to 162 of his second report, pointed out that, even if reservations prejudiced the *integrity* of the treaty, they could never prejudice its *object and purpose*, namely, its very "core"; otherwise they would be impermissible. Moreover, that integrity was typical not only of normative treaties but also of synallagmatic treaties. As to the argument about the non-reciprocal character of normative treaties, the Special Rapporteur found it paradoxical that the criticism levelled at reservations, namely that they did away with reciprocity, should be made in the case of commitments which, by their very nature, were not reciprocal. In any case, the reciprocity element was not entirely absent from normative treaties whereby the States mutually guaranteed that they would apply the same rules. Moreover, the Special Rapporteur considered that the argument about a break in equality between the parties to normative treaties, a break allegedly caused by the fact that reservations could be entered, was just as specious: the inequality would be much more flagrant between a State party and a State which was *not at* all a party to a

normative treaty. Lastly, a State could always restore the initial balance by objecting to the reservation or by taking action under article 20, paragraph 4 (b), of the 1969 Convention and preventing the treaty from entering into force between itself and the reserving State.

(f) *Vienna regime and human rights treaties*

75. In the light of those conclusions, the Special Rapporteur wondered whether, on the other hand, special rules would be applicable to the "special" category of normative treaties formed by human rights treaties. In that regard, he pointed out that, despite the eloquent pleading by human rights specialists for a regime specific to reservations to human rights treaties, none of the arguments offered a convincing basis for such a specific regime. In actual fact, it was the lacunae and the ambiguities of the Vienna regime that were questioned, lacunae and ambiguities of the *general regime* and not its application to certain categories of treaties.

76. The Special Rapporteur pointed out that his answer to the question whether there had been crucial reasons for not applying the Vienna regime to human rights treaties had been in the negative for the following reasons:

(a) The Vienna regime was designed to be applied *universally* and without exception. Moreover, it should not be forgotten that the point of departure, namely the advisory opinion of the International Court of Justice on reservations to the Genocide Convention, concerned a quintessential human rights treaty;

(b) Since the Vienna Conventions, neither the practice of States *inter se*, nor judicial practice nor even the human rights treaty bodies had contested the applicability of the Vienna regime to human rights treaties. Moreover, the majority of the human rights treaties concluded after the Vienna Conventions either contained express clauses on reservations referring to the Vienna Convention or reproducing the Convention's criteria of the "object and purpose" of the treaty, or they contained no clauses on reservations, but entailed the effective application of the Vienna regime as an expression of the "ordinary law," something that was also apparent from the *travaux préparatoires* of those instruments. In that regard, the Special Rapporteur pointed out, even General Comment No. 24 of the Human Rights Committee, which had been challenged on other points, referred on a number of occasions to the Vienna Conventions.

77. However, the Special Rapporteur qualified the preceding paragraph by the following considerations:

(a) It was not inconceivable that States parties to human rights treaties would want to make exceptions or establish special regimes. For that purpose, it would be wise in future for States to stipulate expressly in human rights conventions whether and to what extent non-application of a provision constituted a breach of the "object" of the conventions;

(b) A fruitful dialogue might be established between the reserving State and the objecting State, either spontaneously or on the basis of special provisions inserted in the treaty for that purpose. That technique would strike a balance between the reservations regime and the specificity of human rights;

(c) Human rights monitoring bodies would nonetheless continue to apply the Vienna rules in regard to reservations when no special rules existed.

(g) *The role of monitoring bodies in regard to reservations*

78. The Special Rapporteur emphasized that the third part dealt with the most controversial question, namely the role of the human rights treaty monitoring bodies in regard to the permissibility of reservations.

79. He recalled that there were two entirely opposed positions. One was that the States parties alone were competent to decide on the admissibility and validity of reservations: that was the traditional position of States, of the Legal Counsel of the United Nations, of part of doctrine and even the monitoring bodies themselves up until the mid-1990s.

80. The other position, however, was that not only were the monitoring bodies competent to decide whether reservations were permissible but they could also draw all the necessary consequences of that determination, including the fact that reserving States were bound by all the provisions of the treaty, including the provision in respect of which they had entered the reservation.

81. The Special Rapporteur stated that neither of those positions seemed satisfactory. In his opinion, it was incumbent on the Commission, as an international law body, to provide an answer based *on law*.

82. In the view of the Special Rapporteur two findings would provide grounds for such an answer:

(a) Human rights bodies could and should assess whether reservations were permissible when that was necessary for the exercise of their functions. They could not, however, have more competence in that regard than was necessary for them to discharge their main responsibility. In that respect, he pointed out that bodies to monitor and implement a treaty were not a feature of human rights treaties alone and could and did exist in other fields (disarmament, environment, etc.). Like a dispute settlement body which could and should, in a dispute brought before it, rule on the validity of a reservation, otherwise it could not perform its task, all such control bodies, including human rights bodies, were created or required by the parties to monitor the implementation of the treaty. For that purpose, they had to determine the specific obligations of parties under the treaty, including reservations. If the bodies were jurisdictional (such as the European Court of Human Rights), they had the power to make decisions binding on the parties concerned. If they were consultative in character, their opinion would not be binding, but the States parties should consider the opinion in good faith;

(b) Moreover, the Special Rapporteur was convinced that the competence of such bodies stopped there. It followed that they could not draw any *consequences* from such an assessment in the absence of a decision by the State concerned.

83. In contrast to the positions adopted by some human rights bodies which considered that once the reservation was deemed impermissible the reserving State continued to be bound by the treaty as a whole, the Special Rapporteur emphasized that the treaty was still a *consensual* instrument, drawing its strength from the *will* of States. The reservations made, he said, were "consubstantial" with the State's consent to be bound by the treaty. In international society at the present stage, the State *alone* could know the exact role of its reservation to its consent. It was neither possible nor desirable, said the Special Rapporteur, for *experts* — whose legitimacy drew on the treaty (hence on the will of States) — to replace elected Governments in deciding on the intentions of those Governments.

84. However, on reflection the Special Rapporteur had departed in one respect from the conclusions he had drawn in 1996: those conclusions did not apply to regional bodies vested with powers to make binding decisions (European

Court of Human Rights, Inter-American Court). While he still had doubts about the merits of some decisions by those bodies, he recognized that the stronger solidarity at the regional level than at the universal level could warrant the establishment under regional treaties of machinery with broader powers which reflected precisely those community ties.

85. The Special Rapporteur stated that those regional solutions could not, however, be transposed to a global level: "decisions" of that type by bodies which, like the Human Rights Committee were not given decision-making powers by the States parties, would be contrary to general international law.

86. In that case, the consequences that the reserving State could draw from the findings of monitoring bodies were the following:

(a) The State could, after having examined the finding in good faith, maintain its reservation;

(b) The State could withdraw its reservation;

(c) The State could "regularize" its situation by replacing its impermissible reservation with a permissible reservation;

(d) The State could renounce being party to the treaty.

87. Lastly, the Special Rapporteur objected to the excessive pretensions of the Human Rights Committee in seeking to act as the *sole* judge of the permissibility of reservations. Such a control on the permissibility of reservations, he emphasized, was not the monopoly of the monitoring bodies. States, through objections, could exercise another kind of control and such "duality" of controls would make for still more effective operation of the treaty; moreover, objections by States were often not only a means of exerting significant "pressure" but also a useful guide for the assessment of the permissibility of a reservation by the Committee itself. . . .

157. The text of the Preliminary Conclusions adopted by the Commission is reproduced below:

PRELIMINARY CONCLUSIONS OF THE INTERNATIONAL LAW COMMISSION ON RESERVATIONS TO NORMATIVE MULTILATERAL TREATIES INCLUDING HUMAN RIGHTS TREATIES

The International Law Commission has considered, at its forty-ninth session, the question of the unity or diversity of the juridical regime for reservations. The Commission is aware of the discussion currently taking place in other forums on the subject of reservations to normative multilateral treaties, and particularly treaties concerning human rights, and wishes to contribute to this discussion in the framework of the consideration of the subject of reservations to treaties that has been before it since 1993 by drawing the following conclusions:

1. The Commission reiterates its view that articles 19 to 23 of the Vienna Conventions on the Law of Treaties of 1969 and 1986 govern the regime of reservations to treaties and that, in particular, the object and purpose of the treaty is the most important of the criteria for determining the admissibility of reservations;

2. The Commission considers that, because of its flexibility, this regime is suited to the requirements of all treaties, of whatever object or nature, and achieves a satisfactory balance between the objectives of preservation of the integrity of the text of the treaty and universality of participation in the treaty;

3. The Commission considers that these objectives apply equally in the case of reservations to normative multilateral treaties, including treaties in the area of human rights and that, consequently, the general rules enunciated in the above-mentioned Vienna Conventions govern reservations to such instruments;

4. The Commission nevertheless considers that the establishment of monitoring bodies by many human rights treaties gave rise to legal questions that were not envisaged at the time of the drafting of those treaties, connected with appreciation of the admissibility of reservations formulated by States;

5. The Commission also considers that where these treaties are silent on the subject, the monitoring bodies established thereby are competent to comment upon and express recommendations with regard, *inter alia*, to the admissibility of reservations by States, in order to carry out the functions assigned to them;

6. The Commission stresses that this competence of the monitoring bodies does not exclude or otherwise affect the traditional modalities of control by the contracting parties, on the one hand, in accordance with the above-mentioned provisions of the Vienna Conventions of 1969 and 1986 and, where appropriate by the organs for settling any dispute that may arise concerning the interpretation or application of the treaties;

7. The Commission suggests providing specific clauses in normative multilateral treaties, including in particular human rights treaties, or elaborating protocols to existing treaties if States seek to confer competence on the monitoring body to appreciate or determine the admissibility of a reservation;

8. The Commission notes that the legal force of the findings made by monitoring bodies in the exercise of their power to deal with reservations cannot exceed that resulting from the powers given to them for the performance of their general monitoring role;

9. The Commission calls upon States to cooperate with monitoring bodies and give due consideration to any recommendations that they may make or to comply with their determination if such bodies were to be granted competence to that effect in the future;

10. The Commission notes also that, in the event of inadmissibility of a reservation, it is the reserving State that has the responsibility for taking action. This action may consist, for example, in the State either modifying its reservation so as to eliminate the inadmissibility, or withdrawing its reservation, or forgoing becoming a party to the treaty;

11. The Commission expresses the hope that the above conclusions will help to clarify the reservations regime applicable to normative multilateral treaties, particularly in the area of human rights;

12. The Commission emphasizes that the above conclusions are without prejudice to the practices and rules developed by monitoring bodies within regional contexts.

In Resolution 52/156 (Dec. 15, 1997), the General Assembly took note of the Commission's preliminary conclusions. It noted the ILC's invitation to all treaty bodies set up by normative multilateral treaties to provide, in writing, their comments and observations on the conclusions and drew the attention of governments to the need for comments. As of 2005, the ILC was continuing to draft guidelines and an accompanying commentary on legal issues relating to reservations.

C. *Termination of Treaties*

While some human rights treaties (e.g. the Convention on the Elimination of All Forms of Racial Discrimination and the Convention against Torture) contain provisions permitting parties to withdraw from them after a period of time following notification to the other parties, the Covenants contain no denunciation clauses. Article 56 of the Vienna Convention on the Law of Treaties states the following:

> 1. A treaty which contains no provision regarding its termination and which does not provide for denunciation or withdrawal is not subject to denunciation or withdrawal unless:
>
> (a) it is established that the parties intended to admit the possibility of denunciation or withdrawal; or
>
> (b) a right of denunciation or withdrawal may be implied by the nature of the treaty.
>
> 2. A party shall give not less than twelve months' notice of its intention to denounce or withdraw from a treaty under paragraph 1.

In 1988, the government of the Netherlands considered withdrawing from the Covenant on Civil and Political Rights as a result of disagreement with the Human Rights Committee's case law on Article 26 (see *Broeks v. the Netherlands*, No. 172/1984, CCPR/C/29/D/172/1984, 9 April 1987, and *Zwaan-de Vries v. the Netherlands*, No. 182/1984, CCPR/C/28/D/182/1984, 9 April 1987). After a legal opinion by P.J. Kooijmans (today a judge on the International Court of Justice) concluded that denunciation was impermissible, the government decided not to pursue the matter. In 1997, however, the Democratic People's Republic of Korea (North Korea) circulated a "notification of withdrawal" to other states parties. The Committee quickly adopted the following General Comment:

Human Rights Committee, Continuity of Obligations

General Comment No. 26, UN Doc. A/53/40, annex VII (Dec. 8, 1997)

1. The International Covenant on Civil and Political Rights does not contain any provision regarding its termination and does not provide for denunciation or withdrawal. Consequently, the possibility of termination, denunciation or withdrawal must be considered in the light of applicable rules of customary international law which are reflected in the Vienna Convention on the Law of Treaties. On this basis, the Covenant is not subject to denunciation or withdrawal unless it is established that the parties intended to admit the possibility of denunciation or withdrawal or a right to do so is implied from the nature of the treaty.

2. That the parties to the Covenant did not admit the possibility of denunciation and that it was not a mere oversight on their part to omit reference to denunciation is demonstrated by the fact that article 41(2) of the Covenant does permit a State party to withdraw its acceptance of the competence of the Committee to examine inter-State communications by filing an appropriate notice to that effect while there is no such provision for denunciation of or withdrawal from the Covenant itself. Moreover, the Optional Protocol to the

Covenant, negotiated and adopted contemporaneously with it, permits States parties to denounce it. Additionally, by way of comparison, the International Convention on the Elimination of All Forms of Racial Discrimination, which was adopted one year prior to the Covenant, expressly permits denunciation. It can therefore be concluded that the drafters of the Covenant deliberately intended to exclude the possibility of denunciation. The same conclusion applies to the Second Optional Protocol in the drafting of which a denunciation clause was deliberately omitted.

3. Furthermore, it is clear that the Covenant is not the type of treaty which, by its nature, implies a right of denunciation. Together with the simultaneously prepared and adopted International Covenant on Economic, Social and Cultural Rights, the Covenant codifies in treaty form the universal human rights enshrined in the Universal Declaration of Human Rights, the three instruments together often being referred to as the "International Bill of Human Rights." As such, the Covenant does not have a temporary character typical of treaties where a right of denunciation is deemed to be admitted, notwithstanding the absence of a specific provision to that effect.

4. The rights enshrined in the Covenant belong to the people living in the territory of the State party. The Human Rights Committee has consistently taken the view, as evidenced by its long-standing practice, that once the people are accorded the protection of the rights under the Covenant, such protection devolves with territory and continues to belong to them, notwithstanding change in government of the State party, including dismemberment in more than one State or State succession or any subsequent action of the State party designed to divest them of the rights guaranteed by the Covenant.

5. The Committee is therefore firmly of the view that international law does not permit a State which has ratified or acceded or succeeded to the Covenant to denounce it or withdraw from it.

D. *Are Human Rights Treaties Superior to Other International Legal Regimes?*

Globalization has increased concern about assuring that all relevant international actors fulfill their responsibility to promote and protect human rights. International institutions and scholars have responded with various proposals for strengthening the international human rights regime, among them claims that posit the primacy of human rights law.

The Committee on Economic, Social and Cultural Rights (ESC Committee), for example, has emphasized that "the realms of trade, finance and investment are in no way exempt from these general principles [on respect for human rights] and that international organizations with specific responsibilities in those areas should play a positive and constructive role in relation to human rights." ESC Committee, *Statement on Globalization and Economic, Social and Cultural Rights*, E/C.12/1997/SR.54/Add.1 (May 11, 1998), para. 5. The Committee's language echoes that of the Vienna Declaration and Program of Action, UN Doc. A/CONF.157/23 (1993), which affirmed that "the promotion and protection of human rights and fundamental freedoms is the first responsibility of government." Id., para. 1.

The Sub-Commission on Promotion and Protection of Human Rights has expressly asserted the "centrality and primacy" of human rights obligations in all areas of governance and development, including international and regional trade, investment and financial policies, agreements and practices. Sub-Commission on Promotion and Protection of Human Rights, *Human rights as the primary objective of trade, investment and financial policy*, Res. 1998/12 (Aug. 20, 1998). Subsequently, the Sub-Commission appointed two special co-rapporteurs on globalization and its impact on the full enjoyment of human rights. In their report, they flatly assert that "the primacy of human rights law over all other regimes of international law is a basic and fundamental principle that should not be departed from." Sub-Commission on the Promotion and Protection of Human Rights, *Globalization and its impact on the full enjoyment of human rights*, Preliminary Report of the Special Rapporteurs, J. Oloka-Onyango and Deepika Udagama, UN Doc. E/CN.4/Sub.2/2000/13 (June 15, 2000).

The views of the Commission on Human Rights were expressed (by a vote of 30 to 15, with 7 abstentions) in Res. 2000/82 (Apr. 26, 2000): "[T]he exercise of the basic rights of the people of debtor countries to food, housing, clothing, employment, education, health services and a healthy environment cannot be subordinated to the implementation of structural adjustment policies and economic reforms arising from debt."

Comments and Questions

1. Is it clear that the Vienna Convention on the Law of Treaties applies to the Covenants? If so, which parts?

2. Do you agree that the Human Rights Committee has the power to review the acceptability of reservations to the Covenant? Is this true of all human rights bodies? The International Law Commission's special rapporteur on the topic, Alain Pellet, seems to have some doubt. See the response of the committee to his report in UN Doc. A/54/40 (Jan. 1, 1999), Vol. I, Annex VI.

3. Why should human rights treaties be treated differently from other international legal instruments, many of which have direct or indirect beneficiaries other than states? Can human rights bodies persuasively argue that there is a special regime for human rights treaties with respect to reservations but reject the notion of a special regime regarding denunciations? See E. Lijnzaad, *Reservations to UN Human Rights Treaties: Ratify and Ruin?* (1994).

4. Some of the U.S. reservations to the Covenant on Civil and Political Rights were objected to by Belgium, Denmark, Finland, France, Germany, Italy, the Netherlands, Norway, Portugal, Spain, and Sweden. What is the legal effect of these objections?

5. Following adoption of General Comment No. 26, the North Korean government submitted a long overdue state report and sent a delegation to appear before the Human Rights Committee. Does this suggest agreement with the Committee's opinion on denunciation?

What does the Committee mean in General Comment No. 26 by saying e Covenant does not have a temporary character and that protection of the nshrined in the Covenant, once granted, devolves with the territory of the State? How does this affect the successor states of the former Soviet Union and Yugoslavia, both of whom were parties to the Covenants? Note that Great Britain extended the Covenant to Hong Kong while it still administered the territory (as did Portugal to Macau); does this mean that the government of China was bound to apply the Covenant in Hong Kong despite not having ratified the treaty itself? See the 1984 Joint Declaration by the United Kingdom and China on the future of Hong Kong, Annex I, Article XIII, in which China agrees that "[t]he provisions of the International Covenant on Civil and Political Rights and the International Covenant on Economic, Social and Cultural Rights as applied to Hong Kong shall remain in force." Who is responsible for submitting periodic reports under Article 40 of the Covenant on Civil and Political Rights, China (which is still not a party to the Covenant) or the United Kingdom (which is a party but has no governmental authority over Hong Kong)? Or Hong Kong itself, which is also not a party to the Covenant? The most recent report may be found in UN Doc. CCPR/C/HKG/2005/2 (2005).

7. Can the primacy of human rights be justified as a matter of international law? Is this a matter of customary law or conventional law? Is Article 103 of the UN Charter relevant to the debate?

IV. Final Comments and Questions

1. Given the proliferation of constitutional provisions on a right to environment and regional instruments containing similar provisions, is there any benefit to pressing the issue at the global level? Why does the subject of environmental protection appear to be a matter of such concern to African states? What is the basis of the opposition from some Western or developed countries?

3. Are there any issues related to the environment that do not fit easily within the existing catalogue of human rights? If so, does this support development of a new treaty on the right to a safe and healthy environment? Or does it imply that, whatever one's concerns about the protection of natural beauty or endangered species, such concerns are not properly part of "human" rights?

4. What other rights might be considered appropriate to address in a new global treaty, in light of modern developments and concerns? A right to peace? A right to be free from human trafficking? A right to genetic integrity? See the Council of Europe Convention on Human Rights and Biomedicine, 4 April 1997, E.T.S. 164, together with its two Protocols: Additional Protocol to the Convention for the Protection of Human Rights and Dignity of the Human Being with regard to the Application of Biology and Medicine, on the Prohibition of Cloning Human Beings, 12 Jan. 1998, 168 E.T.S.; and Additional Protocol Concerning Transplantation of Organs and Tissues of Human Origin, 24 Jan. 2002, 186 E.T.S.

5. As Professor Shelton says, supra page 63, "Not every social problem must result in a claim which can be expressed as a human right." There are many social values that vary from state to state or even within states, such as the degree of

equity to be pursued as part of economic policy, government spending priorities, the criminalization of private actions (such as drug use), the role of religion, relationships within the family, and others. Even if wide consensus could be achieved on some of these issues, do you agree with Shelton that certain social or political goods may *not* be suitable for inclusion in a human rights treaty? If everything falls under the rubric of "human rights," does human rights lose all meaning?

Chapter 3

The Development of Human Rights Norms Through Non-Binding Instruments

How and Why Do New International Human Rights Norms Emerge other than by Treaty?

I. Introduction: The Role of "Soft Law" in Human Rights Law Making

As discussed in Chapter 2, human rights law-making takes place primarily through the development of treaties to which states affirmatively commit themselves through formal procedures of signature and ratification or accession. But is international human rights law only made by treaties? Numerous other documents that are in some way endorsed by states or international institutions, but not adopted as treaties, such as UN declarations, also express human rights standards with varying degrees of specificity and over an expanding range of topics. In and of themselves, these documents are not legally binding, but they nonetheless have some measure of authority and impact when they are invoked. Because of their often influential character, UN declarations and other such non-treaty documents proclaiming human rights or related standards are sometimes referred to as "soft" law. But does the "soft" metaphor adequately capture the nature of these documents and their place in decision making by states and others? The answer to this question lies in an examination of the way in which declarations and other non-treaty human rights documents are drafted and adopted and in the role they play in decision making. Implicit in much of the discussion is the distinction between legal and political obligations, and we will see that the line between the two is often blurred — although one should be careful not to ignore that line entirely.

The materials in this chapter explore the process of human rights norm building and application through instruments other than treaties, beginning with an introductory discussion of why one might want to have recourse to "soft law." The chapter then examines the drafting and legal character of the Universal Declaration of Human Rights, the very first human rights declaration to emanate from the United Nations. Succeeding sections offer examples of how soft law norms develop, focusing on indigenous peoples, minorities, self-determination, and standards in the area of criminal justice.

Dinah Shelton, Commentary and Conclusions, in Commitment and Compliance: The Role of Non-Binding Norms in the International Legal System

Dinah Shelton, ed. 449-463 (2000) (extracts, some citations omitted)

International human rights law since the World War II has utilized a combination of binding and non-binding instruments to set forth human rights guarantees and the obligations of states in regard to them. The United Nations Charter contains references to human rights, including the obligation of member states to take joint and separate action in cooperation with the organization to achieve universal respect for, and observance of, human rights and fundamental freedoms. The first instrument adopted by the member states to define the rights referred to in the Charter was the 1948 Universal Declaration of Human Rights (UDHR), a non-binding resolution of the UN General Assembly.

From the beginning, however, the drafters of the UDHR intended that it be the first step, "a common standard of achievement" that would lead to a binding agreement on the subject. The 1966 Covenants on Civil and Political Rights and on Economic, Social and Cultural Rights fulfilled the drafters' expectations by incorporating the UDHR rights in binding international agreements. The UDHR remains, however, and many assert that its norms have become legally binding on all members of the United Nations as an authoritative interpretation of member states' human rights obligations, or that the UDHR is binding on all states as customary international law through state practice and opinio juris.

It is unusual to find human rights norms that exist only in soft law form, given the complex interweaving of treaty and non-binding instruments, global and regional texts. Human rights law also is complicated by the existence of judicial and quasi-judicial bodies that decide cases and build a jurisprudence that itself is a combination of hard and soft law. A decision of the European Court of Human Rights or the Inter-American Court of Human Rights, for example, is legally binding on the state party to the case, but is not binding on other parties to the treaty. In the field of human rights, therefore, it may be useful to attempt to categorize non-binding norms, as follows:

Primary soft law can be considered as those normative texts not adopted in treaty form that are addressed to the international community as a whole or to the entire membership of the adopting institution or organization. Such an instrument may declare new norms, often as an intended precursor to adoption of a later treaty, or it may reaffirm or further elaborate norms previously set forth in binding or non-binding texts. The UN Standard Minimum Rules for the Treatment of Prisoners, adopted by the First United Nations Congress on the Prevention of Crime and Treatment of Offenders, 1955, and approved by the UN Economic and Social Council in 1957 is an example of a primary declarative text, whereas ECOSOC resolution 1984/50 on Safeguards Guaranteeing Protection of the Rights of Those Facing the Death Penalty is a reaffirmation of prior human rights law. The Safeguards text explicitly cites to and calls for application of the fair trial guarantees of Article 14 of the International Covenant on Civil and Political Rights. Sometimes, a non-binding instrument reaffirms a previous non-binding instrument. The United Nations Rules for the Protection of Juveniles Deprived of their Liberty (1990), for example, declare that juveniles should only be deprived of their liberty in accordance with the non-binding UN Standard Minimum Rules for the Administration of Juvenile Justice (Beijing Rules).[1]

In many instances, primary soft law elaborates previously-accepted general or vague norms found in binding agreements or non-binding instruments. The Universal Declaration of Human Rights defines the term human rights as it is used in the United Nations Charter. The UN Declaration on the Rights of the Child in turn calls the Universal Declaration of Human Rights the "basis" for its adoption. The UN Declaration on the Rights of Persons Belonging to National or Ethnic, Religious and Linguistic Minorities is comprehensive in its references. According to its preamble, it elaborates standards on the treatment of minorities in a desire to promote the realization of the principles contained in the UN Charter, the Universal Declaration of Human Rights, the Genocide Convention, the Convention on the Elimination of All Forms of Racial Discrimination, the International Covenant on Civil and Political Rights, the International Covenant on Economic, Social and Cultural Rights, the Declaration on the Elimination of All Forms of Intolerance and Discrimination Based on Religion or Belief, and the Convention on the Rights of the Child, as well as other relevant international regional and global human rights instruments. . . . [T]he American Declaration of

1. See also the United Nations Declaration on the Protection of All Persons from Being Subjected to Torture and Other Cruel, Inhuman or Degrading Treatment or Punishment (1975) which excludes "lawful sanctions to the extent consistent with the Standard Minimum Rules for the Treatment of Prisoners." More sweepingly, the 1974 Declaration on the Protection of Women and Children in Emergency and Armed Conflict cites to treaty law and non-binding texts without distinction, proclaiming that women and children "shall not be deprived of shelter, food, medical aid or other inalienable rights, in accordance with the provisions of the Universal Declaration of Human Rights, the International Covenant on Civil and Political Rights, the International Covenant on Economic, Social and Cultural Rights, the Declaration on the Rights of the Child or other instruments of international law."

the Rights and Duties of Man has played a role in the western hemisphere similar to that of the Universal Declaration of Human Rights on the global level: it constitutes an authoritative interpretation of the treaty references to human rights in the Charter of the Organization of American States.

Secondary soft law includes the recommendations and general comments of international human rights supervisory organs, the jurisprudence of courts and commissions, decisions of special rapporteurs and other *ad hoc* bodies, and the resolutions of political organs of international organizations applying primary norms. Most of this secondary soft law is pronounced by institutions whose existence and jurisdiction is derived from a treaty and who apply norms contained in the same treaty. . . . [E]ven institutions are created by soft law. The Organization of American States established the Inter-American Commission on Human Rights by General Assembly resolution and conferred upon the Commission authority to supervise compliance with the rights and duties contained in the American Declaration of the Rights and Duties of Man, including the power to make recommendations to particular states. Thus, an institution established by soft law received a mandate to apply primary soft law to create secondary soft law. Similarly, the OSCE . . . [discussed in Chapter 8] has no treaty basis and calls on its participating states to adhere to soft law human rights norms. Even less legal authority for creating and applying human rights norms is seen in the case of non-governmental organizations, whose members are self-selecting and whose conduct sometimes lacks the transparency of governmental or inter-governmental entities.

Secondary soft law has expanded in large part due to the proliferation of primary treaty standards and monitoring institutions created to supervise state compliance with the treaty obligations. In some cases, human rights treaty bodies have asserted their implied powers to encourage compliance and have developed a considerable body of secondary soft law. An important source of soft law norms is the set of General Comments issued by many of the UN treaty bodies, including the Human Rights Committee and the Committee on Economic, Social and Cultural Rights [see Chapter 7, page 600]. General Comments interpret and add detail to the rights and obligations contained in the respective treaties. The complaints procedures of international monitoring bodies such as the Racial Discrimination Committee (CERD), the Human Rights Committee, the Inter-American Commission on Human Rights, and the African Commission on Human Rights provide another source of soft law, producing recommendations that are technically not binding, although they constitute a determination of whether or not a violation of the human rights treaty has occurred. Similar "adjudicatory" decisions can be found in resolutions of the UN Commission on Human Rights, the UN General Assembly, and the OAS General Assembly. Although these decisions apply existing human rights norms generally found in treaties, the interpretations and guidance they give make them an important secondary source of human right standards.

Finally, secondary soft law derives from the increasingly important work of specially appointed individuals or working groups. Both in the United Nations and regional organizations, thematic rapporteurs or ad hoc committees have become a common device for monitoring state compliance with particular human rights. Thematic mandates may be based on a particular treaty norm or a primary soft law text. The UN Special Rapporteur on Religious Intolerance, for example, has a mandate based on the 1981 General Assembly Declaration on the Elimination of All Forms of Intolerance and of Discrimination Based on Religion or Belief. Rapporteurs create both primary and secondary soft law. The Special Rapporteur on Summary or Arbitrary Executions worked with the UN Committee on Crime Prevention and Control in developing a resolution on effective prevention and investigation of extra-legal, arbitrary, and summary executions, adopted by ECOSOC in 1989 and approved by the General Assembly. After the resolution was adopted, the Special Rapporteur announced that he would hold governments responsible for any "practice that fails to reach the standards set out in the principles." In his 1993 report, the Special Rapporteur refers to the Declaration on Torture, the Principles on the Use of Force and Firearms by Law Enforcement, and the Standard Minimum rules on the Treatment of Prisoners, and clearly seeks to induce states to comply with all of them.

The UN Working Group on Disappearances recommended the adoption of an international instrument on the topic. After the General Assembly complied by adopting the Declaration on Forced Disappearances, the Working Group sent a questionnaire to all states asking what measures had been taken to incorporate in national legislation the principles set out in the Declaration. Not all governments responded with information, but none refused on the basis that the Declaration was not legally binding.

A. The Use of Non-Binding Instruments

The United Nations has followed the precedent of the UDHR by adopting numerous non-binding texts as a step towards concluding formal treaties. The practice of a preceding declaration was utilized for the Convention on the Elimination of All Forms of Racial Discrimination, the Convention on the Elimination of All Forms of Discrimination Against Women, the Convention Against Torture and Other Cruel, Inhuman and Degrading Treatment or Punishment, and the Convention on the Rights of the Child. In a few instances, no legally-binding instrument has followed, due to lack of agreement: e.g., the 1981 Declaration on the Elimination of All Forms of Intolerance and of Discrimination Based on Religion or Belief and the 1986 Declaration on the Right to Development. In general, however, human rights treaties at the United Nations are preceded by declarations setting forth the normative framework. In some instances, the time lag between adoption of the declaration and the treaty results in strengthening the guarantees, e.g., the rights of the child and the elimination of discrimination against women. Where no treaty is concluded, the declaration may become the de facto standard invoked to judge the behavior of states.

Non-binding instruments are also used to conclude the increasingly frequent global conferences convened by the United Nations. Declarations resulted from two general human rights conferences, Teheran in 1968 and Vienna in 1993. The Vienna Conference also produced a plan of action. In recent years the U.N. has sponsored specialized conferences on social development, population, children, and women. Most of the conferences adopt platforms or plans of action.

Non-binding norms form the only detailed guidance in many areas of criminal justice. These norms have largely emerged from meetings of the United Nations Congresses on Crime Prevention and Treatment of Offenders, but some have been developed by the U.N. Human Rights Commission. There is some effort underway to translate the Standard Minimum Rules on the Treatment of Prisoners into a binding text, but in general the detail involved in many of these texts may make states unwilling to see them placed in a binding agreement. In addition to the Standard Minimum Rules, the texts include rules on treatment of juveniles, codes of conduct for law enforcement officers, prosecutors, judges and lawyers. Rules on the administration of justice generally and on the use of firearms further add to the package. The United Nations Economic and Social Council has now compiled the standards into a manual for law enforcement recommended to every state.

United Nations practice distinguishes various kinds of non-binding instruments as well as binding and non-binding texts. In 1962, the Commission on Human Rights reported to ECOSOC on the impact of human rights declarations ([UN Doc.] E/3616/Rev.1, E/CN.4/832/Rev.1, Commission on Human Rights, Report of the Eighteenth Session, ECOSOC Supp. No. 8 (1962)) after debate arose in the Commission over the form of an instrument on freedom of thought, conscience and religion. The Commission then requested a legal opinion on the difference between a recommendation and a declaration. The Office of Legal Affairs submitted a memorandum in which it said: "[i]n United Nations practice, a 'declaration' is a formal and solemn instrument, suitable for rare occasions when principles of great and lasting importance are being enunciated, such as the Declaration of Human Rights. A recommendation is less formal." The Legal Office added that although a declaration is not binding, "in view of the greater solemnity and significance of a 'declaration' it may be considered to impart, on behalf of the organ adopting it, a strong expectation that Members of the international community will abide by it." *Id.* at para. 105. The opinion also recognized that, in so far as the expectation is gradually justified by state practice, a declaration may by custom become recognized as laying down rules binding upon states. In sum, "in United Nations practice, a 'declaration' is a solemn instrument resorted to only in very rare cases relating to matters of major and lasting importance where maximum compliance is expected." Id. States on the Commission responded to the opinion by deciding to defer a decision on the form of the instrument on freedom of religion until they had determined the normative content. Lack of agreement over substance helped determine the form of the instrument and it took nearly twenty years for agreement to be reached on what became the Declaration on Religious Intolerance. . . .

Conclusions

Soft law is used regularly for international human rights norm-setting, either as an ultimate or an intermediate expression of international consensus. In developing human rights treaties, it is now common to pass through a soft law, declarative stage. Probably even more common is the "secondary" soft law that is not preliminary or declaratory in nature, but is intended to be the ultimate and authoritative determination of a legal question. In this regard, hard law and soft law interact to shape the content of international obligations. Soft law formulates and reformulates the hard law of human rights treaties in the application of this law to specific states and cases. Paradoxically, this secondary soft law may be harder than the primary soft law declaring new standards.

Soft law is clearly useful in enunciating broad principles in new areas of law-making, where details of obligation remain to be elaborated. In addition, soft law can be seen as a necessary mechanism related to the traditional consensual nature of international law formation, which only allows hard law to be made and imposed on those who agree. Even where there is overwhelming consensus on the need for action and on the negative impact that inaction will have on all states, norms cannot be imposed on objectors. Soft law can express standards and broad international consensus when unanimity is lacking in state practice and thus the will to establish hard law is absent. Ultimately, as compliance increases soft law may serve to pressure the few non-consenting states to comply with the majority views.

Perhaps surprisingly, states rarely contest the legitimacy of soft law norms. In 1991, Cuba wrote the Working Group on Arbitrary Detention questioning the legal grounds on which the Group was using the provisions contained "in documents of a merely declaratory nature" or provisions of judicial instruments to which the state in question was not a party to determine the arbitrary nature of a case of detention or imprisonment. The Working Group's response made several claims concerning the juridical basis for using soft law. First, it stated that its mandate extended to the application of "instruments," evidencing an intention to go beyond treaty norms. Second, the Body of Principles on extrajudicial or arbitrary executions, to which Cuba objected, was deemed to be an "instrument declaratory of pre-existing rights" because many of its provisions set forth and developed principles recognized under customary international law. Third, the Working Group cited the decision of the International Court of Justice in the case *Nicaragua v. United States of America* for the proposition that "consent" of members of the UN to the text of declaratory resolutions setting forth customary international law may be "understood as an acceptance of the validity of the rule . . . declared by the resolution." The Working Group decided that the Body of Principles, adopted by consensus in the General Assembly, constituted such a declaration and states had therefore accepted its validity. The Working Group also found that the Covenant on Civil and Political Rights had "declaratory effect" with regard to non-party states.

Whether the norms are binding or non-binding, compliance seems most directly linked to the existence of effective monitoring and independent supervision. The role of non-governmental organizations has been crucial, but without a forum to which to take the results of their investigations and the evidence they gather, they are limited in their effectiveness. In short, it is the synergy between human rights bodies created by inter-governmental organizations and non-governmental organizations that leads to greater compliance by states. The existence of non-binding norms and the consensus that emerges as states begin to comply with them also appears to stimulate the development of legally-binding norms.

The studies indicate that states do comply with non-binding human rights norms some of the time. They also comply with binding human rights norms some of the time. No state is free of human rights problems and it is utopian to think that either international or national human rights norms, binding or non-binding, will ever be complied with by all states all of the time. The use of non-binding instruments in human rights law as a precursor to binding norms probably limits state compliance, because the use of the non-binding form is often a reflection of disagreement over the content of the norm or norms in question. It at least reflects "unfinished business" in defining the details of the rights guaranteed within the instrument. Subsequent adoption of a treaty is significant for all states, as the adoption indicates the emergence of a consensus on the right or rights. Thus, the treaty may lead to greater compliance by non-ratifying states who participated in the drafting process, as well as ratifying states, due to the fact of negotiating an agreed legally binding norm. It may appear, however, that the state is complying with the earlier non-binding norm. Clearly, the non-binding text is useful to begin the process of consensus and in some cases may remain the only available text where no agreement can be reached. In the long run, however, non-binding norms in human rights are generally not as effective as binding commitments and the enforcement possibilities that come with them for victims and their representatives.

II. The Universal Declaration of Human Rights

The Universal Declaration of Human Rights, introduced in the preceding extract, was adopted in 1948 without a dissenting vote by the UN General Assembly, the organization's most broadly representative body. It preceded the many human rights treaties that have emanated from the United Nations and that are discussed in Chapter 2. Although the General Assembly has no formal legislative or law-making power, adoption of the Declaration was a process by which states developed and endorsed a common understanding of basic human rights standards that are to apply universally, building on the general human rights clauses of the UN Charter. The following materials discuss the adoption of the declaration and its evolving influence on law and policy, both domestically and internationally.

A. *The Making of the Universal Declaration*

John P.Humphrey,* The Universal Declaration of Human Rights: Its History, Impact and Juridical Character

In Human Rights: Thirty Years after the Universal Declaration 21-28 (B.G. Ramcharan ed., 1979) (footnotes omitted)

The catalyst to which we owe the Universal Declaration of Human Rights and indeed much of the new international law of human rights which has so radically changed the theory and practice of the law of nations was the gross violations of human rights that were committed in and by certain countries during and immediately before the Second World War. For it was these atrocities that fostered the

* The author served as Director of the Division of Human Rights of the UN from 1946 to 1966 and was a leading participant in the drafting of the Universal Declaration. — Eds.

climate of world opinion which made it possible . . . to make the promotion of respect for human rights and fundamental freedoms "for all without distinction as to race, sex, language or religion" one of the pillars on which the United Nations was erected and a stated purpose of the Organization. It was on these foundations that the new international law of human rights was built. . . .

The most important business of the Commission [on Human Rights] when it met under Mrs. Roosevelt's chairmanship in its first regular session on 27 January 1947, was to make arrangements for the drafting of [an International Bill of Rights]. No decision had yet been taken as to its form. . . . Although the Australian and Indian delegations strongly advocated a convention, the great majority of the governments represented at this first session of the Commission favoured a declaration and it was in that form that the first draft, the so-called Secretariat Outline, was prepared. It was only at its second session that the Commission decided to draft a bill in three parts: a declaration, a multilateral convention (soon known as the Covenant and later as the Covenants after the General Assembly decided that there would be two conventions) and measures of implementation.

The Commission made no attempt at its first session to draft the declaration, but it did appoint a committee consisting of its chairman (Mrs. Roosevelt of the United States), its vice-chairman (P.C. Chang of China) and its rapporteur (Charles Malik of Lebanon) to prepare a first draft. This Committee of three held only one meeting — a tea-party really in Mrs. Roosevelt's Washington Square apartment on the Sunday following the adjournment of the Commission — and soon found itself without a mandate. Nor did it draft any articles, partly because Chang and Malik — two of the most brilliant men ever to sit on the Human Rights Commission and who would later be among the principal architects of the International Bill of Rights — were poles apart philosophically and could seldom agree on anything; but the committee did ask the Director of the Human Rights Division [the author] in the secretariat to prepare a draft declaration. He eventually did so. . . . This draft, which was based on a number of drafts that had been prepared by a number of individuals and organizations, contained forty-eight short articles in which both civil and political and economic and social rights were catalogued and defined. With two exceptions all the texts on which the Director worked came from English-speaking sources and all of them from the democratic West;* but the documentation which the Secretariat later brought together in support of his draft included texts extracted from the constitutions of many countries.

[Humphrey describes the ensuing negotiations around the initial Secretariat draft that took place within and outside a drafting committee that had been reconfigured and expanded to meet the political concerns of certain states.]

* It should be noted that the first draft of a bill of human rights, which was to be included in the UN Charter, came from Cuba, Chile, and Panama in 1945. This text was used by the Commission's drafting committee and by Humphrey, along with an influential text submitted by the Inter-American Juridical Committee. In 1968, French jurist Rene Cassin, who served on the Commission and was later a judge on the European Court of Human Rights, was awarded the Nobel Peace Prize for his work on the Declaration. Further information on the role of Cassin, Malik (Lebanon), Hernan Santa Cruz (Chile), and Alexie Pavlov (USSR) can be found in Johannes Morsink, *The Universal Declaration of Human Rights: Origins, Drafting and Intent* (1999). — Eds.

With the help of the Commission on the Status of Women, the commission's two sub-commissions on freedom of information and the prevention of discrimination, the 1948 Geneva Conference on Freedom of Information, the Specialized Agencies and non-governmental organizations, the Human Rights Commission and its Drafting Committee continued to work on the declaration until the late Spring of 1948. Its work on the two covenants, as they later became, would not be completed until 1954; but on 18 June 1948, at the end of its third session the Commission adopted its draft of the Declaration with twelve of its members voting in favour. Byelorussia, the Soviet Union, the Ukraine and Yugoslavia — anticipating the stand they would later take in the General Assembly — all abstained from voting. The draft declaration was therefore ready for consideration by the Assembly at its third session.

Although the Economic and Social Council through which the Commission's text was transmitted to the General Assembly had so many human rights items on the agenda of its seventh session, including the draft convention on genocide and the Final Act of the Information Conference, that exceptionally it set up a special committee to deal with them, the Council made no changes in the text of the Declaration which when it reached the Assembly was sent to the Third Committee [of the General Assembly]. In the light of the many difficulties which then arose, it was fortunate that the chairman of this committee was Charles Malik who as rapporteur of the Commission was familiar with all the details of the legislative history of the draft. It was a tribute to the work of the Commission that many of the governments represented in the Assembly would have accepted the text as it stood; but in the end the Third Committee devoted eighty-one long meetings to it and dealt with one hundred and sixty-eight resolutions containing amendments. In the circumstances it is remarkable that the text finally adopted was so much like the Commission's text....

Attempts to postpone the adoption of the Declaration were... defeated. It was, however only in the night of 6 December that the Third Committee finished its task and forwarded its report to the plenary session of the Assembly, just in time for that body to adopt the Declaration in the night of 10 December, only two days before the end of the session. There were no dissenting votes but the six communist countries which were then members of the United Nations, Saudi Arabia and South Africa all abstained.

This is no place to review the legislative history of the Declaration or even to analyse its thirty articles. Some of the articles could have been better formulated and the document suffers from the inclusion in it of certain assertions which do not enunciate justiciable rights; but having regard to the very great number of people who in one way or another contributed to the text it is a remarkably well drafted document. There were some important omissions including the failure to include any article on the protection of minorities and to recognize any right of petition even at the national level — a right so fundamental that it is recognized even by some authoritarian countries — let alone by the United Nations.

Remembering that the final arbiters of the text were governments it is perhaps just as well that no serious attempt was made to catalogue or define those duties which are correlative to human rights; but the principle that everyone owes duties to the community is recognized in article 29. This important article also stipulates the conditions under which limitations may be legitimately placed on the exercise of human rights and freedoms, the only permitted limitations being such "as are determined by law solely for the purpose of securing due recognition and respect for the rights and freedoms of others and of meeting the just requirements of morality, public order and the general welfare in a democratic society." The reference here to public order can be compared with advantage to the use in the Covenant on Civil and Political Rights of the expression "public order *(ordre public)*" which insofar as that instrument is concerned in any event introduces the nebulous and dangerous concept of public order in civil law jurisdictions.

The Declaration gives pride of place to the traditional civil and political rights which are catalogued and defined in its first twenty-one articles. There then follows, after an "umbrella article," a list and definitions of economic, social and cultural rights which, in 1948, were still controversial in many countries; witness the principal reason that motivated the division of the Covenant into two parts. It was indeed the inclusion of these rights in the declaration which was one of the reasons for its great historical importance.

Professor Humphrey, whose insider's account of the adoption of the Universal Declaration makes fascinating reading, concludes in another of his many writings on the subject that "[i]ts impact on world public opinion has been as great as if not greater than that of any contemporary international instrument, including the Charter of the United Nations." John Humphrey, *Human Rights and the United Nations: A Great Adventure* 76 (1984). The Declaration consists of 30 articles, which Professor Henkin asserts "are in their essence American constitutional rights projected around the world," Louis Henkin, *International Human Rights and Rights in the United States*, in 1 Human Rights in International Law: Legal and Policy Issues 25, 39 (T. Meron ed. 1984); this statement may not be entirely accurate, however, since the declaration also includes economic and social rights not included in the U.S. Constitution. Compare Stephen P. Marks, *From the "Single Confused Page" to the "Decalogue for Six Billion Persons": The Roots of the Universal Declaration of Human Rights in the French Revolution*, 20 Hum. Rts. Q. 459 (1998). Before proceeding to the materials and cases that follow, take this opportunity to read the Declaration (Documentary Supplement, page 143) in its entirety.

Over one-half of the articles in the Universal Declaration (Articles 3-18) guarantee the civil rights of individuals. Another three articles (Articles 19-21) protect their political rights. Finally, six articles (Articles 22-27) grant individuals certain minimal economic, social, and cultural rights. Since the Declaration was considered by all its drafters to be a standard-setting exercise rather than an instrument with binding legal character, no measures of implementation are included.

B. *The Legal Status of the Declaration*

1. The Historical Perspective

In giving our approval to the declaration today, it is of primary importance that we keep clearly in mind the basic character of the document. It is not a treaty; it is not an international agreement. It is not and does not purport to be a statement of law or of legal obligation. It is a declaration of basic principles of human rights and freedoms,

> to be stamped with the approval of the General Assembly by formal vote of its members, and to serve as a common standard of achievement for all peoples of all nations.

Statement of Mrs. Eleanor Roosevelt, Chairman of the Commission on Human Rights, immediately preceding the General Assembly's vote in 1948 on the Universal Declaration, quoted in 5 M. Whiteman, Digest of International Law 243 (1965).

Egon Schwelb, The Influence of the Universal Declaration of Human Rights on International and National Law

1959 Am. Socy. Intl. Law Proceedings 217

Mr. Alejandro Alvarez the former judge of the International Court of Justice said in his dissenting opinion on Competence of the Assembly for the Admission of a State to the United Nations that

> a treaty or a text that has once been established acquires a life of its own. Consequently, in interpreting it, we must have regard to the exigencies of contemporary life rather than to the intentions of those who framed it.

This dictum can hardly be said to be an accepted statement of present-day international law. One is, however, tempted to add that if there ever has been a development which would induce the student to accept it, it has been the fate of the Universal Declaration of Human Rights in the ten years which followed upon its proclamation by the General Assembly of the United Nations on December 10, 1948.

The *travaux préparatoires* make it clear that the overwhelming majority of the speakers in the various organs of the United Nations did not intend the Declaration to become a statement of law or of legal obligations, but a statement of principles devoid of any obligatory character, and which would have moral force "only." One finds in the debates statements which suggest that the Declaration might be considered a complement to the Charter, as its authoritative or "authentic" interpretation, or a formulation of "the general principles of law recognized by civilized nations" within the meaning of Article 38, paragraph 1(c), of the Statute of the Court. Now the difficulty with these suggestions is that the General Assembly, which adopted the Declaration, does not have the constitutional authority to give an authentic interpretation of the Charter. And as to the question of the "general principles of law," the correct answer is, perhaps, this: that while the substance of most, though by no means all, of the provisions of the Declaration may well be said to be identical with general principles of law recognized by civilized nations, the proposition that the Declaration is a codification of these general principles is not warranted.

With a few exceptions, publicists also agree that the Declaration is a "nonbinding pronouncement." Nevertheless, a complete denial of the legal relevance of the Universal Declaration does not do justice to a document which was adopted — without a dissenting vote — by the governments forming the most representative body of the international community. The General Assembly adopted the Declaration not only as "a common standard of achievement," but also stressed that a "common understanding" of rights and freedoms, to which the pledge of Member States expressed in Article 56 of the Charter applies, was of the greatest importance. Nor can the developments be disregarded which have taken place since December 10, 1948. . . .

There are three main areas in which the influence of the Declaration can be traced.

The first such area comes . . . under the term "invocation" which . . . "consists of making a preliminary appeal to a prescription in the hope of influencing results," if it is admissible, that is, to apply the term "invocation" in connection with an instrument like the Declaration. There are innumerable instances of the use of the Declaration as a yardstick to measure the degree of respect for human rights: by governments, by international conferences, by regional intergovernmental organizations, by specialized agencies and by the United Nations, or as a basis for action or exhortation. . . .

The second area of influence of the Declaration is international treaties and conventions. In this regard we must distinguish between various types of agreements. Some instruments have simply made the Universal Declaration part and parcel of their substantive and immediately applicable law. The earliest and best-known example is the Special Statute for Trieste of 1954. Another example of full incorporation may be found in the Franco-Tunisian Conventions of 1955, in which Tunisia undertook to grant all persons resident in its territory the rights and personal guarantees proclaimed in the Declaration. . . .

An interesting feature of these conventions is the fact that in one form or another, in their preambles they quote from, or expressly refer to, the Universal Declaration of Human Rights. What is the legal relevance of these references to the Declaration? This is a problem which calls for [a more] thorough examination [than can be undertaken here]. The following may be said, however: It is a well-established rule of interpretation, supported by a long line of decisions and advisory opinions of both the Permanent Court and the International Court of Justice, that every word and part of a treaty is presumed to have a meaning and to produce some legal effect. It is the normal function of a preamble to provide an expression of the objectives of a treaty. . . .

There are many instances on record, however, where a preamble, in addition to being an aid in interpreting a treaty, is a direct source of legal obligations not otherwise set forth in the so-called operative articles. . . .

It is impossible to be dogmatic about the effect which the references to the Declaration contained in the preambles to these various conventions may have upon the municipal legal system of states which become parties to them. By necessity, it varies from country to country and from convention to convention. The ratification of these conventions and their becoming part of the municipal law of states parties either ipso facto or by way of transforming legislation, introduces the provisions of the Declaration into the national legal systems with consequences the consideration of which would carry us too far. It can be assumed, for instance, that these principles might achieve relevance, among others, in situations where public policy or *ordre public* governs legal relations.

This brings me to the third area of the impact of the Declaration, i.e., its direct influence on national constitutions and on municipal legislation and, in some instances, on court decisions. It may be objected that the fact that a constitution or municipal enactment uses the phraseology of the Declaration is by no means proof that the rights thereby proclaimed or defined are in fact respected. This, of course, is true.... An audience of American Lawyers will perhaps respond with greater understanding than any other to the suggestion that general principles embodied, and general phraseology used, in a basic document sometimes have a decisive effect on subsequent legal history. The Constitutional law of the United States might be different if the Fifth and Fourteenth Amendments had not prohibited deprivation of life, liberty, or property "without due process of law," or if general expressions such as "the privileges and immunities of citizens" and "equal protection of the laws" had not been used. There are already cases on record where the general language of the Universal Declaration has tended to encourage similar developments.

It is not surprising that constitutions drafted in co-operation with the United Nations, such as those of Libya and Eritrea, show the marked influence of the Universal Declaration, although they fall short of its provisions in one important respect, viz., the right of women to vote. It can be seen from express references to the Declaration in many other constitutions and statutes from various regions of the world, and, in the absence of such references, from extraneous evidence, that the influence of the Declaration is also reflected in many instruments not written under United Nations sponsorship....

The influence of the Universal Declaration is also reflected in the constitutional law of two great European states, the Federal Republic of Germany and France.

The Declaration provides that the family is the natural and fundamental group unit of society and is entitled to protection by society and the state. In the debates of the Commission on Human Rights, this sentence was criticized as being a "sociological concept" and not a legal norm. The idea was taken over, however, by the authors of the Basic Law of the Federal Republic of Germany, which provides in Article 6 that marriage and the family are under the special protection of the state. On the basis of this provision, the Federal Constitutional Court, in a decision of January 17, 1957, in which it traced the provision back to the Universal Declaration, declared unconstitutional and therefore void the provisions of the German Income Tax Act which provided for the joint assessment of the income of husband and wife. The fact that by this assessment married persons were in a less favorable position than unmarried persons, led the Court to the conclusion that such an arrangement amounted to a disturbing interference of the state with marriage and the family and was therefore violative of the constitutional provision. It is not for me to say whether the joint assessment of husband and wife is a good or bad idea. I merely quote this as an example of the influence general provisions and "sociological formulae" may have upon the law in the hands of judges who are ready to exhaust all possibilities to protect the rights of the individual.

The provision of Article 12 of the Universal Declaration that no one shall be subjected to arbitrary interference with his privacy, family, home or correspondence also found its way into the municipal law of the Federal Republic of Germany, this time via Article 8 of the European Convention of Human Rights. The effect of this was illustrated by a judgment of the Federal Court of Administration in 1956. The Court quashed an administrative decision expelling an alien who had a criminal record. It held that the expulsion of the alien, who had a German wife, would interfere with the family life of the alien, his German wife and the wife's illegitimate children.

The Declaration provides that "no one shall be arbitrarily deprived of his nationality." This provision, in a strengthened wording, became Article 16 of the German Basic Law, which is to the effect that no one may be deprived of his German citizenship....

In the preamble to the new French Constitution of 1958 "the French people solemnly proclaims its attachment to the rights of man as defined by the Declaration of 1789, confirmed and complemented by the Preamble of the French Constitution of 1946." In the draft of the preamble as recommended by the Consultative Constitutional Committee, it was proposed that the words "and of the Universal Declaration of Human Rights" be added after the reference to the preamble to the French Constitution of 1946. It is unnecessary to stress the great importance which such reference to the Universal Declaration in the Constitution of a country of the standing of France would have had. In the final text of the Constitution, however, the reference to the Universal Declaration does not appear. Contrary to its predecessor of 1946, the new French Constitution does contain a series of provisions guaranteeing human rights, including at least one which uses the same language as the corresponding provision of the Universal Declaration. This is Article 66 which, in the language of Article 9 of the Universal Declaration, provides that "no one shall be subjected to arbitrary detention." The Constitution further provides that the judicial power, the guardian of individual liberty, shall insure respect for this principle under the conditions provided for by law....

Now a few examples of the Declaration having influenced or having at least been quoted in judicial decisions:...

American Federation of Labor v. American Sash and Door Company involved the constitutionality of an Arizona Constitutional Amendment which prohibited union security arrangements (the closed shop). Mr. Justice Frankfurter, in concurring with the decision of the Court which upheld the Arizona Constitutional Amendment, referred to Article 20(2) of the Universal Declaration providing that "No one may be compelled to belong to an association." Again, it is not for me to say whether this provision of the Declaration applies to trade unions, a matter which is controversial. What we are interested in in this connection is the fact that the Declaration was invoked by one of the justices of the Supreme Court.

In a case which also dealt with trade union matters, the New York Supreme Court, in Wilson v. Hacker, considered whether it may condemn discrimination based upon sex "as a violation of fundamental principle and judge the legitimacy of union activities in the light of the principle." In this connection, the court stated: "Indicative of the spirit of our times are the provisions of the Universal Declaration," and went on to quote the nondiscrimination provision of Article 2 and also Article 23, which provides that everyone has the right to work, to free choice of employment, to just and favorable conditions of work and to protection against unemployment.

The influence of the Declaration is not limited to cases in this country. The Penal Chamber of the Supreme Court of The Netherlands, in a freedom of the press case, dealt with the proposition of the Prosecutor that it had always been the spirit of the Netherlands Constitution that constitutional rights, including the freedom of the press, were not absolute rights and that the modern tendency was to give greater prominence to the public interest. The Supreme Court of The Netherlands held that this contention was disproved by the adoption and proclamation of the Universal Declaration of Human Rights by the General Assembly of the United Nations. Here the Supreme Court interpreted the Constitution by reference to the Declaration.

Belgian and Italian Courts have invoked the provision of the Universal Declaration that no one shall be arbitrarily denied the right to change his nationality, and decided accordingly. The Italian court stated:

> Though not having the force of a binding rule of law, the provisions of the Declaration nevertheless constitute guiding principles of the highest moral value.

The theoretical difference between a rule of law and a rule of morality becomes of little practical importance when the court accepts the latter as a guide for its decision.

A Belgian court in a case concerning the placing of a person in a mental institution, requested an expert opinion on her state of health, giving as the first ground for its decision Article 3 of the Universal Declaration, which states that everyone has the right to life, liberty and security of person.

The Supreme Court of the Philippines ordered the release from custody of a stateless person about to be deported, and placed him under the surveillance of the immigration authorities on the basis, inter alia, that the Universal Declaration proclaimed the right of everyone to life and liberty, to the rights and freedoms set forth in the Declaration without distinction, the right of everyone to an effective remedy and the prohibition of arbitrary arrest, detention and exile.

There are also a few instances in which the Universal Declaration has been referred to by judges of the International Court of Justice, albeit in dissenting opinions:

Judge Azevedo stated in the *Asylum* Case that the new Declaration of Human Rights should not remain a dead letter. Judge Levi Carneiro, in the *Anglo-Iranian Oil Company* Case, invoked Article 17 of the Declaration, which deals with the right to own property and provides that no one shall be arbitrarily deprived of his property. Judge Ad Hoc Guggenheim stressed in the *Nottebohm* Case that to dissociate diplomatic protection from nationality will weaken even further the protection of the individual, which is so precarious under existing international law. He considered that this would be contrary to the basic principle embodied in Article 15(1) of the Declaration, according to which everyone has a right to a nationality.

The state of affairs which has been created by all these developments is certainly not neat or logical. We are faced with a haphazard growth, not with a methodical legislative process; international legislation on human rights has been attempted on a grand scale by the ambitious project of the draft International Covenants on Human Rights [which are discussed in Chapter 2]. . . .

After the delivery of the preceding paper in 1959, the evolution of the status of the Universal Declaration in international law continued apace. By 1968, the twentieth anniversary of its adoption, arguments were being made that the Declaration had become part of customary international law. The non-governmental Assembly for Human Rights meeting in Montreal that year adopted what has become known as the Montreal Statement, which included the assertion that the "Universal Declaration of Human Rights . . . has over the years become a part of customary international law." 9 J. Int. Comm'n Jurists 94, 95 (1968). Also in 1968, the year designated by the United Nations as Human Rights Year, came a similar statement by the UN-sponsored International Conference on Human Rights meeting in Teheran. The Proclamation of Teheran stated that [t]he Universal Declaration of Human Rights . . . constitutes an obligation for members of the international community." UN Doc. A/CONF.32/41 at 3 (May 13, 1968), para. 2.

Note: Customary International Law

Customary international law is among the principal sources of international law in addition to treaties. A norm of customary international law emerges — or *crystallizes* — when a preponderance of states (and other actors with international legal personality) from different regions of the world converge on a common understanding of the norm's content and expect future behavior to conform to the norm. Customary law is "generally observed to include two key elements: a 'material' element in certain past uniformities in behavior and a 'psychological' element, or *opinio juris,* in certain subjectivities of 'oughtness' attending such uniformities in behavior." Myres McDougal et al., *Human Rights and World Public Order: The Basic Policies of an International Law of Human Dignity* 269 (1980). See also Ian Brownlie, *Principles of Public International Law* 6-11 (6th ed. 2003). Article 38 of the Statute of the International Court of Justice identifies in its listing of the sources of law to be applied by the Court "international custom, as evidence of a general practice accepted as law." Complete uniformity in a practice assenting to or acquiescing in a norm is not required, although it must be sufficiently widespread and coherent among states to give rise to expectations of compliance with the norm.

Traditionally, the relevant state practice for the development of customary international law was considered to be limited to or primarily involve the actual physical behavior or episodic conduct of states, for example, a state's actual treatment of foreign diplomats in relation to diplomatic immunity. The now prevalent view, however, is that other forms of practice also contribute the formation of customary international law. Professor Brownlie, for example, includes among the "very numerous" sources of custom the following:

> Diplomatic correspondence, policy statements, press releases, the opinions of official legal advisors, official manuals on legal questions, e.g. manuals of military law, executive decisions and practices, order to naval forces etc., comments by governments on drafts produced by the International Law Commission, state legislation, international and national judicial decisions, recitals in treaties and other international instruments, a pattern of treaties in the same form, the practice of international organs, and resolutions relating to legal questions in the Unite Nations General Assembly.

Brownlie, supra, at 6. Also see Oscar Schachter, *International Law in Theory and Practice* 84-105 (1991) (on the legal effect of resolutions and political texts).

The existence of customary law does not negate the basic principle of international law that a state may not be bound without its consent, however. Although silence in the face of a developing customary norm is presumed to evidence consent, a state will not be bound to such a norm if it clearly and persistently objects to it (unless the norm is one of *jus cogens*, a peremptory or non-derogable norm). See, Brownlie, supra, at 11. While at least one prominent scholar asserts that "some sort of law also imposing obligations on those who were not willing or prepared to be bound, is gradually emerging," Antonio Cassese, *International Law* 124 (2001), any such emerging law does not easily fit within the traditional understanding of customary international law.

Another and somewhat related source of international law is identified in Article 38 of the ICJ Statute as "general principles of law recognized by civilized nations." The distinction between customary international law and general principles of law is ambiguous in modern doctrine. The classic distinction is that, while customary international law evolves from the actual day-to-day practice of states, "general principles" embrace the principles of private and public law administered in domestic courts where such principles are applicable to international relations. See J.L. Brierly, *The Law of Nations* 57-63 (6th ed. H. Waldock ed. 1963). The rubric of general principles, however, is now often understood to include not just such shared principles of domestic law, but also principles reflected on a widespread basis in state practice in the international arena, discernible from numerous international treaties or other standard-setting documents, or which are necessary as logical propositions of legal reasoning. See generally Brownlie, supra, at 15-19; Mark Janis, *An Introduction to International Law* 55-59 (4th ed. 2003).

Also noteworthy are the "subsidiary sources" of international law which endeavor to reveal the content of rules deriving from the primary sources, including custom. In the words of Article 38, these subsidiary sources include "judicial decisions and the teachings of the most highly qualified publicists of the various nations." For U.S. attitudes toward the sources of international law, see Restatement (Third) of the Foreign Relations Law of the United States §102 (1988).

Assertions that the Universal Declaration of Human Rights constitutes or reflects customary international law attempt to fit the Declaration into one of the standard sources of international law and thereby establish its legally binding character. But merely stating that the Universal Declaration of Human Rights is legally binding as customary international law, of course, does not make it so. Although the views of "highly qualified publicists" are a subsidiary source of customary international law, what counts primarily is the actual practice of states, in one form or another, demonstrating uniformity of expectation among them consistent with the Declaration, or states' explicit recognition that the Declaration's norms reflect general principles of law. At the very least, however, the Montreal Statement and the Proclamation of Teheran were important indications that a law-making consensus as to the Declaration's legal status was evolving.

2. Subsequent Developments in the Legal Status of the Declaration

The manner in which the normative impact of Universal Declaration on Human Rights has evolved over the years is demonstrated by the following brief extracts.

> Although the affirmations of the Declaration are not binding qua international convention within the meaning of Article 38, paragraph 1(a), of the Statute of the Court, they can bind States on the basis of custom within the meaning of paragraph 1(b) of the same Article, whether because they constituted a codification of customary law as was said in respect of Article 6 of the Vienna Convention on the Law of Treaties, or because they have acquired the force of custom through a general practice accepted as law, in the words of Article 38, paragraph 1(b), of the Statute. One right which must certainly be considered a preexisting binding customary norm which the Universal Declaration of Human Rights codified is the right to equality, which by common consent has ever since the remotest times been deemed inherent in human nature.

Separate Opinion of Judge Ammoun in the *Namibia* Case, 1971 I.C.J. 16, 76.

> The Universal Declaration of Human Rights was not intended to be binding on states as part of positive international law; not only are resolutions of the General Assembly ordinarily not binding, but the Declaration was to be only one part of the International Bill of Rights which was to include a covenant having substantially the same content as the Declaration and which would be binding on those states that ratified it. If the Declaration had been intended to be binding, a covenant would have been unnecessary. Further, though some delegations attempted to breathe legal life into the Declaration by asserting that it was an authentic interpretation of the human rights provisions of the Charter or that it set forth general principles of law, others insisted more convincingly that it was not binding. In the more than a quarter of a century since its adoption, however, the Declaration has been invoked so many times both within and without the United Nations that lawyers now are saying that, whatever the intention of its authors may have been, the Declaration is now part of the customary law of nations and therefore is binding on all states. The Declaration has become what some nations wished it to be in 1948: the universally accepted interpretation and definition of the human rights left undefined by the Charter.

John Humphrey, *The International Bill of Rights: Scope and Implementation*, 17 Wm. & Mary L. Rev. 527, 529 (1976).

> [Professor Humphrey's] view, first advanced solely by legal scholars but subsequently supported by the resolutions of international conferences, state practice, and even court decisions, now appears to have achieved widespread acceptance. Indeed, the suggestion has been made that the Declaration has "the attributes of jus cogens," surely an overly enthusiastic assertion in the opinion of the present writer if it is intended to imply that *all* the rights enumerated in the Declaration now constitute peremptory norms of international law.

Richard B. Lillich, *Invoking International Human Rights Law in Domestic Courts*, 54 U. Cin. L. Rev. 367, 394-395 (1985) (footnote omitted).

In addition to Professor Humphrey, the expanding group of legal scholars who some time ago argued that the Universal Declaration had developed into customary international law included Professor Louis B. Sohn, who posited that the Universal Declaration is not only "an authoritative interpretation of the Charter obligations but now also a binding instrument in its own right. . . . " Louis B. Sohn, *The Human Rights Law of the Charter*, 12 Tex. Intl. L.J. 129, 133 (1977). But while the Declaration has now been invoked repeatedly by states at the United Nations, before international tribunals, and in the diplomatic context, this is usually done without explicitly ascribing to the Declaration the force of law.

Indeed, in the relatively few instances where states have expressed their views regarding the basis of the obligation to observe human rights under international law, they either have mentioned the provisions of one or more of the human rights treaties or have relied upon the incorporation of the Declaration's articles into the human rights clauses of the UN Charter. See, for example, L.H. Legault, *Canadian Practice in International Law During 1979 as Reflected Mainly in Public Correspondence and Statements of the Department of External Affairs*, 18 Can. Y.B. Intl. L. 301 (1980).

> It is the view of the Canadian Government that the observance of human rights is obligatory under international law. The Canadian Government views the Universal Declaration of Human Rights as a valid interpretation and elaboration of the references to human rights and fundamental freedoms in the Charter of the United Nations. Consequently, the obligation on states to observe the human rights and fundamental freedoms enunciated in the Universal Declaration derives from their adherence to the Charter of the United Nations.

Id. at 326. This view contrasts with the latter half of Professor Sohn's statement — that the Declaration is "a binding instrument in its own right."

Insofar as the Executive Branch of the U.S. government is concerned, explicit recognition that at least *some* articles of the Universal Declaration *reflect* customary international law came in the U.S. Memorial to the International Court of Justice in the *Hostages* case, 1980 I.C.J. 3, where, after marshalling traditional international law precedents to demonstrate "that States have an international legal obligation to observe certain minimum standards in their treatment of aliens," the government added the following brief passage about the nature and scope of fundamental human rights:

> It has been argued that no such standard can or should exist, but such force as that position may have had has gradually diminished as recognition of the existence of certain fundamental human rights has spread throughout the international community. The existence of such fundamental rights for all human beings, nationals and aliens alike, and the existence of a corresponding duty on the part of every State to respect and observe them, are now reflected, inter alia, in the Charter of the United Nations, the Universal Declaration of Human Rights and corresponding portions of the International Covenant on Civil and Political Rights. . . .
>
> In view of the universal contemporary recognition that such fundamental human rights exist . . . Iran's obligation to provide "the most constant protection and security" to United States nationals in Iran includes an obligation to observe those rights. . . .

Memorial of the United States (*U.S. v. Iran*), 1980 I.C.J. Pleadings (Case Concerning United States Diplomatic and Consular Staff in Tehran) 182 (Jan. 12, 1980). As evidence of the fundamental human rights to which all individuals are entitled and which all states must guarantee, the Memorial cites Articles 3, 5, 7, 9, 12, and 13 of the Declaration, at 182 n.36, which cover, respectively, the right to life, liberty, and security of person; the prohibition of torture and cruel, inhuman, or degrading treatment or punishment; the right to equality before the law and to non-discrimination in its application; the prohibition of arbitrary arrest or detention; the right to privacy; and the right to freedom of movement.

Compare this catalogue of "fundamental rights" with that found in the following extract from the Restatement (Third) of the Foreign Relations Law of the United States.

Restatement (Third) of the Foreign Relations Law of the United States §702
1987

§702. Customary International Law of Human Rights

A state violates international law if, as a matter of state policy, it practices, encourages, or condones

(a) genocide,
(b) slavery or slave trade,
(c) the murder or causing the disappearance of individuals,
(d) torture or other cruel, inhuman, or degrading treatment or punishment,
(e) prolonged arbitrary detention,
(f) systematic racial discrimination, or
(g) a consistent pattern of gross violations of internationally recognized human rights.

Although Section 702 remained unchanged from the initial draft in 1982 through the final version in 1987, the Reporters who drafted this section did add a comment that "[t]he list is not necessarily complete, and is not closed: human rights not listed in this section may have achieved the status of customary international law, and some rights might achieve that status in the future." Id. §702 comment a at 162. Possible candidates for customary international law status listed are rights against systematic religious discrimination and gender discrimination, and the right to property, id. at 165-166, all of which are guaranteed by the Universal Declaration.

The Restatement of the Foreign Relations Law of the United States roughly synthesizes the "blackletter" law as practiced by the United States courts and executive agencies engaged in foreign relations. However, U.S. government attitudes, while important and, indeed, perhaps controlling domestically, are only the views of one state and, thus, not necessarily determinative internationally. Cf. generally Bruno Simma and Philip Alston, *The Sources of Human Rights Law: Custom, Jus Cogens, and General Principles*, 12 Austl. Y.B. Intl. L. 12 (1992). The following extract, based upon a six-year study of the practice of numerous UN member states, reveals widespread support for the proposition that a substantial number of the rights contained in the Universal Declaration now reflect customary international law.

International Law Association, Committee on the Enforcement of Human Rights Law, Final Report on the Status of the Universal Declaration of Human Rights in National and International Law

ILA, Report of the Sixty-Sixth Conference 525, 544-549 (Buenos Aires 1995)* (footnotes omitted)

Those who urge acceptance of the Declaration *in toto* as customary law are in a clear minority, and there is insufficient state practice to support such a wide-ranging proposition at present. Unless one wishes to interpret the proposed customary international law norm as merely expressing general agreement with the desirability of the principles in the Declaration, it would appear difficult to make the case that states recognize an international legal obligation to guarantee, e.g., periodic holidays with pay, full equality of rights upon dissolution of a marriage, or protection against unemployment.

However, there would seem to be little argument that many provisions of the Declaration today do reflect customary international law. "Few claim that any state that violates any provision of the Declaration has violated international law. Almost all would agree that some violations of the Declaration are violations of international law." Almost no state has specifically rejected the principles proclaimed in the Universal Declaration, and it constitutes a fundamental part of what has become known as the Universal Bill of Human Rights.

The American Law Institute's *Restatement*... offers one of the most explicit and authoritative opinions as to the content of the customary international law of human rights, at least as of 1987. [The report quotes Section 702, set out at page 156, supra.] The prohibitions against slavery, arbitrary deprivation of life, torture, arbitrary detention, and racial discrimination are explicitly included in the Universal Declaration, as well as other international instruments, and the prohibitions against genocide and gross violations of human rights are certainly implicit in the Declaration's provisions.

It would be presumptuous for the present report to pretend to analyse comprehensively each of the rights set forth in the Universal Declaration. Nevertheless, the evidence of state practice identified by the rapporteur suggests the following tentative conclusions with respect to the various articles of the Declaration.

Articles 1, 2, and 7 express the fundamental right of equal treatment and non-discrimination *with respect to guaranteed human rights* "without distinction of any kind." It would seem difficult to deny the widespread acceptance of such a right to equal treatment under the law, subject to the caveats below.

Of course, even with respect to protected rights, state practice does not support a conclusion that there is full compliance with the principle of equality. Women are prevented from exercising their human rights on an equal footing with men in many states; distinctions based on religious and political beliefs are

* Two of the authors, Professors Lillich and Hannum, served as Chairman and Rapporteur of the Committee, respectively, and were primarily responsible for the preparation of this report. The substance of the report is reprinted in Hurst Hannum, *The Status of the Universal Declaration of Human Rights in National and International Law*, 25 Ga. J. Int'l & Comp. L. 287 (1995/96). — Eds.

found in many constitutions; and the effective guarantee of respective rights and obligations to the wealthy and the poor is often quite different.

One specific kind of discrimination, that based on race, is held by all commentators to be prohibited under customary international law, at least when it is pervasive.

Article 3, guaranteeing "the right to life, liberty and security of person," may be too general to be a useful international norm, although protection of the right to life has been cited frequently as falling within customary international law. The prohibition against murder and causing "disappearances" is included in the Restatement's list, and the prohibition against the arbitrary deprivation of life has been referred to by many other commentators.

The prohibition against slavery in *article 4* is also universally held to form part of customary law; it is further prohibited by a series of widely ratified conventions.

Article 5's prohibition against "torture or . . . cruel, inhuman or degrading treatment or punishment" is perhaps the most widely commented upon right in the Declaration (with the possible exception of the prohibition against racial discrimination). Its place in customary international law is confirmed by the *Restatement*, and many other sources could be cited. The Vienna World Conference on Human Rights "reaffirm[ed] that under human rights law and international humanitarian law, freedom from torture is a right which must be protected under all circumstances."

One of the most comprehensive examinations of the evidence of the status of the prohibition against torture in customary international law is the U.S. case of *Filartiga v. Peña-Irala*, in which the Court of Appeals for the Second Circuit found that the right to be free from torture is one of the rights conferred by international law "upon all people vis-à-vis their own governments." It relied for its conclusion on provisions of the Universal Declaration and a number of other international instruments (most unratified by the United States), national statutes, U.S. government statements, and the opinions of legal experts.

Article 6 states simply that "[e]veryone has the right to recognition everywhere as a person before the law." Although no direct support for this principle is found in scholarly literature, it would seem impossible to deny the status of custom to such a fundamental expression of the essential equality and value of natural persons. The relegation of certain categories of individuals to the status of "non-persons" without rights may unfortunately exist in practice, but no state publicly adheres to such a view.

Article 8's guarantee of an effective remedy before domestic courts for violations of human rights would seem to be an essential prerequisite to ensure the enjoyment of other human rights, but it is not generally included in lists of customary human rights and has not been the subject of significant domestic jurisprudence.

The prohibition in *article* 9 against arbitrary arrest, detention, or exile is included in the *Restatement* list only if it is "prolonged;" other commentators have not made such a fine distinction, although the definition of what is "arbitrary" obviously limits the norm's usefulness in all but the most blatant cases. The International Court of Justice has stated:

> Wrongfully to deprive human beings of their freedom and to subject them to the physical constraint in conditions of hardship is in itself manifestly incompatible with

the principles of the Charter of the United Nations, as well as with the fundamental principles enunciated in the Universal Declaration of Human Rights.

The prohibition against arbitrary detention is closely linked to provisions relating to the right to a fair trial, found in *articles 10 and 11*. A comprehensive survey of provisions relating to criminal justice recently concluded that "at times there seems to be an uncanny resemblance between the terminology of more recent constitutions and that of the Universal Declaration and the ICCPR [International Covenant on Civil and Political Rights]," and many observers include the right to a fair trial (without more specific examination of the components of the right) among those now guaranteed under customary law.

Article 12, which deals, inter alia, with the right to privacy, was cited by the U.S. Government in the *Hostages* case as being encompassed in customary law and is included in other major human rights treaties. However, the content of the right varies considerably among states, and the contours of that realm of personal privacy which is beyond the reach of government is perhaps too vague to be deemed a useful part of customary law at present.

Article 13, which is concerned with freedom of movement and the right to leave and return, also was cited by the United States in the *Hostages* case. Meron believes that these rights should be added to those considered to be part of customary law, but there does not seem to be sufficient consensus on this point at present to draw firm conclusions.

Despite widespread acceptance of the 1951 Convention on the Status of Refugees and the 1967 Protocol thereto, the right to seek (not to receive) asylum set forth in *article 14* has not been identified by commentators or states as falling within customary international law. However, returning a person to a country where he would be tortured or persecuted might well violate a developing customary norm against the *refoulement* of refugees.

German courts have recognized that the right to a nationality set forth in *article 15* is "the expression of customary international law in the sense of article 25 of the Basic Law [German Constitution]." The Inter-American Court of Human Rights referred to article 15 of the Declaration as supporting its conclusion that "[t]he right of every human being to a nationality has been recognized as such by international law." However, no other source for including this specific right within customary law has been found.

A German court has likewise found that "there is a consensus under international law that freedom of marriage is one of the fundamental human rights," citing the European Convention of Human Rights and *article 16* of the Universal Declaration.

The right to property, included in *article 17*, of the Universal Declaration, was omitted from both of the two human rights Covenants. However, a recent UN study on the right to property concludes that the Declaration's standards "became rules of customary international law and which as such were regarded as mandatory in the doctrine and practice of international law." One must assume that the right to property would be included as one of these "mandatory" rules, so long as one excludes from the right broader issues such as the international norms governing expropriation and other controversial topics. The rapporteur did observe that the right to property is not universally recognized, thus casting some doubt on its status or scope as a customary norm. Nonetheless, it would seem difficult to maintain that a state's power to expropriate or seize individual property is wholly unlimited.

Article 18 guarantees the right to freedom of thought, conscience, and religion; its provisions were expanded upon in the 1981 Declaration on the Elimination of All Forms of Intolerance and of Discrimination Based on Religion or Belief adopted by the UN General Assembly. The Declaration's Preamble considers that "religion or belief, for anyone who professes either, is one of the fundamental elements in his conception of life and that freedom of religion or belief should be firmly respected and guaranteed." Although the Special Rapporteur on Iran of the UN Commission on Human Rights has stated that freedom of thought, conscience, and religion has "the character of *jus cogens*," the degree of de facto and de jure suppression of the practice of certain religions makes acceptance of such an assertion problematic. In addition, some Islamic countries have denied that Muslims have a right to change their religion.

Similarly, the widespread restrictions on freedom of opinion and expression, set forth in *article 19* of the Declaration, make it difficult to conclude that this provision is now part of customary international law, unless one accepts that the restrictions to freedom of expression which states believe are permissible can be so broad as to swallow the right itself. Similar observations might be made with respect to *article 20*'s guarantee of the right of peaceful assembly.

Despite the arguments of some that a "right to democracy" may be emerging as a norm of international customary law, it is apparent that many states have not accepted *article 21*'s guarantee of the right to participate in the political life of one's country.

Articles 22 through 27 deal primarily with economic, social, and cultural rights, including social security, the right to work, the right to rest and leisure, the right to an adequate standard of living, the right to education, and the right to participate in cultural life. Despite the fact that the United States, in particular, has often denied the status of "rights" to these norms, they may enjoy wider international support than some of the civil and political rights traditionally emphasized in U.S. jurisprudence. However, they are rarely referred [to] by either commentators or courts in discussions of the content of customary international human rights law.

The following rights would seem to enjoy sufficiently widespread support as to be at least potential candidates for rights recognized under customary international law: the right to free choice of employment; the right to form and join trade unions; and the right to free primary education, subject to a state's available resources. Many rights included within these articles are closely related to other rights, such as the right to life and the prohibition against arbitrary discrimination. The Appeals Board of the Council of Europe has found that "[t]he absence of discrimination based on sex, and equal pay for workers of either sex constitute, at the present time, one of the general principles of law."

Article 28, which calls for "a social and international order" in which the Declaration's rights can be realized is clearly hortatory and insufficiently precise to constitute an international legal norm.

Although it does not set forth a substantive right, *article 29*'s reference to permissible restrictions on rights might be considered as a general principle of international law, if it is interpreted to mean that international human rights may not be restricted arbitrarily. On the other hand, human rights treaties do permit limitations or restrictions on rights to be imposed on grounds other than those specified in article 29, which suggests that the literal terms of the article cannot be taken to represent international custom.

Finally, the savings clause in *article* 30 is found in essentially all subsequent human rights treaties and may be seen as an admonition that the Declaration's provisions must be implemented in good faith, so as not to undermine its very purpose. This may simply reflect the general principle of international law which does not allow a treaty party to act in a way which would defeat the object and purpose of the treaty while purporting to rely on its provisions.

Firm conclusions as to the status of any of the provisions of the Universal Declaration of Human Rights in customary international law cannot be drawn without a much more thorough and comprehensive survey of state practice than is possible in the present report. However, these cursory observations may suggest the rights with respect to which such a survey might be most productive.

The above study found that more than 90 national constitutions since 1948 contain statements of fundamental rights inspired by the Universal Declaration of Human Rights, and Annex 2 of the study lists more than 200 judicial opinions from 27 countries citing the Declaration. At the 1993 World Conference on Human Rights, more than 100 countries reaffirmed "their commitment to the purposes and principles contained in the Charter of the United Nations and the Universal Declaration of Human Rights" and emphasized that the Universal Declaration of Human Rights "is the source of inspiration and has been the basis for the United Nations in making advances in standard setting as contained in the existing international human rights instruments." Vienna Declaration and Programme of Action, World Conference on Human Rights, pmbl, para. 3, 8, UN Doc. A/CONF.157/24 (Part 1) at 20-46 (1993). The General Assembly emphasized the need to observe the Declaration when it created the post of UN High Commissioner for Human Rights, whose mandate is to function within the framework of the Charter and the Universal Declaration of Human Rights, see G.A. Res. 48/141 (Dec. 20, 1993), Pmbl.

Note: Other United Nations and Regional Human Rights Declarations

Since the adoption of the Universal of Declaration of Human Rights, the UN General Assembly has passed resolutions adopting numerous additional declarations articulating human standards on particular subjects of concern. Like the Universal Declaration, which was followed by the two covenants that fill out the International Bill of Human Rights, many of these declarations have been followed by treaties on the same subjects. Various ad hoc conferences convened by the United Nations — such as the 1993 World Conference on Human Rights, the Fourth World Conference on Women in 1995, and the 2001 World Conference Against Racism — have also resulted in UN member states collectively adopting standard-setting and programmatic declarations related to matters of human rights. In addition, specialized agencies of the United Nations, especially the UN Educational, Scientific, and Cultural Organization (UNESCO) and the

International Labour Organization (ILO), have adopted topical statements or declarations on human rights. Even when not followed by treaties, the numerous declarations by the United Nations and its specialized agencies have contributed to a growing corpus of common understandings about human rights and, at least arguably, to new norms of customary international law. Examples of UN declarations or other normative statements are those involving minorities, self-determination, and criminal justice, as well as other declarations and resolutions that are referenced elsewhere in this volume or included in the Document Supplement. For a comprehensive compilation of UN instruments, including non-binding declarations, as of 2002, see United Nations, Human Rights: A Compilation of International Instruments, UN Doc. ST/HR/1/Rev.6, UN Sales No. E.02.XIV.4 (2002).

Regional intergovernmental organizations also have adopted resolutions proclaiming or promoting compliance with human rights standards. States participating in the inaugural session of the 1975 Conference (now Organization) on Security and Cooperation in Europe (CSCE) in Helsinki in 1975, for example, adopted a Final Act setting forth a program of cooperation in multiple spheres and declaring adherence to principles of human rights and, in particular, the Universal Declaration of Human Rights. See Helsinki Final Act, adopted Aug. 1, 1975, reprinted in 14 Int'l Legal Mat. 1292. At a subsequent session, in Copenhagen in 1990, the CSCE adopted a final document that set forth a wide and detailed range of human rights principles to which the participating states expressed commitment. See Final Document of the Copenhagen Meeting of the Conference on the Human Dimension of the CSCE, adopted June 29, 1990, reprinted in 29 Int'l Legal Mat. 1305. While it was explicitly understood by the participating states that texts such as the 1975 Helsinki and 1990 Copenhagen documents were not legally binding, the political impact of their having been adopted by all states by consensus has been considerable.

The Organization of American States (OAS) has been the source of numerous human rights declarations, in addition to promulgating treaties for ratification by the state members of that organization. In a development parallel to the UN's adoption in 1948 of the Universal Declaration of Human Rights, the OAS unanimously passed a resolution earlier that year proclaiming the American Declaration of the Rights and Duties of Man, the first of several human rights declarations to be adopted by OAS member states through the organization's General Assembly. The American Declaration (Documentary Supplement, page 183) in many ways mirrors the catalogue of civil, political, social, economic, and cultural rights subsequently included in the Universal Declaration of Human Rights. In what many describe as an attempt by its drafters to incorporate values of individual responsibility — in addition to values of individual autonomy — deemed common to many Western Hemispheric, especially Latin American, countries, the American Declaration also includes a recitation of various "duties" owed by the individual. These include duties of self-development and productive engagement, to minor children, and to certain minimum obligations of citizenship such as paying taxes and participating in elections.

During the deliberations leading to the adoption of the American Declaration, it was uniformly considered that the Declaration would not impose binding legal obligations on states. See Lawrence LeBlanc, *The OAS and the Promotion and Protection of Human Rights* 13 (1977). However, since its adoption the

American Declaration has functioned as a benchmark for action by the OAS in the area of human rights, particularly in regard to the work of its specialized institutions that are charged with promoting human rights throughout the hemisphere, as discussed below and in Chapter 9. Furthermore, to the extent the American Declaration incorporates many of the same rights expressed in the Universal Declaration of Human Rights that may be considered customary international law, it too may be understood to incorporate or reflect customary international law. According to the Inter-American Court of Human Rights, "by means of an authoritative interpretation, the member states of the Organization have signaled their agreement that the Declaration contains and defines the fundamental human rights referred to in the [OAS] Charter.... For the member states of the Organization, the Declaration is the text that defines the human rights referred to in the Charter." *Interpretation of the American Declaration of the Rights and Duties of Man Within the Framework of Article 64 of the American Convention on Human Rights*, OC–10/89 Inter-Am. Ct. H.R. (Ser. A) No. 10, paras. 43, 45 (1989). An edited version of this Advisory Opinion appears and is discussed in Chapter 9, page 724.

Comments and Questions

1. As the readings indicate, the Universal Declaration of Human Rights is seen as at least partly embodying or reflecting customary international law. The Declaration is alternatively held, as asserted by the Canadian Department of External Affairs, to constitute an authoritative interpretation of the UN Charter's human rights clauses. The Declaration may also be regarded as articulating what are now considered to be general principles of law. What are the differences among these formulations? Do those differences have any practical consequences? See the discussion in Chapter 6 regarding the treatment of treaty and customary international law in U.S. courts.

2. The UN Commission on Human Rights, which consisted of 53 UN member states before it was replaced by a Human Rights Council, and other UN institutions have utilized the norms of the Universal Declaration of Human Rights as a matter of routine in evaluating the many country situations that have come before them. (See Chapter 7 for a discussion of the various UN human rights institutions and procedures.) These bodies typically have applied the Declaration without questioning or establishing its legal character, just as the U.S. Department of State does in its country reports on human rights practices. See, e.g., U.S. Department of State, Country Reports on Human Rights Practices for 1998, Vol. I, at xii (1999) (in two volumes) (highlighting the significance of the Declaration upon its 50th anniversary and reviewing practices in 194 countries in connection with "internationally recognized individual, civil, political, and workers rights, as set forth in the Universal Declaration of Human Rights"). Does this prove that the Universal Declaration is customary international law or some other species of law? Or does it indicate that discussions about the legal character of the Universal Declaration are no longer very relevant, at least in some settings and to the extent that the Declaration does in fact express standards that are rooted in a strong consensus?

3. While the technical legal status of the Universal Declaration may be less significant today, lawyers still need to bear in mind the distinction between

political and legal obligations. That distinction may be unimportant in a political forum, such as the UN Human Rights Council, but it remains vital if one is addressing a domestic or international judicial body. See Chapter 6, infra. The role that "soft law" declarations may play even in judicial or quasi-judicial settings is considered in the next section.

III. The Emergence of New Human Rights Norms: The Rights of Indigenous Peoples and Maya Land Claims in Southern Belize

A. *The Developing Rights of Indigenous Peoples*

Prominent among recent initiatives to develop new human rights declarations are the efforts to conclude UN and OAS declarations that will specifically articulate the rights of indigenous peoples. These efforts have been ongoing since the 1980s, prompted by a worldwide movement of indigenous communities and supportive nongovernmental organizations. A working group of the UN Sub-Commission on the Promotion and Protection of Human Rights developed a draft Declaration on the Rights of Indigenous Peoples, and in 1994 the Sub-Commission approved the draft and submitted it to its parent body, the Commission on Human Rights for further consideration. See Sub-Comm. Res. 1994/45 (Aug. 26, 1994). Parallel proceedings within the Organization of American States have centered on a proposed American Declaration on the Rights of Indigenous Peoples, prepared by the Inter-American Commission on Human Rights and submitted for consideration by the competent OAS organs in 1997. See Annual Report of the Inter-American Commission on Human Rights 1996, O.A.S. Doc. OEA/Ser.L/V/II.95, Doc. 7 rev., ch. IV (1996). These initiatives are part of the international human rights system's response to the demands of communities that historically have fallen victim to patterns and legacies of European empire building and colonial settlement, or to similar invasions, and that now seek to maintain and transmit to future generations their distinctive cultural attributes and associational bonds.

The history of Indians in the Western Hemisphere, aboriginal peoples in Australia and New Zealand, and tribal peoples in Asia and Africa has been one of conflict, conquest, marginalization, and even genocide. In many countries indigenous peoples have been simply treated as impediments to territorial expansion; in others they have been accorded special status, often in order to deny them full participation in the surrounding society.

The status of Indian nations and people was the subject of early discourses by Francisco de Victoria and others considered among the "founders" of international law, as discussed in Chapter 1. France, England, Canada, the United States, and other states entered into treaties with Indian governments. Nonetheless, the conquering Europeans ultimately refused to recognize that indigenous societies were among the "civilized nations" that participated in the formulation of and enjoyed the benefits of international law. See S. James Anaya, *Indigenous Peoples in International Law* 19-34 (2d ed. 2004); see generally Robert Williams, Jr., *The American Indian in Western Legal Thought* (1990).

In the United States, Chief Justice Marshall's acceptance of the doctrine of discovery in *Johnson v. McIntosh*, 21 U.S. (8 Wheat.) 543 (1823), and his later characterization of Indian tribes as "domestic dependent nations" in *Cherokee Nation v. Georgia*, 30 U.S. (5 Pet.) 1 (1831), confirmed that Indian governments were subject to the jurisdiction of the United States. Only a year later, however, Marshall refined his characterization and described Indian tribes as "distinct people, divided into separate nations, independent of each other, and of the rest of the world, having institutions of their own, and governing themselves by their own laws." *Worcester v. Georgia*, 21 U.S. (6 Pet.) 515, 542-543 (183Z). See Russell Barsh and John Henderson, *The Road* 50-61 (1980).

As one author has noted, "Indian law is a complex field, and generalizations are subject to exceptions and can be misleading." Dean Suagee, *Self-Determination for Indigenous Peoples at the Dawn of the Solar Age*, 25 Mich. J. L. Reform 671, 698 (1992). This is not the place to summarize the convoluted history of relations between the U.S. federal government and tribal governments, which generally led to the assertion of ever greater authority by the former over the latter until a change of policy in the 1970s. Congress has asserted "plenary power" to legislate for Indian tribes, but, while affirming that power, the federal courts have held that tribes retain residual governmental powers as an aspect of their original or inherent sovereignty. "Within their reservations, tribes generally retain all powers other than those they gave up in treaties, had taken away by an express act of Congress, or had taken away by implicit divestiture as a result of their dependent status." Id. at 699.

At whatever stage of Indian-federal relations one chooses, however, it is abundantly clear that claims to resources, territory, and governmental powers have remained central to the concerns of Indians and indigenous peoples elsewhere. The inherent conflict of authority — often debated in terms of sovereignty — between national and indigenous governments led the former to claim that relations with indigenous tribes were purely a matter of domestic jurisdiction. As a result, despite the existence of treaties between some indigenous nations and European settler states, indigenous rights came to be regarded as outside the domain of international concern until well into the last century. The International Labor Organization (ILO) had been concerned with the status and condition of indigenous workers since the 1920s, but no multilateral treaty addressed the issue of indigenous rights per se until the adoption in 1957 of ILO Convention No. 107 Concerning the Protection and Integration of Indigenous and Other Tribal and Semi-Tribal Populations in Independent Countries. For background on the ILO's involvement in indigenous issues, see Luis Rodriguez-Piñero, *Indigenous Peoples, Post Colonialism, and International Law: The ILO Regime (1919-1989)* (2005).

The assimilationist orientation of this treaty was eventually challenged and ultimately rejected by the ILO in 1989, when Convention No. 107 was revised by Convention No. 169 Concerning Indigenous and Tribal Peoples in Independent Countries, which entered into force in 1991 (Documentary Supplement, pages 168-169). Convention No. 169 requires, inter alia, that indigenous peoples be consulted whenever laws or administrative regulations affecting them are considered, and that "special measures" be adopted to safeguard indigenous interests. Article 14 of the Convention recognizes "[t]he rights of ownership and possession of the peoples concerned over the lands which they traditionally occupy," and Article 8 declares that indigenous peoples "shall have the right to retain their own customs and institutions, where these are not incompatible with fundamental rights defined by the national legal system and with internationally recognized human rights." The basic theme of the Convention is indicated by the Convention's preamble, which recognizes "the aspirations of [indigenous] peoples to exercise control over their own institutions, ways of life and economic development and to maintain and develop their identities, languages and religions, within the framework of the States in which they live."

Note also should be taken of the shift in terminology from indigenous "populations" to "peoples," the latter being understood to reflect an affirmation of indigenous group identity and collective rights. However, responding to state fears of indigenous self-determination claims, Article 1(3) superfluously provides that "use of the term 'peoples' in this Convention shall not be construed as having any implications as regards the rights which may attach to the term under international law."

Although no specific mechanism to oversee compliance is created by Convention No. 169, states are obliged to report on their implementation of its provisions through the ILO's regular and comprehensive supervisory machinery. See Anaya, *Indigenous Peoples in International Law*, supra 164, at 226-227, 249-252; see generally Lee Swepston, "Human Rights Complaint Procedures of the International Labor Organization,"in *Guide to International Human Rights Practice* (Hurst Hannum ed., 4th ed. 2004).

A much more ambitious attempt to define internationally recognized rights for indigenous peoples has been the initiative to draft a UN declaration on indigenous rights, which began with the creation in 1982 of a Working Group on Indigenous Populations of the UN Sub-Commission on the Prevention of Discrimination and the Protection of Minorities (later the Sub-Commission on the Promotion and Protection of Human Rights). In 1994, a draft declaration was forwarded to the Commission on Human Rights, which in turn established its own working group to study the draft declaration. (The draft text is in the Documentary Supplement, companion CD.) Many governments and representives of indigenous peoples continue to disagree over provisions in the draft concerning, inter alia, self-determination, the extent of indigenous self-government, and indigenous control over land, resources, and development activities. See Report of the working group established in accordance with Commission on Human Rights resolution 1995/32 of 3 March 1995 on its tenth session, UN Doc. E/CN.4/2005/04 (2005). Similar disagreements have persisted with regard to the proposed OAS declaration on indigenous rights, a draft of which was formulated by the Inter-American Commission of Human Rights and which has been under discussion within a special working group of the OAS Committee on Juridical and Political Affairs. See Report of the Chair on the activities of the working group to prepare a draft declaration on the rights of indigenous peoples during the 2004-2005 term, OAS Doc. OEA/Ser.K/XVI, GT/DADIN/doc.224/05 (2005).

In the discussions aimed at the adoption of UN and OAS declarations on the rights of indigenous peoples, advocates and nongovernmental organizations have pressed for language more far reaching than that contained in ILO Convention No. 169 and beyond what most states involved in the discussions have thus far been willing to accept. Nonetheless, these same discussions reflect a certain common ground on the rights of indigenous peoples among states, indigenous peoples themselves, and other actors, a consensus generally in line with Convention No. 169, despite ongoing controversy about the outer limits of those rights. See Report of the working group of the Commission on Human Rights, supra (identifying the multiple points of convergence among the participants in the drafting of the declaration); Anaya, supra, at 63-66 (analyzing the UN discussions around the declaration).

This minimum consensus on indigenous rights is further evidenced in numerous parallel developments, in particular the inclusion of provisions on indigenous peoples in instruments other than Convention No. 169. For example, the Convention on the Rights of the Child affirms in Article 30 that an indigenous child "shall not be denied the right, in community with other members of his or her group, to enjoy his or her own culture, to profess and practice his or her own religion, or to use his or her own language." Resolutions adopted at the 1992 United Nations Conference on Environment and Development include provisions on indigenous people and their communities. The Rio Declaration, and the more detailed environmental program and policy statement known as Agenda 21, reiterate precepts of indigenous peoples' rights and seek to incorporate them within the larger agenda of global environmentalism and sustainable development. Resolutions adopted at subsequent major UN conferences — the 1993 World Conference on Human Rights, the 1994 UN Conference on Population and Development, the 1995 World Summit on Social Development, the Fourth World Conference on Women in 1995, and the 2001 World Conference Against Racism — similarly include provisions that affirm or are consistent with prevailing normative assumptions in this regard. Also noteworthy is the World Bank's recently adopted operational policy to guide its activities in financing development projects in less-developed countries where many of the world's indigenous peoples live. Although its terms fall short of those advocated by indigenous groups, the Bank's operational policy recognizes the "customary rights" of indigenous peoples over lands and resources and affirms the principle of their "free, prior, and informed consultation" in relation to bank-funded projects affecting them. The World Bank Operational Manual: Operational Policies, O.P. 4.10 (July 2005).

These and other developments signify that indigenous peoples are undoubtedly now a matter of international human rights concern and that there already exists a certain core of recognized indigenous rights, however inadequate that recognition may still be absent final approval of the UN and OAS declarations. See generally Patrick Thornberry, *Indigenous Peoples and Human Rights* (2002); *Human Rights of Indigenous Peoples* (Cynthia Cohen ed., 1998); Siegfried Wiessner, *Rights and Status of Indigenous Peoples: A Global Comparative and International Legal Analysis*, 12 Harv. Hum. Rts. L.J. 57 (1999).

B. *The Adjudication of Maya Land Claims by the Inter-American Commission on Human Rights*

Representative of the kinds of claims asserted by indigenous peoples worldwide is the concerted effort by Maya communities of southern Belize to assert rights to their traditional lands in the face of government-permitted logging and

issue

oil development on those lands. The Maya communitites took their case to the Inter-American Commission on Human Rights, whose competence is addressed in detail in Chapter 9, before which they asserted collective land and natural resource rights in terms similar to those set forth in the draft UN and OAS declarations and in ILO Convention No. 169. At the time that the Maya communities presented their petition to the Inter-American Commission and the Commission issued its findings and report, Belize was not a party to ILO Convention No. 169, and the UN and OAS instruments on indigenous rights remained in draft form. The petition ultimately rested on an expansive interpretation of the American Declaration of the Rights and Duties of Man, which is not a treaty and which nowhere specifically mentions indigenous peoples.

S. James Anaya, The Maya Petition to the Inter-American Commission on Human Rights: Indigenous Land and Resource Rights, and the Conflict over Logging and Oil in Southern Belize

In Giving Meaning to Economic, Social, and Cultural Rights 180-185 (Isfahan Merali and Valerie Oosterveld eds., 2001).

In many parts of the world, lands that are rich in natural resources continue to be inhabited by peoples whose origins in the lands predate those of the states that engulf them. In such areas, efforts on the part of states and transnational corporations to develop the natural resources frequently come into conflict with the indigenous inhabitants and their claims to the lands and resources in question. This genre of conflict has implications not just for the physical wellbeing of indigenous people who subsist from fragile ecosystems, but also for the integrity of their cultural and social patterns, which are often dependent on land resources, and for their own economic development potential. Given the frequency and magnitude of conflicts over lands claimed by indigenous peoples, such conflicts increasingly are a matter of concern for policy and decision makers at the international level. The international system for the protection of human rights, in particular, is being tested in its capacity to address indigenous peoples' concerns over lands and natural resources in the face of development efforts by outsiders. The international human rights regime is being pressed to move beyond its traditional concern for the autonomy of the individual and to address claims that are being made by entire groups and that extend into the economic and cultural domains.

A case in point concerns that of the Maya people of southern Belize. In the last several years, the government of Belize, through its Ministry of Natural Resources, has granted at least seventeen concessions for logging on lands totaling approximately 480,000 acres in the Toledo District, the country's most southern political subdivision. The two largest of these concessions, which together cover some 185,000 acres of previously pristine tropical forest, were granted to two, apparently related Malaysian companies that operate in Belize as Atlantic Industries Ltd. and Toledo Atlantic International Ltd. Added to the logging interests is a concession for oil exploration which the Belize Ministry of Energy, Science, Technology and Transportation granted several years ago to AB Energy, Inc., a company based in the United States. The oil exploration concession, which will automatically convert to a concession for oil extraction if commercially viable quantities of petroleum are found, is for 749,222 acres of the lowland portion of the Toledo District.

The rural parts of the Toledo District that are affected by the logging and oil concessions are inhabited primarily by Maya people, descendants of the Maya civilization that flourished throughout substantial parts of Mexico and Central America hundreds of years prior to European colonization in the Western Hemisphere. The Maya live in some thirty-seven villages throughout the Toledo District, and number over 10,000. Through a campaign of several years, Maya leaders and organizations protested to government officials against the concessions and the failure of Belizean law and public administration to adequately recognize and protect Maya rights in lands and natural resources. In late 1997, Maya organizations filed a lawsuit in the Supreme Court of Belize to have the logging concessions enjoined and declared in violation of Maya rights. Government officials never responded with anything more than statements of general and unfulfilled commitments to address Maya concerns, and the lawsuit stalled with no action on the part of the courts.

After having failed in their efforts before Belize authorities at the domestic level, the Maya petitioned the Inter-American Commission on Human Rights, an agency of the Organization of American States. The petition was filed by the Toledo Maya Cultural Council (TMCC) on behalf of the Maya villages of the Toledo District and their members. The TMCC is a Maya non-governmental organization that was formed to advocate for the varied interests of the Maya people in Toledo. It is governed by an executive committee that is elected by delegates of the Maya villages and is comprised of both Mopan and Ke'kchi speaking Maya individuals. In filing the petition the TMCC is assisted by attorneys from the Indian Law Resource Center, a United States-based advocacy organization dedicated to promoting the rights of indigenous peoples.

On the basis of arguments constructed from relevant international human rights instruments, the TMCC petition to the Inter-American Commission on Human Rights asserts that the Maya people have rights to the land and natural resources within much of the area affected by the logging and oil concessions, and that those rights have been violated by the government's actions and inaction. The petition seeks to have the Commission call upon the government of Belize to suspend or cancel the logging and oil concessions until suitable agreements can be negotiated with the Maya people. It also urges the Commission to call for reforms in the legal and regulatory system of Belize in order to provide state recognition and effective protection for Maya rights over lands and resources. The Maya petition to the Inter-American Commission represents the first time Belize finds itself accused of specific violations of human rights before an international human rights body. . . .

The Threat of Environmental Degradation in Southern Belize

Belize is a relatively young country with a diverse population. It gained its independence from Great Britain in 1981 and adopted a constitution that includes principles of democracy and human rights as foundational precepts. It has a small, predominantly English-speaking population of about 200,000, of which somewhat more than 10,000 are Maya. The non-Maya population is comprised of a variety of groups marked by diverse ethnic characteristics that reflect complex immigration and settlement patterns dating back to at least the early period of British rule in the nineteenth century. Although it has become a retirement destination for an increasing number of North Americans and Europeans, Belize shares many of the economic and social difficulties of its Central American and Caribbean neighbors. Unlike many other less developed countries, however, Belize has a well structured system of conservation programs that has earned it a reputation as an environmentally friendly place where natural wonders abound. Tourists from around the world are attracted to Belize's barrier reef — the second largest in the world and one of the healthiest coral habitats anywhere — and to inland resorts that provide access to lush tropical forests and animal sanctuaries.

Most of the environmentally protected areas that draw substantial earnings from tourism, however, are in the northern part of the country, well insulated by distance from the roar of bulldozers and the whir of chainsaws that are felling trees, or from the tremor of seismic blasts and drilling that search for oil, in the southern Toledo District. Environmentalists and forestry experts have identified the logging in Toledo as a major threat to the ecology of the area, which includes a broad diversity of plant and wildlife species. Particular concern has been raised about siltation of the streams that feed into lagoons and sea waters surrounding the delicate reef at its southern extension. The problem, according to close observers of the situation, is not that forestry is inherently bad, but that the government of Belize is unwilling or unable to enforce elementary principles of sustainable forestry that would minimize environmental impacts and avert substantial long-term or permanent damage. The environmental harm that might result from oil development is itself staggering. Oil exploration under the concession to AB Energy is still in its early stage and has not yet had a major impact on the environment. But if oil development proceeds to the production stage, the ensuing consequences may be devastating for the natural environment and the people who live within it. In other less developed countries in which the oil industry has operated, toxins have been released in the process of oil extraction which have caused severe illness and death among human inhabitants; such pollutants, furthermore, have caused degradation in wildlife and plant species. Widespread social ills also have been associated with the penetration of the oil industry and its work force into the habitats of previously insular communities. . . .

While the environmental threat presented by the logging and oil concessions has raised concerns among urban elites in Belize and elsewhere, the Maya people of the Toledo District are the ones most affected by the concessions. The Maya of Toledo live in some thirty-seven villages throughout the District, all of which are either within, or in close proximity to, the lands over which logging and oil development concessions have been granted. Lands around the villages that are used by the Maya for agricultural and other subsistence purposes, including hunting and fishing, are included in the concession areas. From the standpoint of the Maya people who live in the affected areas, the actual and potential further environmental degradation constitutes a threat to their physical wellbeing and subsistence, which are dependent on the territorial space in which the Maya and their ancestors traditionally have lived.

The Assertion of Maya Interests in Lands and Natural Resources

But the issue at hand for the Maya is not just one of concern over the natural environment; it is also, and perhaps more fundamentally, one of ownership and control over the lands and resources at stake. The logging and oil development concessions represent a model of development that succumbs to the profit-motivated interests of forces from outside the target locality that are eager to see the remaining natural resources of less developed countries converted into financial bounty. This model can be witnessed throughout parts of the developing world, particularly in areas inhabited by indigenous peoples, where much of the world's remaining commercially viable stands of tropical timber exist. Governments claim for themselves the prerogative of disposing of natural resources, and they exercise this claimed prerogative in favor of commercial enterprises with, at best, secondary consideration of the legitimate interests of the people who may be affected by the resource development projects. In their petition to the Inter-American Commission on Human Rights, the Maya are directly challenging this model by asserting property rights over lands and forest resources that the government of Belize has encumbered and by attempting to alter the government's course of conduct to accommodate those rights.

The Maya petition asserts land and resource rights on the basis of historical occupancy and ongoing customary land tenure. Early in this century, the British colonial administration established "reservations" for the benefit of several of the Maya villages within lands considered to be "Crown lands." These reservations, now on presumed national lands, continue to exist and include roughly half the Maya villages. In any event, the customary land tenure patterns of even those villages that were granted reservations extend well beyond the reservation boundaries. The petition to the Inter-American Commission asserts rights over the aggregate territory of their customary land tenure independently of any government grant or specific act of recognition.

The Inter-American Commission on Human Rights and Its Capacity to Address Indigenous Peoples' Claims to Lands and Natural Resources

In filing its petition on behalf of Maya villages, the TMCC is testing the capacity of the international system for the protection of human rights, in particular at the regional level, to function as a vehicle for the effective implementation of existing and emergent norms relevant to indigenous peoples. The Inter-American Commission on Human Rights is empowered to promote the observance of human rights among the members of the Organization of American States, and to act on complaints or petitions that allege particular violations of human rights [see Chapter 9]. The TMCC petition represents one of the first cases brought to the Commission in which the central issue is that of control over lands inhabited by indigenous people.

The primary terms of reference for the Inter-American Commission are the American Convention on Human Rights in relation to states that are parties to that convention, and the American Declaration of the Rights and Duties of Man in relation to states — like Belize — that are OAS members but not parties to the American Convention. Neither of these instruments specifically mentions indigenous peoples, indigenous land and resource rights, or rights related to the natural environment. However, the TMCC petition constructs arguments for such rights on the basis of the rights to life, property, and equality under the law, and other human rights affirmed in the American Declaration of the Rights and Duties of Man. The petition builds these arguments in part by linking these generally applicable human rights to developments that have occurred over the last several years at the international level regarding indigenous peoples [including the draft UN and OAS declarations on indigenous rights and ILO Convention No. 169]. International inter-governmental institutions and their relevant agencies, including the Inter-American Commission itself, increasingly have supported rights of indigenous people in relation to ancestral lands and the natural environment. Issues of indigenous lands and environmental concern are now generally viewed, in the international arena, as matters of human rights....

The Maya appear to be aware that the logging and oil development controversy, as well as the larger issue of their land rights, are complex matters that are best worked out through negotiated solutions that seek to accommodate the legitimate interests of all concerned. But, typically of indigenous peoples, they are relatively powerless in the domestic political sphere to move the government toward a framework of negotiation based on recognition and understanding of the Maya people and their relationship with ancestral lands and resources. The Maya are now attempting to use the sphere of international human rights law and invoke scrutiny by an international human rights body to shift the balance of power and terms of debate in their favor. Indigenous peoples throughout the world are confronted by similar problems of state-sponsored industrial encroachment onto their ancestral lands, and many likewise are framing and asserting their interests in terms of international legal entitlement....

Note: The Awas Tingni and Dann Cases

As the Maya petition was being considered by the Inter-American Commission on Human Rights, other indigenous claims were being processed by the Commission and its related institution, the Inter-American Court of Human Rights. In 1998, the Commission issued a confidential report finding Nicaragua in violation of the human rights of the indigenous Mayagna Community of Awas Tingni, because it failed to recognize the traditional land tenure of the community and instead authorized a major logging concession without the community's consent, a scenario similar to that of the Maya communities of Belize. See *Mayagna (Sumo) Awas Tingni Community v. Nicaragua*, Inter-Am Ct. H.R. (ser. C) No. 79, paras. 25-26 (Judgment on merits and reparations of August 31, 2001)(summarizing the report). A major difference between the situations is that, unlike Belize, Nicaragua through its constitution and domestic legislation did recognize in general terms the communal property of indigenous communities. When Nicaragua, a party to the American Convention on Human Rights, did not respond to the Commission's report to the latter's satisfaction, the Commission initiated the procedure available under the Convention and submitted the case to the Inter-American Court. (See Chapter 9 for a description of this procedure.) After a lengthy proceeding, the Court issued a judgment in favor of Awas Tingni largely in agreement with the Commission's position. The Court held that the general right to property articulated in article 21 of the American Convention on Human Rights extends to the protection of traditional indigenous land tenure, even when that land tenure is not authorized by a deed of title or otherwise specifically recognized by the state. In interpreting article 21, the Court stated:

> 143. Article 21 of the American Convention recognizes the right to private property. In this regard, it establishes: a) that "[e]veryone has the right to the use and enjoyment of his property;" b) that such use and enjoyment can be subordinate, according to a legal mandate, to "social interest;" c) that a person may be deprived of his or her property for reasons of "public utility or social interest, and in the cases and according to the forms established by law;" and d) that when so deprived, a just compensation must be paid.
>
> 144. "Property" can be defined as those material things which can be possessed, as well as any right which may be part of a person's patrimony; that concept includes all movables and immovables, corporeal and incorporeal elements and any other intangible object capable of having value. . . .
>
> 146. The terms of an international human rights treaty have an autonomous meaning, for which reason they cannot be made equivalent to the meaning given to them in domestic law. Furthermore, such human rights treaties are live instruments whose interpretation must adapt to the evolution of the times and, specifically, to current living conditions.
>
> 147. Article 29(b) of the Convention, in turn, establishes that no provision may be interpreted as "restricting the enjoyment or exercise of any right or freedom recognized by virtue of the laws of any State Party or by virtue of another convention to which one of the said states is a party."
>
> 148. Through an evolutionary interpretation of international instruments for the protection of human rights, taking into account applicable norms of interpretation and pursuant to article 29(b) of the Convention — which precludes a restrictive interpretation of rights — it is the opinion of this Court that article 21 of the Convention protects the right to property in a sense which includes, among others, the rights of members of the indigenous communities within the framework of communal property, which is also recognized by the Constitution of Nicaragua.
>
> 149. Given the characteristics of the instant case, some specifications are required on the concept of property in indigenous communities. Among indigenous peoples there is a communitarian tradition regarding a communal form of collective property of the land, in the sense that ownership of the land is not centered on an individual but rather on the group and its community. Indigenous groups, by the fact of their very existence, have the right to live freely in their own territory; the close ties of indigenous people with the land must be recognized and understood as the fundamental basis of their cultures, their spiritual life, their integrity, and their economic survival. For indigenous communities, relations to the land are not merely a matter of possession and production but a material and spiritual element which

> they must fully enjoy, even to preserve their cultural legacy and transmit it to future generations.

Id. (notes omitted).

The Court in Awas Tingni determined that indigenous peoples not only have property rights to their traditional lands but that they are also entitled under the Convention to affirmative state measures to secure those rights through land titling or other appropriate mechanism. The Court found that Nicaragua violated Article 21 by not taking such affirmative measures and by granting the logging concession. Id. at paras. 153-155. It further found that, because the Nicaraguan administrative and judicial systems failed to respond adequately to repeated petitions from Awas Tingni for land titling and to halt the concession, Nicaragua violated Article 25 of the Convention, which affirms the right to judicial protection, in connection with Articles 1 and 2, which obligate state parties to adopt measures necessary to secure the enjoyment of fundamental rights. See generally S. James Anaya and Claudio Grossman, *The Case of Awas Tingni v. Nicaragua: A New Step in the International Law of Indigenous Peoples*, 19 Ariz. J. Int'l & Comp. Law 1 (2002).

The "evolutionary interpretation" of the right to property in relation to indigenous lands was expanded in a subsequent decision which addressed a dispute concerning the Western Shoshone people of the Great Basin region of the United States. In the case of *Mary and Carrie Dann v. United States*, the Inter-American Commission extended the interpretation of the right to property of the American Convention on Human Rights advanced in the *Awas Tingni* case to the similar property rights provision of the American Declaration of the Rights and Duties of Man, emphasizing the due process and equal protections prescriptions that attach to indigenous property interests in lands and natural resources. See Report No. 75/02, Case 11.140 (*Mary and Carrie Dann v. United States*), Annual Report of the Inter-American Commission on Human Rights 2002, at 860, OEA/Ser.L/V/II.117 Doc. 5 rev. 1 (2003). The case arose from the refusal of Western Shoshone sisters Mary and Carrie Dann to submit to the permit system imposed by the United States for grazing on large parts of Western Shoshone traditional lands. Faced with efforts by the United States government to forcibly stop them from grazing cattle without a permit and to impose substantial fines on them for doing so, the Danns argued that the permit system contravened Western Shoshone land rights. The United States conceded that the land in question was Western Shoshone ancestral land but contended that Western Shoshone rights in the land had been "extinguished" through a series of administrative and judicial determinations.

The Commission rejected the United States theory of extinguishment as out of step with modern human rights concepts, in light of a lack of procedural fairness in the domestic proceedings upon which that theory relied. See generally John O'Connell, *Constructive Conquest in the Courts: A Legal History of the Western Shoshone Lands Struggle — 1864 to 1991*, 42 Nat. Resources J. 765 (2003). Instead, the Commission found that the United States had "failed to ensure the Danns' right to property under conditions of equality contrary to Articles II [right to equal protection], XVIII [right to fair trial] and XXIII [right to property] of the American Declaration in connection with their claims to property rights in the Western Shoshone ancestral lands." Report 75/02, supra, para. 172.

In applying and interpreting the American Declaration in the *Dann* case, the Commission was explicit in its reliance on developments and trends in the international legal system regarding the rights of indigenous peoples. Significantly the Commission referred to its own Proposed American Declaration on the Rights of Indigenous Peoples, a document it had prepared at the request of the OAS General Assembly. See Annual Report of the Inter-American Commission on Human Rights 1996, ch. IV, OEA/Ser.L/V/II.95, Doc. 7 rev. (1997) (providing the text and the background of the proposed declaration). The Commission affirmed that the "basic principles reflected in many of the provisions" of its proposed declaration, "including aspects of [its] article XVIII, reflect general international legal principles developing out of and applicable inside and outside of the inter-American system and to this extent are properly considered in interpreting and applying the provisions of the American Declaration in the context of indigenous peoples." Report 75/02, supra, para. 129. Article XVIII of the proposed declaration provides for the protection of traditional forms of land tenure in terms similar to those found ILO Convention 169, which the Commission also highlighted in its analysis, id., paras. 127-128. That article states, in part:

> 1. Indigenous peoples have the right to the legal recognition of their varied and specific forms and modalities of their control, ownership, use and enjoyment of territories and property.
>
> 2. Indigenous peoples have the right to the recognition of their property and ownership rights with respect to lands, territories and resources they have historically occupied, as well as to the use of those to which they have historically had access for their traditional activities and livelihood.

The Commission's invocation in the *Dann* case of the Proposed American Declaration on the Rights of Indigenous Peoples — a document still under discussion — along with other international developments led it to articulate the "general international legal principles" that are *now* applicable both within and outside of the Inter-American system in the following terms:

> — the right of indigenous peoples to legal recognition of their varied and specific forms and modalities of their control, ownership, use and enjoyment of territories and property;
>
> — the recognition of their property and ownership rights with respect to lands, territories and resources they have historically occupied; and
>
> — where property and user rights of indigenous peoples arise from rights existing prior to the creation of a state, recognition by that state of the permanent and inalienable title of indigenous peoples relative thereto and to have such title changed only by mutual consent between the state and respective indigenous peoples when they have full knowledge and appreciation of the nature or attributes of such property. This also implies the right to fair compensation in the event that such property and user rights are irrevocably lost.

Report 75/02, supra., para. 130.

With the *Awas Tingni* and *Dann* cases in hand, the Inter-American Commission proceeded to issue its report in the *Maya* case.

Inter-American Commission on Human Rights, Report 40/04, Case 12.053 (Maya Indigenous Communities of the Toledo District of Belize)

Annual Report of the Inter-American Commission on Human Rights 2004, O.A.S. Doc. OEA/Ser.L/V/II.122, Doc. 5 rev. 1 (2005) (footnotes omitted)

I. Summary

1. This report concerns a petition presented to the Inter-American Commission of Human Rights (the "Commission") against the State of Belize (the "State" or "Belize") on August 7, 1998 by the Indian Law Resource Center and the Toledo Maya Cultural Council (the "Petitioners"). The petition claims that the State is responsible for violating rights under the American Declaration of the Rights and Duties of Man (the "American Declaration") that the Mopan and Ke'kchi Maya People of the Toledo District of Southern Belize (the "Maya people of the Toledo District" or the "Maya people") are alleged to have over certain lands and natural resources.

2. The Petitioners claim that the State has violated . . . the American Declaration in respect of lands traditionally used and occupied by the Maya people, by granting logging and oil concessions in and otherwise failing to adequately protect those lands, failing to recognize and secure the territorial rights of the Maya people in those lands, and failing to afford the Maya people judicial protection of their rights and interests in the lands due to delays in court proceedings instituted by them. According to the Petitioners, the State's contraventions have impacted negatively on the natural environment upon which the Maya people depend for subsistence, have jeopardized the Maya people and their culture, and threaten to cause further damage in the future. . . .

45. The Petitioners contend that the State of Belize is responsible for violations of the following human rights of the Maya people under the American Declaration, in conjunction with assorted other international instruments . . . : Articles XXIII (right to property), III (right to religious freedom), VI (right to family and protection thereof), XIV (right to take part in the cultural life of the community), I (right to life), XI (right to preservation of health and well-being) and XX (right to participate in government) all in relation to the logging and oil concessions granted by the government on lands used and occupied by the Maya in the Toledo District; Articles II (right to equality under the law) and XXIII (right to property) and general principles of international law concerning the failure of Belize to recognize and secure Maya territorial rights more broadly; and Article XVIII (right to a fair trial) in respect of the ineffectiveness of efforts by the Maya people to obtain domestic redress for their situation. . . .

IV. Analysis

A. Application and Interpretation of the American Declaration of the Rights and Duties of Man

85. . . . [T]he American Declaration constitutes a source of international legal obligation for all member states of the Organization of American States, including

Belize. [To support this proposition, the Commission cited Advisory Opinion OC-10/89 of the Inter-American Court of Human Rights, which is quoted supra, p. 163.] Moreover, the Commission is empowered under Article 20 of its Statute and Articles 49 and 50 of its Rules of Procedure to receive and examine any petition that contains a denunciation of alleged violations of the human rights set forth in the American Declaration in relation to OAS member states that are not parties to the American Convention.

86. According to the jurisprudence of the inter-American human rights system, the provisions of its governing instruments, including the American Declaration, should be interpreted and applied in context of developments in the field of international human rights law since those instruments were first composed and with due regard to other relevant rules of international law applicable to member states against which complaints of human rights violations are properly lodged.

87. In particular, the organs of the inter-American system have previously held that developments in the corpus of international human rights law relevant to interpreting and applying the American Declaration may be drawn from the provisions of other prevailing international and regional human rights instruments....

88. Accordingly, in determining the present case, the Commission will, to the extent appropriate, interpret and apply the pertinent provisions of the American Declaration in light of current developments in the field of international human rights law, as evidenced by treaties, custom and other relevant sources of international law.

B. THE MAYA COMMUNITIES OF THE TOLEDO DISTRICT OF BELIZE AND INTERNATIONAL HUMAN RIGHTS PERTAINING TO INDIGENOUS PEOPLES

89. In determining the norms and principles of human rights law that are properly applicable in the present case, the Commission first observes that the Petitioners' claims relate to human rights violations that are alleged to have been committed against the members of an indigenous people located in the Toledo District of Belize.

90. According to the information available, the Toledo District is one of two administrative districts in Southern Belize, which together are home to approximately 14,000 Mopan and Ke'kchi-speaking Maya people. The Toledo District encompasses an area of approximately 1,500 square miles, bordered roughly by the Monkey River and the Maya Mountains in the north, the Gulf of Honduras in the East, and Belize's border with Guatemala to the West and South....

95. In this regard, a review of pertinent treaties, legislation and jurisprudence reveals the development over more than 80 years of particular human rights norms and principles applicable to the circumstances and treatment of indigenous peoples. Central to these norms and principles has been the recognition of the need for special measures by states to compensate for the exploitation and discrimination to which these societies have been subjected at the hands of the non-indigenous.

96. In the context of the inter-American human rights system, this Commission has long recognized and promoted respect for the rights of indigenous

peoples of this Hemisphere. In the Commission's 1972 resolution on the problem of "Special Protection for Indigenous Populations — Action to combat racism and racial discrimination," for example, the Commission proclaimed that "for historical reasons and because of moral and humanitarian principles, special protection for indigenous populations constitutes a sacred commitment of the states." This notion of special protection has also been considered in a number of country and individual reports adopted by the Commission and has been recognized and applied in the context of numerous rights and freedoms under both the American Declaration and the American Convention on Human Rights, including the right to life, the right to humane treatment, the right to judicial protection and to a fair trial, and the right to property. . . .

97. The Commission's approach in acknowledging and giving effect to particular protections in the context of human rights of indigenous populations is consistent with developments in the field of international human rights law more broadly. Special measures for securing indigenous human rights have been recognized and applied by other international and domestic bodies, including the Inter-American Court of Human Rights, the International Labour Organisation, the United Nations through its Human Rights Committee and Committee to Eradicate [sic] All Forms of Racial Discrimination, and the domestic legal systems of states.

98. In deciding upon the complaints in the present petition, therefore, the Commission will afford due consideration to the particular norms and principles of international human rights law governing the individual and collective interests of indigenous peoples, including consideration of any special measures that may be appropriate and necessary in giving proper effect to these rights and interests.

C. RIGHT TO PROPERTY

99. In their complaint, the Petitioners contend that the State's practice in granting numerous logging concessions and at least one oil concession on lands used and occupied by the Maya people in the Toledo District has violated the Maya people's right to property under Article XXIII of the American Declaration. The Petitioners also contend that this practice of granting concessions is a component of a more general failure of the State of Belize to recognize and effectively secure the territorial rights of the Maya people, also contrary to their right to property.

100. Article XXIII, of the American Declaration provides:

> Every person has a right to own such private property as meets the essential needs of decent living and helps to maintain the dignity of the individual and of the home. . . .

1. THE RIGHT TO PROPERTY AND INDIGENOUS PEOPLES UNDER CONTEMPORARY INTERNATIONAL HUMAN RIGHTS LAW

112. In evaluating the nature and content of the right to property under Article XXIII of the American Declaration in the context of the present case, several aspects of the evolution of international human rights protections pertaining to indigenous peoples are particularly pertinent.

113. Among the developments arising from the advancement of indigenous human rights has been recognition that rights and freedoms are frequently exercised and enjoyed by indigenous communities in a collective manner, in the sense that they can only be properly ensured through their guarantee to an indigenous community as a whole. The right to property has been recognized as one of the rights having such a collective aspect.

114. More particularly, the organs of the inter-American human rights system have acknowledged that indigenous peoples enjoy a particular relationship with the lands and resources traditionally occupied and used by them, by which those lands and resources are considered to be owned and enjoyed by the indigenous community as a whole and according to which the use and enjoyment of the land and its resources are integral components of the physical and cultural survival of the indigenous communities and the effective realization of their human rights more broadly. . . .

115. The Commission, through its reports on individual petitions and on the general situation of human rights in member states, as well as in its authorization of precautionary measures, has pronounced upon the necessity of states to take the measures aimed at restoring, protecting and preserving the rights of indigenous peoples to their ancestral territories. It has also held that respect for the collective rights of property and possession of indigenous people to the ancestral lands and territories constitutes an obligation of OAS member states, and that the failure to fulfill this obligation engages the international responsibility of the states. According to the Commission, the right to property under the American Declaration must be interpreted and applied in the context of indigenous communities with due consideration of principles relating to the protection of traditional forms of ownership and cultural survival and rights to land, territories and resources. These have been held to include the right of indigenous peoples to legal recognition of their varied and specific forms and modalities of their control, ownership, use and enjoyment of territories and property, and the recognition of their property and ownership rights with respect to lands, territories and resources they have historically occupied.

116. The Inter-American Court [in the *Awas Tingni* case] has taken a similar approach to the right to property in the context of indigenous peoples, by recognizing the communal form of indigenous land tenure as well as the distinctive relationship that indigenous people maintain with their land. . . .

117. Accordingly, the organs of the inter-American human rights system have recognized that the property rights protected by the system are not limited to those property interests that are already recognized by states or that are defined by domestic law, but rather that the right to property has an autonomous meaning in international human rights law. In this sense, the jurisprudence of the system has acknowledged that the property rights of indigenous peoples are not defined exclusively by entitlements within a state's formal legal regime, but also include that indigenous communal property that arises from and is grounded in indigenous custom and tradition. . . .

118. This interpretive approach is supported by the terms of other international instruments and deliberations, which serve as further indicia of international attitudes on the role of traditional system of land tenure in modern systems of human rights protection. The International Labour Organisation Convention (N° 169) concerning Indigenous and Tribal Peoples, for example, affirms

indigenous peoples' rights of ownership and possession of the lands they traditionally occupy, and requires governments to safeguard those rights and to provide adequate procedures to resolve land claims. Additionally, both the Proposed American Declaration on the Rights of Indigenous Peoples and the Draft United Nations Declaration on the Rights of Indigenous Peoples affirm the rights of indigenous people to own, develop, control and use the lands and resources they have traditionally owned or otherwise occupied and used.

119. In this connection, the Commission believes that respect for and protection of the private property of indigenous peoples on their territories is equivalent in importance to non-indigenous property, and, as discussed further below, is mandated by the fundamental principle of non-discrimination enshrined in Article II of the American Declaration. . . .

120. For the organs of the inter-American system, the protection of the right to property of the indigenous people to their ancestral territories is a matter of particular importance, because the effective protection of ancestral territories implies not only the protection of an economic unit but the protection of the human rights of a collective that bases its economic, social and cultural development upon their relationship with the land. It has been the Commission's longstanding view that the protection of the culture of indigenous peoples encompasses the preservation of "the aspects linked to productive organization, which includes, among other things, the issue of ancestral and communal lands." . . .

2. THE SITUATION OF THE MAYA PEOPLE OF THE TOLEDO DISTRICT

121. In the context of the norms and principles outlined above, it is necessary to determine whether the Maya people of the Toledo District are the beneficiaries of a right to property under Article XXIII of the Declaration in respect of lands in the southern region of Belize and, if so, the nature of the State's obligations concerning respect for and protection of this right.

a. The Right to Property and the Traditional Lands of the Maya People in the Toledo District

122. . . . [T]he Commission is satisfied, based upon the information available, that the members of the Mopan and Ke'kchi Maya communities of the Toledo District of Southern Belize constitute an indigenous people whose ancestors inhabited the Toledo District prior to the arrival of the Europeans and the colonial institutions that gave way to the present State of Belize. . . .

127. Based upon the arguments and evidence before it, the Commission is satisfied that the Mopan and Ke'kchi Maya people have demonstrated a communal property right to the lands that they currently inhabit in the Toledo District. These rights have arisen from the longstanding use and occupancy of the territory by the Maya people, which the parties have agreed pre-dated European colonization, and have extended to the use of the land and its resources for purposes relating to the physical and cultural survival of the Maya communities. . . .

131. The Commission also considers that this communal property right of the Maya people is the subject of protection under Article XXIII of the American Declaration, interpreted in accordance with the principles outlined above relating to the situation of indigenous peoples, including the obligation to take special measures to ensure recognition of the particular and collective interest that

indigenous people have in the occupation and use of their traditional lands and resources. In this connection, the Maya people's communal property right has an autonomous meaning and foundation under international law. While the Commission has considered the legislation and jurisprudence of certain domestic legal systems in identifying international legal developments relating to the status and treatment of indigenous people, the communal property right of the Maya people is not dependent upon particular interpretations of domestic judicial decisions concerning the possible existence of aboriginal rights under common law.

132. Accompanying the existence of the Maya people's communal right to property under Article XXIII of the Declaration is a correspondent obligation on the State to recognize and guarantee the enjoyment of this right. In this regard, the Commission shares the view of the Inter-American Court of Human Rights that this obligation necessarily requires the State to effectively delimit and demarcate the territory to which the Maya people's property right extends and to take the appropriate measures to protect the right of the Maya people in their territory, including official recognition of that right [citing the *Awas Tingni* case]. In the Commission's view, this necessarily includes engaging in effective and informed consultations with the Maya people concerning the boundaries of their territory, and that the traditional land use practices and customary land tenure system be taken into account in this process....

135. The Commission therefore concludes that the Mopan and Ke'kchi Maya people have demonstrated a communal property right to the lands that they currently inhabit in the Toledo District, that this communal property right of the Maya people is the subject of protection under Article XXIII of the American Declaration, and that the State has failed to delimit, demarcate and title or otherwise establish the legal mechanisms necessary to clarify and protect the territory on which their right exists. Accordingly, the Commission finds that the State of Belize violated the right to property enshrined in Article XXIII of the American Declaration to the detriment of the Maya people.

b. The Granting of Concessions in the Toledo District

136. The Petitioners have also argued that by granting concessions to companies to extract logging and oil resources from the traditional lands of the Maya people, without properly delimiting and demarcating those lands and without any effective consultation with or agreement by the affected communities, the State has similarly violated the right to property of the Maya people under Article XXIII of the American Declaration....

140. In evaluating this aspect of the Petitioners' complaint, the Commission considers that the right to use and enjoy property may be impeded when the State itself, or third parties acting with the acquiescence or tolerance of the State, affect the existence, value, use or enjoyment of that property without due consideration of and informed consultations with those having rights in the property....

142. The Commission ... observes in this connection that one of the central elements to the protection of indigenous property rights is the requirement that states undertake effective and fully informed consultations with indigenous communities regarding acts or decisions that may affect their traditional territories. As the Commission has previously noted, Articles XVIII and XXIII of the American Declaration specially oblige a member state to ensure that any determination of the extent to which indigenous claimants maintain interests in the lands to which

they have traditionally held title and have occupied and used is based upon a process of fully informed consent on the part of the indigenous community as a whole. This requires, at a minimum, that all of the members of the community are fully and accurately informed of the nature and consequences of the process and provided with an effective opportunity to participate individually or as collectives. In the Commission's view, these requirements are equally applicable to decisions by the State that will have an impact upon indigenous lands and their communities, such as the granting of concessions to exploit the natural resources of indigenous territories.

143. Based upon the record in the present case, the Commission finds that the State granted logging and oil concessions to third parties to utilize property and resources that could fall within the traditional lands of the Maya people of the Toledo District, and that the State failed to take appropriate or adequate measures to consult with the Maya people concerning these concessions. . . .

144. The Commission therefore concludes that logging and oil concessions were granted by the State to third parties to utilize property and resources that could fall within the traditional lands of the Maya people of the Toledo District and that the State failed to take appropriate or adequate measures to consult with the Maya people concerning these concessions. Based upon these acts and omissions, the Commission finds that the State of Belize further violated the right to property enshrined in Article XXIII of the American Declaration to the detriment of the Maya people. . . .

[The Commission went on to also find violations of Article II of the Declaration (equal protection under the law), on the ground that Belize failed to protect Maya customary land tenure under terms equal to the protections provided non-indigenous forms of property, and Article XVIII (right to judicial protection), because of the ineffectiveness of the judicial proceedings initiated by Maya parties to attempt to resolve the land and resource issues. The Commission recommended that Belize adopt legislative and administrative measures to identify and recognize Maya lands and related rights according to Maya customary tenure; that it abstain from any act that might result in its agents, or private parties acting with their permission or acquiescence, that would undermine the property interests of the Maya people; and that it repair the environmental damage caused by the logging concessions.]

Comments and Questions

1. In interpreting the right to property of the American Declaration of the Rights and Duties of Man, is the Inter-American Commission on Human Rights stating a rule of binding international law? If so, in what sense? Recall that the American Declaration is a resolution of the OAS General Assembly, not a treaty. But, like the Universal Declaration of Human Rights, the American Declaration could be deemed to reflect or incorporate customary international law. For their part, the Inter-American Commission and the Inter-American Court on Human Rights have consistently taken the view that the Declaration is an authoritative statement of the human rights that states commit to uphold under the general human rights clauses of the OAS Charter, which is a treaty. See Report Inter-Am. Comm. H.R., 75/02 (*Dann v. United States*), supra, at paras. 162-164; *Interpretation of the*

American Declaration of the Rights and Duties of Man Within the Framework of Article 64 of the American Convention on Human Rights, OC–10/89, Inter-Am. Ct. H.R. (Ser. A) No. 10, paras. 43, 45 (1989).

2. The Inter-American Commission in the *Maya Communities* and *Dann* cases interprets the right to property to extend to indigenous peoples' customary or traditional land tenure systems. Indigenous land tenure systems typically derive from patterns of land use and occupancy prior to the existence of the state and have their origins apart from the state's formal property regime. Is it plausible that states, when they adopted the property rights provision of Article XXIII of the American Declaration in 1948, had in mind protection of traditional indigenous land tenure? If not, on what basis does the Commission read such protection into Article XXIII?

2. In interpreting the American Declaration, the Commission refers to, among other sources, the Proposed American Declaration on the Rights of Indigenous Peoples. Is this use of a draft instrument appropriate, particularly when the Commission itself drafted the text on which it relies? In its response to the Commission's report in the *Dann* case, the United States disputed the Commission's references to the proposed declaration, arguing that, since the instrument is merely a draft of an eventually non-binding declaration, it does not represent general principles of international law and that the assertion of such principles could not be used to convert the American Declaration, which is not a treaty, into a source of legal obligation for the United States. See Report 75/02, supra, at 161-163.

3. In prosecuting the Awas Tingni case before the Inter-American Court of Human Rights, the Commission argued that indigenous peoples' rights to lands and natural resources are now part of customary international law, referring to numerous international developments as well to domestic laws and judicial decisions recognizing such rights. See Final Written Arguments of the Inter-American Commission on Human Rights in the Case of the Awas Tingni Mayagna (Sumo) Indigenous Community Against Nicaragua, Aug. 10, 2000, para. 64, reprinted in 19 Ariz. J. Int'l & Comp. L. 325 (2002). How is this argument different from the assertion that general principles of international law embrace these rights?

4. In assessing whether or not there are in indeed customary or general principles of international law upholding indigenous land rights, what is one to make of the fact that states continue to act contrary to those rights in many parts of the world? One answer is in the view, supported by the jurisprudence of the International Court of Justice, that state behavior that fails to conform to an existing or emerging customary norm does not undermine the norm unless that behavior is persistent and held out by the nonconforming state as acceptable. See Theodor Meron, *Human Rights and Humanitarian Norms in Customary International Law* 58-60 (1989).

IV. Norm Building in Related Areas

A. *Minorities*

Parallel to developments specifically concerning the rights of indigenous peoples is the formulation of "minority rights" in various written instruments.

Indigenous peoples typically are numerical minorities in the countries in which they live and are in non-dominant positions vis-à-vis the larger or majority populations. Yet they are distinct from other groups that share such characteristics and that are commonly identified as national, linguistic, or ethnic minorities. As illustrated by the *Maya Communities* case, indigenous peoples assert claims based on histories of prior occupancy and colonial encounter, unlike the experiences of other non-dominant or minority groups, and their claims go beyond the traditional concerns of minorities for protection of culture, language, and religion. It is thus understandable that indigenous peoples themselves have consistently rejected classification as minorities, both conceptually and politically. But it would be a mistake to overlook the fact that indigenous peoples do have many of the same concerns as groups generally identified as minorities and that the human rights claimed by groups in both categories to a significant extent draw from common core principles, such as non-discrimination and respect for diversity. For a discussion of the theoretical approaches to the status of indigenous peoples, as distinct from minority groups, see Kingsbury, *Reconciling Five Competing Conceptual Structures of Indigenous Peoples' Claims in International and Comparative Law*, in Peoples' Rights 69 (Philip Alston ed. 2001).

Hurst Hannum, The Rights of Persons Belonging to Minorities

In Human Rights: Concepts and Standards 277-94 passim (Janusz Symonides ed. 2000) (emphasis in original; footnotes omitted)

. . . Many vulnerable categories of people have been singled out for protection by the international community in the past 50 years, as more specific norms have been developed to complement the general norms found in the Universal Declaration of Human Rights. Among these categories are workers, refugees, women, prisoners, indigenous peoples, children, disabled persons and migrant workers; prohibitions against discrimination on the basis of race and religion have also been adopted. . . .

Historical Developments

The reluctance to consider minorities as worthy of particular attention is a phenomenon only of the second half of the twentieth century, which has recently begun to change. For example, most early empires considered at least religious minorities worthy of recognition. The "millet" system developed under the Ottoman Empire allowed religious communities a degree of personal and cultural autonomy, although it has been observed that the millets were "the solution devised by a government that did not know what nationality meant and, therefore, was unfamiliar with the majority-minority concept." The development of autonomous, religious-based communities was also consistent with Koranic injunctions of tolerance for other religions, and large non-Muslim communities continued to flourish throughout the Ottoman Empire.

In Europe, international protection of minorities can be traced to the Treaty of Westphalia in 1648, under the terms of which the parties agreed to respect the rights of certain religious minorities within their jurisdiction. However, given the historical congruence of religious and secular authority prior to this period, such agreements could just as easily be seen as recognizing the power of certain political groups rather than guaranteeing religious rights *per se*.

In the nineteenth century, the development of nationalism in Europe was based on the theory that political power was best exercised by groups that shared ethnic or linguistic ties. "Nations" sought to establish a separate political identity, whether by incorporating peoples spread over many countries (Germany, Italy) or by demanding greater political power for groups which had formerly been considered as minorities within existing empires (Greece, Hungary, Serbia, Poland, the Baltic States, and others).

The overriding concern in the nineteenth century with nationalism and the protection of cultural, linguistic and ethnic minorities led to a conscious and comprehensive attempt to protect minorities in the early twentieth century, with adoption of the so-called "minority treaties" at the end of World War I and their monitoring by the League of Nations....

Among the protections commonly included... were the right to equality of treatment and non-discrimination; the right to citizenship (although a minority group member could opt to retain another citizenship if desired); the right to use one's own language; the right of minorities to establish and control their own charitable, religious and social institutions; a State obligation to provide "equitable" financial support to minority schools (in which primary school instruction would be in the minority language) and other institutions; and recognition of the supremacy of laws protecting minority rights over other statutes.

A major advance of this period was the legitimization of international interest in protecting minority rights, evidenced by the supervisory role of the League of Nations in monitoring the treaties....

The existence of German-speaking minorities outside Germany had provided one excuse for Hitler's aggression in the 1930s, and there was thus little concern for the rights of "national minorities" on the part of the victorious Allies after World War II. The Charter of the United Nations does not specifically mention minority rights. Instead, emphasis was placed on the importance of respect for (individual) human rights "for all without distinction as to race, sex, language, or religion" and the principle of (collective) "self-determination of peoples."

The drafters of the UN Charter seemed to assume 1) that European and other minorities would be satisfied if their individual rights, particularly those of equality and non-discrimination, were respected; and 2) that the principle of self-determination would be adequate to resolve the larger problem of colonial territories. Despite the disastrous consequences for the individual victims of, e.g., the Greek-Turkish population "exchange" of 1920-22, migration became the preferred solution for post-1945 European minorities; it was largely the people (especially Germans) who moved, not the boundaries. Unfortunately, there is thus ample historical precedent for the solution of "ethnic cleansing" that re-emerged in the former Yugoslavia in the 1990s.

There were occasional exceptions to this general refusal to consider minority problems *per se*, although such ad hoc initiatives lacked the regular international supervision offered by the League of Nations. The German-speaking minority in the Italian South Tyrol, for example, was the subject of a 1946 agreement between Italy and Austria. The Austrian State Treaty, which re-established Austria within its pre-1938 borders, contains specific provisions for the protection of the Slovene and Croat minorities. The UN proposal for a Free Territory of Trieste and the UN-approved establishment of an autonomous Eritrea federated with Ethiopia were also designed to address minority situations, although each envisioned a greater degree of political autonomy than would traditionally have been reserved to a minority group. . . .

The 1948 Universal Declaration of Human Rights makes no specific mention of minority rights, and a separate part of the same resolution (ominously titled "fate of minorities") noted accurately, if somewhat disingenuously, that "it was difficult to adopt a uniform solution for this complex and delicate question [of minorities], which had special aspects in each State in which it arose." The UN Commission on Human Rights did establish a Sub-Commission on Prevention of Discrimination and Protection of Minorities, but early attempts by the Sub-Commission to address minority issues were essentially rebuffed by the Commission. . . .

Drafting of binding international agreements to implement the Universal Declaration began soon after the Declaration's adoption, and article 27 of the Covenant on Civil and Political Rights does specifically address the issue of minority rights. It provides, in full:

> In those States in which ethnic, religious or linguistic minorities exist, persons belonging to such minorities shall not be denied the right, in community with the other members of their group, to enjoy their own culture, to profess and practise their own religion, or to use their own language.

The Covenant addresses only minimal, traditional, minority rights, that is, cultural, religious and linguistic rights. The fact that rights are granted to "persons belonging to such minorities" rather than to minority groups themselves is an indication of the individualistic orientation of the Covenant on Civil and Political Rights, as well as its reluctance to recognize the rights of groups which had yet to be satisfactorily defined.

Often forgotten in discussions of minority rights is the International Convention on the Elimination of All Forms of Racial Discrimination, which entered into force in 1969 and has been ratified by approximately 150 States. "Racial discrimination" under the convention is defined in article 1 as any distinction "based on race, colour, descent, *or* national or ethnic origin" which impairs the exercise of human rights (emphasis added). Article 2 of the convention requires, *inter alia*, that parties take, in appropriate circumstances, "special and concrete measures to ensure the adequate development and protection of certain racial groups or individuals belonging to them, for the purpose of guaranteeing them the full and equal enjoyment of human rights and fundamental freedoms." An analogous provision is found in the UNESCO Declaration on Race and Racial Prejudice. . .

The Declaration on the Rights of Persons belonging to National or Ethnic, Religious or Linguistic Minorities was finally completed and adopted by the General Assembly in 1992. There is little doubt that progress on the Declaration was greatly aided by the end of East-West rivalry, although it is ironic that the Declaration was completed after the disintegration of its original sponsoring State, Yugoslavia. While it continues the individualistic orientation of article 27 of the

Covenant on Civil and Political Rights by referring to "the rights of persons" belonging to minorities, the Declaration does expand on existing provisions and contains progressive language related to minority participation in the political and economic life of the State. In addition, the Preamble recognizes that protecting minority rights will "contribute to the political and social stability of States in which they live" and, in turn, "contribute to the strengthening of friendship and co-operation among peoples and States." . . .

It was not until 1995 that the Commission on Human Rights created a mechanism to monitor observance of the Declaration, when it authorized the Sub-Commission to establish a five-member working group to "review the promotion and practical realization" of the Declaration, "examine possible solutions to problems involving minorities [and recommend] further measures, as appropriate, for the promotion and protection of the rights of persons belonging to national or ethnic, religious and linguistic minorities."

Other UN initiatives which have contributed to developing standards for the protection of minorities include the adoption of the 1981 Declaration on the Elimination of All Forms of Intolerance and Discrimination Based on Religion or Belief; appointment of special rapporteurs by the Commission on Human Rights and its Sub-Commission in the 1980s to consider specific aspects of religious intolerance and discrimination; and a 1993 report by the Sub-Commission on "the possible ways and means of facilitating the peaceful and constructive solution of problems involving minorities."

Just as Europe was the center of concern with minority rights from the mid-nineteenth century until World War II, it has been Europe which has devoted the most attention to the issue of minority rights since the end of the Cold War in the late 1980s. Perhaps spurred by renewed concerns over "ethnic" conflicts in both Eastern and Western Europe, European governments have attempted to set new standards for minority rights and have at least begun to devise new means of monitoring those standards.

The first indication that agreement on an expanded definition of minority rights was possible came in 1990, when a Final Document was adopted by consensus at the Copenhagen meeting of the Conference on the Human Dimension of the Conference on Security and Cooperation in Europe (CSCE). This remarkable document (which also contains detailed provisions relating to democracy, the rule of law and other human rights) was drafted and agreed to in only six weeks, and it represented the first detailed articulation of minority rights by governments since the post–First World War minorities treaties. It addressed, in particular, minority rights in the areas of language use, education and political participation, each of which is discussed further in the next section.

Two years later, the CSCE (known since 1995 as the Organization on Security and Cooperation in Europe (OSCE)) created the position of High Commissioner on National Minorities, in order to provide "early warning and, as appropriate, early action at the earliest possible stage in regard to tensions involving national minority issues that have the potential to develop into a conflict within the CSCE area, affecting peace, stability, or relations between participating States." Although the High Commissioner's mandate is to prevent conflict rather than protect minority rights *per se*, his interventions thus far appear to have contributed to both goals.

In recent years, it has almost appeared as though the Council of Europe was competing with the CSCE to see which organization could most quickly define rights to protect minorities and establish procedures to implement those rights. In 1992, the Council of Europe adopted and opened for ratification a Charter on the Protection of Minority and Regional Languages. Modelled on the European Social Charter, its provisions offer a wide range of guarantees from among which States may choose the level of obligations they are willing to accept. The following year, the Parliamentary Assembly recommended that a protocol on minority rights be added to the European Convention on Human Rights. A more ambitious Framework Convention on minorities was adopted in 1994. . . . [Both of these treaties entered into force in 1998.]

The Current Content of Minority Rights

Most recent instruments concerning minority rights have taken the form of "soft law," that is, declarations or resolutions which constitute solemn political commitments but which do not constitute binding legal obligations. However, as readily demonstrated by the political impact of the CSCE since 1975 and many other international human rights instruments, political commitments can sometimes be as influential as legally binding treaties. What is significant is that these documents, whether universal or regional, provide evidence that there is an emerging consensus over at least the minimum content of internationally recognized minority rights. This section outlines the substance of those rights.

Two preliminary questions must be addressed before the content of the current rights of minorities can be identified. The first issue is that of defining a "minority" or its members; the second is whether states' obligations with respect to minorities are limited to non-interference and non-discrimination, or whether states may be under a more demanding obligation to take affirmative measures to promote minority cultures. . . .

It should first be recognized that definitional questions are important only if they carry with them legal or political consequences. In the case of minorities, emerging international norms would obviously benefit groups which fall within their scope, while they would be unavailable to groups considered to be only political, regional or social groups. However, there are also some potentially negative consequences to being classified as a minority; for example, "minorities" do not enjoy any right to self-determination, while "peoples" do enjoy that right. . . .

[There is at least a] consensus that any definition of minority must include both objective factors (the existence of shared ethnicity, language, religion or similar cultural traits) and subjective factors (individuals must identify themselves as members of minority group). Whether or not a minority exists is a question of fact and does not depend on a formal determination by the State. . . .

The question of whether "minority rights" are essentially group rights or individual rights may be of theoretical interest, but the practical implications of the debate are more difficult to discern. For example, article 27 of the Covenant and all other intergovernmental instruments relating to minorities apply formally only to "persons belonging to" minorities, but article 1 of the Minorities Declaration does oblige States to protect "the existence and [. . .] identity of minorities within their respective territories," not just individual members of minorities.

The very concept of a "minority" implies a community or group, and the reference in international instruments to the rights of "persons" should be understood primarily as a jurisdictional rather than a substantive limitation. For example, if rights were accorded only to minority groups *qua* groups, difficult questions might arise as to who was entitled to represent the minority and what persons should be considered to be members of the minority. In general it is easier (and more supportive of the underlying rights) to adopt the individually oriented approach of the Covenant and other documents, under which any aggrieved member of a minority may complain about alleged violations of his or her rights....

The second preliminary issue that is relevant to all minority rights is the extent to which states are under a positive obligation to promote such rights, as opposed to a merely negative obligation not to interfere with or impede development of a minority's culture. Article 27 of the International Covenant on Civil and Political Rights is phrased in the negative, that is, minorities "shall not be denied" rights by the State. However, after noting that the rights set forth in article 27 "depend in turn on the ability of the minority group to maintain its culture, language or religion," the Human Rights Committee has stated that "positive measures by States may [...] be necessary to protect the identity of a minority."...

As the number of instruments on minority rights proliferates, it becomes easier to conclude that some state action to promote the rights of persons belonging to minorities may be required. Nonetheless, the scope of such positive obligations on states to promote minority culture remains unclear, and it is perhaps best analyzed by referring to specific provisions concerning, for example, language, access to the media and education....

Turning to the substantive content of specific rights, the most basic obligation on states is to *protect the existence and identity* of minorities and their members. In many instances, this may mean simply guaranteeing the most basic human rights — to life and physical integrity, freedom from arrest and torture, due process, property and freedom of expression. It also implies a prohibition against forced assimilation, a prohibition made explicit in several instruments....

The principles of *equality before the law and non-discrimination* are equally fundamental in all statements of minority rights, and they have by now acquired the status of customary international law binding on all states....

Linked to the principle of equality is the notion that members of minorities are to be equal to members of the majority in fact, as well as in law. This concept, borrowed from the decision of the Permanent Court of International Justice in the "Minority Schools in Albania" case, implies that minorities must enjoy not only formal legal equality, but that they have the right to effective equality of opportunity or result *vis-à-vis* the majority community. This may necessitate that special measures, sometimes known as "positive discrimination" or "affirmative action," be taken to ensure that the minority has the same rights in practice as the majority....

[The author goes on to discuss the rights to freedom of religion, to enjoy one's own culture, to maintain contact with other members of the group, to learn and use one's language, and to education.]

Perhaps the most controversial set of rights concerns the ability of minorities *to participate effectively in decisions* which affect them, a right which was not generally recognized in the treaties supervised by the League of Nations. The earliest formulation of this right was by the CSCE in 1990, when the participating CSCE States agreed to "respect the right of persons belonging to national minorities to effective participation in public affairs, including participation in the affairs relating to the protection and promotion of the identity of such minorities.' The Declaration adopted by the UN General Assembly two years later expands the right of participation to include "cultural, religious, social, economic and public life," although the right to participate in decision-making is limited to "a manner not incompatible with national legislation." Although the text is formulated rather weakly, Article 4(5) of the Minorities Declaration also provides that "states should consider appropriate measures so that persons belonging to minorities may participate fully in the economic progress and development in their country."

The CSCE Copenhagen Document "notes," as one way of achieving the aim of effective participation, the establishment of "appropriate local or autonomous administrations corresponding to the specific historical and territorial circumstances of such minorities and in accordance with the policies of the State concerned." The protocol recommended by the Parliamentary Assembly of the Council of Europe is even more specific, providing that "in regions where they are in a majority the persons belonging to a national minority shall have the right to have at their disposal appropriate local or autonomous authorities or to have a special status."...

Such provisions obviously reach far beyond the scope of "ordinary" human rights, insofar as they mandate that States adopt forms of government which make "effective participation" of minorities possible. Even though no particular constitutional or legislative structure is required, this is a much more delicate task than simply prohibiting torture or providing social security. Of course, "participation" does not necessarily mean "control," and the precise balance between minority and majority rights will need to be determined on a case-by-case basis. At the same time, however, a purely formal democracy in which members of minorities are consistently denied any share in power might well violate the emerging international norms of minority rights.

Concluding Observations

Members of minorities have suffered discrimination, land seizures, forced assimilation, deportation and even death at the hand of intolerant majorities and territorially ambitious governments. Despite such pressures, however, minorities will always exist within state boundaries: it is impossible (and perhaps not even desirable) for every state to be ethnically, linguistically and religiously pure. While one must be careful not to undermine the legitimate rights of the majority, upon which democracy is based, the challenge for the twenty-first century is to do a better job of protecting the more vulnerable, often minority, members of society than was evidenced in the twentieth century....

Ultimately, the challenge of protecting the rights of persons belonging to minorities is to balance the legitimate concerns of majority and minority communities, so that broader political and economic decisions may be reached in an atmosphere of full equality and respect for human rights. The international community has made significant strides in articulating this balance in only a few years. As with other human rights, the task now is to ensure that the political and legal commitments accepted by states are monitored and implemented in good faith.

The General Comment of the Human Rights Committee referred to in the above extract adopts an expansive reading of article 27 of the Covenant on Civil and Political Rights, not dissimilar to the approach adopted by the inter-American institutions with respect to indigenous rights.

Human Rights Committee, General Comment No. 23 (Art. 27)

UN Doc. CCPR/C/21/Rev.1/Add.5, at 2-4 (1994)

5.1 The terms used in article 27 indicate that the persons designed to be protected are those who belong to a group and who share in common a culture, a religion and/or a language. Those terms also indicate that the individuals designed to be protected need not be citizens of the State party. . . .

5.2 Article 27 confers rights on persons belonging to minorities which "exist" in a State party. Given the nature and scope of the rights envisaged under that article, it is not relevant to determine the degree of permanence that the term "exist" connotes. Those rights simply are that individuals belonging to those minorities should not be denied the right, in community with members of their group, to enjoy their own culture, to practice their religion and speak their language. Just as they need not be nationals or citizens, they need not be permanent residents. Thus, migrant workers or even visitors in a State party constituting such minorities are entitled not to be denied the exercise of those rights. As any other individual in the territory of the State party, they would, also for this purpose, have the general rights, for example, to freedom of association, of assembly, and of expression. The existence of an ethnic, religious or linguistic minority in a given State party does not depend upon a decision by that State party but requires [the existence of a minority] to be established by objective criteria. . . .

6.1 Although article 27 is expressed in negative terms, that article, nevertheless, does recognize the existence of a "right" and requires that it shall not be denied. Consequently, a State party is under an obligation to ensure that the existence and the exercise of this right are protected against their denial or violation. Positive measures of protection are, therefore, required not only against the acts of the State party itself, whether through its legislative, judicial or administrative authorities, but also against the acts of other persons within the State party.

6.2 Although the rights protected under article 27 are individual rights, they depend in turn on the ability of the minority group to maintain its culture, language or religion. Accordingly, positive measures by States may also be necessary to protect the identity of a minority and the rights of its members to enjoy and develop their culture and language and to practice their religion, in community with the other members of the group. . . . [A]s long as those measures are aimed at correcting conditions which prevent or impair the enjoyment of the rights guaranteed under article 27, they may constitute a legitimate differentiation under the Covenant, provided that they are based on reasonable and objective criteria. . . .

7. With regard to the exercise of the cultural rights protected under article 27, the Committee observes that culture manifests itself in many forms, including a particular way of life associated with the use of land resources, especially in the case of indigenous peoples. That right may include such traditional activities as fishing or hunting and the right to live in reserves protected by law. The enjoyment of those rights may require positive legal measures of protection and measures to ensure the effective participation of members of minority communities in decisions which affect them. . . .

9. The Committee concludes that article 27 relates to rights . . . is directed to ensure the survival and continued development of the cultural, religious and social identity of the minorities concerned, thus enriching the fabric of society as a whole. Accordingly, the Committee observes that these rights must be protected as such and should not be confused with other personal rights conferred on one and all under the Covenant. States parties, therefore, have an obligation to ensure that the exercise of these rights is fully protected and they should indicate in their reports the measures they have adopted to this end.

The Human Rights Committee has considered minority issues in its examination of states' periodic reports which are mandated by the Covenant, and it has examined a number of complaints concerning alleged violations of Article 27 brought under the First Optional Protocol to the Covenant. These complaints have come from a wide variety of sources and have concerned interference with land, resources, and the use of minority languages. The cases include those filed by the indigenous Sami people against Finland, Norway, and Sweden; Maori against New Zealand; Bretons against France; Sudetenland Germans against the Czech Republic; Afrikaaner and Khoi against Namibia; and indigenous groups against Colombia and Canada. See generally Sia Spiliopoulou, "Protection of Minorities Under Article 27 of the International Covenant on Civil and Political Rights and the Reporting System," in *Writings in Human and Minority Rights* (Frank Horn and Tuula Tervashenka eds., 1994); *Leading Cases of the Human Rights Committee* 375-399 (Raija Hanski and Martin Scheinin eds., 2003).

Note the reference in paragraph 7 of the General Comment to indigenous peoples. The Committee sees the elements of a group's culture as a function of its particular character, so that, in the context of indigenous peoples, the right to culture embraces aspects of indigenous identity, such as the relationship of indigenous peoples with lands and resources. Among the cases that have dealt with indigenous issues are, e.g., *Lovelace v. Canada*, Communication No. 24/1977, Report of the Human Rights Committee, UN Doc. A/36/40, at 166 (views adopted July 1, 1981); *Kitok v. Sweden*, Communication No. 197/1985, Report of the Human Rights Committee, UN Doc. A/43/40 (views adopted July 27, 1988); *Ominayak, Chief of the Lubicon Lake Band v. Canada*, Communication No. 267/1984, Report of the Human Rights Committee, UN Doc A/45/40 (vol. II), at 1 (views adopted March 26, 1990); *Länsman et al. v. Finland*, Communication No. 511/1992, Human Rights Committee, U.N. Doc. CCPR/C/52/D/

511/1992 (views adopted Oct. 26, 1994) (*Länsman I*); *Länsman et al. v. Finland*, Communication No. 671/1995, Human Rights Committee, UN Doc. CCPR/C/58/D/671/1995 (views adopted Oct. 30, 1996)(*Länsman II*); *Mahuika et al. v. New Zealand*, Communication No. 547/1993, Human Rights Committee, UN Doc. CCPR/C/70/D/547/1993 (views adopted October 27, 2000).

Despite the Committee's generally expansive reading of Article 27, as demonstrated by its General Comment, members of minority groups have most often been unsuccessful in pressing their claims. Many cases have been declared inadmissible for failure to exhaust local remedies, which is a requirement under most international human rights complaint procedures. All of the cases against France have been declared inadmissible as to Article 27, because the Committee determined that it is bound by a French reservation to Article 27 stating that the article is "not applicable" (although technically the French statement was entitled a "declaration"). But see *Hopu & Bessert v. France*, Communication No. 549/1993, Human Rights Comm., U.N. Doc. CCPR/E/60/D/549/1993/Rev. 1 (views adoped July 29 1997) (finding France violated rights to family and privacy of articles 17 and 23 of the Covenant by permitting construction of hotel on ancestral burial grounds of indigenous polynesians in Tahiti.) Turkey is the only other state to have filed a substantive reservation to Article 27.

When it has reached the merits of a case, the Committee has set a relatively high threshold for finding a violation. It is not enough that there is an impairment of a minority way of life; it should be a serious deprivation of cultural life. Thus, in *Länsman I*, supra, the Committee decided that Article 27 was not violated by the extent of stone-quarrying permitted by Finland in traditional Sami lands. The Committee also accepted that measures had been taken to minimize the impact on reindeer herding activity and on the environment. In effect, the Committee interpreted Article 27 to mean that, while measures whose impact amount to a denial of the right to culture are not acceptable, those that simply have a "certain limited impact on the way of life of persons belonging to a minority" do not violate the Covenant.

The Committee also has given great weight to the fact that the state made efforts to consult the affected community and take its views into account in making its decision. Some of these consultations had been extensive and resulted in changes in the government's plans, based, for example, on dialogue with leaders of the affected Sami community. It may have appeared to the Committee that the dispute was as much between factions within the indigenous group as between the group and the majority represented by the government.

Finally, the committee has taken a strict view of what constitutes a minority within a state, refusing to view English-speakers in Quebec, for example, as a minority, because they are part of the national majority in Canada even though they are a minority in Quebec. The Committee did find, however, that a measure requiring all commercial signs in Quebec to be in French was a denial of freedom of expression to English-speakers. The practical results for the complainant were the same, whether the case was won based on Article 27 (minority rights) or on Article 19 (free speech). However, by characterizing the case the way it did, the Committee avoided the need to look within states at smaller geographic areas where the ethnic balance may be different from the country as a whole. The Committee might have felt that this was too intrusive in domestic matters or that it would exacerbate tensions to call the majority a minority because of population distribution in particular areas.

B. *Self-Determination*

Inevitably looming in the background of most discussions about the rights of indigenous peoples and minorities is the right of self-determination. But no treaty or resolution adopted by an intergovernmental body to date explicitly affirms that right for these groups, despite persistent efforts (especially by indigenous peoples) to achieve such affirmation through its inclusion in the UN Declaration on the Rights of Indigenous Peoples. The draft for this proposed declaration, which has been under discussion for over two decades, does affirm that "all indigenous peoples have a right of self-determination," but this language has proved unacceptable to many states. The controversy stems from a tendency to see self-determination in its fullest sense as inevitably linked to a right to independent statehood or secession.

The UN Charter affirms the "principle of self-determination and equal rights of peoples," and self-determination is recognized as a "right" of "all peoples" in identical language in the first article of both human rights covenants. However, what became a norm of customary international law in the context of classic decolonization developed initially not through a treaty but on the basis of General Assembly resolutions, which eventually came to be supported by the practice of states.

Although it was not the first resolution to proclaim a right to self-determination, the 1960 Declaration on the Granting of Independence to Colonial Countries and Peoples, G.A. Res. 1514 (Dec. 14, 1960), probably remains the most significant statement on the topic in connection with decolonization. It sets forth the fundamental principle of self-determination, along with an equally fundamental limitation on its application:

> 2. All peoples have the right to self-determination; by virtue of that right they freely determine their political status and freely pursue their economic, social and cultural development. . . .
> 6. Any attempt aimed at the partial or total disruption of the national unity and the territorial integrity of a country is incompatible with the purposes and principles of the Charter of the United Nations.

Since 1960, these principles have been reiterated on numerous occasions, most notably in the authoritative 1970 Declaration on Principles of International Law Concerning Friendly Relations and Co-Operation Among States in Accordance with the Charter of the United Nations, G.A. Res. 2625 (Oct. 13, 1970).

Secessionist movements by ethnic and other groups have occurred often, and these movements typically invoke the right of self-determination. The expansion of secessionist demands outside the colonial context has led increasingly to violent conflict. The post-1989 dissolutions of the Soviet Union, Yugoslavia, Czechoslovakia, and Ethiopia have emboldened groups seeking either independence or self-government and, at the same time, have demonstrated the inability of the international law thus far to provide persuasive normative criteria for resolving such conflicts.

Despite the fact that the right to self-determination is proclaimed in Article 1 of both covenants, the Human Rights Committee has refused to consider alleged violations of that right in the context of individual complaints lodged under the

Optional Protocol to the Covenant on Civil and Political Rights. However, the Committee has examined Article 1 in reviewing state periodic reports. The Committee's General Comment on Article 1 indicates that the right of self-determination is relevant to concerns outside the secessionist or decolonization contexts and requests states to include in their reports, in connection with Article 1, descriptions of "the constitutional and political processes which in practice allow the exercise of this right." General Comment 12 (Art. 1), Report of the Human Rights Committee, UN Doc. A/39/40, Annex VI, para. 4 (1984). This examination has included not only states' internal political processes but also their handling of indigenous peoples' claims. For example, in reviewing Canada's fourth periodic report under the Covenant, the Committee urged upon Canada that "the practice of extinguishing inherent aboriginal rights be abandoned as incompatible with article 1 of the Covenant." Concluding Observations of the Human Rights Committee: Canada, UN Doc. CCPR/C/79/Add.105, para. 7 (1999). In the same vein, the Committee expressed concerns about state laws and policies in Australia and Norway relating to indigenous lands, making references to obligations derived from Article 1. See Concluding Observations of the Human Rights Committee: Norway, UN Doc. CCPR/C/79/Add.112, paras. 16, 17 (1999); Concluding Observations of the Human Rights Committee: Australia, UN Doc. A/55/40, paras. 509-510 (2000). Additionally, even though the Committee still will not entertain alleged violations of Article 1 under the Optional Protocol complaint procedure, it has stated that it may consider Article 1 to interpret other articles of the Covenant. See, e.g., *Mahuika et al. v. New Zealand*, supra page 193, paras. 3, 9.2 (Article 1 could be relevant to complaint under Article 27 in relation Maori claims over fisheries).

Another UN treaty monitoring body, the Committee on the Elimination of Racial Discrimination(CERD), adopted an approach consistent with that of the Human Rights Committee, as evidenced in the following General Recommendation.

Committee on the Elimination of Racial Discrimination, Right to Self-determination, General Recommendation XXI

UN Doc. A/51/18 (Aug. 23, 1996)

1. The Committee notes that ethnic or religious groups or minorities frequently refer to the right to self-determination as a basis for an alleged right to secession. In this connection the Committee wishes to express the following views.

2. The right to self-determination of peoples is a fundamental principle of international law. It is enshrined in article 1 of the Charter of the United Nations, in article 1 of the International Covenant on Economic, Social and Cultural Rights and article 1 of the International Covenant on Civil and Political Rights, as well as in other international human rights instruments. The International Covenant on Civil and Political Rights provides for the rights of peoples to self-determination besides the right of ethnic, religious or linguistic minorities to enjoy their own culture, to profess and practise their own religion or to use their own language.

3. The Committee emphasizes that in accordance with the Declaration on Principles of International Law concerning Friendly Relations and Cooperation among States in accordance with the Charter of the United Nations, approved by the United Nations General Assembly in its resolution 2625 (XXV) of 24 October 1970, it is the duty of States to promote the right to self-determination of peoples. But the implementation of the principle of self-determination requires every State to promote, through joint and separate action, universal respect for and observance of human rights and fundamental freedoms in accordance with the Charter of the United Nations. In this context the Committee draws the attention of Governments to the Declaration on the Rights of Persons Belonging to National or Ethnic, Religious and Linguistic Minorities, adopted by the General Assembly in its resolution 47/135 of 18 December 1992.

4. In respect of the self-determination of peoples two aspects have to be distinguished. The right to self-determination of peoples has an internal aspect, that is to say, the rights of all peoples to pursue freely their economic, social and cultural development without outside interference. In that respect there exists a link with the right of every citizen to take part in the conduct of public affairs at any level, as referred to in article 5(c) of the International Convention on the Elimination of All Forms of Racial Discrimination. In consequence, Governments are to represent the whole population without distinction as to race, colour, descent or national or ethnic origin. The external aspect of self-determination implies that all peoples have the right to determine freely their political status and their place in the international community based upon the principle of equal rights and exemplified by the liberation of peoples from colonialism and by the prohibition to subject peoples to alien subjugation, domination and exploitation.

5. In order to respect fully the rights of all peoples within a State, Governments are again called upon to adhere to and implement fully the international human rights instruments and in particular the International Convention on the Elimination of All Forms of Racial Discrimination. Concern for the protection of individual rights without discrimination on racial, ethnic, tribal, religious or other grounds must guide the policies of Governments. In accordance with article 2 of the International Convention on the Elimination of All Forms of Racial Discrimination and other relevant international documents, Governments should be sensitive towards the rights of persons belonging to ethnic groups, particularly their right to lead lives of dignity, to preserve their culture, to share equitably in the fruits of national growth and to play their part in the Government of the country of which they are citizens. Also, Governments should consider, within their respective constitutional frameworks, vesting persons belonging to ethnic or linguistic groups comprised of their citizens, where appropriate, with the right to engage in activities which are particularly relevant to the preservation of the identity of such persons or groups.

6. The Committee emphasizes that, in accordance with the Declaration on Friendly Relations, none of the Committee's actions shall be construed as authorizing or encouraging any action which would dismember or impair, totally or in part, the territorial integrity or political unity of sovereign and independent States conducting themselves in compliance with the principle of equal rights and self-determination of peoples and possessing a Government representing the whole people belonging to the territory, without distinction as to race, creed or colour. In the view of the Committee, international law has not recognized a general right of

peoples unilaterally to declare secession from a State. In this respect, the Committee follows the views expressed in An Agenda for Peace (paras. 17 and following), namely, that a fragmentation of States may be detrimental to the protection of human rights, as well as to the preservation of peace and security. This does not, however, exclude the possibility of arrangements reached by free agreements of all parties concerned.

The interpretation of the right of self-determination advanced by the CERD views that right as part of the larger universe of human rights and not equaling a right of secession or independent statehood. The implicit message is that self-determination claims, with their potentially profound impact on the very structure of the state, can be better considered from a human rights perspective, rather than being subject exclusively to the geopolitical calculations that have typically guide responses to such claims today. For arguments in favor of such a human rights approach, see S. James Anaya, A *Contemporary Definition of the International Norm of Self-Determination*, 3 Transnatl. L. & Contemp. Probs. 131 (1993); Hurst Hannum, *Rethinking Self-Determination*, 34 Va. J. Int'l L. 1 (1993); Robert McCorquodale, *Self-Determination: A Human Rights Approach*, 43 Int'l & Comp. L. Q.857 (1994).

Among many other works that address the issue of self-determination from a legal perspective are Antonio Cassese, *Self-Determination of Peoples, A Legal Reappraisal* (1995); Hurst Hannum, *Autonomy, Sovereignty, and Self-Determination, The Accommodation of Conflicting Rights* (2d ed. 1996); Karen Knop, *Diversity and Self-Determination in International Law* (2002); Michla Pomerance, *Self-Determination in Law and Practice* (1982); W. Ofuatey-Kodjoe, *The Principle of Self-Determination in International Law* (1977); Diane F. Orentlicher, *Separation Anxiety: International Responses to Ethno-Separatist Claims*, 23 Yale J. Int'l L. 1 (1998); A. Rigo Sureda, *The Evolution of the Right of Self-Determination* (1973); United Nations, The Right to Self Determination, Historical and Current Developments on the Basis of the United Nations Instruments [Aureliu Cristescu, Special Rapporteur], U.N. Sales No. E.80.XIV3 (1981); United Nations, The Right to Self-Determination. Implementation of United Nations Resolutions [Hector Gros Espiell, Special Rapporteur], U.N. Sales No. E.79.XIV.5 (1980).

Comments and Questions

1. How expansive is the Human Rights Committee's interpretation of Article 27 of the Covenant on Civil and Political Rights in its General Comment on that article, supra page 191? Do you think that states intended that Article 27 protect indigenous rights over lands and resources as held by the Committee? Do you think that states intended to grant minority rights to migrant workers and tourists? Does paragraph 6.1 of the General Comment mean that private employers cannot prohibit employees from speaking their own language on the job? What kinds of "positive measures" might be necessary to protect the identity of a minority?

2. The Human Rights Committee's General Comment on Article 27 includes the following distinction between the right of self-determination and rights protected under Article 27:

> 3.1 The Covenant draws a distinction between the right to self-determination and the rights protected under article 27. The former is expressed to be a right belonging to

> peoples and is dealt with in a separate part (Part I) of the Covenant. Self-determination is not a right cognizable under the Optional Protocol. Article 27, on the other hand, relates to rights conferred on individuals as such and is included, like the articles relating to other personal rights conferred on individuals, in Part III of the Covenant and is cognizable under the Optional Protocol.
>
> 3.2 The enjoyment of the rights to which article 27 relates does not prejudice the sovereignty and territorial integrity of a State party. At the same time, one or other aspect of the rights of individuals protected under that article — for example to enjoy a particular culture — may consist in a way of life which is closely associated with territory and use of its resources. This may particularly be true of members of indigenous communities constituting a minority.

Is this distinction consistent with the views taken by the Committee on the Elimination of Racial Discrimination in its General Recommendation on Self-Determination, supra page 195? Is the Human Rights Committee itself faithful to this distinction in its more recent practice?

3. Although two UN rapporteurs have proposed definitions that have been generally accepted, states have resisted reaching formal agreement on a definition of either minorities or indigenous peoples. See United Nations, Study on the Rights of Persons Belonging to Ethnic, Religious and Linguistic Minorities 96 [F. Capotorti, Special Rapporteur], U. N. Sales No. E.91.XIV.2 (1977, reprinted 1991); United Nations, Study of the Problem of Discrimination Against Indigenous Populations, Conclusions and Recommendations 50, 51 [A Martínez Cobo, Special Rapporteur], U.N. Sales No. E.86.XIV.3 (1986). Can one develop meaningful norms in this area without defining such essential terms as minority, indigenous, and peoples?

4. The practice of the Human Rights Committee and CERD's General Recommendation suggest that minority rights, indigenous rights, and rights of self-determination are interrelated categories. How would you describe this interrelationship? What then are the distinctions among the terms minority, indigenous, and peoples in relation to particular groups? Do some groups, such as Indian tribes or nations in the United States, qualify under each of these rubrics? In attempts to categorize groups, what is the relevance of colonization, especially in light of the clear association between the right of self-determination and classical decolonization? Can minorities, whether or not indigenous, qualify as peoples with a right of self-determination and still be considered minorities? One or more of these and related questions are taken up in the following works, in addition to those cited earlier: *The Rights of Peoples* (James Crawford ed. 1988); Jennifer Jackson Preece, *National Minorities and the European Nation-State System* (1998); Maivan Lâm, *At the Edge of the State: Indigenous Peoples and Self-Determination* (2000); Thomas Duncan Musgrave, *Self-Determination and National Minorities* (1997); Patrick Thornberry, *International Law and the Rights of Minorities* (1993).

5. One common theme in discussions about indigenous peoples, minorities, and self-determination is the call for respect for cultural diversity. Note in this regard the UNESCO Universal Declaration on Cultural Diversity, adopted in 2001 by the General Conference of the UN Educational, Scientific and Cultural Organization (UNESCO) and quoted in Chapter 1, page 45.

6. In 1975, the U.S. Congress adopted the Indian Self-Determination and Education Assistance Act, 25 U.S.C. §§13a, 450-450n, 455-458e, 42 U.S. §2004b (1994), which permits tribes to enter into contracts with the federal

government and assume responsibility for various federally administered programs. Does this constitute "self-determination" as that term may be understood in international law?

7. In what sense are the rights of indigenous peoples properly characterized as group or collective human rights? Are human rights by definition individual as opposed to group rights? Compare the discussion of "third generation" rights at pages 91-96 of Chapter 2. Are judicial or quasi-judicial forums less well suited to assessing claims of violations of these rights, as opposed to bodies whose purpose is conciliation or mediation? Note in this regard that, despite the favorable decisions of the Inter-American Commission on Human Rights in the *Dann* and *Maya Communities* cases, discussed at pages 172-183 supra, those decisions had little immediate impact. See Annual Report of the Inter-American Commission on Human Rights 2004, O.A.S. Doc. OEA/Ser.L/V/II.122, Doc. 5 rev. 1 paras. 285-88 (2005). Nicaragua also failed to fully comply with the order of the Inter-American Court of Human Rights in the Awas Tingni case, discussed at page 172-174 supra, to demarcate and title indigenous lands within the time allotted by the court. See Annual Report of the Inter-American Commission on Human Rights 2003, para. 375, OAS Doc. OEA/Ser.L/VII.118 Doc. 5. rev. 2 (2003); Indian Law Resource Center, *The Awas Tingni Case — Fifteen Months Later: The Challenge to the Implementation of the Decision of the Inter-American Court of Human Rights* (Press release, Jan. 16, 2003).

V. The Model or "Soft Law" Approach in the Criminal Justice Area

One area that has been a particular concern of UN declarations and other non-treaty instruments is that of criminal justice. The many instruments in this field constitute a regime of "soft law" that includes prisoners' rights; juvenile delinquency; judicial, prosecutorial, and police conduct; and related fields.

The present legal status of a prisoner has been described by two authorities to "lie in the gray area between slaves and citizens." James Gobert and Neil Cohen, *Rights of Prisoners* 13 (1981). In many states in the United States, a convicted felon permanently loses the right to vote, the right to hold public office, and the right to serve on a jury. Prisoners have minimal rights to freedom of speech and assembly. No laws (either federal or state) provide an adequate minimum wage for work done by prisoners, and no system grants prisoners compensation for injuries suffered on the job. Compensation for prison labor is very low for work that often is, in effect, compulsory. Id. at 196. There is no right to counsel in prison disciplinary proceedings. Moreover, an inmate bringing an action outside prison (with regard to an alleged violation of his rights while incarcerated) assumes a heavier than normal burden of proof. Thus, as the above authorities remark, "no necessary correlation exists between the status of a constitutional right inside and out of prison." Id. at 14. Or, put more graphically, "[p]risons have been such a garbage can of society that they have been a garbage can of the law as well."*

* Unpublished remarks of Professor Herman Schwartz, now Professor of Law at the Washington College of Law, American University, and one of the intermediaries between prisoners and prison officials during the infamous Attica uprising in 1971.

A. *International Norms Governing the Treatment of Prisoners*

The attitude of the international community toward the treatment of prisoners has evolved over the years. Article 5 of the Universal Declaration of Human Rights states a broad, general norm:

> No one shall be subjected to torture or to cruel, inhuman or degrading treatment or punishment.

Article 10(1) of the International Covenant on Civil and Political Rights applies this norm specifically to the treatment of prisoners, while Article 10(3) adopts the view that prisoners can be rehabilitated if treated humanely:

> 1. All persons deprived of their liberty shall be treated with humanity and with respect for the inherent dignity of the human person. . . .
>
> 3. The penitentiary system shall comprise treatment of prisoners the essential aim of which shall be their reformation and social rehabilitation.

While the rehabilitative approach has influenced most recent attempts to codify minimum standards of humane treatment for prisoners on the international and regional levels, it appears to have become less important in the eyes of the U.S. government. In an "understanding" filed at the time it ratified the Civil and Political Covenant, for example, the United States stated that "paragraph 3 of Article 10 does not diminish the goals of punishment, deterrence, and incapacitation as additional legitimate purposes for a penitentiary system." 138 Cong. Rec. S4783 (daily ed. Apr. 2, 1992).

Rather than being adopted through internationally binding treaties, most new norms in the areas of criminal justice and treatment of prisoners have taken the form of non-binding documents setting forth principles, guidelines, and model laws designed to encourage the adoption of comparable national standards.

The basic international prison regulations are the Standard Minimum Rules for the Treatment of Prisoners (Documentary Supplement, companion CD). An initial version of the Rules was drawn up in 1933 by the International Penal and Penitentiary Commission and approved by the Assembly of the League of Nations in 1934. After World War II, the Rules were revised by the UN Secretariat and endorsed by the UN's First Congress on the Prevention of Crime and the Treatment of Offenders in 1955. For a historical perspective on the Rules, see Clifford, *The Standard Minimum Rules for the Treatment of Prisoners*, 66 Am. Socy. Intl. L. Proceedings 232 (1972). In 1957, the UN Economic and Social Council formally approved the Rules. See E.S.C. Res. 663C (July 31, 1957). Drawing the attention of all governments to them, the Council recommended:

(a) That favourable consideration be given to their adoption and application in the administration of penal and correctional institutions.
(b) That the Secretary-General be informed every five years of the progress made with regard to their application.

B. *Status of the Standard Minimum Rules*

While the Rules have been formally approved by the UN Economic and Social Council, they obviously do not have the status of a General Assembly resolution such as the Universal Declaration of Human Rights, much less that of a multilateral treaty. What, then, is their precise legal status? What impact have they had on the prison systems of the UN's member states? What steps have been taken to achieve their implementation? What problems have yet to be solved, and what prospects exist for future progress?

Over the years, the UN has addressed — and is still addressing — the above questions. It continually reviews the Standard Minimum Rules in light of current penological thinking in an effort to achieve greater success with respect to their adoption and implementation. This duty is shared by two components of the UN system little known even to most international human rights lawyers: the Commission on Crime Prevention and Criminal Justice of the Economic and Social Council (which was created in 1991 to replace the former Committee on Crime Prevention and Control) and the quinquennial Congresses on the Prevention of Crime and the Treatment of Offenders. The question of the legal status of the Rules was considered in a working paper prepared by the Secretariat for the Fourth U.N. Congress, which states:

> 40. Acceptance by the United Nations and approval by the Economic and Social Council, however important, are still not sufficient to invest the Standard Minimum Rules with the force of international law. Nevertheless, the fact of this acceptance and adoption does serve to lend an international significance to the Rules superior by far to that enjoyed by international practices and standards which have not been so endorsed. The Secretary-General's request of periodic reporting, moreover, gives to the Rules an official status enjoyed by few matters under the jurisdiction of the United Nations. . . .
>
> 50. It is clear that the Rules already have considerable moral force and are beginning to acquire even greater international standing, especially as they become the subject of reports to the Secretary-General, the focus of a number of different studies and the occasion for the results and findings of inquiries and studies to be submitted to an international Congress, as now. . . .
>
> 51. The issue of the status of the Rules really emerges from the need to promote their recognition and implementation as effectively as possible. Clearly, they can and have inspired better prison regulations and have also improved practice but, ultimately, the Rules are effectively implemented, as indicated already, when they are incorporated into national or municipal law. It may be expected that this process will become more extensive with the increasing support which the Rules are receiving internationally, regionally, and municipally.

Standard Minimum Rules for the Treatment of Prisoners in the Light of Recent Developments in the Correctional Field, Working Paper by the Secretariat, Fourth UN Congress on the Prevention of Crime and the Treatment of Offenders UN Doc. A/CONF.43/3, at 13-18 (1970).

C. *Applying the "Model Law" or "Soft Law" Approach to Specific Subjects*

The "model law" approach of the Standard Minimum Rules and the "soft law" of principles and guidelines have been utilized frequently to develop international norms that protect, directly or indirectly, the rights of prisoners and other aspects of criminal justice systems. The Compendium of United Nations Standards and Norms in Crime Prevention and Criminal Justice, published by the

United Nations in 1992, UN Sales No. E.92.IV.1, includes 48 instruments that set international standards on issues ranging from international cooperation in combating crime and suppression of prostitution to codes of conduct or principles concerning law enforcement officials, judges, prosecutors, lawyers, and health personnel. Forty of these instruments, including four resolutions adopted in 1989 to implement substantive norms, have been adopted since 1980. Following the extraordinarily productive Eighth UN Congress on the Prevention of Crime and the Treatment of Offenders in 1990, the UN General Assembly adopted eight resolutions on crime prevention and criminal justice; an additional 10 resolutions were adopted by the Congress itself or the 1990 session of the Economic and Social Council. Subsequent UN activity in the criminal justice area has resulted in a few additional instruments.

Space constraints prohibit more than a simple listing of some of the most important of these instruments, but their titles indicate the range of issues they address. For convenience, they are grouped under three major headings; the text of all but the most recent of these documents may be found in the UN Compendium, cited supra.

1. Treatment of Prisoners

Principles of Medical Ethics, G.A. Res. 37/194 (Dec. 18, 1982)
Declaration of Basic Principles of Justice for Victims of Crime and Abuse of Power, G.A. Res. 40/34 (Nov. 29, 1985)
Body of Principles for the Protection of All Persons Under Any Form of Detention or Imprisonment, G.A. Res. 43/173 (Dec. 9, 1988)
Standard Minimum Rules for Non-Custodial Measures (The Tokyo Rules), G.A. Res. 45/110 (Dec. 14, 1990)
Basic Principles for the Treatment of Prisoners, G.A. Res. 45/111 (Dec. 14, 1990)
Safeguards Guaranteeing Protection of the Rights of Those Facing the Death Penalty, E.S.C. Res. 1984/50 (May 25, 1984), Annex
Effective Prevention and Investigation of Extra-Legal, Arbitrary, and Summary Executions, E.S.C. Res. 1989/65 (May 24, 1989), Annex

2. Juvenile Offenders

Standard Minimum Rules for the Administration of Juvenile Justice (The Beijing Rules), G.A. Res. 40/33 (Nov. 29, 1985)
Guidelines for the Prevention of Juvenile Delinquency (The Riyadh Guidelines), G.A. Res. 45/112 (Dec. 14, 1990)
United Nations Rules for the Protection of Juveniles Deprived of Their Liberty, G.A. Res. 45/113 (Dec. 14, 1990)

3. Standards for the Administration of Justice

Code of Conduct for Law Enforcement Officials, G.A. Res. 34/169 (Dec. 17, 1979)
Basic Principles on the Independence of the Judiciary, Seventh UN Congress on the Prevention of Crime and the Treatment of Offenders, Report Prepared by the Secretariat, UN Doc. A/CONF. 121/22/Rev. 1, at 58 (1985)

Basic Principles on the Use of Force and Firearms by Law Enforcement Officials, Eighth UN Congress on the Prevention of Crime and Treatment of Offenders, Report Prepared by the Secretariat, UN Doc. A/CONF.144/28, at 110 (1990)

Basic Principles on the Role of Lawyers, Eighth UN Congress on the Prevention of Crime and the Treatment of Offenders, Report Prepared by the Secretariat, UN Doc. A/CONF.144/28, at 117 (1990)

Guidelines on the Role of Prosecutors, Eighth UN Congress on the Prevention of Crime and the Treatment of Offenders, Report Prepared by the Secretariat, UN Doc. A/CONF.144/28, at 188 (1990)

Basic Principles on the Use of Restorative Justice Programmes in Criminal Matters, and Action to Promote Effective Crime Prevention, E.S.C. Res. 2002/12 (July 24, 2002), Annex

For a collection of papers analyzing the various UN instruments in the criminal justice area and their application, see UN Office of Drugs and Crime, The Application of the United Nations Standards and Norms in Crime Prevention and Criminal Justice (2003) (papers presented at and expert group meeting, 10-12 Feb., 2003).

In addition to the normative codes listed immediately above, many of which are designed to provide models for the adoption by states of their own penal or other codes, less formal codes of professional conduct for law enforcement officials may also have an impact in changing behavior. It is important to keep in mind that the purpose of human rights law and activism is to change the reality of the situation on the ground, not simply to promulgate new treaties and laws.

The potential impact of professional ethical codes is discussed in the two extracts that follow.

Nigel Rodley, The Treatment of Prisoners Under International Law

279 (1987)

International Codes of Ethics for Professionals

Introduction

One of the legacies of the Nuremberg and Tokyo war crimes trials was the recognition that, while the organs of the state may be responsible for the most appalling atrocities against those they are supposed to serve and protect, the evil acts themselves are committed not by abstract entities (the police, the judiciary, the military) against other abstract entities (the enemy within or without) but by individual men and women against other men and women. One result of this recognition has been the attribution of individual criminal responsibility to those guilty of some of the more egregious excesses with which this text is concerned [see Chapters 4 and 11].

Important as this formal legal response may be, it cannot be the sole solution to the problem. To paraphrase the Constitution of Unesco: since human rights violations begin in the minds of men, it is in the minds of men that the defenses of human rights must be constructed. The purpose of a code of ethics is to create a set of desired responses in each individual member of the group or profession to which the code is addressed. Since certain groups may be seen to be more vulnerable to, or more exposed to, demands that they (for example) inflict torture on perceived enemies of society, it is clearly necessary to create within such groups an ethos conducive to the rejection of such demands. The groups most directly concerned with torture and other violations of human rights are the police and other law enforcement officials, including the military, but doctors and other health personnel are also often affected, as too may be members of the legal profession.

Alfred Heijder, Codes of Professional Ethics Against Torture

In Amnesty International, Code of Professional Ethics 3, 5-7 (ACT 07/01/84, 1984) (emphasis in original)

FUNCTIONS OF CODES OF PROFESSIONAL CONDUCT

The regulation of professional behaviour has many sources. Most of these sources can be located in four different fields.

First, all professional bodies, and thus each individual member of the professions, work in the context of a given *political system.* This simple observation has disturbing implications in the case of professionals working in or connected with the service of the state. The values, goals and accepted means of the general political system are an important regulating force for professional behaviour. In an official document of the United Nations . . . it is said that corruption within the police depends largely upon the influence, guidance and interest of the total society in the police. Such a statement also holds true for the attitude towards torture. The connivance of other significant persons in the political system is of crucial importance.

Second, within such an overall political system, no one works alone. The work is mostly done in *organizations and functional units.* Every professional has colleagues who exert influence by their opinion on his or her attitudes, behaviour and performance. The influence of social interaction in the professional group is pervasive and omnipresent.

Third, in general, and given certain conditions of information and publicity, *public opinion* is a regulating force too, either in a direct way or via the political system or the opinions of colleagues. In a way and to a certain degree, public opinion sets the boundaries for professional conduct. Hence the strenuous attempts to modify or manipulate public opinion.

Fourth, there are of course the *individual values,* which the professional expresses to a certain degree in his professional behaviour, too.

Each of these four fields — the political system, the professional group, public and individual opinion — can have its own value orientation and its different sets of rules of conduct. The question whether these four fields constitute a hierarchy of values is relevant only in case of conflicting values.

There are two categories of conflicts. First, there may be different values *in one field,* which under certain conditions may conflict. Thus we find in the general political system conflicts between the *raison d'Etat* and morality or between the concept of national sovereignty and individual human rights. Second, conflicts may arise between values not in one field alone but *in different fields.* Thus the general political system will find the preservation of national security an overriding consideration, while professionals such as doctors or lawyers defend human lives and human rights irrespective of the issue of security. In many situations the doctor, lawyer or policeman has to choose among competing values in the face of a variety of situations.

It is obvious that the professionals who are in the service of the state are most exposed to conflicting demands of allegiance. For their skills and expert knowledge are most easily perverted against their original intentions. In cases where such conflicts become manifest and a choice must be made, the individual will look for concrete orientation points to guide his behaviour.

When the individual is part of a professional group, he will be aware of what his colleagues do in the same situation. Since not only general recognition but a prolonged specialized training is a precondition for an occupation being recognized as a profession, he will have undergone during that training a process of anticipatory socialization. He is taught not only the skills of the job but also is oriented to the professional values and norms. The generative traits of a profession call for a measure of professional autonomy against the pressures of the general political system, public opinion and sometimes even one's own value orientation. Codes of professional conduct can be seen as a formalization of the more or less diffuse colleague opinion in the professional field. Sometimes the existence of a full-fledged code is even mentioned as one of the main traits of a profession. A code of professional conduct will help the individual to cope with the problems arising from the different demands of a situation. Its influence may even reach beyond that.

Preliminary to any self-determined act of behavior there is always a stage of examination and deliberation which we may call the definition of the situation. In many instances there is rivalry between the spontaneous definition of the situation made by someone and the definitions which others provide. The prison doctor should not see an enemy of the state on hunger-strike, he should see a patient. The defense lawyer should see a client entitled to a fair trial, not a security risk to be eliminated by judicial means. One aspect of morality is that it provides a generally accepted definition of the situation, expressed in some socially visible form.

There are several defining agencies in society. In fact, the four fields we referred to as sources for rules can be seen as harbouring several defining agencies. Institutions and professional groups offer standardized definitions of the situation, implying that the standard reaction of the individual is not only the expected, reasonable one, but the safe one too. That is why it is so important for doctors, lawyers and law enforcement personnel that their codes of professional conduct should enlarge upon the implications of Article 5 of the Universal Declaration of Human Rights, which addresses itself to "all people and all nations, every individual and every organ of society."

But will a code be an effective force? From a sociological point of view we can say that the reaction to an induced force will vary, depending, among other things, on the person's relation to the inducing agent. Rules and pressure to conform, coming from a friend or colleague, may be accepted in such a way that it acts more like one's own force. A force induced by a stranger or an enemy may be resisted and compliance may arouse conflicts and tensions. Thus a code of professional ethics can be a strong force since it is an acceptable induced force. The acceptance of an induced force sets up additional personal forces in the same direction, while rejection does the same in the opposite direction.

Once a code is established, we can expect — since attitudes and group affiliation are closely connected — that it will play its part in the process of shaping professional attitudes. In this way a code of professional ethics, as a model pattern of behaviour, exerts influence first of all on a conceptual level and only after some time and after some enforcement mechanisms are set in motion, on an operational level. So we can be modestly optimistic about the effectiveness of such codes.

From this general and not exhaustive survey we come to the criteria on which the merits of different proposals should be judged. There are, I suggest, three points on which to focus attention.

1. Is the code more than a declaration of good intentions? Does it formulate real and detailed norms of conduct?
2. Does the code provide for the mechanisms necessary for its implementation and enforcement?
3. Does the code provide for freedom of information about its norms, reports on deviance and efforts to enforce its rules?

Comments and Questions

1. Why are there so few treaties in the area of criminal justice, as opposed to the plethora of declarations, principles, codes, and model laws? Is there something unique about criminal justice that makes it more difficult to develop international norms that will gain wide acceptance?

2. Do you agree with Heijder that codes of conduct can effectively shape behavior? Do you think that professional codes of conduct are likely to be more or less effective than the corporate codes of conduct discussed in Chapter 5?

VI. Final Comments and Questions

1. While the Universal Declaration of Human Rights and other instruments by their terms apply to all segments of humanity, international standard-setting activities often have been aimed at developing norms concerning particular groups. As can be seen from the above materials, standards have been or are being developed to address indigenous peoples, minorities, and prisoners, because of the special vulnerabilities of these groups. International standards have been developed to address other vulnerable groups as well, through UN declarations and other "soft law" instruments. For example, the following declarations have been adopted by the UN General Assembly:

Declaration on the Rights of Mentally Retarded Persons, G.A. Res. 2856 (Dec. 20, 1971)
Declaration on the Rights of Disabled Persons, G.A. Res. 3447 (Dec. 9, 1975)

Declaration on the Human Rights of Individuals Who Are Not Nationals of the Country in which They Live, G.A. Res. 40/144 (Dec. 13, 1985)
Declaration on Social and Legal Principles Relating to the Protection and Welfare of Children, with Special Reference to Foster Placement and Adoption Nationally and Internationally, G.A. Res. 41/85 (Dec. 3, 1986)
Principles for the Protection of the Rights of Persons with Mental Illness and for the Improvement of Mental Health Care, G.A. Res. 46/119 (Dec. 17, 1991), Annex
Declaration of Commitment on HIV/AIDS, G.A. Res. S-26/2 (June 27, 2001), Annex

None of these declarations has been succeeded by a binding convention on the same subject, although UN conventions were adopted after, inter alia, declarations on the rights of the child (declaration 1959, convention 1989), racial discrimination (declaration 1963, convention 1965), discrimination against women (declaration 1967, convention 1979), and the prohibition of torture (declaration 1975, convention 1984).

2. Even outside the area of criminal justice, the United Nations has produced many more non-binding human rights instruments than treaties. Why is this so? Consider the following possible factors:

(a) The general unwillingness of states to subscribe to additional international human rights instruments;

(b) The realization of some states that declarations or model laws and guidelines, being just that, carry with them no international legal obligation;

(c) The greater flexibility that comes with applying non-binding norms and the need to maintain such flexibility in light of the diversity in country situations;

(d) The recognition that, even when an international human rights instrument has been ratified, it has little "legal bite" absent good faith compliance, so that it may be better to agree to declarations of "soft law" which implicitly accept that voluntary compliance is the sine qua non of effective international human rights law.

3. Is it "safer" for states to adopt declarations, guidelines, and principles, on the ground that they are non-binding? Consider the relationship between declarations and customary or general principles of law, discussed supra, 151–161. A declaration may be an initial step toward the formation of customary international law, as is widely understood to have been the case with the Universal Declaration of Human Rights. Can the votes of states in favor of a declaration or model code and the collective act of adopting it themselves be seen as forms of practice contributing to the formation of customary international law? See *TOPCO/CALASIATIC v. Libyan Arab Republic*, International Arbitration Tribunal, Merits (1977), 17 Int'l Legal Mat. 1 (1978) (René Dupuy, arbitrator) (finding applicable customary law in part on the basis of patterns of voting on UN General Assembly resolutions).

A declaration also might confirm or restate already established or developing customary norms or general principles, as was the case with the 1970 Declaration on Principles of International Law Concerning Friendly Relations and Co-Operation Among States in Accordance with the Charter of the United Nations. This also may be the case (at least in part) for any future declaration of the rights of indigenous peoples, if one accepts the view, advanced by the Inter-American Commission on Human Rights, that customary and general principles of law already exist concerning the rights of indigenous peoples.

4. Many of the codes or guidelines adopted by the United Nations in the criminal justice field are extremely detailed, the international equivalents of administrative regulations designed to implement broader principles, such as "humane treatment" for prisoners or guarantees of a "fair trial." This level of specificity contrasts with that of other instruments, for example the relatively brief (nine articles total) UN Declaration on Minorities. What might account for such difference?

5. We can see from the above materials that expert bodies, such as the Inter-American Commission on Human Rights and the UN treaty monitoring bodies, are assuming roles in shaping international human rights standards through their interpretive statements and decisions. What is the legal effect of these statements and decisions? These bodies are made up of individuals acting in their own capacities and not as representatives of states; they are created by states through multilateral treaties or other instruments; and they are authorized only to make recommendations, not to adopt legally binding decisions. Are the statements and decisions of such institutions secondary sources akin to the "judicial decisions and teachings of the most highly qualified publicists" mentioned in Article 38 of the Statute of the International Court of Justice? Are they a form of practice contributing to the formation of customary international law? Note also the relationship between the implementation of international standards and their interpretation and further development by national and international institutions, a topic taken up in subsequent chapters.

Chapter 4

Human Rights in Extremis

How Can Human Rights Be Protected in Civil Strife and Armed Conflict?

Traditional international law made sharp distinctions between peace and war, between civil war and international conflict, between civilians and soldiers. In a time that was based on the rights and duties of states as such, that approach may have made sense. For contemporary international human rights law, however, whose fundamental task is the protection of the rights of individuals, these distinctions often seem woefully artificial. The first three chapters examined the substantial body of international law — conventional, customary, and "soft" law — that has been developed for times of peace. This chapter is concerned with the law that applies in time of conflict, whether internal or international, ranging from sporadic terrorist attacks to sustained war (generally referred to somewhat euphemistically as "armed conflict").

The first section examines human rights law and the derogations from or suspensions of that law that are permissible under certain circumstances. The next three sections consider the "law of war" or "humanitarian law" that applies to armed conflicts; different legal regimes apply depending on whether such conflicts are international or internal. The final two sections consider the possible overlap between these two bodies of law, which have different historical origins and which have operated in quite different institutional settings, particularly in light of the contemporary "war on terror."

As we begin the twenty-first century, humanity does not seem to have made much progress in ridding itself of war. Indeed, war, whether against terrorism or rogue states or internal enemies, is becoming increasingly internationalized, and demands for accountability and punishment have become more frequent and more strident (international criminal responsibility is discussed more fully in Chapter 11). While we wait for peace to break out, it may be important to develop a more coherent, comprehensive, and effective body of international human rights and humanitarian law, so that the traditional barriers between them are broken down and innocent victims are not left without protection. This chapter provides some of the raw materials for that effort.

I. A Mote in the Eye of Freedom: Interrogation at Abu Ghraib Prison, Iraq[1]

On the day after Christmas 2002, the Washington Post published a troubling investigative report exploring interrogation practices employed by U.S. military personnel on captured al Qaeda operatives and Taliban commanders in Afghanistan. It had been over a year since U.S. bombs had begun to fall on Taliban and al Qaeda strongholds in response to the September 11, 2001, terrorist attacks on the World Trade Center and the Pentagon. American firepower had helped the Afghan Northern Alliance rout the Taliban, eliminating the crucial safe haven of the world's best-known terrorist network. Military victory in Afghanistan was only one objective among several of Operation Enduring Freedom, however.

1. Portions of this summary are drawn from Patrick McGreevey, F'06, "Intelligence and Interrogation: The U.S. Legal Perspective on Torture and Cruel, Inhuman and Degrading Treatment — After 9/11, Did the Gloves Come Off?" (May 2005). — Eds.

Scores of Al Qaeda's leading operatives, including Osama bin Laden, and numbers of worldwide "sleeper" cells were still believed to be on the loose and to pose a grave threat to the United States. Exploiting the captured detainees in U.S. custody for any information they had on plans for future attacks or the whereabouts of their cohorts was a critical priority for U.S. national security.

The following report offered the public its first glimpse of the methods America's security apparatus was employing to obtain this information.

Dana Priest and Barton Gellman, *U.S. Decries Abuse but Defends Interrogations; "Stress and Duress" Tactics Used on Terrorism Suspects Held in Secret Overseas Facilities*

Wash. Post, Dec. 26, 2002, at A1

Deep inside the forbidden zone at the U.S.-occupied Bagram air base in Afghanistan, around the corner from the detention center and beyond the segregated clandestine military units, sits a cluster of metal shipping containers protected by a triple layer of concertina wire. The containers hold the most valuable prizes in the war on terrorism — captured al Qaeda operatives and Taliban commanders. . . .

In the multifaceted global war on terrorism waged by the Bush administration, one of the most opaque — yet vital — fronts is the detention and interrogation of terrorism suspects. U.S. officials have said little publicly about the captives' names, numbers or whereabouts, and virtually nothing about interrogation methods. But interviews with several former intelligence officials and 10 current U.S. national security officials — including several people who witnessed the handling of prisoners — provide insight into how the U.S. government is prosecuting this part of the war.

The picture that emerges is of a brass-knuckled quest for information, often in concert with allies of dubious human rights reputation, in which the traditional lines between right and wrong, legal and inhumane, are evolving and blurred.

While the U.S. government publicly denounces the use of torture, each of the current national security officials interviewed for this article defended the use of violence against captives as just and necessary. They expressed confidence that the American public would back their view. The CIA, which has primary responsibility for interrogations, declined to comment.

"If you don't violate someone's human rights some of the time, you probably aren't doing your job," said one official who has supervised the capture and transfer of accused terrorists. "I don't think we want to be promoting a view of zero tolerance on this. That was the whole problem for a long time with the CIA." . . .

U.S. officials oversee most of the interrogations, especially those of the most senior captives. In some cases, highly trained CIA officers question captives through interpreters. In others, the intelligence agency undertakes a "false flag" operation using fake decor and disguises meant to deceive a captive into thinking he is imprisoned in a country with a reputation for brutality, when, in reality, he is still in CIA hands. Sometimes, female officers conduct interrogations, a psychologically jarring experience for men reared in a conservative Muslim culture where women are never in control.

In other cases, usually involving lower-level captives, the CIA hands them to foreign intelligence services — notably those of Jordan, Egypt and Morocco — with a list of questions the agency wants answered. These "extraordinary renditions" are done without resort to legal process and usually involve countries with security services known for using brutal means.

According to U.S. officials, nearly 3,000 suspected al Qaeda members and their supporters have been detained worldwide since Sept. 11, 2001. About 625 are at the U.S. military's confinement facility at Guantánamo Bay, Cuba. Some officials estimated that fewer than 100 captives have been rendered to third countries. Thousands have been arrested and held with U.S. assistance in countries known for brutal treatment of prisoners, the officials said.

At a Sept. 26 joint hearing of the House and Senate intelligence committees, Cofer Black, then head of the CIA Counterterrorist Center, spoke cryptically about the agency's new forms of "operational flexibility" in dealing with suspected terrorists. "This is a very highly classified area, but I have to say that all you need to know: There was a before 9/11, and there was an after 9/ 11," Black said. "After 9/11 the gloves come off."

According to one official who has been directly involved in rendering captives into foreign hands, the understanding is, "We don't kick the [expletive] out of them. We send them to other countries so they can kick the [expletive] out of them." Some countries are known to use mind-altering drugs such as sodium pentathol, said other officials involved in the process....

U.S. National Security Council spokesman Sean McCormack declined to comment earlier this week on CIA or intelligence-related matters. But, he said: "The United States is treating enemy combatants in U.S. government control, wherever held, humanely and in a manner consistent with the principles of the Third Geneva Convention of 1949."

The convention outlined the standards for treatment of prisoners of war. Suspected terrorists in CIA hands have not been accorded POW status.

Other U.S. government officials, speaking on condition of anonymity, acknowledged that interrogators deprive some captives of sleep, a practice with ambiguous status in international law....

U.S. officials who defend the renditions say the prisoners are sent to these third countries not because of their coercive questioning techniques, but because of their cultural affinity with the captives. Besides being illegal, they said, torture produces unreliable information from people who are desperate to stop the pain. They look to foreign allies more because their intelligence services can develop a culture of intimacy that Americans cannot. They may use interrogators who speak the captive's Arabic dialect and often use the prospects of shame and the reputation of the captive's family to goad the captive into talking.

In a speech on Dec. 11 [2002], CIA director George J. Tenet said that interrogations overseas have yielded significant returns recently....

In contrast to the detention center at Guantánamo Bay, where military lawyers, news reporters and the Red Cross received occasional access to monitor prisoner conditions and treatment, the CIA's overseas interrogation facilities are off-limits to outsiders, and often even to other government agencies. In addition to Bagram and Diego Garcia, the CIA has other secret detention centers overseas, and often uses the facilities of foreign intelligence services.

Free from the scrutiny of military lawyers steeped in the international laws of war, the CIA and its intelligence service allies have the leeway to exert physically and psychologically aggressive techniques, said national security officials and U.S. and European intelligence officers.

Although no direct evidence of mistreatment of prisoners in U.S. custody has come to light, the prisoners are denied access to lawyers or organizations, such as the Red Cross, that could independently assess their treatment. Even their names are secret. . . .

According to Americans with direct knowledge and others who have witnessed the treatment, captives are often "softened up" by MPs and U.S. Army Special Forces troops who beat them up and confine them in tiny rooms. The alleged terrorists are commonly blindfolded and thrown into walls, bound in painful positions, subjected to loud noises and deprived of sleep. The tone of intimidation and fear is the beginning, they said, of a process of piercing a prisoner's resistance.

The take-down teams often "package" prisoners for transport, fitting them with hoods and gags, and binding them to stretchers with duct tape.

Bush administration appointees and career national security officials acknowledged that, as one of them put it, "our guys may kick them around a little bit in the adrenaline of the immediate aftermath." Another said U.S. personnel are scrupulous in providing medical care to captives, adding in a deadpan voice, that "pain control [in wounded patients] is a very subjective thing."

The CIA's participation in the interrogation of rendered terrorist suspects varies from country to country. . . .

The Bush administration maintains a legal distance from any mistreatment that occurs overseas, officials said, by denying that torture is the intended result of its rendition policy. American teams, officials said, do no more than assist in the transfer of suspects who are wanted on criminal charges by friendly countries. But five officials acknowledged, as one of them put it, "that sometimes a friendly country can be invited to 'want' someone we grab." Then, other officials said, the foreign government will charge him with a crime of some sort. . . .

According to present and former officials with firsthand knowledge, the CIA's authoritative Directorate of Operations instructions, drafted in cooperation with the general counsel, tells case officers in the field that they may not engage in, provide advice about or encourage the use of torture by cooperating intelligence services from other countries. . . .

Bush administration officials said the CIA, in practice, is using a narrow definition of what counts as "knowing" that a suspect has been tortured. "If we're not there in the room, who is to say?" said one official conversant with recent reports of renditions. . . .

Over the course of the next year and a half, more stories trickled out into the American press, based on the accounts of both interrogators and detainees, suggesting that the rules of the game regarding permissible interrogation methods had indeed changed. The Bush administration maintained that any illegal misconduct was the work of rogue soldiers or interrogators and not a coordinated policy of the U.S. government.

The American public and its congressional representatives seemed largely satisfied with this explanation and focused their attention on the occupation of

Iraq and the bloody insurgency it had spawned. However, in late April 2004, the dark and murky world of intelligence gathering rose to the surface in a sensational manner, and America's reputation in the world incurred serious damage.

On April 28, 2004, the CBS television program *60 Minutes II* broadcast a series of disturbing photographs taken in the fall of 2003 at Abu Ghraib prison, which is twenty miles from Baghdad. The now infamous photographs depicted naked Iraqi detainees being forced to engage in degrading simulated sex acts, while U.S. military personnel looked on with leering smiles, offering the thumbs-up sign. Other photographs captured a hooded detainee standing on flimsy boxes with electrical cords attached to his fingertips and genitalia; a naked detainee prone on the floor with a leash around his neck, held by a female American soldier at the other end; naked detainees cowering as they are threatened with barking military dogs; and the bodies of dead Iraqis packed in ice. The photos became instant international news, and America's moral credibility plummeted around the world.

Abu Ghraib had been notorious under Saddam Hussein's regime for the brutal treatment of prisoners. Now, it seemed, the U.S. was following in Saddam's footsteps.

President George W. Bush denounced the abhorrent behavior, describing it as the acts of a few bad apples which did not represent America or its policies. Yet, the revelations did not stop there.

In the coming weeks, further details emerged regarding America's interrogation policies, other violations already investigated, and a series of confidential warnings from the International Committee of the Red Cross (ICRC) which went largely unheeded. At an ICRC press conference in the week following the Abu Ghraib revelations, the ICRC let it be known that, in conducting inspections at Abu Ghraib between March and November 2003, it had found "a broad pattern [of abuse], not individual acts. There was a pattern and a system." Pierre Krähenbühl, ICRC Director of Operations, press conference, May 7, 2004, http://www.icrc.org/Web/Eng/siteeng0.nsf/iwpList74/7EE8626890D74F76C1256E8D005D3861. In February 2004, two months before the Abu Ghraib abuses became public, the ICRC had

submitted a report to the United States in which inspectors reported witnessing ill-treatment of detainees, including "deliberate physical violence" as well as verbal abuse, forced nudity, and prolonged handcuffing in uncomfortable positions, or short-shackling. These abuses, the ICRC charged in its report, were "tantamount to torture."

The issue of what international law applies to detainees at Abu Ghraib, Guantánamo Bay, and elsewhere, as well as the question of whether the treatment described above violates those norms, are the subject of this chapter.

II. Human Rights in Civil Strife and States of Emergency

Much of this chapter concerns the law of war (or humanitarian law) applicable during international and non-international "armed conflict." The applicability of that law, however, depends on the existence of an "armed conflict." As noted below (page 251 infra), Article 1(2) of Protocol II explicitly states that it does not apply "to situations of internal disturbances and tensions, such as riots, isolated and sporadic acts of violence and other acts of a similar nature;" many states deny the applicability of Common Article 3 to such situations, too.

Nevertheless, situations of civil strife can be serious enough to cause governments to assume drastic emergency powers. Whenever they do, there is always danger that the human rights of individuals may be abused. The "war on terror" instituted by the United States and other countries following the attacks on New York and Washington on September 11, 2001, blurs even further the lines separating peace, civil strife, and armed conflict.

International human rights law applies concurrently with relevant humanitarian law in times of both international and non-international armed conflict, but it is often the *only* international legal regime applicable during civil strife and states of emergency, which governments may declare either during "peacetime" or during situations in which tensions and disturbances within the state fall short of actual armed conflict. Thus, human rights law is important not only for the additional protection it may afford during armed conflicts but also for its role during internal disturbances or other emergencies.

The drafters of the International Covenant on Civil and Political Rights (as well as the European and American Conventions) were aware that human rights could not apply normally in all conceivable situations. Thus, Article 4 of the Covenant concedes the necessity of permitting states to derogate from their normal human rights obligations in times of genuine public emergency, although it also seeks to ensure that the most basic human rights remain respected by listing certain core rights from which no derogation, even in time of emergency, is permitted.

The following reading compares the derogation provisions of the major international instruments.

Joan Fitzpatrick, Human Rights in Crisis, The International System for Protecting Rights During States of Emergency

36-38, 52-66 (1994) (notes omitted)

In a United Nations survey of governments the rights most often mentioned as having been the subject of derogations during emergencies were liberty and security of the person, liberty of movement, protection of privacy, freedom of expression and opinion, and the right of peaceful assembly. Many monitors have noted that excessive invasions of these and other rights have occurred during many emergencies, often in association with deprivations of non-derogable rights, such as the right to life and the prohibition on torture. But, as the International Commission of Jurists observed:

> Some writers have emphasized the effects of states of emergency on individual rights, particularly the right to be free from arbitrary deprivation of freedom and the right to a fair trial. This tends to create a somewhat false image of states of emergency, for one of their most fundamental characteristics is precisely the breadth of their impact on a society. They typically affect trade union rights, freedom of opinion, freedom of expression, freedom of association, the right of access to information and ideas, the right to an education, the right to participate in public affairs . . . not only individual rights but also collective rights and rights of peoples, such as the right to development and the right to self-determination.

The scope of these effects naturally results in a potential concern with states of emergency by all the monitoring bodies with an interest in any of this wide range of rights. These potentially extensive effects have also influenced the debate over the drafting of non-treaty-based substantive standards for government behavior during states of emergency. . . .

Two crucial sets of treaty standards were also drafted at approximately the same time as Common Article 3 [of the Geneva Conventions, discussed infra at 247]. Article 15 of the European Convention was drafted primarily during early 1950 with the benefit of almost three years of discussion by drafters of the Covenant on Civil and Political Rights within the United Nations. The derogation article of the European Convention served as a focal point for the debate between two alternate approaches to treaty drafting, which might be called "general enumeration" and "precise definition." The proponents of general enumeration favored drafting a document with positive definitions of rights and no exceptions or restrictions other than a single general limitations clause, similar to Article 29 of the Universal Declaration. The proponents of precise definition, on the other hand, wanted not only specific limitations clauses in many provisions defining particular rights but also a derogation article for emergencies, arguing that these clauses would actually prevent abusive suspension or denial of rights. During the final stages of the drafting process, the attraction of entrenching a list of non-derogable rights swayed a majority to favor inclusion of the derogation article.

Whereas the drafting of the Covenant on Civil and Political Rights dragged on until 1966, debate on the advisability and specific terms of a derogation article occurred during the relatively compressed period between 1947 and 1952. Article 4 became the focus of the division of opinion between the general-enumeration and precise-definition camps, as had Article 15 in the case of the European

Convention. Another key division, leading to an awkward compromise, developed on the question whether the clause on non-derogable rights should include only those rights most important and central to human dignity and most at risk during typical emergencies, or should be expanded to include all rights that no reasonable government would need to limit substantially in any conceivable emergency.

The drafters of the American Convention on Human Rights, who began work in earnest in the 1960s, had the benefit of earlier-drafted human rights treaties as a model and began with an apparent consensus on the precise-definition approach. Moreover, the OAS had the benefit of a specific study of the problem of the protection of human rights during states of emergency, conducted by the Inter-American Commission on Human Rights. This study was undertaken with three aims, which sound rather familiar to anyone who has worked in this field: (1) to examine the history of states of siege in the Americas to see how human rights had been violated; (2) to determine if it would be possible to articulate general principles that could be binding on all countries in the region and that might be incorporated into the internal laws of those countries; and (3) to determine if there might be international organs that could control the juridical and practical regimes of states of siege. The special interest developed with the OAS on protecting human rights during states of emergency may help explain the rather different form the derogation article takes in the American Convention, as compared to those in the European Convention and the Covenant.

A brief comparison of the three derogation articles in the human rights treaties to the relevant portions of the major humanitarian law instruments reveals some interesting similarities and differences, as well as "lacunae," that have attracted ongoing efforts to formulate additional, more complete standards. Discussion will be limited to the substantive aspects of these emergency provisions, since the ensuing chapters will focus upon measures for their implementation. Certain basic principles are embodied in each of the three derogation articles: a threshold of severity of cause, requirements of notification and/or proclamation, good faith motivation, consistency with other international obligations of the derogating state, proportionality between cause and measures taken, non-discrimination in the application of emergency measures, and entrenchment of a core of non-derogable rights.

1. Severity

While the threshold for a legitimate derogation under the three human rights treaties is largely similar, there are interesting variations in terminology. The Covenant offers the simplest formulation: a public emergency threatening the life of the nation. The European Convention in addition makes explicit reference to "war," but the inclusion of war as a ground for derogation is implicit in the Covenant. The text of Article 27 of the American Convention differs strikingly: "war, public danger, or other emergency that threatens the independence or security of a State Party." On the surface, the American Convention might appear to set a lower threshold than the two earlier treaties, but the drafting history of the provision suggests the contrary.

While "the life of the nation" is clearly intended to have a restrictive meaning, its scope is not self-evident. An emergency that threatens the life of the nation must imperil some fundamental element of statehood or survival of the population — for example, the functioning of a major constitutional organ, such as the judiciary or legislature, or the flow of vital supplies. Threats to a discrete segment of the national territory are particularly problematic, although a risk of detachment or loss of control over an important region, which would have a significant impact an central institutions and the general population, would appear to be sufficient. Though not arising out of political causes, certain natural disasters might meet the criteria for derogation.

War presents its own special problems. As a textual matter, it has been suggested that a reference to "war" in a derogation clause encompasses only external war and not internal armed conflict, though the latter would fit under the general term "emergency." Satisfaction of technical criteria far the existence of a state of war is neither necessary nor sufficient for derogation from human rights treaties, though it bears obvious importance with respect to the applicability of international humanitarian law. Derogation would not be permissible in the case of a war that did not threaten the "life of the nation" or "the independence or security" of the derogating state. For example, involvement in foreign hostilities that did not threaten attack or have a significant impact on domestic institutions, or the mere existence of a state of war without active hostilities, would not meet the threshold of severity to justify substantial restrictions on the domestic enjoyment of fundamental rights.

Despite the benefit of the high threshold set in the earlier two human rights treaties and significant experience within the region of problems arising out of states of emergency, initial proposed drafts of the American Convention would have set a very low threshold of severity for derogation. The version prepared by the Inter-American Council of Jurists (IACJ) permitted derogation in undefined "exceptional situations"; the proposals of Chile and Uruguay also adopted this formula, while making if explicit that each state could define such "exceptional situations" for itself. The IACHR [Inter-American Commission on Human Rights], with the benefit of the Martins study, criticized this terminology and adopted a resolution in 1968 stating that suspension of guarantees should be permissible only "when adopted in case of war or other serious public emergency threatening the life of the nation or the security of the State." . . .

During the Conference, the term "public danger" was inserted. Norris and Reiton explain that while this phrase may seem "strikingly broad," it was intended to cover "public calamity" that was "not necessarily a threat to internal or external security." They question the need for this provision, suggesting that the limitations clauses in particular treaty articles would be adequate to permit governments to deal with such natural disasters.

2. Notification And Proclamation

For the present, it is sufficient to note that all three treaties require formal notification, though the details vary in three respects: (1) while the Covenant and the American Convention require that the other states parties be notified through the intermediary of the secretaries-general of the United Nations and the Organization of American States, respectively, the European Convention simply requires notification to the Secretary-General of the Council of Europe, without mentioning the states parties; (2) the Covenant and the American Convention require that this notice be supplied "immediately," while the European Convention is silent as to timing; and (3) the Covenant requires information concerning the provisions from which the state has derogated, the European Convention demands an explanation of the "measures which it has taken," and the American Convention requires information concerning "the provisions the application of which it has suspended, the reasons that gave rise to the suspension, and the date set for the termination of such suspension."

The Covenant is unique among the three in also requiring proclamation of a public emergency. The aim of this provision was to ensure that derogating states also complied with domestic legal requirements for states of emergency.

3. Good Faith Motivation

This requirement is merely implicit in the derogation articles themselves, though it is express in certain other clauses of the three treaties, which provide that no state party may perform any act aimed at the destruction or undue limitation of rights and freedoms protected by the treaties. Thus, a state of emergency declared in order to destroy a democratic system of government would arguably be invalid.

4. Other International Obligations

Each of the three human rights treaties specifically forbids derogations that are inconsistent with the state's other obligations under international law. Chief among these obligations in relevance would be non-derogable rights in customary and conventional international humanitarian law, as well as the more restrictive or demanding provisions of other human rights treaties and customary human rights law (e.g., any human rights that are jus cogens and thus not subject to suspension or denial under any circumstances). An intriguing question is whether these other international obligations are thereby substantively incorporated into the derogation articles and thus subject to the treaty-based monitoring mechanisms.

5. Proportionality

Along with the threshold of severity, the principle of proportionality is the most important and yet most elusive of the substantive limits imposed on the privilege of derogation. The three treaties impose a similar standard — measures in derogation of treaty rights are permitted only to the extent "strictly required by the exigencies of the situation," although the American Convention also makes explicit the preeminently important requirement that such measures may be imposed only "for the period of time strictly required." The principle of proportionality embodied in the derogation clauses has its roots in the principle of necessity, which also forms one of the key pillars of international humanitarian law. The existence of competent, active, and informed organs of supervision, both at the national as well as at the international level, is vital if the proportionality principle is to have meaning in practice.... [B]oth logistical (access to information and ability to act promptly) and attitudinal (deference to national authorities, e.g., by extension of a "margin of appreciation") factors affect the functioning of the various treaty implementation organs.

6. Non-Discrimination

The Covenant and the American Convention include clauses specifying that derogation measures may not be imposed in a manner that discriminates on the grounds of race, color, sex, language, religion, or social origin. Three interesting issues are raised by these clauses: (1) why no similar provision exists in the European Convention, and whether its absence denotes a real substantive difference among the treaties; (2) what the term "discrimination" is intended to mean; and (3) whether this meaning is affected by the further inclusion of the qualifying term "solely" in the Covenant.

Article 15 of the European Convention is silent on the issue of discrimination in the application of emergency measures. Of course the European Convention, like the other two treaties, elsewhere prohibits discrimination on the grounds listed. But these various non-discrimination provisions outside the derogation articles are generally subject to derogation. The issue of discriminatory treatment of minorities in the application of emergency measures was touched on during the drafting of the European Convention, but it never achieved prominence in the discussions, and no concrete proposals far a non-discrimination clause were made. Nevertheless, arbitrary discrimination against disfavored groups of various types would be difficult to justify as being "strictly required." Thus, there may be no substantive difference between the silence of the European Convention and the explicit non-discrimination clauses of the other two treaties, if only arbitrary distinctions are outlawed by the latter....

The idea that only arbitrary discrimination is outlawed by Article 4(1) is underlined by the deliberate inclusion of the word "solely" in its text. Even without this term, however, the reference to discrimination in Article 4 conveys the implication that only arbitrary and unjustifiable distinctions in the application of emergency measures would be outlawed. Thus, where an identifiable racial or religious group poses a distinct security threat not posed by other members of the community, presumably, emergency measures could be deliberately targeted against the group, despite the non-discrimination clause.

The absence of the word "solely" from the non-discrimination clause in Article 27(1) of the American Convention on Human Rights apparently has no intended significance. The word was included in the draft prepared by the IACHR but "disappeared from the final text, and the records of the conference provide no clue as to the reason." Thus, the three treaties would seem to impose a virtually identical non-discrimination obligation, despite disparate phraseology.

7. Non-Derogable Rights

The three treaties diverge dramatically with respect to defining absolute rights never subject to suspension. The process of defining non-derogable rights has been a markedly progressive one, with each later-drafted instrument expanding the core of non-derogable rights. The European Convention begins with just four, sparely defined: the right to life, excepting deaths resulting from lawful acts of war (Article 2); the ban on torture or inhuman or degrading treatment or punishment (Article 3); the prohibition on slavery or servitude (Article 4(1)); and the prohibition on retroactive criminal penalties (Article 7). . . .

The drafters of the Covenant touched on the basic issue whether defining non-derogable rights should proceed from the perspective of identifying those rights most vital to human integrity and most likely at risk during abusive emergencies, or whether those rights should include all provisions whose suspension could not conceivably be necessary during times of public emergency. Article 4(2) appears to be an uneasy compromise between these two camps, especially with respect to the anomalous inclusion of the ban on imprisonment for contractual debt and the provision on freedom of religion, which has the distinction of being non-derogable, yet subject to limitation at all times.

The American Convention is somewhat more consistent in its approach and includes many rights that are not as central as the right to life or the protection against torture, but whose suspension would not be justifiable in an imaginable emergency. The 1966 study by IACHR member Martins favored the approach of listing rights subject to derogation and suggested making suspendable only the provisions on arbitrary detention and prompt notice of charges, interference with private life and correspondence, and prior restraint on publication; the rights of assembly, association, and movement would not need to be included because they would be subject to limitation even under ordinary circumstances, The IACHR draft presented to the Conference of San Jose did not follow this recommendation, but offered instead a list of non-derogable rights only slightly more expansive than that of the Covenant.

During Conference debate, the suggestion was made that the IACHR draft was too vague, and a working group was appointed to redraft the clause. Their product was a major transformation of the IACHR draft, adding not just numerical references to particular treaty articles that would be non-derogable, but deleting three rights and including five new rights. The handiwork of the working group was later modified by the addition to Article 27(2) of the key phrase "the judicial guarantees essential for the protection of such rights," which includes at least some aspects of the protections against arbitrary detention and for due process of law that would have been nonsuspendable under the original IACHR proposal. [See the discussion of this phrase by the Inter-American Court of Human Rights, infra at pages 228-229.]

The gradual expansion of the list of non-derogable rights in the three major human rights treaties and, particularly, the recognition of a core of fundamental process rights for detainees in the American Convention have stimulated non-treaty-based efforts to articulate standards for protection of human rights during states of emergency. Efforts to refine and perfect these standards continue to the present. An awareness that, in some respects, the principles of international humanitarian law are more advanced than those of the human rights treaties has been an especially important factor in stimulating some of these standard-drafting efforts.

Note: Humanitarian Law as a Limitation on the Right of Derogation: Civil Strife and Internal Armed Conflict Contrasted

When a state is involved in an internal armed conflict, Article 4 of the Covenant permits it to declare a state of emergency and derogate from many of its conventional international human rights obligations. On the other hand, the Geneva Conventions and their two Protocols are not subject to derogation on grounds of public emergency, since the very purpose of their adoption is to provide rules to govern situations of armed conflict. The question raised is thus: "In what way do common article 3 and Protocol II limit the power of a state to suspend its international human rights obligations during the existence of an exceptional danger caused by an internal armed conflict?" Hernan Montealegre, *The Compatibility of a State Party's Derogation Under Human Rights Conventions with Its Obligations Under Protocol II and Common Article* 3, 33 Am. U. L. Rev. 41, 44 (1983).

The answer to this question is that the humanitarian law instruments have great potential for limiting a state's right of derogation. An example of this potential is found in the following extract.

> Among the normative rules subject to ... derogation are the fair trial guarantees of article 14 of the Covenant on Civil and Political Rights, article 6 of the European Convention, and article 8 of the American Convention.
>
> On the other hand, the norms of article 3 common to the 1949 Geneva Conventions and those of 1977 Protocol II are not subject to derogation. Indeed, they were formulated to be applied in armed conflict — obviously a situation of grave public emergency which threatens the life of the nation. With respect to procedural due process, article 3 prohibits "the passing of sentences and carrying out of executions without previous judgment pronounced by a regularly constituted court, affording all the judicial guarantees which are recognized as indispensable by civilized peoples." Therefore, for the [192] nations bound by common article 3, their right to derogate from some of the judicial guarantees of the human rights treaties is inconsistent with their non-derogable obligation under article 3. But, ... common article 3 is only a statement of general principles. It does not spell out categorically what judicial guarantees are deemed indispensable by all the peoples of the West, the communist countries, and the third world.
>
> A solution to the conflict between the right to derogate and the non-derogable obligations of common article 3 is suggested by article 6 of Protocol II, which was adopted by the consensus of the western, communist, and third world states represented at the 1974-1977 Diplomatic Conference. Article 6 provides a respectable catalogue of what these indispensable guarantees are, including an independent and impartial tribunal, a continuing opportunity to exercise all necessary rights and means of defense, notice of charges, conviction only on the basis of individual penal responsibility, protection against ex post facto legislation, presumption of innocence, and the privilege against compulsory self-incrimination. I doubt that there were many military lawyers present when the human rights treaties were drafted, but military lawyers were represented on most delegations at the 1949 and 1977 diplomatic conferences on the Law of Armed Conflict and they did not seem to think that

> there was any reason to dispense with fair trial standards, even in the heat of a civil war.
>
> Presently, only [159] states are bound by Protocol II, and it may be a long time before it attains the same universal acceptance as common article 3. Article 6 of Protocol II serves as an authoritative declaration of the judicial guarantees deemed indispensable by civilized peoples. Therefore, derogations from fair trial guarantees under the human rights instruments are effectively precluded by common article 3 as interpreted by article 6 of Protocol II, and as a result, the parallel norms of the human sights treaties are strengthened and reinforced.

Waldemar A. Solf, *Problems with the Application of Norms Governing Interstate Armed Conflict to Non-International Armed Conflict*, 13 Ga. J. Intl. & Comp. L. 291, 295-296 (1983).

The legal position is different, of course, where a state of emergency is declared in response to civil strife not rising to the level of a non-international armed conflict. Neither Common Article 3 nor Protocol II being applicable in such a situation, a state's derogation could not easily be said to conflict with any obligation under them per se, except to the extent that these humanitarian instruments now reflect customary international law.

Note: Monitoring States of Emergency

Merely determining whether or not a state of emergency exists in a particular state is often a difficult task, as evidenced by the work of a special rapporteur of the UN Sub-Commission on the Promotion and Protection of Human Rights between 1985 and 1997. The rapporteur drew up and updated annually a list of countries that proclaim or terminate a state of emergency; he also studied the legality of such declarations and their impact on human rights and recommended a number of "concrete measures" that would guarantee respect for human rights during emergencies. During the decade of his mandate, the rapporteur identified approximately 60 states or territories in which de facto or de jure emergencies were declared, extended, maintained, or terminated. See Tenth Annual Report and List of States Which, Since 1 January 1985, Have Proclaimed, Extended or Terminated a State of Emergency, U.N. Doc. E/CN.4/Sub.2/1997/19 and Add.1 (1997). Some of the problems faced by the rapporteur are discussed in Fitzpatrick, supra page 217, at 168-173.

Although the UN secretariat continues to update the list, it now relies only on UN sources, based on information provided by states. "It should be understood accordingly that the list cannot purport to be complete." Report of the Office of the High Commissioner for Human Rights, List of States Which Have Proclaimed or Continued a State of Emergency, UN Doc. E/CN.4/Sub.2/2005/6, para. 3 (July 7, 2005).

As discussed in Chapter 7, the Human Rights Committee fulfills its supervisory role with respect to the Covenant on Civil and Political Rights through reviewing state reports and, for those states that have accepted it, examining individual complaints filed under the Optional Protocol. The Committee also has issued two General Comments concerning derogations; while the first (1981) Comment did little more than paraphrase the Covenant, the second (which replaces the first) offers a great deal more detail to guide states in their interpretation of Article 4. It also clarifies that even some rights not listed as nonderogable under Article 4(2) may nonetheless be protected from suspension.

Human Rights Committee, States of Emergency (Article 4)

General Comment no. 29, UN Doc. CCPR/C/21/Rev.1/Add.11 (2001) (notes omitted)

6. The fact that some of the provisions of the Covenant have been listed in article 4 (paragraph 2), as not being subject to derogation does not mean that other articles in the Covenant may be subjected to derogations at will, even where a threat to the life of the nation exists....

11.... States parties may in no circumstances invoke article 4 of the Covenant as justification for acting in violation of humanitarian law or peremptory norms of international law, for instance by taking hostages, by imposing collective punishments, through arbitrary deprivations of liberty or by deviating from fundamental principles of fair trial, including the presumption of innocence....

13. In those provisions of the Covenant that are not listed in article 4, paragraph 2, there are elements that in the Committee's opinion cannot be made subject to lawful derogation under article 4. Some illustrative examples are presented below.

(a) All persons deprived of their liberty shall be treated with humanity and with respect for the inherent dignity of the human person. Although this right, prescribed in article 10 of the Covenant, is not separately mentioned in the list of non-derogable rights in article 4, paragraph 2, the Committee believes that here the Covenant expresses a norm of general international law not subject to derogation. This is supported by the reference to the inherent dignity of the human person in the preamble to the Covenant and by the close connection between articles 7 and 10.

(b) The prohibitions against taking of hostages, abductions or unacknowledged detention are not subject to derogation. The absolute nature of these prohibitions, even in times of emergency, is justified by their status as norms of general international law.

(c) The Committee is of the opinion that the international protection of the rights of persons belonging to minorities includes elements that must be respected in all circumstances. This is reflected in the prohibition against genocide in international law, in the inclusion of a non-discrimination clause in article 4 itself (paragraph 1), as well as in the non-derogable nature of article 18.

(d) As confirmed by the Rome Statute of the International Criminal Court, deportation or forcible transfer of population without grounds permitted under international law, in the form of forced displacement by expulsion or other coercive means from the area in which the persons concerned are lawfully present, constitutes a crime against humanity. The legitimate right to derogate from article 12 of the Covenant during a state of emergency can never be accepted as justifying such measures.

(e) No declaration of a state of emergency made pursuant to article 4, paragraph 1, may be invoked as justification for a State party to engage itself, contrary to article 20, in propaganda for war, or in advocacy of national, racial or religious hatred that would constitute incitement to discrimination, hostility or violence....

16. Safeguards related to derogation, as embodied in article 4 of the Covenant, are based on the principles of legality and the rule of law inherent in the Covenant as a whole. As certain elements of the right to a fair trial are explicitly guaranteed under international humanitarian law during armed conflict, the Committee finds no justification for derogation from these guarantees during other emergency situations. The Committee is of the opinion that the principles of legality and the rule of law require that fundamental requirements of fair trial must be respected during a state of emergency. Only a court of law may try and convict a person for a criminal offence. The presumption of innocence must be respected. In order to protect non-derogable rights, the right to take proceedings before a court to enable the court to decide without delay on the lawfulness of detention, must not be diminished by a State party's decision to derogate from the Covenant.

Although the Committee has addressed critical remarks to states during its examination of their reports, these do not appear to constitute an effective means of determining the legitimacy of derogations. "The widespread failure to comply with the notification requirement according to article 4(3), the exclusively legalistic approach which is often unrealistic, and the unwillingness of some States fully to cooperate with the Committee are among the main setbacks of the reporting procedure." Jaime Oraá, *Human Rights in States of Emergency in International Law* 50 (1992). "The article 40 report process fails as a device for fact-finding in derogation situations because it is unfocused, subject to substantial delays, and unequipped either to produce or to test the veracity of relevant information." Fitzpatrick, supra page 217, at 84. More recently, however, the Committee has begun to take "special decisions" and to request that states in which de facto or de jure emergencies exist provide the Committee with supplemental information, See id. at 94-95. In 1993, the Committee amended its rules of procedure to permit its chairman, after consulting other members, to request such additional reports from states.

The Committee has clearly established the principle that the mere declaration of a state of emergency is insufficient to justify it without further details. In an early case filed against Uruguay under the Optional Protocol, for example, the Committee declared:

> 8.3 Although the sovereign right of a State party to declare a state of emergency is not questioned, yet, in the specific context of the present communication, the Human Rights Committee is of the opinion that a State, by merely invoking the existence of exceptional circumstances, cannot evade the obligations which it has undertaken by ratifying the Covenant. Although the substantive right to take derogatory measures may not depend on a formal notification being made pursuant to article 4, paragraph 3, of the Covenant, the State party concerned is duty-bound to give a sufficiently detailed account of the relevant facts when it invokes article 4, paragraph 1, of the Covenant in proceedings under the Optional Protocol. It is the function of the Human Rights Committee, acting under the Optional Protocol, to

> see to it that States parties live up to their commitments under the Covenant. In order to discharge this function and to assess whether a situation of the kind described in article 4, paragraph 1, of the Covenant exists in the country concerned, it needs full and comprehensive information. If the respondent Government does not furnish the required justification itself, as it is required to do under article 4, paragraph 2, of the Optional Protocol and article 4, paragraph 3, of the Covenant, the Human Rights Committee cannot conclude that valid reasons exist to legitimize a departure from the normal legal regime prescribed by the Covenant.

Landinelli Silva v. Uruguay, Communication No. 34/1978, Report of the Hum. Rts. Comm., U.N. Doc. A/36/40 (1981), reprinted in 2 Y.B. Human Rts. Comm. 1981-1982, at 307, 308 (1989). Also see the Inter-American Commission's 1980 Report on the Situation of Human Rights in Argentina, extracts from which may be found in Chapter 9, page 718.

The European Commission and Court of Human Rights may only address the legitimacy of a derogation in the context of a specific case, which may be brought by an individual or another state. One commentator observes that "[t]he Commission has taken the lead among intergovernmental bodies in developing the formal jurisprudence of states of emergency and has made invaluable contributions to the definition of the elements of permissible and impermissible emergencies. Nevertheless, it also has been cautious and somewhat deferential to governments." Fitzpatrick, supra page 217, at 194. An example of that caution is reflected in the following excerpt from the European Court of Human Rights.

> It falls in the first place to each Contracting State, with its responsibility for "the life of [its] nation", to determine whether that life is threatened by a "public emergency" and, if so, how far it is necessary to go in attempting to overcome the emergency. By reason of their direct and continuous contact with the pressing needs of the moment, the national authorities are in principle in a better position than the international judge to decide both on the presence of such an emergency and on the nature and scope of derogations necessary to avert it. In this matter Article 15(1) (of the European Convention) leaves those authorities a wide margin of appreciation.
>
> Nevertheless, the States do not enjoy an unlimited power in this respect. The Court, which . . . is responsible for ensuring the observance of the States' engagements, is empowered to rule on whether the States have gone beyond the "extent strictly required by the exigencies" of the crisis. The domestic margin of appreciation is thus accompanied by a European supervision.

Ireland v. United Kingdom, European Ct. Hum. Rts. (ser. A), No. 25, at 78-79 (Jan. 18, 1978) (citations omitted).

In contrast to the Human Rights Committee and the European system, the Inter-American Commission on Human Rights has the authority to examine states of emergency on its own initiative, and it has frequently done so. It has also addressed derogations in the context of individual complaints. See generally Fitzpatrick, supra page 91, at 178-189; Oraá, supra page 226, at 51-55.

The Inter-American Court of Human Rights significantly expanded the scope of non-derogable rights that must be protected, even in emergencies, in two advisory opinions it delivered in 1987. The opinions responded to separate requests from the Inter-American Commission and the government of Uruguay to clarify the prohibition in the American Convention on Human Rights against suspending "the judicial guarantees essential for the protection" of the non-derogable rights set forth in Article 27(2) of the Convention. This opinion clearly influenced the Human Rights Committee's 2001 General Comment, excerpted above.

Habeas Corpus in Emergency Situations

Inter-Am. Ct. Hum. Rts., Advisory Opinion OC-8/87 of Jan. 30, 1987, Ser. A No. 8, at 38, 41-42, 48 (1987)

20. It cannot be denied that under certain circumstances the suspension of guarantees may be the only way to deal with emergency situations and, thereby, to preserve the highest values of a democratic society. The Court cannot, however, ignore the fact that abuses may result from the application of emergency measures not objectively justified in the light of the requirements prescribed in Article 27 and the principles contained in other here relevant international instruments. This has, in fact, been the experience of our hemisphere....

27. As the Court has already noted, in serious emergency situations it is lawful to temporarily suspend certain rights and freedoms whose free exercise must, under normal circumstances, be respected and guaranteed by the State. However, since not all of these rights and freedoms may be suspended even temporarily, it is imperative that "the judicial guarantees essential for (their) protection" remain in force. Article 27(2) does not link these judicial guarantees to any specific provision of the Convention, which indicates that what is important is that these judicial remedies have the character of being essential to ensure the protection of those rights.

28. The determination as to what judicial remedies are "essential" for the protection of the rights which may not be suspended will differ depending upon the rights that are at stake. The "essential" judicial guarantees necessary to guarantee the rights that deal with the physical integrity of the human person must of necessity differ from those that seek to protect the right to a name, for example, which is also non-derogable.

29. It follows from what has been said above that the judicial remedies that must be considered to be essential within the meaning of Article 27(2) are those that ordinarily will effectively guarantee the full exercise of the rights and freedoms protected by that provision and whose denial or restriction would endanger their full enjoyment.

30. The guarantees must be not only essential but also judicial. The expression "judicial" can only refer to those judicial remedies that are truly capable of protecting these rights. Implicit in this conception is the active involvement of an independent and impartial judicial body having the power to pass on the lawfulness of measures adopted in a state of emergency....

42. From what has been said before, it follows that writs of habeas corpus and of "amparo" are among those judicial remedies that are essential for the protection of various rights whose derogation is prohibited by Article 27(2) and that serve, moreover, to preserve legality in a democratic society.

43. The Court must also observe that the Constitutions and legal systems of the States Parties that authorize, expressly or by implication, the suspension of the legal remedies of habeas corpus or of "amparo" in emergency situations cannot be

deemed to be compatible with the international obligations imposed on these States by the Convention.

In the second opinion, the Court held that the "essential" judicial guarantees not subject to derogation included, in addition to amparo and habeas corpus, "any other effective remedy before judges or competent tribunals, which is designed to guarantee the respect of the rights and freedoms whose suspension is not authorized by the [American] Convention . . . [and which] should be exercised within the framework and the principles of due process of law." Inter-Am. Ct. Hum. Rts., Advisory Opinion OC-9/87 of Oct. 6, 1987, Judicial Guarantees in States of Emergency, Ser. A No. 9, at 48 (1987). Consider the applicability of these opinions to the situation of detainees at Guantánamo, discussed infra at 767.

Note: Limitation Clauses

The focus on derogations sometimes obscures the fact that numerous articles of the Civil and Political Covenant, while guaranteeing rights, simultaneously permit states parties to limit or restrict those rights for various reasons, even absent the existence of a public emergency. Limitation clauses found in the Covenant permit the restriction of human rights for purposes of the protection of the rights of others (Arts. 12(3), 18(3), 19(3)(a), 21, and 22(2)), national security (Arts. 12(3), 14(1), 19(3), 21, and 22(2)), public safety (Arts. 18(3), 21, and 22(2)), public order (*ordre public*) (Arts. 12(3), 14(1), 18(3), 19(3), 21, and 22(2)), public health (Arts. 12(3), 18(3), 19(3), 21, and 22(2)), and public morals (Arts. 12(3), 14(1), 18(3), 19(3), 21, and 22(2)). Similar provisions are found in the regional human rights treaties.

As Professor Kiss notes,

> It is important to distinguish between derogation from rights in time of public emergency . . . and the permissible limitations on rights [authorized by the Covenant]. Although the circumstance permitting derogations, "public emergency which threatens the life of the nation," resembles one of the grounds for possible limitations, "national security," derogations and limitations differ in character and scope, in the circumstances in which they may be imposed, and in the methods by which they may be effected. Derogations in time of emergency are clearly intended to have only a temporary character; limitations, in contrast, can be permanent. Limitations on guaranteed rights must be provided by law but there is no such requirement for temporary derogations. Certain articles of the Covenant are not subject to derogations, for example Article 18 which provides for freedom of thought, conscience and religion, yet such rights are expressly made subject to possible limitations.

Alexandre Kiss, "Permissible Limitations on Rights," in *The International Bill of Rights: The Covenant on Civil and Political Rights* 290 (L. Henkin ed. 1981). See generally *Symposium: Limitation and Derogation Provisions in the International Covenant on Civil and Political Rights*, 7 Hum. Rts. Q. 1 (1985), which includes the text of the Siracusa Principles on the Limitation and Derogation Provisions in the International Covenant on Civil and Political Rights, adopted by 31 international law experts in 1984.

The International Law Association's Committee on the Enforcement of Human Rights Law produced a lengthy report on Minimum Standards of Human Rights Norms in a State of Exception and ultimately adopted the Paris Minimum Standards of Human Rights Norms in a State of Emergency. ILA, Report of the Sixty-First Conference 1, 56 (Paris 1984); the standards are reprinted in Richard B. Lillich, *The Paris Minimum Standards of Human Rights Norms in a State of Emergency*, 79 Am. J. Intl. L. 1072, 1073 (1985). For an extensive commentary on the Paris Minimum Standards, see Subrata Roy Chowdhury, *Rule of Law in a State of Emergency* (1989).

Comments and Questions

1. The concept of "margin of appreciation" has frequently been criticized as granting too much discretion to states, precisely in situations when human rights are likely to be at risk. Do you agree with the European Court of Human Rights that "national authorities are in principle in a better position than the international judge to decide both on the presence of such an emergency and on the nature and scope of derogations necessary to avert it"? See, e.g., Jeffrey A. Brauch, *The Margin of Appreciation and the Jurisprudence of the European Court of Human Rights: Threat to the Rule of Law*, 11 Colum. J. Eur. L. 113 (2004); Thomas A. O'Donnell, *The Margin of Appreciation Doctrine: Standards in the Jurisprudence of the European Court of Human Rights*, 4 Hum. Rts. Q. 474 (1982).

2.Read President Bush's address in the aftermath of the September 11, 2001, attacks, infra page 268. Does the "war on terror" constitute an "emergency which threatens the life of the nation" under Article 4 of the Covenant on Civil and Political Rights, to which the United States is a party? If so, why has the United States not filed a notice of derogation under Article 4(3)?

III. The Traditional Law of War: International Armed Conflict

Note: *Historical Roots of the Concern for Human Rights in the Law of War*

Beginning at least as far back as the Middle Ages (and probably a good deal further), people have thought about the association between justice and warfare from two basic perspectives: from the standpoint of the decision to resort to war (jus ad bellum) and from the standpoint of the actual conduct of the war once hostilities had begun (jus in bello). By the nineteenth century, international lawyers had more or less abandoned questions of jus ad bellum — of the just war — to philosophers and theologians. Lawyers by then had accepted the view that states had the sovereign right to settle their differences by resort to arms if they so chose. Instead, they concentrated their energies on the questions of jus in bello, on right and wrong ways of making war.

For a long time, little attention was accorded to the development of detailed rules for the protection of civilians. The assumption behind this inattention was that the best way of protecting civilians was by ensuring that the horrors of battle affected only the military forces of the participating states. Civilians were sought (and thought) to be protected by the sharp distinction drawn between them and combatants. If civilians could be kept out of the fray altogether, the reasoning ran, then a detailed body of rules for their protection would be unnecessary. On that supposition, the nineteenth-century pioneers of the modern law of war devoted their attention to developing rules for the humane treatment of soldiers — for the wounded and sick, for prisoners of war, for the banning of particularly inhumane types of weapons, and so forth. Only during the course of the twentieth century did it become apparent that it would be necessary for the law of war to broaden its concerns in certain important ways.

G.I.A.D. Draper, *Human Rights and the Law of War*

12 Va. J. Intl. L. 326, 326-333 (1972)

I. Human Development: Human Rights and the Law of War

The Law of War in its historical development ingested humanitarian restraints and prohibitions relatively late in its long history. At some time in history, probably in the 18th century, the Law of War began to pay some attention to humanitarian considerations. The matter needs careful investigation, but I suspect that the writings of Rousseau, though much maligned, form some clues to the process. In the Contrat Social, published in 1762 and subsequently condemned and publicly burnt in Geneva, Rousseau gave expression to certain ideas which have had considerable ethical, juridical, and political consequences. One such statement was:

> War is not, therefore, any relation between man and man, but a relation between state and state in which individuals are enemies only accidentally, not as men, or even as citizens, but as soldiers. . . .

By the mid-19th century, the humanitarian movement gathered force under the impact of a number of diverse, social, moral, political, scientific, military and economic factors. Religious considerations, so decisive in the early formation of the old Law of Arms, the precursor of our Law of War, were not controlling in the infusion of humanitarian considerations into the 19th century Law of War. It will be recalled that the Red Cross emblem has no Christian connotation, but is merely the heraldic arms of the Swiss Confederation, a white cross on a red background, reversed, as tribute to the origin of the Red Cross movement in that country inspired by Henry Dunant.

The ideas lying behind the first Geneva Convention of 1864, the direct outcome of the appalling suffering on the battlefield of Solferino in 1854, dealing exclusively with the treatment of the sick and wounded as well as medical services and installations, and the powerful de Martens preamble to the Hague Convention No. IV of 1907 on the Law of War on Land, both give us the climate of humanitarian sentiment of the second half of the 19th century. De Martens, a Lutheran by religion, and a German-Balt by parentage, was converted to the Russian Orthodox faith. He became Professor of International Law at the Imperial University of St. Petersburg and held a senior position in the Imperial Foreign Ministry as well as his Chair at the University. He published his main work, in two volumes entitled International Law of Civilized Nations, in 1882. He was one of the moving forces at the First Hague Peace Conference of 1899, convened by his master, Czar Nicholas I. In particular he was the draftsman of the famous Preamble to the Hague Convention No. IV, of 1907, which, in part, reads thus:

> Being animated by the desire to serve, even in this extreme case (the resort to armed conflict), the interest of humanity and the ever progressive needs of civilization;... Until a more complete code of the laws of war can be drawn up, the High Contracting Parties deem it expedient to declare that, in cases not covered by the rules adopted by them, the inhabitants and the belligerents remain under the protection and governance of the principles of the law of nations, derived from the usages established among civilized peoples, from the laws of humanity and from the dictates of the public conscience.

This basic formula is today repeated and inserted in each of the four Geneva Conventions of 1949 for the Protection of War Victims.

The ideas reflected in this formula are still a long way from our modern ideas of Human Rights, but the parentage is surely there....

II. Post War Developments

A. Human Rights

In the main it can be said that in the League of Nations era the direct nexus between the idea of Human Rights and the existing Law of War was not envisaged. No doubt, the great improvement made by the International Committee of the Red Cross and the League of Nations in the establishment of the two Geneva Conventions of 1929, dealing with the better treatment of the Sick and Wounded in the Armed Forces and of Prisoners of War, respectively, and the Geneva Gas Protocol of 1925, a very relevant instrument of law today, furthered the humanitarian endeavor. As yet, however, the idea that individuals should receive specified human rights, simply as human beings and determined by that nature of that central entity, at the hands of International Law, was substantially something for the future. The critical period in this development arrived with the nightmare experiences of World War II and the establishment of the Charter of the United Nations in 1945. It is that appalling experience and that basic instrument of International Law which brings effectively into juxtaposition Human Rights and the Law of War.... The nexus that the framers of the U.N. Charter saw between the gross criminality of State aggression by armed forces and the no less gross denial of human worth within the frontiers of such States rammed home in a way that mankind was not likely to forget the connection between aggressive war and the total disregard of the individual. . . .

A. *Protecting Combatants: The First Three 1949 Geneva Conventions*

Not only was the focus at Nuremberg principally upon war crimes, but it has remained so thereafter. See U.S. Army, *The Law of Land Warfare* 178 (Field Manual 27-10, C 1, 1976): "members of the armed forces will normally be concerned only with those offenses constituting 'war crimes.'" However, it should be noted that such crimes may be committed by any person or persons, civilian as well as military. Id. Since "[e]very violation of the law of war is a war crime," id., just what constitutes the law of war becomes exceptionally important. Although some of it is customary international law, by far the vast bulk of the law of war is derived from law-making treaties, especially the Hague and Geneva Conventions. Id. at 4.

The Geneva Conventions, the focus of this chapter, were adopted in 1949, three years after the completion of the Nuremberg Trials. Three of these Conventions replaced earlier instruments and deal with (1) Wounded and Sick in the Armed Forces in the Field; (2) Wounded, Sick and Ship-wrecked Members of the Armed Forces at Sea; and (3) Prisoners of War.

While much of this chapter is concerned with the treatment of civilians, the Third Geneva Convention is relevant to the treatment that occurred at Abu Ghraib and elsewhere. The most important provisions are the following:

Third Geneva Convention Relative to the Treatment of Prisoners of War

75 U.N.T.S. 135 (Aug. 12, 1949)

Requirement of Humane Treatment

ARTICLE 13

Prisoners of war must at all times be humanely treated. Any unlawful act or omission by the Detaining Power causing death or seriously endangering the health of a prisoner of war in its custody is prohibited, and will be regarded as a serious breach of the present Convention. In particular, no prisoner of war may be subjected to physical mutilation or to medical or scientific experiments of any kind which are not justified by the medical, dental or hospital treatment of the prisoner concerned and carried out in his interest.

Likewise, prisoners of war must at all times be protected, particularly against acts of violence or intimidation and against insults and public curiosity.

Measures of reprisal against prisoners of war are prohibited.

ARTICLE 14

Prisoners of war are entitled in all circumstances to respect for their persons and their honour.

Women shall be treated with all the regard due to their sex and shall in all cases benefit by treatment as favorable as that granted to men.

Prisoners of war shall retain the full civil capacity which they enjoyed at the time of their capture. The Detaining Power may not restrict the exercise, either within or without its own territory, of the rights such capacity confers except in so far as the captivity requires.

Permissible Interrogation of POWS

ARTICLE 17

Every prisoner of war, when questioned on the subject, is bound to give only his surname, first names and rank, date of birth, and army, regimental, personal or serial number, or failing this, equivalent information.

If he willfully infringes this rule, he may render himself liable to a restriction of the privileges accorded to his rank or status. . . .

No physical or mental torture, nor any other form of coercion, may be inflicted on prisoners of war to secure from them information of any kind whatever. Prisoners of war who refuse to answer may not be threatened, insulted, or exposed to any unpleasant or disadvantageous treatment of any kind.

Prisoners of war who, owing to their physical or mental condition, are unable to state their identity, shall be handed over to the medical service. The identity of such prisoners shall be established by all possible means, subject to the provisions of the preceding paragraph.

The questioning of prisoners of war shall be carried out in a language which they understand.

All Forms of Torture and Cruelty Forbidden

ARTICLE 87

Collective punishment for individual acts, corporal punishment, imprisonment in premises without daylight and, in general, any form of torture or cruelty, are forbidden. . . .

Since the United States has provided, in what is now Article 18 of the Uniform Code of Military Justice, 70A Stat. 43, 10 U.S.C. §818 (1994), that "[g]eneral courts-martial also have jurisdiction to try any person who by the law of war is subject to trial by a military tribunal and may adjudge any punishment permitted by the law of war," the law of war in effect has became part of U.S. domestic law (in this case without the necessity of additional federal legislation). Indeed, at the time the

Senate gave its advice and consent to the Geneva Conventions, the Department of Justice stated that "[a] review of existing legislation reveals no need to enact further legislation in order to provide effective penal sanctions for those violations of the Geneva Convention which are designated as grave breaches." Hearing on the Geneva Conventions for the Protection of War Victims Before the Senate Comm. on Foreign Relations, 84th Cong., 1st Sess. 58 (1955). Subsequently, in a 1967 communication to the UN Secretary-General, the United States, citing Article 18, acknowledged that "[t]hus, the law of war is incorporated into United States military law." Quoted from Jordan J. Paust, *My Lai and Vietnam: Norms, Myths and Leader Responsibility*, 57 Mil. L. Rev. 94, 124 (1972). See Ex parte Quirin, 317 U.S. 1, 28 (1942). As Paust points out, "prosecutions of U.S. troops for violations of the law of war have been in military fora and generally for violations of our domestic law as in prosecutions for military offenses under the present Uniform Code of Military Justice." Id. at 117. The Abu Ghraib defendants, for example, were prosecuted under the Uniform Code of Military Justice (UCMJ).

The law of war relevant to this section of the chapter is summarized conveniently in the following eight paragraphs from the U.S. Army's publication *The Law of Land Warfare*, whose purpose is "to provide authoritative guidance to military personnel on the customary and treaty law applicable to the conduct of warfare on land. . . ." Id. at 3.

U.S. Army, *Law of Land Warfare*

Field Manual 27-10, Change 1 (July 15, 1976)

85. Killing of Prisoners

A commander may not put his prisoners to death because their presence retards his movements or diminishes his power of resistance by necessitating a large guard, or by reason of their consuming supplies, or because it appears certain that they will regain their liberty through the impending success of their forces. It is likewise unlawful for a commander to kill his prisoners on grounds of self-preservation, even in the case of airborne or commando operations, although the circumstances of the operation may make necessary rigorous supervision of and restraint upon the movement of prisoners of war.

498. Crimes Under International Law

Any person, whether a member of the armed forces or a civilian, who commits an act which constitutes a crime under international law is responsible therefore and liable to punishment. Such offenses in connection with war comprise:

a. Crimes against peace.
b. Crimes against humanity.
c. War crimes.

Although this manual recognizes the criminal responsibility of individuals for those offenses which may comprise any of the foregoing types of crimes, members of the armed forces will normally be concerned only with those offenses constituting "war crimes."

499. War Crimes

The term "war crime" is the technical expression for a violation of the law of war by any person or persons, military or civilian. Every violation of the law of war is a war crime.

500. Conspiracy, Incitiment, Attempts, And Complicity

Conspiracy, direct incitement, and attempts to commit, as well as complicity in the commission of, crimes against peace, crimes against humanity, and war crimes are punishable.

501. Responsibility for Acts of Subordinates

In some cases, military commanders may be responsible for war crimes committed by subordinate members of the armed forces, or other persons subject to their control. Thus, for instance, when troops commit massacres and atrocities against the civilian population of occupied territory or against prisoners of war, the responsibility may rest not only with the actual perpetrators but also with the commander. Such a responsibility arises directly when the acts in question have been committed in pursuance of an order of the commander concerned. The commander is also responsible if he has actual knowledge, or should have knowledge, through reports received by him or through other means, that troops or other persons subject to his control are about to commit or have committed a war crime and he fails to take the necessary and reasonable steps to insure compliance with the law thereof.

507. Universality of Jurisdiction

a. *Victims of War Crimes.* The jurisdiction of United States military tribunals in connection with war crimes is not limited to offenses committed against nationals of the United States but extends also to all offenses of this nature committed against nationals of allies and of cobelligerents and stateless persons.

b. *Persons Charged with War Crimes.* The United States normally punishes war crimes as such only if they are committed by enemy nationals or by persons serving the interests of the enemy State. Violations of the law of war committed by persons subject to the military law of the United States will usually constitute violations of the Uniform Code of Military Justice and, if so, will be prosecuted under that Code. Violations of the law of war committed within the United States by other persons will usually constitute violations of federal or state criminal law and preferably will be prosecuted under such law. . . . Commanding officers of United States troops must insure that war crimes committed by members of their forces against enemy personnel are promptly and adequately punished.

508. Penal Sanctions

The punishment imposed for a violation of the law of war must be proportionate to the gravity of the offense. The death penalty may be imposed for grave breaches of the law. Corporal punishment is excluded. Punishments should be deterrent, and in imposing a sentence of imprisonment it is not necessary to take into consideration the end of the war, which does not of itself limit the imprisonment to be imposed.

510. Government Officials

The fact that a person who committed an act which constitutes a war crime acted as the head of State or as a responsible government official does not relieve him from responsibility for his act.

Domestic law relating to the interrogation of prisoners of war is found in another Army publication, *Intelligence Interrogation*, whose purpose is "to provide doctrinal guidance, techniques, and procedures governing employment of interrogators as human intelligence collection assets." The manual includes the following provisions:

U.S. Army, *Intelligence Interrogation*

Field Manual 34-52, at 1-6 - 1-8 (Sept. 28, 1992)

Definition of Interrogation

Interrogation is the process of questioning a source to obtain the maximum amount of usable information. The goal of any interrogation is to obtain reliable information in a lawful manner, in a minimum amount of time. . . .

Prohibition Against Use of Force

One of the significant means used by the intelligence staff is the interrogation of the following:

EPWs [enemy prisoners of war].
Captured insurgents.

Civilian internees.
Other captured, detained or retained persons.
Foreign deserters or other persons of intelligence interest.

These persons are protected by the Geneva Conventions for the Protection of War Victims of August 12, 1949, as they relate to captured, wounded and sick enemy personnel ([First Geneva Convention]), retained enemy medical personnel and chaplains ([First Geneva Convention]), enemy prisoners of war ([Third Geneva Convention]), and civilian internees ([Fourth Geneva Convention]). Captured insurgents and other detained personnel whose status is not clear, such as suspected terrorists, are entitled to [prisoner of war] status until their precise status has been determined by competent authority. . . .

The [Geneva Conventions] and US policy expressly prohibit acts of violence or intimidation, including physical or mental torture, threats, insults, or exposure to inhumane treatment as a means of or aid to interrogation.

Such illegal acts are not authorized and will not be condoned by the US Army. Acts in violation of these prohibitions are criminal acts punishable under the UCMJ. . . .

Experience indicates that the use of prohibited techniques is not necessary to gain the cooperation of interrogation sources. Use of torture and other illegal methods is a poor technique that yields unreliable results, may damage subsequent collection efforts, and can induce the source to say what he thinks the interrogator wants to hear.

Revelation of use of torture by US personnel will bring discredit upon the US and its armed forces while undermining domestic and international support for the war effort. It also may place US and allied personnel in enemy hands at greater risk of abuse by their captors. . . .

Torture is defined as the infliction of intense pain to body or mind to extract a confession or information, or for sadistic pleasure.

Examples of physical torture include —

- Electric shock.
- Infliction of pain through chemicals or bondage (other than legitimate use of restraints to prevent escape).
- Forcing an individual to stand, sit, or kneel in abnormal positions for prolonged periods of time.
- Food deprivation.
- Any form of beating.

Examples of mental torture include —

- Mock executions.
- Abnormal sleep deprivation.
- Chemically induced psychosis.

Field Manual 34-52 identifies seventeen permissible interrogation methods, including direct questioning and the use of incentives to encourage detainees to provide information. The 1992 version (which was in use for interrogations of detainees between January 2002, when the first detainees arrived at Guantánamo, until December 2002) differs from its 1987 predecessor, which permitted interrogators to control the lighting, food, heating, clothing, and shelter given to detainees "within the limits of the Geneva and Hague Conventions, as well as the standards of conduct outlined in the [Uniform Code of Military Justice]." Field Manual 34-52 (May 8, 1987), ch. 3.

B. *Protecting Civilians: The Fourth Geneva Convention*

The defendants at Nuremberg, as Draper indicates, were charged not only with violations of the law of war — "war crimes" — but also with two new crimes under international law: "crimes against peace," a concept that provoked much controversy but is beyond the scope of this chapter; and "crimes against humanity," defined by Article 6(c) of the Charter of the International Military Tribunal (the body set up to conduct the Nuremberg Trials) to consist of "murder, extermination, enslavement, deportation, and other inhumane acts committed against any civilian population, . . . or persecutions on political, racial, or religious grounds . . . , whether or not in violation of the domestic law of the county where perpetrated." 82 U.N.T.S. 279, 288. Designed to criminalize severe human rights deprivations that otherwise would have gone unpunished, e.g., Nazi Germany's attempt to exterminate its own Jewish population, crimes against humanity, "though playing a marginal role in the final estimate of the guilt of the accused, affirmed the existence of certain fundamental human rights superior to the law of the State and protected by international criminal sanction even if violated in pursuance of the law of the State." Draper, page 231 supra.

The Fourth Geneva Convention was the first attempt to codify what the Nuremberg Tribunal referred to as "crimes against humanity." The following six articles include some of the Convention's most important provisions.

Fourth Geneva Convention on the Protection of Civilian Persons in Time of War

75 U.N.T.S. 287 (Aug. 12, 1949)

ARTICLE 4 — who's protected

Persons protected by the Convention are those who, at a given moment and in any manner whatsoever, find themselves, in case of a conflict or occupation, in the hands of a Party to the conflict or Occupying Power of which they are not nationals.

Nationals of a State which is not bound by the Convention are not protected by it. Nationals of a neutral State who find themselves in the territory of a belligerent State, and nationals of a co-belligerent State, shall not be regarded as protected persons while the State of which they are nationals has normal diplomatic representation in the State in whose hands they are. . . .

Persons protected by . . . [any of the first three Geneva Conventions] shall not be considered as protected persons within the meaning of the present Convention.

ARTICLE 27

Protected persons are entitled, in all circumstances, to respect for their persons, their honour, their family rights, their religious convictions and practices, and their manners and customs. They shall at all times be humanely treated, and shall be protected especially against all acts of violence or threats thereof and against insults and public curiosity.

Women shall be especially protected against any attack on their honour, in particular against rape, enforced prostitution, or any form of indecent assault.

Without prejudice to the provisions relating to their state of health, age and sex, all protected persons shall be treated with the same consideration by the Party to the conflict in whose power they are, without any adverse distinction based, in particular, on race, religion or political opinion.

However, the Parties to the conflict may take such measures of control and security in regard to protected persons as may be necessary as a result of the war.

ARTICLE 31

No physical or moral coercion shall be exercised against protected persons, in particular to obtain information from them or from third parties.

ARTICLE 32

The High Contracting Parties specifically agree that each of them is prohibited from taking any measure of such a character as to cause the physical suffering or extermination of protected persons in their hands. This prohibition applies not only to murder, torture, corporal punishment, mutilation and medical or scientific experiments not necessitated by the medical treatment of a protected person, but also to any other measures of brutality whether applied by civilian or military agents.

ARTICLE 33

No protected person may be punished for an offence he or she has not personally committed. Collective penalties and likewise all measures of intimidation or of terrorism are prohibited.

Pillage is prohibited.

Reprisals against protected persons and their property are prohibited.

ARTICLE 34

The taking of hostages is prohibited.

The rest of the Convention may be summarized briefly. It provides for the protection of wounded and sick civilians, with particular provision for expectant mothers (Article 14). It encourages opposing armed forces to reach local agreements for the evacuation of civilian populations from zones of combat (Article 17). It contains provisions for the protection of civilian hospitals from attack (Articles 18 to 20) and for the protection of civilian evacuees (Articles 21 and 22). Free passage is to be guaranteed for hospital and medical stores for civilians, together with articles for religious worship (Article 23). There is a specific provision for care of orphans (Article 24). Communication between family members is to be guaranteed (Article 25), and armed forces are to take steps to assist with the reunion of dispersed families (Article 25). Articles 35 to 46 concern aliens found in the territory of parties to an armed conflict. The administration of occupied territories is covered by Articles 47 to 78. Finally, provisions relating to civilian internees are contained in Articles 79 to 135.

The 192 states parties to the Convention (including the United States, which became a party in 1956) are under a general obligation, set forth in Article 1, "to ensure respect for the present Convention in all circumstances." More specifically, states parties are obligated, under Article 146, to enact legislation providing "effective penal sanctions" for persons committing certain specified "grave breaches" of the Convention. Article 147 identifies these grave breaches as "willful killing, torture or inhuman treatment, including biological experiments, willfully causing great suffering or serious bodily injury to body or health, unlawful deportation or transfer or unlawful confinement of a protected person, compelling a protected person to serve in the forces of a hostile Power, or willfully depriving a protected person of the rights of fair and regular trial . . . taking of hostages and extensive destruction and appropriation of property, not justified by military necessity and carried out unlawfully and wantonly." The United States has implemented this obligation through the Uniform Code of Military Justice, extracts from which are set out supra at 234.

C. *Subsequent Developments: Protocol I*

During the early 1970s, the International Committee of the Red Cross (ICRC) convened a diplomatic conference to reaffirm and develop the international humanitarian law applicable in armed conflicts. The result, in 1977, was the adoption of two protocols to the four Geneva Conventions. Protocol I is concerned with international armed conflicts, the traditional subject matter of the law of war, but it defines such conflicts to include those "in which peoples are fighting against colonial domination and alien occupation and against racial regimes in the exercise of their right of self-determination," that is, wars of "national liberation." Protocol Additional to the Geneva Conventions of 12 August 1949, and Relating to the Protection of Victims of International Armed Conflicts (Protocol I), art. 1(4), 1125 U.N.T.S. 3. Protocol II, which will be taken up in the next section, is concerned with internal armed conflicts (i.e., conflicts that take place within the territory of a single country) and, thus, potentially breaks even more new ground. Protocol Additional to the Geneva Conventions of 12 August 1949, and Relating to the Protection of Victims of Non-International Armed Conflicts (Protocol II), 1125 U.N.T.S. 609.

To place these Protocols in context, extracts from an article by the late Judge Baxter, a rapporteur at the conference that drafted them, follow. Thereafter, the key relevant articles of Protocol I are set out. President Ronald Reagan recommended that the United States not ratify Protocol I, and, despite criticisms, this recommendation has been followed by all of his successors in office.

Richard R. Baxter, *Modernizing the Law of War*

78 Mil. L. Rev. 165, 168-173 (1978)

One can understand the work of the Conference on International Humanitarian Law only in the setting of human rights law and humanitarian law in general. Until comparatively recently, the general perception was that there were two separate bodies of law — human rights law applicable to one's own nationals in time of peace and the law with respect to the protection of war victims, incorporated in the Geneva Conventions of 1949 and other treaties and applicable for the most part to individuals depending in one way or another on the adversary. The two bodies of law went their own ways and were supported by quite separate interest groups.

In the last ten years or so, it has come to be realized that human rights are as much at peril in time of war as they are in time of peace and that the law of human rights and the humanitarian law of way are actually closely related. In addition, the humanitarian law of war, which up till now has been applied to "all cases of declared war or of any other armed conflict which may arise between two or more of the High Contracting Parties," has not been brought to bear on two important forms of contemporary conflict.

With the exception of common Article 3 of the Geneva Conventions of 1949, the Geneva law applies only to conflicts between states. Article 3 contains the short bill of rights for non-international armed conflicts and was thought to be a radical transformation of the law when it was incorporated in the Conventions in 1949. But since that time, a large number of internal conflicts have reached a scale akin to that of international armed conflicts whether measured in terms of the number of persons involved or the degree and kinds of force employed. Moreover, a number of international armed conflicts have an important non-international element. The conflict in Vietnam, for example, had both international and noninternational elements, and a strict distinction between the two aspects of the conflict in terms of the law applied proved to be out of the question.

The period since the adoption of the Geneva Conventions of 1949 has also seen the emergence of a new kind of conflict — the war of national liberation. In essence, this is an anticolonial war, which, under the traditional law of war, was governed by whatever law there might be concerning noninternational armed conflicts. When the colony achieved independence, was recognized as a state, and became a party to the Geneva Conventions, then any conflict with the former colonial power was an international armed conflict governed by the totality of the Geneva Conventions. The case for saying that such an anticolonial war is from the outset a conflict that should be governed by the whole of the international law of war is that, if a colony or dependent territory is entitled to independence as a matter of international law, the law should treat such a colony or dependent territory as if it were independent and give it all the benefits of the law governing international armed conflicts. Otherwise the colonial power would profit by its own wrong in refusing to recognize the independence of the colony and in refusing to apply to it the law governing conflicts between two independent states. This is a simplified approach to a complex problem, and there are obvious difficulties that lie in the way of applying the whole corpus of the law of war to conflicts of this character. The developing countries, particularly those that had recently secured their independence, regarded the application of the whole of the law of war to wars of national liberation as the most important reform that ought to be made in the humanitarian law of war....

The legal protection of persons affected by noninternational armed conflicts was seen by the developing and newly independent countries forming a majority of the Conference as much less consequential than the protection of belligerents and civilians in wars of national liberation. In this case, the law swung to the opposite extreme. A new article [Article 1(4)] was steamrollered through the first session of the Conference, which provided in its most significant paragraph that:

> The situations referred to [in Article 2 common to the Geneva Conventions of 1949, namely interstate armed conflicts]...include armed conflicts in which peoples are fighting against colonial domination and alien occupation and against racist regimes in the exercise of their right of self determination, as enshrined in the Charter of the United Nations and the Declaration on Principles of International Law concerning Friendly Relations and Cooperation among States in accordance with the Charter of the United Nations.

By this provision not only Protocol I on International Armed Conflicts itself but also the totality of the Geneva Conventions of 1949 are made applicable to wars of national liberation....

One of the procedural complications occasioned by the provision on wars of national liberation was that a national liberation movement or any other entity or authority constituting the moving party in a war of national liberation would not be a party to the Geneva Conventions of 1949 or to Protocol I. To deal with this difficulty, a clause (Article 96(3)) was inserted whereby an "authority representing a people" engaged in a war of national liberation would undertake to apply the Protocol and the Conventions by a unilateral declaration addressed to Switzerland, the depositary of the Protocol. This declaration would bring the Protocol and Conventions into force between the "authority" and the other party to the conflict.

Note: The Impact of Protocol I

Part IV of Protocol I (Articles 48 to 79) deals with the protection of civilians and contains much of interest. Article 48 sets forth a "basic rule" that the parties to the conflict "shall at all times distinguish between the civilian population and combatants and between civilian objects and military objectives and accordingly shall direct their operations only against military objectives." Articles 51 and 75 set forth more detailed rules to protect civilians from attack.

Protocol Additional to the Geneva Conventions of 12 August 1949, and Relating to the Protection of Victims of International Armed Conflicts (Protocol I)

1125 U.N.T.S. 3 (Dec. 12, 1977)

Article 51 — Protection of the Civilian Population

1. The civilian population and individual civilians shall enjoy general protection against dangers arising from military operations. To give effect to this protection, the following rules, which are additional to other applicable rules of international law, shall be observed in all circumstances.

2. The civilian population as such, as well as individual civilians, shall not be the object of attack. Acts or threats of violence the primary purpose of which is to spread terror among the civilian population are prohibited.

3. Civilians shall enjoy the protection afforded by this Section, unless and for such time as they take a direct part in hostilities.

4. Indiscriminate attacks are prohibited. Indiscriminate attacks are:

(a) those which are not directed at a specific military objective;

(b) those which employ a method or means of combat which cannot be directed at a specific military's objective; or

(c) those which employ a method or means of combat the effects of which cannot be limited as required by this Protocol; and consequently, in each such case, are of a nature to strike military objectives amid civilians or civilian objects without distinction.

5. Among others, the following types of attacks are to be considered as indiscriminate:

(a) an attack by bombardment by any methods or means which treats as a single military objective a number of clearly separated and distinct military objectives located in a city, town, village or other area containing a similar concentration of civilians or civilian objects; and

(b) an attack which may be expected to cause incidental loss of civilian life, injury to civilians, damage to civilian objects, or a combination thereof, which would be excessive in relation to the concrete and direct military advantage anticipated.

6. Attacks against the civilian population or civilians by way of reprisals are prohibited.

7. The presence or movements of the civilian population or individual civilians shall not be used to render certain points or areas immune from military operations, in particular in attempts to shield military objectives from attacks or to shield, favour or impede military operations. The Parties to the conflict shall not direct the movement of the civilian population or individual civilians in order to attempt to shield military objectives from attacks or to shield military operations.

8. Any violation of these prohibitions shall not release the Parties to the conflict from their legal obligations with respect to the civilian population and civilians, including the obligations to take the precautionary measures provided for in Article 57.

ARTICLE 75 — FUNDAMENTAL GUARANTEES

1. In so far as they are affected by a situation referred to in Article I of this Protocol, persons who are in the power of a Party to the conflict and who do not benefit from more favourable treatment under the Conventions or under this Protocol shall be treated humanely in all circumstances and shall enjoy, as a minimum, the protection provided by this Article without any adverse distinction based upon race, colour, sex, language, religion or belief, political or other opinion, national or social origin, wealth, birth or other status, or on any other similar criteria. Each Party shall respect the person, honour, convictions and religious practice of all such persons.

2. The following acts are and shall remain prohibited at any time and in any place whatsoever, whether committed by civilian or by military agents:

(a) violence to the life, health, or physical or mental well-being of persons, in particular:

(i) murder;

(ii) torture of all kinds, whether physical or mental;

(iii) corporal punishment; and

(iv) mutilation;

(b) outrages upon personal dignity, in particular humiliating and degrading treatment, enforced prostitution and any form of indecent assault;

(c) the taking of hostages;

(d) collective punishments; and

(e) threats to commit any of the foregoing acts.

3. Any person arrested, detained or interned for actions related to the armed conflict shall be informed promptly, in a language he understands, of the reasons why these measures have been taken. Except in cases of arrest or detention for penal offences, such persons shall be released with the minimum delay possible and in any event as soon as the circumstances justifying the arrest, detention or internment have ceased to exist.

4. No sentence may be passed and no penalty may be executed on a person found guilty of a penal offence related to the armed conflict except pursuant to a conviction pronounced by an impartial and regularly constituted court respecting the generally recognized principles of regular judicial procedure, which include the following:

(a) the procedure shall provide for an accused to be informed without delay of the particulars of the offence alleged against him and shall afford the accused before and during his trial all necessary rights and means of defence;

(b) no one shall be convicted of an offence except on the basis of individual penal responsibility;

(c) no one shall be accused or convicted of a criminal offence on account of any act or omission which did not constitute a criminal offence under the national or international law to which he was subject at the time when it was committed; nor shall a heavier penalty be imposed than that which was applicable at the time when the criminal offense was committed; if after the commission of the offence, provision is made by law for the imposition of a lighter penalty, the offender shall benefit thereby;

(d) anyone charged with an offence is presumed innocent until proved guilty according to law;

(e) anyone charged with an offence shall have the right to be tried in his presence;

(f) no one shall be compelled to testify against himself or to confess guilt;

(g) anyone charged with an offence shall have the right to examine, or have examined, the witnesses against him and to obtain the attendance and examination of witnesses on his behalf under the same conditions as witnesses against him;

(h) no one shall be prosecuted or punished by the same Party for an offence in respect of which a final judgment acquitting or convicting that person has been previously pronounced under the same law and judicial procedure;

(i) anyone prosecuted for an offence shall have the right to have the judgment pronounced publicly; and

(j) a convicted person shall be advised on conviction of his judicial and other remedies and of the time limits within which they may be exercised.

5. Women whose liberty has been restricted for reasons related to the armed conflict shall be held in quarters separated from men's quarters. They shall be under the immediate supervision of women. Nevertheless, in cases where families are detained or interned, they shall, whenever possible, be held in the same place and accommodated as family units.

6. Persons who are arrested, detained or interned for reasons related to the armed conflict shall enjoy the protection provided by this Article until their final release, repatriation or reestablishment, even after the end of the armed conflict.

7. In order to avoid any doubt concerning the prosecution and trial of persons accused of war crimes or crimes against humanity, the following principles shall apply:

(a) persons who are accused of such crimes should be submitted for the purpose of prosecution and trial in accordance with the applicable rules of international law; and

(b) any such persons who do not benefit from more favourable treatment under the Conventions or this Protocol shall be accorded the treatment provided by this Article, whether or not the crimes of which they are accused constitute grave breaches of the Conventions or of this Protocol.

8. No provision of this Article may be construed as limiting or infringing any other more favourable provision granting greater protection, under any applicable rules of international law, to persons covered by paragraph 1.

Many of the substantive norms set forth in the Protocol (such as those found in Articles 51 and 75, supra) may now constitute norms of customary international law. For example, the "fundamental guarantees" in Article 75 were recognized as forming part of customary international law by a State Department Deputy Legal Adviser; see Michael J. Matheson, *The United States Position on the Relation of Customary International Law to the 1977 Protocols Additional to the 1949 Geneva Conventions*, 2 Am. U. J. Int'l L. & Policy 419 (1987).

Although Protocol I has been widely ratified (there were 163 State Parties as of mid-2005), it is difficult to find clear instances where it has been directly applied by states. The International Fact-Finding Commission provided for in Article 90 of Protocol I was established only in 1991; while over 60 states have accepted its competence to inquire into alleged grave breaches or other serious violations of the 1949 Conventions or Protocol I and to offer its good offices to promote respect for humanitarian norms, none has yet invoked the Commission's services.

President Carter signed Protocol I in 1977, but the official U.S. position since then appears to be that set forth by President Reagan in 1987, when he referred to Protocol I as "fundamentally and irreconcilably flawed. . . . It would give special status to 'wars of national liberation,' an ill-defined concept expressed in vague, subjective, politicized terminology. Another provision would grant combatant status to irregular forces even if they do not satisfy the traditional requirements to distinguish themselves from the civilian population and otherwise comply with the laws of war. This would endanger civilians among whom terrorists and other irregulars attempt to conceal themselves. . . ." Message from the President Transmitting Protocol II Additional to the 1949 Geneva Conventions, and Relating to the Protection of Victims of Noninternational Armed Conflicts, S. Treaty Doc. No. 2, 100th Cong, 1st Sess. III-V (1987).

Comments and Questions

1. The laws of war, while violated on countless other occasions during and since the Vietnam War, nevertheless had a restraining effect on both sides during that conflict. Recall, for instance, that while the North Vietnamese committed numerous atrocities during the 1968 Tet offensive, they backed down from their announced plans to try U.S. airmen as "war criminals" when the United States was able to demonstrate conclusively, within and without the UN, that a serviceman's participation in a war — even arguendo an aggressive one — did not render him criminally responsible. Thus, despite the inhumane treatment many airmen received at the hands of their North Vietnamese captors, they did receive some protection from the law of war — protection that in some instances may have made the difference between life and death. It is also generally agreed that both sides in the 1982 war between the United Kingdom and Argentina over the Malvinas/Falkland Islands made good faith attempts to abide by humanitarian law.

IV. Expanding Traditional Protections: Internal Armed Conflicts

A. *Common Article 3: Its Status and Content*

Daniel Smith, *New Protections for Victims of International Armed Conflicts: The Proposed Ratification of Protocol II by the United States*

120 Mil. L. Rev. 59, 63-65 (1988)

III. THE DEVELOPMENT OF INTERNATIONAL STANDARDS GOVERINING NONINTERNATIONAL ARMED CONFLICTS

The events of World War II led to the four Geneva Conventions of August 12, 1949 for the Protection of Victims of War. At the 1949 Diplomatic Conference, the delegates of many states believed the Geneva Conventions should apply to both civil and international armed conflicts. This position was certainly influenced by Lieber, who believed that rules of warfare could be observed during internal conflicts without giving recognition to the rebel forces. The initial proposal by the International Committee of the Red Cross (ICRC) incorporated this view, and explicitly provided that the application of the Geneva Conventions to internal armed conflicts would not affect the status of the parties. The proposal, however, met stiff resistance from a considerable number of delegates. Many states feared unqualified application of the Conventions to all internal armed conflict would give rebels de facto status as belligerents and possibly even de jure legal recognition. They believed observance of the Conventions would hamper the legitimate repression of rebellions and wanted to limit the laws of war to traditional armed conflicts between states. These states particularly did not want to give rebels prisoner of war status, with its attendant immunity for lawful actions on the battlefield.

Common Article 3 was the compromise between these two views; it provides some minimum protections for victims of internal armed conflicts, while avoiding any recognition of the rebel forces or any rebel entitlement to prisoner of war status. It states:

> In the case of armed conflict not of an international character occurring in the territory of one of the High Contracting Parties, each Party to the conflict shall be bound to apply, as a minimum, the following provisions:
>
> (1) Persons taking no active part in the hostilities, including members of armed forces who have laid down their arms and those placed hors de combat by sickness, wounds, detention, or any other cause, shall in all circumstances be treated humanely, without any adverse distinction founded on race, colour, religion or faith, sex, birth or wealth, or any other similar criteria.
>
> To this end, the following acts are and shall remain prohibited at any time and in any place whatsoever with respect to the above-mentioned persons:
>
> (a) violence to life and person, in particular murder of all kinds, mutilation, cruel treatment and torture;
>
> (b) taking of hostages;
>
> (c) outrages upon personal dignity, in particular humiliating and degrading treatment;
>
> (d) the passing of sentences and the carrying out of executions without previous judgment pronounced by a regularly constituted court, affording all the judicial guarantees which are recognized as indispensable by civilized peoples.
>
> (2) The wounded and sick shall be collected and cared for.
>
> An impartial humanitarian body, such as the International Committee of the Red Cross, may offer its services to the Parties to the conflict.
>
> The Parties to the conflict should further endeavor to bring into force, by means of special agreements, all or part of the other provisions of the present Convention.
>
> The application of the preceding provisions shall not affect the legal status of the Parties to the conflict.

Common Article 3 was a major step toward recognizing the need for basic humanitarian protections for non-combatants in internal armed conflicts. It represented the first internationally accepted law that regulated a state's treatment of its own nationals in internal armed conflicts. The article also established that the laws governing internal armed conflict were of legitimate international concern.

Although Common Article 3 advanced the laws governing internal armed conflicts, it has not been very effective from a practical standpoint. Some governments have explicitly accepted the applicability of Common Article 3 and have attempted to comply with it, but these have been the exception rather than the general rule. Most governments have been reluctant to admit the existence of "armed conflicts" within their states. They still fear the rebels will gain international legal status as insurgents or belligerents if Common Article 3 is applied to the internal strife. To compound this problem, the text of Common Article 3 and its drafting history do not clearly define the term "non-international armed conflict." This has made it easier for states to deny that the provision applies. Finally, Common Article 3 sets forth very general principles rather than the precise standards of conduct necessary to regulate the conduct of states effectively.

Case Concerning Military and Paramilitary Activities In and Against Nicaragua *(Nicaragua v. United States)*

1986 I.C.J. 14, 66-69, 113-114, 129-130 (Judgment of 27 June) (Merits)

[Among the many questions raised in this complicated case was whether the United States incurred legal responsibility for the CIA's preparation and dissemination to the contras in 1983 of a publication, in Spanish, entitled Operaciones sicologicas en guerra de guerillas *(Psychological Operations in Guerrilla Warfare).]*

122. The Court concludes that in 1983 an agency of the United States Government supplied to the FDN [the so-called "contras" who were fighting to overthrow the Sandinista government in Nicaragua] a manual on psychological guerrilla warfare which, while expressly discouraging indiscriminate violence against civilians, considered the possible necessity of shooting civilians who were attempting to leave a town; and advised the "neutralization" for propaganda purposes of local judges, officials or notables after the semblance of trial in the presence of the population. The text supplied to the contras also advised the use of professional criminals to perform unspecified "jobs," and the use of provocation at mass demonstrations to produce violence on the part of the authorities so as to make "martyrs." . . .

218. The court [finds it unnecessary to decide whether common Article 3 applies under the facts of this case,] since in its view the conduct of the United States may be judged according to the fundamental general principles of humanitarian law; in its view, the Geneva Conventions are in some respects a development, and in other respects no more than the expression, of such principles. . . . Article 3 which is common to all four Geneva Conventions of 12 August 1949 defines certain rules to be applied in the armed conflicts of a noninternational character. There is no doubt that, in the event of international armed conflicts, these rules also constitute a minimum yardstick, in addition to the more elaborate rules which are also to apply to international conflicts; and they are rules which, in the Court's opinion, reflect what the Court in 1949 called "elementary considerations of humanity" (Corfu Channel, *Merits*, I.C.J. Reports 1949, p. 22 . . .). The Court may therefore find them applicable to the present

dispute, and is thus not required to decide what role the United States multilateral treaty reservation might otherwise play in regard to the treaties in question.

219. The conflict between the contras' forces and those of the Government of Nicaragua is an armed conflict which is "not of an international character." The acts of the contras towards the Nicaraguan Government are therefore governed by the law applicable to conflicts of that character; whereas the actions of the United States in and against Nicaragua fall under the legal rules relating to international conflicts. Because the minimum rules applicable to international and to non-international conflicts are identical, there is no need to address the question whether those actions must be looked at in the context of the rules which operate for the one or for the other category of conflict. The relevant principles are to be looked for in the provisions of Article 3 of each of the four Conventions of 12 August 1949, the text of which, identical in each Convention, expressly refers to conflicts not having an international character.

220. The Court considers that there is an obligation on the United States Government, in the terms of Article 1 of the Geneva Conventions, to "respect" the Conventions and even "to ensure respect" for them "in all circumstances," since such an obligation does not derive only from the Conventions themselves, but from the general principles of humanitarian law to which the Conventions merely give specific expression. The United States is thus under an obligation not to encourage persons or groups engaged in the conflict in Nicaragua to act in violation of the provisions of Article 3 common to the four 1949 Geneva Conventions, . . .

[The Court held, 14 votes to 1 (Judge Oda dissenting), that the United States, by producing the manual and disseminating it to the contras, had "encouraged the commission by them of acts contrary to general principles of humanitarian law; but does not find a basis for concluding that any such acts which may have been committed are imputable to the United States of America . . ." [1986 I.C.J. at 148.]

B. *Protocol II: Its Scope and Content*

Protocol II, which supplements Common Article 3, emerged from the same Diplomatic Conference of 1974-1977 as did Protocol I. Many states, particularly Third World ones, opposed efforts to regulate internal armed conflicts by international norms. While this position did not prevail at the Diplomatic Conference, Protocol II emerged therefrom a much weaker instrument than the ICRC and most human rights activists had hoped to see drafted.

Richard R. Baxter, *Modernizing the Law of War*

78 Mil. L. Rev. 165, 168-173 (1978)

When the I.C.R.C. began its work on the development of the humanitarian law of war, there were high hopes for a separate new Protocol (or convention) on noninternational armed conflicts. . . . This proved to be too much for the majority of the states participating in the Conference. Opposition to the Protocol first took the form of raising the threshold of violence to which the Protocol would apply. Common Article 3 of the Geneva Conventions simply applies to "armed conflict not of an international character," but the new Protocol II was made to apply to

> all armed conflicts . . . which take place in the territory of a High Contracting Party between its armed forces and dissident armed forces or other organized armed groups which, under responsible command, exercise such control over a pact of its territory as to enable them to carry out sustained and concerted military operations and to implement this Protocol.

What was obviously in the minds of the draftsmen was a conflict resembling the Civil War in Spain rather than the civil wars in Nigeria or the Congo. Through this definition two levels of internal armed conflicts were created, even as to parties to both the Conventions of 1949 and Protocol II — the lower level, governed by Article 3, and the higher level, governed by Protocol II. Such nice legal distinctions do not make the correct application of the law any easier.

The second limitation on the scope of the Protocol came in the fourth session of the Conference when, at the initiative of Pakistan, the drafting of provisions was changed from the form "The parties to the conflict shall. . . ." to statements of the protections which are to be extended to the participants and participants in the conflict. A number of provisions already adopted were simply dropped, and the simplified Protocol II was adopted in its reduced scale. There was some danger that the Protocol would not have survived at all if this radical surgery had not been employed. . . .

Political forces dominated the consideration of "noninternational armed conflicts" and "wars of national liberation." Developing countries, led by those who had experienced civil wars, succeeded in blunting the edge of the movement for a much more ample protection of the victims of civil wars. It was that same bloc of developing countries, supported by the U.S.S.R. and its allies, that succeeded in giving special status to wars of national liberation. . . .

As Baxter notes, one major concession made to states reluctant to develop a legal regime to govern internal wars and civil strife concerned the "threshold" of the Protocol's application. In addition to the definition in Article 1(1), Article 1(2) of Protocol II specifies that it does *not* apply "to situations of internal disturbances and tensions, such as riots, isolated and sporadic acts of violence and other acts of a similar nature, as not being armed conflicts." These conditions effectively bar the Protocol's application to many internal armed conflicts. *

Assuming that the Protocol's conditions are met, its core protective provisions are contained in Article 4, which provides, inter alia, as follows:

Article 4 — Fundamental Guarantees

> 1. All persons who do not take a direct part or who have ceased to take part in hostilities, whether or not their liberty has been restricted, are entitled to respect for

their person, honour and convictions and religious practices. They shall in all circumstances be treated humanely, without any adverse distinction. It is prohibited to order that there shall be no survivors.

2. Without prejudice to the generality of the foregoing, the following acts against the persons referred to in paragraph 1 are and shall remain prohibited at any time and in any place whatsoever:

(a) violence to the life, health and physical or mental well-being of persons, in particular murder as well as cruel treatment such as torture, mutilation or any form of corporal punishment;

(b) collective punishments;

(c) taking of hostages;

(d) acts of terrorism;

(e) outrages upon personal dignity, in particular humiliating and degrading treatment, rape, enforced prostitution and any form of indecent assault;

(f) slavery and the slave trade in all their forms;

(g) pillage;

(h) threats to commit any of the foregoing acts.

Numerous other articles also extend protection to the civilian population, although Protocol II's provisions are much less extensive and specific than those found in Protocol I. See generally Charles Lysaght, *The Scope of Protocol II and Its Relation to Common Article 3 of the Geneva Conventions of 1949 and Other Human Rights Instruments*, 33 Am. U. L. Rev. 4, 24 (1983).

Note: The U.S. Position on Protocol II

Despite concerns about the high threshold of armed conflict necessary to trigger Protocol II, President Jimmy Carter signed it in 1977, and ten years later President Reagan submitted it to the Senate for its advice and consent to ratification with one reservation, two understandings, and one declaration. Only the last is of major importance. It declares that the United States will apply Protocol II to all armed conflicts covered by Common Article 3 (and only such conflicts), which would include all non-international armed conflicts as traditionally defined (but not internal disturbances, riots, and sporadic acts of violence), and that it will encourage all other states to do likewise. Message from the President, supra page 247, at 7. The Legal Adviser to the Directorate of the ICRC called the proposed declaration "a positive step forward that should set an example for other states." Hans Peter Gasser, *An Appeal for Ratification by the United States*, 81 Am, J. Intl. L. 912 (1987). Unfortunately, the United States has still not ratified Protocol II, and there is no evidence that the declaration has started a trend to broaden Protocol II's area of application.

At least one author argues that the scope of humanitarian law protections has been expanded by the International Criminal Tribunal for the former Yugoslavia (which is discussed more fully in Chapter 11), which has interpreted the concept of "internal armed conflict" to include "protracted armed conflict between organized armed groups and government authorities or between such groups." Anthony Cullen, *Key Developments Affecting the Scope of Internal Armed Conflict in International Humanitarian Law*, 183 Mil. L. Rev. 66, 108 (2005).

Note: UN Peacekeeping

International humanitarian law, whether customary or conventional, applies to states (and, to some extent, to other participants in armed conflicts). What, if any, obligations apply to peacekeeping forces operating within a country under the authorization of the United Nations?

The short answer is that the national contingents that make up UN peacekeeping forces remain accountable to their own states for disciplinary and other matters while they are serving with the United Nations. Thus, states are under the same obligation to ensure that their troops respect the laws of war as they would be if they were not wearing the "blue helmets" of UN peacekeepers.

In 1999, Secretary-General Kofi Annan issued a bulletin that reinforced the position that "fundamental principles and rules of international humanitarian law . . . are applicable to United Nations forces when in situations of armed conflict they are actively engaged therein as combatants, to the extent and for the duration of their engagement." Observance by United Nations forces of international humanitarian law, UN Doc. ST/SGB/1999/13 (Aug. 6, 1999), §1.1. The bulletin clarifies that it does not constitute "an exhaustive list" of applicable principles and rules, nor does it replace national laws which bind military personnel in UN operations. Id., §2. It then goes on to address protection of the civilian population, means and methods of combat, treatment of civilians and persons hors de combat, treatment of detainees, and protection of the sick and wounded. With respect to detainees, they are to be treated in accordance with the Third Geneva Convention on prisoners of war, "[w]ithout prejudice to their legal status." Id., §8. Cf. the discussion of the responsibility of international organizations for human rights violations in Chapter 5, page 430.

Comments and Questions

1. As noted above, over 150 states have ratified Protocol II to the 1949 Geneva Conventions, dealing with noninternational armed conflicts. Is there any evidence that combatants in Angola, Liberia, Mozambique, Rwanda, Somalia, Sri Lanka, Sudan, and the former Yugoslavia — to mention only a few recent civil wars that may meet the threshold requirements of Protocol II — abided by its proscriptions? Does it matter that, out of this list, only Rwanda and Yugoslavia have ratified Protocol II? If the other states are not bound, is there no international legal protection for civilians caught up in widespread brutality? See Chapter 11.

2. One objection to Protocol II is that its application might give greater credibility to insurgent or guerrilla forces engaged in a civil war, despite Article 3(1)'s injunction that "[n]othing in this Protocol shall be invoked for the purpose of affecting the sovereignty of a State or the responsibility of the government, by all legitimate means, to maintain or re-establish law and order in the State or to defend the national unity and territorial integrity of the State." Is this a legitimate concern? Is a state prohibited from treating terrorists as common criminals if Protocol II is applicable? Are terrorists bound by the same restrictions as the government, e.g., the requirement to distinguish between combatants and civilians?

3. Given the complexity of humanitarian law, whose application often depends on whether one characterizes a situation as an international or non-international "armed conflict," is it wise for human rights NGOs to enter the field and offer their own opinions? See David Weissbrodt, *The Role of International Organizations in the Implementation of Human Rights and Humanitarian Law in Situations of Armed Conflict*, 21 Vand. J. Transnatl L. 313, 345 (1988): "[N]ongovernmental organizations are not required to cite provisions of humanitarian law except where such citation would appear useful in protecting human rights. In addition, consideration should be given to the use of humanitarian law not as a primary source of applicable norms but as a point of reference. For example, a human rights organization should not say: 'These trial procedures violated common article 3.' Instead, the report might observe: 'Such trial procedures are forbidden even in periods of civil war under common article 3.' ...[T]his more subtle way of citing humanitarian law would make use of the public perception that the Geneva Conventions and Additional Protocols establish the most basic, minimum standard of conduct for governments."

V. Where Does Responsibility Lie for Violations of the Law of War?

Since compliance with the law of war is considered the responsibility of individuals, it is hardly surprising that there have been many attempts by military personnel accused of such violations to shift responsibility onto the shoulders of persons either above or below them in the chain of command. Sometimes the attempt is made to shift the blame upward by contending that the acts in question were ordered by superiors, and that, therefore, the actual perpetrator of the violations should be exonerated and his superior punished instead. Conversely, there have been occasions where commanding officers prosecuted for violations of the law of war have attempted to shift the responsibility downwards, by arguing that the acts in question had been committed by troops in the field without the commander's knowledge or consent. See, e.g., the *Yamashita* case, page 255 infra.

The first of these issues, the question of the defense of superior orders, received attention at the time of the Nuremberg Trials of the leaders of Nazi Germany after World War II. To a great extent, the Charter that established the International Military Tribunal (IMT) foreclosed the issue by expressly providing in Article 2 that "[t]he fact that the defendant acted pursuant to order of his Government or of a superior shall not free him from responsibility, but may be considered in mitigation of punishment if the Tribunal determines that justice so requires." 82 U.N.T.S. 279, 288. Nevertheless, the IMT did elaborate on the question of superior orders several times in its Judgment, most notably when it commented that the rule found in Article 8 was "in conformity with the law of nations. That a soldier was ordered to kill or torture in violation of the international law of war has never been recognized as a defense to such acts of brutality, though, as the Charter here provides, the order may be urged in mitigation of the punishment." The Nuremberg Trial, 6 F.R.D. 69, 111 (1946). Later in its judgment the IMT added that "[s]uperior orders, even to a soldier, cannot be considered in mitigation where crimes as shocking and extensive [as the crimes involved] have been committed consciously, ruthlessly and without military excuse or justification." Id. at 154. "Participation in such crimes," it concluded, "has never been required of any soldier and he cannot now shield himself behind a mythical requirement of soldierly obedience at all costs as his excuse for commission of these crimes." Id. at 177.

This approach to the defense of superior orders has been incorporated into U.S. domestic law. The U.S. Army's The Law of Land Warfare, supra, page 235, provides as follows:

509. Defense of Superior Orders

> a. The fact that the law of war has been violated pursuant to an order of superior authority, whether military or civil, does not deprive the act in question of its character of a war crime, nor does it constitute a defense in the trial of an accused individual, unless he did not know and could not reasonably have been expected to know that the act ordered was unlawful. In all cases where the order is held not to constitute a defense to an allegation of war crime, the fact that the individual was acting pursuant to orders may be considered in mitigation of punishment.
>
> b. In considering the question whether a superior order constitutes a valid defense, the court shall take into consideration the fact that obedience to lawful military orders is the duty of every member of the armed forces; that the latter cannot be expected, in conditions of war discipline, to weigh scrupulously the legal merits of the orders received; that certain rules of warfare may be controversial; or that an act otherwise amounting to a war crime may be done in obedience to orders conceived as a measure of reprisal. At the same time it must be home in mind that members of the armed forces are bound to obey only lawful orders....

The defense of superior orders, as embodied in the above paragraph, was initially at issue in the courts-martials of those involved in the mistreatment of prisoners at Abu Ghraib, taken up later in this chapter.

The issue of whether a commanding officer can absolve himself from blame for violations of the law of war committed by his troops, on the ground that he did not authorize or even know of such violations, involves the concept of "command responsibility." The issue received an authoritative airing in the U.S. Supreme Court case that follows.

In re Yamashita

327 U.S. 1, 5-6, 13-18 (1946)

Chief Justice Stone delivered the opinion of the Court....

From the petitions and the supporting papers it appears that prior to September 3, 1945, petitioner was the Commanding General of the Fourteenth Army Group of the Imperial Japanese Army in the Philippine Islands. On that date he surrendered to and became a prisoner of war of the United States Army forces in Baguio, Philippine Islands.... [P]etitioner was served with a charge prepared by the Judge Advocate General's Department of the Army, purporting to charge petitioner with a violation of the law of war. On

October 8, 1945, petitioner, after pleading not guilty to the charge, was held for trial. . . .

On the same date a bill of particulars was filed by the prosecution, and the commission heard a motion made in petitioner's behalf to dismiss the charge on the ground that it failed to state a violation of the law of war. . . . [T]he motion to dismiss was denied. The trial then proceeded until its conclusion on December 7, 1945. . . . On that date petitioner was found guilty of the offense as charged and sentenced to death by hanging. . . .

The charge. Neither congressional action nor the military orders constituting the commission authorized it to place petitioner on trial unless the charge preferred against him is of a violation of the law of war. The charge, so far as now relevant, is that petitioner, between October 9, 1944 and September 2, 1945, in the Philippine Islands, "while commander of armed forces of Japan at war with the United States of America and its allies unlawfully disregarded and failed to discharge his duty as commander to control the operations of the members of his command permitting them to commit brutal atrocities and other high crimes against people of the United States and of its allies and dependencies, particularly the Philippines; and he . . . thereby violated the laws of war."

Bills of particulars, filed by the prosecution by order of the commission, allege a series of acts, one hundred and twenty-three in number, committed by members of the forces under petitioner's command during the period mentioned. The first item specifies the execution of "a deliberate plan and purpose to massacre and exterminate a large part of the civilian population of Batangas Province, and to devastate and destroy public, private and religious property therein, as a result of which more than 25,000 men, women and children, all unarmed noncombatant civilians, were brutally mistreated and killed, without cause or trial, and entire settlements were devastated and destroyed wantonly and without military necessity." Other items specify acts of violence, cruelty and homicide inflicted upon the civilian population and prisoners of war, acts of wholesale pillage and the wanton destruction of religious monuments.

It is not denied that such acts directed against the civilian population of an occupied country and against prisoners of war are recognized in international law as violations of the law of war. Articles 4, 28, 46, and 47, Annex to the Fourth Hague Convention, 1907, 36 Stat. 2277, 2296, 2303, 2306-7. But it is urged that the charge does not allege that petitioner has either committed or directed the commission of such acts, and consequently that no violation is charged as against him. But this overlooks the fact that the gist of the charge is an unlawful breach of duty by petitioner as an army commander to control the operations of the members of his command by "permitting them to commit" the extensive and widespread atrocities specified. The question then is whether the law of war imposes on an army commander a duty to take such appropriate measures as are within his power to control the troops under his command for the prevention of the specified acts which are violations of the law of war and which are likely to attend the occupation of hostile territory by an uncontrolled soldiery, and whether he may be charged with personal responsibility for his failure to take such measures when violations result. That this was the precise issue to be tried was made clear by the statement of the prosecution at the opening of the trial.

It is evident that the conduct of military operations by troops whose excesses are unrestrained by the orders or efforts of their commander would almost certainly result in violations which it is the purpose of the law of war to prevent. Its purpose to protect civilian populations and prisoners of war from brutality would largely be defeated if the commander of an invading army could with impunity neglect to take reasonable measures for their protection. Hence the law of war presupposes that its violation is to be avoided through the control of the operations of war by commanders who are to some extent responsible for their subordinates....

These provisions [i.e., the Fourth and Tenth Hague Conventions of 1907 and Geneva Red Cross Convention of 1929] plainly imposed on petitioner, who at the time specified was military governor of the Philippines, as well as commander of the Japanese forces, an affirmative duty to take such measures as were within his power and appropriate in the circumstances to protect prisoners of war and the civilian population. This duty of a commanding officer has heretofore been recognized, and its breach penalized by our own military tribunals....

We do not make the laws of war but we respect them so far as they do not conflict with the commands of Congress or the Constitution. There is no contention that the present charge, thus read, is without the support of evidence, or that the commission held petitioner responsible for failing to take measures which were beyond his control or inappropriate for a commanding officer to take in the circumstances. We do not here appraise the evidence on which petitioner was convicted. We do not consider what measures, if any, petitioner took to prevent the commission, by the troops under his command, of the plain violations of the law of war detailed in the bill of particulars, or whether such measures as he may have taken were appropriate and sufficient to discharge the duty imposed upon him. These are questions within the peculiar competence of the military officers composing the commission and were for it to decide. See *Smith v. Whitney*, 116 U.S. 167, 178. It is plain that the charge on which petitioner was tried charged him with a breach of his duty to control the operations of the members of his command, by permitting them to commit the specified atrocities. This was enough to require the commission to hear evidence tending to establish the culpable failure of petitioners to perform the duty imposed on him by the law of war and to pass upon its sufficiency to establish guilt.

Obviously charges of violations of the law of war triable before a military tribunal need not be stated with the precision of a common law indictment. Cf. *Collins v. McDonald* [(258 U.S. 416, 420 (1922)]. But we conclude that the allegations of the charge, tested by any reasonable standard, adequately allege a violation of the law of war and that the commission had authority to try and decide the issue which it raised....

For a lively exchange on the applicability of the above case and the Nuremberg Principles to the Vietnam War, compare Telford Taylor, *Nuremberg and Vietnam: An American Tragedy* 42-43, 159-182 (1970) with Waldemar A. Solf, *A Response to Telford Taylor's "Nuremberg and Vietnam: An*

American Tragedy" in 4 *The Vietnam War and International Law* 421, 433-446 (Richard Falk ed. 1976). Also see Ilias Bantekas, *The Contemporary Law of Superior Responsibility*, 93 Am. J. Int'l L. 573 (1999); *Note, Command Responsibility for War Crimes*, 82 Yale L.J. 1274 (1973).

Note: The Treatment of Command Responsibility in U.S. Domestic Law

Paragraph 501 of the U.S. Army's Law of Land Warfare, supra page 235, basically tracks the Yamashita case in its treatment of command responsibility. The UCMJ itself, however, does not contain a section specifically dealing with the question. This omission causes some complications, as indicated by the following extract from *Note, Command Responsibility for War Crimes*, 82 Yale L.J. 1274 (1973).

> Despite Article 18's incorporation of international law, American war crimes are customarily tried as violations of specific criminal provisions in the UCMJ. Apparently, the prosecution has unfettered discretion to proceed either under these provisions or under Article 18's international law.
>
> While the UCMJ's articles do not expressly mention command responsibility, the offense might conceivably be charged as a form of complicity in the subordinate's crime, as an inferior grade of homicide, or as the inchoate offense of "dereliction of duty." Only complicity would, like Article 18, involve the possibility of capital punishment or life imprisonment. Inferior grades of homicide and "dereliction" carry much lower maximum penalties.
>
> Complicity-through-omission requires that the defendant have had a "duty to interfere" with the crime. While the command relationship does apparently raise this duty, the alleged accomplice must have been at the scene of the crime, must have approved of the crime's perpetration, and must have, through this approval, provided "encouragement" for the perpetration. As for involuntary manslaughter, the Manual for Courts-Martial's broad definition might be read as requiring a commander to eliminate a high risk that his subordinates will commit murder, but the Manual's illustrative examples of the offense do not even hint at such an interpretation. An officer has been convicted of negligent homicide for failing to stop a subordinate's crime, but the Board of Review, in reversing, indicated that an officer must have actual knowledge of the subordinate's crime before incurring a duty to intervene against it. Assimilating command responsibility to traditional notions of homicide is obviously a troublesome project. Officers have quite frequently been convicted of "dereliction of duty" concerning subordinate crimes. While typically the officer was present during the crimes and "did nothing," breach of general supervisory duties has occasionally been punished where subordinate crimes followed, and the Code criminalizes dereliction of any duty created by "custom of the service," an obviously elastic concept.
>
> In short, rather than resolving the conflicts in international law, the UCMJ supplements them with additional theories of command responsibility, also poorly formulated, and fails to indicate which provisions apply in which circumstances.

Id. at 1289-1291.

All of those charged with offenses arising out of the Abu Ghraib scandal pled guilty, with the exceptions of Specialist Charles Graner and, after her initial guilty plea was rejected, Private Lyndie England. The transcript of Graner's testimony at his trial has not been publicly released, but the following statements were made by his attorney, Guy Womack, in January 2005.

Interview with Guy Womack by Chris Matthews

"Hardball with Chris Matthews," MSNBC, Jan. 5, 2005, transcript available at *http://msnbc.msn.com/id/6808711*

[Guy] Womack: . . . Our defense in this case is that he was following lawful orders or what he believed to be lawful orders. That is an absolute defense to all of these charges.

Matthews: Let's get to that absolute defense, as you describe it.

Do you have any written orders from any superior officer, captains or majors or colonels or whatever, telling your client, Charles Graner, to engage in this kind of behavior towards prisoners?

Womack: No.

(CROSSTALK)

Matthews: Do you have any word of mouth? Do you have any evidence of someone who heard someone give him an order to that effect?

Womack: Oh, certainly, absolutely.

Matthews: Well, tell us about it, if you can.

Womack: Yes.

There's evidence of military intelligence officers, both commissioned and noncommissioned, who ordered Specialist Graner specifically to do certain acts. Also, there are witnesses who heard these people give orders implicitly, saying things like, make sure this prisoner has a rough night.

Matthews: Right.

Womack: Make sure this prisoner doesn't sleep, that sort of thing.

Matthews: Do you have the testimony of third parties or the second person in these cases that will back that up in court?

Womack: Yes, absolutely.

Matthews: Do these orders that were given by people orally, do they match up with the picture of his behavior, your client's actual behavior on these videos? In other words, is he shown doing something in line with what he was told to do?

Womack: Yes. Yes.

In virtually every instance, there's an order that matches or that caused the action that's depicted in the videos and in the photographs.

Matthews: Will you bring any Iraqi prisoners in to testify for the defense of your client?

Womack: Yes. There will be two of them.

Matthews: Do they speak English?

Womack: No.

Matthews: So you're going to have to have interpreters in the court to make the case. Are they credible witnesses?

Womack: They are credible. They have already testified by deposition. These are videotaped depositions.

Matthews: I got you.

Womack: We have Iraqi interpreters. And we already have the tapes. They were introduced yesterday.

Matthews: Well, a smart lawyer like yourself knows what he is going to face in court. What will the prosecution claim in contradistinction to your claim and apparently your evidence, at least through witnesses, that your client was following orders?

Womack: They're going to say that the orders were not given or that they were clearly illegal and a reasonable man would not have followed them.

Matthews: Whoa. If a reasonable man would not have followed orders, would that reasonable man not be reasonable in assuming that what everyone else was doing was in fact consistent with the mission, everyone around him?

Womack: I think, if someone had disobeyed the order, they would have been court-martialed for that. Keep in mind that....

(CROSSTALK)

Matthews: Can you prove that? Can you prove it was an order that had to be followed?

Womack: Chris, every order has to be followed, unless you know or reasonably should know that it is unlawful to follow the order. We don't want soldiers debating the legality of orders in combat.

(CROSSTALK)

Womack: These orders appeared to be lawful. Keep in mind that we will have evidence that the unit that was preceding the 372nd had been following the identical orders.

Matthews: OK. How high up the chain of command can you show that he got orders? In other words, did he get orders from captains or majors? What kind of officer, what level of officer or noncommissioned officer gave these orders to your client?

Womack: The highest ranking officer who gave a direct order to Special [sic] Graner was a lieutenant colonel.

Matthews: Whoa. And that person is going to admit that or are they going to have to be proven to have said such a thing?

Womack: No, that's Lieutenant Colonel Jordan. He has invoked his right to remain silent. I've asked the judge to give him a grant of immunity or to order the convening authorities to do that. They have refused.

Matthews: Why? Why don't they want the truth? Why doesn't the judge want the truth by giving immunity?

Womack: Well, the judge says that the government can choose whether or not to give immunity. If they choose not to, he should not invade their....

(CROSSTALK)

Matthews: Do they intend to prosecute that lieutenant colonel or not?

Womack: I don't think they do.

Matthews: And if not, why are they giving him immunity?

Womack: I don't think they will give him immunity. Well, they won't give him immunity. I don't think they will prosecute him, because that would prove that this is a much broader-scope problem than just seven M.P.s. The government doesn't want to admit that.

Matthews: Yes, that would be a lot of people's reasonable assumption, by the way, watching this whole thing. Anyway, thank you. Good luck with your case on Monday with your client, Charles Graner, Specialist Graner.

Womack: Thank you.

Lieutenant Colonel Jordan, who was referred to by Mr. Womack, was neither disciplined nor prosecuted, nor were criminal charges brought against any other officer. Specialist Graner was convicted of conspiracy, dereliction of duty, maltreatment of detainees, assault and committing indecent acts; he was sentenced to ten years' imprisonment. He was also demoted to private and received a dishonorable discharge.

Comments and Questions

1. One of the many panels created to investigate abuses of detainees by U.S. personnel concluded that "commanding officers and their staffs at various levels failed in their duties and that such failures contributed directly or indirectly to detainee abuse. Commanders are responsible for all their units do or fail to do, and should be held accountable for their action or inaction." *Final Report of the Independent Panel to Review DoD Detention Operations* (Schlesinger Report) (Aug. 2004), reprinted in Greenberg and Dratel, infra page 271, at 908, 928. Does this conclusion support charges of war crimes against those in charge of Abu Ghraib?

2. In March 2005, Human Rights First and the American Civil Liberties Union filed a civil suit in the Northern Illinois Federal District Court against Secretary of Defense Rumsfeld on behalf of several detainees allegedly mistreated in violation of domestic and international law in Iraq and Afghanistan, on the theory that Rumsfeld was ultimately responsible for the treatment. See *Ali et al. v. Rumsfeld* (N.D. Ill) (case filed Mar. 1, 2005).

3. Charges also have been brought against soldiers for ill-treatment and deaths of detainees in Afghanistan, where similar issues of insufficient training and command responsibility have been raised. See, e.g., Tom Golden, *Abuse Cases Open Command Issues at Army Prison*, N.Y. Times, Aug. 8, 2005, at A1.

VI. Modern Warfare: Distinguishing Combatants from Civilians

The modern law of war is premised on the possibility and the necessity of distinguishing between combatants and civilians, between military targets and civilian habitats. Certainly nothing is more important insofar as the protection of the human rights of civilians is concerned. At the same time, nothing is more difficult. Moreover, the problem has become increasingly serious in the decades since the adoption of the Fourth Geneva Convention in 1949. The Vietnam War; post-Cold-War "peacekeeping"; the U.S.-led attacks on Kosovo, Afghanistan, and Iraq; internal conflicts in several African countries, Sri Lanka, and Colombia; and the increased focus on international terrorism are only the most vivid illustrations of the fact that the traditional law of war — designed to regulate international armed conflicts between states — may be inadequate to handle the complex issues arising during situations of civil strife, insurgencies, and terrorism.

Sometimes the most important decisions of all — whether particular persons are to live or die — must be made on the spot by the lowest ranking and least trained personnel in the armed services. Is it really fair to assume that when war crimes occur in such a context they are attributable only to the individual soldiers involved? Do conditions of modern warfare resemble the battles between identifiable armies that characterized the first two world wars? How are soldiers supposed to combat irregular fighters who do not wear uniforms, hide their weapons, and deliberately mingle among civilians?

Recall, too, the discussion above of the issue of command responsibility. It is true that soldiers often receive no formal, direct orders on what to do about, for example, prisoners taken during a search and destroy mission. It is also true, however, that more subtle — though none the less effective — messages do filter down from above that can get translated into war crimes in the field. This problem of the filtering downward of an ethos of killing (or torturing), as distinct from any formal orders to kill or torture, can leave the soldier in the field in a nearly hopeless dilemma. He is quite consciously acting to further his superiors' policy. Yet he is not acting under direct orders; so the responsibility for any wrongdoing — or excessive zeal, if you will — stays on his shoulders.

The situation of Lieutenant James T. Duffy, the holder of two Bronze Stars, the Purple Heart, and seven other honorable citations, is a situation in point. Duffy was court-martialed in 1970 for ordering a prisoner to be shot in cold blood. At his trial, Duffy made the following observations.

Lieutenant Duffy's Statement

In *Crimes of War: A Legal, Political-Documentary, and Psychological Inquiry into the Responsibility of Leaders, Citizens, and Soldiers for Criminal Acts in Ways* 248, 249-254 (Richard A. Falk, Gabriel Kolko, and Robert Lifton eds. 1971)

There was only one thing that really upset me (and many other people in the platoon too). That was taking prisoners that we knew were VC [Viet Cong] and having them released by Brigade as innocent civilians. It's not hard to spot a VC after you've spent some time in the field. The only people who live out there are farmers and the VC. The farmers are only women and children and old men. They were always very friendly toward us. We would stop in a house for lunch or dinner and share our food with them, talk, play with the children and really have a good time. I almost never saw any young men in the rice paddies. Whenever we found any young men we immediately questioned them. I can think of only two young men that I ever found in the field and they were just 15 years old and still going to school. The only other young men I ever found in the field were VC who were shooting at us.

Once we ambushed a sampan in the Plain of Reeds, which is a free-fire zone and anybody who moves is fair game. This sampan came down a canal at about 2100 hours. When we opened up, two men were killed and two women were injured. The women were yelling, "Don't shoot, don't shoot, we are VC!" Sergeant Lanasa swam out and rescued the two women and brought them back to shore. The next morning he carried one of them three-quarters of a mile through swamps to an area where we dusted them off for medical treatment and interrogation. We found out two days later that both women had been released by Brigade as innocent civilians. This really upset me and many others in the platoon.... It's hard enough to find the enemy, but to catch and just let them go is ridiculous.

After that incident I decided I was not going to take any more prisoners. If at all possible I was not going to let the situation arise where a prisoner might be taken. I told all my squad leaders and my company commander of this. I told all my men that if they were going to engage someone, not to stop shooting until everyone was dead. I told them if they were going to shoot at somebody, they had better kill him. Nobody ever said anything against this policy and I think most of the men agreed to it. My company commander felt the same way I did about it....

Sometimes innocent civilians are killed out there, but it just can't be helped. We were always careful not to shoot towards any populated areas when we prepped a woodline, and even in a contact we would try not to shoot towards civilians if at all possible. But still you would hit a few, especially at night. Many of the farmers would be out after curfew wandering around, or going over to a friend's house.

They just sort of disregarded the curfew and we have no choice but to engage them, since anybody moving after curfew is supposed to be considered VC. When we kill a man after curfew and he has a valid ID or he is an old man, etc., you can pretty well guess that he was just an innocent civilian out after the curfew (but, of course, you never know for sure because anybody can be a VC, valid ID card or not)....

Whenever we did take prisoners, they were always roughed up and then questioned. When we worked with ARVN's [the South Vietnamese army] or national police, we found that they were excellent interrogators. You could tell that they really hated the VC by the way they beat them when they caught one. They do not mess around at all. I once had a national policeman with me when we chased a VC through a house. The VC got away but the national policemen wanted to take one of the women in the house with us for questioning. That night he beat and kicked that woman for about two hours while he questioned her. When he was finished he came over and told me she was okay, not a VC, and to let her go in the morning. I went along with his decision. I always listened to my Tiger Scouts, ARVN's or national police and would do what they say. They always seem to know who is a VC and who isn't....

I know in my case, platoon leaders never got any guidance on treatment of prisoners. Battalion HQS never said anything about them. There was no SOP [Standard Operating Procedure], there was never a request that we take any prisoners. The only thing we ever heard was to get more body count, kill more VC! We heard that all the time; it was really stressed. My squad leader told me that in his old unit they couldn't come in from the field unless they turned in a body count. Many units "pad" their body count so they can say they killed more than anybody else. The only way anybody judged a unit's effectiveness was by the number of body counts they had. If you had a lot of body counts, everybody would think you were really good. If you didn't have a lot of body counts, they would think you were a poor unit.

I know I was always conscious of how many body counts my platoon had. I keep a record on the wall of my room and had a record painted on the side of my APC [armored personnel carrier]. I was always proud of the fact that my platoon had more kills than any other platoon in the company and that our company led the battalion in kills. The men in the platoon were aware of all this, too, and they were proud of their record. They considered themselves to be the best platoon around. It kept our morale very high when we were leading everyone else for the month.

Some people might have thought it was wrong to judge a unit just by the number of kills they get. I think it is the only way a unit should be judged. That is really the only mission we have in the field, to kill the enemy. As far as I'm concerned that's why we were sent over here and that's what our job is. The only way to see how well a unit is performing its job is to see how many body counts they have. My platoon killed, found or captured about 50 enemy from mid-July to mid-September and I only had one man killed and only two seriously wounded. I always thought that was a pretty good record.

I'm out of the field now and I thank God I made it in one piece. I am not sorry at all that I came over here. I didn't mind all that humping through the mud — I didn't even mind being wounded. That's all part of war; you can't do anything about it. Overall, I have really enjoyed my tour over here in Vietnam and I'm glad I came over. I had a lot of good times in the field, made many friends and have learned an awful lot. I know now just how much we have back in America when I see how hard a life the Vietnamese people live here. Most have known war all their lives. It has killed their sons, even their women and children, and has destroyed their land. They must be very tired of this war. I am glad, though, that we are fighting over here and not in the United States.

I feel that by coming over here I have accomplished a great deal. I feel that I helped a few dozen GI's make it through their tour without being killed and that I was able to help the Vietnamese people, as well as our allied friends, in their fight against Communism. I am only sorry that more Americans back home do not support our efforts over here. I don't think that they really know what it's all about, especially what a soldier has to go through in the field. They do not know what it's like to see Communism face to face. They think we can fight a "moral" war over here. It seems to me that only the bad guys are supposed to get killed, and even then they have to be killed in a nice way. It just doesn't work that way, everything is not black and white, and all the killing is not nice by any means. I always felt that I was living close to death while I was in the field. It was something you had to get used to, seeing dead men, killing some myself and knowing I could be killed in a minute. It became so commonplace that I never worried about it really. That doesn't mean I enjoyed all killing and brutality — I just got used to it.

It's something you have to experience to understand. I think the only ones who really know what's going on in the battlefield are the soldiers who have to go out and kill the enemy to stay alive. They are the ones who know war best. . . .

[Duffy was convicted of involuntary manslaughter and sentenced to six months imprisonment. Was this an appropriate outcome? See *United States v. Duffy*, 47 C.M.R. 658 (1973).]

Is the experience of today's soldiers in Afghanistan, Iraq, and elsewhere much different from that described by Lieutenant Duffy in Vietnam over 30 years ago? Consider the following experiences of U.S. soldiers serving in the UN-authorized "peacekeeping" mission in Somalia in 1994, who came under attack while trying to rescue the crew of a U.S. helicopter that had been shot down.

Mark Bowden, *Black Hawk Down, A Story of Modern War*

At 63, 106, 125, 217 (1999)

From his turret in the rear Humvee, Orthic had seen the flash of the RPG [rocket propelled grenade] tube. He swung his .50 cal around and blasted the spot, mowing down a small crowd that had been standing in front of the shooter.

Then what felt like a baseball bat came down on his right forearm. It felt just like that. He heard the *crack!* and felt the blow and looked down to see a small hole in his arm. The bone was broken.

He shouted, "I'm hit! I'm hit!"

He really did go cyclic on the .50 cal then, just fired continually for maybe as long as a minute, taking down trees and walls and anyone in, around, or behind them, before Sergeant Lorenzo Ruiz stood up in the turret and took the gun. . . .

He leaned his M-16 out the truck window. Although an expert marksman, he was no longer just squeezing off one careful round after the next. There were too many targets, too many people shooting at him. It was as if "Kill-an-American-Day" had been declared in Mog [Mogadishu]. It seemed like every man, woman, and child in the city was out trying to get them. There were people in alleyways, in windows, on rooftops. Spalding kept shooting his rifle dry. Then he would shoot with his 9 mm Beretta pistol with one hand while he replaced the rifle magazine with the other. He just wanted to get the hell out of there. . . .

At every intersection now Somalis just lined up, on both sides of the street, and fired at every vehicle that came across. . . .

The city was shredding them block by block. No place was safe. The air was alive with hurtling chunks of hot metal. They heard the awful slap of bullets into flesh and heard the screams and saw the insides of men' bodies spill out and watched the gray blank pallor rise in the faces of their friends, and the best of the men fought back despair. . . .

. . . Closer to the wrecked helicopter, a woman kept running out into the alley, screaming and pointing toward the house at the southeast corner of the intersection where many of the wounded had been moved. No one shot at her. She was unarmed. But every time she stepped back behind cover a wicked torrent of fire would be unleashed where she pointed. After she'd done this twice, one of the D-boys behind the tail of *Super Six One* said, "If that bitch comes back, I'm going to shoot her."

Captain Coultrop nodded his approval. She did, and the D-boy shot her down on the street.

Then there was the woman in a blue turban, a powerful woman with thick arms and legs who came sprinting across the road carrying a heavy basket in both arms. She was wearing a bright blue-and-white dress that billowed behind her as she ran. Every Ranger at the intersection blasted her. Twombly, Nelson, Yurek, and Stebbins all opened up. Howe fired on her from further up the hill. First she stumbled, but kept on going. Then, as more rounds hit her, she fell and RPGs spilled out of her basket onto the street. The shooting stopped. She had been hit by many rounds and lay in a heap in the dirt for a long moment, breathing heavily. Then the woman pulled herself up on all fours, grabbed an RPG round, and crawled. This time the massive Ranger volley literally tore her apart.

Note: The First Gulf War

The issue of war crimes remains with us. During the 1991 or First Gulf War, which followed Iraq's invasion of Kuwait, most public condemnation was directed against the political and military leaders of the operations rather than individual soldiers — perhaps because the ground phase of the war lasted only 100 hours. However, no prosecutions appear to have been brought by any side to the conflict, and there was no effort to establish a war crimes tribunal, despite early expressions of interest.

Most of the alleged crimes were committed by Iraqi forces and might include the uncontroverted fact of the invasion of Kuwait itself (perhaps more accurately termed a crime against peace) and the firing of Scud missiles at cities in Israel, a state not otherwise involved in the conflict. Other allegations concerned the taking of diplomatic hostages and the treatment of Kuwaitis during the Iraqi occupation, including killing, rape, looting, and destruction of property. See Paul W. Kahn, *Lessons for International Law from the Gulf War,* 45 Stan. L. Rev. 425 (1993); James S. Robbins, *War Crimes: The Case of Iraq,* 18 Fletcher F. World Aff. 45 (No. 2, 1994).

The "coalition forces," led by the United States, were accused of targeting civilian installations (including Iraq's water supply, a "munitions" factory that purportedly produced milk powder, and an air raid shelter in which hundreds of civilians were killed) and of unnecessarily massacring Iraqi soldiers at the end of the brief ground war. The United States also was accused of having encouraged Saddam Hussein's attack on Kuwait and, thus, sharing in guilt for the invasion itself. See Ramsey Clark, *Complaint to the Commission of Inquiry for the International War Crimes Tribunal,* 48 Guild Prac. 33 (1991); John G. Heidenrich, *The Gulf War: How Many Iraqis Died?*, 90 Foreign Policy 108 (1993); Al Kamen, *Iraqi Factory's Product: Germ Warfare or Milk?*, Wash. Post, Feb. 8, 1991, at A1; Charles M. Madigan, *In War, the Bottom Line Is Death,* Chi. Trib., Feb 15, 1991, at 1.

Among the many readings on war crimes and the First Gulf War, see also Ramsey Clark, *The Fire This Time: U.S. War Crimes in the Gulf* (1992); Betsy Baker, *Legal Protections for the Environment in Times of Armed Conflict,* 33 Va. J. Intl. L. 351 (1993); Judith Gail Gardam, *Proportionality and Force in International Law,* 87 Am. J. Intl L. 391 (1993).

Note: Afghanistan and the Second Gulf War

The most serious allegations of war crimes during the U.S. invasion of Afghanistan related to alleged U.S. complicity in the deaths of a large number of Taliban prisoners after the battle for Kunduz in November 2002. See, e.g., Kate Connolly and Rory McCarthy, *New film accuses US of war crimes*, The Guardian, June 13, 2002. Mistaken bombing raids and attacks also continue to kill Afghan civilians, although there have not been widespread allegations of war crimes since the end of major hostilities.

The Second Gulf War, initiated by the United States and another "coalition of the willing" in 2003 against the Saddam Hussein regime in Iraq, also gave rise to serious allegations of war crimes and unjustified killing of civilians, in addition to the ill-treatment at Abu Ghraib. Less attention seems to be paid today to civilian casualties than was the case in previous wars, although one widely-quoted source estimates that approximately 30,000 Iraqi civilians had been killed by the U.S.-led coalition between the onset of the war and late 2005. See *http://www.iraqbodycount.net.*

> It was during Operation Anaconda, the post-Afghan war mop-up effort in the Shahi Kot region of Afghanistan, that Defense Secretary Rumsfeld famously said: "I don't do body counts." General Tommy Franks similarly made the point when the operation ended on 18 March 2002: "You know we don't do body counts." . . .
>
> Based on the Vietnam experience, it is entirely appropriate for military leaders, both civilian and uniform, to remind the nation and its armed forces that "body counts" should not serve as a leading measure of progress toward victory. Vietnam also taught that a rising level of casualties can negatively affect public support for a war effort. In this case, however, the lesson is not that leaders should avoid making casualty estimates or withhold them from public scrutiny. Instead, our armed forces should strive to keep casualties as low as possible, while fully disclosing the facts concerning war's toll, as best they are known. This may breed controversy, but that is the price we must pay for the strengths that democracy affords us. In sum: The Vietnam experience fully justifies the Pentagon's refusal to use "body counts" as the measure of victory; It does not, however, justify a refusal to publically [sic] disclose casualty estimates. . . .

Carl Conetta, *Disappearing the Dead: Iraq, Afghanistan, and the Idea of a "New Warfare,"* Project on Defense Alternatives Research Monograph #9, sec. 7 (2004) (citations omitted)

VII. The "War on Terror": Emergency, Armed Conflict, or Business as Usual?

On the morning of September 11, 2001, America and the world watched in horror as two commercial airplanes, hijacked by terrorists, flew into the twin towers of the World Trade Center, and a third slammed into the Pentagon. A fourth plane crashed into a field in Pennsylvania. In all, nearly 3,000 people died on that fateful day. A week later, President George W. Bush addressed the nation at a joint session of Congress.

George W. Bush, Address to a Joint Session of Congress and to the American People

Sept. 20, 2001, *http://www.whitehouse.gov/news/releases/2001/09/20010920-8.html*

Mr. Speaker, Mr. President Pro Tempore, members of Congress, and fellow Americans:

In the normal course of events, Presidents come to this chamber to report on the state of the Union. Tonight, no such report is needed.

Tonight we are a country awakened to danger and called to defend freedom. Our grief has turned to anger, and anger to resolution. Whether we bring our enemies to justice, or bring justice to our enemies, justice will be done.

On September the 11th, enemies of freedom committed an act of war against our country. Americans have known wars — but for the past 136 years, they have been wars on foreign soil, except for one Sunday in 1941. Americans have known the casualties of war — but not at the center of a great city on a peaceful morning. Americans have known surprise attacks — but never before on thousands of civilians. All of this was brought upon us in a single day — and night fell on a different world, a world where freedom itself is under attack.

Americans have many questions tonight. Americans are asking: Who attacked our country? The evidence we have gathered all points to a collection of loosely affiliated terrorist organizations known as al Qaeda.

This group and its leader — a person named Osama bin Laden — are linked to many other organizations in different countries, including the Egyptian Islamic Jihad and the Islamic Movement of Uzbekistan. There are thousands of these terrorists in more than 60 countries. They are recruited from their own nations and neighborhoods and brought to camps in places like Afghanistan, where they are trained in the tactics of terror. They are sent back to their homes or sent to hide in countries around the world to plot evil and destruction.

Our war on terror begins with al Qaeda, but it does not end there. It will not end until every terrorist group of global reach has been found, stopped and defeated.

Americans are asking: How will we fight and win this war? We will direct every resource at our command — every means of diplomacy, every tool of intelligence, every instrument of law enforcement, every financial influence, and every necessary weapon of war — to the disruption and to the defeat of the global terror network.

This war will not be like the war against Iraq a decade ago, with a decisive liberation of territory and a swift conclusion. It will not look like the air war above Kosovo two years ago, where no ground troops were used and not a single American was lost in combat.

Our response involves far more than instant retaliation and isolated strikes. Americans should not expect one battle, but a lengthy campaign, unlike any other we have ever seen. It may include dramatic strikes, visible on TV, and covert operations, secret even in success. We will starve terrorists of funding, turn them one against another, drive them from place to place, until there is no refuge or no rest. And we will pursue nations that provide aid or safe haven to terrorism. Every nation, in every region, now has a decision to make. Either you are with us, or you are with the terrorists. From this day forward, any nation that continues to harbor or support terrorism will be regarded by the United States as a hostile regime.

Great harm has been done to us. We have suffered great loss. And in our grief and anger we have found our mission and our moment. Freedom and fear are at war. The advance of human freedom — the great achievement of our time, and the great hope of every time — now depends on us. Our nation — this generation — will lift a dark threat of violence from our people and our future. We will rally the world to this cause by our efforts, by our courage. We will not tire, we will not falter, and we will not fail.

A. *Prosecuting Those Persons Responsible for Ill-Treatment at Abu Ghraib*

1. The Dramatis Personae

On January 13, 2004, a guard in the prison, Spc. Joseph Darby, had reported photographs of abuse of detainees taking place on Tier 1A of Abu Ghraib prison to the Army's Criminal Investigative Command. Lt. Gen. Ricardo Sanchez ordered a criminal investigation in response to the complaint. The investigation ordered by Sanchez culminated in a report authored by Maj. Gen. Antonio Taguba, which found numerous cases of prisoner abuse, particularly on Tier 1A, otherwise nown as the "hard site," between October and December 2003. Article 15-6 Investigation of the 800th Military Police Brigade *(Taguba Report),* March 2004, reprinted in Greenberg and Dratel, infra p. 271, at 405. On March 20, 2004, the Army charged six soldiers with abusing inmates at Abu Ghraib.

While condemning the abuses, the Bush administration was unapologetic about the use of interrogation for collecting intelligence. In an op-ed published in the month following the emergence of the Abu Ghraib photographs, John Yoo, Deputy Assistant Attorney General, wrote, "[I]nterrogations of detainees captured in the war on terrorism are not regulated under Geneva. This is not to condone torture, which is still prohibited by the Torture Convention and federal criminal law. Nonetheless, Congress's definition of torture in those laws — the infliction of severe mental or physical pain — leaves room for interrogation methods that go beyond polite conversation." John Yoo, *Terrorists Have No Geneva Rights,* Wall Street Journal, May 26, 2004. Even a year later, the CIA Director of Public Affairs stated, "Lawful interrogation of captured terrorists is a vital tool in saving American lives. It works." Jennifer Millerwise, *Statement by CIA Director of Public Affairs,* March 18, 2005,*http://www.cia.gov/cia/public_affairs/press_release/2005/pr03182005.html.*

Through June 2005, eighteen soldiers had been removed from duty in connection with the Abu Ghraib photographs discussed supra at 215, and nine had been court-martialed. Sentences ranged from dishonorable discharge and forfeiture of two weeks' pay to ten years' imprisonment for Charles Graner, considered to be the ringleader of the abuse.

Officers formally investigated in connection with Abu Ghraib prison scandal were Lt. Gen. Ricardo Sanchez, Commander of Combined Joint Task Force 7; Maj. Gen. Walter Wojdakowski, Deputy Commander, Combined Joint Task Force 7; Maj. Gen. Barbara G. Fast, an intelligence officer of Combined Joint Task Force 7; Col. Marc Warren, Staff Judge Advocate for Combined Joint Task Force 7; Brig. Gen. Janis L. Karpinski, Commander, 800th Military Police

Brigade and head of Abu Ghraib prison in the period when the photographs were taken; and Col. Thomas Pappas, commander of military intelligence personnel at Abu Ghraib.

The Department of Army Inspector General found charges against all officers to be unsubstantiated, except those against Col. Pappas and Brig. Gen. Karpinski. (Col. Warren, as a Staff Judge Advocate, underwent a preliminary screening inquiry conducted by the Department of the Army's Office of the Judge Advocate General for allegations of professional impropriety under lawyers' ethics rules and dereliction in the performance of his duties. The allegations were found to be unsubstantiated.) Allegations of dereliction of duty and shoplifting against Brig. Gen. Karpinski were upheld, but allegations of a material misrepresentation and failure to obey an order were found to be unsubstantiated. Karpinski, who claimed that she was being "scapegoated," was issued a memorandum of reprimand to be filed in her Official Military Personnel File, relieved of her command of the 800th Military Police Brigade, and demoted to Colonel in the U.S. Army Reserve. The Army stated that, "Though Brig. Gen. Karpinski's performance of duty was found to be seriously lacking, the investigation determined that no action or lack of action on her part contributed specifically to the abuse of detainees at Abu Ghraib." U.S. Army News Release, Army releases findings in detainee-abuse investigations, May 5, 2005, *http://www4.army.mil/ocpa/read.php?story_id_key=7293;* Libby Copeland, *Prison Revolt*, Wash. Post, May 10, 2004, at C1 (Karpinski being scapegoated). Col. Pappas was found guilty of two counts of dereliction of duty, one count for allowing dogs to be present during interrogations and one count for failure to ensure that subordinates were adequately informed of, trained in, and supervised in the application of interrogation procedures. He was not found to have ordered the abuse of prisoners but was reprimanded and fined $8,000.

The findings that no officer had ordered abuse and that no policy of torture existed were consistent throughout the U.S. military's investigations of itself. Rather, investigations turned up sadistic soldiers, poor management, confusing policies, and a shortage of trained personnel, in the context of ongoing conflict. Cordon and capture techniques were used to round up a large swathe of the population who were suspected of having ties with the insurgency. Abu Ghraib prison quickly became overcrowded and undermanned, with personnel lacking experience in detention and interrogation.

Abu Ghraib was not unique. Among the investigations ordered by the military in the wake of the Abu Ghraib scandal was one conducted by Lt. Gen. Paul T. Mikolashek, which found 94 incidents of detainee abuse, ranging from theft, physical assault, and sexual assault to death, in U.S. detention centers in Iraq and Afghanistan. See Dept. of the Army Inspector General Detainee Operations Inspection (Mikolashek Report) (July 21, 2004), Greenberg and Dratel, infra page 271, at 630. Among those who died in U.S. custody was Iraqi Gen. Abed Hamad Mowhoush, a "high-priority target." During interrogation conducted on November 26, 2003, Mowhoush was placed inside a sleeping bag with only his feet exposed. He was rolled back and forth while being questioned. One of the interrogators sat on his chest and placed hands over his mouth. Mowhoush died during the interrogation, and an autopsy confirmed evidence of blunt force trauma to the chest and legs. The interrogating officers were given general officer reprimands, prohibited from conducting further interrogations, and referred for consideration of misconduct charges.

The report found that only four of the sixteen facilities inspected had copies of the Geneva Conventions in the detainees' native language, as required. At Abu Ghraib, the inspectors encountered serious overcrowding, with only twelve shower heads for 600 to 700 detainees. Fresh water was not always available, and detainee meals were frequently contaminated with dirt and rodent droppings. Nonetheless, the Mikolashek Report concluded that "we were unable to identify system failures that resulted in incidents of abuse. These incidents of abuse resulted from the failure of indivuduals to follow known standards of discipline and Army Values and, in some cases, the failure of a few leaders to enforce these standards of discipline." Id. at 632. The inspectors recommended that Abu Ghraib be closed and the detainees relocated to Camp Bucca, another U.S.-run detention facility in Iraq. Regarding instructions on interrogation, the Mikolashek Report observed gently, "While the language of the approved policies could be viewed as a careful attempt to draw the line between lawful and unlawful conduct, the published instructions left considerable room for misapplication, particularly under high-stress combat conditions." Id. at 676-677.

Subsequent investigations confirmed that U.S. interrogation policy in Iraq changed frequently. The Jones Report concluded, "At Abu Ghraib, the lack of consistent policy and command oversight regarding interrogation techniques, coupled with changing policies, contributed to the confusion concerning which techniques could be used, which required higher level approval, and what limits applied to permitted techniques." Anthony R. Jones, AR 15-6 Investigation of the Abu Ghraib Prison and 205th Military Intelligence Brigade (Aug. 2004), reprinted in Greenberg and Dratel, infra, at 991, 1011. Another report noted that, in October 2003, "interrogation policy in Iraq had changed three times in less than 30 days." George R. Fay, *AR 15-6 Investigation of the Abu Ghraib Detention Facility and 205th Military Intelligence Brigade* (U) (Fay Report), reprinted in id. at 1018, 1023.

2. The Legal Arguments

A memorandum dated August 1, 2002, and authored by Jay S. Bybee, then Assistant Attorney General at the U.S. Department of Justice, sets out in detail the author's view of U.S. legal obligations with regard to interrogation, as well as the legal definition of torture. The recipient of the memo, Alberto Gonzales, was subsequently appointed Attorney-General in the second Bush Administration. Bybee was appointed a judge on the Ninth Circuit Court of Appeals in 2003.

Memorandum from Assistant Attorney General Jay S. Bybee

August 1, 2002, reprinted in Karen J. Greenberg and Joshua E. Dratel eds., *The Torture Papers* 172-74, 183, 184-85, 191, 196-98, 200, 201-02, 206, 207, 208-09, 213-14 (2005) (citations and references omitted)

U.S. Department of Justice
Office of Legal Counsel

August 1, 2002

Memorandum for Alberto R. Gonzales
Counsel to the President

Re: Standards of Conduct for Interrogation under 18 U.S.C. §§2340-2340A

summary

You have asked for our Office's views regarding the standards of conduct under the Convention Against Torture and Other Cruel, Inhuman and Degrading Treatment or Punishment as implemented by Sections 2340-2340A of title 18 of the United States Code. As we understand it, this question has arisen in the context of the conduct of interrogations outside of the United States. We conclude below that Section 2340A proscribes acts inflicting, that are specifically intended to inflict, severe pain or suffering, whether mental or physical. Those acts must be of an extreme nature to rise to the level of torture within the meaning of Section 2340A and the Convention. We further conclude that certain acts may be cruel, inhuman, or degrading, but still not produce pain and suffering of the requisite intensity to fall within Section 2340A's proscription against torture. We conclude by examining possible defenses that would negate any claim that certain interrogation methods violate the statute.

In Part I, we examine the criminal statute's text and history. We conclude that for an act to constitute torture as defined in Section 2340, it must inflict pain that is difficult to endure. Physical pain amounting to torture must be equivalent in intensity to the pain accompanying serious physical injury, such as organ failure, impairment of bodily function, or even death. For purely mental pain or suffering to amount to torture under Section 2340, it must result in significant psychological harm of significant duration, e.g., lasting for months or even years. We conclude that the mental harm also must result from one of the predicate acts listed in the statute, namely: threats of imminent death; threats of infliction of the kind of pain that would amount to physical torture; infliction of such physical pain as a means of psychological torture; use of drugs or other procedures designed to deeply disrupt the senses, or fundamentally alter an individual's personality; or threatening to do any of these things to a third party. The legislative history simply reveals that Congress intended for the statute's definition to track the Convention's definition of torture and the reservations, understandings and declarations that the United States submitted with its ratification. We conclude that the statute, taken as a whole, makes plain that it prohibits only extreme acts.

In Part II, we examine the text, ratification history, and negotiating history of the Torture Convention. We conclude that the treaty's text prohibits only the most extreme acts by reserving criminal penalties solely for torture and declining to require such penalties for "cruel, inhuman, or degrading treatment or punishment." This confirms our view that the criminal statute penalizes only the most egregious conduct. Executive branch interpretations and representations to the Senate at the time of ratification further confirm that the treaty was intended to reach only the most extreme conduct.

In Part III, we analyze the jurisprudence of the Torture Victims Protection Act, 28 U.S.C. §1350 note (2000) [(TVPA)], which provides civil remedies for torture victims, to predict the standards that courts might follow in determining what actions reach the threshold of torture in the criminal context. We conclude from these cases that courts are likely to take a totality-of-the-circumstances approach, and will look to an entire course of conduct, to determine whether certain acts will violate Section 2340A. Moreover, these cases demonstrate that most often torture involves cruel and extreme physical pain. In Part IV we examine international decisions regarding the use of sensory deprivation techniques. These cases make clear that while many of these techniques may amount to cruel, inhuman or degrading treatment, they do not produce pain or suffering of the necessary intensity to meet the definition of torture. From these decisions, we conclude that there is a wide range of such techniques that will not rise to the level of torture.

In Part V, we discuss whether Section 2340A may be unconstitutional if applied to interrogations undertaken of enemy combatants pursuant to the President's Commander-in-Chief powers. We find that in the circumstances of the current war against al Qaeda and its allies, prosecution under Section 2340A may be barred because enforcement of the statute would represent an unconstitutional infringement of the President's authority to conduct war. In Part VI we discuss defenses to an allegation that an interrogation method might violate the statute. We conclude that, under the current circumstances, necessity or self-defense may justify interrogation methods that might violate Section 2340A.

I. 18 U.S.C. §§2340-2340A

Section 2340A makes it a criminal offense for any person "outside the United States [to] commit[] or attempt[] to commit torture." Section 2340 defines the act of torture as an:

> act committed by a person acting under the color of law specifically intended to inflict severe physical or mental pain or suffering (other than pain or suffering incidental to lawful sanctions) upon another person within his custody or physical control.

18 U.S.C.A. §2340(1); *see id.* §2340A. . . .

[After examining the meaning of "specifically intended" and "severe pain and suffering" within Section 2340, the author summarizes his analysis as follows.]

Section 2340's definition of torture must be read as a sum of these component parts. Each component of the definition emphasizes that torture is not the mere infliction of pain or suffering on another, but is instead a step well removed. The victim must experience intense pain or suffering of the kind that is equivalent to the pain that would be associated with serious physical injury so severe that death, organ failure, or permanent damage resulting in a loss of significant body function will likely result. If that pain or suffering is psychological, that suffering must result from one of the acts set forth in the statute. In addition, these acts must cause long-term mental harm. Indeed, this view of the criminal act of torture is consistent with the term's common meaning. Torture is generally understood to involve "intense pain" or "excruciating pain," or put another way, "extreme anguish of body or mind." In short, reading the definition of torture as a whole, it is plain that the term encompasses only extreme acts.

II. U.N. Convention Against Torture and Other Cruel, Inhuman or Degrading Treatment or Punishment [CAT]. . . .

CAT defines torture as:

> any act by which *severe* pain or suffering, whether physical or mental, is intentionally inflicted on a person for such purposes as obtaining from him or a third person information or a confession, punishing him for an act he or a third person has committed or is suspected of having committed, or intimidating or coercing him or a third person, or for any reason based on discrimination of any kind, when such pain or suffering is inflicted by or at the instigation of or with the consent or acquiescence of a public official or other person acting in an official capacity.

Article 1(1) (emphasis added). Unlike Section 2340, this definition includes a list of purposes for which such pain and suffering is inflicted. The prefatory phrase "such purposes as" makes clear that this list is, however, illustrative rather than exhaustive. Accordingly, severe pain or suffering need not be inflicted for those specific purposes to constitute torture; instead, the perpetrator must simply have a purpose of the same kind. More importantly, like Section 2340, the pain and suffering must be severe to reach the threshold of torture. Thus, the text of CAT reinforces our reading of Section 2340 that torture must be an extreme act.

CAT also distinguishes between torture and other acts of cruel, inhuman, or degrading treatment or punishment. Article 16 of CAT requires state parties to "undertake to prevent . . . other acts of cruel, inhuman or degrading treatment or punishment *which do not amount to torture* as defined in article 1." (Emphasis added.) CAT thus establishes a category of acts that are not to be committed and that states must endeavor to prevent, but that states need not criminalize, leaving those acts without the stigma of criminal penalties. CAT reserves criminal penalties and the stigma attached to those penalties for torture alone. In so doing, CAT makes clear that torture is at the farthest end of impermissible actions, and that it is distinct and separate from the lower level of "cruel, inhuman, or degrading treatment or punishment." This approach is in keeping with CAT's predecessor, the U.N. Declaration on the Protection from Torture. That declaration defines torture as "an aggravated and deliberate form of cruel, inhuman or degrading treatment or punishment." Declaration on Protection from Torture, UN Res. 3457, Art. 1(2) (Dec. 9, 1975). . . .

The text of CAT confirms our conclusion that Section 2340A was intended to proscribe only the most egregious conduct. CAT not only defines torture as involving severe pain and suffering, but also it makes clear that such pain and suffering is at the extreme end of the spectrum of acts by reserving criminal penalties solely for torture. Executive interpretations confirm our view that the treaty (and hence, the statute) prohibits only the worst forms of cruel, inhuman, or degrading treatment or punishment. The ratification history further substantiates this interpretation. Even the negotiating history displays a recognition that torture is a step far removed from other cruel, inhuman or degrading treatment or punishment. In sum, CAT's text, ratification history and negotiating history all confirm that Section 2340A reaches only the most heinous acts. . . .

IV. International Decisions

International decisions can prove of some value in assessing what conduct might rise to the level of severe mental pain or suffering. Although decisions by foreign or international bodies are in no way binding authority upon the United States, they provide guidance about how other nations will likely react to our interpretation of the CAT and Section 2340. As this Part will discuss, other Western nations have generally used a high standard in determining whether interrogation techniques violate the international prohibition on torture. In fact, these decisions have found various aggressive interrogation methods to, at worst, constitute cruel, inhuman, and degrading treatment, but not torture. These decisions only reinforce our view that there is a clear distinction between the two standards and that only extreme conduct, resulting in pain that is of an intensity often accompanying serious physical injury, will violate the latter.

A. European Court of Human Rights

The leading European Court of Human Rights case explicating the differences between torture and cruel, inhuman, or degrading treatment or punishment is *Ireland v. the United Kingdom* (1978). In that case, the European Court of Human Rights examined interrogation techniques somewhat more sophisticated than the rather rudimentary and frequently obviously cruel acts described in the TVPA cases....

The methods at issue in *Ireland* were:

(1) Wall Standing. The prisoner stands spread eagle against the wall, with fingers high above his head, and feet back so that he is standing on his toes such that his [sic] all of his weight falls on his fingers.
(2) Hooding. A black or navy hood is placed over the prisoner's head and kept there except during the interrogation.
(3) Subjection to Noise. Pending interrogation, the prisoner is kept in a room with a loud and continuous hissing noise.
(4) Sleep Deprivation. Prisoners are deprived of sleep pending interrogation.
(5) Deprivation of Food and Drink. Prisoners receive a reduced diet during detention and pending interrogation.

The European Court of Human Rights concluded that these techniques used in combination, and applied for hours at a time, were inhuman and degrading, but did not amount to torture.* In analyzing whether these methods constituted torture, the court treated them as part of a single program. The court found that this program caused "if not actual bodily injury, at least intense physical and mental suffering to the person subjected thereto and also led to acute psychiatric disturbances during the interrogation." Thus, this program "fell into the category of inhuman treatment[.]" The court further

* It should be noted that the European Commission on Human Rights, which considered the case prior to its being appealed to the Court, held unanimously that the five techniques *did* constitute torture. See *Ireland v. United Kingdom*, [1976] Y.B. Eur. Conv. on Human Rights 512-949 (Eur. Comm. on Human Rights) — Eds.

found that "[t]the techniques were also degrading since they were such as to arouse in their victims feeling of fear, anguish and inferiority capable of humiliating and debasing them and possibl[y] breaking their physical or moral resistance." Yet the court ultimately concluded:

> Although the five techniques, as applied in combination, undoubtedly amounted to inhuman and degrading treatment, although their object was the extraction of confession, the naming of others and/or information and although they were used systematically, they did not occasion suffering of the particular *intensity* and *cruelty* implied by the word torture

(emphasis added). Thus, even though the court had concluded that the techniques produce "intense physical and mental suffering" and "acute psychiatric disturbances," they were not sufficient [in] intensity or cruelty to amount to torture....

V. The President's Commander-in-Chief Power

Even if an interrogation method arguably were to violate Section 2340A, the statute would be unconstitutional if it impermissibly encroached on the President's constitutional power to conduct a military campaign. As Commander-in-Chief, the President has the constitutional authority to order interrogations of enemy combatants to gain intelligence information concerning the military plans of the enemy. The demands of the Commander-in-Chief power are especially pronounced in the middle of a war in which the nation has already suffered a direct attack. In such a case, the information gained from interrogations may prevent future attacks by foreign enemies. Any effort to apply Section 2340A in a manner that interferes with the President's direction of such core war matters as the detention and interrogation of enemy combatants thus would be unconstitutional.

A. The War with al Qaeda

At the outset, we should make clear the nature of the threat presently posed to the nation. While your request for legal advice is not specifically limited to the current circumstances, we think it is useful to discuss this question in the context of the current war against the al Qaeda terrorist network. The situation in which these issues arise is unprecedented in American history. Four coordinated terrorist attacks, using hijacked commercial airliners as guided missiles, took place in rapid succession on the morning of September 11, 2001. These attacks were aimed at critical government buildings in the Nation's capital and landmark buildings in its financial center. These events reach a different scale of destructiveness than earlier terrorist episodes, such as the destruction of the Murrah Building in Oklahoma City in 1994. They caused thousands of deaths. Air traffic and communications within the United States were disrupted; national stock exchanges were shut for several days; and damage from the attack has been estimated to run into the tens of billions of dollars. Moreover, these attacks are part of a violent campaign against the United States that is believed to include an unsuccessful attempt to destroy an airliner in December 2001; a suicide bombing attack in Yemen on the *U.S.S. Cole* in 2000; the bombings of the United States Embassies in Kenya and Tanzania in 1998; a truck bomb attack on a U.S. military housing complex in Saudi Arabia in 1996; an unsuccessful attempt to destroy the World Trade Center in 1993; and the ambush of U.S. servicemen in Somalia in 1993. The United States and its overseas personnel and installations have been attacked as a result of Usama Bin Laden's call for a "jihad against the U.S. government, because the U.S. government is unjust, criminal and tyrannical."

In response, the Government has engaged in a broad effort at home and abroad to counter terrorism. Pursuant to his authorities as Commander-in-Chief, the President in October, 2001, ordered the Armed Forces to attack al Qaeda personnel and assets in Afghanistan, and the Taliban militia that harbored them. That military campaign appears to be nearing its close with the retreat of al Qaeda and Taliban forces from their strongholds and the installation of a friendly provisional government in Afghanistan. . . .

Despite these efforts, numerous upper echelon leaders of al Qaeda and the Taliban, with access to active terrorist cells and other resources, remain at large. . . .

Al Qaeda continues to plan further attacks, such as destroying American civilian airliners and killing American troops, which have fortunately been prevented. It is clear that bin Laden and his organization have conducted several violent attacks on the United States and its nationals, and that they seek to continue to do so. Thus, the capture and interrogation of such individuals is clearly imperative to our national security and defense. Interrogation of captured al Qaeda operatives may provide information concerning the nature of al Qaeda plans and the identities of its personnel, which may prove invaluable in preventing further direct attacks on the United States and its citizens. Given the massive destruction and loss of life caused by the September 11 attacks, it is reasonable to believe that information gained from al Qaeda personnel could prevent attacks of a similar (if not greater) magnitude from occurring in the United States. . . .

. . . In wartime, it is for the President alone to decide what methods to use to best prevail against the enemy. . . . *

. . . Congress may no more regulate the President's ability to detain and interrogate enemy combatants than it may regulate his ability to direct troop movements on the battlefield. . . .

VI. Defenses

In the foregoing parts of this memorandum, we have demonstrated that the ban on torture in Section 2340A is limited to only the most extreme forms of physical and mental harm. We have also demonstrated that Section 2340A, as applied to interrogations of enemy combatants ordered by the President pursuant to his Commander-in-Chief power would be unconstitutional. Even if an interrogation method, however, might arguably cross the line drawn in Section 2340, and application of the statute was not held to be an unconstitutional infringement of the President's Commander-in-Chief authority, we believe that under the current circumstances certain justification defenses might be available that would potentially eliminate criminal liability. Standard criminal law defenses of necessity and self-defense could justify interrogation methods needed to elicit information to prevent a direct and imminent threat to the United States and its citizens.

A. NECESSITY

We believe that a defense of necessity could be raised, under the current circumstances, to an allegation of a Section 2340A violation....

The necessity defense may prove especially relevant in the current circumstances. As it has been described in the case law and literature, the purpose behind necessity is one of public policy. According to LaFave and Scott, "the law ought to promote the achievement of higher values at the expense of lesser values, and sometimes the greater good for society will be accomplished by violating the literal language of the criminal law." In particular, the necessity defense can justify the intentional killing of one person to save two others because "it is better that two lives be saved and one lost than that two be lost and one saved." Or, put in the language of a choice of evils, "the evil involved in violating the terms of the criminal law (... even taking another's life) may be less than that which would result from literal compliance with the law (... two lives lost)"....

[T]he harm inflicted by necessity may include intentional homicide, so long as the harm avoided is greater (i.e., preventing more deaths)....

It appears to us that under the current circumstances the necessity defense could be successfully maintained in response to an allegation of a Section 2340A violation. On September 11, 2001, al Qaeda launched a surprise covert attack on civilian targets in the United States that led to the deaths of thousands and losses in the billions of dollars. According to public and governmental reports, al Qaeda has other sleeper cells within the United States that may be planning similar attacks. Indeed, al Qaeda plans apparently include efforts to develop and deploy chemical, biological and nuclear weapons of mass destruction. Under these circumstances, a detainee may possess information that could enable the United States to prevent attacks that potentially could equal or surpass the September 11 attacks in their magnitude. Clearly, any harm that might occur during an interrogation would pale to insignificance compared to the harm avoided by preventing such an attack, which could take hundreds or thousands of lives.

Under this calculus, two factors will help indicate when the necessity defense could appropriately be invoked. First, the more certain that government officials are that a particular individual has information needed to prevent an attack, the more necessary interrogation will be. Second, the more likely it appears to be that a terrorist attack is likely to occur, and the greater the amount of damage expected from such an attack, the more that an interrogation to get information would become necessary. Of course, the strength of the necessity defense depends on the circumstances that prevail, and the knowledge of the government actors involved, when the interrogation is conducted. While every interrogation that might violate Section 2340A does not trigger a necessity defense, we can say that certain circumstances could support such a defense....

B. SELF-DEFENSE

Even if a court were to find that a violation of Section 2340A was not justified by necessity, a defendant could still appropriately raise a claim of self-defense....

The doctrine of self-defense permits the use of force to prevent harm to another person. As LaFave and Scott explain, "one is justified in using reasonable force in defense of another person, even a stranger, when he reasonably believes that the other is in immediate danger of unlawful bodily harm from his adversary and that the use of such force is necessary to avoid this danger." Ultimately, even deadly force is permissible, but "only when the attack of the adversary upon the other person reasonably appears to the defender to be a deadly attack"....

Under the current circumstances, we believe that a defendant accused of violating Section 2340A could have, in certain circumstances, grounds to properly claim the defense of another. The threat of an impending terrorist attack threatens the lives of hundreds if not thousands of American citizens. Whether such a defense will be upheld depends on the specific context within which the interrogation decision is made. If an attack appears increasingly likely, but our intelligence services and armed forces cannot prevent it without the information from the interrogation of a specific individual, then the more likely it will appear that the conduct in question will be seen as necessary. If intelligence and other information support the conclusion that an attack is increasingly certain, then the necessity for the interrogation will be reasonable.... Finally, the fact that previous al Qaeda attacks have had as their aim the deaths of American citizens, and that evidence of other plots have had a similar goal in mind, would justify proportionality of interrogation methods designed to elicit information to prevent such deaths...

CONCLUSION

For the forgoing reasons, we conclude that torture as defined in and proscribed by Sections 2340-2340A, covers only extreme acts. Severe pain is generally of the kind difficult for the victim to endure. Where the pain is physical, it must be of an intensity akin to that which accompanies serious physical injury such as death or organ failure. Severe mental pain requires suffering not just at the moment of infliction but it also requires lasting psychological harm, such as seen in mental disorders like post-traumatic stress disorder.... Because the acts inflicting torture are extreme, there is a significant range of acts that though they might constitute cruel, inhuman, or degrading treatment, fail to rise to the level of torture.

Further, we conclude that under the circumstances of the current war against al Qaeda and its allies, application of Section 2340A to interrogations undertaken pursuant to the President's Commander-in-Chief powers may be unconstitutional. Finally, even if an interrogation method might violate Section 2340A, necessity or self-defense could provide justifications that would eliminate any criminal liability....

Note: Subsequent U.S. Interrogation Policies

A series of memos issued between October 2002 and April 2003 further considered the question of permissible interrogation techniques. The techniques were divided into three categories, depending on their severity. Among the techniques in the first category were yelling at the detainee, deceiving the detainee, and having the interrogator identify himself or herself as coming from a country with a reputation for engaging in torture (also called false flag). The second category included the use of stress positions for up to four hours at a time, solitary confinement for up to thirty days, deprivation of light and noise, deprivation of clothing, interrogations lasting twenty-four hours, and exploiting personal phobias, including fear of dogs. The third category of interrogation methods included death threats, exposure to cold weather or water "with appropriate medical monitoring," using a wet towel or water to induce the misperception of suffocation, and use of "mild non-injurious physical contact, such as grabbing, poking in the chest with the finger, and light pushing." Memorandum from Lieutenant Colonel Jerald Phifer to Commander, Joint Task Force 170 (Oct. 11, 2002), reprinted in Greenberg and Dratel, supra p. 271, at 227-28.

On December 2, 2002, Secretary of Defense Donald Rumsfeld approved the use of Category I and II techniques and "mild, non-injurious physical conduct" techniques from Category III. Memorandum from William J. Haynes II, General Counsel, to Secretary of Defense (Nov. 27, 2002), reprinted in id., at 236. Less than three weeks later, Rumsfeld rescinded use of Category II and III techniques during interrogations at Guantánamo, although they could be used on a case-by-case basis with the Secretary's approval. Memorandum from the Secretary of Defense to Commander USSOUTHCOM (Jan. 15, 2003), reprinted in id., at 239.

A Working Group on the techniques and other policy issues related to detainees concluded on Mar. 6, 2003, that Taliban detainees do not qualify as prisoners of war and that the Geneva Conventions do not apply to other non-state actors detained at Guantánamo; it did note that the United States remained bound by the 1994 Torture Convention. A revised report issued a month later argued that it may be necessary to interrogate detainees "in a manner beyond that which may be applied to a prisoner of war who is subject to the Geneva Conventions." It considers a number of techniques in detail and includes charts that summarize the usefulness of the techniques and their consistency with domestic and international standards. Working Group Report on Detainee Interrogations in the Global War on Terrorism: Assessment of Legal, Historical, Policy, and Operational Considerations (Apr. 4, 2003), reprinted in id., at 286-359. On April 16, 2003, Secretary of Defense Rumsfeld approved a new list of interrogation techniques taken from Categories I and II, some of which required the specific approval of the Secretary of Defense. A useful timeline of the various documents (from which this summary is drawn) is found in Greenberg and Dratel, id., at xxv-xxviii.

In June 2004, after public outrage over the photos from Abu Ghraib and other disclosures of ill-treatment of detainees, the White House "disavowed" the Aug. 1, 2002, Bybee memo, saying that "it had created the false impression that the government was claiming authority to use interrogation techniques barred by international law." Allen and Schmidt, *Justice Document Had Said Torture May Be Defensible*, Wash. Post (June 23, 2004), at A1. As part of what the *Washington Post* called a "public relations offensive," the White House also declassified the bulk of the internal memoranda referred to in this chapter. "The steps followed a string of polls showing sinking public confidence in Bush's handling of the war on terrorism." Id. As late as September 2005, the *New York Times* continued to call for a fuller investigation: "[I]t is simply not acceptable that a few low-level reservists go to jail while the civilian lawyers who wrote the torture policies get promoted and the general who devised the interrogations escapes even the mildest rebuke." Editorial, *Abu Ghraib Unresolved*, N.Y. Times, Sept. 10, 2005, at A26.

Note: Should Torture Always Be Prohibited?

The prohibition against torture, inhuman or degrading treatment or punishment is one of the few absolute protections in international human rights and humanitarian law. Is the above debate just about defining torture (and conveniently ignoring the lesser forms of ill-treatment that are also prohibited), or does it raise broader moral issues that should be addressed? Do you agree with the former executive editor of *The New York Times* that "we've insulated ourselves from the really pertinent, really difficult question: How do we feel about coercive techniques that are commonly, if somewhat cavalierly, held to fall short of torture?... How many lives would have to be demonstrably saved before such intimidation and punishment achieve a kind of moral sanction? If it could be shown with some certainty that, say, 10,000 lives would be saved, few purists would argue against the infliction of pain. If the number was a much smaller multiple of 10 and degree of uncertainty candidly acknowledged, the true murkiness of the issue in the real world would have to be faced." Joseph Lelyveld, *Interrogating Ourselves*, N.Y. Times Magazine (June 12, 2005) at 36, 39, 42.

For further reading, see Mirko Bagaric and Julie Clarke, *Not Enough Official Torture in the World? The Circumstances in Which Torture Is Morally Justifiable*, 39 U.S.F. L. Rev. 581 (2005); Winfried Brugger, *May Government Ever Use Torture? Two Responses From German Law*, 48 Am. J. Comp. L. 661 (2000); Melissa L. Clark, *Israel's High Court of Justice Ruling on the General Security Service Use of "Moderate Physical Pressure": An End to the Sanctioned Use of Torture?* 11 Ind. Int'l & Comp. L. Rev. 145 (2000); Alan Dershowitz, *The Torture Warrant: A Response to Professor Strauss*, 48 N.Y.L. Sch. L. Rev. 275 (2003/2004); Oren Gross, *Are Torture Warrants Warranted? Pragmatic Absolutism and Official Disobedience*, 88 Minn. L. Rev. 1481 (2004); Ardi Imseis, "Moderate" Torture On Trial: Critical Reflections on the Israeli Supreme Court Judgment Concerning the Legality of General Security Service Interrogation Methods, 19 Berkeley J. Int'l L. 328 (2001); Linda M. Keller, Is Truth Serum Torture? 20 Am. U. Int'l L. Rev. 521 (2005); Andrew A. Moher, *The Lesser of Two Evils?: An Argument for Judicially Sanctioned Torture in a Post-9/11 World*, 26 T. Jefferson L. Rev. 469 (2004); John T. Parry and Welsh S. White, *Interrogating Suspected Terrorists: Should Torture Be an Option?* 63 U. Pitt. L. Rev. 743 (2002); Elizabeth S. Silker, *Terrorists, Interrogation, and Torture: Where Do We Draw the Line?* 31 J. Legis. 191 (2004); Marcy Strauss, *Torture*, 48 N.Y. Law Sch. L. Rev. 203, 207 (2004).

Review the protections guaranteed to prisoners of war under the Third Geneva Convention, supra at 233. The treatment authorized by Secretary of Defense Rumsfeld clearly goes beyond these provisions, but it was justified by the consistent U.S. position that the Geneva Convention does not apply to "illegal combatants" captured in Afghanistan or elsewhere. The issue of just what law applies to such persons is addressed in the next section.

B. Guantánamo and "Illegal Combatants"

While the United States has accepted that captured Iraqi soldiers are prisoners of war, protected by the Geneva Conventions, the conflict in Afghanistan

Carlson © 1998 & 2004. *The Milwaukee Journal Sentinel.* Reprinted by Permission of Universal Press Syndicate. All rights reserved.

targeting al Qaeda and the Taliban has tested the applicability of the Geneva Conventions to combatants representing non-state actors. The provisions below from the Third and Fourth Geneva Conventions set forth U.S. obligations, while the subsequent extracts reflect the debate that unfolded within the Bush administration concerning whether or not captured al Qaeda and Taliban fighters (and presumably others taken into custody outside the United States in the "war on terror") qualified as prisoners of war.

Third Geneva Convention Relative to the Treatment of Prisoners of War

75 U.N.T.S. 135 (Aug. 12, 1949)

Article 4

A. Prisoners of war, in the sense of the present Convention, are persons belonging to one of the following categories, who have fallen into the power of the enemy:

(1) Members of the armed forces of a Party to the conflict as well as members of militias or volunteer corps forming part of such armed forces.

(2) Members of other militias and members of other volunteer corps, including those of organized resistance movements, belonging to a Party to

the conflict and operating in or outside their own territory, even if this territory is occupied, provided that such militias or volunteer corps, including such organized resistance movements, fulfil the following conditions:

(a) that of being commanded by a person responsible for his subordinates;

(b) that of having a fixed distinctive sign recognizable at a distance;

(c) that of carrying arms openly;

(d) that of conducting their operations in accordance with the laws and customs of war.

(3) Members of regular armed forces who profess allegiance to a government or an authority not recognized by the Detaining Power.

(4) Persons who accompany the armed forces without actually being members thereof, such as civilian members of military aircraft crews, war correspondents, supply contractors, members of labour units or of services responsible for the welfare of the armed forces, provided that they have received authorization from the armed forces which they accompany, who shall provide them for that purpose with an identity card similar to the annexed model.

(5) Members of crews, including masters, pilots and apprentices, of the merchant marine and the crews of civil aircraft of the Parties to the conflict, who do not benefit by more favourable treatment under any other provisions of international law.

(6) Inhabitants of a non-occupied territory, who on the approach of the enemy spontaneously take up arms to resist the invading forces, without having had time to form themselves into regular armed units, provided they carry arms openly and respect the laws and customs of war.

B. The following shall likewise be treated as prisoners of war under the present Convention:

(1) Persons belonging, or having belonged, to the armed forces of the occupied country, if the occupying Power considers it necessary by reason of such allegiance to intern them, even though it has originally liberated them while hostilities were going on outside the territory it occupies, in particular where such persons have made an unsuccessful attempt to rejoin the armed forces to which they belong and which are engaged in combat, or where they fail to comply with a summons made to them with a view to internment.

(2) The persons belonging to one of the categories enumerated in the present Article, who have been received by neutral or non-belligerent Powers on their territory and whom these Powers are required to intern under international law, without prejudice to any more favourable treatment which these Powers may choose to give and with the exception of Articles 8, 10, 15, 30, fifth paragraph, 58-67, 92, 126 and, where diplomatic relations exist between the Parties to the conflict and the neutral or non-belligerent Power concerned, those Articles concerning the Protecting Power. Where such diplomatic relations exist, the Parties to a conflict on whom these persons depend shall be allowed to perform towards them the functions of a Protecting Power as provided in the present Convention, without prejudice to the functions which these Parties normally exercise in conformity with diplomatic and consular usage and treaties.

C. This Article shall in no way affect the status of medical personnel and chaplains as provided for in Article 33 of the present Convention.

ARTICLE 5

The present Convention shall apply to the persons referred to in Article 4 from the time they fall into the power of the enemy and until their final release and repatriation.

Should any doubt arise as to whether persons, having committed a belligerent act and having fallen into the hands of the enemy, belong to any of the categories enumerated in Article 4, such persons shall enjoy the protection of the present Convention until such time as their status has been determined by a competent tribunal.

Fourth Geneva Convention Relative to the Protection of Civilian Persons in Time of War

75 U.N.T.S. 287

ARTICLE 5

Where in the territory of a Party to the conflict, the latter is satisfied that an individual protected person is definitely suspected of or engaged in activities hostile to the security of the State, such individual person shall not be entitled to claim such rights and privileges under the present Convention as would, if exercised in the favor of such individual person, be prejudicial to the security of such State.

Where in occupied territory an individual protected person is detained as a spy or saboteur, or as a person under definite suspicion of activity hostile to the security of the Occupying Power, such person shall, in those cases where absolute military security so requires, be regarded as having forfeited rights of communication under the present Convention.

In each case, such persons shall nevertheless be treated with humanity and, in case of trial, shall not be deprived of the rights of fair and regular trial prescribed by the present Convention. They shall also be granted the full rights and privileges of a protected person under the present Convention at the earliest date consistent with the security of the State or Occupying Power, as the case may be.

Memorandum from Assistant Attorney General Jay S. Bybee

January 22, 2002, reprinted in Greenberg and Dratel 81, 81-83, 85-86, 87-91, 95-96, 98-100, supra p. 271 (citations omitted) (emphasis in original)

Memorandum for Alberto R. Gonzales
Counsel to the President

and William J. Haynes II
General Counsel of the Department of Defense

Re: Application of Treaties and Laws to al Qaeda and Taliban Detainees

You have asked for our Office's views concerning the effect of international treaties and federal laws on the treatment of individuals detained by the U.S. Armed Forces during the conflict in Afghanistan. In particular, you have asked whether certain treaties forming part of the laws of armed conflict apply to the conditions of detention and the procedures for trial of members of al Qaeda and the Taliban militia. We conclude that these treaties do not protect members of the al Qaeda organization, which as a non-State actor cannot be a party to the international agreements governing war. We further conclude that the President has sufficient grounds to find that these treaties do not protect members of the Taliban militia. This memorandum expresses no view as to whether the President should decide, as a matter of policy, that the U.S. Armed Forces should adhere to the standards of conduct of those treaties with respect to the treatment of prisoners....

... Part I of this memorandum describes the War Crimes Act ["WCA," 18 U.S.C. §2441 (Supp. III 1997)] and the most relevant treaty that it incorporates: the Geneva Convention Relative to the Treatment of Prisoners of War ("Geneva III").

Parts II and III of this memorandum discuss why other deviations from the text of Geneva III would not present either a violation of the treaty or of the WCA. Part II explains that al Qaeda detainees cannot claim the protections of Geneva III because the treaty does not apply to them. Al Qaeda is merely a violent political movement or organization and not a nation-State. As a result, it cannot be a state party to any treaty. Because of the novel nature of this conflict, moreover, a conflict with al Qaeda is not properly included in non-international forms of armed conflict to which some provisions of the Geneva Conventions might apply. Therefore, neither the Geneva Conventions nor the WCA regulate the detention of al Qaeda prisoners captured during the Afghanistan conflict.

Part III discusses why the President may decide that Geneva III, as a whole, does not protect members of the Taliban militia in the current situation. The President has the constitutional authority to temporarily suspend our treaty obligations to Afghanistan under the Geneva Conventions. Although he may exercise this aspect of the treaty power at his discretion, we outline several grounds upon which he could justify that action here. In particular, he may determine that Afghanistan was not a functioning State, and therefore that the Taliban militia was not a government, during the period in which the Taliban was engaged in hostilities against the United States and its allies. Afghanistan's status as a failed State is sufficient ground alone for the President to suspend Geneva III, and thus to deprive members of the Taliban militia of POW status. The President's constitutional power to suspend performance of our treaty obligations with respect to Afghanistan is not restricted by international law. It encompasses the power to suspend some treaties but not others, or some but not all obligations under a particular treaty. Should the President make such a determination, then Geneva III would not apply to Taliban prisoners and any failure to meet that treaty's requirements would not violate either our treaty obligations or the WCA.

Part IV examines justifications for any departures from Geneva III requirements should the President decline to suspend our treaty obligations toward

Afghanistan. It explains that certain deviations from the text of Geneva III may be permissible, as a matter of domestic law, if they fall within certain justifications or legal exceptions, such as those for self-defense or infeasibility. Further, Part IV discusses the President's authority to find, even if Geneva III were to apply, that Taliban members do not qualify as POWs as defined by the treaty.

In Part V, we address the question whether, in the absence of any Geneva III obligations, customary international law requires, as a matter of federal law, that the President provide certain standards of treatment for al Qaeda or Taliban prisoners. We conclude that customary international law, as a matter of domestic law, does not bind the President, or restrict the actions of the United States military, because it does not constitute either federal law made in pursuance of the Constitution or a treaty recognized under the Supremacy Clause.

I. Background and Overview of the War Crimes Act and the Geneva Conventions

It is our understanding that your Department is considering two basic plans regarding the treatment of members of al Qaeda and the Taliban militia detained during the Afghanistan conflict. First, the Defense Department intends to make available a facility at the U.S. Navy base at Guantánamo Bay, Cuba ("GTMO"), for the long-term detention of these individuals who have come under our control either through capture by our military or transfer from our allies in Afghanistan. At the present moment, your Department has confined these individuals in temporary facilities, pending the construction of a more permanent camp at GTMO....

Second, your Department is developing procedures to implement the President's Military Order of November 13, 2001, which establishes military commissions for the trial of violations of the laws of war committed by non-U.S. citizens. The question has arisen whether Geneva III would restrict the proposed rules, or even require that only courts-martial be used to try members of al Qaeda or the Taliban militia for war crimes....

C. Common Article 3 of the Geneva Conventions

[U.S. federal law] defines as a war crime [inter alia] conduct that "constitutes a violation of common article 3" of the Geneva Conventions. Article 3 is a unique provision that governs the conduct of signatories to the Conventions in a particular kind of conflict that is not one between High Contracting Parties to the Conventions. Thus, common article 3 may require the United States, as a High Contracting Party, to follow certain rules even if other parties to the conflict are not parties to the Conventions. On the other hand, article 3 requires State parties to follow only certain minimum standards of treatment toward prisoners, civilians, or the sick and wounded — standards that are much less onerous and less detailed than those spelled out in the Conventions as a whole.

Common article 3 complements common article 2. Article 2 applies to cases of declared war or of any other armed conflict that may arise between two or more of the High Contracting Parties, even if the state of war is not recognized by one of them. Common article 3, however covers "armed conflict not of an international character" — a war that does not involve cross-border attacks — that occurs within the territory of one of the High Contracting Parties.

Common article 3's text provides substantial reason to think that it refers specifically to a condition of civil war, or a large-scale armed conflict between a State and an armed movement within its own territory. First, the text of the provision refers specifically to an armed conflict that a) is not of an international character, and b) occurs in the territory of a state party to the Convention. It does not sweep in all armed conflicts, nor does it address a gap left by common article 2 for international armed conflicts that involve non state entities (such as an international terrorist organization) as parties to the conflict. Further, common article 3 addresses only non-international conflicts that occur within the territory of a single state party, again, like a civil war. This provision would not reach an armed conflict in which one of the parties operated from multiple bases in several different states. . . .

Analysis of the background to the adoption of the Geneva Conventions in 1949 confirms our understanding of common article 3. It appears that the drafters of the Conventions had in mind only the two forms of armed conflict that were regarded as matters of general international concern at the time: armed conflict between nation-States (subject to article 2), and large-scale civil war within a nation-State (subject to article 3). To understand the context in which the Geneva Conventions were drafted, it will be helpful to identify three distinct phases in the development of the laws of war.

First, the traditional laws of war were based on a stark dichotomy between "belligerency" and "insurgency." The category of "belligerency" applied to armed conflicts between sovereign States (unless there was recognition of belligerency in a civil war), while the category of "insurgency" applied to armed violence breaking out within the territory of a sovereign State. International law treated the two classes of conflict in different ways. Inter-state wars were regulated by a body of international legal rules governing both the conduct of hostilities and the protection of noncombatants. By contrast, there were very few international rules governing armed conflict within a state, for states preferred to regard internal strife as rebellion, mutiny and treason coming within the purview of national criminal law, which precluded any possible intrusion by other States. This was a "clearly sovereignty-oriented" phase of international law.

The second phase began as early as the Spanish Civil War (1936-39) and extended through the time of the drafting of the Geneva Conventions until relatively recently. During this period, State practice began to apply certain general principles of humanitarian law beyond the traditional field of State-to-State conflict to "those internal conflicts that constituted large-scale civil wars." In addition to the Spanish Civil War, events in 1947 during the civil war between the Communists and the Nationalist regime in China illustrated this new tendency. Common article 3, which was prepared during this second phase, was apparently addressed to armed conflicts akin to the Chinese and Spanish civil wars. As one commentator [Draper] has described it, article 3 was designed to restrain governments "in the handling of armed violence directed against them for the express purpose of secession or at securing a change in the government of a State, but even after the adoption of the Conventions it remained "uncertain whether [Article 3] applied to full-scale civil war."

The third phase represents a more complete break than the second with the traditional "State-sovereignty-oriented approach" of international law. This approach gives central place to individual human rights. As a consequence, it blurs the distinction between international and internal armed conflicts. This approach is well illustrated by the decision of the International Criminal Tribunal for the Former Yugoslavia in *Prosecutor v. Tadic*, which appears to take the view that common article 3 applies to all armed conflicts of any description other than those between state parties, and is not limited to internal conflicts between a State and an insurgent group. In this conception, common article 3 is not just a complement to common article 2; rather, it is a catch-all that establishes standards for any and all armed conflicts not included in common article 2.

Such an interpretation of common article 3, however, ignores the text and the context in which it was ratified by the United States. If the state parties had intended the Conventions to apply to all forms of armed conflict, they could have used broader, clearer language. To interpret common article 3 by expanding its scope well beyond the meaning borne by its text is effectively to amend the Geneva Conventions without the approval of the State parties to the agreements. Further, as we have discussed, article 3 was ratified during a period in which the traditional, State-centered view of international law was still dominant and was only just beginning to give way to a human-rights-based approach. Giving due weight to the state practice and doctrinal understanding of the time, the idea of an armed conflict between a nation-State and a transnational terrorist organization (or between a nation-State and a failed State harboring and supporting a transnational terrorist organization) could not have been within the contemplation of the drafters of common article 3. Conflicts of these kinds would have been unforeseen and were not provided for in the Conventions. Further, it is telling that in order to address this unforeseen circumstance, the State parties to the Geneva Conventions did not attempt to distort the terms of common article 3 to apply it to cases that did not fit within its terms. Instead, they drafted two new protocols to adapt the Conventions to the conditions of contemporary hostilities. The United States has not ratified these protocols, and hence cannot be held to the reading of the Geneva Convention they promote. Thus, the [prohibition under U.S. federal law] on violations of common article 3 would apply only to internal conflicts between a state party and an insurgent group, rather than to all forms of armed conflict not covered by common article 2.

II. Application of WCA and Associated Treaties to al Qaeda

We conclude that Geneva III does not apply to the al Qaeda terrorist organization. Therefore, neither the detention nor trial of al Qaeda fighters is subject to Geneva III (or the WCA). Three reasons, examined in detail below, support this conclusion. First, al Qaeda is not a State and thus cannot receive the benefits of a State party to the Conventions. Second, al Qaeda members fail to satisfy the eligibility requirements for treatment as POWs under Geneva Convention III.

Third, the nature of the conflict precludes application of common article 3 of the Geneva Conventions.

Geneva III does not apply to a non-State actor such as the al Qaeda terrorist organization. Al Qaeda is not a State. It is a non-governmental terrorist organization composed of members from many nations, with ongoing operations in dozens of nations. Non-governmental organizations cannot be parties to any of the international agreements here governing the laws of war. Common article 2, which triggers the Geneva Convention provisions regulating detention conditions and procedures for trial of POWs, is limited to cases of declared war or armed conflict "between two or more of the High Contracting Parties." Al Qaeda is not a High Contracting Party. As a result, the U.S. military's treatment of al Qaeda members is not governed by the bulk of the Geneva Conventions, specifically those provisions concerning POWs. Conduct towards captured members of al Qaeda, therefore, also cannot constitute a violation of 18 U.S.C. §2441(c)(I).

Second, al Qaeda members fail to satisfy the eligibility requirements for treatment as POWs under Geneva Convention III. It might be argued that, even though it is not a State party to the Geneva Conventions, al Qaeda could be covered by some protections in Geneva Convention III. Article 4(A)(2) of Geneva III defines prisoners of war as including not only captured members of the armed forces of a High Contracting Party, bur also irregular forces such as "[m]embers of other militias and members of other volunteer corps, including those of organized resistance movements." Article 4(A)(3) also includes as POWs "[m]embers of regular armed forces who profess allegiance to a government or an authority not recognized by the Detaining Power." Id. art. 4(A)(3). It might be claimed that the broad terms of these provisions could be stretched to cover al Qaeda.

This view would be mistaken. Article 4 does not expand the application of the Convention beyond the circumstances expressly addressed in common articles 2 and 3. Unless there is a conflict subject to article 2, article 4 simply does not apply. If the conflict is one to which article 3 applies, then article 4 has no role because article 3 does not trigger application of the rest of the provisions of Geneva III. Rather, article 3 provides an alternative set of standards that requires only minimal humanitarian protections. As we have explained, the conflict with al Qadea does not fall within article 2. As a result, article 4 has no application. In other words, article 4 cannot be read as an alternative, and a far more expansive, statement of the application of the Convention. It merely specifies, where there is a conflict covered by article 2 of the Convention, who must be accorded POW status.

Even if article 4, however, were considered somehow to be jurisdictional as well as substantive, captured members of al Qaeda still would not receive the protections accorded to POWs. First, al Qaeda is not the "armed forces," volunteer forces, or militia of a state party that is a party to the conflict, as defined in article 4(A)(1). Second, they cannot qualify as volunteer force, militia, or organized resistance force under article 4(A)(2). That article requires that militia or volunteers fulfill four conditions: command by responsible individuals, wearing insignia, carrying arms openly, and obeying the laws of war. Al Qaeda members have clearly demonstrated that they will not follow these basic requirements of lawful warfare. They have attacked purely civilian targets of no military value; they refused to wear uniform or insignia or carry arms openly, but instead hijacked civilian airliners, took hostages, and killed them; and they themselves do not obey the laws of war concerning the protection of the lives of civilians or the means of legitimate combat. As these requirements also apply to any regular armed force under other treaties governing the laws of armed conflict, al Qaeda members would not qualify under 4(A)(3) either, which provides POW status to captured individuals who are members of a "regular armed force" that professes allegiance to a government or authority not recognized by the detaining power. Members of al Qaeda, therefore, would not qualify for POW treatment under article 4, even if it were somehow thought that they were participating in a conflict covered by common article 2 or if article 4 itself were thought to be jurisdictional in nature.

Third, the nature of the conflict precludes application of common article 3 of the Geneva Conventions. As discussed in Part I, the text of common article 3, when read in harmony with common article 2, shows that the Geneva Conventions were intended to cover either: a) traditional wars between state parties to the Conventions (article 2), b) or non-international civil wars (article 3). Our conflict with al Qaeda does not fit into either category. It is not an international war between nation-States because al Qaeda is not a State. Nor is this conflict a civil war under article 3, because it is a conflict of "an international character." Al Qaeda operates in many countries and carried out a massive international attack on the United States on September 11, 2001. Therefore, the military's treatment of al Qaeda members is not limited either by common article 3 or 18 U.S.C. §2441(c)(3).

III. Application of the Geneva Conventions to the Taliban Militia

Whether the Geneva Conventions apply to the detention and trial of members of the Taliban militia presents a more difficult legal question. Afghanistan has been a party to all four Geneva Conventions since September 1956. Some might argue that this requires application of the Geneva Conventions to the present conflict with respect to the Taliban militia, which would then trigger the WCA. Nonetheless, we conclude that the President has more than ample grounds to find that our treaty obligations under Geneva III toward Afghanistan were suspended during the period of the conflict. Under Article II of the Constitution, the President has the unilateral power to suspend whole treaties or parts of them at his discretion. In this part, we describe the President's constitutional power and discuss the grounds upon which he can justify the exercise of that power.

There are several grounds under which the President could exercise that authority here. First, the weight of informed opinion indicates that, for the period in question, Afghanistan was a "failed State" whose territory had been largely held by a violent militia or faction rather than by a government. As a failed state, Afghanistan did not have an operating government nor was it capable of fulfilling its international obligations. Therefore, the United States could decide to partially suspend any obligations that the United States might have under Geneva III towards the Taliban militia. Second, there appears to be developing evidence that the Taliban leadership had become closely intertwined with, if not utterly dependent upon, al Qaeda. This would have rendered the Taliban more akin to a terrorist organization that used force not to administer a government, but for terrorist purposes. The President could decide that no treaty obligations were owed to such a force. . . .

B. STATUS AS A FAILED STATE

There are ample grounds for the President to determine that Afghanistan was a failed State, and on that basis to suspend performance of our Geneva III obligations towards it. . . .

An initial approach to the question whether Afghanistan was a failed state is to examine some of the traditional indicia of statehood. A State has failed when centralized governmental authority has almost completely collapsed, no central authorities are capable of maintaining government institutions or ensuring law and order, and violence has destabilized civil society and the economy. . . . The State Department [relies on] a four-part test for statehood: i) whether the entity have [sic] effective control over a clearly defined territory and population; ii) whether an organized governmental administration of the territory exists; iii) whether the entity has the capacity to act effectively to conduct foreign relations and to fulfill international obligations; iv) whether the international community recognizes the entity.

We want to make clear that this Office does not have access to all of the facts related to the activities of the Taliban militia and al Qaeda in Afghanistan. Nonetheless, the available facts in the public record would support the conclusion that Afghanistan was a failed State — including facts that pre-existed the military reversals suffered by the Taliban militia and the formation of the new transitional government pursuant to the Bonn Agreement. Indeed, there are good reasons to doubt whether any of the conditions were met.

First, even before the outset of the conflict with the United States, the Taliban militia did not have effective control over a clearly defined territory and population. It is unclear whether the Taliban militia ever fully controlled most of the territory of Afghanistan. At the time that the United States air strikes began, at least ten percent of the country, and the population within those areas, was governed by the Northern Alliance. Indeed, the facts suggest that Afghanistan was divided between different tribal and warring factions, rather than controlled by any central State. . . .

Third, the Taliban militia was unable to conduct normal foreign relations or to fulfill its international legal obligations. . . . The Taliban's continuing role in sheltering and supporting those believed to be responsible for the terrorist attacks of September 11, 2001 placed it in clear breach of international law, which required it to prevent the use of its territory as a launching pad for attacks against other nations. . . .

. . . While a policy decision to violate international law would not be grounds to deny statehood, if al Qaeda — a non-governmental terrorist organization — possessed such power within Afghanistan to prevent its alleged rulers from taking action against it as ordered by the U.N., this would indicate that the Taliban militia did not exercise sufficient control within the territory to fulfill its international obligations.

The Taliban militia's failure to carry out its international obligations became even further apparent during the conflict itself. During the United States' campaign in Afghanistan, Secretary Rumsfeld noted that the Taliban "are using mosques for ammunition storage areas. They are using mosques for command and control and meeting places. They are putting tanks and artillery pieces in close proximity to hospitals, schools, and residential areas." . . . [T]he State Department reported that in August 2000, the Taliban had "executed POWs in the streets of Herat as a lesson to the local population." The State Department also reported on November 2, 2001 that "[t]he Taliban have put the Afghan civilian population in grave danger by deliberately hiding their soldiers and equipment in civilian areas, including in mosques". . . . All of this evidence goes to prove that the Taliban militia refused to follow the laws of armed conflict, which, besides independently providing grounds for a presidential suspension of Geneva III, also demonstrate that Afghanistan had become a failed state and was under the control not of a government but of a violent terrorist group. . . .

[Concluding that the president has the authority not to recognize certain categories of detainees as POWs protected under the Geneva Conventions, the memorandum then turns to an examination of the detention conditions required for POWs under the Third Geneva Convention; it concludes that some deviation from Geneva III is allowed and that "common article 3 is not a catch-all provision". The memo ends with a review of the applicability of customary international law, concluding that "customary international law cannot bind the executive because it is not federal law."]

The following extract sets out a rather different view.

Silvia Borelli, *Casting Light on the Legal Black Hole: International Law and Detentions Abroad in the "War on Terror"*

87 Int'l Rev. Red Cross 39, 45, 48-49, 52-53, 65, 68 (No. 857, Mar. 2005) (citations omitted)

However appealing it is to the mass media or as a rhetorical device used for the purposes of political discourse, the concept of a "war on terror" — i.e. an armed conflict waged against a loosely organized transnational terrorist network — does not stand up when analysed from the viewpoint of international law. . . .

The position of the US is in conflict with the generally accepted principles relative to the application of IHL [international humanitarian law]. The official commentary to the Geneva Conventions posits that there is a "general principle which is embodied in all four Geneva Conventions of 1949", namely that during an armed conflict or a military occupation:

> "Every person in enemy hands must have some status under international law: he is either a prisoner of war and, as such, covered by the Third Convention, a civilian covered by the Fourth Convention, or again, a member of the medical personnel of

the armed forces who is covered by the First Convention. There is no 'intermediate status'; nobody in enemy hands can be outside the law." . . .

Some prisoners in the "war on terror", however, fall outside the protection of the Geneva system. The first and most numerous category is that of persons captured in the context of law enforcement operations carried out by the US and its allies throughout the world after 11 September 2001. As already discussed, those operations cannot be characterized as being part of an "armed conflict" within the meaning that international law attributes to that term. In this respect, the US assertion that "none of the provisions of Geneva [sic] apply to our conflict with al Qaeda," whilst being undeniably correct, is irrelevant: the Geneva Conventions do not apply for the very simple reason that the "war on terror" is not an armed conflict. . . .

In relation to international human rights law, the United States has in the past consistently denied the extraterritorial application of human rights obligations. It has also denied that human rights apply in time of armed conflict, and has recently reiterated both of these positions with regard to the detainees at Guantánamo Bay.

The UK government has taken the more nuanced position that the European Convention on Human Rights is not applicable to the actions of UK troops overseas. In particular, it denied the applicability of the Convention with regard to Iraq on the ground that that country is outside the territorial scope of the Convention, and that in any case British troops did not exercise the required degree of control. . . . [see the discussion of the extraterritorial effect of the European Convention in Chapter 8, page 629].

This brief analysis . . . demonstrates that no matter where they [individuals detained during the "war on terror"] are held, they are always entitled to some measure of protection under international human rights law and, depending on the context in which they were captured, also under IHL. A number of recent decisions, both international and, more importantly, domestic, indicate an incipient reaffirmation of the orthodox understanding of the applicability of the rules of IHL and international human rights law. . . .

. . . It is perhaps overly optimistic to hope that, as a result of a handful of judicial pronouncements, all the States involved will fully accept the applicability of all the relevant international legal norms. However, the recent developments can be interpreted as evidence that legal institutions, and in particular domestic courts, are finally now beginning to recover from the shock of 9/11 to the international and domestic legal systems.

It is now over three years since the first detainees were taken into custody and held in violation of their rights and international law. Declarations of violations of international law may be of little comfort to all those whose rights have been violated over this period. However, when what is at stake is the prevention of violations of norms and values as fundamentally important as those implicated in the detention of individuals abroad in the "war on terror", even the merest glimmer of light shed on the "legal black hole" is to be welcomed.

Three days after the January 22, 2002, Bybee memorandum, White House Counsel Alberto Gonzales, faced with opposition from Secretary of State Colin

Powell, drafted an additional memorandum, supporting and amplifying Bybee's view that the Geneva Conventions should not apply to captured Taliban fighters. Powell noted that "OLC [the Office of Legal Counsel]'s interpretation of this legal issue is definitive. Nevertheless, you should be aware that the Legal Adviser to the Secretary of State has expressed a different view." Memorandum for the President from Alberto R. Gonzales (Jan. 25, 2002), reprinted in Greenberg and Dratel, supra page 271, at 118.

Defending Bybee's January 22, 2002, memorandum, Gonzales reaffirmed the President's view that "the war against terrorism is a new kind of war. It is not the traditional clash between nations adhering to the laws of war that formed the backdrop for [the Geneva Conventions]. The nature of the new war places a high premium on other factors, such as the ability to quickly obtain information from captured terrorists and their sponsors in order to avoid further atrocities against American civilians, and the need to try terrorists for war crimes such as wantonly killing civilians. In my judgment, this new paradigm renders obsolete Geneva's strict limitations on questioning of enemy prisoners and renders quaint some of its provisions requiring that captured enemy be afforded such things as commissary privileges, scrip (i.e., advances of monthly pay), athletic uniforms and scientific instruments." Id. at 119.

In response, Secretary of State Powell the next day drafted a memorandum to Gonzales arguing against the denial of Geneva Convention protection of Taliban detainees. Powell contended that so doing would "reverse over a century of U.S. policy and practice in supporting the Geneva conventions and undermine the protections of the law of war for our troops, both in this specific context and in general.... It [also] has a high cost in terms of negative international reaction, with immediate adverse consequences for our conduct of foreign policy." Memorandum from Colin L. Powell (Jan. 26, 2002), reprinted in id. at 122, 123. A week later, the State Department's Legal Adviser sent a similar memorandum to Gonzales. Referring to Afghanistan, the Legal Adviser advised that "[t]he President should know that a decision that the [Geneva] Conventions do apply is consistent with the plain language of the Conventions and the unvaried practice of the United States in introducing its forces into conflict over fifty years." Memorandum from William H. Taft, IV (Feb. 2, 2002), reprinted in id. at 129.

A few days later, President Bush issued the following memorandum, ending the internal debate within his administration and establishing U.S. policy with regard to the status of both al Qaeda and Taliban detainees.

Memorandum from the President

THE WHITE HOUSE
WASHINGTON
February 7, 2002

MEMORANDUM FOR THE VICE PRESIDENT
THE SECRETARY OF STATE
THE SECRETARY OF DEFENSE
THE ATTORNEY GENERAL

CHIEF OF STAFF TO THE PRESIDENT
DIRECTOR OF CENTRAL INTELLIGENCE
ASSISTANT TO THE PRESIDENT FOR NATIONAL SECURITY AFFAIRS
CHAIRMAN OF THE JOINT CHIEFS OF STAFF

SUBJECT: Humane Treatment of al Qaeda and Taliban Detainees

1. Our recent extensive discussions regarding the status of al Qaeda and Taliban detainees confirm that the application of the Geneva Convention Relative to the Treatment of Prisoners of War of August 12, 1949 (Geneva) to the conflict with al Qaeda and the Taliban involves complex legal questions. By its terms, Geneva applies to conflicts involving "High Contracting Parties", which can only be states. Moreover, it assumes the existence of "regular" armed forces fighting on behalf of states. However, the war against terrorism ushers in a new paradigm, one in which groups with broad, international reach commit horrific acts against innocent civilians, sometimes with the direct support of states. Our Nation recognizes that this new paradigm — ushered in not by us, but by terrorists — requires new thinking in the law of war, but thinking that should nevertheless be consistent with the principles of Geneva.

2. Pursuant to my authority as Commander in Chief and Chief Executive of the United States, and relying on the opinion of the Department of Justice dated January 22, 2002, and on the legal opinion rendered by the Attorney General in his letter of February 1, 2002, I hereby determine as follows:

a. I accept the legal conclusion of the Department of Justice and determine that none of the provisions of Geneva apply to our conflict with al Qaeda in Afghanistan or elsewhere throughout the world because among other reasons, al Qaeda is not a High Contracting Party to Geneva.
b. I accept the legal conclusion of the Attorney General and the Department of Justice that I have the authority under the Constitution to suspend Geneva as between the United States and Afghanistan, but I decline to exercise that authority at this time. Accordingly, I determine that the provisions of Geneva will apply to our present conflict with the Taliban. I reserve the right to exercise this authority in this or future conflicts.
c. I also accept the legal conclusion of the Department of Justice and determine that common Article 3 of Geneva does not apply to either al Qaeda or Taliban detainees, because among other reasons, the relevant conflicts are international in scope and common Article 3 applies only to "armed conflict not of an international character".
d. Based on the facts supplied by the Department of Defense and the recommendation of the Department of Justice, I determine that the Taliban detainees are unlawful combatants and, therefore, do not qualify as prisoners of war under Article 4 of Geneva. I note that, because Geneva does not apply to our conflict with al Qaeda, al Qaeda detainees also do not qualify as prisoners of war.

3. Of course, our values as a Nation, values that we share with many nations in the world, call for us to treat detainees humanely, including those who are not legally entitled to such treatment. Our Nation has been and will continue to be a strong supporter of Geneva and its principles. As a matter of policy, the United States Armed Forces shall continue to treat detainees humanely and, to the extent appropriate and consistent with military necessity, in a manner consistent with the principles of Geneva.

4. The United States will hold states, organizations, and individuals who gain control of United States personnel responsible for treating such personnel humanely and consistent with applicable law.

5. I hereby reaffirm the order previously issued by the Secretary of Defense to the United States Armed Forces requiring that the detainees be treated humanely and, to the extent appropriate and consistent with military necessity, in a manner consistent with the principles of Geneva.

6. I hereby direct the Secretary of State to communicate my determinations in an appropriate manner to our allies and other countries and international organizations cooperating in the war against terrorism of global reach.

[signed] George Bush

There were some indications in mid-2005 that the Bush Administration might adopt a more subtle approach to the fight against terrorism, since referring only to "war"implied to some that the solution was primarily military. One phrase that appeared in the speeches of high-ranking Administration officials at the time, including Secretary of Defense Rumsfeld, was "the global struggle against violent extremism." Whether for legal, political, or emotional reasons, President Bush reiterated his own preference in a speech in August 2005: "Make no mistake about it, we are at war." Stevenson, *President Makes It Clear: Phrase is 'War on Terror'*, New York Times, Aug. 4, 2005, at A12.

C. *Military Commissions*

Note that Article 5 of the Fourth Geneva Convention states that any questions regarding the status of a detainee should be determined by a "competent tribunal." Following the Sept. 11, 2001, attacks, President Bush issued an executive order permitting the detention without trial of suspected terrorists.

Detention, Treatment, and Trial of Certain Non-Citizens in the War Against Terrorism

Military Order of Nov. 13, 2001, 66 Fed. Reg. 57,831 (Nov. 16, 2001)

By the authority vested in me as President and as Commander in Chief of the Armed Forces of the United States by the Constitution and the laws of the United States of America, including the Authorization for Use of Military Force Joint Resolution (Public Law 107-40, 115 Stat. 224) and sections 821 and 836 of title 10, United States Code, it is hereby ordered as follows:

SECTION 1. FINDINGS.

(a) International terrorists, including members of al Qaida, have carried out attacks on United States diplomatic and military personnel and facilities abroad and on citizens and property within the United States on a scale that has created a state of armed conflict that requires the use of the United States Armed Forces.

(b) In light of grave acts of terrorism and threats of terrorism, including the terrorist attacks on September 11, 2001, on the headquarters of the United States Department of Defense in the national capital region, on the World Trade Center in New York, and on civilian aircraft such as in Pennsylvania, I proclaimed a national emergency on September 14, 2001 (Proc. 7463, Declaration of National Emergency by Reason of Certain Terrorist Attacks).

(c) Individuals acting alone and in concert involved in international terrorism possess both the capability and the intention to undertake further terrorist attacks against the United States that, if not detected and prevented, will cause mass deaths, mass injuries, and massive destruction of property, and may place at risk the continuity of the operations of the United States Government.

(d) The ability of the United States to protect the United States and its citizens, and to help its allies and other cooperating nations protect their nations and their citizens, from such further terrorist attacks depends in significant part upon using the United States Armed Forces to identify terrorists and those who support them, to disrupt their activities, and to eliminate their ability to conduct or support such attacks.

(e) To protect the United States and its citizens, and for the effective conduct of military operations and prevention of terrorist attacks, it is necessary for individuals subject to this order pursuant to section 2 hereof to be detained, and, when tried, to be tried for violations of the laws of war and other applicable laws by military tribunals.

(f) Given the danger to the safety of the United States and the nature of international terrorism, and to the extent provided by and under this order, I find consistent with section 836 of title 10, United States Code, that it is not practicable to apply in military commissions under this order the principles of law and the rules of evidence generally recognized in the trial of criminal cases in the United States district courts.

(g) Having fully considered the magnitude of the potential deaths, injuries, and property destruction that would result from potential acts of terrorism against the United States, and the probability that such acts will occur, I have determined that an extraordinary emergency exists for national defense purposes, that this emergency constitutes an urgent and compelling government interest, and that issuance of this order is necessary to meet the emergency.

SECTION 2. DEFINITION AND POLICY.

(a) The term "individual subject to this order" shall mean any individual who is not a United States citizen with respect to whom I determine from time to time in writing that:

(1) there is reason to believe that such individual, at the relevant times,

(i) is or was a member of the organization known as al Qaida;

(ii) has engaged in, aided or abetted, or conspired to commit, acts of international terrorism, or acts in preparation therefor, that have caused, threaten to cause, or have as their aim to cause, injury to or adverse effects on the United States, its citizens, national security, foreign policy, or economy; or

(iii) has knowingly harbored one or more individuals described in subparagraphs (i) or (ii) of subsection 2(a)(1) of this order; and

(2) it is in the interest of the United States that such individual be subject to this order.

(b) It is the policy of the United States that the Secretary of Defense shall take all necessary measures to ensure that any individual subject to this order is detained in accordance with section 3, and, if the individual is to be tried, that such individual is tried only in accordance with section 4.

(c) It is further the policy of the United States that any individual subject to this order who is not already under the control of the Secretary of Defense but who is under the control of any other officer or agent of the United States or any State shall, upon delivery of a copy of such written determination to such officer or agent, forthwith be placed under the control of the Secretary of Defense.

SECTION 3. DETENTION AUTHORITY OF THE SECRETARY OF DEFENSE.

Any individual subject to this order shall be —

(a) detained at an appropriate location designated by the Secretary of Defense outside or within the United States;

(b) treated humanely, without any adverse distinction based on race, color, religion, gender, birth, wealth, or any similar criteria;

(c) afforded adequate food, drinking water, shelter, clothing, and medical treatment;

(d) allowed the free exercise of religion consistent with the requirements of such detention; and

(e) detained in accordance with such other conditions as the Secretary of Defense may prescribe.

SECTION 4. AUTHORITY OF THE SECRETARY OF DEFENSE REGARDING TRIALS OF INDIVIDUALS SUBJECT TO THIS ORDER.

(a) Any individual subject to this order shall, when tried, be tried by military commission for any and all offenses triable by military commission that such individual is alleged to have committed, and may be punished in accordance with the penalties provided under applicable law, including life imprisonment or death.

(b) As a military function and in light of the findings in section 1, including subsection (f) thereof, the Secretary of Defense shall issue such orders and regulations, including orders for the appointment of one or more military commissions, as may be necessary to carry out subsection (a) of this section.

(c) Orders and regulations issued under subsection (b) of this section shall include, but not be limited to, rules for the conduct of the proceedings of military commissions, including pretrial, trial, and post-trial procedures, modes of proof, issuance of process, and qualifications of attorneys, which shall at a minimum provide for —

(1) military commissions to sit at any time and any place, consistent with such guidance regarding time and place as the Secretary of Defense may provide;

(2) a full and fair trial, with the military commission sitting as the triers of both fact and law;

(3) admission of such evidence as would, in the opinion of the presiding officer of the military commission (or instead, if any other member of the commission so requests at the time the presiding officer renders that opinion, the opinion of the commission rendered at that time by a majority of the commission), have probative value to a reasonable person;

(4) in a manner consistent with the protection of information classified or classifiable under Executive Order 12958 of April 17, 1995, as amended, or any successor Executive Order, protected by statute or rule from unauthorized disclosure, or otherwise protected by law, (A) the handling of, admission into evidence of, and access to materials and information, and (B) the conduct, closure of, and access to proceedings;

(5) conduct of the prosecution by one or more attorneys designated by the Secretary of Defense and conduct of the defense by attorneys for the individual subject to this order;

(6) conviction only upon the concurrence of two-thirds of the members of the commission present at the time of the vote, a majority being present;

(7) sentencing only upon the concurrence of two-thirds of the members of the commission present at the time of the vote, a majority being present; and

(8) submission of the record of the trial, including any conviction or sentence, for review and final decision by me or by the Secretary of Defense if so designated by me for that purpose.

SECTION 5. OBLIGATION OF OTHER AGENCIES TO ASSIST THE SECRETARY OF DEFENSE.

Departments, agencies, entities, and officers of the United States shall, to the maximum extent permitted by law, provide to the Secretary of Defense such assistance as he may request to implement this order.

SECTION 6. ADDITIONAL AUTHORITIES OF THE SECRETARY OF DEFENSE.

(a) As a military function and in light of the findings in section 1, the Secretary of Defense shall issue such orders and regulations as may be necessary to carry out any of the provisions of this order.

(b) The Secretary of Defense may perform any of his functions or duties, and may exercise any of the powers provided to him under this order (other than under section 4(c)(8) hereof) in accordance with section 113(d) of title 10, United States Code.

SECTION 7. RELATIONSHIP TO OTHER LAW AND FORUMS.

(a) Nothing in this order shall be construed to —

(1) authorize the disclosure of state secrets to any person not otherwise authorized to have access to them;

(2) limit the authority of the President as Commander in Chief of the Armed Forces or the power of the President to grant reprieves and pardons; or

(3) limit the lawful authority of the Secretary of Defense, any military commander, or any other officer or agent of the United States or of any State to detain or try any person who is not an individual subject to this order.

(b) With respect to any individual subject to this order —

(1) military tribunals shall have exclusive jurisdiction with respect to offenses by the individual; and

(2) the individual shall not be privileged to seek any remedy or maintain any proceeding, directly or indirectly, or to have any such remedy or proceeding sought on the individual's behalf, in (i) any Court of the United States, or any State thereof, (ii) any court of any foreign nation, or (iii) any international tribunal.

(c) This order is not intended to and does not create any right, benefit, or privilege, substantive or procedural, enforceable at law or equity by any party, against the United States, its departments, agencies, or other entities, its officers or employees, or any other person.

(d) For purposes of this order, the term "State" includes any State, district, territory, or possession of the United States.

(e) I reserve the authority to direct the Secretary of Defense, at any time hereafter, to transfer to a governmental authority control of any individual subject to this order. Nothing in this order shall be construed to limit the authority of any such governmental authority to prosecute any individual for whom control is transferred. . . .

The advisability of creating military commissions to try suspected terrorists and others captured during the military campaign in Afghanistan and elsewhere was the subject of much political and legal debate. See, e.g., Ruth Wedgwood, *Military Commissions: Al Qaeda, Terrorism, and Military Commissions*, 96 Am. J. Int'l L. 328 (2002) ("in the middle of a grave conflict with an efficient and undeterrable adversary, military commissions may be the most practicable course"); Harold Honju Koh, *The Case Against Military Commissions*, 96 Am. J. Int'l L. 337 (2002) ("the Military Order undermines the United States' perceived commitment to the rule of law and national confidence in U.S. judicial institutions at precisely the time when that commitment and confidence are most needed"); Joan Fitzpatrick, *Jurisdiction of Military Commissions and the Ambiguous War on Terrorism*,96 Am. J. Int'l L. 345 (2002) ("The legal premises for the November 13 order are dubious and confused.").

In 2004, the U.S. Supreme Court held that detainees in Guantánamo did not fall outside the jurisdiction of U.S. courts, although it did not identify precisely what remedies might be available to such persons to challenge their detention. *Hamdi v. Rumsfeld*, 542 U.S. 507 (2004). In partial response to the decision, the

United States created "combatant status review tribunals" to review detentions. Although a District Court initially rejected those tribunals as insufficient, *Hamdan v. Rumsfeld*, 344 F.Supp. 2d 152 (D.D.C. 2004) (Memorandum Opinion), a court of appeals upheld the legality of the trials in the following opinion.

Hamdan v. Rumsfeld

D.D.C., 415 F.3d 33, 2005 U.S. App. LEXIS 14315 (July 15, 2005) (most internal references omitted)

OPINION: RANDOLPH, Circuit Judge:

Afghani militia forces captured Salim Ahmed Hamdan in Afghanistan in late November 2001. Hamdan's captors turned him over to the American military, which transported him to the Guantánamo Bay Naval Base in Cuba. The military initially kept him in the general detention facility, known as Camp Delta. On July 3, 2003, the President determined "that there is reason to believe that [Hamdan] was a member of al Qaeda or was otherwise involved in terrorism directed against the United States." This finding brought Hamdan within the compass of the President's November 13, 2001, Order concerning the Detention, Treatment, and Trial of Certain Non-Citizens in the War Against Terrorism, 66 Fed. Reg. 57,833. Accordingly, Hamdan was designated for trial before a military commission.

In December 2003, Hamdan was removed from the general population at Guantánamo and placed in solitary confinement in Camp Echo. That same month, he was appointed counsel, initially for the limited purpose of plea negotiation. In April 2004, Hamdan filed this petition for habeas corpus. While his petition was pending before the district court, the government formally charged Hamdan with conspiracy to commit attacks on civilians and civilian objects, murder and destruction of property by an unprivileged belligerent, and terrorism. The charges alleged that Hamdan was Osama bin Laden's personal driver in Afghanistan between 1996 and November 2001, an allegation Hamdan admitted in an affidavit. The charges further alleged that Hamdan served as bin Laden's personal bodyguard, delivered weapons to al Qaeda members, drove bin Laden to al Qaeda training camps and safe havens in Afghanistan, and trained at the al Qaeda–sponsored al Farouq camp. Hamdan's trial was to be before a military commission, which the government tells us now consists of three officers of the rank of colonel. Brief for Appellants at 7.

In response to the Supreme Court's decision in *Hamdan v. Rumsfeld*, 542 U.S. 507, 124 S. Ct. 2633, 159 L. Ed. 2d 578 (2004), Hamdan received a formal hearing before a Combatant Status Review Tribunal. The Tribunal affirmed his status as an enemy combatant, "either a member of or affiliated with Al Qaeda," for whom continued detention was required.

On November 8, 2004, the district court granted in part Hamdan's petition. Among other things, the court held that Hamdan could not be tried by a military commission unless a competent tribunal determined that he was not a prisoner of war under the 1949 Geneva Convention governing the treatment of prisoners. The court therefore enjoined the Secretary of Defense from conducting any further military commission proceedings against Hamdan. This appeal followed.

I.

The government's initial argument is that the district court should have abstained from exercising jurisdiction over Hamdan's habeas corpus petition. Ex parte *Quirin v. Cox*, 317 U.S. 1, 87 L. Ed. 3, 63 S. Ct. 2 (1942), in which captured German saboteurs challenged the lawfulness of the military commission before which they were to be tried, provides a compelling historical precedent for the power of civilian courts to entertain challenges that seek to interrupt the processes of military commissions. The Supreme Court ruled against the petitioners in *Quirin*, but only after considering their arguments on the merits. In an effort to minimize the precedential effect of *Quirin*,the government points out that the decision predates the comity-based abstention doctrine recognized in *Schlesinger v. Councilman*, 420 U.S. 738, 43 L. Ed. 2d 591, 95 S. Ct. 1300 (1975), and applied by this court in *New v. Cohen*, 327 U.S. App. D.C. 147, 129 F.3d 639 (D.C. Cir. 1997). *Councilman* and *New* hold only that civilian courts should not interfere with ongoing court-martial proceedings against citizen servicemen. . . .

Even within the framework of *Councilman* and *New*, there is an exception to abstention: "a person need not exhaust remedies in a military tribunal if the military court has no jurisdiction over him." *New*, 129 F.3d at 644. The theory is that setting aside the judgment after trial and conviction insufficiently redresses the defendant's right not to be tried by a tribunal that has no jurisdiction. The courts in *Councilman* and *New* did not apply this exception because the servicemen had not "raised substantial arguments denying the right of the military to try them at all." New, 129 F.3d at 644 (citing Councilman, 420 U.S. at 759). Hamdan's jurisdictional challenge, by contrast, is not insubstantial, as our later discussion should demonstrate. While he does not deny the military's authority to try him, he does contend that a military commission has no jurisdiction over him and that any trial must be by court-martial. His claim, therefore, falls within the exception to Councilman and, in any event, is firmly supported by the Supreme Court's disposition of *Quirin*.

II.

In an argument distinct from his claims about the Geneva Convention, which we will discuss next, Hamdan maintains that the President violated the separation of powers inherent in the Constitution when he established military commissions. The argument is that Article I, §8, of the Constitution gives Congress the power "to constitute Tribunals inferior to the Supreme Court," that Congress has not established military commissions, and that the President has no inherent authority to do so under Article II. . . .

[O]n the merits there is little to Hamdan's argument. . . .

We therefore hold that through the joint resolution and the two statutes just mentioned, Congress authorized the military commission that will try Hamdan.

III.

This brings us to Hamdan's argument, accepted by the district court, that the Geneva Convention Relative to the Treatment of Prisoners of War may be enforced in federal court.... [The court's discussion and conclusion that the Geneva Convention does not confer upon Hamdan a right to enforce its provisions in U.S. courts is found in Chapter 6, page 469.]

IV.

Even if the 1949 Geneva Convention could be enforced in court, this would not assist Hamdan. He contends that a military commission trial would violate his rights under Article 102, which provides that a "prisoner of war can be validly sentenced only if the sentence has been pronounced by the same courts according to the same procedure as in the case of members of the armed forces of the Detaining Power." One problem for Hamdan is that he does not fit the Article 4 definition of a "prisoner of war" entitled to the protection of the Convention. He does not purport to be a member of a group who displayed "a fixed distinctive sign recognizable at a distance" and who conducted "their operations in accordance with the laws and customs of war." See 1949 Convention, arts. 4A(2)(b), (c) & (d). If Hamdan were to claim prisoner of war status under Article 4A(4) as a person who accompanied "the armed forces without actually being [a] member[] thereof," he might raise that claim before the military commission under Army Regulation 190-8. See Section VII of this opinion, infra. (We note that Hamdan has not specifically made such a claim before this court.)

Another problem for Hamdan is that the 1949 Convention does not apply to al Qaeda and its members. The Convention appears to contemplate only two types of armed conflicts. The first is an international conflict. Under Common Article 2, the provisions of the Convention apply to "all cases of declared war or of any other armed conflict which may arise between two or more of the High Contracting Parties, even if the state of war is not recognized by one of them." Needless to say, al Qaeda is not a state and it was not a "High Contracting Party." There is an exception, set forth in the last paragraph of Common Article 2, when one of the "Powers" in a conflict is not a signatory but the other is. Then the signatory nation is bound to adhere to the Convention so long as the opposing Power "accepts and applies the provisions thereof." Even if al Qaeda could be considered a Power, which we doubt, no one claims that al Qaeda has accepted and applied the provisions of the Convention.

The second type of conflict, covered by Common Article 3, is a civil war — that is, an "armed conflict not of an international character occurring in the territory of one of the High Contracting Parties...." In that situation, Common Article 3 prohibits "the passing of sentences and the carrying out of executions without previous judgment pronounced by a regularly constituted court affording all the judicial guarantees which are recognized as indispensable by a civilized people." Hamdan assumes that if Common Article 3 applies, a military commission could not try him. We will make the same assumption arguendo, which leaves the question whether Common Article 3 applies. Afghanistan is a "High Contracting Party." Hamdan was captured during hostilities there. But is the war against terrorism in general and the war against al Qaeda in particular, an "armed conflict not of an international character"? President Bush determined, in a memorandum to the Vice President and others on February 7, 2002 [see supra pages 294], that it did not fit that description because the conflict was "international in scope." The district court disagreed with the President's view of Common Article 3, apparently because the court thought we were not engaged in a separate conflict with al Qaeda, distinct from the conflict with the Taliban. We have difficulty understanding the court's rationale. Hamdan was captured in Afghanistan in November 2001, but the conflict with al Qaeda arose before then, in other regions, including this country on September 11, 2001. Under the Constitution, the President "has a degree of independent authority to act" in foreign affairs, and, for this reason and others, his construction and application of treaty provisions is entitled to "great weight." While the district court determined that the actions in Afghanistan constituted a single conflict, the President's decision to treat our conflict with the Taliban separately from our conflict with al Qaeda is the sort of political-military decision constitutionally committed to him. To the extent there is ambiguity about the meaning of Common Article 3 as applied to al Qaeda and its members, the President's reasonable view of the provision must therefore prevail.

V.

Suppose we are mistaken about Common Article 3. Suppose it does cover Hamdan. Even then we would abstain from testing the military commission against the requirement in Common Article 3(1)(d) that sentences must be pronounced "by a regularly constituted court affording all the judicial guarantees which are recognized as indispensable by civilized peoples." Unlike his arguments that the military commission lacked jurisdiction, his argument here is that the commission's procedures — particularly its alleged failure to require his presence at all stages of the proceedings — fall short of what Common Article 3 requires. The issue thus raised is not whether the commission may try him, but rather how the commission may try him. That is by no stretch a jurisdictional argument. No one would say that a criminal defendant's contention that a district court will not allow him to confront the witnesses against him raises a jurisdictional objection. Hamdan's claim therefore falls outside the recognized exception to the *Councilman* doctrine. Accordingly, comity would dictate that we defer to the ongoing military proceedings. If Hamdan were convicted, and if Common Article 3 covered him, he could contest his conviction in federal court after he exhausted his military remedies.

VI.

After determining that the 1949 Geneva Convention provided Hamdan a basis for judicial relief, the district court went on to consider the legitimacy of a military commission in the event Hamdan should eventually appear before one. In the district court's view, the principal constraint on the President's power to utilize such commissions is found in Article 36 of the Uniform Code of Military Justice, 10 U.S.C. §836, which provides:

> Pretrial, trial, and post-trial procedures, including modes of proof, for cases arising under this chapter triable in courts-martial, military commissions and other military

> tribunals . . . may be prescribed by the President by regulations which shall, so far as he considers practicable, apply the principles of law and the rules of evidence generally recognized in the trial of criminal cases in the United States district courts, *but which may not be contrary to or inconsistent with this chapter.*

(Emphasis added.) The district court interpreted the final qualifying clause to mean that military commissions must comply in all respects with the requirements of the Uniform Code of Military Justice (UCMJ). This was an error.

Throughout its Articles, the UCMJ takes care to distinguish between "courts-martial" and "military commissions." The terms are not used interchangeably, and the majority of the UCMJ's procedural requirements refer only to courts-martial. The district court's approach would obliterate this distinction. A far more sensible reading is that in establishing military commissions, the President may not adopt procedures that are "contrary to or inconsistent with" the UCMJ's provisions governing military commissions. In particular, Article 39 requires that sessions of a "trial by court-martial . . . shall be conducted in the presence of the accused." Hamdan's trial before a military commission does not violate Article 36 if it omits this procedural guarantee. . . .

VII.

Although we have considered all of Hamdan's remaining contentions, the only one requiring further discussion is his claim that even if the Geneva Convention is not judicially enforceable, Army Regulation 190-8 provides a basis for relief. This regulation, which contains many subsections, "implements international law, both customary and codified, relating to [enemy prisoners of war], [retained personnel], [civilian internees], and [other detainees] which includes those persons held during military operations other than war." AR 190-8 §1-1(b). The regulation lists the Geneva Convention among the "principal treaties relevant to this regulation." §1-1(b)(3); see Hamdi, 124 S. Ct. at 2658 (Souter, J., concurring) (describing AR 190-8 as "implementing the Geneva Convention"). One subsection, §1-5(a)(2), requires that prisoners receive the protections of the Convention "until some other legal status is determined by competent authority." (Emphasis added.) The President found that Hamdan was not a prisoner of war under the Convention. Nothing in the regulations, and nothing Hamdan argues, suggests that the President is not a "competent authority" for these purposes.

Hamdan claims that AR 190-8 entitles him to have a "competent tribunal" determine his status. But we believe the military commission is such a tribunal. . . . We therefore see no reason why Hamdan could not assert his claim to prisoner of war status before the military commission at the time of his trial and thereby receive the judgment of a "competent tribunal" within the meaning of Army Regulation 190-8.

For the reasons stated above, the judgment of the district court is reversed.

So ordered.*

---

* The third judge, who concurred with the Randolph opinion, was John Roberts, appointed later that year by President Bush as Chief Justice of the U.S. Supreme Court. — Eds.

WILLIAMS, Senior Circuit Judge, concurring: I concur in all aspects of the court's opinion except for the conclusion that Common Article 3 does not apply to the United States's conduct toward al Qaeda personnel captured in the conflict in Afghanistan. Because I agree that the Geneva Convention is not enforceable in courts of the United States, and that that any claims under Common Article 3 should be deferred until proceedings against Hamdan are finished, I fully agree with the court's judgment.

There is, I believe, a fundamental logic to the Convention's provisions on its application. Article 2 (P1) covers armed conflicts between two or more contracting parties. Article 2 (P3) makes clear that in a multi-party conflict, where any two or more signatories are on opposite sides, those parties "are bound by [the Convention] in their mutual relations" — but not (by implication) vis-à-vis any non-signatory. And as the court points out, under Article 2 (P3) even a non-signatory "Power" is entitled to the benefits of the Convention, as against a signatory adversary, if it "accepts and applies" its provisions.

Non-state actors cannot sign an international treaty. Nor is such an actor even a "Power" that would be eligible under Article 2 (P3) to secure protection by complying with the Convention's requirements. Common Article 3 fills the gap, providing some minimal protection for such non-eligibles in an "armed conflict not of an international character occurring in the territory of one of the High Contracting Parties." The gap being filled is the non-eligible party's failure to be a nation. Thus the words "not of an international character" are sensibly understood to refer to a conflict between a signatory nation and a non-state actor. The most obvious form of such a conflict is a civil war. But given the Convention's structure, the logical reading of "international character" is one that matches the basic derivation of the word "international," i.e., between nations. Thus, I think the context compels the view that a conflict between a signatory and a non-state actor is a conflict "not of an international character." In such a conflict, the signatory is bound to Common Article 3's modest requirements of "humane[]" treatment and "the judicial guarantees which are recognized as indispensable by civilized peoples."

I assume that our conflicts with the Taliban and al Qaeda are distinct, and I agree with the court that in reading the Convention we owe the President's construction "great weight." But I believe the Convention's language and structure compel the view that Common Article 3 covers the conflict with al Qaeda.

Despite increasing calls in mid-2005 for closing the detention facilities at Guantánamo, there seemed to be little support from the administration or the military for such action. On June 15, 2005, Republican Senator Arlen Specter convened the first Congressional hearing on what procedures should govern the detention of suspected terrorists since the Sept. 11, 2001 attacks. However, J. Michael Wiggins, Deputy Associate Attorney General, testified that "It's our position that legally they [the detainees] could be held in perpetuity." He argued that existing procedures are adequate and that the president must have the power to control foreign prisoners during a war — even if that war could last decades. Charlie Savage, *Republican urges change in detainee rules, Says Con-*

gress should define rights of those held at Guantánamo, Boston Globe, June 15, 2005, at A3.

As of April 2005, Amnesty International estimated that the United States had detained, at least briefly, 70,000 persons around the world as part of the ongoing "war on terror," as follows:

USA: Naval Brig, Charleston, South Carolina — 2 "enemy combatants"
Cuba: Guantanamo Bay naval base — 520 (234 releases/transfers)
Afghanistan: Bagram air base — 300
Afghanistan: Kandahar air base — 250
Afghanistan: other US facilities (forward operating bases) — estimated at scores of detainees
Iraq: Camp Bucca — 6,300
Iraq: Abu Ghraib prison — 3,500
Iraq: Camp Cropper — 110
Iraq: Other US facilities — 1,300
Worldwide: CIA facilities, undisclosed locations — estimated at 40 detainees
Worldwide: In custody of other governments at behest of USA — estimated at several thousand detainees
Worldwide: Secret transfers of detainees to third countries — estimated at 100 to 150 detainees
Foreign nationals held outside the USA and charged for trial — 4
Trials of foreign nationals held in US custody outside the USA — 0
Total number of detainees held outside the USA by the US during "war on terror" — 70,0000

Amnesty International, *Guantánamo and beyond: The continuing pursuit of unchecked executive power,* May 13, 2005, AI Index: AMR 51/063/2005 (sources omitted).

Amnesty International's estimate of 40 detainees at undisclosed locations overseen by CIA turned out to be low, as subsequent press reports disclosed the existence of several such "black sites" around the world, which contained over 100 detainees held totally incommunicado. See Dana Priest, *CIA Holds Terror Suspects in Secret Prisons,* Wash. Post, Nov. 2, 2005, at A1.

D. *Renditions*

At its peak, the camp at Guantánamo Bay housed more than 750 prisoners. Over time, the United States began transferring and releasing detainees from Guantánamo. Through March 2005, approximately 65 prisoners had been transferred from Guantánamo and sent to the following countries: 29 to Pakistan, 5 to Morocco, 7 to France, 7 to Russia, and 4 to Saudi Arabia. See Douglas Jehl, *Pentagon seeks to shift inmates from Cuba base.* New York Times (Mar. 11, 2005).

Rather than easing concerns, this policy of "rendition" sparked new concerns that the U.S. was sending detainees from Guantánamo to countries with long records of torturing prisoners. The Committee on International Human Rights of the Association of the Bar of the City of New York and the Center for Human Rights and Global Justice of New York University School of Law released an outraged report, alleging that this policy amounted to "torture by proxy" and violated both domestic and international law. Association of the Bar of the City of New York and Center for Human Rights and Global Justice, *Torture by Proxy, International and Domestic Law Applicable to Extraordinary Renditions*, Oct. 29, 2004. The following extract addresses some of the legal and policy issues involved.

Joan Fitzpatrick, *Rendition and Transfer in the War Against Terrorism: Guantánamo and Beyond*

25 Loy. L.A. Int'l & Comp. L. Rev. 457, 471, 480-81, 490-92 (2003) (citations omitted)

[T]he current picture regarding seizure and transfer of terrorist suspects is quite mixed. Many persons seized in states outside of Europe with the tacit or formal collaboration of local officials are being irregularly rendered to U.S. detention centers. There, they are held indefinitely without charge or trial and without access to counsel or family. In contrast, persons arrested on terrorist charges in European states are rarely rendered to U.S. custody. Established principles of extradition law continue to apply to such persons and serious prosecutions on ordinary criminal charges are frequently undertaken in cases where extradition is not possible. The attempted reconceptualization of the "war against terrorism" as a matter of humanitarian law, rather than as a matter implicating traditional rules of extradition and criminal law, is not accepted by democratic states....

The applicability of human rights protections to these captives is a matter of vigorous debate. The position of the U.S. Administration appears to be that humanitarian law does not forbid these transfers and that human rights treaties have no application. The territorial scope of human rights treaties is a contested issue and standards may be clarified in light of U.S. practice in the "war against terrorism." Effective mechanisms to assess U.S. compliance, however, appear to be unavailable.

Some of the states transferring captives to U.S. custody are not parties to major human rights treaties and, thus, cannot be held to account for their own violations in depriving the captives the opportunity to contest their transfer based on human rights nonrefoulement principles. The United States appears indifferent to its own treaty obligations not to render persons to states where there are substantial grounds to fear that these persons will be subjected to torture....

The absence of legal authority suggests one of three things. The first possibility, which the Bush Administration might argue, is simply that no legal rules constrain the discretion of U.S. authorities to seize persons any place in the world, to label them as "enemy combatants" on the basis of suspicion of involvement in terrorist activities, or to transport them thousands of miles away to indefinite incommunicado detention. The second possibility is that persons seized in situations that do not constitute a recognizable international armed conflict should be protected by established norms of extradition, refugee, and human rights law. To the extent that any of the current captives are unprivileged combatants seized during a cognizable international armed conflict, a third option exists. This option urges that humanitarian law norms be applied and that the duration of internment be linked to the continuation of active hostilities, the same rule that applies to POWs. . . .

V. Conclusion

In his State of the Union Address on January 28, 2003, President Bush mentioned the 3,000 captives who are the subject of this Article:

> All told, more than 3,000 suspected terrorists have been arrested in many countries. Many others have met a different fate. Let's put it this way — they are no longer a problem to the United States and our friends and allies.
>
> . . .We have the terrorists on the run. We're keeping them on the run. One by one, the terrorists are learning the meaning of American justice.

There are several notable aspects to these remarks. First, the terminology — "terrorists," "arrested," "American justice" — is unusual for a President discussing the wartime internment of captured combatants. This is the language of seizure and rendition of persons suspected of transnational crimes. Second, the apparent reference to terrorist suspects who were summarily executed (perhaps in targeted assassinations such as the one carried out by an unmanned CIA drone in Yemen) is chilling. It suggests a disregard for the humanity and fundamental rights of terrorist suspects that perhaps mirrors actual terrorists' attitudes toward their perceived enemies in the West, but which is antithetical to established human rights principles. Third, the concept of "American justice" reflected in these remarks and in the renditions and detentions of the 3,000 "war against terrorism" captives is both new and alien. The current practices are unprecedented and they conflict with legal values reflected in established principles of extradition, refugee, and human rights norms.

The threat posed by international terrorists is greater and higher on the foreign policy agenda than it was prior to September 11, 2001. The internationalization of the Afghan conflict in October 2001 also complicated the legal picture by plunging counterterrorism into the midst of an international armed conflict and implicating the rules of humanitarian law. But, the time has now come to clarify the rules that should govern the seizure, rendition, detention, and trial of suspected terrorists.

First, combatants captured in the Afghan conflict should be given hearings pursuant to Article 5 of the Third Geneva Convention as soon as possible. . . .

Those who prove to be unprivileged combatants — for example, Al Qaeda fighters who engaged in combat in Afghanistan — should be protected by Article 75 of Protocol Additional I of 1977 as a matter of customary international law. . . . Alternatively, they could be subjected to administrative detention, implemented consistently with the treaty obligations of the United States under the ICCPR.

Those who prove to be noncombatants should be treated in one of two ways. First, civilians captured in the Afghan conflict should receive the full protections of the Fourth Geneva Convention, including the rules relating to internment, transfer, deportation, and repatriation of protected civilians. Second, suspected terrorists seized in situations that do not amount to international armed conflict (for example, in Bosnia and Indonesia) should receive the full protection of extradition, refugee, and human rights norms. If further detention is desired, they must be charged with criminal offenses and granted fair trials in ordinary courts or be subjected to administrative detention. Administrative detention is not wartime internment. It is governed, instead, by the provisions of the ICCPR, including the derogation norms and the absolute prohibition of violation of non-derogable rights.

E. A Congressional Response

The following bill was introduced in the U.S. House of Representatives in June 2005. If enacted, would it meet international human rights standards? Would it require the United States to file a notice of derogation under Article 4 of the Covenant on Civil and Political Rights?

H.R. 3038

109th Cong. (1st Sess. 2005)

A BILL

To affirm the authority of the executive branch to detain foreign nationals as unlawful combatants, to enable a person detained as an unlawful combatant to challenge the basis for that detention and to receive a disposition within 2 years, to provide for the President to establish military tribunals to try such persons, and for other purposes.

Be it enacted by the Senate and House of Representatives of the United States of America in Congress assembled,

SEC. 1. SHORT TITLE. This Act may be cited as the "Guantanamo Detainees Procedures Act of 2005"

SEC. 2. AUTHORITY OF EXECUTIVE BRANCH TO DETAIN PERSONS COVERED BY THIS ACT AS UNLAWFUL COMBATANTS.

(a) FINDING. Congress finds that the executive branch has authority to detain persons covered by this Act as unlawful combatants.

(b) PERSONS COVERED BY THIS ACT. In this Act, the term "person covered by this Act" means an individual who

(1) is accused of knowingly

(A) planning, authorizing, committing, aiding, or abetting one or more terrorist acts against the United States; or

(B) being part of or supporting forces engaged in armed conflict against the United States;

(2) is not a United States person or lawful permanent resident; and

(3) is not a prisoner of war within the meaning of the Geneva Convention Relative to the Treatment of Prisoners of War, done on August 12, 1949.

SEC. 3. RIGHT OF PERSON DETAINED AS UNLAWFUL COMBATANT OR ON SIMILAR BASIS TO CHALLENGE THAT BASIS.

(a) IN GENERAL. Whenever the United States detains a person covered by this Act on the basis of a determination that the person can be detained as an unlawful combatant or can be detained on any similar basis, the person is entitled to a hearing under this section as expeditiously as practicable but not later than 6 months after the date on which the United States first made the determination.

(b) REQUIREMENTS FOR HEARING. A hearing required by subsection (a) must meet the following requirements:

(1) The hearing officer is an active member of one of the Courts of Criminal Appeals of the Armed Forces.

(2) The hearing officer has authority to decide de novo whether the basis of a determination under subsection (a) is valid and to grant appropriate relief if the hearing officer decides that the basis is invalid.

(3) The hearing officer is impartial in fact, and is in a position independent from

(A) the individuals who first determined that the person can be detained; and

(B) the individuals on whose orders the person is being detained.

(4) The person is provided with access to the evidence that tends to support the determination that the person can be detained.

(5) The person is provided with an opportunity to address the hearing officer, and is provided with an interpreter for that purpose.

(c) ADMINISTRATIVE REVIEW. The Secretary of Defense shall conduct administrative review of the activities of a hearing officer under this section.

SEC. 4. RIGHT OF PERSON DETAINED TO DISPOSITION WITHIN 2 YEARS.

(a) IN GENERAL. Whenever the United States detains a person covered by this Act on the basis of a determination that the person can be detained as an unlawful combatant or can be detained on any similar basis, the person is entitled to a disposition under this section not later than 2 years after the date on which the United States first made the determination.

(b) REQUIREMENTS FOR DISPOSITION. A disposition under this section is any one of the following:

(1) Repatriation to the governing authority in the area in which the person was first detained or the person's country of origin, except where there are substantial grounds to believe that the person would be in danger of being subjected to torture.

(2) The commencement, by formal charges, of prosecution in an appropriate court, which may include an extraordinary tribunal under section 5 of this Act, an international criminal tribunal, or a district court of the United States.

(c) EXTENSION.

(1) CERTIFICATION. The period required by subsection (a) for the repatriation of the person or the commencement of formal charges may be extended if the Secretary of Defense certifies, in writing, with respect to the person that the Secretary of Defense has determined that the person is a

continuing threat to the national security of the United States due to a likelihood that the person will undertake terrorist or belligerent acts against the United States based on the person's past conduct, level of authority within the group or organization, statement and actions during confinement, age and health, psychological profile, and other pertinent factors, and the repatriation of the person or the commencement of formal charges will compromise the national security of the United States by curtailing intelligence gathering from the person, jeopardize intelligence sources necessary to prosecute the person, or other extraordinary circumstances justify the extension.

(2) DETAILED BASIS. A certification under this subsection must include a detailed account of the factual basis for that determination.

(3) ACCESS TO CERTIFICATION. A person covered by a certification under this subsection is entitled to an unclassified copy of the certification.

(4) DURATION OF CERTIFICATION. A certification under this subsection is effective for not more than 1 year. The Secretary may make successive certifications with respect to a person so long as each additional certification is made while an imminent threat to national security continues to be posed by the group or organization in which the person is a member or by other persons associated with, or acting on behalf of, the group, organization, or person.

(5) JUDICIAL REVIEW. The United States Court of Appeals for the Armed Forces shall provide judicial review with respect to any issue under this subsection, including whether the determination of the Secretary under paragraph (1) is justified by the factual basis under paragraph (2).

SEC. 5. EXTRAORDINARY TRIBUNALS.

(a) AUTHORITY. The President is hereby authorized to establish tribunals for the trial of persons covered by this Act.

(b) JURISDICTION. Tribunals established under subsection (a) may adjudicate violations of the law of war, international laws of armed conflict, and crimes against humanity targeted against United States persons or residents.

(c) AUTHORITY TO ESTABLISH PROCEDURAL RULES. The Secretary of Defense, in consultation with the Secretary of State and the Attorney General, shall prescribe and publish in the Federal Register, and report to the Committees on the Judiciary of the Senate and the House of Representatives, the rules of evidence and procedure that are to apply to tribunals established under subsection (a).

SEC. 6. PROCEDURAL REQUIREMENTS.

(a) IN GENERAL. The rules prescribed for a tribunal under section 5(c) shall be designed to ensure a full and fair hearing of the charges against the accused. The rules shall require the following:

(1) That the tribunal be independent and impartial.

(2) That the accused be notified of the particulars of the offense charged or alleged without delay.

(3) That the proceedings be made simultaneously intelligible for participants not conversant in the English language by translation or interpretation.

(4) That the evidence supporting each alleged offense be given to the accused, except as provided in subsection (d).

(5) That the accused have the opportunity to be present at trial.

(6) That the accused have a right to be represented by counsel.

(7) That the accused have the opportunity

(A) to respond to the evidence supporting each alleged offense;

(B) to obtain exculpatory evidence from the prosecution; and

(C) to present exculpatory evidence.

(8) That the accused have the opportunity to confront and cross-examine adverse witnesses and to offer witnesses.

(9) That the proceeding and disposition be expeditious.

(10) That the tribunal apply reasonable rules of evidence designed to ensure admission only of reliable information or material with probative value.

(11) That the accused be afforded all necessary means of defense before and after the trial.

(12) That conviction of an alleged offense not be based upon an act, offense, or omission that was not an offense under law when it was committed.

(13) That the penalty for an offense not be greater than it was when the offense was committed.

(14) That the accused

(A) be presumed innocent until proven guilty, and

(B) not be found guilty except upon proof beyond a reasonable doubt.

(15) That the accused not be compelled to confess guilt or testify against himself.

(16) That, subject to subsections (c) and (d), the trial be open and public and include public availability of the transcripts of the trial and the pronouncement of judgment.

(17) That a convicted person be informed of remedies and appeals and the time limits for the exercise of the person's rights to the remedies and appeals under the rules.

(18) That a preliminary proceeding be held within 30 days of detention to determine whether there is jurisdiction under section 4 over the person and the offenses charged. The preliminary proceeding may be continued for an additional 30 days for good cause shown.

(19) That the privilege of the writ of habeas corpus under title 28, United States Code, or under any other provision of law not be infringed.

(20) That the tribunal be comprised of a military judge and not less than five members.

(b) IMPOSITION OF THE DEATH PENALTY. The requirements of the Uniform Code of Military Justice for the imposition of the death penalty shall apply in any case in which a tribunal established under section 5 is requested to adjudge the death penalty.

(c) PUBLIC PROCEEDINGS. Any proceedings conducted by a tribunal established under section 5, and the proceedings on any appeal of an action of the tribunal, shall be accessible to the public consistent with any demonstrable necessity to secure the safety of observers, witnesses, tribunal judges, counsel, or other persons.

(d) CONFIDENTIALITY OF EVIDENCE. Evidence available from an agency of the Federal Government that is offered in a trial by a tribunal established under section 5 may be kept secret from the public only when the head of the agency personally certifies in writing that disclosure will cause

(1) identifiable harm to the prosecution of military objectives;

(2) significant, identifiable harm to intelligence sources or methods; or

(3) substantial risk that such evidence could be used for planning future terrorist attacks.

(e) REVIEW.

(1) PROCEDURES REQUIRED. The Secretary of Defense shall provide for prompt review of convictions by tribunals established under section 5 to ensure that the procedural requirements of a full and fair hearing have been met and that the evidence reasonably supports the convictions.

(2) UNITED STATES COURT OF APPEALS FOR THE ARMED FORCES. The procedures established under paragraph (1) shall, at a minimum, allow for review of the proceedings of the tribunals, and the convictions and sentences of such tribunals, by the United States Court of Appeals for the Armed Forces established under the Uniform Code of Military Justice.

(3) SUPREME COURT. The decisions of the United States Court of Appeals for the Armed Forces regarding proceedings of tribunals established under section 5 shall be subject to review by the Supreme Court by writ of certiorari.

SEC. 7. ANNUAL REPORT ON PERSONS COVERED BY THIS ACT WHO ARE DETAINED AS UNLAWFUL COMBATANTS BY THE UNITED STATES.

(a) REPORT REQUIRED. The Secretary of Defense shall submit to Congress an annual report on persons covered by this Act who are detained as unlawful combatants by the United States.

(b) CURRENT DETAINEES. The report shall include, for each person currently so detained, the following:

(1) The name and nationality of the person.

(2) The period during which the person has been so detained.

(3) A description of the specific process afforded to the person under sections 3 and 4 of this Act and the outcome of those processes.

(c) FORMER DETAINEES. The report shall include, for each person formerly so detained, the following:

(1) The name and nationality of the person.

(2) The terms of the conditional release agreement with respect to the person.

(3) A statement of the basis for the determination of the United States Government that release was warranted.

(4) The period during which the person was so detained, including the release date of the person.

(d) CLASSIFICATION. The report required by this section shall be submitted in unclassified form, but may include a classified annex.

Thomas M. Franck, Editorial Comment, "Criminals, Combatants, or What? An Examination of the Role of Law in Responding to the Threat of Terror"

98 Am. J. Int'l L. 686 (2004)

The criminal laws of liberal democracies require that persons cannot be detained indefinitely unless charged with an offense, given access to legal counsel, and afforded a fair trial at which guilt must be proven by the accusing state beyond a reasonable doubt and without torture, forced confessions, or other cruel or unusual forms of duress. This is the "due process" model applicable to civilians, as groups or individuals, suspected of engaging in unlawful conduct.

International law, too, has developed civilizing checks on unbridled power in the conduct of armed hostilities. This law (jus in bello) permits the state to detain combatants indefinitely — for the duration of a war — but prohibits torture, punishment, or the use of duress to extract information. This "prisoner of war" model applies to persons who engage in combat in recognizable uniform and carry weapons openly. Persons captured as combatants who are not in uniform and carry concealed weapons may forfeit their "prisoner of war" status, thereby becoming subject to trial under the "due process" model. . . .

Still, it is also common ground among most lawyers versed in constitutional and international law that the aforementioned differences between the modern threat of terrorism and more familiar attacks on the legal order by criminals and aggressors affect the inconvenience costs of adherence to the rule of law in both its "due process" and "prisoner of war" models. For several reasons the terrorist défi is different.

First, the "due process" model fails fully to take into account the magnitude of the challenge involved in convicting terrorists as criminals by demonstrating culpability beyond a reasonable doubt. The obstacles include not only the risk to the prosecution of revealing sources and methods, which is likely to be much greater than in an ordinary criminal trial, but also the limitations imposed by criminal law on means of obtaining evidence. Means commonly employed overseas in covert operations, unauthorized wiretaps, for example, may render their fruits inadmissible in domestic criminal proceedings. Moreover, prosecutors are likely to find it difficult to persuade witnesses to come forward to testify, given the heightened danger of retaliation.

Second, no one questions that the costs of releasing a potential terrorist are likely to be greater than those that ordinarily accrue in the event of an accused's discharge for lack of evidence or procedural error. The adage that it is better for a hundred guilty persons to go free than for one innocent person to be incarcerated takes on a different hue in the age of high-technology terror.

In the "prisoner of war" model, too, the normal balance of convenience that supports restraints on authority is skewed by the phenomenon of modern terrorism. The logic behind the Geneva Conventions, for example, is, first, that humane treatment of prisoners of war will encourage other combatants to surrender peaceably. Second, it is assumed that, when one party to a conflict treats its prisoners humanely, the other will reciprocate. Third, it is probably an unspoken conjecture that ordinary prisoners of war do not have much information that is likely, whether revealed or unrevealed, to have a great impact on the outcome of the conflict. Simply stating these underlying assumptions of the law of war is to suggest that they are not so evidently applicable to an international terrorist conspiracy like Al Qaeda. On the other hand, to whatever extent the underlying reasons for normative constraints may be less applicable, that will alter the balance of convenience between upholding and circumventing those constraints. . . .

This seems an appropriate time for scholars to talk with government lawyers and those in the law and policymaking process in searching for adjustments in applicable domestic and international law. Such a search must begin with the assumption that terrorism, as currently practiced, does constitute a new phenomenon: one to which traditional constitutional and international legal constraints may not be wholly responsive. It must equally accept, however, that no adaptation of law — no matter how efficiently responsive to the challenges of a new phenomenon that is both part crime and part combat, yet different from each — should be made at the cost of abandoning the basic concepts of the rule of law that define us and differentiate us from our adversaries. The irreducible core of the rule of law is this: that those who execute the law must never be the sole and final arbiters of that law.

Comments and Questions

1. This chapter has focused on U.S. reactions to terrorism, but the United States is hardly alone in adopting troublesome responses to terrorist attacks. Following the bombing attacks on the London underground in July 2005, the United Kingdom adopted a number of new anti-terrorism laws. See Sarah Lyall, *3 Main British Parties to Back Tougher Antiterrorism Laws*, N.Y. Times, July 27, 2005, at A6; Mara D. Ballaby, *Britain weighing secretive courts in terrorism cases*, Boston Globe, Aug. 10, 2005. Nor are reactions confined to countries that have been direct victims of terrorism. See, e.g., Kevin Sullivan, *Denmark Tries to Act Against Terrorism as Mood in Europe Shifts*, Wash. Post, Aug. 29, 2005, at A9; [Australian Prime Minister] *Howard pushes new anti-terror law*, BBC News, Aug. 9, 2005, *http://news.bbc.co.uk/go/pr/fr/-/1/hi/world/asiapacific/4224936.stm*. Following bomb attacks in southern Thailand, the UN Human Rights Committee criticized the emergency decrees adopted by the Thai government, expressing particular concern over granting immunity to officials enforcing the state of emergency. UN Dept. of Public Information, Human Rights Committee Concludes Eighty-Fourth Session, Press Release HR/CT/669, at 6 (July 29, 2005).

2. Perhaps the most infamous U.S. war crime committed since World War II was the massacre of at least 128 (and probably many more) Vietnamese civilians at the village of My Lai in March 1968. The only person convicted for the killings was Lieutenant William Calley, who was court-martialed and sentenced to 3-1/2 years in prison. A Gallup poll conducted at the time reported that 79 percent of the American public disagreed with the verdict. An Army helicopter pilot, Hugh C. Thompson Jr., who tried to stop the killing and saved perhaps a

dozen Vietnamese was awarded the Soldier's Medal — 28 years after the fact, in 1996. The Calley case is discussed extensively in the third edition of this book, Richard B. Lillich and Hurst Hannum, *International Human Rights: Problems of Law, Policy, and Practice* 839-43, 859-75 (3d ed. 1995).

3. Duffy's complaint supra — that "[t] he only thing we ever heard was to get more body count, kill more VC! . . . My squad leader told me that in his old unit they couldn't come in from the field until they turned in a body count" — reveals rather starkly that the My Lai massacre was nothing more that the logical extension of the body count approach to "pacification" of Vietnam. Might the abuses at Abu Ghraib have been a similar logical extension of the need to acquire intelligence related to the "war on terrorism"? Reread Duffy's observations regarding the fight against communism and substitute the word "terrorism" as appropriate; might a U.S. soldier in Iraq express the same views today?

4. An article in the Air Force Law Review concludes that it would be "incorrect, irresponsible, and unwise for the U.S. to afford POW status to captured members of al-Qaeda and the Taliban as they are not entitled to, and are undeserving of this status. . . . [T]o do so would set a highly injudicious international legal precedent inconsistent with the Rule of Law and the long-term interests of the international community. It would recklessly foster future abuses in armed conflict by undermining directly long-standing rules of war crafted carefully to protect noncombatants by deterring combatants in armed conflicts from pretending to be protected civilians and hiding among them." Joseph P. "Dutch" Bialke, *Al-Qaeda & Taliban Unlawful Combatant Detainees, Unlawful Belligerency, and the International Laws of Armed Conflict*, 55 A.F. L. Rev. 1, 83-84 (2004). Indirect support for this view is found in Stephen R. Ratner, *Revising the Geneva Conventions to Regulate Force by and Against Terrorists: Four Fallacies*, 1 Isr. Def. Forces L. Rev. 8 (2003). Do you agree?

5. Do you agree with Bybee, supra page 271, that conflicts such as those against Afghanistan and the "war against terror" were unforeseen by the drafters of the 1949 Geneva Conventions? Was terrorism, whether state-sponsored or not, unknown before the late twentieth century?

6. David E. Graham, Executive Director for The Judge Advocate General's Legal Center and School, U.S. Army, and former Chief, International and Operational Law Division, Office of The Judge Advocate General, Department of the Army, offered the following explanation of how interrogation techniques approved for use in Guantánamo "migrated" to Abu Ghraib: "I think that certain interrogation techniques migrated from the initial days in Afghanistan, to Guantánamo, and then, from both Guantánamo and Afghanistan, to Iraq. Thus, even in Iraq where the applicable law and standards of treatment and interrogation should have been well known, there was uncertainty in the minds of some with respect to what interrogation techniques were lawful — and which were not. The very painful lesson learned, here, appears, quite clearly, to be that once you cross that interrogation Rubicon, once you sanction interrogation methods that go beyond anything that was ever considered to be of a valid nature previously, one encounters a slippery slope from which it is very difficult, if not impossible, to recover." David E. Graham, "The Treatment and Interrogation of Prisoners of War and Security Detainees: Current Issues," presented to the Miller Center of Public Affairs Forum, University of Virginia: Sept. 3, 2004, and 18th Annual International Military Operations and Law

(MILOPS) Conference, Singapore, Mar. 23, 2005, *http://daphne.apan-info.net/QuickPlace/milops/Main.nsf/h_Index/2AE36A851A82F3B40A256FAC00040363/?OpenDocument.*

7. It should be noted that many military officers opposed attempts by the Bush Administration to loosen rules regarding interrogations on the grounds, inter alia, that such practices could have adverse consequences for U.S. military personnel and did not reflect American values. See, e.g., Neil A. Lewis, *Military's Opposition to Harsh Interrogation Is Outlined,* N.Y. Times, July 28, 2005, at A21; Josh White, *US Lawyers Fought Policy on Interrogations,* Wash. Post, July 15, 2005, at A1.

8. The May 9, 2005, edition of *Newsweek* included a brief item stating that the Pentagon was preparing a report admitting that an American interrogator had flushed a Koran down a toilet at Guantánamo in the course of an interrogation. The story touched off anti-American riots in Afghanistan, and riots soon spread to Pakistan, Gaza, and Indonesia in the week that followed. Seventeen people died and over 100 were injured before calm was restored.

The U.S. military had issued procedures governing the inspection and handling of detainees' Korans in January 2003, which include directions to wear clean gloves prior to handling the Koran, to use two hands, and to treat the book "in [a] manner signaling respect and reverence.... Handle the Koran as if it were a fragile piece of delicate art." Memorandum from Dept. of Defense Joint Task Force Guantánamo, Headquarters, Joint Detention Operation Group, on Guantánamo Standard Operating Procedures on Handling Korans that are Provided to Detainees, Jan. 19, 2003, para. 4, Dept. of Defense website *http://www.defenselink.mil/news/Jun2005/d20050601KoranSOP.pdf.*

When its anonymous source recanted, *Newsweek* retracted its story. While a subsequent investigation by Brig. Gen. Jay Hood found a consistent pattern of respectful handling of the Koran at Guantánamo, he did identify five cases of misuse. If Korans (or Bibles or Torahs) were deliberately misused, would this automatically violate detainees rights? Which ones? If detainees' religious beliefs lead them to object to the exercise of any authority over them by women, should such beliefs also be respected? Are these questions answered by the opinion of the International Committee of the Red Cross that it is customary international law that "[t]he personal convictions and religious practices of persons deprived of their liberty must be respected" in international and non-international armed conflicts? See Jean-Marie Henckaerts and Louise Doswald-Beck, *Customary International Humanitarian Law* 451 (2005).

9. The Foreword to Amnesty International's 2005 Annual Report noted that "the US government has gone to great lengths to restrict the application of the Geneva Conventions and to 're-define' torture. It has sought to justify the use of coercive interrogation techniques, the practice of holding 'ghost detainees' (people in unacknowledged incommunicado detention) and the 'rendering' or handing over of prisoners to third countries known to practise torture. The detention facility at Guantánamo Bay has become the gulag of our times, entrenching the practice of arbitrary and indefinite detention in violation of international law. Trials by military commissions have made a mockery of justice and due process." The reference to "gulag," a term commonly used to describe the Soviet system of prison camps, outraged U.S. government officials; did Amnesty go too far? Also see Physicians for Human Rights, *Break Them Down: Systematic*

Use of Psychological Torture by US Forces (2005). For a formal U.S. explanation of the events at Abu Ghraib and Guantánamo, see *Second Periodic Report of the United States to the Committee on Torture,* UN Doc. CAT/C/48/Add.3 (June 29, 2005).

10. Fitzpatrick suggests that detainees captured in the "war on terrorism" must either be released at the end of hostilities or charged with crimes and granted fair trials in ordinary courts. Recall Lieutenant Duffy's statement concerning the release of Viet Cong prisoners during the Viet Nam War: "It's hard enough to find the enemy, but to catch and just let them go is ridiculous." Are these the only available options?

11. In *Abu Ali v. Ashcroft,* 16 Dec. 2004 (D.D.C.), a U.S. District Court ruled that U.S. courts have jurisdiction to hear a habeas corpus petition from an individual detained by a foreign government where there is unrebutted evidence that the person is in the "constructive custody" of the United States. Such evidence could include the fact that the individual had been taken into custody by U.S. personnel, that U.S. agents were involved in the detention or interrogation abroad, or that the foreign government would release the person into U.S. custody if requested.

12. Among many scholarly articles that examine the situation of Guantánamo and other detainees from the perspective of international and/or constitutional law, see Diane Marie Amann, *Abu Ghraib,* 153 U. Pa. L. Rev. 2085 (2005); id., *Guantánamo,* 42 Col. J. Transnat'l L. 263 (2004); *Human Rights in the 'War on Terror'* (Richard Ashty Wilson ed., 2005); Jordan J. Paust, *Post-9/11 Overreaction and Fallacies Regarding War and Defense, Guantanamo, the Status of Persons, Treatment, Judicial Review of Detention, and Due Process in Military Commissions,* 79 Notre Dame L. Rev. 1335 (2004); Catherine Powell, *The Role of Transnational Norm Entrepreneurs in the U.S. "War on Terrorism,"* 5 Curr. Issues 47 (No. 1, 2004).

VIII. Final Comments and Questions

1. How much of humanitarian law is customary international law? All of the Geneva Conventions? Certain articles thereof? Only Common Article 3? What guidance can be obtained from the ICJ's judgment in the Nicaragua case? Compare the following views of the customary international law status of the Geneva Conventions in the wake of that decision. "I believe that the norms stated in Article 3(1)(a)(c) are of such an elementary, ethical character, and echo so many provisions in other humanitarian and human rights treaties, that they must be regarded as embodying minimum standards of customary law also applicable to non-international armed conflicts. This is also true for the obligation to treat humanely persons who are hors de combat, which is rooted in Hague Regulations 23(e)(d), which undoubtedly reflect customary law, and in the customary obligation contained in the law of human rights to treat with humanity all persons deprived of their liberty. I consider at least the core due process principle stated in Article 3(1)(d) . . . to embody customary law, notwithstanding a recent authoritative enumeration of customary human rights which does not list due process of law." Theodor Meron, *Human Rights and Humanitarian Norms as Customary*

Law 34-35 (1989). "[T]here must be at least very serious doubts whether those conventions could be regarded as embodying customary law. Even the Court's view that the [C]ommon Article 3, laying down a 'minimum yardstick' (para. 218) for armed conflicts of non-international character, are applicable as 'elementary considerations of humanity' is not a matter free from difficulty." 1986 I.C.J. at 537 (Judge Sir Robert Jennings, Dissenting Opinion).

The International Committee of the Red Cross issued a two-volume publication in 2005 designed to answer this question, although the ICRC's conclusions do not, in and of themselves, constitute a definitive legal interpretation. See Henckaerts and Doswald-Beck, supra page 318.

The U.S. military takes a relatively expansive view of what constitues customary international law, which it defines as "the prohibition against any state policy that results in the conclusion that the state practices, encourages, or condones:

1. Genocide,
2. Slavery or slave trade,
3. Murder or causing the disapperance of individuals,
4. Torture or other cruel, inhuman, or degrading treatment or punishment,
5. All violence to life or limb,
6. Taking of hostages,
7. Punishment without fair and regular trial,
8. Prolonged arbitrary detention,
9. Failure to care for and collect the wounded and sick,
10. Systematic racial discrimination, or
11. A consistent pattern of gross violations of internationlly recognized human rights."

Operational Law Handbook (2003) 39-40 (William O'Brien ed., 2003). Most of these norms are taken from the *Restatement of the Foreign Relations Law of the United States*, but numbers 5, 6, 7, and 9 are drawn from other sources, such as the Universal Declaration of Human Rights and Common Article 3 of the 1949 Geneva Conventions.

2. Should the treatment of detainees or the duration of their detention depend on arcane discussions of whether or not an "armed conflict" exists, if the purpose of contemporary human rights law is to protect the individual, wherever he or she may be found? See Derek Jinks, *The Declining Significance of POW Status*, 45 Harv. Int'l L. J. 367, 442 (2004) (arguing that a move toward "protective parity" for detainees has rendered "the unique protective significance of POW status . . . minimal"). Who should decide these issues? The Inter-American Commission on Human Rights issued precautionary measures requesting the United States to ensure that Guantánamo detainees had their status determined by a "competent tribunal" as soon as possible, Inter-Am. Comm'n H.R., 1 Annual Report 2002, OAS Doc. OEA/Ser.L/V/II.117 Doc. 1 rev. 1, para. 80 (Mar. 7, 2003). How do you think the United States responded to the Commission's request?

3. In a case relating to the 1983 invasion of Grenada by U.S. forces, the Inter-American Commission of Human Rights rejected the U.S. argument that "the matter was wholly and exclusively governed by the law of international armed conflict." *Coard et al. v. United States*, Case No. 10.951, Report

No. 109/99, Inter-Am. Comm'n H.R., 2 Annual Report 1999, para. 35 (Apr. 13, 2000). The Commission held, "While international humanitarian law pertains primarily in times of war and the international law of human rights applies most fully in times of peace, the potential application of one does not necessarily exclude or displace the other. There is an integral linkage between the law of human rights and humanitarian law because they share a 'common nucleus of non-derogable rights and a common purpose of protecting human life and dignity,' and there may be a substantial overlap in the application of these bodies of law." Id., para. 39 (citations omitted).

4. Do you agree with Professor Franck that "a search must begin with the assumption that terrorism, as currently practiced, does constitute a new phenomenon: one to which traditional constitutional and international legal constraints may not be wholly responsive"? Is there a gap in international human rights law, international humanitarian law, or both? Cf. Kenneth Watkin, *Controlling the Use of Force: A Role for Human Rights Norms in Contemporary Armed Conflict*, 98 Am. J. Int'l L. 1 (2004): "[S]ystems of accountability developed to regulate the use of force domestically cannot simply be transferred to the international humanitarian law context. Consequently, both states and human rights supervisory bodies may have to readjust their understanding of the role human rights law can play in enhancing the accountability framework regarding the use of deadly force to armed conflict. No gaps in the effort to apply appropriate norms of humanity can be allowed." Id. at 34.

5. During the UN's 2005 World Summit, the Security Council unanimously adopted a resolution condemning terrorism and calling on states to combat it. The resolution also "[s]tresses that States must ensure that any measures taken to implement . . . this resolution comply with all of their obligations under international law, in particular international human rights law, refuge law, and humanitarian law." S.C. Res. 1624 (Sept. 14, 2005). Also see Report of the Independent Expert on the Protection of Human Rights and Fundamental Freedom while countering Terrorism, Robert K. Goldman, UN Doc. E/CN.4/2005/103 (Feb. 7, 2005).

6. "Conflict" is a broad term that ranges from non-violent personal disputes to international wars. What is the role of international human rights law in governing conflict? Identify the different legal norms that apply to the situations discussed in this chapter. Would the protection of combatants and non-combatants alike be better served by a single set of norms applicable to all violent disturbances, civil wars, and international armed conflicts, or does the unique character of armed conflict continue to require specialized norms? Cf. David B. Rivkin Jr. and Lee A. Casey, *That's Why They Call It War*, Wash. Post, Mar. 16, 2003, at B04: "Modern warfare is not a video game, nor can it be organized like some grand 14th-century tournament, with the combatants confined in enclosed fields and the civilian spectators safely on the sidelines. Key military targets are often deliberately placed near, or even in the center of cities to guarantee the maximum collateral damage for CNN's cameras to beam back home and prick our consciences. . . . The more fanciful interpretation of [international humanitarian law] would inhibit all combat, ceding the global arena to unscrupulous countries and groups with a total disregard for legal norms."

7. For additional views on the convergence of (or conflict between) humanitarian and human rights law, see, e.g., Council of Europe, *The Fight against Terrorism: Council of Europe Standards* (3d ed. 2005); *The New Humanitarian*

Law of Armed Conflict (Antonio Cassese ed., 1979); Yoram Dinstein, "Human Rights in Armed Conflict: International Humanitarian Law," in 2 *Human Rights in International Law* 345 (Theodor Meron ed., 1984); G.I.A.D. Draper, *Human Rights and the Law of War,* 12 Va. J. Intl. L. 326 (1972); David Glazier, *Kangaroo Court or Competent Tribunal?: Judging the 21st Century Military Commission,* 89 Va. L. Rev. 2005 (2003); Paul Hoffman, *Human Rights and Terrorism,* 26 Hum. Rts. Q. 932 (2004); Theodor Meron, "Human Rights in Time of Peace and in Time of Armed Conflict," in *Contemporary Issues in International Law* (Thomas Buergenthal ed., 1984); Jelena Pejic, *Procedural Principles and Safeguards for Internment/Administrative Detention in Armed Conflict and Other Situations of Violence,* 858 Int'l Rev. Red Cross 375 (2005); id., *Terrorist Acts and Groups: A Role for International Law?,* 75 Brit. Y.B. Int'l L. 71 (2004); Gabor Rona, *Interesting Times for International Humanitarian Law: Challenges from the "War on Terror,"* 27 Fletcher F. World Aff. 55 (Summer/Fall 2003); A.H. Robertson, "Humanitarian Law and Human Rights," in *Studies and Essays on International Humanitarian Law and Red Cross Principles in Honour of Jean Pictet* 793 (Christophe Swinarski ed., 1984); Dietrich Schindler, *Human Rights and Humanitarian Law: The Interrelationship of the Laws,* 31 Am. U. L. Rev. 935 (1982); Alfred de Zayas, *Human Rights and Indefinite Detention,* 87 Int'l Rev. Red Cross 15 (No. 857, Mar. 2005).

Chapter 5

Who Is Obligated to Promote and Protect Human Rights?

Oil Exploration and Exploitation in the Niger River Delta

Agreeing on the content of human rights guaranteed by international law is not sufficient to ensure that rights can be exercised in practice. The duties that correspond to the right must also be agreed upon and established in law. This chapter examines the range of obligations of states and other actors respecting human rights, including the issue of attributing responsibility for violations of human rights law. Is the state the only entity to have obligations, or do corporations, inter-governmental (and non-governmental) organizations, and individuals also owe duties with respect to human rights? What are the nature and scope of the obligations imposed on states and on other actors?

These questions are studied through the prism of allegations of human rights violations in Nigeria's Niger River delta, the site of extensive oil extraction. This chapter also introduces one of the three regional systems for the protection of human rights, created by the African Charter on Human and Peoples' Rights. The other two major systems, in Europe and the Americas, are considered in Chapters 8 and 9, respectively.

I. The Problem: Oil Exploration and Exploitation in Nigeria[1]

During the past two decades successive governments in Nigeria have been directly involved in oil production through the State oil company, the Nigerian National Petroleum Company (NNPC), which is the majority shareholder in a consortium with Shell Petroleum Development Corporation (SPDC). Inhabitants of the Niger River delta, predominately the Ogoni people, have protested these operations almost continuously.

According to the Ogoni, the oil consortium has exploited oil reserves with no regard for the health or environment of local communities, disposing of toxic wastes into local waterways in violation of applicable international standards. The consortium also neglected and/or failed to maintain its facilities, causing numerous avoidable spills in the proximity of villages. The resulting contamination of water, soil, and air has had serious short and long-term health impacts, including skin infections, gastrointestinal and respiratory ailments, increased risk of cancers, and neurological and reproductive problems. The people in the area were never consulted about the development, nor have they received any of the benefits of the oil exploration and exploitation. The Nigerian Government is said to condone and facilitate these violations by placing the legal and military powers of the state at the disposal of the oil companies.

The Movement for the Survival of the Ogoni People (MOSOP) began a non-violent campaign to oppose the destruction of their environment by oil companies. In response, Shell is alleged to have recruited Nigerian police and military forces to suppress MOSOP and ensure that oil development activities could proceed without hindrance. Shell is said to have provided logistical support, transportation, and weapons to Nigerian authorities.

The government reacted to Ogoni protests with massive violence. In the early 1990s, Nigerian security forces allegedly burned and destroyed several Ogoni

1. The statement of the problem is based on the allegations and findings of fact in *Social and Economic Rights Action Center v. Nigeria* infra, page 355 and *Wiwa v. Royal Dutch Petroleum*, infra page 387.

villages and homes under the pretext of dislodging officials and supporters of MOSOP. Residents of the area were beaten, raped, shot, and sometimes killed during these raids. Some of the attacks involved uniformed forces of the police, the army, the air force, and the navy, armed with armored tanks and other sophisticated weapons. In other instances, the attacks were conducted by unidentified gunmen, mostly at night. The military-type methods and the calibre of weapons used in such attacks strongly suggested to residents the involvement of the Nigerian security forces. The government neither investigated nor prosecuted anyone for the attacks.

Later, the role of the Nigerian Army in the operations which left thousands of villagers homeless became clear, upon the discovery of several memos exchanged between officials of the SPDC and the Rivers State Internal Security Task Force. One such memo called for "ruthless military operations" and "wasting operations coupled with psychological tactics of displacement." At a public meeting recorded on video, Major Okuntimo, head of the Rivers State Internal Security Task Force, described the repeated invasion of villages by his troops, how unarmed villagers running from the troops were shot from behind, and the homes of suspected MOSOP activists were ransacked and destroyed. He stated his commitment to rid the communities of members and supporters of MOSOP. In their raids on villages, Nigerian security forces also destroyed crops and killed farm animals. It became impossible for many villagers to return to their fields and animals. The destruction of farmlands, rivers, crops and animals created malnutrition and starvation among certain communities.

In 1995, Ken Saro-Wiwa, leader of MOSOP, and John Kpuinen, deputy president of the youth wing, were hanged after being convicted of murder by a special tribunal, largely viewed by the outside world as a "show trial." According to observers, witnesses were bribed to testify falsely at the trial, and authorities offered to free the men if protests against Shell stopped. During the trial, members of the Wiwa family, including his mother, were beaten.

Those injured and the families of some of those killed have pursued remedies against the state, the corporate actors and individuals. In Africa, non-governmental organizations filed a complaint against Nigeria with the African Human Rights Commission. In addition, the families of the two MOSOP leaders brought an action in federal court in the United States against Royal Dutch Petroleum Company and Shell Transport and Trading Company, alleging that the corporations and their officers directed and aided the Nigerian government in violating the human rights of the plaintiffs.

II. The Obligations of States

Note: *The African Human Rights System*

Regional systems are a product of the global concern with human rights that emerged at the end of the Second World War. Historical and political factors also encouraged each region to focus on human rights issues. In Europe, the immediate aftermath of World War II was only too clear, and the European system for protecting human rights was created as early as 1950. In the Americas, the 1948

American Declaration on the Rights and Duties of Man actually predated by several months the UN's proclamation of the Universal Declaration of Human Rights, and the Inter-American Commission on Human Rights began actively to address human rights violations in the mid-1960s.

In Africa, the struggles for self-determination, decolonization, and national unity — as well as opposition to systematic racial discrimination in southern Africa — were the first concerns. Thus, creation of formal African institutions to consider human rights regionally did not occur until relatively late, after the continent's former colonies became independent. It may be only coincidental that these new institutions also were adopted at the same time that U.S. President Jimmy Carter was placing human rights firmly on the international agenda in the late 1970s.

The African system has been in operation for a little more than 20 years, and one should recall the somewhat faltering steps of other systems in their early days. Read the African Charter on Human and Peoples' Rights in the Documentary Supplement before considering the following analysis.

Christof Heyns, The African Regional Human Rights System: The African Charter

108 *Penn St. L. Rev.* 679, 680, 681-82, 686, 687, 688-89, 691-92, 693-94, 695-96, 697-98, 700-701 (2004) (footnotes omitted)

. . . [T]he struggle for human rights on the African continent is far from over or complete. The continent is plagued by widespread violations of human rights, often on a massive scale. The process to establish effective institutional structures that will help to consolidate and to protect the hard earned gains of the freedom struggles of the past has become a struggle in its own right. No doubt, the most important task in this regard is to establish legal and political systems on the national level that protect human rights. But regional attempts to change the human rights practices of the continent, and to create safety nets for those cases not effectively dealt with on the national level, are assuming increased importance. . . .

The central document of the African regional system, the African Charter on Human and Peoples' Rights ("African Charter"), was opened for signature in 1981 and entered into force in 1986. It has been ratified by all fifty-three member states of the OAU/AU. . . .

In addition to the African Charter, the African regional human rights system is comprised of the OAU Convention Governing the Specific Aspects of Refugee Problems in Africa ("African Refugee Convention") of 1969, which entered into force in 1974 (44 ratifications); and the African Charter on the Rights and Welfare of the Child ("African Children's Charter") of 1990, which came into force in 1999 (32 ratifications). A special monitoring body for the African Children's Charter has been created. The African Committee on the Rights and Welfare of the Child had its first meeting in 2002 in Addis Ababa, Ethiopia.

The relatively unknown Cultural Charter for Africa of 1976 came into force in 1990 (33 state parties). There are also two African treaties dealing with the environment, although not from a human rights perspective. . . .

. . . Several reasons have been advanced for why only a Commission, and not a Court, was provided for in the African Charter in 1981 as the body responsible for monitoring compliance of state parties with the Charter. On the one hand there is the more idealistic explanation that the traditional way of solving disputes in Africa is through mediation and conciliation, not through the adversarial, "win or lose" mechanism of a court. On the other hand there is the view that the member states of the OAU were protective of their newly found sovereignty, and did not wish to limit it by means of a supra-national court. . . .

The civil and political rights recognised in the African Charter are in many ways similar to those recognised in other international instruments, and these rights have in practical terms received most of the attention of the African Commission. . . .

The way in which the African Charter deals with restrictions on all rights, including civil and political rights, presents a significant obstacle. The African Charter does not contain a general limitation clause (although, as is noted below, article 27(2) is starting to play this role). This means that there are no general guidelines on how Charter rights should be limited — no clear "limits on the limitations," so to speak. A well-defined system of limitations is important. A society in which rights cannot be limited will be ungovernable, but it is essential that appropriate human rights norms be set for the limitations.

A number of the articles of the Charter setting out specific civil and political rights do contain limiting provisions applicable to those particular rights. Some of these internal limitations clearly spell out the procedural and substantive norms with which limitations should comply, while others only describe the substantive requirements that limitations must meet.

A last category of these limitation clauses merely poses the apparently procedural requirement that limitations should be done "within the law." An example of this category of internal limitations is article 9(2), which provides as follows: "Every individual shall have the right to express and disseminate his opinions within the law." This kind of limitation is generally known as "claw-back clauses." Claw-back clauses seem to recognise the right in question only to the extent that such a right is not infringed upon by national law.

If that is the correct interpretation, the claw-back clauses would obviously undermine the whole idea of international supervision of domestic law and practices and render the Charter meaningless in respect to the rights involved. Domestic law will, in those cases, have to be measured according to domestic standards — a senseless exercise. What is given with the one hand is seemingly taken away with the other.

It should be noted . . . that the Charter has a very expansive approach in respect to interpretation. In terms of articles 60 and 61, the Commission has to draw inspiration from international human rights law in interpreting the provisions of the Charter. The Commission has used these provisions very liberally in a number of instances to bring the Charter in line with international practices, and the claw-back clauses are no exception.

In the context of the claw-back clauses, the African Commission has held that provisions in articles that allow rights to be limited "in accordance with law," should be understood to require such limitations to be done in terms of domestic legal provisions, which comply with international human rights standards.

Through this innovative interpretation, the Commission has gone a long way towards curing one of the most troublesome inherent deficiencies in the Charter. However, it remains unfortunate that the Charter, to those who have not had the benefit of exposure to the approach of the Commission, will continue to appear to condone infringements of human rights norms as long as it is done through domestic law. . . .

The socio-economic rights in the Charter have received scant attention from the Commission, but in a prominent case the Commission dealt with the issue and in effect held that the internationally recognised socio-economic rights that are not explicitly recognised in the Charter should be regarded as implicitly included. . . . [*Social and Economic Rights Action Center and the Center for Economic and Social Rights v. Nigeria*, infra page 355.]

There are other, more exotic features of the Charter that have attracted their fair share of academic and political commentary but have figured less in the pronouncements of the Commission.

The Charter, for example, recognises "peoples' rights." All "peoples," according to the Charter, have a right to be equal; to existence and self-determination; and to freely dispose of their wealth and natural resources. Clearly a major part of the motivation for the recognition of "peoples' rights" lies in the fact that entire "peoples" have been colonised and otherwise exploited in the history of Africa and have had to engage in protracted struggles to realise their human rights.

This concept has been referred to in some of the cases before the Commission, including the following two cases.

In a case concerning Katangese secessionists in the former Zaire, a complaint was brought on the basis that the Katangese people had a right, as a people, to self-determination in the form of independence. The Commission ruled against them on the basis that there was no evidence that a Charter provision had been violated because widespread human rights violations or a lack of political participation by the Katangese people had not been proven. This seems to suggest that if these conditions were met, secession by such a "people" could be a permissible option.

In a case concerning the 1994 coup d'etat against the democratically elected government of The Gambia, the Commission held that this violated the right to self-determination of the people of The Gambia as a whole.

The Charter recognises duties in addition to rights. For example, individuals have duties towards their families and society, and state parties have the duty to promote the Charter.

Perhaps the most significant provision under the heading "Duties" is article 27(2), which reads as follows: "The rights and freedoms of each individual shall be exercised with due regard to the rights of others, collective security, morality and common interest." This provision has now in effect been given the status of a general limitation clause by the African Commission. According to the Commission: "The only legitimate reasons for limitations to the rights and freedoms of the African Charter are found in article 27(2). . .".

The Commission's use of article 27(2) as a general limitation clause seems to confirm the view that the concept of "duties" should not be understood as a sinister way of saying rights should first be earned, or that meeting certain duties is a precondition for enjoying human rights. Rather, it implies that the exercise of human rights, which are "natural" or valid in themselves, may be limited by the duties of individuals. Rights precede duties, and the recognition of duties is merely another way of signifying the kind of limitations that may be placed on rights. . . .

1. The Complaints Procedure

Both states and individuals may bring complaints to the African Commission alleging violations of the African Charter by state parties.

The procedure by which one state brings a complaint about an alleged human rights violation by another state has only been used once in a case. Currently that case is pending before the Commission.

The so-called individual communication or complaints procedure is not clearly provided for in the African Charter. One reading of the Charter is that communications could be considered only where "serious or massive violations" are at stake, which then triggers the rather futile article 58 procedure described below. However, the African Commission has accepted from the start that it has the power to deal with complaints about any human rights violations under the Charter, provided the admissibility criteria are met.

The Charter is silent on the question of who can bring such complaints, but the Commission's practice is that complaints from individuals as well as non-governmental organizations are accepted. The individual complaints procedure is used much more frequently than the inter-state mechanism, although not as frequently as one might have expected on a continent with the kind of human rights problems like Africa's. The potential of this mechanism has not nearly been exhausted. . . .

Two of the more controversial articles of the Charter apply to the way in which the Commission is supposed to deal with individual communications. Article 58 provides that "special cases which reveal the existence of serious or massive violations of human and peoples' rights" must be referred by the Commission to the Assembly, which "may then request the Commission to undertake an in-depth study of these cases." When the Commission has followed this route, the Assembly has failed to respond, but the Commission has nevertheless made findings that such massive violations have occurred. Today, the Commission does not seem to refer cases anymore to the Assembly in terms of article 58. . . .

2. Consideration of State Reports . . .

Reporting under the Charter, as in other systems, is aimed at facilitating both introspection and inspection. "Introspection" refers to the process when the state, in writing its report, measures itself against the norms of the Charter. "Inspection" refers to the process when the Commission measures the performance of the state in question against the Charter. The objective is to facilitate a "constructive dialogue" between the Commission and the states.

Reporting has been very tardy, with approximately half of the state parties not submitting any reports. In 2001, the Commission started to issue concluding observations in respect to reports considered.

3. SPECIAL RAPPORTEURS

The Commission has appointed a number of special rapporteurs, with varying degrees of success....

NGOs have a special relationship with the Commission. Large numbers have registered for affiliate status. NGOs are often instrumental in bringing cases to the Commission; they sometimes submit shadow reports, propose agenda items at the outset of Commission sessions, and provide logistical and other support to the Commission, for example by placing interns at the Commission and providing support to the special rapporteurs and missions of the Commission. NGOs often organise special NGO workshops just prior to Commission sessions and participate actively in the public sessions of the Commission. NGOs also collaborate with the Commission in developing normative resolutions and new protocols to the African Charter.

The Charter does not contain a provision in terms of which the Commission has the power to take provisional or interim measures requesting state parties to abstain from causing irreparable harm. However, the Rules of Procedure of the Commission grant the Commission the power to do so. The Commission has used these provisional or interim measures in a number of cases....

V. CONCLUSION

Much remains to be done to make the African human rights system effective. I would venture to say there are a number of determinants for the effectiveness of any regional human rights systems, which include the following.

An adequate level of compliance with human rights norms on the domestic level must occur in a significant number of the state parties. Working national human rights systems are the building blocks of an effective regional system. If the level of respect for human rights norms on the domestic level is low, and domestic courts are not effective in implementing these norms, there can be little hope for supra-national enforcement.

The necessary political will must be present in the regional organisation of which the system forms part, to ensure that the system really works and is not an empty facade. The regional organisation is the primary body through which peer pressure must be channelled. The all-important selection process of Commissioners and Judges must be taken seriously by the regional body. The budgets allocated to human rights organisations also often have an important influence on how effective they are. The system must be properly serviced and able administrators appointed.

Publicity for the work of the monitoring body or bodies of the system is essential. The decisions and resolutions of these bodies must be available, and disseminated on the national and regional level, to have an impact. Publicity is needed so that those who want to comply voluntarily know what is expected of them, but it is also necessary to ensure that shame or peer pressure can be mobilised against recalcitrant states. Peer pressure can change behaviour by inducing shame, or if that does not work, by mobilising stronger forms of sanctions against states. All of this is possible only when there is sufficient publicity. The responsibility to see to it that there is publicity lies on the regional system, the states, and civil society alike.

Trade and other links must exist between the state parties before a regional human rights system can be enforced effectively. Without trade, diplomatic communication, travel, and other links between state parties, the conditions to impose sanctions to affect the behaviour of states do not exist.

The independence, creativity, and wisdom of those who run the system are absolutely crucial. This includes the Commissioners (and judges) and the staff of the Commission (and Court), as well as the officials of the regional organisation.

Resources are important, but the proper management of whatever resources are available is more important.

The African regional human rights system is faced with almost insurmountable challenges: massive violations on a continent of immense diversity, where a tradition of domestic compliance with human rights norms is still to be established. The trade and communication links that are necessary to exercise influence over member states in many cases do not exist.

Moreover, the system itself is also not currently well equipped to face these challenges. The African Charter has severe shortcomings and is in need of reform. The shortcomings in the African Charter relate to the norms recognised (the omission of important civil and political as well as socio-economic rights, the inclusion of concepts that are not easy to translate into legal terms, and the absence of adequate rules in respect to restrictions on rights) as well as the monitoring mechanism itself (none of the main monitoring procedures allowed by the Commission — individual communications, state reports, and special rapporteurs — are provided for explicitly in the Charter, and the provisions concerning secrecy and massive violations should be scrapped). The African Charter should be reformed to keep abreast of the times.

The continuous creation of new mechanisms for the protection of human rights in Africa is not necessarily helping the situation. Instead of focusing on getting the mechanism created by the African Charter, the African Commission, to function properly, new mechanisms are created, such as the African Human Rights Court. Even before the African Human Rights Court is established, the NEPAD African Peer Review Mechanism is developed, and so forth. In themselves all of these mechanisms could be a viable starting point, but the current proliferation of mechanisms means that there is a lack of focus of resources and effort, with the result that none of them might be in a position to make any difference.

The question should be asked which mechanism is mostly likely to make a significant impact on human rights in Africa, and that particular mechanism should be supported and developed until it is functioning properly before other mechanisms are created.

If all the effort that goes into developing new mechanisms goes into the Charter and the Commission, and thereafter the African Human Rights Court, we would be able to point to a specific mechanism that makes a real difference towards consolidating the gains of the struggles of the people of Africa.

In 1998, the OAS adopted a Protocol to the African Charter on the Establishment of an African Court on Human and Peoples' Rights (Documentary Supplement). The Protocol, which entered into force in January 2004, provides that the Commission, a complainant state, or a respondent state may submit cases to the Court concerning the interpretation and the application of the African Charter, the Protocol, or "any other applicable African Human Rights instrument." Optionally, states may declare that they accept the competence of the Court to receive urgent cases and complaints that allege serious, systematic or massive violations of human rights from individuals and non-governmental organizations with observer status; however, to date no state has accepted this optional competence. In July 2004, the AU decided in principle to merge the African Court on Human and Peoples' Rights with the African Court of Justice of the AU, thus delaying the election and inauguration of the human rights tribunal. On May 11, 2005, the African Commission expressed its deep concern about the AU decision, given the different mandates and litigants of the two courts. In its Res.76(XXXVII)05, the Commission called on the Assembly of Heads of State and Government of the African Union to operationalize the African Court on Human and Peoples' Rights at the earliest moment through the election of judges, determination of the seat of the Court and allocation of adequate resources. It also urged the Assembly, when considering determination of the seat of the Court, to consider issues of accessibility by litigants and delegates. Despite calls from the African Commission to expedite creation of the court, it had not yet been established as of mid-2005. See Af. Comm'n Hum. & Peoples' Rts. Res. 76(XXXVII)05 of May 11, 2005.

As the African system has matured, there has been increased scholarly commentary on its activities. See, e.g., *The African Charter on Human and Peoples' Rights: The System in Practice, 1986-2000* (Malcolm Evans and Rachel Murray, eds. 2002); Centre for Human Rights (University of Pretoria), *African Human Rights Law Reports 2000* (2004); Evelyn Ankumah, *The African Commission on Human and Peoples' Rights Practice and Procedures* (1996); Onyangwe, *Obligations of States Parties to the African Charter on Human and Peoples' Rights* 19 Afr. J. Int'l & Comp. L. 625 (1998); Emmanuel Bello, *The Mandate of the African Commission on Human and Peoples' Rights*, 1 Afr. J. Int'l L. 82 (1988); Anselm Chidi, *The Individual Complaints Procedure of the African Commission on Human and Peoples' Rights: A Preliminary Assessment*, 8 Transnat'l L. & Contemp. Probs. 359 (1998); *Compendium of Key Human Rights Documents of the African Union* (2005) (includes a number of cases from the African Commission); Udeme Essien, *The African Commission on Human and Peoples' Rights: Eleven Years After*, 6 Buff. Hum. Rts. L. Rev. 93 (2000); Cees Flinterman and Evelyn Ankumah, "The African Charter on Human and Peoples' Rights," in *Guide to International Human Rights Practice* (4th ed. H. Hannum ed. 2004); Christoph Heyns, *Human Rights Law in Africa* (1997); Gino Naldi & Konstantinos Magliveras, *Reinforcing the African System of Human Rights: The Protocol on the Establishment of a Regional Court of Human and Peoples' Rights*, 16 Neth. Q. Hum. Rts. 431 (1998); George W. Mugwanya, *Human Rights in Africa: Enhancing Human Rights through the African Regional Human Rights System* (2003); Henry Onoria, *The African Commission on Human and Peoples' Rights and the exhaustion of local remedies under the African Charter*, 3 Afr. Hum. Rts. L. J. 1 (2003); Rachel Murray, *The African Commission on Human and Peoples' Rights and International Law* (2000); Oji Umozurike, *The African Charter on Human and Peoples' Rights* (1997); Vincent Nmemielle, *The African Human Rights System: Law, Practices and Institutions* (2001).

A. *The Language of Obligation*

Human rights treaties use a variety of verbs to describe the obligations they impose on states. The Covenant on Civil and Political Rights (ICCPR) and the American Convention on Human Rights require states parties to "respect" and "ensure" the rights proclaimed in the respective treaties. In contrast, under the Covenant on Economic, Social and Cultural Rights, each state party "undertakes to take steps, individually and through international assistance and cooperation, especially economic and technical, to the maximum of its available resources, with a view to achieving progressively the full realization of the rights . . . by all appropriate means, including particularly the adoption of legislative measures." The European Convention on Human Rights obliges states parties to "secure" the rights in the Convention and Protocols, while the African Charter calls on its parties to "recognize" and "give effect" to the rights it enshrines. What do these various terms mean in practice? Do the obligations respecting civil and political rights differ significantly from those concerning economic, social, and cultural rights? Which obligations has Nigeria failed to observe? The following texts illustrate the views of global and regional human rights bodies on the scope of state obligations.

Human Rights Committee, General Comment No. 31, The Nature of the General Legal Obligation Imposed on States Parties to the Covenant on Civil and Political Rights

UN Doc. CCPR/C/21/Rev.1/Add.13 (May 26, 2004)

3. Article 2 defines the scope of the legal obligations undertaken by States Parties to the Covenant. A general obligation is imposed on States Parties to respect the Covenant rights and to ensure them to all individuals in their territory and subject to their jurisdiction (see paragraph 10 below). Pursuant to the principle articulated in article 26 of the Vienna Convention on the Law of Treaties, States Parties are required to give effect to the obligations under the Covenant in good faith.

4. The obligations of the Covenant in general and article 2 in particular are binding on every State Party as a whole. All branches of government (executive, legislative and judicial), and other public or governmental authorities, at whatever level — national, regional or local — are in a position to engage the responsibility of the State Party. The executive branch that usually represents the State Party internationally, including before the Committee, may not point to the fact that an action incompatible with the provisions of the Covenant was carried out by another branch of government as a means of seeking to relieve the State Party from responsibility for the action and consequent incompatibility. This understanding flows directly from the principle contained in article 27 of the Vienna Convention on the Law of Treaties, according to which a State Party "may not invoke the provisions of its internal law as justification for its failure to perform a treaty." Although article 2, paragraph 2, allows States Parties to give effect to Covenant rights in accordance with domestic constitutional processes, the same principle operates so as to prevent States parties from invoking provisions

of the constitutional law or other aspects of domestic law to justify a failure to perform or give effect to obligations under the treaty. In this respect, the Committee reminds States Parties with a federal structure of the terms of article 50, according to which the Covenant's provisions 'shall extend to all parts of federal states without any limitations or exceptions'....

6. The legal obligation under article 2, paragraph 1, is both negative and positive in nature. States Parties must refrain from violation of the rights recognized by the Covenant, and any restrictions on any of those rights must be permissible under the relevant provisions of the Covenant. Where such restrictions are made, States must demonstrate their necessity and only take such measures as are proportionate to the pursuance of legitimate aims in order to ensure continuous and effective protection of Covenant rights. In no case may the restrictions be applied or invoked in a manner that would impair the essence of a Covenant right.

7. Article 2 requires that States Parties adopt legislative, judicial, administrative, educative and other appropriate measures in order to fulfill their legal obligations. The Committee believes that it is important to raise levels of awareness about the Covenant not only among public officials and State agents but also among the population at large.

8. The article 2, paragraph 1, obligations are binding on States [Parties] and do not, as such, have direct horizontal effect as a matter of international law. The Covenant cannot be viewed as a substitute for domestic criminal or civil law. However the positive obligations on States Parties to ensure Covenant rights will only be fully discharged if individuals are protected by the State, not just against violations of Covenant rights by its agents, but also against acts committed by private persons or entities that would impair the enjoyment of Covenant rights in so far as they are amenable to application between private persons or entities. There may be circumstances in which a failure to ensure Covenant rights as required by article 2 would give rise to violations by States Parties of those rights, as a result of States Parties' permitting or failing to take appropriate measures or to exercise due diligence to prevent, punish, investigate or redress the harm caused by such acts by private persons or entities. States are reminded of the interrelationship between the positive obligations imposed under article 2 and the need to provide effective remedies in the event of breach under article 2, paragraph 3. The Covenant itself envisages in some articles certain areas where there are positive obligations on States Parties to address the activities of private persons or entities. For example, the privacy-related guarantees of article 17 must be protected by law. It is also implicit in article 7 that States Parties have to take positive measures to ensure that private persons or entities do not inflict torture or cruel, inhuman or degrading treatment or punishment on others within their power. In fields affecting basic aspects of ordinary life such as work or housing, individuals are to be protected from discrimination within the meaning of article 26.

9. The beneficiaries of the rights recognized by the Covenant are individuals. Although, with the exception of article 1, the Covenant does not mention the rights of legal persons or similar entities or collectivities, many of the rights recognized by the Covenant, such as the freedom to manifest one's religion or belief (article 18), the freedom of association (article 22) or the rights of members of minorities (article 27), may be enjoyed in community with others. The fact that the competence of the Committee to receive and consider communications is

restricted to those submitted by or on behalf of individuals (article 1 of the Optional Protocol) does not prevent such individuals from claiming that actions or omissions that concern legal persons and similar entities amount to a violation of their own rights.

10. States Parties are required by article 2, paragraph 1, to respect and to ensure the Covenant rights to all persons who may be within their territory and to all persons subject to their jurisdiction. This means that a State party must respect and ensure the rights laid down in the Covenant to anyone within the power or effective control of that State Party, even if not situated within the territory of the State Party. As indicated in General Comment 15 adopted at the twenty-seventh session (1986), the enjoyment of Covenant rights is not limited to citizens of States Parties but must also be available to all individuals, regardless of nationality or statelessness, such as asylum seekers, refugees, migrant workers and other persons, who may find themselves in the territory or subject to the jurisdiction of the State Party. This principle also applies to those within the power or effective control of the forces of a State Party acting outside its territory, regardless of the circumstances in which such power or effective control was obtained, such as forces constituting a national contingent of a State Party assigned to an international peace-keeping or peace-enforcement operation.... [Cf. the discussion of jurisdiction in Chapter 8, pages 624-647.]

13. Article 2, paragraph 2, requires that States Parties take the necessary steps to give effect to the Covenant rights in the domestic order. It follows that, unless Covenant rights are already protected by their domestic laws or practices, States Parties are required on ratification to make such changes to domestic laws and practices as are necessary to ensure their conformity with the Covenant. Where there are inconsistencies between domestic law and the Covenant, article 2 requires that the domestic law or practice be changed to meet the standards imposed by the Covenant's substantive guarantees. Article 2 allows a State Party to pursue this in accordance with its own domestic constitutional structure and accordingly does not require that the Covenant be directly applicable in the courts, by incorporation of the Covenant into national law. The Committee takes the view, however, that Covenant guarantees may receive enhanced protection in those States where the Covenant is automatically or through specific incorporation part of the domestic legal order. The Committee invites those States Parties in which the Covenant does not form part of the domestic legal order to consider incorporation of the Covenant to render it part of domestic law to facilitate full realization of Covenant rights as required by article 2.

14. The requirement under article 2, paragraph 2, to take steps to give effect to the Covenant rights is unqualified and of immediate effect. A failure to comply with this obligation cannot be justified by reference to political, social, cultural or economic considerations within the State.

15. Article 2, paragraph 3, requires that in addition to effective protection of Covenant rights States Parties must ensure that individuals also have accessible and effective remedies to vindicate those rights. Such remedies should be appropriately adapted so as to take account of the special vulnerability of certain categories of person, including in particular children. The Committee attaches importance to States Parties' establishing appropriate judicial and administrative mechanisms for addressing claims of rights violations under domestic law. The Committee notes that the enjoyment of the rights recognized under the Covenant

can be effectively assured by the judiciary in many different ways, including direct applicability of the Covenant, application of comparable constitutional or other provisions of law, or the interpretive effect of the Covenant in the application of national law. Administrative mechanisms are particularly required to give effect to the general obligation to investigate allegations of violations promptly, thoroughly and effectively through independent and impartial bodies. National human rights institutions, endowed with appropriate powers, can contribute to this end. A failure by a State Party to investigate allegations of violations could in and of itself give rise to a separate breach of the Covenant. Cessation of an ongoing violation is an essential element of the right to an effective remedy.

16. Article 2, paragraph 3, requires that States Parties make reparation to individuals whose Covenant rights have been violated. Without reparation to individuals whose Covenant rights have been violated, the obligation to provide an effective remedy, which is central to the efficacy of article 2, paragraph 3, is not discharged. In addition to the explicit reparation required by articles 9, paragraph 5, and 14, paragraph 6, the Committee considers that the Covenant generally entails appropriate compensation. The Committee notes that, where appropriate, reparation can involve restitution, rehabilitation and measures of satisfaction, such as public apologies, public memorials, guarantees of non-repetition and changes in relevant laws and practices, as well as bringing to justice the perpetrators of human rights violations.

17. In general, the purposes of the Covenant would be defeated without an obligation integral to article 2 to take measures to prevent a recurrence of a violation of the Covenant. Accordingly, it has been a frequent practice of the Committee in cases under the Optional Protocol to include in its Views the need for measures, beyond a victim-specific remedy, to be taken to avoid recurrence of the type of violation in question. Such measures may require changes in the State Party's laws or practices.

18. Where the investigations referred to in paragraph 15 reveal violations of certain Covenant rights, States Parties must ensure that those responsible are brought to justice. As with failure to investigate, failure to bring to justice perpetrators of such violations could in and of itself give rise to a separate breach of the Covenant. These obligations arise notably in respect of those violations recognized as criminal under either domestic or international law, such as torture and similar cruel, inhuman and degrading treatment (article 7), summary and arbitrary killing (article 6) and enforced disappearance (articles 7 and 9 and, frequently, 6). Indeed, the problem of impunity for these violations, a matter of sustained concern by the Committee, may well be an important contributing element in the recurrence of the violations.... [The issue of impunity is discussed in Chapter 11, pages 974-975.]

19. The Committee further takes the view that the right to an effective remedy may in certain circumstances require States Parties to provide for and implement provisional or interim measures to avoid continuing violations and to endeavour to repair at the earliest possible opportunity any harm that may have been caused by such violations.

20. Even when the legal systems of States parties are formally endowed with the appropriate remedy, violations of Covenant rights still take place. This is presumably attributable to the failure of the remedies to function effectively in

practice. Accordingly, States parties are requested to provide information on the obstacles to the effectiveness of existing remedies in their periodic reports.

The obligation to "respect" and "ensure" appears not only in the CPR Covenant, art. 2, but also in art. 1 of the American Convention on Human Rights. The following case is perhaps the most widely cited judgment on the scope of state duties respecting civil and political rights.

Velásquez Rodríguez Case, *Inter-Am. Ct. H.R.* (ser. C) No. 4 (July 29, 1988)

1. The Inter-American Commission on Human Rights submitted the instant case to the Inter-American Court of Human Rights . . . on April 24, 1986. It originated in a petition (No. 7920) against the State of Honduras . . . , which the Secretariat of the Commission received on October 7, 1981. . . .

3. According to the petition filed with the Commission, and the supplementary information received subsequently, Manfredo Velásquez, a student at the National Autonomous University of Honduras, "was violently detained without a warrant for his arrest by members of the National Office of Investigations (DNI) and G-2 of the Armed Forces of Honduras." The detention took place in Tegucigalpa on the afternoon of September 12, 1981. According to the petitioners, several eyewitnesses reported that Manfredo Velásquez and others were detained and taken to the cells of Public Security Forces Station No. 2 located in the Barrio El Manchén of Tegucigalpa, where he was "accused of alleged political crimes and subjected to harsh interrogation and cruel torture." The petition added that on September 17, 1981, Manfredo Velásquez was moved to the First Infantry Battalion, where the interrogation continued, but that the police and security forces denied that he had been detained. . . .

56. The Court will first consider the legal arguments relevant to the question of exhaustion of domestic remedies and then apply them to the case. . . .

61. The rule of prior exhaustion of domestic remedies allows the State to resolve the problem under its internal law before being confronted with an international proceeding. This is particularly true in the international jurisdiction of human rights, because the latter reinforces or complements the domestic jurisdiction (American Convention, Preamble).

62. It is a legal duty of the States to provide such remedies, as this Court indicated in its Judgment of June 26, 1987, when it stated:

> The rule of prior exhaustion of domestic remedies under the international law of human rights has certain implications that are present in the Convention. Under the Convention, States Parties have an obligation to provide effective judicial remedies to victims of human rights violations (Art. 25), remedies that must be substantiated in accordance with the rules of due process of law (Art. 8 (1)), all in keeping with the general obligation of such States to guarantee the free and full exercise of the rights recognized by the Convention to all persons subject to their jurisdiction (Art. 1). (*Velásquez Rodríguez* Case, Preliminary Objections, para. 91).

63. Article 46 (1) (a) of the Convention speaks of "generally recognized principles of international law." Those principles refer not only to the formal

existence of such remedies, but also to their adequacy and effectiveness, as shown by the exceptions set out in Article 46 (2).

64. Adequate domestic remedies are those which are suitable to address an infringement of a legal right. A number of remedies exist in the legal system of every country, but not all are applicable in every circumstance. If a remedy is not adequate in a specific case, it obviously need not be exhausted. A norm is meant to have an effect and should not be interpreted in such a way as to negate its effect or lead to a result that is manifestly absurd or unreasonable. For example, a civil proceeding specifically cited by the Government, such as a presumptive finding of death based on disappearance, the purpose of which is to allow heirs to dispose of the estate of the person presumed deceased or to allow the spouse to remarry, is not an adequate remedy for finding a person or for obtaining his liberty.

65. Of the remedies cited by the Government, habeas corpus would be the normal means of finding a person presumably detained by the authorities, of ascertaining whether he is legally detained and, given the case, of obtaining his liberty. The other remedies cited by the Government are either for reviewing a decision within an inchoate proceeding (such as those of appeal or cassation) or are addressed to other objectives. If, however, as the Government has stated, the writ of habeas corpus requires the identification of the place of detention and the authority ordering the detention, it would not be adequate for finding a person clandestinely held by State officials, since in such cases there is only hearsay evidence of the detention, and the whereabouts of the victim is unknown.

66. A remedy must also be effective — that is, capable of producing the result for which it was designed. Procedural requirements can make the remedy of habeas corpus ineffective: if it is powerless to compel the authorities; if it presents a danger to those who invoke it; or if it is not impartially applied.

67. On the other hand, contrary to the Commission's argument, the mere fact that a domestic remedy does not produce a result favorable to the petitioner does not in and of itself demonstrate the inexistence or exhaustion of all effective domestic remedies. For example, the petitioner may not have invoked the appropriate remedy in a timely fashion.

68. It is a different matter, however, when it is shown that remedies are denied for trivial reasons or without an examination of the merits, or if there is proof of the existence of a practice or policy ordered or tolerated by the government, the effect of which is to impede certain persons from invoking internal remedies that would normally be available to others. In such cases, resort to those remedies becomes a senseless formality. The exceptions of Article 46 (2) would be fully applicable in those situations and would discharge the obligation to exhaust internal remedies since they cannot fulfill their objective in that case. . . .

76. The record . . . contains testimony of members of the Legislative Assembly of Honduras, Honduran lawyers, persons who were at one time disappeared, and relatives of disappeared persons, which purports to show that in the period in which the events took place, the legal remedies in Honduras were ineffective in obtaining the liberty of victims of a practice of enforced or involuntary disappearances (hereinafter "disappearance" or "disappearances"), ordered or tolerated by the Government. The record also contains dozens of newspaper clippings which allude to the same practice. According to that evidence, from 1981 to 1984 more

applied

than one hundred persons were illegally detained, may of whom never reappeared, and, in general, the legal remedies which the Government claimed were available to the victims were ineffective.

77. That evidence also shows that some individuals were captured and detained without due process and subsequently reappeared. However, in some of those cases, the reappearances were not the result of any of the legal remedies which, according to the Government, would have been effective, but rather the result of other circumstances, such as the intervention of diplomatic missions or actions of human rights organizations.

78. The evidence offered shows that lawyers who filed writs of habeas corpus were intimidated, that those who were responsible for executing the writs were frequently prevented from entering or inspecting the places of detention, and that occasional criminal complaints against military or police officials were ineffective, either because certain procedural steps were not taken or because the complaints were dismissed without further proceedings.

79. The Government had the opportunity to call its own witnesses to refute the evidence presented by the Commission, but failed to do so. Although the Government's attorneys contested some of the points urged by the Commission, they did not offer convincing evidence to support their arguments. The Court summoned as witnesses some members of the armed forces mentioned during the proceeding, but their testimony was insufficient to overcome the weight of the evidence offered by the Commission to show that the judicial and governmental authorities did not act with due diligence in cases of disappearances. The instant case is such an example.

80. The testimony and other evidence received and not refuted leads to the conclusion that, during the period under consideration, although there may have been legal remedies in Honduras that theoretically allowed a person detained by the authorities to be found, those remedies were ineffective in cases of disappearances because the imprisonment was clandestine; formal requirements made them inapplicable in practice; the authorities against whom they were brought simply ignored them, or because attorneys and judges were threatened and intimidated by those authorities.

81. Aside from the question of whether between 1981 and 1984 there was a governmental policy of carrying out or tolerating the disappearance of certain persons, the Commission has shown that although writs of habeas corpus and criminal complaints were filed, they were ineffective or were mere formalities. The evidence offered by the Commission was not refuted and is sufficient to reject the Government's preliminary objection that the case is inadmissible because domestic remedies were not exhausted. . . .

[The Court next considered issues concerning contested evidence and the burden of proof; see Chapter 12, page 1047.]

159. The Commission has asked the Court to find that Honduras has violated the rights guaranteed to Manfredo Velásquez by Articles 4, 5 and 7 of the Convention. The Government has denied the charges and seeks to be absolved.

160. This requires the Court to examine the conditions under which a particular act, which violates one of the rights recognized by the Convention, can be imputed to a State Party thereby establishing its international responsibility.

161. Article 1 (1) of the Convention provides:

Article 1. Obligation to Respect Rights

> 1. The States Parties to this Convention undertake to respect the rights and freedoms recognized herein and to ensure to all persons subject to their jurisdiction the free and full exercise of those rights and freedoms, without any discrimination for reasons of race, color, sex, language, religion, political or other opinion, national or social origin, economic status, birth, or any other social condition.

162. This article specifies the obligation assumed by the States Parties in relation to each of the rights protected. Each claim alleging that one of those rights has been infringed necessarily implies that Article 1 (1) of the Convention has also been violated.

163. The Commission did not specifically allege the violation of Article 1 (1) of the Convention, but that does not preclude the Court from applying it. The precept contained therein constitutes the generic basis of the protection of the rights recognized by the Convention and would be applicable, in any case, by virtue of a general principle of law, iura novit curia, on which international jurisprudence has repeatedly relied and under which a court has the power and the duty to apply the juridical provisions relevant to a proceeding, even when the parties do not expressly invoke them ("*Lotus*," Judgment No. 9, 1927, P.C.I.J., Series A No. 10, p. 31 and Eur. Court H.R., *Handyside* Case, Judgment of 7 December 1976, Series A No. 24, para. 41).

164. Article 1 (1) is essential in determining whether a violation of the human rights recognized by the Convention can be imputed to a State Party. In effect, that article charges the States Parties with the fundamental duty to respect and guarantee the rights recognized in the Convention. Any impairment of those rights which can be attributed under the rules of international law to the action or omission of any public authority constitutes an act imputable to the State, which assumes responsibility in the terms provided by the Convention.

165. The first obligation assumed by the States Parties under Article 1 (1) is "to respect the rights and freedoms" recognized by the Convention. The exercise of public authority has certain limits which derive from the fact that human rights are inherent attributes of human dignity and are, therefore, superior to the power of the State. On another occasion, this court stated:

> The protection of human rights, particularly the civil and political rights set forth in the Convention, is in effect based on the affirmation of the existence of certain inviolable attributes of the individual that cannot be legitimately restricted through the exercise of governmental power. There are individual domains that are beyond the reach of the State or to which the State has but limited access. Thus, the protection of human rights must necessarily comprise the concept of the restriction of the exercise of state power (*The Word "Laws" in Article 30 of the American Convention on Human Rights*, Advisory Opinion OC-6/86 of May 9, 1986. Series A No. 6, para 21).

166. The second obligation of the States Parties is to "ensure" the free and full exercise of the rights recognized by the Convention to every person subject to its jurisdiction. This obligation implies the duty of States Parties to organize the governmental apparatus and, in general, all the structures through which public power is exercised, so that they are capable of juridically ensuring the free and full

enjoyment of human rights. As a consequence of this obligation, the States must prevent, investigate and punish any violation of the rights recognized by the Convention and, moreover, if possible attempt to restore the right violated and provide compensation as warranted for damages resulting from the violation.

167. The obligation to ensure the free and full exercise of human rights is not fulfilled by the existence of a legal system designed to make it possible to comply with this obligation — it also requires the government to conduct itself so as to effectively ensure the free and full exercise of human rights.

168. The obligation of the States is, thus, much more direct than that contained in Article 2, which reads:

ARTICLE 2. DOMESTIC LEGAL EFFECTS

> Where the exercise of any of the rights or freedoms referred to in Article 1 is not already ensured by legislative or other provisions, the States Parties undertake to adopt, in accordance with their constitutional processes and the provisions of this Convention, such legislative or other measures as may be necessary to give effect to those rights or freedoms.

169. According to Article 1 (1), any exercise of public power that violates the rights recognized by the Convention is illegal. Whenever a State organ, official or public entity violates one of those rights, this constitutes a failure of the duty to respect the rights and freedoms set forth in the Convention.

170. This conclusion is independent of whether the organ or official has contravened provisions of internal law or overstepped the limits of his authority: under international law a State is responsible for the acts of its agents undertaken in their official capacity and for their omissions, even when those agents act outside the sphere of their authority or violate internal law.

171. This principle suits perfectly the nature of the Convention, which is violated whenever public power is used to infringe the rights recognized therein. If acts of public power that exceed the State's authority or are illegal under its own laws were not considered to compromise that State's obligations under the treaty, the system of protection provided for in the Convention would be illusory.

(otherwise)

172. Thus, in principle, any violation of rights recognized by the Convention carried out by an act of public authority or by persons who use their position of authority is imputable to the State. However, this does not define all the circumstances in which a State is obligated to prevent, investigate and punish human rights violations, nor all the cases in which the State might be found responsible for an infringement of those rights. An illegal act which violates human rights and which is initially not directly imputable to a State (for example, because it is the act of a private person or because the person responsible has not been identified) can lead to international responsibility of the State, not because of the act itself, but because of the lack of due diligence to prevent the violation or to respond to it as required by the Convention.

173. Violations of the Convention cannot be founded upon rules that take psychological factors into account in establishing individual culpability. For the purposes of analysis, the intent or motivation of the agent who has violated the rights recognized by the Convention is irrelevant — the violation can be established even if the identity of the individual perpetrator is unknown. What is

decisive is whether a violation of the rights recognized by the Convention has occurred with the support or the acquiescence of the government, or whether the State has allowed the act to take place without taking measures to prevent it or to punish those responsible. Thus, the Court's task is to determine whether the violation is the result of a State's failure to fulfill its duty to respect and guarantee those rights, as required by Article 1 (1) of the Convention.

174. The State has a legal duty to take reasonable steps to prevent human rights violations and to use the means at its disposal to carry out a serious investigation of violations committed within its jurisdiction, to identify those responsible, to impose the appropriate punishment and to ensure the victim adequate compensation.

175. This duty to prevent includes all those means of a legal, political, administrative and cultural nature that promote the protection of human rights and ensure that any violations are considered and treated as illegal acts, which, as such, may lead to the punishment of those responsible and the obligation to indemnify the victims for damages. It is not possible to make a detailed list of all such measures, since they vary with the law and the conditions of each State Party. Of course, while the State is obligated to prevent human rights abuses, the existence of a particular violation does not, in itself, prove the failure to take preventive measures. On the other hand, subjecting a person to official, repressive bodies that practice torture and assassination with impunity is itself a breach of the duty to prevent violations of the rights to life and physical integrity of the person, even if that particular person is not tortured or assassinated, or if those facts cannot be proven in a concrete case.

176. The State is obligated to investigate every situation involving a violation of the rights protected by the Convention. If the State apparatus acts in such a way that the violation goes unpunished and the victim's full enjoyment of such rights is not restored as soon as possible, the State has failed to comply with its duty to ensure the free and full exercise of those rights to the persons within its jurisdiction. The same is true when the State allows private persons or groups to act freely and with impunity to the detriment of the rights recognized by the Convention.

177. In certain circumstances, it may be difficult to investigate acts that violate an individual's rights. The duty to investigate, like the duty to prevent, is not breached merely because the investigation does not produce a satisfactory result. Nevertheless, it must be undertaken in a serious manner and not as a mere formality preordained to be ineffective. An investigation must have an objective and be assumed by the State as its own legal duty, not as a step taken by private interests that depends upon the initiative of the victim or his family or upon their offer of proof, without an effective search for the truth by the government. This is true regardless of what agent is eventually found responsible for the violation. Where the acts of private parties that violate the Convention are not seriously investigated, those parties are aided in a sense by the government, thereby making the State responsible on the international plane.

178. In the instant case, the evidence shows a complete inability of the procedures of the State of Honduras, which were theoretically adequate, to carry out an investigation into the disappearance of Manfredo Velásquez, and of the fulfillment of its duties to pay compensation and punish those responsible, as set out in Article 1 (1) of the Convention.

179. As the Court has verified above, the failure of the judicial system to act upon the writs brought before various tribunals in the instant case has been proven. Not one writ of habeas corpus was processed. No judge has access to the places where Manfredo Velásquez might have been detained. The criminal complaint was dismissed.

180. Nor did the organs of the Executive Branch carry out a serious investigation to establish the fate of Manfredo Velásquez. There was no investigation of public allegations of a practice of disappearances nor a determination of whether Manfredo Velásquez had been a victim of that practice. The Commission's requests for information were ignored to the point that the Commission had to presume, under Article 42 of its Regulations, that the allegations were true. The offer of an investigation in accord with Resolution 30/83 of the Commission resulted in an investigation by the Armed Forces, the same body accused of direct responsibility for the disappearances. This raises grave questions regarding the seriousness of the investigation. The Government often resorted to asking relatives of the victims to present conclusive proof of their allegations even though those allegations, because they involved crimes against the person, should have been investigated on the Government's own initiative in fulfillment of the State's duty to ensure public order. This is especially true when the allegations refer to a practice carried out within the Armed Forces, which, because of its nature, is not subject to private investigations. No proceeding was initiated to establish responsibility for the disappearance of Manfredo Velásquez and apply punishment under internal law. All of the above leads to the conclusion that the Honduran authorities did not take effective action to ensure respect for human rights within the jurisdiction of that State as required by Article 1 (1) of the Convention.

181. The duty to investigate facts of this type continues as long as there is uncertainty about the fate of the person who has disappeared. Even in the hypothetical case that those individually responsible for crimes of this type cannot be legally punished under certain circumstances, the State is obligated to use the means at its disposal to inform the relatives of the fate of the victims and, if they have been killed, the location of their remains.

182. The Court is convinced, and has so found, that the disappearance of Manfredo Velásquez was carried out by agents who acted under cover of public authority. However, even had that fact not been proven, the failure of the State apparatus to act, which is clearly proven, is a failure on the part of Honduras to fulfill the duties it assumed under Article 1 (1) of the Convention, which obligated it to ensure Manfredo Velásquez the free and full exercise of his human rights.

183. The Court notes that the legal order of Honduras does not authorize such acts and that internal law defines them as crimes. The Court also recognizes that not all levels of the Government of Honduras were necessarily aware of those acts, nor is there any evidence that such acts were the result of official orders. Nevertheless, those circumstances are irrelevant for the purposes of establishing whether Honduras is responsible under international law for the violations of human rights perpetrated within the practice of disappearances.

184. According to the principle of the continuity of the State in international law, responsibility exists both independently of changes of government over a period of time and continuously from the time of the act that creates responsibility to the time when the act is declared illegal. The foregoing is also valid in the area

of human rights although, from an ethical or political point of view, the attitude of the new government may be much more respectful of those rights than that of the government in power when the violations occurred.

185. The Court, therefore, concludes that the facts found in this proceeding show that the State of Honduras is responsible for the involuntary disappearance of Angel Manfredo Velásquez Rodríguez. Thus, Honduras has violated Articles 7, 5 and 4 of the Convention. . . .

The *Velásquez Rodríguez* judgment speaks of the duty to prevent human rights violations. Such a duty raises the question of what standard of care should be imposed on a government. The following case discusses this issue in respect to the right to life. Thereafter, we turn to the case against Nigeria.

Öneryildiz v. Turkey

Eur. Ct. H.R., App. No. 48938/99 (Nov. 30, 2004) (Grand Chamber) (references omitted). . . .

9. The applicant was born in 1955 and is now living in the district of Şirvan..., the area where he was born. At the material time he was living with twelve close relatives in the slum quarter (gecekondu mahallesi) of Kazim Karabekir in Ümraniye, a district of Istanbul, where he had moved after resigning from his post as a village guard in south-eastern Turkey.

10. Since the early 1970s a household-refuse tip had been in operation in Hekimbaş, a slum area adjoining Kazim Karabekir. On 22 January 1960 Istanbul City Councill . . . had been granted use of the land, which belonged to the Forestry Commission (and therefore to the Treasury), for a term of ninety-nine years. Situated on a slope overlooking a valley, the site spread out over a surface area of approximately 350,000 sq. m and from 1972 onwards was used as a rubbish tip by the districts of Beykoz, Üsküdar, Kadiköy and Ümraniye under the authority and responsibility of the city council and, ultimately, the ministerial authorities.

When the rubbish tip started being used, the area was uninhabited and the closest built-up area was approximately 3.5 km away. However, as the years passed, rudimentary dwellings were built without any authorisation in the area surrounding the rubbish tip, which eventually developed into the slums of Ümraniye. . . .

13. On 9 April 1991 Ümraniye District Council applied to the Third Division of the Üsküdar District Court for experts to be appointed to determine whether the rubbish tip complied with the relevant regulations, in particular the Regulations of 14 March 1991 on Solid-Waste Control. The district council also applied for an assessment of the damage it had sustained, as evidence in support of an action for damages it was preparing to bring against the city council and the councils of the three other districts that used the tip. . . .

According to the experts' report, drawn up on 7 May 1991, the rubbish tip in question did not conform to the technical requirements set forth, inter alia, in regulations 24-27, 30 and 38 of the Regulations of 14 March 1991 and, accordingly, presented a number of dangers liable to give rise to a major health risk for the inhabitants of the valley, particularly those living in the slum areas: no walls or fencing separated the tip from the dwellings fifty metres away from the mountain of refuse; the tip was not equipped with collection, composting, recycling or combustion systems; and no drainage or drainage-water purification systems had been installed. The experts concluded that the Ümraniye tip "exposed humans, animals and the environment to all kinds of risks." In that connection the report, drawing attention first to the fact that some twenty contagious diseases might spread, underlined the following:

> "... In any waste-collection site gases such as methane, carbon dioxide and hydrogen sulphide form. These substances must be collected and... burnt under supervision. However, the tip in question is not equipped with such a system. If methane is mixed with air in a particular proportion, it can explode. This installation contains no means of preventing an explosion of the methane produced as a result of the decomposition [of the waste]. May God preserve us, as the damage could be very substantial given the neighbouring dwellings. ..."

On 27 May 1991 the report was brought to the attention of the four councils in question, and on 7 June 1991 the governor was informed of it and asked to brief the Ministry of Health and the Prime Minister's Environment Office ("the Environment Office").

14. Kadiköy and Üsküdar District Councils and the city council applied on 3, 5 and 9 June 1991 respectively to have the expert report set aside. In their notice of application the councils' lawyers simply stated that the report, which had been ordered and drawn up without their knowledge, contravened the Code of Civil Procedure. The three lawyers reserved the right to file supplementary pleadings in support of their objections once they had obtained all the necessary information and documents from their authorities. As none of the parties filed supplementary pleadings to that end, the proceedings were discontinued.

15. However, the Environment Office, which had been advised of the report on 18 June 1991, made a recommendation (no. 09513) urging the Istanbul Governor's Office, the city council and Ümraniye District Council to remedy the problems identified in the present case. ...

16. On 27 August 1992 Şinasi Öktem, the mayor of Ümraniye, applied to the First Division of the Üsküdar District Court for the implementation of temporary measures to prevent the city council and the neighbouring district councils from using the waste-collection site. He requested, in particular, that no further waste be dumped, that the tip be closed and that redress be provided in respect of the damage sustained by his district.

On 3 November 1992 Istanbul City Council's representative opposed that request. Emphasising the city council's efforts to maintain the roads leading to the rubbish tip and to prevent the spread of diseases, the emission of odours and the destruction of stray dogs, the representative submitted, in particular, that a plan to redevelop the site of the tip had been put out to tender. As regards the request for the temporary closure of the tip, the representative asserted that Ümraniye District Council was acting in bad faith in that, since it had been set up in 1987, it had done nothing to decontaminate the site.

The City Council had indeed issued a call for tenders for the development of new sites conforming to modern standards. The first planning contract was awarded to the American firm CVH2M Hill International Ltd, and on 21 December 1992 and 17 February 1993 new sites were designed for the European and

Anatolian sides of Istanbul respectively. The project was due for completion in the course of 1993.

17. While those proceedings were still pending, Ümraniye District Council informed the mayor of Istanbul that from 15 May 1993 the dumping of waste would no longer be authorised.

18. On 28 April 1993 at about 11 a.m. a methane explosion occurred at the site. Following a landslide caused by mounting pressure, the refuse erupted from the mountain of waste and engulfed some ten slum dwellings situated below it, including the one belonging to the applicant. Thirty-nine people died in the accident. . . .

I. Alleged Violation of Article 2 of the Convention

69. Taking the parties' arguments as a whole, the Court reiterates, firstly, that its approach to the interpretation of Article 2 is guided by the idea that the object and purpose of the Convention as an instrument for the protection of individual human beings requires its provisions to be interpreted and applied in such a way as to make its safeguards practical and effective.

70. In the instant case the complaint before the Court is that the national authorities did not do all that could have been expected of them to prevent the deaths of the applicant's close relatives in the accident of 28 April 1993 at the Ümraniye municipal rubbish tip, which was operated under the authorities' control.

71. In this connection, the Court reiterates that Article 2 does not solely concern deaths resulting from the use of force by agents of the State but also, in the first sentence of its first paragraph, lays down a positive obligation on States to take appropriate steps to safeguard the lives of those within their jurisdiction.

The Court considers that this obligation must be construed as applying in the context of any activity, whether public or not, in which the right to life may be at stake, and a fortiori in the case of industrial activities, which by their very nature are dangerous, such as the operation of waste-collection sites. . . .

74. To sum up, it considers that the applicant's complaint undoubtedly falls within the ambit of the first sentence of Article 2, which is therefore applicable in the instant case. . . .

B. Compliance

(a) General principles applicable in the present case

(i) *Principles relating to the prevention of infringements of the right to life as a result of dangerous activities: the substantive aspect of Article 2 of the Convention*

89. The positive obligation to take all appropriate steps to safeguard life for the purposes of Article 2 entails above all a primary duty on the State to put in place a legislative and administrative framework designed to provide effective deterrence against threats to the right to life.

90. This obligation indisputably applies in the particular context of dangerous activities, where, in addition, special emphasis must be placed on regulations geared to the special features of the activity in question, particularly with regard to the level of the potential risk to human lives. They must govern the licensing, setting up, operation, security and supervision of the activity and must make it

compulsory for all those concerned to take practical measures to ensure the effective protection of citizens whose lives might be endangered by the inherent risks. . . .

(ii) *Principles relating to the judicial response required in the event of alleged infringements of the right to life: the procedural aspect of Article 2 of the Convention*

91. The obligations deriving from Article 2 do not end there. Where lives have been lost in circumstances potentially engaging the responsibility of the State, that provision entails a duty for the State to ensure, by all means at its disposal, an adequate response judicial or otherwise so that the legislative and administrative framework set up to protect the right to life is properly implemented and any breaches of that right are repressed and punished.

92. In this connection, the Court has held that if the infringement of the right to life or to physical integrity is not caused intentionally, the positive obligation to set up an "effective judicial system" does not necessarily require criminal proceedings to be brought in every case and may be satisfied if civil, administrative or even disciplinary remedies were available to the victims.

93. However, in areas such as that in issue in the instant case, the applicable principles are rather to be found in those which the Court has already had occasion to develop in relation notably to the use of lethal force, principles which lend themselves to application in other categories of cases. In this connection, it should be pointed out that in cases of homicide the interpretation of Article 2 as entailing an obligation to conduct an official investigation is justified not only because any allegations of such an offence normally give rise to criminal liability, but also because often, in practice, the true circumstances of the death are, or may be, largely confined within the knowledge of State officials or authorities.

In the Court's view, such considerations are indisputably valid in the context of dangerous activities, when lives have been lost as a result of events occurring under the responsibility of the public authorities, which are often the only entities to have sufficient relevant knowledge to identify and establish the complex phenomena that might have caused such incidents.

Where it is established that the negligence attributable to State officials or bodies on that account goes beyond an error of judgment or carelessness, in that the authorities in question, fully realising the likely consequences and disregarding the powers vested in them, failed to take measures that were necessary and sufficient to avert the risks inherent in a dangerous activity, the fact that those responsible for endangering life have not been charged with a criminal offence or prosecuted may amount to a violation of Article 2, irrespective of any other types of remedy which individuals may exercise on their own initiative; this is amply evidenced by developments in the relevant European standards.

94. To sum up, the judicial system required by Article 2 must make provision for an independent and impartial official investigation procedure that satisfies certain minimum standards as to effectiveness and is capable of ensuring that criminal penalties are applied where lives are lost as a result of a dangerous activity if and to the extent that this is justified by the findings of the investigation. In such cases, the competent authorities must act with exemplary diligence and promptness and must of their own motion initiate investigations capable of, firstly, ascertaining the circumstances in which the incident took place and any shortcomings in the operation of the regulatory system and, secondly, identifying the State officials or authorities involved in whatever capacity in the chain of events in issue.

95. That said, the requirements of Article 2 go beyond the stage of the official investigation, where this has led to the institution of proceedings in the national courts; the proceedings as a whole, including the trial stage, must satisfy the requirements of the positive obligation to protect lives through the law.

96. It should in no way be inferred from the foregoing that Article 2 may entail the right for an applicant to have third parties prosecuted or sentenced for a criminal offence or an absolute obligation for all prosecutions to result in conviction, or indeed in a particular sentence.

On the other hand, the national courts should not under any circumstances be prepared to allow life-endangering offences to go unpunished. This is essential for maintaining public confidence and ensuring adherence to the rule of law and for preventing any appearance of tolerance of or collusion in unlawful acts. The Court's task therefore consists in reviewing whether and to what extent the courts, in reaching their conclusion, may be deemed to have submitted the case to the careful scrutiny required by Article 2 of the Convention, so that the deterrent effect of the judicial system in place and the significance of the role it is required to play in preventing violations of the right to life are not undermined.

(b) Assessment of the facts of the case in the light of these principles

(i) *Responsibility borne by the State for the deaths in the instant case, in the light of the substantive aspect of Article 2 of the Convention*

97. In the instant case the Court notes at the outset that in both of the fields of activity central to the present case — the operation of household-refuse tips . . . and the rehabilitation and clearance of slum areas . . . — there are safety regulations in force in Turkey.

It must therefore determine whether the legal measures applicable to the situation in issue in the instant case call for criticism and whether the national authorities actually complied with the relevant regulations.

98. To that end, the Court considers that it should begin by noting a decisive factor for the assessment of the circumstances of the case, namely that there was practical information available to the effect that the inhabitants of certain slum areas of Ümraniye were faced with a threat to their physical integrity on account of the technical shortcomings of the municipal rubbish tip. . . .

100. The Court considers that neither the reality nor the immediacy of the danger in question is in dispute, seeing that the risk of an explosion had clearly come into being long before it was highlighted in the report of 7 May 1991 and that, as the site continued to operate in the same conditions, that risk could only have increased during the period until it materialised on 28 April 1993.

101. The Grand Chamber accordingly agrees with the Chamber that it was impossible for the administrative and municipal departments responsible for supervising and managing the tip not to have known of the risks inherent in methanogenesis or of the necessary preventive measures, particularly as there were specific regulations on the matter. Furthermore, the Court likewise regards it as established that various authorities were also aware of those risks, at least by 27 May 1991, when they were notified of the report of 7 May 1991.

It follows that the Turkish authorities at several levels knew or ought to have known that there was a real and immediate risk to a number of persons living near the Ümraniye municipal rubbish tip. They consequently had a positive obligation under Article 2 of the Convention to take such preventive operational measures as were necessary and sufficient to protect those individuals, especially as they themselves had set up the site and authorised its operation, which gave rise to the risk in question. . . .

103. . . . [T]he Government also relied on the conclusions of the *Chapman v. the United Kingdom* judgment and criticised the applicant for having knowingly chosen to break the law and live in the vicinity of the rubbish tip.

However, those arguments do not stand up to scrutiny for the following reasons.

104. In the instant case, the Court has examined the provisions of domestic law regarding the transfer to third parties of public property, whether inside or outside the "slum rehabilitation and clearance zones". It has also studied the impact of various legislative initiatives designed to extend in practice the scope ratione temporis of Law no. 775 of 20 July 1966.

The Court concludes from these legal considerations that in spite of the statutory prohibitions in the field of town planning, the State's consistent policy on slum areas encouraged the integration of such areas into the urban environment and hence acknowledged their existence and the way of life of the citizens who had gradually caused them to build up since 1960, whether of their own free will or simply as a result of that policy. Seeing that this policy effectively established an amnesty for breaches of town-planning regulations, including the unlawful occupation of public property, it must have created uncertainty as to the extent of the discretion enjoyed by the administrative authorities responsible for applying the measures prescribed by law, which could not therefore have been regarded as foreseeable by the public.

105. . . . The authorities let the applicant and his close relatives live entirely undisturbed in their house, in the social and family environment they had created. Furthermore, regard being had to the concrete evidence adduced before the Court and not rebutted by the Government, there is no cause to call into question the applicant's assertion that the authorities also levied council tax on him and on the other inhabitants of the Ümraniye slums and provided them with public services, for which they were charged.

106. In those circumstances, it would be hard for the Government to maintain legitimately that any negligence or lack of foresight should be attributed to the victims of the accident of 28 April 1993, or to rely on the Court's conclusions in the case of *Chapman v. the United Kingdom*, in which the British authorities were not found to have remained passive in the face of Mrs Chapman's unlawful actions.

It remains for the Court to address the Government's other arguments relating, in general, to: the scale of the rehabilitation projects carried out by the city council at the time in order to alleviate the problems caused by the Ümraniye waste-collection site; the amount invested, which was said to have influenced the way in which the national authorities chose to deal with the situation at the site; and, lastly, the humanitarian considerations which at the time allegedly precluded any measure entailing the immediate and wholesale destruction of the slum areas.

107. The Court acknowledges that it is not its task to substitute for the views of the local authorities its own view of the best policy to adopt in dealing with the social, economic and urban problems in this part of Istanbul. It therefore accepts the Government's argument that in this respect, an impossible or disproportionate burden must not be imposed on the authorities without consideration being

given, in particular, to the operational choices which they must make in terms of priorities and resources; this results from the wide margin of appreciation which States enjoy, as the Court has previously held, in difficult social and technical spheres such as the one in issue in the instant case.

However, even when seen from this perspective, the Court does not find the Government's arguments convincing. The preventive measures required by the positive obligation in question fall precisely within the powers conferred on the authorities and may reasonably be regarded as a suitable means of averting the risk brought to their attention. The Court considers that the timely installation of a gas-extraction system at the Ümraniye tip before the situation became fatal could have been an effective measure without diverting the State's resources to an excessive degree in breach of Article 65 of the Turkish Constitution or giving rise to policy problems to the extent alleged by the Government. Such a measure would not only have complied with Turkish regulations and general practice in the area, but would also have been a much better reflection of the humanitarian considerations which the Government relied on before the Court. . . .

109. In the light of the foregoing, the Court cannot see any reason to cast doubt on the domestic investigating authorities' findings of fact and considers that the circumstances examined above show that in the instant case the State's responsibility was engaged under Article 2 in several respects.

Firstly, the regulatory framework proved defective in that the Ümraniye municipal waste-collection site was opened and operated despite not conforming to the relevant technical standards and there was no coherent supervisory system to encourage those responsible to take steps to ensure adequate protection of the public and coordination and cooperation between the various administrative authorities so that the risks brought to their attention did not become so serious as to endanger human lives. . . .

110. Such circumstances give rise to a violation of Article 2 of the Convention in its substantive aspect; the Government's submission relating to the favourable outcome of the administrative action brought in the instant case . . . is of no consequence here, for the reasons set . . . out . . . below.

(ii) *Responsibility borne by the State as regards the judicial response required on account of the deaths, in the light of the procedural aspect of Article 2 of the Convention. . . .*

112. . . . It remains to be determined whether the measures taken in the framework of the Turkish criminal-law system following the accident at the Ümraniye municipal rubbish tip were satisfactory in practice, regard being had to the requirements of the Convention in this respect. . . .

113. In this connection, the Court notes that immediately after the accident had occurred on 28 April 1993 at about 11 a.m., the police arrived on the scene and interviewed the victims' families. In addition, the Istanbul Governor's Office set up a crisis unit, whose members went to the site on the same day. On the following day, 29 April 1993, the Ministry of the Interior ordered, of its own motion, the opening of an administrative investigation to determine the extent to which the authorities had been responsible for the accident. On 30 April 1993 the Üsküdar public prosecutor began a criminal investigation. Lastly, the official inquiries ended on 15 July 1993, when the two mayors, Mr Sözen and Mr Öktem, were committed for trial in the criminal courts.

Accordingly, the investigating authorities may be regarded as having acted with exemplary promptness and as having shown diligence in seeking to establish the circumstances that led both to the accident of 28 April 1993 and to the ensuing deaths....

116. In the instant case, in a judgment of 4 April 1996 the Istanbul Criminal Court sentenced the two mayors in question to fines of TRL 610,000 (an amount equivalent at the time to approximately EUR 9.70), suspended, for negligent omissions in the performance of their duties within the meaning of Article 230 §1 of the Criminal Code. Before the Court, the Government attempted to explain why that provision alone had been applied in respect of the two mayors and why they had been sentenced to the minimum penalty applicable. However, it is not for the Court to address such issues of domestic law concerning individual criminal responsibility, that being a matter for assessment by the national courts, or to deliver guilty or not-guilty verdicts in that regard.

Having regard to its task, the Court would simply observe that in the instant case the sole purpose of the criminal proceedings in issue was to establish whether the authorities could be held liable for negligence in the performance of their duties under Article 230 of the Criminal Code, which provision does not in any way relate to life-endangering acts or to the protection of the right to life within the meaning of Article 2.

Indeed, it appears from the judgment of 4 April 1996 that the trial court did not see any reason to depart from the reasoning set out in the committal order issued by the Administrative Council and left in abeyance any question of the authorities' possible responsibility for the death of the applicant's nine relatives. The judgment of 4 April 1996 does, admittedly, contain passages referring to the deaths that occurred on 28 April 1993 as a factual element. However, that cannot be taken to mean that there was an acknowledgment of any responsibility for failing to protect the right to life. The operative provisions of the judgment are silent on this point and, furthermore, do not give any precise indication that the trial court had sufficient regard to the extremely serious consequences of the accident; the persons held responsible were ultimately sentenced to derisory fines, which were, moreover, suspended.

117. Accordingly, it cannot be said that the manner in which the Turkish criminal-justice system operated in response to the tragedy secured the full accountability of State officials or authorities for their role in it and the effective implementation of provisions of domestic law guaranteeing respect for the right to life, in particular the deterrent function of the criminal law.

118. In short, it must be concluded in the instant case that there has been a violation of Article 2 of the Convention in its procedural aspect also, on account of the lack, in connection with a fatal accident provoked by the operation of a dangerous activity, of adequate protection by law safeguarding the right to life and deterring similar life-endangering conduct in future....

[The Court also held by a vote of 15 -2 that there had been a violation of the right to property, contained in Article 1 of Protocol 1 and of the right to a remedy found in Article 13 of the Convention.]

The two preceding cases addressed human rights obligations respecting civil and political rights. In one of its earliest "General Comments," the Committee on

Economic, Social, and Cultural Rights examined the "progressive" obligations of states under the ESC Covenant. The case that follows that comment returns to the problem of oil exploitation in Nigeria and analyzes the scope of state obligations with respect to economic, social, and cultural rights, as well as civil and political rights.

Committee on Economic, Social and Cultural Rights, General Comment No. 3, *The nature of States parties obligations* (Art. 2, para. 1)

UN Doc. E/1991/23 (Dec. 14, 1990) (footnotes omitted)

1. Article 2 is of particular importance to a full understanding of the Covenant and must be seen as having a dynamic relationship with all of the other provisions of the Covenant. It describes the nature of the general legal obligations undertaken by States parties to the Covenant. Those obligations include both what may be termed (following the work of the International Law Commission) obligations of conduct and obligations of result. While great emphasis has sometimes been placed on the difference between the formulations used in this provision and that contained in the equivalent article 2 of the International Covenant on Civil and Political Rights, it is not always recognized that there are also significant similarities. In particular, while the Covenant provides for progressive realization and acknowledges the constraints due to the limits of available resources, it also imposes various obligations which are of immediate effect. Of these, two are of particular importance in understanding the precise nature of States parties obligations. One of these, which is dealt with in a separate general comment, and which is to be considered by the Committee at its sixth session, is the "undertaking to guarantee" that relevant rights "will be exercised without discrimination. . . ."

2. The other is the undertaking in article 2 (1) "to take steps," which in itself, is not qualified or limited by other considerations. The full meaning of the phrase can also be gauged by noting some of the different language versions. In English the undertaking is "to take steps," in French it is "to act" ("s'engage à agir") and in Spanish it is "to adopt measures" ("a adoptar medidas"). Thus while the full realization of the relevant rights may be achieved progressively, steps towards that goal must be taken within a reasonably short time after the Covenant's entry into force for the States concerned. Such steps should be deliberate, concrete and targeted as clearly as possible towards meeting the obligations recognized in the Covenant. . . .

5. Among the measures which might be considered appropriate, in addition to legislation, is the provision of judicial remedies with respect to rights which may, in accordance with the national legal system, be considered justiciable. The Committee notes, for example, that the enjoyment of the rights recognized, without discrimination, will often be appropriately promoted, in part, through the provision of judicial or other effective remedies. Indeed, those States parties which are also parties to the International Covenant on Civil and Political Rights are already obligated (by virtue of arts. 2 (paras. 1 and 3), 3 and 26) of that Covenant to ensure that any person whose rights or freedoms (including the right to equality and non-discrimination) recognized in that Covenant are violated, "shall have an effective remedy" (art. 2 (3) (a)). In addition, there are

a number of other provisions in the International Covenant on Economic, Social and Cultural Rights, including articles 3, 7 (a) (i), 8, 10 (3), 13 (2) (a), (3) and (4) and 15 (3) which would seem to be capable of immediate application by judicial and other organs in many national legal systems. Any suggestion that the provisions indicated are inherently non-self executing would seem to be difficult to sustain. . . .

9. The principal obligation of result reflected in article 2 (1) is to take steps "with a view to achieving progressively the full realization of the rights recognized" in the Covenant. The term "progressive realization" is often used to describe the intent of this phrase. The concept of progressive realization constitutes a recognition of the fact that full realization of all economic, social and cultural rights will generally not be able to be achieved in a short period of time. In this sense the obligation differs significantly from that contained in article 2 of the International Covenant on Civil and Political Rights which embodies an immediate obligation to respect and ensure all of the relevant rights. Nevertheless, the fact that realization over time, or in other words progressively, is foreseen under the Covenant should not be misinterpreted as depriving the obligation of all meaningful content. It is on the one hand a necessary flexibility device, reflecting the realities of the real world and the difficulties involved for any country in ensuring full realization of economic, social and cultural rights. On the other hand, the phrase must be read in the light of the overall objective, indeed the raison d'être, of the Covenant which is to establish clear obligations for States parties in respect of the full realization of the rights in question. It thus imposes an obligation to move as expeditiously and effectively as possible towards that goal. Moreover, any deliberately retrogressive measures in that regard would require the most careful consideration and would need to be fully justified by reference to the totality of the rights provided for in the Covenant and in the context of the full use of the maximum available resources.

10. On the basis of the extensive experience gained by the Committee, as well as by the body that preceded it, over a period of more than a decade of examining States parties' reports the Committee is of the view that a minimum core obligation to ensure the satisfaction of, at the very least, minimum essential levels of each of the rights is incumbent upon every State party. Thus, for example, a State party in which any significant number of individuals is deprived of essential foodstuffs, of essential primary health care, of basic shelter and housing, or of the most basic forms of education is, prima facie, failing to discharge its obligations under the Covenant. If the Covenant were to be read in such a way as not to establish such a minimum core obligation, it would be largely deprived of its raison d'être. By the same token, it must be noted that any assessment as to whether a State has discharged its minimum core obligation must also take account of resource constraints applying within the country concerned. Article 2 (1) obligates each State party to take the necessary steps "to the maximum of its available resources." In order for a State party to be able to attribute its failure to meet at least its minimum core obligations to a lack of available resources it must demonstrate that every effort has been made to use all resources that are at its disposition in an effort to satisfy, as a matter of priority, those minimum obligations.

11. The Committee wishes to emphasize, however, that even where the available resources are demonstrably inadequate, the obligation remains for a State party to strive to ensure the widest possible enjoyment of the relevant rights under the

prevailing circumstances. Moreover, the obligations to monitor the extent of the realization, or more especially of the non-realization, of economic, social and cultural rights, and to devise strategies and programmes for their promotion, are not in any way eliminated as a result of resource constraints. The Committee has already dealt with these issues in its General Comment 1 (1989)....

13. A final element of article 2 (1), to which attention must be drawn, is that the undertaking given by all States parties is "to take steps, individually and through international assistance and cooperation, especially economic and technical...." The Committee notes that the phrase "to the maximum of its available resources" was intended by the drafters of the Covenant to refer to both the resources existing within a State and those available from the international community through international cooperation and assistance. Moreover, the essential role of such cooperation in facilitating the full realization of the relevant rights is further underlined by the specific provisions contained in articles 11, 15, 22 and 23. With respect to article 22 the Committee has already drawn attention, in General Comment 2 (1990), to some of the opportunities and responsibilities that exist in relation to international cooperation. Article 23 also specifically identifies "the furnishing of technical assistance" as well as other activities, as being among the means of "international action for the achievement of the rights recognized...."

14. The Committee wishes to emphasize that in accordance with Articles 55 and 56 of the Charter of the United Nations, with well-established principles of international law, and with the provisions of the Covenant itself, international cooperation for development and thus for the realization of economic, social and cultural rights is an obligation of all States. It is particularly incumbent upon those States which are in a position to assist others in this regard. The Committee notes in particular the importance of the Declaration on the Right to Development adopted by the General Assembly in its resolution 41/128 of 4 December 1986 and the need for States parties to take full account of all of the principles recognized therein. It emphasizes that, in the absence of an active programme of international assistance and cooperation on the part of all those States that are in a position to undertake one, the full realization of economic, social and cultural rights will remain an unfulfilled aspiration in many countries. In this respect, the Committee also recalls the terms of its General Comment 2 (1990).

The Social and Economic Rights Action Center and the Center for Economic and Social Rights v. Nigeria

Case 155/96, African Comm'n H.R., decision of Oct. 27, 2001 (footnotes and references omitted)

10. The communication alleges violations of Articles 2, 4, 14, 16, 18(1), 21, and 24 of the African Charter.

PROCEDURE

11. The communication was received by the Commission on 14th March 1996. The documents were sent with a video.

12. On 13th August 1996 letters acknowledging receipt of the Communication were sent to both Complainants.

13. On 13th August 1996, a copy of the Communication was sent to the Government of Nigeria. . . .

[Between 1996 and 2000 the Commission tried unsuccessfully to obtain a response from the Nigerian government on the allegations in the communication.]

30. During . . . [the spring 2001] session, the Respondent State submitted a Note Verbale stating the actions taken by the Government of the Federal Republic of Nigeria in respect of all the communications filed against it, including the present one. In respect of the instant communication, the note verbale admitted the gravamen of the complaints [which were against the former Abacha regime, not the authorities that finally responded in 2000] but went on to state the remedial measures being taken by the new civilian administration and they included:

> Establishing for the first time in the history of Nigeria, a Federal Ministry of Environment with adequate resources to address environmental related issues prevalent in Nigeria and as a matter of priority in the Niger delta area
>
> Enacting into law the establishment of the Niger Delta Development Commission (NDDC) with adequate funding to address the environmental and social related problems of the Niger delta area and other oil producing areas of Nigeria
>
> Inaugurating the Judicial Commission of Inquiry to investigate the issues of human rights violations. In addition, the representatives of the Ogoni people have submitted petitions to the Commission of Inquiry on these issues and these are presently being reviewed in Nigeria as a top priority matter. . . .

34. At it 30th session held in Banjul, The Gambia from 13th to 27th October 2001, the African Commission reached a decision on the merits of this communication.

Law

Admissibility

35. Article 56 of the African Charter governs admissibility. All of the conditions of this Article are met by the present communication. Only the exhaustion of local remedies requires close scrutiny.

36. Article 56(5) requires that local remedies, if any, be exhausted, unless these are unduly prolonged.

37. One purpose of the exhaustion of local remedies requirement is to give the domestic courts an opportunity to decide upon cases before they are brought to an international forum, thus avoiding contradictory judgments of law at the national and international levels. Where a right is not well provided for in domestic law such that no case is likely to be heard, potential conflict does not arise. Similarly, if the right is not well provided for, there cannot be effective remedies, or any remedies at all.

38. Another rationale for the exhaustion requirement is that a government should have notice of a human rights violation in order to have the opportunity to remedy such violation, before being called to account by an international tribunal. . . . The exhaustion of domestic remedies requirement should be properly understood as ensuring that the State concerned has ample opportunity to remedy

the situation of which applicants complain. It is not necessary here to recount the international attention that Ogoniland has received to argue that the Nigerian government has had ample notice and, over the past several decades, more than sufficient opportunity to give domestic remedies.

39. Requiring the exhaustion of local remedies also ensures that the African Commission does not become a tribunal of first instance for cases for which an effective domestic remedy exists.

40. The present communication does not contain any information on domestic court actions brought by the Complainants to halt the violations alleged. However, the Commission on numerous occasions brought this complaint to the attention of the government at the time but no response was made to the Commission's requests. In such cases the Commission has held that in the absence of a substantive response from the Respondent State it must decide on the facts provided by the Complainants and treat them as given. . . .

41. The Commission takes cognisance of the fact that the Federal Republic of Nigeria has incorporated the African Charter on Human and Peoples' Rights into its domestic law with the result that all the rights contained therein can be invoked in Nigerian courts including those violations alleged by the Complainants. However, the Commission is aware that at the time of submitting this communication, the then military government of Nigeria had enacted various decrees ousting the jurisdiction of the courts and thus depriving the people in Nigeria of the right to seek redress in the courts for acts of government that violate their fundamental human rights. In such instances, and as in the instant communication, the Commission is of the view that no adequate domestic remedies are existent. . . .

42. It should also be noted that the new government in their Note Verbale referenced 127/2000 submitted at the 28th session of the Commission held in Cotonou, Benin, admitted to the violations committed then by stating, "there is no denying the fact that a lot of atrocities were and are still being committed by the oil companies in Ogoni Land and indeed in the Niger Delta area."

The Commission therefore declare the communication admissible.

Merits

43. The present Communication alleges a concerted violation of a wide range of rights guaranteed under the African Charter for Human and Peoples' Rights. Before we venture into the inquiry whether the Government of Nigeria has violated the said rights as alleged in the Complaint, it would be proper to establish what is generally expected of governments under the Charter and more specifically vis-à-vis the rights themselves.

44. Internationally accepted ideas of the various obligations engendered by human rights indicate that all rights—both civil and political rights and social and economic—generate at least four levels of duties for a State that undertakes to adhere to a rights regime, namely the duty to RESPECT, PROTECT, PROMOTE, and FULFIL these rights. These obligations universally apply to all rights and entail a combination of negative and positive duties. As a human rights instrument, the African Charter is not alien to these concepts and the order in which they are dealt with here is chosen as a matter of convenience and in no way should it imply

the priority accorded to them. Each layer of obligation is equally relevant to the rights in question.

45. At a primary level, the obligation to RESPECT entails that the State should refrain from interfering in the enjoyment of all fundamental rights; it should respect right-holders, their freedoms, autonomy, resources, and liberty of their action. With respect to socioeconomic rights, this means that the State is obliged to respect the free use of resources owned or at the disposal of the individual alone or in any form of association with others, including the household or the family, for the purpose of rights-related needs. And with regard to a collective group, the resources belonging to it should be respected, as it has to use the same resources to satisfy its needs.

46. At a secondary level, the State is obliged to PROTECT right-holders against other subjects by legislation and provision of effective remedies. This obligation requires the State to take measures to protect beneficiaries of the protected rights against political, economic and social interferences. Protection generally entails the creation and maintenance of an atmosphere or framework by an effective interplay of laws and regulations so that individuals will be able to freely realize their rights and freedoms. This is very much intertwined with the tertiary obligation of the State to PROMOTE the enjoyment of all human rights. The State should make sure that individuals are able to exercise their rights and freedoms, for example, by promoting tolerance, raising awareness, and even building infrastructures.

47. The last layer of obligation requires the State to FULFILL the rights and freedoms it freely undertook under the various human rights regimes. It is more of a positive expectation on the part of the State to move its machinery towards the actual realization of the rights. This is also very much intertwined with the duty to promote mentioned in the preceding paragraph. It could consist in the direct provision of basic needs such as food or resources that can be used for food (direct food aid or social security). . . .

49. In accordance with Articles 60 and 61 of the African Charter, this communication is examined in the light of the provisions of the African Charter and the relevant international and regional human rights instruments and principles. The Commission thanks the two human rights NGOs who brought the matter under its purview: the Social and Economic Rights Action Center (Nigeria) and the Center for Economic and Social Rights (USA). Such is a demonstration of the usefulness to the Commission and individuals of *actio popularis*, which is wisely allowed under the African Charter. It is a matter of regret that the only written response from the government of Nigeria is an admission of the gravamen of the complaints which is contained in a Note Verbale . . . In the circumstances, the Commission is compelled to proceed with the examination of the matter on the basis of the uncontested allegations of the Complainants, which are consequently accepted by the Commission.

50. The Complainants allege that the Nigerian government violated the right to health and the right to clean environment as recognized under Articles 16 and 24 of the African Charter by failing to fulfill the minimum duties required by these rights. This, the Complainants allege, the government has done by:

— Directly participating in the contamination of air, water and soil and thereby harming the health of the Ogoni population,

— Failing to protect the Ogoni population from the harm caused by the NNPC Shell Consortium but instead using its security forces to facilitate the damage,

— Failing to provide or permit studies of potential or actual environmental and health risks caused by the oil operations

Article 16 of the African Charter reads:

> (1) Every individual shall have the right to enjoy the best attainable state of physical and mental health.
>
> (2) States Parties to the present Charter shall take the necessary measures to protect the health of their people and to ensure that they receive medical attention when they are sick.

Article 24 of the African Charter reads:

> All peoples shall have the right to a general satisfactory environment favourable to their development.

51. These rights recognize the importance of a clean and safe environment that is closely linked to economic and social rights in so far as the environment affects the quality of life and safety of the individual. As has been rightly observed by Alexander Kiss, "an environment degraded by pollution and defaced by the destruction of all beauty and variety is as contrary to satisfactory living conditions and development as the breakdown of the fundamental ecologic equilibria is harmful to physical and moral health."

52. The right to a general satisfactory environment, as guaranteed under Article 24 of the African Charter or the right to a healthy environment, as it is widely known, therefore imposes clear obligations upon a government. It requires the State to take reasonable and other measures to prevent pollution and ecological degradation, to promote conservation, and to secure an ecologically sustainable development and use of natural resources. Article 12 of the International Covenant on Economic, Social and Cultural Rights (ICESCR), to which Nigeria is a party, requires governments to take necessary steps for the improvement of all aspects of environmental and industrial hygiene. The right to enjoy the best attainable state of physical and mental health enunciated in Article 16(1) of the African Charter and the right to a general satisfactory environment favourable to development (Article 16(3)) already noted obligate governments to desist from directly threatening the health and environment of their citizens. The State is under an obligation to respect the just noted rights and this entails largely non-interventionist conduct from the State for example, not from carrying out, sponsoring or tolerating any practice, policy or legal measures violating the integrity of the individual.

53. Government compliance with the spirit of Articles 16 and 24 of the African Charter must also include ordering or at least permitting independent scientific monitoring of threatened environments, requiring and publicizing environmental and social impact studies prior to any major industrial development, undertaking appropriate monitoring and providing information to those communities exposed to hazardous materials and activities and providing meaningful opportunities for individuals to be heard and to participate in the development decisions affecting their communities.

applied

54. We now examine the conduct of the government of Nigeria in relation to Articles 16 and 24 of the African Charter. Undoubtedly and admittedly, the government of Nigeria, through NNPC has the right to produce oil, the income from which will be used to fulfill the economic and social rights of Nigerians. But the care that should have been taken as outlined in the preceding paragraph and which would have protected the rights of the victims of the violations complained of was not taken. To exacerbate the situation, the security forces of the government engaged in conduct in violation of the rights of the Ogonis by attacking, burning and destroying several Ogoni villages and homes. . . .

55. . . . The destructive and selfish role played by oil development in Ogoniland, closely tied with repressive tactics of the Nigerian Government, and the lack of material benefits accruing to the local population, may well be said to constitute a violation of Article 21. Article 21 provides

> All peoples shall freely dispose of their wealth and natural resources. This right shall be exercised in the exclusive interest of the people. In no case shall a people be deprived of it. In case of spoliation the dispossessed people shall have the right to the lawful recovery of its property as well as to an adequate compensation. The free disposal of wealth and natural resources shall be exercised without prejudice to the obligation of promoting international economic co-operation based on mutual respect, equitable exchange and the principles of international law. . . .

57. Governments have a duty to protect their citizens, not only through appropriate legislation and effective enforcement but also by protecting them from damaging acts that may be perpetrated by private parties. This duty calls for positive action on part of governments in fulfilling their obligation under human rights instruments. The practice before other tribunals also enhances this requirement as is evidenced in the case *Velásquez Rodríguez v. Honduras* [see pages 338-345]. In this landmark judgment, the Inter-American Court of Human Rights held that when a State allows private persons or groups to act freely and with impunity to the detriment of the rights recognized, it would be in clear violation of its obligations to protect the human rights of its citizens. Similarly, this obligation of the State is further emphasized in the practice of the European Court of Human Rights, in *X and Y v. Netherlands* [91 ECHR (1985) (Ser. A) at 32]. In that case, the Court pronounced that there was an obligation on authorities to take steps to make sure that the enjoyment of the rights is not interfered with by any other private person.

58. The Commission notes that in the present case, despite its obligation to protect persons against interferences in the enjoyment of their rights, the Government of Nigeria facilitated the destruction of the Ogoniland. Contrary to its Charter obligations and despite such internationally established principles, the Nigerian Government has given the green light to private actors, and the oil companies in particular, to devastatingly affect the well-being of the Ogonis. By any measure of standards, its practice falls short of the minimum conduct expected of governments, and therefore, is in violation of Article 21 of the African Charter.

59. The Complainants also assert that the military government of Nigeria massively and systematically violated the right to adequate housing of members of

the Ogoni community under Article 14 and implicitly recognized by Articles 16 and 18(1) of the African Charter. . . .

60. Although the right to housing or shelter is not explicitly provided for under the African Charter, the corollary of the combination of the provisions protecting the right to enjoy the best attainable state of mental and physical health, cited under Article 16 above, the right to property, and the protection accorded to the family forbids the wanton destruction of shelter because when housing is destroyed, property, health, and family life are adversely affected. It is thus noted that the combined effect of Articles 14, 16 and 18(1) reads into the Charter a right to shelter or housing which the Nigerian Government has apparently violated.

61. At a very minimum, the right to shelter obliges the Nigerian government not to destroy the housing of its citizens and not to obstruct efforts by individuals or communities to rebuild lost homes. The State's obligation to respect housing rights requires it, and thereby all of its organs and agents, to abstain from carrying out, sponsoring or tolerating any practice, policy or legal measure violating the integrity of the individual or infringing upon his or her freedom to use those material or other resources available to them in a way they find most appropriate to satisfy individual, family, household or community housing needs. Its obligations to protect obliges it to prevent the violation of any individual's right to housing by any other individual or non-state actors like landlords, property developers, and land owners, and where such infringements occur, it should act to preclude further deprivations as well as guaranteeing access to legal remedies. The right to shelter even goes further than a roof over ones head. It extends to embody the individual's right to be let alone and to live in peace — whether under a roof or not.

62. The protection of the rights guaranteed in Articles 14, 16 and 18 (1) leads to the same conclusion. As regards the earlier right, and in the case of the Ogoni People, the Government of Nigeria has failed to fulfill these two minimum obligations. The government has destroyed Ogoni houses and villages and then, through its security forces, obstructed, harassed, beaten and, in some cases, shot and killed innocent citizens who have attempted to return to rebuild their ruined homes. These actions constitute massive violations of the right to shelter, in violation of Articles 14, 16, and 18(1) of the African Charter.

63. The particular violation by the Nigerian Government of the right to adequate housing as implicitly protected in the Charter also encompasses the right to protection against forced evictions. The African Commission draws inspiration from the definition of the term "forced evictions" by the Committee on Economic Social and Cultural Rights which defines this term as "the permanent removal against their will of individuals, families and/or communities from the homes and/or which they occupy, without the provision of, and access to, appropriate forms of legal or other protection." Wherever and whenever they occur, forced evictions are extremely traumatic. They cause physical, psychological and emotional distress; they entail losses of means of economic sustenance and increase impoverishment. They can also cause physical injury and in some cases sporadic deaths. . . . Evictions break up families and increase existing levels of homelessness. In this regard, General Comment No. 4 (1991) of the Committee on Economic, Social and Cultural Rights on the right to adequate housing states that "all persons should possess a degree of security of tenure

which guarantees legal protection against forced eviction, harassment and other threats." The conduct of the Nigerian government clearly demonstrates a violation of this right enjoyed by the Ogonis as a collective right.

64. The Communication argues that the right to food is implicit in the African Charter, in such provisions as the right to life (Art. 4), the right to health (Art. 16) and the right to economic, social and cultural development (Art. 22). By its violation of these rights, the Nigerian Government trampled upon not only the explicitly protected rights but also upon the right to food implicitly guaranteed.

65. The right to food is inseparably linked to the dignity of human beings and is therefore essential for the enjoyment and fulfilment of such other rights as health, education, work and political participation. The African Charter and international law require and bind Nigeria to protect and improve existing food sources and to ensure access to adequate food for all citizens. Without touching on the duty to improve food production and to guarantee access, the minimum core of the right to food requires that the Nigerian Government should not destroy or contaminate food sources. It should not allow private parties to destroy or contaminate food sources, and prevent peoples' efforts to feed themselves.

66. The government's treatment of the Ogonis has violated all three minimum duties of the right to food. The government has destroyed food sources through its security forces and State Oil Company; has allowed private oil companies to destroy food sources; and, through terror, has created significant obstacles to Ogoni communities trying to feed themselves. The Nigerian government has again fallen short of what is expected of it under the provisions of the African Charter and international human rights standards, and hence, is in violation of the right to food of the Ogonis.

67. The Complainants also allege that the Nigerian Government has violated Article 4 of the Charter which guarantees the inviolability of human beings and everyone's right to life and integrity of the person respected. Given the wide spread violations perpetrated by the Government of Nigeria and by private actors (be it following its clear blessing or not), the most fundamental of all human rights, the right to life has been violated. The Security forces were given the green light to decisively deal with the Ogonis, which was illustrated by the wide spread terrorisations and killings. The pollution and environmental degradation to a level humanly unacceptable has made living in the Ogoni land a nightmare. The survival of the Ogonis depended on their land and farms that were destroyed by the direct involvement of the Government. These and similar brutalities not only persecuted individuals in Ogoniland but also the whole of the Ogoni Community as a whole. They affected the life of the Ogoni Society as a whole. The Commission conducted a mission to Nigeria from the 7th - 14th March 1997 and witnessed first hand the deplorable situation in Ogoni land including the environmental degradation.

68. The uniqueness of the African situation and the special qualities of the African Charter on Human and Peoples' Rights imposes upon the African Commission an important task. International law and human rights must be responsive to African circumstances. Clearly, collective rights, environmental rights, and economic and social rights are essential elements of human rights in Africa. The African Commission will apply any of the diverse rights contained in the African Charter. It welcomes this opportunity to make clear that there is no right in the African Charter that cannot be made effective. As indicated in the

preceding paragraphs, however, the Nigerian Government did not live up to the minimum expectations of the African Charter.

69. The Commission does not wish to fault governments that are labouring under difficult circumstances to improve the lives of their people. The situation of the people of Ogoniland, however, requires, in the view of the Commission, a reconsideration of the Government's attitude to the allegations contained in the instant communication. The intervention of multinational corporations may be a potentially positive force for development if the State and the people concerned are ever mindful of the common good and the sacred rights of individuals and communities. The Commission however takes note of the efforts of the present civilian administration to redress the atrocities that were committed by the previous military administration as illustrated in the Note Verbale referred to in paragraph 30 of this decision.

FOR THE ABOVE REASONS, THE COMMISSION,

FINDS the Federal Republic of Nigeria in violation of Articles 2, 4, 14, 16, 18(1), 21 and 24 of the African Charter on Human and Peoples' Rights;

APPEALS to the government of the Federal Republic of Nigeria to ensure protection of the environment, health and livelihood of the people of Ogoniland by:

Stopping all attacks on Ogoni communities and leaders by the Rivers State Internal Securities Task Force and permitting citizens and independent investigators free access to the territory;

Conducting an investigation into the human rights violations described above and prosecuting officials of the security forces, NNPC and relevant agencies involved in human rights violations;

Ensuring adequate compensation to victims of the human rights violations, including relief and resettlement assistance to victims of government sponsored raids, and undertaking a comprehensive cleanup of lands and rivers damaged by oil operations;

Ensuring that appropriate environmental and social impact assessments are prepared for any future oil development and that the safe operation of any further oil development is guaranteed through effective and independent oversight bodies for the petroleum industry; and

Providing information on health and environmental risks and meaningful access to regulatory and decision-making bodies to communities likely to be affected by oil operations.

URGES the government of the Federal Republic of Nigeria to keep the African Commission informed of the outcome of the work of:

The Federal Ministry of Environment which was established to address environmental and environment related issues prevalent in Nigeria, and as a matter of priority, in the Niger Delta area including the Ogoni land;

The Niger Delta Development Commission (NDDC) enacted into law to address the environmental and other social related problems in the Niger Delta area and other oil producing areas of Nigeria; and

The Judicial Commission of Inquiry inaugurated to investigate the issues of human rights violations.

As noted by the Commission, the Nigerian government conceded, following the return to civilian government, that violations had occurred. Might the Commission's opinion have been less expansive if the government had contested the allegations? More than a year prior to the Commission's decision, in January 2000, the government created the Justice Oputa Panel, a commission similar to the South African Truth and Reconciliation Commission, to address the human rights abuses perpetrated against the Ogoni and other peoples during the military regimes in the 1990s. Despite this, in a report done in 2004, Amnesty International reported that it remained "very concerned that civil and political as well as economic, social and cultural rights are being violated and abused in the process of the oil exploration and production in the Niger Delta." See Amnesty International, "Nigeria: Are Human Rights in the Pipeline?" Nov. 9, 2004. The Commission has no follow up procedure to monitor compliance with its decision. Would it be useful to create one, as other human rights bodies have done? How would you structure the procedure?

B. Balancing State Obligations to Protect with Individual Freedom and Autonomy

The cases above reveal the importance of positive state action to protect human rights. However, implicit in the nature of law generally is the notion that, while it is legitimate for government to make laws addressing the "public" sphere of life, there remains a sphere of "private" life (explicitly recognized in some international instruments) which should be beyond the reach of the state. The three cases extracted below consider the extent of the right to private life which must be protected by the government, drawing on European jurisprudence. Another view on the public-private distinction is found in the extract by Professor Charlesworth, supra page 36.

Brüggemann and Scheuten v. Germany

Eur. Comm'n H.R., Report, App. No. 5959/75 (Mar. 31, 1978)

[The applicants complained that German laws restricting (although not prohibiting) abortion interfered with their right to private life under Art. 8 of the European Convention.]

55. The right to respect for private life is of such a scope as to secure to the individual a sphere within which he can freely pursue the development and fulfilment of his personality. To this effect, he must also have the possibility of establishing relationships of various kinds, including sexual, with other persons. In principle, therefore, whenever the State sets up rules for the behaviour of the individual within this sphere, it interferes with the respect for private life and such interference must be justified in the light of para (2) of Art. 8.

56. However, there are limits to the personal sphere.... In fact, as the earlier jurisprudence of the Commission has already shown, the claim to respect for private life is automatically reduced to the extent that the individual himself

brings his private life into contact with public life or into close connection with other protected interests....

59.... [P]regnancy cannot be said to pertain uniquely to the sphere of private life. Whenever a woman is pregnant her private life becomes closely connected with the developing foetus.

60. The Commission does not find it necessary to decide, in this context, whether the unborn child is to be considered as "life" in the sense of Art. 2 of the Convention, or whether it could be regarded as an entity which under Art. 8(2) could justify an interference "for the protection of others." There can be no doubt that certain interests relating to pregnancy are legally protected, e.g., as shown by a survey of the legal order in 13 High Contracting Parties [appended to the report]. This survey reveals that, without exception, certain rights are attributed to the conceived but unborn child, in particular the right to inherit....

61. The Commission therefore finds that not every regulation of the termination of unwanted pregnancies constitutes an interference with the right to respect for the private life of the mother....

64.... [T]he Commission has had regard to the fact that, when the European Convention of Human Rights entered into force, the law on abortion in all Member States was at least as restrictive as the one now complained of by the applicants.... There is no evidence that it was the intention of the Parties to the Convention to bind themselves in favour of any particular solution under discussion....

[The Commission unanimously concluded that the German law at the time — which imposed various restrictions on abortions but permitted abortions up to 12 weeks after conception — did not violate the applicants' right to private life. One Commission member who was unable to participate in the vote would have found that the regulations were unjustified under the convention and therefore constituted a violation.]

Open Door and Dublin Well Woman v. Ireland

Eur. Ct. H.R., Ser. A No. 246A (Oct. 29, 1992) (references omitted)

13.... The facts as agreed ... by Dublin Well Woman may be summarised as follows:

(a) It counsels in a non-directive manner pregnant women resident in Ireland;

(b) Abortion or termination of pregnancy may be one of the options discussed within the said counselling;

(c) If a pregnant woman wants to consider the abortion option further, arrangements will be made by the applicant to refer her to a medical clinic in Great Britain;

(d) In certain circumstances, the applicant may arrange for the travel of such pregnant women;

(e) The applicant will inspect the medical clinic in Great Britain to ensure that it operates at the highest standards;

(f) At those medical clinics abortions have been performed on pregnant women who have been previously counselled by the applicant;

(g) Pregnant women resident in Ireland have been referred to medical clinics in Great Britain where abortions have been performed for many years including 1984. . . .

53. The applicants alleged that the Supreme Court injunction, restraining them from assisting pregnant women to travel abroad to obtain abortions, infringed the rights of the corporate applicants and the two counsellors to impart information, as well as the rights of Mrs X and Ms Geragaty to receive information.

67. The Government stressed the limited nature of the Supreme Court's injunction which only restrained the provision of certain information. There was no limitation on discussion in Ireland about abortion generally or the right of women to travel abroad to obtain one. They further contended that the Convention test as regards the proportionality of the restriction was inadequate where a question concerning the extinction of life was at stake. The right to life could not, like other rights, be measured according to a graduated scale. It was either respected or it was not. Accordingly, the traditional approach of weighing competing rights and interests in the balance was inappropriate where the destruction of unborn life was concerned. Since life was a primary value which was antecedent to and a prerequisite for the enjoyment of every other right, its protection might involve the infringement of other rights such as freedom of expression in a manner which might not be acceptable in the defence of rights of a lesser nature. . . .

68. The Court cannot agree that the State's discretion in the field of the protection of morals is unfettered and unreviewable.

It acknowledges that the national authorities enjoy a wide margin of appreciation in matters of morals, particularly in an area such as the present which touches on matters of belief concerning the nature of human life. As the Court has observed before, it is not possible to find in the legal and social orders of the Contracting States a uniform European conception of morals, and the State authorities are, in principle, in a better position than the international judge to give an opinion on the exact content of the requirements of morals as well as on the "necessity" of a "restriction" or "penalty" intended to meet them.

However this power of appreciation is not unlimited. It is for the Court, in this field also, to supervise whether a restriction is compatible with the Convention. . . .

72. While the relevant restriction, as observed by the Government, is limited to the provision of information, it is recalled that it is not a criminal offence under Irish law for a pregnant woman to travel abroad in order to have an abortion. Furthermore, the injunction limited the freedom to receive and impart information with respect to services which are lawful in other Convention countries and may be crucial to a woman's health and well-being. Limitations on information concerning activities which, notwithstanding their moral implications, have been and continue to be tolerated by national authorities, call for careful scrutiny by the Convention institutions as to their conformity with the tenets of a democratic society.

73. The Court is first struck by the absolute nature of the Supreme Court injunction which imposed a "perpetual" restraint on the provision of information to pregnant women concerning abortion facilities abroad, regardless of age or state of health or their reasons for seeking counselling on the termination of pregnancy. The sweeping nature of this restriction has since been highlighted by the case of *The Attorney General v. X and Others* and by the concession made by the

Government at the oral hearing that the injunction no longer applied to women who, in the circumstances as defined in the Supreme Court's judgment in that case, were now free to have an abortion in Ireland or abroad.

74. On that ground alone the restriction appears over broad and disproportionate. Moreover, this assessment is confirmed by other factors. . . .

80. In the light of the above, the Court concludes that the restraint imposed on the applicants from receiving or imparting information was disproportionate to the aims pursued. Accordingly there has been a breach of Article 10.

Pretty v. the United Kingdom

Eur. Ct. H.R., App. No. 2346/02, judgment of 29 April 2002

[The applicant asked the European Court of Human Rights to declare that the United Kingdom's prohibition of assisted suicide violated her rights to life (art. 2), freedom from inhuman and degrading treatment (art. 3), privacy (art. 8), freedom of conscience (art. 9) and non-discrimination (art. 14). The applicant suffered from a progressive and incurable neuro-degenerative disease. At the time of the application she was essentially paralysed from the neck downwards, had virtually no decipherable speech, and was fed by a tube. Her life expectancy was very poor, measurable only in weeks or months. However, her intellect and capacity to make decisions were unimpaired. In her application, she asserted that she wanted to be able to control how and when she died and to be spared suffering and indignity.]

38. . . . Article 2 §1 enjoins the State not only to refrain from the intentional and unlawful taking of life, but also to take appropriate steps to safeguard the lives of those within its jurisdiction. . . . This obligation extends beyond a primary duty to secure the right to life by putting in place effective criminal-law provisions to deter the commission of offences against the person backed up by law-enforcement machinery for the prevention, suppression and sanctioning of breaches of such provisions; it may also imply in certain well-defined circumstances a positive obligation on the authorities to take preventive operational measures to protect an individual whose life is at risk from the criminal acts of another individual. . . . More recently, in the case of *Keenan v. the United Kingdom*, Article 2 was found to apply to the situation of a mentally ill prisoner who disclosed signs of being a suicide risk.

39. The consistent emphasis in all the cases before the Court has been the obligation of the State to protect life. The Court is not persuaded that "the right to life" guaranteed in Article 2 can be interpreted as involving a negative aspect. . . . Article 2 of the Convention is . . . unconcerned with issues to do with the quality of living or what a person chooses to do with his or her life. To the extent that these aspects are recognised as so fundamental to the human condition that they require protection from State interference, they may be reflected in the rights guaranteed by other Articles of the Convention, or in other international human rights instruments. Article 2 cannot, without a distortion of language, be interpreted as conferring the diametrically opposite right, namely a right to die; nor can it create a right to self-determination in the sense of conferring on an individual the entitlement to choose death rather than life. . . .

[The applicant's argument that the suffering which she faced qualified as degrading treatment under Article 3 of the Convention was also rejected, because] it is beyond dispute that the respondent Government have not, themselves, inflicted any ill-treatment on the applicant. Nor is there any complaint that the applicant is not receiving adequate care from the State medical authorities.

[The Court agreed that the concept of "private life" is a broad term not susceptible to exhaustive definition and that "the notion of personal autonomy is an important principle underlying the interpretation of its guarantees." The Court then considered the appropriate balance to be struck:]

62. The Court would observe that the ability to conduct one's life in a manner of one's own choosing may also include the opportunity to pursue activities perceived to be of a physically or morally harmful or dangerous nature for the individual concerned. The extent to which a State can use compulsory powers or the criminal law to protect people from the consequences of their chosen lifestyle has long been a topic of moral and jurisprudential discussion, the fact that the interference is often viewed as trespassing on the private and personal sphere adding to the vigour of the debate. However, even where the conduct poses a danger to health, or arguably, where it is of a life-threatening nature, the case-law of the Convention institutions has regarded the State's imposition of compulsory or criminal measures as impinging on the private life of the applicant within the scope of Article 8 §1 and requiring justification in terms of the second paragraph. . . .

65. The very essence of the Convention is respect for human dignity and human freedom. Without in any way negating the principle of sanctity of life protected under the Convention, the Court considers that it is under Article 8 that notions of the quality of life take on significance. In an era of growing medical sophistication combined with longer life expectancies, many people are concerned that they should not be forced to linger on in old age or in states of advanced physical or mental decrepitude which conflict with strongly held ideas of self and personal identity. . . .

67. The applicant in this case is prevented by law from exercising her choice to avoid what she considers will be an undignified and distressing end to her life. The Court is not prepared to exclude that this constitutes an interference with her right to respect for private life as guaranteed under Article 8 §1 of the Convention. . . .

69. The only issue arising from the arguments of the parties is the necessity of any interference, it being common ground that the restriction on assisted suicide in this case was imposed by law and in pursuit of the legitimate aim of safeguarding life and thereby protecting the rights of others.

70. According to the Court's established case-law, the notion of necessity implies that the interference corresponds to a pressing social need and, in particular, that it is proportionate to the legitimate aim pursued; in determining whether an interference is necessary in a democratic society, the Court will take into account that a margin of appreciation is left to the national authorities, whose decision remains subject to review by the Court for conformity with the requirements of the Convention. The margin of appreciation to be accorded to the competent national authorities will vary in accordance with the nature of the issues and the importance of the interests at stake. . . .

74. . . . [T]he Court finds, in agreement with the House of Lords, . . . that States are entitled to regulate through the operation of the general criminal law activities which are detrimental to the life and safety of other individuals.

. . . The more serious the harm involved the more heavily will weigh in the balance considerations of public health and safety against the countervailing principle of personal autonomy. The law in issue in this case, section 2 of the 1961 Act, was designed to safeguard life by protecting the weak and vulnerable and especially those who are not in a condition to take informed decisions against acts intended to end life or to assist in ending life. Doubtless the condition of terminally ill individuals will vary. But many will be vulnerable and it is the vulnerability of the class which provides the rationale for the law in question. It is primarily for States to assess the risk and the likely incidence of abuse if the general prohibition on assisted suicides were relaxed or if exceptions were to be created. Clear risks of abuse do exist, notwithstanding arguments as to the possibility of safeguards and protective procedures. . . .

76. The Court does not consider therefore that the blanket nature of the ban on assisted suicide is disproportionate. The Government have stated that flexibility is provided for in individual cases by the fact that consent is needed from the DPP to bring a prosecution and by the fact that a maximum sentence is provided, allowing lesser penalties to be imposed as appropriate. The Select Committee report indicated that between 1981 and 1992 in 22 cases in which mercy killing was an issue, there was only one conviction for murder, with a sentence for life imprisonment, while lesser offences were substituted in the others and most resulted in probation or suspended sentences. It does not appear to be arbitrary to the Court for the law to reflect the importance of the right to life, by prohibiting assisted suicide while providing for a system of enforcement and adjudication which allows due regard to be given in each particular case to the public interest in bringing a prosecution, as well as to the fair and proper requirements of retribution and deterrence. . . .

78. The Court concludes that the interference in this case may be justified as necessary in a democratic society for the protection of the rights of others and, accordingly, that there has been no violation of Article 8 of the Convention.

Comments and Questions

1. The Human Rights Committee states that the requirement to "give effect" to the Covenant on Civil and Political Rights "is unqualified and of immediate effect," while enjoyment of most of the rights in the Covenant on Economic, Social, and Cultural Rights is to be achieved progressively. How does a country lacking in resources give "immediate effect" to the right to a fair trial, which requires the expenditure of substantial resources on an entire judicial and criminal justice system? Would a state be justified in funding defense lawyers before it staffed secondary schools or public health clinics?

2. Review General Comment 3 of the ESC Committee, supra pages 353-355. Where does the concept of a "minimum core obligation" come from? Do you agree with the Committee that "international cooperation for development and thus for the realization of economic, social and cultural rights" is an obligation of all States"?

3. Does the nature of state obligations under the Covenant on Civil and Political Rights render civil and political rights more readily justiciable than economic, social, or cultural rights? For a negative response, see Commission

on Human Rights, *Report by the Special Rapporteur on the right to food, Mr. Jean Ziegler, submitted in accordance with Commission on Human Rights resolution 2001/25*, UN Doc. E/CN.4/2002/58, at 11-16 (Jan. 10, 2002). See Chapter 6, pages 501-526.

4. All of the cases presented above raise issues of admissibility, in particular exhaustion of local remedies. What is the extent of the state's obligation to afford remedies? If local remedies are unavailable or unavailing, does this constitute a separate breach of the right to a remedy in the relevant treaty?

5. The Nigerian decision above is the first in which the African Commission details the obligations of states parties to the African Charter. What sources does it invoke in articulating these duties? The African Charter mentions the Charter of the United Nations and the Universal Declaration of Human Rights in connection with the pledge made by the African States to promote international cooperation. In the Charter's Preamble, the African States also reaffirm in sweeping fashion "their adherence to the principles of human and peoples' rights and freedoms contained in the declarations, conventions and other international instruments adopted by the Organization of African Unity, the Movement of Non-Aligned Countries and the United Nations." Do these references permit the Commission to have recourse to UN instruments and the case law of other regional bodies? See African Charter Arts. 60 and 61. Note that the African Commission has adopted several principles established in European and Inter-American case law, such as presuming the truth of the allegations from the silence of government, the notion of continuing violations, continuity of obligations in spite of a change of government, state responsibility for failure to act, and the presumption that the state is responsible for custodial injuries.

6. In the SERAC case, supra page 355, the African Commission found that Nigeria had violated Articles 21 and 24 of the African Charter. These articles set forth "peoples" rights, not individual rights; who are the "peoples" whose rights were violated? Does the African Charter's references to "peoples" refer to the entire population within a state or to distinct ethnic groups within it? See, e.g., Morne van der Linde and Lirette Louw, "Considering the interpretation and implementation of article 24 of the African Charter on Human and Peoples' Rights in light of the SERAC communication," 3 *Af. Hum. Rts. L.J.* 167 (2003). Compare the African Commission's approach with that of the Human Rights Committee, which has refused to consider individual communications that claim violation of the right of all "peoples" to self-determination under Article 1 of the Covenant on Civil and Political Rights.

7. What rule should apply if more than one instrument is in force for a state, and the norms are not identical? In traditional international law, state sovereignty was preserved by interpreting provisions narrowly in favor of the freedom of state action. Is such an assumption compatible with the object and purpose of human rights treaties? Would application of the "rule most favorable to the individual" be more appropriate? Is there a principled basis on which to develop and apply such a choice of law rule?

8. The African Commission's four-part analysis of obligations (protect, preserve, ensure, fulfill) does not appear in any human rights treaty. Nor are the rights to housing and food explicit in the African Charter. Is the Commission re-writing the treaty, or are the implications necessary to implement the rights and duties contained therein?

9. Do you agree with the *Öneryildiz* judgment? Should (gross) negligence by state authorities result in a finding that human rights have been violated? In *Makaratzis v. Greece,* App. No. 50385/99 (Dec. 20, 2004) (Grand Chamber), the European Court of Human Rights held that physical ill-treatment by state officials which does not result in death may, in exceptional circumstances, bring the facts of a case within the scope of Article 2. The facts of the case indicated that policemen had engaged in a high speed car chase with the applicant and repeatedly fired their weapons at him. While they had not intended to kill him, the fact that he did not die was fortuitous, because the conduct had put his life at risk; Article 2 was thus applicable. The conduct of the authorities lacked appropriate structure in domestic law or practice setting out clear guidelines and criteria governing the use of force. Therefore, the authorities had not complied with their positive obligations under Article and the applicant had been the victim of a violation. Does this place too great a burden on the state? For another controversial case where the state was held responsible for failing in its positive obligations under Article 2, see *McCann et al. v. United Kingdom*, 324 Eur. Ct. H.R. (Ser. A) (Sept. 27, 1995) (Grand Chamber). Contrast the U.S. Supreme Court decisions in *DeShaney v. County of Winnebago Dept. of Social Services*, 489 U.S. 189 (1989), and *Town of Castle Park, Colo. v. Gonzales*, 125 S.Ct. 2796 (2005), each of which held that the U.S. Constitution imposes no positive obligations on the government to protect life and personal security.

10. In light of the above judgments, how do you think the European Court of Human Rights would decide the case of *Wackenheim v. France*, H.R. Comm., Comm. No. 854/1999 (July 15, 2002)? The facts, as related by the Committee, began as follows:

> 2.1 The author, who suffers from dwarfism, began in July 1991 to appear in dwarf tossing events organized by a company called Societé Fun-Productions. Wearing suitable protective gear, he would allow himself to be thrown short distances onto an airbed by clients of the establishment staging the event (a discotheque).
>
> 2.2 On 27 November 1991, the French Ministry of the Interior issued a circular on the policing of public events, in particular dwarf tossing, which instructed prefects to use their policing powers to instruct mayors to keep a close eye on spectacles staged in their communes. The circular said that dwarf tossing should be banned on the basis of, among other things, article 3 of the European Convention for the Protection of Human Rights and Fundamental Freedoms.

The applicant brought the case to the Committee, alleging that the ban on his working had an adverse effect on his life and represented an affront to his dignity. He claimed to be the victim of a violation by France of his right to freedom, employment, respect for private life, an adequate standard of living, and discrimination. He claimed that there is no work for dwarves in France and that his job was not an affront to human dignity, because dignity consists in having a job.

The Committee found several of the claims inadmissible for failure to exhaust local remedies, including the right to privacy claim. It found admissible, however, the claim of discrimination and proceeded to decide on the merits the question of whether a ban on dwarf tossing constitutes discrimination:

> 7.3 The Committee recalls its jurisprudence whereby not every differentiation of treatment of persons will necessarily constitute discrimination, which is prohibited

> under article 26 of the Covenant. Differentiation constitutes discrimination when it is not based on objective and reasonable grounds. The question, in the present case, is whether the differentiation between the persons covered by the ban ordered by the State party and persons to whom this ban does not apply may be validly justified.
>
> 7.4 The ban on throwing ordered by the State party in the present case applies only to dwarves.... However, if these persons are covered to the exclusion of others, the reason is that they are the only persons capable of being thrown. Thus, the differentiation between the persons covered by the ban, namely dwarves, and those to whom it does not apply, namely persons not suffering from dwarfism, is based on an objective reason and is not discriminatory in its purpose. The Committee considers that the State party has demonstrated, in the present case, that the ban on dwarf tossing as practiced by the author did not constitute an abusive measure but was necessary in order to protect public order which brings into play considerations of human dignity that are compatible with the objectives of the Covenant.

Do you agree with the Human Rights Committee that there was an objective basis for the differentiation made by the French government because only dwarves can be tossed? What about tossing children? Assuming that Mr. Wackenheim exhausts his local remedies on the issue of the right to privacy and files another complaint, how do you think the merits would be decided by the European Court or by the Human Rights Committee? Based on the *Pretty* and *Wackenheim* opinions, what other protections to uphold human dignity would human rights bodies allow? Could a state ban extreme sports, reality television shows, and circus side shows? Is the real message of *Pretty*, *Wackenheim*, and the abortion cases simply that a great deal of deference will be given to states that have democratically adopted legislation that strikes a reasonable balance between legitimate government concerns and privacy rights?

11. The judgments in the *Velásquez-Rodriquez* and the *Öneryildiz* cases address the issue of investigation and prosecution of the persons responsible for human rights violations. Is it necessary for a state to criminalize all human rights violations? Must it investigate and sanction all violations, even if it does not criminalize them? Consider two recent studies done by the Human Rights Commission. The first study led to adoption by the Commission of the *Basic Principles and Guidelines on the Right to a Remedy and Reparation for Victims of Gross Violations of International Human Rights Law and Serious Violations of International Humanitarian Law*, UN Doc. E/CN.4/2005/59 (2005). The Principles provide, inter alia:

> 3. The obligation to respect, ensure respect for and implement international human rights law and international humanitarian law as provided for under the respective bodies of law, includes, inter alia, the duty to:
>
> (a) Take appropriate legislative and administrative and other measures to prevent violations;
>
> (b) Investigate violations effectively, promptly, thoroughly and impartially and, where appropriate, take action against those allegedly responsible in accordance with domestic and international law;
>
> (c) Provide those who claim to be victims of a human rights or humanitarian law violation with equal and effective access to justice... irrespective of who may ultimately be the bearer of responsibility for the violation; and
>
> (d) Provide effective remedies to victims, including reparation....
>
> 4. In cases of gross violations of international human rights law and serious violations of international humanitarian law constituting crimes under international

law, States have the duty to investigate and, if there is sufficient evidence, the duty to submit to prosecution the person allegedly responsible for the violations and, if found guilty, the duty to punish her or him. Moreover, in these cases, States should, in accordance with international law, cooperate with one another and assist international judicial organs competent in the investigation and prosecution of these violations.

The second study, on impunity, is referred to in Chapter 11, page 974-975. Based on the court judgments and these texts, what events in Nigeria should be investigated and prosecuted?

12. In *Dudgeon v. U.K.*, Ser. A No. 45 (Sept. 23, 1981), the European Court of Human Rights held that a Northern Irish law prohibiting homosexual behavior between consenting adults violated Dudgeon's right to private life, although the Commission and Court accepted that the prohibition accurately reflected the wishes of at least a "substantial body of opinion" in Northern Ireland. What distinguishes the protection of Mr. Dudgeon's right to private life, despite the opposition of a large segment of Northern Irish society, from the refusal to allow Mr. Wackenheim to seek gainful — and apparently harmless — employment because its exercise was opposed by (presumably) a large segment of French society?

III. Corporate Responsibility

The human rights violations that occurred in the context of Nigerian oil exploration and exploitation involved not only government agents but also large multinational corporations. We turn now to their role and potential responsibility under human rights law. The first two readings look at the issue of globalization and consider its short-term and long-term impact on human rights.

Dinah Shelton, *Protecting Human Rights in a Globalized World*

25 B.C. Int'l & Comp. L. Rev. 273, 275-76, 278-80 (2002)
(citations and notes omitted)

Globalization is a multidimensional phenomenon, "comprising numerous complex and interrelated processes that have a dynamism of their own." It involves a deepening and broadening of rapid transboundary exchanges due to developments in technology, communications, and media. Such exchanges and interactions occur at all levels of governance and among non-state actors, creating a more interdependent world.

Globalization is not new, although its forms and the technology that spurs it have changed. Globalization today is most often associated with economic interdependence, deregulation and a dominance of the marketplace that includes a shifting of responsibilities from state to non-state actors. Economic globalization has been accompanied by a marked increase in the influence of international financial markets and transnational institutions, including corporations, in determining national policies and priorities. In addition, information and communications technology has emerged as a dominant force in the global system of production, while trade in goods, services and financial instruments are more prevalent than any time in history....

Global technology and the information revolution have limited the ability of governments to control the right to seek, receive, and transmit information within and across boundaries. Ideas and information can circulate more freely, as can individuals. The number of televisions per 1000 persons doubled between 1980 and 1995 while the number of Internet subscribers exceeds 700 million persons. Free circulation enhances the ability to inform all persons about rights and avenues of redress. It also makes it more difficult for governments to conceal violations and allows activists more easily to mobilize shame in order to induce changes in government behavior. Information technology and the media also can be used, however, to violate human rights when the government is weak. In Rwanda, the radio and television channel Radio-Télévision Libre des Mille Collines was an important avenue for inciting genocide. Internet too has been used for hate speech...

Globalization thus has created powerful non-state actors that may violate human rights in ways that were not contemplated during the development of the modern the human rights movement. This development poses challenges to international human rights law, because for the most part that law has been designed to restrain abuses by powerful states and state agents, not to regulate the conduct of non-state actors themselves or to allow intervention in weak states when human rights violations occur. An increasingly globalized civil society is likely to respond to economic globalization by opposing liberalized trade and investment regimes that are not accompanied by accountability, transparency, public participation, and respect for fundamental rights.

The result may be viewed as a "clash of globalizations." The clash plays out in the international institutional and normative system that has separated human rights matters from economic policy and regulation, creating distinct institutions, laws, and values for each field. Integrating them is no easy task, indeed, some commentators view a conflict as inevitable....

The multiple and sometimes contradictory impacts of globalization are reflected in the complete disagreement of views over the pattern and direction of globalization. Proponents point to a rise in average incomes for the world as a whole. Opponents note that there is persistent inequality and poverty. The World Bank Development Report estimates that, at purchasing power parity, the per capita GDP in the richest 20 countries in 1960 was 18 times that of the poorest 20 countries. By 1995, the gap had widened to 37 times. According to the ILO, only 24 percent of the world's foreign direct investment (FDI) went to developing countries in 1999, down from 38 percent over the period 1993-97, and 80 percent of the recent investment went to only ten developing countries. Wealth concentration is not only seen among countries, but among individuals as well. According to the *UNDP Human Development Report 1999*, the assets of the three wealthiest individuals in the world is more than the combined gross national product of all least developed countries, while the annual sales of one transnational corporation exceeds the combined gross domestic product of Chile, Costa Rica and Ecuador.

Rhoda E. Howard-Hassman, *The Second Great Transformation: Human Rights Leapfrogging in the Era of Globalization*

27 Hum. Rts. Q. 1, 4, 5-6, 13, 31, 32, 33, 36-37, 38-40 (2005) (notes omitted)

Undoubtedly, . . . the process of globalization is causing human rights abuses in the short term, some of them very severe. Before presenting my argument, therefore, I wish to make clear my personal position on the human rights abuses caused by globalization. I believe that in the short as well as the medium and long terms every effort ought to be made to ensure that everyone enjoys her or his full range of human rights, including economic rights. I do not believe that present generations should be told that they must suffer, for the sake of future generations. More pragmatically, I would like to see a world in which every policy change meant to promote globalization was obliged to adhere to the principle that the poorest not be rendered even worse off. . . .

. . . On the other hand, the following analysis is meant to persuade readers that in the long run, globalization may well create a world of increased prosperity, democracy, and protection of human rights.

Karl Polanyi wrote *The Great Transformation* to explain the economic, social, and political changes that occurred in Europe, particularly Britain, from the end of the eighteenth century to the Second World War. . . .

What is happening now is the second great transformation. Globalization is the final assault of capitalism on all those areas of the globe that previously escaped it, either because of explicit communist or socialist politics, because of national policies of protectionism or withdrawal from the world economy, or because capitalism had no interest in the region as a source of capital or resources, a source of workers, or a market. All over what was formally the noncapitalist, or only partly capitalist worlds — what Immanuel Wallerstein called the peripheral and semi-peripheral parts of the world — the social is giving way to the profit motive, as it did in Western Europe two centuries ago. . . .

Whether for good or ill in human rights terms, social relations will change in the new global society. Societies will become more fluid; individuals will be more mobile, social norms will change, and traditional roles will give way to new ideas of how to behave. There will be new relations between the sexes. Persons formerly holding authority will find they are unheeded, while hitherto disreputable individuals will gain credence as role models in a new entrepreneurial world. Guns and drugs will be considered as legitimate objects of exchange, much as they were during the great European expansionist period of colonization. Some people will be confused by these changes and long for a simpler time with a stricter normative order. Among them, some will — and do — fight viciously to retain the older world from which they are being so abruptly torn. In such situations of flux, there will be no necessary short or medium-term correlation between the processes of globalization and the entrenchment of human rights, either positive or negative. Nor will there necessarily be such connection in the long term. As is shown below, no simple model of correlations can predict the human rights future. . . .

. . . A major difference between the first and second Great Transformations is the existence the second time around of the international human rights regime, and the international human rights social movement. . . .

During the West's period of growth, there was no international law to prevent the purchase or theft of people. Thus, the West was able to profit from slavery, as also were those who sold slaves to Westerners. . . .

Similarly, during the period of Western expansion there was no international law prohibiting colonialism. . . .

As there were no laws against slavery or colonialism, so also there were no laws against massive population transfers. During the period of Western expansion, citizens — if they could be called that — in the Western world had few rights. . . .

Finally, in the early modern capitalist world, no international law prohibited genocide and ethnic cleansing. Although there were some protests — from Catholic and other missionaries against the treatment of aboriginal populations in the Americas, for example — by and large colonists could do as they pleased to wipe out the "primitive" populations occupying territories that they sought. . . .

Human rights lawlessness, then, gave industrializing Western powers several privileges that are not enjoyed by industrializing regimes in the early twenty-first century. . . .

Therefore, in a global world now characterized by human rights constraints, less developed countries will be at some disadvantage compared to their Western predecessors, in engaging in the capitalist path. On the other hand, as compared to citizens of the West until well into the twentieth century, citizens of these less developed countries are at an advantage in demanding their rights. . . .

Nevertheless, as global communication erodes geographical remoteness, the universal principle of human rights becomes one upon which local actors can base their demands for justice. If the capitalist-owned mass media ignore a particular human right, the technology of global communications nevertheless allows its pursuit through the formation of independent media groups, chat rooms, and websites. . . .

There are now voluntary international codes of conduct for transnational corporations, evolving in part from the twenty-year-long campaign before the end of apartheid to oblige multinational investors to treat their black South African workers better. There is also a movement among international lawyers to bring transnational investors under the constraints of the international human rights regime. The International Labor Organization has found a new centrality in the elaboration of minimum human rights standards for transnational corporations, even if it does not yet have the authority to impose these standards. The Organization for Economic Co-operation and Development has also elaborated voluntary guidelines for multinational enterprises, including the right of workers to form trade unions.

Giddens notes that civil society organizations such as the environmentalist group Greenpeace and the anti-poverty organization Oxfam are themselves now global institutions. The feminist movement is also international: women from all over the world, from the most remote regions and least advantaged social groups, can meet to discuss common problems, as occurred at the Vienna Conference on Human Rights in 1993 and at Beijing in 1995. . . .

Despite efforts of political and cultural spokespersons of various kinds to shut down the borders, it is increasingly difficult for those who suffer human rights abuses not to hear the voices of human rights defenders. Global solidarity is an important aspect of globalization: in 2000 there were 16,500 trans-border civil society organizations. Thus globalization is not merely a phenomenon coming from "above" in the form of transnational organizations and corporations. It is also a phenomenon originating from below, often in the form of "grass-roots globalization," local organizations in the underdeveloped world that can connect via the Internet, email, or jet-set NGO conferences with international human rights organizations based in the West.

. . . Reflecting the changes that occurred in Polanyi's Britain in the eighteenth and nineteenth centuries, human rights are posited upon the basic civil and political rights that communitarian political systems frequently deny; namely, freedoms of speech, assembly, press, and association. Human rights are also posited upon a zone of personal privacy, in family relations, in economic activities, and in individual decision-making. To some people trying to protect their own societies, religions, and cultures from the homogenizing tendencies of globalization, the global norms that human rights activists propose seem suspiciously like "Western" norms. Some influential individuals in the developing world consider the human rights movement to be propounding a "foreign" global normative system that requires social and cultural, as well as political, legal, and economic change. The charge of cultural imperialism is frequently heard, and the politics of resentment is manipulated to hold back the tide of human rights. . . .

Nevertheless, globalization has spread the idea of human rights world wide. It has speeded up social change. Ideas and rules of human rights leapfrog across oceans and centuries, intersecting with social changes on the ground. Countries such as Taiwan and South Korea have already followed paths to become relatively rights-protective societies. . . . They did so in fifty years, not 200. Thus this model is not confined to the West, despite the West's obvious initial advantages in industrializing.

Globalization is, then, a powerful potential tool for promotion of human rights worldwide. But whether, in the end, it promotes or hinders human rights is not something that can be determined by quantitative studies. . . . Nor can it be determined by adding up the numbers of jobs created and comparing them with the numbers lost. . . . It is no more sensible to pass judgment on globalization as an instrument of social change that it would have been sensible to pass judgment on the Industrial Revolution in 1780 or 1800. Now, as then, the short-term detrimental consequences are obvious. Now, as then, humanitarians must strive to overcome the harms of dispossession, underemployment, and poverty. But now, as then, we do not know the final outcome.

A. *Codes of Conduct*

The effort to limit or prohibit conduct detrimental to human rights committed by private actors is as old as the effort to protect human rights through international and national law. As Chapter 1 discussed, the movement to combat the transatlantic slave trade — a major multinational business from the 16th through the 19th centuries — was among the first global human rights actions. In recent years, several developments have placed international standards of human rights and environmental protection on the agenda of corporations and other business organizations. Consumer awareness has increased, as consumers are paying more attention to issues such as the labor practices of the companies whose products they buy. Privatization has elevated corporate influence on society and with that influence have come increasing demands for transparency and accountability. Some corporations have been publicly implicated in serious human rights violations and have found themselves subject to consumer boycotts, loss of market share, and litigation. In sum, respect for human rights has become one of the key performance indicators for at least some corporations around the world.

During the 1970s, many developing countries supported a multilateral effort to draft principles to regulate international trade and investment. The locus of the effort was the UN Commission and Centre on Transnational Corporations, which were established by ECOSOC in November 1974. In 1975 the Centre began work on a Code of Conduct for Transnational Corporations and prepared numerous studies in connection with this work. In 1985, the Centre concluded that a code of conduct was needed, and the Commission itself reached agreement in 1990 on a draft code. The draft was submitted to the General Assembly, but, after informal consultations, it was apparent that no consensus was possible on the issue, and the effort to adopt a global code failed.

In the past decade, the United Nations reinvigorated the issue of corporate social responsibility through a set of principles known as the Global Compact, which originated in 1999, when UN Secretary-General Kofi Annan encouraged business leaders to adhere to policies that ensure responsible forms of globalization. In announcing the Global Compact, he urged corporations to increase transparency and integrate social responsibility into their business operations. The first two Principles address human rights and provide that businesses should 1) "support and respect the protection of internationally proclaimed human rights" and 2) make sure they are not complicit in human rights abuses. UN Global Compact, *http://www.unglobalcompact.org/Portal/Default.asp?*. Other principles address labor standards, the environment, and combating corruption.

The two human rights principles suggest that business should refrain from acts that could interfere with the enjoyment of human rights and also, more ambitiously, they suggest that business should actively support human rights. There is certainly potential for promotion through investment and promotion of the underlying conditions required for the enjoyment of human rights, but overly aggressive promotional activities could involve business in political decisions that are normally the purview of governments. Similarly, the principle that calls on business to refrain from complicity in human rights abuses raises the question of what constitutes complicity: knowledge, toleration, authorization, or providing practical assistance? The duty to act or not act in specific situations might not always be clear.

The ILO *Tripartite Declaration of Principles concerning Multinational Enterprises and Social Policy* (adopted by the Governing Body of the International Labour Office at its 204th Session (Nov. 1977) as amended at its 279th Session (Nov. 2000)) also aims to encourage the positive contribution of business to labor and human rights standards. The OECD *Guidelines for Multinational Enterprises*, reprinted as amended in 40 I.L.M. 237 (2000), are recommendations to businesses from the 30 OECD member states and eight adhering non-member states concerning conduct in many areas of business ethics. While essentially promotional in character, the OECD Guidelines include a monitoring mechanism consisting of National Contact Points appointed by adhering states. One of their responsibilities is to contribute to the resolution of specific issues that arise relating to the implementation of the Guidelines.

The most recent international attempt to articulate the proper relationship between business and human rights is the *Norms on the Responsibilities of Transnational Corporations and Other Business Enterprises with Regard to Human Rights*, adopted by the Sub-Commission on the Promotion and Protection of Human Rights in 2003. According to their primary author, then-Sub-Commission member David Weissbrodt, "the document was binding in the sense that it applied human rights law under ratified conventions to the activities of transnational corporations and other business enterprises. Moreover, the language of the document emphasized binding responsibilities through the use of the term 'shall' rather than 'should,' and the draft norms included measures for implementation." UN Doc. E/CN.4/Sub.2/2002/13, at 6 (Aug. 6, 2002).

Reaction to the Sub-Commission's work by the Commission on Human Rights was less than enthusiastic, however, and the Commission explicitly noted that it had not requested that the norms be prepared and that "as a draft proposal, [the Sub-Commission report] has no legal standing, and that the Sub-Commission should not perform any monitoring function in this regard." Comm'n H.R., Dec. 2004/116, para. c (April 20, 2004). The Commission nonetheless requested the High Commissioner for Human Rights, inter alia, "to compile a report setting out the scope and legal status of existing initiatives and standards relating to the responsibility of transnational corporations and related business enterprises with regard to human rights." Id., para. b. Extracts from that report follow the Norms themselves, which are set out immediately below.

Sub-Comm'n on the Promotion and Protection of Human Rights, Norms on the Responsibilities of Transnational Corporations and Other Business Enterprises with Regard to Human Rights

UN Doc. E/CN.4/Sub.2/2003/12/Rev.2 (Aug. 26, 2003)

. . .

A. *General obligations*

1. States have the primary responsibility to promote, secure the fulfilment of, respect, ensure respect of and protect human rights recognized in international as well as national law, including ensuring that transnational corporations and other business enterprises respect human rights. Within their respective spheres of activity and influence, transnational corporations and other business enterprises have the obligation to promote, secure the fulfilment of, respect, ensure respect of and protect human rights recognized in international as well as national law, including the rights and interests of indigenous peoples and other vulnerable groups.

B. *Right to equal opportunity and non-discriminatory treatment*

2. Transnational corporations and other business enterprises shall ensure equality of opportunity and treatment, as provided in the relevant international

instruments and national legislation as well as international human rights law, for the purpose of eliminating discrimination based on race, colour, sex, language, religion, political opinion, national or social origin, social status, indigenous status, disability, age — except for children, who may be given greater protection — or other status of the individual unrelated to the inherent requirements to perform the job, or of complying with special measures designed to overcome past discrimination against certain groups.

C. *Right to security of persons*

3. Transnational corporations and other business enterprises shall not engage in nor benefit from war crimes, crimes against humanity, genocide, torture, forced disappearance, forced or compulsory labour, hostage-taking, extrajudicial, summary or arbitrary executions, other violations of humanitarian law and other international crimes against the human person as defined by international law, in particular human rights and humanitarian law.

4. Security arrangements for transnational corporations and other business enterprises shall observe international human rights norms as well as the laws and professional standards of the country or countries in which they operate.

D. *Rights of workers*

5. Transnational corporations and other business enterprises shall not use forced or compulsory labour as forbidden by the relevant international instruments and national legislation as well as international human rights and humanitarian law.

6. Transnational corporations and other business enterprises shall respect the rights of children to be protected from economic exploitation as forbidden by the relevant international instruments and national legislation as well as international human rights and humanitarian law.

7. Transnational corporations and other business enterprises shall provide a safe and healthy working environment as set forth in relevant international instruments and national legislation as well as international human rights and humanitarian law.

8. Transnational corporations and other business enterprises shall provide workers with remuneration that ensures an adequate standard of living for them and their families. Such remuneration shall take due account of their needs for adequate living conditions with a view towards progressive improvement.

9. Transnational corporations and other business enterprises shall ensure freedom of association and effective recognition of the right to collective bargaining by protecting the right to establish and, subject only to the rules of the organization concerned, to join organizations of their own choosing without distinction, previous authorization, or interference, for the protection of their employment interests and for other collective bargaining purposes as provided in national legislation and the relevant conventions of the International Labour Organization.

E. *Respect for national sovereignty and human rights*

10. Transnational corporations and other business enterprises shall recognize and respect applicable norms of international law, national laws and regulations, as well as administrative practices, the rule of law, the public interest, development objectives, social, economic and cultural policies including transparency, accountability and prohibition of corruption, and authority of the countries in which the enterprises operate.

11. Transnational corporations and other business enterprises shall not offer, promise, give, accept, condone, knowingly benefit from, or demand a bribe or other improper advantage, nor shall they be solicited or expected to give a bribe or other improper advantage to any Government, public official, candidate for elective post, any member of the armed forces or security forces, or any other individual or organization. Transnational corporations and other business enterprises shall refrain from any activity which supports, solicits, or encourages States or any other entities to abuse human rights. They shall further seek to ensure that the goods and services they provide will not be used to abuse human rights.

12. Transnational corporations and other business enterprises shall respect economic, social and cultural rights as well as civil and political rights and contribute to their realization, in particular the rights to development, adequate food and drinking water, the highest attainable standard of physical and mental health, adequate housing, privacy, education, freedom of thought, conscience, and religion and freedom of opinion and expression, and shall refrain from actions which obstruct or impede the realization of those rights.

F. *Obligations with regard to consumer protection*

13. Transnational corporations and other business enterprises shall act in accordance with fair business, marketing and advertising practices and shall take all necessary steps to ensure the safety and quality of the goods and services they provide, including observance of the precautionary principle. Nor shall they produce, distribute, market, or advertise harmful or potentially harmful products for use by consumers.

G. *Obligations with regard to environmental protection*

14. Transnational corporations and other business enterprises shall carry out their activities in accordance with national laws, regulations, administrative practices and policies relating to the preservation of the environment of the countries in which they operate, as well as in accordance with relevant international agreements, principles, objectives, responsibilities and standards with regard to the environment as well as human rights, public health and safety, bioethics and the precautionary principle, and shall generally conduct their activities in a manner contributing to the wider goal of sustainable development.

H. *General provisions of implementation*

15. As an initial step towards implementing these Norms, each transnational corporation or other business enterprise shall adopt, disseminate and implement internal rules of operation in compliance with the Norms. . . .

16. Transnational corporations and other business enterprises shall be subject to periodic monitoring and verification by United Nations, other international and national mechanisms already in existence or yet to be created, regarding application of the Norms. . . .

I. Definitions. . . .

23. The phrases "human rights" and "international human rights" include civil, cultural, economic, political and social rights, as set forth in the International Bill of Human Rights and other human rights treaties, as well as the right to development and rights recognized by international humanitarian law, international refugee law, international labour law, and other relevant instruments adopted within the United Nations system.

Report of the United Nations High Commissioner on Human Rights on the Responsibilities of Transnational Corporations and Related Business Enterprises with Regard to Human Rights

UN Doc. E/CN.4/2005/91 (Feb. 15, 2005)

7. Initiatives and standards relevant to corporate and social responsibility have increased rapidly over the last 15 years. The consultation process alone identified over 200 existing initiatives and standards . . . [which] can be categorized as follows:

(a) *International instruments.* International instruments such as treaties and declarations can be directed at States but of relevance to business — such as the Organization for Economic Cooperation and Development Convention on Combating Bribery of Foreign Public Officials in International Business Transactions — and directed specifically at business: such as the International Labour Organization Tripartite Declaration of Principles concerning Multinational Enterprises and Social Policy and the OECD Guidelines for Multinational Enterprises;

(b) *Nationally based standards.* Nationally, legally based standards include constitutional provisions, national laws and national regulations of relevance to business activities. Nationally based standards can also have extraterritorial effect, such as the United States Alien Tort Claims Act;

(c) *Certification schemes.* Certification schemes are programmes established by an organization, group or network requiring adherence to a set of principles. Upon adherence, the scheme is generally monitored independently to ensure compliance. The Worldwide Responsible Apparel Protection (WRAP) certification program, the SA8000 certification scheme and the Kimberley Process Certification Scheme are examples;

(d) *Voluntary initiatives.* Voluntary initiatives include codes of conduct, directive policies, third-party and self-reporting initiatives established by individual companies, groups of companies, intergovernmental organizations or civil society groups and adopted by business on a voluntary basis. The Secretary-General's United Nations Global Compact provides an example of a voluntary initiative backed by the United Nations. Intergovernmental voluntary initiatives include the Voluntary Principles on Security and Human Rights for the extractive and energy sectors and the Extractive Industries Transparency Initiative. Non-governmental voluntary initiatives include the Global Sullivan Principles, the Caux Round Table Principles for Business and International Peace Operations Associations Code of Conduct. In the consultation process, individual companies — BASF, P, Gap, Nexen, Pfizer, Rio Tinto, Shell, SONOFON, Storebrand and Telefonica — provided information on their voluntary initiatives;

(e) *Mainstream financial indices.* These are sets of social and environmental indices based on objective criteria against which companies are monitored as a means of changing the nature of business activities through investors and markets. Examples include the FTSE4Good Index and the Goldman Sachs Energy Environmental and Social Index;

(f) *Tools, meetings and other initiatives.* These initiatives seek to promote greater understanding of and respect for human rights in a variety of forms, including methodologies for undertaking human rights impact assessments, management tools, training manuals, workshops, pilot projects, multi-stakeholder consultations, public-private partnerships and so on. The Business Leaders' Initiative for Human Rights (BLIHR) and the Danish Institute for Human Rights and Business Project provide examples in this category. . . .

27. In considering the responsibilities of business with regard to human rights, it is important to reiterate that States are the primary duty bearers of human rights. While business can affect the enjoyment of human rights significantly, business plays a distinct role in society, holds different objectives, and influences human rights different to States. The responsibilities of States cannot therefore simply be transferred to business; the responsibilities of the latter must be defined separately, in proportion to its nature and activities. . . .

What are the boundaries of the responsibilities of business with regard to human rights?

36. In contrast to the limits on States' human rights obligations, the boundaries of the human rights responsibilities of business are not easily defined by reference to territorial limits. While a small business might have relatively limited influence over the enjoyment of human rights within a particular country, a large company might influence the enjoyment of human rights across boundaries. Defining the boundaries of business responsibility for human rights therefore requires the consideration of other factors such as the size of the company, the relationship with its partners, the nature of its operations, and the proximity of people to its operations.

37. A helpful means to understand the scope and boundaries of the responsibilities of business is the non-legal concept of "sphere of influence." The concept has not been defined authoritatively; however the "sphere of influence" of a business entity tends to include the individuals to whom it has a certain political, contractual, economic or geographic proximity. Every business entity, whatever its size, will have a sphere of influence; the larger it is, the larger the sphere of influence is likely to be. It is relevant to note that the Global Compact asks participating business entities "to embrace, support and enact, within their sphere of influence" its ten principles.

38. The notion of "sphere of influence" could be useful in clarifying the extent to which business entities should "support" human rights and "make sure they are not complicit in human rights abuses" by setting limits on responsibilities according to a business entity's power to act. Importantly, "sphere of influence" could help clarify the boundaries of responsibilities of business entities in relation to other entities in the supply chain such as subsidiaries, agents, suppliers and buyers by guiding an assessment of the degree of influence that one company exerts over a partner in its contractual relationship — and therefore the extent to which it is responsible for the acts or omissions or a subsidiary or a partner down the supply chain. At the same time, "sphere of influence" should help draw the boundaries between the responsibilities of business and the obligations on States so that business entities do not take on the policing role of Government. Finally, the notion of "sphere of influence" could ensure that smaller business entities are not forced to undertake over-burdensome human rights responsibilities, but only responsibilities towards people within their limited sphere of influence. . . .

How can the responsibilities of business with regard to human rights be guaranteed?

43. Ensuring that business respects human rights is first a matter of State action at the domestic level. States have undertaken international obligations to respect the rights of individuals and groups of individuals and to protect those rights against the actions of third parties; those third parties include business entities. Many countries have introduced human rights implementing legislation that regulates business entities in areas such as discrimination and workers' human rights. Courts and quasi-judicial tribunals enforce these laws.

44. Companies also have an important role to play in ensuring that they protect human rights standards in their own operations. Voluntary initiatives on business and human rights can help to promote a culture of respect for human rights from within the company and can give human rights standards practical meaning while motivating positive change in support of human rights. Companies can also promote human rights in their relationships with business partners through the inclusion of contractual terms stipulating respect for human rights as part of a business deal. Similarly, markets mechanisms have a role to play in ensuring respect for human rights through the use of environmental and social indices and public reporting on social responsibility which rates the performance of business entities, which in turn can affect market confidence and motivate better performance.

45. Nonetheless, company and market initiatives have their limits and are not necessarily comprehensive in their coverage nor a substitute for legislative action. Importantly, while voluntary business action in relation to human rights works for the well-intentioned and could effectively raise the standard of other companies, there remains scepticism amongst sectors of civil society as to their overall effectiveness.

46. There is also a question of how to ensure respect for human rights in situations where effective governance or accountability are absent because the State is unwilling or unable to protect human rights — for example due to a lack of control over its territories, weak judiciary, lack of political will or corruption. A lack of appropriate regulation and enforcement by the State could fail to check human rights abuses adequately while also encourage a climate of impunity. A particularly complex issue involves the regulation of companies headquartered in one country,

operating in a second and having assets in a third. There is concern that business entities might evade the jurisdictional power of States in some situations, which could lead to negative consequences for the enjoyment of human rights.

47. Increasing attention is being given to whether and to what extent parent companies should be subject to the law and jurisdiction of their home countries in relation to their operations abroad. The United States Alien Tort Claims Act provides one example of a home country measure which gives courts power to hear civil claims by foreign citizens for injuries caused by actions in violation of the law of nations or a treaty of the United States although other examples also exist. Subjecting parent companies to their home jurisdiction for alleged human rights abuses against claimants of the host country raises questions of respect for the national sovereignty of the host country while also highlighting several complex legal questions which require further examination. Nonetheless, home country regulation could provide an effective means of protecting human rights in situations where accountability gaps exist.

Following submission of the High Commissioner's report, the Commission adopted a resolution in which it recognized that transnational corporations and other business enterprises can contribute to the enjoyment of human rights, *inter alia*, through investment, employment creation and the stimulation of economic growth. Comm'n H.R. Res. 2005/69, pmbl. (April 20, 2005). The resolution requested the Secretary-General to appoint a special representative on the issue of human rights and transnational corporations and other business enterprises, for an initial two-year period, whose mandate will include: a) identifying and clarifying the standards of corporate responsibility and accountability for transnational corporations and other business enterprises with regard to human rights; b) elaborating on the role of States in effectively regulating and adjudicating the role of transnational corporations and other business enterprises with regard to human rights, including through international cooperation; c) researching and clarifying the implications for transnational corporations and other business enterprises of concepts such as "complicity"and "sphere of influence"; d) developing materials and methodologies for undertaking human rights impact assessments of the activities of transnational corporations and other business enterprises; and e) compiling a compendium of best practices of States and transnational corporations and other business enterprises. Id., para. 1. Although there is no reference to the Sub-Commission's norms, they clearly inspired the Commission's response.

B. *Potential Domestic Liability of Corporations for Human Rights Abuses*

As Chapter 6 discusses in detail, the U.S. Alien Tort Statute (ATS), 28 U.S.C. §1350, provides that the federal courts have jurisdiction over actions brought in tort by an alien for violations of a treaty of the United States or the law of nations. In 2004, the United States Supreme Court for the first time interpreted and applied this statute in the case of *Sosa v. Alvarez Machain*, 124 S.Ct. 2739 (2004). In so doing, as the following extract describes, the Court briefly addressed some issues of corporate liability for human rights violations outside the United States.

Ralph Steinhardt, *Laying One Bankrupt Critique to Rest:* Sosa v. Alvarez Machain *and the Future of International Human Rights Litigation in U.S. Courts*

57 Vand. L. Rev. 2241, 2283-87 (2004)

The first significant battle over the interpretation of *Alvarez-Machain* II [*Sosa v. Alvarez Machain*, 124 S.Ct. 2739 (2004)] will come in a variety of cases testing whether corporate actors may be liable under the ATS [Alien Tort Statute] for their complicity in human rights abuses by the government with which they do business. Many such cases have been dismissed on jurisdictional, political, or factual grounds, and others have been derailed under the forum non conveniens doctrine. Especially in the context of cases arising out of World War II against Japanese and Germany government entities or corporations, the treaties ending the war have been interpreted to render additional compensation or reparations a matter for the executive branch. If anything, the corporate cases that have actually been decided reaffirm that the courts have the necessary tools to distinguish non justiciable or frivolous claims from those that are meritorious.

No part of *Alvarez-Machain II* turned on the circumstances under which a corporation faces liability for a breach of international law, but the government and a coalition of business interests had urged the Court to interpret the ATS so as to bar such actions. The Court implicitly rejected the propositions that corporations are *in principle* immune from liability under international law or that the prospect of abusive lawsuits required narrow interpretation of the ATS. Instead, the Court reasoned only that "the determination whether a norm is sufficiently definite to support a cause of action" is "related [to] whether international law extends the scope of liability for a violation of a given norm to the perpetrator being sued, if the defendant is a private actor such as a corporation or individual." For these purposes, the Court contrasted torture, which does require state action in order to be a violation of international law, with genocide which does not. The Court also noted a particular set of pending class actions "seeking damages from various corporations alleged to have participated in, or abetted, the regime of apartheid that formerly controlled South Africa," but rather than decide that all such cases were beyond the reach of the ATS, the Court declared instead that "[i]n such cases, there is a strong argument that federal courts should give serious weigh to the Executive Branch's view of the case's impact on foreign policy."

For centuries, the imposition of individual liability for certain international wrongs (e.g., piracy) has generated little controversy. Certainly the framers of the First Judiciary Act of 1789 had little doubt that private citizens who infringed the rights of ambassadors or diplomats could be sued under Section 1350. Pirates, the exemplar of intended defendants under the ATS, were not always or necessarily considered state actors, but there was never any question that their actions violated international law; indeed, one of the earliest exercises of jurisdiction under the ATS involved an unlawful seizure of property by a non state actor. The statute subsequently provided jurisdiction over a child custody dispute that involved a breach of the law of nations. In settings other than *Alvarez-Machain II*, the executive branch has concluded that corporations are in principle capable of violating the law of nations or a treaty of the United States for purposes of the

ATS, and that conclusion is consistent with well-established international norms to which the United States has given its assent. Specific treaties establish that private actors may be punished for acts of genocide, slavery, and war crimes. These regimes do not distinguish between natural and juridical individuals, and corporations that engage in the slave trade or commit acts of genocide or provide corporate cover for war crimes would not as a matter of law be exempt from liability. "Certain forms of conduct violate the law of nations whether undertaken by those acting under the auspices of a state or only as private individuals."

This suggests that there are at least two distinct circumstances in which a corporation (or any other private actor) might bear international responsibility: (1) a category of per se wrongs, in which the corporation "like any individual" commits one of that narrow class of wrongs identified by treaty or custom as not requiring state action to be considered wrongful; and (2) a category of contextual wrongs, in which the corporation's conduct is sufficiently infused with state action as to engage international standard. To date, no corporation has been found liable under the ATS under either theory, but both remain viable in the aftermath of Alvarez-Machain II, despite the strong position staked out by business groups as amici curiae.

As noted supra page 326, Ken Saro-Wiwa, one of the Ogoni leaders, was executed by the Nigerian government. Some of his relatives filed an action in U.S. courts under the Alien Tort Statute, alleging that the defendant companies directly or indirectly participated in or directed the grave human rights abuses that occurred in the Ogoni region and that are described in the case filed against Nigeria with the African Commission, supra page 355. The district court initially dismissed the action on grounds of *forum non conveniens,* after determining that the United Kingdom was an adequate alternative forum and that a balancing of public interest and private interest factors made the British forum preferable. Plaintiffs appealed, arguing, inter alia, that the district court erred in not affording sufficient weight to the plaintiffs' choice of forum and to the interests of the United States in providing a forum for the adjudication of claims of abuse of international human rights. On appeal, the circuit court affirmed in part and reversed in part, holding that the district court properly exercised jurisdiction over the defendants and should not have dismissed for *forum non conveniens*. 226 F.3d 88 (2d Cir. 2000). When the case was remanded, defendants moved to dismiss for failure to state a claim.

Wiwa v. Royal Dutch Petroleum Co. and Shell Transport & Trading Co. P.L.C.

2002 U.S. Dist. LEXIS 3293, No. 96 CIV. 8386 (KMW) (S.D.N.Y. Feb. 28, 2002) (notes and citations omitted)

Wood, D.J.

Presently before the Court are: (1) defendants' motion to dismiss the actions for lack of subject matter jurisdiction; (2) defendants' motion to dismiss claims for failure to state a claim for which relief may be granted; (3) defendants' motion to abstain on the basis of the act of state doctrine; and (4) defendant Anderson's motion to dismiss on the grounds of *forum non conveniens*. For the reasons stated below, the Court grants defendants' motion to dismiss pursuant to Fed.R.Civ.P. 12(b)(6) with respect to two claims only: Owens Wiwa's Alien Tort Claims Act claims, 18 U.S.C. §1350 ["ACTA"], founded on an alleged violation of his right to life, liberty and security of person, and his ACTA claim for arbitrary arrest and detention. Plaintiffs are given 30 days from the date of this Order to re-plead those claims. Defendants' motion to dismiss is denied in all other respects.

Background

A. The Parties

Plaintiffs are three former citizens and residents of Nigeria, as well as a Nigerian citizen identified only as Jane Doe. Plaintiff Ken Wiwa, who brings this action individually and as executor of the estate of his father, Ken Saro-Wiwa, is a citizen and resident of Great Britain. (Amended Complaint Against Royal Dutch/Shell, dated April 29, 1997). Plaintiff Owens Wiwa, the brother of Ken Saro-Wiwa, remains a Nigerian citizen but resides in Canada. Plaintiff Blessing Kpuinen, who brings this action individually and as administrator of her husband John Kpuinen's estate, remains a Nigerian citizen but resides in the United States. . . .

Defendants Royal Dutch Petroleum Company and Shell Transport and Trading Company [collectively, "Royal Dutch/Shell"] are incorporated and headquartered in the Netherlands and the United Kingdom respectively. . . . Royal Dutch/ Shell wholly owns The Shell Petroleum Company, Ltd., which in turn wholly owns Shell Petroleum Development Company of Nigeria, Ltd. ["Shell Nigeria"]. . . .

Defendant Brian Anderson was the country chairman of Nigeria for Royal Dutch / Shell and managing Director of Shell Nigeria. (Complaint Against Brian Anderson, dated April 4, 2001). . . . According to plaintiffs, Anderson resides in China. According to Anderson, however, he is a citizen of the United Kingdom and Northern Ireland who maintains residences in Hong Kong and France. . . .

B. Plaintiffs' Factual Allegations

Plaintiff's factual allegations are as follows. Ken Saro-Wiwa was the leader of the Movement for the Survival of the Ogoni People ["MOSOP"]; John Kpuinen was the deputy president of MOSOP's youth wing. MOSOP formed in opposition to the coercive appropriation of Ogoni land without adequate compensation, and the severe damage to the local environment and economy, that resulted from Royal Dutch/Shell's operations in the Ogoni region.

Defendants, operating directly and through Shell Nigeria, recruited the Nigerian police and military to suppress MOSOP and to ensure that defendants' and Shell Nigeria's development activities could proceed "as usual." The corporate defendants, through Anderson, provided logistical support, transportation, and weapons to Nigerian authorities to attack Ogoni villages and stifle opposition to Shell's oil-excavation activities. Ogoni residents, including plaintiffs, were beaten, raped, shot, and/or killed during these raids. Jane Doe was beaten and shot during one raid in 1993, and Owens Wiwa was illegally detained.

In 1995, Ken Saro-Wiwa and John Kpuinen were hanged after being convicted of murder by a special tribunal. Defendants bribed witnesses to testify falsely at the trial, conspired with Nigerian authorities in meetings in Nigeria and the Netherlands to orchestrate the trial, and offered to free Ken Saro-Wiwa in return for an end to MOSOP's international protests against defendants. During the trial, members of Ken Saro-Wiwa's family, including his elderly mother, were beaten.

C. PLAINTIFFS' CLAIMS

1. Claims Against Royal Dutch/Shell

Plaintiffs allege that corporate defendants' conduct violated international and common law, and is actionable under the Alien Tort Claims Act ["ACTA"].... Specifically, plaintiffs assert claims for the following tortious acts: (1) summary execution with respect to the hangings of Ken Saro-Wiwa and John Kpuinen; (2) crimes against humanity, in that general acts perpetrated against plaintiffs were "inhumane . . . [and] of a very serious nature . . . committed as part of a . . . systematic attack against [a] civilian population or persecutions on political, racial or religious grounds"; (3) torture with respect to Ken Saro-Wiwa, John Kpuinen, and Jane Doe; (4) cruel, inhuman, or degrading treatment in that the acts allegedly perpetrated against plaintiffs "had the intent and effect grossly humiliating and debasing the plaintiffs, forcing them to act against their will and conscience [sic], inciting fear and anguish, breaking physical or moral resistance, and forcing them to leave their home and country and flee into exile"; (5) arbitrary arrest and detention with respect to Ken Saro-Wiwa, John Kpuinen, and Owens Wiwa; and (6) violation of the rights to life, liberty and security of person and peaceful assembly and association with respect to Ken-Saro Wiwa, John Kpuinen, Owens Wiwa, and Jane Doe. Plaintiffs also assert the following common law claims under New York, Nigerian, and United States law: (7) wrongful death with respect to Ken Saro-Wiwa and John Kpuinen; (8) assault and battery with respect to all plaintiffs; (9) intentional infliction of emotional distress with respect to all plaintiffs; (10) negligent infliction of emotional distress with respect to all plaintiffs; and (11) negligence with respect to all plaintiffs. Plaintiffs Owens Wiwa and Jane Doe also assert (12) a RICO claim.

2. Claims Against Anderson

Plaintiffs' claims against Anderson differ in three respects from their claims against the corporate defendants. First, plaintiffs allege that some of Anderson's conduct violates, not just the ACTA but also the Torture Victim Protection Act of 1991 ["TVPA"], 28 U.S.C. §1350, note (1993). Second, Jane Doe is not a plaintiff in the action against Anderson. Third, plaintiffs do not assert a RICO claim against Anderson.

DISCUSSION

...

B. LIABILITY UNDER THE ACTA AND TVPA

In their motion to dismiss, defendants argue that plaintiffs' claims under the ACTA and the TVPA are deficient in several respects. First, defendants contend that certain of plaintiffs' claims are inadequate because they are not supported by adequately plead [sic] violations of international law, and that plaintiffs have therefore failed to satisfy the third prong of the ACTA statute (which requires them to plead a violation of "the law of nations"). Second, defendants contend that plaintiffs have not made (and cannot make) a claim under either the TVPA or the ACTA because they have failed to satisfy the state action requirements of these statutes. That is, defendants argue that plaintiffs have failed to plead facts supporting their contention that the corporate defendants or defendant Anderson "acted under color of law."

None of these arguments is persuasive, especially when analyzed under the liberal pleading standard applicable to a motion to dismiss....

1. Violations of International Law by Nigerian Authorities and Defendants....

To summarize, the Court finds that plaintiffs have alleged conduct that violates the rights of Jane Doe and Owens Wiwa as secured under international law, and which therefore constitutes actionable conduct under the ACTA, with respect to the following claims: (1) crimes against humanity with respect to Doe and Owens Wiwa; (2) torture with respect to Doe; (3) cruel, inhuman, or degrading treatment with respect to Doe and Owens Wiwa; (4) violation of the right to life, liberty and security of person with respect to Doe; (5) violation of the right to peaceful assembly and association with respect to Doe and Wiwa. Plaintiffs' allegations of arbitrary arrest and detention, and violation of the right to life, liberty and security of the person with respect to Owens Wiwa do not adequately demonstrate violations of international law, and therefore are not actionable under the ACTA. Plaintiffs are given 30 days from the date of this Order and Opinion to re-plead these two claims.

A. LIABILITY OF PRIVATE ACTORS UNDER ATCA AND TVPA

Having determined that plaintiffs have alleged violations of international human rights law, the Court must next consider whether plaintiffs are required to demonstrate state action in order to support their claims and, if so, whether they have met that burden.

(1) Does the State Action Requirement Apply?

The ACTA and TVPA have similar, albeit not identical, state action requirements. Statutory language makes clear that all claims brought under the TVPA must demonstrate that the alleged violations were perpetrated "under actual or apparent authority, or color of law, of any foreign nation." 28 U.S.C. §1350, note, §2(a). Thus, in order for plaintiffs to sustain their claims against Brian Anderson brought pursuant to the TVPA, they must satisfy the state action requirement....

(2) Corporate Defendants' Liability for the Acts of the Nigerian Authorities

To determine whether a private actor acts under color of law in the context of a claim under ATCA and the TVPA, the Court must look to the standards developed under 42 U.S.C. §1983. See *Kadic I*, 70 F.3d at 242. "A private individual acts under color of law within the meaning of section 1983 when he acts together with state officials or with significant state aid." Id. The relevant test in this case is the "joint action" test, under which private actors are considered state actors if they are "willful participant[s] in joint action with the State or its agents." See *Dennis v. Sparks*, 449 U.S. 24, 27 (1980); see also *Unocal I*, 963 F.Supp. at 891 ("[W]here there is a substantial degree of cooperative action between the state and private actors in effecting the deprivation of rights, state action is present.").

In order to meet this burden in the instant case, plaintiffs have presented two theories of "joint action" that would satisfy the state action requirement. First, they contend that the facts alleged demonstrate a substantial degree of cooperative action between corporate defendants and the Nigerian government in the alleged violations of international law. Second, they argue that the facts demonstrate that Shell Nigeria and the Nigerian government engaged in significant cooperative action that violated plaintiffs' rights, and that corporate defendants had sufficient knowledge of this conduct that they may be held liable for Shell Nigeria's conduct. The Court finds that plaintiffs have pled facts that support their first theory of "joint action" and have therefore demonstrated that corporate defendants acted under color of law in the commission of acts alleged by plaintiffs to have violated international law. The Court need not consider plaintiffs' second theory of state action.

applied

In their Amended Complaint, plaintiffs allege various acts that, if proven, would demonstrate "a substantial degree of cooperative action between" corporate defendants and Nigerian officials in conduct that violated plaintiffs' rights. . . .

Defendants argue that plaintiffs must demonstrate that Royal/Dutch Shell acted in concert with the Nigerian government with respect to each human rights violation allegedly committed against each plaintiff, and have failed to do so in their Amended Complaint. The Court disagrees for three reasons. First, plaintiffs have alleged that defendants jointly collaborated with the Nigerian government in committing several of the claimed violations of international law, such as planning the arbitrary arrest and killing of Ken Saro-Wiwa and John Kpuinen, the attempted bribery of Owens Wiwa, and bribery (or attempted bribery) of witnesses to give false testimony against Saro-Wiwa. Second, under section 1983 jurisprudence, individuals engaged in a conspiracy with government actors to deprive others of their constitutional rights act "under color of law" to commit those violations. See *Dennis*, 449 U.S. at 27-28 (dismissal of section 1983 suit is inappropriate where plaintiff alleges that a private individual engaged in a conspiracy with state officials to deprive another of constitutional rights). Section 1983 case law does not require plaintiffs' complaint to allege that private actors and state actors acted in concert to commit each specific act that violates plaintiffs' rights. See, e.g., *Burton v. Wilmington Parking Authority*, 365 U.S. 715, 724-725 (1961) (finding joint conduct between a government agency and private restaurant based on public ownership and maintenance of the restaurant's leased space, and financial benefits derived by the government from the lease arrangement). Third, Rule 8(a)(2) of the Federal Rules of Civil Procedure requires a complaint to include only "a short and plain statement of the claim showing that the pleader is entitled to relief." . . . The allegations in the Amended Complaint concerning the joint conduct of defendants and the Nigerian government are sufficient to satisfy Rule 8(a)(2), and therefore to survive a challenge pursuant to Rule 12. . . .

D. ACT OF STATE DOCTRINE. . . .

To determine whether to apply the act of state doctrine, the Court should "weigh in balance the foreign policy interests that favor or disfavor [its] application." *Republic of Philippines v. Marcos*, 806 F.2d 344, 359 (2d Cir. 1986). . . . In this case, the military regime responsible for the alleged torts has been replaced by a democracy, and the new government has set up a commission to investigate the alleged abuses. Consequently, any finding of improprieties on the part of the previous regime "would more likely be consonant, than at odds, with the present position of the [Nigerian] government" and thus the danger of hindrance or embarrassment is "dim indeed." *Bigio*, 239 F.3d at 453. . . . Thus, the Court finds no basis to conclude that adjudicating plaintiffs' claims would interfere with Nigerian-American relations, and the Court declines to invoke the act of state doctrine.

CONCLUSION

For the reasons set forth above, the Court grants defendants' motion to dismiss the actions pursuant to Fed.R.Civ.P. 12(b)(6) with respect to two claims: plaintiff Owens Wiwa's ACTA claim founded on an alleged violation of his right to life, liberty and security of person, and his ACTA claim for arbitrary arrest and detention. Plaintiffs are given 30 days from the date of this Order to re-plead these claims. Defendants' motion to dismiss is denied in all other respects.

[The *Wiwa* case was still in litigation as of September 2005.]

C. *A Response from Business*

Some industries and individual companies have responded to concern about their social and environmental impacts by drafting their own codes of conduct. In 2003, the Swiss company Swiss Re became the first reinsurer to focus management attention on liability and corporate social responsibility around the world. It began to consider which policy issues were linked to the essential conditions for insurability. Together with the law firm of Foley Hoag, it sponsored a report by the group SustainAbility, aimed at advising businesses of the need to adopt policies of corporate responsibility.

SustainAbility, The Changing Landscape of Liability: A Director's Guide to Trends in Corporate Environmental, Social and Economic Liability

1, 6, 8-9, 20-21, 30 (2004)

Over recent years, our work with companies has highlighted that there is growing awareness of a connection between the linked Corporate Responsibility/Sustainable Development agendas and risk management. . . .

Around the world, boardrooms are grappling with new and expanded concepts of corporate responsibility, accountability, governance and — increasingly — liability. Companies that have long believed themselves safe from the type of crises experienced by Shell over Nigeria or Nike over child labour are now feeling increasingly vulnerable. In a world characterized by instant global communication and decreasing trust in business, disgruntled or outraged stakeholders are holding companies to account for perceived societal or personal damage, often in a court of law. Perhaps most worryingly for business leaders, companies are being challenged for actions and decisions taken outside their direct line of control, occurring decades if not generations ago, and for impacts never before interpreted as their responsibility. This demands, we believe, robust and strategic approaches to risk management by business leaders if they and their companies are to thrive in the 21st century. . . .

A key message . . . is that the longstanding debate over the balance between voluntary and mandatory requirements is increasingly academic. We see that in many areas, soft and hard forms of liability are converging and blurring: corporate social responsibility standards are progressively shifting from the "soft" voluntary codes into "hard" regulation and legislation, and corporate moral liability is being used to challenge companies in the court of public opinion. Legal compliance is, in essence, the entry fee for companies doing business anywhere in the world. But legal compliance on its own may no longer be enough. Companies that cling chiefly to technical compliance as their business strategy are unlikely to prevail in the court of public opinion even if they succeed in the courts of law. Instead, we argue for a proactive, trust-based approach, firmly grounded in a deep understanding of emerging societal expectations for responsible corporate behavior.

[S]ocietal expectations of responsible business behaviour are rising. The range of areas, therefore, in which moral liability can develop is expanding, particularly around

— Transparency and disclosure.
— Following the spirit and the letter of the law.
— Accepting responsibility for legacy issues.
— Responsible divestment.
— Ethical sourcing.
— Economic equity, including fair trade, fair pricing, and fair taxation. . . .

Recommendations for business

For companies operating in areas with human rights concerns, we would recommend a thorough assessment of the political condition and human rights practices of the countries in which they seek to do business. Seek out experts from human rights NGOs who can provide current information as to the country's human rights protections.

Assess the business for current or potential exposure to human rights risks using progressive codes such as those from the International Labor Organization, the UN Norms on the Responsibilities of Transnational Corporations and Other Business Enterprises, or the Global Compact as a reference point. Pay particular attention to the supply chain (including those elements outside of the company's direct control) and to potential legacy issues (e.g. South Africa or Nazi "collaboration").

Make sure the company's business principles, codes of conduct and internal policies are up to date on human rights. Confirm that conformance is not only to the letter but also to the spirit.

Compare human rights standards for consistency in all operations globally. Where local regulations allow lower standards, assess for alignment with internal business principles/codes/policies as well as with current and emerging societal expectations. Explore and test dilemmas and alternative responses with constructive NGOs/opinion formers.

Consider active rather than passive support for human rights where passive covers local norms of working conditions, diversity and gender equality and active extends to endorsing and promoting (for example) the Universal Declaration of Human Rights and using economic power and influence to improve conditions and to fight abuses in the countries in which it operates.

If involved in areas requiring abnormal levels of security by public or private forces at the site of a project, contracts with security should include a requirement to respect human rights. A monitoring system should be established to ensure human rights guidelines are being followed, and disciplinary proceedings should be initiated when rights are violated.

Know which voluntary principles or standards your company is signed up to and commitments your company has made and check for compliance to the letter and the spirit.

Build internal education at all levels of management to new norms and expectations of corporate behaviour in relation to human rights.

Comments and Questions

1. The debate over the role of corporate codes of conduct in efforts to promote and protect human rights has received considerable attention in recent years. See, e.g., Emekia A. Duruigo, *Multinational Corporations and International Law: Accountability and Compliance Issues in the Petroleum Industry* (2003); *Human Rights Standards and the Responsibility of Transnational Corporations* (Michael K. Addo ed. 1999); Sean D. Murphy, *Taking Multinational Corporate Codes of Conduct to the Next Level*, 43 Colum. J. Transnat'l L. 389 (2005); Robin Broad and John Cavanagh, *The Corporate Accountability Movement: Lessons and Opportunities*, 23 Fletcher F. World Aff. 151 (1999); Barbara A. Frey, *The Legal and Ethical Responsibilities of Transnational Corporations* in the Protection of International Human Rights, 6 Minn. J. Global Trade 153 (1997). On the particular problem presented in this chapter see Human Rights Watch, "The Price of Oil: Corporate Responsibility and Human Rights Violations in Nigeria's Oil Producing Communities" (1999).

2. The Nigerian Senate adopted a resolution ordering Shell Petroleum Development Company of Nigeria to pay $1.5 billion as compensation for environmental degradation, health problems, and loss of livelihood in the area being exploited. Is it appropriate for the new government to seek redress for a joint venture in which the prior government was involved? See John Yarney, *Shell Rejects Nigerian Senate Order to Pay Compensation for Environmental Damage*, 27 BNA Int'l Env't Rep. 708 (2004). Why did the Senate not mention human rights violations?

3. Reread Norms 10 and 12, supra page 381. As corporate counsel to a multinational corporation, how would you explain to your employer just what behavior was expected of it? Do the Norms adopted by the UN Sub-Commission impose greater responsibilities on business entities than human rights law imposes on states? Do you think that they are appropriate and would be acceptable to most businesses? States are normally obligated to respect human rights with respect to persons "within their jurisdiction" [see the discussion in Chapter 8, pages 621-647]; should corporations be obliged to respect human rights anywhere within their "sphere of influence"? For a fuller discussion of the Norms by their primary author, see David Weissbrodt and Muria Kruger, *Norms on the Responsibilities of Transnational Corporations and Other Business Enterprises with Regard to Human Rights*, 97 Am. J. Int'l L. 901 (2003).

4. Do you agree that "the longstanding debate over the balance between voluntary and mandatory requirements is increasingly academic"? Do we not need to maintain the distinction between decisions corporations (and other actors) may take because they are politically or economically desirable and those that they are legally obliged to take? If we do not, do we strengthen "soft" norms or weaken "hard" norms? Or both?

5. If it is clear that there are viable theories under which one may hold corporations civilly liable under international law pursuant to the ATS, why has no case thus far imposed liability? How significant is it that, following the *Alvarez-Machain* case, Unocal Corp. settled for substantial damages an Alien Tort case brought by Burmese nationals who had alleged that Unocal was complicit in forced labor and other human rights violations in connection with a pipeline being built in Burma? See *Doe v. Unocal Corp.*, 2002 WL 31063976 (9th Cir. 2002) (upholding a complaint under ATS against Unocal). On February 14, 2003, the Ninth Circuit granted a motion for rehearing *en banc* and ordered that the panel decision could not be cited as precedent within the Circuit. *Doe v. Unocal Corp.*, Nos. 00-56603, 00-57197 (9th Cir. Feb. 14, 2003); see Lisa Girion, *U.S. Court Will Rehear Case Against Unocal*, L.A. Times, Feb. 15, 2003. The suit settled before the en banc ruling. Do you have sufficient information to determine how the *Wiwa* case should be decided on the merits?

6. In the *Wiwa* case, supra page 387, the court found, inter alia, that the rights to peaceful assembly and association were guaranteed under international law. Since the Alien Tort Statute requires pleading a violation of "the law of nations," does this mean that peaceful assembly and association now form part of customary international law?

7. Among the more significant cases seeking to hold corporations accountable for alleged human rights violations, see *In re South African Apartheid Litigation*, 346 F.Supp. 2d 538 (S.D.N.Y. 2004); *Aguinda v. Texaco, Inc.* 303 F.3d 470 (2d Cir. 2002); *Sarai v. Rio Tinto*, 221 F. Supp. 2d 1116 (C.D. Cal. 2002); *Joo v. Japan*, 332 F.3d 679 (D.C. Cir. 2003), vacated and remanded 124 S.Ct. 2835 (2004); *Presbyterian Church of Sudan v. Talisman Energy, Inc.*, 244 F.Supp. 2d 289 (S.D.N.Y. 2003). For commentary on the issue, see Courtney Shaw, *Uncertain Justice: Liability of Multinationals under the Alien Tort Claims Act*, 54 Stan. L. Rev. 1359 (2002); Steven Ratner, *Corporations and Human Rights: A Theory of Legal Responsibility*, 111 Yale L.J. 443 (2001); Elliott Schrage, *Judging Corporate Accountability in the Global Economy*, 42 Colum. J. Transnat'l L. 153 (2003).

IV. Do International Organizations Have Human Rights Obligations?

International organizations are taking on a multitude of new roles, from election observing to establishment of mixed national-international criminal tribunals to de facto governance of states emerging from violent conflict. With these new roles, they are being pushed to be accountable for their own conduct measured by international law. Three issues have been prominent in discussions of human rights and international organizations: the role of international financial institutions, trade and human rights, and the responsibility of the United Nations for its peacekeepers.

A. *International Financial Institutions*

The World Bank and the International Monetary Fund were created in 1944 to assist in the reconstruction of Europe and Asia after the Second World War, although the Bank has since turned its attention to the economic problems of developing countries. The IMF works closely with the Bank on economic policy, but is more concerned with financial markets and stability than with development and poverty. The Bank is founded on Articles of Agreement supplemented with by-laws approved by the member states. A Board of Governors meets once a year to set policy for the Bank while on-going operations are handled by a 24-member Board of Executive Directors that meets weekly. The Bank President acts as the Chair of the Board of Executive Directors. Voting in the Bank is weighted and based upon financial shares that correspond in large part to the global economic rank of the member state. The seven largest industrial states (G-7) hold about 45% of the voting shares at the Bank. Generally, however, decisions are taken by consensus.

The World Bank Group is comprised of five associated institutions: the International Bank for Reconstruction and Development, the International Development Association, the International Finance Corporation, the Multilateral Investment Guarantee Agency, and the International Center for the Settlement of Investment Disputes. The Group uses financial instruments to promote sustainable development, including by loan arrangements, long-term low-interest concessional credits and grants made to the poorest countries, partial risk guarantees, and private sector debt and equity. IBRD and IDA provide loans for public-sector projects, with IDA providing concessional or low-cost loans to the poorest countries and IBRD providing loans to other developing countries and to countries in transition. The IFC finances private sector projects and MIGA provides insurance against the risks of loss private investors face in developing countries.

The Bank's Articles of Agreement do not mention human rights. During the past decade, however, the World Bank has addressed social issues through the development of ten "Safeguard Policies" and through the work of the Inspection Panel established in 1993. In doing so, the Bank recognized the connection between economic issues and social issues. In 1998 the Bank decided to reorganize its Operational Manual around related themes. Key policies were grouped together, including Involuntary Resettlement (OP 4.12, Dec. 2001), Indigenous Peoples (OD 4.20, Sept. 1991), Cultural Property (OP 11.03, Sept. 1986), Safety of Dams (OP 4.37, Sept. 1996), International Waterways (OP 7.50, Oct. 1994), and Projects in Disputed Areas (OP 7.60, Nov. 1994). Disclosure of Information applies to all ten safeguard policies according to the new Disclosure Policy which came into effect in January 2002.

The International Monetary Fund (IMF) Articles of Agreement provide that the mandate of the Fund is economic. The World Bank similarly was designed with a limited, specific purpose in mind. The Fund's purpose is unequivocally targeted to attaining financial stability in the international economic arena and is largely concerned with trade balances, exchange rate stability, and balance of payments. See Jorge Daniel Taillant, *Human Rights and International Financial Institutions* (June 2002), *http://www.cedha.org.ar*. The success of the international financial institutions in reconstructing post-war Europe and assisting development in other regions of the world has given rise to a new set of problems and issues. Today, the Bank recognizes that its primary focus is to help the poorest people and the poorest countries. What is the role of human rights in this new focus?

According to Taillant, "Both institutions have strongly resisted assuming any responsibility for the assurance or guarantee of human rights. The standard argument of the IFIs [International Financial Institutions] on this approach centers on the IFIs unwillingness to place conditionality on countries for not complying with human rights obligations under the treaties they have signed. They do not wish to become human rights policemen. This position is strongly echoed in the IFI's Executive Directors' board rooms where countries like China are vehemently opposed to international bodies reacting to their human rights performance." Many developing countries view such conditionality as pretextual and a means to maintain western economic dominance.

Nonetheless, the UN Commission on Human Rights has suggested that multilateral financial and trade institutions must conform their policies and practices to international human rights norms. In practice this may be accomplished by action taken by the member states. In Resolution 2005/17 (April 14, 2001), the Commission recognized that "in addition to States' separate responsibilities to their individual societies, they have a collective responsibility to uphold the principles of human dignity, equality and equity at the global level as an essential element in the construction and shaping of an ethnical foundation for globalization." Para. 2. The UN Sub-Commission affirmed "the importance and relevance of human rights obligations in all areas of development, including international and regional trade, investment and financial policies and practices, while confirming that this in no way implies the imposition of conditionalities upon aid to development." Sub-Comm'n Res. 2001/5 (Aug. 15, 2001), para. 2. The Sub-Commission urged all governments and "international economic policy forums" to take international human rights obligations fully into account in international economic policy formulation. Id., para. 3.

The World Bank established an Inspection Panel in 1993 because of growing concerns about the accountability of it and other international development agencies in supporting projects and programs. The Panel is an independent investigatory body that receives and investigates complaints from those in the territory of a borrower whose rights or interests have been adversely affect by the Bank's failure to comply with its policies and procedures in the design, appraisal, and implementation of a Bank-financed project. The Panel may investigate complaints upon authorization by the Bank's Board of Executive Directors and assess to what extent the Bank has complied with its own standards. At the first stage, the Panel registers the request and asks Management to respond to the concerns expressed in it. The Panel then assesses whether or not the request meets the eligibility requirements, in particular, whether prima facie the Bank has engaged in a serious violation of its operational policies and procedures resulting or likely to result in material and adverse harm to those making the request and to which Management has failed to respond adequately. On the basis of this assessment, the Panel recommends to the Executive Directors whether or not to authorize an investigation. If authorized, the Panel investigates the merits and reaches findings. The process can result in a remedial action plan requiring management to take action.

In its first five years, the Panel received 17 requests for inspection. Two were outside the mandate; of the 15 remaining, 13 concerned infrastructure, environmental and land reform projects, while two related to adjustment operations. The Panel recommended investigation in six cases but was only authorized to investigate two matters. In four other cases, a type of friendly settlement under Panel verification was reached.

Two outside reviews have led to clarifications and changes in the operation of the Inspection Panel. The first review, in 1996, focused on procedure. The Second Inspection Panel Review, completed in 1999, added to and revised the 1996 conclusions. The results clarify that the initial (admissibility) stage of the procedure must focus on assertions of non-compliance and resulting potential or material harm; it is not a decision on the merits involving a true finding of harm. The issue of non-compliance is antecedent to the issue of harm and supports the notion of the Inspection Panel as a mechanism of accountability rather than a true remedial procedure. Other conclusions focus on the Panel's role in monitoring the Bank's non-compliance with its own policies and procedures. The 1999 review of the panel paid particular attention to the relatively small number of full reviews that had been undertaken by the Panel. The "Clarifications" make clear that the Board will authorize an investigation recommended by the Panel without making any judgment on the merits or without discussion, except in relation to "technical eligibility criteria" or admissibility requirements. The Clarifications emphasize the non-judicial function of the Panel and its absence of authority to interpret the legal instruments involved in the request. If issues of interpretation arise, the Panel is to seek the advice of the Legal Department.

Efforts to extend the Inspection Panel to private sector funding were opposed by the relevant institutions (IFC/MIGA), who instead appointed a Compliance Adviser/Ombudsman with different terms of reference, a more flexible confidential procedure, and emphasis on mitigating damage. The cooperation of the Bank and the private International Finance Corporation means that, in some instances, both procedures may apply to a single project, e.g. the Chad/Cameroon Pipeline and the Bujagali Hydropower Project in Uganda.*

On the World Bank Inspection Panel, see Dana Clark and Jonathan Fox, eds., *Demanding Accountability: Civil Society Claims and the World Bank Inspection Panel* (2003). A history of the evolution of the panel can be found in Ibrahim F.I. Shihata, *The World Bank Inspection Panel* (1994). The Bank's Operational Policies can be found at *http://wbln0018.worldbank.org/institutional/manuals/opmanual.nsf/textonly*.

* The above summary is drawn from Alexandre Kiss and Dinah Shelton, *International Environmental Law* 87-88 (3d ed. 2004).

IBRD/World Bank, Development and Human Rights: The Role of the World Bank

2-4, 5-6, 8, 11, 12, 30 (1998) (emphasis in original)

. . . The World Bank believes that creating the conditions for the attainment of human rights is a central and irreducible goal of development. By placing the dignity of every human being — especially the poorest — at the very foundation of its approach to development, the Bank helps people in every part of the world build lives of purpose and hope. And while the Bank has always taken measures to ensure that human rights are fully respected in connection with the projects it supports, it has been less forthcoming about articulating its role in promoting human rights within the countries in which it operates. . . .

The world now accepts that sustainable development is impossible without human rights. What has been missing is the recognition that the advancement of an interconnected set of human rights is impossible *without development*. Enlightened legislation and vigorous civil society are essential. But they are not enough. Human rights are in a sense both the design *and* the product of people organized through government. They don't just happen. Many public services will only reach the poor if governments are both capable of delivering them, and do so without the obstacles of corruption; laws created to end child labor will be more effective in economic conditions that allow families to live off of the incomes of parents; and legal rights are better pursued in effective court systems.

The Bank contributes directly to the fulfillment of many rights articulated in the Universal Declaration. Through its support of primary education, health care and nutrition, sanitation, housing, and the environment, the Bank has helped hundreds of millions of people attain crucial economic and social rights. In other areas, the Bank's contributions are necessarily less direct, but perhaps equally significant. By helping to fight corruption, improve transparency and accountability in governance, strengthen judicial systems, and modernize financial sectors, the Bank contributes to building environments in which people are better able to pursue a broader range of human rights.

. . . The Bank's Articles of Agreement set out its broad scope of activity in economic and social development. They also establish guidelines that limit the range of its activities. In particular, the Articles state that, in all its decisions, "only economic considerations shall be relevant." Some believe that this restriction prevents the Bank from adequately confronting the issue of human rights. And to be sure, some aspects of human rights do fall outside its mandate. But the Bank's economic and social approach to development advances a comprehensive, interconnected vision of human rights that is too often overlooked. There is also practical, operational value in the way the Articles are drafted. Because lending decisions are based on the quality of the project, and the effectiveness of the programs in reducing poverty, the Bank has been able to escape the costly experience of committing scarce funds based on short-term political or ideological considerations, which have little to do with relieving the burden of poverty.

None of this means that the Bank views other factors — factors that go to the heart of civil and political rights — as any less important to development. It does mean that, constituted as it is, and with the expertise and resources it possesses, the Bank makes its greatest contribution to development — and *simply is able to help more people* — by continuing to focus on the important work of economic and social development. . . .

The first element in the Bank's approach to development is understanding, in each of the countries and communities in which it works, the particular causes — and effects — of poverty. This means talking with people — asking the poor themselves what they need most, and what will make the biggest difference in their lives. Since the Bank introduced poverty assessments nearly 10 years ago, 94 assessments have been prepared for 83 countries, covering approximately 90 percent of the world's poor. . . .

The international community understands better than ever which policies most effectively contribute to economic growth: Openness to trade and investment, stable exchange rates, low inflation, sound fiscal policies, and acquisition of high technology are the basics. . . .

Over the years, these policies have sometimes been the subject of concern for the Bank's partners in civil society, including in the human rights community. Some believe that reform programs — when they result in the cutting of subsidies, the adoption of trade liberalization, and privatization — place undue stress on the poor. And it is true that economic policy reforms can cause real pain to real people. However, these programs have come a long way since the beginning, in terms of cushioning the impact on the poor and expanding the benefits of reform to all people. This is the challenge for governments and lenders.

But the difficulty of the policies should not be mistaken for their necessity. Countries that do not adopt a broad mix of outward-oriented, pro-growth policies risk being left behind in an increasingly global economy, with the poor suffering the most severe consequences. It is not, therefore, economic reform lending that should raise concerns about human rights, but rather, how those programs are implemented, and what measures are taken to ensure that the needs of the poor are not neglected. The Bank has learned a great deal during the past 15 years about how to design social safety nets and other programs to ease the transition into reforms. Those who design sound economic policies must pay particularly close attention to social spending in countries dealing with high external debt obligations. . . .

For the first few decades of its history the Bank addressed development primarily as a technocratic challenge. The implicit model was that good advisers and technical experts would design good policies and good projects, which good governments with adequate resources would then implement for the benefit of society. The Bank has learned, however, that at least as important as the policies and the resources for development are the efficiency and transparency of the institutions that carry out the policies. World Bank President James Wolfensohn made this clear when he underscored the connection between good economic performance and accountable governance: Irrespective of political systems, public decisions must be brought . . . into the sunshine of public scrutiny. Not simply to please the markets but to build the broad social consensus without which even the best-conceived economic strategies will ultimately fail.

This theme is strongly supported by World Bank research, which suggests the strong link between economic performance with accountability and the openness of governance. The World Bank helps its client countries build better governance. This assistance in improving the efficiency and integrity of public sector institutions — from banking regulation to government auditing functions to the court system — has a singularly important impact on creating the *structural* environment in which citizens can pursue and continue to strengthen all areas of human rights. . . .

In the *World Development Report 1997: The State in a Changing World*, the World Bank identified five fundamental tasks that governments must administer to ensure sustainable, widely shared development.

— Establishing the foundation of law

— Maintaining a nondiscriminatory policy environment, including macroeconomic stability

— Investing in basic social services and infrastructure

— Protecting the vulnerable

— Protecting the environment. . . .

For the World Bank, protecting and advancing human rights means helping the world's poorest people escape poverty. But this will require commitment from all sides. It is ironic that today, just as we are learning the keys to reducing poverty, official development assistance is reaching all-time lows. Developing countries are now better able to turn financial resources into effective growth, and invest in the needs of their people. And donors are better able to identify those countries. We know that aid reduces poverty; and now we know how to make aid work better, at lower cost.

Despite the progress made in recent years, and the possibilities held out by modern technology and better policies, 3 billion people are desperately poor. Many suffer unnecessarily from disease and malnutrition, others from the scourge of violence. How we reach out to those in need will determine what is said 50 years from now of the promises we have made.

Kelly Currah et al., *Doing The Rights Thing? The World Bank and The Human Rights of People Living In Poverty*

World Vision Briefing Paper, pp. 7-8, 12-13, 15, 17-19 (2003)

The World Bank is not Amnesty International nor Human Rights Watch. It has already adapted its operational modalities to respond to a wide range of external concerns. So why should the World Bank now take on yet another issue and change the way it views the role of rights within its work?

This briefing does not argue that the Bank should become a human rights organisation nor berate governments on their record of upholding rights. Indeed World Vision opposes the concept of human rights–related conditionality.

Instead, this briefing suggests that embracing existing national commitments on rights could greatly assist countries in achieving the realisation of their rights objectives. The Bank can do much to help countries with their rights objectives through incremental changes to its own programme partnerships with governments.

This briefing is therefore focused on the Bank's role as a partner to national governments. It centres the debate on rights within the context of these partnerships. As a result the definition of rights used in the discussion is narrowed to the legal reality of rights that have been accepted at the national level. . . .

In the process of helping countries to realise their obligations under international human rights treaties the Bank can also benefit its own programmes. More attention to rights could help to build local constituencies for reform and enhance Bank due diligence. An unclear position on national rights objectives only weakens the Bank's mission of promoting economic growth and improving living standards.

Why is it particularly important for the Bank to embrace such national policy commitments? Because the Bank is often at the heart of programmes to reform the capacity and infrastructure of a state. This briefing refers often to the education sector, an area in which the Bank is both a large funder and a significant source of technical expertise. The Bank is therefore intimately involved with those ministries and aspects of national policy that are vital to the realisation of national commitments to key human rights conventions. The Bank also has the very technical skills and expertise that would be essential for governments to build gradual realisation of rights objectives into their strategies.

This does not mean that the Bank is solely responsible for the success or failure of movement towards national rights objectives in key sectors such as education. The government ultimately has primary responsibility (issues such as political will are discussed below). Nevertheless, the Bank makes a choice whether to offer to help governments turn their rhetorical promises into reality. . . .

Offering strategic assistance to partner governments on rights is not just important because it can improve progress towards the realisation of rights. It also makes good sense for the Bank itself. Embracing national commitments on rights offers the Bank two useful tools for its programme lending: the first relates to the sustainability of reform; the second to the Bank's own impact on human development:

1. National policy objectives: The primary responsibility for delivering on human rights commitments rests with governments. By making these commitments, however, governments have created a useful basis of understanding for the potential future entitlements and obligations of citizens. The Bank is an important partner to many governments that have relatively weak capacity to implement social policy through rights-friendly approaches. Governments often themselves are not aware that a greater emphasis on rights can entail simple and incremental changes rather than major policy overhauls. The Bank has a unique role to play in working with governments embarking on this policy journey, and a failure to take up this role may actually hinder governments from doing so.
2. Due diligence: Development is often defined as the improvement of the human condition, and in recent years the Bank has embraced the concept of "human development". Yet the Bank is failing to ensure that its own programming reflects the multi-dimensional needs of the people who are intended to be its beneficiaries, with some alarming results. . . .

The Bank has in the past professed not only that it is concerned about rights but also that its work broadly supports a rights agenda. But without a greater commitment by the Bank, many governments will continue to struggle to achieve their rights commitments. The Bank's unique role in partnering with governments means that its non-commitment is itself a barrier. Yet offering help to national governments on their existing rights commitments would not contravene the Bank's mandate — indeed, it would be much less "political" than some existing Bank activities. . . .

1.3 Rights and Support for the Demand side of Reform

There is currently a major inconsistency in the World Bank's approach to economic reform. The Bank has recognised that the sustainability of reform requires much closer attention to political economy issues and to a sense of national ownership-a recognition that has influenced new initiatives such as Poverty Reduction Strategy Papers (PRSPs). The Bank has also recognised that creating a good climate for investment entails tackling institutional issues such as rule of law and judicial reform.

Despite this understanding on the part of the Bank, its approach to both sets of issues still refuses to recognise their interconnectedness with the question of rights. This can be seen with rule of law, which represents something of a chicken and egg situation in relation to human rights. Rights are rarely fully respected where rule of law is not strong, and yet it is difficult for rule of law to be strong where expectations are lowered by lack of awareness of rights.

If the Bank is serious about promoting accountability and the rule of law, then it must also take more seriously the issue of raising citizens' awareness of nationally owned commitments to rights expressed within the CRC [Convention on the Rights of the Child], CEDAW [Convention on the Elimination of All Forms of Discrimination Against Women] and other conventions. Indeed the Bank should be proactively encouraging governments to introduce their international human rights commitments into domestic legislation.

Rights are inextricably linked to the process of human empowerment. For example, as women become aware of their rights under CEDAW to refuse to undergo genital mutilation, or to seek equality of opportunity with men, it becomes more likely that they are able to press for an environment that respects these rights. The Bank cannot expect citizens to hold anybody to account if they are asking: accountable for what? . . .

As the next section shows, however, the Bank's own position on rights is rather confusing. The Bank seems in some ways to know that proactive work on rights could substantially benefit its objectives, but still resists more systematic assistance to governments in these areas. . . .

Section Two: The Bank's Position on Rights

The World Bank has always readily expressed broad support for the concept of Economic, Social and Cultural (ESC) rights, but has shown less concern for the counterpart Civil and Political (CP) rights.

2.1 The 1998 Report

The Bank has enthusiastically pointed to its financial support for the delivery of clean water, education and health as inevitably advancing the cause of ESC rights. In its 1998 report *Development and Human Rights*, the Bank states that:

> The Bank contributes directly to the fulfilment of many rights articulated in the Universal Declaration. Through its support of primary education, health care and nutrition, sanitation, housing, and the environment, the Bank has helped hundreds of millions of people attain crucial economic and social rights.

That report, however, fails to acknowledge that in order for such provision to help create the environment for attainment of rights (something it describes as a "central and irreducible goal of development"), some degree of deliberate strategy is needed. The case studies in this briefing (Section four) show that the Bank's expenditure of US$31 billion on education over 35 years does not necessarily mean that the Bank has helped education systems become better vehicles through which governments can deliver on rights.

The Bank's failure in 1998 to bring the concept of rights down from the broad and vague to the practical and specific is partly explained by an underlying belief that "development" itself will ultimately, somehow, deliver the rights involved. Using logic eerily reminiscent of the view that economic growth on its own is sufficient for poverty reduction, the Bank suggests that its greatest role may be to facilitate the process of development, rather than to help governments with solid plans.

The 1998 report also struggles to embrace a critical link that exists between ESC and CP rights: the fact that governments have less incentive to fulfil their commitments on the former where the latter are weak. This is evident when the report points to the Bank's mandate as the key impediment to it doing any more than working obliquely around the edges of CP rights (such as its efforts to combat corruption).

This reticence to get involved with CP rights seems to extend even to those cases where governments have an expressed national policy commitment to improve their record in these areas. Indeed, some states have included their desire to improve performance and internalise their international commitments within their Poverty Reduction Strategy Papers, written as part of a Bank/Fund debt relief process. Thus, the Bank's approach has been to view rights only in the broadest of lights, and its own role as limited to supporting a development process that, it assumes, will facilitate the fulfilment of rights. This approach simply will not work. It neither helps citizens wanting to be aware of their entitlements in relation to failing service providers, nor helps states that are seeking to improve service provision to better meet their international rights obligations....

Section Three: Keeping within the Mandate

The Bank has made frequent reference to its mandate, derived from its founding charters, as the reason why it cannot be more proactive in relation to rights.

…[T]he IBRD *Articles of Agreement* (article 4, section 10), the *Articles of Agreement* of the IDA (article 5, section 6), the articles of the IFC (article 3, section 9), and the *Convention Establishing the Multilateral Investment Guarantee Agency* (chapter 5, article 34) all impose some form of prohibition on political activity. The first three of these are worded:

> The Association and its officers shall not interfere in the political affairs of any member; nor shall they be influenced in their decisions by the political character of the member or members concerned. Only economic considerations shall be relevant to their decisions, and these considerations shall be weighed impartially in order to achieve the purposes stated in this Agreement.

Clearly, the wording of this prohibition poses two definitional questions that are central to the issue of the Bank's role in institution-building within the area of human rights. The first question is the precise meaning and interpretation of political interference with respect to human rights. The second is the meaning and interpretation of "economic considerations", and how these might differ from questions of politics.

3.1 Political or Partisan?

Upon closer scrutiny, invoking the danger of being too political as an excuse for the Bank to avoid helping governments on rights is misleading at best. The nature of both development and conditionality are inherently political and as a result the Bank has frequently become political when needed. There are simply no neat dividing lines between the economic and political spheres in the process of development. The proscription imposed at the founding of the Bank was therefore most logically intended to refer to partisan politics….

The Bank is already engaged in other activities that are considerably more political than simply offering assistance to those states struggling to implement their commitments under the CRC. For example, the Bank had planned FY2003 commitments of over $100 million for projects dealing with legal and judicial reform. These projects include not only reform to the judiciary but also direct involvement in changes within legislatures.

The Cambodia Legal and Judicial Reform Project, for example, includes an extensive component aimed at substantially changing the operations of the Phnom Penh legislature. The component in question is aimed at developing capacity in "agencies and institutions; in the case of the National Assembly and Senate, the capacity to consider, initiate, review or adopt legislation." Such projects seem to have a markedly political dimension.

Put simply, the decision of the Bank to categorise human rights issues as being in the political rather than the economic arena was a highly subjective decision, the basis of which many would have reason to question. In the case of ESC conventions there would seem to be a more immediate connection to 'economic' issues than for some existing Bank projects, such as the Cambodian example mentioned above….

3.2 Accountability as an Economic Imperative

The Bank defends the 'economic' credentials of highly political projects involving legislature and judicial reform by pointing out that accountability is critical to the promotion of a conducive environment for investment and growth. By embracing the economic importance of the rule of law, the Bank has pointed to the potential economic benefits of further nurturing a culture of respect for rights. For example, just as there are benefits in respecting and formalising the rights of farmers whose families have tilled the same land for generations without legal title, so there are economic as well as social benefits in protecting the rights of children vulnerable to the worst forms of child labour (as defined in *ILO Convention 182*).

The Bank's current activities to promote the rule of law and responsible legal process cannot be clinically confined to a few individual areas of state competence. The transitory nature of governmental appointments, and of governments themselves, suggests that crucial to effective institution building is the creation of a wider culture of respect for legal process and rights.

In summary, given the considerably more political activities the Bank already undertakes, its insistence that working on human rights is outside its mandate is not tenable. Nor is it logical, given the close inter-connections between rights and other areas of Bank work. Indeed, it is somewhat ironic that the Bank rejects what have become politically neutral and nationally owned objectives on rights while elsewhere engaging heavily in national policymaking processes. Rather, the decision to label fulfilment of the CRC/CEDAW and other conventions as political rather than economic suggests a subjective exercise in political pragmatism, taken more with reference to perceived views of the Bank's Board rather than with reference to the *Articles of Agreement*.

B. *The World Trade Organization*

International financial institutions are not the only organizations whose activities have an impact on human rights. The increasing role of the World Trade Organization has brought with it concerns about the possible impact that liberalized economic policies might have on human rights. Issues of particular concern include protecting labor rights, upholding economic and social rights (such as the right to health, which may conflict with intellectual property protection for pharmaceutical companies), and permitting the use of economic sanctions or boycotts for human rights purposes, e.g., to ban the sale of "conflict diamonds" or implements of torture. The following readings explore some of these issues.

Robert Howse and Makau Mutua, *Protecting Human Rights in a Global Economy: Challenges for the World Trade Organization*

Rights and Democracy (2000), http://www.ichrdd.ca/english/commdoc/bpublications/globalization/wtoRightsGlob.html#

Over the past decade, trade agreements have come under increased scrutiny from the public. More and more people — peasants, trade unionists, human rights activists, small businesses, environmentalists, farmers, students and others — are expressing concern about how trade agreements are affecting their lives. For all the talk of the benefits of globalization and its presumed contribution to economic growth, the undeniable reality is that globally, and within most countries, the gap between the rich and the poor is widening, and hundreds of millions of people are denied the basic human rights provided for by the United Nations. The creation of the World Trade Organization (WTO), outside the auspices of the UN, has aggravated many of civil society's concerns.

There is no consensus on how trade liberalization affects human rights, nor even a well-developed methodology for determining the human rights impacts of trade agreements. Many people in the mainstream trade policy community see no linkage whatsoever with human rights and consider such concerns outside their realm. Likewise, many human rights groups lack familiarity with trade issues. They are puzzled by the language and suspicious of the entire process: from the negotiations of tariffs to the settlement of disputes. The two communities are so far apart that they do not even use the same vocabulary, let alone share a common philosophy.

Both trade and human rights have been codified in highly developed legal regimes, negotiated by governments since the end of World War II. These two legal regimes have developed however in splendid isolation from one another. Both trade law and human rights law narrow the range of policy options that are available to governments. And yet, it seems that the question of whether the two legal regimes are contradictory has rarely been asked. . . .

As the postwar GATT regime evolved into the World Trade Organization in late 1994, so its rules and those of its accompanying agreements evolved into a detailed legal code, which is interpreted and defined through a dispute settlement process. This process, however, has not been transparent and has not viewed dispute resolution through the lens of human rights impacts. Provisions of WTO Agreements on domestic food safety and other technical standards, as well as on intellectual property directly affect the ability of governments to fulfill their human rights obligations to their citizens. This is especially true in the case of social and economic rights, which should be understood in connection with, not in isolation from, civil and political rights.

. . . The preamble of the WTO Agreement, which establishes the framework for the entire WTO system, does not make free trade an end in itself. Rather, it establishes the objectives of the system as related to the fulfillment of basic human values, including the improvement of living standards for all people and sustainable development. As is widely recognized now, both in development literature as well as in numerous documents of international policy, these objectives cannot be reached without respect for human rights. . . .

Although the GATT text — now part of the broader WTO system of treaties — reflects the recognition of non-trade public values, which are meant to prevail in the event of conflict with its free trade rules, institutional isolation has contributed to a very limited interpretation of this principle. Specifically, GATT Article XX,* which was designed to be a fundamental pillar of the international trade regime, has often been construed so restrictively as to almost read it

* GATT article XX provides in relevant part as follows:

"Subject to the requirement that such measures are not applied in a manner which would constitute a means of arbitrary or unjustifiable discrimination between countries where the same conditions prevail, or a disguised restriction on international trade, nothing in this Agreement shall be construed to prevent the adoption or enforcement by any contracting parties of measures: (a) necessary to protect public morals; (b) out of text, or to marginalize it. Compounding the problems created by institutional isolation is the atmosphere of secrecy and the lack of transparency in the dispute settlement and appellate process within the WTO. The GATT has often been interpreted as creating a general right to free trade; however, as emphasized in a few recent decisions of the WTO Appellate Body, the GATT and the other WTO treaties contain fine balances of rights and obligations. And the provisions that limit or balance trade liberalization, protecting other human interests, are as fundamental a part of the international law of trade, as those that support the globalization of markets. They must not be read out or down.

Enlightened interpretation of the GATT and other WTO agreements, however, will not in and of itself address the needs of under-development, inequality and the corresponding violations of fundamental human rights around the world. Trade rules must be looked at in their relationship to other phenomena connected to globalization, such as free capital movements and the practices of the international financial institutions. We must understand the effects of trade laws and policies in the broadest sense, and evolve new laws and policies in a manner that overcomes the isolation between human rights institutions and economic institutions, including those preoccupied with the trading system.

Highlights

— The relationship of trade law and human rights law: In the event of a conflict between a universally recognized human right and a commitment ensuing from international treaty law such as a trade agreement, the latter must be interpreted to be consistent with the former. When properly interpreted and applied, the trade regime recognizes that human rights are fundamental and prior to free trade itself.

— Labour: It is often claimed that the GATT prohibits members from regulating access of imports based on the manner in which those products have been produced, even if such regulations are applied equally to domestic products. However, this view is inconsistent with a close analysis of the jurisprudence, despite its presence in two notorious panel rulings, which were not adopted as legally binding by the GATT membership. The correct reading of the GATT text would permit a country to impose conditions on imports related to the labour practices involved in their production.

— Government Procurement: The current negotiation of government procurement rules with respect to services provides the opportunity to develop the position that human rights-based procurement conditions are consistent with WTO law. As well, the existing Government Procurement Agreement, which concerns trade in goods, should be interpreted so as to permit ethical purchasing policies by governments. Not permitting members of the WTO to impose the kind of requirements on foreign suppliers that they routinely impose on domestic suppliers (such as anti-discrimination requirements) would amount to an obligation to favour foreign suppliers, which the GPA could not possibly be read as to entrench. Further, the public order exception in the GPA must be interpreted in light of the international law of human rights.

---

necessary to protect human, animal or plant life or health; . . . (e) relating to the products of prison labor; (f) imposed for the protection of national treasures of artistic, historic or archaeological value. . . ." — Eds.

— Trade Policy Review: WTO member states are currently subject to a review process which examines their policies and practices in relation to their promotion of free trade. This is inconsistent with the actual full objective of the review process, which is to review policies in their relation to the "functioning of the multilateral trading system." The objective of the trading system is not free trade as such, but rather "ensuring full employment," "optimal use of the world's resources" and "sustainable development." National trade policy and practice should be examined in relation to the achievement of these goals.

— Dispute Settlement: Consideration of the human rights impact of dispute settlement rulings would be facilitated by the acceptance of amicus briefs by panel and appellate body members. In the *Shrimp/Turtle* case, a precedent has been established for the submission of amicus briefs to both the panels and the Appellate Body. Secrecy of pleadings and oral argument in WTO dispute settlement, however, may limit the effectiveness of amicus participation, and these provisions of the Dispute Settlement Understanding should be revisited as soon as possible.

— Global Governance: Interpretation of WTO law has not incorporated the expertise of other institutions governing the various regimes of international law. Nor has there been serious dialogue or interaction between the WTO as an institution and other relevant international institutions. However, the agreement establishing the WTO requires that this be the case. The implementation of this obligation should be the subject of a formal review.

World Trade Organization, Trade and Labour Standards

Press Brief, Jan. 20, 2003

Labour standards are currently not subject to World Trade Organization rules and disciplines but some industrial nations believe the issue should be studied by the WTO as a first step toward bringing the matter of core labour standards into the organization.

These industrial member states believe the right to bargain collectively, freedom of association and workplace abuse (including forced labour and certain types of child labour), are matters for consideration in the WTO. WTO rules and disciplines, they argue, would provide a powerful incentive for member nations to improve workplace conditions.

These proposals have been highly controversial.

Many developing and some developed nations believe the issue has no place in the WTO framework. These nations argue that efforts to bring labour standards into the arena of multilateral trade negotiations are little more than a smokescreen for protectionism. Many officials in developing countries believe the campaign to bring labour issues into the WTO is actually a bid by industrial nations to undermine the comparative advantage of lower wage trading partners.

The controversy over the issue of trade and labour standards is not new. Almost every Minister who spoke at the Ministerial Conference in Marrakesh in 1994 expressed a view on whether there was role for the WTO in this area. The Chairman of that meeting concluded there was no basis at the time for agreement on this issue. Since then there has been debate in the International Labour Organisation on the possibility of including a "social clause" in the WTO to enforce core ILO labour standards. The debate there has also been marked by divergences of view between ILO member governments and more generally across an ILO structure that includes representatives from government, labour and business.

An empirical study produced by the Organization for Economic Cooperation and Development earlier this year on "core workers rights and international trade" has enriched the substance of the debate, but so far at least, it has not narrowed noticeably the differences of view of WTO Members on whether the subject properly belongs in the WTO.

During preparations for the Singapore Ministerial Conference, proposals were made by the United States and Norway for a decision to be taken by Ministers for the WTO to undertake work on promoting core labour standards in the context of global trade liberalization and to report back to Ministers at their 1998 Conference. Both proposals view WTO work in this area as complementing that of the ILO, which they recognize has primary international responsibility in this field. Both countries view the objective as reaching a common understanding among WTO members on how to reinforce the mutually supporting nature of increased trade and improving labour standards.

While some WTO Members expressed support for the approach suggested by the United States and Norway, many others raised serious reservations about any structured discussion of trade and labour standards in the organization.

WTO Director General Renato Ruggiero has suggested four points on which a consensus on this difficult issue might be built. In his consultations with member states, Mr. Ruggiero has found wide support for the four points, which are as follows:

— All WTO member nations oppose abusive work place practices, through their approval of the United Nations Universal Declaration of Human Rights.

— The International Labour Organization holds primary responsibility for labour issues.

— Trade sanctions should not be used to deal with disputes over labour standards.

— Member states agree that the comparative advantage of low wage countries should not be compromised.

Agreement Reached on WTO Waiver for "Conflict Diamonds" Under the Kimberley Process Certification Scheme for Rough Diamonds

WTO NEWS: 2003 NEWS ITEMS, Feb. 26, 2003,
http://www.wto.org/english/news_e/news03_e/goods_council_26fev03_e.htm

The WTO Council for Trade in Goods, on 26 February 2003, agreed to recommend that the General Council grant requesting members a waiver for trade measures taken. The agreed decision recognized "the extraordinary humanitarian nature of this issue and the devastating impact of conflicts fuelled by trade in conflict diamonds on the peace, safety and security of people in affected countries and the systematic and gross human rights violations that have been perpetrated in such conflicts."

The waiver was requested by Australia, Brazil, Canada, Israel, Japan, Korea, Philippines, Sierra Leone, Thailand, United Arab Emirates and United States.

They requested a waiver from GATT rules to give legal certainty to domestic measures taken under the Kimberley Process aimed at curbing the trade in conflict diamonds while supporting legitimate diamond trade.

The WTO waiver decision would exempt — from 1 January 2003 until 31 December 2006 — trade measures taken under the Kimberley Process by these 11 members and other members that would subsequently join from GATT provisions on most-favoured-nation treatment (Article I:1), elimination of quantitative restrictions (Article XI:1) and non-discriminatory administration of quantitative restrictions (Article XIII:1).

Participants in the Kimberley Process, on November 5, 2002, issued the Interlaken Declaration expressing their intent to implement an international scheme of certification for rough diamonds to help break the link between armed conflict and the trade in rough diamonds. The Kimberley Process provides that each participant should "ensure that no shipment of rough diamonds is imported or exported to a non-Participant."

The Chairman of the Goods Council, Ambassador M Supperamaniam of Malaysia, thanked Canada for conducting the informal consultations that led to the agreement on the waiver. He added that this issue had been handled in a cooperative and pragmatic manner by members. It was noted that the waiver is open for other member to join until or even after the decision is adopted by the General Council.

Report of the High Commissioner for Human Rights, *Liberalization of Trade in Services and Human Rights*

Sub-Comm'n on the Promotion and Protection of Human Rights, UN Doc. E/CN.4/Sub.2/2002/9 (June 25, 2002)

The present report . . . introduces the General Agreement on Trade in Services (GATS). While many policies, agreements and laws drive and shape the liberalization of trade in services, GATS is significant as the first multilateral agreement to set a legal framework for the liberalization process. GATS includes general obligations that apply to all services that come within the scope of GATS for all WTO members. The Agreement also allows States to commit voluntarily specific service sectors to liberalization. Each country has a schedule in which these country-specific commitments are made. Importantly, GATS includes the trade principle of non-discrimination known as most favoured nation, as well as national treatment. After setting an outline for GATS, the report examines the obligations of States to promote and protect the human rights most directly affected by the liberalization of trade in services, specifically the right to health (including the right to drinking water), the right to education and the right to development. . . .

[T]he High Commissioner identifies a list of areas requiring further action to promote human rights approaches to the liberalization of trade in services, including the following:

(a) *Ensuring equal access for basic services* — the High Commissioner encourages States to take action to ensure universal supply of essential services, including through the use of affirmative action to ensure provision of services to the poor, isolated and marginalized, taking into account national circumstances and capacities;

(b) *Ensuring Governments' right and duty to regulate* — the High Commissioner encourages interpretations of GATS provisions that acknowledge the need for countries to retain the flexibility to use development tools, such as cross-subsidization or the regulation of corporate governance, in response to national development needs;

(c) *Encouraging interpretations of GATS that are compatible with human rights* — the High Commissioner reminds WTO members of their concurrent obligations under human rights law and encourages the development of rules or tests that acknowledge and protect States' duties concerning human rights when determining or assessing whether a measure is trade-restrictive;

(d) *Undertaking human rights assessments of trade policies* — the High Commissioner highlights the voluntary nature of commitments to liberalize trade in services and stresses the need to make commitments on the basis of sound empirical evidence;

(e) *Providing international cooperation and assistance* — the High Commissioner reminds developed countries of the commitment to provide 0.7 per cent of GDP as official development assistance. Further, the High Commissioner reminds States of their responsibility to negotiate in ways that enable poorer countries to maintain the maximum flexibility to develop policies to meet commitments to the progressive realization of human rights;

(f) *Increasing dialogue on human rights and trade* — the High Commissioner encourages greater consultation between delegates to WTO and delegates representing the same country as members or observers in the Commission on Human Rights on the links between human rights and trade and on particular ways to ensure coherence in policy and lawmaking;

(g) *Future work* — the High Commissioner recommends that the Sub-Commission consider requesting a report on human rights, trade and investment.

The High Commissioner prepared two other reports on trade and human rights that are of interest. One addresses TRIPS (Report of the High Commissioner, *The impact of the Agreement on Trade-Related Aspects of Intellectual Property Rights on human rights*, UN Doc. E/CN.4/Sub.2/2001/13 (June 27, 2001)), and the other examines the agreement on agriculture (Report of the High Commissioner for Human Rights submitted in accordance with Commission on Human Rights resolution 2001/32, *Globalization and its impact on the full enjoyment of human rights*, UN Doc. E/CN.4/2002/54 (Jan. 15, 2002)).

C. *Intellectual Property Issues*

Committee on Economic, Social and Cultural Rights, *Protection of Intellectual Property Under The TRIPS Agreement*

Background paper submitted by the Secretariat of the World Trade Organization, UN Doc. E/C.12/2000/18 (Nov. 29, November 2000)

. . .

IPRs [intellectual property rights] and human rights

8. The TRIPS Agreement is contained in Annex 1C to the WTO Agreement [of Apr. 15, 1994.] The Annex to this paper describes the TRIPS Agreement as aiming "to ensure the adequate protection and effective enforcement of intellectual property rights and the impartial resolution of disputes between WTO members about such matters, to the mutual advantage of both producers and users of intellectual property." The overall objectives of the WTO, as reflected in the Preamble to the WTO Agreement, concern also the TRIPS Agreement. The Preamble recognizes that member countries' trade and economic relations "should be conducted with a view to raising standards of living, ensuring full employment and a large and steadily growing volume of real income and effective demand, and expanding the production of and trade in goods and services, while allowing for the optimal use of the world's resources in accordance with the objective of sustainable development, seeking both to protect and preserve the environment and to enhance the means for doing so in a manner consistent with their respective needs and concerns at different levels of economic development." It also recognizes the "need for positive efforts designed to ensure that developing countries, and especially the least developed among them, secure a share in the growth in international trade commensurate with the needs of their economic development."

9. The objectives of the TRIPS Agreement, as explicitly set out in its article 7, put emphasis on the public interest rationale of intellectual property protection. This article, entitled "Objectives," says that "the protection and enforcement of intellectual property rights should contribute to the promotion of technological innovation and to the transfer and dissemination of technology, to the mutual advantage of producers and users of technological knowledge and in a manner conducive to social and economic welfare, and to a balance of rights and obligations." This corresponds with the objectives article 15.1 (a) and 15.1 (b) of the ICESCR, which recognize the right of everyone to take part in cultural life and to enjoy the benefits of scientific progress and its applications.

10. While the expressly stated objectives of the WTO Agreement and the TRIPS Agreement lay emphasis on promoting social and economic welfare, articles 27.2 of the UDHR and article 15.1 (c) of the ICESCR underline the need to protect the interests of authors and inventors in the results of their intellectual efforts not only for the sake of the broader public interest but because they are recognized as worthy of protection as such. However, it can be argued that the TRIPS Agreement, including the pre-existing IP [intellectual property] conventions incorporated into it, also seeks to give effect at the multilateral level to article 15.1 (c) of the ICESCR, which establishes everyone's "right to the protection of the

moral and material interests resulting from any scientific, literary or artistic production of which he is the author" as a human right. This would appear, for example, to be indicated by the statement in the Preamble to the TRIPS Agreement that recognizes that intellectual property rights are private rights.

11. It should be added that the TRIPS Agreement promotes also other values deemed essential for the realization of human rights. For example, the TRIPS Agreement prohibits discrimination on the basis of nationality in the area of intellectual property rights; this is supportive of the non-discrimination principles contained in the human rights instruments. The Agreement promotes the rule of law at the national level; it requires, *inter alia*, the observance of due process by requiring that judicial procedures are fair and equitable, decisions are in writing and reasoned, and that parties have an opportunity to appeal. The Agreement provides for international cooperation to fight copyright piracy and trade mark counterfeiting, which often have links to organized crime. . . .

18. A more general point that should be made is that the grant of an IP right does not impair the possibility for Governments to regulate production and the use and distribution of products on any public policy grounds, such as concerns about public order, morality, health or environment. This is because a patent and other intellectual property rights do not guarantee the right of the right holder to use the invention or other protected subject matter; they are only concerned with the right of the right holder to prevent others from doing so.

19. A key feature in achieving a proper balance in IP regimes is granting protection only for a limited period, which should be appropriately long to provide the necessary incentive and reward for creative work and innovation. After the expiration of the term of protection, the work or invention falls into the public domain, and everyone is free to use it without restriction. The fact that IP systems provide for a limited period of protection is an indication that in all such systems the protection of the rights of authors and inventors are not absolute but are balanced by considerations of public interest.

20. The TRIPS Agreement provides a fair amount of leeway to member countries to adjust the level of protection by providing limitations and exceptions to exclusive rights. The Agreement contains general clauses that permit limitations and exceptions to exclusive rights, provided that they address specific situations, do not conflict with a normal exploitation of the protected material and do not unreasonably prejudice the legitimate interests of right holders. In addition, the Agreement and the Conventions incorporated in it allow for numerous specific limitations and contain provisions on compulsory licences. . . .

Patent Protection for Pharmaceutical Products

27. The issue of patent protection for pharmaceutical products is one where the problem of finding a proper balance is particularly acute. On the one hand, it is especially important from a social and public health point of view that new drugs and vaccines to treat and prevent diseases are generated and the incentives provided by the patent system are particularly important in this regard. On the other hand, precisely because of the social value of the drugs so generated, there is strong pressure for such drugs to be as accessible as possible as quickly as possible.

28. The TRIPS Agreement represents an effort to find an appropriate balance between these considerations. On the one hand, the Agreement requires that, after the end of the relevant transition period, patent protection for pharmaceutical products should be available for a 20-year term of protection. On the other hand, the Agreement contains a substantial number of provisions which enable Governments to implement their intellectual property regimes in a manner which takes account of immediate as well as longer term public health considerations. These provisions, some of which have already been mentioned, include those relating to certain exemptions from patentability, the possibility to make limited exceptions to exclusive rights, compulsory licensing, parallel importation and the recognition that member countries may adopt measures necessary to protect public health and nutrition (for example, many countries have price or reimbursement controls, generic substitution policies, etc.). These various provisions were the result of several years of hard negotiation and involved important concessions on the part of the major *demandeurs* for the TRIPS negotiations. They recognize and legitimize in public international law the right of countries to qualify patent rights in certain ways.

29. It is important to put the impact of the TRIPS Agreement on access to drugs in developing countries into perspective:

— Most developing countries have provided product patent protection for pharmaceuticals all along or have introduced it prior to the end of the transition period to which they are entitled under the TRIPS Agreement (2005 for developing countries and 2006 for least developed countries). Only a handful of WTO members are using the full transition period.

— Most drugs, including most of those vital for essential health care in developing countries, are not under patent protection anywhere and are in the public domain.

— In many of the poorest countries, for example in Sub-Saharan Africa, patents have not been sought and granted for drugs even where they are patentable under their national laws.

— The effective period of patent protection for pharmaceuticals that use new chemical entities is very much shorter than the nominal 20-year period, especially in developing countries, because of the time taken to obtain marketing approval from the public health authorities.

30. It should also be noted that the TRIPS Agreement does not stand in the way of prices for patented pharmaceuticals being modulated to take into account the capacity to pay of different countries and the populations within them. The WTO Secretariat is examining the issue of differential pricing in the context of its cooperation with the World Health Organization. The two Secretariats are jointly preparing a workshop of interested parties which would seek to examine the legal, institutional and political environment that would favour widespread use of differential pricing.

31. For the private sector to make a significant contribution to developing vaccines and drugs to treat the neglected diseases of the poor, patent protection is necessary. However, it is recognized that patent protection may not be sufficient in many cases where the purchasing power of those afflicted is low. Especially now that developing countries have committed themselves through the TRIPS Agreement to share some of the burden of providing incentives for research and development, it is more than ever important

that, where necessary, the patent system is complemented with other forms of support from the international community for research and development into neglected diseases.

32. It should also be recalled that there is a strong relationship between trade, poverty and health. While improved health is good for development, development and the increased resources that it provides are vital for promoting public health. And the open trading system which the GATT/WTO has sought to establish, of which the TRIPS Agreement is an integral part, is vital for creating opportunities for development.

World Trade Organization, *Declaration on the TRIPS Agreement and Public Health*

Adopted Nov. 14, 2001, WTO Doc. WT/MIN(01)DEC/2 (Nov. 20, 2001)

1. We recognize the gravity of the public health problems afflicting many developing and least-developed countries, especially those resulting from HIV/AIDS, tuberculosis, malaria and other epidemics.

2. We stress the need for the WTO Agreement on Trade-Related Aspects of Intellectual Property Rights (TRIPS Agreement) to be part of the wider national and international action to address these problems.

3. We recognize that intellectual property protection is important for the development of new medicines. We also recognize the concerns about its effects on prices.

4. We agree that the TRIPS Agreement does not and should not prevent Members from taking measures to protect public health. Accordingly, while reiterating our commitment to the TRIPS Agreement, we affirm that the Agreement can and should be interpreted and implemented in a manner supportive of WTO Members' right to protect public health and, in particular, to promote access to medicines for all.

In this connection, we reaffirm the right of WTO Members to use, to the full, the provisions in the TRIPS Agreement, which provide flexibility for this purpose.

5. Accordingly and in the light of paragraph 4 above, while maintaining our commitments in the TRIPS Agreement, we recognize that these flexibilities include:

> In applying the customary rules of interpretation of public international law, each provision of the TRIPS Agreement shall be read in the light of the object and purpose of the Agreement as expressed, in particular, in its objectives and principles.
>
> Each Member has the right to grant compulsory licences and the freedom to determine the grounds upon which such licences are granted.
>
> Each Member has the right to determine what constitutes a national emergency or other circumstances of extreme urgency, it being understood that public health crises, including those relating to HIV/AIDS, tuberculosis, malaria and other epidemics, can represent a national emergency or other circumstances of extreme urgency.
>
> The effect of the provisions in the TRIPS Agreement that are relevant to the exhaustion of intellectual property rights is to leave each Member free to establish its own regime for such exhaustion without challenge, subject to the MFN and national treatment provisions of Articles 3 and 4.

6. We recognize that WTO Members with insufficient or no manufacturing capacities in the pharmaceutical sector could face difficulties in making effective use of compulsory licensing under the TRIPS Agreement. We instruct the Council for TRIPS to find an expeditious solution to this problem and to report to the General Council before the end of 2002. [See the WTO Decision of 30 August 2003 on Implementation of Paragraph 6 of the Doha Declaration on the Trips Agreement and Public Health, Wt/L/540 (Sept. 2, 2003).]

7. We reaffirm the commitment of developed-country Members to provide incentives to their enterprises and institutions to promote and encourage technology transfer to least-developed country Members pursuant to Article 66.2. We also agree that the least-developed country Members will not be obliged, with respect to pharmaceutical products, to implement or apply Sections 5 and 7 of Part II of the TRIPS Agreement or to enforce rights provided for under these Sections until 1 January 2016, without prejudice to the right of least-developed country Members to seek other extensions of the transition periods as provided for in Article 66.1 of the TRIPS Agreement. We instruct the Council for TRIPS to take the necessary action to give effect to this pursuant to Article 66.1 of the TRIPS Agreement.

Commission on Human Rights, *The right of everyone to the enjoyment of the highest attainable standard of physical and mental health*

Report of the Special Rapporteur, Paul Hunt, Mission to the World Trade Organization, UN Doc. E/CN.4/2004/49/Add.1 (Mar. 1, 2004)

Trade impacts on the right to health in numerous ways. States have to ensure that the trade rules and policies they select are consistent with their legal obligations in relation to the right to health. This raises complex and controversial issues. . . . This report attempts to provide an accessible introduction to a few of the technical issues that lie at the intersection of trade and the right to health. The Introduction signals some of the fundamental features of the Special Rapporteur's approach, such as the principle of policy coherence.

Policy Coherence

9. The Special Rapporteur's work is guided by the fundamental principle that national and international human rights law, including the right to health, should be consistently and coherently applied across all relevant national and international policy-making processes, including those relating to trade. This highlights one of the greatest challenges confronting international human rights law: the problem of disconnected Government. Practice shows that one part of Government does not necessarily grasp what another part of the same Government has agreed to do. Increasingly, States recognize this is a problem and some of them are trying to address it by mainstreaming human rights.

10. In this context, the Special Rapporteur notes the endeavours of WTO, the World Bank and the International Monetary Fund (IMF) to ensure greater

coherence between trade, development and finance. This powerful trend has far-reaching implications that are beyond this report. However, the Special Rapporteur wishes to emphasize that enhanced coherence should not be confined to policies that only deal with trade, development and economics. What is needed is a coherent approach to the application of a State's various national and international obligations, including those relating to trade, development, economics and human rights.

The Relationship Between Trade Liberalization and International Human Rights Law

11. International human right law takes a position neither for nor against any particular trade rule or policy, subject to two conditions: first, the rule or policy in question must, in practice, actually enhance enjoyment of human rights, including for the disadvantaged and marginal; second, the process by which the rule or policy is formulated, implemented and monitored must be consistent with all human rights and democratic principles. Thus, if reliable evidence confirms that a particular trade policy enhances enjoyment of the right to health, including for those living in poverty and other disadvantaged groups, and that policy is delivered in a way that is consistent with all human rights and democratic principles, then it is in conformity with international human rights law. However, if reliable evidence confirms that a particular trade policy has a negative impact on the enjoyment of the right to health of those living in poverty or other disadvantaged groups, then the State has an obligation under international human rights law to revise the relevant policy. This does not necessarily mean that the particular policy has to be altogether abandoned — it might mean that it has to be revised in such a way that it begins to have a positive impact on the enjoyment of the right to health of those living in poverty and other disadvantaged groups.

12. This position has a number of important implications that are examined further in this report. Among the most important is that international human rights law requires reliable evidence that a chosen rule or policy is delivering positive right to health outcomes, including for the disadvantaged. If a policy is at the planning stage, international human rights require that reliable assessments be undertaken to anticipate the likely impact of the policy on the enjoyment of the right to health of those living in poverty and other disadvantaged groups. Thus, international human rights law promotes rational and rigorous national and international policy-making that is based upon reliable data. The next section of this report outlines some of the other characteristics of a right to health approach to trade, such as participation and accountability. . . .

II. A Selection of Trade Issues and the Right to Health

A. Intellectual Property and Access to Medicines

41. The Agreement on Trade-Related Aspects of Intellectual Property Rights (the TRIPS Agreement) is the most comprehensive multilateral agreement that sets detailed minimum standards for the protection and enforcement of

intellectual property rights. The forms of intellectual property protection covered by the TRIPS Agreement most relevant to the enjoyment of the right to health include patent protection (over new medical processes and products such as pharmaceuticals), trademarks (covering signs distinguishing medical goods and services as coming from a particular trader), and the protection of undisclosed data (in particular test data). For example, patent protection of a pharmaceutical allows the intellectual property right holder to exclude competitors from certain acts, including reproducing and selling the drug for a minimum period of 20 years. This period of exclusion theoretically allows the right holder to recoup some of the costs involved in medical research. Apart from establishing minimum standards for various forms of intellectual property protection, the Agreement also allows WTO member States to adopt measures to protect public health and nutrition, and to protect against the abuse of intellectual property rights in certain cases. The Agreement makes disputes between WTO members concerning respect for the minimum standards subject to the WTO dispute settlement procedures.

42. Intellectual property protection can affect the enjoyment of the right to health, and related human rights, in a number of ways. Importantly, intellectual property protection can affect medical research and this can bear upon access to medicines. For example, patent protection can promote medical research by helping the pharmaceutical industry shoulder the costs of testing, developing and approving drugs. However, the commercial motivation of intellectual property rights encourages research, first and foremost, towards "profitable" diseases, while diseases that predominantly affect people in poor countries — such as river blindness — remain under-researched. This report returns to this issue under "Neglected diseases" below. Further, intellectual property rights may affect the use of traditional medicines such as those of indigenous peoples. While existing intellectual property protection can promote the health innovations of indigenous and local communities, the particular nature of this knowledge and the knowledge holders might require significant amendment to be made to intellectual legislation for protection to be comprehensive. Further, some traditional medicines have been appropriated, adapted and patented with little or no compensation to the original knowledge holders and without their prior consent, which raises questions for both the right to health and cultural rights.

43. The exclusion of competitors as a result of the grant of a patent can also be used by patent holders as a tool to increase the price of pharmaceuticals. High prices can exclude some sections of the population, particularly poor people, from accessing medicines. Given that the right to health includes an obligation on States to provide affordable essential medicines according to the WHO essential drugs list, intellectual property protection can lead to negative effects on the enjoyment of the right to health. In other words, in some cases intellectual property protection can reduce the economic accessibility of essential medicines. The TRIPS Agreement includes some flexibility in such circumstances by permitting WTO members to authorize third parties to work a patent (i.e. manufacture and sell pharmaceuticals at a lower price) without the authorization of the patent holder, subject to certain limitations including payment of a reasonable fee. Nonetheless, such flexibilities are, in reality, only available to those WTO members that have a domestic pharmaceutical manufacturing capacity.

Article 31 (f) of the TRIPS Agreement allows unauthorized working of the patent where sale is dominant locally. Thus, poorer countries without adequate manufacturing capacity might not be able to benefit from these flexibilities. The Special Rapporteur welcomes the Decision on Implementation of paragraph 6 of the Doha Declaration on the TRIPS Agreement and Public Health (August 2003) allowing countries producing generic copies of patented drugs under compulsory licence to export drugs to countries with no or little drug manufacturing capacity. The Special Rapporteur notes that the protracted negotiations that led to this Decision should have been informed by the human rights responsibility of rich States to engage in international assistance and cooperation in relation to the right to health. The Special Rapporteur underlines that the effectiveness of the Decision will depend on the extent to which it actually does lead to increased access to medicines for the poor. . . .

G. ACCEDING COUNTRIES. . . .

69. The Special Rapporteur reiterates his opinion that international human rights law is neither for nor against any particular trade rule or policy, subject to two conditions. However, he is concerned that pressure in trade negotiations, particularly when exercised by stronger trading partners over smaller acceding countries, might lead to unsustainable commitments to trade liberalization that, in practice, diminish States' capacity to realize the right to health. Powerful States have a human rights responsibility of international assistance and cooperation in relation to the right to health which means, inter alia, that they should respect the obligation of an acceding State to realize the right to health of individuals in its jurisdiction. In other words, during accession negotiations, the various human rights responsibilities of all parties should be kept in mind. At root, human rights remain a check against the possible misuse of power.

Commission on Human Rights Res. 2005/23, *Access to medication in the context of pandemics such as HIV/AIDS, tuberculosis and malaria*

Apr. 15, 2005

. . . *Noting with great concern* that, according to the Joint United Nations Programme on HIV/AIDS (UNAIDS), the HIV/AIDS pandemic claimed an estimated 3.1 million lives in 2004,

Alarmed that, according to the same source, about 40 million people were living with HIV by the end of 2004 and that an estimated 5 million people were newly infected with HIV in 2004, . . .

Alarmed that, according to the global Roll Back Malaria partnership, malaria annually causes more than one million preventable deaths, about 90 per cent of which are in Africa, that malaria is the leading cause of death in young children and that it causes at least 300 million cases of acute illness each year,

Alarmed also that, according to the World Health Organization report of 2004 entitled *Global Tuberculosis Control: Surveillance, Planning, Financing*, tuberculosis kills about 2 million people each year, more than 8 million people around the world become sick with tuberculosis each year, and it is projected that between 2002 and 2020, 36 million people will die of tuberculosis if control is not further strengthened,

Acknowledging the significance of HIV/AIDS in the increase in tuberculosis and other opportunistic infections,

Alarmed that, according to the World Health Organization, one third of the world's population still lacks access to essential medicines and that in the poorest parts of Africa and Asia, over half of the population lacks access to even the most basic essential drugs, . . .

Recalling the Declaration on the Agreement on Trade-Related Aspects of Intellectual Property Rights (TRIPS Agreement) and Public Health adopted at the Fourth Ministerial Conference of the World Trade Organization in Doha in November 2001,

Recalling also the decision on the implementation of paragraph 6 of the Doha Declaration on the TRIPS Agreement and Public Health, adopted by the General Council of the World Trade Organization on 30 August 2003, . . .

1. *Recognizes* that access to medication in the context of pandemics such as HIV/AIDS, tuberculosis and malaria is one fundamental element for achieving progressively the full realization of the right of everyone to the enjoyment of the highest attainable standard of physical and mental health; . . .

6. *Calls upon* States to pursue policies, in accordance with applicable international law, including international agreements acceded to, which would promote:

(*a*) The availability, in sufficient quantities, of pharmaceutical products and medical technologies used to treat and/or prevent pandemics such as HIV/AIDS, tuberculosis and malaria or the most common opportunistic infections that accompany them;

(*b*) The accessibility and affordability for all without discrimination, including the most vulnerable or socially disadvantaged groups of the population, as well as infants and children, of pharmaceutical products or medical technologies used to treat and/or prevent pandemics such as HIV/AIDS, tuberculosis, malaria or the most common opportunistic infections that accompany them;

(*c*) The assurance that pharmaceutical products or medical technologies used to treat and/or prevent pandemics such as HIV/AIDS, tuberculosis, malaria or the most common opportunistic infections that accompany them, irrespective of their sources and countries of origin, are scientifically and medically appropriate and of good quality;

7. *Calls upon* States, at the national level, on a non-discriminatory basis, in accordance with applicable international law, including international agreements acceded to:

(*a*) To refrain from taking measures which would deny or limit equal access for all persons to preventive, curative or palliative pharmaceutical products or medical technologies, including microbicides and male and female condoms, used to treat and/or prevent pandemics such as HIV/AIDS, tuberculosis, malaria or the most common opportunistic infections that accompany them;

(*b*) To adopt and implement, as appropriate, legislation or other measures affecting public health, in accordance with applicable international law, including international agreements acceded to, to safeguard access to such preventive, curative or palliative pharmaceutical products or medical technologies from any limitations by third parties;

(*c*) To adopt all appropriate positive measures, to the maximum of the resources allocated for this purpose, to promote effective access to such preventive, curative or palliative pharmaceutical products or medical technologies;

8. *Also calls upon* States, in furtherance of the Declaration of Commitment on HIV/AIDS, to address factors affecting the provision of drugs related to the treatment of pandemics such as HIV/AIDS and the most common opportunistic infections that accompany them, as well as to develop integrated strategies to strengthen health-care systems;...

12. *Further calls upon* States, at the international level, to take steps, individually and/or through international cooperation, in accordance with applicable international law, including international agreements acceded to, such as:

(*a*) To facilitate, wherever possible, access in other countries to essential preventive, curative or palliative pharmaceutical products or medical technologies used to treat and/or prevent pandemics such as HIV/AIDS, tuberculosis and malaria and the most common opportunistic infections that accompany them, as well as to extend the necessary cooperation, wherever possible, especially in times of emergency;

(*b*) To ensure that their actions as members of international organizations take due account of the right of everyone to the enjoyment of the highest attainable standard of physical and mental health and that the application of international agreements is supportive of public health policies that promote broad access to safe, effective and affordable preventive, curative or palliative pharmaceutical products and medical technologies;

13. *Urges* States to consider, whenever necessary, enacting appropriate national legislation in order to use to the fullest extent the flexibilities contained in the TRIPS Agreement and encourages States to take into account such flexibilities when entering into international trade agreements that may affect public health;

14. *Calls upon* States to conduct an impact assessment of the effects of international trade agreements with regard to public health and to the progressive realization of the right of everyone to the highest attainable standard of health;...

In considering the issues raised by this section, note the efforts to litigate issues of access to health care, in particular, the South African cases discussed in Chapter 6, pp. 511-526.

D. *Peacekeeping*

In 2000, the UN's International Law Commission decided to include the topic "Responsibility of international organizations" in its long-term program of work, a decision approved by the General Assembly, GA Res. 55/152, para. 8 (Dec. 12, 2000). In May 2002, the ILC appointed a Special Rapporteur and established a Working Group on the topic. By 2004, the Commission had before it two reports of the Special Rapporteur (UN Doc. A/CN.4/541 (Apr. 2, 2004)) and had provisionally adopted several draft rules. The text of the articles provisionally adopted so far by the Commission, together with some of the commentary, follow.

Report of the International Law Commission on its 56th Session

UN Doc. A/59/10 (2004), at 98, 100, 102, 109-14

Article 3. General Principles

1. Every internationally wrongful act of an international organization entails the international responsibility of the international organization.
2. There is an internationally wrongful act of an international organization when conduct consisting of an action or omission:(a) Is attributable to the international organization under international law; and(b) Constitutes a breach of an international obligation of that international organization. . . .

Article 6. Excess of Authority or Contravention of Instructions

The conduct of an organ or an agent of an international organization shall be considered an act of that organization under international law if the organ or agent acts in that capacity, even though the conduct exceeds the authority of that organ or agent or contravenes instructions.

Article 7. Conduct Acknowledged and Adopted by an International Organization as its Own

Conduct which is not attributable to an international organization under the preceding draft articles shall nevertheless be considered an act of that international organization under international law if and to the extent that the organization acknowledges and adopts the conduct in question as its own. . . .

The present articles do not say, but only imply, that conduct of military forces of States or international organizations is not attributable to the United Nations when the Security Council authorizes States or international organizations to take necessary measures outside a chain of command linking those forces to the United Nations. This point, which is hardly controversial, was recently expressed by the Director of the Field Administration and Logistics Division of the Department of Peacekeeping Operations of the United Nations in a letter to the Permanent Representative of Belgium to the United Nations, concerning a claim resulting from a car accident in Somalia, in the following terms:

> UNITAF troops were not under the command of the United Nations and the Organization has constantly declined liability for any claims made in respect of incidents involving those troops. . . .

Should instead persons or groups of persons act under the instructions, or the direction or control, of an international organization, they would have to be regarded as agents according to the definition given in paragraph 2 of draft article 4. . . .

When an organ of a State is placed at the disposal of an international organization, the organ may be fully seconded to that organization. In this case the organ's conduct would clearly be attributable only to the receiving organization. The same consequence would apply when an organ or agent of one international organization is fully seconded to another organization. In these cases, the general rule set out in article 4 would apply. Article 5 deals with the different situation in which the lent organ or agent still acts to a certain extent as organ of the lending State or as organ or agent of the lending organization. This occurs for instance in the case of military contingents that a State placed at the disposal of the United Nations for a peacekeeping operation, since the State retains disciplinary powers and criminal jurisdiction over the members of the national contingent. In this situation the problem arises whether a specific conduct of the lent organ or agent has to be attributed to the receiving organization or to the lending State or organization. . . .

The lending State or organization may conclude an agreement with the receiving organization over placing an organ or agent at the latter organization's disposal. The agreement may state which State or organization would be responsible for conduct of that organ or agent. For example, according to the model contribution agreement relating to military contingents placed at the disposal of the United Nations by one of its Member States, the United Nations is regarded as liable towards third parties, but has a right of recovery from the contributing State under circumstances such as "loss, damage, death or injury [arising] from gross negligence or willful misconduct of the personnel provided by the Government." The agreement appears to deal only with distribution of responsibility and not with attribution of conduct. At any event, this type of agreement is not conclusive because it governs only the relations between the contributing State or organization and the receiving organization and could thus not have the effect of depriving a third party of any right that that party may have towards the State or organization which is responsible under the general rules.

The criterion for attribution of conduct either to the contributing State or organization or to the receiving organization is based on the factual control that is exercised over the specific conduct taken by the organ or agent placed at the receiving organization's disposal. . . .

With regard to States, the existence of control has been mainly discussed in relation to the question whether conduct of persons or of groups of persons, especially irregular armed forces, is attributable to a State. In the context of the placement of an organ or agent at the disposal of an international organization, control plays a different role. It does not concern the issue whether a certain conduct is attributable at all to a State or an international organization, but rather to which entity — the contributing State or organization or the receiving organization — conduct is attributable.

The United Nations assumes that in principle it has exclusive control of the deployment of national contingents in a peacekeeping force. This premise led the United Nations Legal Counsel to state:

> As a subsidiary organ of the United Nations, an act of a peacekeeping force is, in principle, imputable to the Organization, and if committed in violation of an

> international obligation entails the international responsibility of the Organization and its liability in compensation.

This statement sums up United Nations practice relating to the United Nations Operation in the Congo (ONUC), the United Nations Peacekeeping Force in Cyprus (UNFICYP) and later peacekeeping forces.

Practice relating to peacekeeping forces is particularly significant in the present context because of the control that the contributing State retains over disciplinary matters and criminal affairs. This may have consequences with regard to attribution of conduct.... Attribution of conduct to the contributing State is clearly linked with the retention of some powers by that State over its national contingent and thus on the control that the State possesses in the relevant respect.

As has been held by several scholars, when an organ or agent is placed at the disposal of an international organization, the decisive question in relation to attribution of a given conduct appears to be who has effective control over the conduct in question. For instance, it would be difficult to attribute to the United Nations conduct of forces in circumstances such as those described in the report of the Commission of inquiry which was established in order to investigate armed attacks on UNOSOM II personnel:

> The Force Commander of UNOSOM II was not in effective control of several national contingents which, in varying degrees, persisted in seeking orders from their home authorities before executing orders of the Forces Command. Many major operations undertaken under the United Nations flag and in the context of UNOSOM's mandate were totally outside the command and control of the United Nations, even though the repercussions impacted crucially on the mission of UNOSOM and the safety of its personnel.

The United Nations Secretary-General held that the criterion of the "degree of effective control" was decisive with regard to joint operations:

> The international responsibility of the United Nations for combat-related activities of United Nations forces is premised on the assumption that the operation in question is under the exclusive command and control of the United Nations [....] In joint operations, international responsibility for the conduct of the troops lies where operational command and control is vested according to the arrangements establishing the modalities of cooperation between the State or States providing the troops and the United Nations. In the absence of formal arrangements between the United Nations and the State or States providing troops, responsibility would be determined in each and every case according to the degree of effective control exercised by either party in the conduct of the operation....

International Law Association, Report of the Seventieth Conference

Third Report Consolidated of the Committee on Accountability of International Organisations, at 772, 797 (2002)

...Practice of international organizations confirms that ultra vires conduct of an organ or agent is attributable to the organization when that conduct is linked with the organ's or agent's official functions. This appears to underlie the position taken by the Office of Legal Affairs of the United Nations in a memorandum concerning claims involving off-duty acts of members of peacekeeping forces: "United Nations policy in regard to off-duty acts of the members of peace-keeping forces is that the Organization has no legal or financial liability for death, injury or damage resulting from such acts [. . . .] We consider the primary factor in determining an 'off-duty' situation to be whether the member of a peace-keeping mission was acting in a non-official/non-operational capacity when the incident occurred and not whether he/she was in military or civilian attire at the time of the incident or whether the incident occurred inside or outside the area of operation [. . . .] [W]ith regard to United Nations legal and financial liability a member of the Force on a state of alert may none the less assume an off-duty status if he/she independently acts in an individual capacity, not attributable to the performance of official duties, during that designated 'state-of-alert' period. [. . .] [W]e wish to note that the factual circumstances of each case vary and, hence, a determination of whether the status of a member of a peace-keeping mission is on duty or off duty may depend in part on the particular factors of the case, taking into consideration the opinion of the Force Commander or Chief of Staff."

While the "off-duty" conduct of a member of a national contingent would not be attributed to the organization, the "on-duty" conduct may be so attributed. One would then have to examine in the case of ultra vires conduct if it related to the functions entrusted to the person concerned.

These theoretical issues have been given new significance by the broad expansion of UN peacekeeping operations. The United Nations has carried out some sixty peacekeeping operations since its creation, to which more than 100 member states have contributed; as of mid-2005, it was engaged in sixteen missions around the world. In 2004, the United Nations rotated some 120,000 military and civilian police personnel and operated fourteen military hospitals and 120 clinics. During these operations, allegations of abuse committed by peacekeepers have arisen, especially (but not exclusively) sexual abuse; these issues are addressed in the next two extracts.

Colum Lynch, *U.N. Sexual Abuse Alleged in Congo, Peacekeepers Accused in Draft Report*

Wash. Post, Dec. 16, 2004, at A26

U.N. peacekeepers threatened U.N. investigators investigating allegations of sexual misconduct in Congo and sought to bribe witnesses to change incriminating testimony, a confidential U.N. draft report says.

The 34-page report, which was obtained by The Washington Post, accuses U.N. peacekeepers from Morocco, Pakistan and Nepal of seeking to obstruct U.N. efforts to investigate a sexual abuse scandal that has damaged the United Nations' standing in Congo.

The report documents 68 cases of alleged rape, prostitution and pedophilia by U.N. peacekeepers from Pakistan, Uruguay, Morocco, Tunisia, South Africa and

Nepal. U.N. officials say they have uncovered more than 150 allegations of sexual misconduct throughout the country as part of a widening investigation into sexual abuse by U.N. personnel that has plagued the United Nations' largest peacekeeping mission, U.N. officials said.

"Sexual exploitation and abuse, particularly prostitution of minors, is widespread and long-standing," says a draft of the internal July report, which has not previously been made public. "Moreover, all of the major contingents appear to be implicated."

The latest disclosure comes as U.N. officials confirmed that a senior U.N. official in Congo was suspended from his job with pay in recent weeks pending an investigation into allegations of "inappropriate conduct." The senior official, a New Zealand national, was accused of being seen drinking with Congolese prostitutes at a bar when the U.N. leadership was trying to address a major sexual abuse scandal, officials said. William Lacy Swing, a former U.S. ambassador who heads the U.N. mission in Congo, declined to discuss the matter except to say the official is no longer in the country.

Swing also declined to discuss specific allegations against national peacekeepers. He conceded, however, that the mission's credibility has been badly damaged in recent months by allegations of sexual misconduct against U.N. personnel in Congo.

"We view this as something very serious that can impede our ability to accomplish our mandate," he said. "There is no question of the dedication of this mission to getting rid of this."

The report alleges that a Moroccan contingent stationed in Bunia threatened a U.N. informant investigating child prostitution. The Moroccan peacekeepers also "spread the word" that a U.N. child-protection advocate looking into allegations of child prostitution and rape by U.N. peacekeepers "had better be careful when she went out at night," the report said.

The report cites cases in which peacekeepers from Morocco, Pakistan and possibly Tunisia "were reported to have paid, or attempted to pay witnesses to change their testimony" regarding alleged sexual abuse. It also charges that Moroccan military officials refused "to provide the names of Moroccan soldiers present at the location" of an alleged rape.

Morocco's ambassador to the United Nations, Mohamed Bennouna, was unavailable for comment last night. A spokesman for Pakistan's mission to the United Nations, Mansoor Suhail, said it is unfair to "defame" the troops before they have faced "a proper investigation and inquiry."

He also noted that Western personnel in Congo and other U.N. missions around the world have also been the target of sexual abuse charges.

"In case the allegations are established, we would like to discipline them," he added. "The Pakistani army's discipline is the strictest."

The U.N. mission in Congo was established five years ago to end the country's war, oversee the withdrawal of seven foreign armies and help prepare for national elections. It employs more than 1,000 civilians and nearly 11,000 peacekeepers from 50 nations.

The crisis has challenged the organization's ability to effectively manage and impose discipline in a large peacekeeping operation. It has also hurt the organization's reputation as it confronts charges of corruption in its management of Iraq's prewar oil-for-food program.

The Washington Post first reported last month on a separate U.N. report that found sexual exploitation by U.N. personnel in Congo "appears to be significant, wide spread and ongoing."

The latest report says that allegations of sexual misconduct were initially leveled in summer 2003 against U.N. personnel based in Kindu and Kisingani. But the U.N. report says the abuse worsened in Bunia, where more than half of the United Nations' troops are stationed.

While most cases of sexual misconduct involved U.N. peacekeepers soliciting prostitutes, the report cites three cases of alleged rape by Nepalese peacekeepers, including the alleged abduction and rape of a 10-year-old girl in a U.N. armored personnel carrier in April.

Report of the Secretary-General, *UN Special Measures for Protection from Sexual Exploitation and Sexual Abuse*

U.N. Doc. A/59/782 (April 15, 2005)

. . .

1. The General Assembly in resolution 57/306 of 15 April 2003 requested the Secretary-General to, inter alia, maintain data on investigations into sexual exploitation and related offences by humanitarian and peacekeeping personnel, and all relevant actions taken thereon. Pursuant to that resolution, the Secretary-General on 9 October 2003 issued his bulletin ST/SGB/2003/13 on special measures for protection from sexual exploitation and sexual abuse. It was addressed to all staff of the United Nations, including staff of separately administered organs and programmes. As defined in the bulletin, "sexual exploitation" means any actual or attempted abuse of a position of vulnerability, differential power, or trust, for sexual purposes, including, but not limited to, profiting monetarily, socially or politically from the sexual exploitation of another. The term "sexual abuse" means actual or threatened physical intrusion of a sexual nature, whether by force or under unequal or coercive conditions. . . .

7. . . . [E]xamination of allegations by the Head of Mission, followed by a preliminary investigation, exists for complaints against uniformed peacekeeping personnel, namely, members of national military contingents, military observers and civilian police (referred to as "experts on mission"). However, for personnel in these categories, the preliminary investigation is followed by a Board of Inquiry investigation. In cases in which individuals are found to have committed sexual exploitation or abuse, the Head of Mission can recommend repatriation to the Under-Secretary-General for Peacekeeping Operations. If he/she approves the recommendation, the Permanent Mission of the uniformed personnel concerned is notified and the expenses of the repatriation are paid by the relevant Member State. Among the 89 allegations against uniformed personnel, the Head of Mission decided that no further action was necessary for 6 allegations, 6 allegations were pending a preliminary investigation, and 4 allegations had been deemed unsubstantiated as at 31 December 2004. Seventy-three allegations against uniformed personnel had been sent to the Board of Inquiry: 15 were pending investigation, 5 had been found unsubstantiated, and allegations had been substantiated in 53 cases as at 31 December 2004. In substantiated cases, the

military personnel were repatriated on disciplinary grounds. The Department of Peacekeeping Operations is following up with Member States to obtain information on disciplinary and/or criminal action taken. . . .

II. Observations

9. The total number of 121 allegations of sexual exploitation and abuse registered in 2004 was more than double the 53 allegations reported in 2003. The increase in allegations is deeply troubling. It should be noted, however, that the recorded increase may result in part from the newly implemented measures to prevent and respond to sexual exploitation and abuse. Focal points have been designated to facilitate receipt of complaints, reporting procedures have become more clearly defined, and managers have clearly and publicly indicated that sexual exploitation and abuse will not be tolerated. In these new work environments, it is to be expected that victims, United Nations personnel and others will be more inclined to come forward with their allegations. . . .

III. Progress in Implementing Special Measures for Protection from Sexual Exploitation and Sexual Abuse. . . .

21. While some progress has been made during the period under review, those efforts have also served to highlight shortcomings in terms of policies, procedures and guidelines that are needed to prevent sexual exploitation and abuse and enforce United Nations standards of conduct in this regard. In particular, much more needs to be done to establish clear, confidential and easily accessible complaints mechanisms and to improve information-sharing between different components of the system. Staff have also requested a clearer understanding of the terms of the Secretary-General's bulletin, guidance on how allegations are to be handled and investigated, and information about the disciplinary consequences attached to breaching the standards laid out in the bulletin. . . .

Comments and Questions

1. May states avoid their human rights responsibilities by transferring power to non-state actors or intergovernmental organizations? Note that Chapter VII of the UN Charter originally envisaged special agreements between the UN and member states to provide for military contingents to be readily available to the UN, under the strategic direction of a Military Staff Committee. Instead, peacekeeping and enforcement forces remain under the control of national officers and policies. How does this affect UN responsibility for abuses committed by peacekeepers? Difficulties in drawing a line between operational and organizational control are underlined in Luigi Condorelli, "Le statut des forces de l'ONU et le droit international humanitaire," 78 Rivista di Diritto Internazionale 881 (1995).

2. The responsibility of international organizations for human rights violations has both an external and an internal dimension. International civil service law largely governs the rights and obligations of staff members within

international organizations. Several international organizations have administrative tribunals, including the UN, the ILO, and the World Bank. The International Labour Organisation's Administrative Tribunal (ILOAT) has jurisdiction over more than three dozen specialized agencies, including UNESCO, WHO, and FAO. Although their competence varies, international administrative tribunals deal with appeals by international civil servants against measures taken by an organization in breach of conditions of appointment and benefits, including workers' rights, discrimination, and sexual harassment. The tribunals may overturn the decisions of employers in some cases and may grant financial compensation. The ILOAT has stated that the law that the Tribunal applies in entertaining claims that are put to it includes not just the written Rules of the defendant organization but the general principles of law and basic human rights. *Franks and Vollering v. EPO*, ILOAT Judgment No. 13333 of Jan. 31, 1994, Consideration 5. See Karel Wellens, *Remedies against International Organizations* (2002); C.F. Amerasinghe, *Law of the International Civil Service* (2 vols. 1994); id., *Case Law of the World Bank Administrative Tribunal* (2 vols. 1989, 1993). On the liability of international organizations generally, see: Ewa Butkiewicz, "The Premises of International Responsibility of Inter-Governmental Organizations," 11 Polish Y.B. Int'l Law 117 (1981-1982); Manuel Perez Gonzalez, "Les organisations internationales et le droit de la responsabilité," 99 *Rev. gén. Droit int'l public* 63 (1988); Moshe Hirsch, *The Responsibility of International Organizations toward Third Parties* (1995); C.F. Amerasinghe, *Principles of the Institutional Law of International Organizations* (1996); Pierre Klein, *La responsabilité des organisations internationales dans les ordres juridiques internes et en droit des gens* (1998); I. Scobbie, "International Organizations and International Relations" in A *Handbook of International Organizations* (Rene-Jean Dupuy ed., 2d ed. 1998); C. Pitschas, *Die völkerrechtliche Verantwortlichkeit der europäischen Gemeinschaften und ihrer Mitgliedstaaten* (2001); Jean-Marc Sorel, "La responsabilité des Nations Unies dans les opérations de maintien de la paix," 3 Int'l L. Forum 127 (2001); M. Bothe, *Streitkräfte internationaler Organisationen* (1968).

3. Most commentary on trade and human rights focuses mainly on the obligations of WTO member states rather than on the WTO itself. Yet, as the decisions on public health and conflict diamonds show, various entities within the organization act in ways that can promote or harm human rights. Does the WTO have any obligation to act consistently with human rights, or is it simply a coordinating body for the policies and laws of its member states?

4. Note that corporate codes of conduct and attempts to make international financial and trade organizations more accountable often address issues that go far beyond traditional human rights concerns, such as protection of the environment, economic development, transparency, and corruption. Is human rights likely to gain or lose as it is increasingly considered in tandem with the promotion of other social goods, such as those just mentioned?

V. The Responsibility of Individuals for Human Rights Violations

Historically, individuals could be objects of international law but were not subjects of that law, i.e., they had no international personality in and of themselves. Of course, individual acts could be criminalized at the international level, a development which is discussed in detail in Chapter 11. But it is important to distinguish duties of the individual to obey national and international criminal law from any duties an individual may have to promote, respect, or ensure the human rights of others.

The African Charter on Human and Peoples' Rights includes an extensive list of duties of the individual, but it was not the first international instrument to refer to individual duties or responsibilities. The American Declaration of the Rights and Duties of Man contains a list of duties, and the first paragraph of Article 29 of the Universal Declaration of Human Rights provides, "Everyone has duties to the community in which alone the free and full development of his personality is possible." The preambles of both covenants also refer generally to "the individual, having duties to other individuals and the community to which he belongs. . . ."

In 1980, UN Sub-Commission member Erica-Irene Daes completed a study on Article 29 of the Universal Declaration and, inter alia, reached the following conclusions with respect to the meaning of such duties and their relationship to human rights.

Erica-Irene A. Daes, *Freedom of the Individual under Law: An Analysis of Article 29 of the Universal Declaration of Human Rights*

UN Sales No. E.89.XIV.5, at 53-60 (1990) (originally issued as UN Docs. E/CN.4/Sub.2/432/Rev.1 and E/CN.4/Sub.2/432/Adds.1-7 (1980))

234. Among the first duties of the individual should be the duty to use his strength to maintain international peace and security. . . .

[The individual also has duties to refrain from propaganda for war and advocacy of racial or religious hatred, stemming from Article 20 of the Covenant on Civil and Political Rights.]

239. The individual also has duties to humanity. This conclusion is mainly derived from the law of nature. Thus, natural law commands the individual not only to strive for his own preservation and protection, but also aid his fellow men in this effort, as only in this way can each really preserve and perfect himself. . . .

242. The individual has a responsibility to observe the rules of international law and in particular the Charter of the United Nations, the International Covenants on Human Rights and other international instruments relating to human rights. . . .

250. It is the duty of the individual to respect, recognize and give priority to the general welfare, or the public or general interest, in so far as they are compatible with the dignity of the individual. The general welfare by itself has no meaning; its purpose is to promote man's dignity and well-being.

251. The general welfare is something quite different from "reason of state." One of the purposes of the State is to safeguard the rights and interests of the individual human being. Man should identify himself with the community but not lose his identity in it. . . .

255. Another concluding observation which could be made is that every individual has a duty to oppose demands of the community that are incompatible with the purposes and principles of the Charter of the United Nations . . . and

other international instruments relating to the protection of human rights and fundamental freedoms or with national democratic constitutions. . . .

257. However, resistance to unlawful acts and measures must, in principle, not overstep the limits of the legal order which that act or measure has contravened. Everyone is under an obligation to refrain from using violence except in self-defence. Also, it is an obligation of every individual, in cases of resistance, to protect the life and the rights of others and to avoid damaging natural ecological systems which serve the public welfare. . . .

259. The individual has an obligation to obey the law and other legitimate commands of the authorities of his country and those of the country in which he may be residing.

260. The obligation of obedience to the law is well known, even from ancient times. But which law should the individual obey? The just and good law. . . .

265. . . . [I]n a model democratic community, where a free democratic political system prevailed, there would be important reasons which vitally affect the individual's duty to obey laws emanating from that system. Among these reasons, the following two are the most important: the fact that a democratic community, in which all have equal power and there is no tendency for the majority to treat the minority with less than equal consideration, is a fair compromise between competing claims to power; and the fact that participating in good faith gives rise to an obligation to act as if one had consented to be bound by the result of the decision-making procedure. Hence these important reasons for obeying the law in a democratic community apply only when no rights essential to the functioning of a fair compromise decision-making procedure have been infringed. Among such rights are, for example, the right of free expression and the right of free participation in elections. . . .

[The author goes on to identify, inter alia, individual duties to protect the "human environment," respect other individuals, protect the bodily integrity and human dignity of others, vote and be elected, and promote culture.]

In 2000, the Commission on Human Rights once more considered the issue of individual duties and appointed a special rapporteur who submitted a preliminary report in 2002 and a final report in 2003, to which he annexed a "pre-draft declaration on human social responsibilities." The Commission asked states to respond to the report and decided in 2005, in a 26-25 vote with one state abstaining, to request Mr. Martinez to prepare a new initial version of his pre-draft declaration taking into account the comments submitted. Comm'n on Hum. Rts., Decision 2005/111 (Apr. 20, 2005). The decision was based on a proposal from China and the "like-minded group." Extracts of the final report and the reaction of some states are set forth below.

Comm'n on Hum.Rts, *Human rights and human responsibilities: Final report of the Special Rapporteur, Miguel Alfonso Martinez, on the Study requested by the Commission in its resolution 2000/63, and submitted pursuant to Economic and Social Council decision* 2002/277

E/CN.4/2003/105, 17 March 2003. . . .

27. It is worth emphasizing from the start that the main purpose of this study — as the Special Rapporteur has understood it even before beginning

his mandate — is very clear and simple: to determine whether it is possible, convenient or necessary today in this field of human rights — both on the domestic plane in each State and on the international level — first, to highlight conceptually and encourage practical actions exclusively concerned with the rights of individuals, without doing the same with respect to their duties towards their society; second, to block any attempt to define what these social responsibilities could possibly be, and, finally, to deny — as a dogma of faith, impossible to challenge — the notion that there exists a link between the rights and duties of each individual. . . .

29. The Special Rapporteur has been able to verify that, in reality, the relationship that exists between the rights of the individual and their social responsibilities — to which the Universal Declaration and the two International Covenants on Human Rights of 1966 refer only vaguely — constitutes an element of particular historical and current relevance in very dissimilar parts of the world, fundamentally in countries "of the South" and in the conceptual thinking of limited intellectual circles in countries "of the North".

30. The Special Rapporteur believes that, to a great degree, the odd lack of attention to this matter is due to the singular focus that these bodies have given to those three important documents that date back several decades and were born in well-known circumstances.

31. For example, in 1948 only 57 of the 191 States that today are Members of the United Nations could contribute their ideas to the contents of the Universal Declaration. Only three of them were African countries. Later, during the preparatory work on the Covenants, it was still highly difficult for the dozens of countries "of the South", recently emerged from the long night of European colonialism and only recently incorporated into the international life as sovereign States, to be able to establish and articulate in a concerted way their positions within the United Nations. . . .

38. Ethics, morality, equity, justice and human solidarity offer rules and principles that are essential to forge (or develop, as the case may be) a new social, individual and collective awareness, so as to invigorate the current established legal institutions to more successfully pursue this task.

39. This new ethical and humanistic awareness has to be, by definition, global and, for that reason, pluralistic and imbued with the spirit of solidarity. It should be as pluralistic as is the world in which we all live. It should be based on solidarity and humanism, and as fully participative as required by the need to effectively achieve and guarantee the full dignity inherent in every human being in every corner of the planet. It cannot be based on an incomplete vision, nor seek solutions to humanitarian problems based on double standards or condone political manipulation in the field of human rights.

40. The road to the creation and consolidation of this new ethic passes different milestones. In the view of the Special Rapporteur, one of the most relevant is the point where one internalizes that when dealing with human rights issues one cannot reject the notion that in addition to *rights*, individuals also have *obligations* (the strictly legal dimension of their life in society) and *duties* (the ethical dimension of their living together with others in the same society). It must be acknowledged, nonetheless, that this thesis is not yet generally accepted. . . .

42. The Special Rapporteur starts out from the premise that the idea that there can be rights without ethical duties or responsibilities, or rights not based on equity and human solidarity, constitutes a patent breach of logic, as well as a social impossibility. The proof is the thousands of millions of human beings in the

world who today suffer from all sorts of deprivations, and the generalized crisis in the economy, the environment and governance that visibly marks today's world should serve as a clear warning to all. Freedoms recognized only generically and in the abstract are simply useless. On the other hand, to argue that social duties can exist without individual rights is not only unimaginable, but absolutely unacceptable under the principles of ethics and equity.

43. For these reasons he considers that all persons have, at the same time, *rights*, *obligations* and *duties* in all aspects of life touching on the promotion, effective realization and protection of *all* human rights. Neither from a legal point of view, nor on the ethical plane, is it possible to conceive of rights without such a logical correlation. Every right, in one way or another, is linked to some obligation or some responsibility, and every time that a duty is fulfilled, it is very likely that the violation of some right is prevented. . . .

48. If it is recognized that all citizens enjoy equal rights, it is fair to admit that all of them are subject to equal duties. Furthermore, would it be rational for someone to proclaim that he or she enjoys certain rights or liberties, without recognizing that others have the duty to respect them? The Special Rapporteur is of the opinion that it is impossible not to perceive that this active link between one and the other constitutes the real and ultimate essence within the social fabric that sustains and guarantees the harmonious survival of the whole human community, no matter what type of political or social organization it as and no matter where it is located on our planet.

49. In addition, awareness of that link will help to avoid that, under certain conditions, the individual moves, imperceptibly but inexorably, towards an unacceptable "freedom of indifference" (in the words of the Inter-Action Council) towards what happens to the rest of humanity.

50. To try, for example, to justify an alleged "right" to the conceptual defence of racism and practical action along those lines by invoking, as a pretext, freedom of opinion, expression and association, appears to the Special Rapporteur as an aberration illustrative of just how far this totally unbridled "freedom" can go without moral constraints.

51. What will this "freedom" be worth when the life of our planet becomes highly precarious or even impossible, when the world's ecological balance has been destroyed as a result of policies and practices of promoting anarchical exploitation of nonrenewable resources for the "development" of a few societies, without any ethical guidelines and based only on profits, the irrational lust for wealth and vulgar riches, at the expense of the habitat of entire peoples (indigenous, in particular) and the future of Humanity?

52. Finally, the Special Rapporteur underlines his conviction that in societies in which some individuals have a greater degree of effective freedom than others, they have correspondingly greater duties than the rest of those with whom they live, and that each individual person has the ethical and moral duty to recognize and exercise the rights that belong to him or her in due form and just degree, according to his/her honest reasoning and good faith (in the words of the Catholic Church). . . .

61. To start, it can be seen that these extralegal *responsibilities* may have very diverse sources of authority; e.g. the provisions of the Universal Declaration itself (arts. 1, final part, 14(2), 29(3) and 30); non-mandatory jurisdictional or legislative acts (article 85 of the Family Code in effect in Cuba), and even from texts at the

constitutional level (e.g. articles 35 of the 1978 Constitution of Spain; 125 of the 1982 Constitution of Honduras; 51A(e) of the Constitution of India; 2 of the 1947 Constitution of Italy; 6 of the present Constitution of Switzerland; and 57 and 58 of the Constitution which came into force in 2000 following a popular referendum in the Bolivarian Republic of Venezuela).

62. On the other hand, the ratio legis for these duties toward the community can be widely varied. First, all individuals have the *duty* to assist the State, within their means, so that it can completely fulfil the basic role that belongs to it. . . .

64. Nevertheless, it should be noted here that certain groups with specific social functions (e.g. the clergy, doctors, journalists and lawyers, to mention just a few) acquire — precisely because of the nature of their work — additional social responsibilities. The same is true for the business class in general and for editors (or owners) of the mass media. The decisions taken by these social groups carry such weight in modem society that, depending on their sector, they may limit, deny, or help large segments of the population gain access to their rights to work, to an adequate standard of living, or to adequate information that would allow them to fully exercise their freedom of opinion and expression.

65. All the duties expressed above are applicable, of course, whether the person acts in his/her capacity as an individual, in association with others, or as a member of a specific social group.

66. For all of the above, the Special Rapporteur considers quite evident both the wide variety and the importance of those responsibilities that, to his understanding, each individual has towards his/her community/society under the present globalization.

67. Therefore, the need to compile all of them in an orderly fashion appears unquestionable to him, and perhaps the Commission could initiate that task on the basis of the text presented in annex I. This work should take place entirely within the United Nations bodies specializing in human rights (in particular in the Commission on Human Rights) given the obvious advantages for participation that these offer to both Governments and NGOs during the entire drafting process of the text. That compilation should lead to the preparation of a draft international standard.

Comm'n on Hum. Rts, *Compilation of the essential aspects of replies received on the pre-draft declaration on human social responsibilities Report of the Office of the High Commissioner for Human Rights*, E/CN.4/2005/99 (7 Feb. 2005)

3. The Governments of Albania, Belgium, the Czech Republic, Finland, Germany, Hungary, Lithuania, Luxembourg, the Netherlands, Poland, Portugal, Romania, Sweden and the United Kingdom of Great Britain and Northern Ireland submitted a joint comment in which they expressed the view that the predraft declaration is contrary to the principles on which the international human rights system is built. The idea that a State can determine which, if any, rights an individual can enjoy in return for the exercise of responsibilities is fundamentally inconsistent with the basic concepts of human rights, according to which human rights are universal and inalienable.

4. The universal and inalienable character of human rights results from Article 55 of the Charter of the United Nations which provides that "the United Nations shall promote universal respect for, and observance of, human rights and fundamental freedoms for all without distinction as to race, sex, language or religion." All human rights derive from the dignity and worth inherent in the human person. Individuals are entitled to enjoy human rights without interference or qualification by a State, other than as necessary and permitted by human rights treaties. The pre-draft declaration may undermine this principle and also the principle that individuals are entitled to enjoy the same human rights without discrimination of any kind. . . .

6. Conditional linkages between responsibilities and human rights cannot be accepted. The debate on strengthening social and cultural "norms and values" should always be conducted on the understanding that human rights are universal and inalienable and therefore cannot and must not be conditionally linked to, or made otherwise dependent on the performance of duties. If members of any society have a range of responsibilities and duties towards each other and towards democratic society as a whole, in no way can these responsibilities affect the obligations of States towards individuals for the promotion and protection of human rights. . . .

12. In the view of the Government of Canada, the main thrust of the pre-draft declaration runs contrary to the purpose of the Commission on Human Rights, which is to promote universal respect for, and observance of, human rights and fundamental freedoms for all without distinction. Human rights serve to protect the inherent dignity and equality of every individual. The primary responsibility for the promotion and protection of human rights rests with the State. States have binding international legal obligations to respect human rights under a number of treaties and under customary international law. States are internationally responsible for compliance with their international human rights obligations, and have created a variety of international mechanisms, such as the human rights treaty bodies, and the Commission on Human Rights and its system of special procedures, to provide a framework for monitoring compliance with human rights.

13. In contrast, the document of the Sub-Commission on the Promotion and Protection of Human Rights would purport to impose responsibilities and duties directly on individuals and link them to the exercise of human rights. Further, the pre-draft declaration would purport to subordinate the enjoyment of human rights to the performance of these duties and to other vague and undefined interests of society. Such language could, if adopted, be used to justify restricting or otherwise violating human rights contrary to international law. . . .

17. The Government of Cuba expressed the view that the notion of rights implicitly and inevitably means that other persons, groups, and the State as a whole have responsibilities or duties concerning the recognition and effective realization of these rights and the creation of an environment conducive to their enjoyment. The pre-draft declaration constitutes an important contribution to resolving the acute discrepancy existing between, on the one hand, the enormous conceptual advances made on the subject of rights and, on the other, the lack of precise definitions concerning what duties result from article 29, paragraph 1, of the Universal Declaration of Human Rights and the last (fifth) common preambular paragraph of the International Covenants on Human Rights. The texts of the Universal Declaration and of the Covenants leave no

doubt that all individuals have duties (or responsibilities) towards the community/ society in which they live. This is the only environment that cannot only afford everyone the possibility of fully developing his or her personality, but also ensure the effective realization of the rights and freedoms enshrined in the Universal Declaration itself.

18. There is a need to specify what the duties (or responsibilities) of every person are towards the community in which he or she lives. A future codification of human social responsibilities should include the following duties: to respect international peace and security; to refrain from any propaganda for war and advocacy of national, racial or religious hatred; to uphold the rules of international law and all human rights for everyone; to oppose actions that are incompatible with the purposes and principles of the Charter of the United Nations; to protect the environment; to respect and promote the right of peoples to self-determination and cultural and religious diversity; to work to promote the economic, social and cultural development of all the world's peoples; to strengthen solidarity and respect between all human beings and peoples of the world; and to promote the establishment of an international order based on the principles of humanity, equity, solidarity and social justice.

19. National efforts should be pursued to incorporate human duties/responsibilities in domestic legislation. International and domestic codification of human social responsibilities can move forward in parallel and mutually reinforce each other. The development of international codification will guide domestic legislation. The obligation to stipulate responsibilities is a key factor for arriving at a system of equitable justice and, ultimately, reconciliation and stability at both the national and the international level.

Comments and Questions

1. Daes explicitly addresses issues of morality and ethics, as well as law, throughout her study. Are the distinctions sufficiently clear? Is she able to define individual duties in a way that does not undermine individual human rights?

2. Is it necessary or appropriate for the Commission on Human Rights to adopt a declaration of human responsibilities? Does it make any difference that the states most strongly supporting the declaration are China and Cuba? Are the objections raised by Canada evident in the extracts from the Martinez report?

3. Review Articles 27-29 of the African Charter. Documentary Supplement. Are they a prerequisite to the enjoyment of the rights set forth in the Charter? Do they limit the rights that may be claimed by, in effect, subordinating rights to an individual's duties to, e.g., "serve his national community by placing his physical and intellectual abilities at its service . . . [n]ot to compromise the security of the State whose national or resident he is . . . [and] preserve and strengthen social and national solidarity" (Article 29(2)(3) and (4))? Recall Heyns' observation, supra page 328, that the African Commission's use of article 27(2) "as a general limitation clause seems to confirm the view that the concept of 'duties' should not be understood as a sinister way of saying rights should first be earned, or that meeting certain duties is a precondition for enjoying human rights. . . . Rights precede duties, and the recognition of duties is merely another way of signifying the kind of limitations that may be placed on rights." For a

positive interpretation of the Charter's concept of duties, see Makau Wa Mutua, "The Banjul Charter and the African Cultural Fingerprint: An Evaluation of the Language of Duties", 35 *Va. J. Int'l L.* 339 (1995).

VI. Final Comments and Questions

As the materials in this chapter have shown, many parties may be implicated in human rights violations. For the past several hundred years, the territorial state has been the primary entity endowed with powers and responsibilities over individuals and groups within its boundaries. It was therefore natural that the state would be held responsible for protecting and promoting human rights, as those rights began to be articulated in the twentieth century. Have changes in the modern world altered the appropriateness of identifying states as the only or primary duty-holders in this respect? What are the likely consequences, if entities such as international organizations, multinational corporations, or even civil society organizations are also obliged to promote and protect human rights? To whom are such entities accountable?

Chapter 6

Domestic Enforcement Mechanisms

Are States' Courts Bound to Apply International Human Rights Norms?

I. Introduction: The Relationship Between International and Domestic Legal Systems

Previous chapters have identified a broad array of international human rights standards, contained in binding multilateral treaties and, to some extent, in customary international law, as well as standards articulated in "soft law" instruments that have not yet ripened into legally binding norms. It is one thing, however, for there to exist a well developed universe of international human rights norms; it is quite another for those norms to affect the lives of real people. In all too many parts of the world, an enormous gap persists between internationally recognized rights and their enjoyment in practice. Even in Western democracies such as the United States that claim strong human rights traditions, infractions of human rights frequently occur. One should recall that the international human rights movement exists precisely because of this gap between the ideal and the reality of life for many.

As we will see in subsequent chapters, mechanisms associated with the United Nations and regional international institutions have been developed to promote the observance of human rights and, in limited circumstances, to provide remedies for human rights violations. Still, states remain the fundamental units of sovereignty and power in the world today; the international system looks to them, not international institutions, as the primary agents responsible for securing the observance of human rights. States have a duty to safeguard human rights and provide remedies when they are violated, a duty that relates to international law on the responsibility of states in regard to unlawful acts and omissions, which is discussed in Chapter 5. This duty is at least implicit in human rights treaties and is similarly discernible in customary human rights law. See generally Theodor Meron, *Human Rights and Humanitarian Norms as Customary Law* 136-245 (1989); B.G. Ramcharan, "State Responsibility for Violations of Human Rights Treaties," *in Contemporary Problems of International Law: Essays in Honour of Georg Schwarzenberger on his Eightieth Birthday* 242-261 (Bin Cheng & Edward D. Brown eds., 1988). In order for this duty to be fulfilled and for human rights norms to be effective, those norms must be — in one way or another — incorporated into states' domestic law and enforced by courts or other authorities with power to mandate corrective action. But to what extent does or can this "domestication" of international human rights law happen?

To help understand the difficulties of incorporating international obligations within the framework of domestic law, it is useful to review the basic distinctions between international and domestic law. Traditionally, the two systems were quite separate: the international legal system was a law of nations, that is, concerned only with the rights and duties of states, not of individuals; each of the various domestic legal systems, therefore, remained completely free to regulate the lives of its own citizens. See 1 Lassa Oppenheim, *International Law: A Treatise* 362-369 (2d ed. 1912).

Furthermore, while domestic legal systems were and generally still are organized in a hierarchical fashion, with laws flowing from a constitution and being promulgated by court decisions, statutes, decrees, and administrative regulations; in the international community there exists no sovereign body whose law-making or conflict-resolving authority is accepted universally. The United Nations may have the functional capacity to fulfill these roles — indeed, the second of these functions, conflict resolution through its political organs or its principal judicial organ, the International Court of Justice, is one reason for its very existence — but the United Nations is not a sovereign body in the sense that nation states are. Its decisions, generally expressed in the form of resolutions, derive their legal force more from the voluntary consensus of member states than from any law-making authority. (But see the legal effects of Security Council resolutions under Article 25 and Chapter VII of the Charter, considered in Chapter 10.)

Resolutions of the UN General Assembly on matters of human rights may contribute to the development of customary international law, as discussed in Chapter 3, but that development is subject ultimately to the acquiescence of states. General principles of international law similarly must rest on their widespread acceptance by states. And treaties, which constitute the other major source of international law, only bind states that have formally agreed to them, except to the extent that treaties may themselves reflect or contribute to binding customary law or general principles of international law.

The distinctions between the international legal system and domestic legal systems have important ramifications. Since the two systems are relatively separate, it is possible for a state's actions to contravene international law while at the same time conforming to its own domestic law. Thus, even if a state violates an obligation to which it freely has committed itself by treaty — for example, not to permit racial discrimination — its citizens may be unable to challenge such violations through its domestic courts. In such cases, the state's domestic law generally will provide that the treaty obligation is owed only to other states that are parties to the agreement, not to the state's own citizens. Alternatively, domestic law simply may provide that the state's law always prevails over the treaty obligation in case of conflict. Under either of these approaches, individuals remain only the objects, not the subjects, of international law as applied within the domestic arena, even when the subject matter of the treaty is of great concern to them. They have only those rights that their domestic legal system accords them. That this traditional view of the relationship between international law and domestic law still holds some sway in the United States was illustrated graphically by the case of *Committee of U.S. Citizens in Nicaragua v. Reagan,* 859 F.2d 929, 935-939 (D.C. Cir. 1988) (rejecting aguments based on international law challenging U.S. statutorily backed support for insurgents in Nicaragua).

The extent to which the traditional view subordinates both conventional and customary international law to domestic legal norms remains a significant problem in the field of international human rights. Jurisprudentially, it conflicts with the major purpose of the post–World War II international human rights movement, namely, to establish that the individual is (at least to some extent) a subject of international law who possesses certain basic human rights that do not depend for their validity upon the domestic law of any particular state.

The first three chapters of the present book trace the developments that led to the inclusion of human rights provisions in the UN Charter, adoption of the Universal Declaration of Human Rights in 1948, and the subsequent adoption of the two Covenants and numerous other human rights treaties. These developments altered the traditional state-to-state character of international law by holding states to standards of conduct concerning the treatment of their own citizens and other individuals under their respective jurisdictions. States are now bound to uphold their legal obligations under applicable treaties or customary law and may incur international responsibility for failing to do so, regardless of any domestic doctrine that subordinates international norms to internal law. See, e.g., *International Responsibility for the Promulgation and Enforcement of Laws in Violation of the Convention (Arts. 1 and 2 of the American Convention on Human Rights)*, Advisory Opinion, Inter-Am. Ct. H.R., Dec. 9, 1994 (Ser. A.) No. 14 (1994). Cf. *Military and Paramilitary Activities in and against Nicaragua (Nicaragua v. United States)*, 1986 I.C.J. (June 27); *Lagrand (Germany v. United States)*, 2001 I.C.J. (June 27); *Avena and other Mexican Nationals (Mexico v. United States)*, 2004 I.C.J. (Mar. 31).

To harmonize their domestic law with their international legal obligations, many states have adopted constitutional provisions that explicitly incorporate and give primacy to human rights treaties to which they subscribe. See infra, pages 527-529. By contrast, within the U.S. constitutional order, treaties (including human rights treaties) have no such primacy, and the status and role of both treaty and customary international law in domestic law remain somewhat ambiguous, as we shall see in the following materials. Still, as we also shall see, international law does exert some influence on domestic decision making in the United States.

The materials in this chapter explore the constraints and possibilities for the enforcement of international human rights norms by domestic courts, and how that enforcement may be aided by legislation or constitutional provisions. An initial case study on the eradication of the death penalty for juvenile offenders in the United States provides a look into U.S. judicial treatment of international human rights law.

II. U.S. Courts and the Right of Juvenile Offenders Not to Be Executed

A. *Finding the Parameters of Domestic Legal Protections in Light of International Norms*

Several states of the United States applied the death penalty to persons convicted of committing capital offenses while under the age of 18, until the Supreme Court rendered its decision in *Roper v. Simmons*.

Roper v. Simmons

543 U.S. 551 (2005)

[At the age of 17 Christopher Simmons was the oldest of three minors who broke into the home of Shirley Crook, forcibly took her to a bridge where they bound her with duct tape and wire, and threw her into the river below where she drowned. Simmons later confessed to the murder. He was tried as an adult and convicted of murder in a Missouri state court. Despite arguments of his lawyer that his age at the time of the murder should count as mitigating factor, Simmons was sentenced to death under Missouri state law. After his conviction, the U.S. Supreme Court decided *Atkins v. Virginia*, 536 U.S. 304 (2002), in which it held that the Eighth and Fourteenth Amendments to the U.S. Constitution prohibit the execution of a mentally retarded person. Simmons filed a petition for state post-conviction relief, arguing that the reasoning of *Atkins* established that the Constitution prohibits the execution of a juvenile who was under 18 when the crime was committed. The Missouri Supreme Court agreed, and subsequently the case was reviewed by the U.S. Supreme Court]. facts, PH

Justice Kennedy delivered the opinion of the Court [in which Justices Stevens, Souter, Ginsberg, and Breyer joined].

...The Eighth Amendment [to the U.S. Constitution] provides: "Excessive bail shall not be required, nor excessive fines imposed, nor cruel and unusual punishments inflicted." The provision is applicable to the States through the Fourteenth Amendment. As the Court explained in Atkins, the Eighth Amendment guarantees individuals the right not to be subjected to excessive sanctions. The right flows from the basic "'precept of justice that punishment for crime should be graduated and proportioned to [the] offense'." 536 U.S., at 311, 153 L. Ed. 2d 335, 122 S. Ct. 2242. By protecting even those convicted of heinous crimes, the Eighth Amendment reaffirms the duty of the government to respect the dignity of all persons.

The prohibition against "cruel and unusual punishments," like other expansive language in the Constitution, must be interpreted according to its text, by considering history, tradition, and precedent, and with due regard for its purpose and function in the constitutional design. To implement this framework we have established the propriety and affirmed the necessity of referring to "the evolving standards of decency that mark the progress of a maturing society" to determine which punishments are so disproportionate as to be cruel and unusual. *Trop v. Dulles*, 356 U.S. 86, 100-101, 2 L. Ed. 2d 630, 78 S. Ct. 590 (1958) (plurality opinion).

In *Thompson v. Oklahoma*, 487 U.S. 815, 101 L. Ed. 2d 702, 108 S. Ct. 2687 (1988), a plurality of the Court determined that our standards of decency do not permit the execution of any offender under the age of 16 at the time of the crime. *Id.*, at 818-838, 101 L. Ed. 2d 702, 108 S. Ct. 2687 (opinion of Stevens, J., joined by Brennan, Marshall, and Blackmun, JJ.). The plurality opinion explained that no death penalty State that had given express consideration to a minimum age for the death penalty had set the age lower than 16....

The next year, in *Stanford v. Kentucky*, 492 U.S. 361, 106 L. Ed. 2d 306, 109 S. Ct. 2969 (1989), the Court, over a dissenting opinion joined by four Justices, referred to contemporary standards of decency in this country and concluded the

Eighth and Fourteenth Amendments did not proscribe the execution of juvenile offenders over 15 but under 18. The Court noted that 22 of the 37 death penalty States permitted the death penalty for 16-year-old offenders, and, among these 37 States, 25 permitted it for 17-year-old offenders. These numbers, in the Court's view, indicated there was no national consensus "sufficient to label a particular punishment cruel and unusual." *Id.*, at 370-371, 106 L. Ed. 2d 306, 109 S. Ct. 2969. . . .

The same day the Court decided *Stanford*, it held that the Eighth Amendment did not mandate a categorical exemption from the death penalty for the mentally retarded. *Penry v. Lynaugh*, 492 U.S. 302, 106 L. Ed. 2d 256, 109 S. Ct. 2934 (1989). . . .

Three terms ago the subject was reconsidered in *Atkins*. We held that standards of decency have evolved since *Penry* and now demonstrate that the execution of the mentally retarded is cruel and unusual punishment. The Court noted objective indicia of society's standards, as expressed in legislative enactments and state practice with respect to executions of the mentally retarded. When *Atkins* was decided only a minority of States permitted the practice, and even in those States it was rare. 536 U.S., at 314-315, 153 L. Ed. 2d 335, 122 S. Ct. 2242. On the basis of these indicia the Court determined that executing mentally retarded offenders "has become truly unusual, and it is fair to say that a national consensus has developed against it." *Id.*, at 316, 153 L. Ed. 2d 335, 122 S. Ct. 2242. . . .

III.

A.

The evidence of national consensus against the death penalty for juveniles is similar, and in some respects parallel, to the evidence *Atkins* held sufficient to demonstrate a national consensus against the death penalty for the mentally retarded. When *Atkins* was decided, 30 States prohibited the death penalty for the mentally retarded. This number comprised 12 that had abandoned the death penalty altogether, and 18 that maintained it but excluded the mentally retarded from its reach. 536 U.S., at 313-315, 153 L. Ed. 2d 335, 122 S. Ct. 2242. By a similar calculation in this case, 30 States prohibit the juvenile death penalty, comprising 12 that have rejected the death penalty altogether and 18 that maintain it but, by express provision or judicial interpretation, exclude juveniles from its reach. *Atkins* emphasized that even in the 20 States without formal prohibition, the practice of executing the mentally retarded was infrequent. . . . In the present case, too, even in the 20 States without a formal prohibition on executing juveniles, the practice is infrequent. . . . [The Court described a trend among states in the years since *Stanford v. Kentucky* to reject the juvenile death penalty.]

As in *Atkins*, the objective indicia of consensus in this case — the rejection of the juvenile death penalty in the majority of States; the infrequency of its use even where it remains on the books; and the consistency in the trend toward abolition of the practice — provide sufficient evidence that today our society views juveniles, in the words *Atkins* used respecting the mentally retarded, as "categorically less culpable than the average criminal." 536 U.S., at 316, 153 L. Ed. 2d 335, 122 S. Ct. 2242.

B.

A majority of States have rejected the imposition of the death penalty on juvenile offenders under 18, and we now hold this is required by the Eighth Amendment.

Because the death penalty is the most severe punishment, the Eighth Amendment applies to it with special force. . . . [T]he death penalty is reserved for a narrow category of crimes and offenders.

Three general differences between juveniles under 18 and adults demonstrate that juvenile offenders cannot with reliability be classified among the worst offenders. First, as any parent knows and as the scientific and sociological studies respondent and his *amici* cite tend to confirm, "[a] lack of maturity and an underdeveloped sense of responsibility are found in youth more often than in adults and are more understandable among the young. . . ."

The second area of difference is that juveniles are more vulnerable or susceptible to negative influences and outside pressures, including peer pressure. . . .

The third broad difference is that the character of a juvenile is not as well formed as that of an adult. The personality traits of juveniles are more transitory, less fixed. . . .

These differences render suspect any conclusion that a juvenile falls among the worst offenders. The susceptibility of juveniles to immature and irresponsible behavior means their "irresponsible conduct is not as morally reprehensible as that of an adult." *Thompson, supra,* at 835, 101 L. Ed. 2d 702, 108 S. Ct. 2687 (plurality opinion). Their own vulnerability and comparative lack of control over their immediate surroundings mean juveniles have a greater claim than adults to be forgiven for failing to escape negative influences in their whole environment. . . .

Once the diminished culpability of juveniles is recognized, it is evident that the penological justifications [of retribution and deterrence] for the death penalty apply to them with lesser force than to adults. . . .

IV

Our determination that the death penalty is disproportionate punishment for offenders under 18 finds confirmation in the stark reality that the United States is the only country in the world that continues to give official sanction to the juvenile death penalty. This reality does not become controlling, for the task of interpreting the Eighth Amendment remains our responsibility. Yet at least from the time of the Court's decision in *Trop,* the Court has referred to the laws of other countries and to international authorities as instructive for its interpretation of the Eighth Amendment's prohibition of "cruel and unusual punishments." 356 U.S., at 102-103, 2 L. Ed. 2d 630, 78 S. Ct. 590 (plurality opinion) ("The civilized nations of the world are in virtual unanimity that statelessness is not to be imposed as punishment for crime"); see also *Atkins, supra,* at 317, n. 21, 153 L. Ed. 2d 335, 122 S. Ct. 2242 (recognizing that "within the world community, the imposition of the death penalty for crimes committed by mentally retarded offenders is overwhelmingly disapproved"); *Thompson, supra,* at 830-831, and n. 31, 101 L. Ed. 2d 702, 108 S. Ct. 2687 (plurality opinion) (noting the abolition of the juvenile death penalty "by other nations that share our Anglo-American heritage, and by the leading members of the Western European community," and observing that "[w]e have previously recognized the relevance of the views of the international community in determining whether a punishment is cruel and unusual"); *Enmund, supra*, at 796-797, n. 22, 73 L. Ed.2d 1140, 102 S. Ct. 3368 (observing that "the doctrine of felony murder has been abolished in England and India, severely restricted in Canada and a number of other Commonwealth countries, and is unknown in continental Europe"); *Coker, supra*, at 596, n. 10, 53 L. Ed. 2d 982, 97 S. Ct. 2861 (plurality opinion) ("It is . . . not irrelevant here that out of 60 major nations in the world surveyed in 1965, only 3 retained the death penalty for rape where death did not ensue").

As respondent and a number of *amici* emphasize, Article 37 of the United Nations Convention on the Rights of the Child, which every country in the world has ratified save for the United States and Somalia, contains an express prohibition on capital punishment for crimes committed by juveniles under 18. United Nations Convention on the Rights of the Child, Art. 37, Nov. 20, 1989, 1577 U. N. T. S. 3, 28 I. L. M. 1448, 1468-1470 (entered into force Sept. 2, 1990); Brief for Respondent 48; Brief for European Union et al. as *Amici Curiae* 12-13; Brief for President James Earl Carter, Jr., et al. as *Amici Curiae* 9; Brief for Former U. S. Diplomats Morton Abramowitz et al. as *Amici Curiae* 7; Brief for Human Rights Committee of the Bar of England and Wales et al. as *Amici Curiae* 13-14. No ratifying country has entered a reservation to the provision prohibiting the execution of juvenile offenders. Parallel prohibitions are contained in other significant international covenants. See [International Covenant on Civil and Political Rights] Art. 6(5), 999 U. N. T. S., at 175 (prohibiting capital punishment for anyone under 18 at the time of offense) (signed and ratified by the United States subject to a reservation regarding Article 6(5), as noted, *supra*, 161 L. Ed. 2d, at 20); American Convention on Human Rights: Pact of San Jose, Costa Rica, Art. 4(5), Nov. 22, 1969, 1144 U. N. T. S. 146 (entered into force July 19, 1978) (same); African Charter on the Rights and Welfare of the Child, Art. 5(3), OAU Doc. CAB/LEG/24.9/49 (1990) (entered into force Nov. 29, 1999) (same).

Respondent and his *amici* have submitted, and petitioner does not contest, that only seven countries other than the United States have executed juvenile offenders since 1990: Iran, Pakistan, Saudi Arabia, Yemen, Nigeria, the Democratic Republic of Congo, and China. Since then each of these countries has either abolished capital punishment for juveniles or made public disavowal of the practice. Brief for Respondent 49-50. In sum, it is fair to say that the United States now stands alone in a world that has turned its face against the juvenile death penalty.

Though the international covenants prohibiting the juvenile death penalty are of more recent date, it is instructive to note that the United Kingdom abolished the juvenile death penalty before these covenants came into being. The United Kingdom's experience bears particular relevance here in light of the historic ties between our countries and in light of the Eighth Amendment's own origins. The Amendment was modeled on a parallel provision in the English Declaration of Rights of 1689, which provided: "[E]xcessive Bail ought not to be required nor excessive Fines imposed; nor cruel and unusually Punishments inflicted." 1 W. & M., ch. 2, §10, in 3 Eng. Stat. at Large 441 (1770); see also *Trop, supra*, at 100, 2 L. Ed. 2d 630, 78 S. Ct. 590 (plurality opinion). As of now, the United Kingdom has abolished the death penalty in its entirety; but, decades before it took this step, it recognized the disproportionate nature of the juvenile death penalty; and it abolished that penalty as a separate matter. In 1930 an official committee recommended that the minimum age for execution be raised to 21. House of Commons Report from the Select Committee on Capital Punishment (1930), 193, p. 44. Parliament then enacted the Children and Young Person's Act of 1933, 23 Geo. 5, ch. 12, which prevented execution of those aged 18 at the date of the sentence. And in 1948, Parliament enacted the Criminal Justice Act, 11 & 12 Geo. 6, ch. 58, prohibiting the execution of any person under 18 at the time of the offense. In the 56 years that have passed since the United Kingdom abolished the juvenile death penalty, the weight of authority against it there, and in the international community, has become well established.

It is proper that we acknowledge the overwhelming weight of international opinion against the juvenile death penalty, resting in large part on the understanding that the instability and emotional imbalance of young people may often be a factor in the crime. See Brief for Human Rights Committee of the Bar of England and Wales et al. as *Amici Curiae* 10-11. The opinion of the world community, while not controlling our outcome, does provide respected and significant confirmation for our own conclusions.

The majority's decision in *Roper v. Simmons* invalidating the death penalty for juvenile offenders rested on a reinterpretation of the Eighth Amendment that was buttressed by an understanding of world opinion, as manifested by the practice of other countries and provisions in a number of multilateral treaties. Simmons' lawyers and several amicus parties had provided extensive argument detailing these and many additional manifestations of international condemnation of the juvenile death. Highlighted were the overwhelming practice of states prohibiting the death penalty for offenders under 18 years of age, the repeated and numerous resolutions and statements against the practice by the UN General Assembly and UN human rights organs, and the global and regional human rights treaties prohibiting the practice. Amici pointed to a widespread international practice that left the United States isolated as the "only nation in the world that has not committed itself by treaty to bar the death penalty" for juvenile offenders. Brief of Amici Curiae Nobel Peace Laureates 9 (July 19, 2004), 2004 WL 1636446. See also Brief of Amici Curiae Former U.S. Diplomats (July 19, 2004), 2004 WL 1636448. On the basis of these multiple sources, the argument was pressed upon the Supreme Court that the prohibition of the juvenile penalty is an international norm of jus cogens, that is, a norm binding on the United States from which it cannot derogate as a matter of international law. See Brief of Amici Curiae the European Union and Members of the International Community 19-21 (July 12, 2004), 2004 WL1619203.

Although it did not explicitly acknowledge that it was legally binding on the United States, the Court did, in effect, identify an international standard against the juvenile death penalty and applied it through a reinterpretation of the Eighth Amendment. This *indirect* method of incorporating an internationals norm into domestic law contrasts with the *direct* application by courts of treaty or customary international rules, and it is the most common use of international norms by courts in the United States.

> Direct incorporation of international law involves use of an international agreement or customary international law directly as law forming the basis for a claim, right, duty, power, civil cause of action, criminal prosecution, or other type of sanction. In such cases, direct incorporation occurs whether or not there is a specific statutory basis for such uses of international law.
>
> Another primary form of incorporation is indirect incorporation involving the use of international law as an interpretive aid. This form of incorporation can involve use of international law indirectly to clarify or supplement the meaning of, for example, the U.S. Constitution, a federal statute, a state constitution or statute, common law, a private contract, or some other legal provision. In this instance, international law is not used directly as the basis for a civil claim or criminal prosecution, but indirectly to inform the meaning of some other law or legal instrument. When international law is used to clarify duties or powers under the U.S. Constitution, it is the Constitution that provides the direct basis for the duty or power addressed and international law is used indirectly as an interpretive aid concerning the identification, limitation, or enhancement of a duty or competence....
>
> Indirect incorporation happens to be the most frequent use of international law throughout United States history. Even treaties that had not been ratified yet by the U.S. have been used indirectly to clarify or provide content of federal law. Since most lawyers and judges in the U.S. have never taken a course in international law, it is not surprising that some of the judges may be more comfortable applying a domestic law as the direct basis for a civil claim, but utilizing international law as an aid to interpret such domestic law.

Jordan J. Paust, International Law as Law of the United States 12-13 (2d ed. 2003) (endnotes omitted).

The outcome in *Roper v. Simmons* — making the juvenile death penalty a thing of the past — was the culmination of years or work by death penalty opponents both in the United States and abroad. Some of the individuals and non-governmental organizations that submitted amicus briefs in favor of Simmons had been involved for years in efforts to see an end to the juvenile death penalty. These efforts included embarking on numerous prior challenges in U.S. federal and state courts on the basis of a combination of constitutional and international law arguments. See, e.g., *Beazley v. Johnson*, 242 F.3d 248 (5th Cir. Tex. 2001), cert. denied, 534 U.S. 945 (2001); *Ex Parte Marcus Pressly*, 770 So. 2d 143 (Ala. 2000), cert denied, 531 U.S. 931 (2000); *Servin v. Nevada*, 117 Nev. 775, 794, 32 P.3d 1277 (2001); *Domingues v. State of Nevada*, 114 Nev. 783, 961 P.2d 1279 (1998), cert. denied 528 U.S. 963 (1999) (edited opinion included infra). The arguments advanced in these cases are exemplified in the following articles: Carrie Martin, *Spare the Death Penalty, Spoil the Child: How the Execution of Juveniles Violates the Eighth Amendment's Ban on Cruel and Unusual Punishment in 2005*, 465 Tex. L. Rev. 695 (2005); Carly Baetz-Stangel, *The Role of International Law in the Abolition of the Juvenile Death Penalty*, 16 Fla. J. Int'l L. 955 (2004). Juvenile death penalty opponents extended their efforts into the international arena, addressing appeals to UN and regional institutions, which in turn responded with statements of condemnation and expressions of concern, in some cases directed specifically at the United States. The UN Commission on Human Rights and its Sub-Commission issued a series of resolutions condemning the execution of juvenile offenders. See infra page 473 (extract of *Roper v. Simmons*, Brief for the Human Rights Committee of the Bar of England and Wales, Human Rights Watch, Human Rights Advocates, and the World Organization for Human Rights as Amici Curiae in Support of Respondents (July 15, 2004)). In the fall of 1997, after years of expressing concern about the practice of executing juvenile offenders in the United States, the UN Special Rapporteur on Extrajudicial, Summary or Arbitrary Executions visited the United States on a special mission to investigate the matter along with the issue of police killings. His report emphasized "that international law clearly indicates a prohibition of imposing a death sentence on juvenile offenders" and called on the United States to follow that prohibition. See Report of the Special Rapporteur on extrajudicial, summary or arbitrary executions: Mission to the United States of America, U.N. Doc E/CN.4/1998/68/Add.3, para 55 (Jan. 22, 1998). Some of the specific challenges to the application of the juvenile death penalty that had failed in domestic courts made their way to the Inter-American Commission on Human Rights, which joined in condemning the U.S. practice as a violation of international law. See *Domingues v. United States*, Case 12.285, Inter-Am. C.H.R., Report No. 62/02 (merits), OEA/Ser.L/V/II.116, Doc. 33 (Oct. 22, 2002); *Napoleon Beazley v. United States*, Case 12.412, Inter-Am. C.H.R., Report No. 101/03 (merits), OEA/Ser./L/V/II.114 Doc. 70 rev. 1 (Dec. 29, 2003); *Gary Graham v. United States*, Case No. 11.193, Inter-Am. C.H.R., Report No. 97/03 (merits), OEA/Ser./L/V/II.114 Doc. 70 rev. 1 (Dec. 29, 2003); *Douglas Christopher Thomas v. United States*, Case No. 12.240, Inter-Am. C.H.R., Report No. 100/03 (merits), OEA/Ser./L/V/II.114 Doc. 70 rev. 1 (Dec. 29, 2003).

Whether or not a causal link can be established, these efforts against the juvenile death penalty and manifestations of international concern about it were followed by or contemporaneous with the developments identified by the Supreme Court in *Roper* as crucial to its reinterpretation of the Eighth Amendment: a diminishment in the number of states in the United States that allowed or practiced the juvenile death penalty and a corresponding shift in public consensus away from allowing the penalty. The Supreme Court's decision in *Roper* was itself part of a gradual evolution in the views among the Court's members toward greater restrictions on the use of the death penalty, as indicated by the prior cases cited by the Court, *Thompson v. Oklahoma* (prohibiting the death penalty for juvenile offenders under the age of 16), and *Atkins v. Virginia* (prohibiting the death penalty for the mentally retarded).

Given its place within a multifaceted advocacy effort that combined domestic and international dimensions and that influenced multiple actors, *Roper* can be seen as part of what Professor Harold Hongju Koh refers to as the "transnational legal process" by which nations "obey" international law.

Harold Hongju Koh, *Review Essay: Why Do Nations Obey International Law*

106 Yale L.J. 2599, 2624, 2645-2646, 2655-2658 (1997)
(most footnotes omitted)

. . . By the 1970s and '80s, the legal landscape had altered significantly. The growth of international regimes and institutions, the proliferation of nonstate actors, and the increasing interpenetration of domestic and international systems inaugurated the era of "transnational relations," defined by one scholar as "regular interactions across national boundaries aris[ing] when at least one actor is a non-state agent or does not operate on behalf of a national government or an intergovernmental organization."[121] Multinational enterprises, nongovernmental organizations, and private individuals reemerged as significant actors on the transnational stage. In particular, the oil crisis of the early 1970s highlighted the interdependence of politics and economics in the new transnational economy, and created the discipline of international political economy. Instead of focusing narrowly on nation-states as global actors, scholars began to look as well at transnational networks among nonstate actors, international institutions, and domestic political structures as important mediating forces in international society. . . .

. . . [Recent scholarship] suggest[s] that the key [today] to better compliance [with international law] is more internalized compliance, or what I have called obedience. But by what process does norm-internalization occur? How do we transform occasional or grudging compliance with global norms into habitual obedience?

As I have already suggested, such a process can be viewed as having three phases. One or more transnational actors provokes an interaction (or series of interactions) with another, which forces an interpretation or enunciation of the global norm applicable to the situation. By so doing, the moving party seeks not simply to coerce the other party, but to internalize the new interpretation of the international norm into the other party's internal normative system. The aim is to "bind" that other party to obey the interpretation as part of its internal value set. Such a transnational legal process is normative, dynamic, and constitutive. The transaction generates a legal rule which will guide future transnational interactions between the parties; future transactions will further internalize those norms; and eventually, repeated participation in the process will help to reconstitute the interests and even the identities of the participants in the process. . . .

As I have described it, transnational legal process presents both a theoretical explanation of why nations obey and a plan of strategic action for prodding nations to obey. How, then, to study this process? Although a full account will require book-length interdisciplinary treatment, let me identify some basic inquiries, using international human rights as an example. In the human rights area, treaty regimes are notoriously weak, and national governments, for reasons of economics or *realpolitik*, are often hesitant to declare openly that another government engages in abuses. In such an area, where enforcement mechanisms are weak, but core customary norms are clearly defined and often peremptory *(jus cogens)*, the best compliance strategies may not be "horizontal" regime management strategies, but rather, vertical strategies of interaction, interpretation, and internalization.

If transnational actors obey international law as a result of repeated interaction with other actors in the transnational legal process, a first step is to empower more actors to participate. It is here that expanding the role of intergovernmental organizations, nongovernmental organizations, private business entities, and

121. Thomas Risse-Kappen, *Bringing Transnational Relations Back In: Introduction*, in *Bringing Transnational Relations Back In* 3 (Thomas Risse-Kappen ed., 1995) (emphasis omitted). . . .

"transnational moral entrepreneurs" deserves careful study. How, for example, do international human rights "issue networks" and epistemic communities form among international and regional intergovernmental organizations, international and domestic NGOs on human rights, and private foundations? How do these networks intersect with the "International Human Rights Regime," namely, the global system of rules and implementation procedures centered in and around the United Nations; regional regimes in Europe, the Americas, Africa, Asia, and the Middle East; single-issue human rights regimes regarding workers' rights, racial discrimination, women's rights; and "global prohibition regimes" against slavery, torture, and the like? Within national governments and intergovernmental organizations, what role do lawyers and legal advisers play in ensuring that the government's policies conform to international legal standards and in prompting governmental agencies to take proactive stances toward human rights abuses?

Second, if the goal of interaction is to produce interpretation of human rights norms, what fora are available for norm-enunciation and elaboration, both within and without existing human rights regimes? If dedicated fora do not already exist, how can existing fora be adapted for this purpose or new fora, such as the International Criminal Tribunal for Rwanda and the former Yugoslavia, be created?

Third, what are the best strategies for internalization of international human rights norms? One might distinguish among social, political, and legal internalization. Social internalization occurs when a norm acquires so much public legitimacy that there is widespread general obedience to it. Political internalization occurs when political elites accept an international norm, and adopt it as a matter of government policy. Legal internalization occurs when an international norm is incorporated into the domestic legal system through executive action, judicial interpretation, legislative action, or some combination of the three. The ABM Treaty controversy thus exemplified the incorporation of a norm (narrow treaty interpretation) into U.S. law and policy through the executive action of the President, acting through his delegate, the U.S. Arms Control and Disarmament Administration. Judicial internalization can occur when domestic litigation provokes judicial incorporation of human rights norms either implicitly, by construing existing statutes consistently with international human rights norms, or explicitly, through what I have elsewhere called "transnational public law litigation." Legislative internalization occurs when domestic lobbying embeds international law norms into binding domestic legislation or even constitutional law that officials of a noncomplying government must then obey as part of the domestic legal fabric.

The relationship among social, political, and legal internalization can be complex. In the Haitian refugee case, for example, U.S. human rights advocates failed to achieve judicial internalization of an international treaty norm, but in tandem with the growing social outrage about the treatment of Haitian refugees, eventually achieved political internalization: a reversal of the Clinton Administration's policy with respect to Haiti. Similarly, beginning with *Filartiga v. Pena-Irala* [extracted and discussed infra, page 479] U.S. human rights litigators began to promote domestic judicial incorporation of the norm against torture in a manner that eventually helped push President Bush to ratify the U.N. Convention against Torture and Congress to enact the Torture Victim Protection Act of 1991. In the United Kingdom, the issue of legislative internalization has similarly been brought to the fore by the first general election in five years, in which the opposition Labour party has promised, if elected, to incorporate the European Convention on Human Rights into U.K. law. This issue has been a major human rights issue in British politics since the Clement Attlee government first ratified the Convention in the early 1950s. Since then, the Convention has been internalized in part through judicial construction. Yet judicial refusal to recognize explicit incorporation has given new impetus to a political internalization movement that at this writing seems likely to bring about legal internalization of the European Convention into U.K. law by an act of Parliament.

Comments and Questions

1. *Roper v. Simmons*, which was decided by a five to four majority, overruled *Stanford v. Kentucky*, 492 U.S. 361 (1989), which had upheld the prerogative of states to apply the death penalty to a juvenile offender between the ages of 16 and 18 at the time of the crime. Justice Scalia, writing for the plurality in that previous case, had declined to give weight to international opinion in determining whether the death penalty for juvenile offenders was inconsistent with Eighth Amendment's prohibition against cruel and unusual punishment: "We emphasize that it is *American* conceptions of decency that are dispositive, rejecting the contention . . . that the sentencing practices of other countries are relevant." 492 U.S. at 370 n.1 (emphasis in original). That rejection of world opinion became the dissenting position in *Roper v. Simmons*. See 125 S.Ct. at 1225-1229 (dissenting opinion of Justice Scalia, joined by Chief Justice Rhenquist and Justice Thomas). But note that Supreme Court Chief Justice John Roberts, during his confirmation hearings before the U.S. Senate after *Roper* was decided, echoed the sentiments of Justice Scalia, arguing further that recourse to foreign sources as precedent inappropriately enhances the discretion of judges. Transcript: Day Three of the Roberts Confirmation Hearings, Wash. Post, Sept. 14, 2005. Do justices Roberts and Scalia have a point? Why, if at all, are the practices of other countries or international opinion relevant to understanding the meaning of the Eighth Amendment to the U.S. Constitution? For an argument that disregarding international standards in this regard is detrimental to U.S. security interests, see Elizabeth Burleson, *Juvenile Execution, Terrorist Extradition, and Supreme Court Discretion to Consider International Death Penalty Jurisprudence*, 68 Alb. L. Rev. 909, 947 (2005). Should practical, instrumentalist concerns such as these affect interpretation of domestic law?

2. In other recent cases, the Supreme Court has made reference to human rights standards as understood internationally or applied in other democracies. In *Lawrence v. Texas*, for example, the Court noted that the right to engage in homosexual conduct has been accepted as an integral part of human freedom in many other countries and referenced jurisprudence of the European Court of Human Rights; it found the right to be within the privacy interest protected by the due process clause of the Constitution. 5 U.S. 576-577 (2003). See also *Washington v. Glucksberg*, 521 U.S. 702, 710 & n.8 (1997) (noting that "almost every western democracy" criminalized physician-assisted suicide and discussing laws in a number of nations in Western Europe); *Grutter v. Bollinger*, 539 U.S. 306, 342 (2003) (Ginsburg, J., concurring) (citing UN conventions and identifying the "international understanding" concerning affirmative action plans). In each of

these cases, members of the Supreme Court identified patterns of normative understanding being adopted and applied transnationally, although they declined to explicitly recognize a binding international norm or apply it directly. Despite not recognizing *binding* international norms, is the United States, by virtue of these decisions, nonetheless "obeying" international law? For an explanation of norm incorporation somewhat similar to that offered by Koh, supra page 449, see *The Power of Human Rights: International Norms and Domestic Change* (Thomas Risse, Stephen C. Ropp, and Kathryn Sikkink eds., 1999).

3. As illustrated by *Roper*, a growing number of U.S. courts have referred explicitly to the UN Charter, the Universal Declaration, or other international human rights instruments to determine the content and contours of various rights guaranteed by U.S. law. This "indirect incorporation" of both conventional and customary human rights law is a promising approach warranting even greater attention and increased use in the future. For an excellent article supporting this approach by the president of the American Civil Liberties Union, see Nadine Strossen, *Recent U.S. and International Judicial Protection of Individual Rights: A Comparative Legal Process Analysis and Proposed Synthesis*, 41 Hastings L.J. 805 (1990). Through the invocation of the established principle of statutory interpretation that "an Act of Congress ought never to be construed to violate the law of nations if any other possible construction remains," *Murray v. Schooner Charming Betsy*, 6 U.S. (2 Cranch) 64, 118 (1804), international human rights norms should have some impact in statutory construction cases, in addition to constitutional cases. See Restatement (Third) of the Foreign Relations Law of the United States §114 (1987). For some time before the Supreme Court's decision in *Roper*, efforts had been made to convince U.S. constitutional law experts that international human rights norms should become a significant factor in constitutional decision-making. See, e.g., Richard B. Lillich and Hurst Hannum, *Linkages Between International Human Rights and U.S. Constitutional Law*, 79 Am. J. Intl. L. 158 (1985). Indeed, teaching materials had been designed to supplement leading U.S. constitutional and criminal law and procedure casebooks have been prepared. See *Materials on International Human Rights and U.S. Constitutional Law* (Hurst Hannum ed., 1985); *Materials on International Human Rights and U.S. Criminal Law and Procedure* (Hurst Hannum ed., 1989). Were they used or referred to in your basic constitutional law and criminal law classes? If not, why not, in view of *Roper* and the cases cited in comment 2, supra?

B. *The Application of Treaty Provisions by Domestic Courts*

Among the several international instruments cited by the Supreme Court in *Roper v. Simmons* to support its decision that the death penalty as applied to juvenile offenders is unconstitutional was the International Covenant on Civil and Political Rights. Article 6(5) of the Covenant provides:

> Sentence of death shall not be imposed for crimes committed by persons before eighteen years of age and shall not be carried out on pregnant women.

The United States became a party to the Covenant on June 8, 1992, years before the Supreme Court's ruling in *Roper*. But while specifically citing Article

6(5) of the Covenant, which explicitly prohibits the juvenile death penalty at issue in *Roper*, the Court did not directly apply it as a rule of decision. Absent from the Court's opinion is any suggestion that Article 6(5) could itself be an independent or alternative legal basis for invalidating state laws allowing execution of juvenile offenders. Article 6(5) of the Covenant effectively is reduced to one of many contributors to a policy backdrop for the Court's interpretation of the Eighth Amendment. In earlier cases in federal and state courts, defendants had sought without success to avoid the death penalty on the basis of Article 6(5) of the Covenant. See, e.g., *Beazley v. Johnson*, 242 F.3d 248, 266-267 (5th Cir. Tex. 2001), cert. denied, 534 U.S. 945 (2001); *State v. Odom*, 137 S.W.3d 572, 598 (Tenn. 2004); *Ex parte Pressley*, 770 So. 2d 143, 148 (Ala. 2000), cert. denied, 531 U.S. 931 (2000); *Domingues v. Nevada*, 114 Nev. 783, 785, 961 P.2d 1279, 1280 (1998), cert. denied, 528 U.S. 963 (1999) (see infra, page 456).

Article VI, Section 2 of the U.S. Constitution affirms that treaties ratified by the United States are part of the "supreme Law of the Land," thereby establishing treaties as part of federal law with supremacy over state law. Thus, the Supreme Court in *United States v. Pink*, 315 U.S. 203, 230 (1942), emphasized that "state law must yield when it is inconsistent with, or impairs the policy or provisions of, a treaty." See generally Jordan J. Paust, *International Law as Law of the United States* 70-71 (2d ed. 2003) (discussing early Supreme Court cases in which "treaty law was accepted as operating directly as supreme federal law in the face of inconsistent state law"). To be sure, U.S. courts have regarded treaties as equal but not superior to federal statutes; thus, if a treaty conflicts with a federal law, the more recent prevails, whichever it is. See *Chinese Exclusion Case*, 130 U.S. 581, 578-99 (1889). Also, like federal statutes, treaties are held subject to constitutional protections for individual rights and other constitutional limitations. See *Reid v. Covert*, 354 U.S. 1, 16-17 (1957). But there can be no argument that the prohibition of the juvenile death penalty of Article 6(5) of the Covenant is itself prohibited by the Constitution. And no federal legislation subsequent to the ratification of the Covenant supplants Article 6(5) by authorizing the imposition of the death penalty on juvenile capital offenders. As in the *Roper* case, authorization for imposing the death penalty on juvenile offenders had been under state, not federal, law. At the time *Roper* was decided, 20 states had laws providing such authorization.

So why have courts in the United States not applied Article 6(5) of the Covenant on Civil and Political Rights to invalidate state laws authorizing the application of the death penalty to juvenile offenders? Treaties like the Covenant are part of United States law to which state law is subordinate, in light of the Supremacy Clause and established Supreme Court doctrine. The most obvious answer lies in the reservations the United States attached to the Covenant upon ratification, as well as the allegedly non-self-executing character of the Covenant. We now turn to these issues.

1. Judicial Treatment of Reservations to Multilateral Treaties

The United States ratified the Covenant on Civil and Political Rights subject to various reservations, understandings, and declarations, as discussed in Chapter 2, page 113. Among these was the affirmation that "the United States reserves the right, subject to its Constitutional constraints, to impose capital punishment on any person (other than a pregnant woman) duly convicted under existing or future laws permitting the imposition of capital punishment, including persons below eighteen years of age." U.S. Senate Resolution of Advice and Consent to the Ratification of the International Covenant on Civil and Political Rights, art. I(2), 138 Cong. Rec. S4781 (1991).

The Supreme Court in *Roper v. Simmons* referred to this reservation in a parenthetical following its reference to Article 6(5), even while invoking the article as evidence of world opinion relevant to an interpretation of the Eighth Amendment prohibition against cruel and unusual punishment. The validity of the reservation has been questioned by the U.N. Human Rights Committee, as discussed in Chapter 2, as well as by a significant number of scholars and human rights advocates. See, e.g., William A. Schabas, *Invalid Reservations to the International Covenant on Civil and Political Rights: Is the United States Still a Party?* 21 Brooklyn J. Int'l L. 277 (1995); Annika K. Carlsten, *Young Enough to Die? Executing Juvenile Offenders in Violation of International Law*, 29 Denv. J. Int'l L. & Pol'y 181, 187-189 (2001). Arguments that the reservation is invalid, based on the Covenant itself and on the general international law applicable to treaty reservations (see Chapter 2), are exemplified succinctly by the following extract.

> Turning first to the language of the treaty, Article 4(2) of the ICCPR [the Covenant on Civil and Political Rights] states that "no derogation from Articles 6, 7, 8 (paragraphs one and two), 11, 15, 16, and 18 may be made under this provision." Although there is no formula to determine under what conditions a reservation may be valid, the Inter-American Court on Human Rights issued an opinion linking the non-derogable provisions of a treaty with the incompatibility principle of the Law of Nations. [See Restrictions to the Death Penalty (Arts. 4(2) and 4(4) American Convention on Human Rights), Advisory Opinion No. OC-3/83 of September 8, 1983.] In this advisory opinion, the court defined the incompatibility doctrine when it stated that a reservation violating a non-derogable right is incompatible with the object and purpose of the treaty and is therefore not permitted. The Human Rights Committee, established under the ICCPR, affirmed that some components of the death penalty reservation may be "incompatible with the object and purpose of the Covenant" causing these reservations to be invalid. [Human Right's Committee's observations on the United States' first report under the Covenant.] The Inter-American Court of Human Rights also discussed the object and purpose of treaties, stating that modern human rights treaties, such as the ICCPR, stand for the protection of "basic rights of individual human beings . . . against the State of their nationality and all other contracting States." [See The Effect of Reservations on the Entry into Force of the American Convention (Arts. 74 and 75), Advisory Opinion No. OC-2/82 of Sept. 24, 1982.] In light of the above opinions, the Senate's reservation is incompatible with the purpose of the treaty and signifies the United States' non-compliance with its international obligations under Article Six.
>
> External to the language of the ICCPR and decisions interpreting specific reservations to Article Six, Article 19(c) of the Vienna Convention on the Law of Treaties establishes that a party may not formulate a reservation that is incompatible with the object and purpose of the treaty. Although the United States has not ratified the Vienna Convention, the State Department recognizes this treaty as a guide to international law and practice.

Christian A. Levesque, *The International Covenant on Civil and Political Rights: A Primer for Raising a Defense Against the Juvenile Death Penalty in Federal*

Courts, 50 Am. U.L. Rev. 755, 784-785 (2001) (footnotes changed into bracketed text).

The foregoing argument, however, has not carried the day in the courts. Before the U.S. Supreme Court in *Roper v. Simmons* determined that the U.S. Constitution itself prohibits capital punishment of juvenile offenders, federal and state courts consistently applied the U.S. reservation to Article 6(5) of the Covenant to avoid that article's prohibition of the juvenile death penalty, as illustrated by the following case decided by the Supreme Court of Nevada.

Domingues v. State of Nevada

114 Nev. 783, 961 P.2d 1279 (1998), cert. denied 528 U.S. 963 (1999) (footnotes omitted)

OPINION By the Court, YOUNG, J.:

This case raises the single issue of whether NRS 176.025 is superseded by an international treaty ratified by the United States, which prohibits the execution of individuals who committed capital offenses while under the age of eighteen. NRS 176.025 allows imposition of the death penalty on a defendant who was sixteen years old or older at the time that the capital offense was committed.

FACTS

On October 22, 1993, sixteen-year-old Michael Domingues murdered a woman and her four-year-old son in the victims' home. In August 1994, a jury found Domingues guilty of one count of burglary, one count of robbery with the use of a deadly weapon, one count of first degree murder, and one count of first degree murder with the use of a deadly weapon. At seventeen years of age, Domingues was sentenced to death for each of the two murder convictions. On May 30, 1996, this court upheld Domingues' convictions and sentence.

On November 7, 1996, Domingues filed a motion for correction of illegal sentence, arguing that "execution of a juvenile offender violates an international treaty ratified by the United States and violates customary international law." Article 6, paragraph 5 of the International Covenant on Civil and Political Rights (ICCPR) provides that: "Sentence of death shall not be imposed..."

DISCUSSION

...Although the United States Senate ratified the ICCPR with a reservation allowing juvenile offenders to be sentenced to death, Domingues asserts that this reservation was invalid and thus this capital sentencing prohibition set forth in the treaty is the supreme law of the land.... We disagree.

We conclude that the Senate's express reservation of the United States' right to impose a penalty of death on juvenile offenders negates Domingues' claim that he was illegally sentenced. Many of our sister jurisdictions have laws authorizing the death penalty for criminal offenders under the age of eighteen, and such laws have withstood Constitutional scrutiny. See *Stanford v. Kentucky*. . . .

NRS 176.025 provides that the death penalty shall not be imposed upon individuals who were under sixteen years of age at the time that the offense was committed. Because Domingues was sixteen at the time he committed a capital offense, we conclude that the death penalty was legally imposed upon him. Accordingly, we affirm the decision of the district court denying Domingues' motion to correct the sentence.

We concur: SHEARING, J., BLAKE, D.J.

SPRINGER, C.J., dissenting:

The International Covenant on Civil and Political Rights, to which the United States is a "party," forbids imposing the death penalty on children under the age of eighteen. International treaties of this kind ordinarily become the "supreme law of the land." Under the majority's interpretation of the treaty, the United States, at least with regard to executing children, is a "party" to the treaty, while at the same time rejecting one of its most vital terms. Under Nevada's interpretation of the treaty, the United States will be joining hands with such countries as Iran, Iraq, Bangladesh, Nigeria and Pakistan in approving death sentences for children. I withhold my approval of the court's judgment in this regard.

ROSE, J., dissenting:

Following a brief hearing, the district court summarily concluded that the death sentence was facially valid in spite of an international treaty signed by the United States which prohibits the execution of individuals who were under eighteen years of age when the crime was committed. I believe this complicated issue deserved a full hearing, evidentiary if necessary, on the effect of our nation's ratification of the ICCPR and the reservation by the United States Senate to that treaty's provision prohibiting the execution of anyone who committed a capital crime while under eighteen years of age.

The penultimate issue that the district court should have considered is whether the Senate's reservation was valid. Article 4 (2) of the treaty states that there shall be no derogation from Article 6 which includes the prohibition on the execution of juvenile offenders. ICCPR, 999 U.N.T.S. at 174. Furthermore, there is authority to support the proposition that the Senate's reservation was invalid. See, e.g., Restatement (Third) of the Foreign Relations Law of the United States §313 (1987); Ved P. Nanda, *The United States Reservation to the Ban on the Death Penalty for Juvenile Offenders: An Appraisal Under the International Covenant on Civil and Political Rights*, 42 DePaul L. Rev. 1311, 1331-32 (1993).

If the reservation was not valid, then the district court should determine whether the United States is still a party to the treaty. If the reservation was a "sine qua non" of the acceptance of the whole treaty by the United States, then the United State's ratification of the treaty could be considered a nullity. See William A. Schabas, *Invalid Reservations to the International Covenant on Civil and Political Rights: Is the United States Still a Party?*, 21 Brook. J. Int'l. L. 277, 318-19 (1995). But, if the United States has shown an intent to accept the treaty as a whole, the result could be that the United States is bound by all of the provisions of the treaty, notwithstanding the reservation. Id.

These are not easy questions and testimony about the international conduct of the United States concerning the subjects contained in the treaty, in addition to expert testimony on the effect of the Senate's reservation may be necessary. A federal court that deals with federal law on a daily basis might be better equipped to address these issues; however, the motion is before the state court and it should do its best to resolve the matter. Accordingly, I would reverse the district court's denial of Domingues' motion and remand the case for a full hearing on the effect of the ICCPR on Domingues' sentence.

Justice Rose's dissent raises, inter alia, the issue of the effect of a determination that the reservation is invalid. The issue of the effect of an invalid reservation to a multilateral human rights treaty is an especially complex one, which is addressed in Chapter 2. Implicit in Justice Rose's dissent is the understanding that such issues are appropriately resolved by a domestic court, with the potential outcome being that a court might void a reservation to a treaty provision and apply that provision.

With such a judicial role in mind, Domingues petitioned for a writ of certiorari to the U.S. Supreme Court, asking the Court to grant review of the Nevada Supreme Court decision and determine that the U.S. reservation to Article 6(5) is invalid. In considering the petition for review, the Court asked the Office of the Solicitor General of the U.S. Department of Justice to weigh in, which it did, defending the validity of the reservation and adding:

> Even if there were merit to [arguments that the reservation is invalid] as a matter of international treaty law, that would not mean that Article 6(5) should be enforced by a domestic court in the face of the United States' reservation. A reservation in which the President and the Senate have concurred is controlling as a matter of domestic law, and prevents the provision of the treaty to which the reservation was taken from being part of the "Treat[y] made . . . under the authority of the United States" that would bind the States under the Supremacy Clause, U.S. Const. Art. VI, Cl. 2. The President, with the concurrence of the Senate, has the constitutional authority to "make" treaties, and the courts have no authority to add provisions to treaties that were not adopted by the other Branches. If other nations are dissatisfied with the reservations attached by the United States to its ratification of a treaty, they may present a diplomatic protest or may decline to recognize themselves as being in treaty relations with the United States, that is a matter between states and not for judicial resolution. Accordingly, where the United States has ratified a treaty subject to a reservation exempting it from a particular provision of the treaty, the courts may not give effect to the provision to which reservation is made on the ground that the reservation violates international law.

Brief for the United States as Amicus Curiae Opposing the Grant of Certiorari, Domingues v. Nevada (U.S. S. Ct. No 98-8327).

The Supreme Court summarily denied the petition for review. See 528 U.S. 963 (1999). Its one sentence order gave no reasons for the denial — in keeping with its practice for denying petitions for writs of certiorari. Yet that denial appeared to close the door to any subsequent judicial questioning of the validity of the reservation to Article 6(5). In his concurring opinion in *Ex Parte Marcus Pressly*, a later case in which another juvenile offender sought to avoid the death penalty, Justice Houston of the Alabama Supreme Court reluctantly agreed to apply the reservation to Article 6(5), in light of the U.S. Supreme Court's denial of the petition for certiorari in *Domingues*:

> The Supreme Court of the United States [in *Domingues*] denied the defendant's petition for certiorari review.... I am aware that an order of the Supreme Court of the United States denying a petition for certiorari review is not to be taken as an expression of an opinion on the merits of the case. *Maryland v. Baltimore Radio Show*, 338 U.S. 912, 94 L. Ed. 562, 70 S. Ct. 252 (1950); *Carpenter v. Gomez*, 516 U.S. 981, 133 L. Ed. 2d 415, 116 S. Ct. 488 (1995); however, I am also aware that when a petition raises a substantial question, the Court sometimes "points out those concerns which, although unrelated to the merits, justify the decision not to grant review." *Carpenter v. Gomez*, 516 U.S. at 981, 716 S. Ct. 488. How much more substantial can a question be than whether a person can be executed for a crime committed in his youth, when the ICCPR [Covenant on Civil and Political Rights], a treaty to which the United States is a signatory, makes such an execution facially illegal? However, the Court did not point out concerns justifying the decision not to grant review that were unrelated to the merits. Therefore, I do not believe it is a quantum leap for me to assume that certiorari review was denied based on the merits of the case.

Ex Parte Marcus, 770 So. 2d 143, 151 (Ala. 2000) (J. Houston concurring). See also *Beazley v. Johnson*, 242 F.3d 248, 266 n. 1 (5th Cir. Tex. 2001), cert. denied, 534 U.S. 945 (2001) (quickly dispensing with an effort to invoke Article 6(5) over the reservation and referencing the denial of the petition for certiorari in *Domingues*).

Justice Rose of the Nevada Supreme Court, who had dissented in *Domingues*, continued to view the judiciary as competent to determine the validity of the reservation to Article 6(5) of the Covenant. But ultimately he agreed that the reservation was valid, in a subsequent juvenile death penalty case, *Servin v. Nevada*, 117 Nev. 775, 794, 32 P.3d 1277 (2001). In that case, the Nevada Supreme Court ruled that the death penalty as applied to Robert Paul Servin, a juvenile offender, was excessive under state law and constitutional standards of proportionality; the majority opinion considered Article 6(5) inapplicable because of the reservation, see 117 Nev. at 787. In concurring with the ruling in Servin, Justice Rose wrote:

> At first blush, the U.S. Senate's reservation to the International Covenant on Civil and Political Rights (ICCPR) seems completely incompatible with the object and purpose of the treaty. However, three factors convince me that the Senate's reservation has continued viability. First, the ICCPR does not expressly prohibit reservations or make reference to the object-and-purpose test. Second, it is reported that there is a "widespread state practice in support of reservations to human rights treaties" and that "approximately one-third of the parties to the ICCPR made reservations to over a dozen substantive provisions." Third, while 11 of the 146 nations objected to the Senate's reservation because it violated the basic purpose of the treaty, none of the objections were raised within the twelve months after the communication of the United States' reservation, and therefore, the reservation is deemed accepted under the Vienna Convention. This court has carefully considered the effect of the Senate reservation as I was concerned about in *Domingues v. State* and I am gratified that we have fully addressed this important issue.

117 Nev. at 794 (Rose, J., concurring).

It is further telling that, in *Roper v. Simmons*, the lawyers for Simmons did not urge the Court to consider Article 6(5) a binding treaty provision, effectively conceding the validity of the U.S. reservation. See Brief for Respondent (Jul. 19, 2004), WL 1947812. Neither for the most part did the several amicus parties that weighed in favor of Simmons urge rejection of the reservation to Article 6(5); instead, they presented a picture of applicable international law and world opinion that did not depend on finding that Article 6(5) was binding on the United States as a party to the Covenant. See Brief of Amici Curiae Nobel Peace Laureates in Support of Respondent, supra page 447. But see Brief of Amici Curiae the European Union and Members of the International Community in Support of Respondent, supra page 447, at 14-17 (asserting that the reservation is invalid). The Court itself did not question the validity of the reservation, although it did count Article 6(5) among the indicators of world opinion (something that attracted caustic criticism by Justice Scalia in his dissent). A rationale, if not justification, for this deference to the reservation was provided in the following article, written before the Court's decision in *Roper*.

Curtis A. Bradley, *The Juvenile Death Penalty and International Law*

52 Duke L.J. 485, 541-544, 557 (2002) (notes omitted)

...[I]in order for an ICCPR-based challenge against the U.S. juvenile death penalty to succeed under international law, a decisionmaker would have to reach two questionable conclusions: that the U.S. reservation violates the object and purpose of the ICCPR, and that the proper remedy under international law is to sever the reservation and enforce the treaty against the United States as if it had never entered the reservation. Even those conclusions, however, would probably be insufficient to provide a *U.S. court* with a basis for disregarding the reservation.

Article II of the Constitution specifies the procedural requirements for treatymaking: the president has the power to make treaties, "by and with the Advice and Consent of the Senate,...provided two thirds of the Senators present concur." The reservations to the ICCPR, including the reservation to the juvenile death penalty provision, comply with these requirements. The president and at least two-thirds of the senators present accepted these reservations, and they were included with the U.S. instrument of treaty ratification that was deposited by the president with the United Nations. Furthermore, there does not appear to be any basis in U.S. law for imposing on this process any additional limitations derived from the customary international law of treaty reservations. Although the Supreme Court has not addressed this issue directly, it has long held that Congress is not required under U.S. law to comply with treaties, and the lower courts uniformly have held that Congress is not required to comply with customary international law. Furthermore, lower courts generally have held that the executive branch is not required to comply with customary international law. There is no reason to believe that U.S. law imposes a requirement of international law compliance on the Senate and president when making treaties when it does not impose this requirement on Congress or the president outside the treaty process.

Consequently, even if a U.S. court accepted the international law arguments, it would not have a basis under U.S. law for disregarding the U.S. reservation.

In fact, enforcement of the juvenile death penalty provision by a U.S. court would not only lack support in U.S. law, it arguably would violate the U.S. Constitution. Under Articles II and VI of the Constitution, the president and two-thirds of the Senate must agree on the terms of a treaty before it becomes part of the "supreme Law of the Land." If a U.S. court disregarded the U.S. reservation and enforced the juvenile death penalty provision, it would be treating as supreme law of the land a treaty provision that had never been approved by the president and Senate. Even if one were to conclude that the proper *international law remedy* was to sever the reservation and enforce the treaty as if the reservation had never been entered, the procedural requirements of the Constitution would remain unsatisfied. This is true even if a court somehow concluded that the U.S. treatymakers would have ratified the treaty without the reservation if they had known that the reservation was invalid under international law, since Article II refers to what the treatymakers *actually* agreed upon, not to what they *would have* agreed upon.

More generally, courts would likely be reluctant to disregard the U.S. reservation because doing so would involve a substantial judicial intervention into the treaty process. U.S. courts have never exercised judicial review to invalidate either the domestic or international effects of a treaty. In part, this is because the text of the Constitution is relatively silent about the scope and exclusivity of the treaty power. U.S. courts also have recognized that, although treaties are legal instruments, their creation and especially their enforcement are heavily informed by political factors. Recognizing the lack of textual guidance and the importance of political contingency in this context, U.S. courts have taken a largely passive role in the institutional developments concerning the making and enforcement of treaties. They usually defer to the accommodations of the political branches (such as the allowance of congressional-executive agreements) or abstain from adjudicating disputes between the political branches (such as over the termination of treaties). Similarly, they consider many matters pertaining to the negotiation, observance, and status of treaties to be "political questions" committed to the discretion of the political branches. They also give "great weight" to the Executive Branch's interpretation of a treaty. And, of course, judicial deference to political branch arrangements is especially strong in situations, as with the reservations to the ICCPR, in which the political branches are in agreement. For all of these reasons, it is highly unlikely that a U.S. court would apply the customary international law of treaty reservations to invalidate the United States' juvenile death penalty reservation to the ICCPR. . . .

I do not intend to suggest in this Article that the juvenile death penalty reflects wise policy or that it should be retained. Nor am I arguing that international practice is irrelevant to this policy question, or even to the Eighth Amendment analysis of what is cruel and unusual. My argument, rather, is that these policy and legal questions must ultimately be decided by the United States, in accordance with its constitutional processes. Claims by advocacy groups and scholars that these decisions have already been made for the United States distort the actual requirements of international law and, in any event, are not likely to be persuasive to U.S. decision makers.

2. The Doctrine of (Non) Self-Executing Treaties

As noted earlier, Article VI, section 2, of the Constitution establishes treaties ratified by the United States to be part of the "supreme Law of the Land." However, under principles first enunciated by Chief Justice Marshall in *Foster v. Nielson*, 27 U.S. (2 Pet.) 253, 314 (1829), the status accorded by courts in the United States to treaty provisions that are admitted to be binding on the country turns on whether or not the provisions are considered self-executing. "It is only when a treaty is self-executing, when it prescribes rules by which private rights may be determined that it may be relied upon for the enforcement of such rights." *Dreyfus v. Von Finck*, 534 F.2d 24, 30 (2d Cir.), cert. denied, 429 U.S. 835 (1976). Thus, even if the reservation to Article 6(5) of the Covenant on Civil and Political Rights did not exist or was somehow considered inoperative, the self-execution hurdle would have to be overcome for that provision — and the other provisions of the Covenant — to be judicially enforceable within the United States.

Note: The Fujii Case

In the leading case of *Fujii v. State*, the California Supreme Court applied the self-execution doctrine to find that the human rights clauses of the UN Charter could not be the basis of a legal challenge to a blatantly discriminatory California statute. The California Alien Property Initiative Act of 1920 (better known as the Alien Land Law) had a long and infamous life. Enacted in the xenophobic atmosphere that prevailed in the United States after World War I, the Alien Land Law distinguished the right to own real property based on class of alienage: Aliens who were eligible for U.S. citizenship were permitted to hold title to real property; aliens ineligible for citizenship (principally Chinese and Japanese, although not specifically designated by the statute) were not permitted to own land. Land acquired by those aliens escheated to the state.

The Alien Land Law made a second distinction of historic interest. If an alien purchased land with consideration supplied by another alien, the law would make different presumptions about the nature of the transaction depending upon whether the alien supplying the consideration was eligible for citizenship (and hence eligible to own land). If he or she was not eligible, the law presumed that the transaction was made with the intention to circumvent the substantive policy behind the statute by setting up an alien eligible to own land as a mere cover for de facto ownership by the ineligible alien. The burden of proof was placed on the party who took title to the land to show that the conveyance was not made simply to avoid the escheat penalty.

The U.S. Supreme Court struck down this second distinction in *Oyama v. California*, 332 U.S. 633 (1948), as violating the equal protection clause of the Fourteenth Amendment. Two points are noteworthy about this decision. First, four of the nine justices ventured the opinion that the provision violated not only the Fourteenth Amendment, but also the United States' obligations under the UN Charter. The second point that should be remembered is that the decision was cast very narrowly; the substantive policy behind the statute — the disqualification of certain aliens from owning land — was not struck down.

Such was the status of the California Alien Land Law at the time that Mr. Sei Fujii entered the drama. Mr. Fujii, who was not eligible for U.S. citizenship under the prevailing federal naturalization laws, purchased and acquired some real property in 1948. He then made use of a provision of California law that entitled him to apply to the District Court of Los Angeles County (where the land was situated) for a determination of whether or not an escheat had occurred under the Alien Land Law. The court held that it had, whereupon Mr. Fujii appealed that ruling to California's District Court of Appeal.

The California court of appeals ruled in favor of Mr. Fujii, determining that the Alien Land Law was invalid under the human rights clauses of Articles 1, 55, and 56 of the UN Charter. The court interpreted the broad language of these clauses of the Charter in light of the specific rights of non-discrimination and property affirmed in Articles 1, 2, and 17 of the Universal Declaration of Human Rights. The court stated:

> The Charter has become the "supreme Law of the Land; and the Judges in every State shall be bound thereby..." U.S. Const., Art. VI., sec. 2. The position in this country in the family of nations forbids trafficking in generalities but demands that every State in the Union accept and act upon the Charter according to its plain language and its unmistakable purpose and intent.

Fujii v. State, 97 A.C.A. 154, 217 P.2d, 481, 486 (1950). The California court of appeals' decision sparked a lively scholarly debate centered on the issue of whether or not the Charter's human rights clauses had been properly considered to be self-executing. Compare, for example, Manley O. Hudson, *Charter Provisions on Human Rights in American Law*, 44 Am J. Int'l L. 543 (1950) (criticizing the court of appeals decision in Fujii); with Quincy Wright, *National Courts and Human Rights — The Fujii Case*, 45 Am. J. Int'l L. 63 (defending that decision as in line with a "long and unbroken tradition" in American jurisprudence). When the case ultimately reached the California Supreme Court in another round of appeal, that court sided with those holding the Charter's human rights clauses not to be judicially enforceable.

Sei Fujii v. State

38 Cal. 2d 718, 242 P.2d 617 (1952)

Gibson, C.J.... [T]he sole question presented on this appeal is the validity of the California alien land law.

It is first contended that the land law has been invalidated and superseded by the provisions of the United Nations Charter pledging the member nations to promote the observance of human rights and fundamental freedoms without distinction as to race. Plaintiff relies on statements in the preamble and in Articles 1, 55 and 56 of the Charter....

It is not disputed that the charter is a treaty and our federal Constitution provides that treaties made under the authority of the United States are part of the supreme law of the land and that the judges in every state are bound thereby. U.S. Const., art. VI. A treaty, however, does not automatically supersede local laws which are inconsistent with it unless the treaty provisions are self-executing.

In the words of Chief Justice Marshall: A treaty is "to be regarded in courts of justice as equivalent to an act of the Legislature, whenever it operates of itself, without the aid of any legislative provision. But when the terms of the stipulation import a contract — when either of the parties engages to perform a particular act, the treaty addresses itself to the political not the judicial department; and the Legislature must execute the contract, before it can become a rule for the court." *Foster v. Neilson*, 1829, 2 Pet. 253, 314, 7 L. Ed. 415.

In determining whether a treaty is self-executing courts look to the intent of the signatory parties as manifested by the language of the instrument, and, if the instrument is uncertain, recourse may be had to the circumstances surrounding its execution... In order for a treaty provision to be operative without the aid of implementing legislation and to have the force and effect of a statute, it must appear that the framers of the treaty intended to prescribe a rule that, standing alone, would be enforceable in the courts....

It is clear that the provisions of the preamble and of Article 1 of the charter which are claimed to be in conflict with the alien land law are not self-executing. They state general purposes and objectives of the United Nations Organization and do not purport to impose legal obligations on the individual member nations or to create rights in private persons. It is equally clear that none of the other provisions relied on by plaintiff is self-executing. Article 55 declares that the United Nations "shall promote:... universal respect for, and observance of, human rights and fundamental freedoms for all without distinction as to race, sex, language, or religion," and in Article 56. The member nations "pledge themselves to take joint and separate action in cooperation with the Organization of the achievement of the purposes set forth in Article 55." Although the member nations have obligated themselves to cooperate with the international organization in promoting respect for, and observance of human rights, it is plain that it was contemplated that future legislative action by the several nations would be required to accomplish the declared objectives, and there is nothing to indicate that these provisions were intended to become rules of law for the courts of this county upon the ratification of the charter.

The language used in Articles 55 and 56 is not the type customarily employed in treaties which have been held to be self-executing and to create rights and duties in individuals. For example, the treaty involved in *Clark v. Allen*, 331 U.S. 503, 507-508, 67 S. Ct. 1431, 1434, 91 L. Ed 1633, relating to the rights of a national of one country to inherit real property located in another country, specifically provided that "such national shall be allowed a term of three years in which to sell the [property]...and withdraw the proceeds..." free from any discriminatory taxation... In *Nielsen v. Johnson*, 279 U.S. 47, 50, 49 S. Ct. 223, 73 L. Ed. 607, the provision treated as being self executing was equally definite. There each of the signatory parties agreed that "no higher or other duties, charges, or taxes of any kind, shall be levied" by one country on removal of property therefrom by citizens of the other country "than are or shall be payable in each state, upon the same, when removed by a citizen or subject of such state respectively." In other instances treaty provisions were enforced without implementing legislation where they prescribed in detail the rules governing rights and obligations of individuals or specifically provided that citizens of one nation shall have the same rights while in the other country as are enjoyed by that country's own citizens....

It is significant to note that when the framers of the charter intended to make certain provisions effective without the aid of implementing legislation they employed language which is clear and definite and manifests that intention. For example, Article 104 provides: "The Organization shall enjoy in the territory of each of its Members such legal capacity as may be necessary for the exercise of its functions and the fulfillment of its purposes." Article 105 provides: "1. The organization shall enjoy in the territory of each of its Members such privileges and immunities as are necessary for the fulfillment of its purposes. 2. Representatives of the Members of the United Nations and officials of the Organization shall similarly enjoy such privileges and immunities as are necessary for the independent exercise of their functions in connection with the Organization." In *Curran v. City of New York*, 191 Misc. 229, 77 N.Y.S.2d 206, 212, these articles were treated as being self-executory....

The provisions in the charter pledging cooperation in promoting observance of fundamental freedoms lack the mandatory quality and definiteness which would indicate an intent to create justiciable rights in private persons immediately upon ratification. Instead, they are framed as a promise of future action by the member nations. Secretary of State Stettinius, Chairman of the United States delegation at the San Francisco Conference where the charter was drafted, stated in his report to President Truman that Article 56 "pledges the various countries to cooperate with the organization by joint and separate action in the achievement of the economic and social objectives of the organization without infringing upon their right to order their national affairs according to their own best ability, in their own way, and in accordance with their own political and economic institutions and processes." Report to the President on the Results of the San Francisco Conference by the Chairman of the United States Delegation, the Secretary of State, Department of State Publication 2349, Conference Series 71, p. 115; Hearings before the Committee on Foreign Relations, United States Senate [Revised] July 9-13, 1945, p. 106. The same view was repeatedly expressed by delegates of other nations in the debates attending the drafting of article 56. See U.N.C.I.O. Doc. 699 II/3/40, May 30, 1945, pp. 1-3; U.N.C.I.O. Doc. 684, II/3/38, May 29, 1945, p. 4; Kelsen, *The Law of the United Nations* [1950], footnote 9, pp. 100-102.

The humane and enlightened objectives of the United Nations Character are, of course, entitled to respectful consideration by the courts and legislatures of every member nation, since that document expresses the universal desire of thinking men for peace and for equality of rights and opportunities. The charter represents a moral commitment of foremost importance, and we must not permit the spirit of our pledge to be compromised or disparaged in either our domestic or foreign affairs. We are satisfied, however, that the charter provisions relied on by plaintiff were not intended to supersede existing domestic legislation, and we cannot hold that they operate to invalidate the alien land law....

[Having thus disposed of the issues relating to the UN Charter, the court proceeded to hold the Alien Land Law invalid on the ground that it violated the equal protection clause of the Fourteenth Amendment.]

The decision in *Fujii* was not appealed to the U.S. Supreme Court, a fact leading some to conclude optimistically that question of whether or not the human rights clauses of the UN Charter are self-executing "remains unsettled for the country as a whole." George A. Finch, *The Need to Restrain the Treaty-Making Power of the United States Within Constitutional Limits*," 48 Am. J. Int'l L. 57, 72 (1954). While this statement remains technically true today, no federal or state court that has addressed the question during the past 60 years has held that the Charter's human rights clauses are self-executing; to the contrary, many courts have held they are *not*. See, e.g., *Frovola v. U.S.S.R.*, 761 F.2d 370, 374 (7th Cir. 1985). For a compilation of such cases, see Richard B. Lillich, *International Human Rights Instruments* 10.9-10.11 (2d ed. Rev. 1995). Further, the rationale in *Fujii* has been transposed to find that other human rights treaties are not self-executing, see, e.g., In re *Alien Children Educ. Litig.*, 501 F. Supp. 544, 590 (S.D. Tex. 1980), aff'd unreported mem. (5th Cir. 1981), aff'd sub. nom *Plyler v. Doe*, 457 U.S. 202 (1982) (OAS Charter non-self-executing); *Bertrand v. Sava*, 684 F.2d 204, 218-219 (2d Cir. 1982) (Refugees Protocol non-self-executing). See generally Richard B. Lillich, *Invoking International Human Rights in Domestic Courts*, 54 U. Cin. L. Rev. 367, 385-393 (1985).

Contrasting with the language of the human rights provisions of the Charter, which the court in *Fujii* found to "lack the mandatory quality and definiteness which would indicate an intent to create justiciable rights," are provisions of the International Covenant on Civil and Political Rights specifying particular rights and corresponding state obligations, including the Covenant's quite specific and mandatory prohibition of the juvenile death penalty in Article 6(5). A reasonable argument could be made that Article 6(5) and other provisions of the Covenant are self-executing. However, the question of whether or not any of the Covenant's provisions are self-executing has not been left entirely — if at all — to judicial resolution.

The U.S. Declarations of Non-Self-Execution

The President attached to his ratification of the Covenant on Civil and Political Rights a "declaration" that the Covenant's substantive provisions "are not self-executing." U.S. Senate Resolution of Advice and Consent to the Ratification of the International Covenant on Civil and Political Rights, art. III(1), 138 Cong. Rec. S4781 (1991). Similar declarations ware attached to U.S. ratification of the International Convention on the Elimination All Forms of Racial Discrimination and the Convention Against Torture and Other Cruel, Inhuman, or Degrading Treatment or Punishment.

Scholars and advocates have argued that the non-self-execution declaration is invalid on the ground that the question of self-execution is a matter of judicial determination that should not be predetermined by the President or Senate. See, e.g., Louis Henkin, *Comment, U.S. Ratification of Human Rights Convention: The Ghost of Senator Bricker*, 89 Am. J. Int'l L. 341, 346-347 (1995) (arguing that the Senate and President's attempt to foreclose judicial enforcement of the Covenant "may be unconstitutional"). An alternative argument is that the declaration is contrary to the object and purpose of the Covenant since rendering the Covenant non-self-executing undermines the judicial remedies contemplated by the Covenant. See, e.g., Jordan J. Paust, *Customary International Law and Human Rights Treaties are Law of the United States*, 20 Mich. J. Int'l L. 301, 322-324 (1999).

Notwithstanding such arguments, the U.S. Supreme Court in *Sosa v. Alvarez-Machain*, 124 S. Ct. 2739, 2763, 2767 (2004), followed a clear trend in the lower federal courts and summarily construed the Covenant to be non-self-executing in light of the declaration. The Court concluded that the Covenant does not "itself create obligations enforceable in the federal courts" and hence could not "establish the relevant and applicable rule of international law" for an action under the federal Alien Tort Statute. Id. at 2767 (an edited version of the opinion in *Sosa* is set forth infra at page 485).

Assuming that the non-self-execution declaration is valid, how far reaching is it? Does it render the Covenant, and other human rights treaties ratified with similar declarations of non-self-execution, without *any* possibility of providing a rule of decision in the domestic courts? Relevant to this question is the following statement from the Clinton administration, made during deliberations on the ratification of the Convention on the Elimination of All Forms of Racial Discrimination.

> . . . By making clear that this convention is not self-executing, we ensure that it does not create a new or independently enforceable private cause of action in U.S. courts. We have proposed and the Senate has concurred in the same approach to previous human rights treaties, such as . . . the International Covenant on Civil and Political Rights (1992).
>
> As was the case with the earlier treaties, existing U.S. law provides extensive protection and remedies. . . . We see no need for the establishment of additional causes of action to enforce the requirements of the convention.

Statement of Conrad Harper, Legal Advisor of the U.S. State Department, to the Senate Committee on Foreign Relations (May 11, 1994).

This statement has been used to argue that the effect of the non-self-execution declaration is not to prevent the substantive provisions of the Covenant on Civil and Political Rights from operating as rules of decision in all judicial proceedings, but only to ensure that the treaty does not itself give rise to any affirmative cause of action in domestic courts. The extension of this argument is that, notwithstanding the declaration, Article 6(5) of the Covenant on Civil and Political Rights may be applied to prevent application of the death penalty to a juvenile defender (assuming that the reservation specific to that article is invalid), since such a defensive use of the Covenant is not the assertion of a cause of action. See Connie de la Vega, *Amici Curiae Urge the U.S. Supreme Court to Consider International Human Rights Law in Death Penalty Case*, 42 Santa Clara L. Rev. 1041, 1056 (2002) (advancing this argument). See generally Paust, *Customary International Law and Human Rights Treaties are Law of the United States*, supra, at 326 (arguing that even "non-self-executing treaties are still law of the United States and can be used [inter alia] . . . defensively in civil or criminal contexts"); Carlos Manuel Vazquez, *The Four Doctrines of Self-Executing Treaties*, 89 Am J. Int'l L. 695 (1995) (distinguishing between treaties that create affirmative causes of action and those that do not but that should still otherwise be judicially enforceable).

However, the sweeping language of the Supreme Court in *Sosa v. Alvarez-Machain* — stating that the Covenant does "not itself create obligations enforceable in the federal courts" — discourages this argument. This language can be read to suggest that the Covenant on Civil and Political Rights cannot for *any* purpose provide a judicially applicable rule of decision, including, but not limited to, establishing an affirmative cause of action. The quoted language read in this way, however, might be considered mere dictum, since in the matter before the Court was whether customary international law established a cause of action that could be pursued under the Alien Tort Statute (see infra page 485). It is strong dictum, nonetheless, supported by a number of cases in which courts have consistently deferred to the non-self-execution declaration and declined to directly apply the Covenant, including instances when the Covenant was defensively invoked. See, e.g., *Beazley v. Johnson*, 242 F.3d 248, 267 (5th Cir. 2001); *United States v. Duarte-Acero*, 296 F. 3d. 1277, 1283 (11th Cir. 2002), cert. denied, 537 U.S. 1038 (2002); *Iguarta de la Rosa v. United States*, 32 F.3d 8, 10 n.1 (1st Cir. 1994), cert. denied, 514 U.S. 1049 (1995); *Ralk v. Lincoln County*, 81 F. Supp. 2d 1372, 1381 (S.D. Ga. 2000); In re *Matter of the Extradition of Cheung*, 968 F. Supp. 791, 803 n. 17 (D. Conn. 1997); *Rivera v. Warden*, 2001 U.S. Dist. LEXIS 24344, 13, 14 (M.D. Pa. June 12, 2001).

Even without relying on the declaration, the federal district court in *White v. Paulsen*, 997 F. Supp. 1380 (E.D. Wash. 1998), found the Covenant on Civil and Political Rights not to be self-executing. The court held that neither the Covenant nor the Convention Against Torture could ground a claim of prisoner mistreatment in connection with 28 U.S.C. §1331, which provides a statutory basis for federal jurisdiction over claims "arising under the Constitution, laws, or treaties of the United States." Taking a rare judicial posture, the court in *White* stated that the non-self-execution declaration "may not carry controlling weight on this issue," 997 F. Supp. at 1387, but the court nonetheless found the substantive provisions of the Covenant to be non-self-executing on the basis of its own analysis of the treaty's text:

> There is no set test for determining whether a treaty is self-executing; different courts have come up with various descriptions of factors relevant to this inquiry. *See, e.g., Frolova v. Union of Soviet Socialist Republics*, 761 F.2d 370, 373 (7th Cir. 1975) (listing six relevant factors). The Ninth Circuit has expressly stated that its subordinate courts must look to relevant "contextual factors," including:
>
> > the purposes of the treaty and the objectives of its creators, the existence of domestic procedures and institutions appropriate for direct implementation, the availability and feasibility of alternative enforcement methods, and the immediate and long-range social consequences of self- or non-self-execution.
>
> *People of Saipan v. United States Dep't of Interior*, 502 F.2d 90, 97 (9th Cir. 1974). Of these four non-exclusive factors, "it is the first factor that is critical to determine whether an executive agreement is self-executing, while the other factors are most relevant to determine the extent to which the agreement is self-executing." *Iran*, 771 F.2d at 1283; *see also Frolova*, 761 F.2d at 373 ("if the parties' intent is clear from the treaty's language courts will not inquire into the remaining factors").
>
> Plaintiffs contend two treaties to which the United States is a party contain self-executing prohibitions on torture that incorporate non-consensual medical experimentation: the previously discussed International Covenant on Civil and Political Rights ("ICCPR"), and the Convention Against Torture and Other Cruel, Inhuman or Degrading Treatment or Punishment... [B]oth of these treaties expressly require that party-states take steps under their municipal laws to enforce the rights described in those treaties, suggesting strongly that parties to these agreements did not intend for them to be self-executing. *See Foster v. Neilson*, 27 U.S. 253, 314, 7 L. Ed. 415 (1829)

("When the terms of [a treaty] import a contract, when either of the parties engages to perform a particular act, the treaty addresses itself to the political, not the judicial department; and the legislature must execute the contract before it can become a rule for the Court."), *overruled on other grounds*, *United States v. Percheman*, 32 U.S. (7 Pet.) 51, 8 L. Ed. 604 (1833).

For example, although Article 2 of the ICCPR expressly addresses the duty of party-states to enforce the rights described in the ICCPR, it does not purport to expressly or implicitly create a private right of action for violations of those rights. On its face, Article 2 creates no express right, discussing only what the party-states have agreed to do to give effect to the rights discussed in the ICCPR. Moreover, the language is couched in terms of further actions that States agree to undertake, thereby suggesting that the agreement is subject to further domestic action rather than self-executing. *Compare with Iran*, 771 F.2d at 1283 (finding statements that United States "agrees to" undertake further actions does not evince intent that agreement be self-executing). Additionally, Article 2 expressly recognizes that the treaty imposes no obligation to take further action if effective remedies exist, non-judicial or otherwise, and also provides that the remedy need not be judicial in nature. Indeed, to the extent that Article 2 addresses itself to a requirement for a judicial remedy, it states only that its parties must "develop the possibilities of a judicial remedy." From this language, it is apparent that the parties to the ICCPR did not intend for its provisions to be self-executing in the sense of automatically creating a private right of action cognizable by citizens of a State. *See also Tel-Oren*, 726 F.2d at 818-19 & n.26 (Bork, J. concurring) (language of Art. 2 of ICCPR implies convention is not self-executing).

White v. Paulsen, 997 F. Supp. at 1385-1387.

Many scholars have argued in favor of a presumption that treaties are self-executing, given the constitutional status of treaties as part of the "supreme law of the land." See, e.g., Jodan J. Paust, *Self-Executing Treaties*, 82 Am J. Intl. L. 760 (1988). A few other scholars have maintained the opposite view, in light of the characteristics that distinguish treaties historically and today from ordinary federal statutes, including their foreign policy dimensions. See, e.g., John C. Woo, *Globalism and the Constitution, Treaties, Non-Self-Execution, and the Original Understanding*, 99 Colum L. Rev. 2095 (1999). Whatever the relative merits of these contending positions, courts now appear reluctant to find multilateral human rights treaties to be judicially enforceable without implementing legislation, as illustrated further by the following recent decision (under review by the Supreme Court as of this writing), in which the court rejected applying the 1949 Geneva Convention in a habeas corpus proceeding.

Hamdan v. Rumsfeld

2005 U.S. App. LEXIS 14315 (D. C. Cir. 2005)

[For a summary of the facts, see extracts from the case in Chapter 4 page 301.]

[We now consider] Hamdan's argument, accepted by the district court, that the Geneva Convention Relative to the Treatment of Prisoners of War, Aug. 12, 1949, 6 U.S.T. 3316 ("1949 Geneva Convention"), ratified in 1955, may be enforced in federal court.

"Treaties made, or which shall be made, under the Authority of the United States, shall be the supreme Law of the Land." U.S. CONST., art. VI, cl. 2. Even so, this country has traditionally negotiated treaties with the understanding that they do not create judicially enforceable individual rights. *See Holmes v. Laird*, 148 U.S. App. D.C. 187, 459 F.2d 1211, 1220, 1222 (D.C. Cir. 1972); *Canadian Transport Co. v. United States*, 214 U.S. App. D.C. 138, 663 F.2d 1081, 1092 (D.C. Cir. 1980). As a general matter, a "treaty is primarily a compact between independent nations," and "depends for the enforcement of its provisions on the interest and honor of the governments which are parties to it." *Head Money Cases, Edye and Another v. Robertson*, 112 U.S. 580, 598, 28 L. Ed. 798, 5 S. Ct. 247, Treas. Dec. 6714 (1884). If a treaty is violated, this "becomes the subject of international negotiations and reclamation," not the subject of a lawsuit. *Id.*; *see Charlton v. Kelly*, 229 U.S. 447, 474, 57 L. Ed. 1274, 33 S. Ct. 945(1913); *Whitney v. Robertson*, 124 U.S. 190, 194-95, 31 L. Ed. 386, 8 S. Ct. 456 (1888); *Foster v. Neilson*, 27 U.S. (2 Pet.) 253, 306, 314, 7 L. Ed. 415 (1829), *overruled on other grounds, United States v. Percheman*, 32 U.S. (7 Pet.) 51, 8 L. Ed. 604 (1883).

Thus, "international agreements, even those directly benefitting private persons, generally do not create private rights or provide for a private cause of action in domestic courts." RESTATEMENT (THIRD) OF THE FOREIGN RELATIONS LAW OF THE UNITED STATES §907 cmt. a, at 395 (1987). The district court nevertheless concluded that the 1949 Geneva Convention conferred individual rights enforceable in federal court. We believe the court's conclusion disregards the principles just mentioned and is contrary to the Convention itself. To explain why, we must consider the Supreme Court's treatment of the Third Geneva Convention of 1929 in *Johnson v. Eisentrager*, 339 U.S. 763, 94 L. Ed. 1255, 70 S. Ct. 936 (1950), and this court's decision in *Holmes v. Laird*, neither of which the district court mentioned.

In *Eisentrager*, German nationals, convicted by a military commission in China of violating the laws of war and imprisoned in Germany, sought writs of habeas corpus in federal district court on the ground that the military commission violated their rights under the Constitution and their rights under the 1929 Geneva Convention. 339 U.S. at 767. The Supreme Court, speaking through Justice Jackson, wrote in an alternative holding that the Convention was not judicially enforceable: the Convention specifies rights of prisoners of war, but "responsibility for observance and enforcement of these rights is upon political and military authorities." *Id.* at 789 n.14. We relied on this holding in *Holmes v. Laird*, 459 F.2d at 1222, to deny enforcement of the individual rights provisions contained in the NATO Status of Forces Agreement, an international treaty.

This aspect of *Eisentrager* is still good law and demands our adherence....

Although the government relied heavily on *Eisentrager* in making its argument to this effect, Hamdan chose to ignore the decision in his brief. Nevertheless, we have compared the 1949 Convention to the 1929 Convention. There are differences, but none of them renders *Eisentrager*'s conclusion about the 1929 Convention inapplicable to the 1949 Convention. Common Article 1 of the 1949 Convention states that parties to the Convention "undertake to respect and to ensure respect for the present Convention in all circumstances." The comparable provision in the 1929 version stated that the "Convention shall be respected ... in all circumstances." Geneva Convention of 1929, art. 82. The revision imposed upon signatory nations the duty not only of complying themselves but also of making sure other signatories complied. Nothing in the revision altered the method by which a nation would enforce compliance. Article 8 of the 1949

Convention states that its provisions are to be "applied with the cooperation and under the scrutiny of the Protecting Powers. . . ." This too was a feature of the 1929 Convention. *See* Geneva Convention of 1929, art. 86. But Article 11 of the 1949 Convention increased the role of the protecting power, typically the International Red Cross, when disputes arose: "In cases of disagreement between the Parties to the conflict as to the application or interpretation of the provisions of the present Convention, the Protecting Powers shall lend their good offices with a view to settling the disagreement." Here again there is no suggestion of judicial enforcement. The same is true with respect to the other method set forth in the 1949 Convention for settling disagreements. Article 132 provides that "at the request of a Party to the conflict, an enquiry shall be instituted, in a manner to be decided between the interested Parties, concerning any alleged violation of the Convention." If no agreement is reached about the procedure for the "enquiry," Article 132 further provides that "the Parties should agree on the choice of an umpire who will decide upon the procedure to be followed."

Hamdan points out that the 1949 Geneva Convention protects individual rights. But so did the 1929 Geneva Convention, as the Court recognized in *Eisentrager*, 339 U.S. at 789-90. The NATO Status of Forces Agreement, at issue in *Holmes v. Laird*, also protected individual rights, but we held that the treaty was not judicially enforceable. 459 F.2d at 1222. . . .

We therefore hold that the 1949 Geneva Convention does not confer upon Hamdan a right to enforce its provisions in court. [The court thus rejected Hamdan's habeas corpus petition which relied on the Convention, and it upheld the validity of the military commission and the proceedings that would try him.]

Comments and Questions

1. How, if at all, do the analyses leading to determinations of non-self-execution in *Fujii* and *Hamdan* differ? Compare also the criteria applied in *White v. Paulsen*, supra page 468, to find the Covenant on Civil and Political Rights non-self-executing. For an analysis of the divergent approaches employed by courts to determine whether or not a treaty is self-executing, see Carlos Manuel Vazquez, *The Four Doctrines of Self-Executing Treaties*, supra page 467.

2. Reread Article 6(5) along with Article 2 of the Covenant on Civil and Political Rights, which is in the Documentary Supplement. Do you agree, as concluded in *White v. Paulsen*, that Article 2, which commits states to take measures domestically to give effect to the rights in the Covenant, is a strong indication that the Covenant is non-self-executing? Or does Article 2 instead suggest that states should ensure the availability of judicial remedies, even in the absence of relevant implementing legislation?

3. In *Asakura v. Seattle*, 265 U.S. 332 (1924), the Supreme Court interpreted the U.S.-Japan treaty of 1911, which provided that citizens of each country enjoyed the right to carry on a trade or business within the other country. Holding that this provision of the treaty was self-executing and created enforceable rights in individuals, the Court opined that "[t]reaties are to be construed in a broad and liberal spirit, and when two constructions are possible, one restrictive of rights which may be claimed under it, and the other favorable to them the latter is preferred." Id. at 342. Are *Fujii*, *Hamdan*, and *White* consistent with this mandate

of a liberal reading of treaties? What factors might explain or justify holding the treaties in those cases to a higher standard of scrutiny, with the result that they were each deemed to be non-self-executing? The fact that each of those treaties — the UN Charter, the Covenant on Civil and Political Rights, and the 1949 Geneva Convention — is a multilateral treaty, as opposed to a bilateral treaty governing aspects of the reciprocal relationship between two countries and their citizens? In the case of the human rights provisions of the UN Charter and the Covenant, the fact that those provisions apply in favor of U.S. citizens whose rights are otherwise defined and protected by domestic law? Note also *People of Saipan ex rel. Guerrero v. U.S. Dept. of Interior*, 502 F.2d 90 (9th Cir.), cert. denied, 420 U.S. 1003 (1974), a case in which citizens of Micronesia sued to enforce the Trusteeship Agreement that the United States had entered into with the United Nations governing its administration of the Trust Territory of the Pacific Islands. In finding that international agreement to be self-executing, the court of appeals acknowledged that "the substantive rights guaranteed through the Trusteeship Agreement are not precisely defined. However, we do not believe that the agreement is too vague for judicial enforcement. Its language is no more general than such terms as 'due process of law,' 'seaworthiness,' 'equal protection of the law,' 'good faith,' or 'restraint of trade,' which courts interpret every day . . ." 502 F.2d. at 99. Is there a distinction between U.S. courts interpreting vague constitutional or statutory language and these same courts construing similarly vague treaty provisions? Should there be?

4. Might justification for applying a high standard to find a treaty judicially enforceable relate to foreign policy and separation of powers considerations? Note the context in *Hamdan*, in which the 1949 Geneva Convention is being invoked in direct opposition to the president's action as part of the "war on terror." If not in the same degree, are foreign policy and separation of powers considerations always present when courts are asked to judicially enforce treaties without implementing legislation? See generally Woo, *Globalism and the Constitution, Treaties, Non-Self-Execution, and the Original Understanding*, supra page 469. In this regard, consider the caution counseled by the Supreme Court in discerning the existence of causes of action in federal court on the basis of customary international law in *Sosa v. Alvarez-Machain*, infra page 485.

5. Do you find the arguments that the U.S. declaration regarding Article 6(5) of the Covenant on Civil and Political Rights is an invalid reservation to be convincing? Isn't the purpose of a reservation precisely to avoid obligations that a ratifying state, for whatever reasons, does not wish to accept? See the discussion of reservations in Chapter 2, page 113.

6. European colonizing states and the United States after them concluded hundreds of treaties with the Indian tribes within the country's borders. Most of these treaties have not been abrogated by subsequent acts of Congress, and they continue to define many of the rights retained by tribes in exchange, usually, for vast areas of land and other concessions. Indian treaties stand essentially on the same footing in U.S. domestic law as treaties with foreign nations. See *Worcester v. Georgia*, 31 U.S. (6 Pet.) 515 (1832). However, Indian treaties have consistently been judicially applied (or ignored), without regard to the non-self-execution doctrine. See, e.g., id (affirming the territorial rights of the Cherokee Nation as defined by the Treaty of Hopewell against incursions by the state of Georgia); *Puyallup Tribe v. Department of Game*, 391 U.S. 392 (1968) (enforcing treaty

right of tribal members to fish "at all usual and accustomed grounds and stations" in off-reservation areas). Why are Indian treaties apparently exempt from scrutiny as to whether or not they possess the criteria of self-execution?

C. *The Judicial Application of Customary International Law*

Advocates and scholars have argued for years that, beyond any treaty obligation arising from Article 6(5) of the International Covenant on Civil and Political Rights, the prohibition of the juvenile death penalty is a norm of customary international law. Support for this position was submitted to the Supreme Court in *Roper v. Simmons* in the following amicus brief, which argues for recognition of a norm against the juvenile death penalty as part of general international law and jus cogens.

Brief for the Human Rights Committee of the Bar of England and Wales, Human Rights Advocates, Human Rights Watch, and the World Organization for Human Rights as Amici Curiae in Support of Respondents

***Roper v. Simmons* (July 15, 2004) (some internal references omitted)**

. . . The practice of executing persons who were under 18 at the time of their offense has been rejected by every nation in the world except the United States. In fact, the prohibition against the juvenile death penalty has reached the level of a jus cogens norm, which is binding on the United States. . . .

Under article 53 of the Vienna Convention, a jus cogens norm is "a norm accepted and recognized by the international community of States as a whole as a norm from which no derogation is permitted and which can be modified only by a subsequent norm of general international law having the same character." The Restatement (Third) of the Foreign Relations Law agrees with this standard and provides that a jus cogens norm is a "norm accepted and recognized by the international community of States as a whole from which no derogation is permitted and which can be modified only by a subsequent norm of general international law having the same character," and that the norm is established where there is acceptance and recognition by a "large majority" of states, even if over dissent by a very small number of states. . . . definition

. . . [T]he prohibition against the execution of persons who were under 18 at the time they committed their crime is generally accepted in international law. Numerous treaties, declarations, and pronouncements by international bodies, as well as the laws of the vast majority of nations, are evidence of that law. Among the treaties are the International Covenant on Civil and Political Rights, article 6(5), the Convention on the Rights of the Child, article 37(a), the Geneva Convention Relative to the Protection of Civilian Persons in Time of War, article 68, and the American Convention on Human Rights, Chapter 2, Article 4, Section 5 (American Convention on Human Rights, Nov. 22, 1969, art. 4, 1144 U.N.T.S. 123).

Similarly, a resolution by the United Nations Economic and Social Council opposed the imposition of the death penalty for juvenile offenders. See Safeguards

Guaranteeing Protection of the Rights of those Facing the Death Penalty, E.S.C. Res. 1984/50, annex. And in 1985, the United Nations General Assembly adopted by consensus the United Nations Standard Minimum Rules for the Administration of Juvenile Justice ("The Beijing Rules"), which also oppose capital punishment for juveniles. G.A. Res. 40/33, annex.

The United Nations Commission on Human Rights since 1997 has passed annual resolutions calling on states "not to impose [the death penalty] for crimes committed by persons below 18 years of age." . . .

Those Commission resolutions passed with a number of dissenting votes, reflecting the fact that they also called for a moratorium on the death penalty generally. Since a number of countries still have the death penalty — which is not prohibited by the International Covenant and the prohibition of which is not as widely accepted as the prohibition on the juvenile death penalty is — many countries opposed the broader moratorium. Other Commission resolutions that mention only the prohibition against the juvenile death penalty, however, passed by consensus. See Rights of the Child, Comm. on Hum. Rts., 59th Sess. Resolution 2003/86, adopted April 25, 2003;[4] Rights of the Child, Comm. on Hum. Rts., 58th Sess. Resolution 2002/92, adopted April 26, 2002; Human Rights in the Administration of Justice, in Particular Juvenile Justice, Comm. on Hum. Rts., 58th Sess. Resolution 2002/47; Rights of the Child, Comm. on Hum. Rts., 57th Sess., Resolution 2001/75, adopted April 25, 2001. While the United States opposed the resolution in 2004, the resolution passed by a vote of 52-1. See Rights of the Child, Comm. on Hum. Rts., 60th Sess. Resolution 2004/48, adopted April 14, 2004. Each of those resolutions requests governments to end the practice of executing juvenile offenders.

The United Nations Sub-Commission on the Promotion and Protection of Human Rights has passed similar resolutions condemning the juvenile death penalty. In 1999, the Sub-Commission specifically noted that the United States is one of only six countries that had executed juvenile offenders since 1990 and that it accounted for 10 of the 19 executions during that time period. The Death Penalty, Particularly in Relation to Juvenile Offenders, U.N. Sub-Comm'n on the Promotion and Protection of Human Rights, 52nd Sess., Resolution 1999/4, adopted August 24, 1999. One year later, the Sub-Commission affirmed "that the imposition of the death penalty on those aged under 18 at the time of the commission of the offence is contrary to customary international law." The Death Penalty in Relation to Juvenile Offenders, U.N. Sub-Comm'n on the Promotion and Protection of Human Rights, 53rd Sess., Resolution 2000/17, adopted August 17, 2000. Again, the latter resolution was adopted without a vote.

Other international bodies have reached the same conclusion. The Inter-American Commission on Human Rights — the body responsible for the protection of fundamental freedoms in the Organization of American States (OAS), an organization which includes the United States — found that a jus cogens norm proscribes the execution of persons who were under 18 at the time of the commission of their crime. . . .

4. An effort by the United States to delete that paragraph lost by a vote of 51-1. See United Nations Press Release, Commission on Human Rights Adopts Resolution on Situation in Iraq; Concludes Substantive Work, April 25, 2003, Afternoon at 9-10.

These treaties, declarations, resolutions, and pronouncements by international bodies demonstrate that the prohibition of the juvenile death penalty is now part of general international law.

. . . The United States is the only country in the world that has not accepted the international norm against the execution of juvenile offenders. The only other countries known to have executed juvenile offenders in the last 10 years have since abolished the practice, acknowledged that such executions were contrary to their laws, or denied that they took place.

The United States' isolated stance on the issue of the juvenile death penalty is evidenced by the status of the Convention on the Rights of the Child. Almost every nation in the world has ratified that Convention. In fact, the only States not to have ratified the Convention are the United States and Somalia — a country lacking a central government. Indeed, the Convention on the Rights of the Child has been the catalyst that has prompted many countries in the past 10 years to change their laws to raise the age of eligibility for the death penalty to 18. The United Nations reported that Barbados, Yemen, and Zimbabwe changed their laws in 1994. Likewise, China changed its age for death penalty eligibility to 18 in 1997. Indeed, by the time of that report in 2000, only 14 countries that had ratified the Convention had not formally changed their laws to incorporate the prohibition on the juvenile death penalty.[5] None of those countries had placed reservations on the Convention's prohibition on the juvenile death penalty, and only six have executed juvenile offenders since 1991: Democratic Republic of the Congo (1 in 2000), Iran (6: 3 in 1992, 1 in 1999, 1 in 2000, 1 in 2001), Nigeria (1 in 1997), Pakistan (2: 1 in 1992, 1 in 1997), Saudi Arabia (1 in 1992), and Yemen (1 in 1993). In addition, Amnesty International documented an execution in Pakistan on November 3, 2001 and one in Iran on January 25, 2004.[6]

In each of the six other countries where juveniles have been executed since 1990, either the laws have been changed or the governments have denied that the executions of juvenile offenders took place. For example, the laws have changed in Yemen, as noted above, and Pakistan promulgated the Juvenile Justice System Ordinance in July 2000, banning the death penalty for anyone under 18 at the time of the crime. Since the passage of the Juvenile Justice System Ordinance, President Musharraf of Pakistan commuted the death sentences of approximately 100 young offenders to imprisonment in response to Amnesty International's Secretary General Irene Khan's request.

Nigeria, as noted in the United Nations report above, has national legislation setting the age at 18. With respect to the execution in 1997, the Nigerian government insisted to the Sub-Commission on the Promotion and Protection of Human Rights last year that the offender was well over 18 at the time of the offense and reiterated that any juveniles convicted of capital offenses have their sentences commuted. Saudi Arabia has adamantly insisted at the Commission on Human Rights that the allegations regarding the execution of a juvenile in 1992 are untrue. While there has been documentation that the executions in Nigeria

5. The countries were Afghanistan, Burundi, Bangladesh, the Democratic Republic of the Congo, India, Iran, Iraq, Malaysia, Morocco, Myanmar, Nigeria (excepting Federal Law), Pakistan, the Republic of Korea, Saudi Arabia, and the United Arab Emirates.

6. Amnesty International also reported that a juvenile offender was executed in China in 2003, because the courts do not take sufficient care to determine the age of offenders.

and Saudi Arabia did take place, the denials by the governments are an indication that those countries have accepted the norm.

While executions of juvenile offenders seem to have taken place with more frequency in Iran, that government also has denied at the Commission on Human Rights that such executions take place. Furthermore, in December 2003, a bill establishing special courts for minors and removing provisions for the execution of child offenders was passed by the Iranian parliament and awaits ratification of the Guardian Council, the highest legislative body in Iran.

Finally, the Democratic Republic of the Congo, which is in the midst of civil war, is also reported to have executed a juvenile offender in 2000, despite a moratorium on the death penalty in that country. However, that execution was carried out by the Military Order Court rather than through the judicial process. In 2001, when four juvenile offenders were sentenced to death by the Military Order Court, the executions were stayed and the sentences commuted following appeals from the international community. Thus, it appears that even during wartime, the Democratic Republic of the Congo intends to comply with the international norm banning the juvenile death penalty.

Hence, the United States stands alone in not accepting the norm against the execution of juvenile offenders. Even if the reports that executions of juveniles took place not only in the United States but in Iran as well, the level of adherence to the norm is similar to those noted in the Restatement (Third) as having had attained peremptory status: rules prohibiting genocide, slave trade and slavery, apartheid and other gross violations of human rights. And while United States courts have found the prohibition against torture to have attained the status of a jus cogens norm, Amnesty International found that 125 countries violated that norm in 2001. In stark contrast, only two or perhaps three countries have violated the norm prohibiting the execution of juvenile offenders in the past year.

The Court in *Roper v. Simmons* agreed with the assessment of a widespread international practice and opinion against the death penalty, although without explicitly declaring the existence of a binding norm of general or customary international law, much less one of jus cogens. See supra page 446. Before the Court in *Roper* overruled precedent to find that Eighth Amendment itself prohibits the juvenile death penalty, state and lower federal courts had rejected finding an alternative basis for the prohibition in either Article 6(5) of the Covenant on Civil and Poltical Rights, in light of the United States reservation to that article, or customary international law. The courts rejected arguments based on customary international law, not because they denied that a relevant norm of customary international law existed, but rather because they determined that such a norm could not be controlling over prior Supreme Court precedent allowing the juvenile death penalty. See, e.g., *Beazley v. Johnson*, 242 F.3d 248, 268-269 (5th Cir. Tex. 2001), cert. denied, 534 U.S. 945 (2001). By reversing the earlier precedent and bringing the United States in conformity with international practice and opinion, albeit ultimately on the basis of the Eighth Amendment, the Supreme Court's decision in *Roper* added to the global practice and reinforced the customary international norm against the juvenile death penalty, and it nullified any persistent objector status the U.S. may have enjoyed in regard to the norm.

The Supreme Court in *Roper* both reinforced the customary norm and effectively applied it indirectly through a reinterpretation of the Eighth Amendment's prohibition against cruel and unusual punishment. As pointed out above, at page 448, such indirect application of an international norm — whether treaty-based or customary — is the most common use of international law by domestic courts. But, like treaty-based ones, norms of customary international law can sometimes also be applied *directly* by domestic courts.

Referring to customary international law in particular, the Supreme Court confirmed in the *Paquete Habana* that "[i]nternational law is part of our law, and must be ascertained and administered by the courts of justice of appropriate jurisdiction, as often as questions of right depending upon it are duly presented for their determination." 175 U.S. 677, 700 (1900). Still, one must ask, under what circumstances are questions that depend upon customary international law "duly presented" to the courts. These qualifying words to this famous utterance of the Supreme Court signify the complexities that often are encountered in efforts to enforce rights in U.S. courts entirely on the basis of customary international law.

Joan Fitzpatrick, *The Role of Domestic Courts in Enforcing International Human Rights Law*

In Guide to International Human Rights Practice 247, 253-254 (Hurst Hannum ed., 3d ed. 1999)

The weight of judicial and scholarly opinion holds that customary international law forms an aspect of federal common law and is thus part of the "supreme Law of the Land" for Article VI purposes. In the earliest days of the Republic, courts in the United States enforced the criminal prohibitions of international law, and the 1789 Alien Tort Claims Act (ACTA) opened the federal courts to civil suits by aliens premised upon the law of nations.

Despite the impressive revival of the ATCA in relation to human rights violations occurring in foreign states [discussed below], plaintiffs rarely invoke customary international human rights law in litigation arising out of events occurring in the United States. The reasons for this relative rarity can be best explicated by considering concrete examples.

Assume that your client had been subjected to a specific use of force by police (for example, direct application of pepper spray to the unprotected eye in order to disrupt a non-violent demonstration) or had been excluded from public elementary education on the basis of her undocumented immigrant status. What obstacles might you encounter in bringing suit, in either federal or state court, against the responsible officials?

Human rights litigation of this type resembles civil rights litigation under the Constitution, statutes, and the common law of tort. Thus sovereign immunity and official immunities will have to be considered in selecting the appropriate defendants and judicial forum. Moreover, there may be alternate grounds (constitutional protections, statutory rights, or state common law) that provide a simpler avenue for relief.

An attorney representing a client asserting a right under customary international law must grapple with both substantive and jurisdictional puzzles. First, the advocate must prove that the actions of the defendants violated a norm of customary law that is specific, universal, and obligatory. While the process by which a norm of customary law may be proved is laid out in long-standing U.S. Supreme Court decisions, this process is complex and may require the expert testimony of recognized international law scholars.

e.g. In the police abuse example above, a litigant would have to prove that such use of pepper spray violates a customary prohibition on torture; cruel, inhuman, or degrading treatment; or other norms concerning humane treatment of persons detained by police. In the case of children excluded from school, the litigant would need to convince the court that, under a customary norm banning discrimination, the exclusion of minor children from education is unjustified and disproportionate to any legitimate governmental objective. Alternatively, an advocate might argue that a customary right to elementary education exists for all children within the national territory.

Even if the existence of the asserted norm in incontestable, an advocate must anticipate the argument that the norm is unenforceable. While the Supreme Court in the *Paquete Habana* recognized customary international law as "part of our law" to be enforced on behalf of injured individuals, the Court also suggested that the enforceability of international rights might be abrogated by contrary controlling acts of the Executive, Congress, or even the judiciary. Thus, an advocate must consider whether federal officials have authorized the act in question and show why such a contrary federal policy should not prevail. In the context of numerous cases involving indefinite detention of Cuban asylum-seekers, for example, U.S. courts have systematically rejected efforts to assert the primacy of the customary international norm against arbitrary detention, relying in part on this dictum from *Paquete Habana*. Where the challenged policies or acts are attributable to state officials, the likelihood that inconsistent federal law or policies may insulate the practice from challenge is diminished.

e.g.

Finally, an advocate must establish that subject matter jurisdiction exists over the claim. This should not present a problem in state court, regardless of the citizenship of the litigants, because customary international law is incontestably a part of common law.

A claim premised solely upon customary international human rights law in federal court, in the absence of diversity of citizenship, requires establishing the asserted norm is one of federal law. The weight of authority holds that [federal court] jurisdiction exists over ATCA claims, regardless of the citizenship of the defendant. Where both plaintiff and defendant in a case arising under customary international law are U.S. citizens, just as where both are aliens, federal question jurisdiction must be shown to exist.

Customary International Law Under the Alien Tort Statute — *Filartiga* and Beyond

As noted in the above extract, customary international law is rarely — if at all — asserted as an independent basis for a cause of action by plaintiffs who are citizens of the United States. But in several cases plaintiffs who are not U.S. citizens have brought customary international law-based claims under the Alien Tort Statute (also referred to as the Alien Tort Claims Act). Extracts from the first such modern case are set forth next.

Filartiga v. Peña-Irala

630 F.2d 876 (2d Cir. 1980)

[Dr. Joel Filartiga and his daughter Dolly, both citizens of Paraguay who were living in the United States and had applied for political asylum, brought this action in the Eastern District of New York against Americo Noberto Peña-Irala (Peña), also a citizen of Paraguay, for wrongfully causing the death of Dr. Filartiga's 17-year-old son, Joelito. The Filartigas contended that Joelito had been kidnapped and tortured to death by Peña, who was then Inspector General of Police in Asuncion, Paraguay, in retaliation for Dr. Filartiga's political activities and beliefs.

The Filartigas brought their action under the Alien Tort Statute, 28 U.S.C. §1350 (1988), a then little-known federal law dating back to the original Judiciary Act of 1789, which provides: "The district courts shall have original jurisdiction of any civil action by an alien for a tort only, committed in violation of the law of nations or a treaty of the United States." The United States not being a party to a treaty proscribing torture, jurisdiction under the statute turned upon whether or not torture now violated "the law of nations," i.e., customary international law. The District Court, in an unreported decision, felt constrained by precedent to dismiss the complaint on the ground that "'the law of nations,' as employed in Section 1350, [excludes] that law which governs a state's treatment of its own citizens." In short, it ruled that torture of a Paraguayan in Paraguay by a Paraguayan official did not violate customary international law. This appeal followed.]

IRVING R. KAUFMAN, Circuit Judge:

Upon ratification of the Constitution, the thirteen former colonies were fused into a single nation, one which, in its relations with foreign states, is bound both to observe and construe the accepted norms of international law, formerly known as the law of nations. Under the Articles of Confederation, the several states had interpreted and applied this body of doctrine as a part of their common law, but with the founding of the "more perfect Union" of 1789, the law of nations became preeminently a federal concern.

Implementing the constitutional mandate for national control over foreign relations, the First Congress established original district court jurisdiction over "all causes where an alien sues for a tort only (committed) in violation of the law of nations." Judiciary Act of 1789, ch. 20, s 9(b), 1 Stat. 73, 77 (1789), codified at 28 U.S.C. §1350. Construing this rarely-invoked provision, we hold that deliberate torture perpetrated under color of official authority violates universally accepted norms of the international law of human rights, regardless of the nationality of the parties. Thus, whenever an alleged torturer is found and served with process by an alien within our borders, §1350 provides federal jurisdiction. Accordingly, we reverse the judgment of the district court dismissing the complaint for want of federal jurisdiction....

Appellants rest their principal argument in support of federal jurisdiction upon the Alien Tort Statute, 28 U.S.C. §1350, which provides: "The district courts shall have original jurisdiction of any civil action by an alien for a tort only, committed in violation of the law of nations or a treaty of the United States." Since appellants do not contend that their action arises directly under a treaty of the United States,* a threshold question on the jurisdictional issue is whether the conduct alleged violates the law of nations. In light of the universal condemnation of torture in numerous international agreements, and the renunciation of torture as an instrument of official policy by virtually all of the nations of the world (in principle if not in practice), we find that an act of torture committed by a state official against one held in detention violates established norms of the international law of human rights, and hence the law of nations.

The Supreme Court has enumerated the appropriate sources of international law. The law of nations "may be ascertained by consulting the works of jurists, writing professedly on public law; or by the general usage and practice of nations; or by judicial decisions recognizing and enforcing that law." *United States v. Smith,* 18 U.S. (5 Wheat.) 153, 160-61, 5 L.Ed. 57 (1820); *Lopes v. Reederei Richard Schroder*, 225 F.Supp. 292, 295 (E.D.Pa.1963). In Smith, a statute proscribing "the crime of piracy (on the high seas) as defined by the law of nations," 3 Stat. 510(a) (1819), was held sufficiently determinate in meaning to afford the basis for a death sentence. The Smith Court discovered among the works of Lord Bacon, Grotius, Bochard and other commentators a genuine consensus that rendered the crime "sufficiently and constitutionally defined." *Smith, supra*, 18 U.S. (5 Wheat.) at 162, 5 L.Ed. 57.

The *Paquete Habana,* 175 U.S. 677, 20 S.Ct. 290, 44 L.Ed. 320 (1900), reaffirmed that

> where there is no treaty, and no controlling executive or legislative act or judicial decision, resort must be had to the customs and usages of civilized nations; and, as evidence of these, to the works of jurists and commentators, who by years of labor, research and experience, have made themselves peculiarly well acquainted with the subjects of which they treat. Such works are resorted to by judicial tribunals, not for the speculations of their authors concerning what the law ought to be, but for trustworthy evidence of what the law really is.

Id. at 700, 20 S.Ct. at 299. Modern international sources confirm the propriety of this approach.

Habana is particularly instructive for present purposes, for it held that the traditional prohibition against seizure of an enemy's coastal fishing vessels during wartime, a standard that began as one of comity only, had ripened over the preceding century into "a settled rule of international law" by "the general assent of civilized nations." *Id.* at 694, 20 S.Ct. at 297; accord, *id.* at 686, 20 S.Ct. at 297. Thus it is clear that courts must interpret international law not as it was in 1789, but as it has evolved and exists among the nations of the world today. See *Ware v. Hylton*, 3 U.S. (3 Dall.) 198, 1 L.Ed. 568 (1796) (distinguishing between "ancient" and "modern" law of nations).

* Appellants "associate themselves with" the argument of some of the amici curiae that their claim arises directly under a treaty of the United States, Brief for Appellants at 23 n.*, but nonetheless primarily rely upon treaties and other international instruments as evidence of an emerging norm of customary international law, rather then independent sources of law.

The requirement that a rule command the "general assent of civilized nations" to become binding upon them all is a stringent one. Were this not so, the courts of one nation might feel free to impose idiosyncratic legal rules upon others, in the name of applying international law. Thus, in *Banco Nacional de Cuba v. Sabbatino*, 376 U.S. 398, 84 S.Ct. 923, 11 L.Ed.2d 804 (1964), the Court declined to pass on the validity of the Cuban government's expropriation of a foreign-owned corporation's assets, noting the sharply conflicting views on the issue propounded by the capital-exporting, capital-importing, socialist and capitalist nations. *Id.* at 428-30, 84 S.Ct. at 940-41.

The case at bar presents us with a situation diametrically opposed to the conflicted state of law that confronted the Sabbatino Court. Indeed, to paraphrase that Court's statement, *id.* at 428, 84 S.Ct. at 940, there are few, if any, issues in international law today on which opinion seems to be so united as the limitations on a state's power to torture persons held in its custody.

The United Nations Charter (a treaty of the United States, see 59 Stat. 1033 (1945)) makes it clear that in this modern age a state's treatment of its own citizens is a matter of international concern. [The court quotes Articles 55 and 56.]

While this broad mandate has been held not to be wholly self-executing, *Hitai v. Immigration and Naturalization Service*, 343 F.2d 466, 468 (2d Cir. 1965), this observation alone does not end our inquiry.[*] For although there is no universal agreement as to the precise extent of the "human rights and fundamental freedoms" guaranteed to all by the Charter, there is at present no dissent from the view that the guaranties include, at a bare minimum, the right to be free from torture. This prohibition has become part of customary international law, as evidenced and defined by the Universal Declaration of Human Rights, General Assembly Resolution 217 (III)(A) (December 10, 1948) which states, in the plainest of terms, "no one shall be subjected to torture."[†] The General Assembly has declared that the Charter precepts embodied in this Universal Declaration "constitute basic principles of international law." G.A.Res. 2625 (XXV) (October 24, 1970)

Particularly relevant is the Declaration on the Protection of All Persons from Being Subjected to Torture, General Assembly Resolution 3452, 30 U.N. GAOR Supp. (No. 34) 91, U.N.Doc. A/1034 (1975), which is set out in full in the margin. The Declaration expressly prohibits any state from permitting the dastardly and totally inhuman act of torture. Torture, in turn, is defined as "any act by which severe pain and suffering, whether physical or mental, is intentionally inflicted by or at the instigation of a public official on a person for such purposes as . . . intimidating him or other persons." The Declaration goes on to provide that "(w)here it is proved that an act of torture or other cruel, inhuman or degrading treatment or punishment has been committed by or at the instigation of a public official, the victim shall be afforded redress and compensation, in

* We observe that this Court has previously utilized the U.N. Charter and the Charter of the Organization of American States, another non-self-executing agreement, as evidence of binding principles of international law. *United States v. Toscanino*, 500 F.2d 267 (2d Cir. 1974). In that case, our government's duty under international law to refrain from kidnapping a criminal defendant from within the borders of another nation, where formal extradition procedures existed, infringed the personal rights of the defendant, whose international law claims were thereupon remanded for a hearing in the district court.

† Eighteen nations have incorporated the Universal Declaration into their own constitutions. 48 Revue Internationale de Droit Penal Nos. 3 & 4, at 211 (1977).

accordance with national law." This Declaration, like the Declaration of Human Rights before it, was adopted without dissent by the General Assembly. Nayar, "Human Rights: The United Nations and United States Foreign Policy," 19 Harv. Int'l L.J. 813, 816 n.18 (1978).

These U.N. declarations are significant because they specify with great precision the obligations of member nations under the Charter. Since their adoption, "(m)embers can no longer contend that they do not know what human rights they promised in the Charter to promote." Sohn, "A Short History of United Nations Documents on Human Rights," in The United Nations and Human Rights, 18th Report of the Commission (Commission to Study the Organization of Peace ed. 1968). Moreover, a U.N. Declaration is, according to one authoritative definition, "a formal and solemn instrument, suitable for rare occasions when principles of great and lasting importance are being enunciated." 34 U.N. ESCOR, Supp. (No. 8) 15, U.N. Doc. E/cn.4/1/610 (1962) (memorandum of Office of Legal Affairs, U.N. Secretariat). Accordingly, it has been observed that the Universal Declaration of Human Rights "no longer fits into the dichotomy of 'binding treaty' against 'non-binding pronouncement,' but is rather an authoritative statement of the international community." E. Schwelb, Human Rights and the International Community 70 (1964). Thus, a Declaration creates an expectation of adherence, and "insofar as the expectation is gradually justified by State practice, a declaration may by custom become recognized as laying down rules binding upon the States." 34 U.N. ESCOR, supra. Indeed, several commentators have concluded that the Universal Declaration has become, in toto, a part of binding, customary international law. Nayar, supra, at 816-17; Waldlock, "Human Rights in Contemporary International Law and the Significance of the European Convention," Int'l & Comp. L.Q., Supp. Publ. No. 11 at 15 (1965).

Turning to the act of torture, we have little difficulty discerning its universal renunciation in the modern usage and practice of nations. *Smith*, supra, 18 U.S. (5 Wheat.) at 160-61, 5 L.Ed. 57. The international consensus surrounding torture has found expression in numerous international treaties and accords. E.g., American Convention on Human Rights, Art. 5, OAS Treaty Series No. 36 at 1, OAS Off. Rec. OEA/Ser 4 v/II 23, doc. 21, rev. 2 (English ed., 1975) ("No one shall be subjected to torture or to cruel, inhuman or degrading punishment or treatment"); International Covenant on Civil and Political Rights, U.N. General Assembly Res. 2200 (XXI)A, U.N. Doc. A/6316 (Dec. 16, 1966) (identical language); European Convention for the Protection of Human Rights and Fundamental Freedoms, Art. 3, Council of Europe, European Treaty Series No. 5 (1968), 213 U.N.T.S. 211 (semble). The substance of these international agreements is reflected in modern municipal — i.e., national — law as well. Although torture was once a routine concomitant of criminal interrogations in many nations, during the modern and hopefully more enlightened era it has been universally renounced. According to one survey, torture is prohibited, expressly or implicitly, by the constitutions of over fifty-five nations, including both the United States and Paraguay. Our State Department reports a general recognition of this principle:

> There now exists an international consensus that recognizes basic human rights and obligations owed by all governments to their citizens. . . . There is no doubt that these rights are often violated; but virtually all governments acknowledge their validity.

Department of State, Country Reports on Human Rights for 1979, published as Joint Comm. Print, House Comm. on Foreign Affairs, and Senate Comm. on Foreign Relations, 96th Cong. 2d Sess. (Feb. 4, 1980), Introduction at 1. We have been directed to no assertion by any contemporary state of a right to torture its own or another nation's citizens. Indeed, United States diplomatic contacts confirm the universal abhorrence with which torture is viewed:

> In exchanges between United States embassies and all foreign states with which the United States maintains relations, it has been the Department of State's general experience that no government has asserted a right to torture its own nationals. Where reports of torture elicit some credence, a state usually responds by denial or, less frequently, by asserting that the conduct was unauthorized or constituted rough treatment short of torture.*

Memorandum of the United States as Amicus Curiae at 16 n.34.

Having examined the sources from which customary international law is derived the usage of nations, judicial opinions and the works of jurists† we conclude that official torture is now prohibited by the law of nations. The prohibition is clear and unambiguous, and admits of no distinction between treatment of aliens and citizens. Accordingly, we must conclude that the dictum in *Dreyfus v. von Finck, supra*, 534 F.2d at 31, to the effect that "violations of international law do not occur when the aggrieved parties are nationals of the acting state," is clearly out of tune with the current usage and practice of international law. The treaties and accords cited above, as well as the express foreign policy of our own government, all make it clear that international law confers fundamental rights upon all people vis-à-vis their own governments. While the ultimate scope of those rights will be a subject for continuing refinement and elaboration, we hold that the right to be free from torture is now among them. . . .

* The fact that the prohibition of torture is often honored in the breach does not diminish its binding effect as a norm of international law. As one commentator has put it, "The best evidence for the existence of international law is that every actual State recognizes that it does exist and that it is itself under an obligation to observe it. States often violate international law, just as individuals often violate municipal law; but no more than individuals do States defend their violations by claiming that they are above the law." J. Brierly, The Outlook for International Law 4-5 (Oxford 1944).

† Earlier in the opinion the court had noted that "[t]he Filartigas submitted the affidavits of a number of distinguished legal scholars, who stated unanimously that the law of nations prohibits absolutely the use of torture as alleged in the complaint." 630 F.2d at 879. Here, the court cites the footnote supporting this statement, which in its entirety reads as follows:

> Richard Falk, the Albert G. Milbank Professor of International Law and Practice at Princeton University, and a former Vice President of the American Society of International Law, avers that, in his judgment, "it is now beyond reasonable doubt that torture of a person held in detention that results in severe harm or death is a violation of the law of nations." Thomas Franck, professor of international law at New York University and Director of the New York University Center for International Studies offers his opinion that torture has now been rejected by virtually all nations, although it was once commonly used to extract confessions. Richard Lillich, the Howard W. Smith Professor of Law at the University of Virginia School of Law, concludes, after a lengthy review of the authorities, that officially perpetrated torture is "a violation of international law (formerly called the law of nations)." Finally, Myres MacDougal, a former Sterling Professor of Law at the Yale Law School, and a past President of the American Society of International Law, states that torture is an offense against the law of nations, and that "it has long been recognized that such offenses vitally affect relations between states."

Id. n.4 — Eds.

In the twentieth century the international community has come to recognize the common danger posed by the flagrant disregard of basic human rights and particularly the right to be free of torture. Spurred first by the Great War, and then the Second, civilized nations have banded together to prescribe acceptable norms of international behavior. From the ashes of the Second World War arose the United Nations Organization, amid hopes that an era of peace and cooperation had at last begun. Though many of these aspirations have remained elusive goals, that circumstance cannot diminish the true progress that has been made. In the modern age, humanitarian and practical considerations have combined to lead the nations of the world to recognize that respect for fundamental human rights is in their individual and collective interest. Among the rights universally proclaimed by all nations, as we have noted, is the right to be free of physical torture. Indeed, for purposes of civil liability, the torturer has become like the pirate and slave trader before him hostis humani generis, an enemy of all mankind. Our holding today, giving effect to a jurisdictional provision enacted by our First Congress, is a small but important step in the fulfillment of the ageless dream to free all people from brutal violence.

Filartiga was the first case to use the over two hundred-year-old Alien Torts Statute to vindicate rights based on the post-UN Charter international law of human rights. It generated considerable international human rights law litigation and was highly praised by numerous legal commentators. See, e.g., Carolyn Patty Blum and Ralph G. Steinhardt, *Federal Jurisdiction over International Human Rights Claims: The Alien Tort Claims Act After Filartiga v. Pena-Irala*, 22 Harv. Intl. L.J. 53 (1981); Human Rights Symposium, 4 Hous. J. Intl. L. 1 (1981); Symposium, Federal Jurisdiction, *Human Rights and the Law of Nations: Essays on Filartiga v. Pena-Irala*, 11 Ga. J. Intl. & Comp. L. 305 (1981); and the articles cited in Bert B. Lockwood, *The United Nations Charter and United States Civil Rights Litigation: 1946-1955*, 69 Iowa L. Rev. 901, 925 (1984). Cf. Comment, *Torture as a Tort in Violation of International Law: Filartiga v. Pena-Irala*, 33 Stan. L. Rev. 353 (1981). For an account by the author of the opinion, see Irving R. Kaufman, "A Legal Remedy for International Torture?," N.Y. Times, Nov. 9, 1980, §6 (Magazine), at 44. For a recent compilation of cases that have arisen under the Alien Tort Statue, a majority of them since Filartiga, see Russell G. Donaldson, Annotation, *Construction and Application of Application of Alien Tort Statute (28 U.S.C. §1350), Providing for Federal Jurisdiction over Alien's Action for Tort Committed in Violation of Law of Nations or Treaty of the United States*, 116 A.L.R. Fed. 387 (1993) (updated 2005).

The decision in *Filartiga*, however, also drew criticism. A leading protagonist of an attack on an expansive reading of the Alien Tort Statute was former Judge Robert H. Bork. In a concurring opinion, he contended, inter alia, that international human rights law could be invoked under the Alien Tort Statute only in those rare instances where the treaty or customary international law norm in question itself grants individuals a private, affirmative "cause of action," in addition to establishing obligations for states. *Hanoch Tel-Oren v. Libyan Arab Republic*, 726 F.2d 774, 798-823 (D.C. Cir. 1984), cert. denied, 470 U.S. 1003 (1985). Contrary to the position it and the Department of State had taken earlier in *Filartiga*, see Memorandum for the United States as Amicus Curiae, *Filartiga v. Peña-Irala*, reprinted in 12 Hasting Int'l & Comp. L. Rev. (1988), the Department of Justice adopted Judge Bork's "cause of action" approach in its amicus brief in *Trajano v. Marcos,* 878 F.2d 1439 (9th Cir. 1989). The government eventually took an even more restrictive view of the Alien Tort Statute, arguing not only that the statute is purely jurisdictional but, further, that it allows only private actions related to the law of nations that Congress itself authorizes or creates by legislation apart from the ATS, a view it tried to advanced in the following case before the U.S. Supreme Court.

Sosa v. Alvarez-Machain

542 U.S. 692 (2004)

Justice SOUTER delivered the opinion of the Court....

I

We have considered the underlying facts before, *United States v. Alvarez-Machain,* 504 U.S. 655, 119 L. Ed. 2d 441, 112 S. Ct. 2188 (1992). In 1985, an agent of the Drug Enforcement Administration (DEA), Enrique Camarena-Salazar, was captured on assignment in Mexico and taken to a house in Guadalajara, where he was tortured over the course of a 2-day interrogation, then murdered. Based in part on eyewitness testimony, DEA officials in the United States came to believe that respondent Humberto Alvarez-Machain (Alvarez), a Mexican physician, was present at the house and acted to prolong the agent's life in order to extend the interrogation and torture. *Id.*, at 657, 119 L. Ed. 2d 441, 112 S. Ct. 2188.

In 1990, a federal grand jury indicted Alvarez for the torture and murder of Camarena-Salazar, and the United States District Court for the Central District of California issued a warrant for his arrest. 331 F.3d 604, 609 (CA9 2003) (en banc). The DEA asked the Mexican Government for help in getting Alvarez into the United States, but when the requests and negotiations proved fruitless, the DEA approved a plan to hire Mexican nationals to seize Alvarez and bring him to the United States for trial. As so planned, a group of Mexicans, including petitioner Jose Francisco Sosa, abducted Alvarez from his house, held him overnight in a motel, and brought him by private plane to El Paso, Texas, where he was arrested by federal officers. *Ibid.*

Once in American custody, Alvarez moved to dismiss the indictment on the ground that his seizure was "outrageous governmental conduct," *Alvarez-Machain,* 504 U.S., at 658, 119 L. Ed. 2d 441, 112 S. Ct. 2188, and violated the extradition treaty between the United States and Mexico. The District Court agreed, the Ninth Circuit affirmed, and we reversed, *id.*, at 670, 119 L. Ed. 2d 441, 112 S. Ct. 2188, holding that the fact of Alvarez's forcible seizure did not affect the jurisdiction of a federal court. The case was tried in 1992, and ended at the close of the Government's case, when the District Court granted Alvarez's motion for a judgment of acquittal.

PH

In 1993, after returning to Mexico, Alvarez began the civil action before us here. He sued Sosa, Mexican citizen and DEA operative Antonio Garate-Bustamante, five unnamed Mexican civilians, the United States, and four DEA agents. 331 F.3d, at 610. So far as it matters here, Alvarez sought damages from the United States under the FTCA [Federal Tort Claims Act], alleging false arrest, and from Sosa under the ATS [Alien Tort Statute], for a violation of the law of nations. The former statute authorizes suit "for . . . personal injury . . . caused by the negligent or wrongful act or omission of any employee of the Government while acting within the scope of his office or employment." 28 U.S.C. §1346(b)(1) [28 USCS §1346(b)(1)]. The latter provides in its entirety that "[t]he district courts shall have original jurisdiction of any civil action by an alien for a tort only, committed in violation of the law of nations or a treaty of the United States." §1350.

The District Court granted the Government's motion to dismiss the FTCA claim, but awarded summary judgment and $25,000 in damages to Alvarez on the ATS claim. A three-judge panel of the Ninth Circuit then affirmed the ATS judgment, but reversed the dismissal of the FTCA claim. 266 F.3d 1045 (2001).

A divided en banc court came to the same conclusion. 331 F.3d, at 641. As for the ATS claim, the court called on its own precedent, "that [the ATS] not only provides federal courts with subject matter jurisdiction, but also creates a cause of action for an alleged violation of the law of nations." *Id.*, at 612. The Circuit then relied upon what it called the "clear and universally recognized norm prohibiting arbitrary arrest and detention," *id.*, at 620, to support the conclusion that Alvarez's arrest amounted to a tort in violation of international law. On the FTCA claim, the Ninth Circuit held that, because "the DEA had no authority to effect Alvarez's arrest and detention in Mexico," *id.*, at 608, the United States was liable to him under California law for the tort of false arrest, *id.*, at 640-641.

We granted certiorari in these companion cases to clarify the scope of both the FTCA and the ATS. 540 U.S. 1045, 540 U.S. 1045, 157 L. Ed. 2d 692, 124 S. Ct. 807 (2003). We now reverse in each. . . .

[The Court's analysis finding that the FTCA did not permit Alvarez's California law tort claim against the United States is omitted.]

III

Alvarez has . . . brought an action under the ATS against petitioner, Sosa, who argues (as does the United States supporting him) that there is no relief under the ATS because the statute does no more than vest federal courts with jurisdiction, neither creating nor authorizing the courts to recognize any particular right of action without further congressional action. Although we agree the statute is in terms only jurisdictional, we think that at the time of enactment the jurisdiction enabled federal courts to hear claims in a very limited category defined by the law of nations and recognized at common law. We do not believe, however, that the limited, implicit sanction to entertain the handful of international law *cum* common law claims understood in 1789 should be taken as authority to recognize the right of action asserted by Alvarez here.

A

. . . The parties and *amici* here advance radically different historical interpretations of [the ATS]. Alvarez says that the ATS was intended not simply as a jurisdictional grant, but as authority for the creation of a new cause of action for torts in violation of international law. We think that reading is implausible. As enacted in 1789, the ATS gave the district courts "cognizance" of certain causes of action, and the term bespoke a grant of jurisdiction, not power to mold substantive law. See, *e.g.*, The Federalist No. 81, pp. 447, 451 (J. Cooke ed. 1961) (A. Hamilton) (using "jurisdiction" interchangeably with "cognizance"). The fact that the ATS was placed in §9 of the Judiciary Act, a statute otherwise exclusively concerned with federal-court jurisdiction, is itself support for its strictly jurisdictional nature. Nor would the distinction between jurisdiction and cause of action have been elided by the drafters of the Act or those who voted on it. As Fisher Ames put it, "there is a substantial difference between the jurisdiction of courts and rules of decision." 1 Annals of Cong. 807 (Gales ed. 1834). It is unsurprising, then, that an authority on the historical origins of the ATS has written that "section 1350 clearly does not create a statutory cause of action," and that the contrary suggestion is "simply frivolous." Casto, The Federal Courts' Protective Jurisdiction Over Torts Committed in Violation of the Law of Nations, 18 Conn. L. Rev. 467, 479, 480 (1986) (hereinafter Casto, *Law of Nations*); cf. Dodge, The Constitutionality of the Alien Tort Statute: Some Observations on Text and Context, 42 Va. J. Int'l L. 687, 689 (2002). In sum, we think the statute was intended as jurisdictional in the sense of addressing the power of the courts to entertain cases concerned with a certain subject.

But holding the ATS jurisdictional raises a new question, this one about the interaction between the ATS at the time of its enactment and the ambient law of the era. Sosa would have it that the ATS was stillborn because there could be no claim for relief without a further statute expressly authorizing adoption of causes of action.* *Amici* professors of federal jurisdiction and legal history take a different tack, that federal courts could entertain claims once the jurisdictional grant was on the books, because torts in violation of the law of nations would have been recognized within the common law of the time. Brief for Vikram Amar et al. as *Amici Curiae*. We think history and practice give the edge to this latter position.

1

"When the *United States* declared their independence, they were bound to receive the law of nations, in its modern state of purity and refinement." *Ware v. Hylton*, 3 Dall. 199, 281, 3 U.S. 199, 3 Dallas 199, 1 L. Ed. 568 (1796) (Wilson, J.). In the years of the early Republic, this law of nations comprised two principal elements, the first covering the general norms governing the behavior of national states with each other: "*the science which teaches the rights subsisting between nations or states, and the obligations correspondent to those rights,*" E. de Vattel, The Law of Nations, Preliminaries §3 (J. Chitty et al. transl. and ed. 1883) (hereinafter Vattel) (footnote omitted), or "that code of public instruction which defines the rights and prescribes the duties of nations, in their intercourse with each other," 1 James Kent Commentaries *1. This aspect of the law of nations

* The United States joined in arguing this position. See Brief for the United States as Respondent in Support of the Petitioner, at 24-40. January 23, 2004. — EDS.

thus occupied the executive and legislative domains, not the judicial. See 4 W. Blackstone, Commentaries on the Laws of England 68 (1769) (hereinafter Commentaries) ("[O]ffenses against" the law of nations are "principally incident to whole states or nations").

The law of nations included a second, more pedestrian element, however, that did fall within the judicial sphere, as a body of judge-made law regulating the conduct of individuals situated outside domestic boundaries and consequently carrying an international savor. To Blackstone, the law of nations in this sense was implicated "in mercantile questions, such as bills of exchange and the like; in all marine causes, relating to freight, average, demurrage, insurances, bottomry . . . ; [and] in all disputes relating to prizes, to shipwrecks, to hostages, and ransom bills." *Id.*, at 67. The law merchant emerged from the customary practices of international traders and admiralty required its own transnational regulation. And it was the law of nations in this sense that our precursors spoke about when the Court explained the status of coast fishing vessels in wartime grew from "ancient usage among civilized nations, beginning centuries ago, and gradually ripening into a rule of international law. . . ." *The Paquete Habana*, 175 U.S. 677, 686, 44 L. Ed. 320, 20 S. Ct. 290 (1900). . . .

2

Before there was any ATS, a distinctly American preoccupation with these hybrid international norms had taken shape owing to the distribution of political power from independence through the period of confederation. The Continental Congress was hamstrung by its inability to "cause infractions of treaties, or of the law of nations to be punished," J. Madison, Journal of the Constitutional Convention 60 (E. Scott ed. 1893), and in 1781 the Congress implored the States to vindicate rights under the law of nations. . . .

The Framers responded by vesting the Supreme Court with original jurisdiction over "all Cases affecting Ambassadors, other public ministers and Consuls." U.S. Const., Art. III, §2, and the First Congress followed through. The Judiciary Act reinforced this Court's original jurisdiction over suits brought by diplomats, see 1 Stat. 80, ch. 20, §13, created alienage jurisdiction, §11 and, of course, included the ATS, §9. See generally Randall, Federal Jurisdiction over International Law Claims: Inquiries into the Alien Tort Statute, 18 N. Y.U. J. Int'l L. & Pol. 1, 15-21 (1985) (discussing foreign affairs implications of the Judiciary Act); W. Casto, The Supreme Court in the Early Republic 27-53 (1995).

3

Although Congress modified the draft of what became the Judiciary Act, see generally Warren, New Light on the History of the Federal Judiciary Act of 1789, 37 Harv. L. Rev. 49 (1923), it made hardly any changes to the provisions on aliens, including what became the ATS, see Casto, Law of Nations 498. There is no record of congressional discussion about private actions that might be subject to the jurisdictional provision, or about any need for further legislation to create private remedies; there is no record even of debate on the section. . . . [D]espite considerable scholarly attention, it is fair to say that a consensus understanding of what Congress intended has proven elusive.

Still, the history does tend to support two propositions. First, there is every reason to suppose that the First Congress did not pass the ATS as a jurisdictional convenience to be placed on the shelf for use by a future Congress or state legislature that might, some day, authorize the creation of causes of action or itself decide to make some element of the law of nations actionable for the benefit of foreigners. The anxieties of the preconstitutional period cannot be ignored easily enough to think that the statute was not meant to have a practical effect. Consider that the principal draftsman of the ATS was apparently Oliver Ellsworth, previously a member of the Continental Congress that had passed the 1781 resolution and a member of the Connecticut Legislature that made good on that congressional request. See generally W. Brown, The Life of Oliver Ellsworth (1905). Consider, too, that the First Congress was attentive enough to the law of nations to recognize certain offenses expressly as criminal, including the three mentioned by Blackstone. See An Act for the Punishment of Certain Crimes Against the United States, §8, 1 Stat. 113-114 (murder or robbery, or other capital crimes, punishable as piracy if committed on the high seas), and §28, *id.*, at 118 (violation of safe conducts and assaults against ambassadors punished by imprisonment and fines described as "infract[ions of] the law of nations"). It would have been passing strange for Ellsworth and this very Congress to vest federal courts expressly with jurisdiction to entertain civil causes brought by aliens alleging violations of the law of nations, but to no effect whatever until the Congress should take further action. There is too much in the historical record to believe that Congress would have enacted the ATS only to leave it lying fallow indefinitely.

The second inference to be drawn from the history is that Congress intended the ATS to furnish jurisdiction for a relatively modest set of actions alleging violations of the law of nations. Uppermost in the legislative mind appears to have been offenses against ambassadors, see *id.*, at 118; violations of safe conduct were probably understood to be actionable, *ibid.*, and individual actions arising out of prize captures and piracy may well have also been contemplated. *Id.*, at 113-114. But the common law appears to have understood only those three of the hybrid variety as definite and actionable, or at any rate, to have assumed only a very limited set of claims. As Blackstone had put it, "offences against this law [of nations] are principally incident to whole states or nations," and not individuals seeking relief in court. 4 Commentaries 68.

4

The sparse contemporaneous cases and legal materials referring to the ATS tend to confirm both inferences, that some, but few, torts in violation of the law of nations were understood to be within the common law....

In sum, although the ATS is a jurisdictional statute creating no new causes of action, the reasonable inference from the historical materials is that the statute was intended to have practical effect the moment it became law. The jurisdictional grant is best read as having been enacted on the understanding that the common law would provide a cause of action for the modest number of international law violations with a potential for personal liability at the time.

IV

We think it is correct, then, to assume that the First Congress understood that the district courts would recognize private causes of action for certain torts in violation of the law of nations, though we have found no basis to suspect Congress had any examples in mind beyond those torts corresponding to Blackstone's three primary offenses: violation of safe conducts, infringement of the rights of ambassadors, and piracy. We assume, too, that no development in the two centuries from the enactment of §1350 to the birth of the modern line of cases beginning with *Filartiga v. Pena-Irala*, 630 F.2d 876 (CA2 1980), has categorically precluded federal courts from recognizing a claim under the law of nations as an element of common law; Congress has not in any relevant way amended §1350 or limited civil common law power by another statute. Still, there are good reasons for a restrained conception of the discretion a federal court should exercise in considering a new cause of action of this kind. Accordingly, we think courts should require any claim based on the present-day law of nations to rest on a norm of international character accepted by the civilized world and defined with a specificity comparable to the features of the 18th-century paradigms we have recognized. This requirement is fatal to *Alvarez's* claim.

A

A series of reasons argue for judicial caution when considering the kinds of individual claims that might implement the jurisdiction conferred by the early statute. First, the prevailing conception of the common law has changed since 1789 in a way that counsels restraint in judicially applying internationally generated norms. When §1350 was enacted, the accepted conception was of the common law as "a transcendental body of law outside of any particular State but obligatory within it unless and until changed by statute." *Black and White Taxicab & Transfer Co. v. Brown and Yellow Taxicab & Transfer Co.*, 276 U.S. 518, 533, 72 L. Ed. 681, 48 S. Ct. 404 (1928) (Holmes, J., dissenting). Now, however, in most cases where a court is asked to state or formulate a common law principle in a new context, there is a general understanding that the law is not so much found or discovered as it is either made or created. . . .

Second, along with, and in part driven by, that conceptual development in understanding common law has come an equally significant rethinking of the role of the federal courts in making it. *Erie R. Co. v. Tompkins*, 304 U.S. 64, 82 L. Ed. 1188, 58 S. Ct. 817 (1938), was the watershed in which we denied the existence of any federal "general" common law, *id.*, at 78, 82 L. Ed. 1188, 58 S. Ct. 817, which largely withdrew to havens of specialty, some of them defined by express congressional authorization to devise a body of law directly, *e.g.*, *Textile Workers v. Lincoln Mills of Ala.*, 353 U.S. 448, 1 L. Ed. 2d 972, 77 S. Ct. 912 (1957) (interpretation of collective-bargaining agreements); Fed. Rule Evid. 501 (evidentiary privileges in federal-question cases). Elsewhere, this Court has thought it was in order to create federal common law rules in interstitial areas of particular federal interest. *E.g.*, *United States v. Kimbell Foods, Inc.*, 440 U.S. 715, 726-727, 59 L. Ed. 2d 711, 99 S. Ct. 1448 (1979). And although we have even assumed competence to make judicial rules of decision of particular importance to foreign relations, such as the act of state doctrine, see *Banco Nacional de Cuba v. Sabbatino*, 376 U.S. 398, 427, 11 L. Ed. 2d 804, 84 S. Ct. 923 (1964), the general practice has been to look for legislative guidance before exercising innovative authority over substantive law. It would be remarkable to take a more aggressive

see p. 481

role in exercising a jurisdiction that remained largely in shadow for much of the prior two centuries.

Third, this Court has recently and repeatedly said that a decision to create a private right of action is one better left to legislative judgment in the great majority of cases. *Correctional Services Corp. v. Malesko*, 534 U.S. 61, 68, 151 L. Ed. 2d 456, 122 S. Ct. 515 (2001); *Alexander v. Sandoval*, 532 U.S. 275, 286-287, 149 L. Ed. 2d 517, 121 S. Ct. 1511 (2001). The creation of a private right of action raises issues beyond the mere consideration whether underlying primary conduct should be allowed or not, entailing, for example, a decision to permit enforcement without the check imposed by prosecutorial discretion. Accordingly, even when Congress has made it clear by statute that a rule applies to purely domestic conduct, we are reluctant to infer intent to provide a private cause of action where the statute does not supply one expressly. While the absence of congressional action addressing private rights of action under an international norm is more equivocal than its failure to provide such a right when it creates a statute, the possible collateral consequences of making international rules privately actionable argue for judicial caution.

Fourth, the subject of those collateral consequences is itself a reason for a high bar to new private causes of action for violating international law, for the potential implications for the foreign relations of the United States of recognizing such causes should make courts particularly wary of impinging on the discretion of the Legislative and Executive Branches in managing foreign affairs. It is one thing for American courts to enforce constitutional limits on our own State and Federal Governments' power, but quite another to consider suits under rules that would go so far as to claim a limit on the power of foreign governments over their own citizens, and to hold that a foreign government or its agent has transgressed those limits. Cf. *Sabbatino, supra*, at 431-432, 11 L. Ed. 2d 804, 84 S. Ct. 923. Yet modern international law is very much concerned with just such questions, and apt to stimulate calls for vindicating private interests in §1350 cases. Since many attempts by federal courts to craft remedies for the violation of new norms of international law would raise risks of adverse foreign policy consequences, they should be undertaken, if at all, with great caution. Cf. *Tel-Oren v. Libyan Arab Republic*, 233 U.S. App. D.C. 384, 726 F.2d 774, 813 (CADC 1984) (Bork, J., concurring) (expressing doubt that §1350 should be read to require "our courts [to] sit in judgment of the conduct of foreign officials in their own countries with respect to their own citizens").

The fifth reason is particularly important in light of the first four. We have no congressional mandate to seek out and define new and debatable violations of the law of nations, and modern indications of congressional understanding of the judicial role in the field have not affirmatively encouraged greater judicial creativity. It is true that a clear mandate appears in the Torture Victim Protection Act of 1991, 106 Stat 73, providing authority that "establish[es] an unambiguous and modern basis for" federal claims of torture and extrajudicial killing, H. R. Rep. No. 102-367, pt. 1, p 3 (1991). But that affirmative authority is confined to specific subject matter, and although the legislative history includes the remark that §1350 should "remain intact to permit suits based on other norms that already exist or may ripen in the future into rules of customary international law," *id.*, at 4, Congress as a body has done nothing to promote such suits. . . .

invitation?

C

We must still, however, derive a standard or set of standards for assessing the particular claim Alvarez raises, and for this case it suffices to look to the historical antecedents. Whatever the ultimate criteria for accepting a cause of action subject to jurisdiction under §1350, we are persuaded that federal courts should not recognize private claims under federal common law for violations of any international law norm with less definite content and acceptance among civilized nations than the historical paradigms familiar when §1350 was enacted. See, *e.g., United States v. Smith*, 18 U.S. 153, 5 Wheat. 153, 163-180, 5 L. Ed. 57 (1820) (illustrating the specificity with which the law of nations defined piracy). This limit upon judicial recognition is generally consistent with the reasoning of many of the courts and judges who faced the issue before it reached this Court. See *Filartiga, supra*, at 890 ("[F]or purposes of civil liability, the torturer has become — like the pirate and slave trader before him — *hostis humani generis*, an enemy of all mankind"); *Tel-Oren, supra*, at 781 (Edwards, J., concurring) (suggesting that the "limits of section 1350's reach" be defined by "a handful of heinous actions — each of which violates definable, universal and obligatory norms"); see also *In re Estate of Marcos Human Rights Litigation*, 25 F.3d 1467, 1475 (CA9 1994) ("Actionable violations of international law must be of a norm that is specific, universal, and obligatory"). And the determination whether a norm is sufficiently definite to support a cause of action[20] should (and, indeed, inevitably must) involve an element of judgment about the practical consequences of making that cause available to litigants in the federal courts.[21]

20. A related consideration is whether international law extends the scope of liability for a violation of a given norm to the perpetrator being sued, if the defendant is a private actor such as a corporation or individual. Compare *Tel-Oren v. Libyan Arab Republic*, 233 U.S. App. D.C. 384, 726 F.2d 774, 791-795 (CADC 1984) (Edwards, J., concurring) (insufficient consensus in 1984 that torture by private actors violates international law), with *Kadic v. Karadzic*, 70 F.3d 232, 239-241 (CA2 1995) (sufficient consensus in 1995 that genocide by private actors violates international law).

21. This requirement of clear definition is not meant to be the only principle limiting the availability of relief in the federal courts for violations of customary international law, though it disposes of this case. For example, the European Commission argues as *amicus curiae* that basic principles of international law require that before asserting a claim in a foreign forum, the claimant must have exhausted any remedies available in the domestic legal system, and perhaps in other fora such as international claims tribunals.

Another possible limitation that we need not apply here is a policy of case-specific deference to the political branches. For example, there are now pending in federal district court several class actions seeking damages from various corporations alleged to have participated in, or abetted, the regime of apartheid that formerly controlled South Africa. See *In re South African Apartheid Litigation*, 238 F. Supp. 2d 1379 (JPML 2002) (granting a motion to transfer the cases to the Southern District of New York). The Government of South Africa has said that these cases interfere with the policy embodied by its Truth and Reconciliation Commission, which "deliberately avoided a 'victors' justice' approach to the crimes of apartheid and chose instead one based on confession and absolution, informed by the principles of reconciliation, reconstruction, reparation and goodwill." Declaration of Penuell Mpapa Maduna, Minister of Justice and Constitutional Development, Republic of South Africa, reprinted in App. to Brief for Government of Commonwealth of Australia et al. as *Amici Curiae* 7a, P 3.2.1 (emphasis deleted). The United States has agreed. See Letter of William H. Taft IV, Legal Adviser, Dept. of State, to Shannen W. Coffin, Deputy Asst. Atty. Gen., Oct. 27, 2003, reprinted in *id.*, at 2a. In such cases, there is a strong argument that federal courts should give serious weight to the Executive Branch's view of the case's impact on foreign policy. Cf. *Republic of Aus. v. Altmann*, 541 U.S. ____, ____, 541 U.S. 677, 159 L. Ed. 2d 1, 124 S. Ct. 2240 (2004) (slip op., at 23-24) (discussing the State Department's use of statements of interest in cases involving the Foreign Sovereign Immunities Act of 1976, 28 U.S.C. §1602 *et seq.* [28 USCS §§1602 *et seq.*]).

Thus, Alvarez's detention claim must be gauged against the current state of international law, looking to those sources we have long, albeit cautiously, recognized.... *The Paquete Habana*, 175 U.S., at 700, 44 L. Ed. 320, 20 S. Ct. 290.

To begin with, Alvarez cites two well-known international agreements that, despite their moral authority, have little utility under the standard set out in this opinion. He says that his abduction by Sosa was an "arbitrary arrest" within the meaning of the Universal Declaration of Human Rights (Declaration), G. A. Res. 217A (III), U. N. Doc. A/810 (1948). And he traces the rule against arbitrary arrest not only to the Declaration, but also to article nine of the International Covenant on Civil and Political Rights (Covenant), Dec. 19, 1996, 999 U. N. T. S. 171, to which the United States is a party, and to various other conventions to which it is not. But the Declaration does not of its own force impose obligations as a matter of international law. See Humphrey, *The UN Charter and the Universal Declaration of Human Rights*, in The International Protection of Human Rights 39, 50 (E. Luard ed. 1967) (quoting Eleanor Roosevelt calling the Declaration "'a statement of principles . . . setting up a common standard of achievement for all peoples and all nations'" and "'not a treaty or international agreement . . . impos[ing] legal obligations'"). And, although the Covenant does bind the United States as a matter of international law, the United States ratified the Covenant on the express understanding that it was not self-executing and so did not itself create obligations enforceable in the federal courts. See *supra*, at ______, 159 L. Ed. 2d, at 750. Accordingly, Alvarez cannot say that the Declaration and Covenant themselves establish the relevant and applicable rule of international law. He instead attempts to show that prohibition of arbitrary arrest has attained the status of binding customary international law.

Here, it is useful to examine Alvarez's complaint in greater detail. As he presently argues it, the claim does not rest on the cross-border feature of his abduction. Although the District Court granted relief in part on finding a violation of international law in taking Alvarez across the border from Mexico to the United States, the Court of Appeals rejected that ground of liability for failure to identify a norm of requisite force prohibiting a forcible abduction across a border. Instead, it relied on the conclusion that the law of the United States did not authorize Alvarez's arrest, because the DEA lacked extraterritorial authority under 21 U.S.C. §878 [21 USCS §878], and because Federal Rule of Criminal Procedure 4(d)(2) limited the warrant for Alvarez's arrest to "the jurisdiction of the United States." It is this position that Alvarez takes now: that his arrest was arbitrary and as such forbidden by international law not because it infringed the prerogatives of Mexico, but because no applicable law authorized it.

Alvarez thus invokes a general prohibition of "arbitrary" detention defined as officially sanctioned action exceeding positive authorization to detain under the domestic law of some government, regardless of the circumstances. Whether or not this is an accurate reading of the Covenant, Alvarez cites little authority that a rule so broad has the status of a binding customary norm today. He certainly cites nothing to justify the federal courts in taking his broad rule as the predicate for a federal lawsuit, for its implications would be breathtaking. His rule would support a cause of action in federal court for any arrest, anywhere in the world, unauthorized by the law of the jurisdiction in which it took place, and would create a cause of action for any seizure of an alien in violation of the Fourth Amendment, supplanting the actions under Rev Stat §1979, 42 U.S.C. §1983 [42 USCS §1983] and *Bivens v. Six Unknown Fed. Narcotics Agents*, 403 U.S. 388, 29 L. Ed. 2d 619, 91 S. Ct. 1999 (1971), that now provide damages remedies for such violations. It would create an action in federal court for arrests by state officers who simply exceed their authority; and for the violation of any limit that the law of any country might place on the authority of its own officers to arrest. And all of this assumes that Alvarez could establish that Sosa was acting on behalf of a government when he made the arrest, for otherwise he would need a rule broader still.

Alvarez's failure to marshal support for his proposed rule is underscored by the Restatement (Third) of Foreign Relations Law of the United States (1987), which says in its discussion of customary international human rights law that a "state violates international law if, as a matter of state policy, it practices, encourages, or condones . . . prolonged arbitrary detention." *Id.*, §702. Although the Restatement does not explain its requirements of a "state policy" and of "prolonged" detention, the implication is clear. Any credible invocation of a principle against arbitrary detention that the civilized world accepts as binding customary international law requires a factual basis beyond relatively brief detention in excess of positive authority. Even the Restatement's limits are only the beginning of the enquiry, because although it is easy to say that some policies of prolonged arbitrary detentions are so bad that those who enforce them become enemies of the human race, it may be harder to say which policies cross that line with the certainty afforded by Blackstone's three common law offenses. In any event, the label would never fit the reckless policeman who botches his warrant, even though that same officer might pay damages under municipal law. *E.g., Groh v. Ramirez*, 540 U.S. 551, 157 L. Ed. 2d 1068, 124 S. Ct. 1284 (2004).

Whatever may be said for the broad principle Alvarez advances, in the present, imperfect world, it expresses an aspiration that exceeds any binding customary rule having the specificity we require. Creating a private cause of action to further that aspiration would go beyond any residual common law discretion we think it appropriate to exercise. It is enough to hold that a single illegal detention of less than a day, followed by the transfer of custody to lawful authorities and a prompt arraignment, violates no norm of customary international law so well defined as to support the creation of a federal remedy.

Comments and Questions

summary

1. In *Alvarez-Machain*, the Court resolved the question of whether the Alien Tort Statute (ATS) itself creates a cause of action for violations of international law or whether it is purely jurisdictional. But while affirming the latter, the Court held that the statute's grant of jurisdiction for non-citizen claims based on international law does not depend on additional action by Congress for the statute to be invoked. The Court affirmed that customary international law is part of the limited universe of federal common law that can appropriately be discerned and applied by the courts and from which a cause of action under the jurisdictional grant of the ATS can arise. Yet, in the end, the Court set a high bar for allowing an ATS claim based on an alleged violation of international law: such a claim must be found "to rest on a norm of international character accepted by the civilized

world and defined with a specificity comparable to the features of the 18th-century paradigms we have recognized." What, in particular, are the eigthteenth-century paradigms? Why did the right against arbitrary detention asserted by *Alvarez* not meet the threshold articulated by the Court? How can you distinguish that right and the prohibition against torture which was found to be actionable under the ATS in *Filartiga*? Did the court implicitly agree that *Filartiga* met the threshold? Note that the Court cited *Filartiga* in stating that its articulated limit for ATS claims "is generally consistent with the reasoning of many of the courts and judges who faced the issue before it reached this Court." Supra, p. 492.

In an article written shortly after the Supreme Court's decision in *Sosa*, Professor Steinhardt surmised that courts in ATS cases prior to that decision already were applying a high burden of proof for finding actionable international norms.

> Despite hyperbolic assertions to the contrary, lower courts had routinely dismissed ATS cases that did not satisfy this high burden of proof even before the decision in *Alvarez-Machain II*. In *Flores v. Southern Peru Copper Corp.* for example, the Second Circuit ruled that environmental torts are not in violation of customary international law. In *Hamid v. Price Waterhouse*, the Ninth Circuit determined that garden-variety fraud is not a violation of the law of nations, and similar conclusions have been reached with respect to transnational defamation, full First Amendment freedoms, and the fairness of state lottery distribution systems.
>
> . . . It is a mistake to assume . . . that courts have or ever had a "free hand" to make up norms of customary law and enforce them through the ATS. To the contrary, courts have sustained jurisdiction under Section 1350 only for certain egregious violations of international human rights law in addition to torture: disappearances; war crimes; genocide; cruel, inhuman, and degrading treatment — including sexual assault; arbitrary detention; and crimes against humanity. Thus, the repeated rhetoric of caution in *Alvarez-Machain* II — referring for example to the enforceability of "only a very limited set of claims" or "the modest number of international law violations with a potential for personal liability" — is a new restriction on ATS litigation only according to those litigants and critics who had overstated its threat.

Ralph G. Steinhardt, *Laying One Bankrupt Critique to Rest: Sosa v. Alvarez-Machain and the Future of International Human Rights Litigation in U.S. Courts*, 57 Vand. L. Rev. 2241, 2263-2265 (2004) (notes omitted). In light of this analysis and the fact that the Court did not explicitly roll back any of the international norms previously recognized as actionable under the ATS, other than the norm against arbitrary detention upheld by the lower court in *Alvarez-Machain*, what is the significance of the Court's decision beyond the specific controversy before it? Is the Court simply solidifying the practice that had developed in the lower courts? Or is it introducing new limitations to ensure that very few, if any, new rights are found actionable absent significant developments in international law or further congressional action? If there are *new* limitations, what are they?

2. In any case, is it fair to say that *Alvarez-Machain* confirms that, in order for an international norm to be actionable under the ATS, it must meet a level of specificity in its definition and depth of worldwide acceptance beyond that which is ordinarily required for finding the existence of a customary international law norm? Consider that, subsequent to the Supreme Court's decision in

Alvarez-Machain, the Eleventh Circuit Court of Appeals in *Aldana v. Del Monte Fresh Produce, Inc.*, 416 F.3d 1242 (11th Cir. 2005), ordered the dismissal of claims for "cruel, inhuman, degrading treatment or punishment" and arbitrary detention in connection with the alleged abduction and mistreatment of union leaders in Guatemala, while allowing a claim of torture arising from the same events to proceed. By contrast, in a suit against Unocal Corporation the plaintiffs appealed the district court decision denying their ATS claim for alleged complicity by the oil company in forced labor practices in Burma and, after the Supreme Court's decision in *Alvarez-Machain*, the defendant oil company agreed to settle the claim for a substantial sum of money. See 403 F.3d 708 (9th Cir. 2005) (stipulated dismissal of the appeal with prejudice). For discussion of corporate responsibility for human rights violation, including in connection with ATS suits, see Chapter 5.

3. The Supreme Court in *Alvarez-Machain* sounded a strong cautionary note against the recognition of new actionable customary international law norms and offered several reasons for judicial restraint in this regard. What specifically are those reasons? Do you agree with them? What are their implications generally for application of international law by domestic courts?

4. Its very name indicates that U.S. citizens cannot avail themselves of the Alien Tort Statute. For a suggestion that "Congress should consider amending [the ATS] to allow lawsuits brought by U.S. citizens as well as aliens," see The Phenomenon of Torture: Hearings on H.J. Res. 605 Before the House Comm. on Foreign Affairs and Its Subcomm. on Human Rights and International Organizations, 98th Cong. 2d Sess. 247 (1984) (statement of Michael H. Posner, Esq., Executive Director of the Lawyers Committee for Human Rights). Other amendments to clarify the ATS also have been recommended. See Kenneth C. Randall, *Further Inquiries into the Alien Tort Statute and a Recommendation*, 18 N.Y.U. J. Int'l L. & Pol. 473, 511-532 (1986). What, if anything, might amending the ATS in this way add to existing federal statutory causes of action for violations of civil rights?

5. While efforts to amend the ATS proved unsuccessful, Congress, over the opposition of the Reagan and first Bush administrations, did enact the Torture Victim Protection Act (TVPA), Pub. L. No. 102-256, 106 Stat. 73, codified at 28 U.S.C. §1350 (1988 & Supp. V 1993). Enacted in 1992, this statute preceded U.S. ratification in 1994 of the Convention against Torture and Other Cruel, Inhuman or Degrading Treatment or Punishment. The TVPA effectively codifies the result in *Filartiga* as to torture and extrajudicial killings and allows U.S. citizens as well as aliens to sue for recovery of damages from individuals who, under actual or apparent authority or color of law of any foreign nation, have committed such wrongs. See generally Robert Drinan and Teresa T. Kuo, *Putting the World's Oppressors on Trial: The Torture Victim Protection Act*, 15 Human Rts. Q. 605 (1993).

The TVPA is a welcome effort to accord U.S. citizens and aliens alike remedies in the enforcement of international human rights in U.S. courts. But as Professor Fitzpatick has observed, it "comes encumbered with three limitations that are not contained in the Alein Tort Claims Act: (1) a specific requirement that 'adequate and available remedies' be exhausted in the state where the violation occurred (section 2(b)); (2) a ten-year statute of limitations on claims (section 2(c)); and (3) a restriction of jurisdiction to individual defendants (section 2(a)), thus excluding foreign states." Joan Fitzpatrick, *Reducing the FSIA Barrier to Human Rights Litigation — Is Amendment Necessary and Possible?*, 1992 Am. Socy. Int'l L. Proceedings 338, 346. Additionally, it has been held that "the Act was not intended to trump diplomatic and head-of-state immunities," *Lafontant v. Aristide*, 844 F. Supp. 128, 138 (E.D.N.Y. 1994) (extrajudicial killing action against exiled president of Haiti dismissed on head of state immunity grounds), and that the TVPA does not impose liability on corporations, *Beanal v. Freeport-McMoran*, 969 F.Supp. 362 (E.D. La. 1997), dismissal aff'd on other grounds, 197 F.3d 161 (5th Cir. 1999).

6. The argument has been made that both U.S. citizens and non-citizens should be able to obtain jurisdiction in federal court for violations of international human rights law on the basis of the federal question statute, 28, U.S.C. §1331 (2005). This statute provides federal district courts with "original jurisdiction of all civil actions arising under the Constitution, laws, or treaties of the United States." Id. See Kenneth C. Randall, *Federal Questions and the Human Rights Paradigm*, 73 Minn. L. Rev. 349, 3386-424 (1988). In *Forti v. Suarez-Mason*, 672 F. Supp. 1531 (N.D. Cal. 1988), the federal district court construed the Alien Tort Statute to provide not just jurisdiction but also a cause of action for certain well defined international torts and alternatively upheld jurisdiction over certain claims for violations of customary international law on the basis of 28 U.S.C. §1331. The court in *Forti* stated, "It has long been settled that federal common law incorporates international law. . . . Thus, a case presenting claims arising under customary international law arises under the laws of the United States for purposes of federal question jurisdiction." 672 F. Supp. at 1544. Cf. *Kadic v. Karadzic*, 70 F.3d 232, 246, cert. denied, 518 U.S. 1005 (1996) (declining to decide whether 1331 provides an independent basis for jurisdiction over alleged violations of international law law, since the claims asserted could be based on the ATS and the TVPA). In light of the Supreme Court's decision in *Alvarez-Machain*, how plausible is the argument that claims for violations of customary international law can be brought under the federal question jurisdiction statute? Can *any* treaty that is self-executing be the basis of jurisdiction under the statute, or must a treaty also be construed to give rise to a cause of action? See *Tel-Oren v. Libyan Arab Republic*, 726 F.2d 774, 778, cert. denied, 470 U.S. 1003 (1985) (J. Edwards, concurring) (the law of nations generally does not create private causes of action to remedy its violations, but leaves to each nation the task of defining the remedies that are available for international law violations). Is there any argument that non-self-executing treaties can ground federal court jurisdiction under 28 U.S.C. §1331?

7. State courts at least theoretically have greater flexibility for fashioning remedies for violations of customary international law than do federal courts, given that they are not constrained by the limited jurisdictional parameters of federal courts within the federal system. In particular, they may more easily blend customary international law into the general common law over which state courts have jurisdiction, without having to conform to the narrow judicial role ascribed to the federal courts in *Alvarez-Machain* of keeping customary international law within the confines of a federal common law limited to "havens of specialty" or "interstitial areas of particular federal interest." Thus, the Maryland Court of Appeals applied the Nuremberg Code to establish the relevant duty in a state common law negligence action, regarding the Code as "'international common

law'" and the "preferred standard for assessing the legality of scientific research on human subjects,'" *Grimes v. Kenney Krieger Institute, Inc.*, 782 A.2d. 807, 814, 835 (Md. 2001) (quoting George J. Annas, *Mengele's Birthmark: The Nuremberg Code in United States Courts*, 7 Journal of Contemporary Health Law & Policy 17, 19-21 (Spring, 1991)). In addition, state legislatures and local authorities are free to incorporate international standards into state and local law, as long as in doing so they do not run afoul of state and federal constitutional parameters or federal preemption. In a bold move, the Hawaii state legislature passed a concurrent resolution "adopting" the draft United Nations Declaration on the Rights of Indigenous Peoples even while that document was still under discussion. See House Concurrent Resolution Adopting the United Nations Declaration on the Rights of Indigenous Peoples, HI H.C.R. 195, 23rd Leg., Reg. Sess. (Haw. 2005). Compare the law passed by the state of Massachusetts prohibiting trade with Burma as a means of enforcing human rights standards against the oppression in that country, a law that was found to be preempted by federal law. See *Crosby v. National Foreign Trade Council*, 530 U.S. 363 (2000), discussed in Chapter 10, page 824.

Note: The State Action and Act of State Doctrines

The Court in *Alvarez-Machain* noted that limitations exist for ATS claims in addition to the constraints on finding international norms that meet the required criteria of specificity. Among these limitations is that ATS plaintiffs must usually establish state action in the alleged violation, while simultaneously avoiding the barriers presented by the act of state doctrine. Ordinarily, "only individuals who have acted under official authority or under color of such authority may violate international law. . . . " In re *Estate of Ferdinand E Marcos Human Rights Litigation* ("Estate I"), 978 F.2d 493, 501-02 (9th Cir. 1992). International law proscribes purely private conduct for only a limited number of wrongs including piracy, slave trading, and certain war crimes. See *Kadic v. Karadzic*, 70 F.3d 232, 239, 243, (2d Cir. 1995), cert. denied, 518 U.S. 1005 (1996). Unless the alleged wrongful conduct falls under one of the limited categories, an ATS plaintiff is required to established that the defendant acted with the kind of linkage to state action — such as in *Filartiga* in which the defendant committed torture while acting as a Paraguayan police official — that typically is required in constitutional or federal statutory civil rights claims. See, e.g., *Wiwa v. Royal Dutch Petroleum Co.*, 2002 U.S. Dis. LEXIS 3293, 43 (S.D. N.Y.) (plaintiffs' allegations of torture and unlawful killing were sufficient to state a claim that private "defendants were 'willful participants in joint action with the state or its agents,' and can hence be treated as state actors for the purpose of the" ATS) (extracts from which may be found in Chapter 5, page 387). See generally Natalie L. Bridgeman, *Human Rights Litigation Under the ATCA as a Proxy for Environmental Claims*, 6 Yale H.R. & Dev. L.J. 1, 8-17 (2003) (summarizing cases under the ATS applying the state action doctrine).

On the other hand, if a claim calls into question the sovereign acts of a foreign government (and not just the actions of individuals acting under color state authority), then the act of state doctrine comes into play. The act of state doctrine is a domestic rule of judicial comity that exists to preclude U.S. courts from sitting in judgment of the official acts of a recognized government of another state performed within its own domestic jurisdiction, especially where there is no clear controlling domestic or international standard for the court to apply. See *Banco National de Cuba v. Sabbatino*, 376 U.S. 398, 428, 430 n. 34 (1964). In *Filartiga*, Judge Kaufman found it unnecessary to decide the question of whether an act of state was being impugned, although in dictum he expressed doubt "whether action by a state official in violation of the Constitution and laws of the Republic of Paraguay, and wholly unratified by that nation's government, could properly be characterized as an act of state." 630 F. 2d at 889.

One might well question whether Judge Kaufman's reasoning goes far enough. Given the rationale of the act of state doctrine, many have argued that it should not preclude U.S. courts from adjudicating claims that actually do impugn actions of foreign governments when those actions involve serious violations of international human rights law. See Richard A. Falk, *The Role of Domestic Courts in the International Legal Order* 9-10, 72 (1964); Malvina Halberstam, *Sabbatino Resurrected: The Act of State Doctrine in the Revised Restatment of U.S. Foreign Relations Law*, 79 Am. J. Int'l L. 68, 86-87 (1985); Richard B. Lillich, *The Role of Domestic Courts in Promoting Human Rights Norms*, 24 N.Y.U. L. Sch. L. Rev. 153, 159-62 (1978). According to the Restatement, "A claim arising out of an alleged violation of fundamental human rights — for instance, a claim on behalf of a victim of torture or genocide — would (if otherwise sustainable) probably not be defeated by the act of state doctrine, since the accepted international law of human rights is well established and contemplates external scrutiny of such acts." Restatement (Third) of the Foreign Relations Law of the United States §443 comment c at 370 (1987). In addition, in holding that the defendant leader of the self-proclaimed Bosnian-Serb republic of Srpska was not shielded by the act of state doctrine against claims of torture and genocide, the court in *Kadic* noted, "it would be a rare case in which the act of state doctrine precluded suit under [the ATS]. *Banco Nacional* [v. *Sabbatino*] was careful to recognize the doctrine in the absence of . . . unambiguous agreement regarding controlling legal principles . . . and applied the doctrine only in a context — expropriation of an alien's property — in which world opinion was sharply divided." 70 F.3d at 250. Other lower federal courts likewise have declined to apply the act of state doctrine in cases involving allegations of violations of well-established international human rights norms. See, e.g., *Republic of the Philippines v. Marcos*, 862 F.2d 1355, 1360-1361 (9th Cir. 1988), cert. denied, 490 U.S. 1035 (1989), *Liu v. Republic of China*, 892 F.2d 1419, 1431-1434 (9th Cir. 1989), cert. denied, 497 U.S. 1058 (1990). Cf. *National Coalition Government of Burma v. Unocal Corp.*, 176 F.R.D. 329, 353-357 (C.D. Cal. 1997) (act of state doctrine a bar to claims under ATS for expropriation of property, trespass, and conversion where no controlling international law, although claims of torture and forced labor not barred by the doctrine).

The Supreme Court has not yet adopted this "human rights exception" to the act of state doctrine. But, at least insofar as the ATS claims are concerned, the Supreme Court in *Alvarez-Machain* may well have rendered the act of state doctrine of limited or no applicability. As already noted, the Court in that case established that the ATS provides jurisdiction for only those claims based on rules of international law whose existence is firmly established and that meet certain criteria of specificity. And, as earlier instructed by the Supreme Court in *Banco*

Nacional v. Sabbatino, 376 U.S. at 428, and as illustrated in *Kadic*, 70 F.3d at 250, the act of state doctrine will ordinarily not apply where the state conduct in question contravenes a well–settled rule of international law.

Note: *Foreign Sovereign Immunity*

While *Filartiga* and *Alvarez-Machain* involved suits against individuals, nothing in the Alien Tort Statute itself prohibits suits against foreign states or their agents that seek to hold the state itself liable. Any suit against a foreign state, however, must be prepared to contend with claims of sovereign immunity (even if the act of state doctrine can be overcome). The Supreme Court has held that the Foreign Sovereign Immunities Act (FSIA) is the sole basis for obtaining jurisdiction over foreign states in U.S. courts; the ATS does not provide an alternative avenue for jurisdiction, nor does it provide an exception to the immunity from suit provided foreign states by the act. See *Argentine Republic v. Amareda Hess Shipping Corp.*, 488 U.S. 428, 434-440 (1989). The FSIA itself does provide for certain exceptions to sovereign immunity, including a "commercial activities" exception, a "tort exception," and a "state-sponsored terrorism" exception. See 28 U.S.C. §1605(a). The first two exceptions apply only in relation to acts occurring within or in substantial connection to U.S. territory, and the third applies only in relation to states that have been formally designated by the United States as state sponsors of terrorism. In *Amerada Hess*, which involved an incident on international waters during the Argentine-British war in the South Atlantic, the Court found the tort exception inapplicable because of a lack of nexus with U.S. territory. 488 U.S. at 439. Compare *Letelier v. Republic of Chile*, 488 F. Supp. 665 (D.D.C. 1980) (federal district court had jurisdiction under the FSIA to hear tort claim against Chile for its alleged role in lethal bombing in District of Columbia).

The thesis has been advanced that, when a foreign state's act violates a jus cogens norm, the state is not entitled to claim sovereign immunity with respect to that act. See Adam C. Belsky, Mark Merva, and Naomi Roht-Arriaza, *Implied Waiver under the FSIA: A Proposed Exception to Immunity for Violations of Peremptory Norms of International Law*, 77 Calif. L. Rev. 365 (1989). This "jus cogens" exception to the FSIA was rejected by the Ninth Circuit, however, which noted that "the FSIA does not specifically provide for an exception to sovereign immunity based on jus cogens." The court concluded that "if violations of jus cogens committed ouside the United States are to be exceptions to immunity, Congress must make them so. The fact that there has been a violation of jus cogens does not confer jurisdiction under the FSIA." *Siderman de Blake v. Argentina*, 965 F.2d 699, 718, 719 (9th Cir. 1992) (finding implied waiver of immunity on other grounds, id. at 720-723), cert. denied, 507 U.S. 1017 (1993). The Court of Appeals for the D.C. Circuit reached the same conclusion in *Princz v. Federal Republic of Germany*, 26 F.3d 1116, 1173-1174 (D.C. Cir. 1994) (2-1), reversing 813 F. Supp. 22, 26, 27 (D.D.C. 1994). For a perceptive critique of *Siderman*, arguing that a "jus cogens exception" should be read into the implied waiver provision of the FSIA, see Comment, *Siderman de Blake v. Republic of Argentina: Can the FSIA Grant Immunity for Violations of Jus Cogens?*, 19 Brook. J. Int'l L. 967 (1993). See also Joan Fitzpatrick, *Reducing the FSIA Barrier to Human Rights Litigation — Is the Amendment Necessary and Possible?*, 1992 Am. Socy. Int'l L.

Proceedings, 338, 345-346 (supporting legislation that would add a "human rights exception" to the FSIA). What are the implications of the Supreme Court's decision in *Alvarez-Machain*, if any, for efforts to have the courts read into the existing FSIA a jus cogens exception?

While the FSIA clearly governs suits against states themselves, another question is the extent to which government officials are entitled to some form of derivative sovereign immunity. Suits against named government officials, rather than against the state or one of its agencies, have not been barred by the FSIA when the suits were for acts by the defendants that were found to have been outside the bounds of their official or lawful authority. See, e.g., *Hilao v. Estate of Marcos*, 23 F. 3d 1467, 1470-1471 (9th Cir. 1994), cert. denied, 513 U.S. 1126, (1995); *Trajano v. Marcos* (In re *Estate of Ferdinand Marcos*, Human Rights Litigation), 978 F.2d 493, 497 (9th Cir. 1992), cert. denied, 508 U.S. 972 (1993); *Xunax v. Gramajo*, 886 F.Supp. 162 (D. Mass. 1985); *Cabiri v. Assassie-Gyimah*, 921 F.Supp. 1189, 1197-98 (S.D.N.Y. 1996). However, a sitting head of state may enjoy immunity independently of the FSIA. Head of state immunity is a federal common law doctrine that arises from customary international law, and it has been found to have survived the enactment of both the FSIA and the Torture Victims Protection Act (See comment 5, supra page xxx), providing heads of state absolute immunity from lawsuits brought against them in the United States, see *Lafontant v. Aristide*, 844 F. Supp. 128 (E.D. N.Y. 1994). In order to assert head of state immunity, however, a government official must be recognized as a head of state by the United States and the foreign state concerned. *United States v. Noriega*, 746 F. Supp. 1506 (S.D. Fla. 1990).

The United Kingdom adopted a statute similar to the FISA, the State Immunity Act, 1978, ch. 33 (Eng.), but both British courts and the European Court of Human Rights have upheld the granting of sovereign immunity when an individual has attempted to sue a foreign government for acts that occurred outside British territory. See *Al-Adsani v. United Kingdom*, Al-Adsani v. United Kingdom Eur. Ct. Hum. Rts., Judgment of Nov. 21, 2001 (Grand Chamber) (extracted in Chapter 8, page xxx). With respect to claims filed against former Chilean President Pinochet, see Chapter 11.

III. The Justiciability of Economic, Social, and Cultural Rights

Judicial enforcement of international norms by domestic courts in the United States turns on considerations of justiciability, considerations which into account the nature of particular norms that may be invoked and the bounds of judicial competency in relation to those norms. The non-self-execution doctrine looks, at least in part, to the existence of treaty provisions that are sufficiently specific and mandatory to be capable of judicial application without further legislative action. Courts effectively have treated reservations to treaty provisions as non-justiciable, eschewing challenges to those reservations and deferring to the political branches. The application of customary international law norms is also subject to constraints related to concerns about the role of courts vis-à-vis the political branches in matters touching upon foreign affairs, so that courts are required to find a high degree of specificity in international consensus and U.S. acquiescence in a customary norm before it can give rise to a cause of action.

In the United States, the most obvious candidates for judicially applicable international treaty or customary norms are those in the area of civil and political rights, given the priority accorded by the United States to these rights in its foreign relations and the long tradition of adjudication of civil and political rights in both the federal and state courts. But as we have seen, even international norms in this area must overcome major hurdles before they will be applied directly by the courts. On the other hand, to the extent that civil and political rights are affirmed in the Constitution or legislation, these rights are for the most part justiciable, and their expression in treaties or customary international law may serve as interpretive guides.

The adjudication of economic, social, and cultural rights is quite another story. Few federal or state laws exist that provide firm entitlements to such rights, except for limited categories of beneficiaries. And the United States has been reluctant to promote such rights in its international relations, most notably declining thus far to ratify the International Covenant on Economic, Social, and Cultural Rights (Documentary Supplement, page 353), one of the pillars of the International Bill of Human Rights. Even if the United States were to ratify this treaty, questions would persist about the extent to which rights affirmed in it correspond with specific obligations that are capable of judicial enforcement. Recall the materials in Chapter 5, page xxx, on the nature and scope of obligations that arise from the ESC Covenant. Such questions about the proper means of enforcing economic, social and cultural rights are a backdrop to the following materials, which focus on the right to health and include a comparative perspective from the Constitutional Court of South Africa.

Committee on Economic, Social, and Cultural Rights, The Right to the Highest Attainable Standard of Health

General Comment no. 14, UN Doc. E/C.12/2000/4 (Aug. 11, 2000) (endnotes omitted)

1. Health is a fundamental human right indispensable for the exercise of other human rights. Every human being is entitled to the enjoyment of the highest attainable standard of health conducive to living a life in dignity. The realization of the right to health may be pursued through numerous, complementary approaches, such as the formulation of health policies, or the implementation of health programmes developed by the World Health Organization (WHO), or the adoption of specific legal instruments. Moreover, the right to health includes certain components which are legally enforceable.

2. The human right to health is recognized in numerous international instruments. Article 25.1 of the Universal Declaration of Human Rights affirms: "Everyone has the right to a standard of living adequate for the health of himself and of his family, including food, clothing, housing and medical care and necessary social services." The International Covenant on Economic, Social and Cultural Rights provides the most comprehensive article on the right to health in international human rights law. In accordance with article 12.1 of the Covenant, States

parties recognize "the right of everyone to the enjoyment of the highest attainable standard of physical and mental health," while article 12.2 enumerates, by way of illustration, a number of "steps to be taken by the States parties . . . to achieve the full realization of this right". Additionally, the right to health is recognized, *inter alia*, in article 5 (e) (iv) of the International Convention on the Elimination of All Forms of Racial Discrimination of 1965, in articles 11.1 (f) and 12 of the Convention on the Elimination of All Forms of Discrimination against Women of 1979 and in article 24 of the Convention on the Rights of the Child of 1989. Several regional human rights instruments also recognize the right to health, such as the European Social Charter of 1961 as revised (art. 11), the African Charter on Human and Peoples' Rights of 1981 (art. 16) and the Additional Protocol to the American Convention on Human Rights in the Area of Economic, Social and Cultural Rights of 1988 (art. 10). Similarly, the right to health has been proclaimed by the Commission on Human Rights, as well as in the Vienna Declaration and Programme of Action of 1993 and other international instruments.

3. The right to health is closely related to and dependent upon the realization of other human rights, as contained in the International Bill of Rights, including the rights to food, housing, work, education, human dignity, life, non-discrimination, equality, the prohibition against torture, privacy, access to information, and the freedoms of association, assembly and movement. These and other rights and freedoms address integral components of the right to health. . . .

I. Normative Content of Article 12

7. Article 12.1 provides a definition of the right to health, while article 12.2 enumerates illustrative, non-exhaustive examples of States parties' obligations.

8. The right to health is not to be understood as a right to be *healthy*. The right to health contains both freedoms and entitlements. The freedoms include the right to control one's health and body, including sexual and reproductive freedom, and the right to be free from interference, such as the right to be free from torture, non-consensual medical treatment and experimentation. By contrast, the entitlements include the right to a system of health protection which provides equality of opportunity for people to enjoy the highest attainable level of health.

9. The notion of "the highest attainable standard of health" in article 12.1 takes into account both the individual's biological and socio-economic preconditions and a State's available resources. There are a number of aspects which cannot be addressed solely within the relationship between States and individuals; in particular, good health cannot be ensured by a State, nor can States provide protection against every possible cause of human ill health. Thus, genetic factors, individual susceptibility to ill health and the adoption of unhealthy or risky lifestyles may play an important role with respect to an individual's health. Consequently, the right to health must be understood as a right to the enjoyment of a variety of facilities, goods, services and conditions necessary for the realization of the highest attainable standard of health. . . .

11. The Committee interprets the right to health, as defined in article 12.1, as an inclusive right extending not only to timely and appropriate health care but also to the underlying determinants of health, such as access to safe and potable water and adequate sanitation, an adequate supply of safe food, nutrition and

housing, healthy occupational and environmental conditions, and access to health-related education and information, including on sexual and reproductive health. A further important aspect is the participation of the population in all health-related decision-making at the community, national and international levels.

12. The right to health in all its forms and at all levels contains the following interrelated and essential elements, the precise application of which will depend on the conditions prevailing in a particular State party:

(a) *Availability*. Functioning public health and health-care facilities, goods and services, as well as programmes, have to be available in sufficient quantity within the State party. The precise nature of the facilities, goods and services will vary depending on numerous factors, including the State party's developmental level. They will include, however, the underlying determinants of health, such as safe and potable drinking water and adequate sanitation facilities, hospitals, clinics and other health-related buildings, trained medical and professional personnel receiving domestically competitive salaries, and essential drugs, as defined by the WHO Action Programme on Essential Drugs.

(b) *Accessibility*. Health facilities, goods and services have to be accessible to everyone without discrimination, within the jurisdiction of the State party. Accessibility has four overlapping dimensions:

Non-discrimination: health facilities, goods and services must be accessible to all, especially the most vulnerable or marginalized sections of the population, in law and in fact, without discrimination on any of the prohibited grounds.

Physical accessibility: health facilities, goods and services must be within safe physical reach for all sections of the population, especially vulnerable or marginalized groups, such as ethnic minorities and indigenous populations, women, children, adolescents, older persons, persons with disabilities and persons with HIV/AIDS. Accessibility also implies that medical services and underlying determinants of health, such as safe and potable water and adequate sanitation facilities, are within safe physical reach, including in rural areas. Accessibility further includes adequate access to buildings for persons with disabilities.

Economic accessibility (affordability): health facilities, goods and services must be affordable for all. Payment for health-care services, as well as services related to the underlying determinants of health, has to be based on the principle of equity, ensuring that these services, whether privately or publicly provided, are affordable for all, including socially disadvantaged groups. Equity demands that poorer households should not be disproportionately burdened with health expenses as compared to richer households.

Information accessibility: accessibility includes the right to seek, receive and impart information and ideas concerning health issues. However, accessibility of information should not impair the right to have personal health data treated with confidentiality.

(c) *Acceptability*. All health facilities, goods and services must be respectful of medical ethics and culturally appropriate, i.e. respectful of the culture of individuals, minorities, peoples and communities, sensitive to gender and life-cycle requirements, as well as being designed to respect confidentiality and improve the health status of those concerned.

(d) *Quality*. As well as being culturally acceptable, health facilities, goods and services must also be scientifically and medically appropriate and of good quality. This requires, *inter alia*, skilled medical personnel, scientifically approved and unexpired drugs and hospital equipment, safe and potable water, and adequate sanitation.

13. The non-exhaustive catalogue of examples in article 12.2 provides guidance in defining the action to be taken by States. It gives specific generic examples of measures arising from the broad definition of the right to health contained in article 12.1, thereby illustrating the content of that right. . . .

II. States Parties' Obligations

General Legal Obligations

30. While the Covenant provides for progressive realization and acknowledges the constraints due to the limits of available resources, it also imposes on States parties various obligations which are of immediate effect. States parties have immediate obligations in relation to the right to health, such as the guarantee that the right will be exercised without discrimination of any kind (art. 2.2) and the obligation to take steps (art. 2.1) towards the full realization of article 12. Such steps must be deliberate, concrete and targeted towards the full realization of the right to health.

31. The progressive realization of the right to health over a period of time should not be interpreted as depriving States parties' obligations of all meaningful content. Rather, progressive realization means that States parties have a specific and continuing obligation to move as expeditiously and effectively as possible towards the full realization of article 12.

32. As with all other rights in the Covenant, there is a strong presumption that retrogressive measures taken in relation to the right to health are not permissible. If any deliberately retrogressive measures are taken, the State party has the burden of proving that they have been introduced after the most careful consideration of all alternatives and that they are duly justified by reference to the totality of the rights provided for in the Covenant in the context of the full use of the State party's maximum available resources.

33. The right to health, like all human rights, imposes three types or levels of obligations on States parties: the obligations to *respect*, *protect* and *fulfil*. In turn, the obligation to fulfil contains obligations to facilitate, provide and promote. The obligation to *respect* requires States to refrain from interfering directly or indirectly with the enjoyment of the right to health. The obligation to *protect* requires States to take measures that prevent third parties from interfering with article 12 guarantees. Finally, the obligation to *fulfil* requires States to adopt appropriate legislative, administrative, budgetary, judicial, promotional and other measures towards the full realization of the right to health.

Specific Legal Obligations

34. In particular, States are under the obligation to *respect* the right to health by, *inter alia*, refraining from denying or limiting equal access for all persons,

including prisoners or detainees, minorities, asylum seekers and illegal immigrants, to preventive, curative and palliative health services; abstaining from enforcing discriminatory practices as a State policy; and abstaining from imposing discriminatory practices relating to women's health status and needs. Furthermore, obligations to respect include a State's obligation to refrain from prohibiting or impeding traditional preventive care, healing practices and medicines, from marketing unsafe drugs and from applying coercive medical treatments, unless on an exceptional basis for the treatment of mental illness or the prevention and control of communicable diseases. Such exceptional cases should be subject to specific and restrictive conditions, respecting best practices and applicable international standards, including the Principles for the Protection of Persons with Mental Illness and the Improvement of Mental Health Care.

In addition, States should refrain from limiting access to contraceptives and other means of maintaining sexual and reproductive health, from censoring, withholding or intentionally misrepresenting health-related information, including sexual education and information, as well as from preventing people's participation in health-related matters. States should also refrain from unlawfully polluting air, water and soil, e.g. through industrial waste from State-owned facilities, from using or testing nuclear, biological or chemical weapons if such testing results in the release of substances harmful to human health, and from limiting access to health services as a punitive measure, e.g. during armed conflicts in violation of international humanitarian law.

35. Obligations to *protect* include, *inter alia*, the duties of States to adopt legislation or to take other measures ensuring equal access to health care and health-related services provided by third parties; to ensure that privatization of the health sector does not constitute a threat to the availability, accessibility, acceptability and quality of health facilities, goods and services; to control the marketing of medical equipment and medicines by third parties; and to ensure that medical practitioners and other health professionals meet appropriate standards of education, skill and ethical codes of conduct. States are also obliged to ensure that harmful social or traditional practices do not interfere with access to pre- and post-natal care and family-planning; to prevent third parties from coercing women to undergo traditional practices, e.g. female genital mutilation; and to take measures to protect all vulnerable or marginalized groups of society, in particular women, children, adolescents and older persons, in the light of gender-based expressions of violence. States should also ensure that third parties do not limit people's access to health-related information and services.

36. The obligation to *fulfil* requires States parties, *inter alia*, to give sufficient recognition to the right to health in the national political and legal systems, preferably by way of legislative implementation, and to adopt a national health policy with a detailed plan for realizing the right to health. States must ensure provision of health care, including immunization programmes against the major infectious diseases, and ensure equal access for all to the underlying determinants of health, such as nutritiously safe food and potable drinking water, basic sanitation and adequate housing and living conditions. Public health infrastructures should provide for sexual and reproductive health services, including safe motherhood, particularly in rural areas. States have to ensure the appropriate training of doctors and other medical personnel, the provision of a sufficient number of hospitals, clinics and other health-related facilities, and the promotion and

support of the establishment of institutions providing counselling and mental health services, with due regard to equitable distribution throughout the country. Further obligations include the provision of a public, private or mixed health insurance system which is affordable for all, the promotion of medical research and health education, as well as information campaigns, in particular with respect to HIV/AIDS, sexual and reproductive health, traditional practices, domestic violence, the abuse of alcohol and the use of cigarettes, drugs and other harmful substances. States are also required to adopt measures against environmental and occupational health hazards and against any other threat as demonstrated by epidemiological data. For this purpose they should formulate and implement national policies aimed at reducing and eliminating pollution of air, water and soil, including pollution by heavy metals such as lead from gasoline. Furthermore, States parties are required to formulate, implement and periodically review a coherent national policy to minimize the risk of occupational accidents and diseases, as well as to provide a coherent national policy on occupational safety and health services.

37. The obligation to *fulfil (facilitate)* requires States *inter alia* to take positive measures that enable and assist individuals and communities to enjoy the right to health. States parties are also obliged to *fulfil (provide)* a specific right contained in the Covenant when individuals or a group are unable, for reasons beyond their control, to realize that right themselves by the means at their disposal. The obligation to *fulfil (promote)* the right to health requires States to undertake actions that create, maintain and restore the health of the population. Such obligations include: (i) fostering recognition of factors favouring positive health results, e.g. research and provision of information; (ii) ensuring that health services are culturally appropriate and that health care staff are trained to recognize and respond to the specific needs of vulnerable or marginalized groups; (iii) ensuring that the State meets its obligations in the dissemination of appropriate information relating to healthy lifestyles and nutrition, harmful traditional practices and the availability of services; (iv) supporting people in making informed choices about their health. . . .

CORE OBLIGATIONS

43. In General Comment No. 3, the Committee confirms that States parties have a core obligation to ensure the satisfaction of, at the very least, minimum essential levels of each of the rights enunciated in the Covenant, including essential primary health care. Read in conjunction with more contemporary instruments, such as the Programme of Action of the International Conference on Population and Development, the Alma-Ata Declaration provides compelling guidance on the core obligations arising from article 12. Accordingly, in the Committee's view, these core obligations include at least the following obligations:

(a) To ensure the right of access to health facilities, goods and services on a non-discriminatory basis, especially for vulnerable or marginalized groups;

(b) To ensure access to the minimum essential food which is nutritionally adequate and safe, to ensure freedom from hunger to everyone;

(c) To ensure access to basic shelter, housing and sanitation, and an adequate supply of safe and potable water;

(d) To provide essential drugs, as from time to time defined under the WHO Action Programme on Essential Drugs;

(e) To ensure equitable distribution of all health facilities, goods and services;

(f) To adopt and implement a national public health strategy and plan of action, on the basis of epidemiological evidence, addressing the health concerns of the whole population; the strategy and plan of action shall be devised, and periodically reviewed, on the basis of a participatory and transparent process; they shall include methods, such as right to health indicators and benchmarks, by which progress can be closely monitored; the process by which the strategy and plan of action are devised, as well as their content, shall give particular attention to all vulnerable or marginalized groups.

44. The Committee also confirms that the following are obligations of comparable priority:

(a) To ensure reproductive, maternal (pre-natal as well as post-natal) and child health care;

(b) To provide immunization against the major infectious diseases occurring in the community;

(c) To take measures to prevent, treat and control epidemic and endemic diseases;

(d) To provide education and access to information concerning the main health problems in the community, including methods of preventing and controlling them;

(e) To provide appropriate training for health personnel, including education on health and human rights.

45. For the avoidance of any doubt, the Committee wishes to emphasize that it is particularly incumbent on States parties and other actors in a position to assist, to provide "international assistance and cooperation, especially economic and technical" which enable developing countries to fulfil their core and other obligations indicated in paragraphs 43 and 44 above.

III. VIOLATIONS

46. When the normative content of article 12 (Part I) is applied to the obligations of States parties (Part II), a dynamic process is set in motion which facilitates identification of violations of the right to health. The following paragraphs provide illustrations of violations of article 12.

47. In determining which actions or omissions amount to a violation of the right to health, it is important to distinguish the inability from the unwillingness of a State party to comply with its obligations under article 12. This follows from article 12.1, which speaks of the highest attainable standard of health, as well as from article 2.1 of the Covenant, which obliges each State party to take the necessary steps to the maximum of its available resources. A State which is unwilling to use the maximum of its available resources for the realization of the right to health is in violation of its obligations under article 12. If resource constraints render it impossible for a State to comply fully with its Covenant obligations, it has the burden of justifying that every effort has nevertheless been made to use all available resources at its disposal in order to satisfy, as a matter of priority, the

obligations outlined above. It should be stressed, however, that a State party cannot, under any circumstances whatsoever, justify its non-compliance with the core obligations set out in paragraph 43 above, which are non-derogable.

48. Violations of the right to health can occur through the direct action of States or other entities insufficiently regulated by States. The adoption of any retrogressive measures incompatible with the core obligations under the right to health, outlined in paragraph 43 above, constitutes a violation of the right to health. Violations through *acts of commission* include the formal repeal or suspension of legislation necessary for the continued enjoyment of the right to health or the adoption of legislation or policies which are manifestly incompatible with pre-existing domestic or international legal obligations in relation to the right to health.

49. Violations of the right to health can also occur through the omission or failure of States to take necessary measures arising from legal obligations. Violations through *acts of omission* include the failure to take appropriate steps towards the full realization of everyone's right to the enjoyment of the highest attainable standard of physical and mental health, the failure to have a national policy on occupational safety and health as well as occupational health services, and the failure to enforce relevant laws.

VIOLATIONS OF THE OBLIGATION TO RESPECT

50. Violations of the obligation to respect are those State actions, policies or laws that contravene the standards set out in article 12 of the Covenant and are likely to result in bodily harm, unnecessary morbidity and preventable mortality. Examples include the denial of access to health facilities, goods and services to particular individuals or groups as a result of de jure or de facto discrimination; the deliberate withholding or misrepresentation of information vital to health protection or treatment; the suspension of legislation or the adoption of laws or policies that interfere with the enjoyment of any of the components of the right to health; and the failure of the State to take into account its legal obligations regarding the right to health when entering into bilateral or multilateral agreements with other States, international organizations and other entities, such as multinational corporations.

VIOLATIONS OF THE OBLIGATION TO PROTECT

51. Violations of the obligation to protect follow from the failure of a State to take all necessary measures to safeguard persons within their jurisdiction from infringements of the right to health by third parties. This category includes such omissions as the failure to regulate the activities of individuals, groups or corporations so as to prevent them from violating the right to health of others; the failure to protect consumers and workers from practices detrimental to health, e.g. by employers and manufacturers of medicines or food; the failure to discourage production, marketing and consumption of tobacco, narcotics and other harmful substances; the failure to protect women against violence or to prosecute perpetrators; the failure to discourage the continued observance of harmful traditional medical or cultural practices; and the failure to enact or enforce laws to prevent the pollution of water, air and soil by extractive and manufacturing industries.

VIOLATIONS OF THE OBLIGATION TO FULFIL

52. Violations of the obligation to fulfil occur through the failure of States parties to take all necessary steps to ensure the realization of the right to health. Examples include the failure to adopt or implement a national health policy designed to ensure the right to health for everyone; insufficient expenditure or misallocation of public resources which results in the non-enjoyment of the right to health by individuals or groups, particularly the vulnerable or marginalized; the failure to monitor the realization of the right to health at the national level, for example by identifying right to health indicators and benchmarks; the failure to take measures to reduce the inequitable distribution of health facilities, goods and services; the failure to adopt a gender-sensitive approach to health; and the failure to reduce infant and maternal mortality rates.

IV. Implementation at the National Level

FRAMEWORK LEGISLATION

53. The most appropriate feasible measures to implement the right to health will vary significantly from one State to another. Every State has a margin of discretion in assessing which measures are most suitable to meet its specific circumstances. The Covenant, however, clearly imposes a duty on each State to take whatever steps are necessary to ensure that everyone has access to health facilities, goods and services so that they can enjoy, as soon as possible, the highest attainable standard of physical and mental health. This requires the adoption of a national strategy to ensure to all the enjoyment of the right to health, based on human rights principles which define the objectives of that strategy, and the formulation of policies and corresponding right to health indicators and benchmarks. The national health strategy should also identify the resources available to attain defined objectives, as well as the most cost-effective way of using those resources. . . .

56. States should consider adopting a framework law to operationalize their right to health national strategy. The framework law should establish national mechanisms for monitoring the implementation of national health strategies and plans of action. It should include provisions on the targets to be achieved and the time-frame for their achievement; the means by which right to health benchmarks could be achieved; the intended collaboration with civil society, including health experts, the private sector and international organizations; institutional responsibility for the implementation of the right to health national strategy and plan of action; and possible recourse procedures. In monitoring progress towards the realization of the right to health, States parties should identify the factors and difficulties affecting implementation of their obligations.

RIGHT TO HEALTH INDICATORS AND BENCHMARKS

57. National health strategies should identify appropriate right to health indicators and benchmarks. The indicators should be designed to monitor, at the national and international levels, the State party's obligations under article 12. States may obtain guidance on appropriate right to health indicators, which should address different aspects of the right to health, from the ongoing work of WHO and

the United Nations Children's Fund (UNICEF) in this field. Right to health indicators require disaggregation on the prohibited grounds of discrimination.

58. Having identified appropriate right to health indicators, States parties are invited to set appropriate national benchmarks in relation to each indicator. During the periodic reporting procedure the Committee will engage in a process of scoping with the State party. Scoping involves the joint consideration by the State party and the Committee of the indicators and national benchmarks which will then provide the targets to be achieved during the next reporting period. In the following five years, the State party will use these national benchmarks to help monitor its implementation of article 12. Thereafter, in the subsequent reporting process, the State party and the Committee will consider whether or not the benchmarks have been achieved, and the reasons for any difficulties that may have been encountered.

REMEDIES AND ACCOUNTABILITY

59. Any person or group victim of a violation of the right to health should have access to effective judicial or other appropriate remedies at both national and international levels. All victims of such violations should be entitled to adequate reparation, which may take the form of restitution, compensation, satisfaction or guarantees of non-repetition. National ombudsmen, human rights commissions, consumer forums, patients' rights associations or similar institutions should address violations of the right to health.

60. The incorporation in the domestic legal order of international instruments recognizing the right to health can significantly enhance the scope and effectiveness of remedial measures and should be encouraged in all cases. Incorporation enables courts to adjudicate violations of the right to health, or at least its core obligations, by direct reference to the Covenant.

61. Judges and members of the legal profession should be encouraged by States parties to pay greater attention to violations of the right to health in the exercise of their functions.

62. States parties should respect, protect, facilitate and promote the work of human rights advocates and other members of civil society with a view to assisting vulnerable or marginalized groups in the realization of their right to health. . . .

As reflected in the above comment, the UN Committee on Economic, Social and Cultural Rights sees the existence of domestic judicial remedies, as well as appropriate international procedures, as important to the realization of the right to health. The following South African case appears to illustrate what the Committee had in mind.

Minister of Health et al. v. Treatment Action Campaign et al.

Constitutional Court of South Africa, Case CCT 8/02, Judgment of July 5, 2002 (some footnotes omitted)

INTRODUCTION

[1] The HIV/AIDS pandemic in South Africa has been described as "an incomprehensible calamity" and "the most important challenge facing South

Africa since the birth of our new democracy" and government's fight against "this scourge" as "a top priority." It "has claimed millions of lives, inflicting pain and grief, causing fear and uncertainty, and threatening the economy." These are not the words of alarmists but are taken from a Department of Health publication in 2000 and a ministerial foreword to an earlier departmental publication.

[2] This appeal is directed at reversing orders made in a high court against government because of perceived shortcomings in its response to an aspect of the HIV/AIDS challenge. The court found that government had not reasonably addressed the need to reduce the risk of HIV-positive mothers transmitting the disease to their babies at birth. More specifically the finding was that government had acted unreasonably in (a) refusing to make an antiretroviral drug called nevirapine[2] available in the public health sector where the attending doctor considered it medically indicated and (b) not setting out a time-frame for a national programme to prevent mother-to-child transmission of HIV.

[3] The case started as an application in the High Court in Pretoria on 21 August 2001. The applicants were a number of associations and members of civil society concerned with the treatment of people with HIV/AIDS and with the prevention of new infections. In this judgment they are referred to collectively as "the applicants." The principal actor among them was the Treatment Action Campaign (TAC). The respondents were the national Minister of Health and the respective members of the executive councils (MECs) responsible for health in all provinces save the Western Cape. They are referred to collectively as "the government" or "government."

[4] Government, as part of a formidable array of responses to the pandemic, devised a programme to deal with mother-to-child transmission of HIV at birth and identified nevirapine as its drug of choice for this purpose.[3] The programme imposes restrictions on the availability of nevirapine in the public health sector. This is where the first of two main issues in the case arose. The applicants contended that these restrictions are unreasonable when measured against the Constitution, which commands the state and all its organs to give effect to the rights guaranteed by the Bill of Rights. This duty is put thus by sections 7(2) and 8(1) of the Constitution respectively:

> "7(2) The state must respect, protect, promote and fulfil the rights in the Bill of Rights. . . .
> 8(1) The Bill of Rights applies to all law, and binds the legislature, the executive, the judiciary and all organs of state."

At issue here is the right given to everyone to have access to public health care services and the right of children to be afforded special protection. These rights

2. Nevirapine is a fast-acting and potent antiretroviral drug long since used worldwide in the treatment of HIV/AIDS and registered in South Africa since 1998. In January 2001 it was approved by the World Health Organization for use against intrapartum mother-to-child transmission of HIV, i.e. transmission of the virus from mother to child at birth. It was also approved for such use in South Africa. The nature and precise date of such approval were contested and this led to some vigorously debated subsidiary issues, dealt with more fully below.

3. The drug is currently available free to government and its administration is simple: a single tablet taken by the mother at the onset of labour and a few drops fed to the baby within 72 hours after birth.

are expressed in the following terms in the Bill of Rights:

> "27(1) Everyone has the right to have access to —
> (a) health care services, including reproductive health care;...
> (2) The state must take reasonable legislative and other measures, within its available resources, to achieve the progressive realisation of each of these rights....
> 28(1) Every child has the right —
> ...(c) to basic nutrition, shelter, basic health care services and social services."

[5] The second main issue also arises out of the provisions of sections 27 and 28 of the Constitution. It is whether government is constitutionally obliged and had to be ordered forthwith to plan and implement an effective, comprehensive and progressive programme for the prevention of mother-to-child transmission of HIV throughout the country. The applicants also relied on other provisions of the Constitution which, in view of our conclusions, need not be considered.

[6] The affidavits lodged by the applicants addressed these two central issues from a variety of specialised perspectives, ranging from paediatrics, pharmacology and epidemiology to public health administration, economics and statistics. The applicants' papers also include the testimony of doctors, nurses and counsellors confronted daily with the human tragedies of HIV-infected mothers and their babies. In addition there are poignant accounts of HIV-positive pregnant women's pleas for access to nevirapine for themselves and their babies at public health institutions where its supply is prohibited....

Factual Background

[10] The two principal issues had been in contention between the applicants and government for some considerable time prior to the launching of the application in the High Court. Thus, when the TAC in September 1999 pressed for acceleration of the government programme for the prevention of intrapartum mother-to-child transmission of HIV, it was told by the Minister that this could not be done because there were concerns about, among other things, the safety and efficacy of nevirapine. Nearly a year later (in August 2000), following the 13th International AIDS Conference in Durban and a follow-up meeting attended by the Minister and the MECs, the Minister announced that nevirapine would still not be made generally available. Instead each province was going to select two sites for further research and the use of the drug would be confined to such sites.

[11] Close to a year later, in a letter dated 17 July 2001 written by their attorney, the applicants placed on record that

> "[t]he Government has decided to make NVP [nevirapine] available only at a limited number of pilot sites, which number two per province. The result is that doctors in the public sector, who do not work at one of those pilot sites, are unable to prescribe this drug for their patients, even though it has been offered to the government for free."

At the same time they pointedly asked the Minister to:

> "(a) provide us with legally valid reasons why you will not make NVP available to patients in the public health sector, except at the designated pilot sites, or

alternatively to undertake forthwith to make NVP available in the public health sector.

(b) undertake to put in place a programme which will enable all medical practitioners in the public sector to decide whether to prescribe NVP for their pregnant patients, and to prescribe it where in their professional opinion this is medically indicated." . . .

[12] Nevirapine had been registered in 1998 by the Medicines Control Council, a specialist body created by the Medicines and Related Substances Control Act 101 of 1965 to determine the safety of drugs before their being made available in South Africa. In terms of this Act registration of a drug by definition entails a positive finding as to its quality, safety and efficacy. In January 2001 the World Health Organization recommended the administration of the drug to mother and infant at the time of birth in order to combat HIV and between November 2000 and April 2001 the Medicines Control Council settled the wording of the package insert dealing with such use. The insert was formally approved by the Council in April 2001 and the parties treated that as the date of approval of the drug for the prevention of mother-to-child transmission of HIV. . . .

[14] The letter from the Minister also lists a number of social, economic and public health implications of breastfeeding by HIV-positive mothers, emphasises the cultural and financial impact of formula-feeding as a substitute and outlines the overall complexity of providing a comprehensive package of care throughout the country. The Minister, although not responding directly to the undertakings sought on behalf of the applicants, quite clearly intimated that neither undertaking was or would be given. The decision was to confine the provision of nevirapine in the public sector to the research sites and their outlets.

[15] It can be accepted that an important reason for this decision was that government wanted to develop and monitor its human and material resources nationwide for the delivery of a comprehensive package of testing and counselling, dispensing of nevirapine and follow-up services to pregnant women attending at public health institutions. Where bottle-feeding was to be substituted for breastfeeding, appropriate methods and procedures had to be evolved for effective implementation, bearing in mind cultural problems, the absence of clean water in certain parts of the country and the increased risks to infants growing up with inadequate nutrition and sanitation. At the same time, data relating to administrative hitches and their solutions, staffing, costs and the like could be gathered and correlated. All of this obviously makes good sense from the public health point of view. These research and training sites could provide vital information on which in time the very best possible prevention programme for mother-to-child transmission could be developed.

[16] This point is also made in the *Protocol for providing a comprehensive package of care for the prevention of mother to child transmission of HIV in South Africa (draft version 4)* issued by government in April 2001. . . .

[17] The crux of the problem, however, lies elsewhere: what is to happen to those mothers and their babies who cannot afford access to private health care and do not have access to the research and training sites? It is not clear on the papers how long it is planned to take before nevirapine will be made available outside these sites. Some of the provinces had not yet established any test sites by the time the application was launched in late August 2001. The first sites were established

only in May 2001 following a meeting the previous month at which government had endorsed the establishment of the sites for a period of two years. These sites were to be selected according to stated criteria, one in an urban and one in a rural community in each province. Whether the programme was to be maintained strictly until the last of the provincial test sites had been functioning for two years or could possibly be extended beyond that period does not appear from the papers. What is plain, though, is that for a protracted period nevirapine would not be supplied at any public health institution other than one designated as part of a research site. . . .

[22] In their argument counsel for the government raised issues pertaining to the separation of powers. This may be relevant in two respects — (i) in the deference that courts should show to decisions taken by the executive concerning the formulation of its policies; and (ii) in the order to be made where a court finds that the executive has failed to comply with its constitutional obligations. These considerations are relevant to the manner in which a court should exercise the powers vested in it under the Constitution. It was not contended, nor could it have been, that they are relevant to the question of justiciability.

ENFORCEMENT OF SOCIO-ECONOMIC RIGHTS

precedent

[23] This Court has had to consider claims for enforcement of socio-economic rights on two occasions.[4] On both occasions it was recognised that the state is under a constitutional duty to comply with the positive obligations imposed on it by sections 26 and 27 of the Constitution. It was stressed, however, that the obligations are subject to the qualifications expressed in sections 26(2) and 27(2). On the first occasion, in *Soobramoney*, the claim was dismissed because the applicant failed to establish that the state was in breach of its obligations under section 26 in so far as the provision of renal dialysis to chronically ill patients was concerned. In *Grootboom* the claim was upheld because the state's housing policy in the area of the Cape Metropolitan Council failed to make reasonable provision within available resources for people in that area who had no access to land and no roof over their heads and were living in intolerable conditions.

[24] In both cases the socio-economic rights, and the corresponding obligations of the state, were interpreted in their social and historical context. The difficulty confronting the state in the light of our history in addressing issues concerned with the basic needs of people was stressed. Thus, in *Grootboom*, Yacoob J said:

> "This case shows the desperation of hundreds of thousands of people living in deplorable conditions throughout the country. The Constitution obliges the State to act positively to ameliorate these conditions. The obligation is to provide access to housing, health-care, sufficient food and water, and social security to those unable to support themselves and their dependants. The State must also foster conditions to enable citizens to gain access to land on an equitable basis. Those in need have a

4. *Soobramoney v. Minister of Health, KwaZulu-Natal* 1998 (1) SA 765 (CC); 1997 (12) BCLR 1696 (CC); *Government of the Republic of South Africa and Others v. Grootboom and Others* 2001 (1) SA 46 (CC); 2000 (11) BCLR 1169 (CC).

corresponding right to demand that this be done. I am conscious that it is an extremely difficult task for the State to meet these obligations in the conditions that prevail in our country. This is recognised by the Constitution which expressly provides that the State is not obliged to go beyond available resources or to realise these rights immediately. I stress however, that despite all these qualifications, these are rights, and the Constitution obliges the State to give effect to them. This is an obligation that Courts can, and in appropriate circumstances, must enforce."

[25] The question in the present case, therefore, is not whether socio-economic rights are justiciable. Clearly they are.[5] The question is whether the applicants have shown that the measures adopted by the government to provide access to health care services for HIV-positive mothers and their newborn babies fall short of its obligations under the Constitution.

Minimum Core

[26] Before outlining the applicants' legal submissions, it is necessary to consider a line of argument presented on behalf of the first and second amici. It was contended that section 27(1) of the Constitution establishes an individual right vested in everyone. This right, so the contention went, has a minimum core to which every person in need is entitled. The concept of "minimum core" was developed by the United Nations Committee on Economic, Social and Cultural Rights which is charged with monitoring the obligations undertaken by state parties to the International Covenant on Economic, Social and Cultural Rights. According to the Committee

> "a State party in which any significant number of individuals is deprived of essential foodstuffs, of essential primary health care, of basic shelter and housing, or of the most basic forms of education is, *prima facie*, failing to discharge its obligations under the Covenant. If the Covenant were to be read in such a way as not to establish such a minimum core obligation, it would be largely deprived of its *raison d'être*. By the same token, it must be noted that any assessment as to whether a State has discharged its minimum core obligations must also take account of resource constraints applying within the country concerned. Article 2(1) obligates each State party to take the necessary steps 'to the maximum of its available resources'. In order for a State party to be able to attribute its failure to meet at least its minimum core obligations to a lack of available resources it must demonstrate that every effort has been made to use all resources that are at its disposition in an effort to satisfy, as a matter of priority, those minimum obligations."[6] . . .

[30] Section 26(1) refers to the "right" to have access to housing. Section 26(2), dealing with the state's obligation in that regard, requires it to "take reasonable legislative and other measures, within its available resources, to achieve the progressive realization of this right." The reference to "this right" is clearly a reference to the section 26(1) right. Similar language is used in section 27

5. *Ex Parte Chairperson of the Constitutional Assembly: In re Certification of the Constitution of the Republic of South Africa, 1996* 1996 (4) SA 744 (CC); 1996 (10) BCLR 1253 (CC) para 78.

6. CESCR General Comment 3, "The nature of States parties obligations (Art. 2, par.1)," 4/12/90 para 10.

which deals with health care services, including reproductive health care, sufficient food and water, and social security, including, if persons are unable to support themselves and their dependants, appropriate social assistance. Subsection (1) refers to the right everyone has to have "access" to these services; and subsection (2) obliges the state to take "reasonable legislative and other measures, within its available resources, to achieve the progressive realisation of each of these rights." The rights requiring progressive realisation are those referred to in sections 27(1)(a), (b) and (c).

[31] In *Soobramoney* it was said:

> "What is apparent from these provisions is that the obligations imposed on the State by ss 26 and 27 in regard to access to housing, health care, food, water and social security are dependent upon the resources available for such purposes, *and that the corresponding rights themselves are limited by reason of the lack of resources.*"

The obligations referred to in this passage are clearly the obligations referred to in sections 26(2) and 27(2), and the "corresponding rights" are the rights referred to in sections 26(1) and 27(1).

[32] This passage is cited in *Grootboom*. It is made clear in that judgment that sections 26(1) and 26(2) "are related and must be read together." Yacoob J said: "The section has been carefully crafted. It contains three subsections." . . .

[33] In *Grootboom* reliance was also placed on the provisions of the Covenant. Yacoob J held that in terms of our Constitution the question is "whether the measures taken by the State to realise the right afforded by s 26 are reasonable."

[34] Although Yacoob J indicated that evidence in a particular case may show that there is a minimum core of a particular service that should be taken into account in determining whether measures adopted by the state are reasonable, the socio-economic rights of the Constitution should not be construed as entitling everyone to demand that the minimum core be provided to them. Minimum core was thus treated as possibly being relevant to reasonableness under section 26(2), and not as a self-standing right conferred on everyone under section 26(1).

[35] A purposive reading of sections 26 and 27 does not lead to any other conclusion. It is impossible to give everyone access even to a "core" service immediately. All that is possible, and all that can be expected of the state, is that it act reasonably to provide access to the socio-economic rights identified in sections 26 and 27 on a progressive basis. In *Grootboom* the relevant context in which socio-economic rights need to be interpreted was said to be that

> "[m]illions of people are living in deplorable conditions and in great poverty. There is a high level of unemployment, inadequate social security, and many do not have access to clean water or to adequate health services. These conditions already existed when the Constitution was adopted . . ."

[36] The state is obliged to take reasonable measures progressively to eliminate or reduce the large areas of severe deprivation that afflict our society. The courts will guarantee that the democratic processes are protected so as to ensure accountability, responsiveness and openness, as the Constitution requires in section 1. As the Bill of Rights indicates, their function in respect of socio-economic rights is directed towards ensuring that legislative and other measures taken by the state are reasonable. As this Court said in *Grootboom*, "[i]t is necessary to

deference

recognise that a wide range of possible measures could be adopted by the State to meet its obligations."

[37] It should be borne in mind that in dealing with such matters the courts are not institutionally equipped to make the wide-ranging factual and political enquiries necessary for determining what the minimum-core standards called for by the first and second amici should be, nor for deciding how public revenues should most effectively be spent. There are many pressing demands on the public purse. As was said in *Soobramoney*:

> "The State has to manage its limited resources in order to address all these claims. There will be times when this requires it to adopt a holistic approach to the larger needs of society rather than to focus on the specific needs of particular individuals within society."

[38] Courts are ill-suited to adjudicate upon issues where court orders could have multiple social and economic consequences for the community. The Constitution contemplates rather a restrained and focused role for the courts, namely, to require the state to take measures to meet its constitutional obligations and to subject the reasonableness of these measures to evaluation. Such determinations of reasonableness may in fact have budgetary implications, but are not in themselves directed at rearranging budgets. In this way the judicial, legislative and executive functions achieve appropriate constitutional balance.

[39] We therefore conclude that section 27(1) of the Constitution does not give rise to a self-standing and independent positive right enforceable irrespective of the considerations mentioned in section 27(2). Sections 27(1) and 27(2) must be read together as defining the scope of the positive rights that everyone has and the corresponding obligations on the state to "respect, protect, promote and fulfil" such rights. The rights conferred by sections 26(1) and 27(1) are to have "access" to the services that the state is obliged to provide in terms of sections 26(2) and 27(2). . . .

Considerations Relevant to Reasonableness

[67] The policy of confining nevirapine to research and training sites fails to address the needs of mothers and their newborn children who do not have access to these sites. It fails to distinguish between the evaluation of programmes for reducing mother-to-child transmission and the need to provide access to health care services required by those who do not have access to the sites.

[68] In *Grootboom* this Court held that "[t]o be reasonable, measures cannot leave out of account the degree and extent of the denial of the right they endeavour to realise. Those whose needs are the most urgent and whose ability to enjoy all rights therefore is most in peril, must not be ignored by the measures aimed at achieving realisation of the right." The fact that the research and training sites will provide crucial data on which a comprehensive programme for mother-to-child transmission can be developed and, if financially feasible, implemented is clearly of importance to government and to the country. So too is ongoing research into safety, efficacy and resistance. This does not mean, however, that until the best programme has been formulated and the necessary funds and infrastructure provided for the implementation of that programme, nevirapine must be withheld from mothers and children who do not have access to the research and training

sites. Nor can it reasonably be withheld until medical research has been completed. A programme for the realisation of socio-economic rights must "be balanced and flexible and make appropriate provision for attention to . . . crises and to short, medium and long term needs. A programme that excludes a significant segment of society cannot be said to be reasonable."

[69] The applicants do not suggest that nevirapine should be administered indiscriminately to mothers and babies throughout the public sector. They accept that the drug should be administered only to mothers who are shown to be HIV-positive and that it should not be administered unless it is medically indicated and, where necessary, counselling is available to the mother to enable her to take an informed decision as to whether or not to accept the treatment recommended. Those conditions form part of the order made by the High Court.

[70] In dealing with these questions it must be kept in mind that this case concerns particularly those who cannot afford to pay for medical services. To the extent that government limits the supply of nevirapine to its research sites, it is the poor outside the catchment areas of these sites who will suffer. There is a difference in the positions of those who can afford to pay for services and those who cannot. State policy must take account of these differences.

[71] The cost of nevirapine for preventing mother-to-child transmission is not an issue in the present proceedings. It is admittedly within the resources of the state. The relief claimed by the applicants on this aspect of the policy, and the order made by the High Court in that regard, contemplate that nevirapine will only be administered for the prevention of mother-to-child transmission at those hospitals and clinics where testing and counselling facilities are already in place. Therefore this aspect of the claim and the orders made will not attract any significant additional costs.

[72] In evaluating government's policy, regard must be had to the fact that this case is concerned with newborn babies whose lives might be saved by the administration of nevirapine to mother and child at the time of birth. The safety and efficacy of nevirapine for this purpose have been established and the drug is being provided by government itself to mothers and babies at the pilot sites in every province.

[73] The administration of nevirapine is a simple procedure. Where counselling and testing facilities exist, the administration of nevirapine is well within the available resources of the state and, in such circumstances, the provision of a single dose of nevirapine to mother and child where medically indicated is a simple, cheap and potentially lifesaving medical intervention.

CHILDREN'S RIGHTS

[74] There is another consideration that is material. This case is concerned with newborn children. Sections 28(1)(b) and (c) of the Constitution provide that "[e]very child has the right —

> (a) . . .
> (b) to family care or parental care, or to appropriate alternative care when removed from the family environment;
> (c) to basic nutrition, shelter, basic health care services and social services."

The applicants and the amici curiae relied on these provisions to support the order made by the High Court.

[75] In *Grootboom* it was held that paragraphs (b) and (c) must be read together.

> "They ensure that children are properly cared for by their parents or families, and that they receive appropriate alternative care in the absence of parental or family care. The section encapsulates the conception of the scope of care that children should receive in our society. Subsection 1*(b)* defines those responsible for giving care while ss 1*(c)* lists various aspects of the care entitlement. It follows from ss 1*(b)* that the Constitution contemplates that a child has the right to parental or family care in the first place, and the right to alternative appropriate care only where that is lacking." . . .

[78] The provision of a single dose of nevirapine to mother and child for the purpose of protecting the child against the transmission of HIV is, as far as the children are concerned, essential. Their needs are "most urgent" and their inability to have access to nevirapine profoundly affects their ability to enjoy all rights to which they are entitled. Their rights are "most in peril" as a result of the policy that has been adopted and are most affected by a rigid and inflexible policy that excludes them from having access to nevirapine.

[79] The state is obliged to ensure that children are accorded the protection contemplated by section 28 that arises when the implementation of the right to parental or family care is lacking. Here we are concerned with children born in public hospitals and clinics to mothers who are for the most part indigent and unable to gain access to private medical treatment which is beyond their means. They and their children are in the main dependent upon the state to make health care services available to them.

Evaluation of the Policy to Limit Nevirapine to Research and Training Sites

[80] Government policy was an inflexible one that denied mothers and their newborn children at public hospitals and clinics outside the research and training sites the opportunity of receiving a single dose of nevirapine at the time of the birth of the child. A potentially lifesaving drug was on offer and where testing and counselling facilities were available it could have been administered within the available resources of the state without any known harm to mother or child. In the circumstances we agree with the finding of the High Court that the policy of government in so far as it confines the use of nevirapine to hospitals and clinics which are research and training sites constitutes a breach of the state's obligations under section 27(2) read with section 27(1)(a) of the Constitution.

[81] Implicit in this finding is that a policy of waiting for a protracted period before taking a decision on the use of nevirapine beyond the research and training sites is also not reasonable within the meaning of section 27(2) of the Constitution.

Does Government Have a Comprehensive Plan to Combat Mother-to-child Transmission of HIV?

[82] The issues relating to the alleged failure to implement a comprehensive national programme for the prevention of mother-to-child transmission are intertwined with the averments concerning the refusal to permit nevirapine to be prescribed at public hospitals and clinics outside the research and training sites. Foundational to all aspects of the case was the challenge to the policy concerning the use of nevirapine. . . .

Summary of the Relevant Evidence

[92] To sum up, the position when the application was launched was this. Two research and training sites had been selected at hospitals in each province to use nevirapine for the prevention of mother-to-child transmission of HIV. These research and training sites were linked to access points at satellite clinics. There were approximately 160 access points. (During the course of the proceedings these had increased to over 200.) At the project hospitals and satellite clinics a full package for the treatment of mother-to-child transmission was to be available. This included testing, counselling, nevirapine if medically indicated, the provision of formula feed as a substitute for breastfeeding, aftercare including the provision of vitamins and antibiotics, and monitoring of the progress of the children. At all other public hospitals and clinics nevirapine would not be available. There was, however, to be a programme for testing and counselling, including counselling on matters related to breastfeeding. Formula feed was available at some hospitals and clinics but it was not a requirement of the programme to combat mother-to-child transmission outside the research and training sites that it be made available to HIV-positive mothers of newborn babies who would like to avoid breastfeeding but cannot afford the formula feed. Although the programme envisaged the progressive establishment of testing and counselling facilities at all hospitals and clinics, progress had been slow in certain parts of the country, particularly in clinics in the Northern Province, Mpumalanga, the Eastern Cape and KwaZulu-Natal. The bulk of the rural population lives in these provinces where millions of people are still without access to clean water or adequate sanitation.

Findings re Government's Programme

[93] In the present case this Court has the duty to determine whether the measures taken in respect of the prevention of mother-to-child transmission of HIV are reasonable. We know that throughout the country health services are overextended. HIV/AIDS is but one of many illnesses that require attention. It is, however, the greatest threat to public health in our country. . . .

[95] The rigidity of government's approach when these proceedings commenced affected its policy as a whole. If, as we have held, it was not reasonable to restrict the use of nevirapine to the research and training sites, the policy as a whole will have to be reviewed. Hospitals and clinics that have testing and

prescriptions for program

counselling facilities should be able to prescribe nevirapine where that is medically indicated. The training of counselors ought now to include training for counselling on the use of nevirapine. As previously indicated, this is not a complex task and it should not be difficult to equip existing counsellors with the necessary additional knowledge. In addition, government will need to take reasonable measures to extend the testing and counselling facilities to hospitals and clinics throughout the public health sector beyond the test sites to facilitate and expedite the use of nevirapine for the purpose of reducing the risk of mother-to-child transmission of HIV.

The Powers of the Courts

[96] Counsel for the government contended that even if this Court should find that government policies fall short of what the Constitution requires, the only competent order that a court can make is to issue a declaration of rights to that effect. That leaves government free to pay heed to the declaration made and to adapt its policies in so far as this may be necessary to bring them into conformity with the court's judgment. This, so the argument went, is what the doctrine of separation of powers demands.

[97] In developing this argument counsel contended that under the separation of powers the making of policy is the prerogative of the executive and not the courts, and that courts cannot make orders that have the effect of requiring the executive to pursue a particular policy.

[98] This Court has made it clear on more than one occasion that although there are no bright lines that separate the roles of the legislature, the executive and the courts from one another, there are certain matters that are pre-eminently within the domain of one or other of the arms of government and not the others. All arms of government should be sensitive to and respect this separation. This does not mean, however, that courts cannot or should not make orders that have an impact on policy.

[99] The primary duty of courts is to the Constitution and the law, "which they must apply impartially and without fear, favour or prejudice." The Constitution requires the state to "respect, protect, promote, and fulfil the rights in the Bill of Rights." Where state policy is challenged as inconsistent with the Constitution, courts have to consider whether in formulating and implementing such policy the state has given effect to its constitutional obligations. If it should hold in any given case that the state has failed to do so, it is obliged by the Constitution to say so. In so far as that constitutes an intrusion into the domain of the executive, that is an intrusion mandated by the Constitution itself....

[100] The rights that the state is obliged to "respect, protect, promote and fulfil" include the socio-economic rights in the Constitution. In *Grootboom* this Court stressed that in so far as socio-economic rights are concerned

> "[t]he State is required to take reasonable legislative *and* other measures. Legislative measures by themselves are not likely to constitute constitutional compliance. Mere legislation is not enough. The State is obliged to act to achieve the intended result, and the legislative measures will invariably have to be supported by appropriate, well-directed policies and programmes implemented by the Executive. These policies and

programmes must be reasonable both in their conception and their implementation. The formulation of a programme is only the first stage in meeting the State's obligations. The programme must also be reasonably implemented. An otherwise reasonable programme that is not implemented reasonably will not constitute compliance with the State's obligations." . . .

[106] We thus reject the argument that the only power that this Court has in the present case is to issue a declaratory order. Where a breach of any right has taken place, including a socio-economic right, a court is under a duty to ensure that effective relief is granted. The nature of the right infringed and the nature of the infringement will provide guidance as to the appropriate relief in a particular case. Where necessary this may include both the issuing of a mandamus and the exercise of supervisory jurisdiction. . . .

[112] [A] brief survey [of foreign jurisprudence] makes clear . . . that in none of the jurisdictions surveyed is there any suggestion that the granting of injunctive relief breaches the separation of powers. The various courts adopt different attitudes to when such remedies should be granted, but all accept that within the separation of powers they have the power to make use of such remedies — particularly when the state's obligations are not performed diligently and without delay. . . .

[114] A factor that needs to be kept in mind is that policy is and should be flexible. It may be changed at any time and the executive is always free to change policies where it considers it appropriate to do so. The only constraint is that policies must be consistent with the Constitution and the law. Court orders concerning policy choices made by the executive should therefore not be formulated in ways that preclude the executive from making such legitimate choices.

Circumstances Relevant to the Order to Be Made

[115] The finding made concerning the restricted use of nevirapine has implications for government's policy on the prevention of mother-to-child transmission of HIV. If nevirapine is now made available at all state hospitals and clinics where there are testing and counselling facilities, that will call for a change in policy. The policy will have to be that nevirapine must be provided where it is medically indicated at those hospitals and clinics within the public sector where facilities exist for testing and counselling. . . .

[122] In the present case we have identified aspects of government policy that are inconsistent with the Constitution. The decision not to make nevirapine available at hospitals and clinics other than the research and training sites is central to the entire policy. Once that restriction is removed, government will be able to devise and implement a more comprehensive policy that will give access to health care services to HIV-positive mothers and their newborn children, and will include the administration of nevirapine where that is appropriate. The policy as reformulated must meet the constitutional requirement of providing reasonable measures within available resources for the progressive realisation of the rights of such women and newborn children. This may also require, where that is necessary, that counsellors at places other than at the research and training sites be trained in counselling for the use of nevirapine. We will formulate a declaration to address these issues.

Transparency

[123] Three of the nine provinces[16] have publicly announced programmes to realize progressively the rights of pregnant women and their newborn babies to have access to nevirapine treatment. As for the rest, no programme has been disclosed by either the Minister or any of the other six MECs, this notwithstanding the pertinent request from the TAC in July 2001[17] and the subsequent lodging of hundreds of pages of affidavits and written legal argument. This is regrettable. The magnitude of the HIV/AIDS challenge facing the country calls for a concerted, co-ordinated and co-operative national effort in which government in each of its three spheres and the panoply of resources and skills of civil society are marshalled, inspired and led. This can be achieved only if there is proper communication, especially by government. In order for it to be implemented optimally, a public health programme must be made known effectively to all concerned, down to the district nurse and patients. Indeed, for a public programme such as this to meet the constitutional requirement of reasonableness, its contents must be made known appropriately.

Relief . . .

[125] It is essential that there be a concerted national effort to combat the HIV/AIDS pandemic. The government has committed itself to such an effort. We have held that its policy fails to meet constitutional standards because it excludes those who could reasonably be included where such treatment is medically indicated to combat mother-to-child transmission of HIV. That does not mean that everyone can immediately claim access to such treatment, although the ideal, as Dr Ntsaluba says [on behalf of the government], is to achieve that goal. Every effort must, however, be made to do so as soon as reasonably possible. The increases in the budget [about which we have been informed] will facilitate this.

[126] We consider it important that all sectors of the community, in particular civil society, should co-operate in the steps taken to achieve this goal. In our view that will be facilitated by spelling out the steps necessary to comply with the Constitution.

[127] We will do this on the basis of the policy that government has adopted as the best means of combating mother-to-child transmission of HIV, which is to make use of nevirapine for this purpose. Government must retain the right to adapt the policy, consistent with its constitutional obligations, should it consider it appropriate to do so. The order that we make has regard to this.

[128] We do not consider it appropriate to deal with the use of formula feed in the order. Whether it is desirable to use this substitute rather than breastfeeding raises complex issues,[18] particularly when the mother concerned may not have easy access to clean water or the ability to adopt a bottle-feeding regimen because of her personal circumstances. The result of the studies conducted at the research

16. Western Cape, Gauteng and KwaZulu-Natal.

17. Quoted in para 11 above.

18. See conclusions and recommendations regarding infant feeding in the WHO Technical Consultation entitled *New data on the prevention of mother-to-child transmission of HIV and their policy implications* approved 15 January 2001.

and training sites may enable government to formulate a comprehensive policy in this regard. In the meantime this must be left to health professionals to address during counselling. We do not consider that there is sufficient evidence to justify an order that formula feed must be made available by the government on request and without charge in every case....

[130] The anxiety of the applicants to have the government move as expeditiously as possible in taking measures to reduce the transmission of HIV from mother to child is understandable. One is dealing here with a deadly disease. Once a drug that has the potential to reduce mother-to-child transmission is available, it is desirable that it be made available without delay to those who urgently need it.

[131] We do not underestimate the nature and extent of the problem facing government in its fight to combat HIV/AIDS and, in particular, to reduce the transmission of HIV from mother to child. We also understand the need to exercise caution when dealing with a potent and a relatively unknown drug. But the nature of the problem is such that it demands urgent attention. Nevirapine is a potentially lifesaving drug. Its safety and efficacy have been established. There is a need to assess operational challenges for the best possible use of nevirapine on a comprehensive scale to reduce the risk of mother-to-child transmission of HIV. There is an additional need to monitor issues relevant to the safety and efficacy of and resistance to the use of nevirapine for this purpose. There is, however, also a pressing need to ensure that where possible loss of life is prevented in the meantime.

[132] Government policy is now evolving. Additional sites where nevirapine is provided with a "full package" to combat mother-to-child transmission of HIV are being added. In the Western Cape, Gauteng and KwaZulu-Natal, programmes have been adopted to extend the supply of nevirapine for such purpose throughout the province. What now remains is for the other provinces to follow suit. The order that we make will facilitate this.

[133] It is necessary that the government programme, as supplemented to comply with the requirements of this judgment, be communicated to health caregivers in all public facilities and to the beneficiaries of the programme. Having regard to the nature of the problem, the steps that have to be taken to comply with the order that we make should be taken without delay....

Orders

[135] We accordingly make the following orders:

1. The orders made by the High Court are set aside and the following orders are substituted.

2. It is declared that:

a) Sections 27(1) and (2) of the Constitution require the government to devise and implement within its available resources a comprehensive and co-ordinated programme to realize progressively the rights of pregnant women and their newborn children to have access to health services to combat mother-to-child transmission of HIV.

b) The programme to be realised progressively within available resources must include reasonable measures for counselling and testing pregnant women for HIV, counselling HIV-positive pregnant women on the options open to them to reduce the risk of mother-to-child transmission of HIV, and making appropriate treatment available to them for such purposes.

c) The policy for reducing the risk of mother-to-child transmission of HIV as formulated and implemented by government fell short of compliance with the requirements in subparagraphs (a) and (b) in that:

i) Doctors at public hospitals and clinics other than the research and training sites were not enabled to prescribe nevirapine to reduce the risk of mother-to-child transmission of HIV even where it was medically indicated and adequate facilities existed for the testing and counselling of the pregnant women concerned.

ii) The policy failed to make provision for counsellors at hospitals and clinics other than at research and training sites to be trained in counselling for the use of nevirapine as a means of reducing the risk of mother-to-child transmission of HIV.

3. Government is ordered without delay to:

a) Remove the restrictions that prevent nevirapine from being made available for the purpose of reducing the risk of mother-to-child transmission of HIV at public hospitals and clinics that are not research and training sites.

b) Permit and facilitate the use of nevirapine for the purpose of reducing the risk of mother-to-child transmission of HIV and to make it available for this purpose at hospitals and clinics when in the judgment of the attending medical practitioner acting in consultation with the medical superintendent of the facility concerned this is medically indicated, which shall if necessary include that the mother concerned has been appropriately tested and counselled.

c) Make provision if necessary for counsellors based at public hospitals and clinics other than the research and training sites to be trained for the counselling necessary for the use of nevirapine to reduce the risk of mother-to-child transmission of HIV.

d) Take reasonable measures to extend the testing and counseling facilities at hospitals and clinics throughout the public health sector to facilitate and expedite the use of nevirapine for the purpose of reducing the risk of mother-to-child transmission of HIV.

4. The orders made in paragraph 3 do not preclude government from adapting its policy in a manner consistent with the Constitution if equally appropriate or better methods become available to it for the prevention of mother-to-child transmission of HIV.

5. The government must pay the applicants' costs, including the costs of two counsel.

6. The application by government to adduce further evidence is refused.

Comments and Questions

1. As discussed in the foregoing case, the right to health, among other economic, social, and cultural rights, are explicitly affirmed in the South African

Constitution. Might a right to health be read into the due process clauses of the Fifth and Fourteenth Amendments to the United States Constitution, in light of relevant provisions of the Universal Declaration on Human Rights and the International Covenant on Economic, Social and Cultural Rights? The due process clauses of the Constitution, which provide that no one shall "be deprived of life, liberty, or property without due process of law," have been construed to protect "fundamental rights," including the right to privacy and, for example, derivative rights of reproductive choice that are not explicitly articulated in the Constitution. Would reading a right to health into the Constitution be more likely if the United States were to ratify the Covenant on Economic, Social and Cultural Rights? Or is ratification of the Covenant impeded because of the absence of such a right in U.S. constitutional and other domestic law?

Note: *The Use of International Human Rights Law in Foreign Jurisdictions*

In the *Treatment Action Committee* case, the South African Constitutional Court construed Articles 27 and 28 of the Bill of Rights enshrined in that country's Constitution, articles concerning the right to health, with reference to General Comment 3 by the UN Committee on Economic, Social, and Cultural Rights (an edited version of which is reproduced in Chapter 5, supra). That General Comment, like the Committee's General Comment 14 on the right to health, supra page 502, interprets the International Covenant on Economic, Social and Cultural Rights, to which South Africa is a party. This use of international standards and opinion in relation to domestic constitutional provisions is akin to that employed by the U.S. Supreme Court in *Roper v. Simmons*, discussed supra, albeit in the context of the very different constitutional right of juvenile offenders to be free from the death penalty.

The South African Constitution, however, does not leave such indirect application of international norms entirely to judicial discretion. Article 39(1)(b) of the Constitution mandates: "When interpreting the Bill of Rights, a court, tribunal or forum . . . must consider international law." In *Government of the Republic of South Africa v. Grootboom*, 2001 (1) SALR 46, 63-64 (CC), the Constitutional Court construed this directive as including even international human rights law that is not binding on South Africa, such as unratified treaties and decisions from the European and inter-American human rights systems. Additionally, Article 39 (1) (b) of the Constitution authorizes (but does not require) the courts to consider foreign law (e.g., constitutional doctrines from United States and elsewhere) Some other constitutions — for example, those of Spain, Romania, and Colombia — also include provisions requiring that constitutional rights be interpreted in a manner consistent with the treaties those countries have ratified. See Constitution of Colombia, Art. 93 (1992, as amended through March 2005); Constitution of of Spain, Art. 10(2) (1978, as amended through Aug. 1992); Constitution of Romania, Art. 20(1) (1991).

Even in the absence of such constitutional mandates, the courts of many other countries interpret domestic constitutional, statutory, or common law in light of applicable international human rights standards. In British commonwealth jurisdictions, in which international law generally has no domestic legal effect unless it is incorporated by legislation, international treaties and other instruments frequently inform the judicial application domestic law in the area of human rights. In courts of the United Kingdom, the European Convention on Human Rights is a significant factor in the development of common law rights. See, e.g., *Derbyshire County Council v. Times Newspapers Ltd.*, 1992 Q.B. 770, 810-817 (European Convention and Civil and Political Covenant relevant in determining scope of common law free speech). See generally Andrew Clapham, "The European Convention on Human Rights in the British Courts: Problems Associated with the Incorporation of International Human Rights," in *Promoting Human Rights through Bills of Rights* 95 (Philip Alston, ed., 1999); Jeremy McBride and L.N. Brown, *The United Kingdom, the European Community and the European Convention on Human Rights*, 1981 Y.B. Eur. L. 167, 177. The Human Rights Act of 1998 incorporated the European Convention into British law, and it now may be invoked directly in domestic courts.

In Canada, courts look to international human rights law for interpretive guidance in construing the Canadian Charter of Rights and Freedoms, in applying statutes, and in identifying the contours of the common law. See, e.g, *Suresh v. Canada (Minister of Citizenship & Immigration)*, [2002] 1 S.C.R. 3, 31-32, 38; *Puspanathan v. Canada*, [1998] 1 S.C.R. 982 (using international human rights bodies' interpretations of the Convention relating to the Status of Refugees to interpret the Immigration Act implementing that Convention); *Mugesara v. Canada*, [2005] S.C.J. No. 39 (looking to international law of genocide to guide interpretation of the Criminal Code); *Baker v. Canada*, [1999] 2 S.C.R. 817 (using the Convention on the Rights of the Child to develop common law on administrative statutory discretion). The Supreme Court of Canada was asked the specific question of whether international or domestic law governs in the event of a conflict in relation to the right of peoples to self-determination, but the court failed to address the issue because no such conflict was determined to exist in that case. See *Quebec Secession Reference* [1998] 2 S.C.R. 217.

Australia's courts similarly look to international human rights norms for interpretive guidance. Perhaps the most prominent instance of this occurred in *Mabo v. Queensland* (No. 2), (1992) 175 C.L.R.1, in which the High Court overturned more than a century of common law doctrine based on the concept of terra nullius, a concept that regarded the land inhabited by Australian aboriginals prior to European settlement as legally vacant and that continued to serve to deny aboriginals rights to traditional lands. Justice Brennan of the High Court wrote that "unjust and discriminatory doctrine of that kind can no longer be accepted." Id. at 42. Instead, he reasoned, the common law in its present formulation should be interpreted in conformity with contemporary values embraced by Australian society and also in light of contemporary international law, which clearly prohibits racial discrimination: "If it were permissible in past centuries to keep the common law in step with international law, it is imperative in today's world that the common law should neither be nor be seen to be frozen in an age of racial discrimination." Id. at 41.

The constitutions of a number of countries explicitly incorporate the human rights affirmed in specified international sources. See Chapter 3, pages 148-149, for a discussion of constitutions incorporating references to the Universal Declaration of Human Rights. The Constitution of Nicaragua, for example, affirms and guarantees enjoyment of the rights affirmed in the international bill of human rights, the

American Declaration of the Rights and Duties of Man, and the American Convention on Human Rights. See Constitution of Nicaragua, Art. 46 (1987, as amended through 2000). See also, e.g., Constitution of Colombia, Art. 93 (incorporating human rights treaties to which Colombia is a party and according them primacy in domestic law); Constitution of Romania, 20 (incorporating the Universal Declaration and ratified human rights treaties, and giving precedence to the treaties over internally created law). Through such constitutional provisions, international human rights norms become more than mere interpretive backdrops; they are given constitutional status and may be directly applicable by courts of appropriate jurisdiction. See, e.g., Colombian Const. Ct. Judgment No.C-139/96 (1996) (applying provisions of ILO Convention No. 169 on Indigenous and Tribal Peoples to declare invalid parts of the Ley de Resguardos, a domestic statute governing Indian reserves).

International human rights norms can be incorporated into domestic law by general constitutional references to international law, such as that which appears in Article VI of the U.S. Constitution referring to treaties as part of the "Supreme Law of the Land." The constitutions of several countries have provisions generally incorporating treaties or other international law into the domestic legal order, but usually without judicial imposition of a self-execution doctrine such as that in the United States which generally limits the domestic legal effect of treaties. The Constitution of the Russian Federation, for example, provides:

> The commonly recognized principles and norms of the international law and the international treaties of the Russian Federation shall be a component part of its legal system. If an international treaty of the Russian Federation stipulates other rules than those stipulated by the law, the rules of the international treaty shall apply.

Constitution of the Russian Federation, Art. 15(4) (1993). The following extract indicates the significance of this provision for judicial decision-making, especially in relation to other provisions of the Russian Constitution concerning human rights.

Supreme Court of the Russian Federation, Decision on the applicability by ordinary courts of the universally recognized principles and norms of international law and the international treaties of the Russian Federation

No. 5 of Oct. 10, 2003 (Plenum), reprinted in 25 Hum. Rts. L. J. 108 (2004)

Pursuant to Article 15(4) of the Constitution of the Russian Federation the generally recognized principles and norms of international law and the international treaties of the Russian Federation are an integral part of its legal system.

. . . International treaties are of paramount importance in the protection of human rights and fundamental freedoms, in which context there is a need for further improvement in the work of courts concerning domestic application of the provisions of international law.

With the aim of ensuring proper and uniform application of international law in the working of courts the Plenum of the Supreme Court of the Russian Federation hereby decides to give the following interpretations:

1. Human and civil rights are acknowledged and guaranteed in the Russian Federation in accordance with universally recognized principles and norms of

international law and pursuant to the Constitution of the Russian Federation (Art. 17(1)).

Pursuant to Article 46(1) of the Constitution of the Russian Federation all persons are guaranteed legal protection of their basic rights and freedoms.

On the basis of the foregoing, and of the provisions of Article 15(4), Article 17(1) and Article 18 of the Constitution of the Russian Federation, human rights and freedoms are directly effective within the jurisdiction of the Russian Federation in accordance with generally recognized principles and norms of international law, and also with the international treaties of the Russian Federation. They define the meaning, content and application of laws, the activity of the legislature, executive and self-administering local authorities, and they secure justice.

The generally recognized principles of international law are to be understood as the fundamental imperative norms of international law applied and recognized by the international community of states as a whole, deviation from which is impermissible.

The principles of universal respect for human rights and conscientious fulfillment of international obligations are of particular importance among the universally recognized principles of international law.

A universally recognized norm of international law is to be understood as a rule of conduct accepted and recognized as legally binding by the international community of states as a whole....

2. Equally with the universally recognized principles and norms of international law the international treaties of the Russian Federation are a integral pat of its legal system....

3. Pursuant to Section 5(3) of the Federal Law "On the international treaties of the Russian Federation" the provisions of officially promulgated international treaties of the Russian Federal that do not require the promulgation of domestic acts for their application come directly into force in the Russian Federation. Appropriate legal acts are adopted to give effect to other provisions of the international treaties of the Russian Federation.

The attributes that indicate the impossibility of direct application of the provisions of an international treaty of the Russian Federation include, in particular, the presence in the treaty of a reference to the obligation of the States Parties to make changes to their domestic legislation.

When a court is examining civil, criminal or administrative cases direct application may be made of an international treaty of the Russian Federation that has come into force and become binding on the Russian Federation and the provisions of which do not require the promulgation of domestic acts for their application and are capable of giving rise to rights and obligations for physical persons and corporations subject to national law....

9. When administering justice the courts should bear in mind that... incorrect application by the court of the universally recognized principles and norms of international law and international treaties of the Russian Federation may provide a ground for the quashing or changing of the ruling. Norms of international law may be incorrectly applied when the court has not applied a norm of international law that should have been applied or when, conversely, it has applied a norm of international law that should not have been applied, or when the court has given an incorrect interpretation of a norm of international law.

10. . . . The Russian Federation, as a party to the Convention for the Protection of Human Rights and Fundamental Freedoms, accepts the jurisdiction of the European Court of Human Rights as binding on matters of the interpretation and application of the Convention and its Protocols in the case of a presumed infringement by the Russian Federation of the provisions of these treaty documents, when the presumed infringement occurred after the entry into force in relation to the Russian Federation. . . . Therefore use by the courts of the above-mentioned Convention must have regard to the practice of the European Court of Human Rights so as to avoid any infringement of the Convention. . . .

Implementation of the decisions concerning the Russian Federation implies that, should the need arise, the State will adopt special measures aimed at eliminating breaches of the human rights covered by the Convention, and the consequences of those breaches for the claimant, as well as general measures to prevent repetition of such breaches. The courts should act within their competence so as to ensure fulfillment of the obligations of the State arising from the participation of the Russian Federation in the Convention. . . .

Should circumstances conducive to breaches of the human rights and fundamental freedoms guaranteed by the Convention have emerged in the hearing of a case, the court is entitled to give an interlocutory ruling (or decision) in which it draws the attention of the appropriate organizations and officials to the circumstances and facts of infringement of the said rights and freedoms requiring the taking of the necessary measures. . . .

16. Should difficulties arise in interpreting the generally recognized principles and norms of international law and of the international treaties of the Russian Federation it is recommended that courts should use the instruments and decisions of international organizations, including the bodies of the United Nations Organization and its specialized agencies. . . .

[The court decides]

17. To recommend to the Judicial Department of the Supreme Court of the Russian Federation:

to ensure, in coordination with the representative of the Russian Federation at the European Court of Human Rights, that courts are informed of the practice of the European Court of Human Rights, especially on decisions affecting the Russian Federation, by sending the authentic texts and Russian translations of them;

to provide courts regularly and promptly with the authentic texts and official translations of the international treaties of the Russian Federation and other instruments of international law.

18. To recommend to the Russian Academy of Justice that it should pay special attention when arranging for the training, retraining and further training of judges and court officials to study of the generally recognized principles and norms of international law and of the international treaties of the Russian Federation, to regular analysis of the sources of international and European law, and to publication of the necessary instruction manuals, commentaries and monographs, and other educational, methodological and learned publications.

IV. *Final Comments and Questions*

1. In the United Kingdom and other British Commonwealth countries, including Canada and Australia, the Executive alone may enter into treaties without formally involving the legislative branch. Does this explain why, in these countries, the courts do not directly apply any treaty that has not been legislatively incorporated into national law? In other countries, such as Colombia, treaties are ratified following legislative approval by an act that is equivalent to a law, and such ratified treaties are directly applicable by the courts. Does the self-execution doctrine in the United States constitute an appropriate middle ground between these two systems, even with its complexities? Note that the U.S. Constitution, Art. II, §2, cl. 2, requires only the advice and consent of the Senate for a treaty to be ratified, not passage by the full Congress through the ordinary law-making process.

2. The Bill of Rights of the U.S. Constitution and numerous federal and state laws protect many of the rights found in international human rights law. As demonstrated by its reservations to the treaties it has ratified and its failure to ratify other treaties, the United States has endeavored to limit its international legal obligations to the rights already or about to be included in domestic law. Is this because human rights protections in U.S. law are generally adequate? Or because of a belief that rights to be legally protected should be determined primarily, if not exclusively, through domestic decision making? If it is the latter, is that a credible argument? Why is it that other countries seem more willing to include international human rights standards in domestic decision making? Does the U.S. Supreme Court's decision in *Roper v. Simmons* represent a welcome trend toward greater attention by the courts to international human rights standards? Or is any such trend overshadowed by the many barriers to direct judicial enforcement of international norms?

Chapter 7

UN Mechanisms for Addressing Violations of Human Rights

What Petition and Other Procedures Are Available for Implementing Human Rights Standards?

I. Introduction

Rights without remedies, Justice Holmes is purported to have remarked, are no rights at all. What remedies exist in the international arena to enforce human rights? Previous chapters have discussed the development of international human rights norms and the corresponding obligations that fall on states to effectively implement them. While arising from dynamics that involve multiple actors extending their influence to the international arena, international human rights law is made operational primarily through procedures that engage the legislative, executive, and judicial institutions of states at the domestic level. But it goes without saying that states all too often fail at this task, the very reason that international law came to embrace human rights in the first place. Thus, the international system over time has not only generated norms, but also has developed mechanisms to oversee their implementation. The procedures thus developed are the subject of this chapter.

The relationship between the domestic and international procedural levels is regulated by the principle of non-interference in matters essentially within the domestic jurisdiction of states, a corollary to the doctrine of state sovereignty reflected in Article 2(7) of the UN Charter. This principle favors decision making at the most local level possible, including decision making on human rights, and it reflects the realities of a world system that is still largely state-centered.

The principle of noninterference in domestic affairs is not absolute, however, and is less a barrier to international concern with human rights than in earlier periods in the development of international law. Today, as we shall see in this chapter, the principle only conditionally shields states from international scrutiny or intervention in human rights matters. International procedures exist to scrutinize state behavior with regard to human rights, and the intrusiveness of such procedures into the domestic realm is not always entirely a function of state consent to the procedures. Offending states, sometimes without their consent, may find themselves subject to a level of international scrutiny depending upon the gravity of noncompliance with applicable norms or the degree to which violations of human rights linger unchecked by domestic institutions and decision makers.

International procedures to advance compliance with human rights take many forms, including diplomatic debates in political fora, formal state-to-state complaints under relevant treaties, and discussions by expert bodies of reports submitted by states. Intergovernmental bodies may focus attention on human rights violations through investigations of particular countries or issues. All of these techniques, it will be noted, are triggered for the most part by the decisions of states individually and collectively. Increasingly, however, the initiatives of individual persons and other non-state actors have a role in the international enforcement of human rights.

Previous chapters have shown that the development of international human rights law closely tracks the recognition of the individual as distinct from the state as a proper subject of international law. Since states frequently are reluctant to protest human rights violations in other states, it is only logical and, indeed, absolutely necessary that not only states, but also individuals be accorded standing to protest such violations. For this reason, it is not surprising that the UN General Assembly, over 50 years ago, declared that "the right of petition is an essential human right, as is recognized in the Constitutions of a great number of countries" G.A. Res. 217B (III) (Dec. 10, 1948).

Several important international agreements, notably the UN Charter and the "Declaration of Santiago" establishing the Inter-American Commission on Human Rights in 1959, have been interpreted to permit the right of petition even in the absence of an express provision to that effect. The right has been codified as well in several other UN treaties, regional conventions, and specialized agreements, and procedures concerning these petitions (or "applications" or "communications," as they are sometimes called) have been created within various international organizations.

This chapter focuses on petition and other human rights implementation procedures that are part of the UN system, including those derived from the general authority provided by the UN Charter to advance human rights, as well as the optional petition and mandatory reporting procedures connected to particular human rights treaties. Procedures created under regional human rights arrangements in Africa, Europe, and the Americas are discussed in Chapters 5, 8, and 9. We begin here with a study of the first "communication" to be lodged under the Resolution 1503 procedure, a procedure that opened the door to UN examination and potential action on individual petitions.

II. The Situation in Greece: An Early Test Case

A. *Resolution 1503: High Expectations*

Despite the fact that the United Nations received thousands of complaints from individuals alleging human rights violations throughout the world for over a decade after 1945, no UN organ would consider such petitions (except in the context of trust and non-self-governing territories, discussed infra, page 562). The UN Commission on Human Rights was established shortly after the United Nations was created as a subsidiary intergovernmental body of the Economic and Social Council to function as the UN's principal human rights forum. But it was only in 1959 that the Commission was authorized to review summaries of communications received by the UN Secretary-General about human rights violations, and even then with the caveat that the Commission had no power to take any action in regard to any complaints concerning human rights. See E.S.C. Res. 728F (XXVIII) (July 30, 1959). Eight years later, in 1967, the Commission and its expert advisory body, the Sub-Commission on Prevention of Discrimination and Protection of Minorities (later renamed the Sub-Commission on the Promotion and Protection of Human Rights), were empowered to discuss and initiate studies of "situations which reveal a consistent pattern of violations of human rights as exemplified by . . . apartheid . . . and racial discrimination" and report and make recommendations to the Economic and Social Council. E.S.C. Res. 1235 (XLII) (June 6, 1967) (Documentary Supplement, page 821).

Finally, in 1970, the Economic and Social Council adopted Resolution 1503 (XLVIII) (May 27, 1970) (Documentary Supplement, page 906), which authorized the Commission and Sub-Commission to examine, in closed sessions, communications concerning situations "which appear to reveal a consistent pattern of gross and reliably attested violations of human rights." This landmark resolution, coupled with a subsequent resolution of the Sub-Commission which set out more specific procedures (Sub-Commission on Prevention of Discrimination and Protection of Minorities Res. 1 (XXIV) (Aug. 18, 1971)), broke the logjam at the United Nations that had until that time prevented it from discussing specific human rights violations, except for those occurring in colonial territories, southern Africa, and (after 1967) the Israeli-occupied territories in the Middle East. The UN was now in the business (or so it might seem) of at least discussing human rights worldwide through individual petitions.

Less than a year after the Sub-Commission adopted the procedures to consider communications under Resolution 1503, the first major petition arrived.

B. *Historical Note*

On April 21, 1967, a military junta of right-wing army colonels successfully seized control of the government of Greece. This coup d'etat was the fifth one in Greece since 1920, exemplifying the political unrest and volatility that often characterized Greece during its first century and a half of independence. The 1967 upheaval had its roots in a 1965 confrontation between King Constantine II and the popular Center Union party of Premier George Papandreou. The famous Aspida case brought these two powerful figures into combat. King Constantine alleged that the leftist organization Aspida (the Shield) was penetrating the army. An investigation by Papandreou's Center Union government reported that the group was harmless and that the King's accusations were a red herring. When Papandreou also demanded that King Constantine's right-wing Defense Minister Garoufalias resign, the King refused to comply and demanded and accepted Papandreou's resignation instead.

Popular support for Papandreou escalated into violence and bloodshed over the following months, and for the next two years the country was torn between two extremes, with caretaker governments continually being reshuffled. During this time, the alleged Aspida plotters, including both George Papandreou and his son Andreas, were indicted on charges of conspiracy to seize power and depose the monarchy. Although the Papandreous eventually were released, the trial served to agitate and polarize the nation even further. Most of the 28 defendants refused to defend themselves, on the ground that the entire Aspida case rested on trumped-up charges. Fifteen officers finally were convicted on March 16, 1967.

Only a few days before the close of the trial, Andreas Papandreou published an article charging that forces in Greece were conspiring to rig the upcoming May elections, thereby keeping his father from being chosen Premier. The dictatorship that Andreas Papandreou rightly predicted would oust the caretaker government of Premier Panayotis Kanellopoulos by military coup seized power in Athens in April 1967.

The five-officer military junta, led by Colonel George Papadopoulos, immediately occupied all government buildings, commandeered all media operations, and closed all borders. It declared a curfew, and all vehicles and pedestrians were banned from the streets. Broadcasts announced that the country was in a state of siege and that many constitutional rights were temporarily suspended, specifically:

> (1) Individuals can be apprehended and arrested without charge. They can be detained for any length of time. (2) There is no bail for political crimes. (3) All citizens, independent of position, can be brought before an emergency court-martial. (4) All gatherings, indoors or outdoors, are forbidden. All gatherings will be dissolved by force. (5) It is forbidden to form a syndicated [union] or group with labor union aims. Strikes are completely forbidden. (6) It is permitted to search houses, political premises, public buildings, all buildings, day and night, without special warrant. (7) It is forbidden to announce or publish any kind of information in any way through the press, radio and television without censorship beforehand. (8) Letters, telegrams and all means of communication will be censored. (9) Crimes, political crimes as well as those of the press, whether they have to do with private life or not, as well as the crimes to be judged by the court of appeal, will be judged by court-martial. (10) Everyone who commits a crime which should be punished by law, even if it is not against the army, will also be judged by court-martial.

Greece Under the Junta 14 (Peter Schwab and George D. Frangos eds., 1970).

Army patrols reportedly rounded up between 2,500 and 6,000 persons, including all the country's major political figures, within 48 hours of the coup. The most prominent among them were kept under arrest in Athens hotels. Other prisoners were detained in hastily built camps or converted soccer stadiums. Newspapers and other publications were shut down or placed under heavy censorship.

The scheduled May elections thus were preempted by mass arrests, censorship, purges, and the imposition of a state of siege, all executed in the name of fighting communism. Numerous reports of the torture of political prisoners, arbitrary arrests, and prolonged detention without charge began filtering through to international human rights organizations. In 1969, and again in 1971, the

Geneva-based International Commission of Jurists reported no change in the regime initially imposed by the military junta.

Greece: Justice in Blinkers

1 Int'l Comm'n Jurists Rev. 6, 6-7 (1969)

Little has changed in Greece since the Colonels seized power two years ago. The regime is still totalitarian. The old Constitution has been repealed and the main provisions of the new Constitution, those governing the fundamental freedoms of citizens, have been suspended. Despite assurances to the contrary, a return to democracy seems as remote as before; the regime seems even to be tightening its grip on the country as opposition to it becomes more overt. A symptom of the deterioration in the situation is the increase in political trials. Most of the accused are quite clearly being tried for their political opinions. The principal victims of this purge are the liberal intellectuals.

The International Commission of Jurists sent Observers to two of these trials. Mr. Michael Ellman, a solicitor from London, was sent to Athens in July 1968 to observe the trial of *Notaras and others* and Professor Edmond Martin-Achard, former President of the Genevan Bar, attended the trial of *Nestor and others*, held at Salonika in November 1968. The main points that Mr. Ellman made in his report are again to be found in that of Professor Martin-Achard, . . . which gives a good picture of how such trials are conducted.

Perhaps the most characteristic and disturbing feature brought out by these reports is the absence of any real legal basis to support the prosecution or the sentences imposed. The Colonels were not even able to resort to their Basic Decrees, a device purporting to give their actions legal validity. They finally fell back on a law dating from the civil war, No. 509 of 1947, which is now their principal instrument for removing opponents under the semblance of legality.

The arbitrary use that is made of this law is indefensible. Acts which are often so innocuous that in a free country they would not even be considered criminal are assimilated to treason. Moreover, Law 509 was an emergency law passed during a civil war to meet a special situation; it should have been repealed long ago. In addition, its purpose was to outlaw communism: the accused must be shown to have committed acts "in implementation of an ideology whose manifest and avowed aim is the forceful overthrow of the established social order and political system." In most of the cases the elements of the offence under Law 509 were not present. But that was no obstacle. The military judges were soldiers not lawyers and saw no reason why they should be prevented by purely legal considerations from convicting the accused and imposing disproportionate sentences upon them.

It is perhaps understandable that the Colonels should be fond of courts martial and should find in martial law a means of acquiring powers which are normally exercised by others. They are enabled to establish an authoritarian government, unembarrassed by opposition from those they rule over. But so long as martial law is in force, it is useless to talk of restoring the proper balance of power and normal political life, and equally useless for the Greeks to expect any guarantee of impartiality from the courts.

Human Rights Report on Greece

7 Int'l Comm'n Jurists Rev. 9, 10 (1971)

The International Commission of Jurists is also deeply concerned about the continuing cases of arbitrary arrests and prolonged detentions without trial in Greece. Among the most notorious of these is the detention of Judge Christos Sartzetakis and other members of the legal profession. The case of Judge Sartzetakis has received wide public attention because of his independence and personal courage. His brilliant handling of the Lambrakis case, at the conclusion of which he committed several senior police and gendarmerie officers to the Criminal Court for trial, was portrayed in the French film "Z." In May 1968, the military regime "suspended" for three days the provision of the Constitution guaranteeing the independence of the judiciary, and then dismissed Sartzetakis and a number of other judges for alleged acts "incompatible with the status of the Judiciary" and "political partiality" in the exercise of their functions. An appeal was lodged before the Council of State in July 1968, which led to the crisis between the Government and the highest administrative Tribunal. By annulling the judges' dismissal, the Council of State entered into an open conflict with the military regime who reacted by dismissing the President of the Council and forcing the resignation of its most distinguished members. Judge Sartzetakis was arrested on Christmas Eve, 1970. He was held by the military police, for nearly a year practically incommunicado with no date set for his trail. Following many powerful representations by legal professions from all over Europe and the United States and by many organizations including the International Commission of Jurists Judge Sartzetakis was at last released on 19 November 1971.

C. *Communication Alleging Violation of Human Rights in Greece*

His Excellency Kurt Waldheim May 19, 1972
Secretary-General of the United Nations
United Nations
New York, N.Y. 10017

Dear Mr. Secretary-General:

On behalf of [five] individuals and [two nongovernmental] organizations, and at their request, I address this letter to you as their Communication Concerning Human Rights in Greece:

You will see that this communication (with its annexes) reveals a consistent pattern of gross violations of human rights and fundamental freedoms by the Greek Government.

Some of the people whom I represent are victims of those violations. All have reliable knowledge that enables them to present clear evidence of the violations.

The object of this communication is to seek implementation of the relevant principles of the United Nations Charter, of the Universal Declaration of Human

Rights, and of other applicable instruments in the field of human rights. Among the rights that in Greece have been and are being grossly violated are these:

The right not to be subjected to torture or to cruel, inhuman or degrading treatment or punishment.
The right to liberty and security of person, and to be free from arbitrary arrest and detention.
The right to a fair and public hearing by an independent and impartial tribunal, and the right when charged with a penal offense to be presumed innocent until proved guilty in a public trial which respects the guarantees necessary for one's defense.
The right to freedom of opinion, expression, peaceful assembly and association.
The right to be free from arbitrary deprivation of nationality.
The right to take part in the government of one's country, directly or through freely chosen representatives, and the right of the Greek people to express their will in genuine elections.
The right to equal protection against discrimination that violates the Universal Declaration of Human Rights.

Annex I to this communication sets forth the clauses of the Universal Declaration of Human Rights that are pertinent. It also summarizes the discussions regarding Greece that took place in the UN Commission on Human Rights during 1968.

Annex II to this communication sets forth evidence of torture and of other gross violations, and it shows that they are part of a consistent pattern. Some of the evidence we set forth was examined formally by the Council of Europe in 1969 and 1970. Those European proceedings and the consequent condemnation of the Greek Government are discussed in Annex II. The Greek government rejected that verdict, however; and thus there has not been any settlement in accordance with the principles set forth in the Universal Declaration of Human Rights or other applicable documents in the field of human rights.

Annex III shows how the torture and other gross violations of human rights in Greece have continued since 1970, notwithstanding the Council of Europe action. Accordingly, the purpose of this letter is to secure, pursuant to ECOSOC Resolutions 728F and 1503, a study or investigation of the pertinent facts.

Therefore, Mr. Secretary-General, we request that you proceed pursuant to ECOSOC Resolutions 728F and 1503, and that you recommend whatever steps may be appropriate to help secure the study or investigation we herein request.

It should be recalled that Greece, as a Member of the United Nations, more than a quarter-century ago pledged itself to take joint and separate action, in cooperation with the Organization, for the achievement of the human rights goals set forth in Article 55 of the United Nations Charter.

Also to be recalled is the awesome pronouncement in the Universal Declaration of Human Rights that it is essential, if man is not to be compelled to have recourse, as a last resort, to rebellion against tyranny and oppression, that human rights should be protected by the rule of law.

Sincerely,
Frank C. Newman, Counsel

D. *The Sub-Commission's Response to the Communication*

Disappointing Start to New U.N. Procedure on Human Rights

9 Int'l Comm'n Jurists Rev. 5, 5-7 (1972)

At its forty-eighth session in 1970 the UN Economic and Social Council laid down in Resolution 1503 a new procedure for dealing with communications to the Secretary-General alleging violations of human rights and fundamental freedoms.

Under this new procedure there are three stages. First, the Sub-Commission on Prevention of Discrimination and Protection of Minorities is authorized to appoint a Working Party "to consider all communications, including replies of governments thereon . . . with a view to bringing to the attention of the Sub-Commission those communications, together with the replies of governments, if any, which appear to reveal a consistent pattern of gross and reliably attested violations of human rights and fundamental freedoms." Secondly, the Sub--Commission is requested to consider the communications brought before it by the Working Group, and any replies of governments and any other relevant information, "with a view to determining whether to refer to the Commission on Human Rights particular situations which appear to reveal a consistent pattern of gross and reliably attested violations of human rights requiring consideration by the Commission." Finally, the Commission on Human Rights, after examining any situation referred to it, it asked to determine (a) "whether it requires a thorough study by the Commission and a report and recommendation thereon to the Council," or (b) "whether it may be subject of an investigation by an adhoc committee to be appointed by the Commission, which shall be undertaken only with the express consent of the State concerned and shall be conducted in constant cooperation with the State and under conditions determined by agreement with it."

On 14 August 1971 the Sub-Commission adopted Resolution 1 (XXIV) setting out the procedures for dealing with the question of the admissibility of communications, and laying down the standards and criteria, and rulings relating to the sources of communications, the contents and nature of allegations, the existence of other remedies, and their timeliness. Admissible communications may originate from individuals or groups who are victims of violations, person having direct knowledge of violations, or non-governmental organizations acting in good faith and not politically motivated and having direct and reliable knowledge of such violations.

This new procedure constitutes a landmark in the history of the implementations of human rights. For the first time within the framework of the United Nations there is a procedure under which private individuals and non-governmental organizations, as well as governments, can raise complaints about violations of human rights within a state and have those complaints investigated and reported upon by an impartial international body.

By its constitution the Sub-Commission on Discrimination and Minorities is intended to be a body of independent experts. They are appointed by governments, but to act in their individual capacity and not as representatives of or spokesmen for their governments. Some governments adhere to the spirit of this procedure, but unfortunately in many cases the persons appointed are government employees and even members of official government missions to the U.N. It is inevitable in these circumstances that political considerations will tend to affect unduly the work of the Sub-Commission, thus following the pattern of its parent body, the Commission on Human Rights, whose members are explicitly government representatives.

The new procedure came into operation for the first time in 1972. The Working Group met in New York for the 10 days immediately preceding the meeting of the Sub-Commission in August. According to a report in the New York Times on September 21, 1972, the Working Group singled out for consideration by the Sub-Commission communications relating to three countries, Greece, Iran and Portugal.

The communication concerning Greece was a very complete dossier filed on May 19 and June 20, 1972, by Professor Frank Newman of the University of California as Counsel for the International Commission of Jurists, the International League for the Rights of Man, the Federation Internationale des Droits de l'Homme, the International Association of Democratic Lawyers, Amnesty International and seven Greek exiles who have personally suffered violations of their human rights; one of them was Lady Amalia Fleming. The communication included a large number of reports and personal affidavits by individuals who had been subjected to arbitrary arrest and detention, torture or cruel or inhuman treatment, persons who had been denied fair trials, who had been denied their right to freedom of opinion, expression, peaceful assembly and association, who had been deprived arbitrarily of their nationality, who had been prevented from expressing their will in genuine elections or in other respects subjected to violation of their human rights.

The Sub-Commission spent two days in private session considering the report of the Working Group and the communications referred to the Sub-Commission. Regrettably they failed to decide whether or not to refer to the Commission on Human Rights the communications brought to their attention by the Working Group. Instead they referred them back to the Working Group for another year. The reason put forward for this was that the Governments of the countries concerned had not replied to the communications. The official report of the Sub-Commission records the decision "that the Working Group shall consider at its next session those communications it was not able to examine at its last session, as well as communications received thereafter, and that *it may reexamine the communications singled out in its report, in the light of replies of governments, if any*" (italics added). The effect of this decision is that the consideration of allegations of gross violations of human rights, involving the liberty, the safety, the freedom from torture and even the lives of many individuals has been shelved for a whole year.

There appears to be no justification for this long delay. The governments concerned had ample opportunity to reply to the communications if they had wished to do so. Under the procedure for dealing with these communications the Secretary-General furnishes each Member State concerned with a copy of any communication concerning human rights which refers explicitly to that state or to territories under its jurisdiction, and the governments are asked when sending replies to say whether they wish their replies to be presented to the Commission in summary form or in full. If the governments concerned had not replied to the communications singled out by the Working Group, the reasonable inference is that they did not wish to do so.

The terms of the resolutions adopted by ECOSOC and by the Sub-Commission also clearly contemplate the reference to the Commission of communications to which there has been no governmental reply. As has been seen, ECOSOC Resolution 1503 (XLVIII) speaks of the Working Group bringing to the attention of the Sub-Commission "those communication, together with the replies of governments, *if any*" and the Sub-Commission are asked to consider those communications "and any replies of governments relating thereto." The Sub-Commission's Resolution 1 (XXIV) says that "Communications shall be admissible only if, after consideration thereof, together with the replies, *if any*, of the governments concerned, there are reasonable grounds to believe . . ." (all italics added).

In view of these clear provisions in the Resolutions laying down the procedure, it is difficult to avoid the conclusion that he decision of the Sub-Commission was affected by undue regard for the susceptibilities of governments.

It is to be hoped that he Commission on Human Rights and the ECOSOC will give clear directions to ensure that this new procedure is not brought into contempt by prevarication and delay.

E. The Reaction of the Greek Regime

The Greek regime eventually replied to the allegations of human rights violations in the Resolution 1503 communication and to similar charges that had been made by several states during sessions of the Commission on Human Rights outside the 1503 procedure.

Letter Dated 12 August 1973 from the Permanent Representative of Greece to the United Nations Addressed to the Secretary-General

U.N. Doc. E/5415 (1973)

Further to my letter of 9 May 1973, which was circulated as Economic and Social Council document E/5333, I have been instructed to express to you the deep regret of the Greek delegation of the fact that certain Member States are engaging in systematic attacks on Greece and its Government in violation both of the fundamental principles of the Charter and of the Economic and Social Council resolutions concerning the sequential procedure to be followed in considering any communication containing accusation of violations of human rights and fundamental freedoms. . . .

. . . My delegation is obliged to note with regret that since the summer of 1972 [the] procedural principles [of Resolution 1503] seem to have been lost sight of in so far as relates to Greece and that the distressing situation resulting from that fact shows a tendency to continue.

It seems quite probable that delegates of certain Member States, who are instructed by their Governments to support complaints against my country, are not sufficiently familiar with the procedural principles in question; what is clear, however, is that the competent division of the Secretariat has the responsibility of ensuring that this procedure is observed under all circumstances.

While it is in no sense attempting to assign blame in this matter, my delegation nevertheless hopes that the Division concerned will be instructed to take action henceforth as a *matter of course* to prevent the use of tactics which might detract from the high degree of objectivity and impartiality which must prevail in the consideration of questions of this kind. In that connection, mention should also be made of a specific incident which greatly disturbed my delegation and which I feel I must bring to your attention. On 21 September 1972, The New York Times published an article headed "U.N. Unit Said to Report Greeks Violate Human Rights" which reported allegations brought to the attention of the Sub-Commission by the Working Group and referred to the Sub-Commission's resolution 2 (XXV) of 28 August 1972. It has not so far been possible to obtain any concrete information indicating how this indiscretion occurred, but, since questions of this nature are to be kept strictly confidential and their premature disclosure can be extremely harmful both to the countries concerned and to the Secretariat, it is most desirable that strict measures should be taken to ensure that such leaks do not occur again. In addition, my delegation wishes to point out that the provisions of Article 2, paragraphs 1, 4, and 7, of the Charter are violated by the slanderous references to Greece and its Government in paragraph 262 of the report of the Commission on Human Rights. The paragraph in question, which we find it difficult to accept as it stands, grossly distorts the basic facts with which it deals, and this distortion was unfortunately not corrected by the Economic and Social Council at its fifty-fourth session.

In the light of what has been said above, this delegation is certain that, in your wisdom and acumen, you will take the necessary steps to put an end to the prejudiced and discriminatory attitude adopted towards Greece by the Commission on Human Rights, whose very reason for being is the elimination of all discrimination. If this unacceptable state of affairs should continue — and we trust that it will not — my delegation will have no choice but to draw the obvious conclusions and determine its attitude towards the Commission accordingly.

At the same time, wishing to prevent my misinterpretation of the reasons which might dictate a decision to by-pass the machinery of the Commission on Human Rights if the situation should deteriorate, the Government of Greece, which has no cause for self-reproach and nothing to hide, feels it would be useful to bring to the attention of all Member States, for the purpose of refuting the oral and written allegations which have up to now been communicated to the Commission, the following information on the laws and regulations applied in Greece in conformity with the provisions of the Universal Declaration of Human Rights and the relevant articles of the Charter:

[Greece then addressed the alleged violations of human rights, denying each of them.]

(Signed) C.P. Panayotacos
Ambassador
Permanent Representative of Greece
to the United Nations

While the official reaction of the Greek regime was to counterattack the UN's handling of the 1503 procedure and then to deny any violations of human rights in Greece, a dramatic turnabout occurred not more than two weeks after Ambassador Panayotaco's letter to the Secretary-General. On August 20, 1973, President George Papadopoulos officially ended martial law and declared a general amnesty for all political prisoners, including Alexandros Panagoulis, who had attempted his assassination in 1968. The Sub-Commission thereupon decided to remove Greece from its agenda and turn its attention to other matters.

F. *The Overthrow of the Greek Regime and the Sub-Commission's Role Therein*

A little over two months after the release of prisoners and the declaration of amnesty, the Papadopoulos regime was overthrown by yet another military coup. An International Commission of Jurists (ICJ) report four months into the regime of General Phaedon Ghizihis concluded that "the new regime in Greece is showing no greater respect for the principles of the Rule of Law than did its predecessor, and there is even less legal basis for it. The authority of the government rests on naked force alone" (ICJ Press Release, 25 March 1974).

On May 17, 1974, a communication similar to that of May 19, 1972, was sent to the UN Secretary-General on behalf of numerous human rights groups concerned with the situation in Greece. Again, the procedures that route such petitions to the Sub-Commission and the Commission on Human Rights failed to produce a condemnation of the well-documented violations of human rights by this new Greek regime.

The Ghizihis regime itself finally was toppled, but only because it precipitated the Cyprus crisis, which nearly plunged it into full scale war with Turkey. Thus, constitutional government returned to Greece at last on August 24, 1974, when Premier Constantine Karamanlis swore in a civilian cabinet. Several officials in the military regime were subsequently convicted of torture and other human rights violations, and Judge Christos Sartzetakis became President of Greece.

During the final year of the Greek military regime, the Sub-Commission maintained its record of silence, prompting the following comments to the Sub-Commission (made five days before the return of civilian rule) by Amnesty International and the International Student Movement for the UN.

Statement by Amnesty International and the International Student Movement for the UN

UN Doc. E/CN.4/Sub.2/SR.708 (1974)

Mr. Chairman, we suggest that August 1974, the second month of crisis on the Island of Cyprus, hardly seems to be the month for continued silence as to gross violations of human rights in Cyprus and in Greece. Today the Secretariat seems to have forgotten that, seven years ago, this Sub-Commission did report to the Human Rights Commission, under par. 2 of ECOSOC resolution 1235, regarding activities of the Greek militarists. There then were two years of silence, pending the condemnation of the Greek colonels by the Council of Europe. There then were four more years of silence (1970, '71, '72, '73). Many friends of the United Nations wondered *why*, since the evidence of torture and other gross violations seemed so persuasive.

Mr. Smirnov, this morning and again this afternoon, correctly stated that this Sub-Commission can be proud of its fine record as to apartheid, and as to racial discrimination generally, in Southern Africa. But Ms. Gillian Walker last year observed that many students, concerned about the United Nations, were asking whether the Greek Case did not illustrate a basic rule of this Sub-Commission, to hear no evil, see no evil, speak no evil, except as to Southern Africa and (occasionally and appropriately) the Middle East.

Last month the Greek militarists, in their desperate and cynical last act, launched in Cyprus their third coup, thus unleashing greeds and fears and passions that now involve the people of three nations in a brutal war that most of us thought was inconceivable.

We will never know for sure whether that war might have been prevented. If during the last four years, however, available United Nations procedures for protecting human rights had been utilized, can anyone say for sure that the Greek militarists would have retained the awful, minimal strength that enabled them insanely to ignite this current crisis? Rarely do we witness a situation where violations of human right leads so directly, so indisputably to war. . . .

III. Analyzing the Procedures and Problems of Resolution 1503

Although the Working Group of the UN Sub-Commission failed to refer the communication concerning the situation in Greece to the Commission on Human Rights, during 1973 it did refer communications involving eight other countries. The Sub-Commission, after much deliberation, referred to the Commission communications describing particular situations in Brazil, Britain, Burundi, Guyana, Indonesia, Iran, Portugal, and Tanzania for consideration. See 11 *Int'l Comm'n Jurists Rev.* 27 (1973). Some observers viewed this development as a noteworthy victory compared with the inertia shown in the case of Greece. However, the Commission refused to initiate either a thorough study or even an ad hoc investigation into any of the eight situations.

Many of the procedural problems in the 1503 process were immediately apparent and are raised in the following statement by the late Professor Frank Newman, who authored the 1503 communication in the Greek case (and who was the co-author of the first edition of the present book).

Frank C. Newman, The New U.N. Procedures for Human Rights Complaints: Reform, Status Quo, or Chamber of Horrors?

Hearings on the International Protection of Human Rights before the Subcomm. on International Organizations and Movements of the House Comm. on Foreign Affairs, 93d Cong. 1st Sess. 715-716 (Comm. Print 1973)

[The relevant resolutions] provide that:

(1) if the communication refers to a Government or to territories under its jurisdiction, it gets a copy and also a chance to reply;

(2) "a brief indication of the substance" of the communication appears on a confidential list prepared for each annual session of the Commission on Human Rights;

(3) that list is accompanied by Governments' replies, "in summary form or in full" as each Government requests;

(4) the list and the replies, including "a brief description" of each communication, are furnished every month to the members of the Sub-Commission.

One also learns from these resolutions that at no time will the author (or lawyer) ever be allowed to see the list or the Government's reply or the brief indication of the substance or the brief description of the communication.

During July/August, "for a period not exceeding ten days immediately before the session of the Sub-Commission [held in August/September]," a 5-person working group elected by the Sub-Commission from its members meets to "consider all communications, including replies of Governments thereon." In 1972 the Secretariat submitted 27,577 communications to the working group; more than 20,000 were considered.

These questions come to mind:

1. May the author (or lawyer) attend those meetings? Testify? Argue?
2. Will the author be notified if the working group's action is favorable? Unfavorable?
3. May the author be told anything about the group's proceedings?
4. May translations be checked, for accuracy and completeness?

The answer to each of those questions is no. The working group's sole function seems to be "bringing to the attention of the Sub-Commission those communications, together with replies of Governments, if any, which appear to reveal a consistent pattern of gross and reliably attested violations of human rights and fundamental freedoms within the terms of reference of the Sub-Commission."

At higher levels is the UN more respectful of authors' concerns? Again the answer is no.... The governing rule is that "all actions... remain confidential until such time as the Commission may decide to make recommendations to the Economic and Social Council." Further, the Sub-Commission's meetings are "private"; the working group's meetings are both "private" and "closed"; and "the results of the Working Group's work shall be communicated to the Sub-Commission confidentially."

Where does all that leave authors (and their lawyers)? In hopelessly complete ignorance, unhappily. They get absolutely none of the protections that due process, natural justice, and similar concepts rightfully are presumed to ensure.

We must look also at the rights of the accused Government. As we have seen it has a chance to "reply." Yet its representatives have no right to attend meetings, testify, or argue. Unless the rules are breached it has no more access than does the author to information regarding what has happened. Iran, for example, was singled out in the working group's secret 1972 report because of several communications thought to reveal a consistent pattern of gross violations. No Iranian was a member of the Sub-Commission. A representative of the Iranian government was an observer at the Sub-Commission's session, but we may not infer that he or she observed the "private meetings." So far as the record shows, Iran still has no notice as to the present status of those critical communications....

Despite the unsatisfactory beginnings of the resolution 1503 procedure, the number of petitions invoking it quickly mounted. Two decades after the adoption of the procedure, a well-informed observer summarized the activity under it and evaluated the procedure as follows.

Philip Alston, *The Commission on Human Rights*

In The United Nation and Human Rights 146-152 (Philip Alston ed., 1992) (footnotes omitted)

In numerical terms the United Nations has never had problems attracting complaints about the behavior of governments. This has remained true despite various efforts to discourage their submission. Even in the late 1940s and early 1950s, when the complaints were virtually ignored, annual figures of 20,000 or so appear not to have been uncommon. From the time when the 1503 procedure began functioning (in 1972) until the mid-1980s an average of 25,000 complaints were received annually. In 1988 and 1989 the numbers rose to 200,000 and 300,000 respectively. Although much of the increase is due to well-orchestrated letter-writing campaigns involving a handful of situations, the numbers still attest to a significant awareness of the procedures combined with an apparent faith, on the part of at least a few groups, in their potential effectiveness.

... [I]n the absence of a decision [by the Commission] to go public, the entire [1503] procedure is shrouded in secrecy, with each of its stages being accomplished in confidential sessions by the bodies concerned. Nevertheless, the details have invariably been leaked to the media for one reason or another and the complete documentation in cases concerning Equatorial Guinea, Uruguay, Argentina, and the Philippines.

In statistical terms, the 1503 procedure has touched an impressive number of countries. On the basis of unofficial sources it seems that at least forty-five countries have been reported to the Commission under the procedure since 1972. More authoritatively, however, it can be said that since the Commission began to officially identify the situations before it, in 1978, thirty-nine States have been subject to scrutiny as of the end of the 1991 session.*

Before seeking to evaluate the procedure, it is essential to review the often-skimpy concrete evidence that is in the public domain. It can be said at the outset, however, that most of the available snapshots provide few grounds for optimism as to the procedure's effectiveness. Thus, for example, the first attempt to put specific situations on the Commission's 1503 agenda, in 1972, rapidly became bogged down at the level of the Sub-Commission which was loathe to act on its own Working Group's recommendation that the focus be on Greece, Iran, and Portugal. The choice of such a list served to put those who had championed the 1503 procedure, in the hope that it would become a potent tool in the struggle against racism and colonialism, quickly on notice that the procedure could equally well be applied to other offenders. While one of the three was a colonial power and another was from the Western group, the latter case involved the sort of violations

* By 2005, the total number of states examined had grown to 84. These countries, which are in all regions of the world, are listed on the website of the Office of the High Commissioner for Human Rights, *http://www.ohchr.org/english/bodies/chr/stat1.htm*. — Eds.

of which many of the Third World regimes might equally stand accused, if not today perhaps tomorrow. Establishing such a precedent, especially right from the outset, would not augur well. In addition, the other accused State was actually from the Third World, thus indicating that the racists and imperialists might not be able to monopolize the spotlight as had been hoped by many of the procedure's original sponsors. The Sub-Commission decided to do nothing for a year so that the governments concerned might be given more time to respond to the allegations if they so wished. The International Commission of Jurists deplored this decision and, in the diplomatic language of the day, accused the Sub-Commission of being "affected by undue regard for the susceptibilities of governments." The subsequent fate of at least one of these cases, that of Greece, is particularly well documented. In brief the Sub-Commission managed to defer any action until 1974, by which time the military government had been overthrown.

Another notorious case in the early years was that of Uganda under President Idi Amin. In 1974, confronted by allegations that Amin had killed 75,000 people since coming to power in 1970, the Sub-Commission placed the case on the Commission's agenda. But because Amin was then chairman of the Organization of African Unity, he had little difficulty in mobilizing the support needed to have the case struck off the Commission's agenda. Although Uganda was again placed on the list, it was not until 1978 that the Commission finally sought to send an envoy to Amin, still on a confidential basis. But before this could have any effect Amin had been overthrown after an invasion by Tanzanian troops. Among the many troubling aspects of this case was the fact that a brutal regime had managed, by virtue of playing the 1503 game, to keep its case off the Commission's public agenda over a four-year period. Another case in respect of which the relevant documentation is now available is that of Uruguay which was on the Commission's 1503 list from 1978 to 1985. Human rights NGOs had reported thousands of cases of arbitrary arrest and torture, a significant number of disappearances and deaths and the destruction of the rule of law. The first violation to be found by the Human Rights Committee under the Optional Protocol had concerned the treatment of a detainee in Uruguay. [The individual complaint procedure under the Optional Protocol to the International Covenant on Civil and Political Rights is discussed infra, page 592.] The Committee began consideration of the case in August 1977.

Faced with an imposing dossier of allegations, the Commission requested the then Secretary-General (Waldheim) to undertake a direct contacts mission to investigate prison conditions. He appointed Javier Perez de Cuellar (later to become UN Secretary-General) as his envoy. Perez de Cuellar's report was soon leaked to the press and provides a dismal insight into the type of fact-finding reports that can be produced when the glare of publicity is eliminated in the context of human rights procedures. It is: aridly descriptive; openly predicated on the assumption that respect for, and co-operation with, the government is the principal ground rule for the mission; determinedly unprobing; apologist in its emphasis on the 'justifications' cited by the government; and entirely at odds with authoritative reports by the International Committee of the Red Cross and other groups in concluding blandly that prisoners were being held under 'normal detention conditions'. In the view of one commentator this episode showed that the 1503 procedure had turned 'dialogue' into an end in itself. "Dialogue," to the United Nations, meant "cooperating," and cooperation brought its reward: the case stayed confidential. If it felt under any pressure, an astute government could always introduce minor changes and present them as "improvements." There was endless room to maneuver for clever diplomats . . . '. In the event the Commission, instead of appointing a Special Rapporteur as had been proposed, accepted an Argentinian amendment to maintain direct contacts with the government. But in doing so it also gave the thumbs down to Perez de Cuellar's report by noting that it had been helpful to the Commission in elucidating the views of the Government, a function which it had hardly been intended to achieve.

Another major failure of the 1503 procedure which has recently been documented in great detail is that of the disappearances in Argentina during the 1970s and early 1980s. At the first try, in 1977, the case failed to get past the Sub-Commission's Working Group. The following year it reached the Sub-Commission but went no further. By 1979 the situation was so grave that the Commission began to seek a public response . . . even though the case had still not reached it under 1503. The latter event occurred in 1980 and it remained on the 1503 agenda until 1985. Following an exhaustive assessment of the procedure in the case of Argentina, Iain Guest concluded that it had, if anything, been positively harmful to the cause of those wishing to put an end to the continuing violations under the military government. This resulted primarily from the ready availability of opportunities to manipulate the procedure at each stage.

In concluding this review of some specific country studies, it must be conceded that the range of 1503 cases in respect of which public documentation is available is not only limited but now also somewhat dated. In recent years, however, the record would not appear to be much better. In the late 1980s and in 1990 NGO observers have tended to be highly critical of the results obtained (or, rather, not obtained) by the procedure, both in general, and in specific cases as China, Iraq, Somalia, Syria, Zaire, etc.

The experience gained with the 1503 procedure over almost twenty years is sufficient to enable some general observations to be made about it. With respect to the range of situations taken up it appears that: (a) alleged violations of economic, social, and cultural rights have never been examined seriously, despite a resolution by the Commission urging that they should be, (b) the Commission has responded to violations of only a limited range of civil and political rights, which in turn has ensured that while Third World countries are disproportionately represented on the 1503 blacklist, developed countries (both West and East) have only very rarely been called to account,* (c) there is probably a *de facto* limit of 6 to 8 on the number of countries that the Commission is prepared to take on at any one time, but since a similar principle applies to the public country-specific procedures, 1503 effectively doubles the number of countries that can be "named"; (d) despite the focus on "situations" some individuals have been directly assisted under the procedure; and (e) many of the situations dealt with under the Commission's public procedures have been raised earlier in the 1503 context.

* As of the early 1990s, the rare exceptions were Albania, the German Democratic Republic, Japan, Portugal, and Turkey; the list now also includes the Czech Republic, Estonia, (reunified) Germany, Latvia, Lithuania, Slovenia, the United Kingdom, and the United States.—Eds.

With respect to the actual functioning of the procedure it is clear that some of the early wrinkles were effectively ironed out in the course of the first decade. In particular, the relationship between the public [examination of situations authorized by ECOSOC Res. 1235 (discussed infra) and the private 1503 procedure], which was often invoked in an effort to confine discussions to the latter domain in the 1970s, was resolved in such a way as to make it clear that only the proceedings themselves and the details of decisions taken were confidential. There is thus no bar to focusing on the same country in both procedures at the same time. Nevertheless, the procedure is designed to move extremely slowly and deliberations are, as a result, too often based on outdated information. As one Filipina activist put it, use of the 1503 procedure to put pressure on the Marcos regime 'was not done with any illusion that immediate specific relief would be forthcoming'. Rather, 'it was used simply as another device to generate adverse propaganda against' the regime. Another criticism of the functioning of the procedure concerns the Commission's apparent failure to structure its working methods under 1503. Consequently, the response in one situation will often bear little relationship to that adopted in another generally comparable one. While no two situations are identical and attempts to draw comparisons are often flawed, there is still room to seek some consistency in responses, to seek a more uniform structure for reports prepared, and to question States representatives in a more systematic fashion. From the records that are available, the 'dialogue' that takes place is usually unadulterated political horse-trading rather than a probing inquiry into the facts and a quest for the most effective potential response. Thus, those who have observed the procedure in practice have noted that the level of debate in the closed sessions is sometimes abysmally low and reveals that delegations have done little, if any, serious preparation.

Providing a general evaluation of the 1503 procedure is difficult but necessary. The question is whether the procedure provides adequate returns in terms of the investments of faith, time, energy, and media attention that have been made in it; whether, on balance, it succeeds in putting enough pressure on enough countries in ways that could not more effectively be achieved by other means. Some of those means might already be in existence; others might more easily be created if the 1503 procedure were to be eliminated.

The first point to be made is that the historical value of the 1503 procedure cannot be doubted. In many ways it laid the groundwork for the development of the potentially effective public (i.e., resolution 1235-based) response to violations which began to come into its own after 1979. It put paid once and for all to the domestic jurisdiction *canard;* it accustomed States to the need to defend themselves and gave them practice in examining (and prosecuting) the performance of others; it galvanized some of the NGOs at a time when some of the other procedures offered even lower rates of return; and it exposed the Commission and Sub-Commission to the real world of violations more effectively than any earlier exercise had. But a valuable historical role does not of itself justify the procedure's retention. . . .

Examination of communications under the 1503 procedure has continued apace since the above observations were made, with little or no perceptible change in those characteristics of the procedure that have either drawn criticism or cautious optimism. In 2000, reforms were undertaken to streamline the procedure by formalizing a mechanism for initial screening of communications, eliminating their consideration by the full Sub-Commission, and otherwise regularizing the steps in the procedure. See E.S.C. Res. 2000/3 (June 16, 2000). But in other respects the procedure remained essentially as before, including with respect to the admissibility of communications and confidentiality. The following extract briefly describes the mechanics of the 1503 procedure as it stood just before the decision to replace of the Commission on Human Rights with the higher level Human Rights Council. See infra, p. 564. These mechanics are unchanged as of this writing except for their adaptation to the organizational restructuring that will come about with the newly established Council.

Nigel S. Rodley and David Weissbrodt, *United Nations Nontreaty Procedures for Dealing with Human Rights Violations*

In Guide to International Human Rights Practice 45, 69-71 (Hurst Hannum ed., 4th ed. 2004)

...The UN Secretariat [through the Office of the High Commissioner for Human Rights (OHCHR)] acknowledges receipt [of a communication] but usually does not otherwise correspond with the author of the communication. Unless the communication is screened out as "manifestly ill-founded," the OHCHR sends it to the government concerned and summarizes it in a monthly confidential list. A Working Group on Communications composed of five Sub-Commission members (one form each of the UN's five geographic regions) meets in private for two weeks in August immediately following the annual sub-commission session to review the confidential lists (the group also has access to the full texts of communications) and any corresponding government replies. Since governments are given a minimum of twelve weeks to reply, a communication transmitted to a government after the third week of May will probably not be considered for another year, unless the Secretariat receives a reply from the government prior to the group's presessional meeting. NGOs should thus submit their communications well before the deadline.

If at least three members of the group agree that a communication appears to reveal a consistent pattern of gross violations of human rights, the group forwards it to the Commission. The Working Group also may keep the matter pending for a year. (Before 2000, the Working Group referred communications to the Sub-Commission, which then decided in closed session which of the situations referred to it by the working group should be forwarded to the next session of the Commission.) The situations in eighty-four different countries have been referred to the Commission since the procedure's creation, although no public announcement is made at this stage about which countries are involved.

A parallel Working Group on Situations, appointed from among the states which are members of the Commission, meets for one week before the Commission's annual session. It examines the country dossiers; determines whether to refer a particular situation to the Commission, keep the matter pending or discontinue consideration; and makes recommendations to the Commission about how to deal with the situations referred by the Sub-Commission. The Commission is free to accept or reject the Working Group's recommendations.

The Commission considers the "situations" (note that it is no longer dealing only with the forwarded "communications") in closed session. Resolution 1503 empowers it to make a "thorough study" or institute an "investigation by an ad hoc committee." No such committee is known to have been created, however, and it would appear (although it has not been publicly confirmed) that only one thorough study has been initiated.

In practice, the Commission has developed a wide range of techniques short of a "thorough study" to investigate a particular situation. The primary ones include (in descending order of their perceived seriousness): (1) referring the situation for consideration by the Commission in public session (this occurred with regard to both Chad and Liberia in 2003); (2) appointing an independent expert/rapporteur (this occurred in 1995, with respect to Chad); (3) asking the Secretary-General to establish direct contacts with the government concerned; (4) asking the government for further information: and (5) and keeping the situation "under review." In each of these cases, the situation is reported on and considered the following year. Of course, the Commission also may simply decide to discontinue consideration.

At the end of the Commission's closed discussions, the Chairperson announces publicly the names of the countries in which situations have been considered and those which have been discontinued. The public is thereby informed of the countries that the Commission is reviewing under the 1503 procedure, but not of the action taken or the nature of the alleged violations. Eventually, the Commission may recommend that ECOSOC put the situation on the public record. ECOSOC has only rarely been called onto do this, either at the request of a new government in the country concerned (e.g., Argentina after democracy was restored under President Raul Alfonsin) or when a country totally refused to cooperate with the Commission (e.g., Equatorial Guinea's refusal to supply any defense to accusations against it). In 1988, ECOSOC failed to act on a Commission recommendation to make the file of Albania public, although it did pave the way for the Commission's public consideration of the situation.

As noted in the above extract, the 1503 procedure resulted in placing Liberia under scrutiny that eventually became part of the Commission's public deliberations. Illustrating a technique sometimes used by the Commission in response to communications under the 1503 procedure, the Commission appointed an independent expert to investigate and report back on the situation. In a rare lifting of the shroud of confidentiality usually provided within the 1503 procedure, which met with little or no resistance from a discredited government embroiled in civil war, the Commission decided to make public the following report of the independent expert "so as to encourage assistance to the Government and the people of Liberia in restoring full respect for human rights and fundamental freedoms." Note by the Secretariat, UN Doc. E/CN.4/2004/8, para. 1 (Sept. 25, 2003) (introducing the report).

Report of the independent expert of the Commission on Human Rights [Charlotte Abaka] on the situation of human rights in Liberia submitted under the 1503 procedure

UN Doc. E/CN.4/2004/8 (Sept. 25, 2003)

INTRODUCTION

1. At its fifty-eighth session, the Commission on Human Rights considered the human rights situation in Liberia under the confidential 1503 procedure and adopted its first confidential decision relating to Liberia on 4 April 2002. The Commission having examined the material relating to the human rights situation in Liberia brought before it under the 1503 procedure . . . decided to appoint an independent expert under the confidential 1503 communications procedure, with the purpose of establishing direct contacts with the Government and the people of Liberia.

2. On 14 October 2002, the Chairperson of the fifty-eighth session appointed Ms. Charlotte Abaka as independent expert on the human rights situation in Liberia. Ms. Abaka has been for the last 12 years a member of the Committee on the Elimination of Discrimination against Women (CEDAW), which she chaired for the last 2 years. The Secretariat informed the Government of Liberia of this decision by a note verbale dated 15 October 2002, through which the agreement of the Government of Liberia was requested to an in situ visit by the independent expert at the beginning of the month of December 2002.

3. . . . [T]he mission to Liberia took place from 16 to 21 December 2002. In this connection, the independent expert welcomes the Government's agreeing to her mission, and appreciates the warm reception that she was given as well as the general spirit of cooperation and the efforts of the Liberian authorities to facilitate the mission. . . .

7. The recent civil war — which is still ongoing in some parts of the country — has devastated Liberia, leaving a sad feeling of desolation. In Monrovia, the capital, the majority of the buildings are now totally destroyed. There has been no reconstruction at all, and the volatile security situation hampers any attempt to invest in infrastructure or development projects, since the financial resources are used for defence or security matters. Five years after the civil war, the country still has no electricity and no running water, even in the nation's capital. Many schools are still closed and in the ones that are open teachers who have not been paid for several months have difficulty in performing their duties. The existing schools are mainly private institutions for which only an elite of students can afford the enrolment fees. The same problems apply to hospitals, clinics and medical services in general. The savage civil war from 1989 to 1997 destroyed most of the infrastructure of the country and all social services remain disrupted. Improvement in the sectors of health, water and sanitation, as well as local community development, is urgently needed. Moreover, the fact that an entire generation of Liberians knows only war and has never received any education is a matter of serious concern for the future. The grievous problem of child soldiers is illustrative of the fate of the young generation. . . .

9. The independent expert also noted during her visit that many of the existing problems originate from long-standing intolerance between the different ethnic groups in the country.

10. The present report reflects information and figures at the disposal of the independent expert as of 31 December 2002.

I. Historical and Political Situation

11. Liberia (111,370 km2) has a population of 3,225,837 (July 2001 estimate). It is bounded by Guinea to the north, Côte d'Ivoire to the east and north-east and Sierra Leone to the north-west. The southern border, with a coastline of almost 600 km, faces the Atlantic Ocean.

12. Liberia is the only West African country never to have had formal colonial status. Early in the nineteenth century rights to the territory were bought by United States philanthropic organizations, which wanted to use the area as a safe haven for the growing free black population of the United States. In 1847 these settlers declared Liberia a republic.

13. For most of the following 130 years the True Whig Party (TWP) — monopolized by the descendants of freed slaves, the Americo-Liberians — was the only significant political organization in Liberia. TWP rule ended on 12 April 1980, when the president, William Tolbert, was overthrown and Samuel Doe set up a 15-member military People's Redemption Council to run the country.

14. The decade following the 1980 coup was marked by growing opposition to Mr. Doe's regime. There was a plethora of actual or alleged coup attempts, which led to executions and widespread detentions. Multiparty elections in October 1985, widely believed to have been rigged, returned Mr. Doe to power with a thin majority.

15. On 24 December 1989, a small group of armed rebels invaded Nimba county from Côte d'Ivoire, led by Charles Taylor. The rebels took advantage of the general climate of ethnic tension in the country, and by June 1990 all but the capital, Monrovia, was in rebel hands.

16. Seven years of civil war were brought to a close in 1996 when disarmament and demobilization finally started at the end of November. International observers monitored the presidential and legislative elections which were held in July 1997. Charles Taylor won the presidential vote by a landslide, while his National Patriotic Party (NPP) secured the majority in the National Assembly.

17. Unfortunately, contrary to expectations that peace would return to the country with the holding of elections in 1997, Liberia has over the years been afflicted by hostilities of varying intensity and the conflict continues, mainly in the northern and western parts of the country.

18. The conflict is particularly intense in Lofa county, where a rebel group called Liberians United for Reconciliation and Democracy (LURD), allegedly based in Guinea, aims to overthrow the current Government. The United Nations Panel of Experts on Liberia, established by Security Council resolution 1306 (2000), estimated that LURD has some 2,000 men fighting on its side. According to the information received, LURD is intensifying its attacks against governmental forces beyond the northern part of the country (Lofa county) to the north-western and central parts (Gbarpolu, Bomi and Bong counties) towards the capital.

II. Economic and Social Factors

19. Liberia is currently one of the world's poorest countries. In 1991 it had a per capita gross national product (GNP) income of US$ 669, which decreased to US$ 390 in 1995 and may be less than US$ 170 today (2001 estimate). On the other hand, Liberia is potentially rich in natural resources, notably iron ore, diamonds, gold, timber and rubber. Indeed, a 1995 World Bank study, which included natural resources in its measurement of total national wealth per head, ranked Liberia 132nd out of 193 countries worldwide — higher than Nigeria, Côte d'Ivoire or Zimbabwe.

20. The Government that was installed in 1997 inherited an enormous national debt burden of US$ 2.8 billion and has not been able to generate the required resources domestically and internationally to revive the economy to its pre-civil war level. There is a widespread feeling among all interlocutors, both official and not, that Liberia was "abandoned" by the international community soon after 1997. This "abandonment", and the imposition of sanctions by the Security Council in March 2001, have been cited by the Government as the major causes of its inability to mobilize both external and domestic resources for reconstruction and humanitarian needs. Sanctions, imposed by Council resolution 1343 (2001) for the alleged support of the Government of Liberia for the Revolutionary United Front in Sierra Leone and other armed groups in the region, included the re-imposition of an arms embargo already established by Security Council resolution 788 (1992), a ban on the import of rough diamonds and selective travel bans.

21. The independent expert was informed that after five years of transition, GDP remains under 50 per cent of its pre-civil war level....

IV. Obstacles to Greater Respect for Human Rights

34. According to the information received, the Government of Liberia has done little to prevent human rights violations and has not brought the perpetrators of such violations to justice. Indeed, the high level of impunity is considered to be one of the key factors in the current alarming rate of human rights violations. Concerns about the independence and impartiality of the judiciary are also reported. The Liberian judicial system still suffers from the negative consequences of the civil war and is in strong need of resources and logistics, while judicial officials would need training in human rights standards.

35. The independent expert was informed that the imposition of a state of emergency on 8 February 2002 by President Taylor led to yet more human rights violations. She was further informed that even after the lifting of the state of emergency in September 2002, serious human rights violations, including restrictions on freedom of expression, arbitrary arrests and detention, torture and ill-treatment, continue to occur in the country....

RIGHT TO LIFE AND SECURITY OF PERSON

38. Armed conflict between government forces and LURD, which began in 1999, continues. According to the information received, both sides are guilty of

deliberate and arbitrary killings of unarmed civilians, rape and other forms of sexual abuse, abductions and forced recruitment of children. Ill-treatment, torture and arbitrary arrest of suspected members of LURD or other purported "dissidents" by Liberian security forces have been widely reported. Abduction and forced recruitment of young men and boys by Liberian security forces are said to be widespread. . . .

TORTURE AND ILL-TREATMENT

41. The independent expert received information indicating that the Liberian security forces have used torture against critics of the Government to intimidate and silence them. Furthermore, the independent expert has been informed that civilians suspected of backing the armed opposition have been tortured by the Anti-Terrorist Unit (ATU), a special security unit, in order to make them confess.

42. Similarly, it is reported that on 21 March 2001 more than 40 Liberian students were arbitrarily detained and tortured and female students were raped after forces of the ATU and the Special Operation Division intervened in the University of Liberia campus to stop a peaceful rally. Subsequently, a number of students — mainly the leaders of the University of Liberia Student Union and the Student Unification Party — have left Liberia.

43. The Special Rapporteur on torture noted in his 2002 report to the Commission on Human Rights (E/CN.4/2002/76/Add.1, para. 916) that, "since mid-2000, more than 100 civilians, including women, have been tortured by the ATU and other Liberian security forces. According to the information received, victims of torture are mainly people suspected of backing the armed incursions by Liberian armed opposition groups from Guinea into Lofa county. . . . People are said to have been tortured while held incommunicado, especially at the military base in Gbatala and the ATU cells behind the executive mansions in Monrovia. According to the information received, armed opponents detained at the military base in Gbatala are held in holes dug in the ground — some of them filled with dirty water — and are regularly beaten including with gun butts, flogged and kicked. It is reported that some have had plastic melted on their bodies or cigarettes put on their skin, that others have been forced to roll in the mud, walk on broken glass with their bare feet or eat hot pepper. Suspects are said to be regularly *tabied*, which means that their arms are tied together so tightly behind their backs that their elbows eventually touch. It is also alleged that women and young girls have been raped by the security forces."

44. The independent expert also wishes to refer to the Special Rapporteur's findings in his report that "since the end of the civil war and the holding of elections in 1997, no institution for protection and promotion of human rights has been established and no training in international human rights standards has been provided to special security units such as the ATU and the Special Operation Division (SOD), which are said to be regularly responsible for torture" (ibid.).

45. The independent expert expresses her concerns about the above and notes that despite the establishment of the national Human Rights Commission as well as of the National Reconciliation and Reunification Commission, these offices have not functioned since their creation owing to lack of human and financial resources.

FREEDOM OF EXPRESSION AND OPINION

46. As mentioned earlier, freedom of expression and opinion were reportedly curtailed not only during the state of emergency, but also after it was lifted on 14 September 2002, particularly targeting those perceived as opponents of the Government, including political opponents, journalists and human rights activists. This is still a serious concern although on occasion independent articles or comments in the newspapers, on the radio or on billboards appear. However, the independent expert was informed several times that this would appear to be a form of "window dressing"....

50. According to the information received, on 29 October 2002, prominent human rights activists, including Dempster Brown, Blamoh Sieh and Peter Nicholson, were arrested and detained without charge for short periods following protests by the Liberian Coalition of Human Rights Defenders (a coalition of 19 human rights organizations) on behalf of their detained colleagues Hassan Bility, Sheikh Sackor and others detained with them. Furthermore, the independent expert was informed that another leading member of the coalition, Aloysius Toe (Justice and Peace Commission), who had been among those arrested in March 2002, went into hiding after the authorities accused him of association with LURD. When Mr. Toe presented himself to the police on 4 November 2002 he was arrested and was finally charged with treason on 17 December 2002.

51. The independent expert has also been informed that on 11 December 2002 several members of two opposition political parties were arrested in Buchanan, Grand Bassa County, and kept in detention awaiting the outcome of an investigation. It is reported that those arrested include the local chairman of the Liberian Unification Party, Byron Brown, George Gayebueh, Emma Morris (Secretary-General and Chairwoman of the Women's Wing of the New Deal Grand Bassa Chapter), Estella Kilby-Pailey (former Chairwoman of the NPP Women's Wing in Grand Bassa County) and Solomon Russel of the United People's Party. The authorities declared that the operation was meant to search for war-related materials based upon intelligence information relating to an alleged imminent attack by rebels.

52. The independent expert observes that this kind of incident might undermine political tolerance and have a negative impact on the forthcoming elections.

53. The independent expert is gravely concerned about the situation of journalists, human rights defenders and others deemed critical of the Government.

V. CHILD SOLDIERS

54. The independent expert has been informed that an estimated 14,000 child soldiers participated in the Liberian civil war from 1990 to 1997. Since the outbreak of the present vicious conflict in early 1999, the re-emergence of the grievous practice of using child soldiers has been recorded. The services of children, not only as porters, couriers, cooks, etc., but also as active combatants have been used by all the warring factions.

55. During the meetings with the independent expert, the Liberian authorities recognized the existence and the gravity of this problem. Unfortunately, they say, parents seem sometimes to turn a blind eye when their children are offered

money to go to the front, considering the extreme poverty families are faced with. In practical terms, children who are often just hanging around with no place to go and nothing to do are recruited in the streets — even in Monrovia — and are brought to the front. . . .

57. The independent expert abhors the use of child soldiers, regardless of the faction that exploits them. The independent expert invites the Liberian authorities to comply with the international norms prohibiting the recruitment and participation of children in armed conflict. Indeed, Liberia is a party to the Convention on the Rights of the Child which states in its article 38, paragraph 2, "States parties shall take all feasible measures to ensure that persons who have not attained the age of 15 years do not take a direct part in the hostilities." . . .

VI. Refugees and Internally Displaced Persons

59. According to the information received, the instability has resulted in a protracted humanitarian crisis in which nearly one quarter of the population is dependant on humanitarian aid and, at the time of writing, this crisis is continuing. . . .

SEXUAL EXPLOITATION OF REFUGEES AND IDPS

64. A particular challenge facing the aid community is related to the protection of IDPs [internally displaced persons], especially from sexual abuse and exploitation. IDPs, already vulnerable owing to uprooting, trauma, indignities and hardship associated with camp life, also regularly fall victim to abuse by armed groups and individuals who infiltrate or attack camps in order to intimidate and rob residents or even injure or kill them. Women, children and adolescents are usually the main targets.

65. The primary responsibility for providing protection rests with the Government which has established a national institutional framework through a ministerial-level Task Force on Protection comprising the Ministers for Foreign Affairs, Justice, Planning, Defence and Internal Affairs. This task force is to develop strategic policy and guidance regarding the protection of civilians and particularly IDPs. Furthermore, aid agencies also carry responsibility for ensuring that protection features are integrated in their programmes and operations.

VII. Final Comments

66. The independent expert notes that the human rights situation in Liberia is far from being satisfactory. Moreover, the ongoing conflict and the resulting humanitarian problem of refugees and displaced persons aggravate the overall circumstances and contribute to the generally worrisome situation. In this connection, the independent expert highlights the importance of the authorization by the Liberian authorities for her in situ mission in December 2002, since cooperation with the Liberian authorities is essential in order to continue a necessary process that would assist the Government of Liberia in promoting respect for human rights, inter alia through the establishment of effective national institutions and structures and respect for the rule of law in full compliance with the fundamental human rights standards. . . .

70. The independent expert welcomes the recognition by the Liberian authorities of the existing lapses in ensuring respect for human rights and the positive attitude of the Government towards collaboration with the Office of the High Commissioner for Human Rights (OHCHR) for further improvement of the human rights situation. In this connection, the Government indicated that it would welcome the presence of human rights officials based in the country to engage in dialogue with the Government in order to raise human rights awareness and education. . . .

VIII. Recommendations

73. With regard to the matters addressed above, the independent expert makes the following recommendations:

74. In order to provide the conditions for the full respect for the promotion and protection of human rights, the independent expert recommends:

(a) That a comprehensive solution be sought addressing all aspects and the root causes of the crisis in Liberia, taking into consideration the overall situation in the Mano River region, including a ceasefire, disarmament of all non-State armed groups and militia, ensuring conditions for free and fair elections, respect for the rule of law, human rights and good governance;

(b) That an international monitoring force be deployed as soon as possible in order to guarantee a safer and more transparent environment which has to be considered a sine qua non condition for free and fair elections;

(c) That the Government of Liberia be assisted in organizing a census of the population for proper demarcation of the constituencies, the voter registration and organization of the polls;

(d) That the Government of Liberia be supported in order to strengthen the independent electoral commission in terms of capacity-building and human and financial resources;

(e) That the Government of Liberia be urged to ensure the effective functioning of its national institutions and human rights mechanisms, in particular the National Human Rights Commission and the National Reconciliation and Reunification Commission;

(f) That attention be paid to the strong need for human rights education and training for the whole population, particularly targeting judicial and law enforcement institutions, including judges, lawyers, law enforcement officials as well as police, security and prison officers and health-care providers.

75. In order to address the concerns regarding the human rights situation in the country, the independent expert recommends:

(a) That the Government of Liberia fully guarantee the fundamental rights of freedom of expression and independence of the media as established in the Universal Declaration of Human Rights, the African Charter of Human and Peoples' Rights and in the main international human rights instruments;

(b) That the Government of Liberia take urgent measures to address the issue of arbitrary arrest and detention of human rights defenders and guarantee the security and physical integrity of all Liberians, irrespective of their political affiliation, religion or ethnicity;

(c) That the grievous practice of using child soldiers throughout the country be stopped immediately;

(d) That the Government of Liberia fully respect common article 3 to the Four Geneva Conventions of 1949 dealing with the treatment of civilians and prisoners of war during armed conflicts;

(e) That the Liberian authorities ensure safety in the refugee and IDP camps all over the country and investigate the allegations of sexual exploitation and abuses taking into account the gender dimension of the violations;

(f) That, with the support of the international community, the Government of Liberia give strong consideration to the improvement of the living conditions of the Liberians, particularly as to nutrition, access to potable water, sanitation and education;

(g) That the Commission on Human Rights renew the mandate of the independent expert for one year taking into account the importance of an in situ mission in 2003 in order to monitor the progress made in greater respect for human rights.

As indicated by the above report, the human rights problems in Liberia arose in the context of a bloody civil war, which had raged almost continuously since 1989 with spillover effects in neighboring countries. Just before the report was published in 2003, but after it was written, the Liberian government entered into a comprehensive peace agreement with the main rebel groups, assisted by a coordinated international mediation effort with UN Security Council oversight and by the field work of the UN Peace-Building Support Office in Liberia, under the authority of the Secretary-General. The Security Council also had imposed an arms embargo and other mandatory measures to stem the violence and related trafficking in diamonds. After the peace agreement, the Security Council created the UN Mission on Liberia, a peacekeeping force to help implement the agreement and whose mandate included contributing to international efforts to protect and promote human rights.

Following up on the expert report on Liberia it had authorized under the 1503 procedure, the Commission on Human Rights appointed the same independent expert for a period of three additional years to continue monitoring the human rights situation in the country and to provide "technical assistance and advisory services" in coordination with the Office of the High Commissioner for Human Rights. See Comm'n H.R. Res. 2003/82 (April 25, 2003). The independent expert's subsequent report noted improved human rights conditions but nonetheless identified serious ongoing problems. See Report of the Independent Expert, [Charlotte Abaka,] on the Situation of Human Rights in Liberia, UN Doc. E/CN.4/2005/119 (January 6, 2005).

As can be seen, the intervention by the Commission in the situation of Liberia initiated under the 1503 procedure has been part of a broader series of actions taken by the United Nations concerning the conflicts in that country. Under these circumstances, one might question what the Commission's intervention under the 1503 procedure has contributed to improving human rights in Liberia, beyond that which the United Nations has otherwise contributed through the Security Council and other agencies involved in the country. In a report published in September 2005, Amnesty International assailed the slow pace of reforms leading up to elections and ongoing systemic human rights problems. Amnesty pointed out, in particular, "[t]he impunity enjoyed by both the perpetrators of serious human rights abuses during the war and by those instigating large-scale acts of violence [which] threatens peace and human rights." Amnesty International, Liberia: Violence, Discrimination, Impunity, AI Index: AFR 34/003/2005 (Sept. 19, 2005). Returning to the issue in 2004, the Commission on Human Rights adopted a resolution expressing "deep concern" at the "serious violations of human rights and humanitarian law that continue to be perpetrated against the civilian population, particularly women and children." Comm'n H.R. Res. 2004/83 (Apr. 21, 2004).

At the very least, the Commission's involvement in Liberia initiated under the 1503 procedure can be seen as shedding important institutional light on the human rights dimension of a serious crisis and adding to the impetus for concerted UN action.

IV. Other UN Mechanisms for Investigating Alleged Human Rights Abuses

A. *Petition Procedures*

The procedure established under ECOSOC Resolution 1503 and discussed in this chapter is the primary, but not the only, direct petition procedure available to individuals and groups to complain to the United Nations about alleged human rights violations. It also is important to bear in mind that the 1503 procedure is not available when a single or isolated violation occurs but is limited to *situations* "which appear to reveal a consistent pattern of gross . . . violations of human rights," as exemplified by the Liberian case.

While most of the other petition procedures have been created pursuant to treaties or conventions, certain additional procedures have been established pursuant to the inherent authority of the UN Charter. See generally Office of the High Commissioner for Human Rights, Complaint Procedures (Fact Sheet No. 7/Rev. 1), *http://www.ohchr.org/english/about/publications/docs/fs7.htm;* Rodley and Weissbrodt, supra page 552.

Article 87(b) of the UN Charter provides that the Trusteeship Council has authority to accept and examine petitions concerning the trust territories. However, with the termination in 1994 of the final trusteeship, the U.S. administered Trust Territory of the Pacific Islands, the Trusteeship Council decided to discontinue its regular meetings, holding open the possibility of meeting in the future if necessary.

The Special Committee on the Situation with regard to the Implementation of the Declaration on the Granting of Independence to Colonial Countries and Peoples (commonly known as the Special Committee on Decolonization or the Committee of 24) was created by the General Assembly in 1961 to oversee implementation of the 1960 Declaration on Decolonization (G.A. Res. 1514 (Dec. 14, 1960)). The Special Committee may receive petitions from individuals and groups and, with the permission of the administering state, conduct on-site visits to territories. In 2005, its mandate extended to 16 non-self-governing territories, ranging from small island possessions of the United Kingdom and United States to the

Western Sahara. The Special Committee submits annual reports to the General Assembly; for example, the 2004 report was issued as UN Doc. A/59/23 (July 2, 2004). See generally UN Dept. of Public Information, Decolonization, the Task Ahead, Publication DPI/1109 (1991).

More important from the perspective of individual rights (as opposed to the collective right of self-determination) is the confidential petition procedure of the Commission on the Status of Women, which functions pursuant to a series of Economic and Social Council resolutions. See E.S.C. Res. 76 (V) (Aug. 5, 1947), 304-I (XI) (July 17, 1950); E.S.C. Res. 1983/27 (May 26, 1983); E.S.C. Res. 1992/19 (July 30, 1992); and E.S.C. Res. 1993/11 (July 27, 1993). A Working Group on Communications, composed of five members of the Commission, meets privately during the Commission's annual session to consider complaints of violations of women's human rights and the corresponding replies of governments. The Working Group prepares a report that summarizes the communications according to specific categories of concern. Individual complainants are not provided copies of the report or government responses. The Commission considers the Working Group report in a closed meeting and then reports to the Economic and Social Council with any recommendations that it may deem appropriate.

Also worth noting is a procedure adopted by the UN Educational, Scientific and Cultural Organization (UNESCO) in 1978, which derives its authority from UNESCO's constitution, distinct from the UN Charter. Pursuant to Decision 104EX/3.3 (1978) of the UNESCO Executive Board, UNESCO's Committee on Conventions and Recommendations may consider petitions that allege violations of human rights within UNESCO's competence, that is, in the fields of education, science, culture, and information. While the Committee's deliberations are confidential, the petitioner is informed of any action taken. The Committee does not act as an adjudicative body; its primary goal is to engage in a dialogue with the government concerned, in the hope of resolving the complaint on a humanitarian basis. Its conclusions are not published, and there is no formal enforcement mechanism, but the secrecy of the procedure is less complete than that under Resolution 1503. See Stephen P. Marks, "The Complaint Procedure of the United Nations Educational, Scientific and Cultural Organization," in *Guide to International Human Rights' Practice* 107 (Hurst Hannum ed., 4th ed. 2004); David Weissbrodt and Rose Farley, "The UNESCO Human Rights Procedure: An Evaluation," 16 *Hum. Rts. Q.* 391 (1994).

The International Labor Organization (ILO), another specialized agency within the UN system, has a fairly comprehensive system of monitoring and supervising implementation of the approximately 185 of its conventions currently in force. In addition, workers or employers organizations may file formal representations or complaints under the ILO constitution, alleging violations of freedom of association by any ILO member. The various ILO petition procedures and reporting systems are described in Lee Swepston, "Complaints Procedures of the International Labour Organization," in *Guide to International Human Rights Practice* (Hurst Hannum ed., 4th ed. 2004).

When they are available, the most effective forums for filing individual petitions often are those created under specific human rights treaties that the concerned state has ratified. Those procedures are discussed in Part V of this chapter and in Chapters 5 (African Charter on Human and Peoples' Rights), 8 (European Convention on Human Rights), and 9 (American Convention on Human Rights).

B. *Non-Petition Procedures*

Formal petition procedures remain the exception rather than the rule, and the confidential nature of the 1503, Women's Commission, and UNESCO procedures may make them inappropriate to redress either widespread cases of massive human rights abuses, where maximum publicity is desired, or little-known individual cases, where the remedy sought is immediate and humanitarian rather than political. As demonstrated by Figure 7.1 (page 565 infra), the United Nations has developed an impressive array of bodies that deal, in some manner or other, with human rights issues.

The most important procedures have been developed at the initiative of, and were implemented by, the UN Commission on Human Rights. The Commission Human Rights was replaced by the Human Rights Council pursuant to a decision of the high-level UN summit convened in September 2005. See 2005 World Summit Outcome, U.N. Doc. A/60/L.1, paras 157-160 (September 15, 2005). The specifics of the Council's formation mandate were left to subsequent negotiations within the General Assembly, which are ongoing as of this writing. The Commission on Human Rights has been a subsidiary body of the Economic and Social Council composed of 53 member states, whereas the newly formed Human Rights Council will be answerable directly to the General Assembly and its membership will include a different number of states. Also, the Council will possibly be a standing body, rather than one like the Commission which has met in annual six-week sessions. Despite these and other differences, the evolution of the Council's methods of addressing violations of human rights will undoubtedly build on the methods and previous experience of the Commission.

The Commission on Human Rights spent most of its early years engaged in standard-setting activities, which led to adoption by the General Assembly of the Universal Declaration of Human Right in 1948 and the two covenants in 1966. It also played a promotional role in calling attention to important human rights issues. Its greatest transformation, however, was its (eventual) willingness to address specific human rights violations, albeit in a highly political context.

The following reading provides an historical overview of the Commission's activities and the major mechanisms it created to address human rights violations, including the general debate and adoption of resolutions authorized under E.S.C. Resolution 1235 and the appointment of various rapporteurs and working groups to consider specific countries or issues.

Philip Alston, The Commission on Human Rights

In The United Nations and Human Rights 139, 155, 158-160, 165, 167-168, 171-173, 175-177, 180-181 (Philip Alston ed., 1992)

The Historical Evolution: An Overivew

Although it is tempting to evaluate the Commission's performance solely on the basis of recent developments, any such assessment is likely to be grossly distorted if it is not placed carefully in historical perspective. In brief, there have been three very distinct phases: (1) 1946-66. during which time the Commission was not

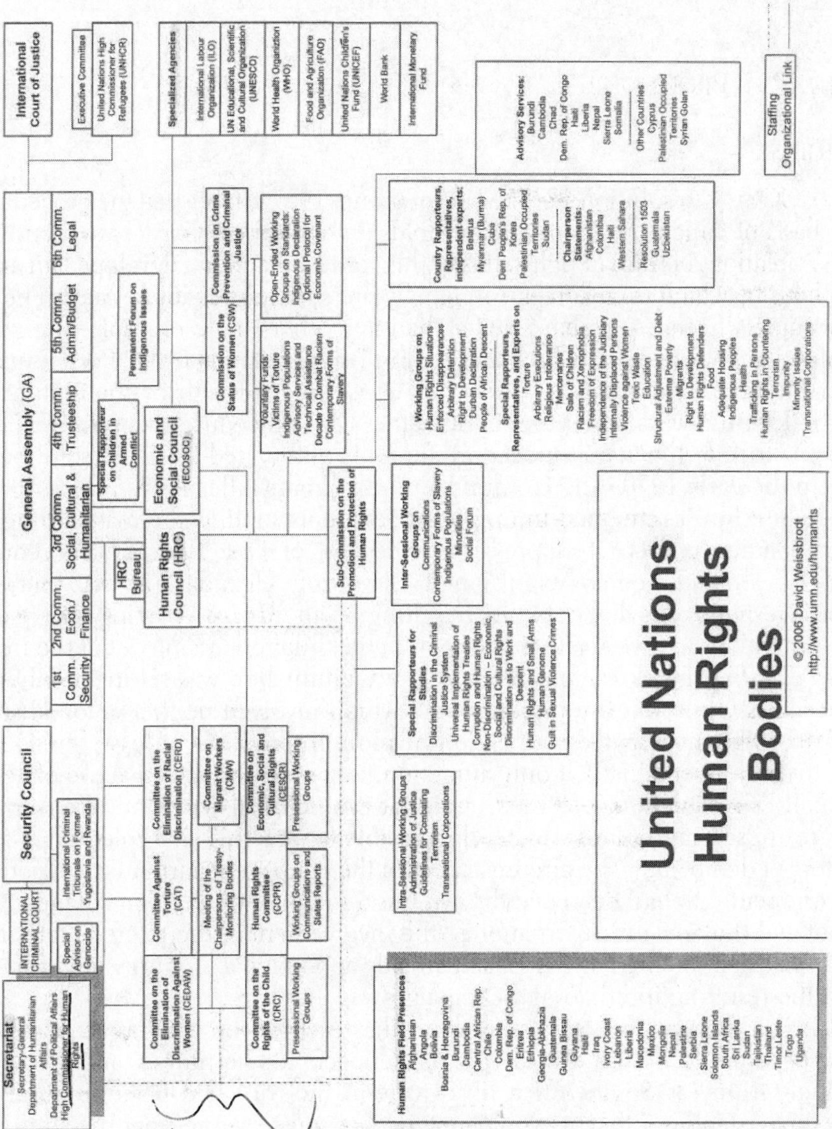
Secretariat
Secretary-General
Department of Humanitarian Affairs
Department of Political Affairs
High Commissioner for Human Rights
INTERNATIONAL CRIMINAL COURT
Special Advisor on Genocide
Security Council
International Criminal Tribunals on Former Yugoslavia and Rwanda
General Assembly (GA)
1st Comm. Security
2nd Comm. Econ./ Finance
3rd Comm. Social, Cultural & Humanitarian
4th Comm. Trusteeship
5th Comm. Admin/Budget
6th Comm. Legal
International Court of Justice
Executive Committee
United Nations High Commissioner for Refugees (UNHCR)
Special Rapporteur on Children in Armed Conflict
HRC Bureau
Human Rights Council (HRC)
Economic and Social Council (ECOSOC)
Permanent Forum on Indigenous Issues
Committee on the Elimination of Discrimination Against Women (CEDAW)
Committee Against Torture (CAT)
Committee on the Elimination of Racial Discrimination (CERD)
Meeting of the Chairpersons of Treaty-Monitoring Bodies
Committee on Migrant Workers (CMW)
Committee on the Rights of the Child (CRC)
Human Rights Committee (CCPR)
Committee on Economic, Social and Cultural Rights (CESCR)
Presessional Working Groups
Working Groups on Communications and States Reports
Presessional Working Groups
Commission on the Status of Women (CSW)
Commission on Crime Prevention and Criminal Justice
Voluntary Funds: Victims of Torture Indigenous Populations Advisory Services and Technical Assistance Decade to Combat Racism Contemporary Forms of Slavery
Open-Ended Working Groups on Standards: Indigenous Declaration Optional Protocol for Economic Covenant
Specialized Agencies
International Labour Organization (ILO)
UN Educational, Scientific and Cultural Organization (UNESCO)
World Health Organiztion (WHO)
Food and Agriculture Organization (FAO)
United Nations Children's Fund (UNICEF)
World Bank
International Monetary Fund
Sub-Commission on the Promotion and Protection of Human Rights
Human Rights Field Presences
Afghanistan
Angola
Bolivia
Bosnia & Herzegovina
Burundi
Cambodia
Central African Rep.
Chile
Colombia
Dem. Rep. of Congo
Eritrea
Ethiopia
Georgia-Abkhazia
Guatemala
Guinea Bissau
Guyana
Haiti
Iraq
Ivory Coast
Lebanon
Liberia
Macedonia
Mexico
Mongolia
Nepal
Palestine
Serbia
Sierra Leone
Solomon Islands
South Africa
Sri Lanka
Sudan
Tajikistan
Thailand
Timor Leste
Togo
Uganda
Intra-Sessional Working Groups
Administration of Justice
Guidelines for Combating Terrorism
Transnational Corporations
Special Rapporteurs for Studies
Discrimination in the Criminal Justice System
Universal Implementation of Human Rights Treaties
Corruption and Human Rights
Non-Discrimination – Economic, Social and Cultural Rights
Discrimination as to Work and Descent
Human Rights and Small Arms
Human Genome
Guilt in Sexual Violence Crimes
Inter-Sessional Working Groups on
Communications
Contemporary Forms of Slavery
Indigenous Populations
Minorities
Social Forum
Working Groups on
Human Rights Situations
Enforced Disappearances
Arbitrary Detention
Right to Development
Durban Declaration
People of African Descent
Special Rapporteurs, Representatives, and Experts on
Torture
Arbitrary Executions
Religious Intolerance
Mercenaries
Sale of Children
Racism and Xenophobia
Freedom of Expression
Independence of the Judiciary
Internally Displaced Persons
Violence against Women
Toxic Waste
Education
Structural Adjustment and Debt
Extreme Poverty
Migrants
Right to Development
Human Rights Defenders
Food
Adequate Housing
Indigenous Peoples
Health
Trafficking in Persons
Human Rights in Countering Terrorism
Impunity
Minority Issues
Transnational Corporations
Country Rapporteurs, Representatives, independent experts:
Belarus
Myanmar (Burma)
Cuba
Dem People's Rep. of Korea
Palestinian Occupied Territories
Sudan
Chairperson Statements:
Afghanistan
Colombia
Haiti
Western Sahara
Resolution 1503
Guatemala
Uzbekistan
Advisory Services:
Burundi
Cambodia
Chad
Dem. Rep. of Congo
Haiti
Liberia
Nepal
Sierra Leone
Somalia
Other Countries
Cyprus
Palestinian Occupied Territories
Syrian Golan
United Nations Human Rights Bodies
© 2006 David Weissbrodt
http://www.umn.edu/humanrts
Staffing
Organizational Link

prepared to address the issue of specific violations at all; (2) 1967-78, when the Commission struggled to evolve procedures which were initially designed to respond only to problems associated with racism and colonialism; and (3) 1979 to the present, when the procedures developed earlier have been applied in an increasingly creative and tailored fashion to an ever-widening range of countries and types of violations. . . .

THE 1235 PROCEDURE

ORIGINS

ECOSOC resolution 1235 (XLII) of 6 June 1967 established the procedure on the basis of which the Commission holds an annual public debate focusing on gross violations of human rights. It is in this context that it has developed an array of methods by which to investigate and apply pressure to individual states. The 1235 procedure illustrates, perhaps better than any other single example, the gradual evolutionary manner in which the Commission's mandate has been expanded over the years. The ways in which violations are dealt with by the Commission in the 1990's, always under the rubric of the '1235 procedure', bears only a passing resemblance to the actual procedure formally authorized by that resolution. . . .

In the early 1970's the Commission heard many allegations under the 1235 procedure but it remained unmoved by incidents such as the mass killings that accompanied efforts to suppress the secession of East Pakistan (subsequently Bangladesh) and the mass expulsion of Asians from Uganda. The case that finally drew a response was that of Chile. In setting up an *Ad Hoc* Working Group of five of its members to investigate the human rights situation arising out of the military *coup d'etat* against President Allende, the Commission was setting another vital precedent. Chile was the first situation, which involved neither colonialism nor racism, to be investigated by the Commission. In principle at least, the door had finally been opened, albeit only a fraction, to permit the effective use of 1235 in virtually any situation, provided only that the political will could be mustered. There are several reasons why Chile was able to play this vital role: it had a long history of democracy; the circumstances of the coup were particularly bloody; the government that had been overthrown was a member of the Non-Aligned Movement and the Socialist International; the involvement of the United States in the coup was documented; the ILO had already appointed a Commission of Inquiry; and the resulting international campaign was intensive.

It is important to note at this point that each of the three precedent-setting investigations [southern Africa, the Israeli-occupied territories and Chile] the (unholy trinity as South Africa liked to term the trio) had been authorized on the 'understanding' that it would not in fact create a precedent. Rather, each situation was presented as though it were *sui generis*. . . . Between 1975 and 1979 an impressive succession of horror stories was presented to the Commission but none was deemed worthy of an inquiry under the 1235 provisions. Idi Amin's atrocities in Uganda, Emperor Bokassa's barbarisms in the Central African Empire, Pol Pot's genocidal regime in Democratic Kampuchea, the annexation of East Timor and the abuse of its people by Indonesia, the systematic disappearances and the widespread terror that accompanied them in Argentina and Uruguay, the brutality of the military regime in Brazil, and many other comparable situations were all ignored in the 1235 context.

THE OPENING-UP OF THE PROCEDURE

By 1979, however, the situation had changed. NGO's such as Amnesty International and others had created a far better informed public opinion and governments were beginning to be subjected to domestic pressure to do something about human rights. [Amnesty International was awarded the Nobel Peace Prize in 1977.] The United Nations forum provided a convenient setting in which to take a stand. The Carter Administration's heavy-handed but none the less pioneering efforts, building upon continuing Congressional efforts, had dramatically elevated the international profile of human rights issues.

The Commission's first tentative move to open up its procedures came in 1978. It asked the government of Democratic Kampuchea to respond to allegations brought against it and requested the Sub-Commission to consider that response and any other material and report to the Commission.... In the same year the Commission... condemn[ed] the Somoza regime in Nicaragua for violations and also sent a telegram to the Guatemalan government expressing concern over the assassination of a former Minister for Foreign Affairs. It also took action under resolution 1235 against Equatorial Guinea.... Taken together these developments opened the door much wider than before and set the scene for a comparatively rapid development of the means by which the United Nations could use the 1235 procedure to respond to violations....

In 1980, the Assembly requested the Commission to take action in cases concerning Bolivia and El Salvador, which it did the following year. From then on, the 1980's witnessed a steady stream of resolutions under the 1235 procedure calling for a variety of 'special procedures' to be undertaken....

[The author identifies a number of country-specific actions taken by the Commission, which include appointment of a special rapporteur, representative, expert, independent expert, working group, or Commission delegation; the maintenance of "direct contacts" by the Secretary-General; review of information by a member of the Sub-Commission; a report to the Commission by the Secretary-General; and a report to the Commission by the Secretary-General or his designated representative. As of mid-2005, country-specific mechanisms under one title or another were in place for 13 countries: Belarus, Burundi, Cambodia, Cuba, Democratic Republic of Korea, Democratic Republic of Congo, Haiti, Liberia, Myanmar, the occupied Palestinian territories, Somalia, Sudan, and Uzbekistan. A current list may be found on the Office of the High Commissioner for Human Rights website, *http://www.ohchr.org/english/bodies/chr/special/countries.htm.]*

...An enormous range of situations has been specifically discussed under the 1235 item, and in some of those cases, the mere expression of serious concern or the threat of a resolution has been sufficient to provoke a constructive response from the government concerned. In addition, the Commission has adopted a number of country-specific resolutions and decisions which stop short of initiating a special procedure. A new technique pioneered in 1991, is for the Chairman to make a formal (pre-agreed) statement on a specific situation. Moreover, the agenda items on self-determination, advisory services, slavery, and other matters have provided important opportunities for discussing specific violations...

DESIGNATION AND SELECTION OF RAPPORTEURS

The implementation of special procedures has been entrusted to a wide range of entities. While 'working groups' and 'special rapporteurs' were initially the favoured means of fact-finding, various other designations have been added over the years. They include 'rapporteurs', 'envoys', 'special representatives', 'experts', 'independent experts', 'delegations', etc. The different terminology was originally intended to reflect an unstated hierarchy according to the gravity of the response. But the Commission's creativity, combined with its inconsistency in this regard, has served to blur the significance of these distinctions, at least in the minds of all but those diplomats who continue to fight with such vigour and enthusiasm to secure one designation rather than another. Of much greater importance today is the agenda item under which the appointment is made. If made under the advisory services item it has been presumed to have a far less negative connotation than if made under the violations item. But the significance of this distinction may also disappear in time if the Commission continues to blur the lines between the two items....

THE MANDATE: PROSECUTORS, SOLUTION SEEKERS OR FACT-FINDERS?

The terms used to describe the formal mandates given to country rapporteurs have varied considerably. But whether they have been asked to "study", "inquire into", "investigate", or "examine" most rapporteurs have tended to assume considerable flexibility and to approach each situation as they see fit. The Commission, for its part, has generally not sought to impose any procedural straitjackets and has been reluctant to criticize the approach adopted by individual rapporteurs. Not surprisingly, this lack of structure has resulted in enormous disparities of style, methodology, content, and focus from one report to another. It has also enabled individual rapporteurs to assume that they have a *carte blanche* in determining the nature of their reports.

For analytical purposes, three principal approaches to country-reporting may be discerned. The first emphasizes the *fact finding and documentation function*. In this view the function of reporting is to record the facts, to provide reliable historical record, and to provide the necessary raw material against the background of which the political organs can determine the best strategy under the circumstances.... The second approach assumes that the *prosecutorial/publicity function* is paramount. Thus the rapporteur's role is not to establish whether violations have occurred but to marshal as much evidence as possible to support a condemnation that, in many instances, will already have been made.... The third approach is to emphasize the *conciliation function*. The rapporteur's role is not to confront the violators but to seek solutions which will improve, even if not necessarily resolve, the situation....

THE COMMISSION'S RESPONSE TO REPORTS

The Commission's response to a rapporteur's report is dictated in part by the approach adopted in the report itself. If extensive conclusions and recommendations are offered by the rapporteur, as is usually the case whether or not the Commission has specifically requested them, the latter's room for manoeuvre is very limited. It cannot readily reach a conclusion which is at odds with that of its fact finder without putting the government concerned in a strong position to denounce the fairness of the process. . . .

The Commission's debates are rarely the occasion for any serious and sustained analysis of the content of the reports it has commissioned. Delegate's speeches are usually taken up by general justifications of the position which that State proposes to take in response to the report. The real action is in the corridors where the contents of the draft resolution is determined. Determined lobbying can also take place in the capitals and the content of the report is at best a minor element in such negotiations. . . .

THE EFFECTIVENESS OF THE 1235 PROCEDURE

Evaluating effectiveness of any procedure in the human rights field is a vexing issue. The principal question concerns the criteria to be applied. Objectives range from general consciousness-raising to the actual saving of lives. It would seem difficult to sustain many strong claims on behalf of the 1235 procedure at the latter end of the spectrum. The response time is too great, the potential sanction too distant (or un-immediate), and the range of other relevant pressures in most situations too vast to be able to say with confidence in any given situation that 1235 made the crucial difference. This is borne out by the few studies which have sought to evaluate the United Nations' impact within the context of specific situations. . . .

THE THEMATIC PROCEDURES

Just as the reinvigoration of the 1235 procedure resulted in part from the horrors of the 1970s and the accompanying unresponsiveness of the UN's human rights organs, so too did the evolution of various 'thematic' procedures. The first of these procedures, the Working Group on Enforced or Involuntary Disappearances, was established in 1980 in response to developments in Argentina and Chile. . . .

Once again, as with the opening up of the 1235 procedure after 1979, the establishment of the Disappearances Group served as a vital precedent that enabled other comparable initiatives to be taken in later years. . . .

Initially, the thematic procedures might have been seen as being located in-between the 1503 and 1235 procedures. Their work was not to be confidential but nor was it to be country-specific in the full sense. The procedure was more co-operative than adversarial in design and condemnations were neither the goal nor the likely result of the exercise. Indeed the term 'fact-finding' was of dubious application to the procedures that were envisaged. But, despite the procedures' initially very modest aspirations, they have over the course of their first decade proven to be far more flexible, innovative, and persistent that either their original detractors or proponents would have dared to think. . . .

MANDATES AND PROCEDURES

Each of the procedures has been endowed with slightly different terms of reference, although the resulting differences have gradually been diminished, if not eliminated, over time. The Disappearances Group was empowered to 'examine questions' relating to the problem, 'to bear in mind the need to be able to respond effectively and to work with discretion'. The latter element was reiterated in 1981 when the Commission specified that such discretion was needed to 'protect persons providing information as well as to limit the dissemination of information provided by Governments'. The Commission also characterized the Group's objectives as 'strictly humanitarian'. By 1990, however, the Group's practice had evolved to the point where its mandate 'to examine questions' was the one to which it gave the greatest emphasis, thus playing down many of the constraints implicit in some of the other language used at one time or other by the Commission to describe its mandate. In this context it has worked at three different levels, examining: (1) individual cases; (2) overall country situations; and (3) the 'dynamics' of the phenomenon of disappearances. In the latter context it has focused on systemic factors such as the role of paramilitary groups, harassment of witnesses and relatives, impunity for perpetrators, and the role of military courts and of amnesties. It has also consistently advocated the adoption of a new international instrument dealing with disappearances.

The injunctions to examine or study the relevant phenomenon and to seek to 'respond effectively' is common to the mandates of most of the thematic rapporteurs....

SOURCES OF INFORMATION

Unlike other United Nations efforts to monitor human rights violations, the thematic procedures have never been hobbled in terms of the sources of information on which they are authorized to rely. The Disappearances Group was empowered to make use of information from any 'reliable sources', a term which placed only a minimal limitation upon it.... The other thematic rapporteurs have been restricted to seeking or obtaining information from NGO's or even from NGOs in consultative status with ECOSOC. But these restrictions have not been permitted to hinder their activities. Thus, for example, a significant number of on-site visits has been undertaken under each of the thematic procedures. Such visits should, and usually do, provide unrivalled opportunities for the collection of information. In the words of one commentator, 'all procedures appear to have had a healthy disregard for formality and to have employed a wider range of sources than officially permitted'....

MEANS OF PRESSURE

While each of the thematic procedures has experimented with different priorities in terms of the various means by which pressure can be exerted upon governments, the type of approaches used by the Disappearances Working Group have been broadly representative. For analytical purposes, five different techniques may be identified: routine requests for information; urgent action requests; country visits; prompt interventions; and reporting to the Commission....

EVALUATING EFFECTIVENESS

[I]t would seem that the thematic procedures have, in a number of important respects, been more effective than either the 1235 or 1503 procedures. In terms of the fact-finding function, as narrowly defined, the country visits being undertaken with increasing frequency under the auspices of the thematic procedures may well turnout to be more effective than the country-specific procedures under resolution 1235. Their working methods, while far from uniform across the different mandates, are generally better developed and more sophisticated than those of their 1235 counterparts. Their missions have been generally better prepared, their co-operation with NGOs and other sources more comprehensive and they have demonstrated a greater willingness to tackle some of the structural dimensions of the problem with which they are dealing. Perhaps none of this should be surprising in view of the ability of the thematic rapporteurs to pick and choose their priorities, their greater insulation from political pressures generated by individual governments, and, in most cases, the stronger Secretariat support that they have received.

In terms of the public relations function, the thematic rapporteurs have also been very effective, especially in comparative terms. They have developed and maintained contacts with a wide range of NGOs, they have reached out systematically to the victims and their supporters, and they have succeeded in generating a better informed public debate around the relevant issues. In particular, most of the procedures have played an important role as catalysts to the development of new international instruments. Finally, in terms of the conciliation function, the thematic procedures have often succeeded in producing highly critical analyses while at the same time reassuring the governments concerned that co-operation was all that they sought.

As implied in the Alston reading, the 1235 procedure is not so much a procedure as an authorization to call attention to allegations of human rights violations anywhere in the world through debate, the adoption of resolutions, and other actions (such as the appointment of a special rapporteur). By its terms, ECOSOC Resolution 1235 applies to the Commission on Human Rights and its Sub-Commission. The authority provided by that resolution and mechanisms developed under or alongside it, including the country-specific and thematic rapporteurs, will likely be inherited by the newly established Human Rights Council which is replacing the Commission.

In addition to the country-specific mechanisms, there are now 26 thematic rapporteurs or working groups operating under the authority of the Commission. Their respective mandates deal with disappearances (1980); extrajudicial, summary, or arbitrary executions (1982); torture (1985); freedom of religion(1986); the sale of children and child prostitution and pornography (1990); arbitrary detention (1991); racism and xenophobia (1993); freedom of opinion and expression (1993); the independence of the judiciary (1994); violence against women (1994); children and armed conflict (1997); poverty (1998); human rights defenders (2000); toxic and dangerous products and wastes (1995); right to education (1998); migrants (1999); economic reform policies and foreign debt (2000); right to housing (2000); right to food (2000); indigenous peoples (2001); physical and mental health (2002); people of African descent (2002); internally displaced persons (2004); human trafficking (2004); mercenaries (2005); and protection of human rights while countering terrorism (2005).

Although all of the above individuals and groups are usefully described as "thematic," their mandates may vary significantly. Compare, for example, the following extracts from the resolutions creating the respective rapporteurs or working groups.

Commission on Human Rights, Torture and Other Cruel, Inhuman or Degrading Treatment or Punishment

Comm'n H.R. Res. 1985/33 (Mar. 13, 1985)

2. *Requests* the Chairman of the Commission to appoint, after consultation with the other members of the Bureau [of the Commission], an individual of recognized international standing as special rapporteur;

3. *Decides further* that the special rapporteur, in carrying out his mandate, shall seek and receive credible and reliable information from Governments, as well as specialized agencies, intergovernmental organizations and non-governmental organizations;

4. *Requests* the Secretary-General to appeal to all Governments to cooperate with and assist the special rapporteur in the performance of his tasks and to furnish all information requested;

5. *Further requests* the Secretary-General to provide all necessary assistance to the special rapporteur;

6. *Invites* the special rapporteur, in carrying out his mandate, to bear in mind the need to be able to respond effectively to credible and reliable information that comes before him and to carry out his work with discretion....

Commission on Human Rights, Question of Arbitrary Detention

Comm'n H.R. Res. 1991/42 (Mar. 5, 1991)

2. *Decides* to create, for a three-year period, a working group composed of five independent experts, with the task of investigating cases of detention imposed arbitrarily or otherwise inconsistently with the relevant international standards set forth in the Universal Declaration of Human Rights or in the relevant international legal instruments accepted by the States concerned;

3. *Decides* that the working group, in carrying out its mandate, shall seek and receive information from Governments and intergovernmental and non-governmental organizations, and shall receive information from the individuals concerned, their families or their representatives;

4. *Invites* the working group to take account, in fulfilling its mandate, of the need to carry out its task with discretion, objectivity and independence.

5. *Requests* the working group to present a comprehensive report to the Commission at its forty-eighth session;

6. *Requests* the Secretary-General to provide all necessary assistance to the working group to enable it to accomplish its task.

Commission on Human Rights, Human Rights and Indigenous Issues

Comm'n H.R. Res 2001/57 (Apr. 24, 2001)

1. *Decides* to appoint, for a three-year period, a special rapporteur on the situation of human rights and fundamental freedoms of indigenous people, with the following functions:

(a) To gather, request, receive and exchange information and communications from all relevant sources, including Governments, indigenous people themselves and their communities and organizations, on violations of their human rights and fundamental freedoms;

(b) To formulate recommendations and proposals on appropriate measures and activities to prevent and remedy violations of the human rights and fundamental freedoms of indigenous people;

(c) To work in close relation with other special rapporteurs, special representatives, working groups and independent experts of the Commission on Human Rights and of the Sub-Commission on the Promotion and Protection of Human Rights . . . ;

2. *Invites* the special rapporteur to take into account a gender perspective while in carrying out her/his mandate, paying special attention to discrimination against indigenous women;

3. *Also invites* the special rapporteur to pay special attention to violations of the human rights and fundamental freedoms of indigenous children;

From the cautious beginnings in the early 1980s, the thematic mechanisms have taken an increasingly aggressive approach toward the task of responding effectively to human rights violations. The Working Group on Arbitrary Detention, for example, for a number of years adopted formal "decisions" each year on specific cases of arbitrary detention. Not surprisingly, some states objected to what they perceived to be an unwarranted assertion of authority by the Working Group, particularly when it began to apply the norms of the Covenant on Civil and Political Rights to states that had not ratified that treaty. Under pressure, the Working Group decided in 1997 to no longer apply international legal instruments to states that were not a party to them and to offer its "views," rather than adopt "decisions," on cases that come before it. Comm'n H.R. Res. 1997/50, paras. 5, 7 (Apr. 15, 1997). Nonetheless, the Working Group continues to take a straightforward approach to its mandate of "investigating cases of deprivation of liberty imposed arbitrarily" and does offer opinions on specific cases. See Id., para. 15. The group's current methods of operation are described in the following extract.

Office of the High Commissioner for Human Rights, The Working Group on Arbitrary Detention

Fact Sheet No. 26, http://www.ohchr.org/english/about/publications/docs/fs26.htm#A46

III. Composition and Mandate of the Group

The Commission on Human Rights has entrusted the Working Group with the following mandate:

(a) To investigate cases of detention imposed arbitrarily or otherwise inconsistently with relevant international standards set forth in the Universal Declaration of Human Rights or in the relevant international legal instruments accepted by the States concerned provided that no final decision has been taken in such cases by domestic courts in conformity with domestic law;

(b) To seek and receive information from Government and intergovernmental and non-governmental organizations, and receive information from the individuals concerned, their families or their representatives;

(c) To present a comprehensive report to the Commission at its annual session.

The Working Group on Arbitrary Detention is the only non-treaty-based mechanism whose mandate expressly provides for consideration of individual complaints. This means that its actions are based on the right of petition of individuals anywhere in the world. . . .

The Group is assisted by the Secretariat throughout the year and holds three sessions per year, each lasting between five and eight working days.

IV. Criteria Adopted by the Working Group to Determine Whether a Deprivation of Liberty is Arbitrary. . . .

V. Procedures Followed by the Working Group

A. The Procedure Involving Investigation of Individual Cases

This procedure comprises the following four stages. . . .

STAGE 1: Bringing the matter to the attention of the Working Group

The Group's involvement is generally triggered by communications sent to it by the individuals directly concerned, their families, their representatives or non-governmental organizations for the protection of human rights, although it may also receive communications from Governments and inter-governmental organizations. . . .

Since 1993, the Commission on Human Rights has authorized the Working Group to take up cases on its own initiative when its attention is drawn to sufficiently substantiated allegations of arbitrary deprivation of liberty.

STAGE 2: Offering the Government an opportunity to refute the allegations

The Group attaches great importance to the adversarial character of its procedure. Consequently, the communication is forwarded to the Government concerned through diplomatic channels with an invitation to communicate to the Working Group within 90 days its comments and observations on the allegations made, both as regards the facts and the applicable legislation and concerning the progress and outcome of any investigations that may have been ordered. If the Government desires an extension of this time limit, it is required to inform the Group of the reasons for requesting one, so that it may be granted a further period of a maximum of two months in which to reply.

The Working Group, whose terms of reference require it to discharge its duties with discretion, does not reveal the identity of the source to the Government to which it forwards the substance of the communication.

STAGE 3: Offering the source an opportunity to make comments on the Government's response

A reply sent by the Government to the Working Group is transmitted to the source for any final comments.

On the other hand, if the Government has not communicated its response within the above-mentioned 90-day deadline, or within the extended deadline, the Working Group may take a position on the case on the basis of all the information available to it.

STAGE 4: The Working Group's opinion

In the light of the information collected under this adversary procedure, the Working Group adopts one of the following measures in private session:

(a) If the person has been released, for whatever reason, following the reference of the case to the Working Group the case is filed; the Group, however, reserves the right to render an opinion, on case-by-case basis, whether or not the deprivation of liberty was arbitrary, notwithstanding the release of the person concerned;

(b) If the Group considers that the case is not one of the arbitrary deprivation of liberty, it shall render an opinion to this effect;

(c) If the Group considers that further information is required from the Government or the source, it may keep the case pending until that information is received;

(d) If the Group considers that it is unable to obtain sufficient information on the case, it may file the case provisionally or definitively;

(e) If the Group decides that the arbitrary nature of the deprivation of liberty is established, it shall render an opinion to that effect and make recommendations to the Government.

The opinion is sent to the Government, together with the recommendations. Three weeks after this notification, the opinion is also conveyed to the source for information.

The opinions are published in an annex to the report presented by the Working Group to the Commission on Human Rights at each of its annual sessions.

B. THE DELIBERATIONS PROCEDURE

The Working Group may also formulate deliberations on matters of a general nature involving a position of principle in order to develop a consistent set of precedents and assist States, for purposes of prevention, to guard against the practice of arbitrary deprivation of liberty. The Group has already adopted various such deliberations, specifically in the . . . areas of house arrest and deprivation of freedom for purposes of rehabilitation through labour; by means of these "deliberations" it defines the criteria on the basis of which deprivation of freedom linked with such situations may become arbitrary.

C. THE URGENT ACTION PROCEDURE

The Working Group has developed an urgent action procedure for cases in which there are sufficiently reliable allegations that a person is being detained arbitrarily and that the continuation of the detention may constitute a serious danger to that person's health or life.... In such cases, an urgent appeal is sent, by the most rapid channel of communication, to the Minister for Foreign Affairs of the State concerned, requesting that his Government should take appropriate measures to ensure that the detained person's right to life and to physical and mental integrity are respected. In addressing such communications, the Working Group emphasizes that such urgent appeals are of purely humanitarian character and in no way prejudge the Working Group's final assessment of whether the deprivation of liberty is arbitrary or not.

D. FIELD MISSIONS

Visits to countries constitute an opportunity for the Working Group, through a direct dialogue with the Government concerned and representatives of civil society, to understand better the situation prevailing in that country, as well as the underlying reasons for instances of arbitrary deprivation of liberty. Discussions conducted during such visits with the judicial, penitentiary and other officials concerned, as well as with detainees, enable the Working Group members to enhance their understanding of the state and the evolution of the national legislation from the perspective of international human rights norms, taking into account the social, political and historical context in each country. Such visits bring about a spirit of cooperation between the country visited and the Working Group. They take place on the basis of an invitation from the Government concerned. This is why the Commission on Human Rights has on numerous occasions encouraged Governments to invite the Working Group to their countries so as to enable the Group to discharge its mandate even more effectively.

In accordance with these principles, the Working Group carries out country visits on a regular basis.

In principle, the Working Group does not visit countries in respect of which provision has already been made for a special rapporteur (or similar machinery), unless the Special Rapporteur appointed for the country in question requests or agrees that it should do so....

The number of thematic mechanisms grew significantly in the 1990s, and with that growth came an elevated amount of activity and variance of work methods among them, along with greater potential for duplication or overlapping. As part if the reforms it adopted in 2000, the Commission on Human Rights merged a number of thematic mechanisms; established criteria to be applied to creating, merging, or terminating mandates; and provided guidelines for the thematic mechanisms to carry on aspects of their work, in particular in regard to urgent appeals, as well as guidelines for the Commission in its consideration of reports. See Report of the inter-sessional open-ended Working Group on Enhancing the Effectiveness of the Mechanisms of the Commission on Human Rights, UN Doc. E/CN.4/2000/112, paras. 5-34 (Feb. 16, 2000), adopted by Comm'n H.R. Dec. 2000/109 (Apr. 26, 2000).

Since 1994, the country and thematic rapporteurs and working group chairs have met annually to share experiences, identify cross-cutting issues and ways of coordinated action on them, and discuss ways of enhancing the effectiveness of their work. The following extract of the twelfth report of the meeting of the country and thematic mechanisms, or special procedures as they are sometimes collectively called, gives an indication of the extent to which their work has grown into an intricate web of activity that engages other UN and affiliated agencies.

Report of the twelfth meeting of special rapporteurs/ representatives, independent experts and chairpersons of working groups of the special procedures of the Commission on Human Rights and of the advisory services programme

UN Doc. E/CN.4/2006/4 (Aug. 3, 2005) (advance edited copy)

46. Participants met with representatives of UNHCR [UN High Commissioner for Refugees], the United Nations Educational, Scientific and Cultural Organization (UNESCO), the United Nations Development Programme (UNDP), the Food and Agriculture Organization of United Nations (FAO) and the World Bank to exchange views on the interaction between the special procedures mandate holders and the organizations and bodies of the United Nations system, including the specialized agencies.

47. The meeting began with presentations by individual agencies. The representative of UNHCR, noting the close link between human rights law and refugee law, underlined the importance of the work of special procedures to the work of UNHCR. At the same time, the representative highlighted the need to strengthen cooperation in order to avoid duplication. The representative of UNESCO referred to the work on human rights within that organization, noting the particular relevance of the work of the Special Rapporteur on the right to education. The representative of UNDP gave an example of excellent cooperation between the United Nations Country Team in Uzbekistan, OHCHR and the Special Rapporteur on torture when he visited the country. All partners had worked closely together in the preparations for the mission, during the mission, as well as on follow-up. The representative noted the importance of constant dialogue with the resident coordinator from an early stage in the preparations for missions. Finally, the representative of the World Bank noted the organization's appreciation for the close cooperation it had had with special procedures, in particular the Special Rapporteur on the right to the highest attainable standard of physical and mental health and the independent expert on the effects of economic reform policies and foreign debt on human rights. However, the representative also noted concern about the appointment of mandate holders, suggesting that time limits could be set on the terms of appointment and that a mid-term evaluation could be undertaken prior to extension of the mandate. A lack of resources continued to be an operational limitation for special procedures. . . .

49. Participants also stressed the importance of sharing information. In particular, there was a need for greater dissemination of information among United Nations agencies on the special procedures themselves and on their role. Similarly, while the sharing of information between United Nations agencies and mandate holders was important for the mandates, representatives of United Nations agencies were sometimes unsure as to whether information could be shared.

50. Several participants discussed the relevance of human rights mainstreaming in United Nations agencies. Economic, social and cultural rights were particularly relevant to United Nations agencies and the World Bank, not least because denial of those rights could lead to violations of civil and political rights. Some participants highlighted the importance of promoting the right to education as a means though which other rights could be realized. Similarly, poverty had important linkages with the phenomena of trafficking and migration. One participant noted that cooperation between special procedures and United Nations agencies was important for the effective integration of human rights in national development plans, the Common Country Assessment/United Nations Development Assistance Framework process and in the development of poverty reduction strategies.

51. Participants also discussed the importance of joint action. There was a need to improve dialogue between United Nations agencies and special procedures, while at the same time safeguarding the critical independence of mandate holders. Similarly, special procedures, as independent experts, could make statements on issues that might be too risky for United Nations agencies, particularly country teams, to make. This could support United Nations work on difficult issues. Special procedures, in turn, depended on the wisdom of United Nations agencies.

Apart from the Human Rights Commission/Council, there are many other UN Charter-based bodies that are concerned with violations of human rights, although there is no formal or direct route of access for individuals or NGOs to submit information to most of these other bodies. Many of these bodies lack the power to act directly in response to information on violations. Of course, the UN General Assembly has plenary power to address human rights, as manifested by its longstanding activity in human rights matters associated with decolonization, the Israel-occupied territories, and South Africa before the end of apartheid. The Security Council also may be concerned with human rights within the framework of its work on peace and security, as illustrated by its attention to human rights concerns in Liberia, supra page 553, and in Darfur (see the discussion in Chapter 10, page 782).

The Economic and Social Council, which was the parent body of the Commission on Human Rights, addresses human rights within its general mandate and as the parent body of the Commission on Crime Prevention and Criminal Justice (see Chapter 3, page 201), the Commission on the Status of Women, and the Permanent Forum on Indigenous Issues. In addition to its communications procedures (supra page 563), the Commission on the Status of Women addresses women's rights in non-case-specific studies and discussions of a range of issues, such as violence against women and the need for equal pay for equal work; this work is summarized in the Commission's annual report to ECOSOC.

The Permanent Forum on Indigenous Issues is a relatively new body, created in 2000, with a mandate to advise and make recommendations to the Economic and Social Council specifically on indigenous peoples' concerns and to promote awareness and coordination of the activities concerning these issues within the U.N. system. See E.S.C. Res. 2000/22 (July 28, 2000). Unlike other major UN bodies that are intergovernmental, the Permanent Forum is composed of independent experts, eight of whom are nominated by states and the other eight of whom are named by the president of the Economic and Social Council in consultation with indigenous peoples. The Permanent Forum opens its meetings to representatives of indigenous peoples and support groups from throughout the world, in addition to a wide range of government and international agency representatives, providing them the opportunity to raise their concerns and make recommendations in the Forum's public sessions. However, the Forum has thus far declined to take any action on the many specific cases of violations of indigenous peoples' human rights that have been brought to its attention.

In addition to the above bodies, the UN Secretary–General carries on a number of human rights activities both directly and through the Office of the High Commissioner on Human Rights (OHCHR). The High Commissioner has the rank of Under-Secretary–General and has principal responsibility for United Nations human rights activities under the direction and authority of the Secretary-General. G.A. Res 48/141 (Dec. 20, 1993). The Office of the High Commissioner, based in Geneva, provides services to the Human Rights Council and its special procedures and other UN bodies concerned with human rights, including the treaty bodies. In recent years, the Office has expanded its field offices to provide technical and advisory services in human rights, often in conjunction with UN country teams; this work is primarily promotional, however, and the "field presences" should not be thought of primarily as on-site monitoring missions. The recent reforms proposed by the Secretary–General suggest that the High Commissioner is to have an expanded role, along with a significantly greater budget, and this may evidence a willingness to make human rights a higher priority throughout the UN system.

Comments and Questions

1. In 1976 John Humphrey, the first Director of the UN's Division of Human Rights, observed,

> Human rights cannot and should not be divorced from politics and in a political organization like the United Nations they always will be discussed in political contexts, but there should be an opportunity in the Organization for complaints of individuals protesting the violation of their rights to be considered objectively on their merits, particularly if there are gross violations following consistent patterns. . . . What is needed is some judicial or quasi-judicial body, composed of independent persons acting in their personal capacity, before which individual complaints could be brought with some hope that they would be examined fairly and objectively.

John P. Humphrey, *The International Bill of Rights: Scope and Implementation*, 17 Wm. & Mary L. Rev. 527, 532-533 (1976).

2. Despite the fact that the Resolution 1503 procedure has not fulfilled the expectations of its most ardent advocates, has it not been a limited success? Consider:

(a) the fact that, while Greece was able to short-circuit European Convention procedures by withdrawing from the Council of Europe before it could be suspended or expelled, neither Greece nor any other state can escape Resolution 1503, which is universal in coverage.

(b) the fact that, by the practice of publicly naming states being considered under the 1503 procedure, the Commission marshals world public opinion against them, which, in the case of Greece, produced an amnesty for political prisoners literally on the eve of the Working Group's meetings in 1973. A later communication concerning Brunei, initially ignored by the government, led directly to the release of a number of individuals who had been kept in detention beyond their sentences.

(c) the fact that the quiet diplomacy (epitomized by the confidential 1503 procedure) may, in some instances, be more effective than public condemnation in encouraging states to reform. For example, a 1503 communication filed against Japan in 1981 alleged widespread official discrimination against members of the Korean minority in Japan and supplied valuable international support for domestic Japanese efforts to remedy the situation.

(d) the fact that well-known NGOs, such as Amnesty International and the International Commission of Jurists, continue to file communications under Resolution 1503, often in conjunction with more public activities concerning the same situation, as part of increasingly sophisticated strategies to improve human rights conditions.

3. In which contexts might the 1503 procedure be most useful in addressing gross violations of human rights, given its confidential nature and the fact that its often prolonged consideration rarely leads to public scrutiny by the Commission? As an NGO, would it be possible to submit a communication under 1503 and at the same time raise the same issues in the public debate under Resolution 1235?

4. The Greek Communication (pages 539-546 supra), while cut from whole cloth (no form books then existing), still constitutes an acceptable model for international human rights lawyers drafting a complaint. Useful suggestions in this regard not only as to Resolution 1503 communications, but also as to the other UN and regional procedures, are contained in *Guide to International Human Rights Practice* (Hurst Hannum ed., 4th ed. 2004) (see especially the Model Communication contained in Appendix C at 331-34). Also see generally *The United Nations and Human Rights: A Critical Reappraisal* (Philip Alston and Frederic Megret eds., 2d ed. 2006); Julie A. Mertus, *The United Nations and Human Rights* (2005).

5. One of the main drawbacks of the Resolution 1503 procedure is that the petitioner must show the existence of a consistent pattern of gross human rights violations. What is a non-gross violation? Is there a consistent pattern if the kind of violations varies over time? Can the 1503 procedure deal effectively with even gross violations that are not of a continuing nature, such as the poison gas attacks on Kurds in Iraq in the late 1980s or the massacre of demonstrators in Beijing's Tiananmen Square in 1989? Would the denial of indigenous land rights, such as that discussed in Chapter 3, qualify as a gross violation?

6. NGOs have gradually become much freer than they were in the 1970s to denounce human rights violations publicly during Commission and Sub-Commission debates under Resolution 1235, and it appears that they will continue to have wide latitude in complaining about human rights violations in the public discussions of the Human Rights Council. The country-specific and thematic mechanisms also provide multiple opportunities for shedding light and channeling scrutiny on human rights violations. Do such activities undermine the value of the 1503 procedure? If the 1503 procedure were abandoned, what procedures would petitioners from states not parties to the European or American

Conventions on Human Rights or to the Optional Protocol to the Covenant on Civil and Political Rights be able to invoke?

7. African-Americans, Native Americans, and other groups have (thus far unsuccessfully) filed complaints against the United States under Resolution 1503. What should the U.S. government's reaction to such complaints be? Can you predict the response, based on the consistent U.S. refusal to accept any optional individual complaint procedure contained in a human rights treaty? How do you think the general public would react to a UN investigation of human rights in the United States?

8. Running through almost every petition procedure is the requirement that the petitioner have exhausted domestic remedies before invoking the jurisdiction of an international body. What relevance does this requirement, which was borrowed from the traditional law governing the responsibility of states for injuries to aliens, have in the human rights context? Is it linked to the conditional principle of non-interference in the domestic affairs of states contained in Article 2(7) of the UN Charter? Or does it simply reflect the fact that the ultimate guarantor of human rights is still the state, not an international institution? See Chapter 5.

9. All of the mechanisms discussed in this chapter thus far are based on the inherent authority of the United Nations to consider human rights issues; none of them imposes a formal legal requirement on states to respond or participate. Nonetheless, states have generally paid close attention to the petition procedures, thematic mechanisms, and public debates, particularly at the level of the Commission on Human Rights. The six-week sessions of the Commission have been attended by approximately 3,000 people, including state delegations (both members and non-members of the Commission), representatives of other UN agencies, and nongovernmental organizations. Lobbying has been often intensive, both inside and outside the Commission chamber. While one may certainly question the sincerity of many statements made during the sessions, it would be difficult to argue that many states believe that the best path is simply to ignore the UN's human rights activities altogether.

One example of the significance of UN debates is offered by the paid announcement on page 582, which was taken from the *Washington Post*, Mar. 5, 1939, at A26, and was placed in major U.S. and European newspapers by the government of (then) Zaire. The announcement obviously ignores the required confidentiality of 1503, but it also suggests that governments find even secret UN procedures to be of some relevance.

10. The Sub-Commission on the Promotion and Protection of Human Rights has been an essential point of access for NGOs, because its (more or less) independent experts and less politically charged atmosphere have facilitated informal contacts among NGOs, Sub-Commission members, and the OHCHR secretariat. The Sub-Commission remains the only UN body to have adopted a resolution expressing even indirect concern over the massacres in Tianamen Square, although the specific incident was not even mentioned and the resolution passed by a vote of only 15 to 9. Sub-Comm'n Res. 1989/5 (Aug. 31, 1989). However, its authority to adopt country-specific resolutions and to participate in the 1503 procedure as a plenary body was ended by the Commission in 2000, see Comm'n H.R. Dec. 2000/19 (Apr. 26, 2000), and it has returned in large part to its original role of undertaking studies and research. Should the Sub-Commission be continued? Before answering, review the Sub-Commission's role with respect to

indigenous rights (Chapter 3, pages 164, 166) and its recent initiative in the area of corporate responsibility for human rights (Chapter 5, page 379).

UNITED NATIONS REPORT: HUMAN RIGHTS SITUATION IMPROVES MARKEDLY IN ZAIRE

The Embassy of the Republic of Zaire in Washington, D.C. is pleased to bring to your attention the conclusions of the United Nations Commission on Human Rights, based on our country's accomplishments in promoting and protecting human rights.

Zaire, true to President Mobutu's guidelines and goals, continues to demonstrate the commitment of its government to the principles of Human Rights and Democracy.

We would like to take this opportunity to salute the cordial and long standing relations between the United States of America and the Republic of Zaire.

H.E. Mushobekwa Kalimba wa Katana
Ambassador E. and P.

OFFICE DES NATIONS UNIES A GENEVE

UNITED NATIONS OFFICE OF GENEVA

DECISION CONCERNING ZAIRE ADOPTED WITHOUT A VOTE AT THE 38TH MEETING (CLOSED) OF THE COMMISSION HELD ON 24 FEBRUARY 1989

The Commission on Human Rights,

Having examined the material concerning the human rights situation in Zaire brought before it under Economic and Social Council resolution 1503 (XLVIII), including the report of the Secretary-General on his direct contacts with the government of Zaire (E/CN.4/1989/R.4),

Noting with appreciation the willingness of the Government of Zaire, with the active participation of Maitre Nimy Mayidika Ngimbi, Commissaire d'Etat aux droits et libertes du citoyen, to co-operate with the Commission by furnishing replies and observations relating to the material which the Commission has before it,

1. **Decides to discontinue consideration of the matter;**
2. **Encourages the Government of Zaire in its efforts to promote and protect human rights;**
3. **Requests the Government of Zaire to inform the Commission at its forty-sixth session, of the results of the action already taken to this and at a special closed meeting;**
4. **Requests the Secretary-General to provide Zaire with all the assistance it desires under the advisory services program in order to help that country in its efforts to strengthen the machinery established for the purpose of protecting and promoting human rights;**
5. **Requests the Secretary-General to communicate this decision to the Government of Zaire.**

V. Monitoring the Implementation of UN Human Rights Treaties

In addition to the Charter-based procedures discussed above, every UN human rights treaty adopted since the mid-1960s has included specific provisions for supervising its implementation. Unfortunately, the effectiveness of many of these procedures has been questioned, and states have been reluctant to adopt implementation measures that truly amount to enforcement. While all of the major UN treaties establish separate monitoring bodies (except the Covenant on Economic, Social, and Cultural Rights, whose oversight body was eventually created by the Economic and Social Council), their mandates are limited and many of the procedures are optional. At the same time, all treaty bodies have the power to write their own rules of procedure, and this authority has sometimes been used to strengthen their oversight capabilities. In addition, some of the treaties, such as the Convention against Torture and the Convention on the Elimination of Discrimination against Women, have been strengthened through the adoption of additional protocols.

The only procedural obligation that is mandatory under all of the treaties is self-reporting by states parties; provisions for inter-state complaints and individual petition procedures are usually optional. Two of the treaty bodies (the Committee against Torture [CAT] and the Committee for the Elimination of All Forms of Discrimination Against Women [CEDAW]) may conduct inquiries into alleged violations of their treaty's terms, but this ability also depends on separate acceptance by states. A final authority given to the treaty bodies is the ability to adopt "general comments" or "general recommendations." While not technically part of their monitoring functions, the adoption of General Comments on the meaning of rights and the scope of obligations contained within the specific treaty has become an important device for interpreting treaty provisions.

These competences are discussed more fully in the following sections.

A. *Monitoring Bodies*

Each of the core UN human rights treaties, except the Covenant on Economic, Social and Cultural Rights, creates a specific monitoring body, usually a committee of independent experts numbering between 10 (CAT) and 23 (CEDAW). The members of each committee are nominated and elected by the states parties. The Human Rights Committee, for example, is composed of 18 members who must be nationals of states parties to the Covenant on Civil and Political Rights (CPR Covenant) (it is not necessary that the state have ratified either of the Covenant's protocols). Like most treaties, the CPR Covenant requires that Committee members be persons of high moral character and recognized competence in the field of human rights. The CPR Covenant also recommends that states consider the "usefulness of the participation of some persons having legal experience." The Convention against Torture is unique in recommending that some of its members also serve the Human Rights Committee. All of the treaties recommend giving consideration to equitable geographic representation and membership by individuals who come from "the different forms of civilization and of the principal legal systems of the world", although the geographical balance of the committees is not formally mandated (as is the case with most intergovernmental organs within the United Nations).

Since members of the committees serve in their personal capacity, most of the committees have adopted ethical guidelines, either in their rules of procedure or as a separate instrument, in order to safeguard the impartiality of the work. The Human Rights Committee, for example, does not permit a member to participate in considering state reports from her or his state or in hearing complaints against that state.

As described below, the procedures for reviewing state compliance have evolved considerably since they began functioning in the 1970s. This has led monitoring bodies to establish sub-committees or special rapporteurs to consider specific matters. The Human Rights Committee, for example, selects three members who have special responsibilities:

— the Special Rapporteur on New Communications registers new complaints under the Optional Protocol and considers requests for interim measures of protection that arise between Committee sessions;

— the Special Rapporteur on Follow-up of Views monitors states' responses to the Committee's decisions on the merits of individual cases; and

— The Special Rapporteur on Follow-up to Concluding Observations monitors state responses to the Committee's observations and recommendations following consideration of state reports.

None of the treaty bodies meets full time. Most hold two to three sessions of two to three weeks a year, but working groups on communications may meet for an additional week in advance of or following the plenary meeting. The Office of the High Commissioner for Human Rights in Geneva provides full-time secretariat support for all of the committees except CEDAW, which is serviced from New York.

The Covenant on Economic, Social and Cultural Rights (ESC Covenant) is unique in not having created a new treaty body. Instead, the Covenant foresaw a system of state reports submitted to ECOSOC. This procedure proved completely unworkable and, in 1985, ECOSOC used the CPR Covenant as a model and created an 18-member expert Committee on Economic, Social and Cultural Rights to consider state reports and issue general comments. The Committee has also elaborated an optional protocol to create some form of complaint procedure, as discussed further below.

B. *State Reporting*

One of the most obvious ways — if not necessarily the most reliable — to discover what is happening in a country is to seek information from the government concerned. State reporting has a long tradition, having been used by the International Labor Organization throughout its history. See *The International Labour Organisation* (Bartocomei de la Cruz et al. eds., 1996). As of 2005, eight major UN-sponsored human rights conventions require states parties to submit periodic reports on matters relevant to the particular treaty: the Convention on Racial Discrimination (1965), the CPR and ESC Covenants (1966), the

Convention Against Apartheid (1973), the Convention on Discrimination Against Women (1979), the Convention Against Torture (1984), the Convention on the Rights of the Child (1989) and the Convention on the Protection of the Rights of All Migrant Workers and Members of their Families (1990). State reporting also is required under several treaties adopted by specialized agencies, e.g., the UNESCO Convention against Discrimination in Education (1960), and some of the regional systems, such as the European Social Charter (1961) (see Chapter 8, page 706).

The treaties do not indicate how treaty bodies should approach the task of considering state reports. By now, however, all of the treaty bodies have adopted broadly the same approach, the main features of which are initiating a constructive dialogue between committee members and state delegations whose report is under consideration, and the adoption of "concluding observations" or comments on the report, which acknowledge progress made and indicate to the state where further action is required. However, there remains considerable variation in the practice of each treaty body with respect to considering state reports. See Compilation of Rules of Procedure adopted by Human Rights Treaty Bodies, UN Doc. HRI/GEN/3/Rev.1 and Add.1 (Apr. 28 and May 7, 2004); Stephanie Farrior, "International Reporting Systems", in *Guide to International Human Rights Practice* (Hurst Hannum ed., 4th ed. 2004).

All of the committees have issued guidelines on reporting to aid states in preparing their reports, which are compiled in UN Doc. HRI/GEN/2/Rev.2 (May 7, 2004) and are revised regularly. The guidelines are designed to ensure that reports are presented in a uniform manner, so that treaty bodies and parties can obtain a complete picture of the situation of each state with respect to the implementation of the relevant treaty. Some committees recommend that states take an article-by-article approach, while others require reporting on clusters of related articles. Some committees elaborate detailed questions to be answered with respect to each article; others allow the state to decide what information is most relevant. A number of committees have different guidelines for initial and periodic reports.

As the reporting burdens have substantially increased on states, the chairpersons of the various human rights treaty bodies have sought to ease the burden, as a means of encouraging compliance. They now require an initial "core report," which details basic information about a state, including its demographics, geography, constitution, legal and political structures, and other general information. This core report needs to be submitted only once and provides information to all the treaty bodies responsible for treaties that the state has ratified. As basic changes occur in a state, the core report should be updated.

Article 40 of the CPR Covenant is a typical reporting provision. It obliges every state party to submit reports to the Human Rights Committee on the measures that the state has adopted to give effect to the rights protected by the Covenant and on the progress made in the enjoyment of those rights. The reports also are to include the factors and difficulties, if any, that affect the state's implementation of the Covenant. An initial report is due one year after the Covenant enters into force for a state, with subsequent reports due at a time individually specified for each state party. In 1997, the Committee changed its rule that required states to submit reports every five years; with the increasing number of parties, it became increasingly impracticable to adhere to this schedule. Document on procedures for the consideration of initial and periodic reports under article 40 of the Covenant, UN Doc. A/43/40, vol. I, Annex VIII (Apr. 9, 1998), para. 7. Now, the Committee indicates in its final observations on a state's report when the next report should be submitted. Supplementary reports also may be requested by the Committee, if it deems it desirable. Since the end of the Cold War, the Committee has begun to request special reports from states in which there is armed conflict or serious internal violence. Such emergency reports have been requested by the Human Rights Committee, for example, from Burundi, Iraq, Peru, Rwanda, and the former Yugoslavia, as a result of the crises in those states.

Over the years, the committees have jointly formulated general guidelines on the form and content of such reports; the committees' procedures have also become similar. As the first committee to begin functioning, the Committee on the Elimination of Racial Discrimination (CERD) set an important precedent when it requested governments to send their representatives to participate in the session at which their state's report was scheduled for consideration, to present the report, and to answer questions from the committee. States agreed to do so, although nothing in the convention explicitly foresaw such a public hearing, and the practice is now standard. Before each committee meets, a working group usually reviews the report to be examined, identifies the issues to be raised with the state, and prepares a list of questions where further information is sought. Normally, it takes two days for a committee to examine a report. The report is normally introduced by the state's representative, after which committee members put questions and engage in what is intended to be a "constructive dialogue." One member of the Committee commented on the nature of this dialogue (Manual on Human Rights Reporting, HR/PUB/91/1 (Rev. 1)(1997), at 262:

> []It has to be underlined that the Committee in its consideration of States reports is neither a judicial nor even a quasi-judicial body. Its role is not to pass judgement on the implementation of the provisions of the Covenant in any given State. The main function of the Committee is to assist States parties in fulfilling their obligations under the Covenant, to make available to them the experience the Committee has acquired in its examination of other states and to discuss with them any issue related to the enjoyment of the rights enshrined in the Covenant in a particular country.

Other aspects of the Committee's review process, including the purpose of reporting, the recourse to outside information, and the status of its general comments on particular reports, are addressed in the following extracts.

Office of the United Nations High Commissioner for Human Rights, Effective Functioning of Human Rights Mechanisms: Treaty Bodies

UN Doc. E/CN.4/2004/98 (Feb. 11, 2004)

Holistic Perspective of Human Rights

7. The revised reporting system is intended to provide a coherent framework within which States can meet their reporting obligations under all of the international human rights treaties to which they are a party as part of a coordinated

and streamlined process. This approach, which was supported by the Secretary-General and the General Assembly, reflects the holistic perspective of human rights established by the Universal Declaration of Human Rights and reaffirmed in the human rights treaties: that human rights are indivisible and interrelated, and that equal importance should be attached to each and every right recognized therein. When reporting, States should consider the implementation of the rights protected in each treaty within the wider context of its implementation of all of their international human rights obligations.

COMMITMENT TO TREATIES

8. The reporting process constitutes a reaffirmation by the State party of its continuing commitment to respect and ensure observance of the rights set out in the treaties to which it is party. This commitment should be viewed within the wider context of the commitment of all States "to promote respect for [the] rights and freedoms [set out in the Universal Declaration of Human Rights] and by measures, national and international, to secure their universal and effective recognition and observance." . . .

REVIEW OF THE IMPLEMENTATION OF HUMAN RIGHTS AT THE NATIONAL LEVEL

9. States parties should see the process of preparing their reports for the treaty bodies not only as the fulfilment of an international obligation, but also as an opportunity to take stock of the state of human rights protection within their jurisdiction for the purpose of policy planning and implementation. The report preparation process offers an occasion for each State party to:

(a) Conduct a comprehensive review of the measures it has taken to harmonize national law and policy with the provisions of the relevant international human rights treaties to which it is a party;

(b) Monitor progress made in promoting the enjoyment of the rights set forth in the treaties in the context of the promotion of human rights in general;

(c) Identify problems and shortcomings in its approach to the implementation of the treaties;

(d) Assess future needs and goals for more effective implementation of the treaties; and

(e) Plan and develop appropriate policies to achieve these goals.

10. The reporting process should encourage and facilitate, at the national level, popular participation, public scrutiny of government policies and constructive engagement with civil society conducted in a spirit of cooperation and mutual respect, with the aim of advancing the enjoyment by all of the rights protected by the relevant convention.

BASIS FOR CONSTRUCTIVE DIALOGUE AT THE INTERNATIONAL LEVEL

11. At the international level, the reporting process creates a framework for constructive dialogue between States and the treaty bodies. The treaty bodies, in providing these guidelines, wish to emphasize their supportive role in fostering effective implementation of the international human rights instruments and in

encouraging international cooperation in the promotion and protection of human rights in general.

Dinah Shelton, Compliance Mechanisms [Periodic Reports]

In United States Ratification of the International Covenants on Human Rights 151, 153-55 (Hurst Hannum and Dana D. Fischer eds., 1993)

There is no explicit provision in the Covenant for consideration of outside information by the [Human Rights] Committee in reviewing State reports; which [during the Cold War] resulted in some dispute within the Committee on the role of specialized agencies and non-governmental organizations. In practice, the specialized agencies have been invited to attend public meetings of the Committee where State reports are considered and to address the Committee on any matter on which it might require information. In addition, the Committee has agreed in rule 67 of its rules of procedure to have the Secretary-General transmit relevant parts of reports to the specialized agencies. It should be noted, however, that the specialized agencies have no right under the Covenant to comment on State reports and may do so only if specifically requested by the Committee. [Since 1995, the relevant bodies, especially the ILO, UNESCO, FAO, WHO, UNHCR, UNICEF, UNDP and the World Bank, have been regularly invited to submit written and oral information on state reports and contribute to the preparation of lists of issues to be discussed with states.]

Although specialized agencies have not presented formal reports, the Committee has made use of the work of other organs of the United Nations. In the case of Chile, it took official notice of General Assembly resolutions and the work of the United Nations' Ad Hoc Working Group on Chile. The result was a request of Chile to file a new report, based on the view that the first report did not reflect the realities of the human rights situation in that country. . . .

[The reporting procedure concludes with the adoption of final observations and recommendations regarding a state's compliance record. In 1992, the Committee decided that:

> comments would be adopted reflecting the views of the Committee as a whole at the end of the consideration of each State party report. That would be in addition to, and would not replace, comments made by members, at the end of the consideration of each State party report. A rapporteur would be selected in each case to draft a text, in consultation with the Chairman and other members, for adoption by the Committee. Such comments were to be embodied in a written text and dispatched to the State party concerned as soon as practicable before being publicized and included in the annual report of the Committee. They were to provide a general evaluation of the State party report and of the dialogue with the delegation and to underline positive developments that had been noted during the period under review, factors and difficulties affecting the implementation of the Covenant, as well as specific issues of concern regarding the application of the provisions of the Covenant. Comments were also to include suggestions and recommendations formulated be the Committee to the attention of the State party concerned.

Report of the Human Rights Committee, UN Doc. A/47/40 (Supp.), at 10 (1994).]

In general, although it appears that some States have been delinquent in presenting their reports, compliance with the reporting requirement has been extensive. Most reports contain detailed information on measures taken to implement the Covenant, and every State has sent a representative to the proceedings to introduce the State report and answer questions. The Committee has develop[ed] links with specialized agencies and other bodies, as well as informal contacts from NGOs, from whom independent information can be obtained. Thus, while State reporting as an effective measure of implementation has been criticized, the Committee appears to be making reasonably full use of its authority to assess impartially the efforts of States Parties to implement the Covenant. When such critical appraisal is permitted and made, including obtaining supplemental information, using outside sources, and commenting on inadequate or inaccurate reporting, a reporting mechanism can be an effective, if limited, enforcement measure.

Not everyone would agree with this relatively positive assessment of the reporting system, and the weaknesses of relying on state reports for fact-finding are perhaps more obvious than the strengths. One highly critical observer concluded in 2001 that "the gap between universal right and remedy has become inescapable and inexcusable, threatening the integrity of the international human rights legal regime. There are overwhelming numbers of overdue reports, untenable backlogs, minimal individual complaints from vast numbers of potential victims, and widespread refusal of states to provide remedies when violations of individual rights are found. . . . The average consideration by each treaty body of a state for six or seven hours once every five years has not maximized constructive interaction." Anne F. Bayefsky, *The UN Human Rights Treaty System: Universality at the Crossroads* xiii, xiv (2001).

It is hardly surprising that a state's own report tends to express a fairly high degree of satisfaction with its efforts in the human rights area. Nor is it surprising that the reports tend to be rather formalistic in character, i.e., to concentrate on the state of the law in the country rather than the state of the facts. Finally, there is the problem that many states are extremely remiss in even submitting their reports as required.

Various reforms have sought to address some of the most cogent criticisms of the reporting process. First, in order to correct misinformation contained in self-serving state reports, committees have strengthened the role of nongovernmental organizations. Initially, any consideration of challenges to the accuracy of state reports or the submission of additional information to treaty bodies by NGOs was very controversial, but over time — particularly after the end of the Cold War — the participation of NGOs has come to be accepted and even welcomed by most of the committees. NGOs, separately or jointly, may offer their own submissions to a committee, either critiquing a government report or providing additional information; they are encouraged to combine and submit a single shadow report and, if they do so, this is usually given greater weight that the report of a single NGO. Since 2002, the Human Rights Committee has permitted NGOs and specialized agencies to be heard in a private meeting of the plenary Committee at the beginning of each session, before state reports are taken up.

The Human Rights Committee also has created a follow-up procedure to monitor compliance with the final paragraph in each of its observations on state reports. In this final paragraph, the Committee identifies a number of priority issues and asks the state party to provide information, no later than one year thereafter, on the measures it has taken to address those specific issues. That information, together with information from other sources, is assessed by the Special Rapporteur on Follow-up to Concluding Observations, who then recommends to the Committee any further action that may be appropriate. The Committee has several options: it can move up the date for the next state report, request further information, or authorize the Special Rapporteur to meet with representatives of the state to discuss specific issues. If the state fails to provide the requested information, the Special Rapporteur also can meet with state representatives. Non-cooperation is reported to the General Assembly.

Finally, the Human Rights Committee in 2001 addressed the problem of state failure to submit reports, deciding that it could examine a state's compliance record even in the absence of any report and, if necessary, in the absence of a delegation from the state concerned. The major factor in deciding which states are to be examined in this fashion is the length of the delay in submitting a report. The procedure was first used in the case of Zaire (now Democratic Republic of Congo), whose report was more than twenty years overdue. This measure has spurred states to submit long-overdue reports, and the backlog of all of the committees has decreased in recent years. Nonetheless, long delays both in the submission and consideration of reports continue to plague the reporting system. For the sobering statistics, see Recent Reporting History under the Principal International Human Rights Instruments, UN Doc. HRI/GEN/4/Rev.4 (May 15, 2004).

For additional analyses of state reporting under the Civil and Political Covenant, see Manfred Nowak, *U.N. Covenant on Civil and Political Rights: CCPR Commentary* 712-753 (2d ed. 2005); Dominick McGoldrick, *The Human Rights Committee* 62-119 (1991).

Although viewed by many observers as weak, even reporting procedures can have unintended consequences, as the following reading indicates.

Congressional Record, S 8400-8401

June 14, 1995

On June 14, 1995, Senator Jesse Helms on behalf of himself and 18 other senators, [including Senators Ashcroft, Frist, and Lott], introduced the following resolution, S. Res. 133, which was transmitted to the Committee on Foreign Relations:

Whereas the Senate affirms the commitment of the United States to work with other nations to enhance the protection of children, the advancement of education, the eradication of disease, and the protection of human rights;

Whereas the Constitution and laws of the United States are the best guarantees against mistreatment of children in our country;

Whereas the laws and traditions of the United States affirm the right of parents to raise their children and to transmit to them their values and religious beliefs;

Whereas the United Nations Convention on the Rights of the Child, if ratified, would become the supreme law of the land, taking precedence over State and Federal laws regarding family life;

Whereas that Convention establishes a (universal standard which must be met by all parties to the Convention, thereby inhibiting the rights of the States and the Federal Government to enact child protection and support laws inconsistent with that standard; and

Whereas the Convention's intrusion into national sovereignty was manifested by the Convention's 1986 committee report, faulting the United Kingdom for permitting parents to make decisions for their children without consulting those children: Now, therefore, be it

Resolved, That it is the sense of the Senate that

(1) the United Nations Convention on the Rights of the Child is incompatible with the God-given right and responsibility of parents to raise their children;
(2) The Convention has the potential to severely restrict States and the Federal Government in their efforts to protect children and to enhance family life;
(3) the United States Constitution is the ultimate guarantor of rights and privileges to every American, including children; and
(4) the President should not sign and transmit to the Senate that fundamentally flawed Convention.

Senator Helms: As for the specifics of this treaty, Mr. President, Article 12 of the Convention on the Rights of the Child requires that States Parties shall assure to the child who is capable of forming his or her own views the right to express those views freely in all matters affecting the child, the view of the child being given due weight in accordance with the age and maturity of the child. What on earth does this mean? Will the U.S. be censured because a parent did not leave it to a child to choose which school to attend? Will the U.S. be censured because a parent did not allow a child to decide whether to accompany the family to church? Will the U.S. be censured because a parent did not consult a child before requiring that he or she complete family chores?

These are not Jesse Helms' hypothetical questions. A report by a Committee, established under the Convention, indicates that failure to consult a child in the previously mentioned areas are potential violations of the Convention. That report stated:

> In relation to the possibility for parents in England and Wales to withdraw their children from parts of the sex education programme in schools, the Committee is concerned that in this and other decisions, including exclusion from school, the right of the child to express his or her opinion is not solicited. Thereby the opinion of the child may not be given due weight and taken into account as required under article 12 of the Convention.

Does this mean, Mr. President that American parents will be forced to allow their children to attend sex education classes? . . . The American people do not need yet another body determining what is in the best interest of U.S. families. The U.N. Convention is incompatible with God-given rights and responsibilities of parents to raise their children. It is grotesque even to imagine handing this important privilege over to U.N. bureaucrats.

The Committee on Foreign Relations did not adopt the proposed resolution, but Senator Helms' diatribe at least suggests that someone is listening to the treaty bodies' observations.

C. *Individual Communications*

The right of individual petition has long been considered the key to effective enforcement of international human rights law. Occasionally it is made mandatory by a human rights instrument, as under the American and European human rights conventions, but more frequently it is optional, as in article 14 of the Racial Discrimination Convention. In the case of the CPR Covenant, a different approach was taken. By a very close vote, it was decided to relegate the right of individual petition to a separate legal text, straightforwardly called the Optional Protocol to the International Covenant on Civil and Political Rights (Documentary Supplement, page 1054). As of September 2005, it had been ratified by 105 of the 154 states parties to the Covenant. The United States, which ratified the Covenant in 1992, has neither signed nor ratified the Optional Protocol.

The following case raises issues of the Committee's jurisdiction and is indicative of how the Committee interprets the rights and obligations in the Covenant.

Toonen v. Australia

Views of the H.R. Committee, Communication No. 488/1992, UN Doc. CCPR/C/50/D/488/1992 (Apr. 4, 1994) (notes omitted)

The Facts as Submitted by the Author

2.1 The author is an activist for the promotion of the rights of homosexuals in Tasmania, one of Australia's six constitutive states. He challenges two provisions of the Tasmanian Criminal Code, namely, sections 122 (a) and (c) and 123, which criminalize various forms of sexual contact between men, including all forms of sexual contact between consenting adult homosexual men in private.

2.2 The author observes that the above sections of the Tasmanian Criminal Code empower Tasmanian police officers to investigate intimate aspects of his private life and to detain him, if they have reason to believe that he is involved in sexual activities which contravene the above sections. He adds that the Director of Public Prosecutions announced, in August 1988, that proceedings pursuant to sections 122 (a) and (c) and 123 would be initiated if there was sufficient evidence of the commission of a crime.

2.3 Although in practice the Tasmanian police has not charged anyone either with "unnatural sexual intercourse" or "intercourse against nature" (section 122) nor with "indecent practice between male persons" (section 123) for several years, the author argues that because of his long-term relationship with another man, his active lobbying of Tasmanian politicians and the reports about his activities in the local media, and because of his activities as a gay rights activist and gay HIV/AIDS worker, his private life and his liberty are threatened by the continued existence of sections 122 (a) and (c) and 123 of the Criminal Code.

2.4 Mr. Toonen further argues that the criminalization of homosexuality in private has not permitted him to expose openly his sexuality and to publicize his views on reform of the relevant laws on sexual matters, as he felt that this would have been extremely prejudicial to his employment. In this context, he contends that sections 122 (a) and (c) and 123 have created the conditions for discrimination in employment, constant stigmatization, vilification, threats of physical violence and the violation of basic democratic rights.

2.5 The author observes that numerous "figures of authority" in Tasmania have made either derogatory or downright insulting remarks about homosexual men and women over the past few years. These include statements made by members of the Lower House of Parliament, municipal councillors (such as "representatives of the gay community are no better than Saddam Hussein" and "the act of homosexuality is unacceptable in any society, let alone a civilized society"), of the church and of members of the general public, whose statements have been directed against the integrity and welfare of homosexual men and women in Tasmania (such as "[g]ays want to lower society to their level" and "You are 15 times more likely to be murdered by a homosexual than a heterosexual . . ."). In some public meetings, it has been suggested that all Tasmanian homosexuals should be rounded up and "dumped" on an uninhabited island, or be subjected to compulsory sterilization. Remarks such as these, the author affirms, have had the effect of creating constant stress and suspicion in what ought to be routine contacts with the authorities in Tasmania.

2.6 The author further argues that Tasmania has witnessed, and continues to witness, a "campaign of official and unofficial hatred" against homosexuals and lesbians. This campaign has made it difficult for the Tasmanian Gay Law Reform Group to disseminate information about its activities and advocate the decriminalization of homosexuality. Thus, in September 1988, for example, the Group was refused permission to put up a stand in a public square in the city of Hobart, and the author claims that he, as a leading protester against the ban, was subjected to police intimidation.

2.7 Finally, the author argues that the continued existence of sections 122 (a) and (c) and 123 of the Criminal Code of Tasmania continue to have profound and harmful impacts on many people in Tasmania, including himself, in that it fuels discrimination and violence against and harassment of the homosexual community of Tasmania.

The Complaint. . . .

3.3 The author submits that no effective remedies are available against sections 122 (a) and (c) and 123. At the legislative level, state jurisdictions have primary responsibility for the enactment and enforcement of criminal law. As the Upper and Lower Houses of the Tasmanian Parliament have been deeply divided over the decriminalization of homosexual activities and reform of the Criminal Code, this potential avenue of redress is said to be ineffective. The author further observes that effective administrative remedies are not available, as they would depend on the support of a majority of members of both Houses of Parliament, support which is lacking. Finally, the author contends that no judicial remedies for a violation of the Covenant are available, as the Covenant has not been incorporated into Australian law, and Australian courts have been unwilling to apply treaties not incorporated into domestic law.

The State Party's Information and Observations

4.1 The State party did not challenge the admissibility of the communication on any grounds, while reserving its position on the substance of the author's claims.

4.2 The State party notes that the laws challenged by Mr. Toonen are those of the state of Tasmania and only apply within the jurisdiction of that state. Laws similar to those challenged by the author once applied in other Australian jurisdictions but have since been repealed.

The Committee's Decision on Admissibility

5.1 During its forty-sixth session, the Committee considered the admissibility of the communication. As to whether the author could be deemed a "victim" within the meaning of article 1 of the Optional Protocol, it noted that the legislative provisions challenged by the author had not been enforced by the judicial authorities of Tasmania for a number of years. It considered, however, that the author had made reasonable efforts to demonstrate that the threat of enforcement and the pervasive impact of the continued existence of these provisions on administrative practices and public opinion had affected him and continued to affect him personally, and that they could raise issues under articles 17 and 26 of the Covenant. Accordingly, the Committee was satisfied that the author could be deemed a victim within the meaning of article 1 of the Optional Protocol, and that his claims were admissible *ratione temporis*.

5.2 On 5 November 1992, therefore, the Committee declared the communication admissible inasmuch as it appeared to raise issues under articles 17 and 26 of the Covenant.

The State Party's Observations on the Merits and Author's Comments Thereon

6.1 In its submission under article 4, paragraph 2, of the Optional Protocol, dated 15 September 1993, the State party concedes that the author has been a victim of arbitrary interference with his privacy, and that the legislative provisions challenged by him cannot be justified on public health or moral grounds. It incorporates into its submission the observations of the government of Tasmania, which denies that the author has been the victim of a violation of the Covenant.

6.2 With regard to article 17, the Federal Government notes that the Tasmanian government submits that article 17 does not create a "right to privacy" but only a right to freedom from arbitrary or unlawful interference with privacy, and that as the challenged laws were enacted by democratic process, they cannot be an unlawful interference with privacy. The Federal Government, after reviewing the *travaux préparatoires* of article 17, subscribes to the following definition of "private": "matters which are individual, personal, or confidential, or which are kept or removed from public observation." The State party acknowledges that based on this definition, consensual sexual activity in private is encompassed by the concept of "privacy" in article 17.6.3 As to whether sections 122 and 123 of the Tasmanian Criminal Code "interfere" with the author's privacy, the State party notes that the Tasmanian authorities advised that there is no policy to treat investigations or the prosecution of offences under the disputed provisions any differently from the investigation or prosecution of offences under the Tasmanian Criminal Code in general, and that the most recent prosecution under the challenged provisions dates back to 1984. The State party acknowledges, however, that in the absence of any specific policy on the part of the Tasmanian authorities not to enforce the laws, the risk of the provisions being applied to Mr. Toonen remains, and that this risk is relevant to the assessment of whether the provisions "interfere" with his privacy. On balance, the State party concedes that Mr. Toonen is personally and actually affected by the Tasmanian laws.

6.4 As to whether the interference with the author's privacy was arbitrary or unlawful, the State party refers to the *travaux préparatoires* of article 17 and observes that the drafting history of the provision in the Commission on Human Rights appears to indicate that the term "arbitrary" was meant to cover interferences which, under Australian law, would be covered by the concept of "unreasonableness." Furthermore, the Human Rights Committee, in its general comment 16 (32) on article 17, states that the "concept of arbitrariness is intended to guarantee that even interference provided for by law should be in accordance with the provisions, aims and objectives of the Covenant and should be . . . reasonable in the particular circumstances." On the basis of this and the Committee's jurisprudence on the concept of "reasonableness," the State party interprets "reasonable" interferences with privacy as measures which are based on reasonable and objective criteria and which are proportional to the purpose for which they are adopted.

6.5 The State party does not accept the argument of the Tasmanian authorities that the retention of the challenged provisions is partly motivated by a concern to protect Tasmania from the spread of HIV/AIDS, and that the laws are justified on public health and moral grounds. This assessment in fact goes against the National HIV/AIDS Strategy of the Government of Australia, which emphasizes that laws criminalizing homosexual activity obstruct public health programmes promoting safer sex. The State party further disagrees with the Tasmanian authorities' contention that the laws are justified on moral grounds, noting that moral issues were not at issue when article 17 of the Covenant was drafted.

6.6 None the less, the State party cautions that the formulation of article 17 allows for some infringement of the right to privacy if there are reasonable grounds, and that domestic social mores may be relevant to the reasonableness of an interference with privacy. The State party observes that while laws penalizing homosexual activity existed in the past in other Australian states, they have since been repealed with the exception of Tasmania. Furthermore, discrimination on the basis of homosexuality or sexuality is unlawful in three of six Australian states and the two self-governing internal Australian territories. The Federal Government has declared sexual preference to be a ground of discrimination that may be invoked under ILO Convention No. 111 (Discrimination in Employment or Occupation Convention), and has created a mechanism through which complaints about discrimination in employment on the basis of sexual preference may be considered by the Australian Human Rights and Equal Opportunity Commission.

6.7 On the basis of the above, the State party contends that there is now a general Australian acceptance that no individual should be disadvantaged on the basis of his or her sexual orientation. Given the legal and social situation in all of Australia except Tasmania, the State party acknowledges that a complete prohibition on sexual activity between men is unnecessary to sustain the moral fabric of Australian society. On balance, the State party "does not seek to claim that the challenged laws are based on reasonable and objective criteria." . . .

6.9 In respect of the alleged violation of article 26, the State party seeks the Committee's guidance as to whether sexual orientation may be subsumed under the term . . . "or other status" in article 26. In this context, the Tasmanian authorities concede that sexual orientation is an "other status" for the purposes of the Covenant. The State party itself, after review of the *travaux préparatoires*, the Committee's general comment on articles 2 and 26 and its jurisprudence under these provisions, contends that there "appears to be a strong argument that the words of the two articles should not be read restrictively." The formulation of the provisions "without distinction of any kind, such as" and "on any ground such as" support an inclusive rather than exhaustive interpretation. While the *travaux préparatoires* do not provide specific guidance on this question, they also appear to support this interpretation. . . .

7.1 In his comments, the author welcomes the State party's concession that sections 122 and 123 violate article 17 of the Covenant but expresses concern that the argumentation of the Government of Australia is entirely based on the fact that he is threatened with prosecution under the aforementioned provisions and does not take into account the general adverse effect of the laws on himself. He further expresses concern, in the context of the "arbitrariness" of the interference with his privacy, that the State party has found it difficult to ascertain with certainty whether the prohibition on private homosexual activity represents the moral position of a significant portion of the Tasmanian populace. He contends that, in fact, there is significant popular and institutional support for the repeal of Tasmania's anti-gay criminal laws, and provides a detailed list of associations and groups from a broad spectrum of Australian and Tasmanian society, as well as a detailed survey of national and international concern about gay and lesbian rights in general and Tasmania's anti-gay statutes in particular. . . .

7.6 As to the discriminatory effect of sections 122 and 123 of the Tasmanian Criminal Code, the author reaffirms that the *combined* effect of the provisions is discriminatory because together they outlaw all forms of intimacy between men. Despite its apparent neutrality, section 122 is said to be by itself discriminatory. In spite of the gender neutrality of Tasmanian laws against "unnatural sexual intercourse," this provision, like similar and now repealed laws in different Australian states, has been enforced far more often against men engaged in homosexual activity than against men or women who are heterosexually active. At the same time, the provision criminalizes an activity practised more often by men sexually active with other men than by men or women who are heterosexually active. The author contends that in its general comment on article 26 and in some of its views, the Human Rights Committee itself has accepted the notion of "indirect discrimination." . . .

7.8 Finally, the author develops his initial argument related to the link between the existence of anti-gay criminal legislation and what he refers to as "wider discrimination," i.e. harassment and violence against homosexuals and anti-gay prejudice. He argues that the existence of the law has adverse social and psychological impacts on himself and on others in his situation and cites numerous recent examples of harassment of and discrimination against homosexuals and lesbians in Tasmania.

7.9 Mr. Toonen explains that since lodging his complaint with the Committee, he has continued to be the subject of personal vilification and harassment. This occurred in the context of the debate on gay law reform in Tasmania and his role as a leading voluntary worker in the Tasmanian community welfare sector. He adds that more importantly, since filing his complaint, he lost his employment partly as a result of his communication before the Committee. . . .

7.11 The author concludes that sections 122 and 123 continue to have an adverse impact on his private and his public life by creating the conditions for discrimination, continuous harassment and personal disadvantage.

EXAMINATION OF THE MERITS

8.1 The Committee is called upon to determine whether Mr. Toonen has been the victim of an unlawful or arbitrary interference with his privacy, contrary to article 17, paragraph 1, and whether he has been discriminated against in his right to equal protection of the law, contrary to article 26.

8.2 In so far as article 17 is concerned, it is undisputed that adult consensual sexual activity in private is covered by the concept of "privacy," and that Mr. Toonen is actually and currently affected by the continued existence of the Tasmanian laws. The Committee considers that sections 122 (a) and (c) and 123 of the Tasmanian Criminal Code "interfere" with the author's privacy, even if these provisions have not been enforced for a decade. In this context, it notes that the policy of the Department of Public Prosecutions not to initiate criminal proceedings in respect of private homosexual conduct does not amount to a guarantee that no actions will be brought against homosexuals in the future, particularly in the light of undisputed statements of the Director of Public Prosecutions of Tasmania in 1988 and those of members of the Tasmanian Parliament. The continued existence of the challenged provisions therefore continuously and directly "interferes" with the author's privacy.

8.3 The prohibition against private homosexual behaviour is provided for by law, namely, sections 122 and 123 of the Tasmanian Criminal Code. As to whether it may be deemed arbitrary, the Committee recalls that pursuant to its general comment 16 (32) on article 17, the "introduction of the concept of arbitrariness is intended to guarantee that even interference provided for by the law should be in accordance with the provisions, aims and objectives of the Covenant and should be, in any event, reasonable in the circumstances." The Committee interprets the requirement of reasonableness to imply that any interference with privacy must be proportional to the end sought and be necessary in the circumstances of any given case.

8.4 While the State party acknowledges that the impugned provisions constitute an arbitrary interference with Mr. Toonen's privacy, the Tasmanian authorities submit that the challenged laws are justified on public health and moral grounds, as they are intended in part to prevent the spread of HIV/AIDS in Tasmania, and because, in the absence of specific limitation clauses in article 17, moral issues must be deemed a matter for domestic decision.

8.5 As far as the public health argument of the Tasmanian authorities is concerned, the Committee notes that the criminalization of homosexual practices cannot be considered a reasonable means or proportionate measure to achieve the aim of preventing the spread of AIDS/HIV. The Government of Australia observes that statutes criminalizing homosexual activity tend to impede public health programmes "by driving underground many of the people at the risk of infection." Criminalization of homosexual activity thus would appear to run counter to the implementation of effective education programmes in respect of the HIV/AIDS prevention. Secondly, the Committee notes that no link has been shown between the continued criminalization of homosexual activity and the effective control of the spread of the HIV/AIDS virus.

8.6 The Committee cannot accept either that for the purposes of article 17 of the Covenant, moral issues are exclusively a matter of domestic concern, as this would open the door to withdrawing from the Committee's scrutiny a potentially large number of statutes interfering with privacy. It further notes that with the exception of Tasmania, all laws criminalizing homosexuality have been repealed throughout Australia and that, even in Tasmania, it is apparent that there is no consensus as to whether sections 122 and 123 should not also be repealed. Considering further that these provisions are not currently enforced, which implies that they are not deemed essential to the protection of morals in Tasmania, the Committee concludes that the provisions do not meet the "reasonableness" test in the circumstances of the case, and that they arbitrarily interfere with Mr. Toonen's right under article 17, paragraph 1.

8.7 The State party has sought the Committee's guidance as to whether sexual orientation may be considered an "other status" for the purposes of article 26. The same issue could arise under article 2, paragraph 1, of the Covenant. The Committee confines itself to noting, however, that in its view, the reference to "sex" in articles 2, paragraph 1, and 26 is to be taken as including sexual orientation.

9. The Human Rights Committee, acting under article 5, paragraph 4, of the Optional Protocol to the International Covenant on Civil and Political Rights, is of the view that the facts before it reveal a violation of articles 17, paragraph 1, *juncto* 2, paragraph 1, of the Covenant.

10. Under article 2, paragraph 3 (a), of the Covenant, the author, as a victim of a violation of articles 17, paragraph 1, *juncto* 2, paragraph 1, of the Covenant, is entitled to a remedy. In the opinion of the Committee, an effective remedy would be the repeal of sections 122 (a) and (c) and 123 of the Tasmanian Criminal Code.

11. Since the Committee has found a violation of Mr. Toonen's rights under articles 17, paragraph 1, and 2, paragraph 1, of the Covenant requiring the repeal of the offending law, the Committee does not consider it necessary to consider whether there has also been a violation of article 26 of the Covenant.

12. The Committee would wish to receive, within 90 days of the date of the transmittal of its views, information from the State party on the measures taken to give effect to the views.

Do you think that *Toonen* might have been decided differently if homosexuality were outlawed throughout Australia, instead of only in Tasmania? Would you expect the Committee to adopt similar views in the cases of Algeria or Mali, both of which are parties to the Optional Protocol, or might arguments based on morality be given different weight in different cultural and religious contexts?

For further reading on the individual petition procedures, see Anne F. Bayefsky, *How to Complain to the UN Human Rights Treaty System* (2002); P.R. Ghandhi, *The Human Rights Committee and the Right of Individual Communication* (1998); Siân Lewis-Anthony and Martin Scheinin, "Treaty-Based Procedures for Making Human Rights Complaints Within the UN System," in *Guide to International Human Rights Practice* (Hurst Hannum ed., 4th ed. 2004); McGoldrick, supra page 590, at 120-246; Nowak, supra page 590, at 819-909; Kirsten A. Young, *The Law and Process of the U.N. Human Rights Committee* (2002).

Note: Should There Be an Optional Protocol to the Covenant on Economic, Social and Cultural Rights?

Since 1990, there has been much discussion about adopting an optional protocol to the Covenant on Economic, Social, and Cultural Rights, which would give the ESC Committee the competence to consider individual communications relating to the rights set forth in the Covenant. After much discussion, the Committee submitted to the Commission on Human Rights in 1996 a Draft Optional Protocol to add a right of individual petition to the ESC Covenant. UN Doc. E/CN.4/1997/105, Annex (Dec. 18, 1996).

The Commission considered the issue for three years, soliciting comments and observations from states and intergovernmental and nongovernmental organizations. The last-mentioned were firmly in favor of the adoption of a draft protocol, while states were much more divided in their opinions. In 2001, the Commission appointed an independent expert to study the question of the draft protocol, and it later established an open-ended working group to continue considering the issue. The mandate of the working group was renewed in 2004 for two years.

States have suggested various options for the proposed protocol:

(1) using as a model the 1988 Additional Protocol to the American Convention on Human Rights in the Area of Economic, Social and Cultural Rights, which allows only a few rights to be subject to the petition procedure;
(2) basing the optional protocol on the collective complaints procedure of the European Social Charter [see Chapter 8, page 706];
(3) taking an "à la carte" approach, allowing states to choose the rights which would fall within the jurisdiction of the ESC Committee; and
(4) adopting a comprehensive protocol covering all the rights in the Covenant.

The UN Office of Legal Counsel has made clear that any petition procedure requires the consent of parties to the Covenant in the form of an amendment or protocol to the Covenant; the Committee could not on its own simply decide to consider communications. Many states favor including in any protocol provisions which also would give a basis in the treaty itself for the Committee on Economic, Social and Cultural Rights, which is not mentioned in the Covenant. While most delegations that support an optional protocol seem to favor a comprehensive agreement, some key states (including Australia, Canada, Japan, Poland, and the United States) have expressed skepticism about any protocol. The United States has asserted that an optional protocol would be ineffective and costly — although, since the U.S. is not a party to the ESC Covenant, one might question the weight that should be given to its views.

D. *Interstate Complaints*

Traditional international law has always envisaged the possibility for one state to initiate proceedings against another state, assuming that both states accept the jurisdiction of an appropriate judicial or arbitral tribunal. Similarly, human rights treaties normally provide for inter-state complaints, whenever one state alleges that another is acting in breach of the relevant treaty. Among the major UN treaties, the Convention against Torture (art. 21), Migrant Workers Convention (art. 76), CERD (arts 11-13), and CPR Covenant (arts. 41-43) provide for the possibility of inter-state complaints; however, only CERD makes this procedure mandatory. Under all of the other treaties, states must separately accept the possibility of inter-state complaints when or after ratifying the treaty. To date, not a single inter-state complaint has been filed under any of these procedures, despite the fact that there are, for example, over 80 parties to CERD and nearly 50 states that have declared their acceptance of inter-state complaints under article 41 of the CPR Covenant. The reluctance of states to raise human rights issues in an international dispute settlement process is similarly reflected by the fact that an ILO procedure for inter-state complaints, provided for in articles 26-34 of the ILO Constitution, has only been used six times since 1919. It is only within the European human rights system (see Chapter 8) that inter-state complaints have been utilized significantly, and even these represent a very small percentage of cases.

Read the relevant articles that allow inter-state complaints. Why do you think that they have never been utilized? Recall the discussion supra of the diplomatic wrangling over human rights in the Commission on Human Rights; why haven't states used the treaty procedures for similar purposes or to bring the equivalent of an acto popularis when human rights obligations are being widely ignored?

For additional commentary on interstate complaints, see Novak, supra page 590, at 753-777; Dinah Shelton, Compliance Mechanisms [Inter-State Communications], in Hannum and Fischer, supra page 588, at 155-157.

E. *General Comments*

The supervisory organs of all the major human rights bodies also issue General Comments (called "General Recommendations" under CERD and

CEDAW). The Human Rights Committee began the practice in the 1980s, with the intent of assisting states in fulfilling their reporting obligations. The treaties do not specify what the subject-matter of General Comments should be, and the various committees have gradually expanded their scope so that they now address technical or reporting issues, the nature of the obligations states have assumed under the treaties, and the committees' interpretation of the substantive meaning of various articles. Strictly speaking, of course, General Comments are not an implementation measure, but the gloss they may put on a treaty's substantive provisions may make it easier to determine a state's obligations thereunder and, if the facts warrant it, file a communication to hold it accountable for violations thereof.

Dozens of general comments or recommendations have been adopted by the treaty bodies, and they are periodically compiled by the United Nations; the most recent such compilation is Compilation of General Comments and General Recommendations adopted by Human Rights Treaty Bodies, UN Doc. HRI/GEN/1/Rev.7 (May 12, 2004) and Add.1 (May 4, 2005); they also may be found on the OHCHR website, *http://www.ohchr.org*. In addition to addressing the form and content of reports, the comments have considered such substantive issues as the right to life; torture; freedom of expression; the protection of aliens, children, and the family; self-determination and minority rights; reservations to human rights treaties; and discrimination.

In 2003, the inter-committee meeting of treaty bodies discussed the possibility of issuing joint general comments, in view of the overlap between provisions of different treaties monitored by different committees. A suggested starting point has been the meaning of the prohibition on discrimination found in all of the treaties; another is the consequence of non-reporting by states parties. See Effective Implementation of Human Rights Instruments on Human Rights, Including Reporting Obligations under International Instruments on Human Rights: Report of the Chairpersons of the Human Rights Treaty Bodies on their Fifteenth Meeting, UN Doc. A/58/350(Sept. 5, 2003).

F. *Strengthening the Treaty System*

Human rights treaties have been drafted largely in response to political pressure from NGOs and interested states. This piecemeal approach has meant that there has been little long-term thinking about the UN system or how to ensure that new instruments and treaty bodies complement existing procedures. For this and many other reasons described in the following readings, the system today suffers from substantial structural problems. As Manfred Nowak has indicated, "the proliferation of UN human rights treaties with different but overlapping reporting obligations and with separate treaty monitoring bodies working on an unpaid, voluntary and part-time basis, together with a trend towards universal ratification of these treaties, has led to an unmanageable and deeply frustrating situation for all involved. Governments complain about the high number of reports they are obliged to draft periodically, and which often are examined many years after their submission, and the expert bodies complain about the lack of discipline among governments and the limited time they are given to examine the numerous reports.... [O]nly a major structural reform can help to solve the ongoing crisis." Nowak, supra page 590, at 718-719. Professor Bayefsky concluded that "the human rights treaty system will remain inefficient and inadequate in the absence of consolidation of the treaty bodies. Some limited amendment is, therefore, unavoidable.... At the same time, consolidation is not a panacea. To work, it must be accompanied by a commitment on the part of states to accept the equally fundamental need for independent and expert membership on the monitoring bodies, coupled with the provision of adequate resources." Bayefsky, supra page 599, at xiv.

These and other issues are addressed in the following report by Professor Philip Alston, former Chair of the ESC Committee, who was appointed by the Secretary-General in the late 1980s to identify measures that might be taken to improve the effective functioning of the UN human rights treaty system. His interim report is contained in UN Doc. A/44/668 (Nov. 8, 1989), and the final report follows.

Final Report on Enhancing the Long-Term Effectiveness of the United Nations Human Rights Treaty System

UN Doc. E/CN.4/1997/74 (Mar. 27, 1996)

10. The . . . present system is unsustainable and . . . significant reforms will be required if the overall regime is to achieve its objectives. This is a function of several developments including the immense expansion of the human rights treaty system in a period of less than two decades, the expanding reach and increasing demands of regional human rights systems, the proliferation of reporting obligations in other contexts, especially in the environmental field, and the increasing pressures upon Governments and the United Nations system to reduce their budgetary outlays and streamline their programmes. The treaty bodies cannot, and nor should they seek to, remain immune to these pressures....

III. Medium-Term And Long-Term Reform Issues

A. Introduction

80. It is now almost eight years since the independent expert first suggested that consideration might be given to the preparation of consolidated reports to the treaty bodies as well as to the eventual consolidation of the existing treaty bodies into "one or perhaps two new treaty bodies." He also called for "a sustained exchange of views" on these proposals (A/44/668, paras. 179 and 182). Since that time, academic and other observers have taken up the challenge while the treaty bodies themselves, the meetings of chairpersons and the policy organs have all remained virtually silent. There is good reason for the silence of the treaty bodies. Their members are in the process of investing considerable time and energy into making the existing procedures work and they can hardly be expected to be enthusiastic about the elimination of either the procedures they are struggling to perfect or of those committees as they currently exist. It is less clear why the policy organs have remained reluctant to engage in the debate. It is suggested that the trends documented in this report have already made such debate urgent

and that, in any event, the unsustainability of the existing system will have compelled radical changes of one type or another within less than a decade. The only real question is whether they will be of an ad hoc, reactive and incomplete nature or whether they will have been planned logically and systematically.

B. THE NATURE OF THE EMERGING CHALLENGE

81. The information and analysis contained in this report support a number of conclusions as to the future evolution of the treaty body system. Over the course of the next decade, close to universal ratification of the six core treaties is likely to be achieved. States will be under increased pressure to honour their reporting obligations and significant technical and financial assistance will be made available to help them to do so. States which do not report will often be subject to review anyway. States will be expected to produce six reports, to engage in six separate "constructive dialogues," to answer to additional ad hoc requests from six committees, and to respond to complaints emanating from perhaps four or more separate communications procedures. They will also be expected to take full account of general comments (or their equivalents) emanating from six different committees and to respond to increasingly detailed concluding observations from the same number of committees.

82. In addition to these obligations, within a decade a significant number of countries may well be required to report under the International Convention on the Protection of the Rights of All Migrant Workers and Members of Their Families. That would add a seventh reporting procedure and yet another committee and will require States parties to report in relation to the most complex, detailed and lengthy of all of the human rights treaties.

83. But a growing burden upon States will not be the only consequence. The treaty bodies will need to at least double their existing meeting time so that the Committee on the Rights of the Child alone would be meeting for close to six months of every year. Committees which already have a very large backlog of unexamined communications will be joined by others in the same situation and together they will need to find the time and the expertise to deal with the more and more complex issues which, in the nature of things, will inevitably be brought before them. The size of the secretariat servicing the treaty bodies would need at least to be doubled just in order to maintain existing levels of service (which almost every treaty body has condemned as entirely inadequate). The costs of conference servicing (especially translation of documents and interpretation) will rise exponentially, thus making major additional demands upon resources that are presently subject to dramatic cuts. Domestic non-governmental organizations would rapidly lose interest in reporting to a different treaty body every year and their international counterparts will be unable to keep up with the demands emanating every year from one treaty body or another in relation to every country. The media, both national and international, are likely to become even less interested than is currently the case in relation to such frequent, and most likely superficial, procedures.

84. The members of the treaty bodies would be required to spend between one-third and one-half of their time in Geneva or New York, for which some (members of the Human Rights Committee, the Committee on the Elimination of Discrimination against Women and the Committee on the Rights of the Child)

will receive US$ 3,000 per year (apart from their daily allowances) and the others (members of the Committee on Economic, Social and Cultural Rights, the Committee on the Elimination of Racial Discrimination and the Committee against Torture) will receive nothing (apart from the same allowances). In light of such demands, committee membership will be feasible only for governmental officials paid by their national authorities (a situation unlikely to guarantee either independence or expertise), academics subsidized by their Governments (since in today's climate of budget cuts and a user-pays approach most universities are unlikely to be prepared to subsidize international service for half the year), or retirees. . . .

D. CONSOLIDATED REPORTS

90. The interim report by the independent expert outlined a proposal for the preparation of a single consolidated report by each State party, which would then be submitted in satisfaction of the requirements under each of the treaties to which the State is a party. That proposal is for individual States to consider and act upon. It does not require endorsement or other formal action by any United Nations body or the treaty bodies. The detailed analytical study called for by the General Assembly in resolution 51/87 will, when completed, assist in the preparation of any such consolidated reports. Ultimately, the questions and concerns that have been raised can only be answered definitively on the basis of concrete efforts to produce and work on the basis of such reports.

E. ELIMINATION OF COMPREHENSIVE PERIODIC REPORTS IN THEIR PRESENT FORM

91. Another proposal, previously foreshadowed by the independent expert but not developed in any detail, would be to eliminate the requirement that States parties' periodic reports should be comprehensive. Such an approach would clearly not be appropriate in relation to initial reports. Similarly, it might be better suited to the situation of some treaty bodies than others, and might not be applied in all cases. The broader the scope of a treaty, the more appropriate it would seem to be to seek to limit the range of issues which must be addressed in a report. In effect, the reporting guidelines would be tailored to each State's individual situation. In many respects, it is a logical extension of an approach followed by the Human Rights Committee since 1989.

92. Since there are various formulas which might be adopted, the following process is only indicative. It would begin with a decision by the committee at session A to draw up a list of questions at session B. In the intervening period it would invite submissions of information from all relevant sources and would request the Secretariat to prepare a country analysis. The pre-sessional working group could then meet, perhaps immediately before or during session B, and draft a specific and limited list of questions. After endorsement by the Committee at session B the list would be forwarded immediately to the State party with a request for a written report to be submitted in advance (in sufficient time to enable translation) of session C or D. Such a procedure would: focus the dialogue on a limited range of issues; entirely eliminate the need to produce a lengthy report covering many issues of little

particular import in relation to the country concerned; ensure that issues of current importance are the principal focus; guarantee that a report would be examined on schedule; enable individuals with expertise in the matters under review to participate in the delegation; reduce the number of ministries directly involved in report preparation; enhance the capacity of expert members of the committees to be well prepared for the dialogue; and provide a strong foundation for more detailed and clearly focused concluding observations. . . .

F. TOWARDS A CONSOLIDATION OF THE TREATY BODIES

94. Some of the arguments for and against this reform have already been explored in the independent expert's 1989 report (A/44/668, paras. 182-183). For that reason, they will not be repeated here. Given the limitations of space it must suffice to note in this context that while the legal and procedural problems inherent in such an initiative would not be negligible, the prior issue is whether there is the political will to begin exploring in any detail the contours of such a reform. If that will were manifest, the technical challenges would be resolvable. It is therefore recommended that consideration be given to the convening of a small expert group, with an appropriate emphasis upon international legal expertise, to prepare a report on the modalities that might be considered in this respect.

G. THE DESIRABILITY OF ADDITIONAL PROACTIVE MEASURES

95. In addition to examining the possibility of steps to reduce the existing number of treaty bodies, it is important for United Nations organs which are involved in the design of new procedures to bear in mind the desirability of limiting the number of additional bodies to be created. Viewed in isolation, and on their individual merits, proposals to establish new, and improved, mechanisms are inevitably attractive. This attraction should, however, be balanced against the impact on the system as a whole of new bodies competing for scarce resources and perhaps, in some respects at least, unnecessarily duplicating the demands upon States parties. . . .

H. AMENDING THE TREATIES

98. Since the submission of the first report on treaty body reform, in 1989, amendments to three of the six treaties have been approved by the respective Meetings of the States Parties and endorsed by the General Assembly. They seek to ensure that the activities of both the Committee on the Elimination of Racial Discrimination and the Committee against Torture are financed from the regular budget of the United Nations (rather than wholly or partly by the States parties as currently provided for in the respective treaties) and to permit the Committee on the Elimination of Discrimination against Women to meet for longer than the two weeks annually specified in the Convention. A fourth proposed amendment would expand the membership of the Committee on the Rights of the Child from 10 to 18. The fact that both the respective Meetings of States Parties, as well as the General Assembly, have approved these amendments is an indication of the need for reform and of the preparedness of Governments to endorse such reforms. . . .

101. Several recommendations emerge from this situation:

(a) All future human rights treaties should provide for a simplified process to be followed in order to amend the relevant procedural provisions. While the specific endorsement of this proposal by the Commission on Human Rights could not be binding in the context of any future negotiations it would constitute a clear policy guideline and help to facilitate the adoption of such flexibility in the future;

(b) A report should be requested from the Legal Counsel which would explore the feasibility of devising more innovative approaches in dealing with existing and future amendments to the human rights treaties;

(c) The General Assembly should request the Meetings of the States Parties to the relevant treaties to discuss means by which the States concerned might be encouraged to attach a higher priority to ratification of the amendments already approved; . . .

IV. Other Issues

A. The Unmentionable Language Question

102. The question of languages has gone largely unaddressed in this report. For the most part, this is merely an accurate reflection of the inability of the United Nations and its Member States to come to grips with one of the most controversial and enduring issues confronting the Organization as a whole. Unfortunately, it is also one which is of particular importance to the treaty bodies. Any attempt by the independent expert to resolve the dilemmas would be both presumptuous and doomed to failure. Nevertheless, it is appropriate to proffer a few pertinent observations.

103. In the first place, the treaty bodies have been compelled by resource constraints and decisions taken elsewhere to privilege the two principal working languages [English and French] of the Secretariat. This is reflected in the production of summary records and press releases, and in the vast majority of drafting exercises. Simultaneous interpretation into languages other than Spanish, unless specifically requested, seems to be increasingly less common in the daytoday work of the treaty bodies. Secondly, the de facto dominance of English as the main working language of the committees has increased very significantly in the past few years. While this may be regrettable in terms of the maintenance of linguistic equality and diversity it is largely a reflection of national trends which are outside the control of the treaty bodies. These trends seem likely to accelerate in the years ahead as a result of the emphasis upon English in business, information technology, science, media and other spheres of activity. Thirdly, for a variety of reasons well beyond the control of the United Nations, English language materials tend to predominate in the rapidly growing volume of information which makes up the background materials available to the treaty bodies in their examination of individual State reports.

104. Official responses within the United Nations to these trends have been somewhat contradictory. On the one hand, the General Assembly has reaffirmed its strong commitment to the principle of linguistic diversity, and the Secretariat has attached renewed emphasis to an old rule by which a document cannot be issued in any language until it is available in all. At the same time, various policies

and practices encourage the treaty bodies to operate with as few languages as possible. The very rapidly increasing number of individuals, groups and agencies obtaining access to the documentation of international organizations by electronic means are, and are virtually certain to continue to be, significantly advantaged if they can work in English rather than in any other language.

105. The official rules are appropriate reflections of a commitment to multilingualism and would, in a context of adequate resources, help to maintain an appropriate balance. But in a situation of dire financial stringency the resulting inflexibility will, on the one hand, wreak havoc and on the other, provoke resort to ever more creative and devious strategies to circumvent unworkable rules. Such strategies invariably add to overall costs and, at least in the longer term, generate a range of inefficient, opaque and counter-productive practices. Understandable resentment of the extent to which extraneous factors have tended to undermine the policy of language equality has tended to stifle efforts to identify a range of medium-term and long-term strategies which might respond to emerging realities in a more nuanced manner.

106. In the context of the treaty bodies the importance of maintaining linguistic diversity is, for many reasons, beyond doubt. By the same token, in the absence of a substantial increase in funds for interpretation, there is a clear need for the different committees to explore ways in which working groups and other non-plenary meetings can be held without official translation. Greater emphasis should be attached to the ability of nominees for election to the treaty bodies to work in at least one, and preferably two, of the three major languages. Ways will have to be found in which the content of materials available in only one language can be drawn upon more efficiently for the benefit of the whole committee. Consideration will need to be given to delegating certain responsibilities to working groups capable of working without translation. While these and other more innovative and flexible steps will probably be considered only reluctantly, necessity will have its way sooner rather than later. . . .

V. Principal Recommendations

110. This section summarizes some of the recommendations made in the report.

111. The goal of achieving universal ratification of the six core treaties has been affirmed frequently. Concrete measures aimed at making it a reality are needed. They should include: (a) consultations with the leading international agencies to explore their potential involvement in a ratification campaign (para. 32); (b) the appointment of special advisers on ratification and reporting and the earmarking of funds for those purposes (paras. 33-34); (c) special measures should be explored to streamline the reporting process for States with small populations (para. 35); and (d) particular attention should be paid to other substantial categories of nonparties.

112. Non-reporting has reached chronic proportions. In addition to considering reforms to the overall system (noted below), a new specially tailored project for the provision of advisory services should be implemented. In responding to cases of persistent delinquency, all treaty bodies should be urged to adopt procedures which lead eventually to the examination of situations even in the absence of a

report (paras. 37-45). Such an approach should reflect thorough research and lead to detailed, accurate and comprehensive "concluding observations" (para. 47).

113. The present reporting system functions only because of the large-scale delinquency of States which either do not report at all, or report long after the due date. If many were to report, significant existing backlogs would be exacerbated, and major reforms would be needed even more urgently (paras. 48-52).

114. Proposed documentation limits are unworkable within the context of existing procedures. The issue needs to be dealt with in a far more transparent manner than has so far been the case and full justification for any cuts need to be provided. The Secretariat should draw up a detailed options paper to enable the committees to consider measured and innovative responses (paras. 53-54).

115. The extent of documentation which is central to the dialogue but which is nowhere officially recorded is an important problem and calls for appropriate measures to be devised by the Secretariat (para. 55). The preparation of summary records is an indispensable element in the system and their timely preparation should be accorded priority. The continued production of bound and edited volumes of Official Records of the Human Rights Committee (previously known as Yearbooks) is difficult to justify at a time of financial stringency (para. 58). Priority should be accorded to transferring the existing data on to electronic databases and ensuring the timely publication, including in electronic form, of all summary records as soon as they are available (para. 59).

116. The new home page of the High Commissioner/Centre for Human Rights constitutes an unduly delayed but very welcome development. It should be maintained and expanded and a strategy to widen access should be devised. Future development of the database should reflect a more systematic, consultative and transparent process than has hitherto been the case. An expert seminar should be convened for that purpose and an external advisory group appointed (paras. 60-64). The ILO should consider making its very valuable database available on the Web to the human rights community and others (para. 65).

117. The public information materials relating to the work of the treaty bodies are highly inadequate. The treaty bodies should be given a direct input into future decision-making in this regard. A public information budget should be made available to support grassroots initiatives designed to disseminate information about the treaty bodies in culturally appropriate and more popular formats and media. Partnerships with academic and other external institutions should be explored in order to enhance the publications programme. An external advisory group should be asked to review the human rights-related publications programme and make recommendations (paras. 66-70). The Secretary-General should report on the actual availability of treaty body related materials at United Nations information centres (para. 71).

118. The advisory services programme has not provided sufficient support for surveys required prior to ratification of a human rights treaty or for the preparation of reports by States in need of assistance. Regional and subregional training courses in relation to reporting are unlikely to produce results commensurate with their cost. A specially designed programme should be devised to address the needs in this area and it should be accorded priority (paras. 72-77).

119. The effectiveness of "special reports" and "urgent procedures" should be carefully evaluated by the committees concerned. At present, the value they add

seems low. In general, the division of labour between the treaty bodies and special mechanisms should be maintained (paras. 78-79).

120. In light of current trends the existing reporting system is unsustainable (paras. 81-84). Four options are available to States: (a) to dismiss the concern as alarmist and take no action; (b) to urge the treaty bodies to undertake far-reaching reforms and adapt to cope with existing and new demands from within existing resources; (c) to provide greatly enhanced budgetary resources to sustain the status quo; (d) to combine some elements of (b) and (c) with the adoption of some far-reaching reforms (paras. 85-89). The latter could include: the preparation of "consolidated reports" (para. 90); elimination of comprehensive periodic reports in their present form and replacement by reporting guidelines tailored to each State's individual situation (paras. 91-93); and a consolidation (reduction) of the number of treaty bodies (para. 94). If the political will exists in relation to the latter, a small expert group should be convened to examine modalities. Proactive measures should also be considered, including amending the migrant workers convention to entrust the supervisory functions to an existing committee and giving more systematic consideration to the institutional implications of the proposed optional protocol to the Convention against Torture (paras. 96-98).

121. The procedural provisions of human rights treaties need to be made more susceptible to amendment. Various recommendations are suggested (para. 101). Constructive attention needs to be given to the taboo subject of working languages (paras. 102-106). Existing arrangements for cooperation with the specialized agencies and other bodies have been improved in some respects but remain very inadequate. The High Commissioner should convene a highlevel meeting to explore better means of cooperation with the treaty bodies (para. 108).

122. Treaty bodies must strive to further improve the quality of their "concluding observations," in terms of their clarity, degree of detail, level of accuracy and specificity (para. 109).

In 2002, the UN Secretary-General called for further reform of the treaty body system. The Office of the High Commissioner for Human Rights responded by organizing consultations with the treaty bodies, states parties, and NGOs to recommend measures to make the treaty body system more effective and efficient. The following two extracts describe the continuing process of reform.

General Assembly Res. 57/202, Effective implementation of international instruments on human rights, including reporting obligations under international instruments on human rights

Jan. 16, 2003 (references omitted)

The General Assembly,

Recalling its resolution 55/90 of 4 December 2000, as well as other relevant resolutions, and taking note of Commission on Human Rights resolution 2002/85 of 26 April 2002,

Reaffirming that the full and effective implementation of United Nations human rights instruments is of major importance to the efforts of the Organization, pursuant to the Charter of the United Nations and the Universal Declaration of Human Rights, to promote universal respect for and observance of human rights and fundamental freedoms,

Considering that the effective functioning of treaty bodies established pursuant to United Nations human rights instruments is indispensable for the full and effective implementation of such instruments,

Reaffirming the contribution of the human rights treaty bodies, within their mandates, to the prevention of violations of human rights, in the context of their consideration of reports submitted pursuant to their respective treaties,

Reiterating its concern about the lack of adequate resources, which impedes the effective functioning of the human rights treaty bodies,

Recalling that the effectiveness of the treaty bodies in encouraging the realization by States parties of their obligations under United Nations human rights instruments requires constructive dialogue aimed at assisting States parties in identifying solutions to human rights problems, which should be based on the reporting process supplemented by information from all relevant sources, which should be made available to all interested parties,

Recalling also the initiatives taken by a number of human rights treaty bodies to elaborate early warning measures and urgent procedures, within their mandates, with a view to preventing the occurrence or recurrence of serious human rights violations,

Reaffirming its responsibility for the effective functioning of the human rights treaty bodies, and reaffirming also the importance of:

(a) Promoting the effective functioning of the periodic reporting by States parties to those instruments,

(b) Securing sufficient financial, human and information resources for the Office of the United Nations High Commissioner for Human Rights to enable the human rights treaty bodies to carry out their mandates effectively, including in regard to their ability to work in the applicable working languages,

(c) Promoting greater efficiency and effectiveness through better coordination of the activities of the United Nations bodies active in the field of human rights, taking into account the need to avoid unnecessary duplication and overlapping of their mandates and tasks,

(d) Addressing questions of reporting obligations and financial implications when elaborating any further instruments on human rights,

1. *Takes note with appreciation* of the report of the Secretary-General and the reports of the persons chairing the human rights treaty bodies on their thirteenth and fourteenth meetings, held at Geneva from 18 to 22 June 2001 and from 24 to 26 June 2002 respectively, and also takes note of the conclusions and recommendations contained in the reports;

2. *Encourages* each human rights treaty body to continue to give careful consideration to the relevant conclusions and recommendations contained in the reports of the persons chairing the human rights treaty bodies on their meetings, and, in this context, encourages enhanced cooperation and coordination among the treaty bodies;

3. *Welcomes* the holding of the first inter-committee meeting of the human rights treaty bodies, from 26 to 28 June 2002, to discuss issues of common concern, including issues relating to the methods of work of the treaty bodies, and encourages those bodies to continue this practice in future on an annual basis;

4. *Encourages* the persons chairing the human rights treaty bodies to continue to invite representatives of States parties to participate in a dialogue within the framework of their meetings, and welcomes broad participation by States parties in the dialogue;

5. *Emphasizes* the need to ensure financing and adequate staff and information resources for the operations of the human rights treaty bodies, particularly in view of the additional demands placed on the system by the new reporting requirements and the increasing number of ratifications and, with this in mind:

(a) Reiterates its request that the Secretary-General provide adequate resources in respect of each human rights treaty body, while making the most efficient use of existing resources, in order to give the treaty bodies adequate administrative support and better access to technical expertise and relevant information;

(b) Calls upon the Secretary-General to seek, in the next biennium, the resources within the regular budget of the United Nations necessary to give the human rights treaty bodies adequate administrative support and better access to technical expertise and relevant information;

(c) Welcomes the plans of action prepared by the United Nations High Commissioner for Human Rights to enhance the resources available to all the human rights treaty bodies and thereby strengthen the implementation of the human rights treaties, and encourages all Governments, United Nations bodies and specialized agencies, non-governmental organizations and interested persons to consider contributing to the appeal for extrabudgetary resources for the treaty bodies made by the High Commissioner until the regular budget funding meets their needs;

8. *Also welcomes* the initiative taken by certain human rights treaty bodies to set page limitations for the initial and periodic reports of States parties, and encourages other treaty bodies to consider setting page limitations;

9. *Requests* each State party to update its core document, incorporating as necessary material common to its multiple reports to the human rights treaty bodies;

10. *Commends* the recent efforts by the human rights treaty bodies, with the assistance of the Office of the High Commissioner, to improve the petition system and to reduce the backlog;

11. *Reiterates* that a priority of the Office of the High Commissioner should be to provide assistance to States parties, upon their request and, if possible, in coordination with other United Nations bodies, Governments and other interested parties, in order:

(a) To assist those States in the process of ratifying United Nations human rights instruments;

(b) To assist States to implement their obligations under such instruments, including the preparation of their initial reports;

15. *Invites* States parties that have not yet submitted their initial reports pursuant to United Nations human rights instruments to avail themselves, where necessary, of technical assistance for this purpose;

17. *Reiterates its concern* about the large number of overdue reports on the implementation by States parties of certain United Nations instruments on human rights, and:

(a) Urges States parties to make every effort to meet their reporting obligations;

(b) Welcomes the efforts made by certain human rights treaty bodies to consider the situations of some States parties with overdue reports;

(c) Welcomes new initiatives by certain human rights treaty bodies actively to follow up concluding observations and comments with States parties, including through the appointment of one of their members as rapporteur for follow-up;

18. *Urges* each State party whose report has been examined by a human rights treaty body to translate, publish and make available in its territory the full text of the concluding observations and comments of the treaty body on its report and to provide adequate follow-up to those observations;

19. *Welcomes* the contribution to the work of the human rights treaty bodies made by the specialized agencies and other United Nations bodies, and encourages the specialized agencies and other United Nations bodies, the various organs of the Commission on Human Rights, including its special procedures, the Subcommission on the Promotion and Protection of Human Rights, the Office of the High Commissioner and the persons chairing the human rights treaty bodies to continue to explore specific measures to intensify this cooperation among themselves and to improve communication and information flow so as to improve further the quality of their work, including by avoiding unnecessary duplication;

20. *Recognizes* the important role played by non-governmental organizations in all parts of the world in the effective implementation of all human rights instruments, and encourages the exchange of information between the human rights treaty bodies and such organizations;...

Office of the United Nations High Commissioner for Human Rights, Effective Functioning of Human Rights Mechanisms Treaty Bodies

UN Doc. E/CN.4/2004/98 (Feb. 11, 2004)

2. Since the adoption of [Commission on Human Rights] resolution 2002/85, there have been a number of developments in the human rights treaty body system. The Optional Protocols to the Convention on the Rights of the Child on the sale of children, child prostitution and child pornography and on the involvement of children in armed conflict, which entered into force on 18 January and 12 February 2002 respectively, attracted further ratification and accession, and the Committee on the Rights of the Child considered the first report submitted in accordance with the Optional Protocol on the involvement of children in armed conflict at its thirty-fourth session in September/October 2003. The amendment to article 43, paragraph 2, of the Convention on the Rights of the Child increasing the membership of the Committee from 10 to 18 members entered into force on 18 November 2002, and an enlarged Committee met for the first time in May 2003. The Optional Protocol to the Convention against

Torture and Other Cruel, Inhuman or Degrading Treatment or Punishment, establishing a system of regular visits by national bodies and a subcommittee on Prevention of the Committee against Torture to visit places of detention, was adopted by the General Assembly in the annex to resolution 57/199 of 18 December 2002. In accordance with its article 87, the International Convention on the Rights of All Migrant Workers and Members of Their Families entered into force on 1 July 2003, and the first meeting of the Committee on the Protection of the Rights of All Migrant Workers and Members of Their Families is scheduled to take place from 1 to 5 March 2004.

3. During the reporting period, treaty bodies have continued to develop their working methods. The Committee against Torture established a pre-sessional working group to facilitate its monitoring activities. The Human Rights Committee and the Committee against Torture introduced procedures to follow up their concluding observations in order to assist in the implementation of human rights treaties in States parties. These innovations — in particular the follow-up procedure of the Human Rights Committee — have been successful, with a high rate of response from the parties to which the procedure has been applied. Informal meetings between individual treaty bodies and States parties to discuss working methods and other issues have been convened by all treaty bodies. All chairpersons of human rights treaty bodies were invited to address the fifty-ninth session of the Commission on Human Rights, and four chairpersons were able to take advantage of this opportunity to brief the Commission on the work of their respective committee.

4. At its thirty-fourth session, which closed on 3 October 2003, the Committee on the Rights of the Child adopted a recommendation on its working methods in which it decided that, for an initial period of two years, it would consider the reports of States parties in two parallel chambers, each consisting of nine members of the Committee, taking account of equitable geographical representation. The Committee's recommendation was brought to the attention of the General Assembly at its fifty-eighth session (A/C.3/58/10). During its thirtieth session, which took place from 12 to 30 January 2004, the Committee on the Elimination of Discrimination against Women (CEDAW) discussed the option of meeting in parallel working groups for consideration of periodic reports, on the basis of a note submitted by the secretariat (CEDAW/C/2004/I/4/Add.2)....

10. As of 31 January 2004, 185 initial reports of States parties required under the various treaties were overdue, of which 114 had been overdue for more than five years. Furthermore, a total of 660 periodic reports from States parties were overdue. Treaty bodies encourage States parties with overdue reports to avail themselves of technical cooperation programmes provided by the United Nations to assist in reporting. With the exception of CEDAW, treaty bodies have adopted the practice of reviewing implementation in States parties whose reports are significantly overdue in the absence of a report....

13. The establishment at the end of 2000 of a dedicated Petitions Team to deal with individual communications submitted under the Optional Protocol to the International Covenant on Civil and Political Rights, the Convention on the Elimination of All Forms of Racial Discrimination and the Committee against Torture ... has resulted in a significant reduction in the delay in processing individual complaints. The average time taken to review a complaint has been reduced during the reporting period by 8 months, from 42 to 36 months, repre-

senting a 20 per cent improvement over the period 2000-2001. The Petitions Team prepared draft decisions and recommendations with respect to approximately 150 individual complaints per year for the consideration of the treaty bodies. Of these, 115 have been considered by the Human Rights Committee, as compared to the 78 cases that were dealt with during the previous two years. The Human Rights Committee convened an additional one week of meetings during its seventy-eighth session in order to reduce the backlog in the consideration of pending registered individual complaints.

14. The delay in dealing with correspondence relating to individual complaints has been significantly reduced, with the only remaining backlog relating to complaints received in Russian, although this backlog is far less than during the period 2000-2001. Over 12,000 pieces of correspondence were dealt with during 2002-2003 as compared with 2000-2001. Speedier processing of correspondence has encouraged the submission of more individual complaints, in particular those directed to the Human Rights Committee, in respect of which the number of cases registered has risen from 102 in 2001-2002 to 170 in 2002-2003.

15. The creation of a database to manage individual complaints has greatly facilitated the case management capacity of the Petitions Team, serving as a tool for providing a clear picture of the status of cases before the treaty bodies. In line with the Secretary-General's reform programme, and in order to streamline the procedures and practices of the treaty bodies, efforts are under way to ensure the functioning of the interactive database on communications between OHCHR and the Division for the Advancement of Women of the Secretariat. The Division processes communications received under the Optional Protocol to the Convention on the Elimination of All Forms of Discrimination against Women, which entered into force in December 2000. The Petitions Team trained staff of the Division in relation to petitions and the database in December 2002.

In June 2004, the meeting of chairpersons of the committees agreed that a state wishing to use an expanded core report covering all matters common to the treaties to which it is party, with additional concise reports on treaty-specific issues, could do so. In June 2005, the UN secretariat produced a revised version of Harmonized Guidelines on Reporting under the International Human Rights treaties, including guidelines on a common core document and treaty-specific Targeted Documents, UN Doc. HRI/MC/2005/3 (June 1, 2005). The revision incorporates many of the changes suggested by the treaty bodies; states parties; UN agencies, funds, and programs; and NGOs.

The high-level summit convened by the United Nations in New York in September 2005 was unable to agree on the membership or mandate of a new Human Rights Council (although it agreed to its creation), but it did address some human rights issues in general terms, resolving to "improve the effectiveness of the human rights treaty bodies, including through more timely reporting, improved and streamlined reporting procedures and technical assistance to States. . . ." 2005 World Summit Outcome, supra page 564, para. 125. Perhaps the most specific and meaningful pledge was to double the budget of the Office of the High Commissioner for Human Rights over the next five years. Id., para. 124.

Comments and Questions

1. The Toonen case raises several issues of jurisdiction and merits. First is the question of whether Toonen could be considered a victim. In this respect, note that the European Court of Human Rights came to a similar conclusion in the case of *Dudgeon v. UK*, 45 Eur. Ct. H.R., App. No. 7525/76 (Oct. 22, 1981). When is the threat of a violation sufficient to make someone a victim for purposes of jurisdiction? Apart from the victim requirement, which issues of admissibility are jurisdictional and which are defenses that can be waived by the state? Note that Australia did not raise any objections to admissibility.

2. What is the legal status of the "views" of the Human Rights Committee adopted under the Optional Protocol?

3. Which of Professor Alston's recommendations, supra page 607, do you think are realistic and stand a chance of being accepted by states parties to the various treaties? To what extent is it appropriate for the General Assembly to make recommendations to treaty bodies on procedural changes? Does it make a difference that every UN member state has now ratified at least one of the seven major treaties? Will substantial changes require amendments to each of the treaties, or can reforms be instituted within existing legal constraints?

4. Note that it still takes on average three years for complaints under the CPR Covenant's Optional Protocol to be reviewed. How does this affect the effectiveness of the procedure? Is such a delay less than, more than, or comparable to the time that it takes the highest domestic court of appeal in your country to hear cases at the national level?

VI. Final Comments and Questions

1. One problem with the UN system is that it is starved for resources. Indeed, the Office of the High Commissioner functions today only because of outside contributions; only about 20 percent of its funding comes from the regular United Nations budget. Might this compromise the priorities set by the High Commissioner? Is the High Commissioner likely to be less willing to criticize a state that has recently provided substantial money, equipment, or personnel to the Office?

2. In the end, in evaluating these procedures and institutions, how much is human rights like Dr. Johnson's dancing dog, about which he is reported to have commented that one should not expect the dog to dance well; one should acknowledge and admire the fact that it can do it at all?

Chapter 8

The European System for the Protection of Human Rights

Can Regional Systems to Protect Human Rights Be More Effective than UN Mechanisms?

Thus far our concern has been primarily with issues relating to the promotion and protection of human rights by the United Nations. This and the next chapter move outside the UN framework to examine human rights protection at the regional level, which occurs primarily through treaty-based mechanisms. Regional human rights systems exist in Europe, the Americas, and Africa. The Arab League has a nascent system since it adopted the Arab Charter for Human Rights in 1994, and continuing efforts are underway to create a regional system or systems within the Asia-Pacific region. This chapter considers the extensive jurisprudence developed under the European Convention for the Protection of Human Rights and Fundamental Freedoms, as well as other human rights activities at the European regional level.

The jurisprudential and practical reasons for creating regional human rights regimes and their origins are set out in Chapter 5, pages 326, in which the African system is considered. The following reading offers a comparative overview of the three existing regional systems.

I. Universal and Regional Norms

Dinah Shelton, *The Promise of Regional Human Rights Systems*

In The Future of International Human Rights 365-66, 369-70, 373,377, 390-91, 393, 396 (B. Weston and S. Marks eds. 2000) (citations omitted)

The seemingly endless debate over universality and diversity in human rights law is inescapable when evaluating regional systems. The issue of normative diversity is complex. Virtually all the legal instruments creating the various regional systems refer to the Universal Declaration of Human Rights (UDHR) and the Charter of the United Nations, providing a measure of uniformity in the fundamental guarantees and a reinforcement of the universal character of the Declaration. The rights contained in the treaties also reflect the human rights norms set forth in other global human rights declarations and conventions, in particular the United Nations Covenants on Civil and Political Rights (CCPR) and Economic, Social and Cultural Rights (CESCR). In addition, as each successive system has been created it has looked to normative instruments and the jurisprudence of those systems founded earlier. Yet, there are clear differences in the regional instruments within the framework of the universal norms. The differences may be less pronounced than appears at first reading, however, because of provisions regarding choice of law and canons of interpretation contained in the regional instruments. The application of these provisions has led to a cross-referencing and mutual influence in jurisprudence that is producing some convergence in fundamental human rights principles....

[Rights have been added,] and in no case has a right been limited or withdrawn by a later instrument. In Europe, for example, even before the signing of the ECHR, the Assembly proposed the inclusion of additional rights, added by Protocol 1. The evolutionary character of the European system, reflected in its [13] protocols and related human rights treaties, is not unique. Regional systems seem to add new rights in a kind of feedback process of mutual inspiration, including such specific guarantees as abolition of the death penalty, action to combat violence against women, the right to a satisfactory environment, and strengthened guarantees in regard to economic, social, and cultural rights.... The dynamic interplay of the systems is characteristic of the non-linear complexity and evolution of modern systems.

All the regional instruments contain limitations clauses whose language is often similar, based on the UDHR. They also contain "clawback" clauses which limit certain rights to the extent provided in national law. The European Convention, for example, provides that the right to marry and to found a family is "according to the national laws governing the exercise of this right" (art. 12). The African and Arab Charters contain extensive "clawback" clauses that could undermine the effectiveness of both systems, although the developing jurisprudence of the African system thus far has insisted on effective enjoyment of the rights....

All of the systems have a growing case law detailing the rights and duties enunciated in the basic instruments. The jurisprudence of the regional human rights bodies has thus become a major source of human rights law. In many instances this case law reflects a convergence of the different substantive protections in favor of broad human rights protections. In other instances, differences in treaty terms or approach have resulted in a rejection of precedent from other systems. In general, the judges and the commissioners have been willing to substantiate or give greater authority to their interpretations of the rights guaranteed by referencing not only their own prior case law but the decisions of other global and regional bodies.

Some decisions cross-reference specific articles of other instruments. The European Court of Human Rights has utilized article 19(2) of the CCPR [Covenant on Civil and Political Rights] to apply article 10 of the European Convention to cover freedom of artistic expression. It has referred to the UN Convention on the Rights of the Child in regard to education and both the CCPR and American Convention in regard to the right to a name as part of European Convention art. 8. Most well known is the *Soering* case, where the Court found implicit in article 3 of the European Convention the obligation of article 3 of the UN Torture Convention not to extradite someone who might face torture.

While the mutual influence of the systems is clear, there are regional differences in the nature of cases filed that have limited the relevance of precedents from other systems. In Europe, until recently, virtually all cases raised questions of law on agreed facts. In addition, a large percentage concerned procedural guarantees in civil and criminal proceedings. In contrast, nearly all the Inter-American cases have concerned the factual determination of state responsibility for the death, disappearance, or other mistreatment of individuals. The result has been an Inter-American focus on issues of standard of proof and burden of proof that rarely arose in the European system until recently. For this reason, most of the references to European jurisprudence are found in the Inter-American Court's advisory opinions on questions of law. The Inter-American Commission has also had to be concerned with the widespread armed conflicts in the region. As a result, it has begun to document human rights violations by non-state actors, making an important contribution to international human rights law....

Roughly half the members states of the Council of Europe have joined since 1990, all of them in Central and Eastern Europe.... The change of membership affects the culture of the system and the nature of cases that are brought.... The Court now faces unprecedented situations of widespread violations where factual determinations of responsibility are crucial. European cases are coming to resemble those found in the Inter-American and the African systems. Both the character of the system and its effectiveness are challenged.

In contrast to other regions, the European system is also faced with institutional proliferation that creates problems and possibilities for advancing human rights protections. In addition to the Council of Europe, the Organization for Security and Cooperation in Europe (OSCE) and the European Communities (EC) are engaged in human rights activities. Their existence and work constitute a fundamental change in the environment of the Council and have helped to transform the regional system....

The result of multiple regional institutions can be both positive and negative. On the positive side, the mutual influence seen among regional institutions can also occur intraregionally, leading to greater human rights protections. Minority protection, for example, has become important since the enlargement of the Council of Europe. Under the influence of Helsinki process, which has high standards for minority protections, the Council has taken action to meet the challenges of ethnic tensions in the region.

[There remain areas] of specialization. The OSCE has a comparative advantage in conflict prevention because the Council of Europe is not a security organization and its mandate is thus more limited. The OSCE has also taken action on some situations where the Council of Europe and the UN have been inactive, such as with regard to citizenship and language laws in Estonia and Latvia, and the language law in Slovakia. On the other hand, the complaints procedure of the European Convention has no parallel in the OSCE. The political character of the OSCE commitments precludes judicial enforcement or complaints procedures, but consequently allows rapid response in periods of crisis. It can thus be seen to supplement, but not replace the pre-existing European system. More generally, the various regional bodies can reinforce the views and messages of the others provided there is good cooperation and careful coordination to avoid forum shopping by governments and contradictory messages from European institutions....

The obvious evolution in norms and procedures does not address the fundamental question of whether regional systems have actually had an impact on respect for human rights, but there can be little doubt in this regard. While compliance is not as good as it should be and much remains to be done, there is considerable evidence that states have responded to judgments of the regional tribunals, changing their laws and practices as a result. In Europe it is relatively easy to demonstrate the effect of the Convention and Court judgments: Austria, for example, has modified its Code of Criminal Procedure; Belgium has amended its Penal Code, its laws on vagrancy and its Civil Code; Germany has modified its Code of Criminal Procedure regarding pre-trial detention, given legal recognition to transsexuals, and taken action to expedite criminal and civil proceedings; The Netherlands has modified its Code of Military Justice and the law on detention of mental patients; Ireland created a system of legal aid; Sweden introduced rules on expropriation and legislation on building permits; Switzerland amended its Military Penal Code and completely reviewed its judicial organization and criminal procedure applicable to the army; France has strengthened the protection for privacy of telephone communications. According to Buergenthal, the decisions of the European Court are routinely complied with by European governments. As a matter of fact, the system has been so effective in the last decade that the Court has for all practical purposes become Western Europe's constitutional court.

II. The Council of Europe and the European Convention on Human Rights

Dinah Shelton, *The Boundaries of Human Rights Jurisdiction in Europe*

13 Duke J. Int'l & Comp. L. 95, 96-102 (2003) (footnotes omitted)

[O]ver 50 years ago, 10 northern and western European countries created the Council of Europe, the first post-war European regional organization. Europe had been the theater of the greatest atrocities of the Second World War and felt compelled to press for international human rights guarantees as part of its reconstruction. Faith in western European traditions of democracy, the rule of law and individual rights inspired belief that a regional system could be successful in avoiding future conflict and in stemming post-war revolutionary impulses backed by the Soviet Union. The Statute of the Council provides that each Member State must "[a]ccept the principles of the rule of law and of the enjoyment by all persons within its jurisdiction of human rights and fundamental freedoms."

A year later, these same states, self-described as "like-minded and hav[ing] a common heritage of political traditions, ideals, freedom and the rule of law," agreed to take the "first steps for the collective enforcement of certain of the rights stated in the Universal Declaration (of Human Rights)" and adopted the Convention for the Protection of Human Rights and Fundamental Freedoms (hereinafter European Convention). Today, membership in the Council is de facto conditioned upon adherence to the European Convention and cooperation with its supervisory machinery, a condition met by all of the [46] Member States. In addition, accession requires free and fair elections based upon national suffrage, freedom of expression, protection of national minorities and observance of the principles of international law. Several new Member States also have entered into additional and specific commitments during the examination of their request for membership.

The drafters of the European Convention focused their attention primarily on developing control machinery to supervise implementation and to enforce the initially short list of guaranteed rights. This focus adhered to the mandate of the Congress that helped create the Council of Europe: "We desire a Charter of Human Rights guaranteeing liberty of thought, assembly and expression as well as the right to form a political opposition; We desire a Court of Justice with adequate sanctions for the implementation of this Charter." A Resolution adopted by the Congress stated its conviction

> that in the interest of human values and human liberty, the (envisaged) Assembly should make proposals for the establishment of a Court of Justice with adequate sanctions for the implementation of this Charter, and to this end any citizen of the associated countries shall have redress before the Court, at any time and with the least possible delay, of any violation of his rights as formulated in the Charter.

The European Convention drafters moved cautiously towards fulfilling the aspirations of the Congress. The original Convention set forth a short list of civil and political rights and a single and opening statement of the obligation of Contracting Parties: "The High Contracting Parties shall secure to everyone within their jurisdiction the rights and freedoms defined in Section I of this Convention." The European Convention initially established two institutions whose mandate was "to ensure the observance of the engagements undertaken by the High Contracting Parties:" the European Commission of Human Rights and the European Court of Human Rights. The former Commission and Court were replaced on November 1, 1998, with the entry into force of Protocol 11 and the inauguration of a new full-time Court. The European Convention also confers some supervisory functions relating to the enforcement of the rights it guarantees on the Committee of Ministers, the governing body of the Council of Europe. Moreover, because the European Convention is a treaty adopted within the framework and under the auspices of the Council of Europe, some of its other organs and institutions also play important roles in facilitating the application and implementation of the European Convention.

The Court today is composed "of a number of members equal to that of the High Contracting Parties" to the European Convention. The judges are elected for a six-year renewable period by the Parliamentary Assembly of the Council of Europe from a list of three nominees submitted by each Member State. The judges serve in their individual capacities and must be persons of "high moral character," who "possess the qualifications required for appointment to high judicial office or be persons of recognized competence." The judges do not have to be nationals of the Member States of the Council of Europe. They serve full-time during their term and may not undertake any activity incompatible with their judicial functions. They must retire at age 70. The permanent Court has its seat in Strasbourg, also the seat of the Council of Europe, and judges are expected to live in the area. The Court has a Registry and legal secretaries to assist it. The Registrar is the chief clerk of the Court.

Although the European Convention initially created an independent Commission and Court, the drafters made the Court's jurisdiction optional. They also established, but again made optional, the world's first individual petition procedure for human rights violations. The "normal" procedure thus envisaged was one of inter-state complaints brought through the Commission to the Committee of Ministers. The Commission would meet in closed sessions, undertake fact-finding, attempt a friendly settlement of the matter, and report its findings to the Committee of Ministers for decision. Only the Commission or the state could refer a matter to the Court, if the state in question had accepted the Court's jurisdiction. Enforcement of judgments of the Court and decisions of the Committee of Ministers lay with the Committee itself, which could suspend a state from its rights of representation or ask it to withdraw from the Council for serious violations of its obligations.

During the intervening half century, this rather modest system has undergone evolutionary, sometimes revolutionary changes. The Council of Europe has adopted [13] protocols to the European Convention and in the process expanded the list of guaranteed civil and political rights. The first Protocol added a right to property, a right to education and the undertaking by the Contracting Parties to hold free and secret elections at reasonable intervals. Protocol No. 4 enlarged the list further by prohibiting deprivation of liberty for failure to comply with contractual obligations, by guaranteeing the right to liberty of movement, and by barring forced exile of nationals and the collective expulsion of aliens. Protocol No. 6 abolished the death penalty except during wartime and Protocol No. 7 requires states to accord aliens various due process safeguards before they may be expelled from a country where they reside. The instrument also provides for rights of appeal in criminal proceedings, compensation in cases of miscarriage of justice, protection against double jeopardy, and equality of rights and responsibilities between spouses. Protocol No. 12 augments the non-discrimination guarantee in Convention Art. 14 by providing that "the enjoyment of any right set forth by law shall be secured without discrimination on any ground," adding that "no one shall be discriminated against by any public authority." Protocol No. 13, adopted by the Committee of Ministers on February 21, 2002, abolishes the death penalty under all circumstances.

Other protocols gradually enhanced the role and status of the individual before the Court and eliminated the discretion of Member States to accept the jurisdiction of the Court and the right of individual petition. In 1990, Protocol No. 9 enabled individuals to take cases to the Court in certain circumstances. Protocol No. 11 fundamentally restructured the system, eliminating the Commission and providing the new full-time Court with compulsory jurisdiction over interstate and individual cases brought against Contracting Parties to the Convention. Today the states are locked into a system of collective responsibility for the protection of human rights, a system in which the jurisdiction of the Court provides the centerpiece. Pursuant to Article 34 of the Convention, the Court now may receive applications from "any person, non-governmental organization or group of individuals claiming to be the victim of a violation . . . of the rights set forth in the Convention or the protocols thereto." [The system has been so successful that today the 1998 reforms instituted by Protocol 11 themselves require amendment. Protocol 14, opened for ratification in 2004 and discussed infra, page 702, is intended to restrict access to the Court to some extent, but it requires unanimous ratification before it will enter into force.]

A. *Jurisdiction*

Like all human rights institutions, the jurisdiction of the European Court of Human Rights is limited by the provisions of the Convention. Among the admissibility requirements (common to most petition systems) are that the available domestic remedies first be exhausted (Article 35(1)); that the application not be anonymous (Article 35(2)(a)) or "substantially the same" as an earlier submission to the court or to a similar international procedure (Article 35(2)(b)); and that the application not be "manifestly ill-founded," i.e., complain of facts which, even if true, would not constitute a violation of the Convention (Article 35(3)). An applicant also must be a "victim" of the alleged violation (Article 34), as the Court will not entertain *in abstracto* or general complaints about human rights violations. The full text of the convention is found in the Documentary Supplement, page 149.

The territorial application of the European Convention has been at issue in a number of cases. Review Article 1, and then consider how the following situation should be addressed.

*Note: Civilian Deaths in Iraq**

The United Kingdom conducted military operations in Iraq in 2003 under the codename "Operation Telic," operations in which British troops formed part of the US-led Coalition that removed Sadaam Hussein's regime from power. Major combat operations in Iraq were declared complete on May 1, 2003. On May 8, 2003, the U.S. and U.K. permanent representatives to the United Nations wrote to the then president of the Security Council stating that they had created a Coalition Provision Authority (CPA) to exercise powers of government and

* This description is based on the statement of facts in *The Queen v. the Secretary of State for Defence* [2004] EWHC 2911 (Admin) Case No. CO/2242/2004 (Q.B.), Dec. 14, 2004.

especially to provide security, allow the delivery of humanitarian aid, and eliminate weapons of mass destruction.

On May 22, 2003, the Security Council unanimously adopted resolution 1483, which noted the letter of May 8 and recognized "the specific authorities, responsibilities, and obligations under applicable international law of these states under unified command." . . .

CPA South was under British responsibility and control, with a British regional coordinator. It covered the southernmost four of Iraq's eighteen provinces, each having a governorate coordinator. British troops were deployed in the same area. The CPA ceased to exist on June 28, when the Iraq Interim Government under the presidency of Ghazi al Yawr became the sole sovereign authority of Iraq with all Iraq ministries legally under full Iraqi control.

Legally, from May 1, 2003 until June 28, 2004, the United Kingdom was an occupying power in Southern Iraq, under the relevant provisions of the Regulations annexed to the 1907 Hague Convention ("the Hague Regulations") and the 1949 Fourth Geneva Convention ("the Fourth Geneva Convention"). When this status formally ended, British troops remained in Iraq at the invitation of the Iraqi Government and under UN auspices.

In this context, the families of six civilian persons are seeking reparations from the U.K. for deaths that occurred in Iraq during the occupation period. Each of the deaths occurred in areas of Iraq in which British forces were stationed. In four of the cases, the deceased were shot and killed by British troops. In one case, the deceased was a bystander shot and killed in the course of an exchange of fire between British troops and Iraqi gunmen, but the government claims evidence is lacking about whether the deceased was killed by a shot fired by a British soldier or by an Iraqi. The sixth case concerns Baba Mousa, who died at age 26 in British custody, three days after he was arrested by British soldiers.

Baba Mousa's father, Daoud Mousa, has been a policeman for over two decades and is a colonel in the Basra police force. According to Daoud Mousa, on the night of September 13/14, 2003, his son had been working as a receptionist at the Ibn Al Haitham Hotel in Basra. Early in the morning of September 14, Daoud Mousa went to the hotel to pick up his son from work. On his arrival he noticed that a British unit had surrounded the hotel. He saw soldiers breaking open a safe. They had a plastic bag in which they put various items that they found in the safe. Daoud Mousa also noticed that three of the soldiers were pocketing money taken from the safe. Daoud Mousa reported what he had seen to the officer in charge, whom he recalls being called "Lieutenant Mike." Lieutenant Mike called the soldiers over, reprimanded them, took their weapons, and ordered them inside an army personnel carrier.

While this was going on, Daoud Mousa noticed that his son and six other hotel employees were lying on the floor of the hotel lobby with their hands behind their heads. Daoud Mousa expressed his concern to Lieutenant Mike, who reassured him that it was a routine investigation that would be over in a couple of hours. On the third day after his son had been detained, Daoud Mousa was visited by a military police unit. He was told that his son had been killed in custody and was asked to accompany them to identify the corpse. Mousa recounted that his son had been severely beaten and his body was literally covered in blood and bruises. He had a badly broken nose. There was blood coming from his nose and mouth. The skin on one side of his face had been torn away to reveal the flesh beneath. There were severe patches of bruising over all of his body. The skin on his wrists had been torn off and the skin on his forehead torn away; there was no skin under his eyes either. Mousa was not allowed to see a copy of the autopsy report, but one of the clerks told him that the cause of death was asphyxiation. One of the other hotel employees described beatings by British soldiers, who kicked and punched them in the abdomen. The prisoners were forced to crouch for hours with their arms out straight in front of them. At the same time they were beaten about the neck, chest, and genital areas. During the detention, Baba Mousa was taken into another room where he received more beatings.

The applicants claim that the guarantees of the European Convention on Human Rights and the obligations of the U.K. as a state party extend to the government's actions as an occupying power in Iraq. In considering how the U.K. courts and potentially the European Court of Human Rights should interpret and apply the Convention in this instance, consider the following cases on the territorial scope of the Convention. Note that, in each instance, the Court must determine what principles govern the interpretation and application of the Convention's guarantees.

Banković and Others v. Belgium and Others

Eur. Ct. Hum. Rts., App. No. 52207/99 (admissibility dec., Dec. 12, 2001) (Grand Chamber) (footnotes omitted)

[The applicants, all citizens of the Federal Republic of Yugoslavia ("FRY"), applied to the Court to hold the governments of Belgium, the Czech Republic, Denmark, France, Germany, Greece, Hungary, Iceland, Italy, Luxembourg, the Netherlands, Norway, Poland, Portugal, Spain, Turkey and the United Kingdom (all of the members of NATO that are also are parties to the European Convention) responsible for deaths and injuries caused by NATO bombings in Belgrade during the 1999 conflict in Kosovo, which is discussed more fully in Chapter 10, pages 847.]

A. The Circumstances of the Case....

2. THE BOMBING OF RADIO TELEVIZIJE SRBIJE ("RTS")

9. Three television channels and four radio stations operated from the RTS facilities in Belgrade. The main production facilities were housed in three buildings at Takovska Street. The master control room was housed on the first floor of one of the buildings and was staffed mainly by technical staff.

10. On 23 April 1999, just after 2.00 am approximately, one of the RTS buildings at Takovska Street was hit by a missile launched from a NATO forces' aircraft. Two of the four floors of the building collapsed and the master control room was destroyed.

11. The daughter of the first and second applicants, the sons of the third and fourth applicants and the husband of the fifth applicant were killed and the sixth applicant was injured. Sixteen persons were killed and another sixteen were seriously injured in the bombing of the RTS. Twenty-four targets were hit in the FRY that night, including three in Belgrade....

B. Relevant International Legal Materials

3. THE DRAFTING HISTORY OF ARTICLE 1 OF THE CONVENTION

19. The text prepared by the Committee of the Consultative Assembly of the Council of Europe on legal and administrative questions provided, in what became Article 1 of the Convention, that the "member States shall undertake to ensure to all persons residing within their territories the rights . . .". The Expert Intergovernmental Committee, which considered the Consultative Assembly's draft, decided to replace the reference to "all persons residing within their territories" with a reference to persons "within their jurisdiction." The reasons were noted in the following extract from the *Collected Edition of the* Travaux Préparatoires *of the European Convention on Human Rights* (Vol. III, p. 260):

> The Assembly draft had extended the benefits of the Convention to 'all persons residing within the territories of the signatory States'. It seemed to the Committee that the term 'residing' might be considered too restrictive. It was felt that there were good grounds for extending the benefits of the Convention to all persons in the territories of the signatory States, even those who could not be considered as residing there in the legal sense of the word. The Committee therefore replaced the term 'residing' by the words 'within their jurisdiction' which are also contained in Article 2 of the Draft Covenant of the United Nations Commission.

20. The next relevant comment prior to the adoption of Article 1 of the Convention, made by the Belgian representative on 25 August 1950 during the plenary sitting of the Consultative Assembly, was to the effect that

> henceforth the right of protection by our States, by virtue of a formal clause of the Convention, may be exercised with full force, and without any differentiation or distinction, in favour of individuals of whatever nationality, who on the territory of any one of our States, may have had reason to complain that [their] rights have been violated.

21. The *travaux préparatoires* go on to note that the wording of Article 1 including "within their jurisdiction," did not give rise to any further discussion and the text as it was (and is now) was adopted by the Consultative Assembly on 25 August 1950 without further amendment (the above-cited Collected Edition (Vol. VI, p. 132). . . .

THE LAW

29. The first to the fifth applicants rely on Articles 2, 10 and 13 on their own behalf and on behalf of their deceased close relatives. The sixth applicant, injured during the strike, relies on these Articles on his own behalf. With the consent of the Court, the parties' written and oral submissions were limited to the admissibility issues, the Governments' further accepting that they would not be arguing that the complaints were manifestly ill-founded.

30. As to the admissibility of the case, the applicants submit that the application is compatible ratione loci with the provisions of the Convention because the impugned acts of the respondent States, which were either in the FRY or on their own territories but producing effects in the FRY, brought them and their deceased relatives within the jurisdiction of those States. They also suggest that the respondent States are severally liable for the strike despite its having been carried out by NATO forces, and that they had no effective remedies to exhaust.

31. The Governments dispute the admissibility of the case. They mainly contend that the application is incompatible *ratione personae* with the provisions of the Convention because the applicants did not fall within the jurisdiction of the respondent States within the meaning of Article 1 of the Convention....

A. Whether the Applicants and Their Deceased Relatives Came Within the "Jurisdiction" of the Respondent States Within the Meaning of Article 1 of the Convention

34. This is the principal basis upon which the Governments contest the admissibility of the application and the Court will consider first this question. Article 1 of the Convention reads as follows:

"The High Contracting Parties shall secure to everyone within their jurisdiction the rights and freedoms defined in Section I of [the] Convention."...

3. THE COURT'S ASSESSMENT

54. The Court notes that the real connection between the applicants and the respondent States is the impugned act which, wherever decided, was performed, or had effects, outside of the territory of those States ("the extra-territorial act"). It considers that the essential question to be examined therefore is whether the applicants and their deceased relatives were, as a result of that extra-territorial act, capable of falling within the jurisdiction of the respondent States (*Drozd and Janousek v. France and Spain*, judgment of 26 June 1992, Series A no. 240, §91, the above-cited *Loizidou* judgments (*preliminary objections* and *merits*), at §64 and §56 respectively, and the *Cyprus v. Turkey* judgment, cited above, at §80).

(a) The Applicable Rules of Interpretation

55. The Court recalls that the Convention must be interpreted in the light of the rules set out in the Vienna Convention 1969 (*Golder v. the United Kingdom* judgment of 21 February 1975, Series A no. 18, §29).

56. It will, therefore, seek to ascertain the ordinary meaning to be given to the phrase "within their jurisdiction" in its context and in the light of the object and purpose of the Convention (Article 31 §1 of the Vienna Convention 1969 and, amongst other authorities, *Johnston and Others v. Ireland* judgment of 18 December 1986, Series A no. 112, §51). The Court will also consider "any subsequent practice in the application of the treaty which establishes the agreement of the parties regarding its interpretation" (Article 31 §3 (b) of the Vienna Convention 1969 and the above-cited *Loizidou* judgment (*preliminary objections*), at §73).

57. Moreover, Article 31 §3(c) indicates that account is to be taken of "any relevant rules of international law applicable in the relations between the parties." More generally, the Court recalls that the principles underlying the Convention cannot be interpreted and applied in a vacuum. The Court must also take into account any relevant rules of international law when examining questions concerning its jurisdiction and, consequently, determine State responsibility in conformity with the governing principles of international law, although it must remain mindful of the Convention's special character as a human rights treaty (the above-cited *Loizidou* judgment (*merits*), at §§43 and 52). The Convention should be interpreted as far as possible in harmony with other principles of

international law of which it forms part (*Al-Adsani v. the United Kingdom*, [GC], no. 35763, §60, to be reported in ECHR 2001).

58. It is further recalled that the *travaux préparatoires* can also be consulted with a view to confirming any meaning resulting from the application of Article 31 of the Vienna Convention 1969 or to determining the meaning when the interpretation under Article 31 of the Vienna Convention 1969 leaves the meaning "ambiguous or obscure" or leads to a result which is "manifestly absurd or unreasonable" (Article 32). The Court has also noted the ILC [International Law Commission] commentary on the relationship between the rules of interpretation codified in those Articles 31 and 32. . . .

(b) The Meaning of the Words "Within Their Jurisdiction"

59. As to the "ordinary meaning" of the relevant term in Article 1 of the Convention, the Court is satisfied that, from the standpoint of public international law, the jurisdictional competence of a State is primarily territorial. While international law does not exclude a State's exercise of jurisdiction extra-territorially, the suggested bases of such jurisdiction (including nationality, flag, diplomatic and consular relations, effect, protection, passive personality and universality) are, as a general rule, defined and limited by the sovereign territorial rights of the other relevant States (citations omitted).

60. Accordingly, for example, a State's competence to exercise jurisdiction over its own nationals abroad is subordinate to that State's and other States' territorial competence. . . . In addition, a State may not actually exercise jurisdiction on the territory of another without the latter's consent, invitation or acquiescence, unless the former is an occupying State in which case it can be found to exercise jurisdiction in that territory, at least in certain respects (citations omitted).

61. The Court is of the view, therefore, that Article 1 of the Convention must be considered to reflect this ordinary and essentially territorial notion of jurisdiction, other bases of jurisdiction being exceptional and requiring special justification in the particular circumstances of each case (see, *mutatis mutandis* and in general, Select Committee of Experts on Extraterritorial Criminal Jurisdiction, European Committee on Crime Problems, Council of Europe, "Extraterritorial Criminal Jurisdiction," Report published in 1990, at pp. 8-30).

62. The Court finds State practice in the application of the Convention since its ratification to be indicative of a lack of any apprehension on the part of the Contracting States of their extra-territorial responsibility in contexts similar to the present case. Although there have been a number of military missions involving Contracting States acting extra-territorially since their ratification of the Convention (*inter alia*, in the Gulf, in Bosnia and Herzegovina and in the FRY), no State has indicated a belief that its extra-territorial actions involved an exercise of jurisdiction within the meaning of Article 1 of the Convention by making a derogation pursuant to Article 15 of the Convention. The existing derogations were lodged by Turkey and the United Kingdom in respect of certain internal conflicts (in south-east Turkey and Northern Ireland, respectively) and the Court does not find any basis upon which to accept the applicants' suggestion that Article 15 covers all "war" and "public emergency" situations generally, whether obtaining inside or outside the territory of the Contracting State. Indeed, Article 15 itself is to be read subject to the "jurisdiction" limitation enumerated in Article 1 of the Convention.

63. Finally, the Court finds clear confirmation of this essentially territorial notion of jurisdiction in the *travaux préparatoires* which demonstrate that the Expert Intergovernmental Committee replaced the words "all persons residing within their territories" with a reference to persons "within their jurisdiction" with a view to expanding the Convention's application to others who may not reside, in a legal sense, but who are, nevertheless, on the territory of the Contracting States (§19 above).

64. It is true that the notion of the Convention being a living instrument to be interpreted in light of present-day conditions is firmly rooted in the Court's case-law. The Court has applied that approach not only to the Convention's substantive provisions (for example, the *Soering* judgment cited above, at §102; the *Dudgeon v. the United Kingdom* judgment of 22 October 1981, Series A no. 45; the X, *Y and Z v. the United Kingdom* judgment of 22 April 1997, *Reports* 1997-II; *V. v. the United Kingdom* [GC], no. 24888/94, §72, ECHR 1999-IX; and *Matthews v. the United Kingdom* [GC], no. 24833/94, §39, ECHR 1999-I) but more relevantly to its interpretation of former Articles 25 and 46 concerning the recognition by a Contracting State of the competence of the Convention organs (the above-cited *Loizidou* judgment (*preliminary objections*), at §71). The Court concluded in the latter judgment that former Articles 25 and 46 of the Convention could not be interpreted solely in accordance with the intentions of their authors expressed more than forty years previously to the extent that, even if it had been established that the restrictions at issue were considered permissible under Articles 25 and 46 when the Convention was adopted by a minority of the then Contracting Parties, such evidence "could not be decisive."

65. However, the scope of Article 1, at issue in the present case, is determinative of the very scope of the Contracting Parties' positive obligations and, as such, of the scope and reach of the entire Convention system of human rights' protection as opposed to the question, under discussion in the *Loizidou* case (*preliminary objections*), of the competence of the Convention organs to examine a case. In any event, the extracts from the *travaux préparatoires* detailed above constitute a clear indication of the intended meaning of Article 1 of the Convention which cannot be ignored. The Court would emphasise that it is not interpreting Article 1 "solely" in accordance with the *travaux préparatoires* or finding those *travaux* "decisive"; rather this preparatory material constitutes clear confirmatory evidence of the ordinary meaning of Article 1 of the Convention as already identified by the Court (Article 32 of the Vienna Convention 1969).

66. Accordingly, and as the Court stated in the *Soering* case:

> Article 1 sets a limit, notably territorial, on the reach of the Convention. In particular, the engagement undertaken by a Contracting State is confined to 'securing' ('*reconnaître*' in the French text) the listed rights and freedoms to persons within its own 'jurisdiction.' Further, the Convention does not govern the actions of States not Parties to it, nor does it purport to be a means of requiring the Contracting States to impose Convention standards on other States.

(c) Extra-Territorial Acts Recognised as Constituting an Exercise of Jurisdiction

67. In keeping with the essentially territorial notion of jurisdiction, the Court has accepted only in exceptional cases that acts of the Contracting States performed, or producing effects, outside their territories can constitute an exercise of jurisdiction by them within the meaning of Article 1 of the Convention.

68. Reference has been made in the Court's case-law, as an example of jurisdiction "not restricted to the national territory" of the respondent State (the *Loizidou* judgment (*preliminary objections*), at §62), to situations where the extradition or expulsion of a person by a Contracting State may give rise to an issue under Articles 2 and/or 3 (or, exceptionally, under Articles 5 and or 6) and hence engage the responsibility of that State under the Convention (the above-cited *Soering* case, at §91, *Cruz Varas and Others v. Sweden* judgment of 20 March 1991, Series A no. 201, §§69 and 70, and the *Vilvarajah and Others v. the United Kingdom* judgment of 30 October 1991, Series A no. 215, §103).

However, the Court notes that liability is incurred in such cases by an action of the respondent State concerning a person while he or she is on its territory, clearly within its jurisdiction, and that such cases do not concern the actual exercise of a State's competence or jurisdiction abroad (see also, the above-cited *Al-Adsani* judgment, at §39).

69. In addition, a further example noted at paragraph 62 of the *Loizidou* judgment (*preliminary objections*) was the *Drozd and Janousek* case where, citing a number of admissibility decisions by the Commission, the Court accepted that the responsibility of Contracting Parties (France and Spain) could, in principle, be engaged because of acts of their authorities (judges) which produced effects or were performed outside their own territory (the above-cited *Drozd and Janousek* judgment, at §91). In that case, the impugned acts could not, in the circumstances, be attributed to the respondent States because the judges in question were not acting in their capacity as French or Spanish judges and as the Andorran courts functioned independently of the respondent States.

70. Moreover, in that first *Loizidou* judgment (*preliminary objections*), the Court found that, bearing in mind the object and purpose of the Convention, the responsibility of a Contracting Party was capable of being engaged when as a consequence of military action (lawful or unlawful) it exercised effective control of an area outside its national territory. The obligation to secure, in such an area, the Convention rights and freedoms was found to derive from the fact of such control whether it was exercised directly, through the respondent State's armed forces, or through a subordinate local administration. The Court concluded that the acts of which the applicant complained were capable of falling within Turkish jurisdiction within the meaning of Article 1 of the Convention.

On the merits, the Court found that it was not necessary to determine whether Turkey actually exercised detailed control over the policies and actions of the authorities of the "Turkish Republic of Northern Cyprus" ("TRNC"). It was obvious from the large number of troops engaged in active duties in northern Cyprus that Turkey's army exercised "effective overall control over that part of the island." Such control, according to the relevant test and in the circumstances of the case, was found to entail the responsibility of Turkey for the policies and actions of the "TRNC." The Court concluded that those affected by such policies or actions therefore came within the "jurisdiction" of Turkey for the purposes of Article 1 of the Convention. Turkey's obligation to secure the rights and freedoms set out in the Convention was found therefore to extend to northern Cyprus.

In its subsequent *Cyprus v. Turkey* judgment (cited above), the Court added that since Turkey had such "effective control," its responsibility could not be confined to the acts of its own agents therein but was engaged by the acts of the local administration which survived by virtue of Turkish support. Turkey's "jurisdiction" under Article 1 was therefore considered to extend to securing the entire range of substantive Convention rights in northern Cyprus.

71. In sum, the case-law of the Court demonstrates that its recognition of the exercise of extra-territorial jurisdiction by a Contracting State is exceptional: it has done so when the respondent State, through the effective control of the relevant territory and its inhabitants abroad as a consequence of military occupation or through the consent, invitation or acquiescence of the Government of that territory, exercises all or some of the public powers normally to be exercised by that Government.

72. In line with this approach, the Court has recently found that the participation of a State in the defence of proceedings against it in another State does not, without more, amount to an exercise of extra-territorial jurisdiction (*McElhinney v. Ireland and the United Kingdom* (dec.), no. 31253/96, p. 7, 9 February 2000, unpublished). The Court said:

> In so far as the applicant complains under Article 6 . . . about the stance taken by the Government of the United Kingdom in the Irish proceedings, the Court does not consider it necessary to address in the abstract the question of whether the actions of a Government as a litigant before the courts of another Contracting State can engage their responsibility under Article 6. . . . The Court considers that, in the particular circumstances of the case, the fact that the United Kingdom Government raised the defence of sovereign immunity before the Irish courts, where the applicant had decided to sue, does not suffice to bring him within the jurisdiction of the United Kingdom within the meaning of Article 1 of the Convention.

73. Additionally, the Court notes that other recognised instances of the extra-territorial exercise of jurisdiction by a State include cases involving the activities of its diplomatic or consular agents abroad and on board craft and vessels registered in, or flying the flag of, that State. In these specific situations, customary international law and treaty provisions have recognised the extra-territorial exercise of "jurisdiction" by the relevant State.

(d) Were the Present Applicants Therefore Capable of Coming within the "Jurisdiction" of the Respondent States?

74. The applicants maintain that the bombing of RTS by the respondent States constitutes yet a further example of an extra-territorial act which can be accommodated by the notion of "jurisdiction" in Article 1 of the Convention, and are thereby proposing a further specification of the ordinary meaning of the term "jurisdiction" in Article 1 of the Convention. The Court must be satisfied that equally exceptional circumstances exist in the present case which could amount to the extra-territorial exercise of jurisdiction by a Contracting State.

75. In the first place, the applicants suggest a specific application of the "effective control" criteria developed in the northern Cyprus cases. They claim that the positive obligation under Article 1 extends to securing the Convention rights in a manner proportionate to the level of control exercised in any given extra-territorial situation. The Governments contend that this amounts to a "cause-and-effect" notion of jurisdiction not contemplated by or appropriate to Article 1 of the Convention. The Court considers that the applicants' submission is tantamount to arguing that anyone adversely affected by an act imputable to a Contracting State, wherever in the world that act may have been committed or its

consequences felt, is thereby brought within the jurisdiction of that State for the purpose of Article 1 of the Convention.

The Court is inclined to agree with the Governments' submission that the text of Article 1 does not accommodate such an approach to "jurisdiction." Admittedly, the applicants accept that jurisdiction, and any consequent State Convention responsibility, would be limited in the circumstances to the commission and consequences of that particular act. However, the Court is of the view that the wording of Article 1 does not provide any support for the applicants' suggestion that the positive obligation in Article 1 to secure "the rights and freedoms defined in Section I of this Convention" can be divided and tailored in accordance with the particular circumstances of the extra-territorial act in question and, it considers its view in this respect supported by the text of Article 19 of the Convention. Indeed the applicants' approach does not explain the application of the words "within their jurisdiction" in Article 1 and it even goes so far as to render those words superfluous and devoid of any purpose. Had the drafters of the Convention wished to ensure jurisdiction as extensive as that advocated by the applicants, they could have adopted a text the same as or similar to the contemporaneous Articles 1 of the four Geneva Conventions of 1949 (see §25 above).

Furthermore, the applicants' notion of jurisdiction equates the determination of whether an individual falls within the jurisdiction of a Contracting State with the question of whether that person can be considered to be a victim of a violation of rights guaranteed by the Convention. These are separate and distinct admissibility conditions, each of which has to be satisfied in the afore-mentioned order, before an individual can invoke the Convention provisions against a Contracting State.

76. Secondly, the applicants' alternative suggestion is that the limited scope of the airspace control only circumscribed the scope of the respondent States' positive obligation to protect the applicants and did not exclude it. The Court finds this to be essentially the same argument as their principal proposition and rejects it for the same reasons.

77. Thirdly, the applicants make a further alternative argument in favour of the respondent States' jurisdiction based on a comparison with the *Soering* case (cited above). The Court does not find this convincing given the fundamental differences between that case and the present as already noted at paragraph 68 above.

78. Fourthly, the Court does not find it necessary to pronounce on the specific meaning to be attributed in various contexts to the allegedly similar jurisdiction provisions in the international instruments to which the applicants refer because it is not convinced by the applicants' specific submissions in these respects (see §48 above). It notes that Article 2 of the American Declaration on the Rights and Duties of Man 1948 referred to in the above-cited *Coard* Report of the Inter-American Commission of Human Rights (§23 above), contains no explicit limitation of jurisdiction. In addition, and as to Article 2 §1 the CCPR 1966 (§26 above), as early as 1950 the drafters had definitively and specifically confined its territorial scope and it is difficult to suggest that exceptional recognition by the Human Rights Committee of certain instances of extra-territorial jurisdiction (and the applicants give one example only) displaces in any way the territorial jurisdiction expressly conferred by that Article of the CCPR 1966 or explains the precise meaning of "jurisdiction" in Article 1 of its Optional Protocol 1966 (§27 above). While the text of Article 1 of the American Convention on Human Rights 1978 (§24 above) contains a jurisdiction condition similar

to Article 1 of the European Convention, no relevant case-law on the former provision was cited before this Court by the applicants.

79. Fifthly and more generally, the applicants maintain that any failure to accept that they fell within the jurisdiction of the respondent States would defeat the *ordre public* mission of the Convention and leave a regrettable vacuum in the Convention system of human rights' protection.

80. The Court's obligation, in this respect, is to have regard to the special character of the Convention as a constitutional instrument of *European* public order for the protection of individual human beings and its role, as set out in Article 19 of the Convention, is to ensure the observance of *the engagements undertaken* by the Contracting Parties (the above-cited *Loizidou* judgment (*preliminary objections*), at §93). It is therefore difficult to contend that a failure to accept the extra-territorial jurisdiction of the respondent States would fall foul of the Convention's *ordre public* objective, which itself underlines the essentially regional vocation of the Convention system, or of Article 19 of the Convention which does not shed any particular light on the territorial ambit of that system.

It is true that, in its above-cited *Cyprus v. Turkey* judgment (at §78), the Court was conscious of the need to avoid "a regrettable vacuum in the system of human-rights protection" in northern Cyprus. However, and as noted by the Governments, that comment related to an entirely different situation to the present: the inhabitants of northern Cyprus would have found themselves excluded from the benefits of the Convention safeguards and system which they had previously enjoyed, by Turkey's "effective control" of the territory and by the accompanying inability of the Cypriot Government, as a Contracting State, to fulfil the obligations it had undertaken under the Convention.

In short, the Convention is a multi-lateral treaty operating . . . in an essentially regional context and notably in the legal space (*espace juridique*) of the Contracting States. The FRY clearly does not fall within this legal space. The Convention was not designed to be applied throughout the world, even in respect of the conduct of Contracting States. Accordingly, the desirability of avoiding a gap or vacuum in human rights' protection has so far been relied on by the Court in favour of establishing jurisdiction only when the territory in question was one that, but for the specific circumstances, would normally be covered by the Convention.

81. Finally, the applicants relied, in particular, on the admissibility decisions of the Court in the above-cited *Issa* and *Öcalan* cases. It is true that the Court has declared both of these cases admissible and that they include certain complaints about alleged actions by Turkish agents outside Turkish territory. However, in neither of those cases was the issue of jurisdiction raised by the respondent Government or addressed in the admissibility decisions and in any event the merits of those cases remain to be decided. Similarly, no jurisdiction objection is recorded in the decision leading to the inadmissibility of the *Xhavara* case to which the applicants also referred (cited above); at any rate, the applicants do not dispute the Governments' evidence about the sharing by prior written agreement of jurisdiction between Albania and Italy. The *Ilascu* case, also referred to by the applicants and cited above, concerns allegations that Russian forces control part of the territory of Moldova, an issue to be decided definitively on the merits of that case. Accordingly, these cases do not provide any support for the applicants' interpretation of the jurisdiction of Contracting States within the meaning of Article 1 of the Convention.

4. The Court's Conclusion

82. The Court is not therefore persuaded that there was any jurisdictional link between the persons who were victims of the act complained of and the respondent States. Accordingly, it is not satisfied that the applicants and their deceased relatives were capable of coming within the jurisdiction of the respondent States on account of the extra-territorial act in question....

For these reasons, the Court unanimously

Declares the application inadmissible.

Issa and Others v. Turkey

Eur. Ct. Hum. Rts, App. No. 31821/96, Nov. 16, 2004

1. The case originated in an application (no. 31821/96) against the Republic of Turkey lodged with the European Commission of Human Rights ("the Commission") under former Article 25 of the Convention for the Protection of Human Rights and Fundamental Freedoms ("the Convention") by six Iraqi nationals, Mrs Halima Musa Issa, Mrs Beebin Ahmad Omer, Mrs Safia Shawan Ibrahim, Mrs Fatime Darwish Murty Khan, Mrs Fahima Salim Muran and Mrs Basna Rashid Omer ("the applicants"), on 2 October 1995....

[The applicants complained of the alleged unlawful arrest, detention, ill-treatment, and subsequent killing of their relatives in the course of a military operation conducted by the Turkish army in northern Iraq in April 1995.]

B. THE GOVERNMENT'S VERSION OF THE FACTS

25. The respondent Government confirm that a Turkish military operation took place in northern Iraq between 19 March 1995 and 16 April 1995. The Turkish forces advanced to Mount Medina. The records of the armed forces do not show the presence of any Turkish soldiers in the area indicated by the applicants, the Azadi village being ten kilometres south of the operation zone. There is no record of a complaint having been made to any of the officers of the units operating in the Mount Medina region....

THE LAW

I. PRELIMINARY ISSUE: THE GOVERNMENT'S PRELIMINARY OBJECTION CONCERNING JURISDICTION AND THE APPLICANTS' ESTOPPEL ARGUMENTS

A. PARTIES' SUBMISSIONS

1. The Government

52. In their post-admissibility observations dated 9 July 2002, the Government submitted that the need had arisen to examine the issue of "jurisdiction" in the instant case, having regard to the Court's inadmissibility decision of 12 December 2001 in the case of *Banković and Others* cited above. They contended that in

its *Banković and Others* decision the Court had departed from its previous case-law on the scope of interpretation of Article 1 of the Convention. Since the jurisdiction issue in the applicants' case had been left unresolved in the admissibility decision, which pre-dated the *Banković and Others* decision, the Court should address itself in the first place to the compatibility *ratione loci* of the application.

2. The Applicants

53. The applicants replied that the Court in the *Banković and Others* case had merely refined and applied existing case-law on Article 1 to the facts of the *Banković and Others* case. In any event, it had already ruled on the admissibility of their complaints. On that account, the Government should be considered estopped from raising a new objection to admissibility at this late stage of the proceedings. The applicants, on the other hand, had addressed the issue of jurisdiction squarely both in their initial application and in their pre-admissibility pleadings. The Government never sought to rebut their claim that Turkey's jurisdiction was engaged on the facts of the case and confined themselves to challenging the admissibility of the application on the grounds set out in Article 35 §1 of the Convention. To allow the Government to re-open admissibility issues at this stage would fundamentally offend against the principles of certainty and finality and would make a mockery of the principle of "equality of arms."

54. Furthermore, both the Government and the Court had already accepted jurisdiction in the present case. The applicants reasoned that, in their submissions to the Court in the *Banković and Others* case, the respondent Governments, including Turkey, expressly agreed with the Court's admissibility decision in *Issa*, describing it as "...a classic exercise of such legal authority or jurisdiction over those persons by military forces on foreign soil" (*Banković and Others*, cited above, §37). Thus, the Turkish Government can be said to have impliedly accepted the force of that argument and its application to the circumstances of the instant case. Likewise, the Court effectively accepted jurisdiction when it ruled on the issue of domestic remedies. For the applicants, it was inconceivable that the Court had not supposed Turkey's jurisdiction when ruling on admissibility. Its detailed examination of the general and political context as well as its cross-references to other judgments against Turkey is only intelligible on the basis that Turkey came within the terms of Article 1.

B. THE COURT'S ASSESSMENT

55. The Government did not explicitly raise the issue of jurisdiction prior to the admissibility decision in the instant case. However, they have at all times denied the factual basis of the applicants' allegations and, by implication, the applicants' specific and crucial contention that the deceased shepherds were under the control and authority of Turkish armed forces operating in northern Iraq at the relevant time and were, accordingly, within the jurisdiction of Turkey. In the Court's opinion, and notwithstanding the requirements of Rule 55 of the Rules of Court, the Government cannot be considered precluded from raising the jurisdiction issue at this juncture. That issue is inextricably linked to the facts underlying the allegations. As such, it must be taken to have been implicitly reserved for the merits stage. It would add that it cannot accept the applicants' arguments that the Court had accepted that Turkey had

jurisdiction when it ruled on the admissibility of the application. It refers in this connection to the fact that the Grand Chamber in its *Banković and Others* decision pointed out that "in any event the merits of [the *Issa* case] remain to be decided." (ibid. §81).

In conclusion, the question of jurisdiction must be seen as a live issue in the case before it and must therefore be examined.

II. Whether the Applicants' Relatives Came within the Jurisdiction of Turkey. . . .

B. The Court's Assessment. . . .

67. The established case-law in this area indicates that the concept of "jurisdiction" for the purposes of Article 1 of the Convention must be considered to reflect the term's meaning in public international law (see *Gentilhomme, Schaff-Benhadji and Zerouki v. France*, nos. 48205/99, 48207/99 and 48209/99, §20, 14 May 2002; *Banković and Others*, cited above, §§59-61, and *Assanidzé v. Georgia*, [GC], no. 71503/01, §137, ECHR 2004 - . . .).

From the standpoint of public international law, the words "within their jurisdiction" in Article 1 of the Convention must be understood to mean that a State's jurisdictional competence is primarily territorial (see *Banković and Others*, cited above, §59), but also that jurisdiction is presumed to be exercised normally throughout the State's territory.

68. However, the concept of "jurisdiction" within the meaning of Article 1 of the Convention is not necessarily restricted to the national territory of the High Contracting Parties (see *Loizidou v. Turkey*, cited above, pp. 2235-2236 §52). In exceptional circumstances the acts of Contracting States performed outside their territory or which produce effects there ("extraterritorial act") may amount to exercise by them of their jurisdiction within the meaning of Article 1 of the Convention.

69. According to the relevant principles of international law, a State's responsibility may be engaged where, as a consequence of military action — whether lawful or unlawful — that State in practice exercises effective control of an area situated outside its national territory. The obligation to secure, in such an area, the rights and freedoms set out in the Convention derives from the fact of such control, whether it be exercised directly, through its armed forces, or through a subordinate local administration (*ibid.* §52). . . .

71. Moreover, a State may also be held accountable for violation of the Convention rights and freedoms of persons who are in the territory of another State but who are found to be under the former State's authority and control through its agents operating — whether lawfully or unlawfully — in the latter State (see, *mutatis mutandis, M. v. Denmark*, application no. 17392/90, Commission decision of 14 October 1992, DR 73, p. 193; *Illich Sanchez Ramirez v. France*, application no. 28780/95, Commission decision of 24 June 1996, DR 86, p. 155; *Coard et al. v. the United States*, the Inter-American Commission of Human Rights decision of 29 September 1999, Report No. 109/99, case No. 10.951, §37, 39, 41 and 43; and the views adopted by the Human Rights Committee on 29 July 1981 in the cases of *Lopez Burgos v. Uruguay and Celiberti de Casariego v. Uruguay*, nos. 52/1979 and 56/1979, at §§12.3 and 10.3 respectively).

Accountability in such situations stems from the fact that Article 1 of the Convention cannot be interpreted so as to allow a State party to perpetrate violations of the Convention on the territory of another State, which it could not perpetrate on its own territory (*ibid.*).

2. Application of the Above Principles

72. In the light of the above principles the Court must ascertain whether the applicants' relatives were under the authority and/or effective control, and therefore within the jurisdiction, of the respondent State as a result of the latter's extra-territorial acts.

73. In this connection, the Court notes that it is undisputed between the parties that the Turkish armed forces carried out military operations in northern Iraq over a six-week period between 19 March and 16 April 1995 (see paragraphs 58 and 63 above). It transpires from the parties' submissions and the documentary evidence contained in the case-file that the crossborder operation conducted at that time was extensive and was aimed at pursuing and eliminating terrorists who were seeking shelter in northern Iraq (see paragraphs 36, 43, 45, 58 and 63).

74. The Court does not exclude the possibility that, as a consequence of this military action, the respondent State could be considered to have exercised, temporarily, effective overall control of a particular portion of the territory of northern Iraq. Accordingly, if there is a sufficient factual basis for holding that, at the relevant time, the victims were within that specific area, it would follow logically that they were within the jurisdiction of Turkey (and not that of Iraq, which is not a Contracting State and clearly does not fall within the legal space (*espace juridique*) of the Contracting States (see the above-cited *Banković* decision, §80).

75. However, notwithstanding the large number of troops involved in the aforementioned military operations, it does not appear that Turkey exercised effective overall control of the entire area of northern Iraq. This situation is therefore in contrast to the one which obtained in northern Cyprus in the *Loizidou v. Turkey* and *Cyprus v. Turkey* cases (both cited above). In the latter cases, the Court found that the respondent Government's armed forces totalled more than 30,000 personnel (which is, admittedly, no less than the number alleged by the applicants in the instant case — see §63 above — but with the difference that the troops in northern Cyprus were present over a very much longer period of time) and were stationed throughout the whole of the territory of northern Cyprus. Moreover, that area was constantly patrolled and had check points on all main lines of communication between the northern and southern parts of the island.

76. The essential question to be examined in the instant case is whether at the relevant time Turkish troops conducted operations in the area where the killings took place. The fate of the applicants' complaints in respect of the killing of their relatives depends on the prior establishment of that premise. The Government have vigorously denied that their troops were active in or around Azadi village in the Spna area (see paragraphs 25 and 58 above). The reasonableness of that assertion must be tested in the light of the documentary and other evidence which the parties have submitted to the Court, having regard to the standard of proof which it habitually employs when ascertaining whether there is a basis in fact for an allegation of unlawful killing, namely proof "beyond reasonable doubt" (*Orhan v. Turkey*, no. 25656/94, §264, 18 June 2002; *Tepe v. Turkey*, no. 27244/95, §125, 9 May 2003; and *İpek v. Turkey*, no. 25760/94, §109, ECHR

2004-.... (extracts)), it being understood that such proof may follow from the coexistence of sufficiently strong, clear and concordant inferences or of similar unrebutted presumptions of fact....

81. On the basis of all the material in its possession, the Court considers that it has not been established to the required standard of proof that the Turkish armed forces conducted operations in the area in question, and, more precisely, in the hills above the village of Azadi where, according to the applicants' statements, the victims were at that time.

3. The Court's Conclusion

82. In the light of the above, the Court is not satisfied that the applicants' relatives were within the "jurisdiction" of the respondent State for the purposes of Article 1 of the Convention.

This finding makes it unnecessary to examine the applicants' substantive complaints under Articles 2, 3, 5, 8, 13, 14 and 18 of the Convention....

The *Banković* and *Issa* cases both concerned military activities taking place in or above foreign states and thus are precedents that must be considered in relation to the British occupation of Iraq. The following case also concerns human rights violations occurring outside the territory of the accused state party, but ones for which that state was not responsible. The facts and the judgment raise two key questions. First, must a state provide remedies for violations that have been committed by another government? Second, are some or all human rights part of jus cogens or peremptory norms and, if so, what are the legal consequences that flow from that designation?

Al-Adsani v. United Kingdom

Eur. Ct. Hum. Rts., Judgment of Nov. 21, 2001 (Grand Chamber), 34 Eur. Hum. Rts. Rev. 11 (2002) (most references omitted)

1. The case originated in an application (no. 35763/97) against the United Kingdom of Great Britain and Northern Ireland lodged with the European Commission of Human Rights under former Article 25 of the Convention for the Protection of Human Rights and Fundamental Freedoms ("the Convention") by a dual British/Kuwaiti national, Mr Sulaiman Al-Adsani ("the applicant"), on 3 April 1997....

3. The applicant alleged that the English courts, by granting immunity from suit to the State of Kuwait, failed to secure enjoyment of his right not to be tortured and denied him access to a court, contrary to Articles 3, 6 §1 and 13 of the Convention....

35.... He submitted that, correctly interpreted, the above provisions taken together required the United Kingdom to assist one of its citizens in obtaining an effective remedy for torture against another State. The grant of immunity from civil suit to the State of Kuwait had, however, frustrated this purpose.

36. The Government submitted that the complaint under Article 3 failed on three grounds. First, the torture was alleged to have taken place outside the United

Kingdom's jurisdiction. Secondly, any positive obligation deriving from Articles 1 and 3 could extend only to the prevention of torture, not to the provision of compensation. Thirdly, the grant of immunity to Kuwait was not in any way incompatible with the obligations under the Convention.

37. The Court reiterates that the engagement undertaken by a Contracting State under Article 1 of the Convention is confined to "securing" ("*reconnaître*" in the French text) the listed rights and freedoms to persons within its own "jurisdiction" (see *Soering v. the United Kingdom*, judgment of 7 July 1989, Series A no. 161, pp. 33-34, §86).

38. It is true that, taken together, Articles 1 and 3 place a number of positive obligations on the High Contracting Parties, designed to prevent and provide redress for torture and other forms of ill-treatment. Thus, in *A. v. the United Kingdom* the Court held that, by virtue of these two provisions, States are required to take certain measures to ensure that individuals within their jurisdiction are not subjected to torture or inhuman or degrading treatment or punishment. In *Aksoy v. Turkey* it was established that Article 13 in conjunction with Article 3 impose an obligation on States to carry out a thorough and effective investigation of incidents of torture, and in *Assenov and Others v. Bulgaria*, the Court held that where an individual raises an arguable claim that he has been seriously ill-treated by the police or other such agents of the State unlawfully and in breach of Article 3, that provision, read in conjunction with the State's general duty under Article 1 of the Convention to "secure to everyone within their jurisdiction the rights and freedoms defined in . . . [the] Convention," requires by implication that there should be an effective official investigation. However, in each case the State's obligation applies only in relation to ill-treatment allegedly committed within its jurisdiction.

39. In *Soering*, cited above, the Court recognised that Article 3 has some, limited, extraterritorial application, to the extent that the decision by a Contracting State to expel an individual might engage the responsibility of that State under the Convention, where substantial grounds had been shown for believing that the person concerned, if expelled, faced a real risk of being subjected to torture or to inhuman or degrading treatment or punishment in the receiving country. In the judgment it was emphasised, however, that in so far as any liability under the Convention might be incurred in such circumstances, it would be incurred by the expelling Contracting State by reason of its having taken action which had as a direct consequence the exposure of an individual to proscribed ill-treatment.

40. The applicant does not contend that the alleged torture took place within the jurisdiction of the United Kingdom or that the United Kingdom authorities had any causal connection with its occurrence. In these circumstances, it cannot be said that the High Contracting Party was under a duty to provide a civil remedy to the applicant in respect of torture allegedly carried out by the Kuwaiti authorities.

41. It follows that there has been no violation of Article 3 of the Convention in the present case.

II. Alleged Violation Of Article 6 §1 Of The Convention

42. The applicant alleged that he was denied access to a court in the determination of his claim against the State of Kuwait and that this

constituted a violation of Article 6 §1 of the Convention, which provides in its first sentence:

> In the determination of his civil rights and obligations or of any criminal charge against him, everyone is entitled to a fair and public hearing within a reasonable time by an independent and impartial tribunal established by law.

43. The Government submitted that Article 6 §1 did not apply to the proceedings, but that, even if it did, any interference with the right of access to a court was compatible with its provisions.

A. APPLICABILITY OF ARTICLE 6 §1 OF THE CONVENTION....

2. The Court's Assessment

46. The Court reiterates its constant case-law to the effect that Article 6 §1 does not itself guarantee any particular content for "civil rights and obligations" in the substantive law of the Contracting States. It extends only to *contestations* (disputes) over "civil rights and obligations" which can be said, at least on arguable grounds, to be recognised under domestic law.

47. Whether a person has an actionable domestic claim may depend not only on the substantive content, properly speaking, of the relevant civil right as defined under national law but also on the existence of procedural bars preventing or limiting the possibilities of bringing potential claims to court. In the latter kind of case Article 6 §1 may be applicable. Certainly the Convention enforcement bodies may not create by way of interpretation of Article 6 §1 a substantive civil right which has no legal basis in the State concerned. However, it would not be consistent with the rule of law in a democratic society or with the basic principle underlying Article 6 §1 — namely that civil claims must be capable of being submitted to a judge for adjudication — if, for example, a State could, without restraint or control by the Convention enforcement bodies, remove from the jurisdiction of the courts a whole range of civil claims or confer immunities from civil liability on large groups or categories of persons.

48. The proceedings which the applicant intended to pursue were for damages for personal injury, a cause of action well known to English law. The Court does not accept the Government's submission that the applicant's claim had no legal basis in domestic law since any substantive right which might have existed was extinguished by operation of the doctrine of State immunity. It notes that an action against a State is not barred *in limine*: if the defendant State waives immunity, the action will proceed to a hearing and judgment. The grant of immunity is to be seen not as qualifying a substantive right but as a procedural bar on the national courts' power to determine the right.

49. The Court is accordingly satisfied that there existed a serious and genuine dispute over civil rights. It follows that Article 6 §1 was applicable to the proceedings in question.

B. COMPLIANCE WITH ARTICLE 6 §1....

52. In *Golder v. the United Kingdom* the Court held that the procedural guarantees laid down in Article 6 concerning fairness, publicity and promptness

would be meaningless in the absence of any protection for the pre-condition for the enjoyment of those guarantees, namely, access to a court. It established this as an inherent aspect of the safeguards enshrined in Article 6, referring to the principles of the rule of law and the avoidance of arbitrary power which underlie much of the Convention. Thus, Article 6 §1 secures to everyone the right to have any claim relating to his civil rights and obligations brought before a court.

53. The right of access to a court is not, however, absolute, but may be subject to limitations; these are permitted by implication since the right of access by its very nature calls for regulation by the State. . . .

54. The Court must first examine whether the limitation pursued a legitimate aim. It notes in this connection that sovereign immunity is a concept of international law, developed out of the principle *par in parem non habet imperium*, by virtue of which one State shall not be subject to the jurisdiction of another State. The Court considers that the grant of sovereign immunity to a State in civil proceedings pursues the legitimate aim of complying with international law to promote comity and good relations between States through the respect of another State's sovereignty.

55. The Court must next assess whether the restriction was proportionate to the aim pursued. It reiterates that the Convention has to be interpreted in the light of the rules set out in the Vienna Convention on the Law of Treaties of 23 May 1969, and that Article 31 §3 (c) of that treaty indicates that account is to be taken of "any relevant rules of international law applicable in the relations between the parties." The Convention, including Article 6, cannot be interpreted in a vacuum. The Court must be mindful of the Convention's special character as a human rights treaty, and it must also take the relevant rules of international law into account. The Convention should so far as possible be interpreted in harmony with other rules of international law of which it forms part, including those relating to the grant of State immunity.

56. It follows that measures taken by a High Contracting Party which reflect generally recognised rules of public international law on State immunity cannot in principle be regarded as imposing a disproportionate restriction on the right of access to a court as embodied in Article 6 §1. Just as the right of access to a court is an inherent part of the fair trial guarantee in that Article, so some restrictions on access must likewise be regarded as inherent, an example being those limitations generally accepted by the community of nations as part of the doctrine of State immunity.

57. The Court notes that the 1978 Act, applied by the English courts so as to afford immunity to Kuwait, complies with the relevant provisions of the 1972 Basle Convention, which, while placing a number of limitations on the scope of State immunity as it was traditionally understood, preserves it in respect of civil proceedings for damages for personal injury unless the injury was caused in the territory of the forum State. Except insofar as it affects claims for damages for torture, the applicant does not deny that the above provision reflects a generally accepted rule of international law. He asserts, however, that his claim related to torture, and contends that the prohibition of torture has acquired the status of a *jus cogens* norm in international law, taking precedence over treaty law and other rules of international law.

58. Following the decision to uphold Kuwait's claim to immunity, the domestic courts were never required to examine evidence relating to the applicant's allegations, which have, therefore, never been proved. However, for the purposes of the present judgment, the Court accepts that the ill-treatment alleged by the

applicant against Kuwait in his pleadings in the domestic courts, namely, repeated beatings by prison guards over a period of several days with the aim of extracting a confession, can properly be categorised as torture within the meaning of Article 3 of the Convention.

59. Within the Convention system it has long been recognised that the right under Article 3 not to be subjected to torture or to inhuman or degrading treatment or punishment enshrines one of the fundamental values of democratic society. It is an absolute right, permitting of no exception in any circumstances. Of all the categories of ill-treatment prohibited by Article 3, "torture" has a special stigma, attaching only to deliberate inhuman treatment causing very serious and cruel suffering.

60. Other areas of public international law bear witness to a growing recognition of the overriding importance of the prohibition of torture. Thus, torture is forbidden by Article 5 of the Universal Declaration of Human Rights and Article 7 of the International Covenant on Civil and Political Rights. The United Nations Convention against Torture and Other Cruel, Inhuman and Degrading Treatment or Punishment requires, by Article 2, that each State Party should take effective legislative, administrative, judicial or other measures to prevent torture in any territory under its jurisdiction, and, by Article 4, that all acts of torture should be made offences under the State Party's criminal law. In addition, there have been a number of judicial statements to the effect that the prohibition of torture has attained the status of a peremptory norm or jus cogens. For example, in its judgment of 10 December 1998 in *Furundzija*, the International Criminal Tribunal for the Former Yugoslavia referred, *inter alia*, to the foregoing body of treaty rules and held that "[b]ecause of the importance of the values it protects, this principle [proscribing torture] has evolved into a peremptory norm or *jus cogens*, that is, a norm that enjoys a higher rank in the international hierarchy than treaty law and even 'ordinary' customary rules." Similar statements have been made in other cases before that tribunal and in national courts, including the House of Lords in the case of *ex parte Pinochet (No. 3)*.

61. While the Court accepts, on the basis of these authorities, that the prohibition of torture has achieved the status of a peremptory norm in international law, it observes that the present case concerns not, as in *Furundzija* and *Pinochet*, the criminal liability of an individual for alleged acts of torture, but the immunity of a State in a civil suit for damages in respect of acts of torture within the territory of that State. Notwithstanding the special character of the prohibition of torture in international law, the Court is unable to discern in the international instruments, judicial authorities or other materials before it any firm basis for concluding that, as a matter of international law, a State no longer enjoys immunity from civil suit in the courts of another State where acts of torture are alleged. In particular, the Court observes that none of the primary international instruments referred to (Article 5 of the Universal Declaration of Human Rights, Article 7 of the International Covenant on Civil and Political Rights and Articles 2 and 4 of the UN Convention) relates to civil proceedings or to State immunity.

62. It is true that in its Report on Jurisdictional Immunities of States and their Property the working group of the International Law Commission noted, as a recent development in State practice and legislation on the subject of immunities of States, the argument increasingly put forward that immunity should be denied in the case of death or personal injury resulting from acts of a State in violation of

human rights norms having the character of *jus cogens*, particularly the prohibition on torture. However, as the working group itself acknowledged, while national courts had in some cases shown some sympathy for the argument that States were not entitled to plead immunity where there had been a violation of human rights norms with the character of *jus cogens*, in most cases (including those cited by the applicant in the domestic proceedings and before the Court) the plea of sovereign immunity had succeeded.

63. The ILC working group went on to note developments, since those decisions, in support of the argument that a State may not plead immunity in respect of human rights violations: first, the exception to immunity adopted by the United States in the amendment to the Foreign Sovereign Immunities Act (FSIA) which had been applied by the United States courts in two cases; secondly, the *ex parte Pinochet (No. 3)* judgment in which the House of Lords "emphasised the limits of immunity in respect of gross human rights violations by State officials." The Court does not, however, find that either of these developments provides it with a firm basis on which to conclude that the immunity of States *ratione personae* is no longer enjoyed in respect of civil liability for claims of acts of torture, let alone that it was not enjoyed in 1996 at the time of the Court of Appeal's judgment in the present case.

64. As to the amendment to the FSIA, the very fact that the amendment was needed would seem to confirm that the general rule of international law remained that immunity attached even in respect of claims of acts of official torture. Moreover, the amendment is circumscribed in its scope: the offending State must be designated as a State sponsor of acts of terrorism, and the claimant must be a national of the United States. The effect of the FSIA is further limited in that after judgment has been obtained, the property of a foreign State is immune from attachment or execution unless one of the statutory exceptions applies.

65. As to the *ex parte Pinochet (No. 3)* judgment, the Court notes that the majority of the House of Lords held that, after the UN Convention and even before, the international prohibition against official torture had the character of *jus cogens* or a peremptory norm and that no immunity was enjoyed by a torturer from one Torture Convention State from the criminal jurisdiction of another. But, as the working group of the ILC itself acknowledged, that case concerned the immunity *ratione materiae* from criminal jurisdiction of a former head of State, who was at the material time physically within the United Kingdom. As the judgments in the case made clear, the conclusion of the House of Lords did not in any way affect the immunity *ratione personae* of foreign sovereign States from the civil jurisdiction in respect of such acts. In so holding, the House of Lords cited with approval the judgments of the Court of Appeal in *Al-Adsani* itself.

66. The Court, while noting the growing recognition of the overriding importance of the prohibition of torture, does not accordingly find it established that there is yet acceptance in international law of the proposition that States are not entitled to immunity in respect of civil claims for damages for alleged torture committed outside the forum State. The 1978 Act, which grants immunity to States in respect of personal injury claims unless the damage was caused within the United Kingdom, is not inconsistent with those limitations generally accepted by the community of nations as part of the doctrine of State immunity.

67. In these circumstances, the application by the English courts of the provisions of the 1978 Act to uphold Kuwait's claim to immunity cannot be said to have amounted to an unjustified restriction on the applicant's access to a court.

It follows that there has been no violation of Article 6 §1 of the Convention in this case.

FOR THESE REASONS, THE COURT

1. *Holds* unanimously that there has been no violation of Article 3 of the Convention;
2. *Holds* by nine votes to eight that there has been no violation of Article 6 §1 of the Convention.

JOINT DISSENTING OPINION OF JUDGES ROZAKIS AND CAFLISCH, JOINED BY JUDGES WILDHABER, COSTA, CABRAL BARRETO AND VAJIĆ

We regret that we are unable to concur with the Court's majority in finding that, in the present case, there has not been a violation of Article 6 of the Convention in so far as the right of access to a court is concerned. Unlike the majority, we consider that the applicant was unduly deprived of his right of access to English courts to entertain the merits of his claim against the State of Kuwait although that claim was linked to serious allegations of torture. To us the main reasoning of the majority — that the standards applicable in civil cases differ from those applying in criminal matters when a conflict arises between the peremptory norm of international law on the prohibition of torture and the rules on State immunity — raises fundamental questions, and we disagree for the following reasons.

1. The Court's majority unequivocally accept that the rule on the prohibition of torture had achieved at the material time, namely at the time when civil proceedings were instituted by the applicant before the English courts, the status of a peremptory rule of international law (*jus cogens*). They refer to a number of authorities which demonstrate that the prohibition of torture has gradually crystallised as a *jus cogens* rule. To this conclusion we readily subscribe and in further support of this we refer to the Statutes of the *ad hoc* Tribunals for the Former Yugoslavia and Rwanda, and to the Statute of the International Criminal Court, which also gives a definition of the crime. State practice corroborates this conclusion.

By accepting that the rule on prohibition of torture is a rule of *jus cogens*, the majority recognise that it is hierarchically higher than any other rule of international law, be it general or particular, customary or conventional, with the exception, of course, of other *jus cogens* norms. For the basic characteristic of a *jus cogens* rule is that, as a source of law in the now vertical international legal system, it overrides any other rule which does not have the same status. In the event of a conflict between a *jus cogens* rule and any other rule of international law, the former prevails. The consequence of such prevalence is that the conflicting rule is null and void, or, in any event, does not produce legal effects which are in contradiction with the content of the peremptory rule.

2. The Court's majority do not seem, on the other hand, to deny that the rules on State immunity; customary or conventional, do not belong to the category of *jus cogens*; and rightly so, because it is clear that the rules of State immunity, deriving from both customary and conventional international law, have never been considered by the international community as rules with a hierarchically higher status. It is common knowledge that, in many instances, States have, through their own initiative, waived their rights of immunity; that in many instances they have contracted out of them, or have renounced them. These instances clearly demonstrate that the rules on State immunity do not enjoy a

higher status, since jus cogens rules, protecting as they do the "ordre public," that is the basic values of the international community, cannot be subject to unilateral or contractual forms of derogation from their imperative contents.

3. The acceptance therefore of the *jus cogens* nature of the prohibition of torture entails that a State allegedly violating it cannot invoke hierarchically lower rules (in this case, those on State immunity) to avoid the consequences of the illegality of its actions. In the circumstances of this case, Kuwait cannot validly hide behind the rules on State immunity to avoid proceedings for a serious claim of torture made before a foreign jurisdiction; and the courts of that jurisdiction (the United Kingdom) cannot accept a plea of immunity, or invoke it *ex officio*, to refuse an applicant adjudication of a torture case. Due to the interplay of the *jus cogens* rule on prohibition of torture and the rules on State immunity, the procedural bar of State immunity is automatically lifted, because those rules, as they conflict with a hierarchically higher rule, do not produce any legal effect. In the same vein, national law which is designed to give domestic effect to the international rules on State immunity cannot be invoked as creating a jurisdictional bar, but must be interpreted in accordance with and in the light of the imperative precepts of *jus cogens*.

4. The majority, while accepting that the rule on the prohibition of torture is a *jus cogens* norm, refuse to draw the consequences of such acceptance. They contend that a distinction must be made between criminal proceedings, where apparently they accept that a *jus cogens* rule has the overriding force to deprive the rules of sovereign immunity from their legal effects, and civil proceedings, where, in the absence of authority, they consider that the same conclusion cannot be drawn. Their position is well summarised in paragraph 66 of the judgment, where they assert that they do not find it established that "there is yet acceptance in international law of the proposition that States are not entitled to immunity in respect of civil claims for damages for alleged torture committed outside the forum State." Hence, "[t]he 1978 Act, which grants immunity to States in respect of personal injury claims not inconsistent with those limitations generally accepted by the community of nations as part of the doctrine of State immunity."

In our opinion, the distinction made by the majority and their conclusions are defective on two grounds.

Firstly, the English courts, when dealing with the applicant's claim, never resorted to the distinction made by the majority. They never invoked any difference between criminal charges or civil claims, between criminal and civil proceedings, in so far as the legal force of the rules on State immunity or the applicability of the 1978 Act was concerned. The basic position of the Court of Appeal — the last court which dealt with the matter in its essence — is expressed by the observations of Lord Justice Stuart-Smith who simply denied that the prohibition of torture was a *jus cogens* rule. In reading the Lord Justice's observations, one even forms the impression that if the Court of Appeal had been convinced that the rule of prohibition of torture was a norm of *jus cogens*, they could grudgingly have admitted that the procedural bar of State immunity did not apply in the circumstances of the case.

Secondly, the distinction made by the majority between civil and criminal proceedings, concerning the effect of the rule of the prohibition of torture, is not consonant with the very essence of the operation of the *jus cogens* rules. It is not the nature of the proceedings which determines the effects that a *jus cogens* rule has upon another rule of international law, but the character of the rule as a peremptory norm and its interaction with a hierarchically lower rule.

The prohibition of torture, being a rule of *jus cogens*, acts in the international sphere and deprives the rule of sovereign immunity of all its legal effects in that sphere. The criminal or civil nature of the domestic proceedings is immaterial. The jurisdictional bar is lifted by the very interaction of the international rules involved, and the national judge cannot admit a plea of immunity raised by the defendant State as an element preventing him from entering into the merits of the case and from dealing with the claim of the applicant for the alleged damages inflicted upon him.

Under these circumstances we believe that the English courts have erred in considering that they had no jurisdiction to entertain the applicant's claim because of the procedural bar of State immunity and the consequent application of the 1978 Act. Accordingly, the applicant was deprived of his right to have access to the English court to entertain his claim of damages for the alleged torture suffered by him in Kuwait, and Article 6 §1, has, in our view, been violated.

Comments and Questions

1. The case of the Iraqi civilians, supra page 624, was before the British courts as of September 2005. In *The Queen* (on the Application of Mazin Jumaa Al Skeini and Others) *v. The Secretary of State for Defence* ([2004] EWHC 2911 (Admin) Case No. CO/2242/2004 (Q.B), Dec. 14, 2004), the Divisional Court concluded that the case of Mr. Baba Mousa's death in the custody of British forces in Iraq falls within the scope of the European Convention and the British Human Rights Act and within the jurisdiction of the United Kingdom; that there was a breach in his case of the procedural investigative obligation arising under articles 2 and 3 of the Convention; but that the other claims, arising out of shootings of Iraqis by British forces in the field, fail on the ground that those shootings occurred outside the jurisdiction of the United Kingdom and thus outside the scope of the Convention and of the Act. How should the case be decided on appeal?

2. Given the problems of extradition, rendition, peacekeeping, and military activities throughout the world (some of which are addressed in Chapters 4 and 10), international tribunals are likely to face a growing number of cases that concern the territorial scope of the relevant instrument and the degree of control being exercised in another state. In addition to the cases cited in the *Banković* decision, see *Ilaşcu and Others v. Moldova and Russia*, App. No. 48787/99, Judgment of July 8, 2004 (Grand Chamber), where the Court held both states responsible for violations of human rights in the Moldovan district of Transdniestria. Moldova was faulted for not doing more to secure the release of illegally detained Moldovans in Transdniestria, but Russia was also found to be responsible, because its occupying troops supported the illegal government which wrongfully detained and tried the victims (similar to the situation of the Turkish occupation of northern Cyprus). In *Öcalan v. Turkey*, no. 46221/99, Judgment of May 12, 2005 (Grand Chamber), the Court accepted that the capture in Kenya of a Kurdish guerilla leader by Turkish forces brought Öcalan within Turkish jurisdiction, although it found no violation with regard to his treatment. (The Court did find that Öcalan's subsequent trial in Turkey did not meet the requirements for a fair trial in various respects.) See generally Tarik Abdel-Monem, "How Far Do the Lawless Areas of Europe Extend? Extraterritorial Application of

the European Convention on Human Rights," 14 *J. Transnat'l L. & Pol'y* 159 (2005); Erik Roxstrum et al., The NATO Bombing Case . . . and The Limits of Western Human Rights Protection, 23 B.U. Int'l L.J. 55 (2005).

3. In *Issa*, the European Court cited the Human Rights Committee and the Inter-American Commission on Human Rights for the proposition that "Article 1 of the Convention cannot be interpreted so as to allow a State party to perpetrate violations of the Convention on the territory of another State which it could not perpetrate on its own territory." Isn't that precisely the effect of the *Issa* and *Banković* decisions? Why do you think that *Issa* was initially declared admissible, even though the acts occurred outside Turkish territory? Could it be that the Court viewed the Turkish incursion into Iraq differently from the NATO bombing of Yugoslavia? Oral arguments in *Banković* took place in Strasbourg approximately six weeks after the terrorist attacks of Sept. 11, 2001; could this have influenced the Court's unanimous decision?

4. During oral arguments in *Banković*, the respondent governments attempted to distinguish *Issa* (which, at the time, had been declared admissible) on the grounds that Turkish forces had initially arrested the alleged victims before killing them, thus bringing them within the "effective control" of Turkey. The *Banković* lawyers responded that this would result in an absurd situation in which a government could be found to have violated the European Convention by arresting a person outside the state's territory, but that simply killing the person would be beyond the reach of the Convention. Since *Issa* was ultimately dismissed on factual grounds, the issue remains unresolved.

5. Read the jurisdictional provisions of the Covenant on Civil and Political Rights and American Convention on Human Rights. How relevant is or should be the jurisprudence of other human rights bodies in determining the *rationae loci* of a human rights tribunal?

6. The International Court of Justice considered the relationship between traditional international immunities and international crimes in the *Arrest Warrant Case (Congo v. Belgium)*, which is discussed in Chapter 11, page 953. Consistent with the European Court's judgment in the *Al-Adsani* case, the I.C.J. did not find that accusations of crimes against humanity trumped the immunity of a sitting foreign minister. What is the impact of labeling a norm *jus cogens* if it does not have a trumping effect?

B. *The Interpretation and Application of Substantive Rights in the European Convention: Freedom of Expression*

Once a case has been found admissible, the European Court must interpret and apply the guarantees within the Convention. While the Court has delivered opinions on a wide range of issues, one of the more controversial and highly litigated issues has been the scope of Article 10, which guarantees freedom of speech, information, and expression. The following three cases illustrate the approach of the court to commercial speech, public affairs broadcasting, and artistic expression. In reading the cases, consider the issues of deference to state authorities, the extent to which the type of speech makes a difference, and how the same issues would be decided in the national courts of your country. Also consider the approach of the court in determining whether an interference with a protected right has occurred and, if so, whether the interference is justified.

Handyside v. United Kingdom

Eur. Ct. H.R., ser. A No. 24, App. No. 5493/72, Dec. 7, 1976 (some references omitted)

As To The Facts

HISTORICAL

9. The applicant, Mr. Richard Handyside, is proprietor of the publishing firm "Stage 1" in London which he opened in 1968. He has published, among other books, *The Little Red Schoolbook* (hereinafter called "the *Schoolbook*"), the original edition of which was the subject of the present case and a revised edition of which appeared on 15 November 1971.

10. The applicant's firm had previously published *Socialism and Man in Cuba*, by Che Guevara, *Major Speeches*, by Fidel Castro, and *Revolution in Guinea*, by Amilcar Cabral. Since 1971 four further titles have appeared, namely *Revolution in the Congo*, by Eldridge Cleaver, a book of writings from the Women's Liberation Movement called *Body Politic, China's Socialist Revolution*, by John and Elsie Collier, and The *Fine Tubes Strike*, by Tony Beck.

11. The British rights of the *Schoolbook*, written by Søren Hansen and Jesper Jensen, two Danish authors, had been purchased by the applicant in September 1970. The book had first been published in Denmark in 1969 and subsequently, after translation and with certain adaptations, in Belgium, Finland, France, the Federal Republic of Germany, Greece, Iceland, Italy, the Netherlands, Norway, Sweden and Switzerland as well as several non-European countries. Furthermore it circulated freely in Austria and Luxembourg.

12. After having arranged for the translation of the book into English the applicant prepared an edition for the United Kingdom with the help of a group of children and teachers. He had previously consulted a variety of people about the value of the book and intended publication in the United Kingdom on 1 April 1971. As soon as printing was completed he sent out several hundred review copies of the book, together with a press release, to a selection of publications from national and local newspapers to educational and medical journals. He also placed advertisements for the book in various publications including *The Bookseller, The Times Educational and Literary Supplements and Teachers World.*

13. On 22 March 1971, the *Daily Mirror* published an account of the book's contents, and other accounts appeared in *The Sunday Times* and the *Sunday Telegraph* on 28 March. Further reports were carried by the *Daily Telegraph* on 29 and 30 March; they also indicated that representations would be made to the Director of Public Prosecutions demanding that action should be taken against the publication of the book. The *Schoolbook* was also the subject of further extensive press comment, some favourable and some not, immediately after and around the time of the seizure referred to below.

14. After receipt of a number of complaints, on 30 March 1971 the Director of Public Prosecutions asked the Metropolitan Police to undertake enquiries. As a result of these, on 31 March 1971, a successful application was made for a warrant under section 3 of the Obscene Publications Acts 1959/1964 to search the premises occupied by Stage 1 in London. The warrant was issued in the applicant's absence but in accordance with the procedure laid down by English law and a

copy of the *Schoolbook* was before the judicial authority which issued the warrant. It was executed on the same day and 1,069 copies of the book were provisionally seized together with leaflets, posters, showcards and correspondence relating to its publication and sale.

15. Acting on the advice of his lawyers the applicant continued distributing copies of the book in the subsequent days. After the Director of Public Prosecutions had received information that further copies had been taken to Stage 1's premises after the search, further successful applications were made on 1 April 1971 (in conditions similar to those described above) to search again those premises and also the premises of the printers of the book. Later that day altogether 139 copies of the book were seized at Stage 1's premises and, at the printer's, 20 spoiled copies of the book, together with correspondence relating to it and the matrix with which the book was printed. About 18,800 copies of a total print of 20,000 copies were missed and subsequently sold, for example, to schools which had placed orders.

16. On 8 April 1971, a Magistrates' Court issued, under section 2 (1) of the Obscene Publications Act 1959, as amended by section 1 (1) of the Obscene Publications Act 1964, two summonses against the applicant for the following offences:

(a) on 31 March 1971 having in his possession 1,069 obscene books entitled "The Little Red Schoolbook" for publication for gain;
(b) on 1 April 1971, having in his possession 139 obscene books entitled "The Little Red Schoolbook" for publication for gain.

The summonses were served on the applicant on the same day. He thereupon ceased distribution of the book and advised bookshops accordingly but, by that time, some 17,000 copies were already in circulation....

[The applicant was tried in summary proceedings before a magistrate, found guilty, and fined £25 on each summons and ordered to pay £110 costs. The court also made a forfeiture order for the destruction of the books by the police.]

19. Whilst the *Schoolbook* was not the subject of proceedings in Northern Ireland, the Channel Islands or the Isle of Man, the same was not true of Scotland.

Indeed a Glasgow bookseller was charged under a local Act. However he was acquitted on 9 February 1972 by a stipendiary magistrate who considered that the book was not indecent or obscene within the meaning of that Act. It does not appear from the file whether the case concerned the original or the revised edition.

Further, a complaint was brought under Scottish law against Stage 1 in respect of the revised edition. It was dismissed on 8 December 1972 by an Edinburgh court solely on the ground that the accused could not have the necessary mens rea. In January 1973 the Procurator Fiscal announced that he would not appeal against this decision; he also did not avail himself of his right to initiate criminal proceedings against Mr. Handyside personally.

THE SCHOOLBOOK

20. The original English language edition of the book, priced at thirty pence a copy, had altogether 208 pages. It contained an introduction headed "All

grown-ups are paper tigers," an "Introduction to the British edition," and chapters on the following subjects: Education, Learning, Teachers, Pupils and The System. The chapter on Pupils contained a twenty-six page section concerning "Sex" which included the following sub-sections: Masturbation, Orgasm, Intercourse and petting, Contraceptives, Wet dreams, Menstruation, Child-molesters or "dirty old men," Pornography, Impotence, Homosexuality, Normal and abnormal, Find out more, Venereal diseases, Abortion, Legal and illegal abortion, Remember, Methods of abortion, Addresses for help and advice on sexual matters. The Introduction stated: "This book is meant to be a reference book. The idea is not to read it straight through, but to use the list of contents to find and read about the things you're interested in or want to know more about. Even if you're at a particularly progressive school you should find a lot of ideas in the book for improving things."

21. The applicant had planned the distribution of the book through the ordinary book-selling channels although it was said at the appeal hearing to have been accepted that the work was intended for, and intended to be made available to, school-children of the age of twelve and upwards.

22. Pending the appeal hearing, the applicant consulted his legal advisers concerning a revision of the Schoolbook to avoid further prosecutions; apparently he tried to consult the Director of Public Prosecutions as well, but in vain. It was decided to eliminate or re-write the offending lines which had been attacked before the Magistrates' Court by the prosecution but to do so necessitated, in some cases, re-writing substantially more than these criticised sentences. There were other alterations made to the text by way of general improvement, for example in response to comments and suggestions from readers and the updating of changed data (addresses, etc.).

23. The revised edition was published on 15 November 1971. After consulting the Attorney General, the Director of Public Prosecutions announced on 6 December 1971 that the new edition would not be the subject of a prosecution. This publication took place after the Quarter Sessions judgment but the revision of the *Schoolbook* had been completed, and the printing of the new version was in train, well before.

DOMESTIC LAW

24. The action against the *Schoolbook* was based on the Obscene Publications Act 1959, as amended by the Obscene Publications Act 1964 (hereinafter called "the 1959/1964 Acts").

25. The relevant extracts from the 1959/1964 Acts, read together, are as follows:

Section 1

> (1) For the purposes of this act an article shall be deemed to be obscene if its effect or (where the article comprises two or more distinct items) the effect of any one of its items is, if taken as a whole, such as to tend to deprave and corrupt persons who are likely, having regard to all relevant circumstances, to read, see or hear the matter contained or embodied in it. . . .

Section 4

(1) A person shall not be convicted of an offence against section 2 of this Act and an order for forfeiture shall not be made under the foregoing section if it is proved that publication of the article in question is justified as being for the public good on the ground that it is in the interests of science, literature, art of learning, or of other objects of general concern.

(2) It is hereby declared that the opinion of experts as to the literary, artistic, scientific or other merits of an article may be admitted in any proceedings under this Act either to establish or to negative the said ground.

26. At the time of the events under review, the authorities frequently adopted a non-contentious procedure ("disclaimer/caution procedure") rather than instituting, as in this case, criminal proceedings. However it could only be used when the individual admitted that the article was obscene and consented to its destruction. The procedure constituted no more than a matter of practice and was abandoned in 1973 following criticisms expressed in a judicial decision.

THE JUDGMENT OF THE INNER LONDON QUARTER SESSIONS

27. At the appeal hearing two principal issues were examined by the court, namely, first, whether or not the Crown had proved beyond reasonable doubt that the *Schoolbook* was an obscene article within the meaning of the 1959/1964 Acts; and secondly, if so, whether or not the applicant had established the defence under section 4 of the 1959/1964 Acts to the effect that he had shown, on a balance of probabilities, that publication of the book was justified as being for the public good.

28. The court first dealt with the issue of obscenity. Following a decision in another case the court noted that it had to be satisfied that the persons who it was alleged were likely to read the article would constitute a significant proportion. It also accepted the meaning of the words "deprave and corrupt" as it had been explained in that other case and about which there had been no dispute between the parties.

29. Following further previous case-law, the court had decided that expert evidence should be admitted on the question of whether the *Schoolbook* was obscene. Such evidence, though not normally admissible for this purpose but only in connection with the defence under section 4 of the 1959/1964 Acts, could be heard in the present case which was concerned with the effect of the article upon children.

The court had therefore heard seven witnesses on behalf of the prosecution and nine on behalf of the applicant, being experts in various fields, in particular those of psychiatry and teaching; the views they had expressed were very different. After they had been heard, the applicant had argued that, when one had the sincere opinion of many highly-qualified experts against the prosecution's case, it was impossible to say that the tendency to deprave and corrupt had been established with certainty. The court was unable to accept this submission: in its judgment of 29 October 1971 it pointed out that there was an almost infinite variation in the relevant background of the children who would be in one way or another affected by the book, so that it was difficult to speak of "true facts" in this case. The views of the applicant's witnesses had been those approaching the extreme of one wing of the more broadly varied outlook on the education and upbringing of children, whereas the evidence given on behalf of the prosecution tended to cover the views of those who, although clearly tending in the opposite direction, were less radical. Particularly, when looking at the evidence on behalf of the applicant, the court had been driven to the conclusion that most of the witnesses were so uncritical of the book looked at as a whole, and so unrestrained in their praise of it, as to make them at times less convincing than otherwise they might have been. In summary the court considered that a good deal of the witnesses had been so single-minded in an extreme point of view as to forfeit in a large measure the power to judge with that degree of responsibility which makes the evidence of any great value on a matter of this sort.

30. Concerning the *Schoolbook* itself, the court first stressed that it was intended for children passing through a highly critical stage of their development. At such a time a very high degree of responsibility ought to be exercised by the courts. In the present case, they had before them, as something said to be a perfectly responsible adult opinion, a work of an extreme kind, unrelieved by any indication that there were any alternative views; this was something which detracted from the opportunity for children to form a balanced view on some of the very strong advice given therein.

31. The court then briefly examined the background. For example, looking at the book as a whole, marriage was very largely ignored. Mixing a very one-sided opinion with fact and purporting to be a book of reference, it would tend to undermine, for a very considerable proportion of children, many of the influences, such as those of parents, the Churches and youth organisations, which might otherwise provide the restraint and sense of responsibility for oneself which found inadequate expression in the book.

The court reached the conclusion that, on the whole, and quite clearly through the mind of the child, the *Schoolbook* was inimical to good teacher/child relationships; in particular, there were numerous passages that it found to be subversive, not only to the authority but to the influence of the trust between children and teachers.

32. Passing to the tendency to deprave and corrupt, the court considered the atmosphere of the book looked at as a whole, noting that the sense of some responsibility for the community as well as to oneself, if not wholly absent, was completely subordinated to the development of the expression of itself by the child. As indications of what it considered to result in a tendency to deprave and corrupt, the court quoted or referred to the following:

A. Passage headed "Be yourself" (p. 77):

> "Maybe you smoke pot or go to bed with your boyfriend or girlfriend — and don't tell your parents or teachers, either because you don't dare to or just because you want to keep it secret.
>
> Don't feel ashamed or guilty about doing things you really want to do and think are right just because your parents or teachers might disapprove. A lot of these things will be more important to you later in life than the things that are 'approved of'."

The objectionable point was that there was no reference there to the illegality of smoking pot which was only to be found many pages further on in an entirely different part of the book. Similarly there was no specific mention at all in the book of the illegality of sexual intercourse by a boy who has attained the age of fourteen and a girl who has not yet attained sixteen. It had to be remembered that the *Schoolbook* was indicated as a work of reference and that one looked up the part which one wanted rather than read it as a whole book.

B. The passage (pp. 97-98) headed "Intercourse and petting" under the main heading "Sex": to lay this before children as young as many of those who the court considered would read the book, without any injunction about restraint or unwisdom, was to produce a tendency to deprave and corrupt.

C. The passage — (pp. 103 to 105) — under the heading of "Pornography" and particularly the following:

> "Porn is a harmless pleasure if it isn't taken seriously and believed to be real life. Anybody who mistakes it for reality will be greatly disappointed. But it's quite possible that you may get some good ideas from it and you may find something which looks interesting and that you haven't tried before."

Unfortunately, the sane and sensible first paragraph quoted above was immediately followed by a passage suggesting to children that in pornography they might find some good ideas which they might adopt. This was to raise the real likelihood that a substantial number of children would feel it incumbent upon them to look for and practise such things. Moreover, just on the previous page there was the following passage: "But there are other kinds — for example pictures of intercourse with animals or pictures of people hurting each other in various ways. Pornographic stories describe the same sort of thing." The court considered that, although it was improbable that young people would be likely to commit sexual offences with animals as a result of this, the possibility that they should practise some other forms of cruelty to one another, for sexual satisfaction, was a real likelihood in the case of a significant number of children if this got into the hands of children at a disturbed, unsettled and sexually excited stage of their lives. Such acts might very well be criminal offences just like smoking pot and sexual intercourse between a boy of at least fourteen and a girl not yet sixteen. The expression "to deprave and corrupt" must include the admission of or the encouragement to commit criminal offences of that kind.

33. The court concluded "in the light of the whole of the book, that this book or this article on sex or this section or chapter on pupils, whichever one chooses as an article, looked at as a whole does tend to deprave and corrupt a significant number, significant proportion, of the children likely to read it." Such children would, it was satisfied, include a very substantial number aged under sixteen.

34. The court finally dealt with the issue of the defence under section 4 of the 1959/1964 Acts. It stated that no doubt there were many features about the book which, taken by themselves, were good. The unfortunate thing was that so frequently the good was intermixed with things that were bad and detracted from it.

For example, much of the information about contraceptives (pp. 98-102) was very relevant and desirable which should be laid before very many children who might not otherwise readily have access to it. But it was damaged by the suggestion, backed by the recommendation to take direct action if the school authorities would not give way, that every school should have at least one contraceptive vending machine (p. 101).

Similarly, the treatment of the subject of homosexuality (pp. 105-107) was a factual, very compassionate, understanding and valuable statement. But again, no matter how good one assessed the value of this section, it was hopelessly damning by its setting and context, and the fact that it, only, contained any suggestion of a stable relationship in relation to sex and that marriage received no such treatment at all. Moreover, there was a very real danger that this passage would create in the minds of children a conclusion that that kind of relationship was something permanent.

Again, there were passages with regard to venereal diseases (pp. 110-111), contraception (pp. 98-102) and abortion (pp. 111-116), containing dispassionately and sensibly, and on the whole completely accurately, a great deal of advice which ought not to be denied to young children. However, on the balance of probabilities, these matters could not outweigh what the court was convinced had a tendency to deprave and corrupt. The court asked itself whether, granted the degree of indecency which it found, the good likely to result from the *Schoolbook* was such that it ought, nevertheless, to be published in the public interest; it regretfully came to the conclusion that the burden on the appellant to show that "publication of the article in question is justified as being for the public good" had not been discharged. . . .

As to the Law. . .

I. On the Alleged Violation of Article 10 of the Convention

42. The applicant claims to be the victim of a violation of Article 10 (art. 10) of the Convention which provides:

> 1. Everyone has the right to freedom of expression. This right shall include freedom to hold opinions and to receive and impart information and ideas without interference by public authority and regardless of frontiers. This Article shall not prevent States from requiring the licensing of broadcasting, television or cinema enterprises.
>
> 2. The exercise of these freedoms, since it carries with it duties and responsibilities, may be subject to such formalities, conditions, restrictions or penalties as are prescribed by law and are necessary in a democratic society, in the interests of national security, territorial integrity or public safety, for the prevention of disorder or crime, for the protection of health or morals, for the protection of the reputation or rights of others, for preventing the disclosure of information received in confidence, or for maintaining the authority and impartiality of the judiciary.

43. The various measures challenged — the applicant's criminal conviction, the seizure and subsequent forfeiture and destruction of the matrix and of hundreds of copies of the *Schoolbook* — were without any doubt, and the Government did not deny it, "interferences by public authority" in the exercise of his freedom of expression which is guaranteed by paragraph 1) of the text cited above. Such interferences entail a "violation" of Article 10 if they do not fall within one of the exceptions provided for in paragraph 2, which is accordingly of decisive importance in this case.

44. If the "restrictions" and "penalties" complained of by Mr. Handyside are not to infringe Article 10, they must, according to paragraph 2, in the first place have been "prescribed by law." The Court finds that this was the case. In the United Kingdom legal system, the basis in law for the measures in question was

the 1959/1964 Acts. Besides, this was not contested by the applicant who further admitted that the competent authorities had correctly applied those Acts.

45. Having thus ascertained that the interferences complained of satisfied the first of the conditions in paragraph 2 of Article 10, the Court then investigated whether they also complied with the others. According to the Government and the majority of the Commission, the interferences were "necessary in a democratic society," "for the protection of . . . morals."

46. Sharing the view of the Government and the unanimous opinion of the Commission, the Court first finds that the 1959/1964 Acts have an aim that is legitimate under Article 10 para. 2, namely, the protection of morals in a democratic society. Only this latter purpose is relevant in this case since the object of the said Acts — to wage war on "obscene" publications, defined by their tendency to "deprave and corrupt" — is linked far more closely to the protection of morals than to any of the further purposes permitted by Article 10 para. 2.

47. The Court must also investigate whether the protection of morals in a democratic society necessitated the various measures taken against the applicant and the *Schoolbook* under the 1959/1964 Acts. Mr. Handyside does not restrict himself to criticising these Acts as such: he also makes — from the viewpoint of the Convention and not of English law — several complaints concerning their application in his case. . . .

48. The Court points out that the machinery of protection established by the Convention is subsidiary to the national systems safeguarding human rights. The Convention leaves to each Contracting State, in the first place, the task of securing the rights and liberties it enshrines. The institutions created by it make their own contribution to this task but they become involved only through contentious proceedings and once all domestic remedies have been exhausted (Article 26).

These observations apply, notably, to Article 10 para. 2. In particular, it is not possible to find in the domestic law of the various Contracting States a uniform European conception of morals. The view taken by their respective laws of the requirements of morals varies from time to time and from place to place, especially in our era which is characterised by a rapid and far-reaching evolution of opinions on the subject. By reason of their direct and continuous contact with the vital forces of their countries, State authorities are in principle in a better position than the international judge to give an opinion on the exact content of these requirements as well as on the "necessity" of a "restriction" or "penalty" intended to meet them. The Court notes at this juncture that, whilst the adjective "necessary," within the meaning of Article 10 para. 2, is not synonymous with "indispensable" (cf., in Articles 2 para. 2) and 6 para. 1, the words "absolutely necessary" and "strictly necessary" and, in Article 15 para. 1, the phrase "to the extent strictly required by the exigencies of the situation"), neither has it the flexibility of such expressions as "admissible," "ordinary" (cf. Article 4 para. 3), "useful" (cf. the French text of the first paragraph of Article 1 of Protocol No. 1), "reasonable" (cf. Articles 5 para. 3 and 6 para. 1) or "desirable." Nevertheless, it is for the national authorities to make the initial assessment of the reality of the pressing social need implied by the notion of "necessity" in this context.

Consequently, Article 10 para. 2 leaves to the Contracting States a margin of appreciation. This margin is given both to the domestic legislator ("prescribed by law") and to the bodies, judicial amongst others, that are called upon to interpret and apply the laws in force.

49. Nevertheless, Article 10 para. 2 does not give the Contracting States an unlimited power of appreciation. The Court, which, with the Commission, is responsible for ensuring the observance of those States' engagements (Article 19), is empowered to give the final ruling on whether a "restriction" or "penalty" is reconcilable with freedom of expression as protected by Article 10. The domestic margin of appreciation thus goes hand in hand with a European supervision. Such supervision concerns both the aim of the measure challenged and its "necessity"; it covers not only the basic legislation but also the decision applying it, even one given by an independent court. In this respect, the Court refers to Article 50 (art. 50) of the Convention ("decision or . . . measure taken by a legal authority or any other authority") as well as to its own case-law.

The Court's supervisory functions oblige it to pay the utmost attention to the principles characterising a "democratic society." Freedom of expression constitutes one of the essential foundations of such a society, one of the basic conditions for its progress and for the development of every man. Subject to paragraph 2 of Article 10, it is applicable not only to "information" or "ideas" that are favourably received or regarded as inoffensive or as a matter of indifference, but also to those that offend, shock or disturb the State or any sector of the population. Such are the demands of that pluralism, tolerance and broadmindedness without which there is no "democratic society." This means, amongst other things, that every "formality," "condition," "restriction" or "penalty" imposed in this sphere must be proportionate to the legitimate aim pursued.

From another standpoint, whoever exercises his freedom of expression undertakes "duties and responsibilities" the scope of which depends on his situation and the technical means he uses. The Court cannot overlook such a person's "duties" and "responsibilities" when it enquires, as in this case, whether "restrictions" or "penalties" were conducive to the "protection of morals" which made them "necessary" in a "democratic society."

50. It follows from this that it is in no way the Court's task to take the place of the competent national courts but rather to review under Article 10 (art. 10) the decisions they delivered in the exercise of their power of appreciation.

However, the Court's supervision would generally prove illusory if it did no more than examine these decisions in isolation; it must view them in the light of the case as a whole, including the publication in question and the arguments and evidence adduced by the applicant in the domestic legal system and then at the international level. The Court must decide, on the basis of the different data available to it, whether the reasons given by the national authorities to justify the actual measures of "interference" they take are relevant and sufficient under Article 10 para. 2.

51. Following the method set out above, the Court scrutinized under Article 10 para. 2 the individual decisions complained of, in particular, the judgment of the Inner London Quarter Sessions.

The said judgment is summarised in paragraphs 27-34 above. The Court reviewed it in the light of the case as a whole; in addition to the pleadings before the Court and the Commission's report, the memorials and oral explanations presented to the Commission between June 1973 and August 1974 and the transcript of the proceedings before the Quarter Sessions were, inter alia, taken into consideration.

52. The Court attaches particular importance to a factor to which the judgment of 29 October 1971 did not fail to draw attention, that is, the intended readership of the *Schoolbook*. It was aimed above all at children and adolescents aged from twelve to eighteen. Being direct, factual and reduced to essentials in style, it was easily within the comprehension of even the youngest of such readers. The applicant had made it clear that he planned a widespread circulation. He had sent the book, with a press release, to numerous daily papers and periodicals for review or for advertising purposes. What is more, he had set a modest sale price (thirty pence), arranged for a reprint of 50,000 copies shortly after the first impression of 20,000 and chosen a title suggesting that the work was some kind of handbook for use in schools.

Basically the book contained purely factual information that was generally correct and often useful, as the Quarter Sessions recognised. However, it also included, above all in the section on sex and in the passage headed "Be yourself" in the chapter on pupils (paragraph 32 above), sentences or paragraphs that young people at a critical stage of their development could have interpreted as an encouragement to indulge in precocious activities harmful for them or even to commit certain criminal offences. In these circumstances, despite the variety and the constant evolution in the United Kingdom of views on ethics and education, the competent English judges were entitled, in the exercise of their discretion, to think at the relevant time that the *Schoolbook* would have pernicious effects on the morals of many of the children and adolescents who would read it.

However, the applicant maintained, in substance, that the demands of the "protection of morals" or, to use the wording of the 1959/1964 Acts, of the war against publications likely to "deprave and corrupt," were but a pretext in his case. The truth of the matter, he alleged, was that an attempt had been made to muzzle a small-scale publisher whose political leanings met with the disapproval of a fragment of public opinion. Proceedings were set in motion, said he, in an atmosphere little short of "hysteria," stirred up and kept alive by ultra-conservative elements. The accent in the judgment of 29 October 1971 on the anti-authoritarian aspects of the *Schoolbook* (paragraph 31 above) showed, according to the applicant, exactly what lay behind the case.

The information supplied by Mr. Handyside seems, in fact, to show that letters from members of the public, articles in the press and action by Members of Parliament were not without some influence in the decision to seize the Schoolbook and to take criminal proceedings against its publisher. However, the Government drew attention to the fact that such initiatives could well have been explained not by some dark plot but by the genuine emotion felt by citizens faithful to traditional moral values when, towards the end of March 1971, they read in certain newspapers extracts from the book which was due to appear on 1 April. The Government also emphasised that the proceedings ended several months after the "campaign" denounced by the applicant and that he did not claim that it had continued in the intervening period. From this the Government concluded that the "campaign" in no way impaired dispassionate deliberation at the Quarter Sessions.

For its part the Court finds that the anti-authoritarian aspects of the *Schoolbook* as such were not held in the judgment of 29 October 1971 to fall foul of the 1959/1964 Acts. Those aspects were taken into account only insofar as the appeal court considered that, by undermining the moderating influence of parents, teachers, the Churches and youth organisations, they aggravated the tendency to "deprave and corrupt" which in its opinion resulted from other parts of the work. It should be added that the revised edition was allowed to circulate freely by the British authorities despite the fact that the anti-authoritarian passages again appeared there in full and even, in some cases, in stronger terms (paragraph 35 above). As the Government noted, this is hard to reconcile with the theory of a political intrigue.

The Court thus allows that the fundamental aim of the judgment of 29 October 1971, applying the 1959/1964 Acts, was the protection of the morals of the young, a legitimate purpose under Article 10 para. 2 (art. 10-2). Consequently, the seizures effected on 31 March and 1 April 1971, pending the outcome of the proceedings that were about to open, also had this aim.

53. It remains to examine the "necessity" of the measures in dispute, beginning with the said seizures. . . .

55. . . . In the Court's view, the absence of proceedings against the revised edition, which differed fairly extensively from the original edition on the points at issue, rather suggests that the competent authorities wished to limit themselves to what was strictly necessary, an attitude in conformity with Article 10 the Convention.

56. The treatment meted out to the *Schoolbook* and its publisher in 1971 was, according to the applicant and the minority of the Commission, all the less "necessary" in that a host of publications dedicated to hard core pornography and devoid of intellectual or artistic merit allegedly profit by an extreme degree of tolerance in the United Kingdom. They are exposed to the gaze of passers-by and especially of young people and are said generally to enjoy complete impunity, the rare criminal prosecutions launched against them proving, it was asserted, more often than not abortive due to the great liberalism shown by juries. The same was claimed to apply to sex shops and much public entertainment.

The Government countered this by the remark, supported by figures, that the Director of Public Prosecutions does not remain inactive nor does the police, despite the scanty manpower resources of the squad specialising in this field. Moreover, they claim that, in addition to proceedings properly so called, seizures were frequently made at the relevant time under the "disclaimer/caution procedure" (paragraph 26 above).

In principle it is not the Court's function to compare different decisions taken, even in apparently similar circumstances, by prosecuting authorities and courts; and it must, just like the respondent Government, respect the independence of the courts. Furthermore and above all, the Court is not faced with really analogous situations: as the Government pointed out, the documents in the file do not show that the publications and entertainment in question were aimed, to the same extent as the *Schoolbook* (paragraph 52 above), at children and adolescents having ready access thereto.

57. The applicant and the minority of the Commission laid stress on the further point that, in addition to the original Danish edition, translations of the "Little Book" appeared and circulated freely in the majority of the member States of the Council of Europe.

Here again, the national margin of appreciation and the optional nature of the "restrictions" and "penalties" referred to in Article 10 para. 2 prevent the Court from accepting the argument. The Contracting States have each fashioned their approach in the light of the situation obtaining in their respective territories; they have had regard, inter alia, to the different views prevailing there about the demands of the protection of morals in a democratic society. The fact that most of them decided to allow the work to be distributed does not mean that the contrary decision of the Inner London Quarter Sessions was a breach of Article 10. Besides, some of the editions published outside the United Kingdom do not include the passages, or at least not all the passages, cited in the judgment of 29 October 1971 as striking examples of a tendency to "deprave and corrupt."

58. Finally, at the hearing on 5 June 1976, the delegate expounding the opinion of the minority of the Commission maintained that in any event the respondent State need not have taken measures as Draconian as the initiation of criminal proceedings leading to the conviction of Mr. Handyside and to the forfeiture and subsequent destruction of the *Schoolbook*. The United Kingdom was said to have violated the principle of proportionality, inherent in the adjective "necessary," by not limiting itself either to a request to the applicant to expurgate the book or to restrictions on its sale and advertisement.

With regard to the first solution, the Government argued that the applicant would never have agreed to modify the *Schoolbook* if he had been ordered or asked to do so before 1 April 1971: was he not strenuously disputing its "obscenity"? The Court for its part confines itself to finding that Article 10 of the Convention certainly does not oblige the Contracting States to introduce such prior censorship.The Government did not indicate whether the second solution was feasible under English law. Neither does it appear that it would have been appropriate in this case. There would scarcely have been any sense in restricting to adults sales of a work destined above all for the young; the *Schoolbook* would thereby have lost the substance of what the applicant considered to be its raison d'être. Moreover, he did not advert to this question.

59. On the strength of the data before it, the Court thus reaches the conclusion that no breach of the requirements of Article 10 has been established in the circumstances of the present case. . . .

Jersild v. Denmark

Eur. Ct. H.R., ser. A No. 298, App. No. 15890/89, Sept. 20, 1994 (Grand Chamber)

. . . 9. Mr Jens Olaf Jersild, a Danish national, is a journalist and lives in Copenhagen. He was at the time of the events giving rise to the present case, and still is, employed by Danmarks Radio (Danish Broadcasting Corporation, which broadcasts not only radio but also television programmes), assigned to its *Sunday News Magazine (Søndagsavisen)*. The latter is known as a serious television programme intended for a well-informed audience, dealing with a wide range of social and political issues, including xenophobia, immigration and refugees.

A. The Greenjackets Item

10. On 31 May 1985 the newspaper *Information* published an article describing the racist attitudes of members of a group of young people, calling themselves "the Greenjackets" ("grønjakkerne"), at Østerbro in Copenhagen. In the light of this article, the editors of the *Sunday News Magazine* decided to produce a documentary on the Greenjackets. Subsequently the applicant contacted representatives of the group, inviting three of them together with Mr Per Axholt, a social worker employed at the local youth centre, to take part in a television interview. During the interview, which was conducted by the applicant, the three Greenjackets made abusive and derogatory remarks about immigrants and ethnic groups in Denmark. It lasted between five and six hours, of which between two and two and a half hours were video-recorded. Danmarks Radio paid the interviewees fees in accordance with its usual practice.

11. The applicant subsequently edited and cut the film of the interview down to a few minutes. On 21 July 1985 this was broadcast by Danmarks Radio as a part of the *Sunday News Magazine*. The programme consisted of a variety of items, for instance on the martial law in South Africa, on the debate on profit-sharing in Denmark and on the late German writer Heinrich Böll. The transcript of the Greenjackets item reads as follows [(I): TV presenter; (A): the applicant; (G): one or another of the Greenjackets]:

(I) In recent years, a great deal has been said about racism in Denmark. The papers are currently publishing stories about distrust and resentment directed against minorities. Who are the people who hate the minorities? Where do they come from? What is their mentality like? Mr Jens Olaf Jersild has visited a group of extremist youths at Østerbro in Copenhagen.

(A) The flag on the wall is the flag of the Southern States from the American Civil War, but today it is also the symbol of racism, the symbol of the American movement, the Ku Klux Klan, and it shows what Lille Steen, Henrik and Nisse are.

(A) Are you a racist?

(G) Yes, that's what I regard myself as. It's good being a racist. We believe Denmark is for the Danes.

(A) Henrik, Lille Steen and all the others are members of a group of young people who live in Studsgårdsgade, called STUDSEN, in Østerbro in Copenhagen. It is public housing, a lot of the inhabitants are unemployed and on social security; the crime rate is high. Some of the young people in this neighbourhood have already been involved in criminal activities and have already been convicted.

(G) It was an ordinary armed robbery at a petrol station.

(A) What did you do?

(G) Nothing. I just ran into a petrol station with a . . . gun and made them give me some money. Then I ran out again. That's all.

(A) What about you, what happened?

(G) I don't wish to discuss that further.

(A) But, was it violence?

(G) Yes.

(A) You have just come out of . . . you have been arrested, what were you arrested for?

(G) Street violence.

(A) What happened?

(G) I had a little fight with the police together with some friends.

(A) Does that happen often?
(G) Yes, out here it does.
(A) All in all, there are 20-25 young people from STUDSEN in the same group. They meet not far away from the public housing area near some old houses which are to be torn down. They meet here to reaffirm among other things their racism, their hatred of immigrants and their support for the Ku Klux Klan.
(G) The Ku Klux Klan, that's something that comes from the States in the old days during — you know — the civil war and things like that, because the Northern States wanted that the niggers should be free human beings, man, they are not human beings, they are animals, right, it's completely wrong, man, the things that happened. People should be allowed to keep slaves, I think so anyway.
(A) Because blacks are not human beings?
(G) No, you can also see that from their body structure, man, big flat noses, with cauliflower ears etc., man. Broad heads and very broad bodies, man, hairy, you are looking at a gorilla and compare it with an ape, man, then it is the same [behaviour], man, it's the same movements, long arms, man, long fingers etc., long feet.
(A) A lot of people are saying something different. There are a lot of people who say, but . . .
(G) Just take a picture of a gorilla, man, and then look at a nigger, it's the same body structure and everything, man, flat forehead and all kinds of things.
(A) There are many blacks, for example in the USA, who have important jobs.
(G) Of course, there is always someone who wants to show off, as if they are better than the white man, but in the long run, it's the white man who is better.
(A) What does Ku Klux Klan mean to you?
(G) It means a great deal, because I think what they do is right. A nigger is not a human being, it's an animal, that goes for all the other foreign workers as well, Turks, Yugoslavs and whatever they are called.
(A) Henrik is 19 years old and on welfare. He lives in a rented room in Studsgårdsgade. Henrik is one of the strongest supporters of the Klan, and he hates the foreign workers, 'Perkere' [a very derogatory word in Danish for immigrant workers].
(G) They come up here, man, and sponge on our society. But we, we have enough problems in getting our social benefits, man, they just get it. Fuck, we can argue with those idiots up there at the social benefit office to get our money, man, they just get it, man, they are the first on the housing list, they get better flats than us, man, and some of our friends who have children, man, they are living in the worst slum, man, they can't even get a shower in their flat, man, then those 'Perkere' families, man, go up there with seven kids, man, and they just get an expensive flat, right there and then. They get everything paid, and things like that, that can't be right, man, Denmark is for the Danes, right? It is the fact that they are 'Perkere', that's what we don't like, right, and we don't like their mentality — I mean they can damn well, I mean . . . what's it called . . . I mean if they feel like speaking Russian in their homes, right, then it's okay, but what we don't like is when they walk around in those Zimbabwe-clothes and then speak this hula-hula language in the street, and if you ask them something or if you get into one of their taxis then they say: I don't know where it is, you give directions right.
(A) Is it not so that perhaps you are a bit envious that some of the 'Perkere' as you call them have their own shops, and cars, they can make ends . . .
(G) It's drugs they are selling, man, half of the prison population in 'Vestre' are in there because of drugs, man, half of those in Vestre prison anyway, they are the people who are serving time for dealing drugs or something similar. They are in there, all the 'Perkere,' because of drugs, right. [That]; must be enough, what's it called, there should not be drugs here in this country, but if it really has to be

smuggled in, I think we should do it ourselves, I mean, I think it's unfair that those foreigners come up here to . . . what's it called . . . make Denmark more drug dependent and things like that. We have painted their doors and hoped that they would get fed up with it, so that they would soon leave, and jumped on their cars and thrown paint in their faces when they were lying in bed sleeping.

(A) What was it you did with that paint – why paint?

(G) Because it was white paint, I think that suited them well, that was the intended effect.

(A) You threw paint through the windows of an immigrant family?

(G) Yes.

(A) What happened?

(G) He just got it in his face, that's all. Well, I think he woke up, and then he came out and shouted something in his hula-hula language.

(A) Did he report it to the police?

(G) I don't know if he did, I mean, he won't get anywhere by doing that.

(A) Why not?

(G) I don't know, it's just kid's stuff, like other people throwing water in people's faces, he got paint in his. They can't make anything out of that.

(A) Per Axholt, known as 'Pax' [P], is employed in the youth centre in Studsgårdsgade. He has worked there for several years, but many give up a lot sooner because of the tough environment. Per Axholt feels that the reasons why the young people are persecuting the immigrants is that they are themselves powerless and disappointed.What do you think they would say that they want, if you asked them?

(P) Just what you and I want. Some control over their lives, work which may be considered decent and which they like, a reasonable economic situation, a reasonably functioning family, a wife or a husband and some children, a reasonable middleclass life such as you and I have.

(A) They do many things which are sure to prevent them from getting it.

(P) That is correct.

(A) Why do you think they do this?

(P) Because they have nothing better to do. They have been told over a long period that the means by which to achieve success is money. They won't be able to get money legitimately, so often they try to obtain it through criminal activity. Sometimes they succeed, sometimes not, and that's why we see a lot of young people in that situation go to prison, because it doesn't work.

(A) How old were you when you started your criminal activities?

(G) I don't know, about 14 I guess.

(A) What did you do?

(G) The first time, I can't remember, I don't know, burglary.

(A) Do you have what one might call a criminal career?

(G) I don't know if you can call it that.

(A) You committed your first crime when you were 14.

(G) Well, you can put it that way, I mean, if that is a criminal career. If you have been involved in crime since the age of 15 onwards, then I guess you can say I've had a criminal career.

(A) Will you tell me about some of the things you have done?

(G) No, not really. It's been the same over and over again. There has been pinching of videos, where the 'Perkere' have been our customers, so they have money. If people want to be out here and have a nice time and be racists and drink beer, and have fun, then it's quite obvious you don't want to sit in the slammer.

(A) But is the threat of imprisonment something that really deters people from doing something illegal?

(G) No, it's not prison, that doesn't frighten people.

(A) Is that why you hear stories about people from out here fighting with knives etc., night after night. Is the reason for this the fact that they are not afraid of the police getting hold of them?

(G) Yes, nothing really comes of it, I mean, there are no bad consequences, so probably that's why. For instance fights and stabbings and smashing up things ... If you really get into the joint it would be such a ridiculously small sentence, so it would be, I mean... usually we are released the next day. Last time we caused some trouble over at the pub, they let us out the next morning. Nothing really comes of it. It doesn't discourage us, but there were five of us, who just came out and then we had a celebration for the last guy, who came out yesterday, they probably don't want to go in again for some time so they probably won't commit big crimes again.

(A) You would like to move back to Studsgårdsgade where you grew up, but we know for sure that it's an environment with a high crime rate. Would you like your child to grow up like you?

(G) No, and I don't think she will. Firstly, because she is a girl, statistics show that the risk is not that high, I mean they probably don't do it, but you don't have to be a criminal because you live in an environment with a high crime rate. I just wouldn't accept it, if she was mugging old women and stealing their handbags.

(A) What if she was among those beating up the immigrants etc. What then?

(G) That would be okay. I wouldn't have anything against that.

(I) We will have to see if the mentality of this family changes in the next generation. Finally, we would like to say that groups of young people like this one in STUDSEN at Østerbro, have been formed elsewhere in Copenhagen.

B. Proceedings in the City Court of Copenhagen

12. Following the programme no complaints were made to the Radio Council, which had competence in such matters, or to Danmarks Radio but the Bishop of Ålborg complained to the Minister of Justice. After undertaking investigations the Public Prosecutor instituted criminal proceedings in the City Court of Copenhagen (Københavns Byret) against the three youths interviewed by the applicant, charging them with a violation of Article 266 (b) of the Penal Code (straffeloven) (see paragraph 19 below) for having made the statements cited below:

> ... the Northern States wanted that the niggers should be free human beings, man, they are not human beings, they are animals.
>
> Just take a picture of a gorilla, man, and then look at a nigger, it's the same body structure and everything, man, flat forehead and all kinds of things.
>
> A nigger is not a human being, it's an animal, that goes for all the other foreign workers as well, Turks, Yugoslavs and whatever they are called.
>
> It is the fact that they are 'Perkere,' that's what we don't like, right, and we don't like their mentality... what we don't like is when they walk around in those Zimbabwe-clothes and then speak this hula-hula language in the street...
>
> It's drugs they are selling, man, half of the prison population in 'Vestre' are in there because of drugs... they are the people who are serving time for dealing drugs...
>
> They are in there, all the 'Perkere,' because of drugs...

The applicant was charged, under Article 266 (b) in conjunction with Article 23 (see paragraph 19 below), with aiding and abetting the three youths; the same charge was brought against the head of the news section of Danmarks Radio, Mr Lasse Jensen.

13. In the City Court counsel for the applicant and Mr Jensen called for their acquittal. He argued that the conduct of the applicant and Mr Jensen could in no way be compared to that of the other three defendants, with whose views they did not sympathise. They sought merely to provide a realistic picture of a social problem; in fact the programme only provoked resentment and aroused pity in respect of the three other defendants, who had exposed themselves to ridicule on their own terms. Accordingly, it was by no means the intention of Danmarks Radio to persuade others to subscribe to the same views as the Greenjackets, rather the contrary. Under the relevant law a distinction had to be drawn between the persons who made the statements and the programme editors, the latter enjoying a special freedom of expression. Having at that time a broadcasting monopoly, Danmarks Radio was under a duty to impart all opinions of public interest in a manner that reflected the speaker's way of expressing himself. The public also had an interest in being informed of notoriously bad social attitudes, even those which were unpleasant. The programme was broadcast in the context of a public debate which had resulted in press comments, for instance in Information, and was simply an honest report on the realities of the youths in question. Counsel, referring inter alia to the above-mentioned article in Information, also pointed to the fact that no consistent prosecution policy had been followed in cases of this nature.

14. On 24 April 1987 the City Court convicted the three youths, one of them for having stated that "niggers" and "foreign workers" were "animals," and two of them for their assertions in relation to drugs and "Perkere." The applicant was convicted of aiding and abetting them, as was Mr Jensen, in his capacity as programme controller; they were sentenced to pay day-fines (dagsbøder) totalling 1,000 and 2,000 Danish kroner, respectively, or alternatively to five days' imprisonment (haefte).

As regards the applicant, the City Court found that, following the article in Information of 31 May 1985, he had visited the Greenjackets and after a conversation with Mr Axholt, amongst others, agreed that the three youths should participate in a television programme. The object of the programme had been to demonstrate the attitude of the Greenjackets to the racism at Østerbro, previously mentioned in the article in Information, and to show their social background. Accordingly, so the City Court held, the applicant had himself taken the initiative of making the television programme and, further, he had been well aware in advance that discriminatory statements of a racist nature were likely to be made during the interview. The interview had lasted several hours, during which beer, partly paid for by Danmarks Radio, was consumed. In this connection the applicant had encouraged the Greenjackets to express their racist views, which, in so far as they were broadcast on television, in itself constituted a breach of Article 266 (b) of the Penal Code. The statements were broadcast without any counterbalancing comments, after the recordings had been edited by the applicant. He was accordingly guilty of aiding and abetting the violation of Article 266 (b) . . .

18. When the Supreme Court has rendered judgment in a case raising important issues of principle it is customary that a member of the majority publishes a

detailed and authoritative statement of the reasons for the judgment. In keeping with this custom, Justice Hermann on 20 January 1990 published such a statement in the *Weekly Law Journal* (*Ugeskrift for Retsvaesen*, 1989, p. 399).

> As regards the conviction of the applicant and Mr Jensen, the majority had attached importance to the fact that they had caused the racist statements to be made public. The applicant's item had not been a direct report on a meeting. He had himself contacted the three youths and caused them to make assertions such as those previously made in Information, which he knew of and probably expected them to repeat. He had himself cut the recording of the interview, lasting several hours, down to a few minutes containing the crude comments. The statements, which would hardly have been punishable under Article 266 (b) of the Penal Code had they not been made to a wide circle ("videre kreds") of people, became clearly punishable as they were broadcast on television on the applicant's initiative and with Mr Jensen's approval. It was therefore beyond doubt that they had aided and abetted the dissemination of the statements.
>
> Acquitting the applicant and Mr Jensen could only be justified by reasons clearly outweighing the wrongfulness of their actions. In this connection, the interest in protecting those grossly insulted by the statements had to be weighed up against that of informing the public of the statements. Whilst it is desirable to allow the press the best possible conditions for reporting on society, press freedom cannot be unlimited since freedom of expression is coupled with responsibilities.
>
> In striking a balance between the various interests involved, the majority had regard to the fact that the statements, which were brought to a wide circle of people, consisted of series of inarticulate, defamatory remarks and insults spoken by members of an insignificant group whose opinions could hardly be of interest to many people. Their news or information value was not such as to justify their dissemination and therefore did not warrant acquitting the defendants. This did not mean that extremist views could not be reported in the press, but such reports must be carried out in a more balanced and comprehensive manner than was the case in the television programme in question. Direct reports from meetings which were a matter of public interest should also be permitted.
>
> The minority, on the other hand, considered that the right to information overrode the interests protected by Article 266 (b) of the Penal Code.

Finally, Justice Hermann noted that the compatibility of the impugned measures with Article 10 of the Convention was not raised during the trial.

II. Relevant Domestic Law

A. The Penal Code

19. At the relevant time Article 266 (b) of the Penal Code provided:

> Any person who, publicly or with the intention of disseminating it to a wide circle ("videre kreds") of people, makes a statement, or other communication, threatening, insulting or degrading a group of persons on account of their race, colour, national or ethnic origin or belief shall be liable to a fine or to simple detention or to imprisonment for a term not exceeding two years.

Article 23, paragraph 1, reads:

> A provision establishing a criminal offence shall apply to any person who has assisted the commission of the offence by instigation, advice or action. The punishment may be reduced if the person in question only intended to give assistance of minor importance or to strengthen an intent already resolved or if the offence has not been completed or an intended assistance failed.

B. THE 1991 MEDIA LIABILITY ACT

20. The 1991 Media Liability Act (Medieansvarsloven, 1991: 348), which entered into force on 1 January 1992, that is after the events giving rise to the present case, lays down rules inter alia on criminal liability in respect of television broadcasts. Section 18 provides:

> A person making a statement during a non-direct broadcast (forskudt udsendelse) shall be responsible for the statement under general statutory provisions, unless:
>
> (1) the identity of the person concerned does not appear from the broadcast; or
>
> (2) [that person]; has not consented to the statement being broadcast; or
>
> (3) [he or she]; has been promised that [he or she]; may take part [in the broadcast]; without [his or her]; identity being disclosed and reasonable precautions have been taken to this effect.

In the situations described in paragraph 1, sub-paragraphs (1) to (3) above, the editor is

> responsible for the contents of the statements even where a violation of the law has occurred without intent or negligence on his part...
>
> Pursuant to section 22:
>
> A person who reads out or in any other manner conveys a text or statement, is not responsible for the contents of that text or statement.

III. Instruments of the United Nations

21. Provisions relating to the prohibition of racial discrimination and the prevention of propaganda of racist views and ideas are to be found in a number of international instruments, for example the 1945 United Nations Charter (paragraph 2 of the Preamble, Articles 1 para. 3, 13 para. 1 (b), 55 (c) and 76 (c)), the 1948 Universal Declaration of Human Rights (Articles 1, 2 and 7) and the 1966 International Covenant on Civil and Political Rights (Articles 2 para. 1, 20 para. 2 and 26). The most directly relevant treaty is the 1965 International Convention on the Elimination of All Forms of Racial Discrimination ("the UN Convention"), which has been ratified by a large majority of the Contracting States to the European Convention, including Denmark (9 December 1971).... [Articles 4 and 5 are then quoted.]

AS TO THE LAW…

27. It is common ground that the measures giving rise to the applicant's case constituted an interference with his right to freedom of expression.

It is moreover undisputed that this interference was "prescribed by law," the applicant's conviction being based on Articles 266 (b) and 23 (1) of the Penal Code. In this context, the Government pointed out that the former provision had been enacted in order to comply with the UN Convention. The Government's argument, as the Court understands it, is that, whilst Article 10 of the Convention is applicable, the Court, in applying paragraph 2, should consider that the relevant provisions of the Penal Code are to be interpreted and applied in an extensive manner, in accordance with the rationale of the UN Convention. In other words, Article 10 should not be interpreted in such a way as to limit, derogate from or destroy the right to protection against racial discrimination under the UN Convention.

Finally it is uncontested that the interference pursued a legitimate aim, namely the "protection of the reputation or rights of others." The only point in dispute is whether the measures were "necessary in a democratic society."

28. The applicant and the Commission were of the view that, notwithstanding Denmark's obligations as a Party to the UN Convention, a fair balance had to be struck between the "protection of the reputation or rights of others" and the applicant's right to impart information. According to the applicant, such a balance was envisaged in a clause contained in Article 4 of the UN Convention to the effect that "due regard" should be had to "the principles in the Universal Declaration of Human Rights and the rights . . . in Article 5 of [the UN] Convention." The clause had been introduced at the drafting stage because of concern among a number of States that the requirement in Article 4 (a) that "[States Parties] shall declare an offence punishable by law all dissemination of ideas based on racial superiority or hatred" was too sweeping and could give rise to difficulties with regard to other human rights, in particular the right to freedom of opinion and expression. In the applicant's further submission, this explained why the Committee of Ministers of the Council of Europe, when urging member States to ratify the UN Convention, had proposed that they add an interpretative statement to their instrument of ratification, which would, inter alia, stress that respect was also due for the rights laid down in the European Convention (Resolution (68) 30 adopted by the Minister's Deputies on 31 October 1968).

The applicant and the Commission emphasised that, taken in the context of the broadcast as a whole, the offending remarks had the effect of ridiculing their authors rather than promoting their racist views. The overall impression of the programme was that it sought to draw public attention to a matter of great public concern, namely racism and xenophobia. The applicant had deliberately included the offensive statements in the programme, not with the intention of disseminating racist opinions, but in order to counter them through exposure. The applicant pointed out that he tried to show, analyse and explain to his viewers a new phenomenon in Denmark at the time, that of violent racism practised by inarticulate and socially disadvantaged youths. Joined by the Commission, he considered that the broadcast could not have had any significant detrimental effects on the "reputation or rights of others." The interests in protecting the latter were therefore outweighed by those of protecting the applicant's freedom of expression. . . .

29. The Government contended that the applicant had edited the Greenjackets item in a sensationalist rather than informative manner and that its news or information value was minimal. Television was a powerful medium and a majority of Danes normally viewed the news programme in which the item was broadcast. Yet the applicant, knowing that they would incur criminal liability, had encouraged the Greenjackets to make racist statements and had failed to counter these statements in the programme. It was too subtle to assume that viewers would not take the remarks at their face value. No weight could be attached to the fact that the programme had given rise to only a few complaints, since, due to lack of information and insufficient knowledge of the Danish language and even fear of reprisals by violent racists, victims of the insulting comments were likely to be dissuaded from complaining. The applicant had thus failed to fulfil the "duties and responsibilities" incumbent on him as a television journalist. The fine imposed upon him was at the lower end of the scale of sanctions applicable to Article 266 (b) offences and was therefore not likely to deter any journalist from contributing to public discussion on racism and xenophobia; it only had the effect of a public reminder that racist expressions are to be taken seriously and cannot be tolerated. . . .

The Government stressed that at all three levels the Danish courts, which were in principle better placed than the European Court to evaluate the effects of the programme, had carried out a careful balancing exercise of all the interests involved. The review effected by those courts had been similar to that carried out under Article 10; their decisions fell within the margin of appreciation to be left to the national authorities and corresponded to a pressing social need.

30. The Court would emphasise at the outset that it is particularly conscious of the vital importance of combating racial discrimination in all its forms and manifestations. It may be true, as has been suggested by the applicant, that as a result of recent events the awareness of the dangers of racial discrimination is sharper today than it was a decade ago, at the material time. Nevertheless, the issue was already then of general importance, as is illustrated for instance by the fact that the UN Convention dates from 1965. Consequently, the object and purpose pursued by the UN Convention are of great weight in determining whether the applicant's conviction, which — as the Government have stressed — was based on a provision enacted in order to ensure Denmark's compliance with the UN Convention, was "necessary" within the meaning of Article 10 para. 2.

In the second place, Denmark's obligations under Article 10 must be interpreted, to the extent possible, so as to be reconcilable with its obligations under the UN Convention. In this respect it is not for the Court to interpret the "due regard" clause in Article 4 of the UN Convention, which is open to various constructions. The Court is however of the opinion that its interpretation of Article 10 of the European Convention in the present case is compatible with Denmark's obligations under the UN Convention.

31. A significant feature of the present case is that the applicant did not make the objectionable statements himself but assisted in their dissemination in his capacity of television journalist responsible for a news programme of Danmarks Radio. In assessing whether his conviction and sentence were "necessary," the

Court will therefore have regard to the principles established in its case-law relating to the role of the press.

The Court reiterates that freedom of expression constitutes one of the essential foundations of a democratic society and that the safeguards to be afforded to the press are of particular importance. Whilst the press must not overstep the bounds set, inter alia, in the interest of "the protection of the reputation or rights of others," it is nevertheless incumbent on it to impart information and ideas of public interest. Not only does the press have the task of imparting such information and ideas: the public also has a right to receive them. Were it otherwise, the press would be unable to play its vital role of "public watchdog." Although formulated primarily with regard to the print media, these principles doubtless apply also to the audiovisual media.

In considering the "duties and responsibilities" of a journalist, the potential impact of the medium concerned is an important factor and it is commonly acknowledged that the audiovisual media have often a much more immediate and powerful effect than the print media. The audiovisual media have means of conveying through images meanings which the print media are not able to impart.

At the same time, the methods of objective and balanced reporting may vary considerably, depending among other things on the media in question. It is not for this Court, nor for the national courts for that matter, to substitute their own views for those of the press as to what technique of reporting should be adopted by journalists. In this context the Court recalls that Article 10 protects not only the substance of the ideas and information expressed, but also the form in which they are conveyed.

The Court will look at the interference complained of in the light of the case as a whole and determine whether the reasons adduced by the national authorities to justify it are relevant and sufficient and whether the means employed were proportionate to the legitimate aim pursued. In doing so the Court has to satisfy itself that the national authorities did apply standards which were in conformity with the principles embodied in Article 10 and, moreover, that they based themselves on an acceptable assessment of the relevant facts.

The Court's assessment will have regard to the manner in which the Greenjackets feature was prepared, its contents, the context in which it was broadcast and the purpose of the programme. Bearing in mind the obligations on States under the UN Convention and other international instruments to take effective measures to eliminate all forms of racial discrimination and to prevent and combat racist doctrines and practices, an important factor in the Court's evaluation will be whether the item in question, when considered as a whole, appeared from an objective point of view to have had as its purpose the propagation of racist views and ideas.

32. The national courts laid considerable emphasis on the fact that the applicant had himself taken the initiative of preparing the Greenjackets feature and that he not only knew in advance that racist statements were likely to be made during the interview but also had encouraged such statements. He had edited the programme in such a way as to include the offensive assertions. Without his involvement, the remarks would not have been disseminated to a wide circle of people and would thus not have been punishable.

The Court is satisfied that these were relevant reasons for the purposes of paragraph 2 of Article 10.

33. On the other hand, as to the contents of the Greenjackets item, it should be noted that the TV presenter's introduction started by a reference to recent public discussion and press comments on racism in Denmark, thus inviting the viewer to see the programme in that context. He went on to announce that the object of the programme was to address aspects of the problem, by identifying certain racist individuals and by portraying their mentality and social background. There is no reason to doubt that the ensuing interviews fulfilled that aim. Taken as a whole, the feature could not objectively have appeared to have as its purpose the propagation of racist views and ideas. On the contrary, it clearly sought — by means of an interview — to expose, analyse and explain this particular group of youths, limited and frustrated by their social situation, with criminal records and violent attitudes, thus dealing with specific aspects of a matter that already then was of great public concern.

The Supreme Court held that the news or information value of the feature was not such as to justify the dissemination of the offensive remarks. However, in view of the principles stated in paragraph 31 above, the Court sees no cause to question the *Sunday News Magazine* staff members' own appreciation of the news or information value of the impugned item, which formed the basis for their decisions to produce and broadcast it.

34. Furthermore, it must be borne in mind that the item was broadcast as part of a serious Danish news programme and was intended for a well-informed audience.

The Court is not convinced by the argument, also stressed by the national courts, that the Greenjackets item was presented without any attempt to counterbalance the extremist views expressed. Both the TV presenter's introduction and the applicant's conduct during the interviews clearly dissociated him from the persons interviewed, for example by describing them as members of "a group of extremist youths" who supported the Ku Klux Klan and by referring to the criminal records of some of them. The applicant also rebutted some of the racist statements for instance by recalling that there were black people who had important jobs. It should finally not be forgotten that, taken as a whole, the filmed portrait surely conveyed the meaning that the racist statements were part of a generally anti-social attitude of the Greenjackets.

Admittedly, the item did not explicitly recall the immorality, dangers and unlawfulness of the promotion of racial hatred and of ideas of superiority of one race. However, in view of the above-mentioned counterbalancing elements and the natural limitations on spelling out such elements in a short item within a longer programme as well as the journalist's discretion as to the form of expression used, the Court does not consider the absence of such precautionary reminders to be relevant.

35. News reporting based on interviews, whether edited or not, constitutes one of the most important means whereby the press is able to play its vital role of "public watchdog." The punishment of a journalist for assisting in the dissemination of statements made by another person in an interview would seriously hamper the contribution of the press to discussion of matters of public interest and should not be envisaged unless there are particularly strong reasons for doing so. In this regard the Court does not accept the Government's argument that the limited nature of the fine is relevant; what matters is that the journalist was convicted.

There can be no doubt that the remarks in respect of which the Greenjackets were convicted were more than insulting to members of the targeted groups and did not enjoy the protection of Article 10. However, even having regard to the manner in which the applicant prepared the Greenjackets item, it has not been shown that, considered as a whole, the feature was such as to justify also his conviction of, and punishment for, a criminal offence under the Penal Code.

36. It is moreover undisputed that the purpose of the applicant in compiling the broadcast in question was not racist. Although he relied on this in the domestic proceedings, it does not appear from the reasoning in the relevant judgments that they took such a factor into account.

37. Having regard to the foregoing, the reasons adduced in support of the applicant's conviction and sentence were not sufficient to establish convincingly that the interference thereby occasioned with the enjoyment of his right to freedom of expression was "necessary in a democratic society"; in particular the means employed were disproportionate to the aim of protecting "the reputation or rights of others." Accordingly the measures gave rise to a breach of Article 10 of the Convention....

FOR THESE REASONS, THE COURT

1. Holds by twelve votes to seven that there has been a violation of Article 10 of the Convention;
2. Holds by seventeen votes to two that Denmark is to pay the applicant, within three months, 1,000 (one thousand) Danish kroner in compensation for pecuniary damage; and, for costs and expenses, the sums resulting from the calculations to be made in accordance with paragraph 45 of the judgment;
3. Dismisses unanimously the remainder of the claim for just satisfaction.

JOINT DISSENTING OPINION OF JUDGES RYSSDAL, BERNHARDT, SPIELMANN AND LOIZOUL

1. This is the first time that the Court has been concerned with a case of dissemination of racist remarks which deny to a large group of persons the quality of "human beings." In earlier decisions the Court has — in our view, rightly — underlined the great importance of the freedom of the press and the media in general for a democratic society, but it has never had to consider a situation in which "the reputation or rights of others" (Article 10 para. 2) were endangered to such an extent as here.

2. We agree with the majority that the Greenjackets themselves "did not enjoy the protection of Article 10." The same must be true of journalists who disseminate such remarks with supporting comments or with their approval. This can clearly not be said of the applicant. Therefore it is admittedly difficult to strike the right balance between the freedom of the press and the protection of others. But the majority attributes much more weight to the freedom of the journalist than to the protection of those who have to suffer from racist hatred.

3. Neither the written text of the interview nor the video film we have seen makes it clear that the remarks of the Greenjackets are intolerable in a society based on respect for human rights. The applicant has cut the entire interview down to a few minutes, probably with the consequence or even the intention of retaining the most crude remarks. That being so, it was absolutely necessary to add

at least a clear statement of disapproval. The majority of the Court sees such disapproval in the context of the interview, but this is an interpretation of cryptic remarks. Nobody can exclude that certain parts of the public found in the television spot support for their racist prejudices.

And what must be the feelings of those whose human dignity has been attacked, or even denied, by the Greenjackets? Can they get the impression that seen in context the television broadcast contributes to their protection? A journalist's good intentions are not enough in such a situation, especially in a case in which he has himself provoked the racist statements.

4. The International Convention on the Elimination of All Forms of Racial Discrimination probably does not require the punishment of journalists responsible for a television spot of this kind. On the other hand, it supports the opinion that the media too can be obliged to take a clear stand in the area of racial discrimination and hatred.

5. The threat of racial discrimination and persecution is certainly serious in our society, and the Court has rightly emphasised the vital importance of combating racial discrimination in all its forms and manifestations. The Danish courts fully recognised that protection of persons whose human dignity is attacked has to be balanced against the right to freedom of expression. They carefully considered the responsibility of the applicant, and the reasons for their conclusions were relevant. The protection of racial minorities cannot have less weight than the right to impart information, and in the concrete circumstances of the present case it is in our opinion not for this Court to substitute its own balancing of the conflicting interests for that of the Danish Supreme Court. We are convinced that the Danish courts acted inside the margin of appreciation which must be left to the Contracting States in this sensitive area. Accordingly, the findings of the Danish courts cannot be considered as giving rise to a violation of Article 10 of the Convention.

Joint Dissenting Opinion of Judges Gölcüklü, Russo and Valticos

We cannot share the opinion of the majority of the Court in the *Jersild* case.

There are indeed two major principles at issue in this case, one being that of freedom of expression, embodied in Article 10 of the Convention, the other the prohibition on defending racial hatred, which is obviously one of the restrictions authorised by paragraph 2 of Article 10 and, moreover, is the subject of basic human rights documents adopted by the General Assembly of the United Nations, in particular the 1965 Convention on the Elimination of All Forms of Racial Discrimination. That Convention manifestly cannot be ignored when the European Convention is being implemented. It is, moreover, binding on Denmark. It must also guide the European Court of Human Rights in its decisions, in particular as regards the scope it confers on the terms of the European Convention and on the exceptions which the Convention lays down in general terms.

In the *Jersild* case the statements made and willingly reproduced in the relevant broadcast on Danish television, without any significant reaction on the part of the commentator, did indeed amount to incitement to contempt not only of foreigners in general but more particularly of black people, described as belonging to an inferior, subhuman race. . . .

While appreciating that some judges attach particular importance to freedom of expression, the more so as their countries have largely been deprived of it in quite recent times, we cannot accept that this freedom should extend to encouraging racial hatred, contempt for races other than the one to which we belong, and defending violence against those who belong to the races in question. It has been sought to defend the broadcast on the ground that it would provoke a healthy reaction of rejection among the viewers. That is to display an optimism, which to say the least, is belied by experience. Large numbers of young people today, and even of the population at large, finding themselves overwhelmed by the difficulties of life, unemployment and poverty, are only too willing to seek scapegoats who are held up to them without any real word of caution; for — and this is an important point — the journalist responsible for the broadcast in question made no real attempt to challenge the points of view he was presenting, which was necessary if their impact was to be counterbalanced, at least for the viewers.

That being so, we consider that by taking criminal measures which were, moreover, moderate ones the Danish judicial institutions in no way infringed Article 10 of the Convention.

Otto-Preminger-Institut v. Austria

Eur. Ct. H.R., ser. A No. 295A, App. No. 13470/87, Sept. 20, 1994

I. The Particular Circumstances Of The Case

9. The applicant, Otto-Preminger-Institut für audiovisuelle Mediengestaltung (OPI), is a private association under Austrian law established in Innsbruck. According to its articles of association, it is a non-profit-making organisation, its general aim being to promote creativity, communication and entertainment through the audiovisual media. Its activities include operating a cinema called "Cinematograph" in Innsbruck.

10. The applicant association announced a series of six showings, which would be accessible to the general public, of the film *Das Liebeskonzil* ("Council in Heaven") by Werner Schroeter (see paragraph 22 below). The first of these showings was scheduled for 13 May 1985. All were to take place at 10.00 p.m. except for one matinée performance on 19 May at 4 p.m.

This announcement was made in an information bulletin distributed by OPI to its 2,700 members and in various display windows in Innsbruck including that of the Cinematograph itself. It was worded as follows:

> Oskar Panizza's satirical tragedy set in Heaven was filmed by Schroeter from a performance by the Teatro Belli in Rome and set in the context of a reconstruction of the writer's trial and conviction in 1895 for blasphemy. Panizza starts from the assumption that syphilis was God's punishment for man's fornication and sinfulness at the time of the Renaissance, especially at the court of the Borgia Pope Alexander VI. In Schroeter's film, God's representatives on Earth carrying the insignia of worldly power closely resemble the heavenly protagonists.
>
> Trivial imagery and absurdities of the Christian creed are targeted in a caricatural mode and the relationship between religious beliefs and worldly mechanisms of oppression is investigated.

In addition, the information bulletin carried a statement to the effect that, in accordance with the Tyrolean Cinemas Act (Tiroler Lichtspielgesetz), persons under seventeen years of age were prohibited from seeing the film.

A regional newspaper also announced the title of the film and the date and place of the showing without giving any particulars as to its contents.

11. At the request of the Innsbruck diocese of the Roman Catholic Church, the public prosecutor instituted criminal proceedings against OPI's manager, Mr Dietmar Zingl, on 10 May 1985. The charge was "disparaging religious doctrines" (Herabwürdigung religiöser Lehren), an act prohibited by section 188 of the Penal Code (Strafgesetzbuch — see paragraph 25 below).

12. On 12 May 1985, after the film had been shown at a private session in the presence of a duty judge (Journalrichter), the public prosecutor made an application for its seizure under section 36 of the Media Act (Mediengesetz — see paragraph 29 below). This application was granted by the Innsbruck Regional Court (Landesgericht) the same day. As a result, the public showings announced by OPI, the first of which had been scheduled for the next day, could not take place.

Those who attended at the time set for the first showing were treated to a reading of the script and a discussion instead.

As Mr Zingl had returned the film to the distributor, the "Czerny" company in Vienna, it was in fact seized at the latter's premises on 11 June 1985.

13. An appeal by Mr Zingl against the seizure order, filed with the Innsbruck Court of Appeal (Oberlandesgericht), was dismissed on 30 July 1985. The Court of Appeal considered that artistic freedom was necessarily limited by the rights of others to freedom of religion and by the duty of the State to safeguard a society based on order and tolerance. It further held that indignation was "justified" for the purposes of section 188 of the Penal Code only if its object was such as to offend the religious feelings of an average person with normal religious sensitivity. That condition was fulfilled in the instant case and forfeiture of the film could be ordered in principle, at least in "objective proceedings" (see paragraph 28 below). The wholesale derision of religious feeling outweighed any interest the general public might have in information or the financial interests of persons wishing to show the film. . . .

16. In its judgment the Regional Court ordered the forfeiture of the film. It held:

> The public projection scheduled for 13 May 1985 of the film *Das Liebeskonzil*, in which God the Father is presented both in image and in text as a senile, impotent idiot, Christ as a cretin and Mary Mother of God as a wanton lady with a corresponding manner of expression and in which the Eucharist is ridiculed, came within the definition of the criminal offence of disparaging religious precepts as laid down in section 188 of the Penal Code.

The court's reasoning included the following:

> The conditions of section 188 of the Penal Code are objectively fulfilled by this portrayal of the divine persons — God the Father, Mary Mother of God and Jesus Christ are the central figures in Roman Catholic religious doctrine and practice, being of the most essential importance, also for the religious understanding of the believers — as well as by the above-mentioned expressions concerning the Eucharist, which is one of the most important mysteries of the Roman Catholic religion, the more so in view of the general character of the film as an attack on Christian religions. . . .
>
> Article 17a of the Basic Law (Staatsgrundgesetz) guarantees the freedom of artistic creation and the publication and teaching of art. The scope of artistic freedom

was broadened (by the introduction of that article) to the extent that every form of artistic expression is protected and limitations of artistic freedom are no longer possible by way of an express legal provision but may only follow from the limitations inherent in this freedom....

Artistic freedom cannot be unlimited. The limitations on artistic freedom are to be found, firstly, in other basic rights and freedoms guaranteed by the Constitution (such as the freedom of religion and conscience), secondly, in the need for an ordered form of human coexistence based on tolerance, and finally in flagrant and extreme violations of other interests protected by law (Verletzung anderer rechtlich geschützter Güter), the specific circumstances having to be weighed up against each other in each case, taking due account of all relevant considerations....

The fact that the conditions of section 188 of the Penal Code are fulfilled does not automatically mean that the limit of the artistic freedom guaranteed by Article 17a of the Basic Law has been reached. However, in view of the above considerations and the particular gravity in the instant case — which concerned a film primarily intended to be provocative and aimed at the Church — of the multiple and sustained violation of legally protected interests, the basic right of artistic freedom will in the instant case have to come second....

19. There have been theatre performances of the original play in Austria since then: in Vienna in November 1991, and in Innsbruck in October 1992. In Vienna the prosecuting authorities took no action. In Innsbruck several criminal complaints (Strafanzeigen) were laid by private persons; preliminary investigations were conducted, following which the prosecuting authorities decided to discontinue the proceedings.

II. The film "Das Liebeskonzil"

20. The play on which the film is based was written by Oskar Panizza and published in 1894. In 1895 Panizza was found guilty by the Munich Assize Court (Schwurgericht) of "crimes against religion" and sentenced to a term of imprisonment. The play was banned in Germany although it continued in print elsewhere.

21. The play portrays God the Father as old, infirm and ineffective, Jesus Christ as a "mummy's boy" of low intelligence and the Virgin Mary, who is obviously in charge, as an unprincipled wanton. Together they decide that mankind must be punished for its immorality. They reject the possibility of outright destruction in favour of a form of punishment which will leave it both "in need of salvation" and "capable of redemption." Being unable to think of such a punishment by themselves, they decide to call on the Devil for help.

The Devil suggests the idea of a sexually transmitted affliction, so that men and women will infect one another without realising it; he procreates with Salome to produce a daughter who will spread it among mankind. The symptoms as described by the Devil are those of syphilis.

As his reward, the Devil claims freedom of thought; Mary says that she will "think about it." The Devil then dispatches his daughter to do her work, first among those who represent worldly power, then to the court of the Pope, to the bishops, to the convents and monasteries and finally to the common people.

22. The film, directed by Werner Schroeter, was released in 1981. It begins and ends with scenes purporting to be taken from the trial of Panizza in 1895. In

between, it shows a performance of the play by the Teatro Belli in Rome. The film portrays the God of the Jewish religion, the Christian religion and the Islamic religion as an apparently senile old man prostrating himself before the Devil with whom he exchanges a deep kiss and calling the Devil his friend. He is also portrayed as swearing by the Devil. Other scenes show the Virgin Mary permitting an obscene story to be read to her and the manifestation of a degree of erotic tension between the Virgin Mary and the Devil. The adult Jesus Christ is portrayed as a low grade mental defective and in one scene is shown lasciviously attempting to fondle and kiss his mother's breasts, which she is shown as permitting. God, the Virgin Mary and Christ are shown in the film applauding the Devil....

As To The Law

I. The Government's Preliminary Objections...

38. The Government's argument is in effect that OPI is not a "victim" of the forfeiture of the film, as opposed to its seizure.

39. A person can properly claim to be a "victim" of an interference with the exercise of his rights under the Convention if he has been directly affected by the matters allegedly constituting the interference.

40. Although the applicant association was not the owner of either the copyright or the forfeited copy of the film, it was directly affected by the decision on forfeiture, which had the effect of making it impossible for it ever to show the film in its cinema in Innsbruck or, indeed, anywhere in Austria. In addition, the seizure was a provisional measure the legality of which was confirmed by the decision on forfeiture; the two cannot be separated. Finally, it is not without significance that the applicant association's manager appears in the Regional Court's judgment of 10 October 1986 in the forfeiture proceedings as a "potentially liable interested party."

The applicant association can therefore validly claim to be a "victim" of the forfeiture of the film as well as its seizure....

Alleged Violation of Article 10....

A. Whether There Have Been "Interferences" With the Applicant Association's Freedom of Expression

43. Although before the Commission the Government had conceded the existence of an interference with the exercise by the applicant association of its right to freedom of expression only with respect to the seizure of the film and although the same point was made in their preliminary objection (see paragraph 35 above), before the Court it was no longer in dispute that if the preliminary objection were rejected both the seizure and the forfeiture constituted such interferences.

Such interferences will entail violation of Article 10 if they do not satisfy the requirements of paragraph 2. The Court must therefore examine in turn whether the interferences were "prescribed by law," whether they pursued an aim that was legitimate under that paragraph (art. 10-2) and whether they were "necessary in a democratic society" for the achievement of that aim.

B. WHETHER THE INTERFERENCES WERE "PRESCRIBED BY LAW"

44. The applicant association denied that the interferences were "prescribed by law," claiming that section 188 of the Austrian Penal Code had been wrongly applied. Firstly, it was in its view doubtful whether a work of art dealing in a satirical way with persons or objects of religious veneration could ever be regarded as "disparaging or insulting." Secondly, indignation could not be "justified" in persons who consented of their own free will to see the film or decided not to. Thirdly, the right to artistic freedom, as guaranteed by Article 17a of the Basic Law, had been given insufficient weight.

45. The Court reiterates that it is primarily for the national authorities, notably the courts, to interpret and apply national law.

The Innsbruck courts had to strike a balance between the right to artistic freedom and the right to respect for religious beliefs as guaranteed by Article 14 of the Basic Law. The Court, like the Commission, finds that no grounds have been adduced before it for holding that Austrian law was wrongly applied.

C. WHETHER THE INTERFERENCES HAD A "LEGITIMATE AIM"

46. The Government maintained that the seizure and forfeiture of the film were aimed at "the protection of the rights of others," particularly the right to respect for one's religious feelings, and at "the prevention of disorder."

47. As the Court pointed out in its judgment in the case of *Kokkinakis v. Greece* of 25 May 1993 (Series A no. 260-A, p. 17, para. 31), freedom of thought, conscience and religion, which is safeguarded under Article 9 of the Convention, is one of the foundations of a "democratic society" within the meaning of the Convention. It is, in its religious dimension, one of the most vital elements that go to make up the identity of believers and their conception of life.

Those who choose to exercise the freedom to manifest their religion, irrespective of whether they do so as members of a religious majority or a minority, cannot reasonably expect to be exempt from all criticism. They must tolerate and accept the denial by others of their religious beliefs and even the propagation by others of doctrines hostile to their faith. However, the manner in which religious beliefs and doctrines are opposed or denied is a matter which may engage the responsibility of the State, notably its responsibility to ensure the peaceful enjoyment of the right guaranteed under Article 9 to the holders of those beliefs and doctrines. Indeed, in extreme cases the effect of particular methods of opposing or denying religious beliefs can be such as to inhibit those who hold such beliefs from exercising their freedom to hold and express them.

In the *Kokkinakis* judgment the Court held, in the context of Article 9, that a State may legitimately consider it necessary to take measures aimed at repressing certain forms of conduct, including the imparting of information and ideas, judged incompatible with the respect for the freedom of thought, conscience and religion of others. The respect for the religious feelings of believers as guaranteed in Article 9 can legitimately be thought to have been violated by provocative portrayals of objects of religious veneration; and such portrayals can be regarded as malicious violation of the spirit of tolerance, which must also be a feature of democratic society. The Convention is to be read as a whole and therefore the interpretation and application of Article 10 in the present case must be in harmony with the logic of the Convention.

48. The measures complained of were based on section 188 of the Austrian Penal Code, which is intended to suppress behaviour directed against objects of religious veneration that is likely to cause "justified indignation." It follows that their purpose was to protect the right of citizens not to be insulted in their religious feelings by the public expression of views of other persons. Considering also the terms in which the decisions of the Austrian courts were phrased, the Court accepts that the impugned measures pursued a legitimate aim under Article 10 para. 2, namely "the protection of the rights of others."

D. WHETHER THE SEIZURE AND THE FORFEITURE WERE "NECESSARY IN A DEMOCRATIC SOCIETY"

1. General Principles

49. As the Court has consistently held, freedom of expression constitutes one of the essential foundations of a democratic society, one of the basic conditions for its progress and for the development of everyone. Subject to paragraph 2 of Article 10, it is applicable not only to "information" or "ideas" that are favourably received or regarded as inoffensive or as a matter of indifference, but also to those that shock, offend or disturb the State or any sector of the population. Such are the demands of that pluralism, tolerance and broadmindedness without which there is no "democratic society" (see, particularly, the *Handyside v. the United Kingdom* judgment of 7 December 1976, Series A no. 24, p. 23, para. 49).

However, as is borne out by the wording itself of Article 10 para. 2, whoever exercises the rights and freedoms enshrined in the first paragraph of that Article undertakes "duties and responsibilities." Amongst them — in the context of religious opinions and beliefs — may legitimately be included an obligation to avoid as far as possible expressions that are gratuitously offensive to others and thus an infringement of their rights, and which therefore do not contribute to any form of public debate capable of furthering progress in human affairs.

This being so, as a matter of principle it may be considered necessary in certain democratic societies to sanction or even prevent improper attacks on objects of religious veneration, provided always that any "formality," "condition," "restriction" or "penalty" imposed be proportionate to the legitimate aim pursued.

50. As in the case of "morals" it is not possible to discern throughout Europe a uniform conception of the significance of religion in society; even within a single country such conceptions may vary. For that reason it is not possible to arrive at a comprehensive definition of what constitutes a permissible interference with the exercise of the right to freedom of expression where such expression is directed against the religious feelings of others. A certain margin of appreciation is therefore to be left to the national authorities in assessing the existence and extent of the necessity of such interference. . . .

2. Application of the Above Principles. . . .

52. The Government defended the seizure of the film in view of its character as an attack on the Christian religion, especially Roman Catholicism. They maintained that the placing of the original play in the setting of its author's trial in 1895 actually served to reinforce the anti-religious nature of the film, which ended with a violent and abusive denunciation of what was presented as Catholic morality.

Furthermore, they stressed the role of religion in the everyday life of the people of Tyrol. The proportion of Roman Catholic believers among the Austrian population as a whole was already considerable — 78% — but among Tyroleans it was as high as 87%.

Consequently, at the material time at least, there was a pressing social need for the preservation of religious peace; it had been necessary to protect public order against the film and the Innsbruck courts had not overstepped their margin of appreciation in this regard.

53. The applicant association claimed to have acted in a responsible way aimed at preventing unwarranted offence. It noted that it had planned to show the film in its cinema, which was accessible to members of the public only after a fee had been paid; furthermore, its public consisted on the whole of persons with an interest in progressive culture. Finally, pursuant to the relevant Tyrolean legislation in force, persons under seventeen years of age were not to be admitted to the film. There was therefore no real danger of anyone being exposed to objectionable material against their wishes.

The Commission agreed with this position in substance.

54. The Court notes first of all that although access to the cinema to see the film itself was subject to payment of an admission fee and an age-limit, the film was widely advertised. There was sufficient public knowledge of the subject-matter and basic contents of the film to give a clear indication of its nature; for these reasons, the proposed screening of the film must be considered to have been an expression sufficiently "public" to cause offence.

55. The issue before the Court involves weighing up the conflicting interests of the exercise of two fundamental freedoms guaranteed under the Convention, namely the right of the applicant association to impart to the public controversial views and, by implication, the right of interested persons to take cognisance of such views, on the one hand, and the right of other persons to proper respect for their freedom of thought, conscience and religion, on the other hand. In so doing, regard must be had to the margin of appreciation left to the national authorities, whose duty it is in a democratic society also to consider, within the limits of their jurisdiction, the interests of society as a whole.

56. The Austrian courts, ordering the seizure and subsequently the forfeiture of the film, held it to be an abusive attack on the Roman Catholic religion according to the conception of the Tyrolean public. Their judgments show that they had due regard to the freedom of artistic expression, which is guaranteed under Article 10 of the Convention and for which Article 17a of the Austrian Basic Law provides specific protection. They did not consider that its merit as a work of art or as a contribution to public debate in Austrian society outweighed those features which made it essentially offensive to the general public within their jurisdiction. The trial courts, after viewing the film, noted the provocative

portrayal of God the Father, the Virgin Mary and Jesus Christ. The content of the film (see paragraph 22 above) cannot be said to be incapable of grounding the conclusions arrived at by the Austrian courts.

The Court cannot disregard the fact that the Roman Catholic religion is the religion of the overwhelming majority of Tyroleans. In seizing the film, the Austrian authorities acted to ensure religious peace in that region and to prevent that some people should feel the object of attacks on their religious beliefs in an unwarranted and offensive manner. It is in the first place for the national authorities, who are better placed than the international judge, to assess the need for such a measure in the light of the situation obtaining locally at a given time. In all the circumstances of the present case, the Court does not consider that the Austrian authorities can be regarded as having overstepped their margin of appreciation in this respect.

No violation of Article 10 can therefore be found as far as the seizure is concerned. . . .

57. The foregoing reasoning also applies to the forfeiture, which determined the ultimate legality of the seizure and under Austrian law was the normal sequel thereto.

Article 10 cannot be interpreted as prohibiting the forfeiture in the public interest of items whose use has lawfully been adjudged illicit. Although the forfeiture made it permanently impossible to show the film anywhere in Austria, the Court considers that the means employed were not disproportionate to the legitimate aim pursued and that therefore the national authorities did not exceed their margin of appreciation in this respect.

There has accordingly been no violation of Article 10 as regards the forfeiture either. . . .

Note: Other Substantive Rights

The European system has developed a rich jurisprudence during its more than 50 years of existence, and the above cases merely give the reader a flavor of the European Court's approach to one set of issues in which individual rights must be balanced against the legitimate interests of the larger community. The following extract offers a very brief summary of some of the other issues with which the system has dealt over the years.

> . . . Most violations have concerned the right to a fair trial. Cases under Article 6 have brought to light many delays in the hearing of cases in breach of the right to "trial within a reasonable time." Other common infringements have concerned the rights to an independent and impartial tribunal, to judicial review of executive action, to due process in disciplinary proceedings and to legal aid. The next most problematic guarantee for states has been that of freedom of the person. Many breaches of Article 5 have concerned various aspects of defendants' rights, such as the information required upon arrest, the right to bail, the length of detention on remand and the practice concerning discretionary life sentences. Other cases have involved the preventive detention of terrorists and the detention of the mentally disordered, vagrants, children and deportees. Claims relying upon the right to respect for family life, privacy, etc. in Article 8 have been almost equally successful. It is in this context that the Court has made most use of its "dynamic" approach to the interpretation of

the Convention and the idea that there may be positive obligations upon states, requiring them, for example, to legislate so as to respect the rights of homosexuals and children born out of wedlock in accordance with current social values. Cases under Article 10 have confirmed the fundamental importance attached to freedom of expression, particularly freedom of the press. Several violations of Article 3 have been found, in such diverse areas as the ill-treatment of persons in detention, judicial corporal punishment and extradition to face the death row phenomenon. At the other extreme, the guarantees of freedom from slavery and forced labour (Article 4), the right to free elections (Article 3, First Protocol) and all of the rights in the Fourth and Seventh Protocols have yet to lead to an adverse ruling. D.J. Harris, M. O'Boyle, and C. Warbrick, *Law of the European Convention on Human Rights* 32 (1995).

Comments and Questions

1. The three cases above concern, respectively, commercial speech, journalism, and artistic expression. Do the Court's judgments distinguish among kinds of speech in deciding on the permissibility of limitations under Article 10(2)? For another judgment upholding the government's discretion to censor artistic expression, see *Muller and Others v. Switzerland*, Eur. Ct. H.R., ser. A No. 133, App. No. 10737/84, May 24, 1988 (paintings seized from an exhibition and held as obscene). Is the apparently high degree of deference to domestic decisions in these cases due to the fact that "it is not possible to find in the domestic law of the various Contracting States a uniform European conception of morals"? *Handyside v. U.K.*, supra page 649, para. 48.

Other judgments of the Court have concerned challenges to convictions for defamation because of political commentary. See e.g., *Lingens v. Austria*, Eur. Ct. H.R., ser. A No. 103, App. No. 9815/82, July 8, 1986; *Oberschlik v. Austria*, Eur. Ct. H.R., ser. A No. 204, App. No. 11662/85, May 23, 1991. How much "margin of appreciation" should be afforded governments in these types of cases? Censorship of journalistic reporting on public affairs resulted in findings of violations in *The Observer and Guardian Newspapers Ltd. v. United Kingdom*, Eur. Ct. H.R., ser. A No. 216, App. No. 13585/88, Nov. 26, 1991; *The Sunday Times v. United Kingdom*, Eur. Ct. H.R., ser. A No. 217, App. No. 13166/87, Nov. 26, 1991; *Thorgeir Thorgeirson v. Iceland*, Eur. Ct. H.R., ser. A No. 239, App. No. 12778/88, June 25, 1992. The Court has also protected "alternative science," finding a violation of Article 10 when the Swiss government prohibited an individual from claiming that consumption of food prepared in a microwave oven is a danger to human health. See *Hertel v. Switzerland*, Eur. Ct. H.R. 1998-VI, App. No. 25181/94, Aug. 25, 1998.

For a comprehensive summary of the case law on Article 10 up to 1999, see Council of Europe, *Case-Law Concerning Article 10 of the European Convention on Human Rights: Forty Years of Case Law 1959-1999* (1999).

2. The Court upheld the application of blasphemy statutes in *Wingrove v. United Kingdom*, Eur. Ct. H.R., Rep. 1996-V, App. No. 17419/90, Nov. 25, 1996. Following this case, Muslims in England sought to have Salman Rushdie's book, *The Satanic Verses* (1989), banned as blasphemous. British authorities reportedly declined, on the basis that the blasphemy law only applies to Christianity. If true, does this violate any of the rights in the European Convention?

3. Does some speech fall outside the protections of Article 10? Does the Court address this issue in the *Jersild* case? The judgment is one of the few in which the European Court considers the Convention in the light of other human rights instruments to which the relevant state is party. The European Convention itself has no hate speech provision, but the Court upheld the conviction of a neo-Nazi for displaying hostility toward a racial or religious group (he had displayed a photograph of the burning World Trade Center with the words "Islam out of Britain — Protect the British People"), *Norwood v. U.K.* (admissibility), App. No. 23131/03, Nov. 16, 2004. If another treaty contains more specific language or affords greater protection to an applicant, should the European Court always interpret the Convention in the light of the other instrument?

4. Are there limits on the right of expression enjoyed by political parties? The following decisions uphold bans on communist, Nazi, and Islamic parties, respectively: *KPD v. Fed. Rep. Germany*, App. No. 250/57, 1 Y.B. 222 (1957); *Kuhnen v. Fed. Rep. Germany*, App. No. 12194/86, 56 DR 205, May 12, 1988; *The Welfare Party and Others v. Turkey*, Eur. Ct. H.R. 2003-II, App. No. 41340/98, Feb. 13, 2003 (Grand Chamber). On the other hand, bans on political parties or dissolutions of parties were found to violate the convention in these cases: *United Communist Party v. Turkey*, Eur. Ct. H.R. 1998-I, App. No. 19392/92, Jan. 30, 1998; *Socialist Party v. Turkey*, Eur. Ct. H.R. 1998-III, App. No. 21237/93, May 25, 1998; *Freedom and Democracy Party v. Turkey*, Eur. Ct. H.R. 1999-VIII, App. No. 23885/94. Dec. 8, 1999; *Yazar and Others v. Turkey*, Eur. Ct. H.R. 2002-II, App. Nos. 22723-25/93, Apr. 4, 2002; *Presidential Party of Mordovia v. Russia*, Eur. Ct. H.R., App. No. 65659/01, Oct. 5, 2004); *Partidul Communistilor* [Nepeceristi] *et Ungureanu v. Romania*, Eur. Ct. H.R., App. No. 46626/99, Feb. 3, 2005. Is Article 17 of the European Convention relevant to these cases? See generally Thomas Ayres, Batasuna Banned: The Dissolution of Political Parties under the European Convention of Human Rights, 27 *B.C. Int'l & Comp. L. Rev.* 99 (2004).

5. In contrast to the European Convention, the American Convention, discussed in the next chapter, explicitly bans prior censorship. How much of a role do the different history and culture of the two continents play in their divergent approaches to free speech?

C. *Seeking Compliance with European Human Rights Norms*

1. Monitoring Judgments of the European Court of Human Rights

Article 46(2) places responsibility for the execution of judgments of the European Court of Human Rights under the responsibility of the Council of Europe's Committee of Ministers. In its judgment in the *Scozzari and Giunta* case, Eur. Ct. H.R. 2000-VIII, App. No. 39221/98, July 13, 2000 (Grand Chamber), a Grand Chamber of the Court summarized states' obligations to take general measures to prevent further violations and individual measures to remedy the effects of the violation on the applicant as follows:

> By Article 46 of the Convention the High Contracting Parties undertook to abide by the final judgments of the Court in any case to which they were parties, execution being supervised by the Committee of Ministers. It follows, *inter alia*, that a judgment in which the Court finds a breach imposes on the respondent state a legal

> obligation not just to pay those concerned the sums awarded by way of just satisfaction, but also to choose, subject to supervision by the Committee of Ministers, the general and/or, if appropriate, individual measures to be adopted in their domestic legal order to put an end to the violation found by the Court and to redress so far as possible the effects. Furthermore, subject to monitoring by the Committee of Ministers, the respondent state remains free to choose the means by which it will discharge its legal obligation under Article 46 of the Convention, provided that such means are compatible with the conclusions set out in the Court's judgment.

Id. para. 249 (reference omitted).

After the Court transmits its final judgment to the Committee of Ministers, the latter invites the respondent state to inform it of the steps taken to pay the amounts awarded by the Court in respect of just satisfaction and, where appropriate, of the individual and general measures it has taken to comply with the judgment. The Committee examines this information and, if it determines that the state has complied in full, the Committee adopts a resolution concluding that its functions under Article 46(2) of the Convention have been exercised. The Committee of Ministers does not adopt a final resolution striking the judgment off its list of cases until the state in question has adopted satisfactory measures.

During its examination of the case, the Committee may adopt various measures to facilitate execution of the judgment. It may adopt interim resolutions, which usually include information on the interim measures already taken and set a provisional calendar for reforms, encourage the respondent state to pursue certain reforms, or insist that it take the measures needed to comply with the judgment.

In certain cases, national legal systems may lack the appropriate legislation to reopen proceedings, which is often necessary where domestic proceedings have been completed or where the violations are in the context of criminal prosecutions. In 2000, the Committee of Ministers adopted a recommendation to member states on the re-examination or reopening of certain cases at domestic level following judgments of the European Court of Human Rights (Recommendation No. R (2000) 2), inviting them to ensure that their legal systems had adequate possibilities for achieving, as far as possible, *restitutio in integrum,* including the reopening of proceedings.

If difficulties are encountered in executing the judgment, the Directorate General of Human Rights often examines possible solutions in greater detail with the authorities concerned.The Committee of Ministers uses diplomatic and other means to persuade states to comply with the Court's judgments, not least by noting any failure to comply and taking appropriate action. In practice, the Committee of Ministers has seldom needed to exert strong pressure on states, but it has happened on occasion. The types of cases and measures taken by the Committee are indicated in the following press release.

Council of Europe Committee of Ministers to supervise the execution of the Human Rights Court's judgments

Press Release 303a (June 6, 2005)

The Council of Europe Committee of Ministers will hold its third human rights meeting of 2005 on 6 and 7 June to supervise the execution of judgments by the European Court of Human Rights (Article 46 of the ECHR).

The Committee will supervise payment of just satisfaction in some 495 cases. It will also look at around 54 cases of individual measures (including grouped cases) to erase the consequences of violations (such as striking out convictions from criminal records, re-opening domestic judicial proceedings, etc.) and at 89 cases involving general measures (including grouped cases) to prevent similar violations (e.g. constitutional and legislative reforms, changes of domestic case-law and administrative practice). The Committee will also start examining 105 new Court judgments and will consider 41 draft final resolutions concluding that States have complied with the Court's judgments. The agenda includes:

— Remedial measures to be taken by Italy and Turkey to grant the applicants rapid and adequate redress for their conviction and imprisonment on the basis of unfair trials (*Dorigo v. Italy and Hulki Güneş v. Turkey* cases);

— Measures to be taken by Moldova and Russia following the *Ilaşcu and Others* judgment (08/07/2004), which considered the applicants' detention in the "Moldavian Republic of Transdniestria" to be arbitrary and unlawful and ordered the immediate release of the applicants still in detention;

— General and/or individual measures to comply with a number of judgments concerning actions of security forces in Turkey and Northern Ireland, including issues relating to the absence of effective investigations into alleged abuses;

— Individual measures to be taken by Latvia to comply with the *Slivenko* judgment (09/10/2003) finding a violation of the right to private life because of the deportation of the applicants, a mother and a daughter, former Latvian permanent residents of Russian origin, to Russia in connection with the withdrawal of Russian military personnel from Latvia;

— General measures to be taken by Turkey to comply with the *Cyprus v. Turkey* judgment (10/05/2001), with a primary focus at this meeting on the issues of missing persons, on some specific questions concerning the living conditions of the Greek Cypriots in the northern part of Cyprus, in particular those related to education and freedom of religion, as well as on the question of the powers of military courts regarding civilians;

— Legislative reform in the United Kingdom to remedy the unpredictable effects of 'binding over' orders arising from the vague notion of "behaviour *contra bonos mores*," at the basis of the violation of the right to freedom of expression found in the *Hashman and Harrup* judgment (25/11/99);

— Progress achieved and further measures envisaged by Italy in the reform of their judicial systems to prevent new violations as regards the excessive length of judicial proceedings;

— Measures to be adopted by Ukraine to erase the consequences of interferences by the Executive in the independence of the judiciary, as required by the *Sovtransavto v. Ukraine* judgment (06/11/2002 (see Interim Resolution DH (2004)14)). . . .

The general record of compliance with Court judgments is excellent, and non-compliance has been exceptional. In recent years, however, there seems to be greater concern with states that either do not comply with judgments or whose compliance is unreasonably delayed. The following resolutions and recommendations of the Council of Europe's Parliamentary Assembly address these concerns, to which we return in section D, infra page 701.

Council of Europe Parliamentary Assembly Resolution 1226 (2000), Execution of judgments of the European Court of Human Rights

Sept. 28, 2000

1. The Assembly considers that the European Convention on Human Rights (hereafter referred to as "the Convention") offers a unique mechanism for the protection of human rights and contributes substantially to maintaining democratic security and to the principle of the rule of law throughout the European continent. In order to maintain this standard of protection, it is essential that states fully comply with their formal undertaking to abide by the final judgments of the European Court of Human Rights (hereafter referred to as "the Court") in cases to which they are parties.

2. The system of the Convention is based in particular on two principles: subsidiarity and solidarity. The principle of subsidiarity implies that the primary responsibility for ensuring the rights and freedoms laid down in the Convention rests with the national authorities. Only if they fail to fulfil their responsibility is the Court called upon to take a decision.

3. The principle of solidarity implies that the case-law of the Court forms part of the Convention, thus extending the legally binding force of the Convention erga omnes (to all the other parties). This means that the states parties not only have to execute the judgments of the Court pronounced in cases to which they are party, but also have to take into consideration the possible implications which judgments pronounced in other cases may have for their own legal system and legal practice.

4. The Committee of Ministers, according to Article 46.2 of the Convention, supervises the execution of the Court's judgments. Furthermore, Article 52 of the Convention provides that "On receipt of a request from the Secretary General of the Council of Europe any High Contracting Party shall furnish an explanation of the manner in which its internal law ensures the effective implementation of any of the provisions of the Convention." However, the Convention does not provide for a sanction in a case where a state does not execute a judgment of the Court. The measures to be taken in such cases are those foreseen in the Statute of the Council of Europe, in particular in its Article 8.

5. The Assembly is concerned that the execution of some judgments is causing considerable problems that threaten to undermine what has been achieved over the fifty years during which the Convention has operated. Some judgments of the Court have still not been executed several years later.

6. The Assembly is of the view that the responsibility for this situation rests mainly with the states parties which must execute the Court's judgments. In that regard, members of national delegations to the Assembly have a role to play. However, the Court, whose judgments are sometimes not sufficiently clear, and the Committee of Ministers, which does not exert enough pressure when supervising the execution of judgments, share part of the responsibility.

7. In spite of some progress made in giving direct effect to the Court's judgments, the present situation gives cause for serious concern. On the one hand, the Court faces an increase in the number of cases due to the accession of a number of new member states; on the other, the situation is aggravated by the numerous

cases which relate to violations of human rights which have already been judged, but the judgments of which have not been followed by the necessary reforms which would avoid further violations.

8. The problems of implementation are at least seven-fold: political reasons; reasons to do with the reforms required; practical reasons relating to national legislative procedures; budgetary reasons; reasons to do with public opinion; judgments which are casuistical or unclear; reasons relating to interference with obligations deriving from other institutions. . . .

11. At Council of Europe level:

1. the Committee of Ministers should:

1. amend the Convention so as to have the power exceptionally to ask the Court for a clarifying interpretation of its judgments in cases where the execution gives rise to reasonable doubts and serious problems regarding the correct mode of implementation;

2. amend the Convention to introduce a system of "astreintes" (daily fines for a delay in performance of a legal obligation) to be imposed on states that persistently fail to execute a Court judgment;

3. ask the governments of High Contracting Parties to make more use of their right to intervene in cases before the Court, so as to promote the clarity of the decisions of the Court;

4. be more strict towards member states which fail in their obligation to execute decisions and take the measures provided for in Article 8 of the Statute in case of continued refusal;

5. ensure that measures taken are effective means of preventing further violations;

6. keep the Assembly informed of progress in the execution of judgments, in particular by more systematic use of interim resolutions setting a timetable for carrying out the reforms necessary within signatory states in view of their execution;

7. instruct the Secretary General to reinforce assistance programmes for the training of judges and lawyers in member states; . . .

2. the Court should:

1. ensure that its judgments are clear and its case-law coherent;

2. oblige itself to indicate in its judgments to the national authorities concerned how they should execute the judgment so that they can comply with the decisions and take the individual and general measures required;

3. more frequently indicate in a judgment whether a previous judgment has not been executed at all, not been completely executed, or not been executed in time by the state concerned.

3. the Assembly decides to: . . .

3. hold regular debates about the execution of judgments, on the basis of the aforementioned permanent record, and in the case of the non-executed judgments referred to in this report, organise a debate within one year of the date of this resolution;

4. adopt recommendations to the Committee of Ministers, and through it to the relevant states, concerning the execution of certain judgments, if it notices abnormal delays, or if the state in question has neglected to execute or deliberately refrained from executing the judgment — if necessary holding an urgent debate to this end;

5. invite the parliamentary delegations of the states concerned to do their utmost to bring about the quick and efficient execution of judgments;

6. invite the minister for justice, or another relevant minister of the responding state to give the Assembly an explanation in person, in case of refusal to execute a judgment or in case of excessive delays;

7. consider as a reason to open a monitoring procedure the case of a member state refusing to implement a decision of the Court;

8. envisage, if these measures fail, making use of other possibilities, in particular those provided for in its own Rules of Procedure and/or of a recommendation to the Committee of Ministers to make use of Article 8 of the Statute. . . .

12. Accordingly the Assembly:

1. invites the High Contracting Parties:

1. to take the necessary action to execute the Court's judgments in order to avoid any recurrence of violations;

2. in the case of a reasonable doubt as to the correct way a judgment should be executed, to make use of their right, in accordance with Article 79, paragraph 1, of the Rules of the Court, to request from the Court an interpretation of its judgment within a year of its delivery;

3. to ensure that new legislation fully complies with the Convention;

4. to take the necessary steps to give direct effect to the Court's judgments so that national courts can apply them;

5. to remedy the applicant's individual situation and to ensure that their legislation provides for the revision of a trial following a judgment of the Court;

6. to adopt interim measures until definitive reforms come into effect;

7. to proceed with the legislative, and if necessary constitutional, reforms required to bring their national legislation fully into conformity with the European Convention on Human Rights and the case-law of the Court. . . .

Council of European Parliamentary Assembly, Resolution 1411 (2004), Implementation of decisions of the European Court of Human Rights

Nov. 23, 2004

1. The Parliamentary Assembly recalls that, since the adoption of its Resolution 1226 (2000) on the execution of judgments of the European Court of Human Rights — in which it examined the reasons why certain decisions of the Court had not been executed and called for a number of measures to be taken to remedy the situation — it has involved itself with the implementation of judgments of the Court. . . .

4. It has devoted two reports to Turkey owing to the large number of cases involved: one report in 2002 and another in 2004.

5. Its Committee on Legal Affairs and Human Rights has compiled a new record of Court judgments which have not been implemented, using the following three criteria: the time elapsed since the Court's decision, the existence of an interim resolution of the Committee of Ministers and the importance of the issues raised.

6. Against this background, it wrote to eight national delegations on 17 February 2003, concerning twenty-one Court decisions in all, asking them to prevail upon their respective governments to implement the unexecuted decisions, setting a two-month deadline for replies. The delegations concerned were Austria, Belgium, France, Italy, Poland, Romania, Switzerland and the United Kingdom. A reminder was sent to three delegations on 30 May 2003 (France, Italy, Romania). Seven delegations replied (Austria, Belgium, Italy, Poland, Romania, Switzerland and the United Kingdom).

7. The Assembly notes that of the twenty-one decisions in question five date from 1996, seven from 1997 and eight from 1998.

8. In six cases, the individual or general measures requested by the Committee of Ministers have been taken (two decisions against Romania, one decision against Switzerland and three decisions against the United Kingdom).

9. In one case, the individual measures have been taken but general measures are still required (Poland).

10. In four cases, the draft legislation required to facilitate implementation of the judgments still has to be enacted by parliament (Austria, Belgium and Italy — the cases of *F.C.B.*, *Dorigo*, *Calogero Diana*, and *Domenichini*).

11. In seven other cases involving Italy, the Italian authorities are contesting the measures they are required to take.

12. In one case against the United Kingdom, negotiations are under way between the authorities and the Council of Europe Secretariat.

13. No reply has been received concerning the two cases against France.

14. The overall assessment of this new exercise once again illustrates the excessive length of time taken to implement the Court's decisions. It also illustrates the difficulty of interpreting the Court's decisions in a number of cases. Lastly, in some cases the authorities in question have shown unwillingness to take action.

15. We might infer from the replies received that the aim pursued, namely to ensure that parliamentary delegations should approach their government with a view to implementation of Court decisions, has not been attained. Delegations would appear merely to take note of their government's explanations and pass them on, without sufficiently trying to induce the authorities to act by way of making use of their parliamentary prerogatives and privileges to hold the government to account and to put pressure on it.

16. The Assembly welcomed the possibility of the Committee of Ministers asking the Court to clarify its decisions in cases of disputes concerning the requested measures, as established by Protocol No. 14, but regrets that its proposal to establish a system of astreintes (daily fines for a delay in the performance of a legal obligation) has been rejected.

17. The Assembly is, however, still convinced that pressure could usefully be put on governments and a debate organised to discuss this matter, if only to ensure that such cases are brought to public attention and enable other governments to benefit from the experience thus acquired. . . .

Particularly problematic have been Italy and Turkey. Italy has been found in violation of the Convention for failure to ensure trials within a reasonable time in over 2,000 cases, and the necessary changes to the Italian judicial system to redress the situation apparently have not been forthcoming. See, e.g., Parliamentary Assembly Recommendation 1684, Implementation of decisions of the European Court of Human Rights (Nov. 23, 2004); Committee of Ministers, Committee on Legal Affairs and Human Rights Working Paper, Court judgments pending before the Committee of Ministers for control of execution for more than five years or otherwise raising important issues, CoE Doc. AS/Jur (2005) 32 (June 9, 2005). The last-mentioned Working Paper also addresses cases against Bulgaria, France, Germany, Greece, Latvia, Moldova, Poland, Russia, Romania, Turkey, United Kingdom, and Ukraine.

Turkey faces institutional problems similar to those of Italy with respect to some judgments, and it has also been very slow in paying just satisfaction awarded by the Court in some cases. The *Loizidou* case (discussed in the *Banković* judgment, supra page 626) was particularly problematic, because it held Turkey responsible for violations of human rights in the Turkish occupied part of Cyprus. The Turkish government insisted long after the judgment that it was not legally responsible for events in the "Turkish Republic of Northern Cyprus" and refused to honor the judgment. Turkey finally paid the 1998 judgment in December 2003.

2. Monitoring Other Human Rights Obligations of Members of the Council of Europe

The end of the Cold War in the late 1980s and the desire of central and eastern European countries to rejoin "Europe" created new opportunities for encouraging states to conform to human rights norms. The political bodies of the Council of Europe attempted to use those opportunities to the maximum, although the following materials demonstrate that the reality of compliance may still lag well beyond the formal commitments that states make.

Other institutions of the Council of Europe participate in efforts to secure human rights in the region. The Parliamentary Assembly has key functions in reviewing nominations to the European Court of Human Rights and in vetting applicant states seeking to join the Council of Europe. The latter process involves an on-site visit and report on the state, leading to a set of commitments by the government of the applicant state. Compliance with these commitments is overseen by the Committee of Ministers, the Parliamentary Assembly, and the Secretariat. In addition, the Parliamentary Assembly's Committee on Human Rights adopts resolutions and declarations on key human rights issues, often leading to the conclusion of new treaties.

The role of the Committee of Ministers, the highest political body of the Council of Europe, is essential. It approves protocols to the Convention and other human rights treaties to be submitted to states for ratification. As noted in the previous section, it is responsible for ensuring compliance with judgments of the European Court of Human Rights. Pursuant to a 1994 declaration on compliance with commitments, set out immediately below, the Committee also has expanded its thematic monitoring. The first theme it adopted for monitoring was freedom of expression and information; other themes include the functioning of democratic institutions, including political parties and free elections; the functioning of judicial systems; local democracy; capital punishment; police and security forces; the effectiveness of judicial remedies; non-discrimination; freedom of conscience and religion; and equality between women and women. The following readings describe some of these compliance mechanisms.

Committee of Ministers, Declaration on Compliance with Commitments Accepted by Member States of the Council of Europe

Adopted on Nov. 10, 1994, Monitor/Inf (2003) 1 Addendum, p. 4

The Committee of Ministers,

Bearing in mind:

— the vocation of the Council of Europe to promote the reinforcement of democratic security in Europe, as stressed by the Vienna Summit (October 1993), where Heads of State and Government also resolved to ensure full compliance with the commitments accepted by all member States within the Council of Europe;

— the commitments to Democracy, Human Rights and the Rule of Law accepted by the member States under the Council's Statute, the European Convention on Human Rights and other legal instruments;

— the importance of the strict compliance with these commitments by every member State;

— the statutory responsibility incumbent upon itself for ensuring full respect of these commitments in all member States, without prejudice to other existing procedures, including the activities of the Parliamentary Assembly and conventional control bodies;

— the need to facilitate the fulfilment of these commitments, through political follow-up, carried out constructively, on the basis of dialogue, co-operation and mutual assistance,

Decides as follows :

1. The Committee of Ministers will consider the questions of implementation of commitments concerning the situation of Democracy, Human Rights and the Rule of Law in any member State which will be referred to it either:

— by member States,

— by the Secretary General, or

— on the basis of a recommendation from the Parliamentary Assembly.

When considering such issues the Committee of Ministers will take account of all relevant information available from different sources such as the Parliamentary Assembly and the CSCE.

2. The Secretary General will forward to the Committee of Ministers to this end information deriving from contacts and co-operation with member States that are liable to call for the attention of the Committee of Ministers.

3. The Committee of Ministers will consider in a constructive manner matters brought to its attention, encouraging Member States, through dialogue and co-operation, to take all appropriate steps to conform with the principles of the Statute in the cases under discussion.

4. The Committee of Ministers, in cases requiring specific action, may decide to:

— request the Secretary General to make contacts, collect information or furnish advice;
— issue an opinion or recommendation;
— forward a communication to the Parliamentary Assembly;
— take any other decision within its statutory powers.

5. The Committee of Ministers will continue to seek greater efficacity in its procedures with a view to ensuring compliance with commitments, in the framework of a constructive dialogue.

Procedure for Implementing the Declaration of 10 November 1994, on Compliance with Commitments Accepted by Member States of the Council of Europe

Adopted by the Committee of Ministers on April 20, 1995, at the 535th meeting of the Ministers' Deputies

In the Declaration adopted on 10 November 1994 on compliance with commitments accepted by member States of the Council of Europe, the Committee of Ministers decided to seek greater efficacity in its procedures with a view to ensuring compliance with commitments, in the framework of a constructive dialogue. It has agreed on the following:

1. The dialogue will be based on the principles of non-discrimination and co-operation. It will not affect existing procedures arising from statutory or conventional control mechanisms.
2. At least three meetings of the Ministers' Deputies at A level, fixed in advance, shall be devoted every year to this question.
3. At the first meeting and subsequently every second year, unless otherwise decided, the Secretary General shall present a factual overview of the compliance with the commitments accepted by member States. The overview should be based on information from member States and all relevant information as set out in paragraph 1 of the Declaration.
4. If, during the deliberations, a need to continue the discussion on the situation in a member State is voiced, the matter will be put on the agenda of the next meeting, referred to in paragraph 2 above.
5. By request made a month before each of these meetings, any Delegation or the Secretary General may ask to put the situation in any member State on the agenda of that meeting, on the basis of its own concerns or with reference to a discussion in the Parliamentary Assembly.
6. The request should be accompanied by specific questions, to enable the Delegations concerned to obtain relevant information.
7. In accordance with Article 21 of the Statute, the discussions should be confidential and held in camera, to encourage a constructive dialogue with the member States concerned.

   The presence of senior officials from the capitals should be encouraged.

8. Conclusions of the meeting may be followed up in accordance with paragraph 3 of the Declaration. If needed, appropriate assistance may be provided to the member States concerned. Progress may be reviewed at subsequent meetings.
9. The Clerk of the Parliamentary Assembly may be invited to be present to provide information on any discussions in Assembly bodies on the States concerned.
10. Nothing in the preceding paragraphs precludes the Ministers' Deputies from taking decisions in accordance with paragraph 4 of the Declaration of 10 November 1994, after a question has been on the agenda for a reasonable number of meetings.

Note: The Case of Georgia

Parliamentary Assembly, Georgia's application for membership of the Council of Europe

Opinion No. 209 (Jan. 27, 1999)

1. Georgia applied to join the Council of Europe on 14 July 1996. By Resolution (96) 33 of 11 September 1996, the Committee of Ministers invited the Parliamentary Assembly to give an opinion on this application, in accordance with Statutory Resolution 51 (30A).

2. The Parliament of Georgia applied for Special Guest status with the Parliamentary Assembly on 4 March 1993 and obtained it on 28 May 1996. Examination of this application was linked to the adoption of Recommendation 1247 (1994) on the enlargement of the Council of Europe, in which the Assembly stated that "in view of their cultural links with Europe, Armenia, Azerbaijan and Georgia would have the possibility of applying for membership provided they clearly indicated their will to be considered as part of Europe."

3. An ad hoc committee of the Assembly observed the parliamentary elections held in Georgia on 5 November 1995 and noted that, in spite of what they considered to be some minor irregularities, "the election had proceeded calmly and apparently in acceptably normal and lawful conditions."

4. Since 1996, Georgia has been participating in various Council of Europe activities under the intergovernmental co-operation and assistance programmes, and in the work of the Parliamentary Assembly and its committees through its delegation of Special Guests.

5. Georgia has ratified the European Cultural Convention and the Convention on the Transfer of Sentenced Persons, and signed the Convention on the Recognition of Qualifications concerning Higher Education in the European Region.

6. The Assembly considers that Georgia is a pluralist democratic society, respectful of human rights and the rule of law, and is able and willing, in the sense of Article 4 of the Statute, to continue the democratic reforms in progress in order to bring all the country's legislation and practice into line with the principles and standards of the Council of Europe.

7. Georgia has experienced two armed conflicts, in Abkhazia (1992-94) and in South Ossetia (1990-93). The Assembly believes that the country has

demonstrated its resolve to settle conflicts by peaceful means, as is well illustrated by the substantial improvement in relations with South Ossetia.

8. The Assembly considers that the adoption of a declaration of friendship with the Abkhaz and Ossetian peoples, as well as increased contact at every level, would help to establish and consolidate a climate of confidence in relations with Abkhazia and South Ossetia.

9. The Assembly calls on Georgian and Abkhaz leaders to accelerate talks on the status of Abkhazia within the internationally recognised borders of Georgia and on the return of all displaced persons to Abkhazia.

10. The Parliamentary Assembly expects Georgia to undertake:

i. with regard to conventions

a. to sign the European Convention on Human Rights (ECHR), as amended by its Protocols Nos. 2 and 11, at the time of accession;

b. to ratify the ECHR and Protocols Nos. 1, 4, 6 and 7 thereto within a year after its accession;

c. to sign and ratify, within a year after its accession, the European Convention for the Prevention of Torture and Inhuman or Degrading Treatment or Punishment and its protocols;

d. to sign and ratify, within a year after its accession, the Framework Convention for the Protection of National Minorities and the European Charter for Regional or Minority Languages;

e. to sign and ratify, within three years after its accession, the European Charter of Local Self-Government, the European Outline Convention on Transfrontier Co-operation and its additional protocols and the Council of Europe conventions on extradition, on mutual assistance in criminal matters, and on laundering, search, seizure and confiscation of the proceeds from crime, and in the meantime to apply the fundamental principles of these instruments;

f. to sign and ratify the Council of Europe's Social Charter within three years after its accession and, in the meantime, to endeavour to implement a policy in accordance with the principles it contains;

g. to sign and ratify the General Agreement on Privileges and Immunities of the Council of Europe and the protocols thereto within a year after its accession;

h. to sign and ratify the Geneva Convention relating to the Status of Refugees and the 1967 Protocol thereto within two years after its accession;

ii. with regard to domestic legislation

a. to create, within four years after its accession, the legal framework for the establishment of a second parliamentary chamber, in conformity with the constitutional requirements;

b. to enact, within two years after its accession, a legal framework determining the status of the autonomous territories and guaranteeing them broad autonomy, the exact terms of which are to be negotiated with the representatives of the territories concerned;

c. to adopt a law on the electronic media within a year after its accession;

d. to adopt a law on attorneys within a year after its accession;

e. to adopt, within two years after its accession, a legal framework permitting repatriation and integration, including the right to Georgian nationality, for the Meskhetian population deported by the Soviet regime, to consult the Council of Europe about this legal framework before its adoption, to begin the process of repatriation and integration within three years after its accession and complete the process of repatriation of the Meskhetian population within twelve years after its accession;

f. to amend the law on the Ombudsman within six months after its accession, so that a report on the Ombudsman's activities shall be presented to Parliament and made public every six months;

g. to take the necessary legislative measures within two years after its accession and administrative measures within three years after its accession in order to permit the restitution of ownership and tenancy rights or the payment of compensation for the property lost by people forced to abandon their homes during the 1990-94 conflicts;

h. to amend, within three years after its accession, the law on autonomy and local government to enable all the heads of councils to be elected instead of being appointed;

i. to adopt, within two years after its accession, a law on minorities based on the principles of Assembly Recommendation 1201 (1993);

iii. with regard to the implementation of reforms

a. to maintain and continue the reforms of the judicial system, the public prosecutor's office and the police force;

b. to continue and reinforce the fight against corruption in the judiciary, the public prosecutor's office and the police force;

c. to adopt the law concerning the transfer of responsibility for the prison system from the Ministry of the Interior to the Ministry of Justice within three months after its accession and to ensure the effective implementation of this law within six months after it has been adopted;

d. to review the scale of sanctions with a view to the reduction of the length of detention and to foresee alternative sentences to prison sentences;

iv. with regard to human rights

a. to ensure strict observance of the human rights of detainees, to abolish within six months after its accession the existing prison system, which puts prisoners with prior political activities in the same cells as other prisoners, and to continue to improve conditions of detention in prisons and pre-trial detention centres;

b. to give human rights training to prison staff and to the police, with the assistance of the Council of Europe;

c. to respect the maximum length of preventive detention;

d. to implement within six months after its accession the right of a detainee to choose his (own) lawyer;

e. to review the cases of persons convicted or detained for their part in the political upheavals of 1991-92 within two years after its accession;

f. to prosecute resolutely and impartially the perpetrators of war crimes committed during the conflicts in Abkhazia and South Ossetia, even within its own armed forces;

v. with regard to the conflict in Abkhazia

a. to continue the efforts to settle the conflict by peaceful means and do everything in its power to put a stop to the activities of all irregular armed groups in the conflict zone and to guarantee the safety of the collective peace-keeping forces of the Commonwealth of Independent States (CIS), the United Nations Observer Mission (UNOMIG) and representatives of all international organisations involved;

b. to facilitate the delivery of humanitarian aid to the most vulnerable groups of the population affected by the consequences of the conflict;

vi. with regard to the monitoring of commitments to co-operate fully with the implementation of the Assembly's Resolution 1115 (1997) on the setting up of an Assembly committee on the honouring of obligations and commitments by member states of the Council of Europe (Monitoring Committee), as well as with the monitoring process set up under the Declaration of the Committee of Ministers dated 10 November 1994 (95th session).

11. On the basis of these commitments the Assembly believes that Georgia is able and willing, in accordance with Article 4 of the Statute of the Council of Europe, to fulfil the conditions of membership of the Council of Europe as set forth in Article 3 of the Statute in the following terms: "Every member of the Council of Europe must accept the principles of the rule of law and of the enjoyment by all persons within its jurisdiction of human rights and fundamental freedoms, and collaborate sincerely and effectively in the realisation of the aim of the Council (of Europe)."

12. With a view to ensuring compliance with these commitments, the Assembly decides, pursuant to Resolution 1115 (1997), to monitor the situation in Georgia closely as from the country's accession.

13. On the basis of the commitments set out above, the Assembly recommends that the Committee of Ministers:

i. invite Georgia to become a member of the Council of Europe;

ii. allocate five seats to Georgia in the Parliamentary Assembly.

Parliamentary Assembly, Resolution 1257 (2001) of Sept. 25, 2001: Honouring of obligations and commitments by Georgia

1. The Assembly welcomes the efforts Georgia has made since its accession on 27 April 1999 towards honouring some of its obligations and commitments, which it accepted in Opinion No. 209 (1999).

2. With regard to the signature and ratification of conventions, the Assembly is pleased to note that:

i. Georgia has ratified, within the deadlines in Opinion No. 209, the European Convention on Human Rights as well as its Protocols Nos. 4, 6 and 7;

ii. to date, Georgia is the only member state which has, on 15 June 2001, ratified Protocol No. 12 to the European Convention on Human Rights;

iii. Georgia has also ratified the European Convention for the Prevention of Torture and Inhuman or Degrading Treatment or Punishment and its Protocols Nos. 1 and 2, the European Convention on Extradition and its protocols, the European Convention on Mutual Assistance in Criminal Matters, the General Agreement on Privileges and Immunities and its protocols, and signed the revised European Social Charter;

iv. Georgia has also ratified the Geneva Convention relating to the Status of Refugees and the 1967 Protocol thereto.

3. The Assembly nevertheless, regrets that Georgia:

i. did not ratify within one year after its accession the Additional Protocol to the European Convention on Human Rights it signed on June 1999, or the Framework Convention for the Protection of National Minorities it signed in January 2000;

ii. has not signed or ratified the European Charter for Regional or Minority Languages, the European Charter of Local Self-Government, the European Outline Convention on Transfrontier Co-operation and its additional protocols, or the European Convention on Laundering, Search, Seizure and Confiscation of the Proceeds from Crime.

4. With regard to domestic legislation, the Assembly recognises that Georgia has adopted laws in many fields, including an electoral code, a law on the Bar, a new law on imprisonment, a general administrative code, a law amending the Law on the Ombudsman and a law amending the Law on Local Self-Government, but is preoccupied by the lack of enforcement and recalls the need for a proper implementation of existing legislation.

5. The Assembly also supports initiatives taken to combat and eradicate endemic and widespread corruption in the country and in this context welcomes the implementation of the National Anti-Corruption Programme.

6. With regard to the implementation of reforms, the Assembly acknowledges that measures have been taken to improve the functioning of the judiciary, especially in respect of the fight against corruption and incompetence in the judiciary, the monitoring of the execution of judgments, and the reform of the prosecutor's office. It also notes positive steps undertaken to reform the penitentiary system, that is, the transfer of the prison administration from the Ministry of the Interior to the Ministry of Justice, the building of a new prison, and measures to fight corruption.

7. In order to solve the persisting problems in the administration of justice, the Assembly calls on Georgia to accelerate these and other reforms under way and to implement them according to Council of Europe standards, in particular as regards the functioning of the judiciary and the conditions of detention in prisons and pre-trial detention centres.

8. With regard to domestic legislation and implementation of reforms, the Assembly urges Georgia to strengthen co-operation with the Council of Europe in order to ensure full compatibility of Georgian legislation with the Organisation's principles and standards, and in particular:

i. to co-operate with the Council of Europe legal experts on a number of bills which have been prepared recently, including a new draft law on the police, a draft law amending the law on the prosecutor's office, a draft law on development of alternative punishment and to ensure that they are enacted by the Georgian Parliament by January 2003 at the latest;

ii. to implement the recommendations made by Council of Europe experts on criminal procedures, the role of the prosecutor's office, police arrest, pre-trial investigation and pre-trial detention;

iii. in close co-operation with the European Committee for the Prevention of Torture and Inhuman or Degrading Treatment or Punishment, to implement the recommendations made following its visit in May 2001;

iv. to submit for expertise the newly adopted Election Code to the European Commission for Democracy through Law (Venice Commission) in order to assess whether the current electoral legislation takes full account of recommendations made in 1999 by the Parliamentary Assembly Ad hoc Committee on the Observation of Elections and by the OSCE Office for Democratic Institutions and Human Rights (ODIHR);

v. to co-operate with the Congress of Local and Regional Authorities of Europe (CLRAE) in a constructive manner, and in particular:

a. to implement recommendations the Congress made in 1999 to enhance local and regional self-government in Georgia, including the adoption of amendments to existing legislation, new legislation and administrative measures, in accordance with the European Charter of Local Self-Government;

b. to transmit for expertise the text of the law amending the Law on Local Self-Government;

c. to accept assistance in the preparation and observation of the forthcoming local elections;

d. to organise without delay a colloquy on regionalisation which could help to clarify Georgian regional structure and territorial organisation.

vi. to step up co-operation within the Group of States Against Corruption (GRECO) with a view to applying its recommendations on the fight against corruption;

vii. to accelerate the work undertaken with the Council of Europe and the UNHCR on the question of the repatriation of the deported Meskhetian population, including ongoing legal expertise of the draft law "on repatriation of persons deported from Georgia in the 1940s by the Soviet regime," with a view to granting them the same status of rehabilitation as that already given to deportees of other ethnicities who were repatriated to Georgia under the Soviet regime.

9. As regards the freedom of the press and mass media, the Assembly calls on Georgia to draft and adopt a law on the electronic media, in order to regulate media activity and to guarantee the independence, pluralism and objectivity of the Georgian electronic media, and to consult the Council of Europe's experts on any new draft legislation.

10. In respect of the Code of Criminal Procedure, the Assembly regrets that the new code which was initially drafted in close consultation with Council of Europe experts was expurgated by numerous amendments adopted by the Georgian Parliament in the weeks following the accession of the country to the Organisation, in May and June 1999, and that a new package of amendments was adopted in June 2001 without previous consultation of Council of Europe experts. It strongly urges the Georgian authorities to substantially improve co-operation with the Council of Europe in this respect.

11. The Assembly regrets that little progress has been made as regards respect for human rights:

i. it expresses its deep concern with regard to allegations of ill-treatment or torture of detainees in police custody and pre-trial detention, cases of arbitrary arrests and detentions, the violation of the rights of persons under police arrest or in pre-trial detention — in particular their right to consult a lawyer and to communicate with their family — complaints on violation of procedural rights, cases of intimidation, violation of the right to privacy, phone tapping, and so on;

ii. it is alarmed by the behaviour of the police and other law enforcement bodies and condemns any disproportionate violence used by security forces against peaceful demonstrators;

iii. it is also strongly concerned about repeated cases of violence by Orthodox extremists against believers of minority religious groups, such as Jehovah's Witnesses and Baptists.

12. The Assembly urges the Georgian authorities to conduct a proper investigation into all cases of human rights violations and the abuse of power, to prosecute their perpetrators irrespective of their functions, and to adopt radical measures to bring definitively the country into line with the principles and standards of the Council of Europe.

13. The Assembly invites the Georgian authorities to authorise publication of the report of the European Committee for the Prevention of Torture and Inhuman or Degrading Treatment or Punishment on its visit to Georgia in May 2001.

14. In respect of commitments related to the status of the autonomous territories and the settlement of territorial conflicts by peaceful means, the Assembly welcomes progress made in granting autonomous status to Adjaria in April 2000, but regrets that no substantial progress has been made on a political settlement of the South Ossetian and Abkhaz conflicts, in spite of the efforts of the Georgian Government.

15. However, the Assembly recognises that the conditions have not been met for the Georgian authorities to fulfil their commitments to enact a legal framework determining the status of the autonomous territories and to elaborate a legal framework for the establishment of a second parliamentary chamber.

16. As regards the Abkhaz conflict, the Assembly:

i. calls on Georgian and Abkhaz leaders to continue their talks on the status of Abkhazia and on the return of all displaced persons who wish to do so, to Abkhazia;

ii. recalls that Georgia must take legislative and administrative measures providing for restitution of property or compensation for property lost by persons forced to abandon their homes in the 1990 to 1994 conflicts.

17. In the light of the above considerations, the Assembly concludes that, although some progress has been made since accession, Georgia is far from honouring its obligations and commitments as a member state of the Council of Europe. The Assembly resolves to pursue the monitoring procedure in respect of Georgia in close co-operation with the Georgian delegation.

Compliance with Commitments and Obligations: The Situation in Georgia

Directorate of Strategic Planning (DSP), Biannual Report (July 2004–February 2005)

Executive Summary

Over the period covered by this report, the Georgian authorities continued to carry out efforts for institutional, legal and socio-economic modernisation of the country. This process has been developing against the background of persisting instability in the break-away-regions of South Ossetia and Abkhazia, re-integration of which is considered as a key priority by the Georgian leadership. In line with efforts to achieve a peaceful solution of conflict in South Ossetia, the Georgian authorities started to work on the future autonomous status of the region in consultation with the CoE Venice Commission. At the end of January 2005, the CoE Parliamentary Assembly adopted Resolution 1415 (2005) containing a comprehensive list of recommendations on outstanding accession commitments by Georgia. Three priority areas remain central for Georgia's democratic evolution: consolidation of democratic institutions (including those related to regionalisation), reform of the judiciary and law-enforcement agencies and the fight against corruption and organised crime.

— Functioning of democratic institutions (including those related to regionalisation): The election of the Supreme Council of Adjara, held in late June 2004, marked a step forward in terms of transparency and political freedom. Nevertheless, the review of the autonomous status of Adjara in line with the Venice Commission's opinion, as recommended by Parliamentary Assembly, is still expected. Reform of the electoral system, including electoral administration, is ongoing, although the Venice Commission has not yet been able to comment on recent draft amendments to the electoral code. Notwithstanding encouraging developments overall, the decentralisation reform is advancing slowly and not always in a coherent way. Particular attention should be paid to the preparation of the local elections envisaged for 2006 and, in particular, to the issue of election of the Mayor of the capital, the details of which are being elaborated.

— Judiciary and law enforcement: Reform of the major judicial institutions raises questions regarding respect for judicial independence. More emphasis should be put on the follow-up to CoE experts' recommendations on the issue. Reform of the Code of Criminal Procedure is pending and its conformity with CoE standards, notably the ECHR, is still to be ensured. Proper application of the plea-bargaining procedure remains an issue of concern. Human rights and professional training of law-enforcement and prison staff should become a priority area of co-operation with the CoE.

— Fight against corruption, organised crime and impunity: An active case-by-case campaign against corruption raised optimism within the Georgian population. However, the time has come for comprehensive anti-corruption policies and profound institutional reforms. Also, it is essential to ensure that the fight against corruption is carried out in full compliance with human rights and rule of law principles. An overall assessment by GRECO is envisaged for June 2005. The second round evaluation report, adopted by MONEYVAL in January 2005, acknowledged progress in the creation of basic anti-money laundering prerequisites. Local and international human rights defenders welcomed the conviction of the priest responsible for incidents of religious violence during the late nineties as a sign of the authorities' commitment to put an end to impunity. However, impunity appears to persist with respect to the alleged ill-treatment of detainees in pre-trial detention centres and prisons. The report of the CPT on its second periodic visit to Georgia has not yet been made public.

— Outstanding conventions: The CoE stands ready to assist the Georgian authorities in the preparation for the ratification of the outstanding CoE conventions, in particular, the Framework Convention for the Protection of National

Minorities, the European Charter for Regional and Minority Languages and the Revised European Social Charter.

— Repatriation of the Meskhetian population deported in 1940-1944: A special Council to deal with this issue under the President of Georgia was established in December 2004 and work on the draft law on repatriation has started. The CoE stands ready to provide assistance in the elaboration of this law.

— Freedom of the media: Pluralism and independence of the electronic media needs to be preserved and reinforced. In this context, the creation of an authentic public service broadcaster, already started by the Georgian authorities following adoption of the relevant legislation, is of the utmost importance. The CoE will provide assistance to this end, if requested.

— Minorities: The authorities are urged to pay careful attention to the concerns of national minorities, so as to avoid a deterioration in inter-ethnic relations.

Comments and Questions

1. How does the record of compliance with individual judgments under the European system compare with that in other regional systems or under UN instruments? Is the difference due to different political contexts, the legally-binding nature of the European Court, or other factors?

2. Human rights violations in Chechnya by Russian forces are notorious, and the Secretary General wrote to the Committee of Ministers that he considered it his duty "to seize the Committee of Ministers of this matter [the situation in Chechnya] by virtue of paragraph 1, second indent, of the 1994 Declaration on compliance with commitments accepted by member states of the Council of Europe." The question was discussed by the Ministers' Deputies, but no action was taken. The Secretary General regularly submits to the Committee of Ministers, in addition to his monthly reports on the work of the Council of Europe experts on Chechnya, additional information regarding the situation of democracy, human rights, and the rule of law in the Chechen Republic. These reports are transmitted to the Assembly for information. See Ministers' Deputies reply of 9 January 2002 to Parliamentary Assembly Recommendation 1536 (2001) on Progress of the Assembly's monitoring procedure (2000-2001, CoE Doc. CM/Del/Dec(2002)779, item 2.6 On 26 June 2000). The Council of Europe's Parliamentary Assembly regretted in 2001 that "little progress has been made as regards respect for human rights" in Georgia (supra page 696). Should Russia and Georgia have been admitted as members of the Council of Europe, if their human rights records were so dismal?

D. *The Present Crisis and the Future of the System*

Since the inauguration of the permanent court on Nov. 1, 1998, several developments have had significant impacts on its practice and jurisprudence. First, the expansion of the system into Central and Eastern Europe has brought new judges and new cases into the system. The caseload had already begun to rise in the 1980s (leading to the reforms introduced by Protocol 11), but the volume expanded at an unprecedented rate beginning in the late 1990s and has nearly doubled since 1999. In 1990, for example, there were 5,279 applications; in 2004, 40,943. The latter figure is comparable to the number of cases registered during the system's first thirty years combined. The Court issued 180 judgments during its first thirty years; in 2004 alone it rendered 718 judgments. Of the total of 4,863 judgments reached by the Court by the end of 2004, nearly one-third of them were delivered in 2003 and 2004.

Two other trends have been observed in recent years. First, the percentage of cases alleging procedural delay of justice in violation of Article 5 or 6(1) continues to be high. While most of these cases in the past came from Italy, a rising number of cases has emerged from other countries. In 2004, out of 718 judgments, 207 cases concerned the length of civil or administrative proceedings; nearly one-third of these concerned Poland. Another 41 judgments concerned lengthy delays in criminal proceedings.

The second trend is qualitative rather than quantitative: the Court has received a growing number of large and politically sensitive cases stemming from armed conflicts and separatist movements. Many of these cases have involved Turkey, which accounted for nearly one-fourth of all judgments in 2004. The Court has also been involved with cases that concern conflicts or their aftermaths in the former Yugoslavia, the Transdniestrian region of Moldova, Chechnya, and the Polish borders redrawn after World War II.

In response to what is widely perceived as a growing crisis, a Ministerial Conference on Human Rights, held in Rome in November 2000, initiated a discussion on "reform of the reform." On May 13, 2004, Protocol No. 14 to the Convention was adopted and opened for ratification. It requires unanimous ratification by parties to the Convention to enter into force, but only 17 states had ratified as of September 2005. A "Group of Wise Persons" also has been appointed "to draw up a comprehensive stragety to secure the long-term effectiveness" of the Convention; the group will submit an interim report to the Committee of Ministers in May 2006.

The immediately following extract explains the purpose of Protocol No. 14; the next extract was adopted by the Committee of Ministers to address some of the problems of systemic violations, an issue also raised by the Parliamentary Assembly, supra pages 686-690, while awaiting the entry into force of Protocol No. 14.

Explanatory report to the [draft] Protocol No. 14 to the Convention for the Protection of Human Rights and Fundamental Freedoms, amending the Convention's control system

Adopted by the Committee of Ministers Steering Committee for Human Rights (CDDH), Doc. CM(2004)65 Addendum 2 prov. (Apr. 15, 2004)

III. Overview of the Changes Made by Protocol No. 14 to the Control System of the European Convention on Human Rights

34. During the initial reflection stage on the reform of the Convention's control system, which started immediately after the 2000 European Ministerial

Conference on Human Rights, a wide range of possible changes to the system was examined, both in the Evaluation Group and the CDDH's Reflection Group. Several proposals were retained and are taken up in this Protocol. Others, including some proposals for radical change of the control system, were for various reasons rejected during the reflection stage. Some of these should be mentioned here. For example, the idea of setting up, within the framework of the Convention, "regional courts of first instance" was rejected because, on the one hand, of the risk it would create of diverging case-law and, on the other hand, the high cost of setting them up. Proposals to empower the Court to give preliminary rulings at the request of national courts or to expand the Court's competence to give advisory opinions (Articles 47-49 of the Convention) were likewise rejected. Such innovations might interfere with the contentious jurisdiction of the Court and they would, certainly in the short term, result in additional, not less, work for the Court. Finally, two other proposals were rejected because they would have restricted the right of individual application. These were the proposal that the Court should be given discretion to decide whether or not to take up a case for examination (system comparable to the certiorari procedure of the US Supreme Court) and that it should be made compulsory for applicants to be represented by a lawyer or other legal expert from the moment of introduction of the application (see however Rule 36, paragraph 2, of the Rules of Court). It was felt that the principle according to which anyone had the right to apply to the Court should be firmly upheld. The proposal to create a separate filtering body, composed of persons other than the judges of the Court, was also rejected, since in this connection, the Protocol is based on two fundamental premises: filtering work must be carried out within the judicial framework of the Court and there should not be different categories of judges within the same body.

35. Unlike Protocol No. 11, Protocol No. 14 makes no radical changes to the control system established by the Convention. The changes it does make relate more to the functioning than the nature of the system. Their main purpose is to improve it, giving the Court the procedural means and flexibility it needs to process all applications in a timely fashion, while allowing it to concentrate on the most important cases which require in-depth examination.

36. To achieve this, amendments are introduced in three main areas:

— reinforcement of the Court's filtering capacity in respect of the mass of unmeritorious applications;

— a new admissibility criterion concerning cases in which the applicant has not suffered a significant disadvantage and which in terms of respect for human rights do not otherwise require an examination on the merits by the Court;

— measures for dealing with repetitive cases.

37. Together, these elements of the reform seek to reduce the time spent by the Court on clearly inadmissible applications and repetitive applications so as to enable the Court to concentrate on those cases that raise important human rights issues.

38. The filtering capacity is increased by making a single judge competent to declare inadmissible or strike out an individual application. This new mechanism retains the judicial character of the decision-making on admissibility. The single judges will be assisted by non-judicial rapporteurs, who will be part of the registry.

39. A new admissibility requirement is inserted in Article 35 of the Convention. The new requirement provides the Court with an important additional tool which should assist it in concentrating on cases which warrant an examination on the merits, by empowering it to declare inadmissible applications where the applicant has not suffered a significant disadvantage and which, in terms of respect for human rights, do not otherwise require an examination on the merits by the Court. It should be stressed that the new requirement does not restrict the right of individuals to apply to the Court or alter the principle that all individual applications are examined on their admissibility. While the Court alone is competent to interpret the new admissibility requirement and decide on its application, its terms should ensure that rejection of cases requiring an examination on the merits is avoided. The latter will notably include cases which, notwithstanding their trivial nature, raise serious questions affecting the application or the interpretation of the Convention or important questions concerning national law or where the complaint has not been examined by a national authority.

40. The competence of the committees of three judges is extended to cover repetitive cases. They are empowered to rule, in a simplified procedure, not only on the admissibility but also on the merits of an application, if the underlying question in the case is already the subject of well-established case-law of the Court.

41. As for the other changes made by the Protocol, it should be noted, first of all, that the Court is given more latitude to rule simultaneously on the admissibility and merits of individual applications. In fact, joint decisions on admissibility and merits of individual cases are not only encouraged but become the norm. However, the Court will be free to choose, on a case by case basis, to take separate decisions on admissibility. . . .

43. Furthermore, the Committee of Ministers may also decide, by a two-thirds majority of the representatives entitled to sit on the Committee, to bring proceedings before the Grand Chamber of the Court against any High Contracting Party which refuses to comply with the Court's final judgment in a case to which it is party, after having given it notice to do so. The purpose of such proceedings would be to obtain a ruling from the Court as to whether that Party has failed to fulfil its obligation under Article 46, paragraph 1, of the Convention. . . .

47. Finally, an amendment has been introduced with a view to possible accession of the European Union to the Convention.

Resolution (2004) 3, on Judgments Revealing an Underlying Systemic Problem

Adopted by the Committee of Ministers on May 12, 2004

The Committee of Ministers, in accordance with Article 15.b of the Statute of the Council of Europe,

Considering that the aim of the Council of Europe is the achievement of greater unity among its members, and that one of the most important methods by which that aim is to be pursued is the maintenance and further realization of human rights and fundamental freedoms;

Reiterating its conviction that the Convention for the Protection of Human Rights and Fundamental Freedoms (hereinafter referred to as "the Convention") must remain the essential reference point for the protection of human rights in Europe, and recalling its commitment to take measures in order to guarantee the long-term effectiveness of the control system instituted by the Convention;

Recalling the subsidiary character of the supervision mechanism set up by the Convention, which implies, in accordance with its Article 1, that the rights and freedoms guaranteed by the Convention be protected in the first place at national level and applied by national authorities;

Welcoming in this context that the Convention has now become an integral part of the domestic legal order of all states parties;...

Considering that the execution of judgments would be facilitated if the existence of a systemic problem is already identified in the judgment of the Court;...

Invites the Court:

I. as far as possible, to identify, in its judgments finding a violation of the Convention, what it considers to be an underlying systemic problem and the source of this problem, in particular when it is likely to give rise to numerous applications, so as to assist states in finding the appropriate solution and the Committee of Ministers in supervising the execution of judgments;

II. to specially notify any judgment containing indications of the existence of a systemic problem and of the source of this problem not only to the state concerned and to the Committee of Ministers, but also to the Parliamentary Assembly, to the Secretary General of the Council of Europe and to the Council of Europe Commissioner for Human Rights, and to highlight such judgments in an appropriate manner in the database of the Court.

Comments and Questions

1. What has caused the most recent crisis in the European system? Is it realistic to expect any greater commitment from European states than is already evidenced by the existence of a full-time human rights court with hundreds of staff attorneys?

2. If you were legal adviser to a European foreign ministry, would you recommend ratification of Protocol No. 14? What other measures could be taken to improve or preserve the effectiveness of the system?

3. Despite recommendations by the Parliamentary Assembly and Committee of Ministers, the Court has been reluctant to indicate the specific measures that a state should take to remedy a violation. What do you think explains the reluctance of the Court to address "systemic problems"? Can any international human rights court deal effectively with "systemic problems" that lead to individual human rights violations?

III. Other Human Rights Activities of the Council of Europe, European Union, and Organization for Security and Cooperation in Europe

Dinah Shelton, *The Boundaries of Human Rights Jurisdiction in Europe*

13 Duke J. Int'l & Comp. L.at pp. 102-09, 119-23 (2003) (references omitted)

The European Social Charter (ESC) with its protocols provides a system for the promotion and protection of economic, social and cultural rights. The Charter was opened for signature on October 18, 1961 and entered into force on February 26, 1965. It was amended by Protocol in 1988 and again in 1991. The 1991 Protocol modifying the supervisory mechanism of the Charter is not yet in force, as it requires ratification by all parties to the Charter. Most of its provisions, however, have been implemented through actions taken by the supervisory organs.

Two additional instruments have continued the evolution of the ESC. A further Protocol provides for a system of collective complaints. Finally, in 1996, a Revised European Social Charter, bringing the earlier documents up to date and adding some new rights, was opened for signature. It will progressively replace the original Charter and, as the consolidated text, is the basic instrument for the future.

The Revised Charter proclaims in Part I categories of "rights and principles," including workers' rights and family and individual rights to social security, health, and medical assistance. Migrant workers, women, children, the elderly, and disabled persons are afforded special protections. Part II of the Revised Charter defines the meaning and elaborates on the general principles set out in Part I. Part III of the Revised Charter specifies the obligations of the States Parties, giving each state a set of options. First, each state undertakes "to consider Part I of this Charter as a declaration of the aims which it will pursue by all appropriate means." Second, the state must accept as binding at least six out of nine articles found in Part II. Third, each State Party has an obligation to select another specified number of rights or sub-categories of rights with which it agrees to comply. This flexible system was drafted to induce the maximum adherence of states while obliging all States Parties to guarantee some of the most basic rights.

The Charter establishes a reporting system and a system of collective complaints to monitor the compliance by states with their obligations. The reporting procedure calls for two types of reports. The first is due every two years and must address the domestic implementation of those Part II rights that the particular state has accepted. The second report, whose periodicity is determined by the Committee of Ministers, addresses the status of Part II rights that the particular State Party did not accept.

The initial review of state reports is by the European Committee of Social Rights (ECSR), a group of nine experts "of the highest integrity and recognized competence in international social questions," elected by the Committee of Ministers. They assess whether the states have respected their undertakings, and render legal opinions on whether the national laws and practices of the States Parties are in compliance with their obligations under the Charter. The ECSR transmits its conclusions to the Governmental Committee of the Council of Europe, which is composed of state representatives. The Governmental Committee presents its findings on compliance to the Committee of Ministers. The Committee of Ministers may then make the necessary recommendations to any of the High Contracting Parties.

The most significant change to the ESC system comes with the additional protocol providing for a system of collective complaints. While opening the process to non-state actors, the mechanism differs considerably from the judicial proceedings of the Court. First, the ESC procedure affords limited standing. It allows complaints of "unsatisfactory application of the Charter" to originate with one of several types of groups: international organizations of employers and trade unions participating in the work of the Governmental Committee; other international non-governmental organizations with consultative status with the Council of Europe and appearing on a special list drawn up by the Governmental Committee; and national organizations of employers and trade unions from the Contracting Party concerned. Each state may also declare that it accepts the right of its national non-governmental organizations to lodge complaints against it. Article 3 of the Protocol specifies that the "international non-governmental organizations and the national non-governmental organizations . . . may submit complaints . . . only in respect of those matters regarding which they have been recognized as having particular competence."

The collective complaints are examined by the ECSR, which first determines admissibility and then examines admissible complaints on the basis of written submissions and possible hearings. The Committee prepares a report on its examination of the complaint and the conclusions reached. The report is transmitted to the Committee of Ministers, the complaining organization, and the States Parties. On the basis of the report, the Committee of Ministers adopts a resolution on the matter, which may contain recommendations to the State concerned. At the time the resolution is adopted, or four months after the Committee of Ministers receives the report, the Parliamentary Assembly also receives the report and makes it public. The State must submit information on its measures to comply with the recommendations made.

In the first two years after the Protocol entered into force, ten complaints were registered. The first application, *International Commission of Jurists v. Portugal*, complained of child labor in violation of Charter Article 7(1). The ECSR transmitted the report containing its decision on the merits to the Committee of Ministers which agreed that a violation had been shown. The Committee then considered several consecutive complaints against France, Italy, Greece and Portugal concerning the right of armed forces to organize and collectively bargain. These cases are noteworthy because of the potential for conflicting jurisprudence between the ECSR and the ECHR; Article 11(2) of the ECHR expressly permits Contracting Parties to limit labor union rights for members of the armed forces. A complaint subsequently filed in the case *International Federation of Human Rights Leagues v. Greece* alleged forced labor. The ECSR transmitted the report finding violations to the Committee of Ministers on December 12, 2000; the latter made recommendations to the Greek government. [As of July 2005, applicants had submitted 32 collective complaints, three of which had been declared inadmissible and five of which were still pending. The 24 decisions on the merits produced 15 findings of violations on a wide range of topics: unsafe or unjust working conditions, corporal punishment of children, discrimination against Roma, denial of access to health care, inadequate educational opportunities for autistic persons, closed shop provisions, forced labor, and child labor. In each case, the Committee of Ministers adopted a resolution taking note of the ECSR's decisions and in many instances referred to the developments that had taken place in the relevant country. With the procedure relatively new, the Committee of Ministers has not yet reported on implementation of its recommendations by the states.]

The European Convention for the Prevention of Torture and its Protocols supplement the ECHR by seeking to prevent the commission of torture through an innovative procedure of visits and inspections to detention facilities. A Committee for the Prevention of Torture (CPT), composed of independent and impartial experts whose number is equal to that of the States Parties, has the power to visit places of detention of any kind, such as prisons, police cells, military barracks, and mental hospitals, to examine the treatment of detainees and, if appropriate, to make recommendations to the state concerned with a view to strengthening the protection of the detainees. A principle of "cooperation" has led the Committee to exercise its functions in strict confidentiality. Publicity occurs only if a state requests publication of the Committee's report, together with its comments, or if a state fails to cooperate with the Committee or refuses to make improvements following the Committee's recommendations.

The Committee carries out periodic visits to all Contracting Parties and may organize such ad hoc visits "as appear to it to be required in the circumstances." The Committee is obliged to notify the state concerned of its intention to carry out such a visit, but no specific period of notice is required. A visit may take place immediately after the notification in exceptional circumstances. Government objections to the time or place of a visit can be justified only on grounds of national defense, public safety, serious disorder, the medical condition of a person or an urgent interrogation in progress relating to a serious crime. In such cases the state must immediately take steps to allow the Committee to visit as soon as possible.

The newer European Charter for Regional or Minority Languages, and the 1995 Framework Convention for the Protection of National Minorities address problems of minority rights. The Framework Convention is so denominated because it is primarily a statement of principles rather than a detailed set of obligations. Supervision of compliance is done through a system of state reporting to the Committee of Ministers, assisted by an expert advisory committee. The Council of Europe has also taken up human rights problems posed by technological change, adopting the Convention for the Protection of the Individual with Regard to the Automatic Processing of Personal Data, the Convention for the Protection of Human Rights and Biomedicine and its Additional Protocol on the Prohibition of Cloning Human Beings. . . .

The 1993 Declaration adopted by the Council of Europe Heads of State and Government, meeting at the Vienna Summit, included a commitment to combat racism, xenophobia, anti-Semitism and intolerance. The follow up involved creation of a new mechanism, the European Commission against Racism and Intolerance (ECRI), established to review Member States' legislation, policies and other measures to combat racism and intolerance and to propose further action at local, national and European levels. ECRI monitors the situation through an in-depth study of the situation in each of the Member States followed by specific proposals designed to solve current problems or remedy deficiencies. Draft texts are communicated to national liaison officers to allow national authorities to respond with observations. After the confidential dialogue, ECRI adopts a final report and submits it to the state concerned through the Committee of Ministers. State reports are made public two months after transmission to the government unless the government expressly objects. ECRI has completed a first round of reviews and aims to do 10 country reports annually during its second monitoring period.

The Parliamentary Assembly has created a monitoring mechanism to verify compliance with obligations and commitments of all Council of Europe Member States. A monitoring committee is responsible for verifying the fulfillment of obligations assumed by Member States under the terms of the Council of Europe Statute, the European Convention and all other Council of European human rights conventions, as well as the honoring of commitments entered into by the States' authorities upon accession to the Council of Europe. The procedure permits the Assembly to sanction persistent non-compliance by adopting resolutions and recommendations, by not approving the credentials of a national parliamentary delegation, or ultimately by recommending action to the Committee of Ministers.

Finally, the Council of Europe created the post of Commissioner for Human Rights on May 7, 1999. The Commissioner is elected by the Parliamentary Assembly from a list of candidates drawn up by the Committee of Ministers and serves a non-renewable six-year term. The functions of the independent and impartial Commissioner are to serve as "a non-judicial institution to promote education in, awareness of and respect for human rights, as embodied in the human rights instruments of the Council of Europe." The functions are thus primarily promotional and preventive; the Commissioner has no power to accept communications. In the exercise of his functions, the first Commissioner undertook a fact-finding visit to the Russian Federation soon after taking office and submitted a report to the Committee of Ministers and the Parliamentary Assembly on the situation in Chechnya.

The European Union

Outside the Council of Europe and following its creation, six of its original States Parties moved to reduce economic barriers between them through establishing the European Communities. The absence of human rights protections posed increasing problems as the role and powers of the European Communities expanded and its legislative and administrative activities had a growing impact on the rights of individuals and companies. In an evolution parallel to that of the Council of Europe, the Communities have subsequently enlarged their membership and increased the power of their institutions, eventually forming, first, the combined European Community (EC) and then the European Union (EU), of which the European Community is one of the Three Pillars. The other two pillars are common foreign and security policy, and police and judicial cooperation in criminal matters, set out in the Treaty of European Union (TEU) Titles V and VI respectively.

Initially, the treaties creating the Communities contained few human rights guarantees, being primarily concerned with economic integration. The ECJ first announced in *Van Gend en Loos*, Case 26/62 [1963] E.C.R. 1 and then in *Costa v. ENEL*, Case 6/64, [1964] E.C.R. 585 the basic principle that EC law prevails over Member States' national laws. The resulting doctrines of direct applicability and direct effect ensured the supremacy of Community law, but it appeared that no human rights system applied to Community institutions in the exercise of their supranational powers. German and Italian courts almost immediately raised concerns about the supremacy of EC law should it run afoul of constitutional protections for human rights.

To fill the human rights gap and ensure the continued supremacy of EC law, the European Court of Justice (ECJ) declared in a series of decisions that respect for fundamental rights forms an integral part of the general principles of law which the Court is required to apply in interpreting the Community treaties. In *Stauder v. City of Ulm*, 29/69, [1969] E.C.R. 419, the ECJ declared that a doctrine of fundamental human rights was enshrined as a general principle of Community law and was protected by the Court. In *Internationale Handelsgesellschaft v. EVGF*, Case 11/70 [1970] E.C.R. 1125, the ECJ announced a principle of autonomous human rights law, i.e., that the validity of EC law would be judged by the EC's own criteria for fundamental human rights. In the *Nold* case, Case 4/73 [1974] E.C.R. 491 the Court of Justice held that

> [F]undamental rights form an integral part of the general principles of law, the observance of which [the Court] ensures. In safeguarding these rights the Court is bound to draw inspiration from constitutional traditions common to the Member States, and it cannot therefore uphold measures which are incompatible with fundamental rights recognized and protected by the Constitutions of those States. Similarly, international treaties for the protection of human rights on which the Member States have collaborated or of which they are signatories, can supply guidelines, which should be followed within the framework of Community law. Id. at 507.

Over time, both the basic legal instruments and the jurisprudence of the Court have evolved to expand the rights of individuals, not just in the economic field, but in regard to political rights as well. In ascertaining the nature of these rights the Court looks to the European Convention on Human Rights, including the case law of the European Court of Human Rights. Thus, for Community acts to be constitutional, they must be compatible with the requirements of the protection of fundamental rights in the Community legal order. Further, to the greatest extent possible, Member States must apply Community law in accordance with their human rights obligations. The ECJ has also held, in the seminal decision *Francovich v. Italy*, Cases C-6/90 and C-9/90 [1991] E.C.R. I-5357, that Member States can be liable for breaching Community law if they fail to implement directives. This vindication of individual rights ensures a remedy against Member States even when the direct source of the violation is a private actor.

This jurisprudence does not mean, however, that the ECJ can review the compatibility of national laws or practices with the ECHR or other human rights law outside the scope of Community law. Such cases should remain within the jurisdiction of the European Court of Human Rights. Even after changes introduced by the TEU and Treaty of Amsterdam, described below, the protection of human rights generally is not listed as one of the express purposes of the EC or one of the powers expressly conferred upon it, meaning national laws as they affect human rights remain outside Community reach so long as they do not impact Community law or policies.

Changes in EC law in favor of human rights have occurred, however. The preamble to the Maastricht Treaty, which transformed the European Community into the European Union, declared that "[t]he Union shall respect fundamental rights, as guaranteed by the European Convention [of] . . . Human Rights . . . and as they result from the constitutional traditions common to the Member States, as general principles of Community law." The inclusion of this language, derived from ECJ judgments, appears to constitute an express acceptance of the ECJ's approach by the Member States of the Union.

The concern for human rights reflected in the Maastricht Treaty preamble is reinforced in Article 2 of the revised Treaty of European Union (Treaty of Amsterdam) which includes among the EU objectives "to strengthen the protection of the rights and interests of the nationals of its Member States through the introduction of a citizenship of the Union" and "to maintain and develop the Union as an area of freedom, security and justice. . . ." Using language from the former Preamble, Article 6(1) provides that the Union "is founded on the principles of liberty, democracy, respect for human rights and fundamental freedoms, and the rule of law," while Article 6(2) requires that the Union respects fundamental rights guaranteed by the European Convention and the constitutional traditions common to the Member States as general principles of Community law. Further, Article 7 specifies a procedure that can result in suspension of membership rights if a "serious and persistent" breach of human rights occurs in a Member State. The Treaty also strengthens the protection against discrimination and makes human rights an objective of the common foreign and security policy. Perhaps most importantly, TEU Article 46(d) gives the ECJ jurisdiction over compliance with Article 6(2), thereby making human rights broadly justiciable so long as the issue presented in the case is linked to Community law.

In a process parallel to that developed by the Council of Europe, the EU Member States have enunciated criteria that must be met by states applying to join. First, the "Copenhagen Guidelines" adopted at the 1993 EC Summit, state:

> The candidates must achieve stability of institutions guaranteeing democracy, the rule of law, human rights, and respect for the protection of minorities; the existence of a functioning market economy as well as the capacity to cope with competitive pressure and market forces within the union; and the ability to take on the obligations of membership, including adherence to the aims of political, economic and monetary union.

Second, the Commission has deemed that the foundational principles listed in the Treaty of Amsterdam Article 6 establish formal criteria for membership.

Despite these advances, the precise obligations of organs of the Communities remain unclear in the absence of an EU Bill of Rights. Accession to the ECHR appears unlikely [although that possibility is envisaged in Protocol No. 14]. The Court of Justice has determined in an advisory opinion, that the Community lacks competence to accede to the European Convention on Human Rights absent amendment of the Treaty. *Accession by the Communities to the European Convention for the Protection of Human Rights and Fundamental Freedoms,* Opinion 2/94, [1996] E.C.R. I-1759. In the advisory opinion, the Court noted that no provision of the Treaty establishing the European Community confers on the Community institutions any general power respecting human rights. Nor can the Treaty's "necessary and proper" clause provide authority, because adherence to the Convention would entail such a substantial change in the Community human rights system that the modifications produced by adherence "would be of constitutional significance and would therefore be such as to go beyond the scope of Article 235." There is little likelihood of Treaty amendment followed by accession, because EU Member States are reluctant to turn over to the larger membership of the Council of Europe the task of balancing individual rights with Community economic and general interests.

The Treaty of Amsterdam nonetheless somewhat strengthens the ECJ's jurisdiction over human rights. Article 46(d), as noted above, confers jurisdiction on the Court to review the acts of the institutions for conformity with Article 6, which requires that the Union respect fundamental rights. The Court is required to ensure that the law is observed in the interpretation and application of the Treaty. Article 46 also expressly enables the Court to examine the compatibility of "action of the institutions" with fundamental rights in regard to police and judicial cooperation in criminal matters.

For most subject areas, the Court's jurisdiction rests on Article 220. This provision allows the Court to examine the compatibility of Member States' legislation with the fundamental rights protected within the Community legal order when such legislation implements Community rules or relies upon Community law to justify national measures affecting the common market. Several exceptions are provided to exclude matters from the Court's jurisdiction, especially as they relate to policing and internal security measures. These subjects may be reviewable by the European Court of Human Rights, but the Court has been deferential to the Community in most of its decisions, finding that the European Community is itself a legal system that secures fundamental rights and provides for control of their observance. Where such control is lacking because the ECJ lacks jurisdiction, the European Court of Human Rights may be more willing to exercise its own jurisdiction to protect human rights.

Although the Treaty of European Union was not amended in the manner the Court suggested (to allow adhesion to the European Convention), the EU decided in June 1999 to draft a European Charter of Fundamental Rights to cover all rights that pertain to the Union's citizens, in effect combining the guarantees of the European Convention on Human Rights, the European Social Charter, and other human rights instruments. The Charter was proclaimed at the meeting of the Council of the European Union in Nice on December 18, 2000, but it was not adopted as a treaty, due to lack of agreement among the Member States. However, the European Parliament has recommended that it be incorporated into the EU Treaty and the Commission has agreed. The Commission's opinion is that the Charter may be regarded at present, even by the ECJ, as an important source of binding principles of fundamental rights....

[The article goes on to summarize the norms found in the Charter, which include a broad range of civil, political, economic, social, and cultural rights.]

In sum, human rights find protection in the EU today through the revised TEU, the jurisprudence of the ECJ, and to some extent, the Charter of Fundamental Rights. Other EC institutions also act in regard to human rights. The EC signs OSCE documents through its president and EC employees sometimes participate in OSCE meetings as delegation members. In addition, the Parliament's Human Rights Sub-Committee produces an annual report on human rights in countries throughout the world....

The Organization for Security and Cooperation in Europe

The Organization for Security and Cooperation in Europe (OSCE), formerly the Conference on Security and Cooperation in Europe (CSCE), has taken on broad human rights functions in Europe. With the participation of the United States and Canada the OSCE is a transatlantic institution. Emerging from efforts to lessen Cold War hostilities, the CSCE opened at Helsinki in July 1973 and concluded two years later with the adoption of the Helsinki Final Act. The Final Act is not a treaty but sets forth political commitments in the areas of security, cooperation and human rights. The Helsinki Final Act (HFA), adopted Aug. 1, 1975, brought human rights into the context of regional peace and security. The HFA consists of four chapters or "baskets." Basket I, entitled "Questions Relating to Security in Europe," consists of two sections ("Principles Guiding Relations Between Participating States," and "Confidence-Building Measures and Certain Aspects of Security and Disarmament"). Basket II deals with "Cooperation in the Field of Economics, of Science and Technology and of the Environment." The subject of Basket III is "Cooperation in Humanitarian and Other Fields." Basket IV, the final chapter of the instrument, spells out the so-called "follow-up" process.

Human rights issues are addressed primarily in the Guiding Principles proclaimed in Basket I and to some extent in Basket III. Of the 10 Guiding Principles set out in the HFA, two deal with human rights. In Principle VII, the participating States undertake to "respect human rights and fundamental freedoms" and to "promote and encourage the effective exercise of civil, political, economic, social, cultural and other rights and freedoms . . . ", respect freedom of religion, the rights of individuals belonging to national minorities, and the "right of the individual to know and act upon his rights and duties in this field." In the last paragraph of Principle VII, the participating States agree to "act in conformity with the purposes and principles of the Charter of the United Nations and with the Universal Declaration of Human Rights. They will also fulfill their obligations as set forth in the international declarations and agreements in this field, including inter alia the International Covenants on Human Rights, by which they may be bound. Principle VIII for its part devotes four paragraphs to the subject of "equal rights and self-determination of peoples."

The various follow-up meetings to the Helsinki Conference strengthened human rights protections, sometimes adding details not found in other regional or global instruments. Follow-up conferences have been held in Madrid (1983), Vienna (1989), Copenhagen (1990) and Budapest (1994). The Madrid meeting focused on the issue of trade union freedoms in light of the advent of the Solidarity movement in Poland. Specific and detailed guarantees regarding freedom of religion, non-discrimination, minority rights, freedom of movement, conditions of detention and capital punishment were added at the Vienna meeting. Copenhagen also resulted in considerable human rights standard-setting, especially concerning national minorities. It was also one of the first documents to refer to the right of conscientious objection to military service, a right not contained in the European Convention on Human Rights. The follow-up conferences also have been used to review compliance with human rights commitments, develop a mechanism for expanding the list of guaranteed rights, and focus public attention on the failure of certain states to live up to their human rights commitments. In this context, various CSCE meetings have made specific references to and commitments regarding national minorities.

The Vienna Concluding Document established the Human Dimension Mechanism for dealing with the non-observance by states of their human dimension commitments. Subsequent OSCE conferences have expanded the scope of the Mechanism in order to make it more effective. It is now a process of bilateral and multilateral negotiations which obliges participating states to respond to requests for information and allows states to bring situations and cases to the attention of other participating states. Thus, when one or more states claim that another state is not living up to its OSCE commitments regarding the human dimension, a diplomatic exchange between the states concerned follows, for which specific time-limits are provided. If the matter is not resolved between them, a state may bring it to the attention of all OSCE states and place the matter on the agenda of OSCE follow-up or human dimension conferences. In addition, the Moscow Mechanism allows appointment of OSCE expert missions or rapporteur missions to investigate questions or problems relating to the human dimension. The Mission may be invited by the state concerned or initiated at the request of six or more participating states. In emergency situations, a participating state may request a meeting of the OSCE Senior Council, which may take action. Finally, an early warning mechanism allows either state involved in a dispute, a group of eleven states not involved in the dispute, the High Commissioner on National Minorities, or the Permanent Council to draw the attention of the Senior Council to any situation having the potential to develop into a crisis. In 1992, the CSCE established the office of the High Commissioner on National Minorities (HCNM) in order to address potential conflicts posed by minority issues [discussed in Chapter 5]...

Still without a constituting treaty, the OSCE tends to focus on human rights issues primarily through diplomatic intervention for conflict-prevention and mediation. The OSCE has also been engaged in developing regional democracy, linking it with human rights. An Office for Democratic Institutions and Human Rights, established in Warsaw, assists the democratization process in OSCE states and monitors the implementation of OSCE commitments regarding the human dimension. Parallel to the OSCE efforts, the Council of Europe created a program in 1990 to strengthen democracy and to facilitate the integration of new Member States into the Council of Europe.

The success of the HCNM led the OSCE in 1997 to establish the post of Representative on Freedom of the Media ("Representative") in order to address "serious problems caused by, inter alia, obstruction of media activities and unfavourable working conditions for journalists." The Representative acts as an advocate, observing relevant media developments in OSCE participating states and promoting compliance with OSCE principles and commitments regarding freedom of expression and free media, including the use of hate speech. The Representative also provides early warning on violations of freedom of expression, concentrating on rapid response to serious non-compliance with OSCE principles and commitments by participating states. Where problems arise, the Representative seeks direct contacts with the participating state and other parties involved, assesses the facts and tries to resolve the issue. The Representative reports to the Permanent Council, recommending further action where appropriate....

The political character of OSCE commitments precludes judicial enforcement or complaints procedures, but allows rapid response in periods of crisis.

Comments and Questions

1. The European Union is an economic-political institution; the Organization for Security and Cooperation in Europe is a loose political gathering of 55 states with very different political orientations. Should either organization be expected to play a major role in enforcing international human rights law? In promoting human rights principles? In at least ensuring that its actions and decisions are consistent with human rights norms?

2. The OSCE has been most effective in the human rights field in promoting minority rights and democratic rights, such as free expression and free and fair elections. Is this because such rights are more "political" than, e.g., the prohibition of torture or the right to education, and thus more appropriate to be addressed through the mechanisms of the OSCE?

3. Many NGOs have also been active in trying to promote human rights as part of the transition to more democratic governments in central and Eastern Europe. Particularly notable is the work of the Open Society Institute's EU Monitoring and Advocacy Program (formerly the EU Acession Monitoring Program), *http://www.eumap.org.*

IV. Final Comments and Questions

1. The draft European Constitution foresees ratification of the European Convention on Human Rights by the European Union. What impact would this be likely to have on the two organizations?

2. The various European human rights institutions (particularly the Council of Europe) have been the subject of a great deal of scholarly writing. Among works that give a broad overview of procedural and substantive law, see Kevin Boyle, "Council of Europe, OSCE, and European Union," in *Guide to International Human Rights Practice* 143 (4th ed. Hurst Hannum ed., 2004); Pieter van Dijk, *Theory and Practice of the European Convention on Human Rights* (3d ed. 1998); D.J. Harris, M. O'Boyle, and C. Warbrick, *Law of the European Convention on Human Rights* (1995); Mark W. Janis, Richard S. Kay, Anthony W. Bradley, and A. W. Bradley, *European Human Rights Law: Text and Materials* (2001); Alistair Mowbray, A.R. Mowbray, and David Harris, *Cases and Materials on the European Convention on Human Rights* (2005); Clare Ovey, Robin C.A. White, and Francis Geoffrey Jacobs: *European Convention on Human Rights* (3d ed. 2002).

On the European Social Charter, see, e.g., Grainne de Burca, Bruno de Witte, and Larissa Ogertschnig, *Social Rights in Europe* (2005); Council of Europe, *Fundamental Social Rights: Case Law of the European Social Charter* (1997); id., *Digest of the Case Law of the ECSR* (2005), *http://www.coe.int/T/F/Droits_de_27Homme/Cse/Digest_bil_mars_05.pdf;* David Harris, *The European Social Charter* (2d ed. 2001).

On the European Union, see, e.g., Paul Kubicek, *The European Union and Democratization* (2003); Nannette Neuwahl, *The European Union and Human Rights* (1995); *The EU and Human Rights* (Philip Alston ed., 1999); Andrew Williams, *EU Human Rights Policies: A Study in Irony* (2004).

On the OSCE, see OSCE Office for Democratic Institutions and Human Rights, *Individual Human Rights Complaints: A Handbook for OSCE Field Personnel* (2003); id., *OSCE Human Dimension Commitments: A Reference Guide* (2001).

On minority rights in Europe, see, e.g., Council of Europe, *Mechanisms for the Implementation of Minority Rights* 83-202 (2004); Gaetano Pentassuglia, *Minorities in International Law* 119-58 (2002); Walter A. Kemp, *Quiet Diplomacy in Action: The OSCE High Commissioner on National Minorities* (2001); *Minority Rights in Europe: European Minorities and Languages* (Snezana Trifunovska and Fernand de Varennes eds., 2003); *Rights of Minorities: A Commentary on the European Framework Convention for the Protection of National Minorities* (Marc Weller ed., 2005).

Chapter 9

Human Rights in the Americas

Responding to Disappearances in Argentina

I. Human Rights in Argentina

The phenomenon of forced or involuntary "disappearance" is not new, but it became the subject of widespread attention in the 1970s and 1980s, particularly in Latin America. Disappearance poses particular hardship for the relatives and friends of the missing person; they live in a state of uncertainty for years and sometimes decades, not knowing the fate or whereabouts of their loved one. Disappearance also poses problems for human rights inter-governmental and non-governmental human rights bodies, because it is designed to conceal and destroy all evidence that would connect the perpetrators to the victims. This chapter examines the practice of the Inter-American Human Rights system in addressing human rights violations, by focusing on the problem of disappearances in Argentina.

Inter-American Commission on Human Rights, Report on the Situation of Human Rights in Argentina

OAS Doc. OEA/Ser.L/V/II.49, doc. 19, corr. 1, April 11, 1980, pp. 14-15, 18-19, 21, 53-56

A long phase of political and social instability began in Argentina in 1930. It gave rise to institutional crises, the establishment of irregular or de facto governments, an internal state of war, state of siege and martial law, attempts at totalitarian or joint rule, changes in the organization of state powers, enactment of repressive legislation and especially in the last ten years, an abrupt increase in terrorist violence by the extreme left and the extreme right, as a means of armed conflict. All of this has been detrimental to the rule of law.

In the last fifty years only two governments have completed their constitutional mandate: that of General Agustin P. Justo, 1932 to 1938, and that of

General Juan Domingo Peron, 1946-1952. Military takeovers have prevented the completion of the other legal mandates during that same period and since 1952 [until 1980], no government has completed its constitutional term of office.

Such conditions have had a direct effect on the constitutional legal order and have made it difficult to realize the representative and republican form of government provided for in Article 1 of the Constitution.

The political organization of the Argentine State... has been substantially altered by the military takeover of March 24, 1976, the date on which the Armed Forces, "in view of the current state of the country," proceeded to "take over the reins of Government of the Republic" in accordance with a public proclamation. To achieve this, they resolved to adopt measures concerning the organization and operation of the state authorities. In the Act for the National Reorganization Process the following measures were included: a) to establish a military junta with the General Commanders of the Armed Forces, "which shall assume the political power of the Republic," b) to declare the terms of office of the President and of the Governors and Vice Governors of the provinces to be null and void, c) to dissolve the National Congress, the provincial legislature, the House of Representatives of the city of Buenos Aires and the Municipal Councils of the provinces or similar bodies, d) to remove the members of the Supreme Court, the Attorney General and the other members of the higher provincial courts, and e) to appoint the citizen who shall serve as President....

With the military takeover of 1976, the constitutional system was altered by the new Government, by provisions which affect the full observance and exercise of human rights, despite the fact that in the Act issued on March 24 of that year, in which the purpose and basic objectives for the National Reorganization Process were set forth, a prime objective was "the validity of Christian moral values, national tradition and the dignity of the Argentine" and "a full enforcement of the juridical and social system."

When the change of government occurred in March 1976, the country was in a state of siege, pursuant to Article 23 of the Constitution, which made possible implementation of severe national security measures in order to eradicate subversion...

By virtue of the Institutional Act of June 18, 1976, the Military Junta assumed "the power and responsibility to consider the actions of those individuals who have injured the national interest," but on grounds as generic as "failure to observe basic moral principles in the exercise of public, political or union offices or activities that involve the public interest." Based on that Act, a number of special laws have been enacted, which, because of the discretionary nature of the powers granted, have led to the use of arbitrary measures, which have been the cause of intimidation and uncertainty....

During [1976-1979], the IACHR... received a large number of claims affecting a considerable number of persons in Argentina. These claims allege that said persons have been apprehended either in their homes, their jobs, or on the public thoroughfares, by armed men, who are occasionally in uniform, in operations and under conditions that indicate, due to the characteristics in which they are carried out, that they are conducted by agents of the State. After these actions have occurred, the persons apprehended disappear, and nothing is ever known of their whereabouts....

The Commission has in its files, lists with names, dates, and other data, as well as several studies that have been carried out regarding this problem. Without giving, for the time being, exact figures on the number of these disappeared persons, the information obtained makes it clear that there exists a situation of extreme irregularity requiring special discussion and analysis....

In ... denunciations or claims received by the IACHR it has been reported that the armed groups that carry out the operations in the homes apprehend the victim and occasionally his spouse and children, carry out a search of the home, looting the belongings of the residents, and as a general rule, take away all members of the family after placing hoods over their heads and eyes.

The persons affected by these operations, included in the lists at the IACHR, are mostly men and women between 20 and 30 years of age, although older persons and minors have also been known to disappear. Some of the children, kidnapped with their parents, have been released and delivered to relatives or have been abandoned in the streets. Other children, however, continue to be listed among the disappeared.

According to the Commission's information the phenomenon of the disappeared affects professionals, students, union workers, employees in various areas of business, journalists, religious leaders, military recruits and business men; in other words, most elements of Argentine society.

II. Evolution of the Human Rights System in the Americas

The Inter-American system as it exists today began with the transformation of the Pan American Union, which dates back to the nineteenth century, into the Organization of American States (OAS). Article 3 of the OAS Charter proclaims the "fundamental rights of the individual" as one of the Organization's basic principles (Documentary Supplement, page xxx).* Concern with human rights not only inspired the Organization of American States to refer to human rights in its Charter but led it to adopt the Inter-American Declaration on the Rights and Duties of Man in May 1948, half a year before the United Nations completed the Universal Declaration of Human Rights.

The Commission may prepare country reports and conduct on-site visits to individual countries, examining the human rights situation in the particular country and making recommendations to the government. Country reports have been prepared on the Commission's own initiative and at the request of the country concerned. The Commission also may appoint special rapporteurs to prepare studies on hemisphere-wide problems.

Like the European system, the Inter-American system has expanded its protections over time through the adoption of additional human rights norms. The major additional instruments are the following:

> American Convention on Human Rights (1969); Inter-American Convention for the Prevention and Punishment of Torture (1985); Additional Protocol to the American

* The OAS Charter has been amended by four protocols: Buenos Aires (1967), Cartagena de Indias (1985), Washington (1992), and Managua (1993).

Convention on Human Rights in the Area of Economic, Social and Cultural Rights (1988); Second Additional Protocol to the American Convention on Human Rights to Abolish the Death Penalty (1990);
Inter-American Convention on the Prevention, Punishment, and Eradication of Violence against Women (1994); Inter-American Convention on Forced Disappearance of Persons (1994); and
Inter-American Convention on The Elimination Of All Forms Of Discrimination Against Persons With Disabilities (1999).

The Commission has been given competence over matters relating to the fulfillment of obligations undertaken by states parties to all human rights conventions adopted in the regional framework, with the exception of the Convention on Persons with Disabilities, which creates a separate supervisory committee.

The early history and basic structure of the inter-American system is summarized in the following extract.

Cecelia Medina, "The Inter-American Commission on Human Rights and the Inter-American Court of Human Rights: Reflections on a Joint Venture"

12 Hum. Rts. Q. 439-447 (1990)

The Inter-American Commission on Human Rights was . . . originally conceived as a study group concerned with abstract investigations in the field of human rights. However, the creators of the Commission did not foresee the appeal this organ would have for the individual victims of human rights violations. As soon as it was known that the Commission had been created, individuals began to send complaints about human rights problems in their countries. Prompted by these complaints, the Commission started its activities with the conviction that in order to promote human rights it had to protect them.

A significant part of the Commission's work was addressing the problem of countries with gross, systematic violations of human rights, characterized by an absence or a lack of effective national mechanisms for the protection of human rights and a lack of cooperation on the part of the governments concerned. The main objective of the Commission was not to investigate isolated violations but to document the existence of these gross, systematic violations and to exercise pressure to improve the general condition of human rights in the country concerned. For this purpose, and by means of its regulatory powers, the Commission created a procedure to "take cognizance" of individual complaints and use them as a source of information about gross, systematic violations of human rights in the territories of the OAS member states.

The Commission's competence to handle individual communications was formalized in 1965, after the OAS reviewed and was satisfied with the Commission's work. The OAS passed Resolution XXII, which allowed the Commission to "examine" isolated human rights violations, with a particular focus on certain rights. This procedure, however, provided many obstacles for the Commission. Complaints could be handled only if domestic remedies had been exhausted, a requirement that prevented swift reactions to violations. Also, the procedure made the Commission more dependent on the governments for information. This resulted in the governments' either not answering the Commission's requests for information or answering with a blanket denial that did not contribute to a satisfactory solution of the problem.

Furthermore, once the Commission had given its opinion on the case, there was nothing else to be done; the Commission would declare that a government had violated the American Declaration of the Rights and Duties of Man and recommend the government take certain measures, knowing that this was unlikely to resolve the situation. The fact that some of the Commission's opinions could reach the political bodies of the OAS did not solve the problem, because thee Commission's opinions on individual cases were never discussed at that level. Consequently, in order not to lose the flexibility it had, the Commission interpreted Resolution XXII as granting the Commission power to "examine" communications concerning individual violations of certain rights specified in the resolution without diminishing its power to "take cognizance" of communications concerning the rest of the human rights protected by the American Declaration. The Commission preserved this broader power for the purposes of identifying gross, systematic human rights violations.

The procedure to "take cognizance" of communications evolved and became the general case procedure and was later used in examining the general human rights situation in a country. This procedure, maturing with the Commission's practice, had several positive characteristics in view of the Commission's purposes. First, it could be started without checking whether the communications met any admissibility requirements or even in the absence of any communication. All that was necessary was for news to reach the Commission that serious violations were taking place in the territory of an OAS member state. Second, the Commission assumed a very active role by requesting and gathering information by telegram and telephone from witnesses, newspapers, and experts, and also requesting consent to visit the country at the Commission's convenience. Third, the Commission could publicize its findings in order to put pressure upon the governments. Finally, the report resulting from the investigation could be sent to the political bodies of the OAS, thereby allowing for a political discussion of the problem which, at least theoretically, could be followed by political measures against the governments involved.

Since financial and human resources were limited, the Commission concentrated all its efforts on the examination of the general situation of human rights in each country. The examination of individual cases clearly took a secondary place, The Commission appeared to process them only because it had a duty to do so and not because of a conviction that its intervention would be helpful. After all, the special procedure for individual cases did not improve the victims' possibilities for redress, and the Commission could attempt to solve the cases through an examination of the general human rights situation in the country.

In short, the Commission was the sole guarantor of human rights in a continent plagued with gross, systematic violations, and the Commission was part of an international organization for which human rights were definitely not the first priority, and these facts made an imprint on the way the Commission looked upon its task. Apparently, the Commission viewed itself more as an international organ with a highly political task to perform than as a technical body whose main task was to participate in the first phase of a quasi-judicial supervision of the observance of human rights. The Commission's past made it ill-prepared to efficiently utilize the additional powers the [1969] Convention [on Human Rights] subsequently granted it. . . .

The Commission's functions [now] include: (1) promoting human rights in all OAS member states; (2) assisting in the drafting of human rights documents; (3) advising member states of the OAS; (4) preparing country reports, which usually include visits to the territories of these states; (5) mediating disputes over serious human rights problems; (6) handling individual complaints and initiating individual cases on its own motion, both with regard to states parties and states not parties to the Convention; and (7) participating in the handling of cases and advisory opinions before the Court. . . .

The Inter-American Court consists of seven judges irrespective of the number of states that have recognized the jurisdiction of the Court. Although the Court is formally an organ of the Convention and not of the OAS, its judges may be nationals of any member state of the OAS whether or not they are parties to the Convention

The Court has contentious and advisory jurisdiction. In exercising its contentious jurisdiction, the Court settles controversies about the interpretation and application of the provisions of the American Convention through a special procedure designed to handle individual or state complaints against states patties to the Convention. Under its advisory jurisdiction, the Court may interpret not only the Convention but also any other treaty concerning the protection of human rights in the American states. The Court may also give its opinion regarding the compatibility of the domestic laws of any OAS member state with the requirements of the Convention or any human rights treaties to which the Convention refers. In addition, the Court is not prevented from giving its opinion regarding any question relating to the content or scope of the rights defined in the Convention or any question that might have to be considered by the Court in the exercise of its contentious jurisdiction or by the Commission's supervision of human rights. The advisory jurisdiction of the Court may be set in motion by any OAS member state, whether or not it is a party to the Convention, or by any OAS organ listed in Chapter X of the OAS Charter, which includes the Commission.

The Court may consider a case that is brought either by the Commission or by a state party to the Convention. For the Commission to refer a case to the Court, the case must have been admitted for investigation and the Commission's draft report sent to the state party. In addition, the state must recognize the Court's general contentious jurisdiction or a limited jurisdiction specified by a time period or case. For a state party to be able to place a case before the Court, the only requirement is that both states must have recognized the Court's contentious jurisdiction.

During the proceedings, the Court has powers to investigate the facts as it deems necessary. The Court ordinarily concludes its consideration of a case by issuing a judgment. If the Court finds that there has been a violation of a right or freedom protected by the Convention, it shall rule "that the injured party, be ensured the enjoyment of his right or freedom that was violated." If appropriate, it may also rule that "the consequences of the measure or situation that constituted the breach of such a right or freedom be remedied and that fair compensation be paid to the injured party." States are under the international obligation to comply with the judgment of the Court in any case to which they are parties. The part of the judgment that stipulates compensatory damages has executory force in the state concerned.

If a state does not comply with the decision of the Court, the Court may inform and make recommendations to the OAS General Assembly. There is no reference in the Convention to any action that the General Assembly might take; the assembly, being a political body, may take any political action it deems necessary to persuade the state to comply with its international obligations.

Although the procedures are essentially similar, the Commission technically has two bases of jurisdiction: all OAS member states are expected to conform to the norms of the American Declaration on the Rights and Duties of Man, while those states that have ratified the American Convention on Human Rights are bound additionally by its provisions. As noted by Medina, acceptance of the jurisdiction of the Inter-American Court of Human Rights, which was created under the convention, is optional.

The following opinion discusses the status of the American Declaration and the Court's role in interpreting it.

Inter-American Court of Human Rights, *Interpretation of the American Declaration of the Rights and Duties of Man within the Framework of Article 64 of the American Convention on Human Rights*

Advisory Opinion OC-10/89, July 14, 1989, Inter-Am. Ct. H.R. (Ser. A) No. 10 (1989), reprinted in Annual Report 1989, at 109, O.A.S. Doc. OEA/Ser.L/V/III, Doc. 14 (1989) (some references omitted)

1. By note of February 17, 1988, the Government of the Republic of Colombia . . . submitted to the Inter-American Court of Human Rights a request for an advisory opinion on the interpretation of Article 64 of the American Convention on Human Rights . . . in relation to the American Declaration of the Rights and Duties of Man. . . .

2. The Government requests a reply to the following question:

> Does Article 64 authorize the Inter-American Court of Human Rights to render advisory opinions at the request of a member state or one of the organs of the OAS, regarding the interpretation of the American Declaration of the Rights and Duties of Man, adopted by the Ninth International Conference of American States in Bogota in 1948?

The Government adds:

> "The Government of Colombia understands, of course, that the Declaration is not a treaty. But this conclusion does not automatically answer the question. It is perfectly reasonable to assume that the interpretation of the human rights provisions contained in the Charter of the OAS, as revised by the Protocol of Buenos Aires, involves, in principle, an analysis of the rights and duties of man proclaimed by the Declaration,

> and thus requires the determination of the normative status of the Declaration within the legal framework of the inter-American system for the protection of human rights."

The applicant Government points out that

> "for the appropriate functioning of the inter-American system for the protection of human rights, it is of great importance to know what the juridical status of the Declaration is, whether the Court has jurisdiction to interpret the Declaration, and if so, what the scope of its jurisdiction is within the framework of Article 64 of the Convention." . . .

4. By note of March 2, 1988, pursuant to Article 52 of the Court's Rules of Procedure, the Secretariat requested written observations on the question from all the member states of the Organization of American States . . . , and through the Secretary General, from the organs listed in Article 51 of the Charter of the OAS, or Article 52 of the Charter as revised by the Protocol of Cartagena de Indias, after its entry into force for the ratifying states. . . .

11. In its written observations, the Government of Costa Rica "believes that notwithstanding its great success and nobility, the American Declaration of the Rights and Duties of Man is not a treaty as defined by international law, so Article 64 of the American Convention does not authorize the Inter-American Court to interpret the Declaration. Nevertheless, that could not in any way limit the Court's possible use of the Declaration and its precepts to interpret other, related juridical instruments or a finding that many of the rights recognized therein have become international customary law."

12. The Government of the United States of America believes: "The American Declaration of the Rights and Duties of Man represents a noble statement of the human rights aspirations of the American States. Unlike the American Convention, however, it was not drafted as a legal instrument and lacks the precision necessary to resolve complex legal questions. Its normative value lies as a declaration of basic moral principles and broad political commitments and as a basis to review the general human rights performance of member states, not as a binding set of obligations. The United States recognizes the good intentions of those who would transform the American Declaration from a statement of principles into a binding legal instrument. But good intentions do not make law. It would seriously undermine the process of international lawmaking — by which sovereign states voluntarily undertake specified legal obligations — to impose legal obligations on states through a process of "reinterpretation" or "inference" from a non-binding statement of principles."

13. For its part, the Government of Peru said that "although the Declaration could have been considered an instrument without legal effect before the American Convention on Human Rights entered into force, the Convention has recognized its special nature by virtue of Article 29, which prohibits any interpretation 'excluding or limiting the effect that the American Declaration of the Rights and Duties of Man and other international acts of the same nature may have' and has thus given the Declaration a hierarchy similar to that of the Convention with regard to the States Parties, thereby contributing to the promotion of human rights in our continent."

14. The Government of Uruguay affirmed that

> i) The Inter-American Court of Human Rights is competent to render advisory opinions on any aspect of the American Declaration of the Rights and Duties of Man in relation to the revised Charter of the Organization of American States and the American Convention on Human Rights, within the scope of Article 64 of the latter.
>
> ii) The juridical nature of the Declaration is that of a binding, multilateral instrument that enunciates, defines and specifies fundamental principles recognized by the American States and which crystallizes norms of customary law generally accepted by those States.

15. The Government of Venezuela asserted that

> as a general principle recognized by international law, a declaration is not a treaty in the true sense because it does not create juridical norms, and it is limited to a statement of desires or exhortations. A declaration creates political or moral obligations for the subjects of international law, and its enforceability is thus limited in contrast to a treaty, whose legal obligations are enforceable before a jurisdictional body.
>
> The Government recognizes that the Declaration is not a treaty in the strict sense. The Court will surely ratify this position, and it should also decide that it is not competent to interpret the American Declaration of the Rights and Duties of Man adopted in Bogota in 1948, given that the Declaration is not a treaty "concerning the protection of human rights in the American states," as required by Article 64 of the American Convention on Human Rights. . . .

29. The Court will now address the merits of the question before it.

30. Article 64(1) of the Convention authorizes the Court to render advisory opinions "regarding the interpretation of this Convention or of other treaties concerning the protection of human rights in the American states." That is, the object of the advisory opinions of the Court is treaties. . . .

31. According to the Vienna Convention on the Law of Treaties of 1969

> 'treaty' means an international agreement concluded between States in written form and governed by international law, whether embodied in a single instrument or in two or more related instruments and whatever its particular designation (Art. 2(1)(a)).

32. The Vienna Convention of 1986 on the Law of Treaties among States and International Organizations or among International Organizations provides as follows in Article 2(1)(a):

> 'treaty' means an international agreement governed by international law and concluded in written form:
>
> (i) between one or more States and one or more international organizations; or
> (ii) between international organizations,
>
> whether that agreement is embodied in a single instrument or in two or more related instruments and whatever its particular designation.

33. In attempting to define the word "treaty" as the term is employed in Article 64(1), it is sufficient for now to say that a "treaty" is, at the very least, an international instrument of the type that is governed by the two Vienna Con-

ventions. Whether the term includes other international instruments of a conventional nature whose existence is also recognized by those Conventions (Art. 3, Vienna Convention of 1969; Art. 3, Vienna Convention of 1986), need not be decided at this time. What is clear, however, is that the Declaration is not a treaty as defined by the Vienna Conventions because it was not approved as such, and that, consequently, it is also not a treaty within the meaning of Article 64(1).

34. Here it must be recalled that the American Declaration was adopted by the Ninth International Conference of American States (Bogotá, 1948) through a resolution adopted by the Conference itself. It was neither conceived nor drafted as a treaty....

35. The mere fact that the Declaration is not a treaty does not necessarily compel the conclusion that the Court lacks the power to render an advisory opinion containing an interpretation of the American Declaration.

36. In fact, the American Convention refers to the Declaration in paragraph three of its Preamble which reads as follows:

> Considering that these principles have been set forth in the Charter of the Organization of the American States, in the American Declaration of the Rights and Duties of Man, and in the Universal Declaration of Human Rights, and that they have been reaffirmed and refined in other international instruments, worldwide as well as regional in scope.

And in Article 29(d) which indicates:

> Restrictions Regarding Interpretation
> No provision of this convention shall be interpreted as:...
> d. excluding or limiting the effect that the American Declaration of the Rights and Duties of Man and other international acts of the same nature may have.

From the foregoing, it follows that, in interpreting the Convention in the exercise of its advisory jurisdiction, the Court may have to interpret the Declaration.

37. The American Declaration has its basis in the idea that "the international protection of the rights of man should be the principal guide of an evolving American law." This American law has evolved from 1948 to the present; international protective measures, subsidiary and complementary to national ones, have been shaped by new instruments. As the International Court of Justice said: "an international instrument must be interpreted and applied within the overall framework of the juridical system in force at the time of the interpretation" *(Legal Consequences for States of the Continued Presence of South Africa in Namibia (South West Africa) notwithstanding Security Council Resolution* 276 *(1970)*, Advisory Opinion, I.C.J. Reports 1971, p. 16 ad 31). That is why the Court finds it necessary to point out that to determine the legal status of the American Declaration it is appropriate to look to the inter-American system of today in the light of the evolution it has undergone since the adoption of the Declaration, rather than to examine the normative value and significance which that instrument was believed to have had in 1948.

38. The evolution of the here relevant "inter-American law" mirrors on the regional level the developments in contemporary international law and especially in human rights law, which distinguished that law from classical international law

to a significant extent. That is the case, for example, with the duty to respect certain essential human rights, which is today considered to be an erga omnes obligation (*Barcelona Traction, Light and Power Company, Limited*, Second Phase, Judgment, I.C.J. Reports 1970, p. 3. For an analysis following the same line of thought see also *Legal Consequences for States of the Continued Presence of South Africa in Namibia (South West Africa) notwithstanding Security Council Resolution* 276 (1970) supra 37, p. 16 ad 57; cfr. *United States Diplomatic and Consular Staff in Tehran*, I.C.J. Reports 1980, p. 3 ad 42).

39. The Charter of the Organization refers to the fundamental rights of man in its Preamble ((paragraph three) and in Arts. 3(j), 16, 43, 47, 51, 112 and 150; Preamble (paragraph four), Arts. 3(k), 16, 44, 48, 52, 111 and 150 of the Charter revised by the Protocol of Cartagena de Indias), but it does not list or define them. The member states of the Organization have, through its diverse organs, given specificity to the human rights mentioned in the Charter and to which the Declaration refers.

40. This is the case of Article 112 of the Charter (Art. 111 of the Charter as amended by the Protocol of Cartagena de Indias) which reads as follows:

> There shall be an Inter-American Commission on Human Rights, whose principal function shall be to promote the observance and protection of human rights and to serve as a consultative organ of the Organization in these matters. An inter-American convention on human rights shall determine the structure, competence, and procedure of this Commission, as well as those of other organs responsible for these matters.

Article 150 of the Charter provides as follows:

> Until the inter-American convention on human rights, referred to in Chapter XVIII (Chapter XVI of the Charter as amended by the Protocol of Cartagena de Indias), enters into force, the present Inter-American Commission on Human Rights shall keep vigilance over the observance of human rights.

41. These norms authorize the Inter-American Commission to protect human rights. These rights are none other than those enunciated and defined in the American Declaration. That conclusion results from Article 1 of the Commission's Statute, which was approved by Resolution No. 447, adopted by the General Assembly of the OAS at its Ninth Regular Period of Sessions, held in La Paz, Bolivia, in October, 1979. That Article reads as follows:

> 1. The Inter-American Commission on Human Rights is an organ of the Organization of the American States, created to promote the observance and defense of human rights and to serve as consultative organ of the Organization in this matter.
> 2. For the purposes of the present Statute, human rights are understood to be:
> a. The rights set forth in the American Convention on Human Rights, in relation to the States Parties thereto;
> b. The rights set forth in the American Declaration of the Rights and Duties of Man, in relation to the other member states.

Articles 18, 19 and 20 of the Statute enumerate these functions.

42. The General Assembly of the Organization has also repeatedly recognized that the American Declaration is a source of international obligations for the

member states of the OAS. For example, in Resolution 314 (VII-O/77) of June 22, 1977, it charged the Inter-American Commission with the preparation of a study to "set forth their obligation to carry out the commitments assumed in the American Declaration of the Rights and Duties of Man." In Resolution 371 (VIII-O/78) of July 1, 1978, the General Assembly reaffirmed "its commitment to promote the observance of the American Declaration of the Rights and Duties of Man," and in Resolution 370 (VIII-O/78) of July 1, 1978, it referred to the "international commitments" of a member state of the Organization to respect the rights of man "recognized in the American Declaration of the Rights and Duties of Man." The Preamble of the American Convention to Prevent and Punish Torture, adopted and signed at the Fifteenth Regular Session of the General Assembly in Cartagena de Indias (December, 1985), reads as follows:

> Reaffirming that all acts of torture or any other cruel, inhuman, or degrading treatment or punishment constitute an offense against human dignity and a denial of the principles set forth in the Charter of the Organization of American States and in the Charter of the United Nations and are violations of the fundamental human rights and freedoms proclaimed in the American Declaration of the Rights and Duties of Man and the Universal Declaration of Human Rights.

43. Hence it may be said that by means of an authoritative interpretation, the member states of the Organization have signaled their agreement that the Declaration contains and defines the fundamental human rights referred to in the Charter. Thus the Charter of the Organization cannot be interpreted and applied as far as human rights are concerned without relating its norms, consistent with the practice of the organs of the OAS, to the corresponding provisions of the Declaration.

44. In view of the fact that the Charter of the Organization and the American Convention are treaties with respect to which the Court has advisory jurisdiction by virtue of Article 64(1), it follows that the Court is authorized, within the framework and limits of its competence, to interpret the American Declaration and to render an advisory opinion relating to it whenever it is necessary to do so in interpreting those instruments.

45. For the member states of the Organization, the Declaration is the text that defines the human rights referred to in the Charter. Moreover, Articles 1(2)(b) and 20 of the Commission's Statute define the competence of that body with respect to the human rights enunciated in the Declaration, with the result that to this extent the American Declaration is for these States a source of international obligations related to the Charter of the Organization.

46. For the States Parties to the Convention, the specific source of their obligations with respect to the protection of human rights is, in principle, the Convention itself. It must be remembered, however, that, given the provisions of Article 29(d), these States cannot escape the obligations they have as members of the OAS under the Declaration, notwithstanding the fact that the Convention is the governing instrument for the States Parties thereto.

47. That the Declaration is not a treaty does not, then, lead to the conclusion that it does not have legal effect, nor that the Court lacks the power to interpret it within the framework of the principles set out above.

Note: Advisory Opinions of the Court

Protocol No. 2 to the European Convention on Human Rights gives the European Court the authority to issue "advisory opinions on legal questions concerning the interpretation of the Convention," upon the request of the Committee of Ministers of the Council of Europe, but under very strict jurisdictional limitations. No such request has ever been made, and, although the power to issue advisory opinions is retained under the reforms of Protocol 11, there seems to be little interest within Europe in utilizing this possibility of expanding the Court's activities. The Inter-American Court of Human Rights, on the other hand, spent most of its first decade issuing advisory opinions, which are authorized by Article 64 of the American Convention. One reason for this is the much broader range of entities authorized to request advisory opinions, which includes all OAS member states, the Commission, and other OAS organs. States accepted the Court's contentious jurisdiction only gradually, and advisory opinions were thus the only "business" the Court could conduct.

As OC-10 indicates, the Court's advisory jurisdiction extends to interpreting "other treaties concerning the protection of human rights in the American states." Despite the potential for conflicting interpretations were the Court to consider non-American instruments, the Court has adopted a broad view of Art. 64 that encompasses "any international treaty applicable in the American States," whether or not OAS members are parties to it, even if the primary object of the treaty is not the protection of human rights. See Advisory Opinion OC-16, *The Right to Information on Consular Assistance* (Oct. 1, 1999). At the same time as this request for an advisory opinion was being considered, the International Court of Justice at the request of Mexico, was hearing the contentious case of *Avena and Other Mexican Nationals (Mexico v. United States)*. Should the Inter-American Court have declined to give the opinion while the I.C.J. case was pending? Note that the I.C.J. declined to rule on the precise question asked of the Inter-American Court, perhaps to avoid an unfortunate conflict of rulings.

Two advisory opinions, in particular, have made a significant contribution to protecting rights during states of emergency by expanding the scope of non-derogable due process rights, such as habeas corpus and amparo. See Inter-Am. Ct. H.R., *Habeas Corpus in Emergency Situations*, Advisory Opinion OC-8/87 of 30 Jan. 1987, Ser. A No. 8, and *Judicial Guarantees in States of Emergency*, OC-9/87 of 6 Oct. 1987 Ser. A No. 9, both of which are dicussed in Chapter 6, page 455.

A state also may request an advisory opinion in order to test the compatibility of its own law with the American Convention, while avoiding the legally binding result that would follow from a judgment by the Court. See Inter-Am. Ct. H.R., *Compulsory Membership in an Association Prescribed by Law for the Practice of Journalism*, OC-5/85 of 13 Nov. 1985, Ser. A No. 5.

On the Court's advisory jurisdiction, see generally Thomas Buergenthal, The OAS and the Protection of Rights, 3 *Emory J. Intl. Dispute Res.* 1, 19-23 (1988); id., The Advisory Practice of the Inter-American Court of Human Rights, 79 *Am. J. Int'l L.* 1 (1985).

Comments and Questions

1. From the extracts of Advisory Opinion OC-10 above, how would you assess the juridical status of the American Declaration? Is it legally binding on member states? If it is binding, why is it binding? Is it customary international law within the region? Does it take on binding qualities because of its link to treaties? Review the discussion of customary law in Chapter 3, pages 152–156.

III. The Response of the System to Disappearances in Argentina

A. *Country Reports*

As noted by Medina, the Inter-American Commission on Human Rights has a number of quite separate functions. In addition to its ability to "take cognizance" of communications, it may "prepare such studies or reports as it considers advisable for the performance of its duties" (American Convention, Article 12; Statute of the Commission, Article 18 (Documentary Supplement CD)). This authority has been utilized to prepare a relatively large number of reports on "the situation of human rights" in particular countries. The reports may be undertaken in response to individual complaints or NGO reports, at the Commission's own initiative, or even at the government's own request (e.g., Panama).

Unless the human rights situation in a country improves, the Commission normally follows up an initial report with subsequent reports. These later reports may focus on particular aspects of human rights, or they may simply update information previously reported. For example, the Commission issued seven reports on Cuba between 1962 and 1983, four reports on Chile between 1975 and 1985, and seven reports on Haiti since 1979. Shorter analyses (perhaps 10-30 pages long) may be included in the Commission's annual report to the OAS General Assembly under the heading "status of human rights in several countries."

The country reports normally include a detailed analysis of the political and legal framework in the country, reports on specific human rights violations, and the Commission's conclusions and recommendations. They are frequently based on on-site investigations by the Commission and its staff, although such visits require the consent of the country concerned. The reports are published and presented to the OAS General Assembly for the latter's information.

The following extracts from the Commission's 1980 report on Argentina give a flavor of the range of issues considered, the Commission's general approach to country reports, and insights into how it conducts on-site investigations.

Inter-American Commission on Human Rights, Report on the Situation of Human Rights in Argentina

OAS Doc. OEA/Ser.L/V/II.49, 11 April 1980, pp. 1-13, 53-56, 116-139.

A. BACKGROUND

1. In recent years, both before and after the March 1976 military takeover, the IACHR has received denunciations of serious violations of human rights in

Argentina, which it has processed according to its regulations. In addition on a number of occasions, it has informed representatives of the Argentine Government of its concern about the increase in the number of denunciations, and about information received from various sources that comprises a pattern of serious, generalized and systematic violations of basic human rights and freedoms.

2. In light of this situation, the IACHR decided to prepare the present report, and when it informed the Argentine Government of this decision, the Commission also advised it of its interest in conducting an on-site observation in Argentina, in the belief that this is the most suitable method of determining precisely and objectively the status of human rights in a particular country at a particular time in history.

3. In a Note dated December 18, 1978, the Argentine Government extended an invitation to the IACHR to conduct an on-site observation, pursuant to its regulations, scheduled, by mutual agreement, for May 1979. However, because of the changes that occurred in the IACHR as a result of the entry into force of the American Convention on Human Rights, it became necessary to postpone the visit, which finally took place from September 6 through 20, 1979.

B. Activities of the Commission During its On-Site Observation

1. A Special Commission was formed pursuant to the pertinent Regulation, and was charged with conducting the on-site observation in Argentina. The Commission consisted of the following members of the Commission: Dr. Andrés Aguilar, Chairman; Dr. Luis Demetrio Tinoco Castro, First Vice Chairman; Dr. Gerardo Monroy Cabra; Professor Carlos A. Dunshee de Abranches; Professor Tom J. Farer, and Dr. Francisco Bertrand Galindo.

The following technical staff of the Executive Secretariat accompanied the Special Commission: Dr. Edmundo Vargas Carreño, Executive Secretary of the Commission; Dr. Edgardo Paz Barnica; Dr. Guillermo Fernández de Soto; Dr. Manuel Velasco Clark and Dr Robert Norris. . . .

2. The on-site observation began on September 6, and was completed on September 20, 1979. The Commission's first step upon arrival in Buenos Aires was to issue a press release. [The press release announced the purpose of the visit: "to conduct an observation of the human rights situation, to receive denunciations of violations of human rights, and to study and examine the situation in order to prepare a report on observance of human rights in Argentina . . ." The Commission announced the addresses of its offices in the press release and invited anyone wishing to state their problems or file denunciations to come forward.]

3. . . . The Commission's activities were conducted as follows, in accordance with the previously approved work schedule:

A. Interviews with Public Authorities

From September 7 through September 20, the Commission met with the President of Argentina, Lieutenant General (Retired) Jorge Rafael Videla; the Military Government Junta, whose members are Lt. Gen. Roberto E. Viola, Brigadier General Omar D. Graffigna and Admiral Armando Lambuschini. The Commission also met with the Minister of the Interior, General Albano

Harguindeguy; the Minister of Foreign Affairs, Brigadier (Retired) Carlos Washington Pastor; the Minister of Justice, Dr. Alberto Rodríguez Varela, and the Minister of Culture and Education, Dr. Juan Rafael Llerena Amadeo.

The Commission also met with the President of the Supreme Court of Justice, Dr. Adolfo Gabrielli, the members of the Federal Chamber of Appeals, presided over by Dr. Raúl Rodríguez Araya, and Federal Judge Dr. Martín Anzoátegui.

During its visit to the city of Córdoba, the Commission met with the Governor of Córdoba, General (Retired) Adolfo Sigwald, the Commandant of the Third Army Corps, General Luciano Benjamín Meléndez, and the Rector of the National University of Córdoba, Dr. Francisco Quintana Ferreira.

In the city of Rosario, the Commission met with the Commandant of the Second Army Corps, General Adolfo Jáuregui, with the Chief of Regional Unit II of the Provincial Police, Lt. Col. Horacio Beradguer, and with Federal Judge Dr. Rafael Carrillo Avila.

It also met with the Chief of the Federal Police, General Juan Bautista Sasiaiñ; the Director of the Federal Penitentiary Service, Colonel Jorge A. Dotti, and with the Chief of Police of the Province of Buenos Aires, General Ovidio P. Ricchieri. Interviews were also conducted with the director of the prisons visited by the Commission.

The members of the Commission explained the objectives of the mission to all these officials, and received offers of full cooperation from the authorities.

B. FORMER PRESIDENTS OF THE REPUBLIC

The Commission felt it advisable to visit all the former presidents of Argentina to discuss the status of human rights in the country. Beginning on Saturday, September 8, the Commission met with Dr. Arturo Frondizi, Lieutenant General (Retired) Roberto M. Levingston; Lieutenant General (Retired) Alejandro Agustín Lanusse, Dr. Héctor J. Cámpora, in asylum in the Embassy of Mexico, and Mrs. Isabel Martínez de Perón, under house arrest in a farm located in San Vicente, Province of Buenos Aires.

Former President Arturo Illía was out of the country and Lieutenant General (Retired) Juan Carlos Onganía excused himself from receiving the Commission.

C. INTERVIEWS WITH MAJOR RELIGIOUS FIGURES

On Wednesday, September 12, the IACHR visited the Cardinal Primate of Argentina, Archbishop of Córdoba and President of the Episcopal Conference of Argentina, at the headquarters of the Episcopal Conference. He stated his views with regard to the situation of human rights in Argentina, and exchanged opinions with the members of the IACHR.

The Commission also had the opportunity to talk with representatives of various religious groups.

D. HUMAN RIGHTS ORGANIZATIONS

In the afternoon of Friday, September 7, the Commission held separate meetings with Argentine human rights organizations, including: the Permanent Assembly for Human Rights; the Argentine League for Human Rights; the Ecumenical Movement for Human Rights; the Mothers of the Plaza de Mayo, and the leaders of the group called Families of "the Disappeared" and Persons detained for Political Reasons (*Familiares de Desaparecidos y Detenidos por Razones Politicas*).

In the days following, the Commission received other groups and delegations from a number of cities in the interior of the country, who had traveled to meet it. These included: the Families of "The Disappeared" from the cities of Mendoza, Rosario and La Plata; the Society of Grandmothers of Disappeared Children; Families of Disappeared Minors; Families of Disappeared and Detained Journalists; Families; Families of Disappeared Conscripts; Families of Disappeared Uruguayans and Chileans, and the Youth Delegation of the Permanent Assembly for Human Rights.

E. REPRESENTATIVES OF POLITICAL ORGANIZATIONS

The Commission held meetings with representatives of the following political organizations: The *Unión Cívica Radical del Pueblo*, Drs. Ricardo Balbín and Raúl Alfonsín; the *Partido Justicialista*, Mr. Deolindo Bittel; the *Confederación Socialista*, Mr. Boris Passik; the *Partido Intransigente*, Messrs. Rafael Marino and May Zubiría; the *Partido Socialista de los Trabajadores*, Mr. Enrique Germán Broquen; the *Partido Comunista*, Mr. Fernando Nadra; the *Federación Demócrata Cristiana*, Messrs. Enrique de Vedia and Francisco Cerro; the *Partido Federalista Argentino*, Mr. Francisco Manrique; the *Partido Socialista Popular*, Mr. Víctor García Costa, and the *Partido Socialista Unificado*, Mr. Simón Alberto Lázara.

Other political groups, such as the "Committee for the Political Defense of Mrs. Perón," and the *Multipartidaria Juvenil*, also met with the Commission.

F. PROFESSIONAL ASSOCIATIONS

The Commission exchanged views with the Argentine Federation of Bar Associations, and with the Buenos Aires Bar Association. These institutions received the Commission in their headquarters on September 8 and September 13, respectively.

The Commission discussed a number of aspects of the legal profession during a visit at its offices from a group of defense lawyers and trade union lawyers.

Meetings were also held with the Central Association of Architects; the Medical Confederation; the Circle of Engineers; the Association of Psychiatrists of the Federal Capital; a group of doctors who had been laid off, the Association of Psychologists of Buenos Aires, and the Psychology Commission for Human Rights.

G. TRADE-UNION ORGANIZATIONS AND SYNDICATES

The Commission met with the Confederations of Education Workers (*Confederación de Trabajadores de la Educación*), and a delegation from the Light and Power Union (*Sindicato de Luz y Fuerza*).

The Commission received the leaders of the *Conducción Única de Trabajadores Argentinos*, "CUTA", an organization that came into being as a result of the merger that occurred at the same time as the Commission's visit, between the *Gremio de los 25* and the *Comisión Nacional de Trabajadores*, "CNT." The first public act of the new trade union organization was its visit to the IACHR.

H. COMMERCIAL, INDUSTRIAL AND BUSINESS ENTITIES

The Commission met with representatives of the following organizations: Comptroller of the Industrial Union; the Rural Society of Argentina; the Junior Chamber of Buenos Aires; the Association of Pulp and Paper Manufacturers; the Argentine Chamber of Commerce; the Federation of Textile Industries of Argentina; the Coordinator of Food Products; the Chamber of Chemical Industries; the Industrial Union of Buenos Aires; the Chamber of Exporters of the Republic of Argentina; the Argentine Commercial Union; the Association of Banks "ADEBA," and the Argentinean Industrial Movement.

I. OTHER MEETINGS HELD

There were also meetings with the Piñero Pacheco Foundation; the University Federation; the Argentine Technological University Federation; the Argentine Israel Associations, DAIA, and the Union of Women of Argentina.

In addition, the Commission met with a number of other individuals whose testimony it was particularly interested in hearing. These included meetings with the author Ernesto Sábato; the trade union leader Lorenzo Miguel; the journalist Jacobo Timerman, and the trade union leader Professor Alfredo Bravo.

Lastly, on Tuesday September 18, the Commission met with the director or representatives of the mass communications media to discuss the topic of freedom of the press.

J. INVESTIGATION OF CERTAIN CASES

In the cities of Buenos Aires, Córdoba, La Plata and Rosario, the Commission did some investigative work inherent in the on-site observation, and received individuals and groups interested in stating problems or filing denunciations about human rights violations.

K. DETENTION CENTERS

The Commission visited the prisons of Villa Devoto; Caseros; Resistencia; Rawson; Unit 9 in La Plata; Olmos and the military detention centers called Magdalena, near La Plata and La Rivera in Córdoba. It also visited the prison in Córdoba and Unit 21 known as the Resocialization Institute (*Instituto de Resocialización*). The Commission also visited the Superintendent of Federal Security or Federal Coordination, the Naval School of Mechanics and Police Station N° 9 in Buenos Aires.

1. *Denunciations received*

In its initial press release, the Commission invited all persons who considered that any of their rights, as defined in the American Declaration, had been violated, to submit the corresponding denunciation. . . .

The total number of denunciations received was 5,580, of which 4,153 are new and are currently being processed pursuant to the Commission's Regulations;1,261 communications referred to cases already opened and in process, and 166 dealt with questions that bore no relation to violations of human rights.

All persons who wished to file a denunciation were duly received.

4. The Argentine Government cooperated with the Commission at all times, provided it with all the facilities it needed for its work, and repeated its commitment to take no reprisals against persons or institutions who provided the Commission with information, testimony, or evidence of whatever nature....

5. On Thursday, September 20, the full Commission met for the second and last time with the President, Lieutenant General (Retired) Jorge Rafael Videla, who was accompanied by the Ministers of the Interior and of Foreign Affairs. In light of its importance, the Commission at that time delivered to the President a document containing preliminary recommendations, the text of which appears below:

RECOMMENDATIONS OF THE INTER-AMERICAN COMMISSION ON HUMAN RIGHTS TO THE GOVERNMENT OF ARGENTINA

The Inter-American Commission on Human Rights, on the occasion of its on-site observation to the Republic of Argentina, takes the liberty of making the following preliminary recommendations to the Government of Argentina:

I. The Disappeared:

The Commission believes that the problem of the disappeared is one of the most serious human rights problems that Argentina faces. The Commission thus recommends the following:

a) That detailed information be provided on the status of the disappeared persons, understood to mean those persons who have been apprehended in operations in which, because of the conditions in which they took place and because of their characteristics, it is presumed that the state authorities participated.

b) That the necessary instructions be given to the proper authorities that minors who have disappeared as a result of the detention of their parents and other relatives, and children born in detention centers, whose whereabouts are unknown, be handed over to their natural parents or other close family members.

c) That the relevant measures be adopted to discontinue the procedures that have led to the disappearance of persons. In this regard, the Commission notes that cases of this nature have occurred recently, and should be clarified as soon as possible, as should all the other cases....

6. On September 20, the Commission concluded its on-site observation in Argentina and issued its final press release.

C. Methodology

1. In preparing this report, the IACHR used information obtained through its own resources, both before, during and after the on-site observation. Special consideration was given to denunciations, testimonies and information received by the IACHR or by the Special Commission that visited Argentina, which were

used in preparing the present document, although the report is not merely an aggregate of these denunciations, testimonies and information.

Careful study also was given to the Argentine legal system, the body of laws handed down by domestic courts and the applicable international human rights instruments. The IACHR consulted various documents that directly or indirectly deal with the status of human rights in Argentina or in some way enable the Commission to increase its understanding of the recent history of that country, which included documents prepared by the Argentine Government and by various Argentine organizations.

2. The IACHR also wishes to record that during its on-site observation, in addition to the information provided by governmental authorities, it received information and heard from officials of institutions representing all sectors of Argentine society, and also heard from all the individuals who wishes to submit complaints or testimony on the Argentine human rights situation.

3. The present report takes into consideration the Argentine Government's observations dated February 29, 1980, on the preliminary report, which had been approved by the Commission, and delivered to the Argentine Government, on December 14, 1979.

The Commission considers it appropriate to make some general comments about those observations, particularly in relation to the individual case histories included in the present report.

In the judgment of the Commission, these case histories are used to illustrate various topics and situations discussed in the report, and an attempt was made to use them in order to present with greater objectivity the situation of human rights in Argentina.

The Commission wishes to point out that its presentation of these case histories does not necessarily entail any prejudgment of them, in those instances where the Commission has not yet taken a resolution. Each individual case mentioned in the present report has been or will be processed according to the Commission's Regulations. The end of the process in each case is a statement or resolution on the merits.

The IACHR has already adopted a resolution on some individual cases included in the present report. In cases where the Argentine Government has requested reconsideration, careful study has been made of the cases in the light of new information supplied by the Government; if they are still included, it is because, in the opinion of the Commission, reconsideration of the case was not justified.

In cases where the Commission has decided to include a denunciation which has not yet been completely processed, it is because the Commission has decided, on the basis of the available evidence, that the charges are *prima facie* true, particularly in cases where the observations of the Argentine Government do not permit the denunciation to be refuted.

Moreover, the report contains not only individual cases, but also refers to information and documents received during the on/site observation, which was conducted precisely in order to collect such information.

With respect to the information collected during the on-site observation, the IACHR considered that the proper procedural moment to make it known to the Government, was, of course, in the preliminary report itself; this gave the Government the opportunity to make whatever observations it considered appropriate.

It should also be noted that in each of the case histories recorded — which are identified in this report by number — the IACHR informed the Argentine Government of the case prior to the Commission's approval of the report, and that in each case, the Government has had an opportunity to make such comments and observations as it considered appropriate.

4. Finally, the Commission wishes to note that in transcribing the pertinent parts of the denunciations contained in the report, it was decided to omit the names of those public officials or security agents who were accused of human rights violations, in cases where the Commission had no direct information. However, the Commission is confident that such an omission will not prevent the Argentine Government from taking the necessary measures, in accordance with its domestic laws, to investigate these denunciations, and in the event abuses or crimes are proven, to punish those responsible with the full force of the law....

E. Different Positions on the Problem of the Disappeared

1. As stated earlier, the Commission has no doubt that the problem of the disappeared detainees is the most serious human rights problem in Argentina. This problem deeply affects the unity and harmony of the Argentine society. Consequently, it is of particular interest to examine the ideas about and reaction to this on the part of those who have been affected and those who have a special responsibility for solving it.

A. Family Members

2. Those who are concerned about the disappeared persons, in other words, their relatives and close friends, have used virtually every available legal procedure to determine the whereabouts of their loved ones. The most frequently used have been *habeas corpus*, denunciations of illegal deprivation of liberty in courts of justice or to the police, and administrative measures in accordance with procedures established at the Ministry of the Interior.

From all of these measures — measures that have been taken repeatedly — thousands of persons have obtained no satisfaction. The Executive has consistently replied that no information about the detainees is on record. Investigations have always failed. And generally speaking, the Judiciary has rejected all remedies interposed, as will be seen further on, or has dismissed the cases.

In their anxiety, families have also turned to the Catholic Church and other religious authorities for help and intervention. They have sought the assistance of international human rights agencies, among them the IACHR. The Commission itself has received thousands of complaints, which it has in process.

3. It is also important to note here the solidarity that has developed among the families of the disappeared. These families have taken coordinated action at the administrative and judicial levels of Argentine human rights organizations for the purpose of obtaining answers from the authorities. One example of this is the group known as "The Mothers of the Plaza de Mayo." This group meets every Thursday in front of the Government House to demand information on the whereabouts of their family members, especially their children.

In an interview held during the on-site observation, one of these mothers, speaking on behalf of her group, stated the following:

> More than two years ago when what has happened to so many happened to me, I also went to the Plaza de Mayo. My pain was as fresh and not yet tempered. Since these things had been going on for some time, I had the naïve hope that we were reaching the end of this drama. Like all new arrivals, they asked me who my "disappeared person" was and for how long he had been gone. My answer was broken by cries: "a daughter and my son-in-law... four months ago..." I heard their replies: "Three of my children a year ago." "Me, a daughter, an invalid, eight months ago." "My parents and my sister... she was pregnant." At that point, the situation that I felt was coming to an end grew for me both in size and time. Today, the women who were the first to go to Plaza de Mayo have persisted for three long years without finding out anything about their children and there are others who have just started. But they do not have the consolation and strength that we have from the solidarity at the Plaza de Mayo.
>
> In this whole affair there was one hated word but one repeated without end, "disappeared." That is the synthesis and definition of our situation.
>
> When we explained why we were there to people passing through the Plaza de Mayo, with some surprise our actual situation moved into the nebulous area of myth. People asked us: "Disappeared?" "But you see them, you know where they are." "No!" "That is what we want to find out." "But aren't they in jail, aren't they being tried?" "No!, that is what we are asking for." Every Thursday and every day, whenever the chance arose, we explained the situation which, because of its highly unusual nature, not even our own fellow countrymen understood, unless they themselves had been either directly or indirectly touched by it.
>
> The Government did not describe the situation or even use the word "disappeared." (Furthermore, in one request they made us delete the word and change the text.) Official references to events involving internal or external politics spoke only of the "dirty war or the undeclared war," believing that this single reference gave sufficient reason for government action....
>
> Gentlemen, members of the Commission, we are in the presence of a massive violation of human rights, of the right to life that our Constitution, the Universal Declaration of Human Rights and the Church seek to protect.
>
> Gentlemen, members of the IACHR, the mothers here present beg of you, on behalf of the mothers of every "disappeared person," to find a solution for this problem.
>
> You should have the right to the files of lists, to obtain the lists of those who turn themselves in voluntarily (although you should give it in secret to their family members); you should obtain the lists of prisoners and disappeared persons which the President has mentioned; you should be given the lists of persons which all the armed forces keep in their quarters; you should have the list of persons killed in confrontations, persons whose names have not appeared in the newspapers, and whose corpses were never turned over to their family members.
>
> We repeat: please take as many measures as you can to bring about a solution to this frightful problem.
>
> Every Argentine citizen should know of it. Some of us have become aware of it through pain, others will become aware of it by learning about it. But we have to understand this truth because it is our commitment to future generations. Otherwise a shadow of sadness will remain forever over the descendants of this shattered generation and peace will not come to so many desolate families. They will always be looking around thinking in what unknown place their son continues to suffer or what tree or what piece of sky attracted his last glance, his last breath, his last thought. They

have been denied even the small place of earth earned at birth for their final resting place.

B. THE GOVERNMENT

4. The Government's position when complaints started to come in from family members, as can be drawn from the reports received by the Commission, was to avoid giving clear answers and to state firmly that it was unaware of the whereabouts of the disappeared. As time went by, and due primarily to the ceaseless campaign waged by the claimants, it has recognized that this fact exists and has set up mechanisms within the Government, through the Ministry of Interior, to attend to complaints and to provide information. Despite this, many answers are still vague.

When the Judiciary requested information from the Executive, in processing a writ of *habeas corpus*, the Executive responded repeatedly that it was unaware of the whereabouts of the individuals involved and stated that they were not detained or at the disposition of any civil or military authority.

5. Fundamentally, four basic reasons have been advanced by the governmental authorities for their disappearance: a) the persons have died in confrontation and, due to the condition of the corpses, could not have been identified; b) they left the country under cover; c) they had been executed by subversive groups because they are deserters; and d) they are living underground.

Ultimately, however, the authorities have also begun to list as one of the causes for the disappearances "excesses or abuses in repression," although they do not refer to any specific situation or concrete case. During the on-site observation, high-ranking government authorities argued before the Commission that the situation in Argentina for the past few years was one of war, a war that they call a "dirty war" or, in the words of President Videla, a "vague war" or an "ill-defined war." According to the Minister of the Interior, this could never be admitted since it would mean, under international law, the recognition of a state of war with all the consequences that such a situation implies. According to these authorities, excesses could have been committed during this "war" in the repression of subversion, thus leading to the disappearance of persons.

6. An even more forthright opinion on this matter was given to the Commander-in-Chief of the Army and Member of the Military Junta of Government, Lieutenant General Roberto Viola, who on Soldier's Day, May 29, 1979, spoke as follows about the aftermath of the campaign against subversion:

> This war, like all wars, has a dimension that is different from the value of life. For that reason it is a war. Dams and barriers are broken. Life and death are gambled away in the pursuit of victory. The worst thing is not the loss of life; the worst thing is to lose the war. For that reason, the Army, which today has restored the value of life, can say to the country that we have carried out our mission. This is the only and, we believe, sufficient explanation. The price of this is known to the country and to the Army, too. This war, like all wars, had an aftermath: tremendous wounds that time and only time can heal. These wounds are the number of casualties: the dead, the wounded, the detainees, the ones who are absent forever. The Army knows it and feels it because it is not inhumane or insensitive. The terrorists, with unbridled arrogance believed that by assassinations they could break the will to win of the Armed Forces and of the immense majority of the population. Unfortunately, the terrorists were men and women, who had been born on this generous soil. They were

wrong; they were deceived and they deceived and darkened the land of their birth. They deceived their supporters, whose anxiety they provoked which nobody today can legitimately assuage. These circumstances will undoubtedly widen the breach left in the wake of the war, because blameless families, affected by the pain, are also Argentine. The Army knows this and feels this. Its only explanation is the liberty, which our homeland entrusted to it for safekeeping.

7. Earlier statements, combined with the actual experiences of the Commission during its on-site observation, and the express recognition by the Government that the war had ended, and that peace and security now prevail in the streets, inevitably led the Commission to the consideration that the Government ought to use all the means within its power to bring peace and tranquility to the thousands of persons who continue seeking the whereabouts of their loved ones.

C. THE GOVERNMENT ANSWERS TO THE IACHR

8. With respect to the Argentine Government's position, a special section is devoted to the answers the Government has been giving to requests for information from the Commission. As a rule, the answers fall under one of the following formulas:

> Persons for whom there is no record of detention and who are the subject of police search conducted by the Ministry of the Interior. . . .
>
> Persons about whose whereabouts and status investigations are being initiated since no complaints were recorded prior to those submitted by the Commission. . . .
>
> List of names for whom measures cannot be taken since the data needed to initiate the necessary inquiries is incomplete. For the purpose of carrying out an investigation, for each case it is necessary to have first and last names, identification documents, domicile and the circumstances specifying the time and place where these disappearances occurred, as well as any other data that may help to clarify the facts. . . .

9. Starting in October, 1978, the Government stopped answering, for a long time, all requests for information about individual cases that the Commission had requested. It was only answering the resolutions adopted by the Commission.

Since August 1979, the Commission has been receiving new answers, which, even though they do not help to locate the disappeared persons, are more detailed than the earlier answers. Many of them explain what investigations have been undertaken or what the results, likewise unproductive, of the *habeas corpus* procedures have been. In some cases, they have provided information about the sentences or subversive ties of the affected parties.

10. Even though Resolutions 314, 371 and 445, adopted by the OAS General Assembly at its seventh, eighth and ninth regular sessions, respectively, recommended to the member states that they cooperate fully with the Commission and provide it with the information needed to facilitate its work, in the opinion of the Commission the Argentine Government has generally responded in an unsatisfactory manner, and in some cases, it has contradicted itself. Only since August 1979, had it been providing more complete information, which the Commission hope is an expression of the Government's concern for a clarification of the situation of the disappeared persons. . . .

E. PUBLIC OPINION

14. Despite the importance and significance of this problem the lack of public information has prevented the development of a general awareness in Argentina of the implications of what has happened.

Initially, most newspapers refused to publish any news on the issue, and even refused to print paid advertisements that included the word "disappeared." Nonetheless, as a result of numerous complaints, and the persistence of the human rights defense agencies, some personal advertisements, denunciations, and list of names of persons who have disappeared have been published.

15. At the time of the Commission's visit, some newspapers expressed their concern over the question, noting the necessity of solving it, and indicated that in the field of human rights, the phenomenon of the disappeared was of the greatest concern. During its visit, the Commission was able to sense a certain indifference, and in a few cases, even incredulity, among some sectors of the population. However, it believes that the visit itself and the broad, objective publication of information during the course of its work, helped the Argentine people form a clear picture of this serious problem, and this in itself represents a valuable contribution toward solving it in the future. . . .

G. Magnitude and Consequence of the Problem of the Disappeared

1. The origin of the phenomenon of the disappeared, the manner in which the disappearances occurred, and the astonishing number of victims, are all intimately connected with the historical events that unfolded in Argentina during the last few years, in particular, the organized campaign against subversion. The violence employed by the terrorist groups was more than matched by that of the State security apparatus, resulting in serious abuses incurred in its attempt to suppress the subversion by dispensing with all moral and legal considerations.

Much of the testimony and information which the Commission has received appears to support the fact that in the campaign against subversion, special units were established with participation, at different levels, of each of the branches of the Armed Forces whose command units were autonomous and independent in their operations.

The activities of these command units were directed against all persons who, actually or potentially, could pose a danger to the security of the State by virtue of their real or presumed ties to the subversive movement.

This campaign, unleashed for the purpose of totally annihilating the subversive movement, had its most sensitive, cruel and inhuman expression in the thousands of disappeared persons, today presumed dead, whom it left in its wake.

It appears evident that the decision to form the command units that were involved in the disappearance and possible extermination of these thousands of persons was adopted at the highest level of the Armed Forces, for the purpose of decentralizing the anti-subversion campaign. As a result, each of the command units had unlimited power to eliminate terrorists or those suspected of being terrorists.

The Commission is morally convinced that, in general, these authorities could not have been ignorant of the events as they were occurring and did not adopt the necessary measures to terminate them.

2. The Commission has received statements to the effect that the Government "has won the war" and that the subversion is now under control. Despite this, however, the problem of the disappeared persons continues. Even though it is true that compared with 1976, 1977 and 1978, there was a smaller number of disappeared detainees in 1979, and that since October 1979, the Commission has received no new claims of disappearances. The fact that the Government has not taken all measures within its reach to clarify earlier situations means, in the opinion of the Commission, that the problem is not being taken care of.

Even while the Commission was on its visit to Argentina there was an operation very similar to earlier ones involving the disappearance of an entire family which was kidnapped by security agents. This situation prompted the Commission immediately to intervene with the Argentine authorities.

3. The Commission is not able to give an exact number of the disappearances in Argentina. Of all the lists of disappeared persons that have been received, the Commission believes that the most reliable, since it agrees with the number of complaints that it has received, is the list turned over to it by the Minister of the Interior, General Albano Harguindeguy. . . . This list includes 5,818 persons who, between January 7, 1975 and May 30, 1979 were "apprehended in their homes, places of work or in public places by armed groups, who *prima facie*, and almost always stating so specifically, acted under the color of authority, using procedures conducted in the open, with a full display of men — uniformed at times — weapons and vehicles and carried out with a promptness and detail that confirm that those involved were working in a manner typical of the security forces." . . .

4. Whatever is the final number of disappeared persons; it is nonetheless impressive and does nothing if not confirm the extraordinary seriousness of this problem.

Furthermore, the lack of clarification of this problem of disappeared persons has affected many families in the Argentine community. The uncertainty and lack of all contact with the victims have upset the families greatly and especially the children who, in some cases, witnessed the kidnappings of their parents and the mistreatment to which they were subject during the raid. Many of these children will never see their parents again and will thus inherit a number of psychological problems from their memory of the circumstances of the disappearance.

On the other hand, many men and women between 18 and 25 years of age are affected by the anxiety and length of time that has passed without any knowledge of their parents or brothers and sisters.

Spouses, both men and women, who have been violently separated, live in an environment of severe mental disturbances, accentuated by the many economic and legal problems that this separation poses for them. Many men and women do not know whether they are widowed or still married. Many of them will never regain personal peace, harmony or security because of the exhaustion produced by their attempts to carry on in a home where the physical and moral absence of the father or the mother is felt every day.

These and other problems cannot be resolved as long as the situation of these thousands of disappeared persons is not clarified in a final and responsible manner.

5. The Commission took special interest in exhausting all possibilities to determine, without any shadow of a doubt, the truth of the present situation of the "disappeared." To this end, it made inquiries at prison establishments, military installations, cemeteries, the resocialization center, all those places where there was the slightest possibility that persons apprehended by police or military groups might be held or might have been buried. All of its efforts have been in vain.

These circumstances, combined with the information received by the Commission, lead the Commission to the painful conclusion that the great majority of the disappeared are dead, the causes of which it is not in a position to determine but which, in any event, involve a great responsibility for their captors or those who kept them detained.

6. After having studied with great thoroughness the response of the Government with respect to all the cases discussed above, the Commission would like to make some general comments:

> The Commission cannot fail to point out that during the period 1976-1979, a great number of persons, ultimately recognized by the Government as official detainees, were initially apprehended and held *incommunicado* in operations identical to those which, according to a great body of testimony received by the Commission, produced the disappearances which remain unexplained.
>
> This information is confirmed by a great number of persons whose detention has been recognized at some point or another by the Government, who have testified to having seen in unofficial detention centers various disappeared persons, and to have seen them at times and under circumstances which coincide with the denunciations received by the Commission.
>
> In a number of cases considered, . . . the explanations of the Government have been extremely inadequate and unconvincing. Most of the Government replies add little of substance, and do not persuasively contradict the occurrence of the alleged events.
>
> In addition, high Government officials have stated that the arrest of persons suspected of subversive activity were carried out on a regular basis by security forces in civilian clothing. Those and other functionaries have implied that the nature of the conflict required the application of measures that violated human rights.
>
> In view of the circumstances, the Commission finds itself compelled to reiterate its conviction that the material facts of the denunciations must be presumed to be true.

In its conclusions and recommendations, the Commission found that governmental authorities and their agents had committed numerous serious violations of fundamental human rights, as recognized in the American Declaration of the Rights and Duties of Man, between 1975 and 1979. In particular, the Commission found violations of the right to life, the right to personal freedom, the right to personal integrity and security, "by means of the systematic use of torture and other cruel, inhuman and degrading treatment, the practice of which has taken on alarming characteristics," and the right to a fair trial and due process. With regard to other rights the Commission noted that while the failure to observe them did not assume the same gravity of the previous cases, their exercise was limited. These included the right to freedom of opinion, expression, and information, labor rights, political rights, and the freedom of religion and worship. The Commission observed that, subsequent to its visit to Argentina, violations of the right to life, liberty, personal integrity, and security, and of the right to a fair trial and due process decreased, and that after October 1979, it received no further denunciations with respect to further disappearance of persons. As regards the "disappeared," the Commission recommended that the government implement the preliminary recommendations (set out supra, page 736) inform the Commission in detail with respect to the situation of these persons. In order to prevent new cases of disappearance, the Commission recommended that the government create a central register of detainees that will enable their family members and other interested persons rapidly to learn of detentions that have taken place, to order that such detentions be carried out by properly identified agents, and to give instructions that the detainees be transferred without delay to places specifically intended for such purpose.

The following extract was written by one of the staff members who took part in the on-site mission to Argentina.

Thomas Buergenthal, Robert Norris, and Dinah Shelton, *Protecting Human Rights in the Americas, Selected Problems* 299-301 (3d ed. 1990)

* Bob Norris (Robert?)

According to the Executive Secretary of the Commission, the government of Argentina had declared that there were no political prisoners in Córdoba. Therefore, during the course of the visit, I was not to visit the Cárcel Penitenciaria in that city; however, I had requested by liaison with the Ministry of Foreign Affairs to provide me with a list of all the prisoners held in the provinces of Córdoba and Tucamán.

Upon arriving in Córdoba on September 7, I arranged to speak with the Minister of Government of that Province with regard to my mission and to the plans I would make for the visit of two Members of the Inter American Commission scheduled to arrive several days later. I explained that we had no plans to visit the penitentiary, but that Commissioners often changed their minds and we should be aware of that possibility. On the basis of previous experience, I described very briefly our normal procedure for visiting jails and other detention centers. The Members would meet with the prison authorities for a briefing, prior to a tour of the locale. They would be interested in interviewing any prisoners who might have a case before the Commission, and they would probably select several prisoners at random for personal interviews with regard to prison conditions. Those interviews would take place in private, and the Members of the Commission might require a temporary office for the purpose. I reminded him that I had requested an alphabetized list of the prisoners in the Province of Córdoba and would need it as soon as possible.

As I conducted interviews with petitioners during the next few days I was informed of the names of several persons who were allegedly being held in the Cárcel Penitenciaria for political reasons. Without mentioning this information, I called the Minister of Government to advise him that the Members would visit the prison and would need the list previously requested.

When the list finally arrived, I carefully went over the names, searching for the "political" cases reportedly detained at the penitentiary. One fact stood out;

not one of those names was on the list! I then called a private individual who I knew could make contact with one of the prisoners and asked him to try to obtain a list of all the persons held in the same cellblock. He was only partially successful; he could not get all the names, but he did bring back several, along with the exact number of men and women being held there. Again I checked the list and none of those names were on it. It was an exciting moment; I had a "gut feeling" that some of those people were "disappeared," and the mission had yet to uncover any of the thousands of people who had been abducted and literally dropped from sight. I was afraid at the same time that someone might tip the authorities off and the prisoners would be moved before the visit of the Commissioners.

The prisoners sent word through my contact that they were worried about the confidentiality of the interviews. They were afraid of being overheard, and they were also afraid that the government might take advantage of the announced visit to send a "fake party," as it had allegedly done in that prison some months before under the guise of a Red Cross visit. I replied, again through the contact, that I would bring plenty of paper and pens in my briefcase so they would not have to talk. They would be sure that it was an official visit by the Commission by asking Are you Dr. . . . ?" My only reply would be to take out my official OAS passport and show them. Any verbal reply should put them on guard.

When the Members of the Commission did arrive, I briefed them on the situation and provided them with a memorandum on how we should proceed if they wished to visit the penitentiary. They accepted and asked me to finalize the arrangements.

On September 13, I accompanied Professor Carlos Dunshee de Abranches (Brazil) and Dr. Luis Tinoco Castro (Costa Rica) to the penitentiary. In our preliminary briefing by the Director of the prison, Professor Abranches asked for a general explanation of prison rules affecting the inmates. When the Director had finished speaking about visiting rights, Professor Abranches inquired whether all prisoners had the same rights. The reply was affirmative. He then noted that, "according to Dr. . . . [the staff member] there is a sign in one part of the prison which refers to "special prisoners." "We have a complete list of the names of those prisoners, eleven women and thirty-one men, but it is an unofficial list, and we would like to have an official list before we visit that cellblock."

We had no such list, of course, but the fact we knew the exact number must have convinced them that we did. The Director turned to one of his assistants and asked: "Didn't you give them a list of the special prisoners?" "No, sir." "Oh, I see. You didn't give them a list of the special prisoners!"

There followed a long moment of silence. Professor Abranches interrupted: "Since there are only a few names involved, we will simply wait here while the list is prepared." The Director then asked an assistant to bring a list. It only required a few minutes as a list was apparently brought from a file in another room. I could hardly believe my eyes. It was a bonanza, containing not only the names, but under whose disposition. Only seven had been presented before a court of law. Many of the others were at the orders of special councils of war, meaning they were being held indefinitely. Most were held by executive decree, but three were at the orders of the local military commandant. Those three had "disappeared" in the typical fashion just a month before!

When we reached the women's section, we asked to be allowed behind the bars into a large area which served as a dining hall. On the other side of the dining area was a long corridor with tiny cells on either side. We asked that the prisoners be released from their cells, and the Director complied. Not all of the women were accounted for. Professor Abranches shouted down the corridor: "Is anyone else there?" We heard a scream "We're here, we're here" and a hand emerged from a small opening in the door of the very last cell on the right. We had "found" two disappeared persons — Irma Cristina Guillert de Palazzesi and Stella Maria Palazzesi de Cavigliasso. The other women later told us that they had been warned not to mention the presence of the two prisoners being held incommunicado. They were not allowed to talk to them at all.

We left Dr. Tinoco to talk to the women and we continued with the Director to the men's section upstairs. There was another surprise in store. Professor Abranches told the prison officials, "Now that we are here, we'll just stay in the cellblock and interview the prisoners here." "But you can use my office; it's all prepared," blurted the Director. "Tell us who you want to see, and we'll take him to the office where you'll have all the facilities necessary." "No, thank you very much," said Professor Abranches, "we'll stop and see you on the way out!"

Again, we had the prisoners released from their cells, into the dining area, which was also behind bars. The guards withdrew, I brought out the paper and pens and explained what type of information we wanted. When everyone had finished, I took a small tape recorder from my briefcase, chose a cell at random, and interviewed a group of prisoners on general prison conditions.

We now return to the Commission's report, in which it addresses some of the counter-arguments advanced by the government.

Report on the Situation of Human Rights in Argentina

OEA/Ser.L/V/II.49, doc. 19 corr. 1, 11 April 1980, pp. 22-27

. . . Practically all the authorities, beginning with the President of the Republic, the members of the Military Government Junta, the Minister of the Interior, and the Minister of Justice, told the Commission that the problem of the observance of human rights in Argentina could not be given precedence over the situation caused by terrorism and subversion. A number of these authorities provided the Commission with various pieces of background information with regard to the activities of terrorist and subversive groups. The Minister of the Interior, General Albano E. Harguindeguy, even had a voluminous document delivered to the Commission which describes various terrorists acts which, in the opinion of the Armed Forces, determined that they would "assume political power in Argentina together with the responsibility for containing the progressive dissolution of the State, the general chaos and the situation of extreme social indifference. . . ."

2. Through these interviews and its own research, the Commission has come to have an adequate understanding of the violence and social unrest that devastated Argentina during the years immediately prior to the government takeover by the current authorities, as well as of the sporadic terrorist acts that still appear to persist.

The importance of this issue and its invocation as a justification for the Government's conduct in the matter of respect for human rights, provide sufficient reason for the Commission to restate in as clear terms as possible, its thinking in this regard. Basically this issue can be analyzed by attempting to answer two questions that were repeatedly put to the Commission, both before and during the on-site observation:

i) Why doesn't the Commission investigate terrorist acts? In other words, why is it that the Commission concerns itself exclusively with actions attributable to governments, and

ii) To what extent does the Commission take terrorism and subversion into account when assessing the conduct of governments as regards the observance of human rights?

a) The lack of jurisdiction of the IACH to investigate acts imputed to terrorists groups or subversive organizations

3. The simple and legally precise answer to the first question is that the sovereign states of the Organization of American States have not chosen to give the Commission jurisdiction to investigate terrorism and subversion. . . .

b) The limits of the State's repressive actions

4. The Commission now wishes to address the second question. Do the existence of terrorists and the threats to subvert the public order influence the Commission's assessments or evaluations with respect to the observance of human rights in a given country? Within the limits to be described below the obvious answer is yes.

The Commission repeatedly has emphasized the obligation of governments to maintain public order and preserve the safety of their inhabitants. To the end, governments must energetically prevent and repress acts of violence, whether they be committed by public officials or private individuals, and regardless of whether their motivation may be considered political or not.

In the life of any nation, threats to the public order or to the personal safety of its inhabitants, by persons or groups that use violence, can reach such proportions that it becomes necessary, temporarily, to suspend the exercise of certain human rights.

The majority of the constitutions of the American States accept such limitations, and even provide for the temporary institution of states of emergency or states of siege in such circumstances. Of course, in order for such measures to be adopted, extremely serious circumstances must intervene, as the institution of such regimes must be in response to the necessity of preserving those rights and freedoms which have been threatened by the disturbance of the public order and personal safety.

However, it is equally clear that certain fundamental rights can never be suspended, as is the case, among others, of the right to life, the right to personal safety, or the right to due process. In other words, under no circumstances may governments employ summary execution, torture, inhumane conditions of detention, or the denial of certain minimum conditions of justice as the means to restore public order. These measures are proscribed in constitutions and in international instruments, both at the regional and at the global level. . . .

Each government that confronts a subversive threat must choose, on the one hand, the path of respect for the rule of law, or, on the other hand, the descent into state terrorism. When a government enjoys broad popular support, the choice of the first method will always be successful, as various countries have demonstrated both in the distant and more recent past.

As has already been pointed out, respect for the rule of law does not preclude, under certain circumstances, the adoption of extraordinary measures. When the emergency situation is truly serious, certain restrictions may be imposed, for example, on the freedom of information, or limitations on the right of association, within the framework established in the constitution. In more extreme cases, persons may be detained for short periods without it being necessary to bring specific charges against them. It is true that such measures can ultimately pose the risk that the rule of law will be lost; but that is not inevitable provided that governments act responsibly; if they register arrests and inform the families of the detainees of the detentions; if they issue strict orders prohibiting torture; if they carefully recruit and train security forces, weeding out sadists and psychopaths; and lastly, if there is an independent judiciary to swiftly correct any abuse of authority.

Comments and Questions

1. Could the Commission have undertaken an on-site mission to Argentina without the consent of the government? Why would a government consent to such an investigation? Did the government think it would convince the Commission of the necessity of the measures it had undertaken? Does it make a difference that the Commission had already undertaken numerous country studies? In other words, does cooperative state practice exercise a compliance pull — the more states that cooperate with the Commission, the harder it is for a state to decline to cooperate? Note that between 1961 and the beginning of 2005, the IACHR had carried out 87 visits to 23 out of the 35 member states. Based in part on its on-site investigations the IACHR has published 62 country and thematic reports.

2. The staff member's notes of finding disappeared persons in prison were not part of the official report. Why not? Does his story affect your views of the value of on-site visits? What about the more than 5,000 petitions that were lodged with the Commission during its visit?

3. The on-site mission to Argentina included all but one of the Commission members. What do the Rules of Procedure say about the composition of a country team? How is it decided what country to study and under what conditions does the Commission undertake an on-site visit? How would you evaluate the methodology of the Commission? See the discussion on fact-finding in Chapter 12.

4. The Commission notes that, following its on-site visit the number of cases reporting disappearances slowed and even halted. How do you evaluate this fact: was the international pressure having an impact or had the government succeeded in eliminating all its opponents? Or were both elements involved?

B. *Individual Petitions*

Dinah Shelton, "The Inter-American Human Rights System"

In *Guide to International Human Rights Practice* 130-38 (4th ed. H. Hannum ed. 2004) (extracts) (notes omitted)

. . . Provided that the formal and substantive requirements are met, a petition may be filed with the Commission against any OAS member state. For states that are not party to the Convention, the recognized rights are those contained in the American Declaration. For parties to the American Convention, the rights contained in the Convention are protected in relation to all events which occur after the date of ratification, including continuing violations that may have begun prior to that date. Petitions also may be filed against a state party that violates its obligations under the Disappearances Convention or Article 7 of the Convention on Violence against Women.

The procedures governing complaints are set forth in the Commission's Statute and Regulations. The procedures are identical for all petitions, including criteria for admissibility, procedural stages, fact-finding, and decision-making, but only petitions arising under the American Convention or Disappearances Convention may be submitted to the Court (and then only if the state in question has accepted the Court's jurisdiction).

The Commission is obliged to attempt a friendly settlement and may undertake a mission on-site if it deems it necessary and appropriate. The petition process may result in a Commission decision on the merits, together with specific recommendations to the state concerned. The Commission may call for the state to pay "appropriate" compensation when it finds a violation has occurred, but it does not itself set the amount of compensation it views as appropriate.

Who May File

Any person, group of persons, or nongovernmental organization legally recognized in one or more of the member states of the OAS may submit a petition to the Inter-American Commission on Human Rights. The petition need not be filed directly by a victim but may be submitted by third parties, with or without the victim's knowledge or authorization. The petition may involve an individual or may indicate numerous victims of a specific incident or practice (a collective petition)....

Exhaustion of Domestic Remedies

The Commission will not admit a petition unless all available and effective domestic remedies have been exhausted in accordance with general principles of international law. This means that domestic avenues of appeal must be pursued, unless it can be shown that no remedy exists or the purported remedies would be inadequate (i.e. incapable of producing the result sought) or ineffective (available in theory but not in practice). The petition therefore must include information on whether remedies under domestic law have been exhausted or whether it has been impossible or futile to proceed....

The Commission has made clear that it is not a "court of fourth instance." The mere fact that the petitioner lost a case in the national courts is not grounds for bringing a petition to the Inter-American system. The Commission will not substitute its judgment for that of the trier of fact nor will it substitute its interpretation of a domestic statute or Constitutional norm for that of a domestic court. However, the Commission will accept a case if the proceedings in domestic court violated human rights guarantees of due process or fair hearing or were ineffective to remedy the violation, for example, if the domestic court lacked the power to strike down legislation incompatible with the Convention.

Timeliness

Exhaustion of remedies is linked to the time limit within which a petition must be filed. Where domestic remedies have been pursued and exhausted, the petition must be filed within six months of the date on which the party whose rights have been violated was notified of the final ruling. This limit may be extended if the state has interfered with the petitioner's ability to file the complaint within the time period. If the requirement of exhaustion of remedies is excused because no remedies are available or effective, the petition must be filed within a reasonable period of time. If a third party is filing a petition for a victim unable to do so, the reasonableness criterion rather than the strict six-month rule may apply. The petition must include information on compliance with the relevant time period.

Duplication of Procedures

The Commission cannot consider a petition if the subject matter is pending settlement in another international governmental organization or "essentially duplicates a petition pending or already examined and settled by the Commission or by another international governmental organization of which the state concerned is a member." However, the Commission will consider the matter if the other procedure examines only the general situation on human rights in the state in question, such as the UN's "1503 procedure," and there has been no decision on the specific facts in the petition submitted to the Commission, or if the other procedure will not effectively redress the violation. Although the situation is unlikely to arise in practice, the Commission also will consider the petition if the petitioner is the victim or a family member and the petitioner in the other proceeding is a third party acting without specific authorization from the victim. . . .

Procedure

Petitions are considered in several distinct stages. Initially, petitions are received and processed by the Commission's Secretariat to see if they meet the requirements for consideration in accordance with Articles 26-28 of the Commission's rules. . . .

Once the petition is complete and the Commission's *prima facie* competence is verified, the petition is registered and given a number, and the relevant parts of the petition are transmitted to the state in question. In transmitting the petition, the Secretariat deletes all details which would tend to identify the petitioner unless the petitioner has given authorization to have his or her identity revealed. The state is normally given two months from the date the petition is transmitted to respond to it. The state may request one additional month to reply, but it is not automatically entitled to an extension of time and its request must be evaluated by the Secretariat.

The Commission may invite further submissions from either party or may hold hearings prior to making a determination on admissibility. The Commission's regulations provide that, once observations have been received or the relevant time period has passed, the Commission must verify the admissibility of the petition; a working group on admissibility meets prior to each session to study the admissibility of petitions and make recommendations to the Commission. Only after the petition is deemed admissible is the petition registered as and considered "a case." In exceptional circumstances, where issues of admissibility are tied to the merits, the Commission may join consideration of the two issues and open the case by means of a written communication to both parties....

Hearings and On-Site Visits

The Commission is authorized to hold a hearing to verify the facts, which is generally done in a chamber of three Commissioners, on its own initiative or at the request of one or more of the parties....

In addition to holding hearings on cases, Commission practice now commonly includes informal visits to a country by the Commissioner who is the Rapporteur for the country along with a staff attorney. The visits typically concern more than one case and are directed at fact-finding, obtaining evidence or engaging the parties in friendly settlements. Where appropriate, the full Commission may undertake an on-site investigation in the country involved, at the request of the petitioner, state, or on its own motion. While on-site investigations are conducted much more frequently in the Inter-American system than in others, they are rarely undertaken solely to investigate a single or individual case. Instead, they are utilized to investigate allegations of widespread human rights violations within the target country, as part of which individual cases may be examined. No more than one or two such visits can be undertaken in a year.

Final Decisions and Reports

The Commission examines all the evidence in the case and prepares a report stating the facts, arguments, and its conclusions regarding the case, including any proposals and recommendations it wishes to make. If the Commission finds there has been no violation, it states this in the report which it transmits to the parties and includes in its Annual Report. When the Commission finds one or more violations, it prepares a preliminary report with any proposals and recommendations it decides to make and transmits the preliminary report to the state in question. This is known as the Article 50 report, after the provision in the Convention that mandates it. The state is given two months to comply with the recommendations and is not authorized to publish the report until the Commission adopts its final decision. The petitioner is notified when the report is transmitted to the state and is given a summary of the findings. The short time limit for compliance and transmittal of information to the petitioner facilitates preparation for taking the case to the Court, if this can be done, within the three month time limit imposed by the Convention.

If the state is party to the American Convention and has accepted the jurisdiction of the Court, the petitioner has one month to indicate a view on whether or not the Commission should submit the case to the Court and, if so, the reasons for this, the availability of evidence, claims concerning reparations, and personal information about the victim and the victim's family members.

1. Provisional Measures

Reggiardo Tolosa Case, Order of the President of the Inter-American Court of Human Rights of November 19, 1993

Inter-Am. Ct. H.R., Annual Report of the Inter-American Court of Human Rights 1993, 95-98, OAS/Ser.L/V/III.29, doc. 4, Jan. 10, 1993

Provisional Measures Requested by the Inter-American Commission on Human Rights in the Matter of the Republic of Argentina
Whereas:

1. In a fax dated October 20, 1993, and received at the Secretariat of the Inter-American Court of Human Rights . . . on November 8 of that same year, the Inter-American Commission on Human Rights . . . submitted to the Court, pursuant to Articles 63(2) of the American Convention on Human Rights . . . and 24 of the Rules of Procedure of the Court . . . , a request for provisional measures in connection with Case 10.959 currently before the Commission. The provisional measures requested relate to "the mental integrity of minors Gonzalo Xavier and Matías Ángel, Argentine citizens," who, according to the petition presented to the Commission on June 23, 1991, by the Grandmothers of the Plaza de Mayo, a non-governmental organization, are the "children of Juan Enrique Reggiardo and María Rosa Ana Tolosa, a married couple who were the victims of a forced disappearance;"

2. The petition was filed with the Commission because the aforementioned minors have not been delivered to their legitimate family and the family demands that they be placed under its care in provisional custody. This demand has not been met to date, a fact that severely endangers the mental integrity of the minors;

3. According to the petition, on February 12, 1987, the National Federal Criminal and Correctional Court of First Instance N° 2 applied the hemogenetic procedure provided by Law 23.511 establishing the National Genetic Data Bank in order to make an identification and determined that the aforementioned minors, who were born during the illegal detention of their mother, are the offspring of disappearance victims Juan Enrique Reggiardo and María Rosa Ana Tolosa;

4. According to the request for provisional measures, Gonzalo Xavier and Matías Angel were born in April 1977, during the captivity of their mother, and were immediately removed and later registered as the children of Samuel Miara, a former assistant police inspector of the Federal Police, and his wife, Beatriz Alicia Castillo. When the minors reached the age of eleven, they became aware of the fact that the Miara couple were not their real parents. In 1985, they were taken to Paraguay, where they lived, confined to their home, until 1989. That year they were brought back to Argentina "and placed for a period of time

with a foster family, pending the results of the immunogenetic tests. Despite evidence as to the true origins of these children, they continue to be held by the persons who abducted them and falsified their real identities;"

5. According to the request for provisional measures, the proceedings before the Commission developed as follows:

> 6. On August 21, 1992, the Commission received a request for provisional measures from the petitioners. Their argument was that the minors were caught in a situation which is being prolonged indefinitely and poses grave psychological risks to them as a result of the suppression of their identities, their being withheld from their family, and their remaining in the hands of persons who have been prosecuted for crimes committed against them. This request was transmitted to the Government.
>
> 7. By note of September 16, 1992, the Government countered that the claim was not admissible because some important issues were still pending a decision by the Judiciary. The Government informed the Commission that on September 7 of that same year, the Office of the Attorney General had requested the Trial Judge to declare the birth certificates of the minors to be null and void and to order their provisional registration under the surname of Reggiardo-Tolosa, or under an assumed surname, until such time as the family problem is resolved. It also reported that the preventive custody of the Miaras had been confirmed by the National Federal Court of Criminal and Correctional Appeals of the Federal Capital because it had found them to be *prima facie* criminally responsible for the crimes of concealment and withholding of minors and misrepresentation of public documents accrediting the identity of persons.
>
> 8. By note of March 11, 1993, the Commission declared the case admissible, taking into account the fact that the minors had been identified as belonging to the Reggiardo-Tolosa couple and the inability of the family members of the minors to file appeals because they are deemed to be parties in the proceedings at which the custody of said minors is to be decided. Pursuant to Article 46(2)(c) of the Convention, the Commission determined that the unwarranted delay in rendering a final judgment exempted the petition from the requirement of exhaustion of domestic remedies. In accordance with Article 29 of its Regulations, the Commission furthermore requested that the Government of Argentina adopt provisional measures to provide without delay for the placement of the minor children in a foster home under temporary custody and to arrange for them to receive appropriate psychological treatment under the supervision of a professional appointed by their family, until such time as their delivery to their legitimate family is settled.
>
> 9. By note of June 2, 1993, the Government of Argentina responded to the request for provisional measures by informing the Commission that, on April 15, the Federal Judge with jurisdiction over Custody Arrangements for Minors had ordered two hearings to be held with the purpose of placing the minor children under temporary custody in a foster home. The Government also reported that the annulment of the birth registration of the Miara minors had been ordered, and that they had been registered under the name of Reggiardo-Tolosa.
>
> 10. Nevertheless, on August 19, 1993, the Commission received a communication from the Association of Grandmothers of Plaza de Mayo, informing it that no steps had been taken to transfer the minors to a foster home. Consequently, they asked the Commission, pursuant to Article 63 of the Convention, to request the Inter-American Court to order provisional measures to ensure that the Argentine Government place the minors in a foster home.

6. The Commission considers that the situation giving rise to the petition is grave because "the longer [it] . . . is allowed to continue without justification, the

more serious the mental condition of the minors becomes" and is further exacerbated by the suppression of their identities and by the fact that they are not being returned to their legitimate family or transferred to a foster home under temporary custody;

7. The Commission also believes that justice has been unjustifiably delayed, for the identity of the minors had already been established in 1989. Nevertheless, they continue to be held by the very persons who are being prosecuted for committing illegal acts against them. The case history of the minors presents a prima facie case of imminent danger to their mental health and the Commission considers that Argentine law does not provide adequate ordinary guarantees to protect their mental identity;

8. The Commission therefore requests that the Court, in application of Article 63(2) of the Convention "require the Government of Argentina to order the immediate transfer of the minor children to ensure that they be placed under temporary custody in a substitute location and be provided adequate psychological treatment until such time as the matter of their delivery to their legitimate family is settled" ...

CONSIDERING THAT:

1. Argentina is a State Party to the American Convention on Human Rights since November 5, 1984, date on which it also accepted the jurisdiction of the Court, in accordance with Article 62 of the Convention;...

4. Despite the fact that the Commission has not yet submitted the case to the Court, the mental integrity of the two minors is at stake and it is important to prevent them from suffering irreparable damage as a result of the situation alleged in the request for provisional measures. This situation is characterized by the gravity and urgency necessary for the request to be acted upon;

5. Argentina has the obligation to adopt all necessary measures to protect the mental integrity of, and prevent irreparable damage to, all persons whose rights might be threatened, in this case those of minors Gonzalo Xavier and Matías Angel;

Therefore:

the President of the Inter-American Court of Human Rights, taking into consideration Article 63(2) of the American Convention on Human Eights and exercising the authority conferred on her by Article 24(4) of the rules of procedure, in consultation with the judges of the Court,

Orders:

1. To enjoin the Government of the Republic of Argentina to adopt without delay whatever measures are deemed necessary to protect the mental integrity of, and avoid irreparable damage to, minors Gonzalo Xavier and Matías Angel Reggiardo-Tolosa, in strict compliance with its obligation to respect and guarantee human rights under Article 1(1) of the Convention, in order to ensure that the provisional measures that the Court may adopt during its next regular session, to be held from January 10 to 21, 1994, will have the requisite effect.

2. To request the Government of Argentina to submit a report on the measures taken pursuant to this order to the President of the Court no later than December 20, 1993, to enable her to bring this information to the attention of the Court.

3. To instruct the Secretariat to promptly transmit to the Inter-American Commission on Human Rights the report to be received from the Government of the Republic of Argentina.

2. Admissibility and Merits

Following the military coup in Argentina, the Commission received thousands of complaints involving disappearances. The government's replies were nearly always the same and the Commission's conclusions followed a pattern as well. The following case is typical.

Res. No. 31/78, Case 2553 (Argentina), decision of Nov. 18, 1978

Ann. Rep. Inter-Am. Comm'n 1979-80, 58-62, OEA/Ser.L/V/II.50, 2 Oct. 1980

1. In a . . . communication dated November 28, 1977, the following denunciation was made:

> "The purpose of this letter is to determine the whereabouts of a female child, named CLARA ANAHÍ MARIANI, born on August 12, 1976 in La Plata."
>
> "It is public knowledge that on November 24, 1976, at approximately 1.30 p.m., an armed confrontation took place between the joint forces and the occupants of a farm located on Calle 30, between 55 and 56, in La Plata. This house was the residence of Daniel E. Mariani, his wife Diana E. Teruggi, and their three-month old daughter, CLARA ANAHÍ."
>
> "According to a newspaper reports and reports from neighbors, the house — where the child was — was completely surrounded by the joint forces before the confrontation which lasted for several hours."
>
> "On the day following the event, an oral report was made to the 5th Police Precinct that the child's name did not appear in the summary proceedings along with the names of those who had died and who had been identified by the police."
>
> "On March 3, 1977, a written reply was received to one of the notes presented to the Chief of Infantry Regiment N° 7, Colonel Conde, reporting that the child's whereabouts were unknown, but that Police Headquarters of Operations Area 113 was continuing the investigation."
>
> "Dr. Sambucetti initiated proceedings N° 36.792 in Juvenile Court N° 2. Reports were obtained from the Children's Hospital, the Fire Departments, the Regional and Police Units. All replies were negative, and the police were informed that no minor had been at the place where the incident occurred."
>
> "After a year of continuous and anguished searching, the child's whereabouts are still unknown. She has not been found alive or dead, and there is no explanation for her disappearance."

2. The Commission is in possession of a newspaper account of the events in reference during which CLARA ANAHÍ MARIANI disappeared, and has also received a number of negative replies from the Argentinean authorities as to the child's whereabouts.

3. In a note dated February 7, 1978, the Commission transmitted the pertinent parts of this denunciation to the Government of Argentina, asking it to provide the corresponding information.

4. In a note dated May 11, 1978, the Government of Argentina replied to the Inter-American Commission on Human Rights in the following terms:

> ...
>
> D. OBSERVATIONS:
>
> ...
>
> 55. MARIANI, Clara Anahí: Investigation conducted by the competent authorities to determine her whereabouts has not produced positive results to date (CASE 2553).

5. In a letter dated March 27, 1978, the pertinent parts of the reply from the Government of Argentina were forwarded to the complainant, and he was asked to make observations to that reply.

6. In a letter of May 4, the complainant contested the reply by the Government of Argentina as follows:

> The reply you received from the Government of Argentina is the same as it gives to all inquiries about people who have disappeared, regardless of their age. I believe that for a military government, which has such an efficient intelligence service, it would not be difficult to establish, if it wanted to, the whereabouts of a baby who was not yet walking and who needed to be bottle-fed to survive.
>
> We feel that CLARA ANAHI is in the hands of the Argentine authorities or that the authorities have disposed of her, for the following reasons:
>
> 1. The child could only have been removed from her home by the same forces that attacked and occupied it, since it was totally *surrounded* before the confrontation, as reported in all newspapers of 11.25.76. Also, all of the neighbors know that every home in the neighborhood was vacated before the event (but no one would testify to this out of fear).
>
> 2. It is a generally held view throughout the country that some babies removed both from their homes where confrontations have occurred and from the places where their parents 'disappear,' or from the prisons where they were born, are given away or sold. CLARA ANAHI must therefore have been 'given away' or 'sold' like so many other children.
>
> Insofar as giving away other people's children is concerned, I can inform you that Monsignor has told us that he had rescued several little children who were in the hands of policemen who had registered them as their own.
>
> The clergy must be aware of this, just like every other person in this land.
>
> ...If there is a witness, for obvious reasons, one cannot rely on his coming forward with information.
>
> A further point which lacks confirmation is that apparently DIANA E. TERUGGI was gunned down when the confrontation began, while she was trying to escape through the back of the house carrying her child with her. They cut her in half, and falling, the child was bathed in her mother's blood and although unconscious, was unharmed. From there, they would have wrapped her up and given her to some important person who disposed of her.
>
> What is known therefore is:
>
> 1. That they took her away from the house alive.
>
> 2. That the intervening forces took her away and that they are therefore responsible for the baby's life, but we cannot demonstrate this.
>
> 3. That she must have been given away or sold.
>
> The names of the military and police officers who were present while DANIEL'S house was being attacked appeared in the newspapers of November 25, 1976. I believe that they must naturally know CLARA ANAHI'S fate. And we also feel

> that they must be able to remember the event well because it was the longest, one of the bloodiest and I believe the only one, where, at the end, they used a bomb generating a temperature of 2000 degrees, to end the resistance. (This is what was said at the Federal Police in La Plata.) . . .

The Commission received the following additional information from the complainant in a note dated August 18, 1978:

> There was hope of finding CLARA ANAHI through the National Juvenile Bureau, but they say that there are no records on file. There are still checking adoptions during the past two years at our request. They don't know what results this might bring; let us hope that they might be able to locate one of the fifteen babies that we are looking for.

7. In a communication dated August 30, 1978, the Commission forwarded the complainant's observations to the Government of Argentina, and asked it to provide the pertinent information.

8. In note SG 235, dated September 18, 1978, the Government of Argentina replied to the complainant's observations, but failed to refer to the events denounced and forwarded to them; it merely reported in the following terms:

> . . . C. Persons on whom investigator proceedings have been started to determine their whereabouts and possible status because there was no record of denunciations earlier than that made by that Commission:
>
> . . . 16. MARIANI Clara Anahí (Case 2553).

9. The pertinent parts of the reply from the Government of Argentina were sent to the complainant in a communication dated October 3, 1978.

10. In a letter dated September 30, 1978, the complainant provided the following additional information:

> I am now able to add to the documentation a newspaper clipping from that fateful date, which mentions the Infantry Corps of the Province of Buenos Aires, which took a very active part in the siege and attack upon the residence of the father of CLARA ANAHI. I believe that its chief, might know to whom the child was given.

11. The Commission has in its possession a photocopy of the writ of *habeas corpus* presented by the claimant.

12. It should be pointed out that the notes from the Government of Argentina dated May 21 and September 18, 1978 are contradictory, in that the first refers to investigations conducted on the case, while the second states that investigator proceedings were being initiated because no denunciation had been filed prior to the one submitted by the Commission. In that connection, the first communication on this case from the Commission to the Government of Argentina is dated February 7, 1978 and according to the Certification issued by Juvenile Court N° 2 of the La Plata Judicial Department, the proceedings — N° 36.792 — began on April 26, 1977.

WHEREAS:

1. In light of the background information given above, it is found that the child CLARA ANAHI MARIANI was taken from her home by Argentinean military

officers in the operation conducted by those forces on November 24, 1976, on 30th Street, 55-56, in the city of La Plata, and her whereabouts since that date are unknown;

2. The notes from the Government of Argentina of May 21 and September 18, 1978 fail to refer to the events specifically denounced and transmitted to it by the Commission in notes of February 7 and August 30, 1978, and are contradictory,

THE INTER-AMERICAN COMMISSION ON HUMAN RIGHTS, RESOLVES:

1. To observe to the Government of Argentina that such acts are very serious violations of the right to liberty and personal security (Art. I) and of the right to protection from arbitrary arrest (Art. XXV) in the American Declaration of the Rights and Duties of Man.

2. To recommend to the Government of Argentina: a. that it return the child CLARA ANAHI MARIANI to her family; b. that it order a complete, impartial investigation to determine the responsibility for the events denounced; c. that it punish those responsible for such acts, in accordance with Argentine law, and d. that it inform the Commission, within a maximum of 30 days, of the measures it has taken to put into practice the recommendations contained in the present Resolution.

3. To communicate this resolution to the Government of Argentina and to the claimant.

4. To include this Resolution in the Annual Report to the General Assembly of the Organization of American States, pursuant to Article 9 (bis) paragraph *c*.iii of the Statute of the Commission.

While the number of petitions arriving before the Commission continues to rise, observers have been critical of many aspects of the procedure. The following study (written before recent reforms in Commission procedure) indicate some of the most common criticisms of the Commission throughout the 1980s and early 1990s.

Association of the Bar of the City of New York, Committee on International Human Rights, "The Inter-American Commission: A Promise Unfulfilled"

48 *The Record* 589, 598-602, 603-604, 606-608, 611-613 (1993)

The current functions of the Commission include making recommendations to member states of the OAS about measures in aid of human rights, requesting the states to prepare reports, responding to inquiries made by made by states concerning human rights, preparing reports, making on-site visits, and preparing protocols and amendments to the American Convention on Human Rights. The Commission thus has administrative, drafting, and even diplomatic functions, in addition to the quasi-judicial function of examining and deciding upon individual petitions. Everyone interviewed about the work of the Commission, those who are its most enthusiastic supporters, as well as its critics, agreed that many of the problems with the work of the Commission concerning individual petitions grow out of this profusion which tends to lead to a confusion of functions. . . .

The problems that confront the Inter-American Commission in cases of individual complaints alleging human rights violations . . . are especially difficult. Just investigating such a case can be daunting, according to accounts from Commission staff and consultants, because of threats to the lives of witnesses, as well as the difficulties of travel and communication over large distances. Further, the Commission's powers under the American Convention, much less its residual jurisdiction under the OAS Charter, do not give it enough authority to obtain redress from a recalcitrant government without strong support from the OAS itself. Nevertheless, the inadequacies of the Commission's work on individual complaints cannot be explained fully by the intractability of the cases. . . . [Neither] the difficulty of the cases or the obstruction of governments [is] alone sufficient to explain why the Commission's decisions are often not persuasive or well-reasoned, nor why they are so long delayed. . . .

To some extent, the shortcomings of the Commission can be explained by pressures from the OAS, either exerted directly through intervention at the Commission, or through budget decisions and control of staffing. It is also true, however, as will appear more fully in the sections that follow, that they result from working methods of the Commission and its staff that can and should be changed.

The Politics and Law of Individual Petitions

Critics described the problems with the Commission's treatment of individual petitions in several ways. It was said that the Commission does not follow its own regulations, that it is confused about its functions, and, most bluntly, that its decisions are politicized. The Committee has concluded that all of these are aspects of one problem: the Commission does not function well as a neutral, quasi-judicial adjudicative body for individual cases.

Some of the functions assigned to the Commission are diplomatic and political. Thus, advising member states about human rights matters, or drafting proposed new human rights instruments, call for political and diplomatic skills. Even preparing a report concerning the overall human rights situation in an entire country doubtless involves political decisions. But in the individual cases, the Commission has an adjudicative function — to determine and state the law and the facts with respect to an individual or group. The Commission, however, often confuses its other functions with its adjudicative role, treating individual complaints as diplomatic and political as much as legal problems. . . .

The manipulation of the Commission's regulations for political and negotiation purposes, with its attendant delays, finally provoked sharp criticism from the Inter-American Court in an opinion [Advisory Opinion OC-12/91 of 6 Dec. 1991] at the end of 1991 that undoubtedly did not did not improve the already strained relations between the Court and the Commission. In that case, the government of Costa Rica sought the advice of the Court concerning whether proposed Costa Rican laws would infringe upon the right to appeal in criminal cases established by the American Convention. The Court declined to give the advice, because there were individual complaints pending before the Commission, never decided or sent to the Court, which might have resolved the question of law through a contentious case. Some of those complaints had been pending since before 1986, during which time the Commission had given Costa Rica repeated opportunities, extending over five years, to resolve the question of law through legislation, while delaying the resolution of the individual cases. The Commission's strategy of delay had denied the complainants the opportunity to determine their rights through individual eases, without yielding any result through the negotiation process. . . .

Its opinions have been criticized for being poorly reasoned; indeed, an examination of decisions in the annual reports shows that sometimes they are little more than collections of events, dates, and conclusions. It is clear that the situation is in part a result of the poor record of obedience to decisions from the respondent states, the failure of the OAS to insist on compliance, and the pressure from some member states to be even more lenient in enforcement. It is doubtless difficult to take decision-making seriously when important decisions result in verbal abuse amounting almost to threats; Uruguay, for example, was most vociferous at the spring, 1992, meeting of the OAS in advocating restrictions on the Commission's work. It is equally clear that the pressures in the OAS can be countered chiefly by the leadership of those states, including the United States, that claim to be committed to the enforcement of international human rights. . . .

PROCEDURAL ERRORS

. . . [M]ost sources interviewed by the Committee agreed that the results of cases could be better if a more nearly judicial attitude were taken toward them. The manipulation and disregard of regulations has led to slipshod handling of cases, with results that encourage disrespect and create legal difficulties for the Commission. The important case concerning the massacre by the army, using axes, machetes and knives, of at least twenty-nine villagers at Cayara in the Ayaeucho region of Peru in 1988, gave rise to a grim comedy of errors. The Commission submitted the case to the Court at the end of May 1991, only to be informed by Peru that the Commission had failed to forward to the government some of the petitioners' responses to the government's arguments, as the Commission was required to do under its regulations. The Commission staff chose to withdraw the case from the Court — an act for which there is no specific provision in the law - and to send the missing papers to the government. When the Commission then re-submitted the case to the Court in 1992, Peru made preliminary objections in effect that the Commission had no power to withdraw and re-submit the case. . . . [The Court agreed with Peru and consequently dismissed the case.]

BUDGET

The budgetary situation of the Inter-American Commission on Human Rights is, in a word, a scandal. The budget is much too small [ranging from 1.6-2.2% of the total OAS budget between 1987 and 1991], viewed either as a percentage of the OAS budget, or from the point of view of the work to be done by the Commission. . . . All sources agreed that while the members of the OAS give lip-service to human rights, many of them who are in fact offended by the attentions of the Commission, [and] work to keep it starved for funds so that it will not be able to function as effectively as it could. . . .

Personnel and Staff

The election process in the OAS has not always produced Commissioners with a strong commitment to human rights; moreover, the Commission is not getting the full benefit of the talents of its present Commissioners. Although the Commission's statute authorizes them to meet for up to eight weeks, in 1991 they met for only four weeks; it seems doubtful that there is budget available for them to meet more than that.... [The Commission continued to meet for only four weeks annually through 1994.]

Furthermore, the present Commission staff of seven human rights specialists, together with the Executive Secretary and the support staff, is far too small to investigate and prepare cases in a region as vast as the Americas. Each lawyer is potentially responsible for complaints from as many as six countries, a situation that verges on the absurd. All sources interviewed by the Committee thought that the legal staff ought to be at least twice as large as it is, and probably larger.

The Commission responded in various ways to critiques like those in the preceding extract. It should be noted, however, that the Commission was also under attack from states whose human rights performance it had criticized, notably Peru during the administration of President Fujimori. The Commission revised its Rules of Procedure in 2001 (Documentary Supplement, page 1017), separating its consideration of admissibility from any decision on the merits in the handling of petitions. It also established a more transparent and consistent set of rules for transmitting cases to the Court. Thirdly, the Commission established a follow-up procedure to monitor compliance with its decisions.

The impact of politics on the Commission may be even more insidious when it is dealing with a government that is not unrelievedly repressive. This situation is illustrated by an individual case that challenged the legality of certain Mexican elections held in 1990. The Commission adopted Report No. 7/93 "on a provisional basis," which it sent to the Mexican government (not to the complainant) but never published. Following the Mexican government's response, the Commission adopted and published a second report, noting, inter alia, that "progress has been made at the legislative level, a fact which is important to note . . . ; some of the new provisions are in response to the recommendations issued by the Commission, and some others, independently of those recommendations, further the aim of ensuring free and genuine elections." . . . The Commission continued by expressing its "hopes that, as it was told by the authorities of that country, these amendments will effectively allow greater 'authenticity, equality, and transparency' in current and future electoral processes, and trusts that the recommendations this Commission has been making for some time to the Mexican authorities will be carried out . . . legislatively and operationally by the competent authorities." Report No. 14/93, Case 10.956 (Mexico), reprinted in Annual Report of the Inter-American Commission on Human Rights 1993, at 259, 291, 292, O.A.S. Doc. OEA/Ser.L/V/II.85, Doc. 9 rev. (1993). No public finding was ever made on the allegations of fraud raised by the initial complainant.

Note: The Concept of Continuing Violations

The restoration of democracy in Argentina in 1983 and subsequent efforts to deal with (or ignore) the crimes committed during the "Dirty War" are considered in Chapter 11, page 967. One of the most significant issues has been whether various amnesty laws adopted during the 1980s were legitimate; such laws were rejected by the Inter-American Commission in 1992 and ultimately by Argentina itself. See Report N° 28/92, Cases 10.147, 10.181, 10.240, 10.262, 10.309 and 10.311 (Argentina), Annual Report of the Inter-American Commission on Human Rights 1992-1993, OAS Doc. OEA/Ser.L/V/II.83, Doc. 14, corr. 1 (1993).

The Commission held, inter alia, that the granting of amnesty and the refusal to account for disappearances and murders that occurred between 1976 and 1983 constituted continuing failures by the government to live up to its obligations under Article 1(1) of the Convention (which Argentina ratified in 1984). With respect to the temporal aspects of an amnesty case, consider *Blake v. Guatemala*, extracts from which are set out below. Guatemala filed three preliminary objections to the Court's jurisdiction over a case of disappearance in that country. The first and most significant argued that the Inter-American Court was incompetent to try the case, inasmuch as Guatemala recognized the compulsory competence of the Court exclusively for cases that occurred after the date on which the declaration was deposited with the Secretariat of the Organization of American States. Blake disappeared on March 28, 1985, and was killed on March 29, 1985, according to the death certificate. Guatemala accepted the jurisdiction of the Court two years later, on March 9, 1987, with the explicit statement that such acceptance applied exclusively to events that "*occurred after the date on which the instrument of acceptance was deposited with the Secretariat of the Organization of American States.*" *Blake* Case (Preliminary Objections), 27 Inter-Am. Ct. H.R. (ser. C) (1998), para. 36 (emphasis in original).

The Government maintained that the violations ended in March 1985, while the Commission contended that the effects are continuous, since the deprivation of Mr. Blake's liberty and his death were discovered many years later and its consequences are still being felt, inasmuch as "they derive from Mr. Blake's kidnapping and subsequent forced disappearance by agents of the Guatemalan State and comprise, in addition to that crime, a series of violations including the cover-up of the disappearance by high-level Government officials and the Guatemalan Armed Forces, as well as the delay and consequent denial of justice by the Guatemalan State." The Court agreed that the acts of deprivation of Mr. Blake's liberty and his murder were indeed completed in March 1985 and that those events cannot be considered *per se* to be continuous. The Court therefore lacked competence to rule on the Government's liability. However, the Court distinguished those facts from the remaining allegations.

Blake v. Guatemala (Preliminary Objections)

Judgment of July 2, 1996, 27 Inter-Am. Ct. H.R. (ser. C) (notes omitted)

34. . . . [S]ince the question is one of forced disappearance, the consequences of those acts extended to June 14, 1992. As the Commission states in its application,

government authorities or agents committed subsequent acts, and this, in the Commission's view, implies complicity in, and concealment of, Mr. Blake's arrest and murder. Although the victim's death was known to the authorities or agents, his relatives were not informed despite their unstinting efforts to discover his whereabouts, and because attempts had been made to dispose of the remains. The Commission also claims that there were further violations of the American Convention connected with these events.

35. In the first cases of disappearance of persons submitted to it this Court maintained that:

> [t]he forced disappearance of human beings is a multiple and continuous violation of many rights under the Convention that the States Parties are obligated to respect and guarantee . . . The practice of disappearance, in addition to directly violating many provisions of the Convention, such as those noted above, constitutes a radical breach of the treaty in that it shows a crass abandonment of the values which emanate from the concept of human dignity and of the most basic principles of the inter-American system and the Convention. The existence of this practice, moreover, evinces a disregard of the duty to organize the State is such a manner a to guarantee the rights recognized in the Convention (*Velásquez Rodríguez Case*, Judgment of July 29, 1988. Series C No. 4, paras. 155 and 158, and *Godínez Cruz Case*, Judgment of January 20, 1989. Series C No. 5, paras. 163 and 166).

36. There is no treaty in force containing a legal definition of forced disappearance of persons which is applicable to the States Parties to the Convention. However, note should be taken of the texts of two instruments, the United Nations Declaration on the Protection of All Persons from Enforced Disappearance, of December 18, 1992, and the Inter-American Convention on Forced Disappearance of Persons, of June 9, 1994. Although the latter has not yet entered into force for Guatemala, these instruments embody several principles of international law on the subject and they may be invoked pursuant to Article 29(d) of the American Convention. In the terms of that article, no provision of this Convention shall be interpreted as *"excluding or limiting the effects that the American Declaration of the Rights and Duties of Man and other international acts of the same nature may have."*

37. Article 17(1) of the United Nations Declaration states that:

> Acts constituting enforced disappearance shall be considered a continuing offense as long as its perpetrators continue to conceal the fate and the whereabouts of persons who have disappeared and as long as these facts remain unclarified.

Article III of the aforementioned Inter-American Convention provides that:

> The States Parties undertake to adopt, in accordance with their constitutional procedures, the legislative measures that may be needed to define the forced disappearance of persons as an offense and to impose an appropriate punishment commensurate with its extreme gravity. This offense shall be deemed continuous or permanent as long as the fate or whereabouts of the victim has not been determined.

38. In addition, in Guatemala's domestic legislation, Article 201 TER of the Penal Code — amending decree No. 33-96 of the Congress of the Republic approved on May 22, 1996 — stipulates in the pertinent part that the crime of

forced disappearance *"shall be deemed to be continuing until such time as the victim is freed."*

39. The foregoing means that, in accordance with the aforementioned principles of international law which are also embodied in Guatemalan legislation, forced disappearance implies the violation of various human rights recognized in international human rights treaties, including the American Convention, and that the effects of such infringements — even though some may have been completed, as in the instant case — may be prolonged continuously or permanently until such time as the victim's fate or whereabouts are established.

40. In the light of the above, as Mr. Blake's fate or whereabouts were not known to his family until June 14, 1992, that is, after the date on which Guatemala accepted the contentious jurisdiction of this Court, the preliminary objection raised by the Government must be deemed to be without merit insofar as it relates to effects and actions subsequent to its acceptance. The Court is therefore competent to examine the possible violations which the Commission imputes to the Government in connection with those effects and actions.

3. Friendly Settlement

The American Convention and the Commission's Rules of Procedure require the Commission to place itself at the disposal of the parties, with a view to reaching a settlement of the dispute grounded in respect for human rights. The friendly settlement procedure requires the consent of both parties, and either of them may terminate it at any stage. The Commission, which acts as the moderator of meetings to facilitate agreement, is increasingly encouraging friendly settlement negotiations. In general, the Commission allows six months to achieve a settlement, although this may be extended with the consent of the parties. If a friendly settlement is undertaken, the Commissioner who is rapporteur for the country, along with a staff attorney, handles the proceeding. At any point in the process, if the Commission finds that either of the parties is not participating in good faith, the procedure may be terminated. If a friendly settlement is reached, the Commission prepares a report which it transmits to the parties and refers to the Secretary-General of the OAS for publication.

Report No. 21/00, Case 12.059, Carmen Aguiar De Lapacó (Argentina)

February 29, 2000, Ann. Rep. of the Inter-Am. Comm'n H.R., OEA/Ser.L/V/II.106 Doc. 6, rev., Apr. 13, 1999 (notes omitted)

[The case arose from a complaint filed with the Commission by the Grandmothers of the Plaza de Mayo and other organizations in 1998, alleging that the refusal of Argentina to determine what had happened to the petitioner's daughter, who was detained and disappeared in 1977, violated her rights. The petitioners contended that the denial of the mother's petition by the Argentine authorities violated the right to judicial guarantees (Article 8(1)), the right to effective judicial protection (Article 25), and the obligation to respect the rights protected by the American Convention on Human Rights (Article 1(1)). The

Commission actively participated in negotiating a friendly settlement between the two parties, which was signed in Buenos Aires in 1999 in the presence of the Commission's President.]

. . .

17. The State and the petitioners signed an agreement for a friendly settlement containing the following admissions and obligations:

With regard to Case 12,059, before the Inter-American Commission on Human Rights, the Argentine Government and Mrs. Carmen Aguiar de Lapacó, with the mediation of Deputy Alicia Pierini, hereby agree to the following:

1. RIGHT TO THE TRUTH: The Argentine Government accepts and guarantees the right to the truth, which involves the exhaustion of all means to obtain information on the whereabouts of the disappeared persons. It is an obligation of means, not of results, which is valid as long as the results are not achieved, not subject to prescription. This right is specifically recognized in relation to the disappearance of Alejandra Lapacó.

2. EXCLUSIVE JURISDICTION OF THE FEDERAL COURTS: The Argentine Government shall adopt the necessary laws to ensure that the national federal criminal and correctional courts throughout the country have exclusive jurisdiction in all cases to determine the truth regarding the fate of persons who disappeared prior to December 10, 1983, with the sole exception of cases involving kidnapping of minors and theft of identity, which shall continue on the basis of their status.

3. SPECIAL ASSISTING PROSECUTORS: The Argentine Government shall arrange for the Office of the Attorney General to assign an ad hoc group of prosecutors, consisting of at least two, to act as third parties, without displacing the regular functionaries, in all cases involving inquiries into the truth and the fate of disappeared persons. In this way, there will be a specialized search and interpretation of data and better centralization and circulation of information among the various cases.

4. SUSPENSION OF LEGAL PROCEEDINGS: The plaintiff shall refrain from pursuing its international proceeding until this agreement is fulfilled. . . .

20. In the opinion of the Commission, it is appropriate to reiterate that pursuant to Articles 48(1)(f) and 49 of the Convention, the purpose of this procedure is "to arrive at a friendly settlement of the matter on the basis of respect for the human rights recognized in this Convention." The fact that the State has agreed to this process is a sign of its good faith to comply with the purposes and objectives of the Convention, on the basis of the principle of *pacta sunt servanda*, under which States should comply in good faith with obligations assumed in treaties. The Commission also wishes to reiterate that the procedure for a friendly settlement established in the American Convention allows for the termination of individual cases in a noncontentious manner and, in cases involving various countries, it has proven to provide an important vehicle for a settlement, one that can be used by both parties (petitioners and the State).

Comments and Questions

1. Given the government's uncooperative attitude during the 1970s, of what use was it to take a disappearance case to the Inter-American Commission at that

time? Despite the lack of results for the individuals concerned, did the cases nonetheless have an impact in strengthening arguments for an on-site visit? Preparing a record for later claims?

2. The power to issue precautionary measures was granted to the Commission when it received the mandate to consider individual petitions in 1965. The most relevant provision, Article 25(1) of the 2001 Rules of Procedure, states, "In serious and urgent cases, and whenever necessary according to the information available, the Commission may, on its own initiative or at the request of a party, request that the State concerned adopt precautionary measures to prevent irreparable harm to persons." Pursuant to the American Convention on Human Rights, the Commission also may request that the Inter-American Court order "provisional measures" in urgent cases which involve danger to persons, even where a case has not yet been submitted to the Court.

As the number of petitions submitted to the Commission has grown each year, so have the number of requests for precautionary measures. During the last several years, the Commission has ordered more measures than any other international human rights body. The Commission granted or extended 53 precautionary measures in 1998 and early 1999, 60 in 1999 and early 2000, 52 during the rest of 2000 and 54 during 2001, making a total of 219 orders in just four years. Furthermore, the number of precautionary measures is well below the number of individuals protected, because the measures can protect either one person or a group of persons, often covering entire populations or communities. In a single request involving Paraguay, for example, the Commission requested that precautionary measures be adopted on behalf of 255 minors who had been held at the Panchito López Reeducation Center for Minors (petition 11.666). After a fire in the facility, the children had been transferred to other facilities, some of which failed to meet the minimum standards needed to guarantee the physical integrity of the minor inmates; others were sent to different parts of the country and were placed in prisons with small, overcrowded cells alongside adults; the relocation was said to aggravate the children's critical situation and make family visits impossible. At what point in a case can the Commission issue or request that the Court issue provisional measures? Does the case have to be deemed admissible first or can the Commission act at an earlier point in the proceedings?

3. On February 25, 2002, the Center for Constitutional Rights, a U.S. based non-governmental organization, filed a request for precautionary measures under article 25 of the Commission's regulations, in respect to detainees held by the United States in Guantanamo Bay, Cuba (see Chapter 4). The Commission accepted the petition and, on March 12, 2002, requested the United States "to take the urgent measures necessary to have the legal status of the detainees at Guantanamo Bay determined by a competent tribunal." What is the legal effect of this request? The Commission has stated that decisions on precautionary measures, when considered "essential to preserving the Commission's mandate," are legally binding. Is this such a case? Note that the International Court of Justice also held for the first time in a recent case that its decisions on precautionary measures are legally binding. See the *LaGrand Case* (*Germany v. United States*), 2001 I.C.J. Rep., paras. 93-109.

The single largest group of precautionary measures has concerned death-row inmates. The Commission has issued some 75 requests for precautionary measures in pending cases, primarily involving Jamaica, Trinidad and Tobago, and the United States. Because the death penalty is not prohibited by the Declaration or Convention, the petitioners in these cases have generally challenged the fairness of the proceedings that resulted in their conviction and sentence.

4. How flexible is the concept of a "continuing violation" of human rights norms? Is there any violation committed in the past that does not continue to affect the victim or his or her relatives, or is there something unique about the phenomenon of disappearances?

5. The Inter-American Commission on Human Rights has only seven members; its legal staff consists of approximately 20 attorneys, of whom close to a quarter are fellows. Europe, in contrast, is home to a full-time human rights court of 45 judges, serviced by a secretariat that numbers in the hundreds. Since adoption of its procedural reforms in 2001, the Inter-American Commission has reported that approximately 900-1,000 cases are "being processed" during any given year, yet the Commission takes formal decisions (to declare a petition admissible or inadmissible, approve a friendly settlement, adopt a report on the merits, or close a case for other reasons) on an average of only 10% of those cases annually. While most observers would agree that the Commission's procedures have improved significantly in recent years, can this situation continue? What reforms might you suggest?

6. More than 20 years have passed since democracy was restored to Argentina in 1983, and dealing with the crimes of that era is still not complete. The issue of what international law obliges a state to do with respect to past crimes is considered more fully in Chapter 11; the case of Argentina is discussed at pages 967 and 970.

C. *Compliance with the Recommendations of the IACHR*

Between 1965, when the IACHR was expressly authorized to examine complaints or petitions regarding specific cases of human rights violations, and 2004, the IACHR examined nearly 10,000 complaints. The total number of complaints received in recent years is shown in the following table. "Complaints" for the purposes of these statistics includes all complaints presented in writing that concern an alleged violation by an OAS member state of the Convention, the Declaration, and/or other pertinent instrument. From Inter-Am. Comm'n H. R., Annual Report 2004, OAS Doc. OEA/Ser.L/V/II.122, Doc. 5 rev. 1 (2005). Note the large spike in cases from Argentina in 2002; 3635 of the petitions were from or on behalf of persons affected by certain banking measures taken by the state.

The Commission's staff has not increased in response to the growing caseload. Instead, following the 2001 revision of the rules of procedure, the Commission began sending virtually all cases in which it finds a violation to the Court, obviating the need for the Commission to publish a reasoned decision on the merits. Given the part-time nature of the Court and its limited staff and budget, this shifting of the workload does not improve the efficiency of the system, although it is possible that it may improve compliance in the long run, if states do tend to comply more readily with judicial decisions than with recommendations of quasi-judicial bodies like the Commission. See Douglas Cassell, "Inter-American

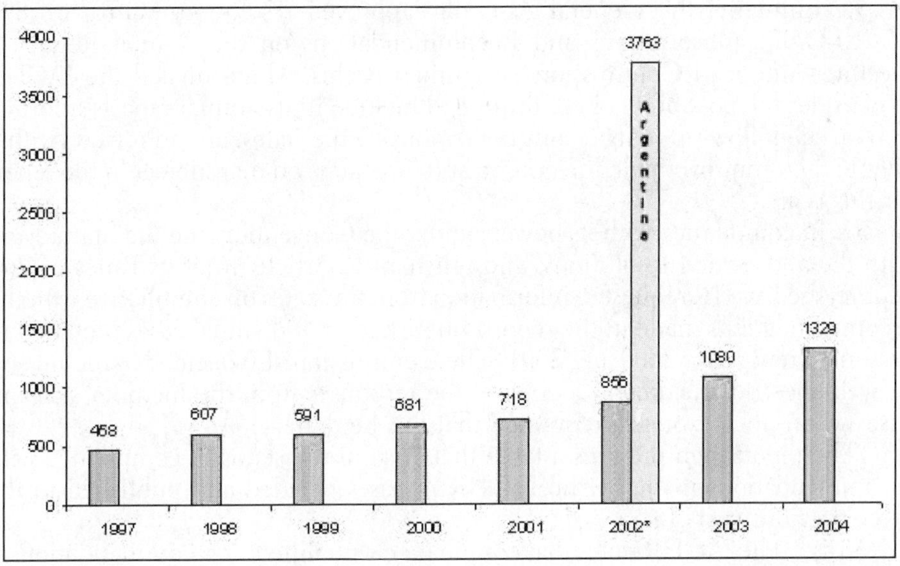

Human Rights Law, Soft and Hard," in *Commitment and Compliance: The Role of Non-Binding Norms in the International Legal System* 393-418 (Dinah Shelton ed., 2000). The following extract considers the continuing concern with compliance.

Inter-American Commission on Human Rights, Annual Report 2004

OAS Doc. OEA/Ser.L/V/II.122, Doc. 5 rev. 1 (2005)

53. Complete compliance with the decisions of the Inter-American Commission is essential for ensuring that human rights have full force in the OAS member states, and for helping strengthen the Inter-American system for the protection of human rights. With that in mind, the IACHR, in this section, analyzes the status of compliance with the recommendations in the reports adopted by the Commission in the last three years. . . .

55. Both the Convention (Article 41) and the Statute of the Commission (Article 18) explicitly grant the IACHR the authority to request information from the member states and to produce such reports and recommendations as it considers advisable. Specifically, Article 46 of the IACHR Rules of Procedure, which took effect on May 1, 2001, provides the following:

> 1. Once the Commission has published a report on a friendly settlement or on the merits in which it has made recommendations, it may adopt the follow-up measures it deems appropriate, such as requesting information from the parties and holding hearings in order to verify compliance with friendly settlement agreements and its recommendations.
>
> 2. The Commission shall report on progress in complying with those agreements and recommendations as it deems appropriate.

56. Similarly, the General Assembly approved resolution AG/RES. 1894 (XXXII-O/02), Observations and Recommendations on the Annual Report of the Inter-American Commission on Human Rights, which invited the IACHR to consider the possibility of continuing to include in its annual reports information on the follow-up of its recommendations by the states, and to review, with a view to their improvement, the criteria and indicators on that subject in the report for this year.

57. In compliance with its powers under the Convention and the Statute and with the above-cited resolutions, and pursuant to Article 46 of its Rules of Procedure, the IACHR requested information from the states on compliance with the recommendations made in the reports published on individual cases included in its annual reports for 2000 and 2001. The Commission also decided to include on its web page (*www.cidh.org*) a copy of the responses from the member states in cases where they expressly requested that this be done.

[The report then presents a table that sets out the status of compliance with recommendations made by the IACHR in cases decided and published in the three previous years.]

58.... The IACHR notes that compliance with different recommendations is meant to be successive and not immediate and that some recommendations require a reasonable time to be fully implemented. The table, therefore, presents the current status of compliance, which the Commission acknowledges as being a dynamic process that may evolve continuously. From that perspective, the Commission evaluates whether or not compliance with its recommendations is complete and not whether it has been started....

59. The three categories included in the table are the following:

— total compliance (those cases in which the state has fully complied with all the recommendations made by the IACHR...);

— partial compliance (those cases in which the state has partially observed the recommendations made by the IACHR either by having complied with only one or some of them or through incomplete compliance with all of them);

— compliance pending (those cases in which the IACHR considers that there has been no compliance with the recommendations because no steps have been taken in that direction; because the state has explicitly indicated that it will not comply with the recommendations made; or because the state has not reported to the IACHR and the Commission has no information from other sources that would suggest otherwise).

[Of the decided cases, the Commission identifies only five states as being in "total compliance"; 42 have partially complied, and compliance is "pending" in 23 states. Among the ten cases concerning the United States, nine are listed as "pending," and compliance with the recommendations in the remaining case is considered to be "partial."]

D. *Resolutions of OAS Political Bodies*

As is true for every international system for the protection of human rights, encouraging (or even coercing) compliance by states found to be in violation of their international obligations remains problematic. The OAS does not have an enforcement body similar to the Committee of Ministers of the Council of Europe. Instead, the Annual Reports of the Commission and the Commission's country reports are sent to the OAS General Assembly, which holds one regular session a year. In addition, the Consultation Meetings of Ministers of Foreign Affairs occasionally take action. The following reading and resolution indicate the potential for action by political bodies.

Thomas Buergenthal, "The Inter-American System for the Protection of Human Rights"

In 2 *Human Rights in International Law* 482-84 (Theodor Meron ed., 1984) (citations omitted)

. . . [F]or a number of years there seemed to be tacit agreement among OAS Member States not to discuss the annual reports that the Commission submitted to the Assembly. Instead, they would routinely and without debate adopt a resolution in which the General Assembly resolved "to take note of the annual report of the Inter-American Commission on Human Rights and to thank the Commission for the important work it has been doing."

The situation began to change in the mid-1970s. The first break with tradition occurred in 1975 when the OAS General Assembly had before it the Commission's annual report for the year 1974 as well as its report on "The Status of Human Rights in Chile." Although the Assembly once against passed its usual resolution on the annual report, it also adopted a separate resolution dealing with the Chilean report, which was preceded by a lengthy and well-publicized debate. . . .

At the next annual OAS General Assembly session, the Assembly adopted a much stronger resolution dealing with the Commission's report concerning violations of human rights in Chile, besides passing another resolution dealing with various specific issues that the Commission had raised in its annual report for the year 1975. This practice has continued, and specific human rights issues raised by annual reports of the Commission have been discussed and acted upon in recent OAS General Assembly sessions. . . .

The gradually stronger resolutions referred to by Buergenthal reached their apex in the following resolution, adopted by the Ministers of Foreign Affairs after the Commission concluded and submitted to the OAS its study of human rights violations by the Somoza regime in Nicaragua.

Resolution of the XVII Meeting of Consultation

Seventeenth Meeting of Consultation of Ministers of Foreign Affairs, Washington D.C., Sept. 21, 1978, OEA/Ser.F/II.17, Doc. 40/79, rev. 2, 23 June 1979, pp. 1–2.

RESOLUTION II

WHEREAS:

— The people of Nicaragua are suffering the horrors of a fierce armed conflict that is causing grave hardships and loss of life, and has thrown the country into a serious political, social and economic upheaval;

— The inhumane conduct of the dictatorial regime governing the country, as evidenced by the report of the Inter-American Commission on Human Rights, is the fundamental cause of the dramatic situation faced by the Nicaraguan people; and

— The spirit of solidarity that guides Hemispheric relations places an unavoidable obligation on the American countries to exert every effort within their power to put an end to the bloodshed and to avoid the prolongation of this conflict which is disrupting the peace of the Hemisphere;

The Seventeenth Meeting of Consultation of Ministers of Foreign Affairs,

DECLARES:

That the solution of the serious problem is exclusively within the jurisdiction of the people of Nicaragua.

That in the view of the Seventeenth Meeting of Consultation of Ministers of Foreign Affairs this solution should be arrived at on the basis of the following:

1. Immediate and definitive replacement of the Somoza regime.
2. Installation in Nicaraguan territory of a democratic government, the composition of which should include the principal representative groups which oppose the Somoza regime and which reflects the free will of the people of Nicaragua.
3. Guarantee of the respect for human rights of all Nicaraguans without exception.
4. The holding of free elections as soon as possible, that will lead to the establishment of a truly democratic government that guarantees peace, freedom, and justice.

The resolution had an impact on Nicaraguan President Anastasio Somoza. In his book, *Nicaragua Betrayed* (1981), he wrote that he announced to all his department commanders that he was going to resign "because our government cannot continue with the OAS resolution which was passed.... By total compliance with this resolution, you people may have a chance." Somoza added, "I wanted all of my people to know that I was not leaving because of fear, I was leaving because I had seventeen nations against me in the OAS and they were demanding my resignation." Id. at 266-67. Somoza went into exile in Miami and was assassinated in September 1980 in Asuncion, Paraguay.

E. *Proceedings before the Inter-American Court*

For the Court to have jurisdiction over an individual case, the state concerned must be a party to the American Convention and have accepted the optional jurisdiction of the Court; proceedings before the Commission must be completed, and the case must be referred by the Commission or the state concerned within three months after the Commission's preliminary report on the matter is transmitted to the parties. An individual petitioner cannot invoke the Court's jurisdiction. (directly)

Under current rules, there is a presumption that all cases should go to the Court if the Commission has found one or more violations and the responsible state has not complied with the Commission's recommendations within the time period specified. A reasoned decision by an absolute majority of the Commission is required to withhold such a case from the Court. Other factors that the Commission may consider include the nature and seriousness of the violation, the need to develop or clarify case law, the future effect of the decision on member states, the quality of the evidence, and the position taken by the petitioner.

Although individuals have no standing to bring cases to the Court, they are represented during all contentious proceedings and participate fully in all stages of Court proceedings before the Court, both written and oral. The first stage consists of a written memorial and counter-memorial. The Court also may ask each side for an offer of proof, to indicate the facts that each item of evidence is intended to prove and how, when, and under what circumstances the party wishes to present the evidence. The 2001 Rules of Court provide for combining arguments on preliminary objections, merits, and reparations in a single hearing, in the Court's discretion, in order to expedite the process. The Court's hearings are normally public but may be closed if the Court so decides. While the Court's deliberations are secret, its judgments and opinions are published.

Unlike the Commission, which can only make recommendations, the Court may order that the violation be remedied and may award compensation to the injured party. Compensation includes indemnification for actual damage, including emotional or moral injury, but does not include punitive damages. Specific orders for non-monetary relief may also be awarded, such as the release of detainees wrongfully held. States are legally obliged to comply with a judgment of the Court, and a remedial order may be enforced in the appropriate domestic courts.

Both the Court and Commission permit amicus curiae briefs to be filed. Such briefs are also important in regard to requests for advisory opinions of the Court, which can have a significant impact on human rights cases in the system.

Reparations

Inter-American Court of Human Rights, *Garrido and Baigorria Case (Reparations)* (Art. 63(1) of The American Convention on Human Rights)

Judgment of August 27, 1998, Ser. C No. 39 (some references omitted)

VI. Obligation to Make Reparations (Article 63(1))

38. In the instant case, Argentina admitted its responsibility for the facts set forth in the Commission's application and it was so recorded in the judgment of February 2, 1996. Hence, the facts recounted in section II of the Commission's application of May 29, 1995, have been established. On the other hand, the parties have differences on other facts having to do with reparations and their scope; it is those differences that the Court is deciding in this judgment.

39. The provision applicable to reparations is Article 63(1) of the American Convention, which states the following:

> 1. If the Court finds that there has been a violation of a right or freedom protected by this Convention, the Court shall rule that the injured party be ensured the enjoyment of his right or freedom that was violated. It shall also rule, if appropriate, that the consequences of the measures or situation that constituted the breach of such right or freedom be remedied and that fair compensation be paid to the injured party.

40. As the Court has stated (*Aloeboetoe et al. Case, Reparations (Art. 63(1), American Convention on Human Rights)*, Judgment of September 10, 1993. Series C No. 15, para. 43), this Article codifies a rule of customary law which is one of the fundamental principles of modern international law, that being the responsibility of States (*Cf. Factory at Chorzow Case, Jurisdiction*, Judgment No. 8, 1927, P.C.I.J., Ser. A, No. 9, p. 21 and *Factory at Chorzow Case, Merits*, Judgment No. 13, 1928, P.C.I.J., Ser. A, No. 17, p. 29; *Reparation for Injuries Suffered in the Service of the United Nations*, Advisory Opinion, I.C.J. Reports 1949, page 184). This is the case law of this Court.... The case law also holds that the obligation embodied in this article is a necessary corollary of the right (decision of rapporteur Max Huber, dated 23.X.1924, in the case of *British Property in the Spanish Zone of Morocco, Compromis*, U.N., Recueil des sentences arbitrales, vol. II, p. 641; *Case Concerning the Barcelona Traction, Light and Power Company, Limited* (Second Phase), Judgment, I.C.J. *Recueil* 1970, p. 33). When an unlawful act imputable to a State occurs, said State becomes internationally responsible for a violation of international law. It is out of this responsibility that a new juridical relationship for the State emerges, which is the obligation to make reparation.

While in both jurisprudence and doctrine there is a certain degree of consensus regarding how the rule enunciated in Article 63(1) of the American Convention is to be interpreted and applied, the Court believes that some clarification is in order.

41. First, some explanation of the terminology employed is useful. Reparation is a generic term that covers the various ways a state may make amends for the international responsibility it has incurred. The specific method of reparation varies according to the damage caused; it may be *restitutio in integrum* of the violated rights, medical treatment to restore the injured person to physical health, an obligation on the part of the State to nullify certain administrative measures, restoration of the good name or honor that were stolen, payment of an indemnity, and so on. When the right to life is violated, as it was in the instant case, given the nature of the right violated, the reparation is primarily in the form of some pecuniary compensation, as has been the practice of this Court. The reparation may also be in the form of measures intended to prevent a recurrence of the offending acts.

42. Given the submissions filed by the victims' families, it is important to point out that the obligation contained in Article 63(1) of the Convention is governed by international law in all of its aspects, such as, for example, its scope, characteristics, beneficiaries, etc. Such was the Court's finding in the *Aloeboetoe et al. Case*.

43. In certain passages of the submissions filed by the victims' families, they seek indemnification that would go beyond the realm of compensation for damages caused, and into the punitive realm. At the January 20, 1998 hearing,

for example, the representative of the victims' relatives demanded "exemplary damages." Such functions are not in the nature of this Court and are not within its power. The Inter-American Court is not a penal court and, in this particular matter, its competence is to determine the reparations that States that have violated the Convention must make. As the word suggests, reparation is achieved through measures that serve to 'repair' the effects of the violation committed. Their quality and their amount depend on the damage done both at the material and at the moral levels. Reparations are not meant to enrich or impoverish the victim or his heirs (*Cf.* del ferrocarril de la bahía de *Delagoa Case*, LA FONTAINE, *Pasicrisie internationale*, Berne, 1902, p. 406).

44. In the cases against Honduras, the Court held that the expression "fair compensation" used in Article 63(1) of the Convention is "compensatory and not punitive" and that international law does not, at this time, use the principle of compensation "to deter or to serve as an example." Also, in the *Fairén Garbi and Solís Corrales Case*, this Court found that "the objective of international human rights law is not to punish those individuals who are guilty of violations, but rather to protect the victims and to provide for the reparation of damages." The Court finds no reason to deviate from these precedents in the instant case....

46. When a federal state's constituent units have jurisdiction over human rights matters, Article 28 of the Convention makes provision for said federal state becoming a party to the Convention. However, from the time of its approval and ratification of the Convention, Argentina has conducted itself as if the federal State had jurisdiction over human rights matters. Hence, it can hardly argue the contrary now, as this would imply a breach of the principle of *estoppel*. As for the "difficulties" invoked by the State at the January 20, 1998 hearing, the Court should note that the case law, which has stood unchanged for more than a century, holds that a State cannot plead its federal structure to avoid complying with an international obligation.

VII. Compensation

47. The Court will now proceed to decide on the reparations sought by the victims' relatives. The first type of reparation requested is compensation. As pointed out earlier in this judgment (*supra* 44), indemnizations are compensatory in nature and hence are to be awarded to the degree and in the measure sufficient to compensate for the material and moral damages suffered. The issue of honoraria and expenses incurred by virtue of these proceedings is examined in this judgment.

48. In the *Aloeboetoe et al. Case, Reparations*, the Court invoked arbitral case law wherein it is a general principle of law that compensation comprise both expenses and loss of earnings....

50. The Court has stated, and now reiterates, that the right to compensation for damages suffered by the victims up to the time of their death is transmitted to their heirs by succession. On the other hand, the damages owed to the victims' next of kin or to injured third parties for causing the victims' death are an inherent right that belongs to the injured parties....

58. To determine the material damages suffered, in the instant case it seems reasonable to identify the expenses incurred and lost earnings that the claimants

sustained. In the instant case, the Court must first ascertain what family, labor, business, farm, industrial or any other type of activity suffered a loss by virtue of the victims' deaths and who the injured parties are. Secondly, it must ascertain who has sustained a loss of income owing to the victim's disappearance. . . .

61. For the reasons set forth in the preceding paragraph, the Court denies the request for payment of material damages, because no such damages were proven.

62. As for the moral damages caused by the disappearance of Adolfo Garrido, the principal person affected is his mother, Ms. Rosa Sara Calderón. As the Court pointed out earlier, these damages do not require evidence as it is clear that the disappearance of her son caused his mother very grave suffering, particularly given the circumstances under which it occurred by reason of the reprehensible conduct of certain public servants in the Province of Mendoza involved in the instant case. One must also consider that as her son's heir, Ms. Rosa Sara Calderón succeeded him in the right to be compensated for the suffering he sustained in life. The Court believes that a fair figure for the total compensation for moral damages owed to Ms. Calderón is US$75,000. . . .

63. The siblings of Adolfo Garrido also claim they are entitled to compensation for moral damages. However, they offered no proof of an affective relationship such that the disappearance of their brother would have caused them grievous suffering. Some live more than 1,000 kilometers from where Mr. Garrido lived and there is no evidence to show that they visited each other frequently or that they took much interest in the life that their brother was leading when they might have. All that has been claimed are sporadic visits made when he was in prison. Quite the contrary, the siblings of Adolfo Garrido only showed serious concern when he disappeared. The Court considers US$6,000 . . . to be fair compensation for moral damages to each of Adolfo Garrido's siblings.

64. The siblings of Raúl Baigorria are also seeking compensation for moral damages caused by the disappearance of their brother. Their situation is analogous to that of the siblings of the other victim. They are not their brothers' heirs. They have not supplied any credible or convincing evidence demonstrating an affective relationship with the disappeared person that goes beyond simple consanguinity. There is no evidence that they visited him in prison or took any interest in him. They only showed an interest in his fate when he disappeared, whereupon they took several measures to ascertain his whereabouts. The Court considers fair compensation to be US$6,000 . . . for each of Raúl Baigorria's siblings.

65. Thus far Mr. Raúl Baigorria's natural children have not been located. They could not claim a right to be compensated for moral damages suffered with their father's disappearance, because it was not shown that they ever knew him or knew of him. But it is undoubtedly the case that as their father's heirs, they succeed him in the right to compensation for the suffering he sustained in life. And as already stated, these moral damages are obvious and do not need to be proven. The Court sets the amount of compensation for moral damages sustained by the victim at US$40,000 . . . with each son receiving half.

VIII. Other Forms of Reparation

66. In addition to compensation, the victims' families are seeking other forms of reparation. First, they ask that forced disappearance of persons be typified

under the penal code as a federal offense. Given the particular circumstances of the instant case, the Court does not consider it necessary to address this matter. Through its agent at the Court's January 20, 1998 public hearing, the State declared that the Government had already introduced in the National Congress a preliminary bill that typified forced disappearance of persons as a crime, in accordance with the Inter-American Convention on Forced Disappearance of Persons.

67. The Commission is requesting as reparations that the Court require that "the Argentine State publicize the report of the *ad hoc* Commission and the findings as widely as possible." At the January 20, 1998 hearing, the agent for Argentina stated that "the commitment to publish [that report] is not only approved, it is done." Under the particular circumstances of the instant case, and inasmuch as this judgment requires that Argentina investigate the facts leading to the disappearance of Mr. Garrido and Mr. Baigorria and punish those responsible (*infra* 73 and 74), no decision on the Commission's request is required.

IX. Duty to Act at the Domestic Level

68. Under the law of nations, a customary law prescribes that a State that has concluded an international agreement must introduce into its domestic laws whatever changes are needed to ensure execution of the obligations it has undertaken. This principle is universally valid and has been characterized in case law as an evident principle (*"principe allant de soi"*; *Exchange of Greek and Turkish populations, Advisory Opinion*, 1925, PCIJ, Series B No. 10, p. 20). Accordingly, the American Convention stipulates that every State Party is to adapt its domestic laws to the provisions of that Convention, so as to guarantee the rights embodied therein.

69. This obligation of the State Party implies that the domestic legal measures must be *effective*. This means the State must adopt all measures necessary so that provisions contained in the Convention have full force and effect within its domestic legal system. Those measures are effective when the community, in general, adapts its conduct to conform to the principles of the Convention and when, if those principles are breached, the penalties provided for therein are effectively applied. . . .

72. . . . The obligation to guarantee and ensure effective exercise is independent of and different from the obligation to make reparation. The difference lies in the following: the reparation provided for in Article 63(1) is an attempt to erase the consequences that the unlawful act may have had for the affected person, his family or close friends. Since the measure is intended to make reparations for a personal situation, the affected party has the right to waive that right. Thus, the Court could not object if an individual, particularly an adult, who was the victim of a human rights violation waived the compensation to which he or she was entitled. On the other hand, even though the aggrieved party may pardon the author of the violation of his human rights, the State is nonetheless obliged to sanction said author, except when the offense involved is prosecutable by a private party. The State's obligation to investigate the facts and punish those responsible does not erase the consequences of the unlawful act in the affected person.

Instead, the purpose of that obligation is that every State party ensure, within its legal system, the rights and freedoms recognized in the Convention.

73. The case law of this Court has consistently been that the State has a legal duty to take reasonable steps to prevent human rights violations and to use the means at its disposal to carry out a serious investigation of violations committed within its jurisdiction, to identify those responsible, to impose the appropriate punishment and to ensure the victim adequate compensation. If a violation goes unpunished in a State, in such a way that the victim's full enjoyment of such rights is not restored as soon as possible, the State has failed to comply with its obligation to ensure the free and full exercise of those rights to the persons within its jurisdiction.

74. It follows, therefore, that Argentina has a legal obligation to investigate the facts leading to the disappearance of Adolfo Garrido and Raúl Baigorria and to bring to trial and punish the authors, accomplices, accessories after the fact, and all those who may have played some role in the events that transpired.

X. Costs

. . .

80. In keeping with the relevant provisions and practice, the Court considers that the costs to which Article 55.1 of its Rules of Procedure refers include the various payments a victim makes or pledges to make in order to be able to have recourse to the inter-American system for protection of human rights. This includes the routine honoraria paid to those who provide the victim with legal assistance. Obviously, the only expenses allowed are those that are necessary and reasonable according to the specifics of each case, and that the victim or his or her representative has actually paid out or promised to pay. . . .

82. In exercise of its jurisdictional powers, it is up to the Court to make a prudent estimate of the specific extent of the costs that should be ordered, taking into account any receipts and vouchers provided, the particular circumstances of the case, the nature of the jurisdiction for the protection of human rights, and the characteristics of the respective proceedings, which are unique and different from those of other proceedings, both at the domestic and international levels. The Court shall determine the reasonable *quantum* of the costs incurred by the victims' families and their attorneys in the proceedings within the Argentine courts, with the Inter-American Commission and before this Court, on an equitable basis, and consider the "sufficient connection" that must exist between those costs and the results achieved.

83. In the Court's view, the method of setting costs as a percentage of the amount of compensation obtained is not adequate. There are other, more important factors to be weighed when assessing the performance of the attorneys in a proceeding before an international tribunal, such as the evidence introduced to demonstrate the facts alleged, full knowledge of international jurisprudence and, in general, everything that would demonstrate the quality and relevance of the work performed.

84. Another factor that needs to be considered to determine the fees of Mr. Varela-Alvarez and Mr. Lavado is that they shared representation of the victims' families with other attorneys at various stages of the process, both in proceedings in the domestic courts and before the Inter-American bodies.

85. Based on the foregoing, the Court sets costs at the sum of US$45,500 . . .; of that amount, US$20,000 . . . is to be the fees for the two attorneys.

Comments and Questions

1. The Court refers frequently to the *Aloeboetoe v. Suriname* case on the issue of reparations. In that case, Suriname accepted responsibility for the kidnapping and deaths of six young men and a 15-year old boy of the Saramaca tribe. The victims were forced to dig their own graves before six of them were killed. The seventh was shot and seriously wounded while trying to escape. He later died of his wounds after testifying about the massacre. On behalf of the victims' families, the Commission sought indemnification for material and moral damages, based on *restitutio in integrum*, other non-monetary reparations, and reimbursement of expenses and costs incurred by the victims' next of kin. The Commission used questionnaire-affidavits, administered with the permission of the Saramaca, to determine appropriate remedies. These were reviewed by an actuary from the accounting firm of Coopers and Lybrand to apply the 'present value added' method to determine projected earnings of the victims. The Commission identified 37 beneficiaries and submitted a total demand for pecuniary damages comprising a lump sum of US$2,557,242 ($557,000 for material damages to the children and an annual payment of $42,000 adjusted, for actual damages to the adult dependants).

In *Aloeboetoe,* the Court faced the difficult problem of identifying those among the family members of the deceased who were entitled to compensation. The case was brought by members of the Saramacas, or Maroons, descendants of African slaves who maintain a traditional culture, including a matriarchal social structure and polygamy. The Court, applying what it called a generally recognized choice of law principle, determined that local law should apply to determine next of kin and beneficiaries of the victims. Surinam law holds that a victim's next of kin includes the legally recognized spouse, the children, and perhaps dependent parents of the victims. The law does not recognize polygamy. In contrast, Saramaca tribal customary law accepts multiple marriages and the duty of adult children to care for their parents. The Court found that Surinam's family law was not effective in the region and was therefore not the local law for purposes of the case. As a result, the multiple wives and children of the victims were recognized by the Court.

2. How are damages for loss of life measured? Is the Court accurately considering the value of a human being? Does the value of human life vary, depending on the country in which the victim or family lives?

3. On what basis are non-monetary awards made? What purpose do they serve? Why does the Court reject the concept of punitive damages? Do you agree that they should be excluded?

4. In the case of *Loayza Tamaya v. Peru* (Reparations), 42 Inter-Am. Ct. H.R. (ser. C), judgment of 27 Nov. 1998, the Court accepted a new heading for damages: interference by the state with the victim's *proyecto de vida* (life plan). How can such an interference be evaluated and damages awarded?

IV. The United States and the Inter-American System

Although the United States has not ratified the American Convention on Human Rights, it remains subject to the jurisdiction of the Commission, as a party to the OAS Charter. The Commission remains the only international governmental body to have conducted a formal on-site investigation of human rights in the United States, which it did when it visited Haitian refugee camps in Florida and Puerto Rico in 1982. See Annual Report of the Inter-American Commission on Human Rights 7981-1982, at 17-18, O.A.S. Doe. OEA/Ser.L/V/II.57, Doc. 6 rev. 1 (1982). The situation of Haitians seeking to apply for asylum in the United States has been the subject of numerous complaints to the Commission, most of which have foundered on the rock of non-exhaustion of domestic remedies.

Many complaints filed against the United States in recent years have concerned the death penalty. See, e.g., a successful challenge to juvenile executions as a violation of Articles 1 and 2 of the American Declaration, Res. 3/87, Case 9647 (United States), reprinted in Annual Report of the Inter-American Commission on Human Rights 1986-87, at 148, OEA/Ser.L/V/II.71, Doc. 9, rev. 1 (1987); and allegations that the death penalty is imposed in a racially discriminatory manner, Res. No. 23/89, Case 10.031 (United States), reprinted in Annual Report of the Inter-American Commission on Human Rights 1989-1940, at 62, OEA/Ser.L/V/II.77, Doc. 7, rev. 1 (1990). Other death penalty cases include Report No. 99/03, *César Fierro*, Case 11.331 (United States), Inter-Am. Comm'n H.R., Annual Report 2003, OAS Doc. OEA/Ser.L/V/II.118, Doc. 5, rev. 2, 29 Dec. 2003; Report No. 100/03 *Douglas Christopher Thomas*, Case 12.240 (United States), Annual Report 2003, id.; Report No. 101/03 *Napoleon Beazley*, Case 12.412 (United States), Annual Report 2003, id.; Report No. 52/02 *Ramón Martínez Villareal*, Case 11.753 (United States) and Report No. 62/02 *Michael Domingues*, Case 12.285 (United States), both reported in Inter-Am. Comm'n H.R., Annual Report of the Commission 2003, OEA/Ser.L/V/II.117, Doc. 1 rev. 1, 7 March 2003.

Other complaints that have led to formal decisions by the Commission on allegations of human rights violations in the United States include an unsuccessful challenge to legalized abortion (the so-called "Baby Boy" case), Res. No. 23181, Case 2141 (United States), reprinted in Annual Report of the Inter-American Commission on Human Rights 1980-1987, at 25, OEA/Ser.L/V/II.54, Doc 9 rev. 1 (1981), and a complaint concerning police misconduct and alleged murder of members of the Move Organization in Philadelphia, which was declared inadmissible for failure to exhaust domestic remedies, Rep. No. 19/92, Case 10.865 (United States), reprinted in Annual Report of the Inter-American Commission on Human Rights 1992-1993, at 142, OEA/Ser.L/V/II.83, Doc. 14, corr.1 (1993). Another case upheld complaints of members of the Western Shoshone that the United States had interfered with their use and occupation of their ancestral lands by appropriating the lands as federal property through an unfair procedure before the Indian Claims Commission.Report No. 75/02, Case 11.140, *Mary and Carrie Dann* (United States), December 27, 2002, reprinted in Inter-Am. Comm'n H.R. 2003, OEA/Ser.L/V/II.117, Doc 1 rev 1, Mar. 7, 2003 (see Chapter 3, page 174).

As of 2005, there seemed little likelihood that the United States would ratify the American Convention on Human Rights in the near future, and the only official U.S. government position on its ratification remains that articulated in

1977 by President Carter. Many of the Carter Administration's objections to substantive provisions of the Convention are similar to those it made with respect to the Civil and Political Covenant, discussed in Chapter 2, page 89 . See Message of the President Transmitting Four Treaties Pertaining to Human Rights, S. Exec. Doc. Nos. 95-C, D, E, and F, 95th Cong. 2d Sess. XVII-XXIII (Feb. 23, 1978).

Note: Voting Rights and Self-Determination in the Americas

One of the most controversial cases involving the United States concerned the political rights of residents of the District of Columbia. The petitioner, Timothy Cooper, acting on behalf of the Statehood Solidarity Committee, alleged that the United States was responsible for violations of Articles II (right to equality before law) and XX (right to vote and to participate in government) of the American Declaration, because citizens of the District of Columbia are unable to vote for and elect members of the U.S. Congress.

Inter-American Commission on Human Rights, Report 98/03, Case 11.204, *Statehood Solidarity Committee* (United States)

Inter-Am. Comm'n H.R., Annual Report of the Commission 2004, OAS Doc. OEA/Ser.L/V/II.122, Doc. 5 rev. 1, 23 (2005).

97. Upon consideration of the parties' observations on the record of the case, the Commission must conclude that the Petitioners' rights to participate in the federal legislature of the United States have been limited or restricted both in law and in fact. As noted, it is agreed that as a matter of domestic constitutional law the Petitioners are not afforded the right to elect members of either chamber of Congress. While the State has contended that the District of Columbia elects a delegate to the House of Representatives who has the right to vote upon legislation in the Committee of the Whole, the record indicates that the delegate is prohibited from casting a deciding vote in respect of any legislation that comes before Congress. On this basis, the State's own courts have proclaimed that the vote extended to the District of Columbia delegate in the Committee of the Whole has no chance of affecting the ultimate result of matters coming before the Committee and is therefore "meaningless." Accordingly, the Commission cannot accept this arrangement as providing the Petitioners with effective participation in their legislature. For similar reasons, the ability of the Petitioners to elect representatives to other levels and branches of government and to participate in public debates on the status of the District of Columbia cannot be considered equivalent to the nature of participation contemplated by Article XX of the Declaration, which, in the Commission's view, entitles the Petitioners to a meaningful opportunity, directly or through freely elected representatives, to influence the decisions of government that affect them, including those of the federal legislature.

98. Therefore, to the extent that each of the Petitioners, unlike similarly situated citizens elsewhere in the United States, does not have the right to vote for a representative in their national legislature who has an effective opportunity to influence legislation considered by Congress, the Commission considers that

they have been denied an equal right under law in accordance with Article II of the Declaration to participate in the government of their country by reason of their place of residence, and accordingly that their right under Articles XX of the Declaration to participate in their federal government has been limited or restricted. . . .

99. The Commission must next consider whether this restriction or limitation on the rights under Article XX and II of the Declaration to vote and to participate in government with equality under law is nevertheless justified when analyzed in the general political context of the State concerned and thereby permissible under these articles of the Declaration. As noted above, this entails evaluating whether the restrictions imposed by the State may be considered to curtail the very essence and effectiveness of the Petitioners' right to participate in their government and whether the State has offered a reasonable, objective and proportionate justification for the restrictions. . . .

101. In entering into this stage of its analysis, the Commission acknowledges the degree of deference that must properly be afforded to states in organizing their political institutions so as to give effect to the right to vote and to participate in government. The Commission should only interfere in cases where the State has curtailed the very essence and effectiveness of an individual's right to participate in his or her government. After considering the information on the record, however, the Commission finds that the restrictions on the Petitioners' rights under Article XX to participate in their national legislature have been curtailed in such a manner as to deprive the Petitioners of the very essence and effectiveness of that right, without adequate justification being shown by the State for this curtailment.

102. The Commission notes in this regard that the political structure of the United States has been developed so as to provide for both state and federal levels of government, each with exclusive areas of jurisdiction under the Constitution. Consistent with this, the U.S. Congress, as the legislative branch of the federal government, has been afforded extensive powers to consider and enact legislation in areas such as taxation, national defense, foreign affairs, immigration and criminal law. It is also clear that these powers and legislative measures are binding upon or otherwise affect residents of the District of Columbia as they do other citizens of the United States. Indeed, as a consequence of Article I, section 8 of the U.S. Constitution and the Organic Act of 1801, Congress has the exceptional authority to exercise all aspects of legislative control over the District, subject to what aspects of that authority Congress may delegate to District authorities through appropriate federal legislation.

103. Despite the existence of this significant and direct legislative authority that Congress exercises over the Petitioners and other residents of the District of Columbia, however, the Petitioners have no effective right to vote upon those legislative measures, directly or through freely chosen representatives, and it is not apparent from the record that Congress is responsible to the Petitioners for those measures by some other means. In this manner, Congress exercises expansive authority over the Petitioners, and yet it is in no way effectively accountable to the Petitioners or other citizens residing in the District of Columbia. This, in the Commission's view, has deprived the Petitioners of the very essence of representative government, namely that title to government rests with the people governed.

104. Both the Petitioners and the State have suggested that the foundation of the denial to the Petitioners of the right to vote for and elect members of Congress lay upon concerns existing at the time the U.S. Constitution was negotiated over 200 years ago that the seat of the federal government may be disproportionately threatened, or the position of a state correspondingly enriched, by placing Congress within a State.

105. The Commission has recognized and given due consideration to the fact that these concerns may have justified depriving residents of the District of elected representation in Congress at the time that the U.S. Constitution was enacted and indeed may have been indispensable to the Constitution's negotiation. However, as with all protections under the American Declaration, the Commission must interpret and apply Articles II and XX in the context of current circumstances and standards. Not only has the State failed to offer any present-day justification for the Petitioners' denial of effective representation in Congress, but modern developments within the United States and the Western Hemisphere more broadly indicate that the restrictions imposed by the State on the Petitioners' right to participate in government are no longer reasonably justified....

107. Numerous political initiatives have been undertaken in the United States in recent years to extend some measure of national representation for D.C. residents, which ... recognize the present-day inadequacy of the Petitioners' status in the federal system of government. These have included, for example, granting District residents in 1960 the right to vote in Presidential elections through the 23rd amendment to the U.S. Constitution, the passage of the District of Columbia Delegate Act in 1970 which provided the District of Columbia with a non-voting delegate in the House of Representatives, and the extension to the D.C. delegate in 1993 of a limited right to vote in Congress' Committee of the Whole.

108. The Commission also considers it significant that according to the information available, no other federal state in the Western Hemisphere denies the residents of its federal capital the right to vote for representatives in their national legislature. In Canada, for example, the City of Ottawa constitutes a part of the Province of Ontario and accordingly its residents are entitled to elect Members of Parliament in the federal House of Commons on the same basis as residents in other provincial electoral divisions. The City of Buenos Aires, while constituting a separate enclave similar to the District of Columbia, is entitled to elect deputies and senators to Argentina's national legislature. Similarly, the residents of Brasilia, Brazil, Caracas, Venezuela, and Mexico City, Mexico, all of which constitute federal enclaves or districts, have voting representation in their national legislatures.

109. Based upon the foregoing analysis, the Commission concludes that the State has failed to justify the denial to the Petitioners of effective representation in their federal government, and consequently that the Petitioners have been denied an effective right to participate in their government, directly or through freely chosen representatives and in general conditions of equality, contrary to Articles XX and II of the American Declaration.

110. It also follows from the Commission's analysis that securing the Petitioners' rights under Articles II and XX of the Declaration does not necessarily require that they be afforded the same means or degree of participation as residents of states in the United States. What the Declaration and its underlying

principles mandate is that the State extend to the Petitioners the opportunity to exercise a meaningful influence on those matters considered by their governing legislature, and that any limitations and restrictions on those rights are justified by the State as reasonable, objective and proportionate, taking due account of the context of its political system. As Article XX of the Declaration suggests, this is generally achieved through the election of representatives to the legislature who may cast a vote on matters before the legislature that has a meaningful possibility of affecting the outcome of those deliberations. Nevertheless, the mechanisms through which the State may afford these opportunities are clearly a matter for the discretion of the State concerned.

V. Proceedings Subsequent to Report 115/01

. . .

112. Report 115/01 was transmitted to the State by note dated October 19, 2001, with a request that the State provide information as to the measures it had taken to comply with the recommendations set forth in the report within a period of two months, in accordance with Article 43(2) of the Commission's Rules.

113. By communication dated December 18, 2001 and received by the Commission on December 19, 2001, the State delivered a response to the Commission's request for information, in which it indicated as follows:

> As the United States has previously indicated, the petition submitted in Case No. 11.204 is inadmissible for the reasons detailed in the numerous submissions to the Commission. The petition in this matter fails to state a claim under the American Declaration on the Rights and Duties of Man ("Declaration"), and on this basis, the United States respectfully requests that the Commission withdraw Report No. 115/01 and order the petition dismissed.
>
> First, petitioners have failed to allege facts that establish a violation of the right to vote as set forth in Article I of the Declaration. The decision to establish the District of Columbia as a federal enclave in which the residents have voting rights that differ from residents of other areas of the United States was not based on any improper grounds as set forth in Article II. Instead, the decision was based on matters of federalism, unrelated to "race, sex, language, creed or any other factor."
>
> Likewise, the petition fails to establish a violation of Article XX of the Declaration. Neither the petition, nor the Commission's Report identifies any standard — either in the Declaration or in international law — that would require participation in government in any particular manner. The framers of the U.S. Constitution, as well as its past and present citizenry, have devised a system of government that affords citizens of the District of Columbia certain rights with regard to participation in governance, both at the district and federal level. This is a matter properly within the discretion of the people of the United States.
>
> Finally, the political system challenged by the petition is simply not appropriate for review, and even less for rejection, by the Commission. These are sensitive issues better left to domestic political processes. There is simply no basis for the Commission to substitute its judgment for the political debate and decision-making of the federal branches of the government of the United States.

114. With respect to the first two observations raised by the State, the Commission considers that these arguments have already been raised before and

examined by the Commission during the admissibility and merits phases of the process and the Commission sees no reason to alter its findings in this connection. With respect to the State's third observation, although the Commission agrees that the issues raised by the Petitioners may constitute sensitive matters ordinarily addressed by domestic processes, it is in large part because the domestic political and legal procedures have failed to resolve the complaints raised by the Petitioners that the Commission has exercised its reinforcing and complementary jurisdiction to evaluate their complaints in light of the United States' international human rights obligations.

115. Based upon the response of the United States, the Commission finds that the State has failed to take measures to comply fully with the Commission's recommendations. On this basis, and having considered the State's observations, the Commission has decided to ratify its conclusions and reiterate its recommendations....

Comments and Questions

1. Compare the Commission's opinion in the District of Columbia case with the discussion of indigenous rights to self-determination in Chapter 3, pages 194–195. Might indigenous peoples file a similar complaint with the Inter-American system? Do you agree with the Commission that it is merely exercising "its reinforcing and complementary jurisdiction" over issues unresolved domestically, or is the U.S. argument that "[t]here is simply no basis for the Commission to substitute its judgment for the political debate and decision-making" of the federal government more persuasive? Do you think that the Commission's opinion makes it more or less likely that the United States will ratify the American Convention and accept the jurisdiction of the Court, so that it could appeal decisions like that involving the District of Columbia? Compare *Matthews v. United Kingdom*, Eur. Ct. H.R. 1999-I, App. No. 24833/94, Feb. 18, 1999 (Grand Chamber) (finding that denying residents of Gibraltar the right to vote for members of the European Parliament violated Protocol I to the European Convention).

V. Final Comments and Questions

1. Note that under the Inter-American and African systems, as opposed to the European, persons filing petitions need not be victims of the alleged human rights violations. NGOs, therefore, may file petitions on behalf of other persons, which they cannot do in Europe. On the other hand, juridical persons like corporations cannot submit petitions in the Americas, whereas in Europe they can. Which system, or blend of systems, seems preferable? Why?

2. The Inter-American Commission's country reports have been rightly praised for their quality and usefulness. However, the Commission has not attempted to establish a periodic reporting process for states similar to that found in the Covenant on Civil and Political Rights (see pages 584–592 of Chapter 7) or the African system. Article 43 of the American Convention permits the Commission to request information from states parties "as to the manner in which their

domestic law, insures the effective application of any provision [of this Convention]." Could an innovative Commission seize upon this language to develop an effective reporting process? Would such a process be valuable, or would it constitute an unwelcome diversion of Commission time and resources away from country reports and individual complaints?

3. The Inter-American Commission on Human Rights has often been criticized for the fact that it is less legalistic than its European counterpart. Given the very different political contexts in which the two bodies operate, and the types of cases they have traditionally received, is this a fair criticism? Is it significant that the Inter-American Commission's competence has always extended to all OAS members, while that of the European Commission was initially restricted to those states that had ratified the European Convention, rather than to all members of the Council of Europe?

4. Compare the substantive rights protected under the American Convention with those protected under the European Convention. Would it still be correct to conclude that "some of the provisions of the American Convention are so advanced that it may be doubted whether there is a country in the Americas that is in full compliance with all of them," as a former president of the Inter-American Court remarked in 1984? See Thomas Buergenthal, The Inter-American System for the Protection of Human Rights, in 2 *Human Rights in International Law: Legal and Policy Issues* 439, 442 ff. (Theodor Meron ed., 1984).

5. A growing body of literature now exists, much of it descriptive in nature, on the Inter-American system. Among the better analytical works are Thomas Buergenthal, Robert Norris, and Dinah Shelton, *Protecting Human Rights in the Americas: Selected Problems* (4th rev. ed, 1995); Cecelia Medina Quiroga, *The Battle of Human Rights: Gross, Systematic Violations and the Inter-American System* (1988); Thomas Farer, "Collectively Defending Democracy in a World of Sovereign States: The Western Hemisphere's Prospect," 15 *Hum. Rts. Q.* 716 (1993); Claudio Grossman, Proposals to Strengthen the Inter-American System of Protection of Human Rights, 32 *German Y.B. Intl. L.* 264 (1990); Dinah Shelton, "The Inter-American Human Rights System," in *Guide to International Human Rights Practice* 119-132 (Hurst Hannum ed., 4th ed. 2004); and *The Inter-American Human Rights System* (David Harris and Stephen Livingstone, eds. 1998).

Chapter 10

Coercing Compliance with Human Rights Norms: Sanctions and Armed Intervention

Can the International Community Prevent Human Rights Violations by Threatening or Using Force?

I. Disaster in Darfur

Sudan is the largest country (in terms of territory) in Africa. It gained its independence in 1956, emerging from a colonial period of joint British-Egyptian administration. Civil war erupted between the northern and southern parts of the country in the same year, as a government dominated by Arab northerners reneged on an agreement to provide for a federal system of government that would permit autonomy to the largely animist and Christian south. Fighting lasted until 1972, when representatives of the north finally agreed to a degree of self-rule for the south. A second civil war — in some ways a continuation of the first — erupted in 1983 when a group calling itself the Sudanese People's Liberation Movement/Army (SPLM/A), led by John Garang, took up arms against the Khartoum government of Jaafar Nimeiri when the latter attempted to impose Shari'a law over the south and also decreed the division of the south into three separate provinces, a move seen as threatening southern power.

The war between the north and the south continued unabated throughout the 1980s and 1990s, leading to at least 1.5 million deaths, as well as massive displacement of civilians and the widespread destruction of infrastructure, ending many people's access to even basic services. Then-Colonel Omar Hassan al-Bashir staged a coup on June 30, 1989, through the National Islamic Front, a fundamentalist political organization which later transformed itself into the National Congress Party. Following the coup, Bashir named himself head of state, head of government, and head of the Sudanese armed forces.

In the midst of this long-running turmoil, the first flickers of peace began to emerge when, in 1993, the leaders of Ethiopia, Eritrea, Kenya, and Uganda formed the Inter-governmental Authority on Development (IGAD) to help facilitate north-south peace negotiations in Sudan. The IGAD initiative identified the essential elements of a workable peace settlement as the relationship between religion and the state, power-sharing, sharing of wealth, and the right of self-determination for the south. The Sudanese Government refused to sign the IGAD declaration of principles until 1997, after a series of military losses to the SPLA. However, serious negotiations were still years away, particularly after the development of new oil fields in southern Sudan in 1999 raised the stakes of any post-settlement political arrangement granting autonomy to the south.

The UN Security Council did impose sanctions on Sudan in the mid-1990s, in response to the suspected harboring by Sudan of terrorists implicated in the attempted assassination of Egyptian president Hosni Mubarak in Addis Ababa in 1995. Resolution 1054 (April 26, 1996) imposed diplomatic sanctions and called on states to reduce the number of staff at diplomatic missions and consular posts and to restrict the movement of those who remained; resolution 1070 (August 16, 1996) would have imposed travel sanctions requiring all states to deny Sudanese aircraft permission to take off from, land in, or fly over their territories. However, the travel ban was to be activated only following a separate Security Council decision, which never came. Even these minimal sanctions were lifted in 2002, although the United States maintained unilateral sanctions against Sudan, citing the country's poor record on terrorism and respect for human rights. No UN sanctions were contemplated to encourage an end to the war or to mitigate the manner in which it was being conducted, although UN relief operations under the name of Operation Lifeline Sudan (a consortium of UNICEF and the World Food Program) have been in operation since April 1989. Operation Lifeline Sudan is dependent on the cooperation of the Khartoum government and the SPLM/A, which has not always been forthcoming and which has forced the suspension of operations on numerous occasions.

On July 20, 2002, the Government of Sudan and the SPLM/A reached an agreement, known as the Machakos Protocol, under which the Government of Sudan agreed to the south's right to seek self-determination after a six-year interim period, while the southern rebels accepted the application of Shari'a law in the north. Thus, real peace between north and south appeared possible, just as the first raids in early 2003 against government military installations in Darfur were occurring.

The background to the situation in Darfur is summarized in the following extract, which was written after a mission to Darfur by Francis Deng, a former Sudanese Minister of State for Foreign Affairs and an expert on the situation of internally displaced persons.

Mission to the Sudan — The Darfur Crisis, Report of the Representative of the Secretary-General on internally displaced persons, Francis M. Deng

UN Doc. E/CN.4/2005/8 (Sept. 29, 2004)

10. Over the last year and a half, Sudan's western region of Darfur has experienced what is widely acknowledged as one of the worst humanitarian crises in the world today. It is estimated that some 1.2 million persons have been internally displaced, and 200,000 people have fled across the borders into Chad as refugees. There have been numerous reports of human rights violations, including extra-judicial killings, and some observers estimate that 30,000-50,000 people have been killed or died from war-related causes since the beginning of the conflict in early 2003. Although the Government contests these numbers, the crisis is undoubtedly monumental.

11. The developments in the Darfur region are often presented as having deep historical roots, marked by complex intertribal conflicts between two sets of tribal groups, nomadic herding tribes, most of whom are said to be Arab, and the farming tribes, mostly Black Africans. The historical tensions and conflicts between these groups have recently been aggravated by the creeping desertification, recurrent drought and competition for scarce resources. Traditionally, relations between the herders and farmers were regulated by conventional arrangements between them and conflicts were managed and resolved by traditional leaders in accordance with the principles of customary law. With the abolition of native administration by the military regime of General Jaafar Mohamed Nimeiri (1969-1985), traditional methods of conflict management and resolution began to be eroded. Although the present regime has tried to revive the system of native administration, the authority of tribal leaders has been weakened to the point where they have virtually lost most of their traditional influence.

12. With the social fabric destroyed, tribes began to organize themselves into armed factions, the most notable of whom are the Arab militias, known for attacking on horses and camels, with modern weapons, targeting Black African civilians. Indeed, the term "Janjaweed", though reportedly ambiguous and elastic, is mostly applied to Arab militias and is said to be a concoction which means, "a daredevil on a horse, carrying a gun". It should be emphasized, however, that Arab and African labels, as noted earlier, reflect perceptions rather than realities, since even those who can claim with some justification to be Arabs are African-Arab hybrids. Historically, being a Muslim, Arabic speaking, culturally Arabized and with some claim to Arab ancestry elevated one to a level of dignity that contrasted sharply to the denigrated and downtrodden status of a Black African, a heathen, and a legitimate target for enslavement. As a result, people passed as Arabs whose visible characteristics betrayed a different African reality. But the more questionable the Arab identity, the more it was claimed and asserted. It should be noted, however, that in Darfur, as indeed throughout the North, Islam and the use of Arabic as the lingua franca had been overriding uniting factors. It should also be noted that there has been considerable intermarriage between the African and Arab tribes in Darfur. In fact, the labels "Arab", "African" or "Black" are new to Darfur and indeed to all regions of the North, which used to be collectively labelled as Arab-Islamic. The change is probably the result of the Black or African consciousness that was initially championed by the liberation struggle in the South, but has spread to regions of the North, notably the Nuba Mountains, Southern Blue Nile, and now Darfur.

13. Although Arab militias in Darfur have been known for years to cooperate with the central Government, even prior to the present regime, the current crisis was triggered by a local rebellion, spearheaded by the predominantly, though not exclusively non-Arab movements JEM and SLM/A, whose declared objective was to redress the marginalization, discrimination and neglect of their communities and their region. It is reported that Arab herders began to encroach on the Black African community lands earlier on and that the encroachment was at times accompanied by the looting of cattle, but that the local government authorities did nothing to address the grievances of the farming communities. This led to feelings of discrimination among these communities and the need to organize a resistance, which, in turn provoked the Arabs to arm themselves even more with the support of the authorities. In addition, the North-South peace process heightened awareness about marginalization of the entire area by the Government and raised expectations about the potential value of rebellion from which the South was apparently gaining.

14. In early 2003, the rebels staged a surprise attack that devastated the government military and police forces in the region, many of whom lacked the will to fight against their own people. Overwhelmed by the rebellion, the Government turned to the Arab militias, the Janjaweed to join ranks in confronting the rebels, and also recruited many Darfurians, predominantly from Arab tribes, into the PDF. Reinforced with arms, training, air cover and backing the government ground forces, fanning the ongoing intertribal tensions and animosities, the Janjaweed attacked with a vengeance, targeting not only the rebels, but also the civilian populations of the non-Arab tribes, particularly the Fur, Masalit and Zaghawa, burning villages, killing, looting, raping, and otherwise terrorizing the people and forcing them off their land, causing the internal displacement of more than a million persons.

15. With most of the internally displaced population clustering in camps and other improvised sites, the world began to witness a grave emergency situation with pressing needs for shelter, food, medicine and sanitation, all of which could not be provided without security and access. Visa requirements and other administrative procedures often impeded access for humanitarian workers and organizations and with the rainy season approaching in a region with poor to non-existent infrastructure, it was feared that the humanitarian crisis was becoming a catastrophe. This was in addition to the persistent attacks and atrocities by the Janjaweed. In the spring of 2004, as many more people were threatened with death and as the world commemorated the 1994 genocide in Rwanda, international attention to the Darfur crisis began to mount. Controversy raged as to whether the crisis constituted ethnic cleansing, genocide, or war crimes and crimes against humanity. Some people warned against time-consuming debate on legal definitions and called instead for prompt action to stop the atrocities, protect the civilian population and save lives.

16. It must be noted that what the world is witnessing in Darfur has been occurring in the southern part of the country for almost the entire period of the civil war, including the burning of villages, killings, destruction and looting of property, the use of tribal Arab militias, the massive displacement of people from their land and abduction of children and women. This has especially been the case since the resumption of hostilities in 1983 between successive Governments in Khartoum and the SPLM/A. Paradoxically, the war in the South appears to be coming to an end as a result of a peace process brokered by the subregional organization the Intergovernmental Authority on Development (IGAD), with strong backing from the international community, in particular, the United States, Norway and the

United Kingdom. A framework for peace, agreed upon by the parties in the Kenyan town of Naivasha on 20 July 2002, followed by a series of protocols, have charted a promising path towards peace in that part of the country, including the areas of the Nuba Mountains, the Southern Blue Nile and Abyei, which, though part of the North, had joined the SPLM/A in the armed struggle.

17. While the international community has played a crucial role in the South, both in response to the humanitarian needs and in the peace process, reaction to the crisis in Darfur has been comparatively more prompt and stronger. Although the international community has not been entirely united in its response, the outcry over the humanitarian and internal displacement crisis in Darfur, the need for assistance, the protection of the internally displaced and the civilian population at large, and respect for human rights and humanitarian principles has certainly been stronger than the response given the tragedy in the southern part of the country. This must be, in significant part, due to the lessons of the genocide in Rwanda, combined with the high profile and sustained media attention. For a while, the Darfur crisis was kept on the back burner of international attention, as the world focused on the promising peace process between the Government and the SPLM/A. Then it became obvious that the two situations could not be kept entirely separate as they could impact upon each other. Besides, the Darfur crisis escalated to a degree that could no longer be sidelined. Heightened international attention on Darfur was perhaps reflected in the visits by the Secretary-General of the United Nations, Kofi Annan, and the United States Secretary of State, Colin Powell, in June 2004, as well as a series of visits and missions by other prominent international personalities and organizations. . . .

Photo: Espen Rasmussen/Gamma

As you read the materials that follow, evaluate the response of the international community to the situation in Darfur. Were sanctions timely and effective? Should armed intervention have been undertaken and, if so, when? Was the eventual dispatch of monitoring troops from the African Union, with the consent of the government of Sudan, the best that could have been expected?

II. Economic Sanctions

A. *The League of Nations*

The story of the League of Nations' experience with sanctions is instructive, if hardly dispositive of the question of the effectiveness of sanctions in general. The founders of the League envisioned economic sanctions as the organization's chief peacekeeping tool. Accordingly, Article 16 of the League Covenant seemed to provide for immediate and automatic economic sanctions against a member state that resorted to war.

Article 16

Should any Member of the League resort to war in disregard of its covenants under Articles 12, 13 or 15, it shall ipso facto be deemed to have committed an act of war against all other Members of the League, which hereby undertake immediately to subject it to the severance of all trade or financial relations, the prohibition of all intercourse between their nationals and the nationals of the covenant-breaking State, and the prevention of all financial, commercial or personal intercourse between the nationals of the covenant-breaking State and the nationals of any other State, whether a Member of the League or not. It shall be the duty of the Council in such case to recommend to the several Governments concerned what effective military, naval or air force the Members of the League shall severally contribute to the armed forces to be used to protect the covenants of the League. . . .

In the fluid world of post-World War I politics, however, it very soon became apparent that a provision of this kind was too inflexible to be accepted within the traditional framework of politics and diplomacy. Thus, the League decided in 1921 that the decision as to when the conditions of Article 16 were met was one that each member state was authorized to make for itself; the article's obligations could not be activated solely by action of the League Council or Assembly. Thus, the League's theoretically mandatory sanctions were, in fact, voluntary.

The first application of Article 16 by the League came in 1935, when it applied sanctions against Italy for its attempted, and ultimately successful, conquest of Ethiopia. Not surprisingly, some of the same issues confronted the League then as confronted the United Nations 30 years later vis-à-vis Rhodesia. The League had a serious problem of sanctions-breaking within its own ranks, particularly by Austria and Hungary; there was also the nagging feeling that perhaps the sanctions were in fact harming those persons whom they were intended to aid. Haile Selassie himself brought this last point poignantly home when he told the League in June 1936 that the major effect of the sanctions seemed to have been to cause Italy to use poison gas to hasten the conquest. For a critical assessment of the League's Italian sanctions, see H.J. Taubenfeld and R. Taubenfeld, *The "Economic Weapon": The League and the United Nations*, 1964 Am. Socy. Intl L. Proceedings 183.

Earlier attempts by the League to respond to Japan's invasion of Manchuria in 1931 were no more successful, and the League's short history does not offer any evidence that economic sanctions were either effective or realistic, given the conditions of the times.

B. *The UN Charter and Southern Rhodesia*

Read Chapter VII of the UN Charter (Documentary Supplement, pages 8-10), which is entitled Action with Respect to Threats to the Peace, Breaches of the Peace, and Acts of Aggression. The key provision is Article 39, which grants to the Security Council authority to act in the name of the United Nations when international peace is threatened:

> The Security Council shall determine the existence of any threat to the peace, breach of the peace, or act of aggression and shall make recommendations, or decide what measures shall be taken in accordance with Articles 41 and 42, to maintain or restore international peace and security.

Articles 41 and 42 deal with sanctions ("measures not involving the use of armed force") and the use of force, respectively.

The legal teeth to the Council's decision are found in two other articles of the Charter:

> *Article 25*
>
> The Members of the United Nations agree to accept and carry out the decisions of the Security Council in accordance with the present Charter.
>
> *Article 103*
>
> In the event of a conflict between the obligations of the Members of the United Nations under the present Charter and their obligations under any other international agreement, their obligations under the present Charter shall prevail.

Finally, you should note the language of Article 2(7), which is quoted in the extract below by Professors McDougal and Reisman.

The binding authority exercised by the Security Council under Chapter VII should be distinguished from the powers of investigation and recommendation given to the Council under Chapter VI. Recommendations are just that, and states need not follow them. When the Council acts with the consent of the state(s) concerned, it normally acts under Chapter VI rather than the coercive Chapter VII.

The first test for the powers of the Security Council came in the mid-1960s, at the height of decolonization. In 1962, the UN General Assembly affirmed that the British colony of Southern Rhodesia was a Non-Self-Governing Territory and called for its independence. G.A. Res. 1760 (Oct. 31, 1962). The following year, it declared that the situation threatened international peace, G.A. Res. 1889 (Nov. 1, 1963), by 73 votes to 2 with 19 abstentions (several abstaining states indicated that they could not agree that the situation posed a threat to the peace within the meaning of Article 39 of the UN Charter).

The United Kingdom (the colonial power) terminated the Federation of Rhodesia and Nyasaland as of January 1, 1964, and the renamed Southern Rhodesia reverted to its former status as a self-governing colony. In late 1964, new Rhodesian Prime Minister Ian Smith declared a state of emergency in Salisbury's overpopulated African townships on the grounds that the rival African nationalist organizations ZANU (led by Reverend Ndabaningi Sithole) and ZAPU (led by Joshua Nkomo) had "indulged in intimidation and violence against each other and against law-abiding Africans." Emergency powers were adopted by the white-dominated government, and, in May 1965, the Security Council declared itself "deeply disturbed" at the worsening situation and requested the United Kingdom to obtain the release of all political prisoners, repeal all repressive and discriminatory legislation, and remove all restrictions on political activity. S.C. Res. 202 (May 6, 1965). One day later, Prime Minister Smith's Rhodesian Front Party gained a massive mandate for independence from the white electorate, which dominated the government under an electoral system that divided voters into two separate voting rolls.

On November 1, 1965, the Smith government announced its Unilateral Declaration of Independence (UDI). The following day, the Security Council condemned UDI, calling on all states not to recognize the "illegal racist minority regime" and to refrain from rendering it any assistance. S.C. Res. 216 (Nov. 12, 1965). The resolution was adopted by a vote of 10 to 1, with one abstention; France considered the matter an internal U.K. problem that the Council should not discuss. There was no support for military intervention under Article 42 of the Charter, and, of course, the United Kingdom, as a permanent member of the Council, could have vetoed any such call. British Prime Minister Harold Wilson had made his opposition to the use of military force clear at a press conference that he gave in Salisbury, Rhodesia, less than two weeks before UDI, during which he cautioned that no one should expect either that the United Kingdom would use force against Rhodesia or that majority rule would come to Rhodesia any time soon.

Nonetheless, with the United Kingdom's acquiescence, the Council did adopt Resolution 217 (Nov. 20, 1965), which called on all states to impose an oil and petroleum embargo and to break all relations with the Smith regime. These voluntary sanctions, Wilson said in January 1966, would bring down the rebel regime "within a matter of weeks rather than months." His prediction could not have been wider of the mark.

By December 1966, the U.K. had recognized that the policy of voluntary sanctions had failed, and the Security Council adopted Resolution 232 (Dec. 16, 1966), imposing mandatory, albeit selective, sanctions against Rhodesia pursuant to Article 41 of the UN Charter. It was the first time that such action had been taken in the UN's history. Under Resolution 232, Rhodesia's principal exports were banned from being imported into any country; also banned was the export to Rhodesia of oil or oil products, arms and military equipment, and aircraft and motor vehicles, as well as equipment or materials for their manufacture, assembly, or maintenance.

Two years later, the Security Council adopted far more comprehensive mandatory sanctions. Resolution 253 (Dec. 16, 1968) decided that all member states "shall prevent":

> The import of all commodities and products originating in Southern Rhodesia;
>
> Any activities by their nationals or in their territories which would promote or are calculated to promote the export of any commodities or products from Southern Rhodesia, and any dealings by their nationals or in their territories in any such products, including in particular the transfer of funds for the purpose of such activities;
>
> The shipment in their vessels or aircraft of any Southern Rhodesian commodities;
>
> The sale or supply of any commodities or products to any person or body in Southern Rhodesia, or to any other person or body for the purposes of any business operated from Southern Rhodesia (except for medical and educational material; publications; news material; and, in special humanitarian circumstances, foodstuffs);
>
> The shipment in their vessels or aircraft or the transport across their territories of any commodities consigned to Southern Rhodesia;
>
> The provision of any funds for investment or any other financial or economic resources; or the remitting of any funds except pension payments or funds for strictly medical, humanitarian, or educational purposes, and, in special humanitarian circumstances, foodstuffs;
>
> The entry into their territories, save on exceptional humanitarian grounds, of any person traveling on a Southern Rhodesian passport or any person ordinarily resident in Southern Rhodesia believed to have encouraged the unlawful acts of the illegal regime;
>
> Operation by their airlines to or from Southern Rhodesia.

Sanctions were tightened by subsequent resolutions in 1973 (S.C. Res. 333 (May 22, 1973)) and 1976 (S.C. Res. 388 (Apr. 6, 1976)).

The significance of these economic sanctions and the role they played in eventually leading to the establishment of black majority rule in what is now Zimbabwe in 1980 is difficult to assess. However, it is important to be aware of the legal controversy that this initial use of mandatory sanctions by the Security Council created; many of these issues are explored in the two readings that follow.

Myers S. McDougal and W. Michael Reisman, *Rhodesia and the United Nations: The Lawfulness of International Concern*

62 Am. J. Intl. L. 1, 1-19 (1968)

The basic substantive argument which has been lodged against the legality of the United Nations' Rhodesian action is that the activities of the white regime in Rhodesia cannot be appropriately characterized as constituting "a threat to the peace" within the meaning of the Charter. Hence, no matter how reprehensible white Rhodesian behavior may be, the basic contingency for the United Nations' measures is absent. . . . A careful appraisal of the relevant policies and of the facts of the case will, however, indicate that the Charter provisions have been misunderstood and that, in the absence of an appropriate understanding of the relevant basic policies, the factual elements have not been properly appreciated.

For the better securing of the most fundamental Charter purpose of maintaining "international peace and security," the framers of the United Nations

Charter deliberately conferred upon the Security Council, in the provisions of Chapter VII, a very broad competence both to "determine the existence of any threat to the peace, breach of the peace, or act of aggression" and to decide upon what measures should be taken to "maintain or restore international peace and security." . . .

The thought which moved the framers, in rejecting all proposed definitions of the key terms "threat to the peace," "breach of peace" and "act of aggression," was that, for effective discharge of the very difficult and delicate task being imposed upon it, the Security Council should be accorded a large freedom to make ad hoc determinations after a full, contextual examination of the peculiar features of each specific situation of threat or coercion. The facts which might in the future endanger international peace and security could be infinitely various, with the significance of any particular feature of the context being a function of many other features, and the measures which might best promote the establishment and maintenance of peace and security in any specific situation could require careful tailoring to fit the unique requirements of that situation. The course of subsequent events has clearly demonstrated the wisdom of this view, and few voices have been heard to suggest that the broad discretion of the Security Council could rationally be curtailed.

Similarly, it was clearly within the expectations of both the framers and the general community that action by the Security Council might have to be anticipatory and was not required to await the full consummation of disaster. Thus, the competence accorded to the Council in Article 39 relates not merely to perfected "breaches of the peace" and "acts of aggression" but explicitly extends also to the prevention and removal of "threats to the peace." . . .

It is not intended, however, to suggest that the broad competence accorded the Security Council to make determinations of "threats to the peace" is absolute, without limit or safeguard. The appropriate exercise of such competence must of course require an evaluation of any alleged "threat" in its relevant context and the relation of such challenged activity to the major Charter purpose of maintaining international peace and security; and the Charter, like other constitutions which confer broad competences for action, establishes certain important procedural safeguards against arbitrary and spurious decisions. . . .

The procedural safeguards established by the Charter are incorporated in the voting procedures prescribed for the Security Council, which require the concurring votes of the permanent members and a special majority of all members. The probabilities of arbitrary or spurious decisions escaping these procedures would not appear great.

The important criticisms of the Rhodesian Resolution . . . relate more to the relevant substantive criteria than to the procedures by which the decision was taken.

The first argument against the lawfulness of the decision is that the actions of the white Rhodesians contain no element of aggression: ". . . whatever the Rhodesians have done has been wholly within their own country and contains no element of aggression." Article 39 does not, however, require "aggression" as a constituent element of a threat to the major inclusive concern. This is not to imply that an act of aggression cannot constitute or precipitate a threat to, or breach of, international peace. The point is that it is not necessary, in order to support a finding of a threat to the peace, that some act of overt aggression should have actually been committed. The aggression argument is thus irrelevant to the determination of a "threat" under Article 39 of the Charter. . . .

The second argument against the lawfulness of the Security Council decision is that the activities of the Rhodesian elites have been entirely in accord with international law. One compelling answer is that the Charter does not require a violation of international law in any sense other than the constitution of a threat to the peace. In point of fact, however, the list of indictments of Rhodesian transgressions against international law is alarmingly long. As far as conventional international law is concerned, the Rhodesian authorities have repudiated a number of Security Council decisions, which, under Article 25 of the Charter, are binding upon all Member States and which, according to Article 2(6), may be applied to nonmembers "so far as may be necessary for the maintenance of international peace and security." They have also repudiated the human rights provisions of the Charter, as authoritatively interpreted by the competent U.N. organs, and the increasingly authoritative Universal Declaration. As far as international customary law is concerned, they have violated the more traditional human rights policies in a degree which, as we have noted, would have in the past served to justify "humanitarian intervention" by individual nation states. It scarcely need be added that circumstances which would justify coercive action undertaken unilaterally by one state must surely be regarded as sufficient to justify organized international action. . . .

The final argument of the critics of the Security Council decision is that, even if the acts of the white Rhodesians are unlawful, they are insulated from international concern by virtue of the fact that they occur only within Rhodesia and affect no one else. This bald contention that the actions of the white Rhodesians occur only within the territorial bounds of Rhodesia is factually incorrect. In the contemporary intensely interdependent world, peoples interact not merely through the modalities of collaborative or combative operations but also through shared subjectivities not merely through the physical movements of goods and services or exercises with armaments, but also through communications in which they simply take each other into account. . . . In the case of Rhodesia, the other peoples of Africa have regarded themselves as affected by the authoritarian and racist policies of the Rhodesian elites. In the context of a world opinion which since World War II has come increasingly to recognize the intimate interdependence of the maintenance of minimum human rights and international peace and security, it would certainly not be easy to demonstrate to these peoples that their expectations of grievous injury from the Rhodesian model are ill-founded. It has been too often confirmed that practices of indignity and strife which begin as internal in physical manifestation in a single community quickly and easily spread to other communities and become international. . . .

II . . .

The invocation of the principle of domestic jurisdiction in the Rhodesian context is, further, ultimately founded on a serious misunderstanding of the contemporary relation between human rights and matters of "international concern." The point is that, even in the absence of a finding of a threat to the peace, the United Nations could have acquired a considerable competence with respect to Rhodesia because of the systematic suppression of human rights practiced there. The concept of domestic jurisdiction in international law has never been impermeable. Actions occurring within the territorial bounds of one state with palpable deprivatory effects upon others have always been subject to claim and decision on the international plane. There has scarcely ever been a case of major proportions in which the principle of domestic jurisdiction has not been invoked; where transnational effects have been precipitated, the principle has rarely barred effective accommodations in accord with inclusive interest. Hence, domestic jurisdiction means little more than a general community concession of primary, but not exclusive, competence over matters arising and intimately concerned with aspects of the internal public order of states. Where such acts precipitate major inclusive deprivations, jurisdiction is internationalized and inclusive concern and measures become permissible. *

The important provision in Article 2(7) of the Charter that "this principle shall not prejudice the application of enforcement measures under Chapter VII" is only the most urgent example of the permeability of domestic jurisdiction to international supervision. . . .

III

It must, accordingly, be concluded that the Security Council decision imposing mandatory sanctions in the Rhodesian situation, contrary to the vigorous criticisms which have been asserted of it, makes an entirely appropriate relation of the facts before the Council to all the relevant basic community policies embodied in the United Nations Charter. In terms of substantive merits, the decision realistically recognizes that in the contemporary world, international peace and security and the protection of human rights are inescapably interdependent and that the impact of the flagrant deprivation of the most basic human rights of the great mass of the people of a community cannot possibly stop short within the territorial boundaries in which the physical manifestations of such deprivations first occur. In terms of the constitutive limitations established by the Charter, the fact that the situation in Rhodesia has been authoritatively found to constitute a threat to international peace makes irrelevant all conceptions of "domestic jurisdiction," and the decision of the Council would not constitute an infringement of the domestic jurisdiction, properly conceived, of Rhodesia, even if Rhodesia were a state entitled to the benefit of the domestic jurisdiction doctrine. Similarly, so far from constituting a violation of the right to self-determination of the great mass of the Rhodesian people, the Security Council resolution is but the most recent expression of a general community concern to preserve that right for them.

Dean Acheson, *The Arrogance of International Lawyers*

2 Intl. Law. 591, 591-99 (1968) (emphasis in original)

Five years ago I was bold enough to scold a meeting of this sort about what I call the arrogance that international law seems to instill in its addicts. To be sure, law in general does this to lawyers in general. One can be tolerantly amused at the veneration which craftsmen in any craft have for the materials of their craft. The cobbler, murmurs, "There's nothing like leather!" But he is too modest to envision as man's highest earthly condition the Rule of Leather. Yet the lawyer does not blush to proclaim it to be the Rule of Law. As he describes it, the rule of law seems to be governance by disembodied principle without the intervention of human hand or voice. Even his own not unimportant role at the bar and on the bench the lawyer turns into the mere voice of the oracle inspired by the Law Principle itself. This miracle finds its most mystical expression in the doctrine of Natural Law, which makes it the efflux of the universe, flowing forth from the Godhead.... When former Justice...Charles Evans Hughes bluntly — and, perhaps, too "Delphically" — said that the Constitution is what the Supreme Court says it is, the lawyers were not too shocked, although they pretended that they were.

Those who devote themselves to international relations in foreign offices at what is disparagingly called "the working level" are understandably and wisely reticent about the role of law. This, however, is not true of academicians who write about it and teach it. Undeterred by the discipline of adversary procedure or by the test of judgment in contested application, motivated by the highest principles and often spurred by a gift for imaginative rhetoric, some of them recall Disraeli's description of Gladstone as "intoxicated by the exuberance of his own verbosity;" I hasten to add that it was the Bar Association en masse, and not the International and Comparative Law Section of it, that voiced the most delusive of all slogans — "World peace through world law."

Those of whom I complain are not the peddlers of spurious panaceas for peace, not those who are over impressed with the role of international law, but those who would impose upon states in the name of law their own subjective conceptions of justice. As is so often the case with the righteous, deeply convinced of the righteousness of their cause, their impulse is to "snatch the knotted cord from the hand of God and deal out murderous blows." These blows are usually directed against the weak by suborning the subjectivities of the strong. This process also furnishes the fig leaf of legal respectability for otherwise naked aggression.

Such support was given to the action of the United Nations Security Council in calling for economic sanctions against Rhodesia and to the attacks upon the World Court's decision dismissing the complaint in the Southwest Africa case. The viciousness of the substitution of the subjective conception of justice for law in these instances is that in both cases it provides means for collective aggression, in both it degrades international adjudication, and in both it departs from the basic conception of international law. This is that it is inter *national*, between sovereign states, based upon accepted practices and agreements of sovereigns. In this latter respect it differs basically from the law taught by the international lawyers' other academic colleagues. To strike at this concept of agreed limitations on sovereignty is to strike at confidence in judicial honesty and restraint, which alone can lead to the slow development of international law from its primitive state.

It will surprise some of my fellow citizens, though hardly anyone here today, to be told that the United States is engaged in an international conspiracy, instigated by Britain, and blessed by the United Nations, to overthrow the government of a country that has done us no harm and threatens no one. This is barefaced aggression, unprovoked and unjustified by a single legal or moral principle.

The charge that Britain brings against Rhodesians is one that George III once brought against Americans and sought unsuccessfully to enforce by arms. It was that the Colonies felt it necessary, as Mr. Jefferson put it, "to dissolve the political bands which [had] connected them with other [people], and to assume among the powers of the earth, the separate and equal station to which the Laws of Nature and of Nature's God entitle them." . . .

How fortunate were the American colonies to have no United Nations to confront in 1776! I need hardly remind you that our Constitution had nothing to say about adult universal suffrage but did have a few pregnant paragraphs continuing the institution of slavery. . . .

Perhaps I might pause for a moment to remind you of the present situation. As everybody knew, this blockade of Rhodesia has not worked. Therefore, Her Majesty's government in accordance with that universal principle which seems to instigate all fanatics that one must redouble effort on finding oneself on the wrong road, has asked the United Nations to extend the blockade and our African friends have raised their cry that the British should come out of the bushes and gain enough courage to fight Rhodesia by arms. The point I am making here is that this highly theoretical and imaginative threat was not posed *by* Rhodesia but *against* Rhodesia. From this premise only the most Humpty-Dumpty reasoning could move to the conclusion that Rhodesia should be punished by international action aimed at overthrowing her government and ending her independence. . . .

One of the troubles of the troubled age in which we live is that too many people are trying to achieve harmony of interest by forcing everyone to harmonize with them. Conscience used to be an inner voice of self discipline; now it is a clarion urge to discipline others. It took a long time to develop the international precept that peace would be furthered by governments' having respect for each other's autonomy. That should apply to them when acting in concert. This is the notion embedded in Paragraph 7 of Article 2 of the Charter. Whatever mistakes they may otherwise have made, the draftsmen of the Charter, at least, did not intend to open the way for endless conflict through unbridled impulses to reform. The new romantic impulse is to overthrow that wise inhibition in favor of a compulsion to reshape the world to fit all sorts of shared subjectivities. . . .

C. *Modern UN Sanctions*

The arguments of McDougal and Reisman have clearly carried the day, and the imposition of mandatory economic sanctions by the Security Council has become almost routine. The path was not smooth, however, and the second imposition of mandatory sanctions — against the apartheid regime in South Africa — occurred only in 1977. S.C. Res. 418 (Nov. 4, 1977). A voluntary arms embargo against South Africa had been imposed in 1963, and subsequent voluntary sanctions were recommended in 1985, but attempts to impose additional mandatory sanctions failed, generally due to exercise of the veto in the Security Council by the United Kingdom, United States, and/or France. With respect to both Rhodesia and South Africa, even mandatory sanctions were widely ignored by a number of countries; it was particularly difficult to stem the flow of oil to Rhodesia. On the impact of these early sanctions, see, e.g., Auglin, "United

Nations Sanctions Against South Africa and Rhodesia," in *The Utility of International Economic Sanctions* (David Leyton-Brown ed., 1987); David A. Baldwin, *Economic Statecraft* (1985); Margaret P. Doxey, *International Sanctions in Contemporary Perspective* (2d ed. 1996); Donald L. Losman, *International Economic Sanctions* (1979); Robin Renwick, *Economic Sanctions* (1981); Harry R. Strack, *Sanctions: The Case of Rhodesia* (1978).

Particularly since the end of the Cold War, sanctions have come to be seen by many as the first response (or perhaps the second, following diplomatic overtures) to the outbreak of armed hostilities or other threats or breaches of international peace. As of January 2005, mandatory Article 41 sanctions had been imposed by the Security Council on Afghanistan, Angola, Côte d'Ivoire, Ethiopia, Eritrea, Haiti, Iraq, Liberia, Libya, Rwanda, Sierra Leone, Somalia, Sudan, and the former Yugoslavia, in addition to the earlier sanctions against Southern Rhodesia and South Africa. While some of these sanctions have been completely lifted, it is worth noting that many have been in place for years, including those against Somalia (since 1992), Rwanda (since 1994), and Sierra Leone (since 1997). Among the sanctions regimes that have been terminated, those imposed on Iraq (after the invasion of Kuwait) were in place for 13 years; Libya, 11 years; Angola (against the rebel group UNITA), nine years; and Liberia, six years (new sanctions were imposed two years later).

As sanctions became more commonplace, their impact on the civilian populations of the target country became a subject of increasing concern. The long-term comprehensive sanctions imposed on Iraq during and after the first Gulf War were particularly heavily criticized and led indirectly to the following two extracts, which are set out after the sanctions resolution itself.

Security Council Resolution 661

Aug. 6, 1990

The Security Council. . . .

Acting under Chapter VII of the Charter of the United Nations,

1. *Determines* that Iraq so far has failed to comply with paragraph 2 of resolution 660 (1990) and has usurped the authority of the legitimate Government of Kuwait;

2. *Decides*, as a consequence, to take the following measures to secure compliance of Iraq with paragraph 2 of resolution 660 (1990) and to restore the authority of the legitimate Government of Kuwait;

3. *Decides* that all States shall prevent:

(a) The import into their territories of all commodities and products originating in Iraq or Kuwait exported therefrom after the date of the present resolution;

(b) Any activities by their nationals or in their territories which would promote or are calculated to promote the export or trans-shipment of any commodities or products from Iraq or Kuwait; and any dealings by their nationals or their flag vessels or in their territories in any commodities or products originating in Iraq or Kuwait and exported therefrom after the date of the present resolution, including in particular any transfer of funds to Iraq or Kuwait for the purposes of such activities or dealings;

(c) The sale or supply by their nationals or from their territories or using their flag vessels of any commodities or products, including weapons or any other military equipment, whether or not originating in their territories but not including supplies intended strictly for medical purposes, and, in humanitarian circumstances, foodstuffs, to any person or body in Iraq or Kuwait or to any person or body for the purposes of any business carried on in or operated from Iraq or Kuwait, and any activities by their nationals or in their territories which promote or are calculated to promote such sale or supply of such commodities or products;

4. *Decides* that all States shall not make available to the Government of Iraq or to any commercial, industrial or public utility undertaking in Iraq or Kuwait, any funds or any other financial or economic resources and shall prevent their nationals and any persons within their territories from removing from their territories or otherwise making available to that Government or to any such undertaking any such funds or resources and from remitting any other funds to persons or bodies within Iraq or Kuwait, except payments exclusively for strictly medical or humanitarian purposes and, in humanitarian circumstances, foodstuffs;

5. *Calls upon* all States, including States non-members of the United Nations, to act strictly in accordance with the provisions of the present resolution notwithstanding any contract entered into or licence granted before the date of the present resolution;

6. *Decides* to establish, in accordance with rule 28 of the provisional rules of procedure of the Security Council, a Committee of the Security Council consisting of all the members of the Council, to undertake the following tasks and to report on its work to the Council with its observations and recommendations:

(a) To examine the reports on the progress of the implementation of the present resolution which will be submitted by the Secretary-General;

(b) To seek from all States further information regarding the action taken by them concerning the effective implementation of the provisions laid down in the present resolution;

7. *Calls upon* all States to co-operate fully with the Committee in the fulfillment of its task, including supplying such information as may be sought by the Committee in pursuance of the present resolution;...

The sanctions imposed by the Security Council against Iraq remained in place for thirteen years. The objectives of the sanctions regime shifted over time: first designed to compel Saddam Hussein (unsuccessfully) to withdraw from Kuwait without resort to force, the United Nations later aimed to force the Iraqi government to comply with weapons inspections. Despite the changing goals of the sanctions regime, what remained constant for several years was the comprehensive nature of the sanctions. The result was drastically limited availability of food and medicines, and diminished capacity for water treatment and electrical systems as the national infrastructure fell into disrepair, often for want of replacement spare parts, which could not be imported into the country. Among the reports emerging during this time was a survey conducted by UNICEF in 1999, which found that under-five child mortality had more than doubled since the imposition of sanctions. See UNICEF, *Iraq surveys show humanitarian emergency*, Press Release (August 12, 1999), *http://www.unicef.org/newsline/99pr29.htm*; the results of the survey were published in Mohamed M. Ali and Iqbal H. Shah, *Sanctions and childhood mortality in Iraq*, 355 The Lancet 1851 (No. 9208, 2000).

Beginning in 1991, the Security Council offered to adjust the sanctions regime to permit Iraq to sell oil in exchange for goods, in order to relieve the suffering of the Iraqi people. The Iraqi government refused, however, claiming that any kind of sanction violated Iraq's sovereignty. It was not until 1996 that Saddam Hussein agreed to participate in what became known as the Oil for Food program. Between 1997 and 2002, Iraq sold more than $67 billion of oil through the program and issued $38 billion in letters of credit to purchase commodities. The program did achieve some success in alleviating the suffering of the Iraqi population — according to the United Nations, average caloric intake rose by nearly 1,000, while the incidence of communicable diseases such as cholera and malaria fell following implementation of the program — but it also provided Saddam Hussein's government with the opportunity to gain billions of dollars in illicit revenue through kickbacks and surcharges. See Joseph A. Christoff, Director, International Affairs and Trade, U.S. General Accounting Office, *Observations on the Oil for Food Program*, Testimony before the Senate Committee on Foreign Relations, April 7, 2004, GAO Pub. GAO-04-651T.

Following the U.S. invasion of Iraq in 2003, the Oil for Food program became the subject of numerous investigations. The U.S. General Accounting Office estimated that Saddam Hussein's regime acquired $10 billion in illegal revenue related to the Oil for Food program, through oil smuggling as well as by adding surcharges to oil sales. Id. Subsequent investigations concerning allegations of corruption at the UN office tasked with operating the program led to the termination of 40 UN staff members for misconduct. Those alleged to have participated in manipulating the Oil for Food Program included multinational corporations, UN officials, and senior foreign government officials of several countries.

Even after the Oil for Food Program was instituted, however, criticisms of the impact of sanctions on Iraq's civilian population were widespread.

Committee on Economic, Social, and Cultural Rights, *The Relationship Between Economic Sanctions and Respect for Economic, Social and Cultural Rights*

General Comment no. 8, UN Doc. E/C.12/1997/8 (Dec. 12, 1997)

1. Economic sanctions are being imposed with increased frequency, both internationally, regionally and unilaterally. The purpose of this general comment is to emphasize that, whatever the circumstances, such sanctions should always take full account of the provisions of the International Covenant on Economic, Social and Cultural Rights. . . .

2. During the 1990s the Security Council has imposed sanctions of varying kind and duration in relation to South Africa, Iraq/Kuwait, parts of the former Yugoslavia, Somalia, the Libyan Arab Jamahiriya, Liberia, Haiti, Angola, Rwanda, and the Sudan. The impact of sanctions upon the enjoyment of

economic, social and cultural rights has been brought to the Committee's attention in a number of cases involving States parties to the Covenant, some of which have reported regularly, thereby giving the Committee the opportunity to examine the situation carefully.

3. While the impact of sanctions varies from one case to another, the Committee is aware that they almost always have a dramatic impact on the rights recognized in the Covenant. Thus, for example, they often cause significant disruption in the distribution of food, pharmaceuticals and sanitation supplies, jeopardize the quality of food and the availability of clean drinking water, severely interfere with the functioning of basic health and education systems, and undermine the right to work. In addition, their unintended consequences can include reinforcement of the power of oppressive elites, the emergence, almost invariably, of a black market and the generation of huge windfall profits for privileged elites which manage it, enhancement of the control of the governing elites over the population at large, and restriction of opportunities to seek asylum or to manifest political opposition. While the phenomena mentioned in the preceding sentence are essentially political in nature, they also have a major additional impact on the enjoyment of economic, social and cultural rights.

4. In considering sanctions, it is essential to distinguish between the basic objective of applying political and economic pressure upon the governing elite of the country to persuade them to conform to international law, and the collateral infliction of suffering upon the most vulnerable groups within the targeted country. . . .

7. The Committee considers that the provisions of the Covenant, virtually all of which are also reflected in a range of other human rights treaties as well as the Universal Declaration of Human Rights, cannot be considered inoperative, or in any way inapplicable, solely because a decision has been taken that considerations of international peace and security warrant the imposition of sanctions. Just as the international community insists that any targeted State must respect the civil and political rights of its citizens, so too must that State and the international community itself do everything possible to protect at least the core content of the economic, social and cultural rights of the affected peoples of that State. . . .

UN Sub-Commission on the Promotion and Protection of Human Rights, The Adverse Consequences of Economic Sanctions on the Enjoyment of Human Rights

Working paper prepared by Mr. Marc Bossuyt, UN Doc. E/CN.4/Sub.2/2000/33 (June 21, 2000)

I. Introduction

1. In its resolution 1997/35 of 28 August 1997, entitled "Adverse consequences of economic sanctions on the enjoyment of human rights", the Sub-Commission expressed concerns about economic sanctions. Framing its concerns in the light of the need to respect the Charter of the United Nations, the Universal

Declaration of Human Rights, the International Covenants on Human Rights and the Geneva Conventions of 1949 and the two Additional Protocols thereto, the Sub-Commission stressed four particular points concerning such measures:

They should always be limited in time (fourth preambular paragraph);
They most seriously affect the innocent population, especially the most vulnerable (fifth preambular paragraph);
They aggravate imbalances in income distribution (sixth preambular paragraph);
They generate illegal and unethical business practices (seventh preambular paragraph)....

10. In practice, sanctions have comprised a wide range of actions, from economic embargoes to restrictions on participation in the Olympic Games. There follows a brief classification of sanctions: economic, travel, military, diplomatic or cultural.

1. ECONOMIC SANCTIONS

11. There are two basic kinds of economic sanctions: trade sanctions and financial sanctions.

(a) **Trade Sanctions**

12. Trade sanctions restrict imports and exports to and from the target country. These restrictions can be comprehensive, as in the case of Iraq, or they can be selective, only restricting certain goods often connected with a trade dispute. Comprehensive trade sanctions are the target of the current criticism of sanctions regimes, because of the humanitarian crises that have erupted in countries against which such sanctions have been imposed.

(b) **Financial Sanctions**

13. Financial sanctions address monetary issues. They can include, as has been addressed at the Interlaken Conferences, blocking government assets held abroad, limiting access to financial markets and restricting loans and credits, restricting international transfer payments and restricting the sale and trade of property abroad. The freezing of development aid also falls into this category. Obviously, there is substantial overlap between financial and trade sanctions, especially when applied comprehensively, since with their foreign assets frozen and access to new funds blocked, Governments will be unable to pay for imports, and trade will suffer.

2. OTHER TYPES OF SANCTIONS

(a) **Travel Sanctions**

14. Travel sanctions can include both sanctions against the travel of certain individuals or groups and sanctions against certain kinds of air transport. The first kind is by nature targeted, as lists of people or groups of people are compiled who are not allowed to leave their country. This type of ban has been imposed on Governments, such as against members of the military junta in Sierra Leone in 1998, and also against non-governmental groups, such as the leaders of the

National Union for the Total Independence of Angola (UNITA) in 1997. Bans on certain types of air travel include the current ban on taking off or landing of any aircraft owned, leased or operated by or on behalf of the Taliban, established by the Security Council in its resolution 1267 (1999).

(b) Military Sanctions

15. Military sanctions may include arms embargoes or the termination of military assistance or training. They are also inherently "targeted", as, domestically, only the armed forces feel their impact. Legal problems may arise, however, when a country's right to self-defence is infringed, as many States subject to arms embargoes have argued.

(c) Diplomatic Sanctions

16. Diplomatic sanctions directly target the rulers of a sanctioned State: diplomats and political leaders may have their visas revoked and may be forbidden to participate in international bodies and organizations. The refusal of the United Nations to allow the participation of the apartheid Government of South Africa in its operations is an example of this type of sanction. Other steps towards diplomatic isolation include the withdrawal of diplomatic personnel and international organizations from the target country.

(d) Cultural Sanctions

17. Finally, cultural sanctions, while having less of a negative impact than other forms of sanctions, can still have undesired results. The athletes of the target nation may be banned from international sports competitions, folk dancers, musicians and other artists may also be banned and restrictions may be placed on educational and tourist travel.

II. Sanctions and International Law: A Law of Limitation

18. The most important implication of international law, especially human rights and humanitarian law, for sanctions is that the right to impose sanctions is not unlimited. Thus, an examination of the standards of international law relevant to sanctions involves looking for the limitations to sanctions inherent in the general operation of international law.

19. Article 39 of the Charter of the United Nations allows the Security Council to take measures such as sanctions only to "maintain or restore international peace and security" following its determination that there exists a threat to or breach of the peace, or an act of aggression. Thus, sanctions may only be imposed upon a Government, "quasi-Government" or other entity that is capable of being a threat to international peace or security or that is in fact threatening international peace and security. While armed groups within a country may pose a threat to international peace and security, a generally unarmed civilian population is, in all likelihood, unable to pose such a threat. Other States not presenting a threat to, or actually breaching, peace and security must not be affected by sanctions imposed on the violating State. . . .

22. In addition to these limitations, other provisions that would limit sanctions are found throughout the Charter.

1. LIMITATIONS IMPLIED BY ARTICLE 24

23. Article 24 requires the Security Council to "act in accordance with the Purposes and Principles of the United Nations". Thus, no act of the Security Council is exempt from scrutiny as to whether or not that act is in conformity with the Purposes and Principles of the United Nations.

2. LIMITATIONS IMPLIED BY ARTICLE 1

24. Article 1, paragraph 1, requires that sanctions or other measures undertaken to maintain international peace and security must be "effective" and must be "in conformity with the principles of justice and international law". Sanctions must be evaluated to ensure that they are not unjust or that they do not in any way violate principles of international law stemming from sources "outside" the Charter. Likewise, sanctions must be constantly reviewed to ascertain whether or not they are effective in maintaining peace and security. Ineffective or unjust sanctions or those that violate other norms of international law may not be imposed, or must be lifted if they have been imposed.

25. Article 1, paragraph 2, requires that sanctions or other measures "respect the principle of equal rights and the self-determination of peoples". Sanctions that cause international dissention, that interfere with a State's legal rights, or that unduly affect a people's right to self-determination may not be imposed or must be lifted if imposed.

26. The United Nations purpose of promoting and encouraging respect for human rights set out in article 1, paragraph 3, necessarily limits sanctions. Article 1, paragraph 3, also requires the United Nations to solve issues of a pressing humanitarian nature, not to cause them. Sanctions, therefore, must not result in undue hardships for the people of a country. Sanctions that directly or indirectly cause deaths would be a violation of the right to life. Other human rights could also be violated by sanctions regimes, such as the rights to security of the person, health, education or employment.

27. Article 1, paragraph 4, requires that sanctions or other measures facilitate the harmonization of national or international action. Sanctions imposed on one country but not on another for the same wrongs would violate this requirement of harmonization. Sanctions imposed unequally on two countries for the same wrongs would also violate the harmony provision.

3. LIMITATIONS IMPLIED BY ARTICLE 55

28. Article 55 of the Charter reinforces the limitations of article 1, paragraph 3, in its requirement that the United Nations promote:

> Higher standards of living and economic and social progress (para. a);
> Solutions to international economic, social, health and other problems (para. b); and
> Respect for and observance of human rights (para. c).

Sanctions regimes that lower economic standards, create health problems or are detrimental to the observance of human rights would violate Article 55. . . .

[The report goes on to discuss provisions in various human rights and humanitarian law instruments that act to limit the scope or application of sanctions. It concludes with a proposed "six-prong" test to evaluate sanctions.]

1. ARE THE SANCTIONS IMPOSED FOR VALID REASONS?

42. Sanctions under the United Nations must be imposed only when there is a threat of or actual breach of international peace and security. Sanctions may not be imposed for invalid political reasons (personal grudges, "East-West" or "North-South" politics, "left-right" politics and the like). Sanctions may not arise from or produce an economic benefit for one State or group of States at the expense of the sanctioned State or other States. Sanctions may not result in undue interference with a State's sovereignty rights under international law.

2. DO THE SANCTIONS TARGET THE PROPER PARTIES?

43. Sanctions may not target civilians who are uninvolved with the threat to peace or international security. Sanctions that would result in an abrogation of Geneva Convention rights are void; there can be no effective, presumed or actual waiver of these rights. Sanctions may not target, or result in collateral damage to, "third party" States or peoples.

3. DO THE SANCTIONS TARGET THE PROPER GOODS OR OBJECTS?

44. Sanctions may not interfere with the free flow of humanitarian goods under the Geneva Conventions and other provisions of humanitarian law. Sanctions may not target goods needed to ensure the basic subsistence of the civilian population (food, drinking water, basic medicines and immunizations), regardless of whether there is an armed conflict. Sanctions may not target essential medical provisions or educational materials of any kind. Even if a target is otherwise legal, the target must still have a reasonable relationship to the threat of or actual breach of peace and international security.

4. ARE THE SANCTIONS REASONABLY TIME-LIMITED?

45. Legal sanctions may become illegal when they have been applied for too long without meaningful results. Sanctions that continue for too long can have a negative effect long after the wrong ceases (the so-called "undue future burden" effect). Sanctions that go on too long may also be viewed as ineffective.

5. ARE THE SANCTIONS EFFECTIVE?

46. Sanctions must be reasonably capable of achieving a desired result in terms of threat or actual breach of international peace and security. Sanctions that are targeted in ways that would not affect the wrongs may be viewed as ineffective.

6. ARE THE SANCTIONS FREE FROM PROTEST ARISING FROM VIOLATIONS OF THE "PRINCIPLES OF HUMANITY AND THE DICTATES OF THE PUBLIC CONSCIENCE"?

47. The reaction of Governments, intergovernmental bodies, non-governmental organizations, scholars and, of course, the public must be taken into account in evaluating sanctions regimes. This prong, the so-called "Martens

Clause test", is important not only in terms of the human rights and humanitarian law from which it derives, but also in terms of the Charter's call for international solidarity and the need to address pressing humanitarian concerns. The public outcry over the sanctions regime in Iraq clearly invokes the Martens Clause test. Individuals and groups are even willing to violate the sanctions and to carry out Gandhi-like passive resistance, including a planned "die-in" for the summer of 2000. Regarding the sanctions imposed on Burundi and Cuba, numerous public officials (United Nations and otherwise) have pointed to their disastrous consequences.

III. Designing "Smarter" Sanctions

A. Theory and Efficacy of Economic Sanctions

48. The "theory" behind economic sanctions is that economic pressure on civilians will translate into pressure on the Government for change. This "theory" is bankrupt both legally and practically, as more and more evidence testifies to the inefficacy of comprehensive economic sanctions as a coercive tool. The traditional calculation of balancing civilian suffering against the desired political effects is giving way to the realization that the efficacy of a sanctions regime is in inverse proportion to its impact on civilians.

49. The case of Iraq by itself points to serious problems in the traditional theory of economic sanctions. In regimes where political decision-making is not democratic, there is simply no pathway through which civilian pressure can bring about change in the Government. In addition, civilian hardship can easily be translated into political advantage by a ruling regime. The targeted Government, especially if it has a strong grip on the media, will push its citizens to unite behind it in defiance of the foreign States. Sanctions can be used by the targeted Government as a scapegoat for its problems and give leaders fuel for political extremism.

50. Under sanctions, the middle class is eliminated, the poor get poorer, and the rich get richer as they take control of smuggling and the black market. The Government and elite can actually benefit economically from sanctions, owing to this monopoly on illegal trade. As many commentators have pointed out, in the long run, as democratic participation, independent institutions and the middle class are weakened, and as social disruption leaves the population less able to resist the Government, the possibility of democracy shrinks. In sum, the civilian suffering that is believed to be the effective factor in comprehensive economic sanctions renders those sanctions ineffectual, even reinforcing the Government and its policies.

51. The Secretary-General recognized this, writing in his Millennium Report:

> "When robust and comprehensive economic sanctions are directed against authoritarian regimes, a different problem is encountered. Then it is usually the people who suffer, not the political elites whose behaviour triggered the sanctions in the first place. Indeed, those in power, perversely, often benefit from such sanctions by their ability to control and profit from black market activity, and by exploiting them as a pretext for eliminating domestic sources of political opposition."

The data support this argument. There is a no small debate around the interpretation of successes and failures of sanctions regimes, but even the most optimistic point to only about a third of all sanctions having even "partial" success, while others looking at the data have come up with a 5 per cent success rate, and a dismal 2 per cent success rate for sanctions against "authoritarian regimes". In addition, it has been noted that financial sanctions alone have a greater success than trade sanctions or combined trade and financial sanctions. Finally, if the purpose of the sanctions is anything beyond merely the "destabilization of the regime", an aim that all Security Council sanctions ostensibly share, researchers have shown that the severity of sanctions is statistically insignificant in determining their success, and that the longer a sanctions regime stays in place, the lower its success. The same researchers demonstrated that when the economic elite are targeted, there is a significant increase in success.

52. Part of the debate on sanctions focuses on ways to mitigate civilian suffering to the point where it does not produce unwanted counter-effects, thus allowing a regime of comprehensive economic sanctions to put pressure on the government. Under the proviso of "humanitarian exemptions", certain necessary humanitarian goods can pass through the sanctions barricade. The primary example of this is the "oil-for-food" programme in Iraq. However, this policy is rife with problems. As was exemplified in Iraq, humanitarian exemptions can in no way fully compensate for the damage done by comprehensive economic sanctions. To quote one analyst:

> "There was general consensus at the seminar that humanitarian exemptions could not provide an adequate safety net against the social and economic dislocation that prolonged trade embargoes cause. Such embargoes have an impact at macro-level. Humanitarian exemptions only mitigate the situation at micro-level and, even when generous, do not constitute a resource flow that can compensate for dramatic overall economic recession."

53. Comprehensive economic sanctions, even qualified by "humanitarian exemptions", do not make any practical sense for changing a recalcitrant State's policies. The traditional theory behind sanctions is disproved by evidence from recent sanctions regimes, and the doctrine of "humanitarian exemptions" amounts to a futile attempt to mitigate disasters. Instead of trying to patch the sunk ship of comprehensive economic sanctions (likened to "medieval military sieges" by one writer) through "humanitarian exemptions", sanctions should be rethought entirely. This is the "smart sanctions" debate set out below.

B. SMART SANCTIONS

54. In response to the tragic consequences of comprehensive economic sanctions on civilians, an increasingly concerted public discourse has arisen around "targeted" or "smart" sanctions. These targeted sanctions are conceived of as directly affecting the political leaders or those responsible for the breach of peace, while leaving the innocent civilian population alone. Properly targeting sanctions, it is hoped, can eliminate civilian suffering while putting significant pressure on the Government itself, thus bringing sanctions regimes into compliance with human rights and humanitarian law and increasing their chances of success.

55. Targeted economic sanctions, especially targeted financial sanctions, have become an international policy focus lately, giving rise to the Interlaken Process centred around two conferences held in Interlaken, Switzerland, in 1998 and 1999, and to a number of other seminars, conferences and research projects around the world. They have been repeatedly endorsed by the Secretary-General, especially in his Millennium Report.

56. Targeted economic sanctions may target the personal foreign assets and access to foreign financial markets of members of the Government, the ruling elite, or members of the military. The assets of government-owned businesses may also be frozen and investment in those businesses prohibited. Imports of luxury goods and other goods generally only consumed by the ruling elite can be banned. It is generally advised that lists be drawn up with the names of political and/or military leaders whose assets are to be frozen and who are subject to travel restrictions; such a list for the imposition of targeted financial sanctions has only been drawn up by the United Nations once, during the sanctions against Haiti, but in that case the list was not even legally binding.

57. Carefully targeted sanctions, it is argued, can also reduce the harm done to third-party States, thus removing incentives to defy the sanctions, as has recently happened in Africa, with many countries ignoring the travel ban against the Libyan Arab Jamahiriya. Use of the six-prong test to ensure proper targeting, clearly defined goals, a definitive exit clause, and regional unanimity, sanctions regimes could be effective while not harming the civilian population. It is up to the international community to demand that the Security Council introduce such changes. . . .

[The report then presents three short case studies that are highly critical of the sanctions regimes in Iraq, Burundi, and Cuba, concluding that all three violate international law.]

103. Any sanctions-imposing body, whether the United Nations Security Council, regional inter-governmental organizations, groups of countries or a single country, should ensure that a sanctions regime passes the six-prong test prior to implementation. A proposed sanctions regime that does not pass the six-prong test should not be imposed, or if imposed should be immediately moderated. . . .

105. When serious allegations of violations under a sanctions regime are brought to the attention of the sanctions-imposing body, that body should be deemed to have received "notice" and accordingly should undertake immediate review of and make appropriate adjustments to the sanctions regime. A sanctions regime deemed to have gone on too long and with inadequate results should be ended. . . .

109. Sanctions regimes that clearly violate international law, especially human rights and humanitarian law, need not be respected. This is especially true when the imposers are clearly on notice of those violations and have undertaken no effective modification. Sanctions are now imposed with no consideration whatsoever of their legal status. In these situations, humanitarian tragedy must be viewed as constituting an "override" to an unduly harsh economic sanctions regime — analogous to the doctrine of force majeure. And, as already set out, the degree of public outcry is a factor in determining whether a sanctions regime is too harsh. . . .

D. *Smart Sanctions*

As suggested at the end of the report by Mr. Bossuyt, the trend today is away from comprehensive and toward more targeted or "smart" sanctions.

Thomas G. Weiss, *Sanctions as a Foreign Policy Tool: Weighing Humanitarian Impulses*

36 J. Peace Research 499 (No. 5, 1999)

. . . Growing misgivings about consistency and transparency have been exacerbated because sanctions often entail such civilian suffering as to overshadow any potential political success. Former UN Secretary-General Boutros-Ghali captured the troubling tensions of a 'blunt instrument' that afflicts vulnerable groups, complicates the work of humanitarian agencies, causes long-term damage to the productive capacity of target nations, and penalizes neighbors. . . .

Policymakers and scholars increasingly are attracted by 'smart' sanctions. . . . Smart sanctions single out groups and individuals responsible for wrongdoing and pinpoint elite needs and desires. With such information, it is possible to fashion policies that frustrate their satisfaction while identifying pro-reform or opposition constituencies pro-reform or opposition constituencies within a targeted country and supporting them.

In theory, political authorities can craft sanctions that apply pressure on wrongdoers and do not unduly and adversely affect civilian populations or weaken opposition movements. Smart sanctions thus would target better the wealthy and powerful to apply coercive pressure while sparing vulnerable populations. Achieving greater political gain with less civilian pain would clearly enhance multilateral moral credibility.

Smarter sanctions include freezing foreign assets, withholding credits and loans, prohibiting investments, and restricting travel, commerce, and communications. . . .

Making Sanctions More Palatable

Is it feasible to mitigate the worst aspects of sanctions on vulnerable groups, especially gendered impacts? Humanitarian exemptions bridge achieving political objectives and protecting the rights of civilians. Provisions for exemptions are included in most Security Council sanctions resolutions, and administrative procedures have improved in recent years with the provision of food and medicine under general (for example, Sierra Leone) or specific regulations (for example, Iraq in the oil-for-food program).

Who should assume responsibility for the consequences of sanctions? Proponents blame reprobate regimes. They bring sanctions upon themselves, have the ability to remove them by changing objectionable policies, and allocate scarce resources to exacerbate suffering. Iraqi children are dying not because sanctions have curtailed financial and commercial transfers, but because Saddam Hussein has poured resources into opulent palaces, rebuilt his military, and continued to develop weapons of mass destruction. Baghdad publishes appalling statistics on child mortality but lets food and medicines rot in warehouses and postpones purchasing vital goods permitted through limited oil sales. Critics, in contrast, see the suffering occasioned by Security Council decisions as the responsibility of member-states. As dislocations are a necessary part of economic coercion, those states approving sanctions can not feign surprise at suffering. Indeed, having embraced sanctions, they are obliged to seek to delimit their human costs. . . .

August Reinisch, *Developing Human Rights and Humanitarian Law Accountability of the Security Council for the Imposition of Economic Sanctions*

95 Am. J. Int'l L. 851, 851-52 (2001) (footnotes omitted)

The end of the Cold War has led the United Nations Security Council to intensify its use of economic sanctions. The generally accepted purpose and emphasis of such sanctions lies in modifying behavior, not in punishment. However, their increased use has also brought to light various shortcomings and problems. Apart from the decades-old debate on their effectiveness, which depends, of course, on such factors as the policy goals set for sanctions, the criteria for measuring their success, the economic development of the target state, and the level of its economic relations with others, a few facts are relatively certain.

Thus, economic sanctions "theory" maintains that economic pressure on civilians will translate into pressure on the government for change, but the targeted leaders, sometimes expressly intended to be ousted by their outraged peoples, have managed to continue pursuing their policies and to stay in power. Part of the reason for this effect derives from the leaders' ability to "retranslate" the message of sanctions into punishment and retribution against the country, which enhances popular support for the regime in "rally around the flag" fashion.

Further, sanctions have unintentionally contributed to the emergence of black markets, creating huge profit-making opportunities for ruling elites and their collaborators. Worst of all, economic sanctions tend to hit the wrong targets; instead of the regime, the population at large and in particular the weakest in society become the true victims. . . .

Can military force be more humane than economic sanctions? . . . Which type of enforcement (Article 41 or 42) entails less suffering for civilians? If sanctions produce as much or more suffering than military force, which is more sensible? If sanctions are painful and virtually certain to be unsuccessful and armed force will be required eventually, is military intervention not desirable sooner rather than later?

. . . A preference to avoid military force no longer appears unequivocally noble should civilian damage from a so-called non-forcible coercive effort be more substantial than from a forcible alternative. . . . [T]he challenge is to determine whether the greatest number over the longer term would be better served by rapid and vigorous military intervention to enforce legitimate international decisions rather than slow, and not necessarily less violent, economic coercion.

Paradoxically, in certain contexts the use of multilateral military force may emerge as a possible more humane option than its supposedly non-forcible relative.

The "more humane option" of military force is considered in section IV of this chapter. In support of the idea that military solutions may be preferable in the long term, see Edward N. Luttwak, *Give War a Chance*, 78 Foreign Aff. 36 (July/Aug. 1999).

Note: Regional or Unilateral Sanctions

States are generally free to formulate their own trade policies (limited by whatever economic treaties they may have accepted) and therefore to impose trade, diplomatic, or other sanctions against other states unilaterally or as part of a regional bloc. There are a number of examples of such sanctions purportedly imposed based on human rights criteria.

Three of these efforts were undertaken by the Organization of American States (OAS). The first was against the Dominican Republic, when the Trujillo family controlled the government. The OAS ordered the breaking of diplomatic relations with the Trujillo regime and also the suspension of all trade in arms and war implements with it. Res. I, Sixth Meeting of Consultation of Ministers of Foreign Affairs, San Jose, Costa Rica, August 16-21, 1960, Final Act, OAS Off. Rec. OEA/Ser.C/II.6 (English) at 8 (1960). Within a year, Trujillo was toppled by an internal insurrection, allegedly supported by the CIA. While sanctions undoubtedly were a factor in events leading to the end of the Trujillo government, there is little evidence that they were decisive.

In 1964, the OAS voted sanctions against Cuba (Res. I, Ninth Meeting of Consultation of Ministers of Foreign Affairs, Washington, D.C., July 21-26, 1964, Final Act, OAS Off Rec. OEA/Ser.D/III.15 (English) at 3 (1964)), which consisted of withholding diplomatic recognition of the Castro regime and a trade embargo, both measures adopted in reaction to the Cuban policy of "exporting revolution" to other Latin American states. The sanctions were less than wholly successful for several reasons. First, there was the heavy support provided by the Soviet Union to Cuba, to the extent of $1.5 million per day at its peak. Second was the steep increase in the price of sugar, Cuba's lone cash crop: sugar prices increased sixfold between 1959 and 1974, although prices have since come down considerably from their 1974 peak. A third problem lay in the fact that the sanctions were not applied uniformly, even within the regional framework. Mexico, for instance, was never part of the effort, and Chile withdrew its support after the election of the Allende government in 1970 (although the junta that overthrew Allende in 1973 reimposed the sanctions). The general enthusiasm of Latin American states for the quarantine faded in the late 1960s and early 1970s, when many states came to believe, rightly or wrongly, that Castro no longer sought to foment revolution in the region. Beginning in 1972, one Latin state after another defected from the sanctioning campaign, with the quarantine being formally lifted in 1975 (Res. I, Sixteenth Meeting of Consultation of Ministers of Foreign Affairs, San Jose, Costa Rica, July 29, 1975, Final Act, OAS Off. Rec. OEA/Ser.C/II.16 (English) at 4 (1975)). Although the United States voted for the lifting of the OAS sanctions against Cuba, it has kept its own sanctions in place and, in recent years, even has strengthened them.

The third OAS sanctions effort began as a response to the military coup that overthrew the democratically elected government of President Aristide in Haiti in late September 1991. On October 3, 1991, the OAS Ministers of Foreign Affairs met and adopted Resolution MRE/Reo.l/qf, OEA/Ser.F/V.1 (1991), which condemned the coup, recognized President Aristide's representatives as the only legitimate representatives of Haiti to the OAS, and recommended that each member state, inter alia, suspend economic, financial, and commercial ties with Haiti. Five days later, the Ministers adopted a follow-up resolution urging member states "to proceed immediately to freeze the assets of the Haitian State and to impose a trade embargo on Haiti, except for humanitarian aid." MRE/Res.2/91, OEA/ser.F/V.I (1991). Subsequent resolutions sought to expand the sanctions and to achieve greater compliance with the trade embargo. Eventually, the UN Security Council invoked Chapter VII of the UN Charter and ordered a limited but mandatory trade embargo, S.C. Res. 841 (June 16, 1993). Still later, invoking both Chapters VII and VIII, it adopted a near-complete trade embargo and authorized member states, "acting nationally or through regional agencies or arrangements, to use such measures commensurate with the specific circumstances as may be necessary under the authority of the Security Council to ensure strict implementation of the provisions of the present resolution and earlier relevant resolutions. . . ." S.C. Res. 917 (May 6, 1994). See the discussion of Haiti, infra page 832.

Another regional — actually subregional — sanctioning effort occurred in Africa in connection with the efforts of the Economic Community of West African States (ECOWAS) to achieve a peaceful resolution of the conflict in Liberia. When the NPFL, the principal party opposing the interim Liberian government, refused to recognize ECOWAS's peacekeeping force as an impartial and neutral force in the conflict, ECOWAS in July 1992 imposed comprehensive economic sanctions against the territory controlled by the NPFL. Report of the Secretary-General on the Question of Liberia, U.N. Doc. S/25402 (Mar. 12, 1993), at 7. The Security Council subsequently adopted two resolutions establishing an embargo on all deliveries of weapons and military equipment to Liberia. S.C. Res. 788 (Nov. 19, 1992); S.C. Res. 813 (Mar. 26, 1993).

Perhaps the most notorious and certainly longest example of regional sanctioning is the effort of the Arab states against Israel, which began in 1945. The Arab League Boycott Office, which is controlled by the Secretariat of the Arab League (subject to guidance from the League Council and the Economic Council), has attempted over the years to bring pressures of various kinds to bear upon Israel, most controversially in the form of "secondary boycotts," that is, the imposition upon companies working in the Arab states of a requirement not only that they themselves observe the boycott by not having dealings with Israel, but also that they not deal with other companies that do business with Israel.

The United States, which considered this boycott an effort to deny rather than to encourage human rights, responded to it in a number of ways. For a comprehensive survey of the Arab League boycott and the response of the United States and other countries thereto, see Andreas Lowenfeld, *Trade Controls for Political Ends*, ch. III (2d ed. 1983). Several Arab countries eventually abandoned the secondary boycotts, and the boycott has had minimal impact since the 1990s.

Finally, while unilateral sanctions imposed for human rights purposes were infrequent until relatively recently, they have now become more common. The efforts of the Carter and successive administrations to bring economic pressure to bear to further human rights are considered in more detail in Chapter 13. Other countries and the European Union increasingly are taking a similar approach.

Comments and Questions

1. Just how "smart" are "smart" sanctions? Arms embargoes seem to be notoriously porous, and limitations on travel or freezing bank accounts provide only indirect pressure on certain individuals, at best. Under what circumstances are such "targeted" sanctions likely to be effective? Compare efforts to address conflicts and resulting human rights violations by, e.g., controlling the sale of so-called "conflict diamonds" used by guerrilla groups to fund civil wars. The Kimberly Process Certification Scheme that was created in 2002 is described at http:*//www.kimberleyprocess.com:8080*, but several of the major rough diamond-trading countries, such as Belgium and The Netherlands, are not participants. For a note on the relationship between trade in uncut diamonds and human rights, see Chapter 5, page 406.

2. Madeleine Albright, then US Ambassador to the United Nations, was asked in May 1996 during an interview on the television show "60 Minutes" about the human cost of ongoing sanctions against Iraq. Lesley Stahl, the interviewer, posed the question, "We have heard that over half a million children have died. I mean, that's more than died in Hiroshima. And, you know, is the price worth it?" Albright replied, "I think this is a very hard choice. But the price, we think the price is worth it." Quoted in Robert Fisk, *The dishonesty of this so-called dossier*, The Independent (London) (Sept. 25, 2002). Do you agree with Albright's assessment that a policy imposing some degree of humanitarian suffering is acceptable in order to maintain regional peace and security? To restore democracy after a fraudulent election? To protect human rights?

3. The high-level UN summit meeting in 2005 reiterated that

> sanctions remain an important tool under the Charter in our efforts to maintain international peace and security without recourse to the use of force and [we] resolve to ensure that sanctions are carefully targeted in support of clear objectives, comply with sanctions established by the Securty Council and are implemented in ways that balance effectiveness to achieve the desired results against the possible adverse consequences, including socio-economic and humanitarian consequences, for populations and third States.

2005 World Summit Outcome, UN Doc. A/60/L.1, para. 106 (Sept. 15, 2005). Would Secretary Albright disagree?

4. For further discussion of the role and impact of sanctions, see David Cortright and George A. Lopez, *Sanctions and the Search for Security: Challenges to*

UN Action (2002); id., *The Sanctions Decade: Assessing UN Strategies in the 1990s* (2000); *Political Gain and Civilian Pain: The Humanitarian Impacts of Economic Sanctions* (Thomas G. Weiss, David Cortright, George A. Lopez, and Larry Minear eds., 1997).

III. U.S. Implementation of International Sanctions

The United Nations itself has no power to order the direct imposition of sanctions; it can only authorize such action (which might otherwise run afoul of various trade agreements). It is up to each state to adopt the necessary domestic legislation, executive orders, or administrative measures to put sanctions in place and, if need be, to enforce compliance with such laws.

Thus, Article 48 of the UN Charter provides:

> 1. The action required to carry out the decisions of the Security Council for the maintenance of international peace and security shall be taken by all the Members of the United Nations or by some of them, as the Security Council may determine.
> 2. Such decisions *shall be carried out by the Members of the United Nations directly* and through their action in the appropriate international agencies of which they are members. (emphasis added)

Note: The Legal Framework

Legislative Reference Service, Library of Congress, The United Nations Participation Act Sections Relating to Economic and Military Action

1-4, June 6, 1967

The United Nations Participation Act of 1945 (22 U.S.C. §287 [2005]) was designed to implement United States participation in the United Nations following Senate ratification of the United Nations Charter. The United Nations Participation Act was amended in 1949 and again in 1965. Sections 5, 6 and 7 [22 U.S.C. §287c] of the United Nations Participation Act relate to economic and military sanctions.

Provisions of the United Nations Charter

Before examining Sections 5, 6 and 7 and the effect of subsequent amendments, attention should be given to the pertinent provisions of the United Nations Charter for economic and military sanctions. Article 25 states:

> The Members of the United Nations agree to accept and carry out the decisions of the Security Council in accordance with the present Charter.

Article 25 in effect makes decisions of the Security Council binding upon members of the United Nations. It should be pointed out, however, that the permanent members of the Council, including the United States, can veto its decisions. Article 41 enables the Security Council to call upon members to apply economic sanctions, interruption of communications, and severance of diplomatic relations. Should the measures provided for under Article 41 prove inadequate, the Security Council is given authority under Article 42 to "take such action by air, sea or land forces as may be necessary to maintain or restore international peace and security. . . ."

Provisions of the United Nations Participation Act

Section 5(a) of the United Nations Participation Act authorizes the President, when called upon pursuant to Article 41 of the Charter by the Security Council, to apply economic sanctions or interruption of communications. Section 5(b) specifies a punishment or a fine of not more than $10,000 or imprisonment of not more than ten years or both to violators or evaders or those who attempt to evade or violate any rule, order, or regulation by the President pursuant to 5(a). Section 5(b) also calls for the forfeit to the United States of "any property, funds, securities, papers, or other articles or documents, or any vessel, together with her tackle, apparel, furniture, and equipment, or vehicle, concerned in such violation." The punishment applies to a natural person, a corporation (with the exception of the ten-year imprisonment), or to the officer, agent, or director of any corporation who knowingly participates in such violation or evasion. Section 5(b) was amended in 1949 to include "aircraft" as being subject to forfeit when concerned in violations of actions taken by the United States in cooperation with the Security Council pursuant to Article 41 of the Charter. This section was not changed by the 1965 amendment.

During the House Foreign Affairs Committee Hearings on the United Nations Participation Act of 1945 it was pointed out by Dean Acheson, then Under Secretary of State, that the effect of section 5 would be to give the President "the authority to do what we have by international treaty agreed to do." Congressman Kee then asked if the President "already has authority to apply other measures, such as severing diplomatic relations." Mr. Acheson responded, "Yes. Under the Constitution the President has that authority. But the interruption of economic relations and communications by rail, sea, radio and telegraph he would not have unless the Congress gave it to him."

The Senate Report on the United Nations Participation Act of 1945 cited precedents in prior legislation delegating to the President the authority to impose embargoes. With reference to Section 5 the following is stated in the Senate Report:

> The committee realizes that the powers proposed to be granted to the President under this section are very great. However, the basic decision in this regard was made when the Charter was ratified and this provision is simply a necessary corollary to our membership in the Organization. The committee also believes that the Security Council must be placed in the most effective position possible to act under article 41 since the prompt and effective application of economic and diplomatic sanctions have all the United Nations (or even the threat or possibility thereof) may avoid the necessity for the use of the armed forces available to the Security Council.

Once the appropriate Executive Order is issued, U.S. compliance with sanctions imposed by the United Nations is the responsibility of the Treasury

Department's Office of Foreign Assets Control. As of mid-2005, the office was concerned with monitoring multilateral or unilateral sanctions related to the former Yugoslavia, Burma, Cuba, Iran, Iraq, Liberia, Libya, North Korea, Sudan (not related to Darfur), Syria, and Zimbabwe, in addition to diamond trading, narcotics trafficking, nonproliferation, and terrorism. See *http://www.treasury.gov/officers/ enforcement/Ofac/sanctions.*

As discussed in Chapter 6, under U.S. law, subsequent federal legislation may override U.S. treaty obligations. This is precisely what happened with respect to the UN sanctions imposed on Southern Rhodesia, when Congress adopted the so-called Byrd Amendment to permit the importation of chrome — considered to be a strategic material essential to the production of various military items — from Rhodesia.

Diggs v. Shultz

470 F.2d 461 (D.C. Cir. 1972), cert. denied, 411 U.S. 931 (1973)

. . . In 1966 the Security Council of the United Nations, with the affirmative vote of the United States, adopted Resolution 232 directing that all member states impose an embargo on trade with Southern Rhodesia, a step which was reaffirmed and enlarged in 1968. In compliance with this resolution, the President of the United States issued Executive Orders 11322 and 11419, 22 U.S.C. 5287c, establishing criminal sanctions for violation of the embargo. In 1971, however, Congress adopted the so-called Byrd Amendment to the Strategic and Critical Materials Stock Piling Act. 50 U.S.C. §98-98h, which provides in part:

> Sec. 10. Notwithstanding any other provision of law . . . the President may not prohibit or regulate the importation into the United States of any material determined to be strategic and critical pursuant to the provisions of this Act, if such material is the product of any foreign country or area not listed as a Communist-dominated country or area . . . for so long as the importation into the United States of material of that kind which is the product of such Communist-dominated countries or areas is not prohibited by any provision of law.

Since Southern Rhodesia is not a Communist-controlled country, and inasmuch as the United States imports from Communist countries substantial quantities of metallurgical chromite and other materials available from Rhodesia, the Byrd Amendment contemplated the resumption of trade by this country with Southern Rhodesia. By direction of the president, the Office of Foreign Assets Control issued to the corporate appellees in this case a General License authorizing the importation of various materials from Southern Rhodesia, and they began importation.

Alleging that the Byrd Amendment did not and could not authorize issuance of such a license contrary to this country's treaty obligations, appellants sought to enjoin further importation, to require official seizure, and to restrain use, of materials already imported under the General License, and to declare the General License null and void. . . .

The District Court, in its comments to the effect that nonjusticiability would necessitate dismissal of the complaint even if standing be found, reasoned as follows: It is settled constitutional doctrine that Congress may nullify, in whole or in part, a treaty commitment. Congress, by the Byrd Amendment in 1971, acted to abrogate one aspect of our treaty obligations under the U.N. Charter, that is to say, our continued participation in the economic sanctions taken against Southern Rhodesia. The considerations underlying that step by Congress present issues of political policy which courts do not inquire into. Thus, appellants' quarrel is with Congress, and it is a cause which can be pursued only at the polls and not in the courts.

In this court appellants do not seriously contest the first of these propositions, namely, the constitutional power of Congress to set treaty obligations at naught. They seek, rather, to show that, in the Byrd Amendment, Congress did not really intend to compel the Executive to end United States observance of the Security Council's sanctions, and that, therefore, it is the Executive which is, without the essential shield of Congressional dispensation, violating a treaty engagement of this country....

We think that there can be no blinking the purpose and effect of the Byrd Amendment. It was to detach this country from the U.N. boycott of Southern Rhodesia in blatant disregard of our treaty undertakings. The legislative record shows that no member of Congress voting on the measure was under any doubt about what was involved then; and no amount of statutory interpretation now can make the Byrd Amendment other than what it was as presented to the Congress, namely, a measure which would make and was intended to make the United States a certain treaty violator....

Diggs v. Shultz remains the law of the land, although federal courts may still try to interpret U.S. legislation consistently with U.S. international obligations whenever possible. Compare United States v. Palestine Liberation Organization, 695 F.Supp. 1456 (S.D.N.Y. 1988) (holding that legislation that mandated closure of the PLO office in violation of the UN Headquarters Agreement was invalid, since it did not specifically state its intention to violate the treaty). The Byrd Amendment was, in effect, repealed by a 1977 amendment to the United Nations Participation Act, codified at 22 U.S.C. §287c(a) (2005).

Some of the policy implications of U.S. imposition of regional and unilateral sanctions — as opposed to those mandated by the United Nations — are considered in the following extract.

Kenneth Roth, Executive Director of Human Rights Watch, The Role of U.S. Sanctions Policies in Promoting Human Rights

Testimony before the Senate Task Force on Economic Sanctions, September 8, 1998, available at *http://www.hrw.org/press98/sept/sanct909.htm*

Thank you, Chairman McConnell, for your invitation to Human Rights Watch to address the Task Force on the issue of U.S. sanctions policies and the promotion and protection of human rights....

[T]he U.S. must consider the human rights impact of imposing — or not imposing — [sanctions as a foreign policy tool]. Just to cite a few examples of their usefulness, the multilateral imposition of sanctions contributed to the end of the apartheid regime in South Africa, while unilateral U.S. sanctions helped build pressure on and hasten the downfall of the Argentine military junta, Jean-Claude Duvalier and Idi Amin. And only this summer, in a different context, we saw the threat of sanctions help to resolve the negotiations involving Holocaust-era assets held in Switzerland. . . .

I. Sanctions as an Important Tool of U.S. Foreign Policy

Human Rights Watch believes that, as set out in the Foreign Assistance Act, a principal goal of United States foreign policy should be to promote the increased observance of human rights by all countries. To this end, the United States government should, on the one hand, seek sustainable long-term improvements through assistance programs which promote human rights, the rule of law and democratic development, and, on the other hand, use active diplomacy — including frank exchanges with the government concerned, and unilateral and multilateral public criticism — to address human rights violations. When diplomatic pressure fails to curb egregious abuses, however, the U.S. and other nations claiming to uphold human rights must retain the ability to employ limited and targeted sanctions to express their condemnation of violations, press for a change in abusive government policies, and avoid complicity in abuses.

Sometimes even the threat of sanctions, if consistently and credibly applied, can avoid the need for their imposition. At times, however, the actual application of sanctions is necessary. Their prompt imposition in such cases can serve the interests of the U.S. and the international community by promoting an environment of respect for human rights, and by helping to prevent a worsening of repression and resulting disorder which can create destabilizing refugee flows or in which military or other extreme measures may become necessary. . . .

II. Considerations for Effective Sanctions Policies

The term "sanctions" covers a multitude of penalties that can be imposed on an abusive regime, including conditions on aid or trade benefits and restrictions on trade. Our experience has taught us that certain types of sanctions, under certain conditions, offer the greatest promise of success in countering abusive human rights practices. A number of policy prescriptions flow from this experience:

SANCTIONS SUPPORTED BY DOMESTIC CONSTITUENCY IN TARGETED COUNTRY.

When human rights activists seeking freedoms in their own countries ask the international community to impose sanctions, the choice is clearest. The United States must listen to Burmese voices today, as it listened to South African voices in 1986 and Polish voices in 1981. Sanctions imposed in response to their pleas reinforce and legitimize their efforts. Domestic support also undermines any effort by the targeted regime to blame the U.S. or the international community for the negative economic impact of sanctions. . . .

TARGETED SANCTIONS.

We advocate sanctions that are targeted, and designed to have the greatest impact on an abusive regime by depriving it of the tools and means of repression, while avoiding or minimizing any negative impact on the general civilian population.

First in the hierarchy of sanctions are arms embargoes and restrictions on military assistance that a brutal regime would likely use to perpetrate further abuses. . . .

We particularly urge the use of "smart sanctions" which narrowly target decision-makers, and which do not permit them to shift the burden to the general population. These include freezing the assets of abusive leaders or governments and denying visas and residency permits to such officials. Another "smart" targeted sanction is active support for the criminal prosecution of abusive officials. . . . Another targeted sanction is the restriction on trade benefits that are most likely to benefit an abusive ruling elite, such as sanctions against an industry that is dominated by an abusive central government or from which the government derives substantial resources. . . .

SANCTIONS TIED TO CLEAR BENCHMARKS.

We have found that sanctions that are tied to clearly defined benchmarks are most effective. The sanctions should be inspired by principle, not political expedience, and this should be reflected in benchmarks rooted in international norms and standards, which, if reached, would trigger a lifting of sanctions. . . . In 1991, Congress put a temporary hold on $95 million in aid to Peru on human rights grounds and within a month disappearances dropped dramatically. . . .

By contrast, we have objected to the form of sanctions currently imposed on Cuba because they reflect an all-or-nothing approach, with no promise of loosening until the government changes, rather than rewarding concrete steps toward democratization and respect for human rights. . . .

When thus tied to clear, realistic, and principled criteria, sanctions serve as a carrot as well as a stick and are more likely to achieve the desired results. . . .

MULTILATERAL VERSUS UNILATERAL SANCTIONS.

We prefer the use of multilateral sanctions because they are more effective and have greater international legitimacy. . . . At the same time, when a multilateral effort is not possible, unilateral sanctions can be useful to stigmatize a government's abusive actions, as leverage to induce change, or to avoid U.S. complicity in abuses. As an example, we support unilateral sanctions imposed on Sudan, including the recent trade ban. . . . At times, even a small symbolic message, or the mere credible threat of unilateral sanctions, can be a source of meaningful leverage when the U.S. is a key financial or political supporter of a government. In the 1980's, the threat of the withdrawal of U.S. aid to El Salvador, for example, was often brandished to produce specific positive actions by the government. . . .

Note: *Think Globally, Act Locally: Local and State-sponsored Sanctions*

When concern about human rights abuses or repressive governments becomes widespread, citizens may not wish to wait for their national government to act. Pressures are often brought on private parties — businesses, universities, sports organizations, and others — to cease doing business with "outlaw" regimes. The military regime in Myanmar (Burma) has been the target of many such initiatives. The following case suggests that such activities, at least at the governmental level, are unlikely to be as effective in the U.S. as they have been in the past.

Crosby v. National Foreign Trade Council

530 U.S. 363 (2000) (footnotes omitted)

JUSTICE SOUTER delivered the opinion of the Court.

The issue is whether the Burma law of the Commonwealth of Massachusetts, restricting the authority of its agencies to purchase goods or services from companies doing business with Burma, [FN: The Court of Appeals noted that the ruling military government of "Burma changed [the country's] name to Myanmar in 1989," but the court then said it would use the name Burma since both parties and amici curiae, the state law, and the federal law all do so. National Foreign Trade Council v. Natsios, 181 F.3d 38, 45, n. 1 (CA1 1999). We follow suit, noting that our use of this term, like the First Circuit's, is not intended to express any political view. See ibid.] is invalid under the Supremacy Clause of the National Constitution owing to its threat of frustrating federal statutory objectives. We hold that it is.

I

In June 1996, Massachusetts adopted "An Act Regulating State Contracts with Companies Doing Business with or in Burma (Myanmar)," 1996 Mass. Acts 239, ch. 130 (codified at Mass. Gen. Laws §§7:22G-7:22 M, 40 F 1/2 (1997). The statute generally bars state entities from buying goods or services from any person (defined to include a business organization) identified on a "restricted purchase list" of those doing business with Burma. §§7:22H(a), 7:22J. Although the statute has no general provision for waiver or termination of its ban, it does exempt from boycott any entities present in Burma solely to report the news, §7:22H(e), or to provide international telecommunication goods or services, ibid., or medical supplies, §7:22I.

"'Doing business with Burma'" is defined broadly to cover any person

> "(a) having a principal place of business, place of incorporation or its corporate headquarters in Burma (Myanmar) or having any operations, leases, franchises,

majority-owned subsidiaries, distribution agreements, or any other similar agreements in Burma, or being the majority-owned subsidiary, licensee or franchise of such a person;"
"(b) providing financial services to the government of Burma, including providing direct loans, underwriting government securities, providing any consulting advice or assistance, providing brokerage services, acting as a trustee or escrow agent, or otherwise acting as an agent pursuant to a contractual agreement;"
"(c) promoting the importation or sale of gems, timber, oil, gas or other related products, commerce in which is largely controlled by the government of Burma, from Burma;"
"(d) providing any goods or services to the government of Burma." §7:22G.

In September 1996, three months after the Massachusetts law was enacted, Congress passed a statute imposing a set of mandatory and conditional sanctions on Burma. See Foreign Operations, Export Financing, and Related Programs Appropriations Act, 1997, §570, 110 Stat. 3009-166 to 3009-167 (enacted by the Omnibus Consolidated Appropriations Act, 1997, §101(c), 110 Stat. 3009-121 to 3009-172). . . .

First, [~~the federal Act~~] bans all aid to the Burmese Government except for humanitarian assistance, counternarcotics efforts, and promotion of human rights and democracy. §570(a)(1). The statute instructs United States representatives to international financial institutions to vote against loans or other assistance to or for Burma, §570(a)(2), and it provides that no entry visa shall be issued to any Burmese government official unless required by treaty or to staff the Burmese mission to the United Nations, §570(a)(3). These restrictions are to remain in effect "until such time as the President determines and certifies to Congress that Burma has made measurable and substantial progress in improving human rights practices and implementing democratic government." §570(a).

Second, the federal Act authorizes the President to impose further sanctions subject to certain conditions. He may prohibit "United States persons" from "new investment" in Burma, and shall do so if he determines and certifies to Congress that the Burmese Government has physically harmed, rearrested, or exiled Daw Aung San Suu Kyi (the opposition leader selected to receive the Nobel Peace Prize), or has committed "large-scale repression of or violence against the Democratic opposition." §570(b). . . .

Third, the statute directs the President to work to develop "a comprehensive, multilateral strategy to bring democracy to and improve human rights practices and the quality of life in Burma." §570(c). He is instructed to cooperate with members of the Association of Southeast Asian Nations (ASEAN) and with other countries having major trade and investment interests in Burma to devise such an approach, and to pursue the additional objective of fostering dialogue between the ruling State Law and Order Restoration Council (SLORC) and democratic opposition groups. . . .

On May 20, 1997, the President issued the Burma Executive Order, Exec. Order No. 13047, 3 CFR 202 (1997 Comp.). He certified for purposes of §570(b) that the Government of Burma had "committed large-scale repression of the democratic opposition in Burma" and found that the Burmese Government's actions and policies constituted "an unusual and extraordinary threat to the national security and foreign policy of the United States," a threat characterized as a national emergency. The President then prohibited new investment in Burma "by United

States persons," Exec. Order No. 13047. . . . The order generally incorporated the exceptions and exemptions addressed in the statute. §§3, 4. Finally, the President delegated to the Secretary of State the tasks of working with ASEAN and other countries to develop a strategy for democracy, human rights, and the quality of life in Burma, and of making the required congressional reports. §5.

II

Respondent National Foreign Trade Council (Council) is a nonprofit corporation representing companies engaged in foreign commerce; 34 of its members were on the Massachusetts restricted purchase list in 1998. . . .

In April 1998, the Council filed suit in the United States District Court for the District of Massachusetts, seeking declaratory and injunctive relief against the petitioner state officials charged with administering and enforcing the state Act (whom we will refer to simply as the State). The Council argued that the state law unconstitutionally infringed on the federal foreign affairs power, violated the Foreign Commerce Clause, and was preempted by the federal Act. [The Court traces the procedural history, observing that the U.S. Court of Appeals for the First Circuit affirmed the District Court's findings against Massachusetts on all three grounds.]

The State's petition for certiorari challenged the decision on all three grounds and asserted interests said to be shared by other state and local governments with similar measures. . . . [The court notes that at least 19 municipal governments have enacted analogous laws.]

III

A fundamental principle of the Constitution is that Congress has the power to preempt state law. Art. VI, cl. 2. . . .

Applying this standard, we see the state Burma law as an obstacle to the accomplishment of Congress's full objectives under the federal Act. We find that the state law undermines the intended purpose and "natural effect" of at least three provisions of the federal Act, that is, its delegation of effective discretion to the President to control economic sanctions against Burma, its limitation of sanctions solely to United States persons and new investment, and its directive to the President to proceed diplomatically in developing a comprehensive, multilateral strategy towards Burma.

A

First, Congress clearly intended the federal act to provide the President with flexible and effective authority over economic sanctions against Burma. It is simply implausible that Congress would have gone to such lengths to empower the President if it had been willing to compromise his effectiveness by deference to every provision of state statute or local ordinance that might, if enforced, blunt the consequences of discretionary Presidential action.

And that is just what the Massachusetts Burma law would do in imposing a different, state system of economic pressure against the Burmese political regime. As will be seen, the state statute penalizes some private action that the federal Act (as administered by the President) may allow, and pulls levers of influence that the federal Act does not reach. But the point here is that the state sanctions are immediate . . . and perpetual, there being no termination provision. . . . This unyielding application undermines the President's intended statutory authority by making it impossible for him to restrain fully the coercive power of the national economy when he may choose to take the discretionary action open to him, whether he believes that the national interest requires sanctions to be lifted, or believes that the promise of lifting sanctions would move the Burmese regime in the democratic direction. Quite simply, if the Massachusetts law is enforceable the President has less to offer and less economic and diplomatic leverage as a consequence. . . .

C

Finally, the state Act is at odds with the President's intended authority to speak for the United States among the world's nations in developing a "comprehensive, multilateral strategy to bring democracy to and improve human rights practices and the quality of life in Burma." §570(c). . . .

[T]he state Act undermines the President's capacity, in this instance for effective diplomacy. It is not merely that the differences between the state and federal Acts in scope and type of sanctions threaten to complicate discussions; they compromise the very capacity of the President to speak for the Nation with one voice in dealing with other governments. We need not get into any general consideration of limits of state action affecting foreign affairs to realize that the President's maximum power to persuade rests on his capacity to bargain for the benefits of access to the entire national economy without exception for enclaves fenced off willy-nilly by inconsistent political tactics. When such exceptions do qualify his capacity to present a coherent position on behalf of the national economy, he is weakened, of course, not only in dealing with the Burmese regime, but in working together with other nations in hopes of reaching common policy and "comprehensive" strategy. . . .

[I]n response to the passage of the state Act, a number of this country's allies and trading partners filed formal protests with the National Government, see 181 F.3d at 47 (noting protests from Japan, the European Union (EU), and ASEAN), including an official Note Verbale from the EU to the Department of State protesting the state Act. . . .

[T]he EU and Japan have gone a step further in lodging formal complaints against the United States in the World Trade Organization (WTO), claiming that the state Act violates certain provisions of the Agreement on Government Procurement, H. R. Doc. No. 103-316, 1719 (1994) and the consequence has been to embroil the National Government for some time now in international dispute proceedings under the auspices of the WTO. In their brief before this Court, EU officials point to the WTO dispute as threatening relations with the United States. . . .

V

Because the state Act's provisions conflict with Congress's specific delegation to the President of flexible discretion, with limitation of sanctions to a limited scope of actions and actors, and with direction to develop a comprehensive, multilateral strategy under the federal Act, it is preempted, and its application is unconstitutional, under the Supremacy Clause.

The judgment of the Court of Appeals for the First Circuit is affirmed.

It is so ordered.

Comments and Questions

1. One of the major issues with respect to domestic enforcement of sanctions is how far they should reach. Should they be restricted to those companies present or incorporated in the territory of the enforcing state, or should they extend extraterritorially to subsidiaries of the enforcing state's companies? See the previous edition of this book and sources cited therein for a discussion of this issue with respect to Rhodesia. Richard B. Lillich and Hurst Hannum, *International Human Rights: Problems of Law, Policy, and Practice* 520-22 (3d ed. 1995).

2. How does one judge whether unilateral sanctions have been worthwhile? What political or other determinations should be made before a decision to impose sanctions is taken? Is it proper to consider the impact of sanctions on the economy of the sanctioning country, as well as the potential impact on the sanctioned state? Is there any value to purely symbolic sanctions?

IV. Armed Intervention

A. *Intervention by the United Nations*

Note that the standards for the UN's authority to use force pursuant to Article 42 of the Charter are exactly the same as for the imposition of sanctions, i.e., the existence of "any threat to the peace, breach of the peace, or act of aggression," as set forth in Article 39. There is no obligation to employ sanctions before the resort to force, although the latter is obviously a more drastic measure that will be resorted to only in the most serious situations. As a matter of law, however, the consensus that has developed which permits the Security Council to impose mandatory sanctions against a country for human rights abuses taking place within it would appear to be applicable to a decision by the Council to use or authorize the use of force, if it deems that the situation warrants it.

In analyzing the ethical and legal circumstances under which armed intervention might be justified — or even required — it is essential to distinguish among the various purposes that intervention is designed to serve. The United Nations has a long history of sending "peacekeepers" to monitor ceasefires, historically only with the consent of the states concerned. It also has authorized the use of force as a reaction to aggression, as it did when Iraq invaded Kuwait in 1990. However, while condemnation and demands to change conduct are directed at human rights–violating states relatively frequently, much less common has been specific (or even implicit) authorization of the use of force on grounds that could honestly be described as primarily "humanitarian" or to protect "human rights." *

The two arguable exceptions to the UN's reluctance to authorize the use of force for human rights purposes are Somalia and Haiti.

1. Somalia

Sean D. Murphy, *Humanitarian Intervention: The United Nations in an Evolving World Order*

217-43 (1996) (footnotes omitted)

In 1988, civil war broke out in Somalia, with various factions and clans seeking the ouster of President Mohamed Siad Barre. After Barre was overthrown in January 1991, these factions and clans turned on each other, killing thousands of people, uprooting hundreds of thousands more from their homes, destroying the country's infrastructure, and crippling its economy. . . . By December 1992, the United Nations estimated Somali deaths at more than 300,000; furthermore, 900,000 Somalis had fled to neighboring Kenya, Ethiopia, and Djibouti, and to Yemen and Saudi Arabia.

International efforts to address the situation in Somalia moved very slowly. . . .

On January 23, 1992, the UN Security Council unanimously passed Resolution 733, stating that it was "concerned" that the continuation of the situation in Somalia constituted a threat to international peace and security [and imposing an arms embargo]. . . .

On December 3, 1992, the Security Council passed Resolution 794 authorizing a U.S.-led force to enter Somalia to safeguard relief work. The resolution, which merits quoting at some length, stated in part the following:

Recognizing the unique character of the present situation in Somalia and mindful of its deteriorating, complex and extraordinary nature, requiring an immediate and exceptional response,

Determining that the magnitude of the human tragedy caused by the conflict in Somalia, further exacerbated by the obstacles being created to the distribution of humanitarian assistance, constitutes a threat to international peace and security, . . .

Expressing grave alarm at continuing reports of widespread violations of international humanitarian law occurring in Somalia, including reports of violence and threats of violence against personnel participating lawfully in impartial humanitarian relief activities; deliberate attacks on non-combatants, relief consignments and vehicles, and medical and relief facilities; and impeding the delivery of food and medical supplies essential for the survival of the civilian population,

Dismayed by the continuation of conditions that impede the delivery of humanitarian supplies to destinations within Somalia, and in particular reports of looting of relief supplies destined for starving people, attacks on aircraft and ships bringing in humanitarian relief supplies, and attacks on the Pakistani UNOSOM contingent in Mogadishu, . . .

Determined further to restore peace, stability and law and order with a view to facilitating the process of a political settlement under the auspices of the United Nations, aimed at national reconciliation in Somalia, and encouraging the Secretary-General and his Special Representative to continue and intensify their work at the national and regional levels to promote these objectives,...

7. *Endorses* the recommendation by the Secretary-General in his letter of 29 November 1992 (S/24868) that action under Chapter VII of the Charter of the United Nations should be taken in order to establish a secure environment for humanitarian relief operations in Somalia as soon as possible;

8. *Welcomes* the offer by a Member State [the United States] described in the Secretary-General's letter to the Council of 29 November 1992 (S/24868) concerning the establishment of an operation to create such a secure environment;

9. *Welcomes* also offers by other Member States to participate in that operation;

10. *Acting* under Chapter VII of the Charter of the United Nations, authorizes the Secretary-General and Member States cooperating to implement the offer referred to in paragraph 8 above to use all necessary means to establish as soon as possible a secure environment for humanitarian relief operations in Somalia;

11. *Calls* on all Member States which are in a position to do so to provide military forces and to make additional contributions, in cash or in kind, in accordance with paragraph 10 above and requests the Secretary-General to establish a fund through which the contributions, where appropriate, could be channelled to the States or operations concerned;

12. *Authorizes* the Secretary-General and the Member States concerned to make the necessary arrangements for the unified command and control of the forces involved, which will reflect the offer referred to in paragraph 8 above;...

[20.] *Invites* the Secretary-General and his Special Representative to continue their efforts to achieve a political settlement in Somalia.

U.S. Marines arrived in Mogadishu [the capital of Somalia] on December 8 and immediately seized control of the airport, seaport, and surrounding areas. Some 19 other states supported the intervention with personnel, equipment, and funding. As foreseen in Resolution 794, these states assumed the operational responsibilities for the mission, with the United States providing a report directly to the Security Council on the early stages of the operation of what became known as the Unified Task Force (UNITAF).

By late January 1993, 24,000 U.S. marines had been deployed throughout southern Somalia, largely ending the civil strife that had prevented relief efforts in that area for so many months; total UNITAF forces peaked in early 1993 at 38,300. The deployment was the largest humanitarian-military relief operation in UN history....

On its face, Resolution 794 left various matters unanswered, such as the exact command and control of the forces, whether they would carry UN insignia, and what degree of force would be used against the Somali factions....

A further ambiguity related to the exact mission of the intervening forces. Everyone agreed that creating a secure environment for humanitarian relief operations was the basic objective, but numerous peripheral issues arose as to how that objective might be achieved. For instance, it was unclear whether the mission of the forces included the disarming of the Somalian factions.... The

United States initially skirted the issue of disarming the factions; once deployed, U.S. forces proceeded by disarming gunmen openly displaying weapons but not seeking to seize cashes held by factional leaders. Nevertheless, U.S. forces ultimately began seeking out, seizing, and destroying certain weapons where feasible and requiring that other weapons be placed in stockpiles subject to UN inspection. . . .

The UN Takes Over from UNITAF

In March 1993, the Secretary-General proposed that, by May 1, UNITAF transfer command to a UN force to consist of up to 28,000 troops under a UN commander. This second phase of UN operations in Somalia (known as UNOSOM II) was authorized unanimously by the Security Council in Resolution 814 of March 26, 1993, marking the first time "blue helmets" were to be deployed with the power to engage in combat to enforce their mandate, as opposed to simply "keep the peace" by their presence. Although many would continue to refer to it as a "peacekeeping" operation, it was well understood that UNOSOM II's mandate was unlike that of any peacekeeping force previously deployed. UNOSOM II was given extensive authority to control heavy weapons of the Somali factions, to seize small arms, to de-mine various areas, to protect relief workers, and to aid in the return and resettlement of displaced persons. . . .

At the time of the transfer of control to UNOSOM II, the intervention by foreign forces in Somalia was considered by the international community and many Somalis to be a tremendous success, at least in terms of reducing violence in Somalia and preventing widespread starvation. Schools were being reopened, food-for-work programs were underway rather than just free food distribution, and commercial enterprises were being encouraged. The question was whether this success could continue and be built upon by UN-led forces under UNOSOM II.

Before long it was clear that maintaining such success would be difficult. . . .

The sheer logistical difficulty for the United Nations in coordinating such a large operation thus itself proved to be a major problem. . . .

On June 5, violence broke out in Mogadishu, leaving 24 UN Pakistani forces dead and 56 wounded — the highest casualty toll suffered by UN forces in a single incident since 1961 in the Congo — as well as scores of Somalis, both combatants and noncombatants. . . .

The Security Council responded by passing a resolution condemning the attacks and affirming that the Secretary-General was authorized under Resolution 814 to "take all measures necessary against all those responsible for the armed attacks [and] to establish the effective authority of [UNOSOM II] throughout Somalia, including to secure the investigation of their actions and their arrest and detention for prosecution, trial, and punishment." Additional UN forces from France and the United States, including attack planes, were deployed to Somalia. . . .

[Beginning in August, U.S. forces made several unsuccessful attempt to capture the most powerful Somali warlord, Mohammed Aideed, who had been responsible for the attack on the Pakistanis. The last of those attempts, on October 3, resulted in the deaths of 18 elite U.S. forces, nearly 100 wounded, and one captured (who was subsequently released), along with the deaths of at least hundreds of Somalis; these events were captured in the book and film, *Black Hawk Down*, a brief extract from which may be found in Chapter 4, page 265. Soon thereafter, President Clinton announced that U.S. troops would be withdrawn by March 1994; his lead was followed by other Western states. In February 1994, UNOSOM II's mandate was restricted to protection of humanitarian aid deliveries, primarily outside Mogadishu (S.C. Res. 897, Feb. 4, 1994). A year later, UNOSOM II and all other foreign troops were withdrawn from Somalia.]

ASSESSMENT OF THE INTERVENTION. . . .

The reason for the interventions was not self-defense but, rather, to create the conditions under which relief operations could prevent widespread death from civil violence, starvation, and lack of basic medical supplies. . . . [I]t generally was recognized that the United States had no strategic or economic interest in Somalia. In explaining the U.S. purpose in proposing UN intervention, U.S. President George Bush characterized the deployment as "necessary to address a major humanitarian calamity, avert related threats to international peace and security, and protect the safety of Americans and others engaged in relief operations." . . .

The December 1992 intervention in Somalia by U.S. military forces in conjunction with forces from other countries was expressly debated and authorized by the Security Council. . . .

The Security Council asserted that it was taking action against a "threat to international peace and security." It is notable, however, that Resolutions 794 and 814 do not refer to the effects of the Somali crisis on neighboring countries, such as the flow of refugees. There were in fact significant flows of refugees to neighboring countries, but the dominant issue discussed by the Security Council members when passing Resolutions 794 and 814 was not the threat of these flows (which had existed for some time) but, rather, the need to address immediately the internal catastrophe of violence and starvation inflicted on the Somali people. . . .

The statements of governments and nongovernmental groups during 1992-93 indicate acceptance of the legality of the intervention, although at various times there was criticism of the conduct of the operation. There is no indication in the debates or statements by the relevant political actors of an acceptance that the United States or other states could have proceeded to intervene in Somalia without Security Council authorization. . . .

Regardless of how one assesses the nature of the problems encountered by UNOSOM II, all would agree that the financial costs of such an operation are tremendous. From December 1992 to June 1994, the United Nations spent close to $2 billion dollars [sic] on its humanitarian activities in Somalia. This, too, presents a serious problem for humanitarian intervention. To address a humanitarian crisis on the scale of what happened in Somalia requires a massive deployment of forces and relief, which entails very high financial costs that the United Nations and its members are likely to accept only in exceptional circumstances.

2. Haiti

A military junta ousted Haiti's freely elected President, Jean-Bertrand Aristide, from office in 1991 and for the next three years ruled that impoverished country with the proverbial iron fist, relying upon murder, disappearances, torture, and intimidation to maintain itself in power. OAS efforts and UN sanctions had relatively little effect upon the military and business establishment. Thus, by mid-1994, the question of whether a humanitarian intervention should be mounted and, if so, what type — UN, OAS, or U.S. unilateral — was much debated. Compare Trainor, *Clinton Should Send in the Troops to Haiti,* Boston Globe, May 16, 1994, at 11, with *Editorial, No Good Reason to Invade Haiti,* N.Y. Times, July 13, 1994, at A18. Eventually, the Clinton Administration took the matter to the UN Security Council and secured the adoption of Resolution 940, to authorize what some would argue is the most far-reaching UN humanitarian intervention to date. Compare the extracts set forth below to those in Resolution 794 on Somalia, set out supra at pages 829.

Security Council Resolution 940

July 31, 1994

. . . *Gravely concerned* by the significant further deterioration of the humanitarian situation in Haiti, in particular the continuing escalation by the illegal de facto regime of systematic violations of civil liberties, the desperate plight of Haitian refugees and the recent expulsion of the staff of the International Civilian Mission (MICIVIH), which was condemned in its Presidential statement of 12 July 1994 (S/PRST/1994/32), . . .

Taking note of the letter dated 29 July 1994 from the legitimately elected President of Haiti (S/1994/905, annex) and the letter dated 30 July 1994 from the Permanent Representative of Haiti to the United Nations (S/1994/910), . . .

Reaffirming that the goal of the international community remains the restoration of democracy in Haiti and the prompt return of the legitimately elected President, Jean-Bertrand Aristide, within the framework of the Governors Island Agreement, . . .

Determining that the situation in Haiti continues to constitute a threat to peace and security in the region,

1. *Welcomes* the report of the Secretary-General of 15 July 1994 (S/1994/828) and takes note of his support for action under Chapter VII of the Charter of the United Nations in order to assist the legitimate Government of Haiti in the maintenance of public order;

2. *Recognizes* the unique character of the present situation in Haiti and its deteriorating, complex and extraordinary nature, requiring an exceptional response; . . .

4. *Acting* under Chapter VII of the Charter of the United Nations, authorizes Member States to form a multinational force under unified command and control and, in this framework, to use all necessary means to facilitate the departure from Haiti of the military leadership, consistent with the Governors Island Agreement, the prompt return of the legitimately elected President and the restoration of the legitimate authorities of the Government of Haiti, and to establish and maintain a secure and stable environment that will permit implementation of the Governors Island Agreement, on the understanding that the cost of implementing this temporary operation will be borne by the participating Member States; . . .

9. *Decides* to revise and extend the mandate of the United Nations Mission in Haiti (UNMIH) for a period of six months to assist the democratic Government of Haiti in fulfilling its responsibilities in connection with:

(a) sustaining the secure and stable environment established during the multinational phase and protecting international personnel and key installations; and

(b) the professionalization of the Haitian armed forces and the creation of a separate police force;...

13. *Requests* the Member States acting in accordance with paragraph 4 above to report to the Council at regular intervals, the first such report to be made not later than seven days following the deployment of the multinational force;...

17. *Affirms* that the Council will review the measures imposed pursuant to resolutions 841 (1993), 873 (1993) and 917 (1994), with a view to lifting them in their entirety, immediately following the return to Haiti of President Jean-Bertrand Aristide....

Both of the letters referred to in the second preambular paragraph were from Haitian President Aristide, who was living in exile in Florida. They requested the United Nations "to take prompt and decisive action" to implement the so-called Governors Island Agreement, which was to return Aristide to power, and specifically noted the "agreement" of President Aristide with the draft text that was adopted as Resolution 940. Does this acceptance of the intervention by the internationally recognized government of Haiti lessen the precedential value of the subsequent use of force?

Faced with imminent invasion, and after the last-minute mediation of former U.S. President Jimmy Carter, the military-led government did not oppose the landing of approximately 20,000 U.S.-led forces in September 1994, when Aristide was returned to power. Since that U.S.-led force withdrew in 1995, there have been five separate UN peacekeeping missions to Haiti. The International Crisis Group summarizes the next few years as follows:

> Aristide agreed to hold presidential elections 1995 and hand over presidency at end of constitutional term (i.e. not to serve three years he had spent in exile). His successor, Lavalas candidate Rene Preval, took office February 1996 and was soon confronted by sharp divisions within Lavalas coalition, resulting in creation of Aristide's own party, Fanmi Lavalas, and lengthy political crisis. May 2000 legislative elections saw overwhelming victory of Fanmi Lavalas amidst serious fraud accusations; as result, main opposition parties boycotted November 2000 presidential elections (marked by extremely low turnout) allowing Aristide to obtain 92 per cent of vote. Irregularities in 2000 electoral process, denounced by OAS, led to severe reduction in western aid to Haiti.
>
> In spite of repeated efforts by OAS to negotiate political solution to crisis, it escalated after several incidents — including alleged attempted coup December 2001 and subsequent attacks against residences and offices of main opposition leaders. Aristide managed to hold on in face of growing economic impoverishment and serious deterioration of human rights situation. Political opposition, joined by civil society Group of 184, progressively intensified campaign of demonstrations asking for Aristide's resignation 2003. February 2004, armed group called Front de Résistance (composed mainly of former Aristide supporters based in Gonaives and former

> military and paramilitary leaders) took control of main northern cities and threatened to enter capital Port-au-Prince. Faced with threat of large-scale clashes, and gradual decline of international support, President Aristide left country 29 February on U.S.-arranged flight. Upon arrival in Central African Republic, Aristide claimed U.S. and France had ousted him. Same day, at request of interim president, UN Security Council authorized rapid deployment of Multinational Interim Force to stabilize country. Political transition process, backed by international community, culminated with installation of transitional government led by Prime Minister Latortue. 1 June [2004] MIF transferred authority to UN peacekeeping force (MINUSTAH).

International Crisis Group, Conflict history: Haiti, *http://www.crisisgroup.org/home/index.cfm?action=conflict_search&l=1&t=1&c_country=46*. The most relevant provisions of Resolution 1542 are set forth below:

Security Council Resolution 1542

April 30, 2004

. . . *Deploring* all violations of human rights, particularly against the civilian population, and urging the Transitional Government of Haiti ("Transitional Government") to take all necessary measures to put an end to impunity and to ensure that the continued promotion and protection of human rights and the establishment of a State based on the rule of law and an independent judiciary are among its highest priorities, . . .

Reiterating its call upon the international community to continue to assist and support the economic, social and institutional development of Haiti over the long term, and welcoming the intention of the Organization of American States (OAS), the Caribbean Community (CARICOM), and of the international donor community, as well as international financial institutions, to participate in those efforts, . . .

7. Acting under Chapter VII of the Charter of the United Nations with regard to Section I below, decides that MINUSTAH shall have the following mandate:

I. Secure and Stable Environment:

(a) in support of the Transitional Government, to ensure a secure and stable environment within which the constitutional and political process in Haiti can take place;

(b) to assist the Transitional Government in monitoring, restructuring and reforming the Haitian National Police, consistent with democratic policing standards, including through the vetting and certification of its personnel, advising on its reorganization and training, including gender training, as well as monitoring/mentoring members of the Haitian National Police;

(c) to assist the Transitional Government, particularly the Haitian National Police, with comprehensive and sustainable Disarmament, Demobilization and Reintegration (DDR) programmes for all armed groups, including women and children associated with such groups, as well as weapons control and public security measures;

(d) to assist with the restoration and maintenance of the rule of law, public safety and public order in Haiti through the provision inter alia of operational support to the Haitian National Police and the Haitian Coast Guard, as well as with their institutional strengthening, including the re-establishment of the corrections system;

(e) to protect United Nations personnel, facilities, installations and equipment and to ensure the security and freedom of movement of its personnel, taking into account the primary responsibility of the Transitional Government in that regard;

(f) to protect civilians under imminent threat of physical violence, within its capabilities and areas of deployment, without prejudice to the responsibilities of the Transitional Government and of police authorities;

II. Political Process:

(a) to support the constitutional and political process under way in Haiti, including through good offices, and foster principles and democratic governance and institutional development;

(b) to assist the Transitional Government in its efforts to bring about a process of national dialogue and reconciliation;

(c) to assist the Transitional Government in its efforts to organize, monitor, and carry out free and fair municipal, parliamentary and presidential elections at the earliest possible date, in particular through the provision of technical, logistical, and administrative assistance and continued security, with appropriate support to an electoral process with voter participation that is representative of the national demographics, including women;

(d) to assist the Transitional Government in extending State authority throughout Haiti and support good governance at local levels;

III. Human Rights:

(a) to support the Transitional Government as well as Haitian human rights institutions and groups in their efforts to promote and protect human rights, particularly of women and children, in order to ensure individual accountability for human rights abuses and redress for victims;

(b) to monitor and report on the human rights situation, in cooperation with the Office of the United Nations High Commissioner for Human Rights, including on the situation of returned refugees and displaced persons;

8. Decides that MINUSTAH in collaboration with other partners shall provide advice and assistance within its capacity to the Transitional Government:

(a) in the investigation of human rights violations and violations of international humanitarian law, in collaboration with the Office of the High Commissioner for Human Rights, to put an end to impunity;

(b) in the development of a strategy for reform and institutional strengthening of the judiciary....

Unfortunately, instability, violence, stagnant economic development, and lack of political will have continued to plague Haiti since the initial intervention in 1994. Legislative and presidential elections were to be held in late 2005, with a new government to assume office in February 2006. Assessments in the months prior to this transition must lead one to question the impact of the efforts of the United Nations, regional organizations, and other actors — and at least give pause to those who believe that nation-building or peacebuilding can be easily accomplished.

The Secretary-General's periodic report on MINUSTAH observed that "the political discourse has yet to address concretely the substantive concerns facing the country or to offer a clear vision for the future of Haiti beyond the upcoming elections. As a result, the political class remains polarized. . . . The security situation in Port-au-Prince [the Haitian capital] remains volatile. . . . The human rights situation remained alarming. Cases of summary execution, prolonged pre-trial detention, arbitrary arrest, disregard for due process, ill-treatment, and rape continued to be reported. Impunity continued to exist." Report of the Secretary-General on the United Nations Stabilization Mission in Haiti, UN Doc. S/2005/313, paras. 4, 12, 29 (May 13, 2005).

A mission of the Security Council (an unusual event) that visited Haiti a month before the Secretary-General's report confirmed the bad news, concluding that "almost all national actors across the political spectrum acknowledged that Haiti was in a deep political, social and economic crisis. . . . Regardless of the approach, the mission found that there was broad agreement that a solution to the country's current situation would not be reached in the short term. . . . [T]he mission received reports that a culture of impunity remained pervasive, marked by arbitrary arrest, wrongful detention, inhumane prison conditions, excessive use of force, and extrajudicial executions. . . . The mission learned that the commission that should investigate allegations against the police had yet to be established." Report of the Security Council mission to Haiti, 13 to 16 April 2005, UN Doc. S/2005/302, paras. 11, 12, 42 (May 6, 2005).

While it is impossible to explore the many explanations for the political and economic quagmire from which Haiti seems unable to escape, the following opinion piece suggests at least some needed changes.

Todd Howland, Op-ed, *In Haiti, Rhetoric Trumps Human Rights*

Boston Globe, Aug. 16, 2005, at A15

The US-inspired peacekeeping approach being utilized by the United Nations in Haiti is a failure. . . .

At present, the international community intervenes in a crisis using two tools: The first is sending in the UN's blue helmets. These missions are approved by the Security Council and paid for by member states according to a pre-agreed payment schedule. It is only natural that the states paying the most, like the United States and Japan, seek to limit the number and breadth of these missions.

To that end, the United States limits UN peacekeeping missions to putting blue helmets on the ground. Thus, peacekeepers normally spend over 99 percent on themselves. The result is situations like Haiti, where the peacekeeping mission's annual budget for its personnel's health care is greater than the annual budget of the Haitian Ministry of Health.

While security does not grow out of the barrel of a gun, many cling to the idea that the international community needs to establish security first and then undertake development. This might work for the conflicts of the past, where a ceasefire between competing armies could achieve a modicum of security. Today, chaos is common, so simultaneous work on security and development is needed.

Peacekeeping missions should measurably improve the full spectrum of human rights and be given the budget to do so. . . .

The US-inspired UN failure in Haiti has numerous causes, but the US unwillingness to change its outdated money-flow modus operandi to peacekeeping operations in order to maximize their transformative potential highlights shows that it is not just the UN that needs reform.

3. The Consequences of Non-Intervention: Rwanda

If UN-authorized "humanitarian" interventions in Somalia and Haiti can be classified as failures, the case of Rwanda suggests that non-intervention can be no less problematic. To place the situation described in the following extract in its geopolitical and chronological context, recall that the killing of U.S. Marines in Mogadishu occurred in October 1993 and that U.S. forces withdrew from Somalia in March 1994; President Aristide was deposed in Haiti in September 1991, and the resolution authorizing the use of force to restore him to power in Haiti was adopted in July 1994. The conflict in former Yugoslavia did not end until late 1995.

It may also be relevant that an estimated 50,000 people were killed in neighboring Burundi immediately after the October 1993 assassination of the first Hutu president of that country, and 200,000-300,000 Burundians have died in Hutu-Tutsi violence since then. The first resolution adopted by the Security Council after the assassination in Burundi was in January 1996, when the Council declared "its readiness . . . (a) To consider the imposition of measures under the Charter of the United Nations, including a ban on the supply of all arms and related matériel to Burundi and travel restrictions and other measures against those leaders in Burundi who continue to encourage violence; and (b) To consider what other steps may need to be taken." S.C. Res. 1040, para. 8 (Jan. 29, 1996).

Report of the Independent Inquiry into the Actions of the United Nations during the 1994 Genocide in Rwanda

1, 2-3, 4-5, 9, 12, 15, 16, 18-22, 26, 27, 28, 30-33, 38, UN Doc. S/1999/1257 (Dec. 16, 1999) (emphasis in original)

I. Introduction

Approximately 800,000 people were killed during the 1994 genocide in Rwanda. The systematic slaughter of men, women and children which took place over the course of about 100 days between April and July of 1994 will forever be remembered as one of the most abhorrent events of the twentieth century. Rwandans killed Rwandans, brutally decimating the Tutsi population of the country, but also targetting moderate Hutus. Appalling atrocities were committed, by militia and the armed forces, but also by civilians against other civilians. . . .

The failure by the United Nations to prevent, and subsequently, to stop the genocide in Rwanda was a failure by the United Nations system as a whole. The fundamental failure was the lack of resources and political commitment devoted to developments in Rwanda and to the United Nations presence there. There was a persistent lack of political will by Member States to act, or to act with enough assertiveness. This lack of political will affected the response by the Secretariat and decision-making by the Security Council, but was also evident in the recurrent difficulties to get the necessary troops for the United Nations Assistance Mission for Rwanda (UNAMIR). Finally, although UNAMIR suffered from a chronic lack of resources and political priority, it must also be said that serious mistakes were made with those resources which were at the disposal of the United Nations. . . .

II. Description of Key Events

ARUSHA PEACE AGREEMENT

On 4 August 1993, following years of negotiations, the Government of Rwanda and the Rwandese Patriotic Front (RPF) signed the Arusha Peace Agreement. . . .

THE ESTABLISHMENT OF UNAMIR. . . .

On 5 October, the Council unanimously adopted resolution 872 (1993), which established UNAMIR. The Council did not approve all the elements of the mandate recommended by the Secretary-General, but instead decided on a more limited mandate. Notably absent was the suggestion that UNAMIR assist in the recovery of arms. Instead, the resolution decided that UNAMIR should contribute to the security of the city of Kigali, i.e., within a weapons-secure area established by the parties in and around the city . . .

The mandate included the following other elements:

- to monitor observance of the cease-fire agreement, which called for the establishment of cantonment and assembly zones and the demarcation of the new DMZ and other demilitarization procedures;
- to monitor security situation during the final period of the transitional government's mandate, leading up to the elections;
- to assist with mine clearance, primarily through training programmes;
- to investigate, at the request of the parties, or on its own initiative, instances of non-compliance with the provisions of the Protocol of Agreement on the Integration of the Armed Forces of the Two Parties, and to pursue any such instances with the parties responsible and report thereon as appropriate to the Secretary-General;
- to monitor the process of repatriation of Rwandese refugees and the resettlement of displaced persons to verify that it is carried out in a safe and orderly manner;
- to assist in the coordination of humanitarian assistance in conjunction with relief operations, and
- to investigate and report on incidents regarding the activities of the gendarmerie and police. . . .

Developments in Rwanda during November and December 1993 gave the new peacekeeping operation cause for concern. The political process faced a stalemate. It was also becoming increasingly clear that the political difficulties were taking place against a backdrop of ever more evident violence. According to the United Nations, about 60 people were killed in violent incidents in November and December. UNAMIR's reports from this period provide graphic descriptions of the ruthlessness with which these killings were carried out. Already at this stage, the optimistic atmosphere which had surrounded the signing at Arusha was beginning to be sobered by considerable concern about the armed activity in Rwanda, including the existence of armed militia. Moreover, the assassination of President Melchior Ndadaye of Burundi in late October, and the violent aftermath and the refugee flows which ensued, provided another worrying backdrop to the beginning of the peacekeeping operation which had not been foreseen when the mission was set up....

POLITICAL DEADLOCK AND A WORSENING OF THE SECURITY SITUATION....

...On 14 February (the United Nations Blue Book on Rwanda dates it 14 March), the Belgian Foreign Minister, Mr Willy Claes, wrote a letter to the Secretary-General, arguing in favour of a stronger mandate for UNAMIR. Unfortunately, this proposal does not appear to have been given serious attention within the Secretariat or among other interested countries....

...Annan [Kofi Annan, then head of the UN's Department of Peacekeeping Operations] emphasized that public security was the responsibility of the authorities and must remain so. "As you know, resolution 792 [sic] (1993) only authorized UNAMIR to 'contribute to the security of the city of Kigali, i.e., within a weapons secure area established by repeat by the parties'."...

[On April 6, 1994, a plane carrying the presidents of Rwanda and Burundi was shot down by as yet unknown persons. Killings in Kigali, the Rwandan capital, began almost immediately thereafter. Among the early casualties were 12 Belgian peacekeepers, who were killed and mutilated after surrendering their weapons.]

Dallaire [Romeo Dallaire, the Canadian force commander of UNAMIR] informed the Belgian Senate commission [during a subsequent investigation] that an armed operation to rescue the Belgians was not feasible because of the high risk of casualties to those who would intervene, and the high potential for failure of the operation. Describing the shortcomings and lack of resources of UNAMIR, Dallaire did not believe he had forces capable of conducting an intervention in favour of the Belgians: "The UNAMIR mission was a peacekeeping operation. It was not equipped, trained or staffed to conduct intervention operations."...

THE CONTINUED ROLE OF UNAMIR....

Dallaire painted the following picture of the dilemma facing the UN under the scenarios being discussed: "The consequences of a withdrawal by UNAMIR will definitely have an adverse affect [sic] on the morale of the civil population, especially the refugees, who will feel that we are deserting them. However, in actual fact, there is little that we are doing at the present time except providing security, some food and medicine and a presence. Humanitarian assistance has not really commenced.... The refugees at locations like Hotel Mille Collines, the Red Cross, St Michels Cathedral etc. in RGF territory are in danger of massacre, but have been in this danger without result so far for the last week even with UNAMIR on the ground."

By 19 April, the Secretariat's line had changed significantly: the draft of a report by the Secretary-General to the Security Council which had been prepared now included three options: to strengthen UNAMIR, to reduce its strength or to withdraw completely. The cable with which the draft was sent to Kigali states that "the option of strengthening UNAMIR was decided upon in the evening here leading to our belated request to you to hold up the movement of personnel scheduled for departure tomorrow."...

On 21 April, the Council voted unanimously to reduce UNAMIR to about 270 and to change the mission's mandate. The resolution stated that the Council was "appalled at the ensuing large-scale violence in Rwanda, which has resulted in the deaths of thousands of innocent civilians, including women and children."...

NEW PROPOSALS ON THE MANDATE OF UNAMIR

By the end of April, however, the disastrous situation in Rwanda made the Secretary-General recommend a reversal of the decision to reduce the force level. Boutros-Ghali's letter to the Security Council of 29 April (S/1994/518) provided an important shift in emphasis — from viewing the role of the United Nations as that of neutral mediator in a civil war to recognising the need to bring to an end the massacres against civilians, which had by then been going on for three weeks and were estimated to have killed some 200,000 people. The Secretary-General stated that the mandate contained in resolution 912 (1994) did not give UNAMIR the power to take effective action to halt the massacres. The Council was asked to reconsider its previous decisions and to consider "what action, including forceful action, it could take, or could authorize Member States to take in order to restore law and order." In a biting final remark, the Secretary-General wrote that he was aware "that such action would require a commitment of human and material resources on a scale which Member States have so far proved reluctant to contemplate."...

Notes on the discussions within the Security Council in the days following the Secretary-General's letter show a body divided on a number of issues: on whether an intervention should take place, and if so, how to describe the strength of the action (countries such as Brazil, China and the United Kingdom are reported to have argued against too strong an "interventionist" wording regarding the role of the United Nations), the possible role of regional actors, the question of the arms embargo...

UNAMIR II ESTABLISHED

The Council adopted resolution 918 (1994) on 17 May 1994. The resolution included a decision to increase the number of troops in UNAMIR, and imposed an arms embargo on Rwanda....

The newly appointed High Commissioner for Human Rights, Mr José Ayala Lasso, visited Rwanda on 11-12 May 1994. The High Commissioner visited Kigali and Byumba and spoke both to representatives of the so-called Interim Government and the RPF. His report to the Commission on Human Rights was published on 19 May 1994 (E/CN.4/S-3/3). While Ayala Lasso stated that more than 200,000 civilians had been killed and called for strong condemnation of those killings, the High Commissioner stopped at characterizing the situation as one where "extremely serious violations of human rights had taken place" and were continuing. His recommendations were directed at both parties. Ayala Lasso did not mention the word genocide other than in a reference to the Convention as one international human rights instrument to which Rwanda was a party. Ayala Lasso proposed the appointment of a Special Rapporteur on Human Rights in Rwanda, assisted by human rights monitors. . . .

The Secretary-General's report outlined a plan for the three-phased deployment of UNAMIR II, whereby phases 1 and 2 were to be initiated immediately in a synchronized manner. The plan foresaw different scenarios for deployment, including a situation where cease-fire was not in place. The two primary tasks of UNAMIR II were described as (a) To attempt to assure the security of as many assemblies as possible of civilians who are under threat and (b) To provide security, as required, to humanitarian relief operations.

The report's final observations were bitter: "The delay in reaction by the international community to the genocide in Rwanda has demonstrated graphically its extreme inadequacy to respond urgently with prompt and decisive action to humanitarian crises entwined with armed conflict. Having quickly reduced UNAMIR to a minimum presence on the ground, since its original mandate did not allow it to take action when the carnage started, the international community appears paralysed in reacting almost two months later even to the revised mandate established by the Security Council. We must all realize that, in this respect, we have failed in our response to the agony of Rwanda, and thus have acquiesced in the continued loss of human lives." . . .

OPERATION TURQUOISE

In a letter dated 19 June to the Security Council (S/1994/728), the Secretary General outlined the results of the efforts to put in place UNAMIR II, which at that time still only had a total force of 503. The Secretary-General stated that the first phase of deployment of UNAMIR II in the best of circumstances would only be able to take place in the first week of July. Mentioning the ongoing killings, the Secretary-General went on to suggest that the Council consider the offer by France to conduct a multinational operation under Chapter VII "to assure the security and protection of displaced persons and civilians at risk in Rwanda." . . .

The Security Council held consultations on the French initiative on 20-22 June. France introduced a draft resolution on 20 June. The Secretary-General participated in informal consultations on 22 June. According to the United Nations notes from the consultations, the Secretary-General argued in favour of an urgent decision to authorize the French-led operation. Later that day, the Council adopted resolution 929 (1994), the vote resulting in 10 votes in favour and 5 abstentions (Brazil, China, New Zealand, Nigeria, Pakistan). . . .

On 18 July, the RPF had gained control over the whole of Rwanda except the humanitarian zone controlled by Operation Turquoise. The RPF declared a unilateral cease-fire.

III. Conclusions

The Independent Inquiry finds that the response of the United Nations before and during the 1994 genocide in Rwanda failed in a number of fundamental respects....

1. THE OVERRIDING FAILURE

The overriding failure in the response of the United Nations before and during the genocide in Rwanda can be summarized as a lack of resources and a lack of will to take on the commitment which would have been necessary to prevent or to stop the genocide. UNAMIR, the main component of the United Nations presence in Rwanda, was not planned, dimensioned, deployed or instructed in a way which provided for a proactive and assertive role in dealing with a peace process in serious trouble. The mission was smaller than the original recommendations from the field suggested. It was slow in being set up, and was beset by debilitating administrative difficulties. It lacked well-trained troops and functioning materiel. The mission's mandate was based on an analysis of the peace process which proved erroneous, and which was never corrected despite the significant warning signs that the original mandate had become inadequate. By the time the genocide started, the mission was not functioning as a cohesive whole: in the real hours and days of deepest crisis, consistent testimony points to a lack of political leadership, lack of military capacity, severe problems of command and control and lack of coordination and discipline.

A force numbering 2,500 should have been able to stop or at least limit massacres of the kind which began in Rwanda after the plane crash which killed the Presidents of Rwanda and Burundi. However, the Inquiry has found that the fundamental capacity problems of UNAMIR led to the terrible and humiliating situation of a UN peacekeeping force almost paralysed in the face of a wave of some of the worst brutality humankind has seen in this century....

5. FAILURE TO RESPOND TO THE GENOCIDE

a. After the Presidential plane was shot down, the situation in Kigali quickly descended into chaos. Roadblocks were set up, massacres of Tutsi and opposition and moderate politicians began. Soon, the RPF broke out of its complex, and were strengthened by forces from outside the capital. In addition to the killings of civilians, fighting broke out between the Presidential Guards and the RPF. UNAMIR was faced with hundreds of calls for help, from politicians, staff members and others. Thousands of people sought refuge at sites where UNAMIR was present, including about 5,000 people who had gathered at the field hospital already by 8 April.

When the genocide began, the weaknesses of UNAMIR's mandate became devastatingly clear. The natural question is why a force numbering 2,500 could not stop the actions of the militia and RGF soldiers who began setting up roadblocks and killing politicians and Tutsi in the early hours after the crash. Could UNAMIR not have deterred, by its presence and a show of determination, the terrible sequence of violence that followed?

The correspondence between UNAMIR and Headquarters during the hours and days after the plane crash shows a force in disarray, with little intelligence about the true nature of what is happening and what political and military forces are at play, with no clear direction and with problems even communicating among its own contingents. The mission was under rules of engagement not to use force except in self defence. It had taken upon itself to protect politicians, but then in certain cases did not do so in the face of threats by the militia....

The decision by the Security Council on 21 April to reduce UNAMIR to a minimal force in the face of the killings which were by then known to all, rather than to make every effort to muster the political will to try and stop the killing has led to widespread bitterness in Rwanda. *It is a decision which the Inquiry finds difficult to justify. The Security Council bears a responsibility for its lack of political will to do more to stop the killing.*

b. The lack of will to act in response to the crisis in Rwanda becomes all the more deplorable in the light of the reluctance by key members of the International Community to acknowledge that the mass murder being pursued in front of global media was a genocide. The fact that what was occurring in Rwanda was a genocide brought with it a key international obligation to act in order to stop the killing. The parties to the 1948 Convention took upon themselves a responsibility to prevent and punish the crime of genocide. This is not a responsibility to be taken lightly. Although the main action required of the parties to the Convention is to enact national legislation to provide for jurisdiction against genocide, the Convention also explicitly opens the opportunity of bringing a situation to the Security Council. Arguably, in this context, the members of the Security Council have a particular responsibility, morally if not explicitly under the Convention, to react against a situation of genocide.

7. THE SHADOW OF SOMALIA

It has often been said that UNAMIR was an operation which was created in the shadow of Somalia [see supra pages 829]. In particular the deaths of the Pakistani and US peacekeepers in Somalia in 1993 had a deep effect on the attitude towards the conduct of peacekeeping operations. For instance, the UN commission of inquiry set up to study these tragic deaths in Somalia, whose report came out just as preparations were being made to strengthen UNAMIR in the wake of the genocide, concluded that "the UN should refrain from undertaking further peace enforcement actions within the internal conflicts of States" (S/1994/653)....

8. FOCUS ON ACHIEVING A CEASE-FIRE....

The persistent attempts to view the situation in Kigali after the death of the President as one where the cease-fire had broken down and therefore needed to be restored through negotiations, rather than one of genocide in addition to the fighting between the RGF and RPF, was a costly error of judgment. It was an error committed by the Secretariat, the leadership of UNAMIR and the Members of the Security Council. Several Council members have criticized the quality of the analysis provided to them by the Secretariat in this instance. For a number of the non-permanent members at the time, a key to realizing the genocidal perspective to the killings in Rwanda was information provided to them by the NGO community.... Secretariat under the leadership of the Secretary-General.

10. THE LACK OF POLITICAL WILL OF MEMBER STATES

Another reason for the main failure of the international community in Rwanda was the lack of political will to give UNAMIR the personnel and materiel resources the mission needed. Even after the Security Council decided to act to try and stop the killing, and reversed its decision to reduce UNAMIR, the problems that the Secretariat had faced since UNAMIR's inception in getting contributions of troops from Member States persisted....

A general point about the need for political will is that such will must be mobilised equally in response to conflicts across the globe. *It has been stated repeatedly during the course of the interviews conducted by the Inquiry that the fact that Rwanda was not of strategic interest to third countries and that the international community exercised double standards when faced with the risk of a catastrophe there compared to action taken elsewhere....*

19. FINAL OBSERVATIONS....

...Faced in Rwanda with the risk of genocide, and later the systematic implementation of a genocide, the United Nations had an obligation to act which transcended traditional principles of peacekeeping. In effect, there can be no neutrality in the face of genocide, no impartiality in the face of a campaign to exterminate part of a population....

The Inquiry agrees with the Secretary-General that "[W]hen the international community makes a solemn promise to safeguard and protect innocent civilians from massacre, then it must be willing to back its promise with the necessary means."

In addition to the failure of the United Nations to respond to the Rwandan genocide, blame has been placed on the United States for actively impeding a more effective international response. See, e.g., Samantha Power, A *Problem from Hell: America and the Age of Genocide* (2002), chap. 10; Alison des Forges, *Leave None* to *Tell the Story: Genocide in Rwanda* (1999). There is disagreement as to what the impact of armed intervention might have been, given the short duration and ferocity of the country-wide genocide, in which an estimated 800,000 people were killed in approximately 12 weeks. However, there is a minimum consensus that at least 100,000-200,000 lives might have been saved, even with a relatively minimal intervention strategy. See Alan J. Kuperman, *Rwanda in Retrospect*, 79 For. Affairs 94 (Jan./Feb. 2000) and *Responses*, id. at 141–44 (May/June 2000) and 81 For. Affairs 206–08 (Nov./Dec. 2002); Alan J. Kuperman, *The Limits of Humanitarian Intervention: Genocide in Rwanda* (2001).

The issue of punishment for those guilty of genocide and other crimes in Rwanda is addressed in Chapter 11, pages 898-906.

B. *Unilateral or Regional Intervention*

Perhaps the most fundamental provision of the UN Charter is its prohibition not just against war (as in the League of Nations Covenant) but against the use of force. Article 2(4) of the Charter reads:

All Members shall refrain in their international relations from the threat or use of force against the territorial integrity or political independence of any state, or in any other manner inconsistent with the Purposes of the United Nations.

States are permitted to use force in self-defense under Article 51 of the Charter:

> Nothing in the present Charter shall impair the inherent right of individual or collective self-defense if an armed attack occurs against a Member of the United Nations, until the Security Council has taken measures necessary to maintain international peace and security. Measures taken by Members in the exercise of this right of self-defense shall be immediately reported to the Security Council and shall not in any way affect the authority and responsibility of the Security Council under the present Charter to take at any time such action as it deems necessary in order to maintain or restore international peace and security.

Article 52 confirms that collective self-defense and other regional arrangements (such as NATO and ECOWAS) are permissible, but regional bodies have no additional legal right to use force not possessed by their members individually. Article 53(1) of the Charter directs the Security Council "where appropriate, [to] utilize such regional arrangements or agencies for enforcement action under its authority. But no enforcement action shall be taken under regional arrangements or by regional agencies without the authorization of the Security Council. . . ." No other article specifically authorizes the unilateral or regional use of force for any other purpose.

As demonstrated by the reluctance of the Security Council to impose even economic sanctions on Sudan as a means of urging it to protect the population of Darfur, the overuse of force by the United Nations — or even the authorization of the use of force by others, which has become the more common manner of approving intervention — is unlikely to become a problem any time soon. While many developing countries, in particular, are uneasy with the prospect of a more interventionist Security Council, it would be difficult to question the Council's competence to adopt such an approach. After all, the first use of sanctions against Southern Rhodesia was to protect the human rights of the disenfranchised majority in that country (albeit in a colonial context that may be distinguished, in the minds of some, from the situation of human rights abuses in an independent state).

The greater fear on the part of many states is intervention without Security Council authorization, and it is this key issue that presents the starkest challenge for human rights advocates: if the United Nations does not act, under what circumstances may states, acting either alone or in concert with others, use military force for "humanitarian" or "human rights" purposes? The NATO bombing campaign in Kosovo in 1999 brought this dilemma to a head. While it is beyond the scope of this chapter to consider the Kosovo situation in the detail that it deserves, there is much for both sides of the intervention debate to take from the NATO campaign.

1. The Consequences of Intervention: Kosovo

Timothy Garton Ash has described the history of Kosovo as "a Serb-Albanian struggle for control . . . that goes back at least 120 years." Timothy Garton Ash, *Anarchy and Madness*, 27 N.Y. Rev. of Books (No. 2, Feb. 10, 2000), *http://www.nybooks.com/articles/220*. In a very small nutshell, Kosovo is a majority-Albanian territory that was part of the original Kingdom of the Serbs, Croats, and Slovenes (as Yugoslavia was first known), when it was founded in 1918. It is considered by many Serbs to be the cradle of Serb civilization and was the site of a famous battle in 1389 — still well-remembered by Serbs — in which the Serbs were defeated by Ottoman forces. There have been constant tensions between Serbs and Albanians within Kosovo, and the majority Albanian population consistently demanded a greater degree of political independence throughout the Yugoslav era.

The 1974 Yugoslav constitution established Kosovo as an autonomous province within Serbia, despite Kosovar desires to be a full republic separate from Serbia. In fact, the degree of autonomy exercised by Kosovo was functionally equivalent to that of a republic, but the distinct de jure status would play a role as Yugoslavia disintegrated in the late 1980s and early 1990s.

As part of his climb to power, Slobodan Milosevic (then leader of Serbia and now on trial before the International Criminal Tribunal for Yugoslavia in The Hague) effectively took over the leadership positions in Kosovo in 1989; in 1990, Serbia suspended Kosovo's autonomous status and instituted direct rule from Belgrade. This was met by massive, non-violent resistance from Albanians in Kosovo, who developed a parallel quasi-government that continued to operate separately from the formal Serb-led governmental authorities in Kosovo throughout the 1990–99 period.

While the Dayton Agreement ended the other wars of Yugoslav dissolution in Croatia and Bosnia and Herzegovina in 1995, it entirely ignored the issue of Kosovo. Kosovo remained largely untouched by the war in Bosnia, remaining under the repressive control of Belgrade. The following extract continues the narrative, leading eventually to the 1999 NATO bombing campaign against Serbia and creation of a de facto UN protectorate over Kosovo.

Independent International Commission on Kosovo, Kosovo Report

41–42, 43, 44, 50, 67, 71, 72, 74, 76–78, 82–83, 88, 97 (2000) (notes omitted)

The revocation of Kosovo's autonomy spawned an increase in human rights abuses and discriminatory government policies designed to Serbianize the province. These included discriminatory language policies: the closure of Albanian language newspapers, radio, and television; the closure of the Albanian Institute; and the change of street names from Albanian to Serbian. In particular, the introduction of a new Serbian curriculum for universities and schools:

> resulted in the closing down of the Educational Administration of Kosovo (. . .) and of other institutions and facilities in the field of education (. . .) [M]ore than 18,000 teachers and other staff of Albanian-language classroom facilities (. . .) were summarily dismissed when they rejected the textbooks of the uniform curricula.

Thousands of Albanians were dismissed from public employment; according to the independent Kosovar Albanian Association of Trades Unions, 115,000 people out of a total 170,000 lost their jobs. Attempts were also made to colonize the province. Special privileges were granted to Serbs who resettled or returned to Kosovo, including loans and free plots of land. Legislation was also passed which made it illegal for Kosovar Albanians to buy or lease property from Serbs, and refugees from Croatia were sent reluctantly to Kosovo. Above all, there were widespread human rights abuses — arbitrary arrest, torture, detention without trial. Albanians were accused of "verbal crimes" and taken to police stations for "informative talks." The scale of these abuses has been documented by Amnesty International, Human Rights Watch and the Council for the Defense of Human Rights in Kosovo. It is said that at least one member of every Albanian family had been called to a police station, or had spent some time in jail, or was waiting for a trial. . . .

In 1990 the various strands of Albanian political movements — former officials and former revolutionaries — came together to form a mass movement which was to operate a self-organized parallel system in Kosovo. On July 2, 1990, three days before the Kosovo Assembly was dissolved, 114 of the 123 Albanian delegates in the Kosovo Assembly met on the steps of the Assembly building, which had been locked. There were enough of them to constitute a quorum and they issued a declaration giving the Albanians the status of a nation entitled to their own republic. On September 7 they met again at Kacanik/Kacanik and agreed on the proclamation of a constitutional law for a "Republic of Kosovo," including provisions for a new assembly and elected presidency. After the Slovene and Croatian declarations of independence in June 1991, the demand for a republic was changed to a demand for independence. In September 1991, a self-organized referendum on independence took place. It is said that 87% of voters took part, including some minorities, and the vote was 99% in favor. And in May 1992 Kosovo-wide elections were held, using private homes as polling stations, for a new republican government and assembly. . . .

From the mid-1990s, the situation began to deteriorate. At the very moment when many ordinary Kosovar Albanians were losing patience with the strategy of passive resistance and were becoming exhausted from the struggle to sustain the parallel system under such difficult conditions, the Dayton Agreement over Bosnia was signed in which no mention was made of Kosovo. For many Kosovar Albanians, it seemed as though the strategy had failed. The conclusions to be drawn from Dayton, to quote Veton Surroi, were that "ethnic territories have legitimacy" and that "international attention can only be obtained by war." . . .

At the beginning of 1998, Kosovo was on the brink of open conflict. . . .

. . . Spring 1998 brought a widespread wave of small or non-coordinated attacks on Serbian police installations, as well as fighting between armed Serbian and Albanian villages in some areas. The KLA [Kosovo Liberation Army] claimed to have spread its control over the countryside with Serbian forces controlling the towns and the main roads. During this time several independent regional KLA groups competed for influence and often refused to share information or resources. Disunity among KLA factions remained a factor until the international armed intervention began. Simultaneously, FRY [Federal Republic of Yugoslavia] forces expanded their campaign of repression. Yugoslav army officials announced the killing of Kosovar Albanians trying to cross into Kosovo from

Albania. The conflict was now escalating province-wide, engulfing the border regions as well as the interior. . . .

Starting in April and continuing into the summer of 1999, increases in attacks on civilians were reported against all parties involved in the widening conflict. The Humanitarian Law Center (HLC) began registering an increased variety of abuses committed against Serbs, and in some cases Roma, including disappearances, abduction, and arbitrary detentions. In a number of cases, KLA activities were directly linked to abuses, causing Serb residents to flee their homes and villages. . . .

This increase in KLA abuses, while notable, was far outstripped by the rise in abuses perpetrated by FRY security and paramilitary forces. . . .

While precise details were not available, as of the beginning of August, reports estimated that between 200,000 and 300,000 Kosovar Albanians had been displaced from their homes as a result of sustained Yugoslav attacks, which included shelling of cities and villages. These figures include internal displacement as well as large numbers fleeing into refuge in Montenegro, Albania, and Macedonia. Property damage resulting from these attacks was also extensive.

During this period, European diplomats referred to the destruction as an excessive use of military force. Responding to this summer long escalation, the president of the UN Security Council issued a statement at the end of August calling for an immediate ceasefire.

UNHCR displacement figures for August 1998 state that there were 260,000 internally displaced people (IDP), and 200,000 refugees outside of Kosovo. Whether all of the refugees and internally displaced people left their homes to avoid combat, or as a result of a campaign of expulsion remains a debated topic. . . .

On October 13, 1998, however, NATO authorities voted to authorize air strikes if security forces were not withdrawn from Kosovo within 96 hours. After a period of intense negotiations, US Special Envoy Richard Holbrooke, representing the Contact Group [an ad hoc group consisting of the United States, United Kingdom, France, Italy, Germany, and Russia], and Serbian President Slobodan Milosevic reached an agreement, based on the demands in [UN Security Council] Resolution 1199, and obviously under the threat of the NATO activation order. While the agreement was never published, its major points addressed the reduction in forces and deployment of monitors. This agreement was submitted to the UN Security Council for approval. Milosevic agreed with negotiators to pull back security forces, allow access to aid groups, and accept the OSCE Kosovo Verification Mission (OSCE-KVM), a team of 2000 civilian observers who would monitor the enforcement of the agreement. . . .

The violence against the civilian population in Kosovo throughout 1998 was accompanied by a series of other systematic and institutional violations of civil rights by Serbian and FRY authorities, further establishing a hostile environment for the civilian population. The two most notable violations were political trials that lacked due process, and efforts to suppress any free and independent media. . . .

Serbia initially implemented the agreement and withdrew its forces accordingly. The KLA, by contrast, took advantage of the new situation and renewed military action. In fact, KLA forces moved in to take up positions vacated by the redeployed Serbian forces. . . .

[The conflict continued between October 1998 and December 1999, although on a smaller scale, despite the presence of the OSCE monitors. In January 1999, the killing by Serb forces of 45 people at the village of Racek, verified by the OSCE mission, proved to be the spark that led to NATO intervention two months later. Attempts to impose or negotiate a solution by the Contact Group at talks held in Rambouillet, France, failed. On March 19, 1999, OSCE announced that it was withdrawing the KVM; five days later, NATO's bombing began.]

It is important to note that for the entire period of internal war, between February 1998 and March 1999, preceding the bombing campaign, the Commission has had considerable difficulty pinpointing statistics on the levels of lethal violence committed against civilians in Kosovo. A precise quantification of abuses, particularly killings, was difficult if not impossible to determine because detailed, verified data was not readily available. Major human rights groups have consistently expressed the need for greater rigor in the collection and presentation of Kosovo data. As mentioned earlier, the UNHCR reported that 300 people were killed between February and May 1998, and the Council for Defense of Human Rights and Freedoms asserts that 750 people were killed between May and August 1998. But neither set of numbers indicates how many of the victims were KLA members and how many were civilians. The Commission has been unable to identify any dependable figure on killings between September 1998 and March 1999, despite the substantial OSCE monitoring presence during most of these months. Therefore the Commission cannot make a reliable estimate of the number of deaths in this period. However, apart from the shocking exception of the Recak/Racak massacre, it is reasonable to assume that the number of civilian killings was significantly lower during the presence of KVM monitors than during the earlier months. . . .

The war quickly took a direction that surprised and shocked the world. The FRY military and paramilitary forces launched a vicious campaign against the Kosovar Albanian population. The FRY government maintained throughout the conflict that it was only conducting military activities against the KLA, and blamed all human rights violations, especially the forced displacement of Kosovar Albanians, on NATO and the KLA. However, virtually every other international, governmental and non-governmental organization that has studied the facts has reached the opposite conclusion. There is widespread agreement that FRY forces were engaged in a well-planned campaign of terror and expulsion of the Kosovar Albanians. This campaign is most frequently described as one of "ethnic cleansing," intended to drive many, if not all, Kosovar Albanians from Kosovo, destroy the foundations of their society, and prevent them from returning.

There are two important questions here that have been much discussed. The first is whether there was a FRY military plan ("Operation Horseshoe") to expel the Albanian population. There has been an intensive debate on whether such a plan did exist, and if so, what relevance it had. The issue is still open, but it is very clear that there was a deliberate organized effort to expel a huge part of the Kosovar Albanian population and such a massive operation cannot be implemented without planning and preparation. The second related issue is the allegation that the NATO bombing campaign in fact provoked this FRY campaign, and that NATO consequently created a humanitarian disaster instead of stopping it.

The latter allegation is difficult to assess. We cannot know what would have happened if NATO had not started the bombing. It is however certainly not true that NATO provoked the attacks on the civilian Kosovar population — the responsibility for that campaign rests entirely on the Belgrade government. It is nonetheless likely that the bombing campaign and the removal of the unarmed monitors created an internal environment that made such an operation feasible. . . .

[After 12 weeks of NATO bombing, the Serbian Parliament agreed to a peace plan on June 3; the NATO bombardment was halted a week later. On June 10, the UN Security Council adopted Resolution 1244, which created a UN Mission in Kosovo that has been the de facto government in Kosovo since that time.]

Was NATO's campaign a success or a failure? That question cannot be answered easily, since it was, in fact, both. It forced the FRY government to withdraw its army and police from Kosovo and to sign an agreement closely modeled on the aborted Rambouillet accord. It stopped the systematic oppression of the Kosovar Albanians. NATO had demonstrated its military clout as well as the ability to maintain its political cohesion in the face of a challenge that could have torn the Alliance apart.

But, the intervention failed to achieve its avowed aim of preventing massive ethnic cleansing. More than a million Kosovar Albanians became refugees, around 10,000 lost their lives; many were wounded, raped or assaulted in other ways. There was widespread destruction. The Kosovar Albanian population had to endure tremendous suffering before finally achieving their freedom. Milosevic remained in power, however, as an indicted war criminal. . . .

The Commission concluded that NATO's military intervention was "illegal, but legitimate," indicating moral approval but confirming that NATO's use of force was illegal under international law. Id. at 186. Although generally sympathetic to NATO's actions, the Commission noted that "[t]he rationale for military intervention by NATO thus rested not on the immediate scale of humanitarian catastrophe in early 1999, but rather on a weaving together of past experiences and future concerns." Id. at 159.

Despite its difficulty in quantifying deaths or other human rights abuses, the Commission observed that abuses in Kosovo "were comparable with those of numerous other recent counter-insurgency wars, for example Colombia or Turkey." Id. at 136. From January 1998 to April 1999, Human Rights Watch identified 320 persons killed by the FRY and 98 killed by the KLA, although it called its list "far from exhaustive." Human Rights Watch, *Kosovo War Crimes Chronology*, available at *http://www.hrw.org/hrw/campaigns/kosovo98/timeline.htm*. A report by the OSCE monitoring mission referred to the massacre of 45 people at Recak as "indicative of what was to follow" after the bombing began, but it stated that "[t]he more frequent occurrence in the period of the OSCE-KVM's presence in Kosovo [October 1998-March 1999] was, however, killings on an individual basis." OSCE, Kosovo/Kosova, *As Seen, As Told* (Dec. 1999), p. 69, available at *http://www.osce.org/documents/mik/1999/11/1620_en.pdf*.

How important are the number of deaths? During the course of the war, the U.S. Secretary of Defense, William Cohen, stated that 100,000 Kosovo men of military age were missing and "may have been murdered." David Scheffer, the

U.S. State Department official responsible for war crimes, said that over 225,000 men and boys between 14 and 59 were unaccounted for. See Jonathan Steele, *Motivated to Believe the Worst*, Manchester Guardian (Aug. 18, 2000).

Estimates for total deaths during the NATO campaign, most of them Albanians killed by Serbs, range from 5,000-10,000. See, e.g., Steven Erlanger and Christopher S. Wren, *Early Count Hints at Fewer Kosovo Deaths*, Wash. Post (Nov. 11, 1999), at A6. However, NATO was widely criticized for its high-altitude bombing tactics — there was not a single NATO casualty during the 78-day campaign — and Human Rights Watch estimated that approximately 500 civilians were killed by NATO air strikes. Human Rights Watch, Civilian Deaths in the NATO Air Campaign (Feb. 2000).

One year after the end of the NATO campaign, the UN's special rapporteur on the former Yugoslavia stated that "[d]ozens and perhaps hundreds of individuals have been killed since June 1999 on account of their ethnicity" — this time, almost all the victims were Serbs or other minorities. Report of the Special Rapporteur of the Commission on Human Rights [Jiri Dienstbier] on the Situation of human rights in Bosnia and Herzegovina, the Republic of Croatia and the Federal Republic of Yugoslavia, UN Doc. A/55/282 (Oct. 20, 2000), para. 101. UNHCR reported that approximately 500 persons were killed from June 1999 to June 2000. Id., para. 104. In March 2000, Dienstbier, a former Czech Foreign Minister, stated at the Commission on Human Rights that most of Kosovo was "ethnically-cleansed of non-Albanians, divided, without any legal system, ruled by illegal structures of the Kosovo Liberation Army and very often by competing mafias." *West should hit KLA extremists in Kosovo — UN sleuth*, Reuters (Mar. 29, 2000).

In fall 2000, Slobodan Milosevic fell from power in Serbia; he was sent to the International Criminal Tribunal for Yugoslavia in The Hague, where his trial began in July 2001 for alleged crimes committed in Kosovo, Bosnia and Herzegovina, and Croatia (Case No. IT-02-54). In February 2005, he was joined in The Hague by Kosovo Prime Minister and former KLA commander Ramush Haradinaj, who was charged with 17 counts of crimes against humanity and 20 counts of war crimes during the period March-September 1998 (Case No. IT-04-84-I).

A few weeks after the bombing commenced, the Federal Republic of Yugoslavia brought a case to the International Court of Justice against those members of NATO that were subject to the Court's jurisdiction, alleging that the bombing violated the international prohibition against the use of force. Perhaps unfortunately, the Court dismissed the case on jurisdictional grounds without reaching the merits, holding that Yugoslavia was not a member of the United Nations at the time the application was filed and therefore was not a party to the Statute of the Court. Case concerning the Legality of the Use of Force (Serbia and Montenegro v. Belgium) (Preliminary Objections), Judgment of Dec. 15, 2004. While the judgment was unanimous, it also was highly controversial; seven members of the court filed a separate opinion specifically rejecting the grounds on which the majority of the court relied.

Note: The Second Gulf War

The primary reasons advanced by the Bush administration for the invasion of Iraq in March 2003 was Iraq's failure to abide by UN resolutions and the purported threat to the United States from Iraq's (ultimately non-existent) weapons of mass destruction. There have also been numerous occasions when Iraq has been linked by administration spokespersons to the larger "war on terrorism" or even to the attacks on September 11, 2001.

At the same time, the invasion of Iraq could be seen to have elements of "humanitarian" intervention, as well, and there is no doubt that the regime of Saddam Hussein committed gross violations of human rights throughout its reign, as stated frequently by the Bush administration. Indeed, many have argued that the Iraqi government committed genocide against the Kurds in 1988, in retaliation for the fact that many Kurds sided with Iran in the 1980-88 Iran-Iraq war. See Human Rights Watch, *Genocide in Iraq: The Anfal Campaign Against the Kurds* (1993). As President Bush stated in a speech to the American Enterprise Institute approximately a month before the invasion of Iraq in March 2003:

> The first to benefit from a free Iraq would be the Iraqi people, themselves. Today they live in scarcity and fear, under a dictator who has brought them nothing but war, and misery, and torture. Their lives and their freedom matter little to Saddam Hussein — but Iraqi lives and freedom matter greatly to us.
>
> Bringing stability and unity to a free Iraq will not be easy. Yet that is no excuse to leave the Iraqi regime's torture chambers and poison labs in operation. Any future the Iraqi people choose for themselves will be better than the nightmare world that Saddam Hussein has chosen for them. . . .
>
> The United States has no intention of determining the precise form of Iraq's new government. That choice belongs to the Iraqi people. Yet, we will ensure that one brutal dictator is not replaced by another. All Iraqis must have a voice in the new government, and all citizens must have their rights protected. . . .
>
> The world has a clear interest in the spread of democratic values, because stable and free nations do not breed the ideologies of murder. They encourage the peaceful pursuit of a better life. . . . A new regime in Iraq would serve as a dramatic and inspiring example of freedom for other nations in the region. . . .

Office of the White House Press Secretary, *President Discusses the Future of Iraq* (Feb. 26, 2003), *http://www.whitehouse.gov/news/releases/2003/02/20030226-11.html*.

Could persuasive arguments be made for the invasion of Iraq on purely humanitarian or human rights grounds? Is the 48-nation "coalition of the willing" that supported the U.S. invasion of Iraq (which initially included, inter alia, Australia, Denmark, Hungary, Iceland, Italy, Japan, Netherlands, Poland, Portugal, Spain, Turkey, and the United Kingdom) any less respectable than the NATO coalition that attacked Kosovo? Which dictator was responsible for more death and destruction, Slobodan Milosevic or Saddam Hussein? Is that the only relevant question, or do the motives of the intervenors also count?

C. *Proposed Criteria for Armed Intervention*

Even if one believes that customary international law permits humanitarian intervention, it would be difficult to argue that there is consensus around the criteria for when such intervention would be both justified and legal.

In December 2000, the government of Canada established an International Commission on Intervention and State Sovereignty, consisting of 12 prominent individuals and co-chaired by Gareth Evans, former foreign minister of Australia and president of the International Crisis Group, and Mohammed Sahoun, a senior Algerian diplomat and special advisor or representative of the UN Secretary-General at various times for Somalia, the Great Lakes region, and the Eritrea-Ethiopia conflict. The report was originally intended to provide a basis for serious discussion and the possible adoption of a UN resolution on the topic of intervention, but the events of "9/11" and the subsequent wars in Afghanistan and Iraq overtook Canada's intentions. It remains one of the more thoughtful contemporary approaches to the issue of humanitarian intervention, although it has not been formally endorsed or accepted by the world community.

The Responsibility to Protect

Report of the International Commission on Intervention and State Sovereignty (2001)

1. The Policy Challenge

THE INTERVENTION DILEMMA

1.1 "Humanitarian intervention" has been controversial both when it happens, and when it has failed to happen. Rwanda in 1994 laid bare the full horror of inaction. The United Nations (UN) Secretariat and some permanent members of the Security Council knew that officials connected to the then government were planning genocide; UN forces were present, though not in sufficient number at the outset; and credible strategies were available to prevent, or at least greatly mitigate, the slaughter which followed. But the Security Council refused to take the necessary action. That was a failure of international will — of civic courage — at the highest level. Its consequence was not merely a humanitarian catastrophe for Rwanda: the genocide destabilized the entire Great Lakes region and continues to do so. In the aftermath, many African peoples concluded that, for all the rhetoric about the universality of human rights, some human lives end up mattering a great deal less to the international community than others.

1.2 Kosovo — where intervention did take place in 1999 — concentrated attention on all the other sides of the argument. The operation raised major questions about the legitimacy of military intervention in a sovereign state. Was the cause just: were the human rights abuses committed or threatened by the Belgrade authorities sufficiently serious to warrant outside involvement? Did those seeking secession manipulate external intervention to advance their political purposes? Were all peaceful means of resolving the conflict fully explored? Did the intervention receive appropriate authority? How could the bypassing and marginalization of the UN system, by "a coalition of the willing" acting without Security Council approval, possibly be justified? Did the way in which the intervention was carried out in fact worsen the very human rights situation it was trying to rectify? Or — against all this — was it the case that had the North Atlantic Treaty Organization (NATO) not intervened, Kosovo would have been at best the site of an ongoing, bloody and destabilizing civil war, and at worst the occasion for genocidal slaughter like that which occurred in Bosnia four years earlier? . . .

1.5 The basic lines in the contemporary policy debate, one constantly being re-engaged at UN headquarters in New York and in capitals around the world, have been clearly enough drawn. For some, the international community is not intervening enough; for others it is intervening much too often. For some, the only real issue is in ensuring that coercive interventions are effective; for others, questions about legality, process and the possible misuse of precedent loom much larger. For some, the new interventions herald a new world in which human rights trumps state sovereignty; for others, it ushers in a world in which big powers ride roughshod over the smaller ones, manipulating the rhetoric of humanitarianism and human rights. The controversy has laid bare basic divisions within the international community. In the interest of all those victims who suffer and die when leadership and institutions fail, it is crucial that these divisions be resolved. . . .

THE CHANGING INTERNATIONAL ENVIRONMENT

1.10 The issues and preoccupations of the 21st century present new and often fundamentally different types of challenges from those that faced the world in 1945, when the United Nations was founded. As new realities and challenges have emerged, so too have new expectations for action and new standards of conduct in national and international affairs. Since, for example, the terrorist attacks of 11 September 2001 on the World Trade Center and Pentagon, it has become evident that the war against terrorism the world must now fight — one with no contested frontiers and a largely invisible enemy — is one like no other war before it. . . .

1.12 The current debate on intervention for human protection purposes is itself both a product and a reflection of how much has changed since the UN was established. The current debate takes place in the context of a broadly expanded range of state, non-state, and institutional actors, and increasingly evident interaction and interdependence among them. It is a debate that reflects new sets of issues and new types of concerns. It is a debate that is being conducted within the framework of new standards of conduct for states and individuals, and in a context of greatly increased expectations for action. And it is a debate that takes place within an institutional framework that since the end of the Cold War has held out the prospect of effective joint international action to address issues of peace, security, human rights and sustainable development on a global scale. . . .

1.19 An unhappy trend of contemporary conflict has been the increased vulnerability of civilians, often involving their deliberate targeting. Sometimes the permanent displacement of civilian populations has been a primary objective of the conflict; there has also been increasing concern about the deliberate use of systematic rape to provoke exclusion from a group. Efforts to suppress armed (and sometimes unarmed) dissent have in too many cases led to excessive and disproportionate actions by governments, producing in some cases excessive and unwarranted suffering on the part of civilian populations. In a few cases, regimes have launched campaigns of terror on their own populations, sometimes in the name of an ideology; sometimes spurred on by racial, religious or ethnic hatred; and sometimes purely for personal gain or plunder. In other cases they have supported or abetted terror campaigns aimed at other countries which have resulted in major destruction and loss of life.

1.20 Intra-state warfare is often viewed, in the prosperous West, simply as a set of discrete and unrelated crises occurring in distant and unimportant regions. In reality, what is happening is a convulsive process of state fragmentation and state formation that is transforming the international order itself. Moreover, the rich world is deeply implicated in the process. Civil conflicts are fuelled by arms and monetary transfers that originate in the developed world, and their destabilizing effects are felt in the developed world in everything from globally interconnected terrorism to refugee flows, the export of drugs, the spread of infectious disease and organized crime.

1.21 These considerations reinforce the Commission's view that human security is indeed indivisible. There is no longer such a thing as a humanitarian catastrophe occurring "in a faraway country of which we know little." On 11 September 2001 global terrorism, with its roots in complex conflicts in distant lands, struck the US homeland: impregnable lines of continental defence proved an illusion even for the world's most powerful state. At the same time, around 40 per cent of the victims of the World Trade Center attacks were non-Americans, from some 80 countries. In an interdependent world, in which security depends on a framework of stable sovereign entities, the existence of fragile states, failing states, states who through weakness or ill-will harbour those dangerous to others, or states that can only maintain internal order by means of gross human rights violations, can constitute a risk to people everywhere. . . .

1.23 Building a stable order after intervention for human protection purposes remains an equally great challenge. Finding a consensus about intervention is not simply a matter of deciding who should authorize it and when it is legitimate to undertake. It is also a matter of figuring out how to do it so that decent objectives are not tarnished by inappropriate means. As is widely recognized, UN peace-keeping strategies, crafted for an era of war between states and designed to monitor and reinforce ceasefires agreed between belligerents, may no longer be suitable to protect civilians caught in the middle of bloody struggles between states and insurgents. The challenge in this context is to find tactics and strategies of military intervention that fill the current gulf between outdated concepts of peacekeeping and full-scale military operations that may have deleterious impacts on civilians. . . .

1.35 The defence of state sovereignty, by even its strongest supporters, does not include any claim of the unlimited power of a state to do what it wants to its own people. The Commission heard no such claim at any stage during our worldwide consultations. It is acknowledged that sovereignty implies a dual responsibility: externally — to respect the sovereignty of other states, and internally, to respect the dignity and basic rights of all the people within the state. In international human rights covenants, in UN practice, and in state practice itself, sovereignty is now understood as embracing this dual responsibility. Sovereignty as responsibility has become the minimum content of good international citizenship.

1.36 This modern understanding of the meaning of sovereignty is of central importance in the Commission's approach to the question of intervention for human protection purposes, and in particular in the development of our core theme, "the responsibility to protect," which is introduced and explained in the next chapter. . . .

2.3 Any new approach to intervention on human protection grounds needs to meet at least four basic objectives:

- to establish clearer rules, procedures and criteria for determining whether, when and how to intervene;
- to establish the legitimacy of military intervention when necessary and after all other approaches have failed;
- to ensure that military intervention, when it occurs, is carried out only for the purposes proposed, is effective, and is undertaken with proper concern to minimize the human costs and institutional damage that will result; and
- to help eliminate, where possible, the causes of conflict while enhancing the prospects for durable and sustainable peace. . . .

THE NORM OF NON-INTERVENTION

2.7 Sovereignty has come to signify, in the Westphalian concept, the legal identity of a state in international law. It is a concept which provides order, stability and predictability in international relations since sovereign states are regarded as equal, regardless of comparative size or wealth. The principle of sovereign equality of states is enshrined in Article 2.1 of the UN Charter. Internally, sovereignty signifies the capacity to make authoritative decisions with regard to the people and resources within the territory of the state. Generally, however, the authority of the state is not regarded as absolute, but constrained and regulated internally by constitutional power sharing arrangements.

2.8 A condition of any one state's sovereignty is a corresponding obligation to respect every other state's sovereignty: the norm of non-intervention is enshrined in Article 2.7 of the UN Charter. A sovereign state is empowered in international law to exercise exclusive and total jurisdiction within its territorial borders. Other states have the corresponding duty not to intervene in the internal affairs of a sovereign state. If that duty is violated, the victim state has the further right to defend its territorial integrity and political independence. In the era of decolonization, the sovereign equality of states and the correlative norm of non-intervention received its most emphatic affirmation from the newly independent states. . . .

SOVEREIGNTY AS RESPONSIBILITY

2.15 Thinking of sovereignty as responsibility, in a way that is being increasingly recognized in state practice, has a threefold significance. First, it implies that the state authorities are responsible for the functions of protecting the safety and lives of citizens and promotion of their welfare. Secondly, it suggests that the national political authorities are responsible to the citizens internally and to the international community through the UN. And thirdly, it means that the agents of state are responsible for their actions; that is to say, they are accountable for their acts of commission and omission. The case for thinking of sovereignty in these terms is strengthened by the ever-increasing impact of international human rights norms, and the increasing impact in international discourse of the concept of human security. . . .

EMERGING PRACTICE

2.24 The debate on military intervention for human protection purposes was ignited in the international community essentially because of the critical gap between, on the one hand, the needs and distress being felt, and seen to be felt, in the real world, and on the other hand the codified instruments and modalities for managing world order. There has been a parallel gap, no less critical, between the codified best practice of international behaviour as articulated in the UN Charter and actual state practice as it has evolved in the 56 years since the Charter was signed. While there is not yet a sufficiently strong basis to claim the emergence of a new principle of customary international law, growing state and regional organization practice as well as Security Council precedent suggest an emerging guiding principle — which in the Commission's view could properly be termed "the responsibility to protect."

2.25 The emerging principle in question is that intervention for human protection purposes, including military intervention in extreme cases, is supportable when major harm to civilians is occurring or imminently apprehended, and the state in question is unable or unwilling to end the harm, or is itself the perpetrator. The Security Council itself has been increasingly prepared in recent years to act on this basis, most obviously in Somalia, defining what was essentially an internal situation as constituting a threat to international peace and security such as to justify enforcement action under Chapter VII of the UN Charter. This is also the basis on which the interventions by the Economic Community of West African States (ECOWAS) in Liberia and Sierra Leone were essentially justified by the interveners, as was the intervention mounted without Security Council authorization by NATO allies in Kosovo.

2.26 The notion that there is an emerging guiding principle in favour of military intervention for human protection purposes is also supported by a wide variety of legal sources — including sources that exist independently of any duties, responsibilities or authority that may be derived from Chapter VII of the UN Charter. These legal foundations include fundamental natural law principles; the human rights provisions of the UN Charter; the Universal Declaration of Human Rights together with the Genocide Convention; the Geneva Conventions and Additional Protocols on international humanitarian law; the statute of the International Criminal Court; and a number of other international human rights and human protection agreements and covenants. Some of the ramifications and consequences of these developments will be addressed again in Chapter 6 of this report as part of the examination of the question of authority.

2.27 Based on our reading of state practice, Security Council precedent, established norms, emerging guiding principles, and evolving customary international law, the Commission believes that the Charter's strong bias against military intervention is not to be regarded as absolute when decisive action is required on human protection grounds. The degree of legitimacy accorded to intervention will usually turn on the answers to such questions as the purpose, the means, the exhaustion of other avenues of redress against grievances, the proportionality of the riposte to the initiating provocation, and the agency of authorization. These are all questions that will recur: for present purposes the point is simply that there is a large and accumulating body of law and practice which supports the notion that, whatever form the exercise of that responsibility may properly take, members of the broad community of states do have a responsibility to protect both their own citizens and those of other states as well. . . .

SHIFTING THE TERMS OF THE DEBATE

2.29 The Commission is of the view that the debate about intervention for human protection purposes should focus not on "the right to intervene" but on "the responsibility to protect." The proposed change in terminology is also a change in perspective, reversing the perceptions inherent in the traditional language, and adding some additional ones:

- First, the responsibility to protect implies an evaluation of the issues from the point of view of those seeking or needing support, rather than those who may be considering intervention. Our preferred terminology refocuses the international searchlight back where it should always be: on the duty to protect communities from mass killing, women from systematic rape and children from starvation.
- Secondly, the responsibility to protect acknowledges that the primary responsibility in this regard rests with the state concerned, and that it is only if the state is unable or unwilling to fulfill this responsibility, or is itself the perpetrator, that it becomes the responsibility of the international community to act in its place. In many cases, the state will seek to acquit its responsibility in full and active partnership with representatives of the international community. Thus the "responsibility to protect" is more of a linking concept that bridges the divide between intervention and sovereignty; the language of the "right or duty to intervene" is intrinsically more confrontational.
- Thirdly, the responsibility to protect means not just the "responsibility to react," but the "responsibility to prevent" and the "responsibility to rebuild" as well. It directs our attention to the costs and results of action versus no action, and provides conceptual, normative and operational linkages between assistance, intervention and reconstruction. . . .

3. The Responsibility to Prevent

A COMMITMENT TO PREVENTION

3.1 This Commission strongly believes that the responsibility to protect implies an accompanying responsibility to prevent. And we think that it is more than high time for the international community to be doing more to close the gap between rhetorical support for prevention and tangible commitment. The need to do much better on prevention, and to exhaust prevention options before rushing to embrace intervention, were constantly recurring themes in our worldwide consultations, and ones which we wholeheartedly endorse. . . .

THE DECISION TO INTERVENE

Extreme Cases Only

4.10 In extreme and exceptional cases, the responsibility to react may involve the need to resort to military action. But what is an extreme case? Where should we draw the line in determining when military intervention is, prima facie, defensible?

4.11 The starting point, here as elsewhere, should be the principle of non-intervention. This is the norm from which any departure has to be justified. All members of the United Nations have an interest in maintaining an order of sovereign, self-reliant, responsible, yet interdependent states. In most situations, this interest is best served if all states, large and small, abstain from intervening or interfering in the domestic affairs of other states. Most internal political or civil disagreements, even conflicts, within states do not require coercive intervention by external powers. The non-interference rule not only protects states and governments: it also protects peoples and cultures, enabling societies to maintain the religious, ethnic, and civilizational differences that they cherish. . . .

5. The Responsibility to Rebuild

POST-INTERVENTION OBLIGATIONS

Peace Building

5.1 The responsibility to protect implies the responsibility not just to prevent and react, but to follow through and rebuild. This means that if military intervention action is taken — because of a breakdown or abdication of a state's own capacity and authority in discharging its "responsibility to protect" — there should be a genuine commitment to helping to build a durable peace, and promoting good governance and sustainable development. Conditions of public safety and order have to be reconstituted by international agents acting in partnership with local authorities, with the goal of progressively transferring to them authority and responsibility to rebuild. . . .

6. The Question of Authority

6.1 There is an international responsibility to protect populations at risk, and this Commission has argued that it extends to a responsibility to react by appropriate means if catastrophe is occurring, or seems imminent. In extreme cases, that responsibility to react includes military intervention within a state, to carry out that human protection. We have spelled out in Chapter 4 the tough threshold and precautionary criteria that must be satisfied in these cases: just cause, right intention, last resort, proportional means and reasonable prospects. The criteria have to be tough, because the action proposed is itself extreme: military intervention means not only an intrusion into a sovereign state, but an intrusion involving the use of deadly force, on a potentially massive scale. But whose right is it to determine, in any particular case, whether a military intervention for human protection purposes should go ahead? . . .

6.13 Because the prohibitions and presumptions against intervention are so explicitly spelled out in the Charter, and since no "humanitarian exception" to these prohibitions is explicitly provided for, the role of the Security Council becomes of paramount importance. There are a number of questions that can reasonably be asked about its authority and credibility, and we address them below: its legal capacity to authorize military intervention operations; its political will to do so, and generally uneven performance; its unrepresentative membership; and its inherent institutional double standards with the Permanent Five veto power. There are many reasons for being dissatisfied with the role that the Security Council has played so far.

6.14 But all that said, the Commission is in absolutely no doubt that there is no better or more appropriate body than the Security Council to deal with military intervention issues for human protection purposes. It is the Security Council which should be making the hard decisions in the hard cases about overriding state sovereignty. And it is the Security Council which should be making the often even harder decisions to mobilize effective resources, including military resources, to rescue populations at risk when there is no serious opposition on sovereignty grounds. That was the overwhelming consensus we found in all our consultations around the world. If international consensus is ever to be reached about when, where, how and by whom military intervention should happen, it is very clear that the central role of the Security Council will have to be at the heart of that consensus. The task is not to find alternatives to the Security Council as a source of authority, but to make the Security Council work much better than it has. . . .

THE IMPLICATIONS OF INACTION

6.36 Interventions by ad hoc coalitions (or, even more, individual states) acting without the approval of the Security Council, or the General Assembly, or a regional or sub-regional grouping of which the target state is a member, do not — it would be an understatement to say — find wide favour. Even those countries involved in the Kosovo intervention, and prepared to passionately defend its legitimacy by reference to all the threshold and precautionary criteria we have identified in this report, for the most part acknowledge its highly exceptional character, and express the view that it would have been much preferable to have secured the Security Council's — or failing that the General Assembly's — endorsement. One view that has some currency is that an ex post facto authorization, of the kind that has occurred for the African regional instances mentioned above, might conceivably have been obtained in the Kosovo and Rwanda cases, and may offer a way out of the dilemma should any such case occur again in the future.

6.37 As a matter of political reality, it would be impossible to find consensus, in the Commission's view, around any set of proposals for military intervention which acknowledged the validity of any intervention not authorized by the Security Council or General Assembly. But that may still leave circumstances when the Security Council fails to discharge what this Commission would regard as its responsibility to protect, in a conscience-shocking situation crying out for action. It is a real question in these circumstances where lies the most harm: in the damage to international order if the Security Council is bypassed or in the damage to that order if human beings are slaughtered while the Security Council stands by.

6.38 In the view of the Commission, there are two important messages for the Security Council in all of this.

6.39 The first message is that if the Security Council fails to discharge its responsibility in conscience-shocking situations crying out for action, then it is unrealistic to expect that concerned states will rule out other means and forms of action to meet the gravity and urgency of these situations. If collective organizations will not authorize collective intervention against regimes that flout the most elementary norms of legitimate governmental behaviour, then the pressures for intervention by ad hoc coalitions or individual states will surely intensify. And there is a risk then that such interventions, without the discipline and constraints of UN authorization, will not be conducted for the right reasons or with the right commitment to the necessary precautionary principles.

6.40 The second message is that if, following the failure of the Council to act, a military intervention is undertaken by an ad hoc coalition or individual state which does fully observe and respect all the criteria we have identified, and if that intervention is carried through successfully — and is seen by world public opinion to have been carried through successfully — then this may have enduringly serious consequences for the stature and credibility of the UN itself. . . .

[The Synopsis included in the Commission's report summarizes the Commission's Principles for Military Intervention as follows:]

(1) The Just Cause Threshold

Military intervention for human protection purposes is an exceptional and extraordinary measure. To be warranted, there must be serious and irreparable harm occurring to human beings, or imminently likely to occur, of the following kind:

A. **large scale loss of life**, actual or apprehended, with genocidal intent or not, which is the product either of deliberate state action, or state neglect or inability to act, or a failed state situation; or

B. **large scale 'ethnic cleansing'**, actual or apprehended, whether carried out by killing, forced expulsion, acts of terror or rape.

(2) The Precautionary Principles

A. **Right intention**: The primary purpose of the intervention, whatever other motives intervening states may have, must be to halt or avert human suffering. Right intention is better assured with multilateral operations, clearly supported by regional opinion and the victims concerned.

B. **Last resort**: Military intervention can only be justified when every non-military option for the prevention or peaceful resolution of the crisis has been explored, with reasonable grounds for believing lesser measures would not have succeeded.

C. **Proportional means**: The scale, duration and intensity of the planned military intervention should be the minimum necessary to secure the defined human protection objective.

D. **Reasonable prospects**: There must be a reasonable chance of success in halting or averting the suffering which has justified the intervention, with the consequences of action not likely to be worse than the consequences of inaction.

(3) Right Authority

A. There is no better or more appropriate body than the United Nations Security Council to authorize military intervention for human protection purposes. The task is not to find alternatives to the Security Council as a source of authority, but to make the Security Council work better than it has.

B. Security Council authorization should in all cases be sought prior to any military intervention action being carried out. Those calling for an intervention should formally request such authorization, or have the Council raise the matter on its own initiative, or have the Secretary-General raise it under Article 99 of the UN Charter.
C. The Security Council should deal promptly with any request for authority to intervene where there are allegations of large scale loss of human life or ethnic cleansing. It should in this context seek adequate verification of facts or conditions on the ground that might support a military intervention.
D. The Permanent Five members of the Security Council should agree not to apply their veto power, in matters where their vital state interests are not involved, to obstruct the passage of resolutions authorizing military intervention for human protection purposes for which there is otherwise majority support.
E. If the Security Council rejects a proposal or fails to deal with it in a reasonable time, alternative options are:
  I. consideration of the matter by the General Assembly in Emergency Special Session under the "Uniting for Peace" procedure; and
  II. action within area of jurisdiction by regional or sub-regional organizations under Chapter VIII of the Charter, subject to their seeking subsequent authorization from the Security Council.
A The Security Council should take into account in all its deliberations that, if it fails to discharge its responsibility to protect in conscience-shocking situations crying out for action, concerned states may not rule out other means to meet the gravity and urgency of that situation — and that the stature and credibility of the United Nations may suffer thereby.

(4) Operational Principles

A. Clear objectives; clear and unambiguous mandate at all times; and resources to match.
B. Common military approach among involved partners; unity of command; clear and unequivocal communications and chain of command.
C. Acceptance of limitations, incrementalism and gradualism in the application of force, the objective being protection of a population, not defeat of a state.
D. Rules of engagement which fit the operational concept; are precise; reflect the principle of proportionality; and involve total adherence to international humanitarian law.
E. Acceptance that force protection cannot become the principal objective.
F. Maximum possible coordination with humanitarian organizations.

The theme of the "responsibility to protect" was taken up in two subsequent UN documents, although neither went so far as to suggest that there might be any unilateral or multilateral right of military intervention without Security Council approval. Both documents were written to prepare the way for significant reform of the United Nations during 2005-2006, although it remains to be seen whether there will be any progress in recognizing or defining the concept of humanitarian intervention. The first document charitably understates the problem:

> The Charter of the United Nations is not as clear as it could be when it comes to saving lives within countries in situations of mass atrocity. It "reaffirm(s) faith in fundamental human rights" but does not do much to protect them, and Article 2.7 prohibits intervention "in matters which are essentially within the jurisdiction of any State." There has been, as a result, a long-standing argument in the international community between those who insist on a "right to intervene" in man-made catastrophes and those who argue that the Security Council, for all its powers under Chapter VII to "maintain or restore international security," is prohibited from authorizing any coercive action against sovereign States for whatever happens within their borders. . . .

A More Secure World: Our Shared Responsibility, Report of the Secretary-General's High-level Panel on Threats, Challenges and Change (2004), originally issued as UN Doc. A/59/565 (2004), para. 199. The report goes on to endorse "the emerging norm that there is a collective international responsibility to protect, exercisable by the Security Council authorizing military intervention as a last resort, in the event of genocide and other large-scale killing, ethnic cleansing or serious violations of international humanitarian law which sovereign Governments have proved powerless or unwilling to prevent." Id., para. 203. Also see Report of the Secretary-General, In Larger Freedom: Towards Development, Security and Human Rights For All (2005), originally issued as UN Doc. A/59/2005 (Mar. 15, 2005).

The high-level summit convened to discuss UN reform in September 2005 affirmed that "we [the "international community"] are prepared to take collective action, in a timely and decisive manner, through the Security Council, in accordance with the Charter, including Chapter VII, on a case-by-case basis and in cooperation with relevant regional organizationms as approrpriate, should peaceful means be inadequate and national authorities manifestly fail to protect their populations from genocide, war crimes, ethnic cleansing and crimes against humanity." 2005 World Summit Outcome, UN Doc. A/60/L.1, para. 139 (Sept. 15, 2005). Notably missing, however, was any reference to more specific criteria or the possibility of actions by states outside the context of the United Nations.

Comments and Questions

1. UN peacekeepers have been strongly criticized for their failure to stop the killing of approximately 7,000 Bosnian men and boys after the fall of Srebrenica in June 1995. See Report of the Secretary-General Pursuant to General Assembly Resolution 53/35 (1998), The fall of Srebrencia, UN Doc. A/54/549 (Nov. 15, 1999). In reading this and other criticisms of the failure to intervene, however, bear in mind that the decisions made at the time can only be fairly judged in light of the information available at the time, not with the benefit of hindsight. In Rwanda, for example, we know in retrospect that the genocide committed in April-June 1994 went far beyond earlier massacres of Tutsis by Hutus and vice versa. However, given the lack of international response to the killings of tens of

thousands of Burundians only a few months earlier and the history of conflict between the two groups since the 1960s, was the lack of response prior to or during the first weeks of the genocide either surprising or without any possible justification? How do you think the Organization of African Unity would have responded if UN troops (especially Belgians) had been increased and given the mandate to forcefully pursue radical Hutus prior to the outbreak of violence in April 1994?

2. It has been estimated that approximately 1,000 people were killed in Kosovo in the year before the NATO bombing — mostly Albanians killed by Serbs — and that roughly the same number were killed in the year following the end of the bombing — mostly Serbs killed by Albanians. Review the facts as they existed in Kosovo in 1998-99 and compare them with the situations in Somalia in 1992, Rwanda in 1994, and Darfur in 2003. Does the situation in Kosovo meet the various criteria proposed by the International Commission on Intervention and State Sovereignty? Do you agree with the Commission's limitation of the threshold test for military intervention to cases in which there is "large scale loss of life, actual or apprehended, [or] large scale 'ethnic cleansing,' actual or apprehended"? Note that the latter, according the Commission, includes "the systematic physical removal of members of a particular group from a particular geographical area; acts of terror designed to force people to flee; and the systematic rape for political purposes of women of a particular group (either as another form of terrorism, or as a means of changing the ethnic composition of that group)." Is "ethnic cleansing" simply another term for "mass expulsion"? If you believe that the Commission's threshold is too demanding, what other human rights violations do you think would justify the use of military force?

3. Is there now a right of unilateral or regional humanitarian intervention — as opposed to intervention authorized by the UN Security Council — under customary international law?

> Numerous authors point to the Kosovo intervention as state practice supportive of a new customary rule, with statements by the United States and several of its allies articulating humanitarian motives presented as evidence of an accompanying *opinio juris*. . . . [H]owever, this is insufficient to bring about a change in customary international law as it is traditionally understood. In order to be taken seriously, these arguments must be interpreted as implying that the rules concerning the formation of custom have themselves changed, or are in the process of changing. For example, are acts, as opposed to statements, today accorded more weight than previously? Does the practice of the powerful now count for more, as compared to the practice of the weak? Or does a lower threshold now exist with regard to the development of customary rules of a humanitarian or human rights character? . . .
>
> The novel conception of international law that is being constructed and reinforced by a limited group of Anglo-American international lawyers is possible only by ignoring the wider circle of states and international lawyers around the world. A broader analysis, in contrast, reinforces traditional assumptions and procedures — and thus leads to very different conclusions on issues such as unilateral humanitarian intervention. . . .
>
> Even if there has been some evidence of a shift in views since the end of the Cold War, the term "humanitarian intervention" remains particularly controversial in Africa. . . .
>
> . . . A widespread view among African commentators is that debate on this topic has become mired in the question of Kosovo-style interventions. Such a model is

> simply inappropriate to the African context, not least because the West has demonstrated that it is now unwilling to commit the resources to fight such a high-tech war (or, indeed, virtually any war) on African soil. . . .
>
> Perhaps what we are seeing, then, is not so much an effort to change all of international law as an effort to create new, exceptional rights for the United States alone, not only with regard to treaties, but also with regard to treaty interpretation and customary international law — and thus to the use of force.

Byers and Chesterman, "Changing the rules about rules? Unilateral humanitarian intervention and the future of international law," in *Humanitarian Intervention: Ethical, Legal, and Political Dilemmas* 187-88, 190, 191, 195 (J. Holzgrefe and R. Keohane eds. 2003).

The so-called Group of 77 (which now includes 133 developing states) has specifically rejected the notion that unilateral humanitarian intervention is permissible under international law; see Ministerial Declaration, 23rd Annual Meeting of the Ministers for Foreign Affairs of the Group of 77, Sept. 24, 1999, para. 69, available at *http://www.g77.org/Docs/Decl1999.html*, and Declaration of the Group of 77 South Summit, April 10-14 2000, para. 54, UN Doc. A/55/74 (2000).

Is it possible that a regional custom authorizing unilateral or NATO military intervention is developing or has developed only in Europe?

4. One prominent U.S. scholar (and former member of the UN Human Rights Committee) concluded as follows in the months immediately following the bombing of Kosovo. Do you share Professor Henkin's skepticism?

> In my view, unilateral intervention, even for what the intervening state deems to be important humanitarian ends, is and should remain unlawful. But the principles of law, and the interpretations of the Charter, that prohibit unilateral humanitarian intervention do not reflect a conclusion that the "sovereignty" of the target state stands higher in the scale of values of contemporary international society than the human rights of its inhabitants to be protected from genocide and massive crimes against humanity. The law that prohibits unilateral humanitarian intervention rather reflects the judgment of the community that the justification for humanitarian intervention is often ambiguous, involving uncertainties of fact and motive, and difficult questions of degree and "balancing" of need and costs. The law against unilateral intervention may reflect, above all, the moral-political conclusion that no individual state can be trusted with authority to judge and determine wisely.

Louis Henkin, *Editorial Comment, NATO's Kosovo Intervention: Kosovo and the Law of "Humanitarian Intervention,"* 93 Am. J. Int'l L. 824, 824-25 (1999).

5. Secretary of State Colin Powell cited the use of force against Kosovo without Security Council authorization as precedent for the later unauthorized invasion of Iraq; does his position have any validity?

6. The UN Secretary-General has said, "[W]hen the international community makes a solemn promise to safeguard and protect innocent civilians from massacre, then it must be willing to back its promise with the necessary means." Of course, one response is to back up such a promise; isn't it an equally valid moral alternative not to make the promise in the first place, if you know that it is unlikely to be kept? And just what is the "international community," to which writers refer so frequently?

V. The International Response to Darfur

The JEM and SLM/A attacks in the Darfur region began in February 2003, and by autumn the UN High Commissioner for Refugees (UNHCR) began to appeal for support for the Sudanese refugees from Darfur spilling over the border into Chad. In November 2003, the UN Office for the Coordination of Humanitarian Affairs (OCHA) warned of a "humanitarian crisis" and estimated that there were over 500,000 internally displaced persons from Darfur. Press reports about the situation from UNHCR or OCHA appeared almost weekly, and by March 2004 even actress and UNHCR Goodwill Ambassador Angelina Jolie was calling for support for the refugees in Chad. At the end of March, eight UN human rights special rapporteurs issued a joint statement that they were "gravely concerned" about reports of ethnic cleansing and violence in Darfur. The special rapporteur on arbitrary, summary, and extrajudicial executions warned the Commission on Human Rights in early April of the deteriorating situation in Sudan. And, of course, human rights NGOs were also calling attention to the situation. See, e.g., Amnesty International, *Sudan: Urgent call for Commission of Inquiry in Darfur as situation deteriorates*, AI Index: AFR 54/004/2003 (Feb. 21, 2003); id., *Darfur: Too many people killed for no reason*, AI Index: AFR 54/008/2004 (Feb. 3, 2004); Fedération Internationale des Droits de l'Homme, *Situation des droits de l'homme alarmante et grave crise humanitaire au Darfour* (Apr. 13, 2004); Human Rights Watch, *Darfur in Flames: Atrocities in Western Sudan* (Apr. 2, 2004); International Crisis Group, *Darfur Rising: Sudan's New Crisis* (Africa Report No. 76, Mar. 25, 2004).

April 2004 marked the tenth anniversary of the beginning of the genocide in Rwanda.

Acting without a formal request from the Commission, Acting High Commissioner for Human Rights Bertrand Ramcharan sent a fact-finding mission to Chad and (after a delay of two weeks awaiting permission from the Sudanese government) Darfur in April 2004, headed by the Director of the High Commissioner's office at UN headquarters in New York. Formally, the report of the mission was submitted in May as a letter to the Chairman of the Commission on Human Rights, which was by than no longer then in session (see UN Doc. E/CN.4/2005/3 (May 7, 2004)). The unusual directness of its analysis was reflected in the Acting High Commissioner's briefing to the Security Council on the day the report was released.

Acting High Commissioner for Human Rights Bertrand Ramcharan, Statement to the UN Security Council

May 7, 2004

Mr. President,
Distinguished members of the Security Council,
Friends and Colleagues,

You have just heard an eloquent and impassioned assessment, from my colleague Jim Morris, of the humanitarian situation currently prevailing in

Darfur and, by extension, across the border in refugee camps and sites in Chad.

I come before you to help complete the picture, for the crisis in Darfur is not simply humanitarian in nature. It was not caused by terrible forces of nature outside of human control. It is first and foremost conflict and egregious human rights abuses which have led to such an appalling tragedy. That this is entirely man-made only serves to compound that tragedy. . . .

The report [referred to above] makes for grim reading. It details a litany of violations of fundamental human rights and international humanitarian law in Darfur.

In particular, it notes that the following violations seem to be taking place in Darfur on a systematic basis:

- Indiscriminate attacks on civilians by forces of the Government of Sudan and militias, commonly referred to as Janjaweed, allied to them;
- Rape and other forms of sexual violence;
- Destruction of property and pillage;
- Forced displacement;
- Disappearances; and
- Clear signs that certain ethnic groups in Darfur — primarily the Zaghawa, Fur and Masaalit — are being persecuted and discriminated against, largely out of the perception that it is from these groups that the rebels are constituted and supported.

Several points deserve particular highlighting.

First, that to the displaced, there was no real distinction between the Sudanese military and the Janjaweed. Numerous witness testimonies allege that the two operated in close coordination with each other in carrying out attacks on civilians. The mission was left in no doubt that the Janjaweed were constituted and coordinated by the Government of Sudan as an effective means of crushing the rebellion and its perceived support base.

Second, the rebels — the SLA and the JEM — whom, it should be noted, initiated the conflict, have been in violation of human rights and humanitarian law. The report before you refers to an incident in which rebels launched an attack using a hospital as cover, and of a recent execution of a tribal leader by the rebels, apparently because he accepted humanitarian assistance from the Government.

Third, the very worrying ethnic dimension to this conflict. In short, what appears to have been a rebellion comprising certain specific ethnic groups of African origin has been met with Government action utilizing militia from ethnic groups of Arab origin. The two have traditionally competed with each other for scarce land resources. The impact of desertification in the Darfur region of Sudan has only served to make this competition more intense.

Finally, the violence is ongoing. In particular, the internally displaced in Darfur continue to exist in a climate of terror, often in siege-like conditions at the mercy of the Janjaweed who surround them. These people have no protection. Female IDPs, in particular, are vulnerable. My colleagues heard in detail of an environment in which the fear of rape, and numerous instances of rape, was suffocating.

In short, impunity reigns. In this situation, and with the wet season fast approaching, this crisis could very well become a tragedy.

This current state of affairs cannot be permitted to continue.

In my report, I lay down a number of recommendations, which I commend to you today, with a view to addressing — and ending — the human rights violations in Darfur. Among them include the following.

The Government of Sudan must end all links with the Janjaweed. It must publicly and unequivocally condemn all actions and crimes committed by these militia.

It must bring to justice all those who have violated human rights and international humanitarian law.

Humanitarian workers must be given full and unimpeded access to all areas in Darfur. All parties to the conflict must permit this access.

The Government of Sudan must develop and quickly implement meaningful policies of national reconciliation for Darfur. It must move quickly and unequivocally to end impunity and promote the rule of law in that region.

The internally displaced must be afforded full protection. This must happen now. The Government of Sudan has a legal responsibility to protect all of its citizens.

Refugees and IDPs must be afforded the opportunity voluntarily to return to their homes without fear and in safety. They should be able to reacquire their lands. Restitution, or fair compensation and reparations should be extended to all victims of the conflict in Darfur.

An international Commission of inquiry, given the gravity of the situation, should be established and mandated to produce a public report on its findings. The Commission should be mandated to look into the activities of all belligerents in the conflict and their compliance with international law.

International human rights monitors should be deployed to Sudan, to ensure that effective protection is afforded to all persons there.

Your Excellencies,

The people of Darfur are crying out. They need protection. They need it now. It is incumbent on the Government of Sudan to ensure that they receive this protection in full, that these abuses are not repeated and that there is accountability for past crimes.

The international community must help ensure that this is done and that the very real, painfully acute, humanitarian needs in Darfur are met.

The people of Darfur are crying out. We, the peoples, must listen. We have a chance to do right by them. We must not fail.

Thank you.

Three days before the report was made public and Mr. Ramcharan briefed the Council, Sudan was re-elected for another two-year term as a member of the UN Commission on Human Rights, as one of four unopposed candidates from Africa.

The government of Sudan has consistently denied ties with the Janjaweed, particularly allegations that the Janjaweed have acted as a proxy militia for the government. For example, Sudanese Foreign Minister Najeib al-Khair Abdel Wahab said, "The situation in Darfur is neither that of ethnic cleansing nor mass genocide. It is primarily a case of resource conflict." *Sudanese officials reject UN charges of ethnic cleansing in Darfur*, Agence France Presse, May 8, 2004.

Nonetheless, the government frequently promised to protect the victims in Darfur; eventually, it agreed to the deployment of monitors from the African Union to the Darfur region.

The Darfur conflict erupted just as protracted peace negotiations between Khartoum and the Sudanese People's Liberation Army (SPLA) to end the decades-long civil war between the central government and rebels in the south were entering their final stages. The government in Khartoum regularly cited the delicate progress of the north-south peace talks when confronted with threats of sanctions or intervention from the international community in response to reports of atrocities in Darfur. Eventually, a comprehensive peace agreement between the Khartoum government and the southern SPLM/A rebels was signed in January 2005.

Following the failure of Sudan to control the Janjaweed, the Security Council, acting under Chapter VII, finally imposed an arms embargo on "all non-governmental entities and individuals" in the Darfur region — but not on Sudanese government forces — and required states to take "the necessary measures" to prohibit restricted items from reaching Darfur. S.C. Res. 1556 (July 30, 2004).

Even with its watered-down language, Sudan's ambassador to the United Nations, Elfatih Mohamed Ahmed Erwa, told the Security Council that he was "overwhelmed with sorrow and sadness over the hasty resolution." He noted that the Sudanese government had, shortly before the resolution was passed, already arrested 200 members of the Janjaweed, sentencing some to death, and had sent female officials to investigate widespread allegations of rape. The ambassador also suggested that the aggressive US position towards sanctions against Sudan was motivated to give the Bush administration an election-year diversion from troubles in Iraq. The Sudanese army described Resolution 1556 as a "declaration of war on the Sudan and its people." BBC, *Sudan Army's Anger Over UN War*, August 2, 2004.

Ten days before this resolution, on July 22, 2004, a concurrent resolution was introduced in the U.S. Congress, H.R. Con. Res. 467 and S. Con. Res. 133, which "declare[d] that the atrocities unfolding in Darfur, Sudan, are genocide." The resolution urged the Bush administration to follow its lead in declaring the emergency in Darfur to be genocide and further "urge[d] the [Bush] Administration to seriously consider multilateral or even unilateral intervention to stop genocide in Darfur, Sudan, should the United Nations Security Council fail to act." It also "call[ed] upon the Administration to impose targeted sanctions, including visa bans and the freezing of assets of the Sudanese National Congress and affiliated business and individuals directly responsible for the atrocities in Darfur. . . ."

Six weeks later, Secretary of State Colin Powell testified before the Senate Foreign Relations Committee.

The Crisis in Darfur, Statement of Secretary of State Colin Powell before the Senate Foreign Relations Committee

September 9, 2004, available at *http://www.state.gov/secretary/rm/36042.htm*

. . . And finally there is the matter of whether or not what is happening in Darfur is genocide.

Since the U.S. became aware of atrocities occurring in Sudan, we have been reviewing the Genocide Convention and the obligations it places on the Government of Sudan. In July, we launched a limited investigation by sending a team to refugee camps in Chad. They worked closely with the American Bar Association and the Coalition for International Justice and were able to interview 1,136 of the 2.2 million people the UN estimates have been affected by this horrible violence. . . .

When we reviewed the evidence compiled by our team, along with other information available to the State Department, we concluded that genocide has been committed in Darfur and that the Government of Sudan and the jinjaweid bear responsibility — and genocide may still be occurring. . . .

Article VIII of the Genocide Convention provides that Contracting Parties "may call upon the competent organs of the United Nations to take such action under the Charter of the United Nations as they consider appropriate for the prevention and suppression of acts of genocide or any of the other acts enumerated in Article III." . . .

Today, the U.S. is calling on the UN to initiate a full investigation. To this end, the U.S. will propose that the next UN Security Council Resolution on Sudan request a UN investigation into all violations of international humanitarian law and human rights law that have occurred in Darfur, with a view to ensuring accountability. . . .

The totality of the evidence from the interviews we conducted in July and August, and from the other sources available to us, shows that:

The jinjaweid and Sudanese military forces have committed large-scale acts of violence, including murders, rape and physical assaults on non-Arab individuals;

The jinjaweid and Sudanese military forces destroyed villages, foodstuffs, and other means of survival;

The Sudan Government and its military forces obstructed food, water, medicine, and other humanitarian aid from reaching affected populations, thereby leading to further deaths and suffering; and

Despite having been put on notice multiple times, Khartoum has failed to stop the violence.

Mr. Chairman, some seem to have been waiting for this determination of genocide to take action. In fact, however, no new action is dictated by this determination. We have been doing everything we can to get the Sudanese government to act responsibly. So let us not be preoccupied with this designation of genocide. These people are in desperate need and we must help them. Call it a civil war. Call it ethnic cleansing. Call it genocide. Call it "none of the above." The reality is the same: there are people in Darfur who desperately need our help.

I expect that the government in Khartoum will reject our conclusion of genocide anyway. Moreover, at this point genocide is our judgment and not the judgment of the International Community. Before the Government of Sudan is taken to the bar of international justice, let me point out that there is a simple way for Khartoum to avoid such wholesale condemnation. That way is to take action.

The government in Khartoum should end the attacks, ensure its people — all of its people — are secure, hold to account those who are responsible for past atrocities, and ensure that current negotiations are successfully concluded. That is the only way to peace and prosperity for this war-ravaged land.

Specifically, Mr. Chairman, the most practical contribution we can make to the security of Darfur in the short-term is to increase the number of African Union monitors. That will require the cooperation of the Government of Sudan.

In the intermediate and long term, the security of Darfur can be best advanced by a political settlement at Abuja and by the successful conclusion of the peace negotiations between the SPLM and the Government of Sudan. . . .

The resolution passed without a dissenting vote on September 22, 2004, H.R. Con. Res. 467, 108th Cong. As Powell predicted, Sudan rejected the application of the "genocide" label to the violence in Darfur. At the same time, Powell's statement also infuriated human rights groups, which were incensed that the U.S. refused to take military action, even though it admitted that genocide was underway in Sudan.

As summer wore into fall, the international response to the ongoing crisis in Darfur consisted largely of humanitarian relief, administered in cooperation with the Sudanese government. The Sudanese government did just enough to fend off sanctions, including lifting restrictions on humanitarian relief, deploying 10,000 police officers to the region, and taking initial steps to disarm the Janjaweed. Peace talks between the north and south continued to advance.

A little over a week after U.S. Secretary of State Colin Powell used the term genocide in testimony to the U.S. Congress to describe the atrocities taking place in Darfur, the UN Security Council again addressed the issue of Darfur and threatened to "consider" sanctions against Sudan if the government did not take further steps to disarm the Janjaweed and bring perpetrators of human rights violations in Darfur to justice. S.C. Res. 1564 (Sept. 18, 2004). China, Russia, Algeria and Pakistan all abstained from voting on the resolution, opposing even the threat of sanctions.

During the 2004 U.S. presidential election campaign, Senator John Kerry and President Bush were asked why neither of their campaigns advocated sending American troops to Darfur. Their response follows.

Transcript of the Candidates' First Debate in the 2004 Presidential Campaign

Commission on Presidential Debates, *http://www.debates.org/pages/trans2004a.html*

. . . [Moderator Jim Lehrer:] Senator Kerry, you mentioned Darfur, the Darfur region of Sudan. Fifty thousand people have already died in that area. More than a million are homeless. And it's been labeled an act of ongoing genocide. Yet neither one of you or anyone else connected with your campaigns or your administration that I can find has discussed the possibility of sending in troops. Why not?

Kerry: . . . [W]ith respect to Darfur, yes, it is a genocide. And months ago, many of us were pressing for action.

I think the reason that we're not saying send American troops in at this point is severalfold.

Number one, we can do this through the African Union, providing we give them the logistical support. Right now all the president is providing is humanitarian support. We need to do more than that. They've got to have the logistical capacity to go in and stop the killing. And that's going to require more than is on the table today.

I also believe that it is — one of the reasons we can't do it is we're overextended. . . .

But I'll tell you this, as president, if it took American forces to some degree to coalesce the African Union, I'd be prepared to do it because we could never allow another Rwanda.

It's the moral responsibility for us and the world.

Lehrer: Ninety seconds.

Bush: . . . In terms of Darfur, I agree it's genocide. And Colin Powell so stated.

We have committed $200 million worth of aid. We're the leading donor in the world to help the suffering people there. We will commit more over time to help.

We were very much involved at the U.N. on the sanction policy of the Bashir government in the Sudan. Prior to Darfur, Ambassador Jack Danforth had been negotiating a north-south agreement that we would have hoped would have brought peace to the Sudan.

I agree with my opponent that we shouldn't be committing troops. We ought to be working with the African Union to do so — precisely what we did in Liberia. We helped stabilize the situation with some troops, and when the African Union came, we moved them out.

My hope is that the African Union moves rapidly to help save lives. And fortunately the rainy season will be ending shortly, which will make it easier to get aid there and help the long-suffering people there.

In order to encourage peace negotiations between the Government of Sudan and the SPLM/A, the Security Council held an extraordinary session in Nairobi in November 2004, only the fourth time that the Council had met outside of New York since 1945. At the special session, the Security Council adopted Resolution 1574 (Nov. 19, 2004), which focused on the progress made in peace talks between the Government of Sudan and the SPLM/A. An international response addressing the situation in Darfur was linked to the achievement of peace between the north and south. Neither sanctions nor military intervention are mentioned; instead, generous amounts of development assistance are offered in the form of "an assistance package for the reconstruction and economic development of Sudan, including official development assistance, possible debt relief and trade access," upon conclusion of a final peace agreement. Id., para. 3.

After the signing of the north-south peace agreement in January 2005, the Council adopted three resolutions on Sudan within a week in March. The first resolution was primarily concerned with the north-south conflict and created a

United Nations Mission in Sudan (UNMIS); it also emphasized that "there can be no military solution to the conflict in Darfur" and asked that the Secretary-General continue his monthly reports on Darfur to the Council. S.C. Res. 1590, paras. 7, 12 (Mar. 24, 2005). UNMIS peacekeepers were mandated to oversee the implementation of the north-south ceasefire but would not be deployed to Darfur, where only African Union (AU) forces would operate.

The second resolution established a committee to identify individuals "who [inter alia] impede the peace process, constitute a threat to stability in Darfur and the region, [and] commit violations of international humanitarian or human rights law or other atrocities." S.C. Res. 1591, para. 3(c) (Mar. 29, 2005). States were to prevent entry into or travel through their territories to such persons and freeze all of their financial assets that might be found in their territories. Id., para. 3(e). There was still no mention of sanctions against the government of Sudan, although the Council did state that it "deplores strongly" the failure of Sudan to comply with its commitments and warned that it would consider "further measures as provided for in Article 41 of the Charter" if the situation continued to deteriorate. Id., para. 8.

The Council had created an International Commission of Inquiry on Darfur in September 2004, which delivered its report in January 2005. The commission concluded that "the Government of the Sudan and the Janjaweed are responsible for serious violations of international human rights and humanitarian law amounting to crimes under international law. . . . These acts were conducted on a widespread and systematic basis, and therefore may amount crimes against humanity." UN Doc. S/2005/60 (Feb. 1, 2005), at 3. The third resolution adopted by the Council decided to refer the situation in Darfur to the International Criminal Court. S.C. Res. 1593 (Mar. 31, 2005). A proposed oil embargo against Sudan was not included, after China indicated it would veto any resolution to that effect.

These resolutions — particularly the reference to the ICC — sparked demonstrations in Khartoum, where tens of thousands of Sudanese marched in protest, calling the resolution "unjust" foreign interference and claiming that any alleged crimes should be tried by Sudanese courts. *Sudanese March against UN War Crimes Resolution*, Reuters AlertNet, April 6, 2005.

Meanwhile, an estimated 2.4 million people remained displaced from their homes in Darfur. Perhaps 200,000 had died from violence, exposure, or malnutrition since the beginning of the violence, and the International Crisis Group estimated that at least 10,000 civilians continued to die each month in Darfur as a result of ongoing turmoil, including sporadic military action by the SLA and JEM. See International Crisis Group, *A New Sudan Action Plan* (2005). NGO reaction is perhaps best summed up by the title of a press statement issued by Human Rights Watch on February 25, 2005: "Darfur: New Atrocities as Security Council Dithers."

In April 2005, the African Union pledged to boost its 2,300-member monitoring operation in Darfur to 7,700 by September 2005. This force was to comprise 5,500 soldiers, 1,600 civilian police, and 700 military observers. US Department of State, Sudan Background Note, May 2005. After the deployment of nearly 7,000 AU peacekeeping troops and a decrease in violence for several months, near the end of 2005 "the Bush administration, aid officers and other experts acknowledge[d] that the international efforts to stanch the bloodshed cannot succeed." Joel Brinkley, Surge in Violence in Sudan Erodes Hope, N.Y. Times, Nov. 7, 2005, at A8. The government of Sudan reportedly paid $30,000 to hire a U.S. lobbyist, Robert Cabelly, to put its views forward; the State Department said that Mr. Cabelly would "provide a perspective on United States concerns and policy that would be useful in advancing the peace process." Id.

Comments and Questions

1. President Bush, Secretary of State Colin Powell, and presidential candidate John Kerry labeled the situation in Darfur "genocide," yet none of them believed that such a designation required any specific action by the United States (or, presumably, any other country). Are they correct? Read Article 1 of the Genocide Convention; does the obligation to "prevent and punish" the crime of genocide imply either the right or the duty to invade another country to stop it? Is it more likely that the drafters of the convention in 1948 took a traditional view of the right of a sovereign state to be free from outside intervention? While Article 8 implies that the United Nations could authorize the use of force to stop genocide, is there any such implication with respect to unilateral action?

2. Estimates of deaths in Darfur range from 60,000 to 400,000; does it matter? Is this an issue more relevant to mobilizing political support for intervention, as opposed to a serious question of how many deaths it should require to "trigger" an intervention? See Mark Lacey, *The Mournful Math of Darfur: The Dead Don't Add Up*, New York Times (May 18, 2005). Cf. Bob Dylan, *Blowin' in the Wind* (1962)

How many times must a man look up
Before he can see the sky?
Yes, 'n' how many ears must one man have
Before he can hear people cry?
Yes, 'n' how many deaths will it take till he knows
That too many people have died?
The answer, my friend, is blowin' in the wind. . . .

3. Apparently, many people, in addition to John Kerry and George W. Bush (see supra page 872), support the use of force to prevent at least genocide or other widespread killing — so long as someone else does the intervening. See, e.g., International Crisis Group, *Do Americans Care about Darfur*? (Africa Briefing No. 26, June 1, 2005), in which an opinion poll found that 79% of Americans surveyed agreed that "the international community has a responsibility — short of sending US troops — to take action to stop these attacks from taking place in Darfur." When asked if U.S. soldiers should be inserted on the ground, however, only 38 percent said yes; 55 percent opposed such a proposal. In 1999, 71 percent of those polled believed that countries had not only a right but a duty to intervene "when a government commits terrible atrocities against its own people," although "intervention" was not defined as necessarily meaning the use of military force,

and there was no comparable question about the use of U.S. soldiers. The Harris Poll #67, Nov. 12, 1999.

Should a government intervene militarily in another country without support from a majority of the people in the intervening country?

4. The UN report on Rwanda, supra page 843, opines that "[a] force numbering 2,500 should have been able to stop or at least limit massacres of the kind which begain in Rwanda after the plane crash," but many disagree with this facile conclusion. See Kuperman, supra page 845. How should the United Nations balance the need for its forces to be able to respond to potential mass murder against its traditional role as a peacekeeper accepted by both parties to a conflict? Would the world have felt so guilty about doing nothing during the Rwandan genocide if there were not UN peacekeepers already in the country? As noted above, there was very little outcry over the 50,000 or more who were killed the preceding October in Burundi.

5. Note the conclusion of the Independent Commission on Kosovo that the NATO intervention was not a response to any immediate humanitarian catastrophe but was rather based on "a weaving together of past experiences and future concerns." Is this a standard that you think is sufficient to invade or bomb another country without UN approval? Is this even a standard?

V. Final Comments and Questions

1. The "responsibility to protect" is said to devolve on the "international community" when a state is unable or unwilling to protect its own population. Is the United Nations the best representative of the "international community"? If the United Nations refuses to act, for any reason, can we simply replace it as the representative of a truly global community with a subregional or regional organization? With "like-minded" states? With a single neighboring state?

2. Do you agree that the "responsibility to protect" includes the "responsibility to rebuild"? Does a potential intervenor have to be ready to "build a durable peace . . . [and promote] good governance and sustainable development"? Do you think that such an obligation will make intervention more or less likely in the future? There is a plethora of literature addressing the issue of nation — or state-building in post-conflict situations, much of it highly critical of past efforts. See, e.g., *Civil War, Insecurity and Intervention* (Barbara F. Walter and Jack Snyder eds. 1999); *Ending Civil Wars: The Implementation of Peace Agreements* (Stephen John Stedman, Donald Rothchild and Elizabeth M. Cousens eds., 2002); Seth G. Jones, *Establishing Law and Order After Conflict* (2005); Roland Paris, *At War's End: Building Peace After Civil Conflict* (2004); Barbara F. Walter, *Committing to Peace: The Successful Ending of Civil Wars* (2001).

Also consider the observations of Lakhdar Brahimi, a senior Algerian diplomat who has served as the UN Secretary-General's special representative or adviser to, inter alia, Lebanon, Haiti, Afghanistan, and Iraq:

> . . . [O]f course, one would expect matters of war and peace ultimately to be difficult and complicated. The problem is that our expectations and agendas are not becoming any more realistic. Instead, they have become more ambitious and multi-faceted, seeking to promote justice, national reconciliation, human rights, gender equality, the rule of law, sustainable economic development and democracy, all at the same time, from day one, now, immediately, even including in the midst of conflict.

Statement by Mr. Lakhdar Brahimi on the Occasion of the Awarding of the Dag Hammarskjöld Medal by the German UN Association, July 8, 2004, *http://www.un.org/apps/news/infocusnewsiraq1.asp?NewsID=767&sID=19*.

3. Is the real goal of "humanitarian intervention" to end civil wars, as opposed to protecting noncombatants or other victims of today's internal conflicts? Is this possible? For a suggestion that war, while not inevitable, was certainly common even during prehistorical times, see Lawrence H. Keeley, *War Before Civilization: The Myth of the Peaceful Savage* (1996).

4. Hovering not too far above the debate over when sanctions should be imposed or military intervention should occur is the issue of whether these are even legal questions. Should one simply accept that there will be situations in which, as the International Commission on Kosovo concluded, acts can be "illegal, yet legitimate"? Should one push for a better articulation of existing norms or seek a consensus around new norms? Consider the following extract, which may be cynical, realistic, heretical — or simply a throwback to former Secretary of State Acheson, supra pages 799 — depending on one's perspective:

> In the face of the collapse of the legalist order governing the use of force, the international system has moved rapidly to a parallel universe of two systems, one *de facto*

> and the other *de jure*. The two exist side by side. In one universe a *de jure* regime continues the traditional pacific dispute settlement process established by the [UN] Charter. Its membership is universal. It consists of the unlike-minded states of the United Nations that share grievances, employ the "good offices" of the Secretary General, and engage in "preventive diplomacy" to avert conflict. The ordering principle of this system is sovereignty. Rules are made by the consent of states deemed to be sovereign equals. In the background is the "invisible college" of international lawyers, as they like to refer to themselves, who remind participant states of when they can and cannot use force under an elaborate body of inflexible rules that are honored more in the breach than in the observance....
>
> In the other universe is a *de facto* system. It is a geopolitical regime over which the strong preside. It bears little resemblance to the formal regime of the Charter. Its ordering principle is not consent but power. Its rules are made not by students' international law journals but by NATO activation orders and the Pentagon's rules of engagement. Its membership is selective. Its participants are the like-minded states of NATO and other Western democracies.... When international order is threatened, whether by aggression or — as lately — by genocide, they are the ones to restore it. For them, international lawyers sojourning from the other universe may as well be invisible because nations do not act the way international lawyers think they act and would like them to act. Governmental officials know that and have better ways to spend their time than arguing about whether a given use of force would violate a "peremptory norm" of customary international law or merely an outdated treaty prohibition. When British Foreign Secretary Robin Cook told U.S. Secretary of State Madeleine Albright that he had "problems with our lawyers" over using force [in Kosovo] without Security Council approval, she responded: "Get new lawyers."...
>
> The term that might leap to a reader's mind is "realism." But this description of my thesis would be only half right. Most realists believe that power rather than law does and *should* control. I argue that power does control the use of force today, but that control by law ultimately would be preferable. The conditions that would permit effective legalist restraints on force simply do not now exist.

Michael J. Glennon, *Limits of Law, Prerogatives of Power: Interventionism after Kosovo* 177-78, 2-3 (2001) (notes omitted) (emphasis in original).

5. Among the many works not already cited that deal with humanitarian or human rights intervention (as opposed to the use of force for other reasons, such as self-defense), see Eileen F. Babbitt, *Principled Peace: Conflict Resolution and Human Rights in Intra-state Conflict* (forthcoming 2006); Mirko Bagaric and John R. Morss, *Transforming Humanitarian Intervention from an Expedient Accident to a Categorical Imperative*, 30 Brooklyn J. Int'l L. 421 (2005); Lee F. Berger, *State Practice Evidence of the Humanitarian Intervention Doctrine: The ECOWAS Intervention in Sierra Leone*, 11 Ind. Int'l & Comp. L. Rev. 605 (2001); *Beyond Westphalia? State Sovereignty and International Intervention* (Gene M. Lyons and Michael Mastanduno eds., 1995); Michael Bonser, *Humanitarian Intervention in the Post-Cold War World: A Cautionary Tale*, 8 Canadian For. Policy 57 (2001); Bartram S. Brown, *Humanitarian Intervention at a Crossroads*, 41 William & Mary L. Rev. 1683 (2000); Michael L. Burton, *Legalizing the Sublegal: A Proposal for Codifying a Doctrine of Unilateral Humanitarian Intervention*, 85 Georgetown L. J. 417 (1996); Simon Chesterman, *Just War or Just Peace? Humanitarian Intervention and International* Law (2001); Tom Farer, *Intervention in Unnatural Humanitarian Emergencies: Lessons of the First*

Phase, 18 Hum. Rts. Q. 1 (1996); id. et al., Roundtable: *Humanitarian Intervention After 9/11*, 19 Int'l Relations 211 (No. 2 2005); Christopher Greenwood, *Humanitarian Intervention: Law and Policy* (2001); Stanley Hoffman, *The Ethics and Politics of Humanitarian Intervention* (1997); *Humanitarian Intervention: Ethical, Legal, and Political Dilemmas* (J.L. Holzgrefe and Robert O. Keohane eds., 2003); *Humanitarian Intervention and the United Nations* (Richard B. Lillich ed., 1973); Ian Johnstone, *The Plea of "Necessity" in International Legal Discourse: Humanitarian Intervention and Counter-terrorism*, 43 Colum. J. Transnat'l L. 337 (2005); Brian Lepard, *Rethinking Humanitarian Intervention* (2002); Richard B. Lillich, *The Role of the UN Security Council in Protecting Human Rights in Crisis Situations: UN Humanitarian Intervention in the Post-Cold War World*, 3 Tulane J. Int'l & Comp. L. 2 (1995); Ved P. Nanda, *Tragedies in Northern Iraq, Liberia, Yugoslavia, and Haiti — Revisiting the Validity of Humanitarian Intervention under International Law — Part I*, 20 Denver J. Int'l L. & Policy 305 (1992); Ved P. Nanda, Thomas F. Muther, and Amy E. Eckert, *id. — Part II*, 26 Denver J. Int'l L. & Policy 827 (1998); Mary Ellen O'Connell, *The UN, NATO, and International Law after Kosovo*, 22 Hum. Rts. Q. 57 (2000); Frederick J. Petersen, *The Façade of Humanitarian Intervention for Human Rights in a Community of Sovereign Nations*, 15 Ariz. J. Int'l & Comp. L. 871 (1998); W. Michael Riesman, *Humanitarian Intervention and Fledgling Democracies*, 18 Fordham Int'l L. J. 794 (1995); Adam Roberts, *The So-called "Right" of Humanitarian Intervention*, 3 Yearbook Int'l Humanitarian L. 3 (2000); Fernando R. Teson, *Humanitarian Intervention: An Inquiry into Law and Morality* (2d ed. 1997); Nicholas J. Wheeler, *Saving Strangers: Humanitarian Intervention in International Society* (2000).

Chapter 11

International Criminal Law

Can We Deter Human Rights Violations by Using the Criminal Justice Process?

I. Introduction

At the outset, one must distinguish between crimes and human rights violations. Human rights violations normally implicate the responsibility of a government; criminal liability, whether domestic or international, attaches to an individual. Human rights violations are not automatically crimes; indeed, most violations — e.g., suppression of freedom of speech, discrimination, interference with property, violations of fair criminal procedure, failure to ensure adequate housing or health care, interference with freedom of religion — are not criminal acts under either domestic or international law. Similarly, many international crimes — e.g., piracy, terrorism, hijacking, drug trafficking, money laundering — are simply crimes com-

Carlson Carton as Pinochet

mitted by individuals and do not implicate human rights norms. It is only a relatively small number of acts (such as torture and some murders) that may be considered to be both violations of international human rights law (when committed under color of governmental authority) and international crimes.

International crimes, whether defined by treaty or customary law, may be punished by international and/or domestic tribunals. After the introductory material on General Pinochet, the next section of this chapter reviews the historical development of international criminal law that led to the precedent-setting creation of the International Criminal Court (ICC) in 1998. The ICC itself is then examined in the fourth section, including some of the criticisms of the ICC, many leveled by the United States. The fifth section examines the issue of universal jurisdiction, i.e., the assertion of jurisdiction over certain kinds of crimes by an individual state, no matter where or against whom those crimes might be committed. Next, the somewhat different issue of treaty-based transnational crimes is briefly examined, where the issue is not so much a global desire to punish particularly heinous crimes but rather the mutual interest of states in punishing "ordinary" crimes with a transnational element, such as drug trafficking, terrorism, and even environmental crimes. The final section addresses domestic prosecution for domestic crimes, particularly the issue of granting amnesty or impunity to members of repressive regimes guilty of "human rights" crimes.

II. The 1973 Coup in Chile and Its Aftermath

A. *Pinochet in Power*

Augusto Pinochet, the man who was to become dictator of Chile, took power on September 11, 1973, in a violent coup d'état that overthrew the democratically-elected government of the socialist president, Salvador Allende. Pinochet, who had been Commander-in-Chief of the Chilean army under Allende, and his military junta quickly consolidated their power by suspending the constitution and dissolving Congress. A state of siege was declared, and, within hours of the coup, thousands of people associated with the deposed Allende government or thought to be sympathetic to the socialist cause were rounded up by military forces and taken to detention centers around the country. Torture in these centers became commonplace under the new regime, with interrogations including beatings, electrocutions, mock executions, Russian roulette, sexual assault, asphyxiation, holding forced positions for long periods of time, sleep deprivation, being forced to witness or listen while others were tortured, and exposure to extreme temperatures. People were allegedly thrown out from planes into the Pacific Ocean or the Andes mountains. It is estimated that 1,200 suspected left-wing sympathizers were killed or "disappeared" in the first three months following the coup, and thousands more met the same fate as Pinochet consolidated his grip on power. An estimated 27,000 Chileans were tortured during Pinochet's seventeen-year rule, with a further 3,000 executed or "disappeared."

On June 27, 1974, Pinochet assumed the title of Supreme Chief of the Nation.

Tens of thousands of people fled Chile in the wake of Pinochet's seizure of power, to live as exiles in neighboring countries. Leaving Chile was no guarantee of safety from Pinochet's regime for suspected opponents, however. During Pinochet's rule, right-wing military dictatorships also held power in Argentina, Bolivia, Brazil, Paraguay, and Uruguay. Through a long-running program called Operation Condor, the governments agreed to share information with one another on suspected dissidents, particularly Marxists. Disappearances and murders of prominent Marxist sympathizers were common during this time.

In 1976, Orlando Letelier, the Foreign Minister under Allende and former Chilean ambassador to the United States, was spectacularly murdered when the car in which he was riding exploded on Embassy Row in Washington, D.C. Two years earlier, a similar assassination by car bomb had taken place in Buenos Aires, in which General Carlos Prats, Pinochet's predecessor as army commander, was killed. In 1978, the Pinochet government passed an amnesty law, Decree Law 2191, aimed at preventing any prosecution in relation to human rights abuses committed since the time of the 1973 coup.

In 1988, after 15 years in power, Pinochet agreed to a plebiscite on his continued rule. Fifty-five percent of those voting chose "No," as against forty-two percent voting in favor of Pinochet staying in power. Pinochet stepped down as President on March 11, 1990, at age 74, and was succeeded by Patricio Aylwin. Despite relinquishing the presidency, Pinochet retained his title of Commander-in-Chief of the Army until 1997, a position from which he continued to exercise considerable political power. Thereafter, he was named Senator-for-Life, an unelected position granted under a 1980 constitutional provision to former presidents who had spent at least six years in office. As a senator, Pinochet enjoyed parliamentary immunity, and he continued to wield influence in Chilean politics when he traveled to London under a diplomatic passport for back surgery on a herniated disc in the fall of 1998.

For a description of human rights abuses during the Pinochet regime, see, e.g., Comisión Nacional sobre Prisión Política y Tortura, Síntesis Informe (Vecher Report) (2004); John Dinges, *The Condor Years: How Pinochet and His Allies Brought Terrorism to Three Continents* (2004); Peter Kornbluh, *The Pinochet File: A Declassified Dossier on Atrocity and Accountability* (2003); Hugh O'Shaughnessy, *Pinochet, The Politics of Torture* (2000); Patricia Verdugo, *Chile, Pinochet, and the Caravan of Death* (2001); and the reports of the Inter-American Commission on Human Rights on the Situation of Human Rights in Chile: Inter-Am. Comm'n H.R., OEA/Ser.L/V/II.34, Report on the Situation of Human Rights in Chile, Doc. 21 corr. 1 (1974); id., OEA/Ser.L/V/II.37, Doc. 19 corr. 1 (1976); id., OEA/Ser.L/V/II.40, Doc. 10 (1977); and id., OEA/Ser.L/V/II.66, Doc. 17 (1985).

B. *Pinochet Indicted*

While recovering from back surgery in a private clinic outside London, and after a social visit with former British Prime Minister Margaret Thatcher the week before, Augusto Pinochet was arrested on October 16, 1998, under an international warrant issued by Judge Baltasar Garzón of Spain; the charges included murder and 94 counts of torture of Spanish citizens between the years 1973 and 1990. Judge Garzón also sought to question Pinochet about his role in Operation Condor, the coordinated campaign among the military regimes in South America to track down and often kill left-wing opponents of their regimes.

- Thatcher's husband was an arms dealer

Human rights groups exulted at the indictment, which was trumpeted as "evidence of a growing consensus in the international community that human rights transcend national boundaries, limiting the immunity of former heads of state and even the prerogatives of sovereignty." Human Rights Watch, *When Tyrants Tremble* 2 (1999). The Institute for Policy Studies, the think tank at which Orlando Letelier had been working when he was assassinated, called Pinochet's indictment "one of the most important events in international law since Nuremberg." (Jonas, *The Ripple Effect of the Pinochet Case*, 11 Hum. Rts. Brief 36 (2004).

The government of Chile expressed its vehement opposition to the arrest of Pinochet and to any possibility of extradition or trial. Legal wrangling in the United Kingdom ensued, as the House of Lords debated whether, as a former head of state, Pinochet was immune from prosecution. A panel of Law Lords first found, largely on the basis of customary international law, that Pinochet's status as a former head of state did not provide immunity from prosecution. Regina v. Bow Street Metropolitan Stipendiary Magistrate, ex parte Pinochet Ugarte, 4 All E.R. 897 (H.L. 1998). The court subsequently annulled its initial ruling, after Pinochet's lawyers successfully argued that one of the judges, Lord Hoffman, was biased due to his ties to Amnesty International. Id., 1 All E.R. 577 (H.L. 1999) (Lord Hoffmann had for years been head of AI's charitable wing, Amnesty International Charity Limited, and his wife worked for Amnesty International.) After reconsidering arguments, the court in March 1999, without Lord Hoffman, reaffirmed its ruling but limited the crimes for which Pinochet could be extradited to acts of torture committed after 1988, the date on which Great Britain had ratified the Convention Against Torture and incorporated it into domestic law. Id., 2 All E.R. 97 (H.L. 1999).

Pinochet remained under house arrest in England for 16 months. As the time of extradition approached, the British Home Secretary, Jack Straw, ruled that Pinochet (then 83 years old) was medically unable to stand trial and should therefore not be extradited to Spain. Instead, on March 2, 2000, Pinochet was permitted to return to Chile.

During his period of house arrest, the political climate in Chile changed dramatically. In 2000, the Santiago Court of Appeals voted to strip Pinochet of his parliamentary immunity, based on an application from Chilean Judge Juan Guzmán, who sought to indict Pinochet for the disappearance of over 70 political opponents in 1973, an incident which had gained notoriety as the "Caravan of Death." The Chilean Supreme Court agreed (despite the fact that the Chilean Senate had voted to grant Pinochet an additional basis for immunity, as a "former President of the Republic"), and, shortly after Pinochet's return from London, he was placed under house arrest in Chile. Without parliamentary immunity, Pinochet soon faced dozens of lawsuits filed by Chilean plaintiffs in Chilean courts, alleging abuses at the hands of his regime. Nevertheless, in July 2002, the Supreme Court suspended the Caravan of Death case on the grounds that Pinochet suffered from vascular dementia and was thus medically unfit to stand trial. Shortly thereafter, Pinochet resigned his Senate seat.

In May 2004, the Court of Appeals reversed the decision on Pinochet's dementia, in part due to an interview he gave to a Miami-based television station, in which he appeared alert and lucid (stating that he was not and had not been a dictator, and that he had no reason to ask for forgiveness). In December 2004, the Court of Appeals charged Pinochet in the 1974 assassination of General Prats; in March 2005, however, the Supreme Court reversed, ruling that Pinochet was immune from prosecution in that particular case.

Pinochet's legal troubles continued with the revelation in July 2004 by a U.S. Senate committee investigation that Riggs Bank, an American bank based in Washington, D.C., had held and laundered between $4-8 million for Pinochet, setting up offshore shell corporations and shielding his account from regulators. In October 2004, Chile's Servicio de Impuestos Internos (Internal Revenue Service) filed a lawsuit against Pinochet, charging fraud and tax evasion.

Despite the plethora of civil and criminal cases pending against him, Pinochet had yet to stand trial (as of mid-2005) for any of the human rights abuses committed during his regime. However, in the aftermath of Pinochet's arrest in London, over 300 Chilean military officers have been indicted for acts committed during the dictatorship. Dozens have been convicted.

Among many writings on the Pinochet case and its impact, see Andrea Bianchi, *Immunity Versus Human Rights: The Pinochet Case*, 10 Eur. J. Int'l L. 237 (1999); Curtis A. Bradley and Jack Goldsmith, *Pinochet and International Human Rights Litigation*, 97 Mich. L.R. 2129 (1999); Michael Byers, *The Law and Politics of the Pinochet Case*, 10 Duke J. Comp. U Int'l L. 415 (2000); Human Rights Watch, *When Tyrants Tremble: The Pinochet Case* (1999); *The Pinochet Case: A Legal and Constitutional Analysis* (Diana Woodhouse ed. 2000); *The Pinochet Papers: The Case of Augusto Pinochet in Spain and Britain* (Reed Brody and Michael Ratner eds.) (2000); Naomi Roht-Arriaza, *The Pinochet Effect: Transnational Justice in the Age of Human Rights* (2005); David Sugarman, *Pursuing Pinochet: A Global Quest for Justice* (forthcoming); Marc Weller, *On the Hazards of Foreign Travel for Dictators and Other International Criminals*, 75 Int'l Aff. 599 (1999).

The attempts to bring Augusto Pinochet to account for the crimes committed during his 15 years in power in Chile form the context in which this chapter's issues should be considered.

III. Efforts to Bring the International Criminal Justice Process to Bear upon Human Rights Violators

Perhaps because of the distinction between human rights and crimes noted at the beginning of this chapter, the criminal justice process has been used to punish human rights violators only sporadically. True, the commission of a traditional international crime — such as piracy on the high seas — subjected the offending individual to the criminal sanction of any state able to bring him to justice, since (the offense being international) jurisdiction was universal; see the discussion infra at page 940. Moreover, as Chapter 4 has shown, persons committing war crimes frequently have been brought to book before domestic courts — generally courts-martial established by their own states. At the end of World War II, an ad hoc international tribunal sitting at Nuremberg applied legal standards set out in a special charter during the trials of Nazi war criminals for crimes against peace, war crimes, and crimes against humanity. (See Chapter 4, page 233.) In many ways, Nuremberg was and remains the highwater mark insofar as the use of the international criminal process is concerned, although the recently established International Criminal Court (see infra page 912) may become an even more important factor in the future.

Immediately after Nuremberg, efforts were made to codify certain large-scale or particularly grave human rights violations as international crimes, the commission of which would render the offender subject to trial in various domestic or international courts. This period saw the UN General Assembly's adoption of the Genocide Convention, followed by the International Law Commission's formulation of the Nuremberg Principles (5 U.N. GAOR Supp. (No. 12) at 11-14, U.N. Doc. A/1316 (1950)) and the Draft Code of Offenses Against the Peace and Security of Mankind (9 U.N. GAOR Supp. (No. 9) at 11-12, U.N. Doc. A/ 2693 (1954)). Even at this early stage, the United Nations considered the possible establishment of an international criminal court (Report of the Committee on International Criminal Jurisdiction, 9 U.N. GAOR Supp. (No. 12) at 23-26, U.N. Doc. A/2645 (1954)). In 1957, however, the General Assembly decided to defer consideration of such a court until it had completed the Draft Code and agreed on a definition of aggression, G.A. Res. 1187 (Dec. 11, 1957). This decision effectively delayed any consideration of an international criminal court for nearly two decades, since the General Assembly took until 1974 to agree on an official definition of aggression, G.A. Res. 3314 (Dec. 14, 1974).

Early efforts to establish international criminal liability for certain "human rights crimes" are discussed in the following two extracts. This history is important, if one is to understand both the possibilities and potential pitfalls of exercising international criminal jurisdiction in the future, as well as the long-standing resistance to its implementation.

Antonio Cassese, *International Criminal Law*

37-38, 40, 41 (2003)

Traditionally, individuals have been subject to the exclusive (judicial and executive) jurisdiction of the State on whose territory they live. Hence, their possible violations of international rules (for example, ill-treatment of foreigners, attacks on foreign diplomats, wrongful expulsion of foreigners by State officials, etc.) were prosecuted and punished by the competent authorities of the State where these acts had been performed (under the doctrine of territorial jurisdiction). Clearly, such prosecution and punishment only occurred if the State authorities were entitled to do so under their national legislation, and provided they were willing so to proceed. If they did not, the State of which the victim had the nationality was authorized to internationally claim from the delinquent State that it either punish the perpetrators or pay compensation. As what was involved was the responsibility of the State (for failure to bring to trial and punish the offenders), the individuals who had *materially* breached international rules could not be called to account by the foreign State, unless they were their nationals (think of the case of a Russian killing a Russian diplomat in Berlin). . . .

A few exceptions existed. One of them was piracy, a practice that was widespread in the seventeenth and eighteenth centuries, and has recently regained some importance, albeit limited to one area of the world, East Asia. (An authoritative definition of piracy can now be found in Article 101 of the 1982 Convention on the Law of the Sea.) All States of the world were empowered to search for and prosecute pirates, regardless of the nationality of the victims and of whether the proceeding State had been directly damaged by piracy. The pirates were regarded as enemies of humanity (*hostes humani generis*) in that they hampered the freedom of the high seas and infringed private property. . . .

The creation of the [International Military Tribunal] and the subsequent trial at Nuremberg of the major German criminals (followed in 1946 by the Tokyo Trial), marked a crucial turning point. First, two new categories of crime were envisaged: crimes against peace and crimes against humanity. Secondly, until 1945 (with the exception of the provisions of the 1919 Treaty of Versailles relating to the German Emperor, which however remained a dead letter), senior State officials had never been held personally responsible for their wrongdoings. Until that time States alone could be called to account by other States, plus servicemen (normally low-ranking people) accused of misconduct during international wars. In 1945, for the first time in history, the principle was laid down — and carried through, in contrast to what had happened in 1919 — that other State representatives (high-ranking officers, politicians, prominent administrators or financiers, as well as men in charge of official State propaganda) could also be made answerable for gross misconduct in time of armed conflict. . . .

After the adoption, in 1948, of the Convention on Genocide (which laid down genocide as a discrete crime), the 1949 Geneva Conventions.... represented a momentous departure from customary, for the Conventions also laid down the principle of universality of jurisdiction (a contracting State could bring to trial a person held in its custody and accused of a "grave breach", regardless of his nationality, of the nationality of the victim, and of the place where the alleged offence had been committed). It is probable that the exceedingly bold character of this regulation contributed to its remaining ineffective for many years.

The Geneva Conventions were followed by the two Additional Protocols in 1977, the Convention against Torture in 1984 (which significantly contributed to the emergence of torture as a distinct crime), and a string of treaties against terrorism since the 1970s (which contributed to the evolution of an international crime of terrorism).

John Carey, *UN Protection of Civil and Political Rights*

63-69 (1970)

[The author's chapter on Protection by Criminal Adjudication begins with a description of the growing trend in the 1960s to define certain acts as international crimes. He then proceeds to set out various ideas that had been presented for improving and developing procedures of enforcement.]

In 1967 Sean MacBride, Secretary-General of the International Commission of Jurists, speaking for his own and other non-governmental organizations, proposed at the UN Seminar in Zambia on apartheid, racial discrimination and colonialism in southern Africa

> that a register or record office be established at United Nations Headquarters for the purpose of registering all complaints of acts of brutality and other acts amounting to crimes against humanity committed in South Africa, South West Africa, Southern Rhodesia, Angola and Mozambique... by anyone in these territories purporting to act in pursuance of the racial or colonial laws or practices being applied in those areas.

The British author Colin Legum proposed that Mr. MacBride's own organization

> open a register of people accused of committing atrocities in defiance of [a Convention on Crimes Against Humanity]. Men like Inspector Lambron, head of the Greek security police, Asphalia, and the torturers in South Africa, Portugal and other countries, should have dossiers on them prepared against the day when conditions change and they become available for prosecution. The mere threat of such a possibility might make torturers think twice before they commit their loathsome brutalities.

Mr. MacBride later proposed a Universal Court of Human Rights to deal with crimes against humanity.

> For a start, violations of the United Nations and the Red Cross Conventions could be made indictable offences before an International Tribunal to punish crimes against humanity. Such a Tribunal could, in addition, be given general power to pass

> judgment on crimes that violate "... the law of nations, the laws of humanity and the dictates of the public conscience." Gradually, later, a code of Crimes against Humanity could be evolved and embodied in an international convention, but the Tribunal with the jurisdiction indicated would be set up now.

A geographically narrower proposal appeared in the Montreal Statement of the Assembly for Human Rights on March 22-27, 1968, which concluded that "criminal courts and procedures might be established for dealing with gross violations of human rights" in South West Africa, whose "unique status provides a special opportunity to experiment with further implementation procedures."

The pace for proposals for criminal jurisdiction was escalated when the UN Human Rights Commission's Special Rapporteur on apartheid and racial discrimination suggested to the Commission in early 1968 that it recommend to the Assembly asking the South African Government to repeal its discriminatory laws:

> In case the present situation continued to prevail, the General Assembly would declare the leaders and responsible officials of the South African Government criminals at large who could be apprehended and tried by the courts of any State under the charge of the commission of crimes against humanity. In case of conviction the penalty would be the severest (penalty) which could be imposed under the laws of the country concerned.

This proposal was not dealt with explicitly by the Commission. The Special Rapporteur went further with his proposal for a Grand Jury of Legal Experts for South West Africa:

> The Commission could recommend to the General Assembly that it establish, in connection with the Assembly's decisions to administer South West Africa (Resolutions 2145 (XXI) and 2248 (S-V)), a Grand Jury of Legal Experts for South West Africa for the protection of the life, personal safety and rights of the inhabitants of the Territory. Such a body of legal experts would determine prima facie violations of international law, crimes against humanity and other serious offenses committed by individual South African Government officials against the inhabitants of the territory for which the Assembly has assumed special responsibility. It could be given a variety of police powers including the powers to issue arrest warrants, lists of wanted men and requests that they be brought to justice by Member States of the United Nations. By acting in person it could have some deterrent effect on South African officialdom in so far as torture, brutality and the execution of death sentences are concerned. Later the terms of reference of this same body may be extended to cover Southern Rhodesia and South Africa as well, in case the Assembly's call for repeal, amendment and replacement of legislation is not heeded.

An American viewpoint on the usefulness of international criminal proceedings was expressed by the Human Rights Committee of the American Branch of the International Law Association, which reached the following conclusions:

> ***Prima Facie Findings Without Trial***
>
> Grand-jury-type proceedings might be useful in cases where the accused were not available to be tried. The spotlight of public opinion could be focused sharply through orderly measures taken in the drastic context of criminality. Those accused

might feel compelled to respond, with public statements if not formal appearance, where the spotlight shone from an impartial source, depoliticized as far as possible.

Criminal "Trials" Without Presence of Defendants

The reasons for prima facie findings apply even more strongly in favor of proceedings in which such findings are subjected to "trial." A greater impact on public opinion should result from facts found after hearing both sides. If the accused neither appeared nor submitted statements, a hearing of sorts for both sides could be obtained through an active tribunal seeking evidence on its own, on the order of an American administrative body or European "juge d'instruction." ...

While international criminal jurisdiction lagged, the practice of national prosecution of crimes of "universal jurisdiction" was used occasionally to fill the gap. Building on the long-standing precedent subjecting pirates to punishment by any state, other serious wrongs have been made universally punishable by convention. Chief among these are the four 1949 Geneva Conventions for the protection of war victims, to which the United States is one of many parties. . . .

With respect to the relative merits of international and national courts for prosecution of international crimes, the Human Rights Committee of the International Law Association's American Branch concluded that

> while universal criminal jurisdiction has been widely accepted, not only in the four 1949 Geneva Conventions but also in the 1958 Convention on the High Seas (for piracy), its lack of use causes concern. Like state vs. state complaints, found in I.L.O. experience to be seldom used and then most likely for political purposes, universal criminal jurisdiction may be a rusty tool, seized at times in haste and crudely wielded. Unilateral prosecution of offenses against the whole international community would seem less desirable than machinery whose guidance is multilateral. Politically motivated prosecutions could then be better controlled. Political prevention of otherwise desirable prosecutions, which might occur, would be a lesser evil than uncontrolled political prosecution.

The growing interest in criminal process to protect basic rights, matched in the United States by concern over personal accountability for international crimes connected with the Viet Nam conflict, is not difficult to comprehend. Frustration at the impregnability of white supremacy bastions like South Africa . . . is bound to add appeal to the notion of punishing apartheid's individual practitioners who, though presently immune through safe location, would, if ever caught, be as subject to punishment as are their own present victims. The actual capture of Adolph Eichmann encourages speculation about others accused of human rights crimes. . . .

Can it be wrong, in the light of Nuremberg, to plan for prosecution on international authority of today's oppressors? The answer is not categorical but qualified. The qualifications concern geographical jurisdiction, the nature of the tribunal, the type of findings made, and the consequence for the accused.

Much has changed since the above words were written in 1970, but the difficulty in addressing even a universally condemned "human rights crime," such as apartheid, is illustrated by the rather limited, if innovative, ideas noted by Carey. The next extract traces the progress of international criminal law in the past two decades and identifies some of the contemporary issues that remain to be faced.

Steven R. Ratner and Jason S. Abrams, *Accountability for Human Rights Atrocities in International Law*

8-9, 10-11, 155, 156-57 (2001) (references omitted) (emphasis in original)

The most recent *étape* toward promoting individual accountability under international law resulted from two distinct developments beginning in the early 1980s. First, the transition from autocratic rule to some form of democracy in numerous countries, beginning in South America but extending the Eastern Europe and parts of Africa, Central America, and Asia, has caused new governments to devise strategies for coming to terms with the human rights abuses of prior regimes and, in some cases, guerrilla opposition groups. In most cases, where societies have decided to seek accountability, they have charted their own course under domestic law, creating mechanisms tailored to their individual circumstances. This pattern has led to criminal trials, truth commissions, and other methods — although impunity through *de jure* or *de facto* amnesties remains the policy in many states. In two cases, El Salvador and Guatemala, the peace accords ending the conflict itself provided for an international truth commission. Whether or not these developments suggest the emergence of a duty on states to hold human rights abusers accountable, they clearly highlight the increasing acceptance by states of the need for such a reckoning and the diverse range of mechanisms available.

Secondly, the horrendous atrocities committed in the former Yugoslavia and Rwanda in the early and mid-1990s goaded many governments, prompted by the United States, to seek criminal accountability for them through the creation of two international tribunals. The former situation has concerned primarily violations of international humanitarian law, the latter crimes outside armed conflict. And both have entailed significant atrocities by persons not traditionally regarded as governmental agents. . . .

[D]etermining the extent to which international law recognizes individual responsibility necessitates an inquiry that takes account of the law's need both to elaborate the crime and to prescribe the role for states. This process requires examining three subsidiary issues that in essence correspond to different strategies for providing international criminal responsibility. First, to what extent does international law *directly provide for judicial (or other) culpability*? Secondly, to what extent does international law *obligate* some or all states or the global community at large to try and punish, or otherwise sanction, offenders? And thirdly, to what extent does international law *authorize* these same actors to try and punish, or otherwise sanction, offenders?

[After a discussion of substantive international criminal law, the authors go on to consider the broader context in which state policies on criminal law are determined.]

Although arguments based on legal duties in treaties or custom should and do influence decision-makers, they hardly determine the policies of states and international organizations regarding accountability, criminal or otherwise. Ultimately, their responses to various atrocities will rely principally on independent moral, social, and political considerations. As an initial matter, international actors contemplating holding individuals accountable must explicitly consider the *purpose* behind such a policy. Ideally, accountability following serious violations of international human rights and humanitarian law may serve a number of goals [such as providing closure and justice for victims, promoting national reconciliation, deterrence, rehabilitation of offenders, retribution, and "serving as a righteous expression of moral condemnation of heinous offenses." Societies must then determine the priorities to give to these goals and how to achieve them.] . . .

First, and most basically, governments and non-governmental actors will need to assess the advantages and disadvantages of criminal vs. non-criminal forms of accountability. In this context, various parties will claim, for example, that trials will lead to instability or cannot be undertaken with proper regard for due process, and that nonprosecutorial mechanisms may actually promote human rights more effectively. Claims that accountability will undermine the political order must always be regarded with some skepticism, as those in power are clearly capable of exaggerating such threats for selfish ends. Claims that trials will be undertaken without regard for due process need to be taken more seriously because of the importance or respecting the human rights of the targets of investigations. Accountability cannot be isolated from a political dynamic in which competing factions within states seek to manipulate the past in order to justify both their prior activities and current programs. Moreover, in the context of ethnic-based strife, criminal trials might provide some closure for victims, but fail to promote any long-term reconciliation for the society of the perpetrators' community believes its concerns were ignored.

Secondly, if trials are determined as useful to advance the relevant goals for the society, decision-makers have increasingly confronted the question of whether these trials should be held through the domestic judiciary or in an international or foreign courtroom. Trials closest to the affected society, victim, perpetrators, and evidence clearly advance the purposes of accountability best. Yet . . . the unwillingness of some governments to prosecute, the inadequacies of domestic judicial systems, and the desire by some powerful states to remove trials from national courts have led to the creation of various international criminal tribunals. The extent to which actors outside an affected society should defer to that society's decisions and standards of justice remains highly problematic.

Thirdly, and intertwined with the other considerations, the affected society, perhaps in conjunction with international actors, will need to make a determination regarding the number of targets involved in any accountability process. For some human rights abuses, the number of perpetrators may be small; for mass atrocities, whether committed over many years (South Africa) or in just a few weeks (Rwanda), the numbers of people may be in the hundreds of thousands. In the latter cases, both the desirability and feasibility of mass criminal trials seems highly questionable.

As noted by Ratner and Abrams, political developments in the 1980s and 1990s made possible more serious consideration of expanding the scope of international criminal law, which had progressed little in preceding decades, despite the efforts of NGOs such as the International Association of Penal Law and its President, M. Cherif Bassiouni. See, e.g., M. Cherif Bassiouni, *International Criminal Law: A Draft International Criminal Code* (1980); id., *International Criminal Law* (1986); and id., *A Draft International Criminal Code and Draft Statute for an International Criminal Court* (1987).

A. *The Yugoslav War Crimes Tribunal*

The Security Council failed to establish an Iraqi War Crimes Tribunal after the 1991 Gulf War, and efforts by the UN's International Law Commission to draft a statute for an international criminal court were proceeding at a snail's pace. By 1992, however, the situation in the former Yugoslavia, especially in Bosnia and Herzegovina, had produced a strong demand within and outside the United Nations for the creation of a Yugoslav war crimes tribunal to hold criminally responsible those persons involved in "ethnic cleansing," war crimes, and numerous other human rights violations. As Professor Meron persuasively argued,

> [r]eaffirming the Nuremberg tenets and the principle of accountability should deter those in Yugoslavia and elsewhere who envisage "final solutions" to their conflicts with ethnic and religious minorities. A war crimes tribunal could also educate the general public not to accept egregious violations of human rights and humanitarian norms. Above all, there is a moral imperative to rigorously prosecute the offenders, given the deliberate, systematic and outrageous nature of the violations in the former Yugoslavia.

Theodor Meron, *The Case for War Crimes Trials in Yugoslavia*, 72 Foreign Aff. 122 (1993). How what became known as the International Tribunal for the Former Yugoslavia (ICTY) was established, the international crimes over which it has jurisdiction, and the rules of procedure and evidence that guide its operations are described and explained in the extract that follows.

Diane Orentlicher, *Yugoslavia War Crimes Tribunal*

ASIL Focus 1-4 (No. 1, 1993)

While the IT's [International Tribunal's] work is firmly anchored in the law of Nuremberg, the decision establishing the Tribunal raises novel questions of international law, and the IT itself will consider a raft of complex legal issues. But the most significant challenges will be eminently pragmatic. How, with a three-sided war still underway in Bosnia-Herzegovina, can the prosecution gather sufficient evidence to convict those responsible for war-related atrocities? Will the prosecution be able to persuade survivors of rape, a war crime committed on a massive scale during the conflict, to testify? Above all, will the Tribunal be able to arrest those who bear primary responsibility for crimes committed during the conflict? Ultimately, the credibility and effectiveness of the Tribunal will turn on its success in addressing these challenges.

Security Council Action

On May 25, 1993 the Security Council unanimously adopted Resolution 827. Acting under Chapter VII of the UN Charter, the Council decided "to establish an international tribunal for the sole purpose of prosecuting persons responsible for serious violations of international humanitarian law committed in the territory of the former Yugoslavia between 1 January 1991 and a date to be determined by the Security Council upon the restoration of peace...," and also adopted the Statute of the Tribunal.

Earlier resolutions had laid the foundation for this historic step. The Security Council had, for example, repeatedly reaffirmed that those who commit or order others to commit "grave breaches" of the Geneva Conventions of 1949 during the Balkan conflict are individually responsible for these war crimes [S.C. Res. 764 (1992)]. In October 1992, the Secretary-General announced the appointment, pursuant to a Security Council resolution, of a Commission of Experts that would document violations of humanitarian law committed in the former Yugoslavia [S.C. Res. 780 (1992)].

Then, in Resolution 808 of February 22, 1993, the Council decided that an international tribunal should be established "for the prosecution of persons responsible for serious violations of international humanitarian law committed in the territory of the former Yugoslavia since 1991."...

Legal Basis of Tribunal

The first substantial issue raised by Resolution 808 was whether the ad hoc tribunal should be established by treaty or, instead, through a Security Council resolution. Following the recommendation of the Secretary General, the Security Council established the IT as an enforcement measure under Chapter VII of the UN Charter. As such, the decision had to be (and was) predicated on a Security Council determination that the situation giving rise to its action constituted a threat to the peace, breach of the peace, or an act of aggression.

Although the Council had previously determined that the situation in the former Yugoslavia constitutes a threat to international peace and security, its decision to establish a tribunal under Chapter VII was not without controversy. Some States, including China, feared that this represented an unwarranted intrusion on sovereignty. Others, such as Brazil, suggested that the establishment of an international tribunal might exceed the Security Council's competence, and took pains to insist that Resolution 827 and the Statute for the IT "are... not meant to establish new norms or precedents of international law," a "legislative" act thought to be beyond the Council's competence. Instead, the IT would only apply "existing norms of international humanitarian law."...

The Secretary-General's report to the Security Council makes clear that, whatever theoretical issues the Security Council's action might raise, the decision was driven by pragmatic concerns. Noting that an international tribunal would ordinarily be established by treaty, the Secretary-General observed that this approach would require "considerable time," and "there could be no guarantee that ratifications will be received from those States which should be parties to the treaty if it is to be truly effective."

The most significant consequence of the Security Council's approach will likewise be practical: Member States of the United Nations are legally required to comply with the decision establishing the IT. (This, of course, is a key reason why some countries thought establishment of the IT by any route other than treaty an undue infringement on sovereignty.) This obligation may prove to be critical in addressing one of the most daunting challenges that the prosecution will face — obtaining jurisdiction over indicted suspects. Among the obligations that the IT Statute imposes on Member States is a duty to comply with any orders of the Tribunal relating to the arrest or detention of persons. That obligation may help assure, at the very least, that suspected war criminals effectively become prisoners in their own countries, lest they risk arrest abroad. In this respect, the Security Council's action may help mitigate the risk that the IT will appear ineffectual by virtue of its inability to obtain personal jurisdiction over key defendants.

Jurisdiction Ratione Materiae

Nowhere is the IT's debt to Nuremberg more apparent than in the statutory provisions establishing the Tribunal's subject matter jurisdiction. Each of the crimes subject to the IT's jurisdiction was encompassed in the jurisdictional provisions of the Nuremberg and Tokyo tribunals, although in several respects the Statute of the IT reflects contemporary definitions of those crimes. (The most controversial crime subject to the jurisdiction of the IMT — crimes against peace — has no analogue in the IT Statute.)

[The author goes on to summarize the substantive law of the tribunal, which extends to violations of humanitarian law, including war crimes; crimes against humanity; and genocide.]

Jurisdiction Ratione Personae

Consistent with the Nuremberg principles, the Statute of the IT assures that those who have ordered or instigated crimes, or who knew or had reason to know about crimes by subordinates and failed to take necessary and reasonable steps to prevent or punish them, are criminally liable. The Statute also incorporates the Nuremberg principle that a person generally is not relieved of criminal responsibility for a crime because it was committed pursuant to superior orders, though such orders can be considered in mitigation of punishment. In these and other respects, the Statute reaffirms the principle of individual responsibility — the bedrock concept underlying international criminal law.

One respect in which the Statute of the IT departs from the Nuremberg precedent is its provision for jurisdiction over natural persons only. The Nuremberg Charter, in contrast, provided that membership in certain criminal organizations, such as the SS, could be considered criminal.

Challenges

Other advances since Nuremberg include the IT Statute's provision that no defendant may be tried in absentia, and the fact that available penalties do not include the death penalty. In contrast, the IMT sentenced Martin Bormann to death in absentia.

But for all its improvements over Nuremberg, the circumstances of the IT's creation imperil its effective operation. While the Nuremberg trial was widely faulted as "victors' justice," the circumstances of that prosecution assured that individuals bearing substantial responsibility for Nazi crimes could be arrested and brought to trial. In striking contrast, those who are most responsible for war crimes committed in the former Yugoslavia may insist on impunity as a condition for ending the war. Even if the UN resists the temptation to capitulate to such demands, it will be hard-pressed to obtain personal jurisdiction over those individuals.

Prosecutions before the IT will also face substantial evidentiary challenges. . . .

Conclusion

Resolution 827 represents an historic step, a watershed in international law and policy. If successful, the Tribunal that it authorizes will add new impetus to long-standing proposals for a permanent international criminal court. Perhaps of more lasting consequence, the work of the Tribunal will reaffirm a principle that has been deeply compromised by the unchecked sweep of "ethnic cleansing" in the former Yugoslavia: there can be no impunity for crimes against humanity.

The International Criminal Tribunal for the former Yugoslavia (ICTY) had a somewhat rocky start, and the war in Bosnia and Herzegovina continued for another two and one-half years after the Security Council voted the tribunal into being. Its existence did not prevent the massacre of approximately 7,000 men and boys in Srebrenica in July 1995, nor did it deter Serbian forces from violating the laws of war when conflict broke out in the province of Kosovo in 1998-1999. Ten of the persons indicted by the tribunal remain at large, including the former leader of the Serbs in Bosnia, Radovan Karadzic, and the person allegedly responsible for the Srebrenica massacre, Ratko Mladic.

Nevertheless, most observers would conclude that, after more than a decade, the ICTY has been reasonably successful. As of July 2005, 162 individuals had been indicted by the tribunal, 126 of whom appeared in proceedings; 21 indictments were withdrawn. Among the 42 persons whose proceedings have been completed, 37 were convicted and given sentences ranging from three to 40 years; five persons were found not guilty. Fifty-five accused, including the former president of Yugoslavia, Slobodan Milosevic,[1] are in custody either awaiting or on trial. Many of the trials have been lengthy, and the ICTY expended nearly $1 billion between 1994 and 2005 and eventually grew to a staff of over 1,000. The ICTY's judgments have set new precedents in a number of important respects, including the first convictions for the crime of genocide and affirmation that systematic rape is a crime against humanity; they and other information may be found on the Tribunal's website, *http://www.un.org/icty*, from which the statistics in this paragraph were taken.

1. Milosevic died in custody in the Hague on March 12, 2006. — Eds.

B. *The International Tribunal for Rwanda*

The massacre of perhaps 800,000 people that took place in Rwanda in 1994 also spurred calls for international trials of the perpetrators; these calls were all the more irresistible, given the establishment of the ICTY only a year earlier to address massacres in Europe. (Chapter 10 discusses the Rwandan situation in greater detail, pages 838.) The Security Council responded by creating a second ad hoc tribunal, the International Criminal Tribunal for the Prosecution of Persons Responsible for Genocide and Other Serious Violations of International Humanitarian Law Committed in the Territory of Rwanda and Rwandan Citizens Responsible for Genocide and Other Such Violations Committed in the Territory of Neighbouring States Between 1 January and 31 December 1994 (ICTR). S.C. Res. 955 (Nov. 8, 1994). While most of the provisions in the Tribunal's 32-article Statute are taken in haec verba from the Statute of the Yugoslav War Crimes Tribunal, and the ICTY Prosecutor initially served as Prosecutor for the ICTR, the ICTR is an independent body based in Arusha, Tanzania.

While there was an "armed conflict" when the Rwandan genocide was occurring, most of the crimes prosecuted by the ICTR had nothing to do with the battles between Rwandan government forces and the Tutsi-led Rwandan Patriotic Front. Thus, the ICTR is somewhat more of a "human rights" tribunal, as opposed to a mechanism to enforce the international humanitarian law discussed in Chapter 4.

Given the scale of the killings in Rwanda, it was not practicable to prosecute all those involved, even if they could have been brought to justice. The ICTR therefore concentrated its resources on trying the leaders of the genocide, and judgments delivered thus far involve the former Prime Minister (who pleaded guilty to genocide and received a sentence of life imprisonment), four ministers, one prefect, five mayors, and several others who held leadership positions during the 1994 killings. Those awaiting trial include, inter alia, eight additional ministers, one parliamentarian, and two prefects. See the Tribunal's website, *http://ictr.org*.

As of May 2005, the ICTR had handed down 19 judgements involving 25 accused; another 25 accused are on trial, and ten indictees remain at large. The ICTR has been criticized for its slow pace and high cost; the following extract identifies some of the ICTR's problems five years after its creation.

Christina M. Carroll, *An Assessment of the Role and Effectiveness of the International Criminal Tribunal for Rwanda and the Rwandan National Justice System in Dealing with the Mass Atrocities of 1994*

18 B.U. Int'l L.J. 163, 181-85 (2000) (notes omitted)

The ICTR has been criticized for not achieving its mandate swiftly enough. Although the ICTR has a multi-million dollar budget, the ICTR has completed only 4 trials, while the work on the 48 other cases is still underway. One of the reasons for the delays, however, is that the ICTR is a nascent criminal court. Creating a tribunal from the ground up is a difficult task, and thus until the ICTR becomes accustomed to its work, it will not be capable of processing cases in as efficient a manner as well-established tribunals and domestic judicial systems. Due to its infancy, the ICTR has suffered from a number of physical, legal, and procedural impediments that have led to delays.

First, the ICTR has suffered from inadequate technical resources and staff. For example, the ICTR has had difficulty staffing the Office of the Prosecutor with professionals, attorneys, and investigators fluent in both English and French. At times, only one person was responsible for the large task of coordinating appeals from the Trial Chamber to the Appeals Chamber. In addition, there are inadequate monetary resources to bring every individual involved in the 1994 atrocities to trial. The Registry, which sets the judicial calendar, and the three trial chambers are struggling to schedule trials for all the indictees newly in custody; the ICTR cannot entertain over forty complicated international humanitarian law cases simultaneously with three trial chambers....

Second, in the early stages, the ICTR suffered from allegations of corruption and mismanagement. In 1997 the United Nations Office of Internal Oversight Services investigated and reported on the mismanagement of the Tribunal.... The Oversight Report stated that "in the Tribunal's Registry not a single administrative area functioned effectively: Finance had no accounting system and could not produce allotment reports, so that neither the Registry nor United Nations Headquarters had budget expenditure information; lines of authority were not clearly defined; internal controls were weak in all sections; personnel in key positions did not have the required qualifications . . .".... Other offices have had similar, although less serious, problems with inexperienced or unqualified staff. The Oversight Report also found that delays resulted from the slow construction of the courtrooms.

Third, having no police authority of its own, the ICTR operates at the whim of other countries to produce suspects for detention and trial....

The ICTR also relies on other countries to facilitate witnesses in traveling to the ICTR to testify; delays often occur when the witnesses have difficulty obtaining the required travel documents. Trial delays have also occurred when the prosecution and defense have had difficulty locating witnesses at the time of trial or when the safety of witnesses is in jeopardy. Because the ICTR only operates a temporary detention center in Tanzania, it also relies on the cooperation of other countries for the enforcement of prison sentences.

Fourth, the ICTR judges create the procedural rules that will govern future proceedings as they go along. Under the ICTR statute, the judges are empowered to create the ICTR's rules of evidence and procedure. This is a gargantuan task that is open to criticism by those who are disadvantaged by any change in the continuously evolving rules. After the tribunal has a body of case law and rules from which to proceed, its task should become somewhat easier and more efficient.

Finally, hundreds of motions filed by both the prosecution and the defense have led to delays. Many of these motions concern the disqualification of judges. Due to the way in which the Rules of Procedure and Evidence were initially drafted, the same judges were not allowed to hear various parts of the case, such as detention, indictment, and trial, concerning the same accused. Due to the low number of judges to handle the caseload, however, some judges were assigned to hear more than one stage in a case. Thus, many cases were delayed for months because of interlocutory appeals concerning re-composition of trial chambers.

3. Legitimacy

In addition to the issue of practical impediments to the success of the ICTR are more serious questions of whether the ICTR is perceived as legitimate. . . . The tribunal's understandably slow initial pace may call its integrity into question if it persists for too long. Early procedural errors and delays may be leading to due process violations. For example, lengthy detentions of defendants before charges are brought or before trial may violate the right to a speedy trial. Additionally, the ICTR has made several warrantless arrests. The charges of financial corruption and incompetent management in 1997 also did not help its image. If such problems continue, the ICTR will fail to achieve accountability in a fair manner for the international community and the Rwandan people who are relying on it as a source of justice.

In addition, the ICTR will not be perceived as legitimate if it does not render justice in an even-handed and neutral manner. Under the ICTR statute, the ICTR is given the power to prosecute "persons" responsible for serious violations of international humanitarian law during 1994; thus the tribunal has the jurisdiction not only to try Hutus involved in the large massacres of Tutsis from April to July 1994, but also any Tutsis who violated international humanitarian law in 1994. The Commission of Experts, established by the United Nations in 1994 to investigate crimes in Rwanda, concluded in their report that although they were unable to uncover any evidence that Tutsis had intended to destroy the Hutu ethnic group within the meaning of the Genocide Convention of 1948, there was overwhelming evidence to prove that Tutsis has committed crimes against humanity and serious violations of international humanitarian law. The ICTR, however, has only indicted and tried Hutu individuals charged with genocide and crimes against humanity perpetrated toward Tutsis. . . .

4. Factors Outside the Control of the ICTR: Continuing Instability in the Region

Another factor that stands in the way of the ICTR's success is simply beyond the control of the tribunal. Due to the limits on its temporal jurisdiction, the ICTR has no power to prosecute individuals involved in the continuing waves of violence and human rights abuses that plague the region. . . .

The spokesman and Legal Adviser to the ICTY offered a different view a couple of years later:

Kingsley Chiedu Moghalu, *The Evolving Architecture of International Law: Image and Reality of War Crimes Justice: External Perceptions of the International Criminal Tribunal for Rwanda*

26 Fletcher F. World Aff. 21, 25-26, 27-31, 33-35, 38, 42-43 (Fall 2002)

. . . [T]he image of the ICTR has been harmed by unjustified criticism by the media, NGOs, and other interest groups. . . .

The problem of inadequate coverage of the ICTR is starkly contrasted by the far more frequent and substantive global media coverage of ICTY. More than 500 journalists from various countries were present at the ICTY to cover the opening of the trial of Slobodan Milosevic, former president of the Federal Republic of Yugoslavia, on February 12, 2002. In contrast, approximately 80 journalists were physically present at the ICTR at Arusha to cover the tribunal's verdict in the first ever judgment by an international court for the crime of genocide on September 2, 1998. This was the largest number of journalists to have covered a trial live at the tribunal.... The ICTR was also the first international criminal tribunal to convict a head of a government (Rwanda's former prime minister, Jean Kambanda) for the crime of genocide, and to bring other high-ranking political and military figures into custody. It was also the first court to hold that rape is in certain circumstances an intrinsic part of genocide and the first to convict an individual for rape as a crime against humanity. These groundbreaking decisions have established legal guideposts for national courts and other international criminal tribunals including the soon-to-be-established permanent International Criminal Court.

Political Priority and Visibility

The reasons for the comparatively inadequate publicity of the ICTR appear, at first sight, to be largely political. The governments in the capitals of North America and Europe, where the global media are mainly based, are actively involved in the pursuit of justice in the Balkans from a geographical, political, and military perspective. Their troops are involved in the North Atlantic Treaty Organization (NATO) peacekeeping and peace enforcement operations in the Balkans, and also are directly involved in the hunt for war criminals. With the politicians and the armed forces of the governments so directly involved in issues relating to ICTY, the media and public opinion in these countries naturally follow....

... The upshot of the media's unbalanced coverage of the two tribunals is the creation of a perception that the ideal of obtaining universal justice is more important in some areas of the world than others....

The visibility of the ICTR within the African continent, in terms of its coverage by African media, is also low....

The Image of the Tribunal

The image of the tribunal is now generally positive. Among those who follow its work, the ICTR is generally respected, though there are several important nuances in the way it is perceived, which must be explored. The tribunal's image also has fluctuated over different periods. In this context, the tribunal should be assessed from the perspective of two sets of important constituencies or stakeholders of its work: the geographical and the thematic. The geographical stakeholders are Rwanda, the wider African continent, and the wider international community. The thematic stakeholders consist mainly of governments, NGOs, and the media....

The International Tribunal as Seen From Rwanda

Assessing the tribunal's image from the viewpoint of geographical stakeholders, it is clear that its image is increasingly positive where it is most important — in Rwanda. Relations between the ICTR and Rwanda were rocky in the tribunal's early years. This was largely because the tribunal's Statute does not provide for the death penalty. There was also an initial perception — based on understandable impatience for justice on the part of victims and a lack of appreciation of the tribunal's procedures and characteristics as an international court that respects the highest human rights standards — that the tribunal was ineffective.

All of these perceptions in Rwanda have recently undergone a subtle, positive shift. One major reason for this shift was the tribunal's successes in apprehending the "big fish," accused persons whom most Rwandans knew were effectively beyond the reach of the domestic judicial system. Judgments in several cases, including the 1998 conviction of former Prime Minister Kambanda based on his confession to the crimes of genocide and crimes against humanity, changed the perception that the tribunal was ineffective. Another reason was the tribunal's Outreach Program, whose efforts have had an important impact: Rwandans now have a positive impression of the ICTR. . . .

There remains, however, a significant strain of skepticism about the ICTR in Rwanda. This skepticism owes itself not so much to the performance of the tribunal, but to wider policy and popular debates about the contextual relevance of international criminal justice to the societies, in which the crimes they are adjudicating occurred. . . . Many Rwandans believe that trials at the tribunal place an excessive emphasis on respect for the rights of the accused persons and not enough on those of the victims and survivors. . . .

While the relationship between the ICTR and Rwanda has generally been a good one in the past few years, it is a relationship that has some inherent frictions imbued in it for the reasons cited above and others. Recent allegations by survivors groups in Rwanda that the tribunal is mistreating Rwandan witnesses illustrate this reality. These allegations are unsubstantiated but important because of the perceptions they create. In reality, and to those with a closer knowledge of the tribunal, they reflect the clash of cultures that frequently takes place in the tribunal's courtrooms. Witnesses for the prosecution, who come predominantly from inside Rwanda and are sometimes already traumatized by the effects of the crimes in question, sometimes encounter robust cross-examination from defense attorneys. Cross-examination, a courtroom procedure typical of the "adversarial" common law system, does not exist in the "inquisitorial" civil law system that is utilized in Rwandan courts. The right of the defense to establish the possible innocence of their client or weaknesses in the prosecution's case is thus seen as "mistreatment" by a witness who may indeed have been a survivor of grave crimes. Such a witness will obviously have difficulty understanding how or why he or she could be questioned in an aggressive manner. Of course, it remains the responsibility of the presiding judge to control judicial proceedings in a manner that safeguards the dignity of witnesses and prevents the abuse of cross-examination by counsel. . . .

The Global Viewpoint

In other African countries, with the exception of a few, not much is known about the activities of the tribunal, and much of what is known is not positive because most of the media outlets there are not able or willing to make independent, original assessments of the court. . . .

The image of the tribunal in the wider international community is generally positive. However, that image is variable among thematic constituencies such as the media (some positive, others less so), NGOs (mostly negative), and governments (mixed but evolving in a more positive direction than was previously the case). The tribunal's image in academia and among professional associations is firmly positive. The reason for the tribunal's now essentially positive image, despite the absence of strong enthusiasm for it in some global media institutions and NGOs, is the sheer weight of its achievements. Its precedent-setting judgments for the crime of genocide and its success rate in apprehending high-ranking suspects are facts that cannot be overlooked by any serious observer. . . .

Lifting The Veil: Why Coverage Is Critical and Inadequate

There are a number of important reasons why the International Criminal Tribunal for Rwanda is frequently the subject of negative reporting and calculated attacks by the media, NGOs, and even by some public officials. It is necessary to understand these reasons in order to prevent baseless criticism where possible and establish a more positive image for the tribunal. It is also important to recognize the tribunal's inherent limitations in this regard.

Yesterday's News and Outdated Perceptions

First, some criticisms of the tribunal are accurate and valid. . . .
The early management crisis no longer is a major point of current criticism of the ICTR, which is largely focused on other aspects of its work. . . .

A "Slow" Pace: The Nature of International Justice, or Justice Delayed?

A third reason for the frequent critical coverage of the ICTR is a strong perception of its judicial work as being slow and unproductive relative to the resources expended on it by the international community. . . .

This criticism that the pace of justice at the tribunal is too slow, one of the most important critiques of the ICTR, reflects a crisis of expectations that international criminal justice faces in general. There is a wide gulf between what the victims and the global public expect of the ICTR and ICTY and the reality of what they can accomplish when their complex operational imperatives and difficulties — engendered by their international nature — are considered. In the case of the ICTR, the management and institutional difficulties in its early years, difficulties that are principally attributable to a lack of an adequate infrastructure at the headquarters of the tribunal when it was established, exacerbated this crisis of expectations. It is not clearly understood by the victims of the Rwandan atrocities and other observers that the ICTR was not established to prosecute the more than 100,000 individuals suspected of involvement in the genocide and who are detained in Rwandan prisons. That is a task that is the responsibility of the

Rwandan domestic judicial system. Rather, the tribunal was set up to apprehend and bring to justice the high-ranking individuals suspected of masterminding and directing the massacres. Thus, it is unlikely that the tribunal will try more than 100-150 suspects on the whole. . . .

There certainly have been many avoidable delays in the judicial work of the tribunal in the past. Yet the apparent "slow" pace of the work is due to many unavoidable factors that are built into its very complex nature as an international judicial institution, making it very different from anything to which its observers are accustomed. Trial proceedings are conducted in three languages (English, French, and Kinyarwanda). While there is simultaneous interpretation from French into English and vice versa, interpretation into and from Kinyarwanda vis-a-vis English and French is still largely consecutive and not simultaneous. This situation often triples the amount of time witness testimony takes because a significant number of witnesses testify in the Kinyarwanda language. . . . Every document involved in the judicial proceedings must be translated into English and French, the official working languages of the tribunal. Add all these complexities and more to the fact that the tribunal's Rules of Procedure and Evidence, though a hybrid, rely heavily on the time-consuming common law adversarial system, and the result is a process that has in-built guarantees for fair trials, but in-built delays as well. . . .

. . . The few numbers of trial judges (nine) relative to the numbers of detainees awaiting trial is the most important reason for the slow pace of the completion of trials.

Pride and Prejudice: World-Views and Double Standards

But the most important reason why the ICTR receives a steady stream of criticism and critical reporting is the stereotypical, biased, and long-standing negative image and neglect of the African continent in the global media. There are strong indications, judging from the admissions of some journalists in the international press, that there is more to their reporting of Africa than meets the ordinary eye. The predominantly negative reporting — and general lack of adequate coverage outside of the negative — is attributable to a mixture of ignorance, misunderstanding, and calculated editorial decision making by the editors of various global media. The ICTR is an international tribunal and a United Nations institution. It would be wrong to view it as an "African" tribunal, though it is located in Africa and the head of its management (the registrar) has since its inception been African, just as the ICTY is located in Europe and a European has always headed its management. Perhaps because of its African affiliation, the ICTR has not escaped the well-known prejudice that attaches to the continent in general. Its understandable but highly publicized problems in its start-up phase simply reinforced this more fundamental disadvantage.

Thus, the Rwandan genocide, portrayed as "tribal chaos and anarchy" in order to locate it within the prevailing stereotype of the African continent as one in perpetual crisis, was given wide global media coverage. The search for justice for the genocide by an international court sitting in Africa has not, however, attracted a fraction of that coverage. This perpetuates the worldview in which Africa does not matter. . . .

Being associated with Africa, a certain mindset is immediately triggered by such a perception. The tribunal is seen and portrayed from this perspective as necessarily beset by problems through distorted emphases in assessments of the institution even when the reality differs markedly from the perception. Such portrayals send a subliminal message: this is Africa, where nothing (supposedly) works — what else is to be expected? Conversely, the frequently hagiographic portrayal of the ICTY as a properly functioning international court sends a subconscious or calculated message: this is Europe, where things work; the massacres in the former Yugoslavia were a reprehensible aberration and their perpetrators can only be brought to efficient justice at The Hague....

VICTORS' JUSTICE?

Yet another contributing factor to the image of the ICTR is the criticism that its prosecutions are one-sided, directed against the Hutu extremists who perpetrated the genocide of the Tutsi and moderate Hutu....

The reality, however, is that in fractured societies, attempts will be made to deflect efforts to exact individual accountability with propaganda that seeks to undermine the perception of the impartiality of justice. It is, as noted above, sometimes the case that crimes within the mandate of an international tribunal may have been committed preponderantly, even if not exclusively, by individuals from specific groups, against those of another. In Rwanda, for example, the genocide, by definition, sought to exterminate the Tutsi group who were its main victims. But the ICTR also has a mandate that includes crimes against humanity and serious violations of Article 3 common to the Geneva Conventions. The prosecutor of the tribunal has publicly stated that she is investigating the possible involvement of individuals who were members of the RPA in these crimes and that indictments will be issued where there is evidence of the alleged commission of such crimes. It is a matter of future observation how this aspect of the work of the ICTR will unfold, and how it will affect the image of the tribunal and the reconciliation process in Rwanda. Initial indications are that it may become controversial — which would not be surprising — but ultimately beneficial to national reconciliation in Rwanda....

CONCLUSION

The perception of the tribunal by the global public and other constituencies is important to its ultimate success or failure. The phenomenon of impunity cannot be effectively tackled if the world, including potential perpetrators of crimes such as genocide, crimes against humanity, and war crimes, either does not know what the ICTR is doing or does not have a positive perception of its work. Without political support by states and other constituencies, no international criminal tribunal can succeed at its task. This fact is a product of the very nature of these institutions. The tribunal has made significant progress in this sphere of its work. But more remains to be done to overcome the serious and inherent limitations it faces.

The fundamental questions to ask regarding the ICTR are: why was the tribunal established? If the tribunal had not been established, would the domestic courts of Rwanda have been able to bring the high-ranking perpetrators of the violations of humanitarian law in that country to justice? The obvious answer to the latter question is in the negative. The ICTR is in the process of accomplishing this goal for which Rwandan courts were ill equipped due to a lack of capacity, while the courts of other states were also ill equipped due to lack of jurisdiction or political will. It must be concluded that the ICTR is succeeding in its historic task, even if imperfectly, by reason of its pioneering nature. . . .

Neither the ICTY nor ICTR has completed its work, although both are scheduled to do so by 2010. See S.C. Res. 1503 (Aug. 28, 2003). However, many of the positive and negative aspects of the tribunals' work are likely to be reflected in the early work of the International Criminal Court as well.

C. *Other Country-specific Tribunals*

Criminal tribunals with at least some formal element of international involvement have been created in East Timor, Bosnia and Herzegovina, Kosovo, Cambodia, and Sierra Leone. See generally *Internationalized Criminal Courts and Tribunals: Sierra Leone, East Timor, Kosovo, and Cambodia* (Cesare P.R. Romano, Andre Nollkaemper, and Jann K. Kleffner eds., 2004). In some cases, this involvement is simply the appointment of a number of "international" judges to serve on what are otherwise national courts, as is the case in Bosnia and Herzegovina. In the two cases discussed below, international involvement has been more substantial.

Note: The Special Court for Sierra Leone

It is estimated that, over the course of Sierra Leone's long, brutal conflict, 75,000 people, mostly noncombatants, were killed. The fighting began in March 1991, as the Revolutionary United Front (RUF), headed by Foday Sankoh, led an insurgency ostensibly designed to overthrow the government of Sierra Leone, but also to gain control of the country's diamond mines and other mineral resources. Charles Taylor, then president of Liberia and head of the National Patriotic Front of Liberia (NPFL), provided arms and training to the RUF in exchange for diamonds, the proceeds of which helped to fuel Taylor's own conflict in Liberia. The fighting caused massive displacement of civilians, and it was estimated that more than a quarter of Sierra Leone's population fled their homes in the course of the conflict. Human Rights Watch, *Bringing Justice: The Special Court for Sierra Leone* (Sept. 2004).

In May 1997, the Armed Forces of Sierra Leone seized power from the elected government of Sierra Leone through a coup d'état, thereafter forming the Armed Forces Revolutionary Council (AFRC), headed by Johnny Paul Koroma, which then fought alongside the rebel RUF forces. In defense of the government, the Civil Defense Force (CDF), composed of loose groups of traditional hunters and led by Sam Hinga Norman, rose up to fight on behalf of the state against the RUF and the AFRC. The Lomé Peace Accords of July 7, 1999, between Foday Sankoh and Ahmed Tejan Kabbah, president of the Republic of Sierra Leone, temporarily ended the conflict, although fighting soon broke out again and continued for another two years.

Once peace was finally restored, Sierra Leone requested assistance from the United Nations to try those responsible for the most egregious crimes committed during the war. The result was creation of the Special Court for Sierra Leone, Agreement between the Government of Sierra Leone and the United Nations on the Establishment of a Special Court for Sierra Leone (Jan. 16, 2002), *http://scsl.org/scsl-agreement.html*. The Special Court was created as an alternative to the Sierra Leone judicial system, which lacked the capacity to prosecute all of those accused of crimes during the decade-long conflict. In addition, the judiciary was held in low regard by the population, which saw it as politicized and corrupt. The Special Court, a stand-alone institution, was given primacy over the domestic court system, following the precedents of the ICTY and ICTR.

The Special Court was intended to incorporate lessons learned from the ICTY and ICTR experiences. In order to keep costs down and to speed up the process of obtaining justice, the Special Court was given only a three-year mandate. The jurisdiction of the Special Court was limited to crimes committed after November 1996, since an amnesty covered crimes prior to that date. While choosing to respect the amnesty lessened the Court's caseload, it also excluded more than half the period of the civil war.

Article 1 of the Special Court's Statute limits the Court's jurisdiction to those who "bear the greatest responsibility" for atrocities perpetrated in the war. Recognizing the impracticality of identifying and trying each individual accused of atrocities, only the most senior leaders of the various armed groups were to be indicted by the Special Court; the majority of the population would have to seek some measure of resolution through a Truth and Reconciliation Commission (TRC), which operated parallel to the Special Court. In this hybrid arrangement, the Special Court has the power to prosecute, while the TRC is a fact-finding body. To this end, the TRC heard testimony and published a report in November 2004 upon the conclusion of its investigation. (See Chapter 12.)

Unlike the ICTR and the ICTY, cooperation with the Special Court was not mandated by the Security Council under Chapter VII of the UN Charter. Thus, the Court remained dependent on the goodwill of other states to cooperate with its requests, including the service of warrants and the search, arrest, and surrender of suspects.

Thirteen people have been indicted by the Special Court, nine of whom are in custody and either on trial or awaiting trial. Foday Sankoh, Sam Bockarie (a senior leader of the RUF), and Johnny Paul Koroma (leader of the AFRC) were indicted, but Sankoh and Bockarie died before their cases could begin; Koroma's whereabouts are unknown, and he also may be dead.

On March 3, 2003, Charles Taylor, the former president of Liberia, was indicted by the Special Court on 17 counts of crimes against humanity and other serious violations of international humanitarian law. The indictment cites Taylor's relationship with Foday Sankoh, head of the RUF, and asserts that Taylor manipulated the domestic upheaval in Sierra Leone in order to secure access to Sierra Leone's diamond mines. Among the numerous violations of Common Article 3 of the Geneva Conventions with which the indictment charges Taylor are unlawful killings, collective punishments, sexual violence, the use of child soldiers, abductions and forced labor, looting and burning, and attacks on UNAMSIL personnel [UN peacekeepers].

In May 2004, the Appeals Chamber of the Special Court rejected the argument made by Taylor's lawyers that he was protected by sovereign immunity, since he was a sitting head of state at the time that the indictment was issued. However, Taylor remains at large in Nigeria, which granted him asylum after he was forced from power in Liberia in late 2003. Nigeria has thus far refused to surrender Taylor to the Special Court, claiming that granting him asylum is necessary for continued peace in Liberia. In November 2005, however, a Nigerian court held that Taylor was liable to be sued for damages by his alleged victims from Liberia.

Note: "Extraordinary Chambers" in Cambodia

During the time of Khmer Rouge rule under Pol Pot from 1975 to 1979, it is estimated that between 1.5 and two million people, out of a population of perhaps seven million, were killed. The Cambodian "killing fields" were subsequently widely documented in, e.g., Elizabeth Becker, *When the War Was Over: The Voices of Cambodia's Revolution and Its People* (1986); Nayan Chanda, *Brother Enemy: The War After the* War (1986); David P. Chandler, *Voices from S-21: Terror and History in Pol Pot's Secret Prison* (1999); *Genocide in Cambodia: Documents from the Trial of Pol Pot and Ieng Sary* (Howard J. De Nike et al. eds, 2000); Ben Kiernan, *The Pol Pot Regime* (1996); Haing Ngor, *A Cambodian Odyssey* (1987); François Ponchaud, *Cambodia: Year Zero* (1978); Ratner and Abrams, supra page 892, at 267-83 (from which this brief historical summary is partially drawn). Although there was disagreement over whether or not the Khmer Rouge committed genocide, there was little doubt by the mid-1980s that massive killings had occurred. (For arguments in favor of bringing a case against Cambodia under Article 9 of the Genocide Convention, see Hurst Hannum, *Genocide in Cambodia: The Sounds of Silence*, 11 Hum. Rts. Q. 82 (1989). For a contrary view, see, e.g., Ratner and Abrams, supra page 892, at 284-88.)

Cold War politics made it impossible to deal with the crimes of the Khmer Rouge at the time; the communist bloc supported the Vietnamese-installed regime of Hun Sen, which took power after the Vietnamese routed the Khmer Rouge in 1979, while the West supported an unlikely government-in-exile coalition, which included the Khmer Rouge. The 1991 Paris Agreements, which ended the Vietnamese occupation and led to elections in May 1993, included no provision regarding accountability, with the exception of oblique references to the "non-return to the policies and practices of the past." (For the texts, see Letter dated 30 October 1991 from the Permanent Representatives of France and Indonesia to the United Nations addressed to the Secretary-General, UN Doc. A/46/608-S/23177, Annex (Oct. 30, 1991).)

The new government (still headed by Hun Sen a decade later) outlawed the Khmer Rouge in 1994, and a combination of defections and the reintegration of former Khmer Rouge fighters into the Cambodian army effectively neutralized the Khmer Rouge by the mid-1990s. An amnesty was granted to the number two person in the Khmer Rouge, Ieng Sary, in 1996; Pol Pot died of natural causes in 1998.

The United Nations began pressing for some form of accountability for Khmer Rouge atrocities in the late 1990s, and the Secretary-General's Special Representative for Human Rights in Cambodia persuaded the Cambodian government in 1997 to request the United Nations to assist it in bringing members of the Khmer Rouge to justice. This position was rejected the following year by Hun Sen, who returned to power following a coup in 1997 and tainted elections in 1998. Following sustained pressure from the international community and at least a portion of civil society within Cambodia, however, the government finally agreed in June 2003 to create a mixed tribunal, formally designated as "Extraordinary Chambers" and created under Cambodian law. The draft agreement is annexed to G.A. Res. 57/228B (May 22, 2003).

The Extraordinary Chambers are composed of Cambodian and "international" judges, the latter nominated by the UN Secretary-General; Cambodian judges form a majority of both the trial and appellate chambers, but at least one of the international judges must join in any decision. There are co-investigating judges and co-prosecutors, one Cambodian and one international. The substantive jurisdiction of the Chambers extends to genocide (as defined in the 1948 Genocide Convention), crimes against humanity (as defined in the ICC Statute), grave breaches of the 1949 Geneva Conventions, and other crimes as defined in the 2001 Cambodian law that created the Chambers.

It was not until May 2005 that the United Nations announced that it had received sufficient financial pledges from states to enable the Chambers to begin their work. See John Aglionby, *Khmer Rouge to Face UN Tribunal*, The Guardian (May 2, 2005). The agreement remains controversial, and many remain skeptical that the tribunal will ever function effectively; it appears unlikely that any more than a dozen (if that many) former Khmer Rouge officials will be prosecuted.

Comments and Questions

1. Among many books and articles discussing the jurisprudence and practice of the ICTY, see Hirad Abtahi, *The Protection of Cultural Property in Times of Armed Conflict: The Practice of the International Criminal Tribunal for the Former Yugoslavia*, 14 Harv. Hum. Rts. J. 1 (2001); Christin B. Coan, *Rethinking the Spoils of War: Prosecuting Rape as a War Crime in the International Criminal Tribunal for the Former Yugoslavia*, 26 N.C.J. Int'l L. & Com. Reg. 183 (2000); Melissa J. Epstein, *The Customary Origins and Elements of Select Conduct of Hostilities Charges Before the International Criminal Tribunal for the Former Yugoslavia: A Potential Model for Use by Military Commissions*, 179 Mil. L. Rev. 68 (2004); Pierre Hazan, *Justice in a Time of War: The True Story Behind the International Criminal Tribunal for the Former Yugoslavia* (2004); Rachel Kerr, *International Criminal Tribunal for the Former Yugoslavia: An Exercise in*

Law, Politics, and Diplomacy (2004); Christopher Scott Maravilla, *Rape as a War Crime: The Implications of the International Criminal Tribunal for the Former Yugoslavia's Decision in* Prosecutor v. Kunarac, Kovac, & Vukovic *on International Humanitarian Law*, 13 Fla. J. Int'l L. 321 (2001); Gabrielle Kirk McDonald, *Reflections on the Contributions of the International Criminal Tribunal for the Former Yugoslavia*, 24 Hastings Int'l & Comp. L. Rev. 155 (2001); James McHenry, *Justice for Foca: The International Criminal Tribunal for Yugoslavia's Prosecution of Rape and Enslavement as Crimes against Humanity*, 10 Tulsa J. Comp. & Int'l L. 183 (2002); Guenael Mettraux, *Crimes Against Humanity in the Jurisprudence of the International Criminal Tribunals for the Former Yugoslavia and for Rwanda*, 43 Harv. Int'l L.J. 237 (2002); William Miller, *Slobodan Milosevic's Prosecution by the International Criminal Tribunal for the Former Yugoslavia: A Harbinger of Things to Come for International Criminal Justice*, 22 Loy. L.A. Int'l & Comp. L. Rev. 553 (2000); Virginia Morris and Michael P. Scharf, *Insider's Guide to the International Criminal Tribunal for the Former Yugoslavia: A Documentary History and Analysis* (1995); William A. Schabas, *Was Genocide Committed in Bosnia and Herzegovina? First Judgments of the International Criminal Tribunal for the Former Yugoslavia*, 25 Fordham Int'l L.J. 23 (2001); Michael P. Scharf, *The Tools for Enforcing International Criminal Justice in the New Millennium: Lessons from the Yugoslavia Tribunal*, 49 DePaul L. Rev. 925 (2000); Symposium: *The ICTY at Ten: A Critical Assessment of the Major Rulings of the International Criminal Tribunal over the Past Decade*, 37 New Eng. L. Rev. (Summer 2003); David Tolbert, *The International Criminal Tribunal for the Former Yugoslavia: Unforeseen Successes and Foreseeable Shortcomings*, 26 Fletcher F. World Aff. 7 (Fall 2002); Patricia M. Wald, *To "Establish Incredible Events by Credible Evidence": The Use of Affidavit Testimony in Yugoslavia War Crimes Tribunal Proceedings*, 42 Harv. Int'l L.J. 535 (2001); id., *The International Criminal Tribunal for the Former Yugoslavia Comes of Age: Some Observations on Day-to-Day Dilemmas of an International Court*, 5 Wash. U. J.L. & Pol'y 87 (2001); Paul R. Williams and Patricia Taft, *The Role of Justice in the Former Yugoslavia: Antidote or Placebo for Coercive Appeasement?* 35 Case W. Res. J. Int'l L. 219 (2003); Richard Ashby Wilson, *Judging History: The Historical Record of the International Criminal Tribunal for the Former Yugoslavia*, 27 Hum. Rts. Q. 908 (2005).

On the ICTR, see Christina M. Carroll, *An Assessment of the Role and Effectiveness of the International Criminal Tribunal for Rwanda and the Rwandan National Justice System in Dealing with the Mass Atrocities of 1994*, 18 B.U. Int'l L. J. 163 (2000); Mark A. Drumbl, *Law and Atrocity: Settling Accounts in Rwanda*, 31 Ohio N.U.L. Rev. 41 (2005); Alexandra A. Miller, *From the International Criminal Tribunal for Rwanda to the International Criminal Court: Expanding the Definition of Genocide to Include Rape*, 108 Penn St. L. Rev. 349 (2003); Kingsley Cheidu Moghalu, *International Humanitarian Law from Nuremberg to Rome: The Weighty Precedents of the International Criminal Tribunal for Rwanda*, 14 Pace Int'l L. Rev. 273 (2002) id., *Rwanda's Genocide: The Politics of Global Justice* (2005); Alex Obote Odora, *Prosecution of War Crimes by the International Criminal Tribunal for Rwanda*, 10 U. Miami Int'l & Comp. L. Rev. 43 (2001); William A. Schabas, *Hate Speech in Rwanda: The Road to Genocide*, 46 McGill L.J. 141 (2000); Stephanie K. Wood, *A Woman Scorned for the "Least Condemned" War Crime: Precedent and Problems with Prosecuting Rape as a Serious War Crime in the International Criminal Tribunal for Rwanda*, 13 Colum. J. Gender & L. 274 (2004).

On Sierra Leone, see Michael A. Corriero, *The Involvement and Protection of Children in Truth and Justice-Seeking Processes: The Special Court for Sierra Leone*, 18 Y.Y.L. Sch. J. Hum. Rts. 337 (2002); Shana Eaton, *Sierra Leone: The Proving Ground for Prosecuting Rape as a War Crime*, 35 Gdo. J. Int'l L. 873 (2004); Elizabeth M. Evenson, *Truth and Justice in Sierra Leone: Coordination between Commission and Court*, 104 Colum. L. Rev. 730 (2004); Human Rights Watch, *Bringing Justice: the Special Court for Sierra Leone, Accomplishments, Shortcomings, and Needed Support* (Sept. 2004, vol. 16, No. 8(A)); International Center for Transitional Justice, *The Special Court for Sierra Leone: The First Eighteen Months* (March 2004); Laurence Juma, *The Human Rights Approach to Peace in Sierra Leone: The Analysis of the Peace Process and Human Rights Enforcement in a Civil War Situation*, 30 Denv. J. Int'l L. & Pol'y 325 (2002); Michael O'Flaherty, *Sierra Leone's Peace Process: The Role of the Human Rights Community*, 26 Hum. Rts. Q. 29 (2004); Joshua A. Romero, *The Special Court for Sierra Leone and the Juvenile Solider Dilemma*, 2 Nw. UK. J. Int'l Hum. Rts. 8 (2004); William A. Schabas, *The Relationship between Truth Commissions and International Courts: The Case of Sierra Leone*, 25 Human Rights Q. 1035 (2003); Nancy Kaymar Stafford, A *Model War Crimes Court: Sierra Leone*. 10 ILSA J Int'l & Comp L 117 (2003); Nsongurua J. Udombana, *Globalization of Justice and the Special Court for Sierra Leone's War Crimes*, 17 Emory Int'l L. Rev. 55 (2003).

On prosecutions in Cambodia, see Amnesty International, *Amnesty International's position and concerns regarding the proposed "Khmer Rouge" tribunal* (April 2003, AI Index: ASA 23/005/2003); Daniel Kemper Donovan, *Joint U.N.-Cambodia Efforts to Establish a Khmer Rouge Tribunal*, 44 Harv. Int'l L.J. 551 (2003); Human Rights Watch, *Serious Flaws: Why the U.N. General Assembly Should Require Changes to the Draft Khmer Rouge Tribunal Agreement* (April 2003); Scott Luftglass, *Crossroads in Cambodia: The United Nations' Responsibility to Withdraw Involvement from the Establishment of a Cambodian Tribunal to Prosecute the Khmer Rouge*, 90 Va. L. Rev. 893 (2004); Ratner and Abrams, supra page 892, at 265-328; Steven R. Ratner, *The Cambodia Settlement Agreements*, 87 Am. J. Int'l L. 1 (1993).

2. Creation of the ICTY was preceded by a five-member Commission of Experts, chaired by Professor Bassiouni, that was created to gather evidence of grave breaches of the Geneva Conventions and other violations of international humanitarian law in the territory of the former Yugoslavia. See Final Report of the Commission of Experts Established Pursuant to Security Council Resolution 780 (Oct. 6, 1992), U.N. Doc. S/1994/674 Annex (May 27, 1994). The Final Report concludes by noting, "Establishing the truth is the best method of enhancing deterrence. In fact, early investigation of the facts, in any context of criminal activity, increases the effectiveness of future prosecution. The combination of investigation and prosecution makes deterrence more effective, thereby reducing possible violations in the future. Without effective investigations and prosecutions, the converse is true." Id. at 84. Do you think that war crimes and crimes against humanity have decreased since creation of the ICTY in 1995? Since creation of the International Criminal Court, discussed in the next section, in 2002?

IV. The International Criminal Court

On July 17, 1998, 120 states signed the Statute of the International Criminal Court (ICC), at the conclusion of the UN Diplomatic Conference of Plenipotentiaries convened in Rome to create the court. To the surprise of some, ratifications of the Statute followed relatively quickly, and it entered into force on July 1, 2002. As of mid-2005, there were approximately 100 parties to the Statute.

The following extract was co-authored by Canadian diplomat Philippe Kirsch, who chaired the Rome Conference and became the first President of the Court. It briefly describes the background to the Rome Conference and outlines the basic provisions of the ICC Statute.

Philippe Kirsch and Valerie Oosterveld, *Negotiating an Institution for the Twenty-First Century: Multilateral Diplomacy and the International Criminal Court*

46 McGill L.J. 1141, 1143, 1145-53, 1155-58 (2001) (citations omitted)

I. The Road to Rome: Adoption of the Rome Statute

Before discussing the Rome Statute itself, it is important to reflect on the fact that it was adopted after decades of unsuccessful attempts. . . .

The cold war brought about decades of inaction on the creation of an ICC. There were several reasons for this impasse. First, many assumed that aggression would fall within the mandate of an ICC, as in the Nuremberg and Tokyo Charters. The major powers could not agree, however, on a definition of aggression, which prevented the completion of the Code of Offences Against the Peace and Security of Mankind, which in turn hindered the establishment of the jurisdictional basis of the ICC. Second, the creation of any international institution requires states to surrender a bit of sovereignty, however small, and the mutual suspicions of the major powers were not conducive to surrendering any control. Third, conflicts were often considered de facto wars between the major powers. Allowing an international court to try crimes committed during any of these conflicts was seen as trying the major powers themselves. There was, therefore, no support for restarting the discussion to create an ICC.

Trinidad and Tobago returned the issue of establishing an ICC to the international stage in 1989. By that time, the end of the cold war had changed the situation. Trinidad and Tobago requested the study of the idea of an ICC, but with a view to trying drug traffickers. The General Assembly requested that the ILC [International Law Commission] consider the issue, and in 1992 the ILC requested and received the mandate to elaborate a draft ICC statute from the General Assembly.

In 1993 the United Nations Security Council established an ad hoc tribunal to try those who had committed breaches of international humanitarian law in the Former Yugoslavia. One year later a similar tribunal was also established to deal with crimes committed in Rwanda. The creation of the International Criminal Tribunals for the Former Yugoslavia and Rwanda ("ICTY" and "ICTR", respectively) sent a strong signal to the international community. There was some recognition that an international court was necessary, even if it had to be established on an ad hoc basis. In addition, the creation of the two tribunals gave a working model, showing that an ICC was intellectually and procedurally possible. Finally, the creation of the two tribunals also demonstrated that the political will lacking throughout the cold war was now present. This last development recognized a shift from the cold war assumption that international and domestic politics would always prevail over international law and justice.

This progress seemed to energize the discussions on the ICC within the General Assembly and the ILC. In 1994 the ILC presented a draft ICC statute to the General Assembly and recommended that "it convene an international conference of plenipotentiaries to study the draft Statute and to conclude a convention on the establishment of an International Criminal Court." The ILC Draft Statute was broader than the original proposal of Trinidad and Tobago, covering the crimes of genocide, aggression, serious violations of the laws and customs applicable in armed conflict, crimes against humanity, and treaty crimes (such as drug trafficking, apartheid, and the use of torture). While the ICC Draft Statute was positively received, many states felt preparatory work was needed before convening the Diplomatic Conference. They created an Ad Hoc Committee on the Establishment of an International Criminal Court, which met in 1995. A Preparatory Committee was subsequently established, the mandate of which was to prepare a draft text for ultimate consideration at a Diplomatic Conference. The creation of the Preparatory Committee was an important step, as it represented a change of attitude from studying the idea of an ICC in the abstract to drafting the ICC statute in reality. The Preparatory Committee met in six sessions from 1996 to 1998.

From the early 1990s to 1998, there was much international discussion of the role of ad hoc tribunals versus the role of a permanent ICC. There was broad recognition that, even when international justice worked through the establishment of ad hoc tribunals, it remained inherently selective. There are, of course, differences between the various tribunals established since World War II, but the common denominator is that their mandates have been limited to specific situations. Many crimes were committed elsewhere that required justice, but about which nothing was done. By the same token, major powers and their nationals were largely sheltered from any possibility of being subject to the jurisdiction of the ad hoc tribunals. The problem of selectivity also contributed to the perception that the Security Council should not retain exclusive control over international justice.

It is important to understand this ongoing dialogue, because it affected the eventual establishment of the ICC. Most states and commentators agreed that there was a need to put an end to the long-established culture of impunity demonstrated in too many areas of the world. They also observed that existing instruments, however effective in specific situations, must be supplemented by an institution that would better reflect the needs of the international community as a whole. This led to a momentum, sustained by an increasing number of states and civil society organizations, strong enough to make the acceptance of the creation of an ICC irresistible, even on the part of states originally not supportive of the idea.

This is not to say that the ICC received only support. There were many objections expressed between 1989 and 1998, which, interestingly, were somewhat different in tone and type than the ones expressed during the cold war. While debates on sovereignty and the crime of aggression continued much as they had developed in the 1950s to 1970s, attention turned to procedural issues. First, there was the concern that one or another kind of criminal law approach would dominate the ICC. Nationalistic pride in domestic criminal law led various countries to introduce proposals that strongly resembled their national procedures. This led to debates, as substantive and procedural criminal law rules in some countries clashed with rules in other countries. This raised the related challenge of how nations would reach consensus on issues as difficult as subject matter jurisdiction, and pretrial, trial, and appeal procedures. Second, there was concern about the cost of an ICC. While many agreed that there would be some savings in establishing an ICC as opposed to a series of ad hoc tribunals, they also feared that the cost of the ICC would be high and that the burden of paying for the ICC would not be shared fairly. Third, reservations were expressed about the establishment of yet another international institution. Though the ICTY and the ICTR had demonstrated that effective bodies could be created within the framework of the United Nations, the previous track record for creating ineffective, excessively bureaucratic bodies caused supporters to pause.

On 17 July 1998 these obstacles were overcome and the Rome Statute was adopted. One hundred and twenty states voted for the statute, seven voted against [China, Iraq, Israel, Libya, Syria, Sudan, and United States], and twenty-one abstained. The fact that the Rome Statute was adopted at all, after so many decades of failure and against considerable resistance, is a success in itself. It is a victory of the vast majority of states and of civil society organizations, who were convinced that selective justice was not enough, and that it was necessary to have an independent and permanent court, with a comprehensive mandate.

II. Provisions of the Rome Statute

While the adoption of the Rome Statute was hailed around the world, many asked whether the statute itself was a success. On the one hand, it met many fundamental objectives of the vast majority of states and civil society organizations present at the Diplomatic Conference, specifically with respect to the kinds of crimes included within the statute, the kinds of conflicts these crimes could be charged under, and the breadth of the protection of victims and witnesses. On the other hand, it also contained compromises. Some felt that certain jurisdictional provisions created loopholes that could allow war criminals to remain unprosecuted, while others felt that it contained potentially unworkable procedures or inadequate provisions.

The Rome Statute covers the major international crimes: genocide, crimes against humanity, and war crimes. These were consistently referred to as "core crimes" throughout the negotiations, as they were considered to represent the most serious crimes of concern to the international community as a whole. It was understood that inclusion of these three crimes would promote broad acceptance of the ICC by states, and thereby enhance its effectiveness, strengthening the credibility and moral authority of the Court. In addition, states argued that the magnitude, the occurrence, and the inevitable international consequences of these crimes necessitated their inclusion. The Rome Statute also deals with important humanitarian aspects that past discussions had tended to overlook. It recognizes rape, sexual slavery, and other forms of sexual violence as war crimes and crimes against humanity, and includes enlisting or using children under fifteen in any conflict as a war crime.

The Rome Statute also covers aggression, subject to an agreement on its definition and on conditions for the exercise of the ICC's jurisdiction over that crime.... Near the close of the conference, when it became clear that no broad-based agreement would be reached on the crime, the non-aligned states proposed to include the crime of aggression in the statute but to leave the elaboration of a definition to a later stage. The Court would not exercise jurisdiction over this crime until a definition was agreed upon.... [Such agreement has not yet been reached.]

A widely-praised aspect of the Rome Statute is that it covers internal armed conflicts. Many states noted before and at the Diplomatic Conference the growth of the number and intensity of internal armed conflicts, so that they represent the majority of wars in the world today. While a major motivation behind the creation of the Court was to address these conflicts, it was also the focus of tremendous resistance prior to and at the Diplomatic Conference.

Many states argued that the ICC would not operate effectively if it could not deal adequately with the experiences of all victims and witnesses. They called for a holistic approach to staffing, elections, procedures, protection, and reparations. With respect to staffing and elections, many states felt that it was important to recognize the advances in "gender mainstreaming" undertaken at the United Nations since the 1995 UN World Conference on Women in Beijing, and therefore an article providing for the "fair representation of female and male judges" was adopted. In addition, many recognized that the presence of certain expertise amongst at least some of the judges and staff would assist the Court in undertaking informed prosecutions with respect to crimes such as rape, slavery, and forced recruitment that particularly target women and children. To facilitate this, articles providing that "judges with legal expertise on specific issues, including, but not limited to, violence against women or children" should be elected to the Court and a similar direction for the staffing of the Court were included.... To complement these articles on the composition and administration of the Court, the Rome Statute includes a particularly well-developed set of provisions relating to the participation of victims and the ability of the Court to make orders against a convicted person for reparations.

In the fundamental area of jurisdiction, the Diplomatic Conference decided that there would be different ways to trigger the jurisdiction of the Court, exceeding the expectations of many participants. Proceedings can be initiated by any state party, by the Security Council, and notably, by the prosecutor of the Court. The Rome Statute provides for automatic acceptance of the Court's jurisdiction by state parties without any need to make a second decision in the context of specific situations (with the exception of article 124, discussed below). The ICC is not subordinated to the Security Council in the way that was anticipated in the draft prepared by the ILC, which would have prevented the Court from exercising jurisdiction if the Security Council dealt with a particular matter. Under the Rome Statute, the Security Council can only delay proceedings in restricted circumstances. The decision by the Security Council is limited to the possibility of delaying a proceeding, so that any veto to such a proposal, instead of blocking jurisdiction, means that the case proceeds. Also, the Rome Statute does not permit reservations, and there is no statute of limitations.

The Rome Statute did not meet all the expectations of those who wanted a strong framework. For example, certain crimes were not included, most notoriously the use of chemical or biological weapons. Certain qualifications were added to the introduction to crimes against humanity and war crimes, as well as to specific acts listed within these crimes. Certain defences were accepted that many felt did not represent the current state of international humanitarian law. The fact that aggression could not be included in the same way as other crimes created intense dissatisfaction because many consider it to be the "crime of all crimes". The many safeguards introduced throughout the Rome Statute led some to worry that the process created could slow down the Court's functions unduly or become Byzantine. Other provisions have also raised concerns for the future, such as the amendment provisions.

The most criticized provisions are probably in the area of jurisdiction included near the end of the Diplomatic Conference. Article 124, giving state parties the possibility to refuse the jurisdiction of the Court over war crimes committed on their territory or by their nationals for a period of seven years after entry into force for those states, is a case in point. Another example is the jurisdictional system generally, under which, except in cases where the Security Council refers a situation to the Court, the Court exercises jurisdiction only with the consent of the state of the nationality of the accused or the state of the territory where the crime was committed. This, it has been said, is far from the regime of universal jurisdiction many hoped for, or even a variation thereof. The two grounds of jurisdiction selected are the classical grounds in international criminal law, but this system makes it more difficult for the Court to exercise jurisdiction, particularly in situations that do not have an international element. That is, of course, until there is widespread ratification of the statute. Those criteria would then lose their importance because a majority of state parties would meet them....

IV. Post-Rome Developments: Growing Support for the ICC

The task of the Rome Diplomatic Conference was to adopt the statute of an ICC. For the Court to function properly, however, it required the preparation of a number of additional instruments, which the Diplomatic Conference clearly was not in a position to do. For this reason, the Final Act of the Rome Conference provided for the creation of a Preparatory Commission ("PrepCom") to ensure a smooth and quick operational transition once the ICC statute enters into force. The PrepCom makes recommendations for consideration and adoption by the Assembly of States Parties, which will have decision-making capacity. Once the Assembly of States Parties comes into being, the PrepCom will cease to exist....

...On 30 June 2000,...the PrepCom completed and adopted by general agreement two essential instruments: the Elements of Crimes ("EOC") and the Rules of Procedure and Evidence ("RPE"). The EOC are designed to elaborate on crimes listed in the Rome Statute for the guidance of judges. The RPE articulate the procedures of the ICC with more precision, dealing with such matters as composition and administration of the Court; investigation, trial proceedings, and appeals; penalties, co-operation of states with the Court, and enforcement of judgments; and jurisdiction, admissibility, and applicable law.

The adoption of the EOC and RPE by consensus was a remarkable achievement. This development means two things. With respect to the EOC, it reflects the fact that there is now general agreement on the crimes themselves, which was not necessarily the case at the end of the Diplomatic Conference; indeed, the PrepCom solved some problems left over after Rome, without deviating from the statute. More generally, overall consensus shows that states made extraordinary efforts to reach general agreement on difficult matters, such as the introduction to crimes against humanity and a rule concerning the request for surrender in cases requiring the consent of the sending state under an international agreement, designed to accommodate the United States. . . .

The role of "civil society" referred to by Kirsch and Oosterveld is, if anything, understated. An ad hoc global coalition of human rights and other NGOs encouraged convening the Rome Conference and participated actively in the proceedings. Some NGO representatives acted as advisers to government delegations, and there is no doubt that their influence was significant. Since the Statute was adopted, NGOs have been in the forefront of lobbying for its ratification by states (cf. the activities of the Coalition for the International Criminal Court, described on its website at *http://www.iccnow.org*).

To some observers, the idea of an international criminal tribunal seems obviously overdue and unquestionably represents an advance in the protection of the rights of individuals everywhere. To others, however, the ICC is viewed as unworkable, distracting, and potentially threatening. Consider the following debate, which occurred soon after the Statute was adopted. A.C. Grayling is professor of philosophy at Birkbeck College, University of London; David Rieff is a staff writer for the *New York Times Magazine* whose recent books include *At the Point of a Gun: Democratic Dreams and Armed Intervention* (2005); *A Bed for the Night: Humanitarianism in Crisis* (2003); and *Slaughterhouse: Bosnia and the Failure of the West* (1995).

Global Rights? [A Debate between A.C. Grayling and David Rieff]

Prospect Magazine [London] (No. 38, February 1999)
***http://www.prospect-magazine.co.uk*, at 14-17**

Dear David,

The treaty signed last summer, establishing an International Criminal Court (ICC) aimed at bringing to justice individuals responsible for "crimes against humanity," has been welcomed by almost everyone in the field of human rights. You do not welcome the ICC; arguing that it is the wrong answer to the challenges posed by crimes such as ethnic cleansing, and you say that it will create disillusionment because, like its sponsor, the UN, it will be another international institution which promises more than it can deliver.

Your argument is based on the practical difficulties which the ICC is likely to experience in bringing offenders to justice. There is, you argue, no practical alternative to force as a means of stopping the kind of thing that happened in Bosnia and Rwanda — and in your view the only provider of the right kind of force is the US military. You point out that although the ICC is, as presently constituted, limited in its competence (so that Pinochet and Saddam Hussein lie beyond its reach), it interferes enough with national sovereignty to alarm those in the US who prefer isolationism.

I agree that the ICC's constitution and the current state of the world present big practical obstacles to the court. But that is no objection to its existence and the hope it offers. The establishment of the ICC is only one step in a journey which began with the adoption of the Universal Declaration of Human Rights 50 years ago. The Universal Declaration and its two associated Conventions (Geneva and Genocide) are now widely influential in international and domestic jurisdictions. Everyone has been conscious of the need for these human rights instruments to have teeth; the ICC is the first big step in realising that goal. As a culture of law in the international arena grows, so the ICC will grow in stature and effectiveness too.

I scarcely believe that you can disagree with the principle of the ICC: that there should be for the world community what any civilised national community has, namely, a properly constituted means of dealing with crime and wrongdoing. The trials at Nuremberg and Tokyo after the second world war provided precedents for bringing individuals to justice for violations of human rights, but those tribunals, and the one currently in operation for crimes in Bosnia, are ad hoc: a permanent, properly constituted institution is preferable.

At no point has the main claim of the ICC's advocates been that its existence will prevent all crimes against humanity, although it will certainly prevent some — we should not underestimate its deterrent effect on a would-be Pinochet or Pol Pot if he thought that at some stage he could be called to account. But it offers the alternative of justice in place of revenge for wrongs done; it offers the possibility of redress to those wronged; it offers a contribution to processes of reconciliation after conflicts; and it offers a chance to establish truth — or at least something better than rumour and legend — in the record of conflict in tragedies such as Bosnia and Rwanda.

Objecting to the ICC on grounds of the practical difficulty it faces is rather like objecting to Montgolfier's balloon because it is not (yet) a Boeing 747. Have patience: just as the introduction of law to the Wild West was (so Hollywood tells us) a difficult, slow process, so much more is the process of making the international arena a lawful domain.

Others complain that a process of "judicial creep" will eventually extend the ICC's powers to competence over, say, drug smuggling, environmental pollution, and beyond. Where, they ask, will it stop? I answer that some of these extensions would be a good thing, given the interdependence of the world economy. But I reject the implicit "slippery slope" argument; it is not beyond the wit of man to see where the jurisdiction of an ICC is most effectively applied, and where not.

It is easy to mock endeavours to improve the world — it is an honourable journalistic recreation to knock Big Ideas as a way of testing them — but my guess is that, in a generation or two, the work of the ICC will be established, and will make your option — which is that nothing but the international equivalent of a punch on the nose will ever be efficacious — seem primitive.

Yours,
AC Grayling

4th January 1999

Dear AC,

I am not a cynic; I am a pessimist. Leaving aside some of the practical questions about the ICC's effectiveness, I do think that some of its supporters have evaded the tougher questions of the consequences of its creation, particularly as it may affect other parts of their own agenda. In the US, some of the same human rights organisations which spearheaded lobbying efforts for the ICC have been relentless in their demands that the US intervene militarily in places such as Rwanda and Bosnia to halt genocide, and have championed various proposals to accompany humanitarian relief efforts with military force. But in the future the US military will be more resistant to pressures for it to deploy in some future Rwanda as a result of the existence of the ICC than it has been in the past.

If you are right, and the establishment of the ICC really does represent what you call the first big step towards giving teeth to the principles enshrined in the Universal Declaration of Human Rights, then perhaps, even if my fears are warranted, they are a small price to pay for something of such epochal significance. The problem is that I am not convinced that it is. My own suspicion is that for all the big talk of transformations of consciousness in the world in the 50 years since the Declaration came into existence, this brave new world of rights and principles is largely a fiction, a utopian tale woven by human rights activists and lawyers.

I discerned something of that faith when you said: "I scarcely believe that you disagree . . . that there should be for the world community what any civilised national community has, namely, properly constituted means of dealing with crime and wrong." But I do disagree; and this, rather than practical exigencies, lies at the root of my lack of sympathy for the ICC. To begin with, I don't believe there is such a thing as the world community. I am quite serious here. National communities, ethnic groups and tribes all share fundamental assumptions. Their laws are the products of long histories. In many instances, these laws have been forged after long and bloody struggles. In contrast, the world community is largely a legal and bureaucratic concept. To me, it has no deep legitimacy and little real history. The UN is not a world government; it is an association of sovereign states, an uneasy mix of talking-shop, alleviation machine and bureaucratic boondoggle.

Most of those who champion the ICC understand the limitations of the UN perfectly well, and are trying to take the first steps towards, if not world government, then at least the further subduing of national sovereignty through the back door of international law. But as someone who has seen the UN at work in Bosnia and Rwanda, I am not convinced that this brave new world of international civil servants, NGO activists, human rights workers and lawyers, is preferable to the old Westphalian system. For all its faults, I prefer democratic nation-states where officials can be thrown out by the voters.

The ICC may accomplish great things, although the claims of its adherents — which you seem to share — that it can help bring about truth and reconciliation, end the culture of impunity, and discourage at least some genocidal impulses, seem overblown, just as your faith that there exists any alternative to force in a situation such as Bosnia or a Rwanda, seems utterly contradicted by reality.

Kind regards,
David Rieff

5th January 1999

Dear David,

I do indeed take the view you repudiate, namely that humankind is one big (currently unhappy) family, and consider your opposing view about the naturalness of smaller units — nation, ethnic group — to be both false and harmful.

First, we live now in a globalised and interdependent world. This has been increasingly the case since 1945, and that is why there is now so much effective international law in the commercial and maritime domains. The existence of so many effective international institutions, from Unicef to the International Court of Justice in The Hague (to say nothing of NATO), shows that supra-national groupings, and by extension the international community itself, are concrete realities. You imply that the feebleness of the UN proves the contrary; but although the UN is indeed paralysed by division, and hamstrung by lack of funds, it has not existed for long — and global consciousness is growing fast, as proved by the very fact that the ICC treaty has been signed.

Second, the nation-state in which you place so much faith is an entity with a short and troubled history. I certainly do not think that state boundaries, almost all drawn on the world map by wars, confer sacred status on the groups of people living within them. If you have a point in this connection, it concerns democracy; but the descendants of Germans in Pennsylvania, Frenchmen in Louisiana, Spaniards in California and Englishmen, Dutchmen and Irishmen in New England all have a vote in the same elections in a country as big as all the states of Europe put together; so it would seem that large political entities of diverse peoples can be democratic — why put an upper limit on the number?

In the past, slowness of communication made political units small. It took time and effort to introduce the rule of law over large communities, and there were many failures. The ideal of bringing humanity under a single rule of law is utopian; but as with anything indisputably good, the task is to strive to approximate it as closely as possible.

Yours,
AC

6th January 1999

Dear AC,

Malraux said that utopianism was admirable, but only so long as it proceeded from a realistic understanding of the world as it actually is. I don't think your argument for the ICC proceeds from any such understanding. You take your wishes for reality and, in doing so, champion an institution the implications of which you are unwilling to face.

It seems that because tribal, racial and national feeling seem so wicked and destructive to you, you are hoping that a world community, and the civilising legal and ideological norms which might accompany it, can come into existence, if only to save us from ourselves.

But I am not sure that globalisation is quite the fait accompli that you claim. Nor am I persuaded that the parallel you draw between international commercial law and criminal law is valid. By asserting the existence, and eventual victory, of this new global consciousness, you are making the very practical assumption, much loved by activists and international lawyers, that if you establish a new norm hoi polloi will eventually migrate to it.

To me, the sovereignty-subduing, human rights-upholding worldview that you champion is itself another "ism" — the ideology of the post-national new class, the people who are as comfortable in Tokyo as in Paris and for whom the nation-state, ethnic feeling, patriotism and the like seem like dangerous atavisms.

Where are the democratic safeguards in your new world order? A politician can be recalled; a UN bureaucrat or a judge cannot. The lack of accountability of the International Committee of the Red Cross, the "guardians" of international humanitarian law, surely would give anyone pause. Who guards the guardians of your better world?

You want to limit sovereignty. Very well. The reasons for that are clear enough, and we would agree on many. But what do you want to replace it with, and why do you believe so firmly that it is either possible or desirable to create a structure of international law for a world community that may never exist? To me, this seems like an abdication of politics.

Best wishes,
David

7th January 1999

Dear David,

I agree with Malraux; so let us look at the world as it actually is. It staggers under a burden of conflicts and inequities. Only a minority of its population — mainly we in the comfortable west — live peacefully and well; but a mere generation ago even we were bombing one another's civilian populations — or rounding them up to "cleanse" or gas them.

Many people in Europe, horrified by the bloody results of nationalistic rivalry and racist ideology in our century, are trying to forge new international arrangements in our continent, under which its residents are people first and members of a particular nationality second, and under which each individual has the hope of protection by or redress against, his fellow humans if he is the victim of wrongdoing. The arguments for the ICC and other internationalising arrangements generalise this worthy impulse to the world at large. The aim is to provide everyone on the planet with peaceful, civilised means for preventing, or at least lessening, conflict and tyranny. I accept that this internationalism — this faith in binding all the world's people together under agreed conceptions of rights and laws — constitutes an ideology. But any view we take about how to organise ourselves — including your tried and failed nation-state — is construable as such. There is no harm in that; we cannot do without one or another theory. We just have to ensure that it is a good one, and keep it under lively scrutiny.

I agree that there must be democratic controls on the institutions which administer that law. But you seem to believe that the world is too big a place for democracy; so you must think there is an upper limit to how large a law-governed community can be. The US is big; is it too big, or just the right size? When did it become the right size? Will it still work as a democracy when its population has doubled? China has a fifth of the world's population. If it could conceivably be a democracy, why could the world as a whole not be one?

I do not think it likely that the world will ever be one country with one government, but that does not mean that its peoples cannot jointly create and operate institutions such as the ICC. Indeed, as I have said, such institutions already exist and function effectively in large numbers, and this is the trend of the future. Sending large numbers of young men to kill each other as a way of settling disputes seems so primitive in comparison, reminiscent of schoolyard fisticuffs — but with missiles and nuclear warheads. As someone said, we are cleverer now than when we fought with spears, but not wiser. The ICC and similar institutions are coming into existence because the world can no longer afford the old ways.

Best wishes,
AC

8th January 1999

Dear AC,

We both believe our world is staggering "under conflicts and inequities." What divides us are two related issues. Is there anything to be done and, if so, what should decent people expend their energies struggling for? Even asking the first question will seem unduly pessimistic, perhaps even immoral, to you. In these politically correct, sentimentalising times in the rich world, where the goal of both public and private discourse often seems to be to occlude reality, it is not an acceptable thing to ask. Which is why asking it is more essential than ever. If, as you say, we are no wiser than we were centuries ago, how can you claim that the kind of transformations you believe institutions such as the ICC herald have any hope of coming to pass?

Even leaving aside the larger issue of whether we as human beings have it in our nature to abandon violence and cruelty — remember Freud's terrifying insight about war being a human need — two other questions loom large. Is law the appropriate instrument with which to begin such a radical transformation of consciousness? And are we just spreading a European consensus to other parts of the world, attempting to impose norms for which the historical bases of legitimacy have not yet been established?

If, for example, during the Wars of Religion, some extra-terrestrial force could have descended and compelled the catholics and protestants of France to stop killing each other, the edict would have made no sense at all to the belligerents. In the wars of post-colonial succession now taking place in Africa, they don't make sense either.

That is the problem with law-based schemes of human improvement: they take no account of history. What you and other advocates of this new international order fail to recognise is that the consensus for building a post-national Europe could only come in the aftermath of the two world wars in which the states of Europe immolated themselves — and even then took another 50 years to achieve the modest form of the EU. To argue that by passing laws, or concluding treaties, this hard-won consensus can be generalised — even if it is the best and most humane way for societies to order themselves — is to show an arrogance towards the historical experiences of other peoples. It may be 1999 by the calendar everywhere, but it is not the same 1999 in the forests of the eastern Congo as it is on the Flanders fields. Anyone who really wants to make the world a better place — not merely feel better about his or her place in that world — must begin by recognising that fact.

Best wishes,
David

Beyond the political debate highlighted by the Graling-Rieff exchange, a number of legal questions have been raised about the ICC. Review the Statute (Documentary Supplement, page xxx) carefully, particularly the provisions on jurisdiction. As noted by Kirsch and Oosterveld, the substantive scope of the ICC extends to genocide, war crimes, and crimes against humanity, each of which is defined in some detail; since no agreement has yet been reached on the definition of the crime of aggression, that crime may not yet be addressed by the Court. The Statute reflects many of the basic norms of criminal law that have been included in humanitarian law for some time, e.g., *ne bis in idem* (prohibition against double jeopardy, Article 20), *nullum crimen sine lege* (no one may be convicted for an act that was not a crime at the time it was committed, Article 22), irrelevance of an individual's government or other position to his or her criminal liability (Article 27), command responsibility (Article 28), and rejection of the defense of superior orders (Article 33). It also sets out a number of provisions to guarantee a fair trial (Articles 63-67) that will be familiar to human rights lawyers.

The court's jurisdiction is limited not only by the Statute's careful definition of crimes but by a number of other provisions, which were essential to the Statute's adoption in Rome. First, the ICC may only exercise jurisdiction if the alleged crime was either committed in the territory of a state that is a party to the Statute or committed by a national of a state party (Article 12). Thus, if the Statute had been in force during the time of the Pinochet regime, the ICC would only have had jurisdiction if Chile had been a party to the Statute (since Chile was both the territorial state and the state of nationality); mere physical jurisdiction over a potential defendant (e.g., Pinochet's presence in the territory of a party to the Statute) is insufficient. However, it is possible for a non-party to accept the exercise of jurisdiction by the court with respect to a particular crime, if it is either the territorial state or the state of nationality. Both of these issues are addressed in the article by Goldsmith, infra page xxx.

Second, the ICC may undertake an investigation or prosecution through the referral of a situation by a state party (Articles 13 and 14); a referral from the UN Security Council (Article 13); or on the Prosecutor's own initiative, subject to the authorization of a Pre-Trial Chamber of the court (Articles 13 and 15). The Security Council may delay the court's investigation or prosecution of a case for renewable period of one year, if it so requests in a resolution adopted under Article VII of the Charter (Article 16).

Finally, unlike the ICTY, the ICC has complementary rather than primary jurisdiction over crimes that fall within its mandate, thus ensuring that a state itself has the first opportunity to investigate and prosecute alleged genocide, crimes against humanity, or war crimes. Pursuant to Article 17 (which should be read carefully), the ICC will defer to national investigation and/or prosecution, unless the state concerned is unable or unwilling to carry out a genuine investigation or prosecution or is acting in bad faith.

A. U.S. Attitudes Toward an International Criminal Court

Over the years, the U.S. attitude toward the establishment of an international criminal court with jurisdiction over, inter alia, war crimes and crimes against humanity has been lukewarm, at best. Cf. Michael P. Scharf, *The Jury Is Still Out on the Need for an International Criminal Court*, 1 Duke J. Comp. & Intl. L. 135 (1991). For example, one of the arguments against U.S. ratification of the Genocide Convention, first raised during the early 1950s, was that U.S. citizens conceivably could be tried for the crime in foreign courts where they would not have the benefit of U.S. constitutional safeguards. Compare Parker, *An International Criminal Court: The Case for Its Adoption*, 38 A.B.A. J. 641 (1952) with Finch, *An International Criminal Court: The Case Against Its Adoption*, 38 A.B.A. J. 644 (1952). Article 6 of the Convention raises this possibility by providing that "[p]ersons charged with genocide . . . shall be tried by a competent tribunal of the State in the territory of which the act was committed, or by such international penal tribunal as may have jurisdiction with respect to those Contracting Parties which shall have accepted its jurisdiction."

The Senate sought to reduce the likelihood of a U.S. citizen being tried abroad by attaching the following understanding to its advice and consent to the convention's ratification: "nothing in Article VI affects the right of any state to bring to trial before its own tribunals any of its nationals for acts committed outside a state." Senate Comm. on Foreign Relations, Report on the International Convention on the Prevention and Punishment of the Crime of Genocide, S. Exec. Rep. 2, 99th Cong., lst Sess. 23 (1985). This understanding makes it clear that the United States reserves the right to try "its nationals for acts of genocide regardless of where the acts took place. Were, for example, a United States citizen accused of genocidal acts abroad, the United States could meet its obligations under Article VI by prosecuting him under United States law." Id. at 24. Of course, the U.S. citizen alleged to have committed genocide abroad can count on a U.S. trial only if he is physically within the jurisdiction of the United States; if he is physically within the state where the conduct allegedly occurred, that state would have jurisdiction to try him for the crime under its own criminal justice system.

Support for an international court grew somewhat in the post-cold-war era. Following the First Gulf War, the Senate unanimously passed a resolution urging President George Bush to confer with the United Nations and other states "to establish an International Criminal Court or an International Military Tribunal to try and punish all individuals involved in the planning or execution of the above referenced crimes, including Saddam Hussein." S. Res. 76, 101st Cong., 1st Sess., 137 Cong. Rec. S3345, S3346 (daily ed. Mar. 14, 1991). The President, however, did not follow through.

The reasons for President Bush's reticence are suggested in the following exchange (1993 Am. Socy. Intl. L. Proceedings 241-242):

> Professor Buergenthal[1]: When I ended my talk, I pointed out that a great deal of law still needs to be developed in order to make individual responsibility a reality, and I think this is certainly true of the procedural area. Let me follow up in this connection. I have come to the conclusion, after years and years in the human rights area, and after sitting on the Inter-American Court of Human Rights, that unless you go after individuals, governments are subject to being blackmailed by certain powerful groups. They are forced to pardon them, absolving them of responsibility; thus, there is no incentive to stop violations. The only way to deal with that issue is to let potential rights abusers know ahead of time that they will be held criminally responsible for large-scale violations of human rights on the international level.
>
> Mr. Bolton[2]: In the case of Iraq [in 1991], although the Security Council authorized the collection of information about human rights abuses, we took a very explicit decision then not to set up a war crimes tribunal, for two reasons: (1) We were hoping the Iraqi top military officials would have the sense to stage a coup and get rid of

1. Professor Buergenthal is now a Judge on the International Court of Justice. — EDS.

2. Mr. Bolton served as Assistant Secretary of State for International Organizations under the first Bush Administration, Under Secretary of State for Arms Control and International Security

Saddam, and we didn't want them on trial at the very time we were hoping they would do so, because if they were tried in absentia and convicted, what incentive would they have? (2) The second reason was that we didn't know how trying them in absentia would fly in many parts of the world where people would be convinced that, absent the defendants themselves, they couldn't possibly receive a fair trial.

Professor D'Amato: I think there was a third reason too — the allegations of war crimes committed by the allies.

Mr. Bolton: That had nothing to do with it.

The reluctance to allow U.S. citizens to be tried by foreign courts pales into insignificance when compared to the unwillingness of the Senate to contemplate such trials by an international criminal court. This unwillingness, reflected repeatedly over the years, found legal expression in another understanding that the Senate attached to its advice and consent to the ratification of the Genocide Convention: "with regard to the reference to an international penal tribunal in Article VI of the Convention, the United States declares that it reserves the right to effect its participation in any such tribunal only by a treaty entered into specifically for that purpose with the advice and consent of the Senate." Id. at 25. Of course, that condition was met by adoption of the ICC Statute in 1998, which the United States has not ratified.

B. *The United States Signs and "Unsigns" the ICC Statute*

December 31, 2000, was the last date on which the ICC Statute was open for signature (although after that date any state could still accede to the Statute, as is true for almost all other treaties). Although the United States had voted against adopting the Statute in Rome in 1998, President Clinton symbolically signed the Statute less than a month before he left office.

President Clinton, Statement on Signature of the International Criminal Court Treaty

Dec. 31, 2000, reprinted at *http://www.amicc.org/docs/Clinton_sign.pdf*

The United States is today signing the 1998 Rome Treaty on the International Criminal Court. In taking this action, we join more than 130 other countries that have signed by the December 31, 2000 deadline established in the Treaty. We do so to reaffirm our strong support for international accountability and for bringing to justice perpetrators of genocide, war crimes, and crimes against humanity. We do so as well because we wish to remain engaged in making the ICC an instrument of impartial and effective justice in the years to come.

The United States has a long history of commitment to the principle of accountability, from our involvement in the Nuremberg tribunals that brought Nazi war criminals to justice, to our leadership in the effort to establish the International Criminal Tribunals for the Former Yugoslavia and Rwanda. Our action today sustains that tradition of moral leadership.

Under the Rome Treaty, the International Criminal Court (ICC) will come into being with the ratification of 60 governments, and will have jurisdiction over the most heinous abuses that result from international conflict, such as war crimes, crimes against humanity and genocide. The Treaty requires that the ICC not supersede or interfere with functioning national judicial systems; that is, the ICC Prosecutor is authorized to take action against a suspect only if the country of nationality is unwilling or unable to investigate allegations of egregious crimes by their national. The U.S. delegation to the Rome Conference worked hard to achieve these limitations, which we believe are essential to the international credibility and success of the ICC.

In signing, however, we are not abandoning our concerns about significant flaws in the Treaty. In particular, we are concerned that when the Court comes into existence, it will not only exercise authority over personnel of states that have ratified the Treaty, but also claim jurisdiction over personnel of states that have not.

Signature will enhance our ability to further protect U.S. officials from unfounded charges and to achieve the human rights and accountability objectives of the ICC. In fact, in negotiations following the Rome Conference, we have worked effectively to develop procedures that limit the likelihood of politicized prosecutions. For example, U.S. civilian and military negotiators helped to ensure greater precision in the definition of the crimes within the Court's jurisdiction.

But more must be done. Court jurisdiction over U.S. personnel should come only with U.S. ratification of the Treaty. The United States should have the chance to observe and assess the functioning of the Court, over time, before choosing to become subject to its jurisdiction. Given these concerns, I will not, and do not recommend that my successor submit the Treaty to the Senate for advice and consent until our fundamental concerns are satisfied.

Nonetheless, signature is the right action to take at this point. I believe that a properly constituted and structured International Criminal Court would make a profound contribution in deterring egregious human rights abuses worldwide, and that signature increases the chances for productive discussions with other governments to advance these goals in the months and years ahead.

President Clinton never submitted the Statute for the Senate's advice and consent, and the former Senator from North Carolina, Jesse Helms, called Clinton's signature "outrageous" and referred to the ICC as "unprecedented assault on American sovereignty. . . . This decision will not stand." Helms was correct in his prediction, and even the symbolic commitment to the principle of an international criminal court was abandoned two years later. Shortly before the Rome Statute entered into force on July 1, 2002, the Bush Administration forwarded the following letter to the Secretary-General of the United Nations, formally notifying him that the United States did not intend to become a party to the Rome Statute.

Letter from Under-Secretary of State John R. Bolton to the Secretary-General of the United Nations

May 6, 2002

UNDER-SECRETARY OF STATE FOR ARMS CONTROL AND INTERNATIONAL SECURITY WASHINGTON

May 6, 2002

Dear Mr. Secretary-General:

This is to inform you, in connection with the Rome Statute of the International Criminal Court adopted on July 17, 1998, that the United States does not intend to become a party to the treaty. Accordingly, the United States has no legal obligations arising from its signature on December 31, 2000. The United States requests that its intention not to become a party, as expressed in this letter, be reflected in the depositary's status lists relating to this treaty.

Sincerely,

John R. Bolton
(signed)

The Administration's position was explained in a speech given by the Under Secretary of State for Political Affairs on the same day the above letter was sent to the Secretary-General.

Under-Secretary of State of Political Affairs Marc Grossman, American Foreign Policy and the International Criminal Court

Remarks to the Center for Strategic and International Studies, Washington, DC, May 6, 2002, *http://www.state.gov/p/9949.htm*

. . . Here's what America believes in:

— We believe in justice and the promotion of the rule of law.

— We believe those who commit the most serious crimes of concern to the international community should be punished.

— We believe that states, not international institutions are primarily responsible for ensuring justice in the international system.

— We believe that the best way to combat these serious offenses is to build domestic judicial systems, strengthen political will and promote human freedom.

We have concluded that the International Criminal Court does not advance these principles. Here is why:

— We believe the ICC undermines the role of the United Nations Security Council in maintaining international peace and security.

— We believe in checks and balances. The Rome Statute creates a prosecutorial system that is an unchecked power.

— We believe that in order to be bound by a treaty, a state must be party to that treaty. The ICC asserts jurisdiction over citizens of states that have not ratified the treaty. This threatens US sovereignty.

— We believe that the ICC is built on a flawed foundation. These flaws leave it open for exploitation and politically motivated prosecutions. . . .

Historical Perspective

Like many of the nations that gathered in Rome in 1998 for the negotiations to create a permanent International Criminal Court, the United States arrived with the firm belief that those who perpetrate genocide, crimes against humanity, and war crimes must be held accountable and that horrendous deeds must not go unpunished. . . .

A Flawed Outcome

But the International Criminal Court that emerged from the Rome negotiations, and which will begin functioning on July 1 will not effectively advance these worthy goals.

First, we believe the ICC is an institution of unchecked power. In the United States, our system of government is founded on the principle that, in the words of John Adams, "power must never be trusted without a check." Unchecked power, our founders understood, is open to abuse, even with the good intentions of those who establish it.

But in the rush to create a powerful and independent court in Rome, there was a refusal to constrain the Court's powers in any meaningful way. Proposals put forward by the United States to place what we believed were proper checks and balances on the Court were rejected. In the end, despite the best efforts of the U.S. delegation, the final treaty had so many defects that the United States simply could not vote for it.

Take one example: the role of the UN Security Council. Under the UN Charter, the UN Security Council has primary responsibility for maintaining international peace and security. But the Rome Treaty removes this existing system of checks and balances, and places enormous unchecked power in the hands of the ICC prosecutor and judges. The treaty created a self-initiating prosecutor, answerable to no state or institution other than the Court itself. . . .

Second, the treaty approved in Rome dilutes the authority of the UN Security Council and departs from the system that the framers of the UN Charter envisioned.

The treaty creates an as-yet-to-be defined crime of "aggression," and again empowers the court to decide on this matter and lets the prosecutor investigate and prosecute this undefined crime. This was done despite the fact that the UN Charter empowers only the Security Council to decide when a state has committed an act of aggression. Yet the ICC, free of any oversight from the Security Council, could make this judgment.

Third, the treaty threatens the sovereignty of the United States. The Court, as constituted today, claims the authority to detain and try American citizens, even through our democratically-elected representatives have not agreed to be bound by the treaty. While sovereign nations have the authority to try non-citizens who have committed crimes against their citizens or in their territory, the United

States has never recognized the right of an international organization to do so absent consent or a UN Security Council mandate.

Fourth, the current structure of the International Criminal Court undermines the democratic rights of our people and could erode the fundamental elements of the United Nations Charter, specifically the right to self defense.

With the ICC prosecutor and judges presuming to sit in judgment of the security decisions of States without their assent, the ICC could have a chilling effect on the willingness of States to project power in defense of their moral and security interests.

This power must sometimes be projected. The principled projection of force by the world's democracies is critical to protecting human rights — to stopping genocide or changing regimes like the Taliban, which abuse their people and promote terror against the world.

Fifth, we believe that by putting U.S. officials, and our men and women in uniform, at risk of politicized prosecutions, the ICC will complicate U.S. military cooperation with many friends and allies who will now have a treaty obligation to hand over U.S. nationals to the Court — even over U.S. objections....

Our Philosophy

While we oppose the ICC we share a common goal with its supporters — the promotion of the rule of law. Our differences are in approach and philosophy. In order for the rule of law to have true meaning, societies must accept their responsibilities and be able to direct their future and come to terms with their past. An unchecked international body should not be able to interfere in this delicate process.

For example: When a society makes the transition from oppression to democracy, their new government must face their collective past. The state should be allowed to choose the method. The government should decide whether to prosecute or seek national reconciliation. This decision should not be made by the ICC....

The existence of a functioning ICC will not cause the United States to retreat from its leadership role in the promotion of international justice and the rule of law.

The United States will:

— Work together with countries to avoid any disruptions caused by the Treaty, particularly those complications in US military cooperation with friends and allies that are parties to the treaty.

— Continue our longstanding role as an advocate for the principle that there must be accountability for war crimes and other serious violations of international humanitarian law.

— Continue to play a leadership role to right these wrongs.

— The armed forces of the United States will obey the law of war, while our international policies are and will remain completely consistent with these norms.

— Continue to discipline our own when appropriate.

— We will remain committed to promoting the rule of law and helping to bring violators of humanitarian law to justice, wherever the violations may occur.

— We will support politically, financially, technically, and logistically any post-conflict state that seeks to credibly pursue domestic humanitarian law.

— We will support creative ad-hoc mechanisms such as the hybrid process in Sierra Leone — where there is a division of labor between the sovereign state and the international community — as well as alternative justice mechanisms such as truth and reconciliation commissions.

— We will work with Congress to obtain the necessary resources to support this global effort.

— We will seek to mobilize the private sector to see how and where they can contribute.

— We will seek to create a pool of experienced judges and prosecutors who would be willing to work on these projects on short notice.

— We will take steps to ensure that gaps in United States' law do not allow persons wanted or indicted for genocide, war crimes, or crimes against humanity to seek safe haven on our soil in hopes of evading justice.

And when violations occur that are so grave and that they breach international peace and security, the United States will use its position in the UN Security Council to act in support of justice....

The U.S. "unsigning" of the ICC Statute was condemned by many observers, most citing the "arrogance" of the United States being unwilling to submit its own military personnel to the same norms that bind other states. Somewhat more diplomatically, the European Union expressed "disappointment and regret" at an action that it believed "may have undesirable consequences on multilateral treaty-making and generally on the rule of law in international relations." Letter dated 16 May 2002 from the Permanent Representative of Spain to the United Nations addressed to the Secretary-General, UN Doc. A/56/950, Annex (May 20, 2002). U.S. exceptionalism is given further expression in the following extract, written by a University of Chicago law professor who would later become Special Counsel to the General Counsel of the U.S. Department of Defense.

Jack Goldsmith, *The Self-Defeating International Criminal Court*

70 U. Chi. L. Rev. 89, 89-92, 95-99, 101-02 (2003) (citations omitted)

[T]he ICC as currently organized is, and will remain, unacceptable to the United States. This is important because the ICC depends on U.S. political, military, and economic support for its success. An ICC without U.S. support — and indeed, with probable U.S. opposition — will not only fail to live up to its expectations. It may well do actual harm by discouraging the United States from engaging in various human rights–protecting activities. And this, in turn, may increase rather than decrease the impunity of those who violate human rights.

I lay out the mechanisms of ICC futility and perversity as follows. Part I shows why the ICC will be incapable of punishing serious human rights abusers. Part II shows how the ICC will likely lead to less rather than more punishment for human rights abusers. Part III asks why the ICC framers might have designed a self-defeating institution. The Conclusion qualifies the analysis and points to larger lessons.

I. Futility

The ICC was created in 1998 at an international conference dominated by weak and middle powers and by nongovernmental organizations (NGOs)....

The ICC can exercise its independent jurisdiction over perpetrators of international crimes if the crimes are committed (a) by a national of a signatory party, or (b) on the territory of a signatory party. Two important consequences follow. The first is territorial liability over non-signatories. The ICC has jurisdiction over crimes committed by a non-signatory nation in the territory of a signatory nation. The second is the traveling dictator exception. Leaders of non-signatory nations can commit crimes in their territories without fear of prosecution. Even if human rights abusers from non-signatory nations vacation in The Hague, they cannot be arrested and tried by the ICC.

Why would the ICC founders reject jurisdiction over nonsignatory nations who commit crimes in their own territory, but embrace jurisdiction when those countries commit a crime in the territory of a signatory nation? This result was a compromise. Many nations wanted the ICC to have universal jurisdiction, which would have abolished the traveling dictator exception by allowing any signatory nation to arrest anyone who committed an international crime anywhere. But other nations objected to universal jurisdiction as having an uncertain basis under international law and as an excessive threat to national sovereignty. The United States went further, objecting both to universal jurisdiction and to non-signatory liability for crimes committed in a signatory nation. Most nations in Rome disagreed with the United States. The final compromise — one designed both to satisfy some U.S. objections and to maximize ratifications — jettisoned the relatively controversial universal jurisdiction idea but retained the relatively (but only relatively) uncontroversial non-signatory liability for crimes committed in a signatory state. The framers also went further in the direction of non-signatory liability by allowing a non-signatory nation to consent to the ICC's jurisdiction with respect to "the crime in question" committed on its territory by another non-signatory nation.

This is the fatal compromise that I believe will ensure that the ICC fails in its aim of ending — or even diminishing — impunity for international crimes. One reason why is obvious. The most salient class of human rights violators during the past century has been oppressive leaders who abuse their own people within national borders. Under the traveling dictator exception, the ICC does not touch this class of offenders, even if they travel abroad. Unless oppressive regimes ratify the ICC (something few are expected to do), the ICC simply fails to address the most serious human rights abuses.

There is an important qualification to the traveling dictator exception. If the Security Council refers a case involving an ICC non-signatory to the ICC under Chapter VII of the UN Charter, it can override national sovereignty and legitimate a prosecution against a non-signatory or some other state otherwise outside ICC jurisdiction. However, such a referral remains subject to the permanent member politics that so worried ICC supporters. And even when Security Council inertia can be overcome for purposes of establishing ICC jurisdiction, the ICC itself lacks the institutional resources to ensure that the defendants actually show up in The Hague....

The ICC has no inherent enforcement powers. It depends completely on member states to arrest and transfer defendants. So the efficacy of even Security Council–initiated prosecutions in this context depends on the uncertain resolve of nations to use military or economic force to extricate an oppressive leader from his country. . . .

II. PERVERSITY

I now turn to consider how the ICC might actually diminish human rights protections. This perverse result could occur because the ICC's actions may have a chilling effect on U.S. human rights–related activities.

The main reason why the United States opposes the ICC is the fear that its unique international policing responsibilities will expose it to politically motivated prosecutions before an unaccountable court. To be sure, the ICC's safeguards to prevent rogue prosecutions are all ultimately subject to ICC interpretation. The most notable safeguard is complementarity. Complementarity requires that the ICC dismiss a case under investigation "unless the State is unwilling or unable genuinely to carry out the investigation or prosecution." But the ICC has the final word on what counts as a "genuine" investigation based on its judgment whether the domestic proceedings are "inconsistent with an intent to bring the person concerned to justice." The perceived efficacy of complementarity and other ICC safeguards turns on the level of trust a nation has toward the ICC. The United States has little. This lack of trust is magnified by the ICC's assertion of jurisdiction over non-signatory nations and the more favorable immunities the ICC provides to signatory nations (most notably, the option for a seven-year immunity from war crimes prosecution).

These are genuine bases for U.S. concern, but they strike me as secondary. The real concern is that the indeterminateness of international criminal law makes it easy to imagine the ICC and the United States having genuine, principled disagreements about whether a particular act is an international crime.

The most likely basis of disagreement relevant to the United States concerns war crimes arising from military strikes. The ICC has jurisdiction, for example, over a military strike that causes incidental civilian injury (or damage to civilian objects) "clearly excessive in relation to the concrete and direct overall military advantage anticipated." Such proportionality judgments are almost always contested. The prosecutor for the NATO dominated ICTY, for example, seriously considered prosecuting U.S. and NATO officials for (among other things) high-altitude bombings in Kosovo that accidentally killed civilians. The prosecutor's staff apparently advised her to pursue these charges, and her memorandum declining to do so seems tendentious because it takes all of NATO's factual assertions, in their best light, as true. Especially during a war in which irregular combatants hide among civilians, it is easy to imagine a prosecution on this basis. And who knows what might be included in the prohibitions on "severe deprivation of physical liberty in violation of fundamental rules of international law," or on "destroying or seizing the enemy's property unless . . . imperatively demanded by the necessities of war," or on "inhumane acts of a similar character [to crimes against humanity that] intentionally cause great suffering, or serious injury to body or to mental or physical health."

There are many other bases for prosecution of U.S. officials. Nonetheless, the ICC's procedural safeguards, when combined with the threat of U.S. retaliation, make it unlikely that a U.S. official will actually end up in the ICC dock. Why, then, is the United States so worried about the ICC? How can an institution that will have little effect on rogue nations affect the calculations of the world's most powerful nation?

There are two plausible answers. First, U.S. troops do not hide behind U.S. borders. Hundreds of thousands of them are spread across the globe and can much more readily be nabbed and whisked away to The Hague. The possibility of capture is thus much more salient for U.S. troops or officials. Even a remote chance that one of them may be prosecuted will understandably concern U.S. leaders. Second, even if no U.S. official ends up in The Hague, the ICC can affect the United States by merely investigating alleged crimes and engaging in official public criticism and judgment of U.S. military actions.

Whatever the source of U.S. opposition, the fact that opposition runs deep is clear. The otherwise-internationalist Clinton administration opposed the treaty that emerged from Rome, and although Clinton nonetheless signed the treaty on the last day possible, he also called it flawed and advised President Bush not to send it to the Senate for ratification. In the spring of 2002, the U.S. officially informed the UN that "the United States does not intend to become a party to the treaty" and that "accordingly, the United States has no legal obligations arising from its signature on December 31, 2000." The Bush administration has openly opposed the treaty since then. Most notably, in the summer of 2002, it played a game of chicken with the UN over the exposure of UN peacekeepers to ICC jurisdiction. The game was resolved when the Security Council, in the face of significant criticism from ICC supporters, exercised its prerogative under the ICC treaty to immunize UN peacekeepers from ICC investigation for twelve months. [See UN S.C. Res. Resolution 1422 (July 12, 2002).]

Just as important, the Senate has been steadfastly opposed to the ICC since the July 1998 vote to create it.... In 2002, Congress enacted the American Servicemembers' Protection Act (ASPA) [116 Stat 899, Pub L No 107-206]. ASPA is sometimes dubbed "The Hague Invasion Act" because it authorizes the President to use "all means necessary and appropriate" to bring about the release from captivity of U.S. or Allied personnel detained or imprisoned by or on behalf of the Court. ASPA also prohibits any cooperation with (including financial support for) the ICC. It bars military aid to nations that support the ICC (except for NATO countries and other major allies). And it requires the President to certify that U.S. forces that participate in peacekeeping will be safe from ICC prosecution. ASPA also gives the President a number of options to waive its requirements.

We can now finally begin to see the perverse effects of the ICC. The first component of the central ICC compromise leaves in place international human rights' dependence on United States political support, funding, and military might. The second component of the fatal compromise exposes the United States, a non-signatory nation, to liability for crimes committed in signatory nations or in non-signatory nations that temporarily invoke Article 12(3). But this latter part of the compromise will lead the United States to limit its human rights enforcement activities. And the first enforcement activities to go will be ones involving human rights crises that lack a powerful U.S. welfare enhancing justification....

Conclusion: Other Effects and Larger Lessons

There are many possible objections to my arguments. In this conclusion I address two, and then reflect on the broader significance of ICC perversity.

The first objection is that I have overlooked other unanticipated consequences of the ICC that may affect my analysis. For example, I have relied heavily on the "indispensability" of U.S. might to the success of international tribunals. But it is possible that U.S. opposition to the ICC will provoke the EU to reorganize itself to assume this role. Or perhaps U.S. opposition to the ICC might undermine European support in a confrontation against Iraq or, more broadly, in the war on terrorism, thereby either harming U.S. security or causing the United States to rethink its position about the ICC. Or maybe the ICC will effect no change. The United States is busy securing Article 98 and related agreements [see infra pages 936] that might give it adequate comfort with the ICC. If this happens, the United States may embrace the ICC enthusiastically, and in a few years it may look like the Security Council–dominated permanent criminal tribunal the United States sought in the first place.

I doubt that these consequences — especially the first two — will come to pass. Even the most optimistic predictions about the EU do not involve the development of a military or political capacity to use significant force outside of Europe. It is hard to see how the United States' ICC stance would affect multilateral security cooperation, since each nation's contribution tends to be based on case-specific national security assessments and little more. And even if the United States gets blanket Article 98 protection, it will likely continue to view the ICC with at least some suspicion. . . .

The second objection is that my analysis of the ICC's perversity effects is lopsided. I have taken the U.S. position as static and focused on the decision strategies of the ICC victors. This is a fair point. There are at least two significant actors here — the dominant parties at the ICC and the United States. The United States' position was not static, and there are at least two questions one should explore for a more complete analysis of what happened in Rome. The first would begin with the fact that in the early- and mid-1990s, the Clinton Administration and the Senate strongly supported an international criminal court. One might even say that the United States was instrumental in bringing about the Rome conference. Clearly what emerged from Rome was an unintended consequence of this early U.S. support. Second, one could examine the United States' preferences and bargaining strategies at Rome to see how it ended up with a court it could not accept.

This raises a related point. I have argued that the ICC as constituted will likely harm human rights on balance. One could respond that it is not the ICC that causes this harm, but rather the United States' opposition to the ICC. I have assumed that the United States' opposition to the ICC is non-derogable, and that the ICC framers could have reached a different result. But ICC proponents could be just as adamant in their position, and perhaps more so, than the United States, and the ICC may be more difficult to move than the United States.

These are valid points, to an extent. The thrust of my argument has been that the ICC will likely fail; in some sense this failure is attributable to all parties, and my analysis no more suggests that ICC proponents should cave to U.S. demands than it suggests that the U.S. should cave to ICC demands. My analysis does, however, assume a baseline of national sovereignty. The United States has no duty either to join a treaty regime not in its interest or to commit its troops and diplomatic prestige in contexts that it views to be harmful on balance to its welfare. It is unrealistic for an international institution to expect the United States to acquiesce in the new legal jeopardy imposed on it without its consent, and to continue with a human rights enforcement role that exacerbates its legal jeopardy. To the extent that the ICC framers did this, the error is (from the baseline of sovereignty) theirs alone. . . .

The ICC is an intricate, and in some respects impressive, legal edifice. But a legal edifice devoted to international peace and stability is worthless without some plausible mechanism of enforcement. The price for a more plausible enforcement mechanism in the ICC context is to make the United States functionally immune, at least in the ICC (as opposed to domestic and other fora), from the enforcement of international criminal law. The ICC's refusal to countenance this may seem quite reasonable. And yet from a consequentialist perspective, the halfloaf of justice that accords with the interests of the nations that can enforce it may be all we can hope for and certainly seems better than little or no justice at all. . . .

C. *Exempting the United States from ICC Jurisdiction*

As noted in both of the immediately preceding extracts, the United States has consistently refused to allow its citizens to be tried by any international court. In order to prevent having any of its nationals fall within the jurisdiction of the ICC, the U.S. began a campaign to reach bilateral agreements with states which were party to the Rome Statute. Under these accords, termed "Article 98 agreements" after the article in the ICC Statute that permits them, states that are parties to the Rome Statute agree that they will not surrender U.S. nationals to the ICC without American consent. As of May 2005, the U.S. had obtained 100 such agreements. See Cosmos Eubany, *Justice for Some? U.S. Efforts Under Article 98 to Escape the Jurisdiction of the International Criminal Court*, 27 Hastings Int'l & Comp. L. Rev. 103, 115-27 (2003); Erik Rosenfeld, *Application of U.S. Status of Forces Agreements to Article 98 of the Rome Statute*, 2 Wash. U. Global Stud. L. Rev. 273, 280 (2003).

Statute of the International Criminal Court

Final Act of the United Nations Diplomatic Conference of Plenipotentiaries on the Establishment of an International Criminal Court, UN Doc. A/CONF.183/10 (July 17, 1998)

Article 98

COOPERATION WITH RESPECT TO WAIVER OF IMMUNITY AND CONSENT TO SURRENDER

1. The Court may not proceed with a request for surrender or assistance which would require the requested State to act inconsistently with its obligations under international law with respect to the State or diplomatic immunity of a

person or property of a third State, unless the Court can first obtain the cooperation of that third State for the waiver of the immunity.

2. The Court may not proceed with a request for surrender which would require the requested State to act inconsistently with its obligations under international agreements pursuant to which the consent of a sending State is required to surrender a person of that State to the Court, unless the Court can first obtain the cooperation of the sending State for the giving of consent for the surrender.

David J. Scheffer, *Original Intent at The Global Criminal Court*

Wall Street Journal Europe (Sept. 20, 2002)

As the Clinton administration's chief negotiator of the treaty on the International Criminal Court, I have lost my patience with the largely Euro-American debate about special agreements designed to protect American suspects from surrender to the court. These agreements are permitted by Article 98 of the treaty for a reason, but they also have their limitations.

The administration of President George W. Bush wants to sign Article 98 agreements with European and other governments to insure American nationals are immune from the jurisdiction of a court the U.S. now doesn't recognize. The European Union initially resisted, claiming any deals might weaken the court, yet now sounds more open to compromise.

The technical legal issue of securing such agreements has become caught up, and distorted, by the trans-Atlantic tussle over the court. It is worth recalling that the original intent of Article 98 agreements was to ensure that Status of Forces Agreements (SOFAs) between the United States and scores of countries would not be compromised and that Americans on official duty could be specially covered by agreements that fit Article 98's terms. I first put that requirement on the table in early 1995 in Madrid.

SOFAs are the U.S. military's security blanket for its global deployments of military personnel. They ensure that U.S. courts have the right to investigate and prosecute American personnel who, though present on foreign soil, are covered by U.S. law. The negotiated provisions of SOFAs vary from country to country, but the general principle of America's right of primacy over its personnel is sacred in these agreements.

Similar provisions protecting the rights of the "sending state" in criminal cases also populate diplomatic mission agreements and agreements for U.N.-established or authorized peacekeeping operations, such as those in Afghanistan and Sierra Leone. Such protection, offered in the extraordinary circumstances of international peace and security, gives the sending state the confidence to deploy its official personnel without them being subjected to unwarranted criminal charges, particularly in a wartorn foreign society.

Throughout five years of treaty negotiations, the Article 98 safeguard was a major U.S. objective and it was successfully achieved. When Article 98 refers to the "sending state," it means the state that deploys an individual (including its top civilian officials) on official duty. Significantly, Article 98 does not prevent the new court from investigating and even indicting an American official. But if there is an Article 98 agreement with another country, that country would not be able to surrender an indicted official covered by that agreement to the court without Washington's consent.

The EU reportedly has offered this type of protection to Washington. It is an improvement over earlier efforts to erroneously interpret Article 98 and limit its protection only to Americans deployed on peacekeeping missions.

However, the Bush administration overreaches if it attempts, with Article 98 agreements, to immunize any U.S. national living abroad or traveling for any reason from surrender to the court and to blanket the entire world with such agreements. The negotiating objective never was to protect American mercenaries or any other citizen engaged in unofficial actions. (We would have used "state of nationality" rather than "sending state" if that had been our intent.) As I often said as a negotiator, rogue citizens act at their own risk. Nor was it ever our intent to set up a global network of Article 98 agreements, even where they are not plausibly needed. But nothing prevents a specific SOFA or a negotiated Article 98 agreement from protecting retired officials for crimes allegedly committed on official duty. . . .

Note: The Early Work of the ICC

The judges and Prosecutor of the ICC, which is based in The Hague, were elected in early 2003. During its first two years, the ICC opened formal investigations into three situations and conducted preliminary analyses of several additional situations; four of these were based upon voluntary referrals from states and one upon a referral from the UN Security Council.

In April 2004, the government of the Democratic Republic of Congo (DRC) requested the Prosecutor to open an investigation into human rights violations in the DRC in connection with the country's long-running civil war. The Court began investigating crimes committed in the DRC after July 1, 2002 (when the Rome Statute came into force), focusing in particular on reports from intergovernmental and non-governmental organizations alleging systematic torture, rape, forced displacement, and the illegal use of child soldiers in the Ituri region of northeastern DRC.

The second investigation concerned violence in northern Uganda related to the decade-long insurgency conducted by the Lord's Resistance Army (LRA). This investigation was opened in July 2004, following a referral from the government of Uganda. Although there seems to be little doubt that international crimes have been committed in northern Uganda, the investigation itself and the role of the ICC have become controversial. Since both the alleged perpetrators and most of the victims are members of the Acholi tribe, many Acholi would prefer to resolve the conflict by traditional means. Questions have been raised about whether ICC involvement might make reaching a ceasefire or peace agreement with the LRA more difficult, and the mediator accepted by both the government and LRA has threatened to resign if indictments of LRA leaders are issued by the ICC. Compare, e.g., Amnesty International, *Uganda: Government cannot prevent the International Criminal Court from investigating crimes*, Press Release AFR/59/008/2004 (Nov. 16, 2004), with Marc Lacey, *Atrocity Victims in Uganda Choose to Forgive*, N.Y. Times (Apr. 18, 2005); see generally International Crisis Group,

Building a Comprehensive Peace Strategy for Northern Uganda (June 2005). The ICC indicted five LRA commanders in October 2005.

In March 2005, the Prosecutor was requested by the UN Security Council to investigate alleged crimes in the Darfur region of Sudan. S.C. Res 1593 (Mar. 31, 2005). The referral followed the report of a UN-appointed Commission of Inquiry on violations of humanitarian and human rights law in Darfur, which, inter alia, generated a confidential list of individuals who might be liable for crimes in Darfur. In July 2005, the ICC Prosecutor reported to the Security Council that he had determined that the case was admissible, based on the lack of prosecutions in Sudan for alleged crimes, even though the government of Sudan had created a Specialised Tribunal for Darfur in mid-June 2005. International Criminal Court, Report of the Prosecutor . . . to the Security Council pursuant to UNSCR 1593 (2005). (The situation in Darfur and the UN's reactions to it are discussed further in Chapter 10.)

By late 2005, the Prosecutor's office also was "collecting information on eight other situations of concern." Report of the International Criminal Court, UN Doc. A/60/177, para. 35 (Aug. 1, 2005). These included the Central African Republic, which referred the situation in that country to the court in January 2005, and Côte d'Ivoire, which the following month referred issues concerning alleged crimes committed after an attempted coup in the country in February 2002. Côte d'Ivoire is not a party to the Court's Statute, so it accepted the ad hoc jurisdiction of the ICC under Article 12(3) of the Statute.

Comments and Questions

1. Reread carefully the definitions of crimes contained in Articles 6-8 of the ICC Statute. Does the United States have legitimate fears that its military personnel abroad might be indicted by the ICC? How is the situation different from that of a U.S. citizen who commits a crime in Mexico and thereby becomes subject to Mexican criminal law and jurisdiction? Should the United States be sufficiently comforted by the notion of complementarity expressed in Article 17 of the Statute? Does the American Servicemember's Protection Act referred to in the Goldsmith extract tie the President's hands, in any event?

2. There is no specific provision in the ICC Statute for "voluntary" referrals to the Court, and some observers have questioned both the legality and wisdom of such referrals regarding the Democratic Republic of Congo, Uganda, and the Central African Republic. See Mahnoush H. Arsanjani and W. Michael Riesman, *The Law-in-Action of the International Criminal Court*, 99 Am. J. Int'l L. 385, 390, 393 (2005) ("[A] system of voluntary referral could open the way to using the Court as a backup to national judicial systems that are otherwise competent and to the selective externalization of difficult cases, relieving governments of the pressure to develop and expand their national judicial systems to process the crimes enumberated in the Statute. . . . [H]owever hideous the crimes committed, one wonders what contribution to the settlement of the dispute accrues from transferring the problem [in the Democratic Republic of Congo], at this juncture, to the International Criminal Court, a body that was neither intended nor equipped to resolve, through judicial means, a longstanding political problem of a government."). Compare Payam Akhavan, *The Lord's Resistance Army Case:*

Uganda's Submission of the First State Referral to the International Criminal Court, 99 Am. J. Int'l L. 403, 415 (2005) ("[T]here is no basis, in law or policy, for the assertion that states cannot voluntarily relinquish jurisdiction in favor of the ICC.").

3. All of the situations thus far referred to the ICC involve armed conflict or, at a minimum, guerrilla warfare. Further, most discussions of pros and cons of the ICC assume the existence of an armed conflict, rather than being concerned with the actions of a Pinochet, Marcos, or Duvalier within his own country. Given this emphasis, is the ICC a "human rights" court or a "humanitarian law" court? While the answer to this question may be primarily semantic, it might also be useful in distinguishing between the human rights concerns addressed in most of this book and the somewhat different issues considered in this chapter and Chapter 4.

4. Among many works on the ICC, in addition to those already cited, see Olympia Bekou and Robert Cryer, *The International Criminal Court* (2005); John R. Bolton, *The United States and the International Criminal Court: The Risks and Weaknesses of the International Criminal Court from America's Perspective*, 64 Law & Contemp. Prob. 167 (2001); Bruce Broomhall, *International Justice & the International Criminal Court: Between Sovereignty and the Rule of Law* (2003); Antonio Cassese et al., *The Rome Statute of the International Criminal Court: A Commentary* (2002); *Editorial Comments on the USA and the ICC*, 2 J. Int'l Crim. J. 2-37 (2004); Joel F. England, *Response of the United States to the International Criminal Court: Rejection, Ratification or Something Else?*, 18 Ariz. J. Int'l & Comp. Law 941 (2001); Jessica Gavron, *Amnesties in the Light of Developments in International Law and the Establishment of the International Criminal Court*, 51 Int'l Comp. & Law Q. 91 (2002); Gerhard Hafner et al., A *Response to the American View as Presented by Ruth Wedgwood*, 10 Eur. J. Int'l L. 108 (1999); Ralph Henham, *Some Issues for Sentencing in the International Criminal Court*, 52 Int'l & Comp. Law Q. 81 (2003); Michael A. Newton, *Comparative Complementarity: Domestic Jurisdiction Consistent with the Rome Statute of the International Criminal Court*, 167 Mil. L. Rev. 20 (2001); William A. Schabas, *Introduction to the International Criminal Court* (2d ed. 2004); Ruth Wedgwood, *The International Criminal Court: An American View*, 10 Eur. J. Int'l L. 93 (1999).

V. Universal Jurisdiction

Universal jurisdiction reflects the principle that some crimes are so heinous and are of such concern to the international community that states are entitled to prosecute alleged perpetrators no matter where the crime was committed and no matter the nationality or residence of either victim or perpetrator. While universal jurisdiction has long been asserted regarding piracy, the possibility of national trials for those accused of "international" crimes has seemed much more realistic since the arrest of Chile's Pinochet, described supra at page 885. As demonstrated in the following readings, this expansion of jurisdiction may be viewed as either a welcome response to criminals who would otherwise enjoy impunity or an unwarranted and dangerous assertion of authority by countries with neither the knowledge, capability, nor willingness to reach fair judgments.

Menno Kamminga, *Lessons Learned from the Exercise of Universal Jurisdiction in Respect of Gross Human Rights Offenses*

23 Hum. Rts. Q. 940, 941-42, 943-44, 941-53, 954, 955, 956-58, 959, 960, 963, 964-65 (2001) (citations omitted)

... Much has changed since the then Legal Adviser of the International Committee of the Red Cross wrote in 1986 that universal jurisdiction was of "no practical value" for war crime trials....

II. What Is Universal Jurisdiction?

Under the principle of universal jurisdiction a state is entitled or even required to bring proceedings in respect of certain serious crimes, irrespective of the location of the crime, and irrespective of the nationality of the perpetrator or the victim. This paper is concerned with jurisdiction to adjudicate, specifically the exercise of criminal jurisdiction by domestic courts in respect of gross human rights offenses. It does not cover enforcement jurisdiction or the exercise of jurisdiction for the purpose of obtaining civil law remedies. The term "gross human rights offences" is employed as shorthand for certain serious violations of international humanitarian law and international human rights law that qualify as crimes under international law.

It follows from this definition that, with one or two exceptions, the post–Second World War trials usually cited as examples of the exercise of universal jurisdiction in fact do not deserve this label. The military tribunals sitting in Germany, Italy, the Netherlands, and on Kwajalein Island that tried the "non-major" war criminals generally failed to indicate any explicit legal basis at all for their exercise of jurisdiction. However, they usually tried offenses committed against their own nationals. The assumption of jurisdiction in these cases was therefore based on the passive personality principle, especially if it is assumed that this principle also enables the exercise of jurisdiction with regard to crimes committed against nationals of a belligerent's ally. . . .

Nevertheless, the exercise of universal jurisdiction in respect of gross human rights offenses raises a series of legal and practical problems that have hardly begun to be considered. The purpose of this article is to take stock of the case law so far, to identify the difficulties that have arisen, and to consider how they might be overcome. . . .

By qualifying certain crimes as being subject to universal jurisdiction the international community signals that they are so appalling that they represent a threat to the international legal order. Justice requires that there should be no safe haven for the perpetrators of such crimes. Domestic courts and prosecutors bringing the perpetrators to justice are not acting on behalf of their own domestic legal system but on behalf of the international legal order. The increasing exercise of universal jurisdiction in respect of gross human rights offenders is a reflection of the smaller world in which we live in which people feel affronted not merely by crimes committed within their own territories or against their own fellow citizens but also by heinous crimes perpetrated in distant states against others. They therefore regard it as appropriate that the machinery of justice in their state is used to bring the perpetrators to trial.

A different argument sometimes put forward, as a justification for the exercise of universal jurisdiction is its supposed deterrent effect. However, as always in the field of criminal justice, this effect should not be overstated. . . .

IV. Human Rights Offenses Subject to Universal Jurisdiction

The work of the International Law Commission offers a convenient starting point for the identification of the crimes that are subject to universal jurisdiction under international law. In its 1996 Draft Code of Crimes against the Peace and Security of Mankind, the ILC suggested that genocide, crimes against humanity, crimes against United Nations and associated personnel, and war crimes are subject to universal jurisdiction. According to the Draft Code a state party in the territory of which an individual is found who is alleged to have committed one of these crimes shall extradite or prosecute that individual. The Draft Code does not define genocide, crimes against humanity, and war crimes. These concepts have recently been authoritatively defined, however, in Articles 6-8 respectively of the Statute of the ICC. Strictly speaking, the purpose of these latter provisions is merely to designate the crimes that are within the jurisdiction of the ICC. A reasonable assumption however, is that the offenses listed here will "take on a life of their own as an authoritative and largely customary statement of international humanitarian and criminal law, and may thus become a model for national laws to be enforced under the principle of universality of jurisdiction." In addition to these crimes, torture not amounting to a crime against humanity is a crime subject to universal jurisdiction pursuant to the UN Convention against Torture. . . .

[The author goes on to discuss these four categories of offenses, concluding that customary international law provides for the exercise of universal jurisdiction in the cases of genocide, crimes against humanity, and grave breaches of the 1949 Geneva Conventions that occur during international armed conflict. He suggests that Article 8 of the ICC Statute "will also be regarded as an authoritative pronouncement on the violations of the law of war that qualify as war crimes under customary international law. A corollary then is that these offenses are covered by the principle of universal jurisdiction." at 947. Torture is discussed infra, page 961.]

VI. Obstacles to the Exercise of Universal Jurisdiction

A comparative analysis of the cases in which proceedings have so far been brought against persons suspected of having committed gross human rights offenses reveals several obstacles of a legal or practical nature that typically arise. Some of these difficulties may arise in any trial of crimes under international law. They include problems such as those relating to statutes of limitations, command responsibility, superior orders, and gender issues. A recent codification of the applicable rules of international law on these issues may be found in the Statute of the ICC. Some difficulties are, however, typical for the trial of crimes on the basis of universal jurisdiction and they will be considered here in some more detail. They include the lack of adequate implementing legislation, lack of specialized machinery, immunities, amnesties, evidentiary problems, and ineffective international supervision.

A. Lack of Adequate Implementing Legislation

In the Lotus case the Permanent Court of International Justice observed that the territoriality of criminal law is not an absolute principle of international law. The Court pointed out that every state remained free to adopt the principles for the exercise of criminal and civil jurisdiction which it regarded as most suitable, as long as it did not overstep the limits which international law placed upon its jurisdiction. In practice, however, states have tended to be more restrictive and this has certainly been the case with regard to the exercise of criminal jurisdiction on the basis of universality. States have been reluctant to provide for such jurisdiction in the absence of a specific permission in international law. Moreover, domestic courts have shown themselves unwilling to try defendants on the basis of universal jurisdiction in the absence of unambiguous provisions in domestic legislation allowing them to do so. This is not only because courts are reluctant to meddle in the internal affairs of another state but also because they do not want to come into conflict with the maxim nulla poena sine lege. . . .

Only a few dozen states appear to have provided their courts with the specific competence to try certain gross human rights offenses under the principle of universal jurisdiction. Even in those states legislation tends to be quite a patchwork. Frequently, for example, laws implementing the Genocide Convention do not provide for the possibility to exercise jurisdiction on the basis of universal jurisdiction. This is because the Genocide Convention does not specifically require states parties to do so. Similarly, the absence of treaty provisions on the exercise of universal jurisdiction regarding crimes against humanity and crimes committed in non-international armed conflict explains why only few states have legal provisions allowing them to exercise universal jurisdiction with regard to these offenses. Domestic courts therefore frequently refuse to exercise universal jurisdiction in respect of these crimes on the grounds that domestic legislation does not provide them with a sufficient legal basis. Australian, French, and Swiss courts, amongst others, have taken this view....

In sum, very few states have adequate implementing legislation enabling the exercise of universal jurisdiction in respect of gross human rights offenses....

B. LACK OF SPECIALIZED INSTITUTIONS

Investigating and prosecuting crimes on the basis of universal jurisdiction requires special skills, both in terms of knowing how to investigate crimes committed abroad and in terms of the specialized knowledge of international criminal law that is needed....

C. IMMUNITIES

Because human rights offenses tend by definition to be committed by persons acting on behalf or with the consent or acquiescence of the state, a question which is likely to arise in proceedings on the basis of universal jurisdiction is whether a person accused of such offenses is exempt from criminal responsibility because he has acted in an official capacity. As a matter of fact, the point that official status does not constitute a defense in criminal proceedings in respect of crimes under international law has been specifically provided for in the Nuremberg Charter and the Statutes of the ICTY and the ICTR [and the ICC]....

... In fact, it would appear that the notion of immunity from criminal liability for crimes under international law perpetrated in an official capacity, whether by existing or former office holders, is fundamentally incompatible with the proposition that gross human rights offenses are subject to universal jurisdiction....

D. AMNESTIES

An issue on which there is no case law yet but which is likely to arise sooner or later is whether domestic courts in third states are bound by amnesties awarded in the territorial state.

It has been argued that awarding amnesties to perpetrators of gross human rights offenses is in itself prohibited under international law. If this proposition is correct, such amnesties are null and void and they cannot prevent proceedings in another state. International practice offers considerable, but not yet entirely conclusive, support for this line of argument.... In July 1999, the UN Secretary-General announced that he would sign the Sierra Leone Peace Agreement (which provides in Article 9 for a sweeping "absolute and free pardon and reprieve to all combatants and collaborators in respect of anything done by them in pursuit of their objectives"), but subject to the important proviso that the "amnesty and pardon shall not apply to international crimes of genocide, crimes against humanity, war crimes and other serious violations of international humanitarian law."

On the other hand, not all international practice on this matter points in the same direction. The United Nations itself has been far from consistent in its attitude to amnesties for perpetrators of gross human rights offenses. Perhaps more significantly, South Africa's Constitutional Court has held in *AZAPO v. South Africa* that the country's truth and reconciliation process, including its amnesty procedure, is not incompatible with international law and this ruling has found some support in the literature. Reliance is sometimes also placed on Article 6(5) of Protocol II to the Geneva Conventions which provides:

> At the end of the hostilities, the authorities in power shall endeavour to grant the broadest possible amnesty to persons who have participated in the armed conflict, or those deprived of their liberty for reasons related to the armed conflict, whether they are interned or detained.

As the International Committee of the Red Cross has pointed out, this provision merely states that combatants should not be punished for legitimate acts of hostility. It does not provide a legal basis for awarding amnesties to persons who have violated international law.

But even if it is assumed that at least some types of amnesties are not incompatible with international law, the bottom line is that in any case amnesties lack extra-territorial effect. They therefore do not affect treaty obligations or entitlements under customary international law to bring gross human rights offenders to justice wherever they are.... [The issue of amnesties is discussed further in Orentlicher, infra page 968.]

E. EVIDENTIARY PROBLEMS

One of the greatest difficulties in bringing proceedings on the basis of universal jurisdiction may be of a practical nature. How does one obtain the necessary evidence to enable a defendant's conviction for offenses committed abroad? The authorities of the territorial state can be expected to be reluctant to render assistance, even when they are obliged to do so, for the simple reason that they may bear co-responsibility for the offenses. In some cases, they may strongly object and actively try to frustrate investigations. Even with the backing of the Security Council, the ICTY and the ICTR have found it difficult to obtain the necessary co-operation from the authorities of the territorial states. Another problem is that witnesses often have to be traced in distant states. Even when they can be found they may be reluctant to testify for fear of reprisals against themselves or their families. Furthermore, numerous documents will need to be translated. Investigations on the basis of universal jurisdiction therefore tend to be considerably more expensive and time-consuming than investigations based on the territoriality principle....

The extent to which states have complied with requests for foreign assistance in the investigation and prosecution of human rights offenses subject to universal jurisdiction is not known. Anecdotal evidence, however, suggests that the situation is far from satisfactory.... Most convictions on the basis of universal jurisdiction appear to have been based essentially on eyewitness testimony that happened to be available in the prosecuting state without any significant assistance from the authorities of the territorial state. . . .

VII. Safeguards Against the Abuse of Universal Jurisdiction

From the point of view of the defendant, the exercise of universal jurisdiction presents some special difficulties that deserve to be taken quite seriously.

To begin with, the decision to initiate proceedings on the basis of universal jurisdiction may be objected to. States exercising jurisdiction on this basis may be accused of jurisdictional imperialism because universal jurisdiction is only likely to be exercised in powerful states with regard to crimes committed in less powerful states. At first sight, the cases summarized in the Appendix would appear to support this accusation. [The article includes an Appendix summarizing the recent exercise by states of universal jurisdiction.] The large majority of universal jurisdiction cases have been conducted in OECD states with respect to crimes committed outside these states. On the other hand, international obligations to prosecute gross human rights offenses on the basis of universal jurisdiction are relatively straightforward and are contained in treaties that have been widely ratified. It can hardly be held against states that they are prepared to comply with their international obligations, especially if they have initiated proceedings against their own nationals in connection with similar offenses.

There are, nevertheless, inherent risks to the fairness of proceedings far removed from the site of the crime and against a defendant who may not understand the language and the culture in which he is being brought to justice. It should therefore be stressed that like any defendant in criminal proceedings, the defendant being tried on the basis of universal jurisdiction is fully entitled to fair treatment in accordance with applicable international human rights standards. . . .

VIII. Concluding Observations. . . .

States that profess to be serious about the exercise of universal jurisdiction in respect of gross human rights offenses should begin by ensuring that their domestic legislation specifically enables their courts to exercise jurisdiction in respect of all crimes identified in the Statute of the ICC, without any restrictions ratione loci, ratione temporis or ratione personae. A suitable occasion for this is when they are reviewing their laws to bring them into line with the Statute of the International Criminal Court. Next, they should consider whether their laws of evidence do not in fact prevent successful proceedings on the basis of universal jurisdiction, e.g., by restricting reliance on written depositions. Furthermore, in view of the specialist knowledge of international (criminal) law and of international legal cooperation that is required, serious consideration should be given to the establishment of specialist investigation and prosecution units that could also be charged with liaising with international criminal tribunals and courts.

The most frequently asked question about universal jurisdiction in respect of gross human rights offenses is whether its exercise is obligatory or merely permissive. The short answer is that states parties to the Geneva Conventions and the UN Convention against Torture have undertaken an obligation to exercise universal jurisdiction in respect of grave breaches and torture, respectively. Under customary international law states are moreover entitled to exercise universal jurisdiction in respect of genocide, crimes against humanity, war crimes and torture.

The exercise of universal jurisdiction in respect of gross human rights offenses is not for the faint-hearted. Territorial states are unlikely to react kindly to it. This is of course because the introduction of such proceedings implies a clear failure on their part to comply with their international obligations. It should therefore cause no surprise that Chile protested vehemently against the detention of Augusto Pinochet in the United Kingdom, that Mauritania responded by cutting all military cooperation and introducing visa restrictions in response to the arrest of one of its military officers in France, and that Congo introduced proceedings against Belgium before the International Court of Justice in response to the international arrest warrant issued against its Foreign Minister. In view of such strong reactions, prosecutors are unlikely to bring universal jurisdiction proceedings lightly. The possibility of abuse is one of the key arguments of the opponents of universal jurisdiction. In fact, the cases surveyed for this paper reveal no evidence whatsoever of frivolous or politically motivated prosecutions.

Henry A. Kissinger, *The Pitfalls of Universal Jurisdiction*

80 For. Aff. 86 (No. 4, 2001)

In less than a decade, an unprecedented movement has emerged to submit international politics to judicial procedures. It has spread with extraordinary speed and has not been subjected to systematic debate, partly because of the intimidating passion of its advocates. To be sure, human rights violations, war crimes, genocide, and torture have so disgraced the modern age and in such a variety of places that the effort to interpose legal norms to prevent or punish such outrages does credit to its advocates. The danger lies in pushing the effort to extremes that risk substituting the tyranny of judges for that of governments; historically, the dictatorship of the virtuous has often led to inquisitions and even witch-hunts.

The doctrine of universal jurisdiction asserts that some crimes are so heinous that their perpetrators should not escape justice by invoking doctrines of sovereign immunity or the sacrosanct nature of national frontiers. . . .

The very concept of universal jurisdiction is of recent vintage. The sixth edition of Black's Law Dictionary, published in 1990, does not contain even an entry for the term. The closest analogous concept listed is hostes humani generis ("enemies of the human race"). Until recently, the latter term has been applied to pirates, hijackers, and similar outlaws whose crimes were typically committed outside the territory of any state. The notion that heads of state and senior public officials should have the same standing as outlaws before the bar of justice is quite new.

. . . Even with respect to binding undertakings such as the genocide convention, it was never thought that they would subject past and future leaders of one nation to prosecution by the national magistrates of another state where the violations had not occurred. Nor, until recently, was it argued that the various U.N. declarations subjected past and future leaders to the possibility of prosecution by national magistrates of third countries without either due process safeguards or institutional restraints.

Yet this is in essence the precedent that was set by the 1998 British detention of former Chilean President Augusto Pinochet....

Disapproval of the Allende regime does not exonerate those who perpetrated systematic human rights abuses after it was overthrown. But neither should the applicability of universal jurisdiction as a policy be determined by one's view of the political history of Chile....

Perhaps the most important issue is the relationship of universal jurisdiction to national reconciliation procedures set up by new democratic governments to deal with their countries' questionable pasts. One would have thought that a Spanish magistrate would have been sensitive to the incongruity of a request by Spain, itself haunted by transgressions committed during the Spanish Civil War and the regime of General Francisco Franco, to try in Spanish courts alleged crimes against humanity committed elsewhere.

The decision of post-Franco Spain to avoid wholesale criminal trials for the human rights violations of the recent past was designed explicitly to foster a process of national reconciliation that undoubtedly contributed much to the present vigor of Spanish democracy. Why should Chile's attempt at national reconciliation not have been given the same opportunity? Should any outside group dissatisfied with the reconciliation procedures of, say, South Africa be free to challenge them in their own national courts or those of third countries?

It is an important principle that those who commit war crimes or systematically violate human rights should be held accountable. But the consolidation of law, domestic peace, and representative government in a nation struggling to come to terms with a brutal past has a claim as well....

Another grave issue is the use in such cases of extradition procedures designed for ordinary criminals. If the Pinochet case becomes a precedent, magistrates anywhere will be in a position to put forward an extradition request without warning to the accused and regardless of the policies the accused's country might already have in place for dealing with the charges. The country from which extradition is requested then faces a seemingly technical legal decision that, in fact, amounts to the exercise of political discretion whether to entertain the claim or not.

Once extradition procedures are in train, they develop a momentum of their own. The accused is not allowed to challenge the substantive merit of the case and instead is confined to procedural issues: that there was, say, some technical flaw in the extradition request, that the judicial system of the requesting country is incapable of providing a fair hearing, or that the crime for which the extradition is sought is not treated as a crime in the country from which the extradition has been requested — thereby conceding much of the merit of the charge. Meanwhile, while these claims are being considered by the judicial system of the country from which extradition is sought, the accused remains in some form of detention, possibly for years. Such procedures provide an opportunity for political harassment long before the accused is in a position to present any defense. It would be ironic if a doctrine designed to transcend the political process turns into a means to pursue political enemies rather than universal justice.

Diane Orentlicher, *Whose Justice? Reconciling Universal Jurisdiction with Democratic Principles*

92 Geo. L.J. 1057, 1059-60, 1133-34 (2004) (citations omitted)

In the years since Pinochet's arrest, a raft of countries have walked through the door the Pinochet case opened. Inspired by the Pinochet precedent, victims of human rights violations in Chad instituted criminal proceedings against former leader Hissène Habré in Senegal and Belgium. In June 2001, a Belgian jury broke new ground when it convicted four Rwandans for their roles in the 1994 genocide in Rwanda in a case that relied on universal jurisdiction. In the past decade, criminal complaints or investigations have been instituted before courts in Austria, Canada, Denmark, France, Germany, the Netherlands, Senegal, Spain, Switzerland, and the United Kingdom for atrocities in Europe, Africa and South America. And while the United States has been reluctant to institute prosecutions based on universal jurisdiction, its courts have seen a surge in civil litigation based on this principle. More controversially, criminal complaints have been filed in Belgium — until recently, the world capital of universal jurisdiction — against current or former leaders of Chad, Cuba, Iraq, Iran, the Democratic Republic of Congo, the Ivory Coast, the Palestinian Authority, Israel, the United States, and other countries. . . .

But if Pinochet and other recent cases have breathed new life into universal jurisdiction, they have also spawned intensive debate about the scope of its legitimate use. Critics charge that bystander justice threatens democratic values because it allows foreign judges to make law for societies to whom they are largely unaccountable. In their view, a deeper challenge to democratic values is inherent in universal jurisdiction: its exercise assertedly wrests decisions about how to confront past atrocities away from the societies to whom these questions belong and may undermine tenuous transitions to democracy.

These concerns deserve to be taken seriously. Critics of universal jurisdiction properly emphasize the primacy of local efforts to confront past crimes: societies that have endured the depredations of dictatorship bear a special burden of reckoning and repair. Home-grown justice represents at least partial payment of a country's debt to citizens previously denied protection of the law and inspires confidence that, in the future, the nation will not once again succumb to wholesale repression. Skeptics also have some ground to wonder whether bystander justice can surmount the peculiar challenge of judicial accountability inherent in its use. Through continuous interaction with fellow citizens, judges operating in a domestic setting remain publicly accountable in myriad ways that anchor the legitimacy of their interpretive work. Similar resources for legitimation of judicial authority are manifestly more elusive in a transnational setting.

Yet the conclusion to which these concerns have led some critics — wholesale rejection of universal jurisdiction — rests upon deeply flawed assumptions. To begin, leading proponents of the view that universal jurisdiction is fundamentally undemocratic overlook a crucial point: many states have consented to its exercise, and for perfectly valid reasons. Societies recovering from the ravages of mass atrocity have been the first to sign up for transnational enforcement regimes that can provide a backstop in the event their nations once again descend into the abyss of lawless violence. In doing so, they are exercising the prerogatives of democracy — and seeking to safeguard its future....

More challenging questions of accountability arise by virtue of the fact that courts exercising universal jurisdiction operate at a remote distance from communities deeply affected by their judgments. But these challenges are hardly insurmountable. Straightforward measures can enhance the transparency of courts exercising universal jurisdiction and bridge the distance between them and the communities most affected by their judgments. Significantly, too, a transnational community of jurists now disciplines the work of courts that exercise universal jurisdiction, operating as a professional bulwark against the misuse of judicial power....

But if the Pinochet case highlights the democracy-enhancing potential of universal jurisdiction, the proceedings in Europe also suggest the value of clarifying the circumstances in which national courts should exercise universal jurisdiction. The legitimacy of bystander justice may be in greatest doubt when national prosecutors and judges seek to extend their writ beyond established boundaries of state assent, whether expressed through participation in a relevant treaty, ad hoc consent, or customary international law. While their most obvious effect is to constrain prosecutors and judges, clearly-framed mandates also empower courts to assert universal jurisdiction in circumstances where its legitimacy should not be doubted.

Note: The Belgian Experience

Almost every recent article on universal jurisdiction refers to Belgium, which in 1993 adopted a law asserting universal jurisdiction over grave breaches of international humanitarian law; that law was expanded in 1999 to include genocide and crimes against humanity. Law of 16 June 1993 concerning the Punishment of Grave Breaches of the International Geneva Conventions of 12 August 1949 and of Protocols I and II of 8 June 1977 Additional Thereto, Moniteur Belge, Aug. 5, 1993, p. 17751, as amended by the Law of 19 February 1999 concerning the Punishment of Serious Violations of International Humanitarian Law, Moniteur Belge, Mar. 23, 1999, p. 9286, translated and reprinted in 38 I.L.M. 921 (1999). Articles 1-6 of the law define grave breaches of international humanitarian law, genocide, and crimes against humanity and set out the prison terms for their violation. Sovereign immunity is specifically excluded as a ground for a defense. The key jurisdictional provision is Article 7, which provides, "The Belgian courts shall be competent to deal with breaches provided for in the present Act, irrespective of where such breaches have been committed."

In 2001, Belgium tried four Rwandans under the law — two nuns, a professor, and a businessman who was a former government minister — for participation in the 1994 genocide that took place in Rwanda. All four were found guilty and received sentences ranging from twelve to twenty years' imprisonment. Although the case was hailed as a triumph of universal jurisdiction, the accused had been living in Belgium during the investigation of their case, and, as the former colonial power, Belgium clearly had at least some connection with events in Rwanda.

Under Belgian law, private persons may institute criminal proceedings before an investigating judge. Quickly, Belgian courts soon faced politically-sensitive lawsuits filed against, inter alia, Ariel Sharon, Yasser Arafat, Fidel Castro, Saddam Hussein, former Iranian president Hashemi Rafsanjani, and others. When, in March 2003, seven Iraqi families sought to initiate an investigation of former president George H.W. Bush and other U.S. officials for war crimes allegedly committed during the 1991 Gulf War in Iraq, the United States began pressuring Belgium to amend or repeal its law. The United States argued, inter alia, that Belgium was jeopardizing its status as the site of NATO's headquarters, since officials might be deterred from attending NATO meetings for fear of indictment and arrest.

Pressure mounted both domestically and internationally, and Belgium finally repealed the 1993 law in August 2003. The Law of August 5, 2003, concerning Serious Violations of International Humanitarian Law, Moniteur Belge, Aug. 8, 2003, actually expanded the categories of crimes covered, by including, inter alia, forced disappearances, apartheid, crimes included in Article 8(2)(f) of the ICC Statute, and "other inhuman acts of similar character which intentionally cause great suffering or serious harm to physical integrity or physical or mental health" (editors' translation). However, the law specifically excludes from its purview sitting heads of state, heads of government, and ministers of foreign affairs; other persons "whose immunity is recognized by international law"; persons who enjoy immunity based on a treaty to which Belgium is a party; and persons officially invited by the Belgian government or by "an international organization established in Belgium and with which Belgium has concluded a headquarters agreement," e.g., NATO. Jurisdiction is asserted for the enumerated crimes only when the accused is Belgian or has his or her primary residence in Belgium; if the victim is a Belgian national or had lived "habitually and legally" in Belgium for at least three years at the time that the crimes were committed; or if Belgium is required by treaty to exercise jurisdiction over the case. Finally, only the Federal Prosecutor may bring cases involving violations of the crimes defined under the new law.

Steven R. Ratner, Editorial Comment, *Belgium's War Crimes Statute: A Postmortem*

97 Am. J. Int'l L. 888, 888-89, 891-92, 893, 896 (2003)

The life and death of Belgium's universal jurisdiction law is a textbook case of the inter-section of law and power in the international arena. A government, its consciousness raised by the increased global attention to individual responsibility for human rights atrocities, enacts a broad statute opening its courts to prosecutions of suspected murderers, torturers, and war criminals around the world. Stung by its peacekeepers' failure to prevent genocide in Rwanda, a former colony, Belgium eventually utilizes the law to try and convict a handful of accomplices to those atrocities. But politically troublesome cases trickle in, as opposing sides in the Middle East seek to have their day in Brussels; and another state, the Democratic Republic of the Congo (DRC), successfully brings an action in the World Court challenging arrest warrants against a former DRC official. The United States government eventually signals opposition to the statute, leading to its nearly instantaneous modification; when the United States says it is still too broad, the government guts the idea entirely.

To many observers, the Belgian story is a Manichean battle of the highest order: idealism vs. pragmatism; law vs. power; a community–minded state vs. a hegemon; human rights vs. foreign policy imperatives; international justice vs. impunity. From this perspective, the outcome could hardly be clearer: a loss for idealism, law, community, human rights, and international justice — a surrender by Belgium to the forces that wish to keep thugs protected for the sake of smooth diplomatic intercourse.

Yet, the real picture is much more complex. In fact, the Belgian case can serve as a laboratory for the future of universal jurisdiction. It highlights the myriad of international actors who have a direct interest in these laws and the steps they will take to advance their claims. Most important, it affords critical lessons regarding what is now the central question surrounding universal jurisdiction: Do its benefits to human rights and public order outweigh its costs? Seen in this light, the Belgian saga is a defeat for a certain vision of universal jurisdiction, but a way forward for yet another. . . .

In the end, Belgium has changed its law in three critical ways since its 1993 and 1999 incarnations: (1) universal jurisdiction was replaced by a required link with Belgium in terms of the nationality or residence of the plaintiff or accused; (2) immunity from prosecution was recognized for leading foreign governmental officials while in office, and immunity from arrest applied to all persons on official visits; and (3) the role of the public prosecutor was increased where only the victim is Belgian. At the same time, the law does not close the Belgian courts to all victims of human rights abuses outside Belgium. Cases for the three specified crimes may proceed if (1) the requisite tie to Belgium is present; (2) the other states with a link to the crime do not have an independent system of justice; and (3) the accused is not one of the immunized governmental officials specified in the law, but is another sort of governmental official or former official, or has always been a private citizen. Moreover, the new law still does not require the accused to be present in Belgium for an investigation. Finally, Belgian courts are open for prosecution of other crimes if Belgium has an obligation under treaty or customary law to submit cases to its authorities for proceedings. . . .

The key questions for observers of *la débacle belge* should be the following: Is it possible to distinguish between cases that prosecutors and judges using universal jurisdiction statutes should investigate and those they should not? If not, should such states open their door or close it? If so, where is the line, and who should draw it? . . .

Universal jurisdiction does not operate in a vacuum. The process whereby one state investigates and then seeks the arrest of a sitting or former official of another state for acts undertaken while that person was an official — however clearly criminal those acts are under well-accepted definitions of international crimes — raises interstate tensions in ways that even the most vociferous criticism by one state of another's human rights practices does not. It is the difference between state responsibility and individual responsibility, one of the central challenges for the future of international criminal law.

[The author then suggests a number of factors that should be weighed by a state in deciding whether to pursue a case, including the presence of the accused in the state asserting jurisdiction (forum state); the severity of the atrocities; the strength of the evidence against the accused; whether the case can be seen as apolitical; the absence of an effective judiciary in the state where the crimes took place, combined with the presence of an effective judiciary in the forum state; special links between the territorial state and forum state; the political powerlessness of the defendants; and the absence of opposition from any state to the forum state's exercise of jurisdiction.]

Even if one believes that cases should be dismissed for various reasons, some would suggest that the final determination should rest with the investigating judge. I would not preclude the possibility that the investigating judge, rather than the prosecutor, should make the final screening determination. Human rights NGOs note that Augusto Pinochet would never have been investigated had it not been for the independence of investigating Judge Baltasar Garzon; when political officials became involved in the person of the United Kingdom's then home secretary Jack Straw, the case ended with Pinochet's return to Chile. But why be so confident that an independent judge will weigh the various factors better than a prosecutor? The issue requires further reflection, but whoever makes the final call must make the factors noted above part of his or her decision.

One of the persons against whom proceedings were brought in Belgium was the Minister for Foreign Affairs of the Democratic Republic of Congo (DRC), Abdulaye Yerodia Ndombasi. When Belgium issued an international warrant for his arrest for alleged serious violations of international humanitarian law, the DRC challenged the warrant before the International Court of Justice, on the grounds that Belgium had violated "the rule of customary international law concerning the absolute inviolability and immunity from criminal process of incumbent foreign ministers." 2002 I.C.J. 121, para. 10. Extracts from the Court's decision are set out below.

Case Concerning the Arrest Warrant of 11 April 2000 (*Democratic Republic of the Congo v. Belgium*)

2002 I.C.J. 121 (Feb. 14, 2002)

[The Court first considered and rejected several preliminary objections by Belgium founded, inter alia, on the fact that Mr. Yerodia was no longer a member of the DRC government.]

51. The Court would observe at the outset that in international law it is firmly established that, as also diplomatic and consular agents, certain holders of high-ranking office in a State, such as the Head of State, Head of Government and Minister for Foreign Affairs, enjoy immunities from jurisdiction in other States, both civil and criminal. For the purposes of the present case, it is only the

immunity from criminal jurisdiction and the inviolability of an incumbent Minister for Foreign Affairs that fall for the Court to consider....

53. In customary international law, the immunities accorded to Ministers for Foreign Affairs are not granted for their personal benefit, but to ensure the effective performance of their functions on behalf of their respective States....

54. The Court accordingly concludes that the functions of a Minister for Foreign Affairs are such that, throughout the duration of his or her office, he or she when abroad enjoys full immunity from criminal jurisdiction and inviolability. That immunity and that inviolability protect the individual concerned against any act of authority of another State which would hinder him or her in the performance of his or her duties.

55. In this respect, no distinction can be drawn between acts performed by a Minister for Foreign Affairs in an "official" capacity, and those claimed to have been performed in a "private capacity," or, for that matter, between acts performed before the person concerned assumed office as Minister for Foreign Affairs and acts committed during the period of office. Thus, if a Minister for Foreign Affairs is arrested in another State on a criminal charge, he or she is clearly thereby prevented from exercising the functions of his or her office. The consequences of such impediment to the exercise of those official functions are equally serious, regardless of whether the Minister for Foreign Affairs was, at the time of arrest, present in the territory of the arresting State on an "official" visit or a private visit, regardless of whether the arrest relates to acts allegedly performed before the person became the Minister for Foreign Affairs or to acts performed while in office, and regardless of whether the arrest relates to alleged acts performed in an "official" capacity or a "private" capacity. Furthermore, even the mere risk that, by travelling to or transiting another State a Minister for Foreign Affairs might be exposing himself or herself to legal proceedings could deter the Minister from travelling internationally when required to do so for the purposes of the performance of his or her official functions.

* * *

56. The Court will now address Belgium's argument that immunities accorded to incumbent Ministers for Foreign Affairs can in no case protect them where they are suspected of having committed war crimes or crimes against humanity....

58. The Court has carefully examined State practice, including national legislation and those few decisions of national higher courts, such as the House of Lords or the French Court of Cassation. It has been unable to deduce from this practice that there exists under customary international law any form of exception to the rule according immunity from criminal jurisdiction and inviolability to incumbent Ministers for Foreign Affairs, where they are suspected of having committed war crimes or crimes against humanity.

The Court has also examined the rules concerning the immunity or criminal responsibility of persons having an official capacity contained in the legal instruments creating international criminal tribunals, and which are specifically applicable to the latter [citations omitted]. It finds that these rules likewise do not enable it to conclude that any such an exception exists in customary international law in regard to national courts....

60. The Court emphasizes, however, that the immunity from jurisdiction enjoyed by incumbent Ministers for Foreign Affairs does not mean that they

enjoy impunity in respect of any crimes they might have committed, irrespective of their gravity. Immunity from criminal jurisdiction and individual criminal responsibility are quite separate concepts. While jurisdictional immunity is procedural in nature, criminal responsibility is a question of substantive law. Jurisdictional immunity may well bar prosecution for a certain period or for certain offences; it cannot exonerate the person to whom it applies from all criminal responsibility.

61. Accordingly, the immunities enjoyed under international law by an incumbent or former Minister for Foreign Affairs do not represent a bar to criminal prosecution in certain circumstances. First, such persons enjoy no criminal immunity under international law in their own countries, and may thus be tried by those countries' courts in accordance with the relevant rules of domestic law.

Secondly, they will cease to enjoy immunity from foreign jurisdiction if the State which they represent or have represented decides to waive that immunity.

Thirdly, after a person ceases to hold the office of Minister for Foreign Affairs, he or she will no longer enjoy all of the immunities accorded by international law in other States. Provided that it has jurisdiction under international law, a court of one State may try a former Minister for Foreign Affairs of another State in respect of acts committed prior or subsequent to his or her period of office, as well as in respect of acts committed during that period of office in a private capacity.

Fourthly, an incumbent or former Minister for Foreign Affairs may be subject to criminal proceedings before certain international criminal courts, where they have jurisdiction....

[The Court concluded that the issue and circulation of the arrest warrant did infringe Mr. Yerodia's immunity and therefore "constituted a violation of an obligation of Belgium towards the Congo, in that it failed to respect the immunity of that Minister and, more particularly, infringed the immunity from criminal jurisdiction and the inviolability then enjoyed by him under international law." Para. 71.]

In their joint separate opinion, Judges Higgins, Kooijmans, and Buergenthal addressed the question of whether Belgium was entitled to exercise universal jurisdiction at all, an issue avoided by the majority opinion. The opinion may reflect the human rights background of all three judges: Higgins was a member of the Human Rights Committee; Kooijmans served as Chairman of the UN Commission on Human Rights and was Special Rapporteur on Torture for six years; and Buergenthal was President of the Inter-American Court of Human Rights and also a member of the Human Rights Committee.

Case Concerning the Arrest Warrant of 11 April 2000 (*Democratic Republic of the Congo v. Belgium*) (joint separate opinion of Judges Higgins, Kooijmans, and Buergenthal)

2002 I.C.J. 121 (Feb. 14, 2002)

2. In its Judgment the Court says nothing on the question of whether — quite apart from the status of Mr. Yerodia at the relevant time — the Belgian magistracy

was entitled under international law to issue an arrest warrant for someone not at that time within its territory and pass it to Interpol. It has, in effect, acceded to the common wish of the Parties that the Court should not pronounce upon the key issue of jurisdiction that divided them, but should rather pass immediately to the question of immunity as it applied to the facts of this case.

3. In our opinion it was not only desirable, but indeed necessary, that the Court should have stated its position on this issue of jurisdiction....

5. Only if it is fully appreciated that there are two distinct norms of international law in play (albeit that the one — immunity — can arise only if the other — jurisdiction — exists) can the larger picture be seen. One of the challenges of present-day international law is to provide for stability of international relations and effective international intercourse while at the same time guaranteeing respect for human rights. The difficult task that international law today faces is to provide that stability in international relations by a means other than the impunity of those responsible for major human rights violations. This challenge is reflected in the present dispute and the Court should surely be engaged in this task, even as it fulfils its function of resolving a dispute that has arisen before it....

[After examining a number of treaties that provide for jurisdiction over persons not within the territory of a state, including treaties on genocide, humanitarian law, torture, drugs, hostage-taking, and aircraft hijacking, the opinion summarizes its "short historical survey" as follows:]

41. The parties to these treaties agreed both to grounds of jurisdiction and as to the obligation to take the measures necessary to establish such jurisdiction. The specified grounds relied on links of nationality of the offender, or the ship or aircraft concerned, or of the victim.... These may properly be described as treaty-based broad extraterritorial jurisdiction. But in addition to these were the parallel provisions whereby a State party in whose jurisdiction the alleged perpetrator of such offences is found, shall prosecute him or extradite him. By the loose use of language the latter has come to be referred to as "universal jurisdiction", though this is really an obligatory territorial jurisdiction over persons, albeit in relation to acts committed elsewhere....

44.... [W]e note that the inaccurately termed "universal jurisdiction principle" in these treaties is a principle of obligation, while the question in this case is whether Belgium had the right to issue and circulate the arrest warrant if it so chose....

45. That there is no established practice in which States exercise universal jurisdiction, properly so called, is undeniable. As we have seen, virtually all national legislation envisages links of some sort to the forum State; and no case law exists in which pure universal jurisdiction has formed the basis of jurisdiction. This does not necessarily indicate, however, that such an exercise would be unlawful. In the first place, national legislation reflects the circumstances in which a State provides in its own law the ability to exercise jurisdiction....

47. The contemporary trends, reflecting international relations as they stand at the beginning of the new century, are striking. The movement is towards bases of jurisdiction other than territoriality....

48. In civil matters we already see the beginnings of a very broad form of extraterritorial jurisdiction. Under the Alien Tort Claims Act, the United States, basing itself on a law of 1789, has asserted a jurisdiction both over human rights

violations and over major violations of international law, perpetrated by non-nationals overseas. . . . [See Chapter 6, page 478.]

[51.] At the same time, the international consensus that the perpetrators of international crimes should not go unpunished is being advanced by a flexible strategy, in which newly-established international criminal tribunals, treaty obligations and national courts all have their part to play. We reject the suggestion that the battle against impunity is "made over" to international treaties and tribunals, with national courts having no competence in such matters. Great care has been taken when formulating the relevant treaty provisions not to exclude other grounds of jurisdiction that may be exercised on a voluntary basis. . . .

53. This brings us once more to the particular point that divides the Parties in this case: is it a precondition of the assertion of universal jurisdiction that the accused be within the territory? . . .

59. If, as we believe to be the case, a State may choose to exercise a universal criminal jurisdiction in absentia, it must also ensure that certain safeguards are in place. They are absolutely essential to prevent abuse and to ensure that the rejection of impunity does not jeopardize stable relations between States. . . .

A State contemplating bringing criminal charges based on universal jurisdiction must first offer to the national State of the prospective accused person the opportunity itself to act upon the charges concerned. . . .

Further, such charges may only be laid by a prosecutor or juge d'instruction who acts in full independence, without links to or control by the government of that State. . . .

* * *

60. It is equally necessary that universal criminal jurisdiction be exercised only over those crimes regarded as the most heinous by the international community [such as piracy, war crimes, and crimes against humanity]. . . .

71. As to the matter of immunity, although we agree in general with what has been said in the Court's Judgment with regard to the specific issue put before it, we nevertheless feel that the approach chosen by the Court has to a certain extent transformed the character of the case before it. By focusing exclusively on the immunity issue, while at the same time bypassing the question of jurisdiction, the impression is created that immunity has value per se, whereas in reality it is an exception to a normative rule which would otherwise apply. . . .

[75.] [A] trend is discernible that in a world which increasingly rejects impunity for the most repugnant offences, the attribution of responsibility and accountability is becoming firmer, the possibility for the assertion of jurisdiction wider and the availability of immunity as a shield more limited. The law of privileges and immunities, however, retains its importance since immunities are granted to high State officials to guarantee the proper functioning of the network of mutual inter-State relations, which is of paramount importance for a well-ordered and harmonious international system.

[The opinion concludes by agreeing with the majority that, in the circumstances of the case before them, the Belgian arrest warrant did interfere with the immunity due the Congolese Foreign Minister. However, the authors disagree with the majority's conclusion that Foreign Ministers enjoy the same immunity as heads of state and suggest that immunity may not exist if a foreign minister is on "private" travels.]

Comments and Questions

1. Although piracy is often cited as the quintessential international crime subject to universal jurisdiction, at least one scholar questions that widely accepted assumption. See Alfred P. Rubin, *The Law of Piracy* (1988):

> It can be concluded that "universal jurisdiction" was at best a rule of international law only for a limited period of time and under political circumstances that no longer apply; at worst it was merely a British attribution to the international legal order of substantive rules forbidding "piracy" and authorizing all nations to apply their laws against it on the high seas, based on a model of imperial Rome, and British racial and commercial ambitions that never did reflect deeper realities, as part of the rationalization of imperialism never really persuasive outside of England alone.

Id. at 343.

2. Prosecutors operating in a purely domestic context normally have a great deal of discretion in determining when and if to seek indictments and against which alleged criminals they should proceed. In jurisdictions such as the United States, it is common to grant immunity to or agree to lesser sentences for lower-level criminals, in exchange for their testimony against co-defendants or more important criminals. Given the potential diplomatic impact and the evidentiary concerns noted by Kamminga, should not potential forum states have at least the degree of discretion we allow domestic prosecutors, if the forum state has no territorial or personal link to the alleged crime? For a discussion of how these issues might be balanced, see International Council on Human Rights, *Hard cases: bringing human rights violators to justice abroad* (1999).

3. Are former Secretary of State Kissinger's arguments against universal jurisdiction an honest attempt to insert a realist perspective into the debate, or might they be more self-serving? Cf. Christopher Hitchens, *The Trial of Henry Kissinger* (2001). According to Hitchens, Kissinger has been sought for questioning by investigating judges in France, Spain, and Argentina. See *Christopher Hitchens versus David Rieff, Pinochet, Milosevic . . . Henry Kissinger*? 66 Prospect (Aug. 2001).

4. Also pending before the I.C.J. is a case brought by the DRC against France, which addresses issues similar to the case extracted supra, but written pleadings are not scheduled to be completed before August 2007. Certain Criminal Proceedings in France (*Democratic Republic of the Congo v. France*).

5. The opinion by Higgins, Kooijmans, and Buergenthal in *DRC v. Belgium*, supra page 955, suggests that the exercise of universal jurisdiction if the accused is not within the territory of the forum state should be predicated on the exercise of "certain safeguards," including that the state of nationality be offered the opportunity to act on the charges and that the charges "may only be laid by a prosecutor or juge d'instruction who acts in full independence, without links to or control by the government of" the forum state. Are these safeguards any more authoritative than those suggested by Ratner, supra page 951? From what international legal norms are they derived, if any?

6. As noted by Ratner, supra page 951, Belgium's revised law on international crimes is not without effect. In June 2005, two Rwandan businessmen were found guilty of participating in the 1994 genocide and sentenced to prison. *Nzabonimana est condamnéà 12 ans, Ndashikirwa à 10 ans*, La Libre Belgique, June 30,

2005. In addition, Belgium continued to investigate allegations of torture and other crimes against former Chadian dictator Hissène Habré, under a "grandfather clause" in the 2003 statute that allowed cases to proceed if the plaintiff was a Belgian citizen or resident at the time the complaint was filed and if an investigation had already been initiated. In September 2005, Belgium issued an international arrest warrant for Habré. For background on the Habré case, which included a failed attempt to try Habré in Senegal (to which he fled in 1990), see Human Rights Watch, *The Victims of Hissène Habré Still Awaiting Justice* (July 2005); Stephen P. Marks, "The Hissène Habré Case: The Law and Politics of Universal Jurisdiction," in *Universal Jurisdiction: National Courts and the Prosecution of Serious Crimes under International Law* (Stephen Macedo ed., 2004).

7. In July 2005, British courts convicted an Afghan warlord (who had been living in the U.K. since 1998) of "torture and hostage-taking" and sentenced him to twenty years' imprisonment. The presiding judge said that the defendant, Faryadi Zardad, had "transgressed the basic rights of humanity." Cahal Milmo, *British court makes history with conviction of Afghan warlord*, The Independent, July 19, 2005. In September 2005, two other former Afghan generals who had been living in The Netherlands were charged with torture and war crimes. Marlise Simons, 2 *Afghans Face Dutch War-Crimes Charges From 80's Soviet Era*, N.Y. Times, Sept. 29, 2005.

Similarly, in the first case of its kind, a Dutch court in April 2004 convicted a DRC colonel of torture, under a Dutch statute that gives the Netherlands universal jurisdiction over torture; legislation adopted in 2003 expanded the crimes to include gdnocide, crimes against humanity, and war crimes, but jurisdiction may be exercised only if the accused is physically present in the Netherlands. See *International Decisions, Prosecutor v. N., Case No.* A07178, 99 Am. J. Int'l L. 686 (2005).

8. An attempt by the Center for Constitutional Rights in 2004 to prosecute Secretary of Defense Rumsfeld and others for atrocities in Abu Ghraib and elsewhere under a German statute that asserts universal jurisdiction over certain war crimes was rejected by the German federal prosecutor; the prosecutor acted within his discretion not to bring a case if the possible prosecution was outweighed by other principles. See Jan Arnmo Hessbruegge, *An Attempt to Have Secretary Rumsfeld and Others Indicted for War Crimes under the German Volkerstrafgesetzbuch*, ASIL Insight (Dec. 2004), at. 1; American Society of International Law, International Law in Brief (Oct. 31, 2005), *http://www.asil.org/ilib/2005/10/ilib051031.htm#ju4*.

VI. The "Piecemeal" Convention Approach Coupled with Domestic Enforcement

A more widely accepted alternative to universal jurisdiction has been to provide what might be called "transnational" jurisdiction through treaties. This approach dates back to the 1949 Geneva Conventions, which obligate states to punish "grave breaches" of humanitarian law no matter where such crimes are committed. However, more typical provisions may be found in a number of conventions that address international or transnational crimes which, by their nature, may be of interest to more than one state, such as terrorism, tax evasion, trafficking in drugs and persons, and hostage-taking. On the other hand, treaties on slavery, apartheid, and torture address quintessentially "human rights" issues, which traditionally would be of direct concern only to the state on whose territory violations occur.

A. *Slavery and Apartheid*

The historical development of the prohibition against slavery is discussed in Chapter 1. As noted therein, slavery has been an international crime at least since the late nineteenth century and is today prohibited by general human rights treaties as well as the 1926 Slavery Convention, its 1953 Protocol, and the 1956 Supplementary Convention on the Abolition of Slavery.

The International Convention on the Suppression and Punishment of the Crime of Apartheid, adopted Nov. 30 Nov. 1973, entered into force July 18, 1976, 1015 U.N.T.S. 243, was one of the clearest modern declarations of an international crime. Article I declares that apartheid is "a crime against humanity" and that inhuman acts resulting from it are "crimes violating the principles of international law." Article V, in addition to providing more explicitly that domestic courts may try offenders under the principle of universal jurisdiction, adds the provision (nearly identical with the one found in Article 6 of the Genocide Convention) that trial also may occur before "an international penal tribunal having jurisdiction with respect to those States Parties which shall have accepted its jurisdiction." This latter option is today more than theoretical, since apartheid is included among the crimes against humanity that fall within the jurisdiction of the International Criminal Court.

Nonetheless, at least one recognized authority on international criminal law believes that apartheid does not rise to the status of an international crime, because the more than 100 parties to the Apartheid Convention do not include any "Western" country and because the issue seems to be inherently limited in time and space. Cassese, supra page 888, at 25. Other analysts have stated that apartheid's status as a crime under customary law "is a matter of some conjecture." Ratner and Abrams, supra page 892, at 122.

The current relevance of the convention would seen to be limited, at best. "The Convention was drafted hastily and was clearly meant to apply to one state alone. For this reason, its definitions may be both too vague and too specific for application beyond South Africa. . . . To our knowledge, the ban on apartheid (in treaty or custom) has not been invoked by victims, their advocates, or international bodies in responding to the plight [of a number of groups that might conceivably fall within the convention's proscription]. . . . It thus seems best to regard the Apartheid Convention as a potential source of law for imputing criminal responsibility for certain patterns of racial discrimination, but one which states have not yet shown much inclination to apply." Id. at 122-23. Human rights NGOs that rail against impunity elsewhere seem satisfied with the "truth and reconciliation" approach adopted by South Africa upon the achievement of majority rule in the mid-1990s, an issue that is mentioned supra, page 945.

B. *Torture*

The Convention Against Torture and Other Cruel, Inhuman or Degrading Treatment or Punishment, adopted Dec. 10, 1984, entered into force June 28, 1987, 1465 U.N.T.S. 85 (1987), which the United States ratified in 1994, is the paradigmatic blend of human rights and international criminal law. It is one of the great successes of Amnesty International and other NGOs that a practice both abhorred and ignored when AI began its international campaign against torture in 1973 became the subject of a General Assembly Resolution in only two years, G.A. Res. 3452 (Dec. 9, 1975); was the subject of a second resolution a few years later (Principles of Medical Ethics Relevant to the Role of Health Personnel, Particularly Physicians, in the Protection of Prisoners and Detainees against Torture and Other Cruel, Inhuman or Degrading Treatment or Punishment, G.A. Res. 37/194 (Dec. 18, 1982)); and finally became a convention that has been ratified by approximately 140 countries.

The Torture Convention is typical of treaties that create criminal liability outside the field of the laws of war. After defining the crime in Article 1, it sets forth the specific obligations of states not only to abolish torture within their own territory but to ensure that no torturer escapes responsibility, no matter where the crime was committed. The following are the relevant articles.

Article 2

1. Each State party shall take effective legislative, administrative, judicial or other measures to prevent such acts of torture in any territory under its jurisdiction. . . .

Article 4

1. Each State Party shall ensure that all acts of torture are offences under its criminal law. The same shall apply to an attempt to commit torture and to an act by any person which constitutes complicity or participation in torture.

2. Each State Party shall make these offences punishable by appropriate penalties which take into account their grave nature.

Article 5

1. Each State Party shall take such measures as may be necessary to establish its jurisdiction over the offences referred to in article 4 in the following cases:

(a) When the offences are committed in any territory under its jurisdiction or on board a ship or aircraft registered in that State;

(b) When the alleged offender is a national of that State;

(c) When the victim is a national of that State if that State considers it appropriate.

2. Each State Party shall likewise take such measures as may be necessary to establish its jurisdiction over such offences in cases where the alleged offender is present in any territory under its jurisdiction and it does not extradite him pursuant to article 8 to any of the States mentioned in paragraph 1 of this article.

3. This Convention does not exclude any criminal jurisdiction exercised in accordance with internal law.

Article 6

1. Upon being satisfied, after an examination of information available to it, that the circumstances so warrant, any State Party in whose territory a person alleged to have committed any offence referred to in article 4 is present shall take him into custody or take other legal measures to ensure his presence. The custody and other legal measures shall be as provided in the law of that State but may be continued only for such time as is necessary to enable any criminal or extradition proceedings to be instituted. . . .

Article 7

1. The State Party in the territory under whose jurisdiction a person alleged to have committed an offence referred to in article 4 is found shall in the cases contemplated in article 5, if it does not extradite him, submit the case to its competent authorities for the purpose of prosecution.

2. These authorities shall take their decision in the same manner as in the case of any ordinary offence of a serious nature under the law of that State. In the cases referred to in article 5, paragraph 2, the standards of evidence required for prosecution and conviction shall in no way be less stringent than those which apply in the cases referred to in article 5, paragraph 1.

3. Any person regarding whom proceedings are brought in connection with any of the offences referred to in article 4 shall be guaranteed fair treatment at all stages of the proceedings.

Article 8

1. The offences referred to in article 4 shall be deemed to be included as extraditable offences in any extradition treaty existing between State Parties. States Parties undertake to include such offences as extraditable offences in every extradition treaty to be concluded between them.

2. If a State Party which makes extradition conditional on the existence of a treaty receives a request for extradition from another State Party with which it has no extradition treaty, it may consider this Convention as the legal basis for extradition in respect to such offences. Extradition shall be subject to the other conditions provided by the law of the requested State.

3. States Parties which do not make extradition conditional on the existence of a treaty shall recognize such offences as extraditable offences between themselves subject to the conditions provided by the law of the requested State.

4. Such offenses shall be treated, for the purpose of extradition between States Parties, as if they had been committed not only in the place in which they occurred but also in the territories of the States required to establish their jurisdiction in accordance with article 5, paragraph 1.

In addition, Article 3 prohibits the expulsion, return, or extradition of any person to a state where there are "substantial grounds" to believe that the returnee would be in danger of being tortured.

Torture has been an integral part of almost every case brought against former dictators and security force members on the basis of universal jurisdiction. Examine Article 5(1) closely; does it create truly universal jurisdiction, or would the links with the prosecuting state that are mentioned justify the exercise of jurisdiction even without the convention? Is Article 5(2) more "universal"? Does it go further than the jurisdiction asserted by the International Criminal Court?

C. *Terrorism*

The international community has never been able to define terrorism in general terms, as evidenced by continuing recourse to the adage that "one person's terrorist is another person's freedom fighter." That reluctance may be weakening, and the 2004 report of the UN Secretary-General's High-Level Panel on Threats, Challenges, and Change reached consensus on defining terrorism as "any action . . . that is intended to cause death or serious bodily harm to civilians or non-combatants, when the purpose of such act, by its nature or context, is to intimidate a population, or to compel a Government or an international organization to do or to abstain from doing any act." United Nations, *A more secure world: Our shared responsibility* (2004), para. 164(d). The General Assembly created an Ad Hoc Committee in 1996 to consider the issue, G.A. Res. 51/210 (Dec. 17, 1996), but failure to agree on a definition has stalled adoption of an omnibus Comprehensive Convention on Terrorism for a decade. See Thalif Deen, *U.N. Member States Struggle to Define Terrorism*, Inter-Press News Service, July 25, 2005.

Another approach is to simply to define specific acts as illegal, without attempting to define "terrorism" in general. There are now over a dozen multilateral conventions dealing with terrorist acts (the most recent of which was adopted in 2005), in addition to bilateral or other treaties that countries have adopted to address specific circumstances. The UN Office on Drugs and Crime summarizes the common factors in each of these conventions as follows (although one should, of course, consult each treaty for specific provisions):

> These conventions and protocols were negotiated from 1963. . . . Most are penal in nature with a common format. Typically the instruments:
>
> 1) Define a particular type of terrorist violence as an offence under the convention, such as seizure of an aircraft in flight by threat or violence;
> 2) Require State Parties to penalize that activity in their domestic law;
> 3) Identify certain bases upon which the Parties responsible are required to establish jurisdiction over the defined offence, such as registration, territoriality or nationality;
> 4) Create an obligation on the State in which a suspect is found to establish jurisdiction over the convention offence and to refer the offence for prosecution if the Party does not extradite pursuant to other provisions of the convention. This last element is commonly known as the principle of "no safe haven for terrorists". It has ben stressed by the Security Council in Resolution 1372 of 28 September 2001, as an essential anti-terrorism obligation of Member States.

http://www.unodc.org/unodc/en/terrorism_convention_overview.html (emphasis deleted).

Thirteen major conventions adopted under the auspices of the United Nations or other global international organizations are listed below. Together they create a relatively comprehensive system for establishing jurisdiction over terrorist suspects no matter where they are found, but the problem is clearly more one of enforcement than theoretical legal commitment.

Ratification of these treaties has been relatively widespread, ranging in mid-2005 from approximately 180 parties to the older Tokyo, Hague, and Montreal Conventions to 100-150 parties for some of the more recent conventions.

Convention on Offences and Certain Other Acts Committed On Board Aircraft, adopted Sept. 14, 1963, entered into force, Dec. 4, 1969, 20 U.S.T. 2941, T.I.A.S. No. 6768, 704 U.N.T.S. 219 ("Tokyo Convention")

Convention for the Suppression of Unlawful Seizure of Aircraft, adopted Dec. 16, 1970, entered into force Oct. 14, 1971, 22 U.S.T. 1641, T.I.A.S. No. 7192, 860 U.N.T.S. 105 ("Hague Convention")

Convention for the Suppression of Unlawful Acts Against the Safety of Civil Aviation, adopted Sept. 23, 1971, entered into force Jan. 26, 1973, 24 U.S.T. 564, T.I.A.S. No. 7570, 974 U.N.T.S. 177 ("Montreal Convention")

Convention on the Prevention and Punishment of Crimes Against Internationally Protected Persons, adopted Dec. 14, 1973, entered into force Feb. 20, 1977, 28 U.S.T. 1975, T.I.A.S. No. 8532, 1035 U.N.T.S. 167

International Convention Against the Taking of Hostages, adopted Dec. 17, 1979, entered into force June 3, 1983, T.I.A.S. No. 11081, 1316 U.N.T.S. 205

Convention on the Physical Protection of Nuclear Material, opened for signature Mar. 3, 1980, entered into force Feb. 7, 1987, I.A.E.A. Legal Series No. 12 (1982), 18 Int'l L. Mat. 1919 (1979)

Protocol for the Suppression of Unlawful Acts of Violence at Airports Serving International Civil Aviation, supplementary to the Convention for the Suppression of Unlawful Acts against the Safety of Civil Aviation (Extends and supplements the Montreal Convention on Air Safety), adopted Feb. 24, 1988, entered into force Aug. 6, 1989, 27 Int'l L. Mat. 627 (1988)

Convention for the Suppression of Unlawful Acts Against the Safety of Maritime Navigation, adopted Mar. 10, 1988, entered into force Mar. 1, 1992, I.M.O. Doc. SUA/CON/15 (1988), 27 Int'l L. Mat. 668 (1988)

Protocol for the Suppression of Unlawful Acts Against the Safety of Fixed Platforms Located on the Continental Shelf, adopted Mar. 10, 1988, entered into force Mar. 1, 1992, 27 Int'l L. Mat. 685 (1988)

Convention on the Marking of Plastic Explosives for the Purpose of Detection, adopted Mar. 1, 1991, entered into force June 21, 1998, 2123 U.N.T.S. xxx

International Convention for the Suppression of Terrorist Bombings, adopted Dec. 15, 1997, entered into force May 23, 2001, UN GA Res. 52/164 (1997)

International Convention for the Suppression of the Financing of Terrorism, adopted Dec. 9, 1999, entered into force Apr. 10, 2002, UN GA Res. 54/109

International Convention for the Suppression of Acts of Nuclear Terrorism, adopted Apr. 13, 2005, UN GA Res. 59/290 (not yet in force)

Most of these treaties require implementation through the adoption of corresponding domestic legislation. For example, under the Hostage Taking Act, 18 U.S.C. §1203 (1994), the United States successfully prosecuted a Lebanese resident-citizen for the hijacking of a Jordanian civilian aircraft in the Middle East with three U.S. nationals aboard. *United States v. Yunis*, 681 F. Supp. 896, 904-905 (D.D.C. 1988). The district court held, inter alia, that aircraft piracy and hostage-taking were international crimes justifying the assertion of jurisdiction. Id. at 900-901.

D. *Other Transnational Crimes*

Space limitations prohibit an exhaustive discussion of all international crimes, many of which include provisions similar to that of the Torture Convention, supra page 961. See, e.g., Jordan J. Paust et al., *International Criminal Law: Cases and Materials* 1051-1122 (2d ed. 2000); Edgar M. Wise, Ellen S. Podgor, and Roger S. Clark, *International Criminal Law: Cases and Materials* 121-208 (2004). One question to consider is whether and how policies and practices adopted to deal with "ordinary" crimes — such as drug trafficking, money laundering, art fraud, and financial crimes — might be adapted to deal with "human rights" crimes. In any event, criminalizing certain behavior often raises deep political, social, and economic issues — just as human rights norms reflect (some might say impose) assumptions about the social and economic "root causes" of violations.

Some transnational crimes have more obvious human rights implications than others, such as treaties that deal with human trafficking, particularly of women and girls. "White slavery" treaties date from the 1904 International Agreement for the Suppression of the White Slave Traffic, adopted May 18, 1904, 1 L.N.T.S. 83, and include the International Convention for the Suppression of the White Slave Traffic, adopted May 4, 1910, 3 L.N.T.S. 278; International Convention for the Suppression of the Traffic in Women and Children, adopted Sept. 30, 1921, 9 L.N.T.S. 415; and International Convention for the Suppression of the Traffic in Women of Full Age, adopted Oct. 11, 1933, 150 L.N.T.S. 431. All of these treaties were amended by protocols adopted in the late 1940s and have been supplemented by the Convention for the Suppression of the Traffic in Persons and of the Exploitation of the Prostitution of Others, opened for signature Mar. 21, 1950, entered into force July 25, 1951, 96 U.N.T.S. 272.

Sex trafficking, in particular, has received a great deal of international attention in the past decade, and the United Nations in 2000 adopted a Protocol to Prevent, Suppress and Punish Trafficking in Persons, Especially Women and Children, Supplementing the United Nations Convention Against Transnational Organized Crime, G.A. Res. 55/25 (Nov. 15, 2000). In 2005, the Council of Europe adopted a Convention on Action against Trafficking in Human Beings, adopted May 16, 2005, Europ. T.S. No. 197.

While they do not themselves create international crimes, some human rights treaties also call upon states to criminalize human trafficking. See Convention on the Elimination of All Forms of Discrimination Against Women, adopted Mar. 1, 1980, entered into force Sept. 3, 1981, 1249 U.N.T.S. 14 (Art. 6), and the Optional Protocol to the Convention on the Rights of the Child on the sale of children, child prostitution and child pornography, adopted May 25, 2000, entered into force Jan. 18, 2002, G.A. Res. 54/263. See generally Mohammed Mattar, *Trafficking in Persons: An Annotated Legal Bibliography*, 96 Law Libr. J. 669 (2004).

Comments and Questions

1. The full title of the Torture Convention includes reference to "other cruel, inhuman or degrading treatment or punishment," although most of the treaty's provisions deal only with torture. Article 16(1) provides:

> Each State Party shall undertake to prevent in any territory under its jurisdiction other acts of cruel, inhuman or degrading treatment or punishment which do not amount to torture as defined in article 1, when such acts are committed by or at the instigation of or with the consent or acquiescence of a public official or other person acting in an official capacity. In particular, the obligations contained in articles 10, 11, 12 and 13 shall apply with the substitution for references to torture of references to other forms of cruel, inhuman or degrading treatment or punishment.

Why did the drafters of the treaty not extend its provisions to all of the prohibited forms of ill-treatment?

2. The principle of *aut prosequi aut dedere* (prosecute or extradite) is central to the Torture Convention and most other international criminal conventions. Does a state have a free choice between the two options? Should deference be given to extradition to a state with close ties to either victims or perpetrators, as opposed to a state without such ties? What if the states of the victim, perpetrator, and territory of the crime are all different? (This is not such a far-fetched scenario; one could easily imagine, for example, a Belgian citizen being tortured or killed by Rwandan forces or paramilitaries within the territory of the Democratic Republic of Congo. To which country should a fourth state extradite an alleged perpetrator that it arrests pursuant to Article 6?)

VII. The Exercise of National Jurisdiction under Domestic Law: Amnesties and Prosecutions

Of course, all of the crimes discussed in this chapter are likely to be crimes under domestic law as well as international law. If the crimes are committed within the territory of a state, domestic courts will have jurisdiction to try and punish the perpetrator.

Reread the account of attempts to try General Pinochet for crimes committed by his regime in Chile between 1973 and 1988, supra page 885. Although pursuit of Pinochet was no doubt given new political impetus by the efforts of Spanish judge Garzón and the judgment of the British Law Lords, the most serious threat from General Pinochet's perspective comes from the many domestic charges filed against him, both criminal and civil. Compare the Chilean experience with that in neighboring Argentina, which suffered from a similar, albeit shorter, military dictatorship at the same time that Pinochet was in power in Chile.

Note: Human Rights Prosecutions in Argentina

A military dictatorship held power in Argentina from 1976-1983. As in Chile, the military regime routinely rounded up dissidents and suspected left-wing sympathizers. Many were tortured, and thousands died or disappeared. A 1984 government investigation concluded that 11,000 people died or disappeared at the hands of military officers, soldiers, and police during Argentina's "dirty war," although human rights groups asserted that the true figure of the disappeared could be up to three times as many. A particularly chilling practice was the kidnapping of babies born to mothers who were imprisoned by the military regime. It was estimated that approximately 500 babies were taken from their imprisoned mothers, with the military falsifying birth records and passing the children off for adoption. Informe de la Comisión Nacional sobre la Desaparición de Personas, *http://www.nuncamas.org/english/library/nevagain/nevagain_001.htm.*

Several of the highest-ranking military officers were tried and convicted of crimes when democracy was restored in Argentina in 1983. However, the military resisted the investigations and twice threatened to mutiny. President Raúl Alfonsin, fearing insurrection, ended the investigations and obtained from Congress two amnesty laws which protected the military from future prosecution. The first law was the Full Stop (Punto Final) Law No. 23,492 of 1986, which established a sixty-day deadline for initiating any new human rights prosecutions. A second law, the Due Obedience Law No. 23,521 of 1987, protected lower-ranking officers from prosecution, on the grounds that soldiers are legally compelled to carry out orders, under the doctrine of "due obedience." Both laws were upheld by the Argentine Supreme Court in 1987. In 1990, President Carlos Menem, acting from a professed desire to further national reconciliation, granted a pardon to all military officials who had been indicted or convicted for acts during the period of military rule.

Beginning in 1998, perhaps because democracy seemed more stable, Argentine courts began to indict military officers for the kidnapping of prisoners' babies, as well as for alleged participation in the transnational, anti-leftist Operation Condor, acts which were not covered by the amnesty laws. In August 2003, the Argentine Congress annulled the earlier amnesty laws and adopted legislation to facilitate the prosecution of crimes against humanity. Under President Nestor Kirchner, who took office in May 2003, Argentina formally ratified the UN Convention on the Non-Applicability of Statutory Limitations to War Crimes and Crimes Against Humanity, adopted Nov. 26, 1968, entered into force Nov. 11, 1970, 754 U.N.T.S. 73.

On June 14, 2005, Argentina's Supreme Court overruled its earlier judgment and declared the two amnesty laws adopted in the 1980s unconstitutional and contrary to Argentina's obligations under international human rights treaties. Military figures from the years of the dictatorship again face the threat of prosecution.

In Chile, Argentina, Uruguay, and many other countries emerging from periods of dictatorship and/or gross violations of human rights, the question arises as to whether there is an *obligation* to try those guilty of the most serious crimes or whether issuing amnesties, pardons, or simply declining to prosecute alleged criminals is a viable and internationally justifiable alternative. The following extract makes the case for recognizing a limited international obligation to prosecute.

Diane Orentlicher, *Settling Accounts: The Duty to Prosecute Human Rights Violations of a Prior Regime*

100 Yale L.J. 2537, 2541-42, 2544-45, 2546-47, 2550, 2551-52, 2583-84, 2595-96, 2599-2601, 2607, 2608, 2615 (1991) (citations omitted)

I. WHY PUNISH?

The debate over post-transition prosecutions has focused on their potential role in ending cycles of state violence and promoting consolidation of democratic transitions. These considerations have, in turn, informed a broader debate about the role that international law should play in shaping governments' policy toward violations of a prior regime.

A. THE CASE FOR PROSECUTIONS

The fulcrum of the case for criminal punishment is that it is the most effective insurance against future repression. By laying bare the truth about violations of the past and condemning them, prosecutions can deter potential lawbreakers and inoculate the public against future temptation to be complicit in state-sponsored violence. Trials may, as well, inspire societies that are reexamining their basic values to affirm the fundamental principles of respect for the rule of law and for the inherent dignity of individuals.

Above all, however, the case for prosecutions turns on the consequences of failing to punish atrocious crimes committed by a prior regime on a sweeping scale. If law is unavailable to punish widespread brutality of the recent past, what lesson can be offered for the future? A complete failure of enforcement vitiates the authority of law itself, sapping its power to deter proscribed conduct. This may be tolerable when the law or the crime is of marginal consequence, but there can be no scope for eviscerating wholesale laws that forbid violence and that have been violated on a massive scale. Societies recently scourged by lawlessness need look no farther than their own past to discover the costs of impunity. Their history provides sobering cause to believe, with William Pitt, that tyranny begins where law ends. . . .

B. THE CASE AGAINST PROSECUTIONS

The chief argument against a general rule requiring prosecutions is that fragile democracies may not be able to survive the destabilizing effects of politically charged trials. Many countries emerging from dictatorship are polarized and unstable, and may be further fractured by prosecutions of the prior regime's depredations. Under these circumstances, some urge, democratic consolidation can be furthered by implementing a policy of reconciliation embodied in an amnesty law covering past violations. . . .

C. THE ROLE OF INTERNATIONAL LAWS

As thus framed, the policy debate has tended to view the imperatives of the rule of law as somehow fundamentally at odds with political reality. This approach is unwarranted. The law itself can accommodate the constraints surrounding transitional societies while securing crucially important values. Addressing the dilemma of tenuous democracies through law assures that an appropriate balance is struck between the demands of justice and potentially conflicting values, such as political stability....

By drawing a bright line between crimes that must be punished and those for which amnesties are permissible, international law helps answer an agonizing question confronting many transitional societies: How is it possible to seek accountability without setting off an endless chain of divisive recriminations?...

II. The Duty to Punish Under Current International Law

Increasingly,... international law has required states to punish certain human rights crimes committed in their territorial jurisdiction. Several human rights treaties require States Parties to criminalize particular abuses, such as genocide and torture, investigate violations and seek to punish the wrongdoers. On their face the more comprehensive treaties, such as the International Covenant on Civil and Political Rights, are silent about a duty to punish violations of the rights they ensure. But authoritative interpretations of these treaties make clear that a State Party fails in its duty to ensure the cluster of rights protecting physical integrity if it does not investigate violations and seek to punish those who are responsible. Moreover a state's failure to punish repeated or notorious violations breaches the customary obligation to respect the same set of preeminent rights....

A wide range of activities of the United Nations and other intergovernmental organizations reinforce the view that punishment plays a necessary part in states' duty under customary law to ensure the rights to life, freedom from torture, and freedom from involuntary disappearance. For example, reports prepared by Special Rapporteurs, Special Representatives, and Working Groups appointed by the Commission on Human Rights of the United Nations to report on human rights conditions in particular countries or on particular types of human rights violations have repeatedly condemned governments' failure to punish torture, disappearances, and extra-legal executions.... [T]hese reports have asserted that a state's failure to punish repeated violations of physical integrity encourages further violations. Although these reports are not authoritative interpretations of international law, resolutions of the U.N. General Assembly have endorsed many of the reports' conclusions regarding punishment of persons responsible for torture, disappearances, and extra-legal executions.

If international law generally requires states to punish serious violations of physical integrity, must a successor government attempt to prosecute every such violation committed with impunity during a recent dictatorship? Or does international law provide a basis for "mitigating" the duty in light of the peculiar constraints prevailing in transitional societies?

In addressing these questions, it is important to begin by making clear what is not at issue. First, the fact that a democratically elected government succeeds a repressive regime has no bearing on the state's international obligations. It is well-established that a change in government does not relieve a state of its duties under international law. Accordingly, if an outgoing government failed to discharge its duty to punish atrocious crimes, its successor is generally bound to fulfill the obligation.

Second, that prosecutions may be inexpedient politically is no excuse for a government's failure to discharge its legal obligations. International law does not, of course, require states to take action that poses a serious threat to vital national interests. But a state cannot evade its duty to punish atrocious crimes merely to appease disaffected military forces or to promote national reconciliation. However desirable the objectives, the government must find other means to achieve them. Ratification of an amnesty law through some form of democratic procedure would not alter this conclusion; nations cannot extinguish their international obligations by enacting inconsistent domestic law. . . .

Somewhat more difficult issues are raised by the question whether international law can accommodate the peculiar constraints faced by nations that have recently emerged from a protracted period of lawlessness. In a country like Argentina, where some 9,000 persons are estimated to have disappeared during the military juntas' "dirty war against subversion," a requirement that the government attempt to prosecute everyone who may be criminally liable could place impossible demands on the judiciary. Even a well-functioning judicial system would be incapable of discharging such a burden; much less can this be expected following the wholesale collapse of judicial process. . . .

1. Application of Customary International Law

The duty to punish human rights crimes imposed by customary law canreadily accommodate the constraints faced by transitional societies. . . . [C]ustomary law would be violated by complete impunity for repeated or notorious instances of torture, extra-legal executions, and disappearances, but would not require prosecution of every person who committed such an offense. Prosecution of those who were most responsible for designing and implementing a system of human rights atrocities or for especially notorious crimes that were emblematic of past violations would seemingly discharge governments' customary-law obligation not to condone or encourage such violations, provided the criteria used to select potential defendants did not appear to condone or tolerate past abuses.

2. Application of Comprehensive Human Rights Conventions

More complex issues are raised by the question whether a government of a state that has ratified the International Covenant, the European Convention, or the American Convention must attempt to prosecute all serious violations of the right to physical integrity committed, following the convention's entry into force for the state, by or with the acquiescence of a previous regime. Decisions interpreting these conventions include some indications that States Parties are in general expected to investigate every violation of the rights to life, freedom from torture, and freedom from involuntary disappearances, and to prosecute those who are responsible. A rigid application of the general rule that a state's international obligations persist despite a change in government might, then, require successor governments to prosecute virtually every violation of those three rights that has not yet been punished. Yet, for reasons suggested above, such a requirement could produce untenable results.

Pursuant to general canons of construction, the comprehensive treaties should be interpreted in a manner that avoids imposing impossible obligations or duties whose discharge would prove harmful. A functional analysis of the general rule requiring prosecution of torture, extra-legal killings, and disappearances provides a principled basis for such an interpretation.

As noted earlier, the duty to punish these three crimes is squarely grounded on a deterrence rationale. Believing criminal sanctions to be the most effective means of securing rights deemed of paramount importance, bodies such as the Human Rights Committee and the Inter-American Commission have found investigation leading to punishment to be the most appropriate response to violations of those rights. The deterrence rationale supporting their decisions generally favors prosecution of each violation, since criminal laws are most likely to deter potential violators when the threat of punishment is as nearly certain as possible. For this reason, the conventions can fairly be interpreted to require successor governments to investigate and seek to punish each violation committed on their own watch. Similarly, the prior government should have made good faith efforts to prosecute each violation committed during its tenure. But the same logic would not compel prosecution of all offenders once massive violations have occurred with impunity. In these circumstances, full enforcement is neither capable of preventing the crimes that have already occurred, nor necessary effectively to deter potential lawbreakers of the future. A bounded program of exemplary punishment could have a significant deterrent effect, and thus achieve the aim justifying the general duty to punish atrocious crimes.

In contrast, a failure to punish any of the past violations would thwart the deterrence objective underlying the general duty to punish. If a government established complete impunity for atrocious crimes committed on a sweeping scale, its action would, as the Restatement reasoned, have the effect of tolerating or condoning the past violations and thereby encouraging similar ones. This result is plainly incompatible with states' convention-based duty to undertake affirmative measures to prevent violations of physical integrity.

While limitations on prosecutions may be compatible with states' international obligations, a policy that exonerates large numbers of persons who committed atrocious crimes offends common standards of justice and diminishes respect for the law. The best means of accommodating competing values might be to combine a finite program of prosecutions with legislation establishing a statute of limitations governing further prosecutions. Such legislation would minimize the destabilizing effects of trials while affirming the rule of law. . . .

The three comprehensive conventions analyzed in Part II allow States Parties to derogate from their duties in time of public emergency that threatens the life of the nation when various conditions are satisfied. Under no circumstances, however, are derogations from the rights to life and freedom from torture permitted. When applicable, the customary doctrines of state of necessity and force majeure similarly preclude the wrongfulness of a state's failure to comply with its international obligations in exceptional circumstances. But the prohibitions of torture, disappearances, and extra-legal executions have the status of peremptory norms: they can never be abrogated.

The question arises, then, whether states' duty to prosecute these crimes should also be treated as nonderogable on the basis that prosecution of violators is necessary to secure the peremptory rights. Authoritative interpretations of the conventions analyzed in Part II offer no clear guidance on this question; the issue has never been squarely addressed. A plausible case can be made in support of either possible position. . . .

Still, in view of the consistent recognition by international bodies that prosecution is necessary to secure certain nonderogable rights, a rule of law allowing states to derogate from the duty to prosecute violations of those rights would produce untenable results. Such a rule would have international law assert on the one hand that the rights to life, freedom from torture, and e freedom from forced disappearances are nonderogable, and on the other hand that, under certain circumstances, states need not do that which is necessary to secure the rights. . . .

Conclusion

In a wide array of countries the specter of torture, political murder, and forced disappearance has been dispelled by the dawning of freedom and the revival of judicial process. But the transitions have rarely been smooth, and the fledgling democracies face formidable challenges as they seek to balance the demands of justice against the continuing threat of destabilizing force.

In these circumstances, can the insertion of this or that provision in an international treaty possibly make a difference? For a new government precariously perched atop a restless and long-oppressed polity, with the torturers still controlling the guns, the threat of a coup may seem all too real. International law seems not so much remote as beside the point.

And yet. If the international community cannot prevent, at least it must not condone. Its words of censure or approval eventually filter through. For over a decade the dissidents of Eastern Europe recited the human rights promises of the Helsinki Final Act. With every recital the legitimacy of the governments that had made and broken those promises crumbled a little more.

Note: Non-judicial Alternatives

A number of alternatives exist to the criminal punishment of individual perpetrators of "human rights crimes," some of which are suggested by Carey, supra page 889. Truth commissions of various kinds have been created in a number of countries and are discussed more fully in Chapter 12. Their mandates vary widely, and they may or may not substitute for criminal prosecution. As demonstrated by the case of Sierra Leone, truth commissions may exist alongside prosecutorial mechanisms (although the relationship is not always comfortable). See, e.g., Priscilla Hayner, *Fifteen Truth Commissions — 1974 to 1994: A Comparative Study*, 16 Hum. Rts. Q. 597 (1994).

Are human rights violations less likely to be committed in the future if past violations are officially documented? Are the reports of government commissions necessarily more persuasive and significant than well-researched reports by NGOs or intergovernmental organizations, such as the country reports issued by the Inter-American Commission on Human Rights (see Chapter 9, page 731)?

Another alternative to criminal prosecution is described in the extract below.

Arthur Asiimwe, *Rwanda Estimates 1 Million Face Genocide Charges*

Reuters, Jan. 14, 2005

An estimated 1 million Rwandans — an eighth of the population — are expected to be tried in traditional "gacaca" [pronounced "gachacha"] village courts for alleged participation in the 1994 genocide, an official said on Friday.

Domitilla Mukantaganzwa, executive secretary of the National Service of Gacaca Jurisdictions, said trials in some areas might start next month, with proceedings beginning in the rest of the country in 2006.

"Drawing from the experience and figures accruing from the pilot trials, we estimate a figure slightly above 1 million people that are supposed to be tried under the gacaca courts," she told Reuters.

Her comment indicates the vast scale of the task awaiting the courts, gearing up to hear accusations against hundreds of thousands of people now living at liberty, often alongside neighbors whose relatives they are suspected of killing.

The courts, a revamped version of a traditional form of justice, were launched in 2002 on an exploratory basis to speed up trials of suspects charged in conventional courts with taking part in the slaughter of 800,000 Tutsis and moderate Hutus from April to June 1994.

Almost 11 years after the massacres, the backlog of suspects awaiting trial in conventional courts remains enormous.

There are 80,000 people behind bars and many would be likely to die before their cases would be heard under the existing justice system. Although many will be transferred eventually to gacaca courts for trial, exact numbers have not been decided.

In the past two years, thousands of other suspects have been questioned by 751 village courts, sitting as investigative panels, to see if there was a case to answer. Those sessions are now complete and trials resulting from these investigations might start in February 2005, Mukantaganzwa said.

On Monday, investigative hearings will be launched in a further 8,262 courts, she said, adding that trials in these courts would start only next year.

"The investigations have only been limited in the areas where pilot trials were held, but this time round (from Monday) the exercise will be rolled out to all parts of the country," Mukantaganzwa said. "We hope all this should be over by year end to have full trials commence (in 2006)."

Ringleaders of the killings, however, will be tried by conventional courts.

Grass Courts

Focusing on confession and apology, the gacaca courts are also intended to ease the way to national reconciliation.

Under gacaca, those who confess and plead guilty before a set date will have their sentences reduced.

Gacaca (meaning grass) courts were traditionally used by village communities who would gather on a patch of grass to resolve conflicts between two families, employing the heads of each household as judges.

Critics have said the investigative panels convened so far have often appeared to lack order, and rights group Amnesty International has said that "gacaca may become a vehicle for summary and arbitrary justice that fails defendants and genocide survivors alike."

Rwandan officials admit that gacaca is flawed, but they argue there is no alternative and the international donor community, which is funding gacaca, seems to agree.

Gacaca will be a world away from the robed lawyers and air-conditioned hallways of the International Criminal Tribunal for Rwanda in the northern Tanzanian town of Arusha, where proceedings are carried out behind bullet-proof glass. . . .

A subsequent report indicated that thousands of Rwandans had fled the country to avoid being judged by the gacaca courts. Arthur Asiimwe, *Thousands Flee Rwandan Genocide Hearings*, Reuters, Apr. 24, 2005. Amnesty International and other human rights NGOs have criticized the gacaca process as being inconsistent with international human rights norms. Amnesty International, *Gacaca: A question of justice*, AI Index AFR 47/007/2002 (Dec. 17, 2002). Could the gacaca courts be justified as derogations necessitated by the inability of Rwanda's regular courts to try 100,000 defendants? If not, what are the alternatives?

Comments and Questions

1. Do you agree with Orentlicher that international law mandates at least some prosecutions? Are "criminal sanctions . . . the most effective means of securing rights deemed of paramount importance"? Is her contention that prosecutions are essential because of their deterrent value borne out in practice? Orentlicher concedes that "[i]nternational law does not, of course, require states to take action that poses a serious threat to vital national interests." Does this have the effect of undermining her entire argument? Cf. Ellen Lutz and Kathryn Sikkink, *The Justice Cascade: The Evolution and Impact of Foreign Human Rights Trials in Latin America*, 2 Chicago J. Int'l L. 1 (2001).

2. Professor Orentlicher was subsequently appointed special rapporteur on issues of impunity by the UN Commission on Human Rights. She developed a draft set of principles, which may be found in Comm'n H.R., Report of the Independent Expert to Update the Set of Principles to Combat Impunity, UN Doc. E/CN.4/2005/102/Add.1 (Feb. 8, 2005), among whose provisions are the following:

> Principle 1. General obligations of states to take effective action to combat impunity
>
> Impunity arises from a failure by States to meet their obligations to investigate violations; to take appropriate measures in respect of the perpetrators, particularly in the area of justice, by ensuring that those suspected of criminal responsibility are prosecuted, tried and duly punished; to provide victims with effective remedies and to ensure that they receive reparation for the injuries suffered; to ensure the inalienable right to know the truth about violations; and to take other necessary steps to prevent a recurrence of violations. . . .

> Principle 19. Duties of states with regard to the administration of justice
>
> States shall undertake prompt, thorough, independent and impartial investigations of violations of human rights and international humanitarian law and take appropriate measures in respect of the perpetrators, particularly in the area of criminal justice, by ensuring that those responsible for serious crimes under international law are prosecuted, tried and duly punished.
>
> Although the decision to prosecute lies primarily within the competence of the State, victims, their families and heirs should be able to institute proceedings, on either an individual or a collective basis, particularly as *parties civiles* or as persons conducting private prosecutions in States whose law of criminal procedure recognizes these procedures. States should guarantee broad legal standing in the judicial process to any wronged party and to any person or non-governmental organization having a legitimate interest therein. . . .
>
> Principle 35. General principles [regarding non-recurrence of violations]
>
> States shall ensure that victims do not again have to endure violations of their rights. To this end, States must undertake institutional reforms and other measures necessary to ensure respect for the rule of law, foster and sustain a culture of respect for human rights, and restore or establish public trust in government institutions. Adequate representation of women and minority groups in public institutions is essential to the achievement of these aims. Institutional reforms aimed at preventing a recurrence of violations should be developed through a process of broad public consultations, including the participation of victims and other sectors of civil society.

Do you agree that the right to know the truth is an "inalienable" right? That adequate representation of women and minorities is essential to ensure that rights are not violated?

3. What if states themselves decide that forgiveness (i.e., amnesty) is better than prosecution? Voters in Uruguay approved a general amnesty in a controversial 1989 plebiscite, five years after the end of military rule; the much-discussed truth and reconcilation process in South Africa offered individualized amnesty to most apartheid-era political criminals; many of those most affected by the conflict in northern Uganda would probably reject national as well as international trials for the perpetrators, both as a means of ending the war and as a reflection of traditional values; and Algerian voters appear in 2005 to have approved a broad general amnesty for those who committed all but the worst crimes in a civil war that may have claimed 100,000 lives. While it is easy to condemn self-serving amnesties passed while criminals are still in power or continue to exercise influence, should the international community automatically reject amnesties if they are granted with knowledge of the atrocities that were committed and through a democratic process?

4. Thirty years have passed since the crimes committed by the Khmer Rouge, the Argentine colonels, and Augusto Pinochet. Under domestic law, there is generally no statute of limitation on murder and similarly serious crimes, but might there be temporal political limits on punishment? In many (not all) instances of widespread "human rights crimes," the crimes were committed or implicitly condoned by broad segments of society; is it always that easy (or appropriate) to select only the leaders or the "worst" perpetrators for punishment? Is the continuing (if diminishing) pursuit of Nazi criminals from the 1940s relevant to your answer? Cf. Mark A. Drumbl, *Collective Violence and Individual Punishment: The Criminality of Mass Atrocity*, 99 Nw. U. L. Rev. 539 (2005).

5. Many of the issues related to national trials for "human rights" crimes have been subsumed under the rather confusing rubric of "transitional justice." See, e.g., Miriam J. Aukerman, *Extraordinary Evil, Ordinary Crime: A Framework for Understanding Transitional Justice*, 15 Harv. Hum. Rts. J. 39 (2002); Roman Boed, *An Evaluation of the Legality and Efficacy of Lustration as a Tool of Transitional Justice*, 37 Colum. J. Transnat'l L. 357 (1999); Jon Elster, *Closing the Books: Transitional Justice in Historical Perspective* (2004); Priscilla Hayner, *Unspeakable Truths* (2001); Martha Minnow, *Between Vengeance and Forgiveness: Facing History after Genocide and Mass Violence* (1998); Eric A. Posner and Adrian Vermeule, *Transitional Justice as Ordinary Justice*, 117 Harv. L. Rev. 761 (2004); Rudi G. Teitel, *Transitional Justice (2000); id., Theoretical and International Framework: Transitional Justice in a New Era*, 26 Fordham Int'l L.J. 893 (2003); Report of the Secretary-General, The rule of law and transitional justice in conflict and post-conflict societies, UN Doc. S/2004/616 (Aug. 3, 2004); *Transitional Justice* (Neil J. Kritz ed., 3 vols. 1995).

In September 2003, the Secretary-General articulated the classic dilemma of peace versus justice (narrowly construed) in a statement to the Security Council:

> Ending the climate of impunity is vital to restoring public confidence and building international support to implement peace agreements. At the same time, we should remember that the process of achieving justice for victims may take many years, and it must not come at the expense of the more immediate need to establish the rule of law on the ground. . . .
>
> At times, the goals of justice and reconciliation compete with each other. Each society needs to form a view about how to strike the right balance between them. . . .
>
> We also know that there cannot be real peace without justice. Yet the relentless pursuit of justice may sometimes be an obstacle to peace. If we insist, at all times, and in all places, on punishing those who are guilty of extreme violations of human rights, it may be difficult, or even impossible, to stop the bloodshed and save innocent civilians. If we always and everywhere insist on uncompromising standards of justice, a delicate peace may not survive.
>
> But equally, if we ignore the demands of justice simply to secure agreement, the foundations of that agreement will be fragile, and we will set bad precedents.
>
> There are no easy answers to such moral, legal and philosophical dilemmas.

UN Press Release SG/SM/8892, SC/7881 (24 Sept. 2003).

VIII. Final Comments and Questions

1. The question of in absentia trials, permitted at Nuremberg and not obviously prohibited by international law, remains an issue open to debate. When jurisdiction cannot be obtained over individuals wanted for trial for the commission of international crimes, in absentia trials establish a record, generate a judgment, and, at the very least, may affect the movement of those persons convicted. Note, however, that neither the ICTY, ICTR, nor ICC permits in absentia trials (although an indictment may be confirmed by an ICC Pre-Trial Chamber in the absence of the accused). Would in absentia trials violate a

defendant's right to a fair trial guaranteed by Articles 10 and 11 of the Universal Declaration and Article 14 of the Civil and Political Covenant?

2. What are the standards by which an international trial should be judged? For a stinging criticism of the Milosevic trial at the ICTY, see John Laughland, *International law is an ass*, The Spectator, Nov. 19, 2005, who characterizes the multi-year trial as "a travesty of justice." "However, even more than the gross abuses of due process which it is committing, the Milosevic trial has shown the futility of trying to submit political decisions to the judgment of criminal law. Because it seeks to comprehend war as the result of the decisions of individuals, and not as the consequence of conflict between states, modern international humanitarian law sees trees but no wood." Id. Do you agree? Or is punishing individuals an acceptable, if imperfect, response to widespread criminality?

3. Do you think that the "criminalization" of human rights violations is a step forward in the protection and promotion of rights? Does it privilege a certain category of violations of physical security, as opposed to equally important economic, social, cultural, and political rights? Obtaining sufficient resources to promote human rights is never easy; would the $100 million or more likely to be spent annually on the ICC be better spent in expanding the work of the UN High Commissioner for Human Rights? Is it realistic to do both?

4. Approaching the issue from the opposite perspective, what is gained by treating crimes as human rights violations? Is trafficking in persons likely to be more effectively combatted by INTERPOL and law enforcement agencies or by UN human rights bodies and NGOs? Again, is there room for both, or might crime prevention and/or human rights priorities be skewed? Why do human rights NGOs and the UN High Commissioner regularly denounce terrorist attacks but not drug trafficking, murder, or other criminal acts? Is there any relationship, besides protecting the rights of suspects, between preventing terrorism and human rights?

5. In his discussion of the ICC, David Rieff criticizes "law-based schemes of human improvement; they take no account of history." Is this a fair observation, in a world where adopting a new international treaty or creating a new international institution is increasingly seen as an answer to complex political and social problems? Does the discussion of slavery in Chapter 1 support or counter Rieff's criticism?

Chapter 12

The Problem of Fact-Finding and Evidence

How Are Human Rights Violations Investigated?

I. The Challenge: To Find Out What Is Really Happening

Previous chapters demonstrated how various international human rights bodies have dealt with human rights violations: for example expressions of concern by the UN Commission on Human Rights over widespread violations of civil and political rights in Liberia (Chapter 7) and condemnation by the Inter-American Commission on Human Rights of disappearances and other human rights violations in Argentina (Chapter 9). It should be appreciated, however, that such cases begin with only *allegations* of violations of human rights. Each human rights body had to uncover relevant facts before it could reach a conclusion on whether or not violations had occurred. Without detailed and reliable knowledge about what is actually happening in countries around the world, protection of human rights cannot be effective.

What are the methods by which international human rights institutions discover what is happening "on the ground"? What are the most effective fact-finding techniques? What sorts of bodies are best equipped to conduct accurate fact-finding? To what extent are there general standards in this area? What role do nongovernmental organizations play in the fact-finding process? How is the reliability of gathered evidence determined? What standards of proof should be applied in human rights investigations? These are some of the questions that are explored in this chapter.

The need for action in this area was recognized as long ago as 1968, when the Montreal Conference on International Human Rights lamented "the absence of effective and impartial fact-finding mechanisms." Montreal Statement of the Assembly for Human Rights, March 22-27, 1968, 9 J. Int'l Comm'n Jurists 94, 106 (1968). Since that time, significant strides have been made. New problems, in turn, have arisen. The concern is no longer whether the United Nations and other bodies can or should engage in human rights fact-finding. Rather, it is *how* they can most effectively do so.

Some observers have advocated a strongly centralized system of fact-finding at the UN. A notable proposal along these lines was advanced by the Netherlands in 1964, which suggested that the UN establish a permanent organ for fact-finding activities. It would consist of a standing body of approximately 15 persons, which would have the option of forming chambers. This body would be at the permanent disposal of the UN and its specialized agencies, with a separate mandate for each inquiry that it undertook. Its reports would be adopted by majority vote, with dissenting opinions permitted.

This proposal was not adopted, and UN fact-finding has taken a much different form. Instead of a single, specialized body, the UN has devised, over the years, a plethora of different fact-finding strategies under the auspices of a variety of different bodies. This fact-finding "system" has grown up over a period of decades in a rather ad hoc, haphazard fashion. As a result, some of the basic questions about effective fact-finding have failed to receive the attention they deserve.

It is impossible, within the compass of a single chapter, to provide a comprehensive survey of human rights fact-finding. Instead, the readings identify some of the more important or innovative activities in this area and also examine some of the major legal issues that have arisen in connection with them.

II. Gathering the Facts: Allegations of Judicial Persecution of Mapuche Leaders in Chile

A. *Fact-Finding by Nongovernmental Organizations*

Nongovernmental organizations play an important role in investigating and documenting human rights violations and bringing them to the attention of international institutions, states, and the public at large. However, NGOs have such a wide variety of interests and levels of resources that it is difficult to generalize about their activities. Still, much of the initial information relied upon by the United Nations and regional institutions in regard to human rights comes from NGOs. Groups like Amnesty International, Human Rights Watch, and others have developed sophisticated techniques for monitoring human rights around the world and for communicating violations to international human rights bodies. Another NGO leader in the field of human rights fact-finding is the Paris-based Federation Internationale des Droits de l'Homme (FIDH)(International Federation for Human Rights), which authored the following report concerning Mapuche indigenous people in Chile.

International Federation for Human Rights, Chile — The Mapuche People: Between Oblivion and Exclusion

Report No. 358/2 (Aug. 22, 2003) (endnotes omitted)

The FIDH is an international non-governmental organization composed of 115 member organizations from 90 different countries, which has a comprehensive approach to human rights issues. It has carried out several observation missions related to indigenous peoples.

The FIDH carried out an observation mission in Chile in 1997, where it analyzed the Ralco hydroelectric plant's construction as well as its impact on the Mapuche–Pehuenche peoples. In 2003, there is still concern about the situation of human rights for the Mapuche people. This is partly due to the situation arising from forest exploitation in the VIII, IX and X Chilean regions, which is having a negative impact on the life and survival of the Mapuche peoples and communities that are settled there. Another cause for concern is the progress that is being made regarding the construction of the aforementioned hydroelectric plant.

Between 21 April and 1 May 2002, the FIDH conducted an international investigative mission in Chile. This mission was aimed at analyzing the human rights situation in the Mapuche communities as related to forest exploitation and the Ralco project, both of which are important sectors in the Chilean domestic economy. It bears emphasizing that, in this report, human rights have been analyzed from a comprehensive perspective, since there is a direct link between the necessary conditions for the enforcement of economic, social and cultural rights, individual human rights and the organization and/or mobilization processes undertaken by the Mapuche communities.

The mission's team was composed of Nicole Du Roy, a French journalist, and Paulina Palacios, an Ecuadorean lawyer. They carried out field visits and interviews with representatives from warring Mapuche communities as well as Mapuche prisoners, communities, regional and national authorities from different States.

The mission began in Temuco, in the IX Region, where its team met with:

Ramiro Pizarro, Regional Governor,
Researchers from the Institute of Indigenous Studies at the Universidad de la Frontera
Esmirna Vidal, District Attorney for the IX Region
Leonardo de la Prida, District Attorney for Purén — IX Region
José Quidel, Mapuche Autonomous Work Commission (*Comisión de Trabajo Autónoma Chilena*), COTAM
Emilio Guerra, Chilean Wood Corporation (*Corporación Chilena de la Madera*), CORMA
Sandra Jilmes and Jaime López, from the Mapuche Criminal Defense Team
Mapuche organizations and representatives from the LIWEN Center

Furthermore, the Institute of Indigenous Studies at the Universidad de la Frontera organized the seminar entitled, "Mapuche Megaprojects and Rights," (*Megaproyectos y Derechos Mapuche*) held in Temuco. Speakers: Rosamel Millaman, Pablo Mariman, José Ayllwin, Rodrigo Lillo, Jaime Madariaga, Jenive Cavieres, Christian Opaso, María Angélica Reuman and Alfredo Seguel

In Valdivia, Nicole Du Roy and Paulina Palacios met with:

Augusto Naulpam, Juan Hueque Francisco Huaichaman and Juan Caniulaf from the Council of Chiefs (*Consejo de Longkos*) for the Mapuche Huilliche People in Pikunwijimapu
Ana María Olivera, Spokesperson (*Werken*) for the Chiloén communities
Delegate from the Quellon community Anselmo Paillamanque, Chief and Spokesperson (*Werken*) for the Osorno communities

In Santiago, Chile:

Jaime Andrade, National Coordinator of Indigenous Politics for the Chilean government and MIDEPLAN's Assistant Secretary Mauricio Solines,

Chilean Attorney General's Office
Patricio Aylwin, President for the Governmental Commission for Historical Truth and New Treatment (*Comisión de Verdad Histórica y Nuevo Trato*)

In Los Angeles:

Esteban Krause, Biobio Provincial Governor
Claudia Parada, responsible for indigenous affairs in Biobio
Gerardo Jires, Attorney for the Provincial government

At the Traiguen municipal prison, they met with the following prisoners: Pascual Pichun, Chief (Longko) of the Antonio Ñerripil community, Alejandro Pichun, Rafael Pichun, and Aniceto Norin.

In the Antonio Ñerripil community, they met with: Juan Pichùn, Pedro Naquel Millan, Machi María Ancamilla Nahuanpi, María Collonao and Flora Collonao.

In Lumaco, they met with leaders from the Ñancuchew Association: Remigio Chureo, Alfonso Reiman, Galvarino Reiman and Dina del Carmen Cayuqueo.

In Tirua: Abraham Santi Calbullanco and Mayor Adolfo Millabur.

In Cañete: Luis Llanquileo, Emilio Ushalao, Juan Segundo, Juan Cárialo, Delegate from the Los Maitenes Community, Delegate the Los Alamos Community, Eliana Cuces, Carmen Lautaro and Rodrigo Peñailillo, Provincial Governor of Arauco.

In Ralco: Hilda del Rosario Riquelme, Aurelia Mariuan Mora, Meulen Huencho and Juan Ricardo Gallina Rodríguez, Leader from the "Las Peñas" relocated community.

In the Ralco Lepoy community: Aurelia, Rosario, Chao Chao, Nicolasa, Berta, Mercedes Julia Huantiao.

In the Quepuka Ralco community: Rebels and leaders from the community.

In the Collipulli municipality: Ariel Tori, Antonio Quideron and Víctor Ancalaf.

The Coordinator for the Mapuche Warring Communities in Tanguipulli: Jaime Alegría Lefian, Palmeria Catriman Huilliman, Domitila Catriman Huilliman and Ciro Alegría.

Members from the Mapuche Arauco Malleco Coordinating Committee: José Llanquilef, Cecilia Salazar, Angélica Ñancupil and José Llanquileo.

They also held a meeting with an environmentalist group: Carlos Ruiz, Jenive Cavieres, Juan Pablo Orrego, Elías Paillán, Malù Sierra, Leonel Lienlaf, Víctor Toledo, Roberto Col and Claudia Padilla, Public Health Ministry.

At the Universidad Arcis, they met with: Roberto Zeledón, Sergio Fuenzalida and José María Bulnes, advocates for the Pehuenche indigenous people from the Alto Biobio region.

Lastly, in Valparaíso, at the Chilean legislative headquarters, they met with: Enrique Zurita and Jaime Naranjo from the Senatorial Human Rights Commission and Deputy Alejandro Navarro.

The mission would like to thank all of them for the information they shared with its representatives and would like to give a special thanks to the Defense Committee for Peoples' Rights (Comité de Defensa de los Derechos del Pueblo) and the Institute of Indigenous Studies at the Universidad de la Frontera, for providing contacts, preparing the agenda and accompanying the FIDH mission team....

1. Historical Background and Origin of the Current Conflict

...

In Valdivia, a dozen men and women described to the FIDH mission the hostility imposed upon them by forestry companies in the region. These communities filed judicial claims to obtain the restitution of their lands, taken over mainly by private landowners during General Pinochet's dictatorship. Furthermore, the Longkos (community leaders) recall that Spanish settlers recognized the Mapuches' rights to some lands and mentioned the Chiloe case. In 1826, Chiloe was annexed by the Chilean Republic, which refused to recognize Mapuche property titles. Little by little, the Chilean settlers, the new colonists, sold their lands to large companies, many of which were not Chilean. The current indigenous law has not provided for the return of these lands to the indigenous people. Today, in Chiloe, roundtables bring together diverse groups for negotiations surrounding the recovery of these lands. "We did not defend our land, they say, so that it could be sold to other countries through multinationals."

Like the Mapuches from Valdivia, the Mapuches from Collipulli have tried to access the judicial system. "We have documents that date back to the Spanish times recognizing the border of the high Biobio river. The Chilean State recognized this border. However, they sold our lands at the cost of our lives. This is why today we strongly claim our territory."

However, in the above described legal and/or judicial initiatives, the negotiations turned into endless bureaucratic problems; no definite solution was reached and the communities' aspirations turned into frustration....

As a result of massive indigenous protests against the celebration of the 500-year anniversary of the so-called discovery of America and the demands already made by the Mapuches, Law 19.253 [the "Indigenous Act"] was passed in 1993. To silence the Mapuche claims, this law created a fund that would allow indigenous peoples to buy lands from forestry companies. According to the authorities involved, 75,000 hectares of land have been returned to the Mapuche communities thanks to the fund. In reality, however, interested companies have lobbied to limit the fund's budget. Therefore, the recovery of usurped Mapuche land, as of today, continues to be an unsolved problem. The indigenous legislation in force is ineffective and greatly weakens the recognition of more integral demands of Mapuches rights. In addition to this, the National Corporation for Indigenous Development (CONADI), an organization founded by that same law and responsible for promoting and executing State action in the area of indigenous policies, was unable to tackle the problem of usurped lands and found itself quickly superseded by the events.

During this period, communities often confronted forestry companies occupying their land in a direct but peaceful fashion, claiming their legitimate rights. However, the only response to these actions was violent repression on the part of authorities, who safeguarded the interests of major companies under the pretext of defending private property. The government has criticized Mapuche actions, accusing them of terrorism. In 1994, 144 Mapuches were found guilty of crimes of illicit association and usurpation of lands. The Chilean government considers that communities that take action are disturbing social tranquility and peace in the country. Moreover, the government has refused to engage in dialogue with the Mapuches stating that it will not converse under pressure, thereby denying, in fact, the issue surrounding the disputed lands. In 1996, the 144 Mapuche prisoners filed an appeal with the Interamerican Commission on Human Rights of the OAS, accusing the Chilean government of political and ethnical persecution as well as disrespect for the Mapuche's civil rights. . . .

[I]t is clear that the conflict over land titles between Mapuche communities and Chilean forestry companies is a very complex issue. Some communities have been turning for years to the Chilean judicial system to solve the problem. However, the courts have refused to rule on the matter. Consequently, after waiting for almost a decade for a legal decision to be pronounced, these communities decided to occupy the lands they consider to be theirs. Although certain courts may consider these occupations illegal, the FIDH believes that in many cases they are in response to legitimate concerns. The government should assume responsibility for this problem and seek a fair and viable solution to the critical question of the land titles under debate so that a solution can be brought the Mapuche conflicts in that part of Chile. . . .

3. Judicial Persecution of Mapuche Leaders and Members of Mapuche Communities

At the judicial level, there has been a noticeable trend towards the criminalization of the Mapuche conflict. The Chilean government, under President Ricardo Lagos' administration, has taken on a policy of repression against the Mapuche and its organizations. Land-recovery actions and demands for rights have been met with a number of legal actions and complaints on the part of forestry companies, as a result of which many Mapuche rebels are now subject to trial and imprisonment.

. . . The research shows that in August 2002, 91 Mapuches were accused on the grounds of their various activities and their participation in several operations carried out against forestry companies. They were indicted for the following crimes: illegal association (35 cases), threatening or showing disrespect for authority (14), second-degree kidnapping (11), theft (10), arson (9), misappropriation (5), causing disturbance (2), second-degree damage (1), and legal exaction (1). With respect to their legal status, 80% are not in custody, but subject to preventive measures, 18% are in preventive detention, and 2% subject to the preventive measure of house arrest.

The FIDH believes that there is a direct relationship between the demands for land, supportive State programs and actions, direct participation and consultation with the Mapuche, and the judicial actions taken against leaders, longkos, werkenes, or ordinary members of Mapuche organizations. Those especially subject to persecution are Mapuches who have in fact conceived their actions in relation to their territorial demands. It should be noted that communities in conflict claim political prisoner status for their imprisoned leaders. For example,

Victor Ancalaf Llaupe, was arrested in November 2002 for political activities defending Mapuche rights.

Similarly, lawyers acting for Mapuche prisoners are also threatened and even have their telephones tapped. Since our mission ended, there has been a notable case involving lawyer Pablo Ortega, who represents a very large proportion of the Mapuche prisoners and defendants. The tapping of Ortega's telephone is a violation of the Mapuche's rights to have a defense and to the confidentiality of the lawyer/client relationship; it also aims at intimidating the lawyer. In relation to those events, a case was brought before the Guarantee Tribunal on 24 December 2002.

It is striking that those currently being detained for allegedly committing offenses connected to the Mapuche conflict and forest exploitation are covered by a combination of different legal regimes: either the Anti-terrorist Act, Act No. 12.927 (also known as the "Domestic Security Act"), or the general classification of several crimes against private property provided for in the Chilean Criminal Code. For the FIDH mission, this fact seemed crucial: the Mapuches do not benefit from any legal guarantees, as there have been a number of cases in which the same offense is prosecuted more than once as different crimes under different laws.

Moreover, it was also brought to the attention of the FIDH mission by a number of concerned witnesses that the proposed criminal procedural reforms, being introduced gradually region by region in Chile may prove to be an instrument for the repression of the Mapuche people. . . .

Some positive aspects of the aforementioned reform should be mentioned, such as the intent to develop an institution known as the Mapuche "Criminal Defense Office," to be staffed by lawyers and intercultural facilitators or interpreters.

This particular plan is very much so in its early stages. However, as a reform that is "favorable to the accused," it does offer a response to a number of fears expressed by Mapuche prisoners and their defenders. However, the reforms have also been criticized and denounced by the Mapuche as just another form of oppression.

To illustrate this theory, the mission looked at the cases of the four Mapuche "political detainees" imprisoned in Traiguen. The cases are symbolic of the persecution of Mapuche leaders within the context of a system of criminal procedure that claims to respect basic legal guarantees. During the month of December 2001, the home of Juan Agustín Figueroa's farm manager was burned down. Those accused of this offense are Pascual Huentequeo Pichun Paillalao, Longko [traditional leader] of the Temulemu community, and Don Segundo Aniceto Norin Catriman, Longko of the Diádico community, and an employee of CONADI. Both are being detained at Traiguen. The sons of Longko Pichun, Rafael, 21, and Alejandro, 18, were also imprisoned. Both students at the Catholic University of Temuco, they were arrested on 12 April 2002, accused of having setting fire to a forestry company truck.

These trials are riddled with irregularities of form and substance. First, the Longkos were not given any sort of trial before being imprisoned. Secondly, although there are no precedents, the provisions of the Domestic Security Act and the Anti-terrorist Act have been applied. Their files also show a total lack of evidence concerning the facts of which they are accused. The prosecutor bringing the case tried to force them to sign a statement admitting their guilt. They refused to do so. The prosecutor then told the prisoners that they would be sentenced to 15 to 20 years in prison for refusing to sign the statement. The sons of Longko Pichun were imprisoned in the rapid investigations room. The police had not been at the scene of the fire, which broke out some kilometers from the house in which the two brothers were arrested. Also, the statements of the truck driver, main witness to the facts, are contradictory. He first stated that he had not seen who started the fire, but then declared that he was certain that he had spotted Rafael and Alejandro. The only "evidence" provided by the police was that the clothes worn by the two young men contained traces of oil when they were arrested.

After visiting the detainees, the mission also visited the community of Temulemu, and noted the profound impact of Chief Pichun's imprisonment on his community. The living conditions of his family were extremely harsh. The older son also told us about acts of provocation and intimidation against the Mapuche within the companies where they work and the humiliations imposed by their managers. It should be pointed out that the four detainees began a hunger strike in August 2002 to denounce the injustices and irregularities of their trials. After their health began to deteriorate, they were transferred to the Traiguen hospital in September.

With respect to this and other similar cases, it should be noticed that they have been conducted under a regular criminal procedure. However, the whole spirit behind the reforms (which is to provide mechanisms to make effective the human rights of detainees) is violated when such provisions are applied within the Anti-terrorist Act. This Act was enacted as part of the repressive policies of a former dictatorial regime, and brought into question by the international community, for its disrespect for human rights.

Chilean magistrates are required to observe the provisions of the Indigenous Act. However, in this case, the detainees and their defenders testified that the fact that the two Mapuche longkos were not native Spanish speakers was not taken into consideration. This is a violation of the basic principles of the rule of law and comprehensible defense, based upon freedom, consent, and the full understanding of the proceedings by those being investigated. Under the Indigenous Act, protection is clearly provided for indigenous peoples, their cultures, families and communities. In the case in question, however, such protection was not provided....

According to Adolfo Millabur, Mayor of Tirua, who was interviewed by the FIDH mission, and who is one of a few Mapuche city counselors:

> *The Anti-terrorist Act, adopted under the Pinochet dictatorship, is antidemocratic. All it takes for the procedure to be applied is to express your disagreement with a certain aspect of policy. Luckily for me, I am protected by my Mayoral status. I am convinced that it was private armed security guards who set fire to the truck to incriminate the Pichun boys. Between the Mapuche and the forestry companies, there is permanent conflict. The police are spread on Mapuche land and the smallest dispute is brought before the courts. There is no possibility of finding a peaceful compromise. The country is not concerned about the indigenous problem. We need political will on the part of the government to search for a solution to the Mapuche problem. Instead, the government cultivates hatred and the police are above the law, even though their abuses are proven. Today, the Chilean State is negotiating trade accords with the European Community*

in order to sell timber, the country's main source of wealth. At a time when we hear so much about fair trade, the Mapuche are simply claiming a small part of the vast lands owned by the forestry companies, lands which belonged to them in the pre-Colonial period.

The FIDH report goes on to conclude, inter alia, that the Chilean government has failed in its duty to adequately address Mapuche land claims and instead has sided with non-indigenous property interests and fostered a climate of repression against the Mapuche. FIDH Report No. 358/2, supra, at 41-42. The report's conclusions highlight the prosecution of Mapuche leaders under the Anti-Terrorism Act, identifying this as part of a "repressive judicial policy" that is fraught with "procedural and material irregularities." Id. at 42. In a subsequent report, Human Rights Watch and a Chilean NGO jointly detailed shortcomings in the criminal proceedings against Mapuche leaders and condemned their prosecution and conviction under the anti-terrorism regime as illegitimate, in light of the context and nature of the alleged criminal behavior. See Human Rights Watch and Observatorio de Derechos de los Pueblos Indígenas, Undue Process: Terrorism Trials, Military Courts, and the Mapuche in Southern Chile (Oct. 2004, HRW Vol. 16, No. 5(B)).

What weight should be accorded these NGO findings? The answer turns in significant part on the methodology of the fact-finding.

Diane Orentlicher, *Bearing Witness: The Art and Science of Human Rights Fact-Finding*

3 Harv. Hum. Rts. J. 83, 85, 92-108, 135 (1990)

As the influence of NGO human rights reporting has grown, NGOs' underlying research methodology has come under heightened scrutiny and, at times, pointed attack. In an age when acquiring the status of "human rights pariah" carries unprecedented costs internationally, governments whose rights violations are publicized frequently respond by challenging the credibility of the fact-finding methodology. United States officials, too, have publicly attacked the credibility of organizations that released reports chronicling abuses committed by strategic allies of the United States government.

In this setting, perhaps no asset is more important to a human rights NGO than the credibility of its fact-finding and, in particular, it reputation for meticulous methodology. Despite the unprecedented attention to issues of human rights methodology, however, the leading NGOs have not adopted uniform methodological standards; most have not even adopted comprehensive, formal standards for use by their own staffs. And while NGO reporting has drawn the close scrutiny of various parties, critiques of NGO methodology do not reflect a coherent set of commonly accepted standards. . . .

. . . Broadly stated, the chief objective of human rights NGOs is to promote compliance with international human rights standards. As self-appointed watchdogs, NGOs have no "authority" to compel governments to bring their practices into compliance with those standards; NGOs can aspire only to *persuade* governments to respect the rights of individuals subject to the governments' jurisdictions.

To this end, NGOs appeal to governments believed to be responsible for abuses to cease the violations. NGOs also frequently marshall external sources of pressure, such as the intervention of other governments or intergovernmental bodies. Fact-finding lies at the heart of these efforts, and the fact-finding "works" when it convinces the target audience that the published allegations are well founded.

. . . [I]t is possible to identify factors that figure prominently in public assessments of NGO fact-finding. The most frequently cited criteria fall into two categories. One relates to the integrity of an NGO's fact-finding methodology; the other takes account of various factors that are thought to indicate whether the NGO has an institutional bias — other than a bias in favor of human rights — that may taint the credibility of its conclusions. . . .

The obstacles to fact-finding posed by the state's nearly exclusive control of essential information are often compounded by other, related circumstances. In a context of widespread state lawlessness, for example, witnesses and victims often are afraid to provide testimony to human rights investigators, fearing retaliation by government forces. Moreover, a substantial number of countries in which gross violations are practiced on a systematic basis are closed to foreign investigators. In many countries, political repression is so severe that independent human rights monitors either cannot operate internally or do so under enormous constraints and at great personal risk. And in countries with serious systematic abuses, a bridled press often does not — because it cannot — provide independent accounts of human rights violations.

Thus, the circumstances in which human rights investigation is undertaken typically place substantial limitations on fact-finding. Though such constraints may be unavoidable, their effect on NGO methodology can invite challenge from a critical audience. . . .

Second, the role of interpretation in the preparation of country reports contributes to their vulnerability to challenge. While it may be a truism that there are no "pure facts" and that any attempt to describe factual conditions entails substantial interpretation, the role of interpretation is particularly large in the context of human rights country reports. Because country reports aspire to describe broad patterns, the finder of fact must attempt not only to verify individual incidents of abuse, but also to reach more sweeping judgments about the extent of the violations, the nature of government (and, where relevant, insurgent) responsibility for the abuses, and the significance of apparent trends. . . .

A third aspect of human rights fact-finding further increases the potential for different conclusions to emerge from the same facts: the investigator must measure facts against an abstract standard. Most NGOs evaluate states' compliance with internationally recognized human rights standards. Some NGOs also assess state practices in light of protections embodied in domestic law. Thus, in seeking to verify a reported violation, NGOs must attempt to determine both what actually happened, and whether the facts, under all the attendant circumstances, constitute a violation of relevant standards. These determinations often require difficult judgment calls, and it is scarcely surprising that different analysts sometimes reach different judgments about the legality of particular conduct. . . .

Challenges to the institutional credibility of NGOs have focused on two charges in particular. . . .

The first charge is that a survey of an NGO's work betrays a high degree of selectivity in the countries that are monitored, and that the selection is driven by a decided political slant. When applying this measure, critics often make reference to both the range of countries which an NGO has scrutinized and the evenhandedness of the organization's application of international standards to different countries' human rights records. Thus, even NGOs that attempt to monitor countries of every political orientation have been criticized for "going easier" on countries of one political shading than another. Sometimes the apparent disparity has been largely a matter of tone — a difference in the moral fervor of an NGO's respective condemnations of similar violations by different governments. But in human rights reporting, in which shadings of language convey varying levels of opprobrium, tone is substance. . . .

The second charge is that an NGO's work on a particular country betrays a political bias against the government and in favor of its opponents. The criticism often arises with respect to reports that examine countries in which the most serious abuses occur in a context of civil war. In these circumstances, government officials have frequently charged that an NGO report is biased if it criticizes only abuses by government forces, and not those of their armed adversaries.

This charge played a prominent role in the Reagan Administration's efforts to discredit human rights reports that documented gross violations by several strategic allies of the United States. Early in its first term, the Administration began to press the view that, to be credible, NGOs that report on violations in a country in a state of armed conflict must monitor the practices of the rebels as well as the government forces.

There are, however, principled reasons for NGOs to monitor violations attributable only to government forces, and most domestic NGOs as well as many international NGOs follow this practice. These organizations base their work on international human rights law, which establishes international responsibility for violations only on the part of governments, in contrast to the laws of war (also known as humanitarian law), which generate international responsibility for violations by all sides to an armed conflict. [See generally Chapter 4.] Thus an NGO that bases its mandate exclusively on international human rights law is faithful to the law by focusing on government conduct. . . .

Beyond such considerations as whether NGOs monitor both sides to an armed conflict or whether they monitor governments of the right and left with equal vigor, more subtle factors affect public perceptions of NGOs' credibility. Governments that are the subject of scrutiny as well as other audiences often evaluate NGO reporting according to its "fairness" in a particular sense: whether it acknowledges contextual factors that place violations "in perspective." Thus, for example, the Israeli government is more likely to credit a report describing its violations in the West Bank and Gaza if the report acknowledges that human rights conditions are deplorable in other areas of the Middle East. Similarly, even if a human rights NGO's mandate does not extend to monitoring abuses committed by armed rebels, its account of a government's violations is likely to seem more credible to that government if the report acknowledges in a more-than-perfunctory fashion the threat posed by the insurgents. Indeed, human rights reports that criticize abuses committed by governments responding to an armed insurgency now routinely acknowledge not only the government's right to respond militarily and, under certain circumstances, to derogate from some human rights, but also express opprobrium of violations committed by the insurgents. . . .

A key point to be made here is that human rights reports are not merely abstract factual accounts. The reports are advocacy tools, designed to promote change in government practices. As such, their presentation of facts is designed to respond to factors likely to affect the report's impact. . . .

A variety of factors account for NGOs' general reluctance to develop standardized methodologies. Most importantly, many human rights professionals believe that the nature of the human rights violations they monitor requires broad flexibility in fact-finding strategies. As noted earlier, NGO fact-finding has focused on abuses which governments deliberately cloak in secrecy. Many human rights professionals believe that adopting rigid methodological standards would limit their ability to adapt their fact-finding efforts to the particular constraints of particular circumstances, and could preclude them from undertaking effective advocacy with respect to countries that engage in the most severe and systematic abuses.

In addition, some human rights professionals believe that the articulation of general fact-finding standards inadvertently could increase the risks faced by domestic human rights monitors. Such monitors frequently work under conditions of extreme danger, and government attacks on the credibility of their methodology often heighten those risks, serving in effect as a public "death warrant." In this setting, some human rights professionals fear that governments might cite, with dangerous consequences, a domestic NGO's failure to adhere to established uniform standards to harm the organization's credibility. . . .

While there are valid reasons for eschewing narrow methodological standards, NGOs should nonetheless aspire to the highest standards possible under prevailing circumstances. Indeed, their institutional objectives would be defeated if their reports failed to persuade their target audiences that the factual conclusions were well-founded. To meet this "burden of persuasion," each report must satisfy a threshold standard of credibility. . . .

. . . While flexible evidentiary standards are appropriate to NGO human rights fact-finding methodology, NGO reports should make out a prima facie case for their factual allegations by developing highly probative — if inconclusive — evidence. If the NGO's methodology is persuasive, the government responsible for alleged violations is likely to face substantial pressure to "answer for itself," while the concerned public is unlikely to accept a bald denial as an adequate response. . . .

[The article then considers in detail various "methodological strategies" that NGOs might adopt to investigate and confirm human rights violations.]

Emerging criteria for judging institutional credibility present especially difficult challenges for NGOs. Their concerns as advocacy organizations may prompt NGOs to take some actions, such as addressing essentially political contextual factors peculiar to a country or pressing for a ban on foreign aid to a government that violates human rights, that might jeopardize the organizations' appearance of political evenhandedness and disinterestedness. While such dilemmas cannot be eliminated — they are inherent in the advocacy nature of human rights organizations — NGOs should be mindful of the trade-offs entailed in some forms of advocacy, and take whatever measures they can to minimize the risks.

The debate over NGO fact-finding methodology is no mere academic one, as illustrated by the international scrutiny brought to bear on the Chilean government over the situation of the Mapuche through the FIDH and Human Rights

Watch reports. These reports weighed heavily in the examination of the situation by the UN Special Rapporteur on the Situation of Human Rights and Fundamental Freedoms of Indigenous People, as discussed infra. One approach to the issue of NGO fact-finding would be to consider the standards that have been developed or proposed for fact-finding by the United Nations and other intergovernmental organizations (IGOs) (discussed infra, pages 1017–1027). However, as the following reading points out, there are important differences between NGO and IGO fact-finding, and it may be difficult to apply the same standards to both. The reading also summarizes the conclusions of a 1983 conference, which remain relevant to contemporary discussions. Some additional recommendations are offered in the second reading.

Hans Thoolen and Berth Verstappen, Human Rights Missions: A Study of the Fact-Finding Practice of Non-Governmental Organizations

24-26, 31-32 (1986)

. . . A central question is whether and to what extent the existing procedural standards for on-site investigations by IGO's can be applied to NGO fact-finding. When taking account of the different contexts in which the fact-finding activities of both types of organizations take place, there seem to be good reasons to be hesitant in doing so.

The mandate of most IGO's covers more than human rights, and the conduct of human-rights fact-finding missions is but a small part of their activities. On the other hand, NGO fact-finding usually is conducted within the framework of an organization that is entirely or to a large degree concerned with the issue of human rights. Generally, in IGO fact-finding the divergence between the fact-finding body and the initiating organization is often somewhat greater.

NGO's lack the resources available to IGO's. It is assumed that they feel stronger financial restraints, are more limited in their staff, mostly have less members on a mission, and usually can't afford to send a mission for several weeks, or provide it with staff for secretarial and interpretation activities. In addition, as NGO's have no diplomatic channels and contacts at their disposal, answers to questions or requests for appointments with the government may suffer considerable delay.

A distinction between IGO and NGO fact-finding, frequently said to be of considerable impact, is that IGO fact-finding emerges within intergovernmental context. IGO fact-finding missions are based on cooperation between governments within the framework of the IGO, and therefore should have less problems in getting access to the territory of a member state. This distinction is correct but does not take into account that NGO's operate on a much more informal basis than IGO's. IGO missions are "heavier" because two entities of a governmental character are meeting. Such missions are conducted at a formal governmental level, official contacts (protocol) are much more preponderant than in NGO fact-finding. NGO's can be more flexible in the conduct of their investigations. They do not have to wait for lengthy diplomatic negotiations, but can send observers in their personal capacity or even "as tourists." Besides, if IGO missions should have less problems in getting access to the territory of a member state, the question can be raised what price had to be paid for that access during preliminary negotiations with the government concerned. Thus, the basic distinction between IGO and NGO fact-finding concerning the cooperation of the government concerned, could be of less importance than one would be inclined to accept at first sight.

Differences between IGO and NGO fact-finding seem to lie in the fields of:

— the difference in the mandate of the sending organization, and, related to this, the difference in objectives for sending a mission.

— the difference in the way in which the decision to send a fact-finding mission is taken. For IGO fact-finding, this is often a lengthy process, in which strong account has to be taken of the extreme sensitivity of governments to foreign intrusion in their internal affairs, especially in the field of human rights. Also NGO's will often establish advance contacts with the government concerned, but in general this is a less complex under-taking.

— the difference in the relationship between the sending organ and the members of the mission.

— the relatively limited availability of expertise, time and financial resources of NGO's.

— the amount of cooperation of the government concerned, and the facilities which it is required or willing to give.

— the formal character of IGO fact-finding versus the informal character of NGO fact-finding. NGO's will often have better opportunities to make use of informal contacts in advance of the mission and in the country to be visited.

— more generally speaking and taking all this into account, there seems to be a strong need for a greater amount of flexibility in NGO fact-finding guidelines.

In general, it does not seem possible for NGO's to simply adopt IGO procedures as a whole. Nevertheless, the considerable fact-finding experience of IGO's should be considered and utilized by NGO's where appropriate. In particular to the extent that NGO's seek to influence government conduct in the area of human rights, IGO procedural rules and guidelines may be instructive and helpful to NGO's. . . .

In June 1983, the Netherlands Institute of Human Rights (SIM), an NGO based in Utrecht, organized a conference on fact-finding and specialized research in the field of human rights. Having in mind the existing lack of procedures for NGO fact-finding missions, the conference focused primarily on fact-finding by NGO's. The above mentioned IGO rules and NGO Studies were the main topic of discussion by over 40 participants from all parts of the world, of both intergovernmental and non-governmental organizations.

It was generally accepted that more detailed guidelines could be expected from IGO's than from NGO's. Nevertheless, it was agreed that there existed sufficient resemblance between IGO and NGO fact-finding to identify certain basic principles. . . .

The summary report by David Weissbrodt provides a broad framework within which it is strongly advised that fact-finding is conducted; this framework is based on the experience of both IGO's and NGO's, as well as individual expertise. The main features of this framework are:

— the members of the mission should be independent, objective and impartial.

— guidelines should be established by the sending NGO or the members of the mission.

— the reports should contain terms of reference and a description of working methods.

— the terms of reference should provide a reasonably clear objective for the fact-finding effort, but might also include a catch-all omnibus clause to provide some flexibility.

— mission delegates should be carefully selected, the relevant considerations including capacities and experience of the members and various aspects of the situation and country under investigation.

— organizations should inform the government of the country to be visited of the terms of reference and members of the mission.

— within the framework of its terms of reference and guidelines, fact-finders should be free to receive, test and evaluate evidence from diverse sources available. The way in which this is done must be explained in the report if not otherwise available.

— in evaluating evidence, reference should be made to relevant articles of international human-rights law.

— the sending NGO should give the government concerned a reasonable opportunity to comment upon the substance of the report, or at least the report should be made available to the government concerned just prior to the publication.

— unless otherwise provided in the terms of reference or guidelines, the report might include conclusions, advisees, and/or recommendations.

— the organizations should have the responsibility to consider what follow up is required, including the publicity for the report. The way of presentation of the report and the issuing of a summary or press release might be considered. NGO reports should be distributed broadly to governments, IGO's and NGOs.

Hurst Hannum, *Fact-Finding by Non-Governmental Human Rights Organizations*

In Fact-Finding Before International Tribunals 293, 301-303 (Richard B. Lillich ed., 1992)

As noted above, there has been no consensus among NGOs on the minimum requirements for accurate fact-finding, although most would no doubt share the ideal aspirations expressed in various formulations designed to guide potential fact-finders. Nevertheless, there do seem to be several practices that would enable observers better to judge the reliability and accuracy of NGO press releases, statements, and reports.

First, every comprehensive NGO report on a particular country should include a clear statement both of the scope of the report (human rights in general? only violations of humanitarian law? only violations by the government? only a specific category of violations?) and of its methodology. Beyond the common practice of listing meetings and interviews, a full statement of the sources for other materials and the particular assistance offered by any other NGO's should be offered. If a report is based on an onsite mission, fuller information should be provided about the mission members and their expertise (beyond a mere listing of names and titles). The person who actually prepared the report should be identified, even if it is ultimately the responsibility of the NGO.

Second, particularly in those situations where an NGO is performing a watchdog or early-warning function rather than claiming to present well-documented facts, the source(s) of the information must be clear, unless there is a legitimate fear of reprisals. The distinction between NGOs as watchdogs and NGOs as impartial fact-finders should be maintained with greater clarity and neither function will necessarily suffer as a result.

Third, the distinction between NGOs as fact-finders and NGOs as political advocates must be deepened. No U.S.-based NGO escaped confusing these issues in dealing with Central America, and each was hurt whenever a political opponent looking for bias could find it. A few organizations successfully manage both functions; Amnesty International, for example, has generally been able to keep its advocacy of fair trials and abolition of the death penalty separate from its more factual conclusions as to the human rights situation of particular persons or countries.

Fourth, NGO fact-finding will continue to be seen as biased against governments unless NGOs are willing, where appropriate, to support unpopular causes, i.e., governments and government supporters. Given its early and vocal criticism of the human rights practices of the South Korean government, for example, the fact that an election observer team of the International Human Rights Law Group found the 1987 South Korean elections to be essentially fair — although the pro-government candidate won — contributed significantly to the recognition of the legitimacy of that election. NGOs may occasionally forget that the protection of human rights is largely concerned with defending the political process or the rights of individuals; it does not legitimize the preference of outside observers for one political or economic system over another.

Despite the lack of common fact-finding procedures, despite the occasional (and unavoidable) confusion of advocacy and reporting, human rights NGOs have, as a group, enjoyed a remarkable degree of credibility and trust. While allegations of political bias or "softness" towards countries of a particular political persuasion continue to be made against human rights groups, there are no important examples of countries being unfairly targeted for attack on human rights grounds. Given the increasing use of the phrase "human rights" by any group that disagrees with government policy, this record is all the more impressive.

Unfortunately, but inevitably, "a remarkable degree of credibility and trust" does not mean infallibility. The consequences of getting the facts wrong are demonstrated by the following summary of certain events in Kuwait in the aftermath of the 1990 Iraqi invasion, prior to the First Gulf War, in which a coalition of states led by the United States defeated the Iraqi forces and forced their withdrawal from Kuwait. The summary is drawn from a curriculum on International Conflict and the Media, prepared by the American Forum for Global Education.

Andrew F. Smith, International Conflict and the Media, A Curriculum Guide: Incubator Baby Incident

http://www.globaled.org/curriculum/cm18a.html and http://www.globaled.org/curriculum/cm18h.html **(reading reference numbers omitted)**

Incubator Baby Incident

The London *Daily Telegraph*, on September 5, 1990, reported the claim by the exiled Kuwaiti housing minister, Yahya al-Sumait, that "babies in the premature unit of one hospital had been removed from their incubators so that these, too, could be carried off." The story was repeated on Reuters, an electronic press service. Two days later the *Los Angeles Times* published the Reuters story about the atrocity accounts of a San Francisco woman identified as "Cindy" and her traveling companion "Rudy" who had been evacuated from occupied Kuwait. "Iraqis are . . . taking hospital equipment, babies out of incubators. Life-support systems are turned off."

Nayirah's Testimony

On October 10, 1990, the congressional Human Rights Caucus provided an opportunity for Amnesty International to present their evidence against Iraq on Capitol Hill. The Caucus is not a committee of Congress and therefore does not require that a witness take an oath. An anonymous fifteen year old "Nayirah" [was] allegedly a Kuwaiti with first-hand knowledge of the crimes witnessed by "Cindy" from San Francisco. Nayirah reportedly could not give her last name because of fear of reprisals against her family. She testified tearfully:

> "I volunteered at the al-Addan hospital. While I was there, I saw the Iraqi soldiers come into the hospital with guns, and go into the room where 15 babies were in incubators. They took the babies out of the incubators, took the incubators, and left the babies on the cold floor to die. It was horrifying."

All major television networks, CNN and many local television stations replayed this testimony. Many newspapers reported on the hearing, and offer Nayirah's testimony.

President Bush

President Bush watched the hearings of the congressional Human Rights Caucus. In these hearings "Nayirah" reported on the Iraqis taking baby incubators in Kuwait. He was delighted with them. On October 15, 1990, President Bush reported that he had met with the Emir of Kuwait, who had told the President horrible tales about "newborn babies thrown out of incubators and the incubators then being shipped to Baghdad." He referred to the story five more times during the next five weeks, once in an interview with David Frost.

The U.N. Security Council

On November 27, 1990, the U. N. Security Council heard "Dr. Issah Ibrahim," who explained that after the Iraqis took over "the hardest thing was burying the babies. Under my supervision, 120 newborn babies were buried the second week of the invasion. I myself buried 40 newborn babies that had been taken from their incubators by soldiers." An unidentified Kuwaiti refugee supported the testimony. The next day newspapers all over America reported on the testimony of this witness.

Middle East Watch's Report

Middle East Watch, a New York based human rights group, also pursued these reports. They cited a Dr. Ahmed al-Shatti who related the stories of Iraqi torture at a press conference in Jiddah, Saudi Arabia, on October 14, 1990. The doctor was unable to document his claims, but other physicians gave similar reports. A Kuwaiti physician, Dr. Ali al-Hawil, said that between sixty to seventy babies had died in the Kuwait City maternity hospital after soldiers dismantled the premature-babies unit. He claimed that he and his colleagues buried fifty babies on August 20.

Amnesty International's Report

On December 19, 1990, Amnesty International published an 84-page report on the Human Rights violations in occupied Kuwait. The report stated, "In addition, over 300 premature babies were reported to have died after Iraqi soldiers removed them from incubators, which were then looted." The report cited three supports for this allegation. First, it reported that an unnamed Red Crescent doctor as saying that 312 premature babies at Maternity Hospital in al Sabah Medical Complex died after being taken from incubators and that he personally had buried 72. Second, the report also quoted the previous statement made before the Human Right Caucus offered by the anonymous fifteen year old "Nayirah." Third, the report mentioned a woman who had quadruplets at al Razi Hospital, who had gone home and then returned to find them out of their incubators. They died a day later at home. On January 8, 1991, U.S. executive director of Amnesty International reported the story in testimony before the House Committee on Foreign Affairs. . . .

Incubator Story Disputed

Some newspapers challenged the story. On September 30, 1990, the *Seattle Times* published an interview with a Palestinian physician contradicting the incubator allegations. On December 10, *USA Today* reported:

> A doctor just out of Kuwait challenges assertions by President Bush and Kuwait exiles that invading Iraqi soldiers had dumped babies out of incubators.
>
> "Babies are dying in hospitals because Iraq's invasion has driven away staff who could save their lives," says Icelander Gisll Sigurdsson, who left Kuwait three weeks ago.
>
> The incubator charge has been levied by Bush repeatedly when he recounts Iraqi atrocities.
>
> "That news was not true," Sigurdsson said in Amman, Jordan. "However there were lots of babies who died because of lack of staff over the last few weeks."

Source: *USA Today*, December 10, 1990, p. 7A.

Sifting for the Truth on Both Sides

> Truth is the first casualty, people always say gloomily at the prospect of war. Just how rapidly this happens can be illustrated by the case of the premature Kuwait

babies, supposedly left to die last August by Iraqis who then removed the incubators to Baghdad. It has become the tale used by the Kuwait government in exile, as well as by President Bush, who invoked Iraqi horrors inflicted upon the innocent children of Kuwait in his speech. It should be said right away that there are thousands of examples of such Iraqi brutality and denial of elementary human rights, not just in Kuwait but in Iraq. But the story of baby mass murder is untrue.

Does it matter that the Iraqis, amid their looting and murders, did not kill scores if not hundreds of babies by stealing their incubators? It does matter. War brings a deluge of propaganda designed to gull us and to protect government. The incubator myth shows how quick we are to believe something when it grabs so savagely at our instincts.

Source: Adapted from Alexander Cockburn, "Sifting for the Truth on both Sides," *Los Angeles Times*, January 17, 1991.

After the War

After the war, John Martin of ABC News interviewed Dr. Mohammed Matar, director of Kuwait's primary health care system and his wife Dr. Fayeza Youssef, chief of obstetrics at the maternity hospital. They reported that the story was not true and was simply propaganda. Dr. Fahima Khafaji, a pediatrician in the maternity hospital, reported that the Iraqis did not do so at her hospital.

On January 6, 1992, John R. MacArthur, publisher of *Harper's Magazine*, revealed that "Nayirah," who offered testimony before the Congressional Human Rights Caucus on October 15, 1990, was really the daughter of Saud al-Sabah, Kuwait's ambassador to the United States. It was also disclosed that Hill and Knowlton, a large public relations firm, had helped prepare her testimony, and that she had rehearsed before video cameras in the firm's Washington headquarters.

The testimony presented before the United Nations Security Council on November 27 by the unidentified Kuwait refugee turned out to be Fatima Fahed, wife of the Kuwait minister of planning and a prominent Kuwait television personality. Dr. Issah Ibrahim, who also offered testimony at the Security Council, was really Dr. Ibrahim Behbehani, a dentist. When questioned after the war, he admitted that he had not seen babies taken from the incubators.

A subsequent private investigation by Kroll Associates — a firm paid by the Kuwait government — found a single, brief incident, in which perhaps a half dozen infants were removed from incubators during the occupation. They offered no evidence to support this position.

On February 4, 1992, the U.S. Ambassador to Kuwait, Edward W. Gnehm, claimed that there were three witnesses to the removal of babies from incubators. He railed against the "smug and cynical" human rights investigators and journalists who had challenged the story. He, however, refused to release the names of the witnesses. Two days later, Middle East Watch staff examined Gnehm's statement and concluded there was no hard evidence.

Amnesty International subsequently retracted its claims, although the "incubator baby" story remains a stain on AI's otherwise excellent record for careful fact-finding. The organization suffered a blow to its credibility, but the quality and reliability of its reporting both before and after the incubator story have ensured that AI remains among the most trusted sources for facts about particular human rights situations. An NGO with a less solid track record might not have survived.

For the transcript of a radio debate between the person who ran the public relations for Hill and Knowlton and one of her critics, see A Debate on One of the Most Frequently Cited Justifications for the 1991 Persian Gulf War: Did PR Firm Hill & Knowlton Invent the Story of Iraqi Soldiers Pulling Kuwaiti Babies From Incubators?, Dec. 2, 2003, http://www.democracynow.org/article.pl?sid=03/12/02/1540237#transcript. See generally Robert Charles Blitt, *Who Will Watch the Watchdogs? Human Rights Nongovernmental Organizations and the Case for Regulation*, 10 Buff. Hum. Rts. L. Rev. 261 (2004); cf. Human Rights Watch, The Damaging Debate on Rapes of Ethnic Chinese Women (Sept. 1, 1998). ("There may well be problems with some of the data initially collected, and rights advocates probably need to exercise more than usual caution in ensuring the credibility of their sources. . . . [T]he focus on rape has obscured several [more important] issues. . . .)

B. *Fact-Finding by the UN and Other Inter-Governmental Organizations*

Many of the same human rights concerns that were identified during the FIDH mission to Chile and included in its report on the Mapuche, supra page 981, came under examination by the UN Special Rapporteur on the Situation of Human Rights and Fundamental Freedoms of Indigenous People, when the Special Rapporteur visited Chile the year after the FIDH mission. The following extract includes the Special Rapporteur's assessment of the criminal prosecution of Mapuche leaders within the broader human rights context.

Report of the Special Rapporteur on the situation of human rights and fundamental freedoms of indigenous people, Mr. Rodolfo Stavenhagen (Addendum: Mission to Chile)

U.N. Doc. E/CN.4/2004/80/Add.3 (Nov. 17, 2003)

INTRODUCTION

1. Pursuant to Commission on Human Rights resolution 2001/57 of 24 April 2001, which established his mandate, and at the invitation of the Chilean Government, the Special Rapporteur visited Chile from 18 to 29 July 2003. His visit coincided with the final phase of the work of the Historical Truth and New Deal Commission, with whose members the Special Rapporteur was able to talk at length.

2. The Special Rapporteur would like to express his gratitude to the Government of Chile for its invitation and cooperation and to the Ministry of Development and Planning (MIDEPLAN) for organizing so efficiently the part of the schedule devoted to contacts with government institutions. He would also like to express his appreciation to the office of the Regional Representative/Adviser for

Latin America and the Caribbean of the United Nations Development Programme (UNDP) in Chile for their excellent work in organizing a full and well-planned schedule of meetings and in taking care of the arrangements and logistics for the mission. He would also like to thank the many indigenous organizations that gave their time and provided useful information. Finally, he would like to thank the Inter-American Institute of Human Rights for its cooperation and, in particular, the Institute's Diego Iturralde for his support during the mission. . . .

I. Schedule For The Visit

5. The schedule for the visit included talks with national and regional government officials in Santiago, Temuco, Iquique and Arica. In Santiago, the Special Rapporteur met with the President, Mr. Ricardo Lagos; the Minister-Secretary General of the Presidency, Mr. Francisco Huenchumilla; the Minister for Foreign Affairs, Ms. Soledad Alvear; the Minister of the Interior, Mr. Jose Miguel Insulza; and the Under-Secretary at the Ministry of Development and Planning, Mr. Jaime Andrade. The Special Rapporteur also had meetings with members of the President's Strategic Analysis Group, members of the Indigenous Policies and Programmes Coordinating Group, which includes representatives of various ministries with responsibility for issues that affect indigenous people, and with the President and members of the Senate Commission on the Constitution, Legislation, Justice and Regulations. He also had several meetings with Mr. Patricio Aylwin, President of the Historical Truth and New Deal Commission, and members of the Commission.

6. On his trip around the various regions, the Special Rapporteur visited indigenous communities, met with local officials and with members of civil and grass-roots organizations, and had meetings with representatives of indigenous peoples in Temuco, Ralco, Iquique, San Pedro de Atacama and Santiago. Although he was unable to travel to Easter Island, the Special Rapporteur met with representatives of the Rapa Nui people in Santiago, where they told him of their concerns and hopes and explained the implications of the island's future special status. . . .

B. SOCIAL GRIEVANCES AND CONFLICTS

28. The Special Rapporteur was informed about the growing number of conflicts in the Mapuche area, including in Regions VIII, IX and X. Most of the conflicts reported stem from Mapuche land claims and generally involve one of three types of protest:

(a) The organization of pressure groups acting on behalf of those who have unsuccessfully applied for additional land or for the restitution of their land;

(b) The occupation of disputed land, as a means of applying direct pressure and gaining publicity;

(c) The occupation of land that is not the object of any ongoing legal claim, involving actions that are serious by definition (such as setting fire to forest plantations or buildings, destroying equipment and fences or blocking communication routes) and clashes with the police.

29. As will be appreciated, the distinctions between these three types of protest are not clear-cut and in some cases a transition from one to another can be observed, depending on whether there are delays or problems in finding solutions to the demands for additional land and for restitution of land. It should also be pointed out that the third, and most serious, type of conflict occurs mostly in the provinces which have higher concentrations of indigenous people and higher poverty rates and which were adversely affected between 1973 and 1990 by the reversal of the measures taken to implement land reform.

> During his visit to Temuco, the Special Rapporteur was able to talk to relatives of a 17-year-old youth, Alex Lemun, who died on 13 November 2002 from his injuries after being shot by the police (*carabineros*) during a clash. Reports say that Alex Lemun died after being shot several times during a demonstration calling for the return of the Santa Alicia estate, which is controlled by a large lumber company. Alex Lemun was a member of the Arauco Malleco Coordinating Committee.
>
> The Special Rapporteur regrets that the necessary steps have not yet been taken to punish those responsible or compensate the family, and calls on the Government to take the necessary steps to resolve this matter. It is a matter of concern that the police officer responsible for the young man's death was released in September 2003.

30. Since the Indigenous Peoples Act was adopted, it has been possible to deal with these problems through administrative procedures conducted by CONADI, which are generally aimed at negotiating with the parties and acquiring the disputed land for subsequent allocation to the indigenous people. However, this solution has been gradually becoming less effective for various reasons, including the limited resources of the Land Fund, the gradual rise in the asking price for land that is to be expropriated or sold — either because of improvements made (to plantations or buildings) or because of speculation related to the growing demand from indigenous people — and the constantly growing number of land claims.

31. Because it is becoming increasingly difficult to find and apply timely solutions and because pressure, mainly in the form of the seizure of lands by the Mapuche, is growing, the preferred course is to take these problems to the criminal courts. In the last few years there has been an increase in the number of criminal cases brought against the leaders of Mapuche communities and organizations. These cases are reportedly related to offences against private or public property and attacks on police officers during protests or the occupation of land and buildings. In addition, several informants expressed concern about the large and permanent police presence in the communities, where inquiries were sometimes accompanied by physical and verbal abuse, leaving the population in a state of fear.

32. In recent years, Chile has reformed its rules on criminal procedures. The reform includes the following measures: a division of the tasks of investigation, defence and judging/sentencing between the Public Prosecutor's Office, the Public Defender's Office and the judge or court; the elimination of secrecy during the pre-trial proceedings; the introduction of oral proceedings during the trial; the possibility of taking preventive measures other than pre-trial detention; and the possibility of handing down sentences suited to the social and cultural circumstances of the accused as an alternative to imprisonment.

33. As pointed out to the Special Rapporteur by the national authorities in this branch of government, the reform establishes a procedure that guarantees the rights of the parties better than the inquisitorial procedure that predominated in previous legislation. In particular, the new system provides for the use of a person's mother tongue and the presence of a translator; guarantees that defence counsel will be provided by the State; allows a number of cultural and social factors to be taken into account as mitigating circumstances; requires any evidence provided by community authorities to be evaluated; and permits alternative punishments to imprisonment.

34. The reform of criminal procedure is being introduced gradually throughout Chilean territory. Region IX is one of the first two regions where it is being put into practice. . . .

35. In the past year, under the reformed criminal procedure, proceedings have been started against a group of Mapuche leaders with links to a de facto coordinating group for the offence of "conspiring to commit a terrorist act" and other offences (mostly setting fire to forests, buildings and equipment). For this reason, a large number of leaders have been in pre-trial detention since December 2002. According to the information given to the Special Rapporteur, this offence is defined in the Counter-Terrorism Act, which has been in force since the military Government took power in 1973 and which provides for the prosecution of illicit acts intended to terrorize the population. The provisions of the Act modify some aspects of criminal procedure, permitting some elements of secrecy in the pretrial investigation phase, eliminating preventive measures other than pre-trial detention, and increasing sentences. The possibility of protecting witnesses, which is permitted under the Anti-Terrorism Act, cancels out some of the advantages of oral proceedings and introduces a serious imbalance in the weight given to oral testimony as opposed to documentary and material evidence.

36. Finally, under the legislation still in force, all acts involving a member of the police or armed forces as the alleged perpetrator or victim of an offence are outside the jurisdiction of the ordinary criminal courts (and thus the scope of the Public Prosecutor's Office and Public Defender's Office) and are referred to military courts, which follow their own procedures.

37. In the opinion of some experts, this combination of a new criminal procedure, the counter-terrorist law and military jurisdiction creates a situation in which the right to due process is weakened, and this affects, in a selective way, a clearly identified group of Mapuche leaders. This is a matter of concern, regardless of the seriousness of the acts in which they may have been involved, with regard to respect for their right to due process.

> The Special Rapporteur visited Ms. Mireya Figueroa, an indigenous Mapuche woman from the Tricauco community in Region IX, in the women's prison in Temuco. She had been held for over six months while awaiting trial, accused, according to a letter sent to the Special Rapporteur in July 2003, of a terrorist attack, arson and conspiracy. During the meeting, she reported several irregularities in the case, including flaws in the investigatory process that undercut several procedural guarantees.
>
> The Special Rapporteur, in his meetings with officials, expressed his concern about the irregularities in the case of Mireya Figueroa and also about the length of time she had been waiting for trial, all of which raised doubts about the protection of her fundamental rights.

38. The situation described above is perceived by most traditional leaders of indigenous communities and by the activists in their organizations as an attempt to criminalize their protests, which they see as a just claim for land and a basically political demand for a new deal from the State....

> During his visit to Temuco, the Special Rapporteur received information on a case involving two *lonkos* (community leaders) that arose in the context of the recent reform of criminal procedure. In a conflict over land, the *lonkos* Pascual Pichun and Aniceto Norin from Region IX (Araucania), were accused in December 2001 of setting fire to a well-known pine forest on the Nancahue estate belonging, it is said, to a famous national politician. They were arrested under the Counter-Terrorism Act and other offences were added to the charges against them. After over a year of pre-trial detention, the court acquitted them of the charges of "terrorist attacks and threats" for lace of evidence, after the statements made by the "faceless witness" produced by the prosecution were set aside.
>
> In July 2003, the Supreme Court of Justice accepted an appeal for annulment submitted by the plaintiff and the State prosecutor and ordered a new trial of the *lonkos*. In September they were sentenced to a prison term of five years and one day for posing a "terrorist threat."
>
> The Special Rapporteur cannot help but express concern at such an extraordinary situation, which as arisen in the context of a social conflict and in which the right to due process could be violated and the impartiality of a respected body such as the Supreme Court of Justice could be called into question.

Recommendations

...Administration of justice

69. Under no circumstances should legitimate protest activities or social demands by indigenous organizations and communities be outlawed or penalized.

70. Charges for offences in other contexts ("terrorist threat", "criminal association") should not be applied to acts related to the social struggle for land and legitimate indigenous complaints.

71. The Special Rapporteur recommends that the case of the *lonkos* on trial, Pascual Pichun de Temulemu and Aniveto Norin de Didaico (from Region IX, Araucania), should be reviewed, in strict accordance with the guarantees of due process established in international human rights standards.

72. The implementation of the reform of criminal procedure should take into account international human rights standards, including due process for all indigenous people accused of social defence or protest activities (particularly with regard to the use of "faceless" witnesses and the pre-trial detention of suspects).

73. In any judicial or administrative proceedings involving indigenous persons, the latter should be assisted by trained bilingual translators and, where necessary, a competent court-appointed defence lawyer with knowledge of indigenous cultures.

74. In any judicial or administrative proceedings involving indigenous persons, indigenous legal customs should be respected.

75. The Special Rapporteur recommends that the Chilean Government should consider declaring a general amnesty for indigenous human rights

defenders on trial for social and/or political activities in the context of the defence of indigenous lands.

An on-site visit, such as the above mission to Chile, is one of the fact-finding tools used regularly by the thematic rapporteurs and working groups of the UN Commission on Human Rights (soon likely to be attached to the Human Rights Council). The mandates and functions of these thematic mechanisms are discussed in Chapter 7, pages 567-578. Of course, on-site missions can occur only with the consent of the government concerned. In addition, as is evident from the above report, fact-finding is often combined with analysis and recommendations. On-site fact-finding complements more passive methods of investigation, including examination of information submitted by NGOs and by governments.

Consideration of mandatory government reports is one of the principal means of fact-finding utilized by the UN treaty-monitoring bodies, such as the Human Rights Committee and the Committee on the Elimination of Racial discrimination, as discussed in Chapter 7, pages 584-592. Although governments are not generally required to submit information to other UN human rights bodies, most do so when requested or when they are under scrutiny for alleged human rights violations. The government of Chile submitted the following document in response to the above report by the Special Rapporteur on indigenous rights.

Government of Chile, Report I — Recommendations of the Special Rapporteur on the Situation of Human Rights and Fundamental Freedoms of Indigenous Chileans

(Feb. 2005) (unpublished; unofficial translation)

The present report is a summary showing the actions taken by the State of Chile for the betterment of the conditions and level of recognition of its indigenous peoples. Methodologically, it follows the order of recommendations given by the Special Rapporteur. . . .

The Area of Administration of Justice

With respect to recommendations 69 and 75: No democratic State should accept the use of violence as a way to address social problems. In Chile there are mechanisms and institutional channels to address social problems, for both indigenous and non-indigenous peoples. The judicial actions are aimed at punishing all those who commit crimes. Sanctioning those who commit a crime does not imply "criminalizing" a social or political problem.

According to the information submitted by the Ministry of the Interior, there are a total of 48 cases — which include crimes of arson, taking over of property, and robbery, among others — in Regions VIII, IX, and X. The government has prosecuted those who are found responsible. Twelve cases have been processed against indigenous actors, three of whom have been convicted.

The attribution of crimes to certain people by the Justice Tribunals has been done on the basis of the nature of crimes and the result of investigations carried out — rather than on the basis of the ethnic origin of those charged. . . .

The Government and Justice Tribunals have applied the antiterrorist law in very specific cases, those in which the acts committed constitute the kind of crimes that the legislation sanctions. Nevertheless, the Government is currently analyzing types of crimes covered by the antiterrorist law according to its new policies in the area criminal justice, since it is aware that the legislation is overly broad; hence its revision is necessary.

The Special Rapporteur recommends that the cases of the *lonkos,* Pascual Pichùn of Temulemu and Aniceto Norin of Didaico (Region IX of Araucanía), be reviewed, with strict adherence to the due process guarantees established in international human rights norms. The *lonkos* appealed to the Inter-American Commission on Human Rights at the beginning of 2004, denouncing various violations of due process in an investigation conducted by the Public Ministry and the subsequent trial before the Justice Tribunals. They also allege that the State of Chile has not respected their rights guaranteed in Article 8 of the American Convention of Human Rights, specifically the rights of presumption of innocence and *non bis in idem.*

Chile has responded to the Commission, stating that throughout each of these proceedings the indicted persons have had been afforded by the State a legal defense by qualified counsel free of charge. At the same time, in accordance with the new criminal procedure rules, each step in this and all cases related to the investigation and adjudication of these crimes has been made public, always in the presence of the persons charged. In addition to having a technical legal defense, they have been able to express themselves directly to the Tribunal of Guarantees and the Tribunal of Hearings in the *mapudungun* language, assisted by a interpreter, as have several of the witnesses. In this way, the claimants [Norin and Pichùn] have had all the guarantees of due process in a public and adversarial system.

As reflected in the Chilean government's response to the Special Rapporteur, information submitted by governments often is short on incriminating detail and is conveyed in a way to show the state in the best possible light. While governments remain important sources of information, the need for independent fact-finding is apparent.

The scrutiny brought to bear by the independent fact-finding of the Special Rapporteur and NGOs in relation to the Mapuche situation has shown some results. In July of 2005, the Special Rapporteur sent a letter to Chile's President Ricardo Lagos, expressing concern about new indictments of Mapuche leaders under the Antiterrorism Act which had been initiated since his on-site visit in 2003. The FIDH sent a delegation to observe the trials of the accused and issued press releases condemning the proceedings as a repressive tactic to quell Mapuche activism in connection with legitimate claims. Subsequently the trial court dismissed the indictments against the defendants on the grounds that the antiterrorism legislation did not apply, construing "terrorism" narrowly to encompass only those acts that put human life at risk. However, the *lonkos* Pascual Pichùn and Aniceto Norín, who the Special Rapporteur had specifically mentioned in his report, remained imprisoned, serving the five year and a day sentences handed down for earlier indictments. Other six Mapuche leaders and activists continued to serve sentences under the Chilean antiterrorist law, and many others remained imprisoned under ordinary criminal legislation.

Chile is by no means new to being the target of international human rights fact-finding. In the aftermath of the 1973 coup and the massive human rights violations that allegedly accompanied it, the Commission on Human Rights in 1975 established a Working Group to Inquire into the Situation of Human Rights in Chile. This country-specific investigation became the precedent for numerous subsequent initiatives by the Commission to examine human rights conditions in specific countries, as discussed in Chapter 7, page 566. Among the more recent targets of scrutiny is Myanmar (formerly Burma). The Commission created a Special Rapporteur for Myanmar in 1992 and, as is typical of country rapporteurs, he proceeded to conduct on-site visits to the country as a principal means of fact-finding. The following extract is from the report of his third visit, out of a total of six visits undertaken as of 2005.

Report on the situation of human rights in Myanmar, submitted by Mr. Paulo Sérgio Pinheiro, Special Rapporteur

U.N. Doc E/CN.4/2003/41 (Dec. 27, 2002)

I. Activities of The Special Rapporteur

A. Fact-Finding Mission

3. The Special Rapporteur conducted his third fact-finding mission to Myanmar from 17 to 28 October 2002. As during his previous missions, he received full cooperation from the Government, for which he expresses once again his sincere appreciation. He was able to carry out his programme in its entirety and enjoyed complete freedom of movement and access to private persons and others of interest. . . .

4. While in Yangon, the Special Rapporteur met with the Secretary 1 of the State Peace and Development Council (SPDC); the Foreign Minister and his Deputy; the Home Minister; the Head of Department of the Office of Military Intelligence; the Chief of the Bureau of Special Investigation; the Directors-General of the Prisons and the Police Departments; the Chiefs of the Special Branch and the Criminal Investigation Departments; and members of the governmental Human Rights Committee. The Special Rapporteur visited Insein Central Prison, where he interviewed confidentially 16 prisoners, including recent political prisoners and those whom he had met during his previous visit in February 2002. He also had meetings with the General Secretary and members of the Central Executive Committee of the National League for Democracy (NLD), representatives of ethnic and other political parties, the United Nations country team, the diplomatic community, international civil society organizations, members of the international and local business community, as well as religious leaders and recently released political prisoners.

5. The Special Rapporteur travelled to Hpa-an (capital) and Kya-in-seikkyi township in Kayin (Karen) State from 23 to 25 October, where he met with local civilian and military authorities and visited the state court and district- and

township-level police offices, including lock-ups. He also met with representatives of two ceasefire groups, and Buddhist and Christian religious leaders. On his way to Yangon, the Special Rapporteur stopped in Mawlawmyine, capital of Mon State, where he met with the Commander of the South-Eastern Command responsible for Mon and Kayin States and visited the local NLD office. Finally, on 27 October, he also travelled to Bago Division to visit Thayarwaddy prison where he interviewed 11 prisoners.

6. The Special Rapporteur followed his mission to Myanmar with a four-day visit to Thailand (29 October-1 November), during which he had meetings with the Deputy Permanent Secretary of the Ministry for Foreign Affairs, United Nations officials, and representatives of the diplomatic community, the media and nongovernmental organizations (NGOs). He also travelled to Chiang Mai to hear the preliminary results of research developed by his team in the context of his mission to gather directly, and in a systematic manner, first hand testimonies from victims of, and witnesses to, human rights violations, and other persons who may have direct knowledge of the circumstances or context of such violations in the Shan, Kayin (Karen), Kayah (Karenni) and Mon ethnic areas of Myanmar. The purpose of this research project was to provide a solid background based on first-hand empirical survey to enable the Special Rapporteur to build up his own knowledge and understanding of the situation in these areas.

7. On his way to and from Myanmar, the Special Rapporteur had consultations with the Special Envoy of the Secretary-General to Myanmar. . . .

II. Enjoyment of Basic Freedoms and Human Rights

A. Freedoms of Association

12. A very important step by the SPDC was the release of Daw Aung San Suu Kyi, which, according to her, has been unconditional. Following her release on 6 May 2002, the General Secretary of the NLD and her party have enjoyed some freedom of movement, assembly and expression within their precincts and the framework of their party activities. She has been able to travel extensively in the country without restriction. She has started to reorganize the party, to meet her followers, to deliver public speeches, and to open new offices (so far, 66 NLD offices have been opened throughout the country). So far, none of her followers, be they party organizers, activists or sympathizers, has been subjected to intimidation or harassment, though surveillance continues unabated, but in a somewhat more courteous manner devoid of direct pressure. Military intelligence personnel systematically monitor the NLD and all other political activities. Such personnel continue to be conspicuously present in front of the NLD office, monitoring movements in and out, photographing visitors, and often visiting them to question them about their contacts and discussions. What these security agencies seem to want is to know what is going on in order to maintain complete control of the situation and avoid any activity that may "get out of hand." They appear to be haunted by the spectre of social unrest.

13. While it is clear that the political space is being gradually reopened for the NLD to revive its activities, the extent to which it will be opened remains to be seen. The Special Rapporteur presumes that the regime that applies to the NLD is

also valid for the eight other political parties which, in addition to the pro-Government National Unity Party, were not deregistered after the 1990 elections. The Special Rapporteur met representatives of several of these parties, none of which has resumed its legitimate activities, citing fear as the reason.

14. The Special Rapporteur also met representatives of parties that were deregistered and that refer to themselves as "national politicians" in order to be allowed to participate in what the SPDC calls "national politics." This term seems to refer to political activities sanctioned by the SPDC, in contrast to "party politics" which contest its legitimacy. The Special Rapporteur also met with the United Nationalities Alliance, an informal umbrella organization founded in July 2002 by eight nationality parties that participated in the 1990 election....

C. POLITICAL PRISONERS

17. The SPDC appears to have accepted the figure established by the International Committee of the Red Cross (ICRC) of 1,448 "security detainees" (as of 21 October 2002) whose detention involves a political or security element, even if they were convicted for criminal offences. Apparent consensus within the SPDC regarding numbers and categories of such detainees provides a clearer basis for mutual understanding. The Special Rapporteur called for their release before the end of the year, or at the latest by his next mission. He was informed that this would be unlikely but that releases would continue. The Special Rapporteur also reiterated his call that those who are imprisoned for their real or imputed peaceful opinions or activities (who appear to constitute the vast majority) should be released, immediately and unconditionally. Concerning those against whom there is credible evidence of involvement in violent acts, their release could be considered through an amnesty in the context of national reconciliation....

D. CONDITIONS IN PRISONS

21. As during previous missions, all the prisoners interviewed by the Special Rapporteur... confirmed that their general detention conditions had improved in recent years. This reflects the positive commitment of the authorities and the constructive cooperation with the ICRC since May 1999. The Special Rapporteur was pleased to learn from prisoners themselves that there had been no retaliation against persons interviewed during his previous missions, in accordance with the assurances received from the SPDC. He is only concerned that some of those interviewed persons were questioned by military intelligence personnel afterwards about the reason and content of his discussion with them. This practice may be perceived as an attempt to intimidate them and discourage some of them, or others, from further cooperation with him.

22. The Special Rapporteur also welcomes the fact that physical ill-treatment of political prisoners, such as beatings, had stopped where it previously occurred, and that elderly prisoners, such as U Win Tin and Dr. Salai Than Tun, have received regular medical attention and daily doctor's visits. The Special Rapporteur took note that the Prison Department is seriously considering giving political prisoners access to writing and reading materials other than religious books and to facilitate access to educational materials for those who wish to pursue their studies. Obviously, their release would resolve these problems.

23. Several areas where further attention would be required include the quality of food, the reported beating of common prisoners and the access to qualified medical attention and treatment, especially in cases of emergency. Since July 2002, four political prisoners have died in detention (Mai Aik Pan, U Aung May Thu, U Sai Pa and U Maung Ko). These deaths were allegedly due to delays in getting clearance from authorities regarding access to urgent medical assistance. This brings to 74 the total number of deaths in detention of political prisoners since 1988. The Special Rapporteur understands that in the case of common prisoners, the situation is worse and that their death rate in prison and labour camps is abnormally high. This is an issue which he intends to follow up on during his next mission. He was also informed that, on several occasions, very sick common criminals had been temporarily taken out of prison just prior to his visit or a visit by the ICRC, so that their poor state of health would not be noticed. This reportedly took place in Myitkyina, Insein and Thayarwaddy prisons. . . .

E. FREEDOM OF RELIGION

29. The Special Rapporteur has the impression that against the background of a general respect the practice of religion, there are local or regional variations. Respect for religious freedom appears to be better in places closer to central authorities than in remote or counter-insurgency areas. He has no clear answer why. Perhaps it is because of insufficient control by the central Government of local authorities or neglect with regard to the respect due certain faiths. Chronic problems involving Muslims, especially but not only in Rakhine State, continue to be reported. The Special Rapporteur is aware of the involvement of officials of the Office of the United Nations High Commissioner for Refugees (UNHCR) in this respect and plans to look at the issue more closely during his next mission.

30. During his mission the Special Rapporteur met with ministers and community leaders of several Christian churches as well as with Buddhist monks. He heard that to build a church or a community centre Christians need to get permission from the authorities. It appears that even if they are authorized to do so by central authorities, they must still go through all the administrative levels down to township where difficulties are frequent; in case of refusal they have to follow their complaint all the way up again through the same levels. . . .

III. Independent Investigation of Allegations of Human Rights Violations in Ethnic Areas

35. One of the major consequences of insurgency on the border between Myanmar and Thailand since the 1980s has been the generation of internally displaced persons (IDPs). Insurgency involves the entire population. This kind of warfare affects civilians as the distinction between combatants and non-combatants is very difficult to make. What is dramatic is the fact that the civilian population in the areas of ethnic insurgency in Myanmar, in spite of their individual choices, are inevitably drawn in to the conflict. The army tends to see the refugees/IDPs as enemies and the refugee camps as rear-guard from which to

attack the country. In consequence, every investigation of human rights violations in the war zones is considered as a war of words against the SPDC.

36. The Special Rapporteur thinks that it is time to overcome this impasse whereby any consideration of well-founded allegations of human rights violations automatically is seen with suspicion as an accusation against the SPDC. He thinks that the peaceful exposure of violations will be a contribution to national reconciliation and peace that may open the path to accountability, a basic requirement for building the rule of law.

37. Serious human rights violations have undoubtedly occurred and continue to occur in the areas where armed groups operate. These violations have been primarily attributed to the army. There is also evidence that groups operating from neighbouring countries and with outside support show little regard for the life and security of civilians. Their continued armed activities in these areas provoked counter-insurgency measures by the army, which has had devastating consequences for the local population.

38. The question of independent investigation of allegations of human rights violations in the ethnic counter-insurgency areas was one of the specific issues addressed by the Special Rapporteur during the reporting period. Special attention was paid to the issue of investigating allegations that Shan women had been systematically raped by Myanmar military personnel in the report "Licence to Rape," published by the Shan Human Rights Foundation (SHRF) and the Shan Women's Action Network (SWAN) in May 2002. In this regard, during his last mission, he received detailed briefings on three investigations into the recent allegations of rape in Shan State conducted by the Myanmar authorities for a period of three months. He was also invited to travel to Shan State, which he opted to decline as a short visit would have been inappropriate for conducting a serious assessment of the alleged violations there. On his way back from Myanmar, the Special Rapporteur met with the authors and researchers of the above report and his research team interviewed a number of victims of and witnesses to incidents of rape in Thailand.

39. In preparing for his mission, the Special Rapporteur had followed the matter closely. He first noted that the SPDC rejected the allegations as fabrications without looking into them at press conferences held on 12 and 30 July; a press briefing on 23 August was an example of "double thinking" in the sense that the Deputy Foreign Minister concluded that "preliminary" findings had shown that the allegations had been fabricated by the authors of the report in connivance with the Shan United Revolutionary Army (SURA), at the same time pledging to "leave no stone unturned" in the investigation; and lastly, the two members of the National Working Group on Women's Affairs who visited OHCHR on 11 October stated that they had not seen the original Shan rape report.

40. The details of the three investigations given to the Special Rapporteur during his mission were as follows:

(a) The first investigation report (by a "special team of security personnel") concluded (after meeting 94 officers and soldiers from 24 battalions, 27 members of the judiciary, police and hospital staff, 6 NGOs and 195 villagers) that "preliminary investigations and findings show that almost all of the allegations were highly exaggerated and their main purpose was to hurt the prestige of Myanmar and the Myanmar Armed Forces";

(b) The second report (by the Chairman of the "Myanmar National Women Committee to Combat Trafficking" (the Deputy Minister for Home Affairs) under "the guidance of Gen. Khin Nyunt") concluded that "there is no proof" to support the "allegation of the SURA narco-terrorists" after a five-day investigation mission in "43 localities";

(c) The third report (by a team of the Myanmar National Working Committee on Women's Affairs led by Dr. Daw Khin Win Shwe (Gen. Khin Nyunt's wife)) concluded after a five-day visit during which it met 650 government officials in two districts and 250-300 village elders in two village tracts, that "it is clear that the accusations are unfounded." There were "no rape cases committed by military personnel between 1996 and 1999 and in 2002," but there were "three cases in 2000 and 2001" the perpetrators of which were sentenced to 5 to 10 years.

41. The Special Rapporteur also received briefings regarding two specific allegations, namely, the execution of five villagers in Kalein Padaw village, Thanbyuzayat township, Mon State and of 12 villagers in Htee Law Bler village, Kya-inseikkyi township, Kayin State, conducted by the SPDC from July to October 2002.

42. While recognizing these important efforts, the Special Rapporteur explained to the SPDC that, having been undertaken by military and other SPDC personnel, the investigations lacked the independence required to be convincing and credible. The actual investigations were apparently conducted by personnel with no special skills or experience in investigating human rights allegations, and who were probably unaware of the minimum standards required for a credible inquiry. From the reports, one can assume that they were conducted in such manner that very few people would probably dare to testify out of fear of reprisals against them or their families (prearranged, large, collective and public meetings with local officials, village elders and villagers, organized by security/military personnel with military escorts; village elders were allegedly requested to gather villagers or risk being fined; villagers were asked to sign a document denying the allegations of rape). To the Special Rapporteur's knowledge, very few efforts were made to interview individual villagers in a manner that would ensure the confidentiality of the interview and the protection of the witnesses afterwards. It is not clear — except in one case — whether effective interpretation was provided to ensure proper communication. Language problems, including translation of names of places and individuals (both victims and soldiers), may have been a complicating factor. The implied methodology and the factual evidence described do not support the conclusions of the investigations.

43. Having explained that, the Special Rapporteur proposed that the SPDC explore several options to establish a credible mechanism for investigating these and numerous other allegations of violations in ethnic minority areas and underlined the importance of making an early commitment to that effect. . . .

On-site fact-finding also may be undertaken by UN agencies apart from the thematic and country-specific mechanisms of the Human Rights Commission/Council. The UN Secretary-General sometimes appoints a personal envoy to conduct a fact-finding mission, as Secretary-General Kofi Annan recently did to examine allegations of human rights violations in Togo. The Office of the

High Commissioner for Human Rights, in addition to assisting with fact-finding by the thematic and country mechanisms of the Human Rights Commission/ Council and by the Secretary-General, engages in fact-finding through its various field offices and pursuant to ad hoc initiatives. It also supports fact-finding missions authorized by the Security Council, such as the International Commission of Inquiry for Darfur established in 2004 (see Chapter 10, page 869). The Security Council has established fact-finding missions to investigate human rights conditions in a number of other places, including creating a group to examine the situation in the former Yugoslavia, as a precursor to establishing the criminal tribunal to adjudicate crimes committed there (see Chapter 11, page 897). The General Assembly also has created human rights missions, going back to its establishment of special bodies to investigate conditions in South Africa and the Israeli-occupied territories.

At the regional level, the Inter-American Commission on Human Rights conducts on-site visits as a regular feature of its human rights monitoring work and issues detailed reports based on those visits. The fact-finding and reporting practices of the Inter-American Commission are discussed in detail in Chapter 9. The African Commission on Human and Peoples' Rights similarly, although thus far with much less frequency, has undertaken on-site fact-finding, including missions to Togo, Sudan, Senegal, Nigeria, and Mauritania. See Chapter 5, page 326, and Rachel Murray, "Evidence and Fact-Finding by the African Commission," in *The African Charter on Human and Peoples' Rights: The System and its Practices, 1986-2000* (Malcolm D. Evans and Rachel Murray eds., 2002).

As a general rule, unless mandated by the Security Council, an on-site visit requires the consent of the state concerned. Requests for "invitations" from governments for on-site visits often are granted, but not always. For example, since his last on-site visit to Myanmar in November 2003, repeated requests by the UN Special Rapporteur for that country have been denied. Thus, instead of being able to engage in the kind of on the ground fact-finding reflected in the above report, the Special Rapporteur for Myanmar has been forced to rely on information gathered from outside the country. See Interim report of the Special Rapporteur of the Commission on Human Rights on the situation of human rights in Myanmar, U.N. Doc. A/60/221 (Aug. 12, 2005).

The requirement of state consent to on-site visits by representatives of international organizations is one of several criticisms in the following extract by Professor Bassiouni, who chaired the commission created by the Security Council to investigate war crimes in the former Yugoslavia.

M. Cherif Bassiouni, Appraising UN Justice-Related Fact-Finding Missions

5 Wash. U. J.L. & Pol'y 35 (2001)(footnotes omitted)

Shakespeare wrote that a rose by any other name is still a rose. But in the United Nations (UN), a fact-finding mission, notwithstanding its name, is not necessarily a fact-finding mission. . . .

The United Nations is a vast organization whose multiple processes bring about fact-finding missions. Some of these processes are established by norms;

others by custom and practice, but many of the processes are ad hoc. The courses of these processes are not always linear, consistent, or predictable, and frequently they will take unexpected turns."....

The human rights component of the UN system reflects the values of justice, while systemically it functions as a political process, thus conditioning the upholding of these values to political oversight. In past decades, what Secretary-General Kofi Annan frequently refers to as the "international civil society" compelled realpolitik to take into account the values of justice. It is not for the sake of these values but rather to offer persons pursuing political ends utility in the form of conflict management and conflict settlement. Seen from this perspective, justice becomes another card for the realpolitician to play and eventually barter away, in a mostly hidden manner, when in pursuit of achieving a political goal. This reality, more than anything else, impacts upon the effectiveness and impartiality of fact-finding missions....

Because the values of truth and justice have become part of the tools of realpolitik, nothing can be done to overtly contradict these values. Consequently, less than obvious ways must be devised to ensure that these missions will, when politically convenient, give only the appearance of pursuing these values while at the same time not generating politically unwanted results. This is essentially, but not exclusively, accomplished in three ways:

1. appointing compliant and understanding non-UN staff persons as heads and members of these missions;
2. relying on a politically-sensitized and cooperative staff; and
3. using the financial resources and bureaucracy to guide the work and outcomes of these missions.

These factors are interrelated in that the heads and other appointees to these missions are politically determined; the bureaucracy has a large influence in the making of these choices; the bureaucracy needs to please the influential member-states because they determine budgets and impact on promotions and staff assignments; appointees are rewarded by the bureaucracy for compliance with their guidance through greater cooperation, which is necessary for the success of the given mission; and present appointees receive support from the bureaucracy for prospective appointments. This explains in part why there is such a recurrence of the same appointees to these missions and why certain members are assigned to work and guide them. The latter factor may also be positive, in that the selection of recurring staff to support these missions provides for more experience and expertise, thereby contributing to the success of the mission....

One need not look for hidden conspiracies to explain certain strained or unexplainable outcomes; rather, they can be explained by the political dynamics of a system that is fueled by political considerations, personal ambition, venality, and other human frailties. The foregoing also explains why certain efficacy measures that would greatly enhance the accomplishment of these missions are not put in place. If they were, they would help clarify what is at times intended to be murky. One example is illustrative of this regrettable situation. After fifty years, there is no standard operating procedure for fact-finding missions. Admittedly, any standard operating procedure needs to be tailored to the situation. But no manual exists to describe how an investigation should be conducted and there is no standard, though adaptable, computer program to input collected data. Worst of all, there is no continuity. In short, there is nothing to guide, instruct, or assist the heads and appointees to these missions of how to better carry out their mandates. It strains one's belief that in fifty years the most elementary aspects of standardized organization, planning, documentation, and reporting have not been developed. Thus, each mission has to reinvent the wheel and, in an organizational sense, has to reinvent itself as a mission. The results are usually poor or mediocre performance, except where particularly competent persons are appointed to these missions, and in these rare cases it is their entrepreneurial and other qualities that bring about the mission's success. But the contributions of dedicated and hardworking UN staffers should not be overlooked in assessing the success of these missions. This situation also means that there is little consistency and predictability as to the methods and outcomes. Thus, there is no way of comparing the results of different, though substantively similar, missions. This principle applies equally well to ongoing missions that produce multiple reports, where it is at times difficult to compare working methods pursued during the mission and the results they produce.

The lack of standardized methods, particularly as to empirical research and field investigation, means that there is no basis to test the validity of the research in order to assess the plausibility of the conclusions. It is safe to say that no scientific research methodology would consider the above-described approach as anything but selective, insufficient, unreliable, and, at best, anecdotal. It should also be noted that portions of mandates issued by UN organs, bodies, and agencies are at times overlapping and almost always ad hoc. Among the results of these partially overlapping mandates are:

1. confusion as to the boundaries of the overlapping mandates;
2. potential contradictions in the conclusions; and
3. potential mutual reliance of these missions in reporting on the overlapping areas, thus creating a false impression of confirmation and reliability.

As a result of the ad hoc issuance of these mandates:

1. there is no predictability as to the situations that will warrant issuance of such mandates;
2. the decisions to issue, extend, amend and terminate these mandates seem essentially contingent upon political and extraneous circumstances; and
3. there is infrequent continuity in follow-up on missions that have reached the end of the mandates.

These observations are evident in the workings of mandates issued by the Security Council, the General Assembly, the Commission on Human Rights, the Subcommission on the Prevention of Discrimination and Protection of Minorities, and the Treaty-bodies. Each one of these appointing organs or bodies relies on a separate formula, uses a different label, provides for different operational methods, and offers different levels of support and resources. However, they have common powers: to establish and terminate the mandate; to define its scope and duration; to appoint its heads and other members; and to determine or condition its operational capabilities.

The Commission on Human Rights has rapporteurs and independent experts; the Subcommission has special rapporteurs; the Security Council has Commissions, and the Secretary-General has Personal Representatives. Most of the Commission and Subcommission fact-finding missions have limited resources, sometimes none at all, and are supported by one or, at best, two staffers, mostly on a part-time basis. These missions seldom have the resources or the ability to do effective field work or empirical research. Consequently, they rely heavily on the NGOs, government reports, and the media. Many rapporteurs, or whatever their actual designation may be, produce reports even though they never set foot in the territory where their investigation takes place. Thus, the experts who over the years had to investigate human rights violations in South Africa during the apartheid regime, Iran, Iraq, and Israel were not allowed into these countries, yet they still reported on them.

The Security Council may establish a Commission because it sees the need, at that time, for that issue to go through a particular process. The Rwanda Commission was one such case, whose mandate and duration were limited. It lasted three months and made a single one-week visit to Rwanda. Its function was essentially window dressing. At the time, the Security Council wanted to follow its precedent of the Yugoslavia Commission that preceded the International Criminal Tribunal for the Former Yugoslavia (ICTY) and that called for its establishment as stated in Resolution 808. Thus, it seemed to the Security Council more suitable, before establishing the International Criminal Tribunal for Rwanda (ICTR), to have a commission that would call for it. But there was another reason: It was necessary to gain time before the Security Council established the ICTR in order to work out the logistics of the prospective tribunal.

... Fact-finding missions also come in other high-level processes. The Secretary-General may appoint a Personal Representative to undertake such a mission, as does the High Commissioner on Human Rights and the High Commissioner on Refugees. These High Commissioners may themselves go out on such missions. But these missions are not real fact-finding missions. They are political missions that need a more neutral or acceptable label to pursue what is essentially a laudable effort to reduce tensions, cause violence to abate, or help restore and preserve peace. Sometimes they are designed to simply show responsiveness to public outcry in certain egregious situations. In these cases they are more akin to public-relations missions.

Fact-finding and investigation are a means to an end. With respect to the values of truth and justice, the end is accountability of the perpetrators, particularly the leaders of jus cogens crimes of genocide, crimes against humanity, war crimes, torture, slavery and slave-related practices, and apartheid. But accountability has yet to be clearly established as one of the goals of fact-finding missions. Indeed, to date the UN has not promulgated guidelines for accountability.

Probably the most significant fact-finding operation in UN history was the work of the Commission established by the Security Council pursuant to Resolution 780 in 1992 to investigate war crimes in the former Yugoslavia. The Commission worked for two years, during which it conducted thirty-five field investigations, established the most extensive database for gathering evidence and information about violations of international humanitarian law, identified over 800 places of detention, estimated 50,000 cases of torture and 200,000 deaths, estimated two million displaced persons as a result of ethnic cleansing that was documented in connection with some 2,000 towns and villages where the practices took place, and conducted the world's first and most extensive investigation into systematic rape. The latter produced over 500 affidavits of victims who identified their perpetrators. Interviews were conducted with 223 victims and witnesses; gathered information led to the identification of close to 1,500 cases; and other information revealed the possibility of an additional 4,500 or so victims.

Most significantly, the Commission, which received from the Security Council the broadest mandate since the establishment of the International Military Tribunal at Nuremberg, received no funding from the UN to conduct its investigations. The funding had to be raised from states' voluntary contributions, states' contributed personnel, private sources of funding, and ultimately the support of DePaul University, which gave this author the space, overhead costs, and staff to establish the database in Chicago. Over a period of two years, over 140 lawyers and law students worked at the database that produced close to 80,000 documents and 300 hours of videotapes. It was on that basis that the Commission was able to produce its Final Report and Annexes. The report exceeded 3,300 pages and was the longest report made by the Security Council. The history of the Commission was tormented and difficult, as it faced opposition by some governments and those in the UN bureaucracy who wanted to advance the political agendas of those governments. That explains the lack of resources that the UN allocated for the investigation, though it did provide the costs of some staff and some limited space at the UN Headquarters in Geneva.

Ultimately, however, it was the Commission's work that gave the Security Council the basis to establish the ICTY. The politics of justice continued in the Security Council's selection of the ICTY prosecutor. It was also reflected in the early administrative termination of the Commission, even though the Security Council never adopted a resolution to that effect. Nevertheless, if it had not been for the work of the Commission, the ICTY Prosecutor who took office almost fourteen months after the establishment of the Tribunal would not have been able to start his work as fast and as efficiently.

The Commission's task was enormous. A war was going on; there was no precedent to guide its work; it had almost no resources available, and it lacked the political backing or the political will of a unified Security Council to which the UN bureaucracy is responsible. More importantly, at the time, the world was emerging from almost a half-century of the Cold War, punctured by many regional and internal conflicts of different dimensions and scope. The idea of impartial, effective, politically independent, and fair international criminal justice was not even on the radar screen of most governments. In a sense, there was a psychological iron curtain that prevented even the consideration of such a system of international criminal justice. The Commission's work tore down this psychological iron curtain. Since then, international criminal justice has become part of the values of the international community, though it is still confronted by the exigencies of realpolitik.

On a more practical level, extraordinarily, the UN has not yet developed a system, despite the experience of the Commission and what followed in the area of fact-finding. Thus, every new Commission, fact-finding body, or mandate for individual fact-finding is ad hoc. There is no institutional memory, and there is no system by which the experiences of the past can be used to benefit the future. It is beyond logical explanation to find that the UN has established no model or standard database and that no model or standard process for field investigations exist, including no protocols for mass grave exhumations or reconstruction of events, and no large-scale interviews of victims and witnesses.

The Commission had established all of that, and while it surely could have been improved, it was simply overlooked and nothing of any systematic nature was ever done. One explanation, of course, is that the lack of existing systems and processes, as well as standardized methods of operation, are certain to delay the work of any fact-finding body or individual, except when there is a political will to give such fact-finding greater momentum. In these cases, interested governments provide the resources, the evidence, and contribute personnel. Thus, fact-finding is held hostage to the political will of major governments. The means to accomplish that end are financial and bureaucratic. The absence of systems, procedures, methods of operation, and funding all contribute not only to delay, but to the inability to achieve the purposes of justice-related fact-finding.

C. *The Need for General Standards for Fact-Finding by Intergovernmental Organizations*

Considering the many kinds of fact-finding that international organizations undertake, the inherent sensitivity of most of the investigations, and the high degree of autonomy the fact-finders have in choosing their methodology, it can hardly be expected that the fact-finders' activities will please everyone. On the one hand, there is a danger that the fact-finding process might be unfairly biased against the states concerned. On the other hand, there is the opposite danger: that fact-finders will tread too warily or be manipulated by governments into painting too rosy a picture, as cautioned by Professor Bassiouni.

There has been an awareness for some time for the need for general standards on fact-finding. Over the years various steps have been taken to this end. These steps are summarized in the following extract from a document by the Office of the High Commissioner for Human Rights. In an effort to consolidate standards for fact-finding by persons working under UN auspices, referred to as UN human rights officers (HROs), the document first includes a synthesis of the relevant principles and it prescribes methodology.

Office of the High Commissioner for Human Rights, Training Manual on Human Rights Monitoring

U.N. Sales No. E.01.XIV.2 (2001) (emphasis in original)

Chapter VII: INFORMATION GATHERING

A. THE INFORMATION GATHERING PROCESS

1. The **principal objective of monitoring is to reinforce State responsibility** to protect human rights. Human rights monitors collect *prima facie* information about human rights problems and illustrative patterns of violations. The process of collecting such information requires considerable effort. While the word "monitoring" might superficially imply a passive process of observing and reporting,

HROs [Human Rights Officers] will need to establish a more **active information-gathering approach**. HROs rarely are direct witnesses to serious violations, so that they can accurately report incidents they see. Instead, HROs learn of such incidents from victims or other witnesses. Accordingly, monitoring requires careful techniques for **collecting accurate and precise information**. Information-gathering requires thorough **inquiries, follow-up, and analysis**; sound information is essential to producing well-documented reports, which can then be used to encourage action by the authorities.

2. Indeed, HROs do not restrict their work simply to observing and reporting, because the human rights operation's objective is generally to help redress human rights problems and prevent future violations. The human rights operation should have a presence at all levels of the society. The local authorities should be aware that the operation reports not only human rights violations which have occurred but also the follow-up action taken by local authorities to redress the situation. Hence, the monitoring and reporting carried out by HROs can help to put pressure on local authorities to address and follow up on particular human rights problems. Often, this **follow up action** will not only **redress** human rights violations, but also serve to **prevent** human rights violations in the future.

3. After identification of the human rights problems to be monitored under the mandate, human rights monitoring is principally pursued by means of **inquiries** to amass the elements of information, allowing *prima facie* assessments on the existence or non-existence of violations. These inquiries include a number of phases and dimensions:

(a) **identifying which problems to pursue** under the mandate;

(b) **developing contacts** and **establishing a presence** in the community;

(c) **collecting testimonies** and complaints;

(d) pursuing an inquiry meant to **verify information** concerning the violation, as well as the **response of the authorities**, including the military, police, and the legal system as relevant;

(e) **if** at this point, it is established that **no** human rights **violation** occurred, the **case is closed**;

(f) **if** the inquiry establishes that there has been **a violation**, the HROs will make **recommendations** and will take **steps** required by their mandate. (Note that different levels of information may be needed to take increasingly assertive action.) . . .

(g) during the entire process, HROs will seek to **assure that the responsible authorities are acting diligently and efficiently**. They will especially monitor the conduct of the police and/or military in respecting human rights and the respect of legal procedures in regard to arrest, detention, and trial as well as the guarantee of security for witnesses. . . .

Chapter XVIII: BACKGROUND OF UNITED NATIONS MONITORING STANDARDS

4. In order for HROs to collect information and gain an understanding about the situation, officers must **develop contacts with knowledgeable individuals**, human rights **organizations**, other nongovernmental organizations, **local government officials**, and other relevant actors working in their area. Lawyers and

journalists may be particularly good sources of information because they are usually aware of relevant developments. HROs should be sensitive to the fact that violations against certain vulnerable groups — for example women — may be more difficult to detect through traditional channels for information gathering. They may therefore need to expand their search in order to ensure that certain groups or categories of persons are given proper attention and sufficient information is gathered on possible violations against them. Developing contacts requires active efforts to contact individuals and organizations, to arrange periodic meetings, etc. Further, HROs must use the sources that they cultivate. They should repeatedly return to their on-site contacts for more information.

5. In this context HROs should develop **relations with local Government** officials, including police and military officials, judges and other officials concerned with the administration of justice. Such contacts and a visible presence will help to discourage violations. Such governmental contacts will help identify which officials can be helpful when different problems arise. In addition, HROs should **regularly visit** prisons, hospitals, morgues, and areas where the population is most at risk (such as slums, working class districts, and rural communities).

6. As mentioned above, **nongovernmental organizations** (NGOs) can usually provide much valuable information and can assist the human rights operation in many ways. . . .

Human rights operations should promptly **identify the NGOs** active in the country to determine which can provide information, which can handle matters outside the mandate of the operation (*e.g.*, child abuse, food assistance), which can help with human rights education and promotion, etc.

7. It is important to **develop contacts before a crisis situation** arises. Once the problem has arisen it will be more difficult to develop the relationships necessary for contacts to be useful.

8. In developing and using contacts, HROs should **assess the perspective of the contacts**. Ideally, officers should identify at least some contacts who have the least apparent bias as to human rights issues which may arise. In any case, HROs need to understand and compensate for the bias of contact persons who may provide information.

C. COLLECTING TESTIMONY

9. Information-gathering requires actively pursuing all credible leads regarding human rights abuses. HROs must be **available and ready to move at any time to receive information** from a person who considers himself or herself to be a victim of a violation. When HROs learn of a situation (such as a demonstration, verified enforced disappearance, forced eviction, or mass arrest), they should take steps to gather relevant information from indirect sources and then to identify and interview witnesses. HROs should consider carefully whether going to the scene of an event will assist with the inquiry or might endanger sources of information and, in case of doubt, always consult with other relevant persons in the operation. In general, it is wise to be somewhat circumspect about visiting the site of an incident until the HRO knows enough to determine whether the benefit will considerably outweigh any potential risk to the officer or sources of information. . . .

D. RECEIVING COMPLAINTS

11. Often individuals identify themselves by coming forward in search of protection or recourse for past violations of human rights. The **number of individual communications reaching the HROs depends on their credibility with the local population**, NGOs, churches, and other organizations. The need for credibility and information provides another reason why officers should develop good relations with human rights and other organizations working in their area.

12. The **objective of an inquiry is to ascertain the circumstances and acts that led to an alleged violation,** for example suspicious death, an illegal detention, internal displacement, a discriminatory eviction, or other human rights violation. Such an inquiry is necessary, whatever the category of violation communicated to the HROs. The **response**, however, **will vary according to the kind of violation** which must be established, for example, death of a victim; disappearance; torture; cruel, inhuman or degrading treatment; serious and frequent threats to individual liberty and security; discriminatory discharge from employment; violence against women; or the exercise of the right of expression and association. The nature of the response **will also vary depending upon the degree of certainty indicated by the information** available. For example, a relatively small amount of information may only require discreet inquiries with regular contacts. A greater degree of information may require more direct inquiry with other witnesses. More information may indicate the need for the preparation and ultimately the undertaking of an on-site visit. If HROs encounter an urgent and grave situation, the response may by necessity be quicker and less circumspect.

13. After a significant amount of information has been collected, HROs may need to make **inquiries with the authorities** as to their response. Depending upon the response of the authorities to the inquiry and the situation, **more information may be needed or other steps** should be considered, for example, appeals to higher level officials in the local Government, invoking the assistance of higher level officers within the human rights field operation, various forms of publicity, etc. Several such follow-up measures must be determined by the head of the field operation. . . .

E. VERIFICATION OF INFORMATION

18. After having received a communication, the HROs must **check the information received**. It is essential to verify the accuracy of the reported human rights violations before taking any steps. The officers should verify the substance of the complaint with any human rights organization or association having knowledge of the matter. Further, the officers may request assistance from any human rights organization or entity with knowledge of the case under scrutiny.

19. In addition, the HROs should determine whether the family, friends, and neighbours of the apparent victim, as well as **other witnesses, can corroborate** the facts in the complaint. The witnesses should be **individually interviewed** as promptly as possible and should be assured that the HROs will **remain in frequent contact** with them. They must be informed that the HROs will endeavour to assure their protection during and after the inquiry, but that their safety cannot be guaranteed. Additionally, the witnesses should be asked whether they wish to remain anonymous. . . .

F. ANALYSIS OF INFORMATION

20. A recurring problem with fact-finding regarding human rights abuses is difficulty in evaluating the information obtained during on-site visits or interviews. HROs, after all, lack the capacity to verify every detail of the information they receive. Indeed, it is rare for the HRO to "get to the bottom" of most violations as would occur in the criminal justice system. In general, however, the HRO seeks to develop at least a ***prima facie* analysis based upon the degree of relevance, veracity, reliability, and probity of the information** which has been collected.

21. The most commonly applied rule of reliability in human rights fact-finding is the principle that **information should be consistent with material collected from independent sources**. Related to the idea of consistency of information collected is the concept that reliability can be assessed by the degree to which a particular **piece of information fits in context** with other materials which have been amassed. Hence, the HRO must consider not only the specific information gathered, but also the officer's sense of whether the whole story seems credible when all the pieces of the puzzle are put together.

22. Another aspect of reliability relates to the degree of certainty which should be applied. The completeness expected from the HROs' fact-finding procedures will vary considerably depending upon the purpose for collecting the information. Instead of a specific "burden of proof" as might be applicable in the criminal justice system, there exists a **continuum of degree of certainty and quantity of information in relation to the action to be taken**.

23. For example, if the HRO attempts to gather complaints and other information so as to inform a lower level Government official of the allegations with the hope that the Government will initiate an investigation, the degree of care and completeness of the fact-finding procedure might be necessarily abbreviated. This lower level of certainty would only require the need for further inquiry at different levels of visibility. It should be recalled, however, that even an inquiry does carry some degree of implied criticism and visibility. The highest level of certainty would be required for the most coercive and visible actions. Hence, for a finding that human rights abuses have been perpetrated, the most complete process and a greater level of certainty would be required. To identify a perpetrator publicly the human rights operation may need to possess very substantial information (possibly even enough to meet the beyond-a-reasonable-doubt standard applied in the criminal justice system), because such a public identification may result in prosecution or possibly reprisals. In any case, such an identification of the perpetrator would represent a significant policy issue for the leadership of the human rights operation and would not be determined by the individual HRO.

G. EVALUATING DIRECT TESTIMONY

24. HROs can use a wide range of **techniques to corroborate** the direct testimony of victims and eyewitnesses. During the interview itself, the interviewer should test the **internal consistency and coherence of the testimony**. The interviewer can probe for inconsistencies by returning to the same subject several times but with different questions. The HRO should be careful to note, however, that often communication difficulties can create inconsistencies. The interviewee should be given the opportunity to provide clarifying information.

25. In general, oral testimony is evaluated based upon the demeanor and overall credibility of the witness. The HRO should, however, be sensitive to the fact that cultural differences and the nature of the testimony may create embarrassment and difficulty in communication. . . .

26. HROs should remember to factor into their analysis the perspective or bias of a witness. For example, a victim may exaggerate in order to justify their conduct and to get revenge against the person who injured them. Political tendencies may obscure or reorder the truth. Refugees may exaggerate the persecution they may have suffered in order to qualify for refugee status or simply to justify their decision to flee. Ideally, the HRO will be able to obtain consistent information from individuals with different political backgrounds and life experiences. The HROs' **use of reliable and uninvolved contacts**, as well as their own good sense, are particularly helpful in this context.

H. OTHER FORMS OF INFORMATION

27. While direct testimony from victims and eyewitnesses is the principal source of information for HROs, officers can **also use second-hand testimony**. When using the second-hand testimony of remote witnesses, however, field officers should remain aware that indirect information is **more unreliable than direct testimony**. The reliability of hearsay or second-hand information from several unrelated sources, though, will increase its probative value. Nonetheless, the officers should carefully consider hearsay or second-hand testimony before accepting it as fact.

28. Other forms of information can provide corroboration for allegations of human rights abuses. HROs can use **physical and psychological symptoms** observed during the interview and/or medical examination **as indicators of reliability**. If possible, HROs should seek the assistance of medical professionals for assessing medical and psychological symptoms of victims. . . .

29. Other **physical corroboration of allegations can occur during on-site visits**, which provide an opportunity to verify witnesses' descriptions of buildings and rooms and possibly to take photographs — particularly when there is a concern that the scene may be changed before the criminal justice professionals can arrive. . . .

I. EVIDENCE FOR CRIMINAL PROSECUTIONS

33. HROs should be aware of contexts in which the information they encounter may potentially be useful for criminal prosecutions — either in **international criminal tribunals** for such places as the Former Yugoslavia, Rwanda, and any other place where the jurisdiction of the International Criminal Court may arise in the future — or by **national courts**. In general, the lawyers and investigators for such tribunals prefer to do their own investigations and have difficulty relying upon information collected by others. Hence, if personnel from a relevant tribunal or court are available, **HROs should promptly inform them of information which might fall within their mandate**. Rule 70 of the Rules of Procedure and Evidence of the international criminal tribunals on the Former Yugoslavia and Rwanda permits the tribunal's prosecutor to receive confidential information and prohibits the prosecutor from revealing the identity of the informant or

the information without previously obtaining the informant's permission. While no Rules of Procedure for the International Criminal Court exist yet, article 54 of its Statute authorizes the Prosecutor to agree not to disclose, at any stage of the proceedings, documents or information that the Prosecutor obtains on the condition of confidentiality and solely for the purpose of generating new evidence, unless the provider of the information consents and take necessary measures to ensure the confidentiality of information, the protection of any person or evidence.

Most of the evidence collected for such tribunals comes from interviewing witnesses, visits to crime scenes, collection of physical evidence, and searches for documents. Evidence for criminal prosecutions usually needs to be more carefully handled than information obtained for human rights reports. Physical evidence must not only be preserved but the chain of custody must be carefully recorded, so that the evidence can later be verified. As indicated above, HROs should avoid disrupting criminal justice investigations and should generally avoid gathering physical evidence. Such issues raise significant policy decisions which can only be determined by the leadership of the human rights operation and not by individual HROs. Such policy decisions may wish to distinguish between the needs of (1) national or local criminal justice procedures, (2) reporting by any truth and justice commission, and (3) investigation for any relevant international criminal tribunal. . . .

34. Similarly, the leadership of the human rights operation may decide that HROs should be particularly careful in interviewing witnesses who later may be required to testify in national and/or international criminal proceedings. The records of such interviews may be produced in the trial and thus must be very carefully prepared. If a witness has evidence which should be adduced in a criminal proceeding, the **human rights operation** may wish to defer interviewing the witness so as to avoid influencing the testimony and **should inform prosecutors of potential witnesses** or may wish to work closely with the officials who are responsible for investigating the criminal offence.

In all cases, in order to decide a policy on these matters the leadership of the human rights operation will need to consult with relevant staff of the tribunals, and any policy decided will have to be consistent with applicable rules of procedure. . . .

Chapter XVIII: Evolution of United Nations Monitoring Standards

2. Various sets of rules of procedure exist to help guide fact-finders. The first international codification of fact-finding procedure was the **Hague Convention for the Pacific Settlement of Disputes of 1907**, 36 Stat. 2199, T.S. No. 536. It provided for a **commission of inquiry** that would be constituted by agreement between two disputing states and set out rules of procedure for the inquiry. Though the Hague Convention's inquiry mechanism received little use, the procedural rules continue to serve as a model for fact-finding which informed the development of the present Manual.

3. In 1970 the Secretary-General issued **Draft Model Rules of fact-finding procedure for UN bodies dealing with violations of human rights**. Although these Draft Model Rules were adopted in 1974 in substantially abbreviated form by the UN Economic and Social Council, they have served as the framework for rules of fact-finding commissions. The 25 Draft Model Rules are divided into

eleven sections covering applicability, constitution of the ad hoc body, agenda of meetings, officers, secretariat, languages, voting and conduct of business, cooperation with member States, oral and written testimony and other sources of information, records, and reports. The rules allow a commission to make recommendations and issue a minority report. They also permit the concerned State to submit evidence, to appoint a representative, and to put questions to witnesses, but they do not allow the State to make recommendations for the agenda or to place obstacles in the way of the attendance of witnesses. Consent of the concerned State is required for the ad hoc body to enter that State. All evidence is admissible, although its use is subject to the discretion of the commission. Witnesses are placed under oath and commission members swear to perform their duties "honourably, faithfully, impartially and conscientiously." A hearing may be conducted by one or more members.

4. A more recent statement of general standards can be found in the **Declaration on Fact-finding by the UN in the Field of the Maintenance of International Peace and Security**, U.N. Doc. A/RES/46/59, Annex (**1992**). . . .

5. As experience has evolved in the various UN, OSCE, and other international human rights field operations, further monitoring standards have been developing. Those standards and practices have been summarized, for example, in *La Guía Metodológica para el Trabajo de la División de Derechos Humanos de la Misión de Observadores de las Naciones Unidas para El Salvador* (Guidelines for the Work of the Human Rights Division of the United Nations Observer Mission for El Salvador (ONUSAL) (1992)); International Civilian Mission in Haiti — UN/OAS (MICIVIH), *Manuel d'Haiti* (1993), UN Mission in Guatemala (MINIGUA), *Manuel de Verification* (1994), Human Rights Field Operation in Rwanda, HRFOR Field Guidance (1996); High Commissioner/Centre for Human Rights, Field Guide for International Police Task Force Monitors of the Peace Implementation Operation in Bosnia and Herzegovina and CIVPOL Officers of the United Nations Transitional Administration in Eastern Slavonia (1996). Those standards, practices, and experiences have been the immediate basis for the present Manual.

6. Although each human rights field operation receives its own mandate from the Security Council or by agreement with the host Government, **several operations have received mandates similar to the United Nations Observer Mission for El Salvador** (ONUSAL):

> The Mission's mandate shall include the following powers:
>
> a. To verify the observance of human rights in El Salvador;
>
> b. To receive communications from any individual, group of individuals or body in El Salvador, containing reports of human rights violations;
>
> c. To visit any place or establishment freely and without prior notice;
>
> d. To hold its meetings freely anywhere in the national territory;
>
> e. To interview freely and privately any individual, group of individuals or members of bodies or institutions;
>
> f. To collect by any means it deems appropriate such information as it considers relevant.

While such a procedural mandate appears to be quite comprehensive and adequate, the **challenge** facing most human rights operations has been actually **employing these techniques in practice when faced with opposition from local authorities** who are unaware of the mandate and covert resistance from national authorities who wish to test the resolve of the UN human rights field operation....

Despite the effort of the Office of the High Commissioner of Human Rights to present a coherent picture of guidelines and methodology to govern UN fact-finding, it is apparent that no one set of comprehensive standards has been adopted by the United Nations. Mention is made in the above document of the Draft Model Rules issued by the Secretary-General in 1970. These Draft Model Rules were considered by a working group of the Commission on Human Rights, which substantially watered them down to muster the necessary consensus in 1974. Even then, the UN took little notice of the effort. The rules were forwarded by the Commission to its parent body, ECOSOC, which simply drew the attention of UN member states to their existence. It did not even go so far as to recommend that UN human rights fact-finding bodies take them into account in their work.

After that chastening experience, the initiative in the area passed to non-UN bodies. The most productive work has been done by the International Law Association (ILA), a group of international lawyers acting in their personal capacities. The Human Rights Committee of the ILA drew up a set of rules for fact-finding by international organizations, which the Association adopted at its meeting in Belgrade in 1980. For the report of the Committee, see Lillich, *Human Rights: Report of the Committee,* Report of the 59th Conference of the International Law Association 83 (Belgrade 1980). The Belgrade Rules, as they are known, remain important guidelines in this area.

Belgrade Minimal Rules of Procedure for International Human Rights Fact-Finding Missions

Reprinted in 75 Am. J. Int'l L. 163, 163-165 (1981)

I. Terms of Reference (Mandate)

1. The organ of an organization establishing a fact-finding mission should set forth objective terms of reference which do not prejudge the issues to be investigated. These terms should accord with the instrument establishing the organization.

2. The resolution authorizing the mission should not prejudge the mission's work and findings.

3. While terms of reference should not unduly restrict the mission in the investigation of the subject and its context, they should be so specific as to indicate the nature of the subject to be investigated.

II. Selection of Fact Finders

4. The fact-finding mission should be composed of persons who are respected for their integrity, impartiality, competence and objectivity and who are serving in their personal capacities.

5. Where the mandate of the mission concerns one or several specific states, in order to facilitate the task of the mission, the government or governments concerned, whenever possible, should be consulted in regard to the composition of the mission.

6. Any person appointed a member of the fact-finding mission should not be removed from membership except for reasons of incapacity or gross misbehaviour.

7. The chairman and the rapporteur of the fact-finding mission should not be replaced during the term of the mission except for reasons of incapacity or gross misbehaviour.

8. Once a fact-finding mission has been established and its chairman and members appointed, no persons should be added to the mission as members except to fill vacancies in the mission.

III. Collection of Evidence

9. At the commencement of the mission, all material relevant to the purpose of the mission should be made available to it, with the assistance of the organization concerned.

10. Fact-finding missions should operate with staff sufficient to permit the independent collection of data and should be assisted by such independent experts as the mission may deem necessary.

11. Fact-finding missions may invite the submission of evidence that is in writing and contains specific statements of fact that are in their nature verifiable.

12. The state concerned should have an opportunity to comment in writing on data referred to in paragraph 10 and statements referred to in paragraph 11.

13. Both the petitioners, such as states, non-governmental organizations, or groups of individuals, and the states concerned may present lists of witnesses to the fact-finding mission. The fact-finding mission should make its own determination as to which witnesses it will hear.

14. Petitioners ought ordinarily to be heard by the fact-finding mission in public session with an opportunity for questioning by the states concerned.

15. The fact-finding mission shall in advance require the state concerned to provide adequate guarantee of non-retaliation against individual petitioners, witnesses and their relatives.

16. In case a guarantee, as referred to in paragraph 15, is provided to the satisfaction of the fact-finding mission, the latter should, on hearing witnesses, either provide an opportunity for the state concerned to be present and to question witnesses, or make available to the state concerned a record of the witnesses' testimony for comment.

17. The fact-finding mission may withhold information which, in its judgment, may jeopardize the safety or well-being of those giving testimony, or of third parties, or which in its opinion is likely to reveal sources.

18. On the basis of data generated by its staff, written statements, and testimony of witnesses, the fact-finding mission should make its own determination as to whether it needs to conduct an on-site inspection.

IV. The On-Site Investigation

19. The fact-finding mission should draw up its programme of work, including the list of witnesses it wishes to interview at the site of the investigation, places it wishes to visit, and the sequence, timing and location of its activities on the site.

20. The fact-finding mission may operate as a whole or in smaller groups assigned to conduct specific parts of the investigation.

21. The fact-finding mission should insist on interviewing any persons it deems necessary, even if incarcerated.

V. Final Stage

22. After conclusion of the on-site investigation, members of the fact-finding mission should draw up a set of preliminary findings and submit these, together with supplementary questions where appropriate, to the state concerned, giving it an opportunity, within a reasonable time, to present comments and/or to rectify the matter investigated.

23. A final report shall be prepared by the chairman reflecting the consensus of the fact-finding mission. In the absence of a consensus, the mission's report should contain the findings of the majority as well as any views of dissenting members.

24. In case a decision is made to publish the report, it should be published in its entirety.

25. The Organization establishing the fact-finding mission should keep under review the compliance of states with their undertaking regarding nonreprisal against petitioners, witnesses, their relatives and associates.

D. Fact-Finding by Judicial and Quasi-Judicial Bodies

In the Anglo-American legal system, judicial bodies typically play only a passive role in fact-finding. It is the task of the parties to a lawsuit to gather the evidence and then present it to the court — often, of course, in contradictory versions — which will then proceed to evaluate it and render a decision. Courts and juries, then, are triers, not finders, of fact. In civil law systems of justice, however, the position is significantly different. There the judicial authorities participate in the investigation of the facts, by means of such institutions as a body of examining magistrates. Since the judiciary, in this kind of system, does not merely passively receive information presented to it, but actively inquires into the facts itself, the process is said to be "inquisitorial" in character (in contrast to the "adversarial" character of the Anglo-American system).

This civil law approach has exercised an important influence over the international legal system, including in the sphere of human rights. Accordingly, a number of international bodies of a judicial or quasi-judicial nature possess fact-finding, as well as adjudicatory, functions. The International Court of Justice, for example, is authorized by Article 50 of its Statute to "entrust any individual, body, bureau, commission, or other organization . . . with the task of carrying out an enquiry. . . ." The Court has not, however, made use of this authority during the past half-century.

There are many international human rights bodies with fact-finding capabilities, although (with the exception of the regional human rights courts) most would be described as only quasi-judicial in character. All fact-finding procedures are based on specific grants of authority contained within the instruments establishing the various bodies or amplifying their authority, but even similar treaty or other language may lead to quite different practices.

At the universal level, the Human Rights Committee is mandated to "consider communications received under the . . . [Optional] Protocol in the light of all written information made available to it by the individual [submitting the communication] and by the State Party concerned." Thus far, the Committee has relied exclusively on written submissions in determining its "views" on the merits of allegations; it has apparently not attempted to gather facts independently, nor has it held oral hearings on any case.

The Committee Against Torture is authorized under Article 20 of the Convention Against Torture and Other Cruel, Inhuman or Degrading Treatment or Punishment to appoint one of its members to undertake a "confidential inquiry" whenever it "receives reliable information which appears to it to contain well-founded indications that torture is being systematically practiced." The Committee "shall seek the co-operation of the State Party concerned," but no on-site visit may be undertaken without the specific consent of the state. The Committee has completed such visits to Turkey, Egypt, Mexico, Sri Lanka, and Peru.

The fact-finding practices of regional human rights bodies vary considerably, but in exercising adjudicatory or quasi-adjudicatory functions they all rely primarily on the review of documentary evidence presented by the parties. More so than other regional bodies, the Inter-American Commission on Human Rights sometimes engages in independent fact-finding and on-site visits in adjudicating complaints, as it did in connection with the case brought against Belize by Maya communities, a case discussed in Chapter 3 at pages 167-172. With respect to states that are parties to the American Convention on Human Rights, Article 48 of the Convention and Article 40 of the Rules of Procedure permit the Commission to conduct an on-site investigation "[i]f it deems it necessary and advisable . . . for the effective conduct of which it shall request and the States concerned shall furnish all necessary facilities." Non-parties to the American Convention must give specific permission for an on-site investigation, but, once permission is given, states are subject to the same obligation to furnish "all necessary facilities . . . and not to take any reprisals of any kind" against persons who cooperate with or provide information to the Commission. Rules of Procedure of the Inter-American Commission on Human Rights, Article 54. The Commission also holds oral hearing in most cases. However, the hearings typically are less than one hour long and allow for little more than arguments and counter arguments by representatives of petitioners and states.

When the Commission submits a case to the Inter-American Court of Human Rights, the Commission takes on a more active fact-finding role, typically in coordination with the petitioners who initiated the case. See generally Cecilia Medina, *The Inter-American Commission on Human Rights and the Inter-American Court of Human Rights: Reflections on Joint Venture*, 12 Hum. Rts. Q. 439 (1990). The Court itself engages in fact-finding through a review of documents and oral hearings. It has also made use of experts, from handwriting experts to anthropologists with expertise concerning indigenous peoples. The Inter-American Court has interpreted its fact-finding role more broadly than has the European Court of Human Rights. Article 45 of the Inter-American Court's Rules of Procedure permits it to "obtain . . . any evidence which it considers helpful." This includes hearing any witness or expert witness, requesting the production of evidence by the parties, calling upon any entity or authority to obtain evidence for the Court, and designating one or more of its members to conduct evidentiary hearings away from the Court's seat in Costa Rica.

Oral testimony by witnesses has been an important part of fact-finding by the Inter-American Court. Members of the Court themselves frequently engage in the questioning of witnesses. The following is an extract of the transcript of the oral hearing in the merits phase of the *Awas Tingni* case, a case introduced in Chapter 3, page 172. In contrast with the less than hour-long hearings typically convened by the Inter-American Commission, the hearing before the Court in the merits phase of the *Awas Tingni* case lasted two and a half days — short by the standards of trials in domestic litigation, but long in comparison with the oral hearings of other international human rights bodies. The following testimony by two leaders of the Awas Tingni community was complemented by that of other indigenous leaders of Nicaragua's Atlantic Coast region and of expert witnesses, including anthropologists and geographers, who endorsed the community's land claim.

Inter-American Court of Human Rights, Case of the Mayagna (Sumo) Community of Awas Tingni: Transcript of the public hearing on the merits, November 16, 17, and 18, 2000, at the seat of the Court (unofficial translation)

Published in 19 Ariz. J. Int'l & Comp. Law 129, 131-152 (2002)

PRESIDENT [OF THE COURT] CANÇADO TRINDADE:

. . . Before the testimony of the first witness, the Secretary of the Court must swear in each of the witnesses before questioning. Thus, I ask that the Secretary to call the first witness to testify. . . .

SECRETARY VENTURA ROBLES

Mr. Jaime Castillo.

PRESIDENT CANÇADO TRINDADE:

Mr. Modesto José Frank Wilson will serve as interpreter [from the Mayagna language into Spanish] . . .

WITNESS JAIME CASTILLO FELIPE (through the interpreter)

My name is Jaime Castillo, I was born in Awas Tingni the 15th of June, 1964.

PRESIDENT CANÇADO TRINDADE

Nationality and number of identification document?

WITNESS JAIME CASTILLO FELIPE

I am from Awas Tingni.

PRESIDENT CANÇADO TRINDADE

Number of identification document?
WITNESS JAIME CASTILLO FELIPE
The identification number is 607-150664-0003.
PRESIDENT CANÇADO TRINDADE
Place of domicile?
WITNESS JAIME CASTILLO FELIPE
I am from Awas Tingni. . . .
PRESIDENT CANÇADO TRINDADE
The witness will now be sworn in.
Do you solemnly swear and testify, with all honor and conscience to tell the truth, the whole truth, and nothing but the truth?
WITNESS JAIME CASTILLO FELIPE
Yes sir.
PRESIDENT CANÇADO TRINDADE
Will the Inter-American Commission representative please tell the Court the name of the person who will question the witness and please proceed.
INTER-AMERICAN COMMISSION
Dr. Bertha Santoscoy.
PRESIDENT CANÇADO TRINDADE
You may proceed.
INTER-AMERICAN COMMISSION
Thank you Honorable Court. . . .
Tell me, what is your mother tongue?
WITNESS JAIME CASTILLO FELIPE
Sumo Mayagna
INTER-AMERICAN COMMISSION
Are you of the Mayagna people or ethnic group?
WITNESS JAIME CASTILLO FELIPE
Yes.
INTER-AMERICAN COMMISSION
And the other members of the Awas Tingni Community are Mayagna?
WITNESS JAIME CASTILLO FELIPE
We are all Sumos, Mayagna. Excuse me?
INTER-AMERICAN COMMISSION
Tell me, Mr. Castillo, have you held a leadership position within the Community? If so, which one and when?
WITNESS JAIME CASTILLO FELIPE
From 1991 to 1996 I used, or was, *Síndico* of the Community.
INTER-AMERICAN COMMISSION
Tell the Court, Mr. Castillo, what being *Síndico* implies.
WITNESS JAIME CASTILLO FELIPE
The *Síndico* is the Community's representative who deals with all the problems about the territory and also conflicts that can come up around the Community, in coordination with communal authorities, before governmental authorities.
INTER-AMERICAN COMMISSION
Could you tell us, Mr. Castillo, on what do you and the members of the Awas Tingni Community subsist?
WITNESS JAIME CASTILLO FELIPE

We subsist on hunting, farming and other activities, on fishing and others.

INTER-AMERICAN COMMISSION

Tell us, who is the owner of the lands where you realize these activities you referred to, hunting, fishing, farming?

WITNESS JAIME CASTILLO FELIPE

We are the owners, which is why we have maintained it by working it and maintain it until now.

INTER-AMERICAN COMMISSION

Why do you say you are owners?

WITNESS JAIME CASTILLO FELIPE

I say that because we have lived more than three hundred years, we have worked all the time and part of that is shown by our having places, historic sites and part of the work accomplished in the land. That is why we are owners of the land.

INTER-AMERICAN COMMISSION

Tell us, Mr. Castillo, during the time you were *Síndico,* did you do anything to obtain the titles or demarcation of the lands in favor of the Community?

WITNESS JAIME CASTILLO FELIPE

At beginning I went before government agencies such as INRA, at that time MARENA. At that time I submitted documents and maps on the case. Following that, the authorities in the region, sent me a letter, transferred the case to Managua and also from Managua they sent a letter to Mr. Alberto Escobar regarding the response, the possible response that we never know what it said.

INTER-AMERICAN COMMISSION

Tell us, you spoke of the INRA, what does the INRA mean?

WITNESS JAIME CASTILLO FELIPE

Agrarian Reform Institute.

INTER-AMERICAN COMMISSION

Now, what were the results of your actions, of your efforts before the INRA?

WITNESS JAIME CASTILLO FELIPE

After all, I visited many times, but they told me to come back another day and another day but to date never responded.

INTER-AMERICAN COMMISSION

You have told us that you went before the INRA, could you tell us if you also went before the regional government of the RAAN?

WITNESS JAIME CASTILLO FELIPE

Yes, I also visited the regional government. . . .

INTER-AMERICAN COMMISSION

And what did you assert in that request?

WITNESS JAIME CASTILLO FELIPE

The contents of the request were that I asked that they give me title to the Community because, well, we had always had the hope, we hoped to have that communal title.

INTER-AMERICAN COMMISSION

What was the response they gave you to that request?

WITNESS JAIME CASTILLO FELIPE

The response was that the authorities of that exact moment were going to study it and that they were going to respond to us later but they never did. At that time

I submitted maps, census of the Awas Tingni population and also a document that Dr. Theodore Macdonald that he had made of the territory....

INTER-AMERICAN COMMISSION

Thank you very much, Mr. Castillo

PRESIDENT CANÇADO TRINDADE

Thank you very much to the Commission's delegation and also for keeping within the time allotted.

I will now call on the representative of the Illustrious State of Nicaragua, if they would like to question the witness, please indicate who will question this witness.

STATE OF NICARAGUA

Good afternoon, Mr. President, good afternoon Judges of this High Tribunal, Honorable Inter-American Commission, ladies and gentlemen.

We appear before you to refute each one of the unfounded violations of the American Convention that the Inter-American Commission has attributed to the Republic of Nicaragua.

Rosenaldo Castro will use our time to conduct the questioning....

...Mr. Castillo, are you Mayagna, mestizo, or Miskito?

WITNESS JAIME CASTILLO FELIPE

I am Mayagna.

STATE OF NICARAGUA

Mr. Castillo, do you know, that in 1995 a census was taken in the Republic of Nicaragua in which the zone know as Caño Awas Tingni was counted, in which there is a habitation settlement and in which it was established that 40% of the population is not Sumo [Mayangna]?

INTER-AMERICAN COMMISSION

Mr. President, I object. The State representative's question is not a question, the State's delegate is giving testimony. He is not asking something concrete. The witness is not an expert in the area.

PRESIDENT CANÇADO TRINDADE

Neither is it testimony, I think that it is a question but that it can be restated in other terms. Please...

STATE OF NICARAGUA

The question is whether he knows that a census exists, right, that he establishes that, yes or no?

INTERPRETER

Excuse me, 40% is not....

STATE OF NICARAGUA

40% of the population of Awas Tingni of 600 persons are not of the Mayagna ethnic group according to the official census of Nicaragua, does he know that, yes or no?

WITNESS JAIME CASTILLO FELIPE

It is certain that those people exist, but they are minimal because they have arrived there to live or as part of a couple.

STATE OF NICARAGUA

In what year was the town or village of Awas Tingni built?

WITNESS JAIME CASTILLO FELIPE

Exactly in Awas Tingni we've been there more than 50 years, but before that in Tuburus, there we lived all the time, that we have no idea since when because we don't know.

STATE OF NICARAGUA

Could you be more precise? We are asking in what year it was established.

WITNESS JAIME CASTILLO FELIPE

I don't know.

PRESIDENT CANÇADO TRINDADE

Yes? — a point of order from the Commission

INTER-AMERICAN COMMISSION

I think that the question would be better restated if the witness were asked: "How many generations, for how many generations have the Awas Tingni been there?"

PRESIDENT CANÇADO TRINDADE

The witness already answered the State's question.

WITNESS JAIME CASTILLO FELIPE

I have no idea.

STATE OF NICARAGUA

The witness has not answered. I would like, Your Honor, I would like with all due respect, em, the State of Nicaragua is asking the question, we would like that the questions of the State of Nicaragua be respected given that the Commission did not ask this question during its time.

PRESIDENT CANÇADO TRINDADE

Yes, you may proceed.

STATE OF NICARAGUA

Thank you very much. Mr. Castillo, the community that your fathers or ancestors comprised, was it issued title at any time?

WITNESS JAIME CASTILLO FELIPE

The elders say, those that no longer exist, that now few know of the history earlier than 300 years ago.

STATE OF NICARAGUA

Nicaragua does not take the answer as a response. Nicaragua is asking whether the witness knows if his ancestors had obtained any property title or not, yes or no?

INTER-AMERICAN COMMISSION

Your Honor, the witness has given an answer to the question.

PRESIDENT CANÇADO TRINDADE

Could you please repeat your answer to the question?

WITNESS JAIME CASTILLO FELIPE

No, I don't have any idea, I don't answer.

PRESIDENT CANÇADO TRINDADE

The question is answered, he has no knowledge of titles.

STATE OF NICARAGUA

. . . Mr. Castillo, could you tell us what distance you normally cover to hunt and fish?

WITNESS JAIME CASTILLO FELIPE (through interpreter)

In all the area over which we have the run of the land, we make use of different activities, without other options to work them there.

STATE OF NICARAGUA

Excuse me, what distance do you cover to hunt, to fish?

WITNESS JAIME CASTILLO FELIPE
I do not specify distances, but rather all the area which belongs to us, so I'm interested right now in saying from here to there.
STATE OF NICARAGUA
Really, the State of Nicaragua is interested in knowing that distance.
WITNESS JAIME CASTILLO FELIPE
In this case it is the government's obligation to go and recognize or know the terrain and not be asking the distance without seeing things.
STATE OF NICARAGUA
Let's make it, eh . . . we would like to emphasize that the witness refuses to answer.
PRESIDENT CANÇADO TRINDADE
Maybe the question could be restated in relation to the extension of the area in which he moves around . . .
STATE OF NICARAGUA
It is very difficult . . . he refuses . . .
PRESIDENT CANÇADO TRINDADE
In a last attempt at an effort to obtain a response to that question, in hours it takes to walk, how much time does it take to move to engage in work or the activities of the type of fishing to which the State referred?
INTER-AMERICAN COMMISSION
Mr. President.
PRESIDENT CANÇADO TRINDADE
In time.
INTER-AMERICAN COMMISSION
Mr. President, with all due respect, it seems the witness has answered in the form in which he can. He does not know the distance in centimeters, blocks, nor in the manner in which the government wants the response given.
PRESIDENT CANÇADO TRINDADE
He still has not been asked the question in terms of time. If he does not know, the opportunity to answer the question will be terminated.
WITNESS JAIME CASTILLO FELIPE
Our normal hunting distance is a trip of 15 days that we go to work or go to hunt and after we return knowing where the surrounding territories are.
PRESIDENT CANÇADO TRINDADE
The question is answered.
STATE OF NICARAGUA
The question is answered, Your Honor, and lets pass to the next one within the time allotted. In order to fish or hunt in a zone with abundant fauna, in a zone with many rivers and fish, the very tributary in which Mr. Castillo lives, Mr. Castillo, is it necessary for you to walk so much to get a fish to feed your children?
WITNESS JAIME CASTILLO FELIPE
In order to maintain the territory in order, even if there is an abundance of animals, types of animals, the Community does not expend its resources, but rather selects what it is going to consume, and in that way it uses a broad expanse of territory but it does not destroy and only recognizes the existence of its surrounding riches.. . .
PRESIDENT CANÇADO TRINDADE
Thank you very much to the delegation of the Illustrious State of

Nicaragua. I now consult the Honorable Judges of the Court as to whether they want to ask any questions . . . Judge de Roux?

JUDGE DE ROUX RENGIFO

I have a question.

PRESIDENT CANÇADO TRINDADE

You have the floor. . . .

JUDGE DE ROUX RENGIFO

Yes, I would like to ask the witness whether the community of Awas Tingni is in any condition to determine who are the people that comprise it in such a manner as to be able to make a list from which no name would be missing nor would there be a single name too many.

WITNESS JAIME CASTILLO FELIPE

Eh, that is a lot, I don't have a good enough memory to mention 1080 persons, 1018, 1018 at this time.

JUDGE DE ROUX RENGIFO

Yes, I would like to clarify. It's not that he would name them for us now. Rather, that he tell us whether at a certain point the Community is in any condition to indicate precisely which persons comprise it.

WITNESS JAIME CASTILLO FELIPE

Perfectly. . . .

JUDGE DE ROUX RENGIFO

Another question. I would like for the witness to indicate whether in the context of the Community, among the Community, the persons who are part of it have parcels of land assigned to them for individual cultivation or if the cultivation is done collectively.

WITNESS JAIME CASTILLO FELIPE

The use of resources is collective and it is organized in such a way that one has to work freely where one wants, but the entire expanse of territory is communal, no one has owner of it.

JUDGE DE ROUX RENGIFO

Thank you, gentlemen. Thank you, President.

PRESIDENT CANÇADO TRINDADE

Thank you Judge de Roux. Judge Garcña Ramñrez, you have the floor. . . .

JUDGE GARCIA RAMIREZ

Thank you, Mr. President. I would like to know the information that the witness could give about the rights that each member of the community has in relation with the lands the Community occupies as a whole.

WITNESS JAIME CASTILLO FELIPE

Please repeat.

JUDGE GARCIA RAMIREZ

What are the rights that each member of the community has in relation to the lands that the Community occupies as a whole? My basic assumption is this: the lands are occupied and taken advantage of by the entire Community. No one is individually an owner of then, the owner is the Community as a whole, if I understood correctly the response to the previous question. If that is so, I would like to know what the rights are that each individual has in relation to those lands.

WITNESS JAIME CASTILLO FELIPE
The right is singular because they demonstrate that, that there are places, sites that we have worked so there, there is no difference that someone determines who has the right, the difference, that does not exist, it is common....
PRESIDENT CANÇADO TRINDADE
[Mr. Castillo] may leave the stand. Mr. Secretary, please call the next witness to testify.
SECRETARY VENTURA ROBLES
Mr. Charlie Mclean....
PRESIDENT CANÇADO TRINDADE
Will the representative of the Inter-American Commission indicate to the Court the name of the person who will question the witness and proceed to the questioning?
INTER-AMERICAN COMMISISON
Thank you very much, Mr. President, James Anaya* will ask the questions....
INTER-AMERICAN COMMISISON
How many persons live in the Community, make up the Awas Tingni Community?
WITNESS CHARLIE MCLEAN
Currently, there are 1016 inhabitants.
INTER-AMERICAN COMMISISON
How do you know that that exact number lives there?
WITNESS CHARLIE MCLEAN
Through a census, house by house, we have taken the number of inhabitants.
INTER-AMERICAN COMMISISON
Who took the census?
WITNESS CHARLIE MCLEAN
The members of the Community; the leaders.
INTER-AMERICAN COMMISISON
You were among them, those who took the census?
WITNESS CHARLIE MCLEAN
Yes.
INTER-AMERICAN COMMISISON
What would you say in response to what the State says, that the number is much lower, that there are only 300 or 400 people?
WITNESS CHARLIE MCLEAN
We, previously, we had a census but very small, after it came, in many years the people have multiplied.
INTER-AMERICAN COMMISISON
Have you held a leadership position in the Community?
WITNESS CHARLIE MCLEAN
Yes.
INTER-AMERICAN COMMISISON
What position have you held?
WITNESS CHARLIE MCLEAN
Manager of the Forest.

* Professor Anaya, one of the editors of this volume, was lead counsel for the Awas Tingni community and was appointed by the Commission as its assistant in the case, as permitted by the Commission's Rules of Procedure, when the Commission submitted the case to the Court. — Eds.

INTER-AMERICAN COMMISISON

And can you explain to us, what is the Manager of the Forest?

WITNESS CHARLIE MCLEAN

He is the manager of the forest, he takes care of the forest, responds all dangers, he cannot discriminate, most of all that is the person responsible for the forest; he takes care of the little wild animals, the little fish, and many other things. . . .

INTER-AMERICAN COMMISISON

All right, at this time with the permission of the Court we're going to show a picture. I will ask our assistant to show the picture on the screen.

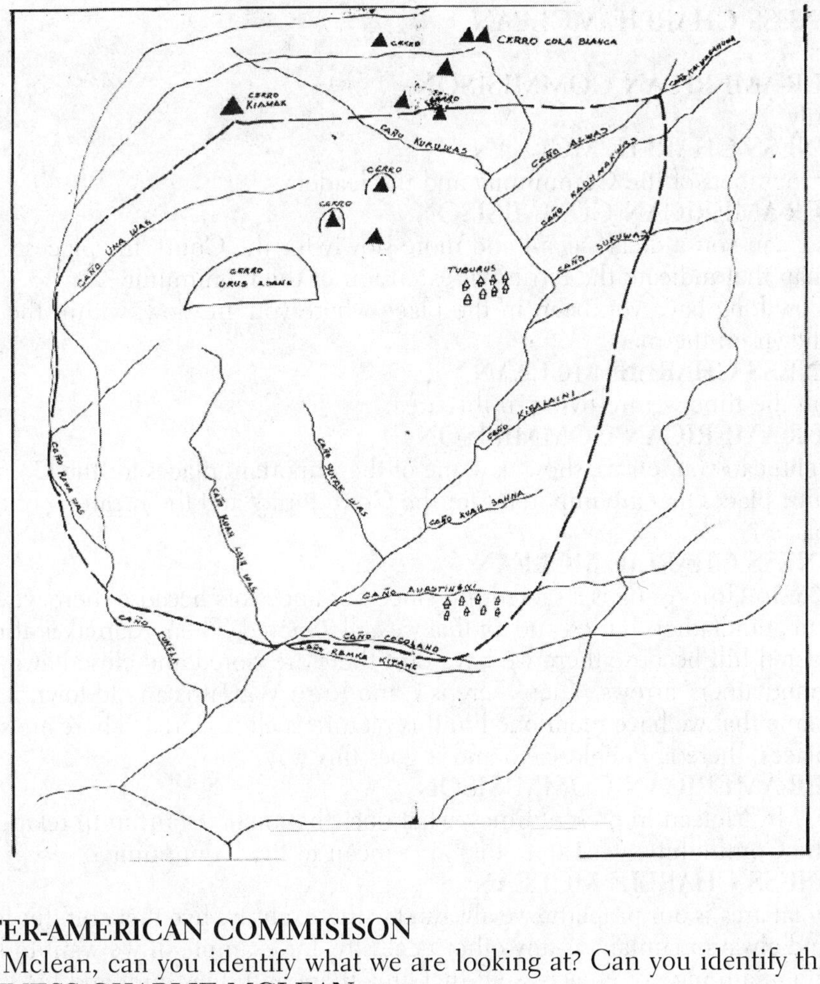

INTER-AMERICAN COMMISISON

Mr. Mclean, can you identify what we are looking at? Can you identify this?

WITNESS CHARLIE MCLEAN

Yes.

INTER-AMERICAN COMMISISON

And what is it?

WITNESS CHARLIE MCLEAN

That picture is the area we are claiming. This area drawn by the black line is drawn all around Awas Tingni.

INTER-AMERICAN COMMISISON
Who made this map?
WITNESS CHARLIE MCLEAN
I personally made, together with the leaders of the Community.
INTER-AMERICAN COMMISISON
And when did you make it?
WITNESS CHARLIE MCLEAN
In 1991.
INTER-AMERICAN COMMISISON
Did you have any help from anyone outside of the Community in making this map?
WITNESS CHARLIE MCLEAN
No.
INTER-AMERICAN COMMISISON
So only
WITNESS CHARLIE MCLEAN
Only members of the Community and the leaders.
INTER-AMERICAN COMMISISON
Please, can you indicate again and more slowly for the Court, the places of the map that indicate the territorial extension of the Community?. . .
For how long have you been in the place where you are now, within the area shown on the map?
WITNESS CHARLIE MCLEAN
Eh, all the time we are living in this area.
INTER-AMERICAN COMMISISON
All right, can you tell us, show us some of the important places for the Community, places that are important for the Community and the meaning of those places?
WITNESS CHARLIE MCLEAN
Yes, Cerro Urus Asang is a sacred hill since our ancestors because there we have our grandfathers buried and for that we call it sacred. Then, Kiamak is also is a sacred hill because there we have our, there are stored and closed away our grandfathers' arrows. Then there is Caño Kuru Was, it is an old town. Every name that we have mentioned in this picture is all is sacred. There are some places, there is Pueblo viejo and it goes this way.
INTER-AMERICAN COMMISISON
Okay, Mr. Mclean in present times, what does the total area mean in relation to the Community, what does that area mean to the Community?
WITNESS CHARLIE MCLEAN
The total area is our property, we always stay there, always live there off this forest and always maintain as any other necessity, for example, if we want to hunt mountain pig, we go across all that area there and then hunt and fish there and we also go there, after we have other ways of obtaining *pipante* [a canoe], there is that we receive . . .
PRESIDENT CANÇADO TRINDADE
Thank you, Inter-American Commission delegation. I will now give the floor to the representative of the Illustrious State of Nicaragua, so that if he wishes to ask questions, he may indicate the person who will do the questioning.

STATE OF NICARAGUA

Yes, Mr. President, I [Edmundo Castillo Salazar] will conduct the examination. . . .

Mr. Mclean, do you know that in the area of the maps that you have presented us, either that prepared by you or by the anthropologist Macdonald, there are other communities with title from 40 years ago, such as Francia Sirpi and Santa Clara and Esperanza?

WITNESS CHARLIE MCLEAN

Yes, there are neighboring communities, but we have always maintained firmly, it is our property, and also, Mr. Macdonald has prepared consistent with what we did in the first map that is by hand, after transferred to a new map, that is more professional, so now it follows; as far as the neighbors, yes they exist, but we firstly had a conflict, small conflict but now we have corrected, discussed, and now we are all peaceful, we are in agreement among four communities with us.

STATE OF NICARAGUA

Mr. Mclean, you requested the surface area all, to your benefit. Why then did you affirm that you are in a friendly relationship, if you want to strip them of all of their titled lands?

INTER-AMERICAN COMMISISON

Again, Mr. President, excuse me, but the premise is incorrect, there is no title of the kind that's being referred to.

PRESIDENT CANÇADO TRINDADE

I would like to ask the State's delegate if maybe he could limit his question to the first part.

STATE OF NICARAGUA

I withdraw the question, Mr. President. I would just like the record to reflect that there are titled communities in the area claimed by Awas Tingni and I continue my questioning.

Do you know that those communities were titled 40 years ago, in a time as ancestral as the date on which you founded Awas Tingni in 1945?

PRESIDENT CANÇADO TRINDADE

Please, let us come to an understanding, because it is not possible to conduct questioning in this manner.

Let us leave the questions specifically about titling for the summations of the parties and limit ourselves to asking the witness whether or not he knows of one thing or another, but the specific questions let us leave them for the summary arguments of the parties, please. . . .

Comments and Questions

1. What standard or burden of proof did the International Federation for Human Rights (FIDH) apply in its investigation of the human rights situation of the Mapuche people in Chile? Can you tell from its report at supra page 981? Should NGOs include in their reports detailed information about their fact-finding methodology and the standard of proof that they employ?

2. The need to protect witnesses is a frequent concern of NGO and IGO fact-finders. Under what circumstances should the identities of witnesses be concealed? Do anonymous denunciations undermine the credibility of reports? On a related matter, should NGO and IGO reports name individual perpetrators, or does it violate the presumption of innocence to name individuals who have not been charged with a crime or subject to a civil complaint?

3. Do you want to know the background and expertise of the fact-finders named by FIDH to look into the situation of the Mapuche? Should the bios of fact-finders be part of the report? Given that many victims of violations may be traumatized by their experiences, what type of training or interview protocols should be imposed before fact-finders are sent into the field? Consider, for example, the situation of rape victims in Bosnia or the Sudan.

4. While NGOs and other fact-finders try to present the "facts" as accurately as possible, does the degree of certainty they require depend on the purpose for which the facts are being used? Is there a difference between the level of confidence in the facts one should have, depending on whether they are being reported in an "urgent action" or "early warning" format or in a lengthy report? Is it sufficient for an NGO (or a human rights officer with OHCHR) to report publicly prima facie evidence of violations that may, upon further investigation, prove to be unfounded?

5. Which of the reports concerning the Mapuche situation do you think carried more weight for the government of Chile, the report by the FIDH or the one by the UN Special Rapporteur on indigenous people? Why? Because of factors having to do with fact-finding methodology or something else?

6. As pointed out at the beginning of this chapter, it is often the case that human rights problems are brought initially to the attention of international organizations by NGOs. To what extent is it proper for a human rights body of an international organization to rely on information submitted by an NGO? Is the answer to this question entirely a function of the reputation of the NGO? Is it ever proper for intergovernmental human rights bodies to rely entirely on information provided by NGOs? What implications do issues of resource allocation have for the answer to the previous question?

7. The Belgrade Rules appear, on their face, to be oriented toward country, as opposed to thematic, fact-finding. How, if at all does the fact-finding by country-specific rapporteurs differ from that of thematic rapporteurs? Is the mandate of the thematic rapporteurs to find facts or to resolve a problem on a humanitarian basis, as the Special Rapporteur on indigenous people attempted to do in regard to criminal prosecution of Mapuche leaders in Chile? Might there be a conflict between these two goals? See the discussion in Chapter 7, pages 569-578.

8. The Belgrade Rules were designed to apply to fact-finding by intergovernmental organizations (IGOs) but not by NGOs. It might be argued that it is actually more important that NGOs have a clear set of guidelines in this regard, on the ground that there is more scope for bias on the part of NGOs, many of which are forthrightly "special interest" groups. Would one really have expected objective fact-finding about, say, the situation in South Africa from an anti-apartheid organization? It may be contended, of course, that NGOs should have *some* standards but not necessarily the same ones as IGOs. How persuasive do you find that argument? Is not the process of objective and conscientious fact-finding basically the same, no matter who is doing the investigating?

9. To what extent does the funding source for NGO fact-finding affect the credibility of the findings? Is the answer the same for IGO funding (note that only about 20% of the budget of the UN High Commissioner's Office comes from the regular UN budget)? Should organizations always disclose their funding sources in their reports? Even if funding does not affect particular findings, might it play a role in determining which countries or issues an NGO investigates?

10. In the *Awas Tingni* case, instead of hearing live testimony the Inter-American Court could simply have asked for written statements by the community leaders and others who testified? What was the value to the Court of the live testimony of the Awas Tingni leaders Jaime Castillo and Charlie McLean, supra? Could the Court instead have achieved its fact-finding objective as to them through written statements? Was Nicaragu more or less advantaged by having them testify in a live hearing? What did the Awas Tingni community itself gain, if anything, from the opportunity to present live testimony over the opportunity to submit documentary evidence? Why aren't live hearings of the type in the *Awas Tingni* case used very much outside the proceedings of the Inter-Amercian Court of Human Rights? Is it simplay a matter or resources? If not what other factors apply?

III. Evaluating the Facts

A. *Admissibility and Evaluation of Evidence*

Gathering facts is an important — and sometimes, as we have seen, controversial — activity. Once it is done, however, difficult problems may still remain. What "facts" should be considered by international human rights bodies and how should they evaluate their *significance*?

Lawyers are accustomed to working with rules of evidence, which determine when facts or allegations of facts are admissible in court. In international human rights law, however, the purpose of gathering the evidence is not necessarily to present it to a judicial body. Often the purpose is to disseminate the findings as widely as possible, with a view to rousing public opinion. Is it, then, possible to devise rules about the admissibility of evidence in the area of human rights fact-finding? If so, then what should they be?

The simple answer seems to be that international human rights bodies are not particularly concerned with formal rules of evidence. Of course, treaties may impose limitations on the kind of evidence that may be considered, for example, by prohibiting the use of information submitted anonymously, but otherwise international bodies enjoy an unfettered right to consider any evidence they consider relevant. The European Court of Human Rights has probably stated the general rule followed by all intergovernmental human rights fact-finding bodies:

> . . . The Court is not bound, under the [European] Convention or under the general principals applicable to international tribunals, by strict rules of evidence. In order to satisfy itself, the Court is entitled to rely on evidence of every kind, including, in so far as it deems them relevant, documents or statements emanating from Governments, be they respondent or applicant, or from their institutions or officials. . . . [T]he Court, being master of its own procedure and of its own rules . . . , has complete

> freedom in assessing not only the admissibility and the relevance but also the probative value of each item of evidence before it.

Ireland v. United Kingdom, European Court of Human Rights, Judgment of 18 January 1978, Ser. A. No 25, paras. 209, 210.

This flexible approach is reflected in the evaluation by the Inter-American Court of Human Rights of the testimony and voluminous documentary evidence presented in the *Awas Tingni* case, which included maps produced by the community with the assistance of professional cartographers (in addition to the sketch map referred to in the testimony by Charlie McLean), ethnographic studies, newspaper clippings, correspondence with government officials, and government documents related to the granting of logging concessions. It also may explain the court's tolerance for Nicaragua's cross examination of community leaders on the basis of factual assertions (census data, competing land titles) not in evidence, see supra pages 1032,1039.

The Case of the Mayagna (Sumo) Awas Tingni Community v. Nicaragua

Inter-Am. Ct. H.R., Judgment of Aug. 31, 2001, Ser. C No. 79 (footnotes omitted)

EVALUATION OF THE EVIDENCE

. . .

87. Given that the purpose of evidence is to demonstrate the veracity of the facts alleged, it is extremely important to establish the criteria applied by an international human rights court in evaluating items of evidence.

88. The Court has discretional authority to evaluate testimony or statements made, both in writing and by other means. For this, it can adequately evaluate evidence following the rule of "competent analysis," which allows the judges to arrive at a conclusion on the veracity of the facts alleged, taking into account the object and purpose of the American Convention.

89. So as to obtain the greatest possible number of items of evidence, this Court has been very flexible in admitting and evaluating them, following the rules of logic and based on experience. A criterion which has already been mentioned and applied previously by the Court is non-formalism in evaluation of evidence. The procedure established for contentious cases before the Inter-American Court has its own characteristics that differentiate it from that which is applicable in domestic legal processes, as the former is not subject to the formalities of the latter.

90. For this reason, "competent analysis" and the non-requirement of formalities in admission and evaluation of evidence are fundamental criteria for its evaluation, as evidence is assessed rationally and as a whole.

91. The Court will now assess the value of the items of evidence tendered by the parties in the instant case.

92. Regarding the documentary evidence tendered by the Commission and by the State, which was neither disputed nor challenged, nor were questions raised on its authenticity, this Court attaches legal value to that evidence and admits it into evidence in the instant case.

93. The documents "Awas Tingni — An Ethnographic Study of the Community and its Territory," prepared by Theodore Macdonald in February, 1996; "Ethnographic expert opinion on the document prepared by Dr. Theodore Macdonald," written by Ramiro García Vásquez, and several maps of the territory occupied by the Awas Tingni Community, were challenged as regards their content. The Court takes into account the various positions of the parties regarding said documents; nevertheless, the Court believes it useful to admit them into evidence in the present case.

94. Regarding the newspaper clippings tendered by the Commission, the Court believes that even though they are not properly documentary evidence, they can be appraised insofar as they reflect publicly or well-known facts, statements by high-level State agents, or corroborate what is established in other documents or testimony received during the proceedings. . . .

98. The body of evidence of a case is indivisible and is formed by the evidence tendered throughout all stages of the proceedings. For this reason, the documentary evidence tendered by the State and by the Commission during the preliminary objections stage is admitted into evidence in the present case.

99. The State did not submit the documents requested by the Court on July 31, 2001, as evidence to facilitate adjudication of the case . . . [The Court had asked the Court to produce copies of land titles of communities neighboring Awas Tingni, which the government alleged existed in an attempt to argue competing rights in those other communities to the lands claimed by Awas Tingni.] In this regard, the Court makes the observation that the parties must submit to the Court the evidence requested by the Court, whether documents, testimony, expert opinions, or other types of evidence. The Commission and the State must supply all required evidentiary items — *ex officio*, as evidence to facilitate adjudication of the case, or upon a request by a party — for the Court to have as many elements of judgment as possible to determine the facts and as a basis for its decisions. In this regard, it must be taken into account that in proceedings on violations of human rights it may be the case that the applicant does not have the possibility of tendering evidence which can only be obtained with the cooperation of the State.

100. Regarding the expert opinions and testimonial evidence heard, which was neither challenged nor disputed, the Court admits it into evidence only insofar as it is in accordance with the object of the respective examination.

101. In the brief submitting its final arguments, the State expressed that:

> Almost all the expert witnesses presented by [t]he Commission recognized that they had no direct knowledge of the claim to ancestral lands made by the Awas Tingni Indigenous Community; in other words, they recognized that their professional opinions were based on studies carried out by other persons. The few experts presented by [t]he Commission who might have some direct knowledge of the claim to ancestral rights made by Awas Tingni, recognized the preliminary and, therefore, inconclusive nature of their essays. As those studies are not conclusive, they should not be admitted as scientific evidence to substantiate an accusation of non-titling of ancestral lands.

102. Regarding the above, the Court has discretionary authority to evaluate statements and pronouncements submitted to the Court. For this purpose, the Court will conduct an appropriate appraisal of the evidence, following the rules of "competent analysis . . .".

[Based on this analysis, the Court concluded that "the State has violated the right of the members of the Mayagna Awas Tingni Community to the use and enjoyment of their property, and that it has granted concessions to third parties to utilize the property and resources located in an area which could correspond, fully or in part, to the lands which must be delimited, demarcated, and titled." The court's further conclusions are summarized in Chapter 3, pages 173-174.]

B. *The Burden and Standard of Proof*

One of the most crucial problems of evaluating evidence is determining by what standard the allegations are to be judged as proved? Who has the burden of proof, and what must be done to discharge it? Should proof be required beyond a reasonable doubt, as in the domestic criminal-law system of the United States? Or is proof according to a preponderance of the evidence (i.e., a "more probable than not" standard) sufficient? Or should the burden of proof merely be stated to be whatever the fact-finder finds persuasive under the circumstances? Should the standard of proof be the same for NGOs as for IGOs? In the *Awas Tingni* case, the Inter-American Court of Human Rights applied a "competent analysis" standard – which appears to be something like a preponderance of the evidence – with the burden on the Inter-American Commission on Human Rights to establish the validity of the community's land claim and violations of relevant provisions of the American Convention on Human Rights in connection with that claim.

The following readings deal with various aspects of the burden-of-proof question and the standards for evaluating evidence. The first extract considers the matter from a general perspective. The four cases that follow offer the views of the Inter-American Court of Human Rights, the UN Human Rights Committee, and the European Court of Human Rights.

Bertrand G. Ramcharan, Evidence

In International Law and Fact-Finding in the Field of Human Rights 64, 77-80 (Bertrand Ramcharan ed. 1982) (notes omitted)

V. The Burden And Standard Of Proof

The burden of persuasion of a fact means the burden which is discharged when the tribunal which is to determine the existence or non-existence of the fact is persuaded by sufficient evidence to find that the fact exists. The burden of producing evidence of a fact means the burden which is discharged when sufficient evidence is introduced to support a finding that the fact exists. According to one source, fact-finding bodies enjoy considerable flexibility on matters such as the burden and standard of proof: "the question of burden of proof and the degree of probability required to establish facts is obviously of some importance. In some cases the Commission was able to make firm findings on facts . . . ; in others it was only able to form a view on a balance of probabilities . . . ; and in others it was unable to reach a definite conclusion. . . . A court or arbitral tribunal, in considering such points, might well have to decide that the burden of proof lay on one or other party and then decide the issue according to whether the burden of proof so found had been satisfied. A Commission of Inquiry is freer in this respect." The flexible approach here suggested is supported in the practice of the European Court of Human Rights. In its Judgement in the Case of Ireland against the United Kingdom (1978), the Court, dealing directly with 'questions of proof,' stated: In order to satisfy itself as to the existence or not in Northern Ireland of practices contrary to Article 3, the Court will not rely on the concept that the burden of proof is borne by one or other of the two Governments concerned. In the cases referred to it, the Court examines all the material before it, whether originating from the Commission, the Parties or other sources, and if necessary, obtains material *proprio motu*. However, upon the establishment of a *prima facie* case that breaches of human rights have occurred, a burden of proof may rest upon the Government concerned to show that this was not the case. In its views delivered in November 1979, on communication No. 2/9, the Human Rights Committee decided "to base its views on... facts which have either been essentially confirmed by the State Party or are unrepudiated or uncontested except for denials of a general character offering no particular information or explanations" and added that the "state party has adduced no evidence that [the complainant's] allegations of ill treatment have been duly investigated in accordance with the laws.... A refutation of these allegations in general terms is not enough. The State Party should investigate the allegations in accordance with its laws." Similarly, in its views delivered in May 1980 on communication No. 2/8, the Committee stated that "specific responses and pertinent evidence (including copies of the relevant decisions of the courts and findings of any investigations which have taken place into the validity of the complaints made) in reply to the contentions of the author of a communication are required. The Government did not furnish the Committee with such information. Consequently, the Committee cannot draw appropriate conclusions on the basis of the information before it."

Turning to the standard of proof, the American Law Institute Model Code of Evidence provided that "wherever 'finds' is used in these rules, it is the equivalent of 'finds by a preponderance of the evidence....' 'Preponderance of evidence' means evidence of greater convincing force.... Obviously no trier can know what is the historical fact when there is a dispute about it; all that the trier can do is to find where the preponderance of probability lies." As a general rule the standard of proof applied by fact-finding bodies should be a balance of probabilities. Probability in this sense may be defined as an evaluation of the likelihood of a past event having happened, given the facts and assumptions expected or adopted for the purposes of evaluation. However; in certain adversarial contexts, the standard "beyond all reasonable doubt may be applied." In the Greek Case as well as in the case of *Ireland v. the United Kingdom*, the European Commission on Human Rights adopted the standard "beyond reasonable doubt." However, in the latter case, the Irish Government argued before the European Court of Human Rights that this was an excessively rigid standard. The Court agreed with the Commission's approach and adopted the standard "beyond reasonable doubt" but added that "such proof may follow from the co-existence of sufficiently strong, clear and concordant inferences or of similar unrebutted presumptions of fact. In this context, the conduct of the Parties when evidence is being obtained has to be taken into account."

VI. Evaluation

...It may be stated as a general principle that the evaluation of evidence is a matter that rests exclusively within the competence of the fact-finding body....

VII. Conclusions

The conclusions reached in the present chapter may be summarized as follows:

(1) the rules of evidence applicable to any fact-finding exercise depend in the first place upon any relevant provisions in the constitutive instrument initiating the exercise. If the constitutive instrument gives the fact-finding body the power to draw up its own rules of procedure, then the fact-finding exercise will be governed by such rules of evidence as are included in the rules of procedure.

(2) In the absence of any, or sufficiently express, provisions in the constitutive instrument, fact-finding bodies should be guided by the following general principles, both in drawing up their rules of procedure and in their practical operations:

(a) The standard of proof is usually a "balance of probability." Probability in this sense may be defined as an evaluation of the likelihood of a past event having happened, given the facts and assumptions expected or adopted for the purposes of the evaluation. However, in adversarial contexts, the standard "beyond all reasonable doubt" may be applied.

(b) Fact-finding exercises in the field of human rights often being more inquisitorial than adversarial there is usually no onus or burden of proof upon any particular complainant. However, upon the establishment of a *prima facie* case that breaches of human rights have occurred, a burden of proof may rest upon the government concerned to show that this was not the case or that government agents were not responsible for such violations.

(c) Flexible admissibility criteria should be applied. A fact-finding body is free to employ for enlightening itself all the kinds of evidence that it deems necessary. It has the unlimited right of admitting all methods of proof that may be considered in conscience as sufficient and necessary.

(d) As regards the communication of evidence to the government concerned, a fact-finding body should, as a general rule, communicate to the government concerned for its comments such evidence as it may receive. However, it always possesses a discretion as to whether or not to communicate a particular piece of evidence to the government, and may decide not to do so, in order to protect the source of information or to protect other persons from reprisals.

(e) As regards the evaluation of evidence this is a matter that rests exclusively within the competence of the fact-finding body, or after it has submitted its report, upon its parent organ (if any).

The next case, Velásquez Rodríguez, was one of the earliest and most significant contentious cases decided by the Inter-American Court; it is quoted in Chapter 5, page 338, with respect to the issues of the extent of a state's obligation to protect human rights and exhaustion of domestic remedies. The following extract deals with the evidence and its evaluation.

Velásquez Rodríguez v. Honduras

Inter-Am. Ct. H.R., Judgment of July 29, 1988, Ser. C No. 4

28. The Court held hearings on the merits and heard the final arguments of the parties from September 30 to October 7, 1987. There appeared before the Court . . .

c) Witnesses presented by the Commission to testify as to "whether between the years 1981 and 1984 (the period in which Manfredo Velásquez disappeared) there were numerous cases of persons who were kidnapped and who then disappeared, and whether these actions were imputable to the Armed Forces of Honduras and enjoyed the acquiescence of the Government of Honduras . . ."

d) Witnesses presented by the Commission to testify as to "whether between the years 1981 and 1984 effective domestic remedies existed in Honduras to protect those persons who were kidnapped and who then disappeared in actions imputable to the Armed Forces of Honduras . . ."

e) Witnesses presented by the Commission to testify on specific facts related to this case: . . . ,

29. After having heard the witnesses, the Court directed the submission of additional evidence to assist it in its deliberations. Its Order of October 7, 1987 reads as follows:

A. Documentary Evidence

1. To request the Government of Honduras to provide the organizational chart showing the structure of Battalion 316 and its position within the Armed Forces of Honduras.

B. Testimony

1. To call as a witnesses, Marco Tulio Regalado and Alexander Hernández, members of the Armed Forces of Honduras.

C. Reiteration of a Request

1. To the Government of Honduras to establish the whereabouts of José Isaías Vilorio and, once located, to call him as a witness. . . .

31. In response to that Order, on December 14, 1987 the Government: a) with respect to the organizational structure of Battalion 316, requested that the Court receive the testimony of its Commandant in a closed hearing "because of strict security reasons of the State of Honduras"; b) requested that the Court hear the testimony of Alexander Hernández and Marco Tulio Regalado "in the Republic of Honduras, in a manner to be decided by the Court and in a closed hearing to be set at an opportune time . . . because of security reasons and because both persons are on active duty in the Armed Forces of Honduras"; and c) reported that José Isaías Vilorio was "working as an administrative employee of the National Office of Investigations, a branch of the Public Security Forces, in the city of Tegucigalpa."

32. By note of December 24, 1987, the Commission objected to hearing the testimony of members of the Honduran military in closed session. This position was reiterated by note of January 11, 1988.

33. On the latter date, the Court decided to receive the testimony of the members of the Honduran military at a closed hearing in the presence of the parties....

82. The Commission presented testimony and documentary evidence to show that there were many kidnappings and disappearances in Honduras from 1981 to 1984 and that those acts were attributable to the Armed Forces of Honduras (hereinafter "Armed Forces"), which was able to rely at least on the tolerance of the Government. Three officers of the Armed Forces testified on this subject at the request of the Court.

83. Various witnesses testified that they were kidnapped, imprisoned in clandestine jails and tortured by members of the Armed Forces (testimony of Inés Consuelo Murillo, José Gonzalo Flores Trejo, Virgilio Carías, Milton Jiménez Puerto, René Velásquez Días and Leopoldo Aguilar Villalobos)....

87. José Gonzalo Flores Trejo testified that he and Inés Consuelo Murillo were kidnapped together and taken to a house presumably located in San Pedro Sula, where his captors repeatedly forced his head into a trough of water until he almost drowned, kept his hands and feet tied, and hung him so that only his stomach touched the ground....

88. The Government argued that the testimony of the witness, a Salvadoran national, was not credible because he attempted to convince the Court that his encounters with Inés Consuelo Murillo were of a casual nature. The Government added that both individuals were involved in illicit activities.

89. Virgilio Carías, who was President of the Socialist Party of Honduras, testified that he was kidnapped in broad daylight on September 12, 1981, when 12 or 13 persons, armed with pistols, carbines and automatic rifles, surrounded his automobile. He stated that he was taken to a secret jail, threatened and beaten, and had no food, water or bathroom facilities for four or five days. On the tenth day, his captors gave him an injection in the arm and threw him, bound, in the back of a pick-up truck. Subsequently, they draped him over the back of a mule and set it walking through the mountains near the Nicaraguan border, where he regained his liberty (testimony of Virgilio Carías).

90. The Government indicated that this witness expressly admitted that he opposed the Honduran government. The Government also maintained that his answers were imprecise or evasive and argued that, because the witness said he could not identify his captors, his testimony was hearsay and of no evidentiary value since, in the Government's view, he had no personal knowledge of the events and only knew of them through others.

91. A Honduran attorney, who stated that he defended political prisoners, testified that Honduran security forces detained him without due process in 1982. He was held for ten years in a clandestine jail, without charges, and was beaten and tortured before he was brought before the court (testimony of Milton Jiménez Puerto).

92. The Government affirmed that the witness was charged with the crimes of threatening national security and possession of arms that only the Armed Forces were authorized to carry and, therefore, had a personal interest in discrediting Honduras with his testimony.

93. Another lawyer, who also said that he defended political detainees and who testified on Honduran law, stated that personnel of the Department of Special Investigations detained him a broad daylight in Tegucigalpa on June 1, 1982,

blindfolded him, took him to a place he was unable to recognize and kept him without food or water for four days. He was beaten and insulted. He said that he could see through the blindfold that he was in a military installation (testimony of René Velásquez Díaz).

94. The Government claimed that this witness made several false statements regarding the law in force in Honduras and that his testimony "lacks truth or force because it is not impartial and his interest is to discredit the State of Honduras." . . .

100. A former member of the Armed Forces, who said that he belonged to Battalion 316 (the group charged with carrying out the kidnappings) and that he had participated in some kidnappings, testified that the starting point was an order given by the chief of the unit to investigate an individual and place him under surveillance. According to this witness, if a decision was made to take further steps, the kidnapping was carried out by persons in civilian clothes using pseudonyms and disguises and carrying arms. The unit had four double-cabin Toyota pick-up trucks without police markings for use in kidnappings. Two of the pick-ups had tinted glass (testimony of Florencio Caballero. See also testimony of Virgilio Carías).

101. The Government objected, under Article 37 of the Rules of Procedure, to the testimony of Florencio Caballero because he had deserted from the Armed Forces and had violated his military oath. By unanimous decision of October 6, 1987, the Court rejected the challenge and reserved the right to consider his testimony. . . .

104. The current Director of Intelligence denied that the Armed Forces had secret jails, stating that it was not its **modus operandi**. He claimed that it was subversive elements who do have such jails, which they call "the peoples' prisons." He added that the function of an intelligence service is not to eliminate or disappear people, but rather to obtain and process information to allow the highest levels of government to make informed decisions (testimony of Roberto Nùñez Montes). . . .

106. The Commission submitted many clippings from the Honduran press from 1981 to 1984 which contain information on at least 64 disappearances, which were apparently carried out against ideological or political opponents or trade union members. Six of those individuals, after their release, complained of torture and other cruel, inhuman and degrading treatment. There clippings mention secret cemeteries where 17 bodies had been found. . . .

VI

119. The testimony and documentary evidence, corroborated by press clippings, presented by the Commission, tend to show:

a. That there existed in Honduras from 1981 to 1984 a systematic and selective practice of disappearances carried out with the assistance or tolerance of the government;

b. That Manfredo Velásquez was a victims of that practice and was kidnapped and presumably tortured, executed and clandestinely buried by agents of the Armed Forces of Honduras, and

c. That in the period in which those acts occurred, the legal remedies available in Honduras were not appropriate or effective to guarantee his rights to life, liberty and personal integrity.

120. The Government, in turn, submitted documents and based its argument on the testimony of three members of the Honduran Armed Forces, two of whom were summoned by the Court because they had been identified in the proceedings as directly involved in the general practice referred to and in the disappearance of Manfredo Velásquez. This evidence may be summarized as follows:

a. The testimony purports to explain the organization and functioning of the security forces accused of carrying out the specific acts and denies any knowledge of or personal involvement in the acts of the officers who testified;

b. Some documents purport to show that no civil suit had been brought to establish a presumption of the death of Manfredo Velásquez; and,

c. Other documents purport to prove that the Supreme Court of Honduras received and acted upon some writs of habeas corpus and that some of those writs resulted in the release of the persons on whose behalf they were brought.

121. The record contains no other direct evidence, such as expert opinion, inspections or reports.

VII

122. Before weighing the evidence, the Court must address some questions regarding the burden of proof and the general criteria considered in its evaluation and finding of the facts in the instant proceeding.

123. Because the Commission is accusing the Government of the disappearance of Manfredo Velásquez, it, in principle, should bear the burden of proving the facts underlying its petition.

124. The Commission's argument relies upon the proposition that the policy of disappearances, supported or tolerated by the Government, is designed to conceal and destroy evidence of disappearances. When the existence of such a policy or practice has been shown, the disappearance of a particular individual may be proved through circumstantial or indirect evidence or by logical inference. Otherwise, it would be impossible to prove that an individual has been disappeared.

125. The Government did not object to the Commission's approach. Nevertheless, it argued that neither the existence of a practice of disappearances in Honduras nor the participation of Honduran officials in the alleged disappearance of Manfredo Velásquez had been proven.

126. The Court finds no reason to consider the Commission's argument inadmissible. If it can be shown that there was an official practice of disappearances in Honduras, carried out by the Government or at least tolerated by it, and if the disappearance of Manfredo Velásquez can be linked to that practice, the Commission's allegations will have been proven to the Court's satisfaction, so long as the evidence presented on both points meets the standard of proof required in cases such as this.

127. The Court must determine what the standards of proof should be in the instant case. Neither the Convention, the Statute of the Court nor its Rules of

Procedure speak to this matter. Nevertheless, international jurisprudence has recognized the power of the courts to weigh the evidence freely, although it has always avoided a rigid rule regarding the amount of proof necessary to support the judgment (Cf. Corfu Channel, Merits, Judgment, I.C.J. Reports 1949; Military and Paramilitary Activities in and against Nicaragua (*Nicaragua v. United States of America*), Merits, Judgment, I.C.J. Reports 1986, paras. 29-30 and 59-60).

128. The standards of proof are less formal in an international legal proceeding than in a domestic one. The latter recognize[s] different burdens of proof, depending upon the nature, character and seriousness of the case.

129. The Court cannot ignore the special seriousness of finding that a State Party to the Convention has carried out or has tolerated a practice of disappearances in its territory. This requires the Court to apply a standard of proof which considers the seriousness of the charge and which, notwithstanding what has already been said, is capable of establishing the truth of the allegations in a convincing manner.

130. The practice of international and domestic courts shows that direct evidence, whether testimonial or documentary, is not the only type of evidence that may be legitimately considered in a reaching a decision. Circumstantial evidence, indicia, and presumptions may be considered, so long as they lead to conclusions consistent with the facts.

131. Circumstantial or presumptive evidence is especially important in allegations of disappearances, because this type of repression is characterized by an attempt to suppress all information about the kidnapping or the whereabouts and fate of the victim.

132. Since this Court is an international tribunal, it has its own specialized procedures. All the elements of domestic legal procedures are therefore not automatically applicable.

133. The above principle is generally valid in international proceedings, but is particularly applicable in human rights cases.

134. The international protection of human rights should not be confused with criminal justice. States do not appear before the Court as defendants in a criminal action. The objective of international human rights law is not to punish those individuals who are guilty of violations, but rather to protect the victims and to provide for the reparation of damages resulting from the acts of the States responsible.

135. In contrast to domestic criminal law, in proceedings to determine human rights violations the State cannot rely on the defense that the complainant has failed to present evidence when it cannot be obtained without the State's cooperation. . . .

VIII

140. In the instant case, the Court accepts the validity of the documents presented by the Commission and by Honduras, particularly because the parties did not oppose or object to those documents nor did they question their authenticity or veracity.

141. During the hearings, the Government objected, under Article 37 of the Rules of Procedure, to the testimony of witnesses called by the Commission. By decision of October 6, 1987, the Court rejected the challenge, holding as follows:

b. The objection refers to circumstances under which, according to the Government, the testimony of these witnesses might not be objective.

c. It is within the Court's discretion, when rendering judgment, to weigh the evidence.

d. A violation of the human rights set out in the Convention is established by facts found by the Court, not by the method of proof.

f. When testimony is questioned, the challenging party has the burden of refuting that testimony.

142. During cross-examination, the Government's attorneys attempted to show that some witnesses were not impartial because of ideological reasons, origin or nationality, family relations, or a desire to discredit Honduras. They even insinuated that testifying against the State in these proceedings was disloyal to the nation. Likewise, they cited criminal records or pending charges to show that some witnesses were not competent to testify (**supra** 86, 88, 90, 92, 101, 110 and 116).

143. It is true, of course, that certain factors may clearly influence a witness' truthfulness. However, the Government did not present any concrete evidence to show that the witnesses had not told the truth, but rather limited itself to making general observations regarding their alleged incompetency or lack of impartiality. This is insufficient to rebut testimony which is fundamentally consistent with that of other witnesses. The Court cannot ignore such testimony.

144. Moreover, some of the Government's arguments are unfounded within the context of human rights law. The insinuation that persons who, for any reason, resort to the Inter-American system for the protection of human rights are disloyal to their country is unacceptable and cannot constitute a basis for any penalty or negative consequence. Human rights are higher values that "are not derived from the fact that (an individual) is a national of a certain state, but are based upon attributes of his human personality" (American Declaration of the Rights and Duties of Man, Whereas clauses, and American Convention, Preamble).

145. Neither is it sustainable that having a criminal record or charges pending is sufficient in and of itself to find that a witness is not competent to testify in Court. As the Court ruled, in its decision of October 6, 1987, in the instant case,

> under the American Convention on Human Rights, it is impermissible to deny a witness, **a priori**, the possibility of testifying to facts relevant to a matter before the Court, even if he has an interest in that proceeding, because he has been prosecuted or even convicted under internal laws.

146. Many of the press clippings offered by the Commission cannot be considered as documentary evidence as such. However, many of them contain public and well-known facts which, as such, do not require proof; others are of evidentiary value, as has been recognized in international jurisprudence . . . , insofar as they textually reproduce public statements, especially those of high-ranking members of the Armed Forces, of the Government, or even of the Supreme Court of Honduras, such as some of those made by the President of the latter. Finally, others are important as a whole insofar as they corroborate testimony regarding the responsibility of the Honduran military and police for disappearances. . . .

148. Based upon the above, the Court finds that the following facts have been proven in this proceeding: (1) a practice of disappearances carried out or tolerated

by Honduran officials existed between 1981 and 1984; (2) Manfredo Velásquez disappeared at the hands of or with the acquiescence of those officials within the framework of that practice; and (3) the Government of Honduras failed to guarantee the human rights affected by that practice.

The Velásquez Rodríguez case was one of three cases concerning disappearances in Honduras brought simultaneously to the Inter-American Court. The second case, *Godinez Cruz*, Judgment of Jan. 20, 1989, Ser. C No. 5, resulted in a judgment identical to that of Velasquez. However, in the third case, *Fairen Garbi and Solis Corrales*, Judgment of Mar. 15, 1989, Ser. C No. 6, the government introduced entry and exit documents signed by the couple who disappeared. The court appointed a handwriting expert who verified the signatures as those of the disappeared. The court therefore concluded that wherever the couple went and whatever happened to them, it had not occurred in Honduras.

In a later case, concerned with alleged torture and death in custody rather than disappearances, the court seemed somewhat more reluctant to presume too much from unclear facts.

Gangaram Panday v. Suriname

Inter-Am. Ct. Hum. Rts., Judgment of Jan. 21, 1994, Ser. C No. 16

49. The Court has maintained that "... in proceedings to determine human rights violations the State cannot rely on the defense that the complainant has failed to present evidence when it cannot be obtained without the State's cooperation." In the exercise of its judicial functions and when ascertaining and weighing the evidence necessary to decide the cases before it, the Court may, in certain circumstances, make use of both circumstantial evidence and indications or presumptions on which to base its pronouncements when they lead to consistent conclusions as regards the facts of the case, particularly when the respondent State has assumed an uncooperative stance in its dealings with the Court.

50. The record shows that, by order of the President dated July 10,1992, the Government was required to provide the official texts of the Constitution and of the substantive and criminal procedure laws governing cases of detention in its territory on the date on which Asok Gangaram Panday was detained. The Government did not produce the texts in question for the record, nor did it give any explanation for the omission.

51. In view of the foregoing, the Court infers from the position taken by the Government that Mr. Asok Gangaram Panday was illegally detained by members of the Military Police of Suriname when he arrived from Holland at Zanderij Airport....

52. As for the torture to which Mr, Asok Gangaram Panday was allegedly subjected during the time he was kept in detention by the Military Police authorities, ... the Court considers that no conclusive or convincing indications result from the evaluation [of the forensic and other evidence] that would enable it to establish the truth of the charge that Mr Asok Gangaram Panday was subjected to

torture during his detention. . . . Accordingly, the Court cannot conclude . . . that in the instant case there exists a presumption that Article 5(2) of the Convention protecting the right to humane treatment was violated. . . .

62. Nevertheless, [with respect to the cause of the complainant's death in custody] it could be argued that the fact that the Court, by inference, considers that the victim's detention was illegal, should also lead it to conclude that there was a violation of the right to life by Suriname on the grounds that, had Suriname not detained that person, he probably would not have lost his life. However, the Court believes that on the matter of the international responsibility of States for violations of the Convention, "[w]hat is decisive is whether a violation . . . has occurred with the support or the acquiescence of the government, or whether the State has allowed the act to take place without taking measures to prevent it or to punish those responsible. . . ." The circumstances surrounding this case make it impossible to establish the responsibility of the State in the terms described above because, among other things, the Court is fixing responsibility for illegal detention by inference but not because it has been proved that the detention was indeed illegal or arbitrary or that the detainee was tortured. . . .

64. The Court notes that, in principle, the confirmation of a single case of violation of human rights by the authorities of a State is not in itself sufficient ground to presume or infer the existence in that State of widespread, large-scale practices to the detriment of the rights of other citizens.

Of course, the ability to prove (or disprove) facts may vary, depending on which party is in the better position to provide evidence. When human rights violations occur while the alleged victim is in the custody of the government, it is the government that may be in the best position to offer additional evidence to an international body. The next two extracts, from the UN Human Rights Committee and the European Court of Human Rights, address this issue.

Bleier v. Uruguay

Human Rights Committee, Communication No. 30/1978, Views of May 29, 1982 [Report of the Hum. Rts. Comm., UN Doc. A/37/40, at 130, 135 (1982), reprinted in 2 Y.B. Hum. Rts. Comm. 1981-1982, at 396, 398 (1989)]

13.3. With regard to the burden of proof, this cannot rest alone on the author of the communication, especially considering that the author and the State party do not always have equal access to the evidence and that frequently the State party alone has access to relevant information. It is implicit in article 4, paragraph 2, of the Optional Protocol that the State party has the duty to investigate in good faith all allegations of violation of the Covenant made against it and its authorities, especially when such allegations are corroborated by evidence submitted by the author of the communication, and to furnish to the Committee the information available to it. In cases where the author has submitted to the Committee allegations supported by substantial witness testimony, as in this case, and where further clarification of the case depends on information exclusively in the hands of the State party, the Committee may consider such allegations as substantiated in the absence of satisfactory evidence and explanations to the contrary submitted by the State Party.

Sevtap Veznedaroglu v. Turkey

Eur. Ct. H.R., App. No. 32357/96 (Apr. 11, 2000)(references omitted)

I. The Circumstances of the Case

8. The facts of the case as submitted by the applicant are summarised below. The Government dispute the applicant's account.

9. The applicant was at the relevant time a research student in public law at Diyarbakir University and married to a lawyer who had been the provincial president of the Diyarbakir Human Rights Association in 1990. According to the applicant she was constantly followed by the police on account of her husband's position.

10. On 4 July 1994, at about 3 P.M., the applicant was arrested by 8 policemen at her home on suspicion of membership of the Kurdistan Workers Party ("PKK"), an illegal organisation.

11. The applicant was taken to the forensic doctor to be examined. Following the doctor's examination she was blindfolded and taken to an unknown destination where she was placed in a cell. After a certain period of time, she was again blindfolded and taken to another room to be interrogated.

12. The applicant was interrogated by approximately 15 policemen and accused of forming links with and of working for the PKK abroad. She was then undressed and hung by her arms. She was given electric shocks to her mouth and sexual organs. After half an hour she was taken down as she had fainted. The interrogators, while threatening her with death and rape, told her not to work on human rights matters. She was then taken to her cell. The next day she was again tortured and threatened with death and rape. The torture continued for four days. During the first two days of her custody the applicant was not given anything to eat. Thereafter she was only given a piece of bread and a few olives.

13. During her detention the applicant was requested to sign some documents. She was told that she would be tortured and raped if she did not agree to sign them. The applicant signed the documents. In the documents, by way of explanation for the marks of torture on her body, it was stated that the applicant had fallen while indicating a place used by the PKK. The policemen applied cream to the applicant's injuries.

14. On 13 July 1994 the police officers brought her to the forensic doctor who drew up a report which stated: "Upon the examination of Sevtap Veznedaroğlu, violet-coloured bruises were identified on the left upper arm 1 by 1 cm and on the right tibia 3 by 1 cm".

15. On 15 July 1994 the applicant, accompanied by police officers, was taken to the Diyarbakir State Hospital where she was examined by a forensic doctor. In his report dated 15 July 1994 the doctor noted the presence of the same bruising on the applicant's arm and leg as indicated in the earlier report of 13 July 1994. The report concluded that the applicant's health was not at risk and that she was fit to work.

16. On 15 July 1994 the applicant was brought before the public prosecutor at the Diyarbakir State Security Court. Her file contained the medical reports dated 4, 13 and 15 July 1994. The applicant maintained before the public prosecutor that she had signed the confession statement under pressure and as a result of

being tortured while in detention. The public prosecutor recorded in the file that the applicant did not acknowledge the statement which she gave to the police.

17. On the same day the applicant appeared before a substitute judge attached to the Diyarbakir State Security Court. The applicant repeated to the judge that she did not acknowledge the statement taken from her by the police "since she had been tortured and held under duress for many days . . . and that the police had held her wrist and forced her to sign the police statement." The applicant's statement was recorded in the minutes of the hearing before the judge. The judge directed that the applicant be released from custody. The public prosecutor for his part ordered that the applicant stand trial before the Diyarbakir State Security Court on a charge of being a member of the PKK.

18. On 18 July 1994 the applicant was given a certificate by the Medical Faculty Hospital of Dicle University indicating that she was unable to work for 20 days. According to the medical report the applicant was suffering from broncho-pneumonia.

19. On 30 October 1995 the applicant was acquitted by the Diyarbakir State Security Court on the ground of lack of evidence. The applicant was not in court on that day. In its ruling the court noted as follows the declarations made by the applicant during a court hearing held on 13 October 1994 and which was recorded in the minutes.

> "Although the accused admitted to the offence with which she was charged in her statements to the police, at a later stage during the proceedings before the judicial organs she claimed that she had made them under duress and even torture and had signed them without having read them."

. . .

AS TO THE LAW

I. ALLEGED VIOLATION OF ARTICLE 3 OF THE CONVENTION

. . .

25. The Government repudiated the applicant's claim. They stressed that following the communication of the applicant's complaint an investigation was conducted into the authenticity of the medical certificate allegedly drawn up by the Dicle University Medical Faculty granting her 20 days' sick leave. That investigation revealed that there was good reason to suggest that the figure "20" had been falsified, all the more so since it was difficult to understand why such a long period of sick leave would be granted on the strength of two bruises. Significantly, the applicant had been authorised to take sick leave on the grounds that she was suffering from pneumonia. Furthermore, the investigation also established that there was no record in the hospital of the certificate having been issued to the applicant. The Government asserted that it must be concluded that the medical certificate, the only concrete evidence submitted by the applicant, was falsified and should therefore be discounted.

26. For the Government, the applicant only made a bare allegation about having been tortured. She failed to substantiate the complaint in any way and

there was no evidence whatsoever which confirmed that she had been given electric shocks and hung up by the arms as alleged. In the absence of any corroborating evidence, the public prosecutor cannot be faulted for not investigating the complaint.

27. The applicant disputed the Government's accusation that the medical certificate had been falsified. She referred to a letter dated 12 January 1998 in which the President of the Department of Internal Medicine informed the Head of the Dicle University Medical Faculty that the applicant had been examined on 18 July 1994 standing up and for that reason no medical record had been kept of her examination. A copy of that letter was sent to the Diyarbakir State Security Court and to the responsible Ministry on their request following the communication of her application to the respondent Government.

28. The Court recalls that Article 3 of the Convention enshrines one of the fundamental values of democratic society. Even in the most difficult of circumstances, such as the fight against terrorism or crime, the Convention prohibits in absolute terms torture or inhuman or degrading treatment or punishment. Unlike most of the substantive clauses of the Convention and of Protocols Nos. 1 and 4, Article 3 makes no provision for exceptions and no derogation from it is permissible under Article 15 even in the event of a public emergency threatening the life of the nation.

29. The Court also recalls that ill-treatment must attain a minimum level of severity if it is to fall within the scope of Article 3. The assessment of this minimum is relative: it depends on all the circumstances of the case, such as the duration of the treatment, its physical and/or mental effects and, in some cases, the sex, age and state of health of the victim. In respect of a person deprived of his liberty, recourse to physical force which has not been made strictly necessary by his own conduct diminishes human dignity and is in principle an infringement of the right set forth in Article 3.

30. The Court notes that the Government do not deny that the applicant sustained bruising to her person during her time in custody. However, they point to the minor nature of these injuries and stress that they are at variance with the severity of the treatment allegedly suffered. The Court for its part finds it impossible to establish on the basis of the evidence before it whether or not the applicant's injuries were caused by the police or whether she was tortured to the extent claimed. It is not persuaded either that the hearing of witnesses by the Court would clarify the facts of the case or make it possible to conclude, beyond reasonable doubt, that the applicant's allegations are substantiated.

31. However it would observe at the same time that the difficulty in determining whether there was a plausible explanation for the bruising found on her body or whether there was any substance to her allegations on the nature of the treatment she allegedly endured rests with the failure of the authorities to investigate her complaints.

32. In this latter connection the Court reiterates that, where an individual raises an arguable claim that he has been seriously ill-treated by the police or other such agents of the State unlawfully and in breach of Article 3, that provision, read in conjunction with the State's general duty under Article 1 of the Convention to "secure to everyone within their jurisdiction the rights and freedoms defined in... [the] Convention," requires by implication that there should be an effective official investigation capable of leading to the identification and

punishment of those responsible. If this were not the case, the general legal prohibition of torture and inhuman and degrading treatment and punishment, despite its fundamental importance, would be ineffective in practice and it would be possible in some cases for agents of the State to abuse the rights of those within their control with virtual impunity.

33. The Court notes that, on 15 July 1994, the applicant alleged before the public prosecutor and the substitute judge attached to the Diyarbakir State Security Court that she had been tortured (see paragraphs 16 and 17 above). The file presented to the public prosecutor contained the results of the medical examinations carried out on the applicant on 4, 13 and 15 July 1994. The medical reports dated 13 and 15 July 1994 indicated fresh bruising to the applicant's arm and leg. The substitute judge noted in the minutes of the hearing the applicant's statement that she had been tortured in custody.

34. In the opinion of the Court the applicant's insistence on her complaint of torture taken with the medical evidence in the file should have been sufficient to alert the public prosecutor to the need to investigate the substance of the complaint, all the more so since she had been held in custody between 4 July 1994 and 15 July 1994. However, no steps were taken either to obtain further details from the applicant or to question the police officers at her place of detention about her allegations. The substitute judge also dismissed her allegations without further enquiry (see paragraph 16 above).

35. The Court considers that in the circumstances the applicant had laid the basis of an arguable claim that she had been tortured. It is to be noted also that the applicant persisted in her allegations right up to the stage of trial (see paragraph 19 above). The inertia displayed by the authorities in response to her allegations was inconsistent with the procedural obligation which devolves on them under Article 3 of the Convention. In consequence, the Court finds that there has been a violation of that Article on account of the failure of the authorities of the respondent State to investigate the applicant's complaint of torture....

For These Reasons, The Court Unanimously

1. *Holds* that there has been a violation of Article 3 of the Convention on account of the failure of the authorities of the respondent State to investigate the applicant's complaint of torture;

2. *Holds*

(a) that the respondent State is to pay the applicant, within three months from the date on which the judgment becomes final according to Article 44 §2 of the Convention, the following sums to be converted into Turkish liras at the rate applicable at the date of payment:

(i) 2,000 (two thousand) US dollars as compensation for non-pecuniary damage;

(ii) 1,000 (one thousand) US dollars for legal fees together with any value-added tax that may be chargeable;

(b) that simple interest at an annual rate of 6% shall be payable from the expiry of the above-mentioned three months until settlement;

3. *Dismisses* the remainder of the applicant's claims for just satisfaction.

Partly Dissenting Opinion of Mr Bonello

1. The Court has unanimously found a violation of Article 3 on account of the failure by the Turkish authorities to investigate the applicant's complaint of torture, but has held that it is "impossible to establish on the basis of the evidence before it, whether or not the applicant's injuries were caused by the police or whether she was tortured to the extent claimed." In other words, the Court dismissed the applicant's claim and was not satisfied, on the 'evidence' that she had suffered torture or inhuman treatment. I disagree.

2. Before the applicant's interrogation by policemen in an undisclosed station, she was examined by a forensic doctor, and there is no allegation that her body showed any trace of trauma.

3. The applicant claims that, during interrogation, she was undressed, hung up by her arms, given electric shocks in her mouth and genitals, threatened with death and rape. This routine was repeated on the following three days. During the first two days she was left without any food at all.

4. The applicant further alleged that, under threat of death and rape, she signed a 'confession' admitting membership of an outlawed organisation, the PKK. The statement which the applicant signed also included a disclaimer to the effect that the bruises on her body had been caused by a fall.

5. Two doctors examined the applicant separately over a week after the interrogation ended, but when still in police custody; they found violet coloured bruises on her upper arm and on her right tibia.

6. The applicant complained both to the public prosecutor and to the State Security Court, before being released from detention, that she had been tortured by the police and that the 'confession' had been extracted under torture.

7. The applicant was tried on a charge of being a member of the PKK. Despite her signed confession, the State Security Court acquitted her on the ground of lack of evidence, having noted the applicant's claim that the confession had been obtained by duress and torture.

8. I believe that the majority, concluding that the applicant had not proved that she had been tortured and that the injuries to her person were caused by the police, disregarded several basic and vital elements of the rules of evidence that should inspire any court.

9. Firstly, this Court has repeatedly held that: "Where an individual, when taken in police custody, is in good health, but is found to be injured at the time of release, it is incumbent on the State to provide a plausible explanation of how those injuries were caused, failing which a clear issue arises under Article 3 of the Convention". This plainly posits that, in the presence of injuries which were not there at the time of arrest, it is *not* for the applicant to substantiate her allegations of torture or inhuman treatment. The onus of proof shifts to the State to provide a 'plausible explanation' of those injuries. In the present case the State has done nothing by way of explanation. The shift in the onus of proof is the first evidential norm neglected in the judgment.

10. Secondly, a cardinal requirement relating to the standard of proof was similarly discounted. In the present case the Court did not expressly assert that the applicant had an obligation to prove her allegations of torture "beyond reasonable doubt". But *that* is the standard of proof hitherto ordained by the Court in allegations of torture and inhuman treatment; it is evident that, in the wake of this

evidentiary imperative, the Court expected the applicant to prove her allegations "beyond reasonable doubt".

11. Independently of the failure by the majority to apply the rule that it was incumbent on the State to discharge the burden of evidence (v. §9), I find the standard of proof — beyond reasonable doubt — required by the Court in torture cases to be legally untenable and, in practice, unachievable.

12. Proof "beyond reasonable doubt" reflects a maximum standard relevant and desirable to establish *criminal* culpability. No person shall be judicially deprived of liberty, or otherwise penally censured, unless his guilt is manifest "beyond reasonable doubt." I subscribe to that stringent standard without hesitation. But in other fields of judicial enquiry, the standard of proof should be proportionate to the aim which the search for truth pursues: the highest degree of certainty, in criminal matters; a workable degree of probability in others.

13. Confronted by conflicting versions, the Court is under an obligation to establish (1) on whom the law places the burden of proof, (2) whether any legal presumptions militate in favour of one of the opposing accounts, and (3) "on a balance of probabilities," which of the conflicting versions appears to be more plausible and credible. Proof "beyond reasonable doubt" can, in my view, only claim a spurious standing in 'civil' litigation, like the adversarial proceedings before this Court. In fact, to the best of my knowledge, the Court is the only tribunal in Europe that requires proof "beyond reasonable doubt" in non-criminal matters.

14. Expecting those who claim to be victims of torture to prove their allegations "beyond reasonable doubt" places on them a burden that is as impossible to meet as it is unfair to request. Independent observers are not, to my knowledge, usually invited to witness the rack, nor is a transcript of proceedings in triplicate handed over at the end of each session of torture; its victims cower alone in oppressive and painful solitude, while the team of interrogators has almost unlimited means at its disposal to deny the happening of, or their participation in, the gruesome pageant. The solitary victim's complaint is almost invariably confronted with the negation "corroborated" by many.

15. For the Court to expect from torture victims any 'hard' evidence, beyond the eloquence of their injuries, is to reward and invigorate the 'inequality of arms' inherent in most torture scenarios.

16. Thirdly, the Court has, in my view, side-tracked the key question of credibility. I ask if, relying on its memory in handling so many cases of torture, the Court has compelling reasons to award more faith and credit to security forces which have an unenviable track-record to live down, rather than to those who claim to be their victims. No allegation has been made against the personal integrity and uprightness of the applicant, other than the damning circumstance that she was the wife of a human rights activist. The test, in the event, should have been: on a balance of credibility, who is likelier to have provided the court with a more reliable version of the incidents? The security forces?

17. Fourthly, it is difficult to envisage what "proof" the Court expected from the applicant in order to substantiate her claim that she was repeatedly tortured by being forcibly undressed, suspended, threatened with death and rape and deprived of food. These amusements are particularly ungenerous with those tangible signs dear to forensic experts. So, again, the only reasonable test ought to have been: on a balance of credibility, which of the two parties rests more convincingly on the side of truth?

18. Personally, I would have little hesitation with the answer. The majority seem to have thought otherwise. And its conclusion is unassailable — if you start your assessment of credibility from the premise that the applicant (whose personal integrity and honour are not in dispute), is neither to be trusted nor believed, while the security forces, repeatedly found guilty by this Court of killings, torture and inhuman behaviour, are.

19. Finally, the Court has unanimously affirmed that the respondent State breached Article 3 in that it failed to investigate the applicant's complaints of torture. In other words, the Court has held the respondent State guilty of defaulting in its obligation to unearth evidence by means of a determined fact-finding exercise. But then, after having established that the dearth of evidence is the defendant's fault, the Court visited the consequences of this failure on the applicant. She has been penalised for not coming up with evidence that the Convention *obliges* the State to procure. Hard as I try, I cannot see this as a consequent technique of decision-making.

Comments and Questions

1. Ramcharan is of the view that human rights fact-finding bodies "may apply flexible admissibility criteria," a view reflected in the practice of the Inter-American Court of Human Rights. Does this amount, in effect, to concluding that there should be no rules as to admissibility of evidence? Ramcharan also observes that "the evaluation of evidence is a matter that rests exclusively within the competence of the fact-finding body." Does this approach amount to allowing the fact-finder unbridled discretion in evaluating facts? If so, might this undermine faith in the objectivity of the fact-finder?

2. In the *Awas Tingni* case, what exactly did the court find in relation to the community's land claim? Did the Court resolve the claim, determine that the community had a valid claim that the state of Nicaragua needed to address, or something else? In the end, what weight did the Court afford the testimony of the community's leaders?

3. How often should human rights courts conduct their evidentiary hearings on-site? Would it have been helpful or feasible for the Inter-American Court to travel to the disputed territory in the *Awas Tingni* case or to Honduras in *Velásquez Rodríguez*? Where issues of fact are presented, how important are oral proceedings in evaluating the credibility of witnesses? Does it make a difference that many witnesses do not speak a language understood by the judges?

4. Cooperation of the government seems to be a key issue in every case in which there is a factual dispute. Is it appropriate to draw conclusions from the government's failure to address a particular issue? Do you agree with the thrust of Judge Bonello's partly dissenting opinion in the *Veznedaroğlu* case? Note that most treaties that provide for individual complaints require the state to "cooperate fully" with any investigation. Might a human rights body find a separate violation if such cooperation is not forthcoming, or is shifting the burden of proof in such circumstances an appropriate response?

IV. Final Comments and Questions

1. The UN General Assembly and the Security Council are political bodies. Do you think that it is appropriate for such bodies to engage in fact-finding — a process that would seem, by its nature, to demand the highest degree of impartiality? Should one harbor the same misgivings about fact-finding by rapporteurs appointed by the Human Rights Council, which, after all, consists of member states rather than independent human rights experts? The obvious danger is that certain states that are politically unpopular in UN circles will receive a disproportionate share of the attention. How serious do you think this consideration is? Do you agree with Professor Bassiouni's assessment, supra pages 1012-1017, that the political nature of the United Nations and its bureaucracy inevitably makes UN fact-finding unstable and fraught with difficulties?

2. Which of the various fact-finding strategies identified in this chapter do you think are the most effective? Judging from the extracts from the decisions and reports of various human rights bodies and NGOs, which strategies do you think are likely to produce the most — and the most reliable — information? Is it better to have an array of different fact-finding mechanisms and techniques, as we now have at the United Nations, or would it have been preferable to have adopted the Dutch proposal from the 1960s for a centralized and specialized UN fact-finding organ? If you were asked by the Secretary-General of the UN to produce a report on the subject of improvements in UN human rights fact-finding, what kinds of suggestions would you make?

3. This chapter has addressed the standards that should be applied to fact-finding, but there are many more practical issues that NGOs concerned with investigating human rights violations must address. What substantive, political, financial, or other issues should an NGO consider before embarking on an on-site mission or other fact-finding initiative? See Hurst Hannum, "Implementing Human Rights: An Overview of Strategies and Procedures," in *Guide to International Human Rights Practice* 19-39 (Hurst Hannum ed., 4th ed. 2004).

Chapter 13

Human Rights and Foreign Policy

The United States–China Relationship

Most problems in this coursebook have focused primarily on legal issues: the many regimes, institutions, procedures, and practices that comprise what has come to be known as international human rights law. Lawyers, of course, have played a major role in the creation and clarification of this body of law and its slow but increasingly effective application in recent years. Human rights, however, also can be furthered through the foreign policy process. Indeed, in many instances it is the most promising way to improve the lives of individuals in a given country. The attitude that the United States or other states take toward a repressive regime might have far more impact upon the lives of people living under that regime than, for example, numerous petitions filed with the United Nations or regional human rights bodies.

For more than thirty years, due to congressional initiatives and presidential policies, human rights have been a formal part of U.S. foreign policy. Exactly what part, and by what means, are questions posed in this chapter. Other problems have looked at U.S. ratification of human rights treaties (Chapter 2), domestic enforcement of human rights (Chapter 6), and the U.S. role in the Inter-American system (Chapter 9). This chapter focuses primarily on bilateral relations with other states and, as one example, asks the reader to consider the role that promotion of human rights should play in U.S. relations with China.

The chapter focuses on U.S. foreign policy because it is well documented and has been the subject of a great deal of commentary. However, almost all of the issues that are raised in internal U.S. policy debates, as well as Sino-American relations, are relevant to relationships between other countries, as well. The reader should consider the questions raised in the following readings in the context of his or her own country, whether it is large or small, and whatever its human rights record.

I. Human Rights and U.S. Foreign Policy

Kenneth Cmiel, *The Emergence of Human Rights Politics in the United States*

86 J. Am. History 1231-1250 (Dec. 1999) (references omitted)

Human rights has a long intellectual pedigree, yet the contemporary human rights movement only took off in the 1970s. Particularly crucial were the years 1973 to 1978. Most literature on the human rights activism of the decade focuses on the foreign policy of the Jimmy Carter administration. But whatever the strengths and inconsistencies of Carter's initiatives, they were not as important for the long term as the emergence of new sources of funding for human rights work or the growth of such nongovernmental organizations (NGOs) as Amnesty International or Human Rights Watch. Nor were they as important for the long term as the human rights legislation passed by Congress before Carter became president. The work of Congress and the NGOs guaranteed that human rights would be a part of the discussion not only in the seventies, but for the rest of the twentieth century.

In the years just prior to the Carter presidency, there was a phenomenal burst of human rights activism in the United States. Signal events contributed: the 1973 military coup in Chile, the publication of Aleksandr I. Solzhenitsyn's massive *Gulag Archipelago* a few months later, the Helsinki Accords in 1975. But more generally, as the Vietnam War wound down, human rights emerged as a new way to approach world politics.

The 1970s activism mostly attacked state-sponsored repression. It was the classic civil and political rights that mattered: freedom of expression, fair trials, protection from torture, the rights to emigrate or peacefully organize. Many human rights activists understood economic and social security rights to be important, but most, nonetheless, made basic civil rights the priority. But by making these concerns global rather than merely domestic, the 1970s human rights perspective etched a sharp alternative to competing ideas about international affairs. It dismissed as morally bankrupt the Cold War theories of containment that drew the line between anticommunist friends and Communist foes. It also, especially between 1973 and 1976, presented a sharp and explicit challenge to the cynical realpolitik of Richard M. Nixon's and Henry A. Kissinger's détente. Exposing the death squads of Latin American military dictatorships or the viciousness of SAVAK, the shah of Iran's secret police, was as important to human rights activists as stories of Communist oppression.

Dozens of new groups started up in the United States, and the few human rights organizations that already existed grew exponentially. Established foundations and church groups began devoting attention to the topic. The number of courses on the subject in colleges and law schools jumped. Reporters, both print and electronic, became more intrigued with the story....

Amnesty International, no doubt the most famous human rights organization, provides an example. AI was founded in London in 1961. The United States section, Amnesty International USA (AIUSA), was organized four years later. The organization had its successes, yet it lived a precarious life at first. The international organization almost collapsed in 1967, thanks to internal bickering. Three years later the United States section almost folded, deep in debt. But the next decade told a very different story. Between 1970 and 1976, the number of dues-paying members in the United States went from 6,000 to 35,000. AIUSA had one paid, half-time staff member in 1970. The organization, such as it was, was run by a volunteer board of directors. A decade later, however, there were fourteen paid staffers with offices in New York City; San Francisco, California; Chicago, Illinois; Colorado, and Washington, D.C. The international organization grew similarly in those years. In 1977, it was awarded the Nobel peace prize.

Amnesty International was just one of more than two hundred groups working on human rights in the United States by the end of the seventies. The Lawyers Committee for Human Rights [now Human Rights First]... dates itself to 1975. Human Rights Watch, now arguably the most important human rights NGO, started in 1978. Human Rights Internet dates from 1976; the Ford Foundation began funding human rights work in 1973. The list could go on. There were a handful of human rights lobbying groups in Washington in the early seventies. By the end of the decade there were over fifty.

Congress was also getting interested. Such House liberals as Democrats Don Fraser of Minnesota and Tom Harkin of Iowa led the way. Fraser chaired the first congressional hearings on the topic of human rights in 1973. More followed. But if key liberals were at the center, there emerged an ideologically eclectic group willing to support one human rights initiative or another. Deeply conservative Republicans, such as John Ashbrook of Ohio, and anticommunist Democrats, such as Henry "Scoop" Jackson of Washington, could also be counted on as allies. Between 1974 and 1976, Congress passed legislation tying foreign aid, both military and economic, to human rights performance. Particularly important were several amendments that Harkin introduced in 1975 and 1976. In them, Congress agreed to stop economic assistance to any country that routinely violated certain human rights and to oblige United States representatives to the Inter-American Development Bank and the African Development Fund to vote down any loans to regimes guilty of gross violations of human rights. (This was later extended to World Bank loans.) Also important was the Jackson-Vanik Amendment (1974) tying most-favored-nation trade status to respect for the right to emigrate. All this legislation remains in force today....

...The first publication of a congressional hearing on human rights came in 1974. In the next two years, the Government Printing Office issued reports on human rights abuses in South Korea, Iran, Haiti, India, the Philippines, Africa, Central America, North Korea, Uruguay, Paraguay, and Chile — the cumulative results of numerous different congressional hearings. When Congress passed legislation tying foreign aid and trade status to human rights performance, State Department officials in countries receiving United States economic or military aid were required to report back to Washington on local human rights situations. After Henry Kissinger initially tried to circumvent the procedure, Congress in 1976 wrote into law a requirement that the reports had to be published. Two years later, the first published State Department report on human rights around the world appeared....

The new information networks brought activists into contact across borders, spurring still more activism. In 1971, the International League for Human Rights became the first organization in the West to establish ongoing ties with a human rights group behind the Iron Curtain. The league agreed to affiliate with the Moscow Human Rights Committee, whose most famous member was the dissident physicist Andrei Sakharov. The league lobbied in the West for the group. Weekly phone calls were instituted, keeping both sides abreast of the latest news. Similarly, when Andrei Tverdokhlebov, another Russian physicist, explored founding an Amnesty International group in Moscow in 1973, he received much of his information from the Madison Avenue AIUSA group in New York City. The first contact came when the United States group simply telephoned Tverdokhlebov. And the Ford Foundation, funding South American academics who had lost their jobs under the military dictatorships, worked almost entirely through private international contacts. The foundation used its network of caseworkers to identify possible grant recipients around the globe. In this way it not only funded some of the most articulate opponents of military rule in Chile and Argentina; the foundation also contributed to the growing body of research documenting the assault on civil liberties in those nations.

By the middle of the seventies, the information revolution on human rights was in full swing and the network of activists increasingly agile. Communication circuits that had not existed ten years before were confidently pushing politically charged information around the globe. NGO activists also had a growing number of allies among politicians, who were more likely to receive media attention. In

1975, when several members of the House of Representatives complained about Georgetown University's decision to give an honorary degree to the shah of Iran's sister, they used Amnesty International research to make their case....

An especially important turning point in the United States was the 1975-1976 human rights legislation. It forced Washington to take human rights information seriously. AI opened a Washington office in 1976. Within a year it was a whirlwind of activity. Staff monitored hearings and consulted with members of Congress and State Department officials. They briefed sympathetic business and religious leaders who were about to meet with ambassadors of countries with brutal human rights records. Even conservative members of Congress were now meeting with Amnesty International. A Washington lawyer and AIUSA board member could speak of the "excellent new access to the State Department." In 1976, Henry Kissinger, a strong foe of human rights initiatives, had at least to give public lip service to the issue, urging the Chilean military dictatorship to mend its ways. He even met with AI activists to discuss the issue.

It was the quantity and quality of the facts gathered that mattered. Human rights NGOs collected troubling information that could be trusted and could not be ignored. In 1976, the *Washington Post* observed that the human rights legislation would probably not have passed except for "the large volume of detailed information that has become available to American lawmakers about just how badly many of Washington's client states are abusing their own citizens." John Salzberg, staff consultant on human rights to the House of Representatives, found the human rights NGOs to be the most credible witnesses they had, better than missionaries, exiled nationals, pro- and antipartisans, and State Department officials. Salzberg singled out Amnesty International, the International Commission of Jurists, and the International League for Human Rights as noteworthy contributors to congressional investigations.

On their end, activists were discovering that they could better a human rights situation by talking with politicians in Washington. Here, too, Harkin's legislation proved critical. Suddenly, the United States might veto a World Bank loan because of a bad human rights record. It might reduce or withhold military aid. Already in 1977, eighteen different countries were adversely affected by the new legislation. In 1978, Argentina lost all its military aid. Economically dependent countries had to take seriously Washington's talk about human rights....

Politicians who talked about the issue not only reported on specific cases but also raised awareness. Reporters who picked up the issue did so as well. Throughout the decade, even before Carter became president, there was growing media interest....

All this contributed to public awareness. In 1968 human rights might have been a noble phrase, but it was not yet a politics that the public recognized. Ten years later it was. The NGOs were maturing; the information networks were in place; important legislation had been passed. And the idea of human rights was developing a warm public image. Survey researchers in 1977 discovered that there was a strong and visceral positive reaction to the mention of "human rights." Pat Caddell, the pollster for Jimmy Carter, found focus groups overwhelmingly in support of Carter's discussions of human rights, irrespective of political party. Even when they did not like Carter they liked his human rights talk. Other independent polling confirmed this. "Human rights is suddenly chic," noted

Roberta Cohen of the International League for Human Rights. "For years we were preachers, idealists or busybodies," she added, "and now we are respectable."

The cumulative result of the new human rights talk, in all its manifestations, was that the very phrase "human rights" developed an aura around it. It was something to be taken seriously. . . .

Human rights factors always have figured in the U.S. foreign policy process. In 1787, Thomas Jefferson wrote James Madison that "a bill of rights is what the people are entitled to against every government on earth." The Monroe Doctrine originally was enunciated to support the liberty of newly independent states in the Americas against feared efforts of European powers to reassert their colonial mastery of the Western Hemisphere. During the late nineteenth century, several U.S. Presidents spoke out strongly against Czarist oppression of Russian Jews. The genocide committed by the Ottoman Empire against the Armenians early in the twentieth century prompted President Woodrow Wilson to condemn the Turks, and in 1917 he called on Congress to declare war on Germany because "the world must be made safe for democracy." President Franklin Roosevelt, shortly before World War II, restated the United States' commitment to human rights in the famous Four Freedoms address, and, when the UN was formed in the aftermath of that war and the horrors of the Holocaust, the United States took the lead in an attempt to create an international structure to promote and protect human rights.

This "idealist" approach to the international community has often confronted the arguments of the "realists," but never more than during the ideological struggles of the Cold War, when combating communist expansion became an almost exclusive objective. During the 1950s, the United States effectively abdicated its leadership role in the international human rights movement, but the reasons were as much linked to the practice of de jure segregation as to concerns about communism. This lack of concern carried over into the 1960s, when the United States became increasingly preoccupied with its domestic civil rights problems and its deepening involvement in Vietnam. Vice-Presidents calling on Greek colonels and Secretaries of State embracing Brazilian dictators were the order of the day. By the early 1970s, international human rights considerations had become, in Professor Farer's apt phrase, "the stepchildren of United States foreign policy." Tom J. Farer, *United States Foreign Policy and the Protection of Human Rights*, 14 Va. J. Intl. L. 623 (1974). (Farer added that "there is nothing particularly American about this attitude. It appears to characterize foreign policy elites in most states." Id.)

In the immediate post-Vietnam, post-Watergate period, however, a new and renewed interest in international human rights appeared in the United States. The Senate approved U.S. ratification of its first post-war human rights agreement in 1976, when it ratified the 1952 Convention on the Political Rights of Women, 193 U.N.T.S. 135, entry into force for the U.S. Apr. 8, 1976, 27 U.S.T. 3301, T.I.A.S. No. 8289. While this was a relatively minor agreement that did little more than grant women the right to vote and hold public office, the ratification nonetheless represented a breakthrough after the 1950s debate on the Bricker Amendment (see Chapter 6, page 466). 1973 saw the seminal hearings held by Congressman Donald Fraser's House Subcommittee on International Organizations (International Protection of Human Rights: Hearings Before the Subcomm.

on International Organizations and Movements of the House Comm. on Foreign Affairs, 93d Cong., 1st Sess. (1973)) and in that Subcommittee's remarkable report the following year (Human Rights in the World Community: A Call for U.S. Leadership, Report of the Subcommittee on International Organizations and Movements of the 93d Cong., 2d Sess. (Comm. Print 1974)). The above hearings and report had their counterpart in the academic world, when the Virginia Journal of International Law published a *Symposium on Human Rights and United States Foreign Policy*, 14 Va J. Intl. L. 591-701 (1974). The following reading, taken from that Symposium, reveals the issues as they were seen in the pre-Carter period, but they are issues that are still relevant to the subject of this chapter.

Richard B. Bilder, *Human Rights and U.S. Foreign Policy: Short-Term Prospects*

14 Va. J. Intl. L. 597, 597-609 passim (1974)

An attempt to assess or predict the role of human rights in U.S. foreign policy involves a number of conceptual and empirical problems which deserve at least brief comment.

First, it is questionable whether the U.S. Government has any unified attitude with respect to the appropriate significance of international human rights considerations in foreign policy matters. "Foreign policy" is a broad abstraction, comprising many separate policies, decisions, actions and reactions. In certain areas of concern, such as national security, U.S. foreign policy may follow a relatively clearly defined and consistent pattern. But in other areas, policy decisions may be ad hoc and sometimes inconsistent, and thus difficult to fit into a single pattern. U.S. international human rights decisions seem to fall principally into the latter category. Decisions relating to general participation in institutional aspects of international human rights activities, such as U.N. or inter-American programs, will involve different considerations than decisions concerning human rights issues potentially relevant to relations with a particular foreign country. The United States may have one stance with respect to ratification of human rights conventions, another towards the establishment of the position of U.N. Human Rights Commissioner, and still others regarding human rights problems in a variety of different countries such as the Soviet Union, Greece, Vietnam, the Dominican Republic, or Rhodesia. We may therefore have to phrase our enquiry in terms of the significance of human rights concerns in different kinds of foreign policy decisions rather than in foreign policy as a whole.

Second, even if we surmise that human rights considerations may have been relevant to a particular foreign policy decision, it may prove very difficult to isolate and measure empirically the particular "role" or "input" of these considerations in that decision. Foreign policy decisions are frequently the result of a complex interaction of many diverse domestic, international and bureaucratic interests and pressures. It may not be easy for the involved officials themselves to assess or articulate accurately all the reasons why they reached their decision. Moreover, due to bureaucratic inaccessibility, diplomatic reticence or government secrecy, evidence indicating the actual influence of various factors may be hard to obtain.

Where we are seeking to determine the influence of what are likely to be relatively secondary factors, such as human rights considerations, these problems may be magnified. In many instances, the best we may be able to say is that, in the broadest terms, human rights considerations seem to have had a relatively "major," "significant," or "negligible" role in the relevant decision.

Third, even if we are able to make a rough assessment of the relative role of human rights in a particular decision, this may furnish only limited guidance as to official attitudes towards human rights generally. The role played by human rights considerations in any single decision will be a function of their influence relative to the influence of all of the other interests and pressures involved in the decision. Thus, to make any useful general judgment, we have to look at the decisional matrix as a whole. There may be contexts in which even the most oppressive government, evincing little concern for human rights objectives, may find it expedient to make decisions supporting these objectives. This would be the case, for example, where strong political interests happen to coincide with what purport to be human rights aims, or if (as in the case of voting for a U.N. human rights decision irrelevant to that country's own situation) there are virtually no costs or countervailing reasons for not supporting such aims. Thus, U.S. condemnation of apartheid in Rhodesia may be a relatively weak test of real U.S. human rights attitudes, since the political costs of such condemnation are comparatively minor and the political gains of currying favor with Black African countries are thought to be high. Conversely, even a genuine and deeply-held official commitment to international human rights objectives may on occasion be submerged by exceptionally strong countervailing interests and pressures. For example, U.S. failure to condemn Soviet repressive policies may not in itself be conclusive evidence of overall U.S. attitudes, since the Administration clearly views the potential costs of any such condemnation, in terms of its overriding objective of detente, as extremely high. . . .

Fourth, the historic character of American foreign policy makes generalization and prediction as to the role of human rights particularly uncertain. U.S. foreign policy has long embodied various coexisting themes. It seems undeniable that one of these themes has been moralism and humanitarianism: a desire to do good in the world by spreading the blessings of the American way of life and its concept of civil and political liberties. It is clear that, for many Americans, U.S. involvement in Vietnam had such a moral and human rights basis. But another theme has been pragmatism, a businessman's sense of the world's harsh realities. Sometimes one theme has clearly dominated our foreign policies, sometimes the other. There is some evidence to suggest that, as American power is perceived as relatively more limited, our foreign policy has tended to shift towards the more pragmatic side of the spectrum. More frequently, however, our policy has represented an uneasy compromise between these two. Even where pragmatism and realpolitik are clearly at the center of the stage, the theme of moralism often lurks in the wings, pressing to get into the act and make its presence felt.

Finally, it is difficult to predict the role of human rights in U.S. foreign policy without knowing who will be the officials making relevant decisions. Our foreign policy will be more or less responsive to human rights considerations depending upon whether the President is Wilson, Kennedy, or Nixon; whether the Secretary of State is Dulles, Rusk, or Kissinger; whether the U.S. representative to the United Nations who deals with human rights matters is Eleanor Roosevelt or perhaps a less committed or influential person. Even relatively low-ranking officials — a Deputy Assistant Secretary of State, for example, or an individual Senator or Congressman — may by virtue of particular interest, energy, persuasive ability or strategic position, exert a significant influence either for or against U.S. involvement in inter-national human rights efforts.

In summary, we can generalize about the role of human rights in U.S. foreign policy only with caution. There are inherent difficulties both in deciding what constitutes human rights considerations and in measuring the influence of such considerations in particular decisions. Human rights considerations may play different or even inconsistent roles in different aspects of our foreign policy depending upon the total configuration of relevant interests and the personalities of the individuals involved. Further, the tension between the moral and humanitarian theme and the pragmatic theme in American foreign policy is a continuing one, and neither can be ignored if our policy is to be understood. Perhaps the most that we may be able to say is that human rights considerations frequently play at least some role in U.S. foreign policy, though rarely a determinative one. What this "some role" is likely to mean will depend upon the circumstances. . . .

In the above reading, Professor Bilder pessimistically predicted that "human rights considerations seem likely to play only a relatively limited role in U.S. foreign policy during the next few years." Professor Henkin, writing in the same Symposium, agreed that "[r]adical transformations in U.S. attitudes are not in sight." Louis Henkin, *The United States and the Crisis in Human Rights*, 14 Va. J. Intl. L. 653, 666 (1974). He added, however, that "[m]uch that I have described might change dramatically," and, with the election in 1976 of Jimmy Carter to the presidency, change it did. Before turning to the dramatic changes wrought during the first two years of his Administration, however, attention should be drawn to the important legislative groundwork laid by Congress in the final years of the Nixon/Ford administration.

A. *Congressional Action: Laying the Foundation*

Richard B. Lillich, *U.S. Foreign Policy, Human Rights, and Foreign Trade and Investment in Private Investors Abroad — Problems and Solutions*

In International Business in 1979, at 281, 288-291 (Southwestern Legal Foundation, 1979)

With the withdrawal of U.S. troops from South Vietnam in 1973 came a reassessment of the underpinnings of U.S. foreign policy. The realpolitik of the Kissinger era, in the view of the distinguished historian and former foreign policy adviser Arthur Schlesinger, Jr.:

> frustrated those in the Wilsonian tradition who felt that American foreign policy should be founded on ideals. It frustrated equally those in the school of FDR who

did not doubt that foreign policy must be founded on national interest but considered ideals an indispensable constituent of American power. Official indifference to the Soviet dissidents [who, Schlesinger maintains, "forced the human rights issue on the world"], symbolized by President Ford's refusal in mid-1975 to receive Solzhenitsyn, seemed to reveal a vacuum at the center of American foreign policy.

Nature, it is said, abhors a vacuum, and in this instance it was Congress that proceeded to fill it. Beginning with a "sense-of-the-Congress" provision in 1973 to the effect that "the President should deny any economic or military assistance to the government of any foreign country which practices the internment or imprisonment of that country's citizens for political purposes," it enacted a series of statutes linking foreign assistance or trade benefits to the status of human rights in foreign countries. One of the earliest and most controversial instances was the Jackson-Vanik Amendment to the Trade Reform Act of 1974, which prohibits, inter alia, the granting of most-favored-nation treatment to nonmarket economy countries that deny or restrict the right of their citizens to emigrate. Designed to place economic pressure upon the Soviet Union and other Communist countries to secure their compliance with Article 13(2) of the Universal Declaration and Article 12(2) of the U.N. Covenant on Civil and Political Rights, which guarantee the right to emigrate, this amendment initially was relatively successful in the case of Rumania and had an impact upon Soviet emigration patterns as well.

Also enacted in 1974 was a new Section 502B to the Foreign Assistance Act of 1961, a "sense-of-the-Congress" provision stating that "except in extraordinary circumstances, the President shall substantially reduce or terminate security assistance to any government which engages in a consistent pattern of gross violations of human rights." Two years later, Congress eliminated the "sense-of-the-Congress" language and mandated the President to terminate military assistance to countries so violating human rights unless "extraordinary circumstances" exist which make it in the "national interest" to continue such aid. [Documentary Supplement, page 312.] This national security exception, first invoked by President Ford in late 1976, may be . . . overridden by a joint resolution of Congress.

Having taken up military assistance in 1974, Congress tackled economic aid the following year by adding Section 116[b] to the Foreign Assistance Act of 1961, which requires the President to terminate such assistance to recipient countries, under criteria roughly similar to the ones contained in Section 502B, "unless such assistance will directly benefit the needy people in such country." [Documentary Supplement, page 822.] Again, this "needy people" exception, often relied upon by the President, is subject to Congress's override, this time by concurrent resolution.

The policy of seeking compliance with internationally recognized human rights norms by the use of economic levers gained momentum in 1976 when Congress enacted several other related statutes. . . . [Thus,] at the end of 1976, a substantial amount of legislation, all initiated by Congress in the face of outright opposition by, or at best tepid approval of, the Nixon-Ford administrations was in place and ready for the Carter administration's use.

B. *Presidential Human Rights Policies and Their Critics, 1975-2005*

1. Almost at the Beginning: President Carter

"It is not altogether clear how Carter personally came to human rights," Professor Schlesinger has written. "The phrase does not appear in the chapter on foreign policy in his memoir, *Why Not the Best?* (1975). Nor was the issue prominent in his presidential campaign." Arthur M. Schlesinger Jr., *Human Rights and the American Tradition*, 57 Foreign Aff. 503, 513 (1978). Suffice to say that between the election and inauguration day, Carter and his advisers concluded that human rights was "the perfect unifying principle" needed to give U.S. foreign policy the moral thrust that it had lacked during the Nixon-Ford period. Id. at 514. Thus, in his inaugural address, the President singled out human rights as a key element in his proposed new foreign policy, declaring that "our commitment to human rights must be absolute.... Because we are free, we can never be indifferent to the fate of freedom elsewhere. Our moral sense dictates a clearcut preference for those societies who share with us an abiding respect for individual human rights:" 1 Pub. Papers of the Presidents 2, 3 (1977). He developed this theme in his March 17, 1977, address to the United Nations (76 Dept. State Bull. 329, 332-333 (1977)):

> The search for peace and justice means also respect for human dignity. All the signatories of the UN Charter have pledged themselves to observe and to respect basic human rights. Thus, no member of the United Nations can claim that mistreatment of its citizens is solely its own business. Equally, no member can avoid its responsibilities to review and to speak when torture or unwarranted deprivation occurs in any part of the world.
>
> The basic thrust of human affairs points toward a more universal demand for fundamental human rights. The United States has a historical birthright to be associated with this process.
>
> We in the United States accept this responsibility in the fullest and the most constructive sense. Ours is a commitment and not just a political posture. I know perhaps as well as anyone that our own ideals in the area of human rights have not always been attained in the United States, but the American people have an abiding commitment to the full realization of these ideals. And we are determined, therefore, to deal with our deficiencies quickly and openly. We have nothing to conceal....
>
> This issue is important in itself. It should not block progress on other important matters affecting the security and well-being of our people and of world peace. It is obvious that the reduction of tensions, the control of nuclear arms, the achievement of harmony in the troubled areas of the world, and the provision of food, good health, and education will independently contribute to advancing the human condition.
>
> In our relationships with other countries, these mutual concerns will be reflected in our political, our cultural, and our economic attitudes....
>
> I believe that this is a foreign policy that is consistent with my own Nation's historic values and commitments. And I believe that it is a foreign policy that is consonant with the ideals of the United Nations.

The theme was developed further by Secretary of State Vance in the major address that follows.

Cyrus R. Vance, *Human Rights and Foreign Policy*

76 Dept. State Bull. 505, 505-508 (1977) (emphasis in original)

. . . I speak today about the resolve of this Administration to make the advancement of human rights a central part of our foreign policy. Many here today have long been advocates of human rights within our own society. And throughout our Nation that struggle for civil rights continues.

In the early years of our civil rights movement, many Americans treated the issue as a "Southern" problem. They were wrong. It was and is a problem for all of us. Now, as a Nation, we must not make a comparable mistake. Protection of human rights is a challenge for all countries, not just for a few.

Our human rights policy must be understood in order to be effective. So today I want to set forth the substance of that policy and the results we hope to achieve.

Our concern for human rights is built upon ancient values. It looks with hope to a world in which liberty is not just a great cause but the common condition. In the past it may have seemed sufficient to put our name in international documents that spoke loftily of human rights. That is not enough. We will go to work, alongside other people and governments, to protect and enhance the dignity of the individual.

Let me define what we mean by "human rights."

1. First, there is the right to be free from governmental violation of the integrity of the person. Such violations include torture; cruel, inhuman, or degrading treatment or punishment; and arbitrary arrest or imprisonment. And they include denial of fair public trial, and invasion of the home.
2. Second, there is the right to the fulfillment of such vital needs as food, shelter, health care, and education. We recognize that the fulfillment of this right will depend, in part, upon the stage of the nation's economic development. But we also know that this right can be violated by a Government's action or inaction — for example, through corrupt official processes which divert resources to an elite at the expense of the needy, or through indifference to the plight of the poor.
3. Third, there is the right to enjoy civil and political liberties — freedom of thought, of religion, of assembly; freedom of speech; freedom of the press; freedom of movement both within and outside one's own country; freedom to take part in government.

Our policy is to promote all these rights. They are all recognized in the Universal Declaration of Human Rights, a basic document which the United States helped fashion and which the United Nations approved in 1948. There may be a disagreement on the priorities these rights deserve, but I believe that, with work, all these rights can become complementary and mutually reinforcing. . . .

Since 1945 international practice has confirmed that a nation's obligations to respect human rights is a matter of concern in international law. Our obligation under the UN Charter is written into our legislation. For example, our Foreign Assistance Act now reads: "A principal goal of the foreign policy of the United States is to promote the increased observance of internationally recognized human rights by all countries." In these ways our policy is in keeping with our tradition, our international obligations, and our laws.

In pursuing a human rights policy, we must always keep in mind the limits of our power and of our wisdom. A sure formula for defeat of our goals would be a rigid, hubristic attempt to impose our values on others. A doctrinaire plan of action would be as damaging as indifference.

We must be realistic. Our country can only achieve our objectives if we shape what we do to the case at hand. In each instance we will consider these questions as we determine whether and how to act:

1. First, we will ask ourselves, what is the nature of the case that confronts us? For example, what kind of violations or deprivations are there? What is their extent? Is there a pattern to the violations? If so, is the trend toward concern for human rights or away from it? What is the degree of control and responsibility of the Government involved? And, finally, is the Government willing to permit independent, outside investigation?
2. A second set of questions concerns the prospects for effective action. Will our action be useful in promoting the overall cause of human rights? Will it actually improve the specific conditions at hand? Or will it be likely to make things worse instead? Is the country involved receptive to our interest and efforts? Will others work with us, including official and private international organizations dedicated to furthering human rights? Finally, does our sense of values and decency demand that we speak out or take action anyway, even though there is only a remote chance of making our influence felt?
3. We will ask a third set of questions in order to maintain a sense of perspective. Have we steered away from the self-righteous and strident, remembering that our own record is not unblemished? Have we been sensitive to genuine security interests, realizing that outbreak of armed conflict or terrorism could in itself pose a serious threat to human rights? Have we considered all the rights at stake? If, for instance, we reduce aid to a Government which violates the political rights of its citizens, do we not risk penalizing the hungry and poor who bear no responsibility for the abuses of their Government?

If we are determined to act, the means available range from quiet diplomacy in its many forms through public pronouncements to withholding of assistance. Whenever possible, we will use positive steps of encouragement and inducement. Our strong support will go to countries that are working to improve the human condition. We will always try to act in concert with other countries through international bodies.

In the end a decision whether and how to act in the case of human rights is a matter for informed and careful judgment. No mechanistic formula produces an automatic answer.

It is not our purpose to intervene in the internal affairs of other countries, but as the President has emphasized, no member of the United Nations can claim that violation of internationally protected human rights is solely its own affair. It is our purpose to shape our policies in accord with our beliefs and to state them without stridency or apology when we think it is desirable to do so.

Our policy is to be applied within our own society as well as abroad. We welcome constructive criticism at the same time as we offer it.

No one should suppose that we are working in a vacuum. We place great weight on joining others in the cause of human rights.

The UN system is central to this cooperative endeavor. That is why the President stressed the pursuit of human rights in his speech before the General Assembly last month. That is why he is calling for U.S. ratification of four important human rights covenants and conventions, and why we are trying to strengthen the human rights machinery within the United Nations. . . .

Regional organizations also play a central role in promoting human rights. The President has announced that the United States will sign and seek Senate approval of the American Convention on Human Rights. We will continue to work to strengthen the machinery of the Inter-American Commission on Human Rights. This will include efforts to schedule regular visits to all members of the Organization of American States, annual debates on human rights conditions, and the expansion of the inter-American educational program on human rights.

The United States is seeking increased consultation with other nations for joint programs on economic assistance and more general efforts to promote human rights. We are working to assure that our efforts reach out to all, with particular sensitivity to the problems of women. . . .

The United States looks to the use of economic assistance — whether bilateral or through international financial institutions — as a means to foster basic human rights. . . .

We are implementing current laws that bring human rights considerations directly into our decisions in several international financial institutions. At the same time, we are working with the Congress to find the most effective way to fulfill our parallel commitment to international cooperation in economic development.

In accordance with human rights provisions of legislation governing our security assistance programs, we recently announced cuts in military aid to several countries.

Outside the government, there is much that can be done. We welcome the efforts of individual American citizens and private organizations — such as religious, humanitarian, and professional groups — to work for human rights with commitments of time, money, and compassion.

All these initiatives to further human rights abroad would have a hollow ring if we were not prepared to improve our own performance at home. So we have removed all restrictions on our citizens' travel abroad and are proceeding with plans to liberalize our visa policies.

We support legislation and administrative action to expand our refugee and asylum policies and to permit more victims of repressive regimes to enter the United States. . . .

What results can we expect from all these efforts?

We may justifiably seek a rapid end to such gross violations as those cited in our law: ". . . torture, or cruel, inhuman or degrading treatment or punishment, or prolonged detention without charges . . ." Just last week our Ambassador at the United Nations, Andrew Young, suggested a series of new ways to confront the practice of torture around the world.

The promotion of other human rights is a broader challenge. The results may be slower in coming but are no less worth pursuing, and we intend to let other countries know where we stand.

We recognize that many nations of the world are organized on authoritarian rather than democratic principles — some large and powerful, others struggling to raise the lives of their people above bare subsistence levels. We can nourish no illusions that a call to the banner of human rights will bring sudden transformations in authoritarian societies.

We are embarked on a long journey. But our faith in the dignity of the individual encourages us to believe that people in every society, according to their own traditions, will in time give their own expression to this fundamental aspiration....

We seek these goals because they are right, and because we too will benefit. Our own well-being, and even our security, are enhanced in a world that shares common freedoms and in which prosperity and economic justice create the conditions for peace. And let us remember that we always risk paying a serious price when we become identified with repression.

Nations, like individuals, limit their potential when they limit their goals. The American people understand this. I am confident they will support foreign policies that reflect our traditional values. To offer less is to define America in ways we should not accept.

America fought for freedom in 1776 and in two World Wars. We have offered haven to the oppressed. Millions have come to our shores in times of trouble. In times of devastation abroad, we have shared our resources.

Our encouragement and inspiration to other nations and other peoples have never been limited to the power of our military or the bounty of our economy. They have been lifted up by the message of our Revolution, the message of individual human freedom. That message has been our great national asset in times past. So it should be again.

The new Carter human rights policy provoked immediate controversy and concerns about how it would be applied. The next reading reveals some of those concerns. It is followed by two commentaries that look back at the Carter policy from twenty years later, demonstrating that the controversy has by no means ended.

Henry A. Kissinger, *Continuity and Change in American Foreign Policy*

15 Society 97, 99-102 (1977)

Morality and Pragmatism

...I would now like to turn to one of the basic challenges of foreign policy, the perennial tension between morality and pragmatism. Whenever it has been forced to wield its great power, the United States has also been driven to search its conscience. How does our foreign policy serve moral ends? How can the

United States carry out its role as humane example and champion of justice in a world in which power is still often the final arbiter? How do we reconcile ends and means, principle and survival? How do we keep secure both our existence and our values? These have been the moral and intellectual dilemmas of the United States for two hundred years.

From the time of the Declaration of our Independence, Americans have believed that this country has a moral significance for the world. The United States was created as a conscious act by men and women dedicated to a set of political and ethical principles they held to be of universal meaning. Small wonder, then, that Santayana declared that "being an American is, of itself, almost a moral condition."

At the same time, since Tocqueville it has been observed that we are a pragmatic people, commonsensical, undogmatic, undoctrinaire — a nation with a permanent bent to the practical and an instinct for what works. We have defined our basic goals — justice, freedom, equality, and progress — in open and libertarian terms, seeking to enlarge opportunity and the human spirit rather than to coerce a uniform standard of behavior or a common code of doctrine and belief.

This duality of nature is not at war with reality. For in international politics our morality and power should not be antithetical. Any serious foreign policy must begin with need for survival. And survival has its practical necessities. A nation does not willingly delegate control over its future. For a great power to remit its security to the mercy of others is an abdication of foreign policy. All serious foreign policy therefore begins with maintaining a balance of power — a scope for action, a capacity to affect events and conditions. Without that capacity a nation is reduced to striking empty poses.

But, equally, our nation cannot rest its policy on power alone. Our tradition and the values of our people ensure that a policy that seeks only to manipulate force would lack all conviction, consistency, and public support. This is why the United States has been most successful in our relations with the world when we combined our idealism and our pragmatism — from the days when our Founding Fathers manipulated the monarchical rivalries of Europe to secure our independence and launch the great democratic experiment to the creative American initiatives after the Second World War such as the Marshall Plan. Our modern efforts to achieve strategic arms limitation, peace in the Middle East and southern Africa, the opening to China, recasting international economic relations based on the principle of interdependence — these have also served both moral and practical ends and can be sustained only by a combination of moral conviction and practical wisdom.

Enhancing Human Rights

These considerations come to bear powerfully on the question of the relationship between human rights and foreign policy. The world needs to know what this country stands for. But we cannot rest on this; we must know how to implement our convictions and achieve an enhancement of human rights together with other national objectives. Neither the issue nor the concern are [sic] new. . . .

The central moral problem of government has always been to strike a just and effective balance between freedom and authority. When freedom degenerates into anarchy, the human personality becomes subject to arbitrary, brutal, and capricious forces — witness aberrations of terrorism in even the most humane societies. Yet when the demand for order overrides all other considerations, man becomes a means and not an end, a tool of impersonal machinery. Human rights are the very essence of a meaningful life, and human dignity is the ultimate purpose of civil governments. Respect for the rights of man is written into the founding documents of almost every nation of the world. It has long been part of the common speech and daily lives of our citizens. . . .

And yet, while human rights must be an essential component of our foreign policy, to pursue it effectively over the long term we must take the measure of the dangers and dilemmas along the way. First, any foreign policy must ultimately be judged by its operational results. "In foreign relations," Walter Lippmann once wrote, "as in all other relations, a policy has been formed only when commitments and power have been brought into balance."

To be sure, the advocacy of human rights has in itself a political and even strategic significance. But in the final reckoning more than advocacy will be counted. If we universalize our human rights policy, applying it indiscriminately and literally to all countries, we run the risk of becoming the world's policeman — an objective the American people may not support. At a minimum we will have to answer what may be the question for several friendly governments: how and to what extent we will support them if they get into difficulties by following our maxims. And we will have to indicate what sanctions we will apply to less well-disposed governments which challenge the very precepts of our policy.

If, on the other hand, we confine ourselves to proclaiming objectives that are not translated into concrete actions and specific results, we run the risk of demonstrating that we are impotent and of evoking a sense of betrayal among those our human rights policy seeks to help. Such a course could tempt unfriendly governments to crack down all the harder on their dissidents, in order to demonstrate the futility of our proclamations this indeed has already happened to some extent in the Soviet Union.

Nor can we escape from the dilemma by asserting that there is no connection between human rights behavior and our attitude on other foreign policy problems — by "unlinking," as the technical phrase goes, human rights from other issues. For this implies that there is no cost or consequence to the violation of human rights, turning our proclamation of human rights into a liturgical theme — decoupled, unenforced, and compromised. Or else we will insist on our values only against weaker countries, in Latin America or Asia, many of which may even be conducting foreign policies supportive of our own. This would lead to the paradox that the weaker the nation and the less its importance on the international scene, the firmer and more uncompromising would be our human rights posture.

Second, precisely because human rights advocacy is a powerful political weapon, we must be careful that in its application we do not erode all moral dividing lines. We must understand the difference between governments making universal ideological claims and countries which do not observe all democratic practices — either because of domestic turmoil, foreign danger, or national traditions — but which make no claim to historical permanence or universal relevance. In the contemporary world it is the totalitarian systems which have managed the most systematic and massive repression of human rights. . . .

The ultimate irony would be a posture of resignation toward totalitarian states and harassment of those who would be our friends and who have every prospect of evolving in a more humane direction. We must take care, finally, that our affirmation of human rights is not manipulated by our political adversaries to isolate countries whose security is important for the future of freedom, even if their domestic practices fall short of our maxims. The membership of the UN Human Rights Commission, composed as it is of a number of nations with extremely dubious human rights practices, does not augur well for an objective approach to this issue in the United Nations. Cuba and other Communist governments, as well as the more repressive regimes of the less developed world, have no moral standing to bring other nations to international account. We should not hesitate to say so.

Third, there is the ominous prospect that the issue of human rights if not handled with great wisdom could unleash new forces of American isolationism. This could defeat the administration's goal of using it to mobilize support for continued American involvement in world affairs. That the human rights issue could develop a life of its own, regardless of the administration's prudent sense of its aims and limits, is already evident from some developments in Congress. . . .

Fourth and most fundamentally, we should never forget that the key to successful foreign policy is a sense of proportion. Some of the most serious errors of our foreign policy, both of over commitment and withdrawal, have occurred when we lost the sense of balance between our interests and our ideals. It was under the banners of moralistic slogans a decade and a half ago that we launched adventures that divided our country and undermined our international position. A few years later young people were parading in front of the White House carrying coffins and candles and accusing their government of loving war; the national leadership was denounced as excessively, indeed imperialistically, involved in the internal affairs of other nations. A few years later still, the government was attacked for sacrificing our ethical values on the altar of detente and being insufficiently concerned with the domestic behavior of other nations. Neither we nor the rest of the world can any longer afford such extreme fluctuations. . . .

The administration is surely right in insisting that human rights is a legitimate and recognized subject of international discourse; it is an object of international legal standards — importantly as a result of American initiatives by administrations of both parties. At the same time, we must recognize that we serve the cause of freedom also by strengthening international security and maintaining ties with other countries defending their independence against external aggressions and struggling to overcome poverty, even if their internal structures differ from ours.

We cannot afford to subordinate either concern to the other. Morality without security is ineffectual; security without morality is empty. To establish the relationship and proportion between these goals is perhaps the most profound challenge before our government and our nation. . . .

U.S. Institute for Peace, *Human Rights in the Pursuit of Peace: A 20 Year Assessment*

United States Institute of Peace Special Report (June 16, 1999)

Roberta Cohen: The Carter Administration

...The Carter administration was the first to integrate human rights concerns into executive branch decision making.... He based this decision on several assumptions:

— The United States had a right and responsibility under international law to promote human rights. Carter proceeded from the assumption that no member of the United Nations could claim that mistreatment of its own citizens was its own business. This was a departure from the policies of former Secretary of State Henry Kissinger, who believed that it was dangerous to make the domestic policy of foreign countries a direct objective of American foreign policy.

— Human rights goals could be effectively pursued along with other foreign policy objectives. Carter rejected the linkage argument used by Kissinger, which held that promoting human rights jeopardized other foreign policy goals. The United States would press for human rights objectives simultaneously with political, economic, and military objectives in its bilateral relations.

— U.S. efforts on behalf of human rights would help expand democracy and freedom abroad, and the United States' own well-being and security would be enhanced in the process. "Stronger allies make better friends" has almost become a mantra today, but it was not something one heard twenty years ago.

The policy was intended to be applied across the board. Its integrity, in fact, was felt to depend on its universal application. At the same time, U.S. law gave special attention to those governments with which the United States had a military and economic relationship. The law required the United States to take human rights considerations into account when providing military and economic assistance. There was also an understanding that extraordinary circumstances or national security interests could restrict the policy's application.

The main tool in carrying out the human rights policy was vigorous, quiet diplomacy. For the first time, U.S. officials from the president down regularly raised serious human rights violations and cases in their discussions with foreign governments. The focus was on life-threatening violations such as torture, disappearances, summary executions, and arbitrary detention, and on broader civil and political freedoms, whether freedom of speech or press, freedom of religion, or freedom from racial discrimination, and it encompassed the lifting of emergency decrees, transitions to civilian rule, and more open political processes. Whether with Chile, Uruguay, the Philippines, Indonesia, Nigeria, South Africa, or the Soviet Union, human rights concerns became part of the diplomatic dialogue. In the last half of 1979 alone, the Carter administration made over 100 representations to Soviet officials on human rights, family reunification, and other related cases.

A second tool was raising human rights publicly. This was more controversial. It was done to make U.S. positions clear; to serve as a restraining influence; and in the case of the Soviet Union, to tell the truth. In one noteworthy case, Secretary of State Cyrus Vance made a statement before the Organization of American States (OAS), where he publicly denounced abduction and torture as unacceptable responses to terrorism and warned that by entering this netherworld of terrorist behavior, the governments concerned would lose their moral authority. The United States was also vocal in international and regional forums at the UN, in the Helsinki Forum with the Soviet bloc, and at the OAS. In addition to making strong statements and resolutions, the Carter administration worked hard to develop and strengthen international and regional machinery so that it would fact-find, publish reports, and find ways to hold governments accountable.

The human rights reports were another tool of public diplomacy. They became more candid, more credible, and more comprehensive as time went on. . . . Symbolic gestures were a tool actively used. For example, a reduction in military-to-military contacts was used to send a message to Guatemala, a presidential letter was sent to Andrei Sakharov, and meetings were conducted with prominent dissidents in South Korea and Paraguay. The United States also developed close and cooperative relationships with human rights nongovernmental organizations (NGOs).

In addition, positive measures were used. Economic aid was channeled to governments working to improve their records. Sales of technology or other products sometimes went hand in hand with human rights improvements. Presidential visits, such as to South Korea, were made with the understanding that there would be human rights reforms. Small grants were introduced by the U.S. Agency for International Development (USAID) for projects to promote civil and political freedoms. Finally, sanctions were applied on human rights grounds. . . . What sanctions essentially sought to do was to disassociate the United States from the practices of those governments' security forces [deemed to be human rights violators] and gain influence with the more progressive political forces in the country. Sometimes the mere threat of sanctions gave important support to U.S. diplomacy. . . . In many cases, however, national security concerns simply prevented the use of sanctions. . . .

In the economic area, the United States voted "no" or abstained on multilateral development bank loans in at least 100 cases. The "no" votes were mostly symbolic since most loans went forward because other nations voted to support them. But the possibility of a negative vote did make governments pause, and weigh their actions, and did sometimes cause governments to withdraw requests for loans. The Carter policy extended sparingly to the Export-Import Bank because the stakes for U.S. business were too high.

Not all the tools used to apply the human rights policy worked well; nor were they applied consistently and across the board. The Human Rights Bureau may have been dedicated to integrating human rights into decision making, but there was a lot of resistance and competing pressures in the State Department and other parts of the government. In some cases, genuine strategic or political interests moved human rights to a back seat. In the case of China, the Carter administration first had to develop a relationship before human rights could be brought into the equation. In other cases, clientism, or cozy relationships with foreign governments at any cost, impeded the human rights policy. That even extended to East

Germany, where desk officers argued that writing up the Berlin Wall as an economic development measure in the human rights reports would prove more palatable to the East German government.

The Cold War presented a more serious challenge. To prevent El Salvador from falling to leftist insurgency, the United States supported El Salvador's security forces, which were clearly linked to death squads in that country. Too little effort was made to insist on reforms in those forces, and too many lies began to be told about their true nature. In South Korea, too, human rights initiatives, including for then-political prisoner Kim Dae Jung, were often thwarted on the grounds that they could undermine the government's security vis-à-vis North Korea. It is worth noting, however, that when Kim Dae Jung was elected president last year, one of the first foreigners he invited to his inauguration was Patt Derian, former assistant secretary of state for human rights. The Central Intelligence Agency (CIA) also engaged in actions that directly undercut the human rights policy, although at the time we were not always fully aware of them. The human rights policy was also conveniently scapegoated at different times for a variety of foreign policy failures, notably Iran, to which we sold billions of dollars in military equipment in support of the Shah.

Despite all the compromises, however, there were important achievements. The most significant was that the policy put human rights squarely on the international agenda. There was hardly a government that did not feel challenged to consider the human rights question. It gave impetus to national policy debates, to the formation of human rights organizations, to stimulating the development of a worldwide human rights movement. It made the aspiration for human rights a goal for peoples all over the world. Human rights emerged as a major theme of discussion in international and regional organizations. For the first time, these organizations began to take action on human rights issues. The legacy of human rights will be Carter's historic contribution to the world.

The United States became the world's leader in the promotion of human rights, which restored a more traditional perception of the United States as a champion of freedom. It also gained for the United States the political high ground in its ideological competition with the Soviet Union. The vision of maintaining human dignity and enlarging human freedom was a far more compelling claim against the appeal of Marxism than simply preserving economic interests and selling arms.

The policy gave hope to many advocates of freedom around the world. It also was effective in saving lives. In some countries, large numbers of prisoners were released: 30,000 in Indonesia, 600 in Paraguay. In other countries, citizens were allowed to emigrate: 50,000 Soviet Jews in 1979. Prison conditions improved in some countries. State-sponsored disappearances were exposed and became fewer, as in Argentina. The use of torture was reduced. There were countries with more systemic change where states of siege were lifted, restrictions on press freedom eased, judicial reforms enacted, elections held, and steps taken toward political liberalization. The policy contributed to the promotion of majority rule in white minority Rhodesia, and it contributed to the restoration and strengthening of democratic and civilian rule in countries as diverse as the Dominican Republic, Peru, Nigeria, and Nepal. Basically, the policy chipped away at the instruments of repression in a lot of different countries and began to promote the kind of expectations that we now take for granted when it comes to human rights and democratization. Finally, Carter policy institutionalized human rights in the U.S. government. No matter how one packages this policy and presents it, a foundation was laid during Carter's presidency. Despite some ill-conceived efforts to do away with it, a policy that promotes human rights and democracy internationally is considered to be an American interest and it prevails.

Charles H. Fairbanks, Jr.: Critique of the Carter Administration

There is no doubt that President Carter achieved something important in giving human rights principal stature in the world, and he proclaimed at the very beginning of his administration that human rights would be the cornerstone of his foreign policy.

The Carter administration, however, accepted the doctrine among Third World tyrants that, for most of the world, civil and political rights come as luxuries that are far away in the future. To have taken that position was playing into the hands of the most fashionable rhetoric of despotism during the 1970s. The secondary importance of political and civil rights, as compared with economic and social rights, was an element of doctrine in the Carter administration that threatened the whole human rights agenda. Because of that, many people who supported Reagan felt that the Carter administration was much harder on friendly authoritarian regimes than on unfriendly totalitarian regimes....

The Carter administration was not uninterested in changes of regime. It was quite active in the cases of Iran and Nicaragua, where what one might call conservative or pro-American authoritarian regimes were in real trouble and fell. The problem lay in the fact that where the Carter administration's conception of human rights policy was most effective, it tended to be counterproductive. In the cases of Iran and Nicaragua, U.S. human rights policies really did contribute to weakening the old regime and getting it replaced by a new regime, which, particularly in the Iranian case, turned out to be far worse.

To be fair, no one had been thinking about the question, at that time, of whether a successor regime would be far worse, a problem that was not limited to the Carter administration. This problem, however, was compounded by the fact that in the Carter administration there was not an effort to focus on the question of what the human rights orientation of opposition movements was. It was not treated in the human rights reports, for example. Overall, there was a tendency of the Carter administration's human rights policy to be a policy of self-abnegation, which was partly how the administration really understood things or some people within it. Policies were limited by the instruments available to the administration.

The last weakness of the Carter administration's policies is something that appeared only with the collapse of the communist regimes at the end of the 1980s and beginning of the 1990s. In talking about democracy building, there was an assumption of the existence of a state that can be handed over from one regime to another. Both the Bush and Clinton policies on transition from communism assumed that. What we call reform in the former Soviet space has really been catastrophic in most places, although not in Central and Eastern Europe. One of the reasons is the weakness of the state, which market reforms such as privatization may have aggravated. I think Russia is today, as El Salvador was in the 1980s, a place where there are private forces linked to the government that the weak state neither wants to control nor could control. This is a problem for the future.

Orville H. Schell Jr., *Carter on Rights — A Re-Evaluation*

N.Y. Times, Oct. 25, 1984, at A27

The hero's welcome accorded to former President Jimmy Carter when he visited South America this month was a tribute to his identification with human rights. It is also an opportunity to re-evaluate the complaint, still heard with some frequency, that the human rights policies of his Administration damaged the strategic interests of the United States by alienating the military governments of otherwise friendly and important allies. In fact, as Mr. Carter's visit showed, nothing could be further from the truth.

Jeanne J. Kirkpatrick, whose writings on this subject earned her appointment by President Reagan as chief delegate to the United Nations, focused her arguments on Latin America and cited Bolivia as an example. In the last month of the Carter Administration, she criticized the preoccupation with human rights that led President Carter to take steps to undo a military coup in that country.

Detecting "a significant Communist/Castroite component" in the coalition supporting the elected President, Hernan Siles Zuazo, she criticized Mr. Carter's intensity in opposing the coup and asserted that five years earlier "the U.S. would have welcomed a coup," 10 years earlier "the U.S. would have sponsored it," and 15 years earlier, "we would have conducted it." The Carter Administration's effort to throw its weight behind Mr. Siles Zuazo, and against a coup, showed its "indifference to strategic concerns."

As it happens, Mr. Siles Zuazo has served as President of Bolivia for the last three years, and by now not even the Reagan Administration believes that his democratic government threatens United States strategic interests. In fact, much in keeping with the approach charted by the Carter Administration, the Reagan Administration acted a few months ago to help head off a military coup in Bolivia. Sadly, but not surprisingly, no one in Washington gave any credit to the Carter human rights policy.

Bolivia was not on Mr. Carter's itinerary on this trip. His stops did, however, include the two most strategically significant countries in South America, Brazil and Argentina. Among those who greeted him in Brazil was Leonel Brizola, now Governor of Rio de Janeiro, who credited Mr. Carter with saving his life. Among those who greeted him in Argentina was Jacobo Timerman, who has returned from exile and has become editor of the country's largest circulation evening newspaper. He also credited Mr. Carter with saving his life. The Argentine President, Raul Alfonsin, though not so vitally affected by Mr. Carter's human rights policy, made clear by his welcome how much he believed the Carter policy did for Argentina.

It now seems evident that, although the Carter Administration may have alienated repressive military regimes by criticizing their human rights abuses, it produced long-lasting friendships in countries where successor governments are restoring democracy and respect for human rights. That is hardly a disservice to our strategic interests. Indeed, if the Reagan Administration is right that the trend in Latin America is toward democratic development, speaking out against human rights abuses may even be considered a way to promote the long-term strategic interests of the United States.

2. Selective Rights, Selective Application: The Reagan Administration

The head of President-Elect Reagan's Department of State transition team told Foreign Service officers to expect "a fundamental change of course" in U.S. foreign policy. The new policy, he was reported to have said, was to be "avowedly nationalistic," one that would avoid "the abstractions," such as undue emphasis on human rights, that supposedly characterized President Carter's foreign policy. See John M. Goshko, *Foreign Policy Shift Seen by Reagan Aide*, Intl. Herald-Tribune, Dec. 19, 1980, at 3, col. 1. Contemporaneously, the President-Elect himself served notice that his Administration would apply a distinction between totalitarian and authoritarian regimes, articulated by Professor and later U.S. Ambassador to the United Nations Jeanne Kirkpatrick, when deciding whether to speak out against repressive regimes. The following readings first describe the new policy, then critique and satirize it. The policy evolved in response. In the end, a Reagan official looks back along with a critic.

International Commission of Jurists, *Human Rights and U.S. Foreign Policy*

32-35 (1984)

In a much noted article, which brought her views on distinctions between "authoritarian" and "totalitarian" regimes to Ronald Reagan's attention, Professor Kirkpatrick wrote:

> The failure of the Carter administration's foreign policy is now clear to everyone except its architects.... [In] Iran and Nicaragua, the Carter administration..., actively collaborated in the replacement of moderate autocrats friendly to American interests by less friendly autocrats of extremist persuasion....
>
> [T]he [Carter] administration's conception of national interest borders on doublethink.... [Its] foreign policy fails...for lack of realism about the nature of traditional versus revolutionary autocrats.... Only intellectual fashion and the tyranny of Right/Left thinking prevent intelligent men of goodwill from perceiving the facts that traditional authoritarian governments are less repressive than revolutionary autocracies, that they are more susceptible of liberalization, and they are more compatible with U.S. interest.

Professor Kirkpatrick's...opinions, endorsed by other neo-conservative intellectuals in the Reagan camp, profoundly influenced the new Administration's international stance. Tough-minded firmness toward totalitarian adversaries and a more conciliatory approach to authoritarian allies, it was indicated, would rectify the Carter vacillations that had encouraged Soviet aggression and tilted the balance of global power against the United States.

Early Reagan Administration Positions

The new policy-makers lost little time in announcing their position. At his confirmation hearing, Secretary of State-designate Alexander Haig declared, "International terrorism will take the place of human rights in our [foreign policy] concern." National security adviser Richard Allen asserted that the new Administration would "not place as much ideological emphasis on human rights."

Professor Kirkpatrick, appointed U.S. Permanent Representative to the United Nations, reiterated her opposition to the Carter human rights program "Because it was utopian, because it was conducted outside of the political and historical context, and because it didn't work.... Our position in the Western Hemisphere has deteriorated to the point where we must now defend ourselves against the threat of a ring of Soviet bases being established on and around our borders. I'm not saying that the Carter human rights policy was the only factor in bringing this about, but it certainly played a role.... The central goal of our foreign policy should not be the moral elevation of other nations, but the preservation of a civilized conception of our own national interest."...

The changes in administration tone and verbiage were matched by changes in substance and policy. The high-level Inter-Agency Committee, created to consider human rights factors in foreign economic policy, was disbanded. The administration urged that Argentina, Chile, Guatemala and Uruguay, all previously denied military and economic aid because of human rights violations, should have such assistance reinstated. U.S. delegates at the international development banks were directed not only to reverse the U. S. opposition to loans for authoritarian Latin American governments, but also for the Philippines and South Korea. In the United Nations and other international agencies, U.S. representatives emphasized Soviet human rights violations while largely ignoring comparably repressive actions by friendly authoritarian regimes; at the 37th session of The Commission on Human Rights in February, 1981, the United States voted with Argentina, Brazil and Ethiopia in an unsuccessful attempt to abolish the United Nations Working Group on Enforced or Involuntary Disappearances established the previous year. And the strategic post of Assistant Secretary of State for Human Rights remained conspicuously empty amid mounting rumors that the Human Rights Bureau would be either discarded or left to wither on the State Department vine.

Finally, in the late spring of 1981, Ernest Lefever was proposed by the White House as the new Assistant Secretary of State for Human Rights and Humanitarian Affairs. The American human rights community, normally a loose assembly of discrepant and even vying organizations, joined in a rare display of unity to mobilize Congressional and public opinion against the nomination. Despite overt Presidential endorsement, the Senate Foreign Relations Committee on June 5th voted 13-4 to reject the Lefever appointment and to provide the President with his first major defeat on a foreign policy issue.

President Reagan never withdrew the Lefever nomination. Indeed, even after the Senate Foreign Relations Committee overwhelmingly rejected his nomination, the White House continued to insist that he was "the man for the job." See Jerome J. Shestack, *The Rise and Decline of Human Rights in United States Foreign Policy*, 15 Colum. Human Rts. L. Rev. 19, 32-33 (1984). The candidate himself withdrew his name a month later. 37 Cong. Q. Almanac 153, 18-A (1981).

WHAT IS THE DIFFERENCE BETWEEN TOTALITARIAN AND AUTHORITARIAN?
WELL, A TOTALITARIAN GOVERNMENT ARRESTS, TORTURES AND MURDERS
UN
UN
AN AUTHORITARIAN GOVERNMENT, ON THE OTHER HAND...
LEAVES MANY OF THESE FUNCTIONS TO THE PRIVATE SECTOR
WASSERMAN© '81

Art Buchwald, *Moderate Repression*

Intl. Herald-Tribune, Dec. 20-21, 1980, at 16, cols. 1-2

WASHINGTON — The Reagan administration has a new approach to human rights which, while it won't affect anyone in the United States, may have some important ramifications for political prisoners around the world. The philosophy of the new approach was expressed recently by Prof. Jeanne Kirkpatrick of Georgetown University, who is a very influential Reagan adviser.

"If we are confronted with the choice between offering assistance to a moderately repressive autocratic government, which is also friendly to the United States, and permitting it to be overrun by a Cuban-trained, Cuban-armed, Cuban-sponsored insurgency, we would assist the moderate autocracy," Ms. Kirkpatrick was quoted as saying.

Nobody in his or her right mind would argue with that. The big question is, how far a moderately repressive autocratic government (MRAG) can go to keep the opposition down? New human rights guidelines will have to be written for the MRAG countries.

Right now the ambassadors of moderately repressive autocratic governments are being called home for Christmas to advise their juntas on what the new U.S. administration will expect of them in the human rights field.

"Colonels, I am happy to report that we can expect all the support we need from the United States to put down the political opposition, providing we can prove our repressive government is being threatened by Cuban intervention."

"Suppose we can't prove it?"

"They'll take our word for it, if we can produce confessions from our political opponents."

"Does that mean we can still resort to torture to exact the confessions?"

"In moderation. Obviously, a certain amount of torture has to be used but we can't overdo it."

"Can we still beat political prisoners with truncheons?"

"Of course that is acceptable. But attaching electrical wires to a person's intimate parts can only be done under the supervision of a doctor."

"What about dunking them in water until they almost drown?"

"If it's done with compassion. But I think we better stay away from pulling out the fingernails, at least at the beginning of the Reagan term."

"Can we continue summary executions without trials?"

"Nobody in the Reagan transition team has spoken out against them. From all I can gather, the U.S. will no longer interfere in our justice system."

"Thank God. Does that mean we can still throw writers, editors and students into prison without have our military aid cut off?"

"I believe that the U.S. would encourage it as long as we can prove they are a threat to the regime."

"Will the secret police be able to get the latest equipment to put down terrorism in our country?"

"That goes without saying. If the United States wants to keep us as a friend, they're going to give us the tools to keep another regime from taking over."

"They're finally making some sense in Washington. As I see it, as long as we torture our opponents in moderation and repress our people for their own good, and only shoot the people who deserve it, we can have good relations with the United States again."

"Colonels, I don't know about the rest of you, but as head of the Moderate Repressive Junta I recommend we give human rights a try."

International Commission of Jurists, *Human Rights and U.S. Foreign Policy*

35-38 (1984)

CHANGE IN THE ADMINISTRATION POSTURE

The strong opposition to the Lefever nomination from diverse sources — Congressional, public interest, academic and religious — precipitated a clamorous public debate. It revealed that the issue of human rights had a vocal constituency within and outside the Congress far deeper and wider than the new Washington policy-makers had anticipated. The Carter program against which they had leveled their most scathing criticisms had proven to have generated extensive support at home and abroad which could not be casually disregarded. A decided moderation in the tone and nature of official rhetoric ensued which amounted to a virtual repudiation of earlier policy declarations.

In June, soon after the Lefever rejection, Secretary of State Haig delivered a major address in Washington entitled "Human Rights and American Interests" to the Trilateral Commission. "Human rights are not only compatible with our national interests," he informed his audience, "they are the major focus of our foreign policy."

That same month, national security adviser Richard Allen assured a New York rally protesting the treatment of Jews in the Soviet Union that the Reagan foreign policy was "inescapably linked to human rights." . . .

In August, in a New Delhi speech on American foreign policy to an audience of Indian diplomats and scholars, Ambassador Kirkpatrick attacked what she described as the "myth" that the Reagan Administration was unconcerned about human rights.

The task of fashioning new directions in a complex international society had turned out to be neither so simple nor so easy as had been anticipated by the Reagan policy-makers. Academic abstractions conceived in secluded study centers were proving oddly discordant with the harsh realities of an untidy world. Emergent developments in disparate parts of the world were already impinging on U.S. foreign policy that gave pause to those who had once advanced sweeping ideological generalizations on categoric differences between authoritarian and totalitarian regimes as final policy truths. . . .

New Directives for Human Rights

But, nine months after the Reagan Administration had taken office, the symbolically important post of Assistant Secretary for Human Rights was still unfilled and the Bureau of Human Rights was virtually inoperative. . . .

A memorandum dated October 27, 1981, written by Assistant Secretary for International Organization Affairs Elliott Abrams . . . was sent to Secretary Haig which recommended a basic administration policy revision. The memorandum, Assistant Secretary Abrams later said, "crystallized recognition of a growing realization of the need for change. A consensus in key policy-making circles was built to introduce a revised approach and develop a more positive acceptance of human rights." The document, approved by Secretary Haig, affirmed:

> Human rights is at the core of our foreign policy because it is central to what America is and stands for. . . . Congressional belief that we have no consistent human rights policy threatens to disrupt important policy initiatives. . . . Our human rights policy must be at the center of our response. Overall foreign policy, based on a strong human rights policy, will be perceived as a positive force for freedom and decency. This policy must be applied even-handedly. If a nation, friendly or not, abridges freedom, we should acknowledge it. . . . Human rights is not advanced by replacing a bad regime with a worse one, or a corrupt dictator with a zealous communist politburo.

> A human rights policy means trouble, for it means hard choices which may adversely affect certain bilateral relations. At the very least, we will have to speak honestly about our friends' human rights violations and justify any decisions wherein other considerations (economic, military, etc.) are determinative. There is no escaping this without destroying credibility of our policy, or otherwise we would simply be coddling friends and criticizing foes.
>
> Despite the cost of such a human rights policy, it is essential.... While we need a military response to the Soviets to reassure our friends and allies, we also need an ideological response.... We seek to improve human rights performance wherever we reasonably can. We desire to demonstrate, by acting to defend liberty and identifying its enemies, that the difference between East and West is a crucial policy distinction of our times.

The memorandum recommended the appointment of Elliott Abrams as Assistant Secretary of State for Human Rights and Humanitarian Affairs, and noted that "H.A. [Humanitarian Affairs] should be designated the lead agency on human rights, not only for the Department but also for the Government, with a specific role providing policy guidance on human rights [to other relevant agencies]."

The Abrams nomination was reinforced by an unusual White House disclaimer which denied charges that human rights had been derogated in the Administration's foreign policy. "The promotion of liberty," President Reagan asserted, "has always been a central element of our nation's foreign policy. In my administration, human rights considerations are important in all aspects of our foreign policy." Then, in sharp contrast to the acrimonious debate that enveloped the Lefever nomination, the Senate Foreign Relations Committee on November 17 unanimously approved the Abrams appointment.

U.S. Institute of Peace, *Human Rights in the Pursuit of Peace: A 20 Year Assessment*

United States Institute of Peace Special Report (June 16, 1999)

ELLIOTT ABRAMS: THE REAGAN ADMINISTRATION

President Reagan's human rights policy started off on the wrong foot. The post of assistant secretary for human rights was left vacant for about eleven months after Reagan was inaugurated, and most administration officials thought that human rights policy was central to what they viewed as the failed foreign policy of the Carter administration.

Human rights policy to these officials meant antagonizing allies without giving much thought to whether their successors would be better and without considering what it meant to be a friend or enemy of the United States. Moreover, human rights policy was seen as a tool of the Left used to hurt abusers on the Right, but rarely applied with equal gusto to people like Fidel Castro. But that changed. Changes in senior officials had a positive impact, primarily George Schultz's arrival as secretary of state about a year and a half into the administration, and the appointment of an assistant secretary for human rights and of a deputy assistant secretary in 1981....

First, the Bureau was careful to examine what it could do as part of the U.S. government and to distinguish this from what the human rights movement could do. It did not view itself as equivalent to, or confuse itself with, movement activists, nor did the Bureau confuse itself with the cause of human rights. Sometimes it was vocally critical of a regime, and sometimes it was not, depending on its view of the tactics most likely to advance the cause. Bureau officials believed that the U.S. government had one function to perform and the NGOs a different one.

Second, Bureau officials viewed themselves as part of the government and part of the State Department and did not see themselves as working in opposition to it. It was important to maintain good relations with other bureaus of the department, particularly the regional bureaus, and other agencies outside the State Department so as to restore the influence of the Bureau. In this, we succeeded.

Third, the Bureau's most useful activity was not to protest abuses or to isolate the United States from them. Rather, the goal was to improve respect for human rights, and that sometimes meant working, for example, alongside a government like that of President José Napolean Duarte in El Salvador to reduce abuses. There was less inclination, therefore, to cut off military-to-military contacts, because so often the military were the human rights abusers. Opportunities needed to be available in order to influence and change their behavior. Guatemala is an interesting case here. The reason that human rights abuses declined more substantially in El Salvador than in Guatemala was that the United States was present. We had tremendous influence in El Salvador, and we used it. In Guatemala, where we had essentially no aid and no military presence, we were unable to encourage them to reduce human rights abuses nearly as much.

Sustained progress required the building of institutions. Thus, the promotion of democracy became central to Reagan policy, as he made clear in his famous speech to Parliament in London (the Westminster speech), where he outlined what eventually became the National Endowment for Democracy with its four subordinate institutions. Reagan policy began to focus more on building institutions than on protesting human rights abuses, in part because we believed that the NGOs were very good at the protests but not very good at the institution-building.

Fourth, it was clear that the greatest threat to human rights in the world in the early and mid-1980s was Soviet communism. Abuses were rampant nearly everywhere in the world, but there was only one great power organized along totalitarian lines and aggressively seeking to expand totalitarian systems. Thus, the fight against communism was not a hindrance to or marginal to the struggle for human rights. It was critical to that struggle. As we head into the next century, that has changed. One of the interesting questions we must now examine is: What is replacing communism as a threat to liberty within the context of the formulation of U.S. human rights policy? Perhaps it is ethnic and religious intolerance.

. . . If one were going to do a case study of distinct change in Reagan policy, however, maybe the best single case would be the Philippines, where the administration began without a human rights policy. In fact, it is fair and accurate to say that when President Ferdinand Marcos made his 1982 visit to Washington, the term "human rights" was not uttered in his presence. The Department generally took the view that human rights was something that could not be mentioned in front of this man because it was too offensive to him. Later, the administration and President Reagan himself came to have a very different view of the situation in the Philippines and supported efforts to remove Marcos.

The Bureau was very active in Latin America, particularly in Chile. It was in no small part Reagan administration pressure that forced or led General Pinochet into holding the plebiscite that led to his departure. Historically it is a fact that when President Reagan entered office, virtually all of Latin America was under military rule. When he left office, almost none of it was. This is partly because the Reagan administration, given its own ideological stance, had the ability to delegitimize regimes — most military regimes, particularly those of Pinochet and Stroessner — which argued that their oppression was the only alternative to communism. When the Reagan administration disputed this opinion and held that democracy was in fact the alternative to communism, that their regimes were the problem, not the solution, their intellectual and moral defenses slowly disappeared. And soon they too were gone.

. . . That did not mean there would be no debate about how human rights fit into foreign policy and which tactics would be more effective. In fact it meant precisely the opposite. It meant that henceforth there would always be debate about how human rights and foreign policy are integrated. The subject of human rights is here to stay at the center of American foreign policy. . . .

Jack Donnelly: Critique of the Reagan Administration

To say that the Reagan administration got off on the wrong foot is certainly correct. It consciously, however, chose to put that foot forward. President Reagan entered office intent less on fixing Carter's mistakes than on expunging human rights from U.S. foreign policy (and replacing it on international agendas with antiterrorism). The assistant secretary position remained vacant largely because of disinterest in filling it. George Schultz's arrival as secretary was a change in personnel that brought a welcome shift in policy.

It is also correct that there was a relatively coherent, if narrow, human rights policy during Reagan's last six years in office. I would even suggest that the administration's most significant legacy was turning human rights into an ordinary part of U.S. foreign policy. In 1980, the central question was whether human rights belonged in American policy. By 1988, the question across the political spectrum was what the substance of U.S. international human rights policy ought to be.

Much of the credit for this change, however, belongs with Congress and human rights advocates, whose pressure the Reagan administration largely resisted. This was most evident in Central America, where the administration did the absolute minimum on human rights needed to allow it to pursue its other, often rights-abusive, foreign policy objectives. . . . Furthermore, given the belief expressed in the Kirkpatrick doctrine that totalitarian regimes were incapable of fundamental change, the administration's efforts to focus attention on Soviet bloc governments meant concentrating its efforts where it expected the least impact — and where United States responsibility for violations was lowest as well. Whatever its other attractions, this certainly did not provide a sound focus for a human rights policy.

Two other prominent shortcomings of the Reagan administration, however, illustrate problems shared to varying degrees by Carter, Bush, and Clinton — and thus might be called elements of a characteristic American myopia on human rights. The first is an exaggerated faith in elections, which too often are presented as a solution rather than a start — and in places like Guatemala and El Salvador during the Reagan administration, very modest starts indeed. Liberalization was (and continues to be) confused with democratization and even democracy. Democracy, understood largely in electoral terms, was (and continues to be) conflated with, or even valued above, human rights. Consider, for example, the current title of the assistant secretary, where human rights has moved behind democracy (and barely in front of labor).

The second problem is a reluctance to recognize economic and social rights. (Even the Carter administration typically spoke of basic needs rather than economic and social rights.) The United States has increasingly preferred the gospel of markets, which the Reagan administration preached with special vigor. But in our (in many ways justifiable) zeal for markets, we often lose sight of their profound human rights defects which usually are tragically evident in the economic chiropractic of structural adjustment. Even if the "average" consumer benefits "in the long run," in the short run, many flesh-and-blood men, women, and children suffer, often intensely.

My final comment pertains to the familiar observation that Reagan set the parameters on the "Right" for future debates, much as Carter set those on the "Left." Without denying the distance between these points, it is also worth noting the similarities across the two administrations — and the Bush and Clinton administrations as well — especially in practice, and especially in the second half of their presidencies. They all (although to varying degrees) reveal a deep reluctance to sacrifice even minor economic interests, let alone security interests, for human rights; have been narrowly targeted on the rights to life and personal security (plus elections); and have relied largely on verbal and symbolic initiatives. These similarities reflect both a narrow vision of and a low priority for human rights. . . .

Note: Key Differences in Human Rights Policy Under Carter and Reagan

The above readings provide ample ammunition for arguments for and against the Reagan Administration's human rights policy. This Note highlights three key differences between the Reagan and Carter approaches to international human rights and their invocation in the foreign policy process.

First, the Reagan Administration redefined international human rights specifically to exclude economic and social rights. Ambassador Kirkpatrick launched a scathing attack on such rights, which are mentioned in the Universal Declaration and set out in great detail in the International Covenant on Economic, Social, and Cultural Rights (signed by President Carter on 5 October 1977 but never ratified), claiming somewhat patronizingly that "no great reflection produced them," and that they were no more than a "letter to Santa Claus," based upon "a vague sense that Utopia is one's due." Jeanne J. Kirkpatrick, *Establishing a Viable Human Rights Policy*, 143 World Aff. 323, 332 (1981). While these rights may partake of the aspirational, they have been deemed rights by the international community in numerous norm-setting international human rights instruments and, hence, are part of the international law of human rights. For criticism of attempts to eliminate social and economic rights, see Jerome J. Shestack, *An Unsteady Focus: The Vulnerabilities of the Reagan Administration's Human Rights Policy*, 2 Harv. Hum. Rts. YB. 25, 39-45 (1989). Few observers would disagree with his conclusion that "[t]he Reagan Administration's failure to address economic and social rights either in its own or multilateral initiatives was a serious deficiency in its human rights record." Id. at 44.

Second, although the Reagan Administration sought to soft-pedal Ambassador Kirkpatrick's totalitarian/authoritarian distinction after the severe criticism it received during the first half of 1981, the Administration never really backed away from it. Indeed, it continued to endorse and apply it. Surveying the Administration's human rights performance in 1984, three leading NGOs noted critically that

> the Administration was vigorous in denouncing abuses in countries aligned with the Soviet Union or otherwise considered to be hostile by the United States. For the most part, those denunciations were well-deserved. Our only complaint about them is that they were not as effective as they might have been had they been part of an even-handed effort to promote human rights worldwide. Accordingly, the moral force of the U.S. denunciation was sharply reduced. This lack of evenhandedness made it possible for the countries criticized by the U.S. to respond by pointing to human rights abuses in countries defended by the United States. In addition, the U.S. was frequently ineffectual in enlisting support from other governments in denouncing abuses because those governments perceived the U.S. as using human rights as a way of pursuing other agendas.
>
> In the case of governments aligned with the United States, the Administration's policy and practice were entirely different. In general, the Administration avoided denunciations of even the grossest abuses. . . .

Americas Watch, Helsinki Watch, and the Lawyers Committee for Human Rights, *The Reagan Administration's Human Rights Record in 1984*, at 1-2 (Jan. 1985). This double standard did little to enhance the credibility of the Reagan Administration's human rights policy. In the waning days of the President's second term, he explicitly repudiated this approach, finally rejecting the totalitarian/authoritarian distinction that had driven over seven years of his Administration's human rights policy. Leslie H. Gelb, *U.S. Vows to Resist Despots of Right as Well as of Left*, N.Y Times, Mar. 14, 1988, at A1.

The third shift centers on the response of the executive branch to Congressional mandates. As noted above, from the mid-1970s, Congress had crafted a number of laws designed to restrict the flow of U.S. economic and military assistance to states engage in gross violations of human rights. The purpose of such laws is to encourage the Executive Branch to put pressure on such states to improve their human rights records or, at the very least, to distance the United States from their human rights violations. Even under the Carter Administration, these attempts to influence U.S. human rights policy had relatively little effect. In an insightful first-hand study, a former (1978-1980) Deputy Assistant Secretary of State for Human Rights and Security Assistance observed that "[t)he history of section 502B is a case study of executive frustration of congressionally mandated foreign policy and underlines the need, particularly with this kind of legislation, for clearer directives, less discretion, and more assiduous congressional oversight." Roberta Cohen, *Conditioning U.S. Security Assistance on Human Rights Prac-*

tices, 76 Am. J. Intl. L. 246, 277 (1982). However, under the Reagan Administration these laws and other "country-specific" legislation were ignored or misapplied so frequently that the will of Congress was completely thwarted. The following reading, by a U.S. representative to the Commission on Human Rights during the Carter Administration, considers this frequent criticism of the Reagan Administration's human rights policy.

Jerome J. Shestack, *An Unsteady Focus: The Vulnerabilities of the Reagan Administration's Human Rights Policy*

2 Harv. Hum. Rts. YB. 25, 36-39 (1989)

In Congress, the Reagan Administration's lack of credibility was highlighted by its resistance to . . . laws linking United States security and economic aid to a nation's human rights policy. . . .

Neither the Carter Administration nor the Reagan Administration invoked the provisions of section 502B. But there were differences. The Carter Administration did not cut off security assistance under section 502B; however, without formally invoking section 502B, it used executive authority to deny security assistance to a number of nations. The Reagan Administration, however, did not follow section 502B, nor did it independently withhold security assistance to various right-wing governments engaged in patterns of human rights violations. . . .

The Carter Administration tried to comply with section 116 and reduced some aid levels because of human rights violations. The Reagan Administration, however, declined to implement section 116. In 1983, Assistant Secretary for Human Rights and Humanitarian Affairs Elliott Abrams said, "We are reluctant to use economic aid as a tool for our [human rights] policy." This reluctance became the policy. Except in a few cases involving leftist regimes, the Reagan Administration did not restrict aid because of human rights violations. . . .

Frustrated by the Reagan Administration's use of specious arguments to bypass general human rights legislation, Congress resorted to country-specific legislation. Such legislation addressed specific countries and established certain human rights conditions as the qualifications for security assistance. For example, the International Security and Development Cooperation Act of 1981 required the President regularly to certify that the Government of El Salvador had met four conditions: concerted and significant efforts to protect human rights; improved prevention of serious human rights abuses by the army; economic and political reforms; and progress towards free elections. However, in 1981, despite reports that Salvadoran forces murdered thousands of civilians, Reagan certified that El Salvador had met the four conditions. Congress was skeptical. Successive certifications were somewhat more forthcoming about human rights conditions but still were far from candid. Misuse of the certification process undermined the credibility of State Department witnesses before congressional committees.

Frustrated once again, Congress turned to "action-specific" legislation which responded to specific occurrences. For example, in November 1983, the Specter Amendment provided for a partial withholding of aid to El Salvador until the verdict was obtained (in May 1984) in the trial of the 1980 murder of four churchwomen from the United States. Congress found these action-specific measures easier to monitor than the more general certification procedures.

The point of this review is not to assess the pros and cons of the congressional limitations or of the certification process. The point is that Congress regarded the Administration's certifications as evasions of human rights legislation. Congress enacted a plethora of "country-specific" and "action-specific" statutes conditioning foreign aid on the satisfaction of human rights objectives because the Administration appeared unwilling to follow more general congressional directives. The Administration regularly complained about congressional interference in the specifics of foreign policy. But it was the Administration's blatant bypass of human rights legislation properly within the congressional prerogative that compelled these congressional directives.

3. Turning Down the Volume: The First President Bush

U.S. Institute for Peace, *Human Rights in the Pursuit of Peace: A 20 Year Assessment*

United States Institute of Peace Special Report (June 16, 1999)

JAMES BISHOP: THE (FIRST) BUSH ADMINISTRATION

Most of the policies, tools, and techniques that the Bush administration employed were developed in earlier administrations. One of the achievements of the Bush administration was that it made a concerted effort to improve working relations with the principal American human rights organizations. Bureau officials not only listened to them and sought their advice, but invited them to speak at the human rights training programs, which the Bureau established at the Foreign Service Institute for employees of all U.S. government agencies being assigned abroad.

The Bush administration's relationship with the NGO community improved to such a degree that in January 1993, representatives of Amnesty International and Human Rights Watch spoke appreciatively of the Bureau during congressional testimony. With regard to the tools employed by the Bush administration to stem or prevent abuses, Bush policy emphasized engagement by speaking extensively with foreign ambassadors, special envoys, and occasionally heads of state, and by issuing public statements from the podiums of the White House, State Department, and relevant international organizations. In the State Department, the human rights reports were strengthened, focusing additional attention on abuses of women and children and on infringements of religious liberty. The Bureau also denounced abuses of Gypsies and guest workers in Europe (to the dismay both of some of our allies and several of our senior U.S. envoys).

The Bureau also waged a battle within the administration to ensure that human rights were given prominence in the conduct of U.S. relations with problem states, and that sanctions were imposed when serious abuses took place. In quiet discussions with foreign governments, we set benchmarks as conditions for a normalization of relations in Southeast Asia and for resumption of suspended assistance in Kenya, Malawi, Guatemala, Mauritania, and elsewhere. We worked with our foreign counterparts to strengthen nascent human rights commissions in Mexico, Russia, Tunisia, and Morocco.

Having held the human rights portfolio at the U.S. mission to the United Nations, where he was one of Ambassador Jeanne Kirkpatrick's deputies, Assistant Secretary for Human Rights Richard Schifter was committed to seeing the UN Human Rights Commission focus on human rights abuses per se, rather than continue to duplicate the political debate more properly within the mandates of the Security Council and the General Assembly. The Bureau's credibility in this area was enhanced by the Bush administration's success in persuading the Senate to ratify the International Covenant on Civil and Political Rights and the House of Representatives to begin work on implementing language for the torture convention. In the UN Human Rights Commission, Schifter paid special attention to the annual election of new members and tried to influence the outcome. Building on personal relationships with envoys from developing countries he had established in Washington, New York, and Geneva, Schifter encouraged them to break ranks with proponents of regional solidarity, frequently egregious human rights violators themselves. He cultivated envoys from the states emerging from the Soviet empire and from the transformed governments of Eastern Europe.

Inevitably, there were frustrations, but there were also successes, including condemnation of Sudan by the General Assembly for its dismal human rights performance. For the first time in its history, the UN Human Rights Commission held extraordinary sessions focused on violations of human rights in Bosnia. Schifter tried with little luck to reform the notoriously inefficient UN Human Rights Commission in Geneva, but his attention to the selection of rapporteurs to investigate serious abuses paid off significantly when his friend Max van der Stoel was selected to investigate those of Saddam Hussein's regime. The former Dutch foreign minister's very detailed reports help preserve international opposition to the Iraqi government. The Bureau, which at that time was called Human Rights and Humanitarian Affairs, sometimes used the humanitarian mandate — lost when the Clinton administration reorganized the Bureau — to call attention to humanitarian crises others in the administration preferred to ignore. Bureau officials were outspoken in pressing for military intervention in Somalia. Over the objections of the Bureau of International Organizations and of Secretary James Baker himself when he became aware of what was afoot, the Bureau joined the State Department's Africa Bureau and USAID's Office of Foreign Disaster Assistance in pressing for UN military intervention. When it became evident that hundreds of thousands were still dying because the UN force was too small and too poorly resourced to be militarily effective, the Bureau pressed for U.S. military intervention. Unfortunately, when U.S. military forces were dispatched, they were sent, contrary to our advice, to Mogadishu, instead of to the famine-stricken south central region of Somalia. When thousands of Haitians began boarding rafts and unseaworthy boats, the Bureau accepted the evidence that most were economic migrants while urging that screening procedures be improved on the U.S. vessels intercepting them. There was much concern about the presumed effect of American sanctions, and, in retrospect, the Bureau was perhaps too easily persuaded by the humanitarian agencies that U.S. food and medical assistance was compensating for the impact of sanctions on the country's poorest.

Bosnia was both a humanitarian and a human rights crisis. The Bureau's most significant activity was to initiate collection of evidence of human rights abuses from the victims. Reports of debriefings by Foreign Service officers of concentration camp survivors, torture victims, and raped women were summarized, edited to protect the identity of the vulnerable, and then transmitted to the United Nations.

These reports became the beginnings of the evidentiary base now being used by the War Crimes Tribunal.... With the end of the "red menace," the "green banner" of Islam was seen by some within the administration as a major threat to American interests. To avoid self-fulfilling prophecy, the Bureau brought speakers into the State Department to help educate colleagues to the nuances of Islamic fundamentalism....

In responding to human rights violations by military establishments abroad, the Bush administration used both conventional and innovative approaches. When the Thai military suppressed pro-democracy demonstrations with loss of life, Bureau officials pressed successfully for suspension of joint exercises and high-level military visits. Ultimately democratic forces triumphed. Wholesale destruction of Kurdish villages by Turkish troops led the Bureau to call for a ban on transfer of U.S. military equipment that would be used for counterinsurgency purposes. Worried that angered Turkish politicians might restrict use of Turkish air bases, from which the no-fly zone in northern Iraq was being enforced, the U.S. embassy in Ankara insisted that the equipment in question really was for potential use against the Syrians or Iranians. Although the Bureau had reports from the military attaches clearly stating the counterinsurgency intent, we lost, and the Turks were given more surplus American military helicopters....

In several of the high-profile human rights issues, the Bush administration took considerable heat from a dissatisfied human rights community. In one case, the Bureau resisted an aid cutoff in Peru, in the belief that, in the absence of aid, the human rights situation would deteriorate should a terrorist overthrow of the government take place. In retrospect, I believe that the administration made the right decision in having stood by the Fujimori government as it defended the population from the Sendero Luminoso.

The Bureau did not fight the renewal of most favored nation treatment for China, believing that normal trade relations would foster improved human rights conditions. The Bureau did attempt to condition it on human rights reforms, dismantling the sanctions regime imposed after Tiananmen Square. While the subsequent history of this issue shows that the pace of reform has been very disappointing, it also suggests that opportunism underlay much of the criticism the administration took from its domestic political opponents....

... Some of the policies did not achieve their anticipated objectives, but Bush policy was honest and consistent. Some may have disagreed with certain policy decisions, but what they saw was what they got, not a smokescreen designed to obscure U.S. policy or the absence thereof. Using innovative tools, President Bush pushed human rights further to the forefront of U.S. foreign policy implementation.

No discernable pattern emerged with respect to the role of human rights in the foreign policy process during President George Bush's four years in office. Unlike the Carter Administration, where both the President and his Secretary of State spoke out forcefully for human rights shortly after assuming office, the Bush Administration's principal officials made no major speeches and adopted no new or innovative policies. That President Bush would continue the status quo of the last years of the Reagan Administration could be gleaned from his reappointment of Ambassador Richard Schifter as Assistant Secretary of State for Human Rights and Humanitarian Affairs. His views on the role of human rights in the foreign policy process had been widely publicized (see, e.g., Richard Schifter, *Building Firm Foundations: The Institutionalization of United States Human Rights Policy in the Reagan Years*, 2 Harv. Human Rts. Y.B. 3 (1989)), and apparently the President felt comfortable with them. "Fine tuning" rather than striking new policies was the order of the day.

Although there were exceptions — the successful effort to achieve ratification of the Civil and Political Covenant, ironically long opposed by Ambassador Schifter, was one — the Bush Administration pursued few new initiatives in the human rights area and responded in languid fashion to one of the major human rights crises during its four years in office: the massacre of protesting Chinese civilians in Tiananmen Square. President Bush's patently inadequate response to the massacre is confirmed by the remarkedly candid account of none other than Ambassador Schifter, given years later at a symposium at Harvard Law School (East Asian Legal Studies, *Human Rights and Foreign Policy* 13-15 (1994)).

> During the late 1970s, the United States government largely ignored China's human rights problems. Throughout the Reagan Administration, "our expectation was that China was on a course that would inevitably result in a loosening of restrictions and compel increased adherence to human rights. Together with our concern to maintain the PRC's goodwill during the Cold War, that caused us not to let human rights concerns intrude into our relations with China." In essence, through both the Carter and Reagan years, "we did try to report accurately on human rights in China, but we did nothing about them."
>
> "Then came Tiananmen Square." The initial response of the American government suggested that human rights concerns had become "sufficiently infused into U.S. policy for the bureaucracy to respond effectively." Various statutorily required measures, including an end to the sale of military equipment and a curtailment of most World Bank lending to China, went into effect. "From the general behavior of my colleagues, including those in the State Department's East Asian Bureau, I had the distinct impression in early June 1989 that we were going to pursue human rights concerns regarding China as we had regarding the Soviet Union."
>
> Mr. Schifter, in what he characterized as the first public description of his thoughts about the "evolution of China policy under the Bush Administration," underscored that this new, more vigorous policy did not come about for the reason that "the China desk officer sat in the Oval Office." President Bush "most assuredly found the arrest and torture of students for the advocacy of democracy to be abhorrent, but he simply did not believe that it was sound policy for the United States to risk its relationship with the leaders of China. He never fully realized that the schoolboys and schoolgirls of the years that he had spent in Beijing had become adults, that many of them had been exposed to the ideas of democracy and respect for human rights, and that they had come to believe in and fight for them." Both the President and his National Security Advisor, Brent Scowcroft, "were sympathetic to the Kissinger approach to foreign policy, one that simply did not factor human rights considerations in policy formulation."
>
> The result, continued Mr. Schifter, "was that we sent mixed signals to China. We did what the law required, but we made no effort to coordinate a comprehensive China human rights policy with our allies as we had through the CSCE process with

regard to the Soviet Union." Most-favored-nation (MFN) status was not suspended. "But let us keep in mind that the law, under its terms at that time, was directed purely to emigration policy." US-led efforts on the multilateral front produced the initial restrictions on World Bank lending, but "after a while that unraveled. Whether we fought hard to prevent it from unraveling, I do not know for sure. I doubt that we did."

What was striking in the midst of this approach was that the "basic commitment to a human rights policy had by then sufficiently imbued the Foreign Service to keep alive a concern in spite of the clear lack of interest at high levels." The concern about China was further nourished by members of Congress from both parties, as well as the general public. "I do want to say that Asia Watch did a very good job in that regard, so that the Administration could not simply shrug off the human rights problems of China."

As a consequence, the idea of sending a "message to Beijing that we cared" did not fade away. The ongoing Congressional concern about renewal of MFN status "began after a time to have its impact on the Chinese," given how important the American market is for China's exports. The Chinese therefore agreed to receive Mr. Schifter in December of 1990 and again in November of 1991 for serious talks, as well as to continue these discussions in Washington through their embassy. Due to this, Mr. Schifter believes, "the number of people convicted was smaller and the sentences were shorter than they would have been without expressions of concern from the United States." Nevertheless, more could have been accomplished if we "had pressed harder and particularly if our allies had joined us in our protestations."

The lesson of the above tale is twofold: first, the human rights concerns initially pressed by President Carter had become institutionalized by the U.S. foreign policy bureaucracy in the late 1980s; second, despite this fact, little can be achieved in the way of pressuring a human rights violator to improve its record if there is "a clear lack of interest at high levels."

4. Searching for a Policy: The Clinton Administration

During the 1992 presidential campaign, candidate Bill Clinton never really addressed the role of human rights in the foreign policy process. He rarely used the phrase "human rights" in his foreign policy speeches but rather spoke of the need for a "pro-democracy foreign policy" that would foster democratic regimes (always with "market economies") abroad.

Initially, the new (or renewed) focus on democratization and its link to human rights drove a reorganization at the Department of State, which saw the former Bureau of Human Rights and Humanitarian Affairs transformed into the Bureau of Democracy, Human Rights, and Labor, one of four offices under the direction of a new Undersecretary of State for Global Affairs. Institutionally as well as symbolically, this change of names and commingling of duties caused some concern among the international human rights community, which feared that the focus on democratization might come at the expense of human rights. While neither President Clinton nor any other government official provided an authoritative elaboration of the link between democracy and human rights, the following two readings — testimony by Undersecretary of State Wirth and a speech by Assistant Secretary of State for Democracy, Human Rights, and

Labor Shattuck — give guidance as to the Administration's thinking in this regard and the role it considered human rights concerns should have in the foreign policy process.

Human Rights Policy Under the New Administration, Statement of the Honorable Timothy E. Wirth, Counselor, U.S. Department of State

Hearing and Markup of H. Res. 188 and H. Con. Res. 106, Before the Subcomm. on International Security, International Organizations and Human Rights of the House Comm. on Foreign Affairs, 103d Cong., 1st Sess. 6-8 (1993)

... Promoting respect for human rights worldwide is one of the pillars of this administration's foreign policy. By fostering pluralism and democracy around the world, we also lay the foundation for stability and economic progress that benefits us as well as others. By working to ensure that other governments respect the rights of their citizens, we create a safeguard against threats to international peace and security. ...

The desire to enjoy the full range of human rights is universal. We respect the national ethnic, religious, and cultural differences that make countries unique. However, where you live should not determine whether you will be imprisoned, tortured, or killed merely for expressing your beliefs.

While a growing number of countries do respect these rights, they continue to be under severe challenge in many other countries, including Bosnia, Burma, China, Cuba, Iran, Iraq, North Korea, and Sudan.

The U.N. World Conference on Human Rights, which ... will take place over the next 2 weeks, June 14 to 25, represents an important opportunity for the Clinton administration and for the U.S. Government to show U.S. support for the popular movements for freedom and democracy that are emerging all over the world in this post-cold war era. ...

We cannot afford to take a business as usual approach to human rights. The administration has made human rights a key component of its foreign policy. And we intend to follow up that policy with activism to advance the cause of human rights. And one of the most important ways that we can do this is to strengthen the U.N. systems for dealing with human rights.

We have worked closely with nongovernmental human rights organizations to develop an action plan to improve the United Nation's effectiveness in addressing and resolving human rights problems. And that draft action plan has been made available to members of the committee.

This plan figures prominently in our strategy for the conference next week in Vienna. And I would like to summarize briefly for you some of the components of that plan.

First, we want to ensure greater effectiveness of the U.N. Human Rights Center, and its advisory services and reporting activities.

Second, we hope to better target U.N. assistance toward helping nations establish the rule of law, eliminate torture, and resolve ethnic, religious, and racial conflict.

Third, we believe that we must integrate more fully the rights of women and children system-wide throughout the United Nations, and support the appointment of a Special Rapporteur on Violence against Women.

Fourth, we believe that the capacity of the United Nations to promote democracy will be increased by assisting in the conduct of elections and improving the administration of justice.

Fifth, we believe that human rights considerations should be integrated in the U.N. activities, such as peacekeeping, refugee protection, conflict resolution, and development of humanitarian programs.

And finally, we believe that an office of a U.N. High Commissioner for Human Rights should be created as a means of improving the effectiveness of the United Nations in implementing human rights standards....

We must, of course, look beyond the world conference to the longer term. The ambitious American agenda will not be completed in Vienna, nor should we expect it to be. However, we can work with other nations to reaffirm our commitment to those fundamental principles; to implement them around the world; and to isolate, Mr. Chairman, those renegade countries who are backsliding and who are using this conference and using other discussions of national sovereignty as a way of covering up and hiding their own egregious human rights abuses....

John Shattuck, *Human Rights and Democracy in Asia*

5 U.S. Dept. State Dispatch 480, 480-481 (July 18, 1994)

U.S. Policy on Human Rights and Democracy

Protecting human rights and promoting democracy are integral elements of U.S. foreign policy for two distinct but closely related reasons. First, respect for human rights in the processes of government and law reflects fundamental values, which not only have played a major role in shaping America's world view but also represent binding and universal principles as expressed in the Universal Declaration of Human Rights and, more recently, at last year's Vienna conference. Second, human rights protection serves far-reaching, long-term interests of the U.S., its trading partners and allies, and, indeed, the entire international community.

We know from historical experience that democracies are more likely than other forms of government to respect human rights; to settle conflicts peacefully; to observe international law and honor agreements; to go to war with great reluctance and rarely against other democracies; to respect the rights of ethnic, racial, and religious minorities; and to provide the social and political basis for free market economies.

Open societies make for better and more stable trading partners because they tend to honor agreements and provide reliable systems of justice. By contrast, repressive regimes foster instability in the long run and put investment at great risk of expropriation or loss.

By contrast, the costs to the world of repression and authoritarianism are painfully clear. In the 20th century, the number of people killed by their own governments under authoritarian regimes is four times the number killed in all this century's wars combined. Repression pushes refugees across borders and triggers wars, and unaccountable governments are heedless of environmental destruction.

We do not seek to replicate America's unique society around the world. Rather, we promote accountable government, a free press, effective judiciaries, and the rule of law. We encourage the development of civil society — of civic, religious, trade, and social groups — that creates breathing room for society to develop apart from the state and affords individuals and communities the greatest opportunity for growth.

The Clinton Administration is incorporating human rights and democracy into the mainstream of our foreign policy. We encourage institutions of accountability that will hold violators to account. Examples include the UN War Crimes Tribunal for the former Yugoslavia, the Truth Commission in El Salvador, and administration of justice programs in many countries, including in Latin America, Russia, and other states of the former Eastern bloc.

We are working to build new multilateral institutions to address racial, ethnic, and religious conflict — institutions that can work to defuse conflicts before they lead to gross violations of human rights. We are especially involved in pursuing cooperation with regional groups to create mechanisms of conflict resolution and are actively engaged in supporting initiatives by the OAU, OAS, and the CSCE. We are integrating, for the first time, women's rights into all aspects of our human rights policy.

We are working to meet U.S. international human rights obligations by pressing for the ratification of a number of pending international treaties and conventions. Thanks to our efforts, the Senate recently ratified the convention on the elimination of race discrimination, which had been languishing for years.

We led the effort in the UN to create a UN High Commissioner for Human Rights, and we are working with other states to improve the functioning of the UN Human Rights Commission. Finally, and perhaps above all, we are strengthening our relationship with non-governmental organizations striving to promote democracy and human rights around the globe.

While the above two readings rightly stress the importance of promoting democracy and protecting human rights, they are less than crystal clear about the relationship between and relative importance of the two concepts. Many members of the human rights community, it was reported, were "uncomfortable with a dual approach and argue that human rights alone, not democracy promotion, should be the centerpiece of the Clinton administration's foreign policy." Thomas Carothers, *Democracy and Human Rights: Policy Allies or Rivals*?, 17 Wash. Q. 109, 110 (1994). The prime difference, these human rights advocates pointed out, is one of law versus politics.

> For many in the human rights movement there is a very significant difference in formal status between human rights and democracy: human rights are international legal norms whereas democracy is a political ideology. In their view, U.S. government pressure on a foreign government to improve its human rights behavior is a form of entirely legitimate intervention in the internal affairs of that country because human rights norms are binding under international law on all states. By contrast,

> they consider that U.S. pressure on a foreign government to become democratic is of questionable legitimacy because democracy is just one of a number of competing political ideologies, not a binding obligation. Democracy promotion by the U.S. government, they hold, constantly runs the risk of veering off into neo-imperialism.

Id. at 111.

According to the former executive director of Human Rights Watch, "the Reagan-Bush emphasis on democracy often seemed not only a means of manipulating human rights for political purposes, . . . but also a pretext for not taking a strong stand on systematic violations of core human rights in countries identified [often too optimistically] as democratic." Arieh Neier, *Asia's Unacceptable Standard*, Foreign Pol'y 42, 48 (No. 92, Fall 1993). To some extent, the human rights camp remains split as to whether to embrace pro-democracy initiatives in addition to traditional human rights concerns. As Neier maintains:

> The Universal Declaration of Human Rights does commit the countries of the world to representative government, and the International Covenant on Civil and Political Rights commits the 120 [now approximately 150] countries that are party to it to periodic free and fair elections. Nevertheless, there is division within the movement about whether human rights organizations should promote democracy. Some fear that associating themselves with the espousal of democracy would align them with the political opponents of nondemocratic governments and, thereby, diminish their credibility in criticizing violations of core human rights. Others consider that support for the right of citizens to take part in self-government is legitimate in that it is analogous to, and an extension of, their efforts on behalf of the freedom of expression recognized in international law. Even those within the movement who fall into the latter camp readily agree, however, that promoting democracy is far less central than stopping torture, murder, and disappearances.

Id.

Whatever the attitude of U.S. NGOs, promoting both democracy and human rights seems to be a wise choice politically, for it permits U.S. administrations to justify their actions on both fronts on national security grounds. See Thomas Carothers, *The Democracy Nostrum*, 11 World Poly. J. 47, 47-48 (No. 3, 1994):

> The notion of democracy promotion as security policy is of particular appeal to the Clinton team as a quintessential "New Democrat" idea. New Democrats are drawn to democracy promotion by their liberal instinct to do good in the world. Yet tempered by the experiences of the Carter human rights policies of the late 1970s, they want their do-good, moralistic instincts to withstand the judgmental fires of hardheaded realism. Casting democracy promotion as a form of war prevention, as a security enhancement, neatly squares this circle. Democracy promotion becomes a bridge spanning the traditional divide between liberal moralism and conservative realism.

President Clinton took a number of human rights initiatives that differentiated his Administration from those of his immediate predecessors: (1) he appointed a Secretary of State, an Undersecretary of State, and an Assistant Secretary of State all committed to an active and aggressive human rights policy; (2) he reversed the Reagan-Bush attitude toward economic, social, and cultural rights, once again recognizing that such rights are an integral part of the corpus of international human rights law; (3) he continued the process of seeking ratification of the backlog of human rights treaties pending for nearly 20 years; (4) he demonstrated a willingness to work with the United Nations in achieving human rights objectives, such as the establishment of the Yugoslav and Rwandan War Crimes Tribunal and the UN-authorized humanitarian intervention in Haiti; and (5) he encouraged the Department of State, after a 12-year hiatus, to reestablish good working relationships with the principal U.S. NGOs. Despite this record, there were those who saw considerable backsliding.

Mary McGrory, *Human Rights Retreat*

Wash. Post, July 7, 1994, at A1

In ways both great and small, the Clinton administration is signaling its retreat from human rights. When our "putting people first" president renewed most favored nation standing for China and practically apologized to Beijing for ever tying trade to human rights, he all but announced that the Republicans were right about human rights: It is a drag, it is inconvenient, it costs money.

Last week the Senate gave human rights the death of a thousand cuts, or to be more precise, a vote of 59 to 35 against a practical application in East Timor. The case is minuscule compared to China. Sen. Patrick J. Leahy (D-Vt.) offered a modest proposal that the United States specifically prohibit the use of U.S.-provided arms in East Timor, the wretched island where Indonesia is diligently practicing ethnic cleansing in the hope of eliminating local resistance to an Indonesian takeover.

It figured that an administration that had swallowed the China camel was not about to strain over the gnat of East Timor.

Sen. J. Bennett Johnston (D-La.) led the victory against human rights. He got a notable assist from Deputy Secretary of Defense John M. Deutch and a last-minute letter from Secretary of State Warren Christopher, who called the Leahy initiative "unnecessary and inconsistent."

"We have raised our human rights concerns at the highest levels in meetings with Indonesia," wrote Christopher. Does it sound familiar? Yes, it is the "quiet diplomacy" that was so popular, and so ineffectual, during the Reagan-Bush years.

Johnston made the also familiar argument about size. Indonesia is big. It is the fourth-largest nation on Earth, he pointed out, the largest Muslim nation in the world. It has a correspondingly large market. Its feelings would be hurt if we indicated we disapproved of its bloody suppression of an island people.

Sen. Alan K. Simpson (Wyo.), the Republican whip, called Leahy's suggestion "arrogant intrusion." Of course, any attempts at behavior modification are invasions of sovereignty, and advocates of human rights don't deny it. The point of the policy was that the world's leading democracy feels that "a decent respect for the opinions of mankind," as it says in the Declaration of Independence, is a transcendent foreign policy consideration.

As the senators were busy proving the opposite, the Indonesian government was demonstrating the shortcomings of quiet diplomacy. Three periodicals were closed, and in the wake of the action, peaceful demonstrators were attacked by riot police and more than 50 people were arrested.

Auth © 1996 The Phildephia Inquirer. Reprinted by permission of Universal Press Syndicate.

Johnston conceded that "not everything taking place in Indonesia is encouraging . . . but Indonesia has made huge steps forward in human rights" without saying what they were.He also said that "if we are going to take sanctions against every country in the world that is criticized by Amnesty International . . . the list of our friends will be short indeed."

Another country severely criticized by Amnesty International as an egregious violator of human rights is being smiled upon by the Clinton administration. Turkey, which is abusing Kurds within its borders and building up an appalling record of death-by-torture — 24 last year — is being reprimanded only by human rights groups.

"The bottom lines are very similar to the Reagan and Bush years," says James O'Dea, director of Amnesty International's Washington office. "What Clinton is doing with Turkey is what Ronald Reagan did when he stepped up security assistance to El Salvador in the face of death squad killings: . . ."

In a five-page letter to Turkish Prime Minister Tansu Ciller, the president devoted one-half sentence to human rights. The House suggested cutting security assistance to Turkey by 25 percent; the president called the prime minister and bade her not to worry.

Turkey, like Indonesia, is considered in Clinton realpolitik a valuable ally in a strategic location.

Kerry Kennedy Cuomo, director of the Kennedy Human Rights Foundation, calls the action on Indonesia "a disaster — I don't see how it promotes democracy."

The president seems determined to exhibit hardheadedness in foreign policy, to put trade and "democracy-building" as top priorities. He rarely discusses human rights and with good reason. The evidence is building that if you don't put human rights at the top, it slides right off the screen.

Yet, when challenged, the administration people say they do too advocate human rights and a source on the National Security Council suggests that the decision on Indonesia, at least, will be revisited.

If it isn't, the cynicism the president so deeply deplores will be on the rise again.

5. National Security, Regime Change, and Human Rights: George W. Bush

For the United States — and particularly for new President George W. Bush — the events of September 11, 2001, were a watershed event. Many in the country argued that the United States needed to subordinate human rights at home and abroad to the requirements of national security, assuming that there was an inherent conflict between the two objectives. For others, addressing human rights deprivations throughout the world was a means to prevent terrorism from gaining further adherents. The administration placed considerable emphasis on pursuing democratic reform and market economy, belatedly using human rights deprivations as one justification for invading Iraq. The following readings describe the Bush Administration's policy and reactions to it.

Assistant Secretary of State for Democracy, Human Rights and Labor Lorne W. Craner, Supporting Human Rights and Democracy: The U.S. Record 2003-2004

Testimony before the House Committee on International Relations, Washington, DC, July 7, 2004, http://www.state.gov/g/dr/rls/rm/34255.htm

. . . In the three months since the release of the most recent Country Reports, much has happened. I would like to begin with the abuses at Abu Ghraib Prison. As an individual, and as the State Department's Assistant Secretary charged with advancing human rights abroad, I have been particularly appalled by the abuses that occurred there. They are unworthy of America. I've been pleased to see the Department of Defense pledge to take action against those individuals involved in such atrocious behavior, and take steps to ensure that similar acts do not occur again. Already, criminal prosecutions are underway, in addition to several different administrative investigations, and positive changes have been announced at Abu Ghraib. [Cf. the discussion of Abu Ghraib in Chapter 4, page 211.]

I've been asked if Abu Ghraib robs us of our ability to talk about human rights abroad. It's a reasonable question. How can we talk about human rights if we fail to uphold the highest standards? On May 17th when Deputy Secretary Armitage first released this new report, he noted that when President Bush expressed his deep disgust and regret about events at Abu Ghraib, it wasn't just his personal reaction as a man of principle. It was also his reaction as the head of state of a country that holds itself to a higher standard, both at home and in our conduct in the world. We will indeed find and expose the truth, and will hold all who bear responsibility for these shameful episodes fully accountable. And we will do everything in our power to ensure that such actions do not occur again. This is all that we ask other countries to do. In doing so, we are showing the world that we hold ourselves to the same standards of accountability for human rights abuses to which we hold them.

To those who wonder if we still possess the will to press for internationally accepted human rights standards and norms I would point to our actions on Darfur.... [The situation in Darfur is considered in Chapter 10.]

...This — coupled with the myriad human rights programs that the U.S. Government provides all around the world — is why we continue to create a constructive legacy that promotes and protects human rights and democracy. In places like Darfur — and Burma and Zimbabwe and Belarus and elsewhere — who would benefit, and who would pay the price if we self-consciously turned inward and ignored human rights abuses outside of our country?

Today, I am very pleased to formally present to Congress our report on "Supporting Human Rights and Democracy: The U.S. Record 2003-2004." This report provides examples of how we are engaged worldwide with people and institutions dedicated to advancing freedom, and how we are trying to help others around the world who want the same institutions we have: institutions that protect human rights and punish those who would violate them. The purpose of this report is to answer the question, "What are we doing about all those abuses in the Country Reports?"

Unlike the 196 individual Country Reports, this report highlights U.S. efforts to promote human rights and democracy in (by legislative mandate) those 101 countries and entities with the most serious human rights abuses. We take care to include places of concern for "extra judicial killings, torture, or other serious violations of human rights," as called for in the Foreign Relations Authorization Act of Fiscal Year 2003. To make this report consistent with the criteria in the legislation, this year's report also includes a number of additional countries and a few deletions from last year's edition.

Each report typically begins with a summary of the human rights conditions in the country referred to. This snapshot is not a complete picture of everything we know about the human rights conditions in the country; that is the purpose of the mother Country Reports.... This report is an overview of our efforts, not an exhaustive account of all U.S. Government efforts....

We employ a wide range of strategies to promote human rights and democracy. In societies that enjoy some measure of openness, we can and do employ a wider range of strategies to promote human rights and democracy. Many who follow these issues closely will recognize strategies that are "tried and true," that are part of our standard tool kit. Other strategies described in the report are innovative and represent the cutting-edge of democracy and human rights promotion, and we've highlighted some in this report: a school to enhance the leadership skills of East African women so that they can run for political office; the first independent printing press in Kyrgyzstan so that journalists can advance media freedom; halfway houses for former child soldiers in Colombia so that they can get off the battlefield and begin normal lives; a training academy for NGOs and others in Yemen to help enhance their democratic process.

Our ability to develop a mix of programs unique to each country where we are active is the result of careful study of the human rights situation and ideas generated by our collaboration with local activists and non-governmental organizations in these countries. By combining approaches that encompass the old and new, the tested and experimental, and top-down and bottom-up, we have the capability to address different situations more effectively....

In addition to all of the efforts I have already laid out, we also continue to engage and remain active at the UN Commission on Human Rights. . . .

In some cases we achieved our objectives at the Commission, evidenced by the passage of resolutions condemning human rights abuses in Cuba, North Korea, Burma, and Turkmenistan. In other cases, we met resistance from countries that would prefer to obscure their records, countries that claim that we have no right to raise concerns about human rights within their borders. But their protests did not, and do not, deter our effort to ensure that human rights are not swept under the rug.

Some ask: "Does it all work?" The answer is obvious: the support we've given for the past quarter century all over the world has helped usher in some of the most dramatic political changes in history. Twenty-five years ago, there were around 40 democracies in the world. Today, there are more than 120. In the 1980s in Latin America and in Eastern Europe, the U.S. Government sought to ensure that democratic reformers were given the oxygen they needed to bring about changes in countries like Chile, El Salvador, Poland, Taiwan and Hungary. In the 1990s, the United States supported South Africa's democracy movement, which helped produce a new era of freedom in a country that some believed would descend into chaos. And for the last decade, we've worked with opposition leaders and NGOs in places like Cuba and Burma and Zimbabwe, and also in places like Georgia, where last year, the time and the energy and the heart of our effort, and the effort of so many others, culminated in the peaceful Revolution of Roses.

Many challenges remain, and we in this Administration have not shrunk from taking them on. . . .

Don Feder, *Human Rights Not a Foreign Policy Concern*

Boston Herald, Mar. 11, 2002

The State Department's 26th annual country report on human rights should have come with a caveat: The purpose of U.S. foreign policy is protecting the security of Americans, not crusading for goodness abroad.

Harsh? Perhaps.

But it's a cold world out there, filled with wolves snapping at our heels. To thwart them, at times we have to ally ourselves with unsavory characters. (Think of Stalin in World War II or Central American juntas in the '80s.) The way they treat their people should be the concern of ministers and moralists, not diplomats.

The State Department spent thousands of pages analyzing human rights in almost 190 countries. The net result of all this breast-beating will be zilch. America's foreign policy will continue to be guided by military necessity, trade or other considerations unrelated to secret police and torture cells.

On those occasions when human rights played a major role in shaping our foreign policy, the results were catastrophic.

In the '70s, President Jimmy Carter (whose administration could have doubled as a revival meeting) decided the Shah of Iran was being beastly to dissident Shiite clerics. The U.S. hedged on its support for a loyal ally. Iran ended up in the arms of lunatic theocrats who've destabilized the region and spread terror abroad. Give me a pro-American autocrat any time.

Under ex-president and human-rights poser Bill Clinton, we twice intervened in Yugoslavia, creating a nation in Bosnia and a Western protectorate in Kosovo, reportedly to end ethnic cleansing. Bosnia has been infected with Moslem fanaticism. Kosovo's Albanians engaged in ethnic cleansing themselves. Both have harbored terrorists.

Somalia, Haiti — these are not high points in U.S. diplomacy.

Efforts like the State Department survey distract us from what should be the sole focus of our foreign policy — protecting the human rights of Americans by guaranteeing their security.

The report devotes 103 pages to the People's Republic of China. But the problem with the PRC isn't its brutal suppression of dissent or toxic treatment of the Falun Gong meditators.

China is an aggressive power, hostile to the West, that's developing a deep-water navy and helping Third World thugs acquire weapons of mass destruction. It could end up starting World War III over its obsession with Taiwan. Beijing's human-rights abuses concern us as individuals. Its military/foreign policy concerns us as a nation.

The Foggy Bottom boys approvingly note improvements in Afghanistan following the end of Taliban rule. Again, the challenge Afghanistan posed for the civilized world was the fact that it had become bin Laden's boot camp — a raging infection pumping its poison into the international bloodstream — not its Neanderthal attitude toward women.

In its section on "Israel and the Occupied Territories," the report reads like a parody. The only democracy in the Middle East, a nation that has always respected minority rights, is condemned for not conducting its fight for survival strictly according to the Marquess of Queensberry's rules.

The reports cites "credible anecdotal evidence" that as many as several thousand Palestinians have encountered abusive treatment at Israeli checkpoints.

Well, excuse me while I brush away the tears. Every few days, one of these blokes blows himself up on a busy street, slaughtering civilians in the process, or sprays bullets into a crowded restaurant.

When news of Sept. 11 reached Ramallah, Palestinians did an end-zone victory dance in the streets — thereby condoning the ultimate human rights abuse inflicted on 3,000 innocents.

The State Department's solicitude for a people that revels in mass murder makes as much sense as European whining because the Guantanamo vermin don't have POW status. Exterminators don't read roaches their rights before they start spraying.

As individuals, we can and should protest human-rights abuses wherever they occur. Washington should try to effect change in governments susceptible to our influence. But like our special forces fighting in Afghanistan, the first order of business is to assure our nation's survival. Human rights will not improve if America fails.

Michael Ignatieff, *Is the Human Rights Era Ending?*

N.Y. Times, Feb. 5, 2002, at A25

Since the end of the cold war, human rights has become the dominant moral vocabulary in foreign affairs. The question after Sept. 11 is whether the era of human rights has come and gone.

If that sounds alarmist, consider some of the evidence. Western pressure on China to honor human rights, never especially effective, has stopped altogether. Chinese support for the war on terror has secured Western silence about repression in the Xinjiang region. China now says it has a problem there with Islamic fundamentalists and terrorists, and it is straining to link them to Al Qaeda.

Meanwhile, Chancellor Gerhard Schröder of Germany, presented with evidence of Qaeda involvement in Chechnya, calls for a "differentiated evaluation" of Russian policy there. This new evaluation seems certain to involve forgetting that Moscow's war against terror has actually been waged against a whole people, costing tens of thousands of lives.

A similar chill is settling over world politics. Australia's government uses the threat of terrorism to justify incarcerating Afghan refugees in a desert compound. Tajikistan and Uzbekistan have leveraged their provision of bases and intelligence into a carte blanche for domestic repression. Egypt, which for many years has used detention without trial, military courts and torture to keep control of militants, now demands an even freer hand. Sudan, which was under attack from a coalition of liberals and black churches determined to end slavery and stop Khartoum's war against the south, is now accepted as an ally against Osama bin Laden. And President Robert Mugabe of Zimbabwe has decided that his longtime political opponents are really "terrorists."

Human Rights Watch has condemned these developments as opportunism, but something more durable than that may be at work. Rome has been attacked, and Rome is fighting to re-establish its security and its hegemony. This may permanently demote human rights in the hierarchy of America's foreign policy priorities.

Of course, just because the United States has other priorities doesn't have to mean that, in global terms, the era of this movement is over. Human rights has gone global by going local, anchoring itself in struggles for justice that can survive without American inspiration or leadership. The movement does not have its headquarters in Washington. But if Washington turns away, the movement loses the one government whose power can be decisive in stopping human rights abuses. . . .

Some veterans of the human rights campaigns of the cold war refuse to admit that the climate is any worse now than it was then. But in the Reagan years, the movement merely risked being unpopular. In the Bush era, it risks irrelevance.

Divided between horror at the attacks and alarm at being enlisted as moral cheerleaders in a war on terror, many European human rights groups are sitting on the sidelines. American groups like Human Rights Watch have turned themselves into war reporters, subjecting American military conduct to tough scrutiny on issues ranging from prisoner detention to collateral damage. Still others have teamed up with civil libertarians to defend rights and freedoms at home.

But the movement will have to engage soon in the battle of ideas: it has to challenge directly the claim that national security trumps human rights. The argument to make is that human rights is the best guarantor of national security. The United States, to encourage the building of secure states that do not harbor or export terror, will have to do more than secure base agreements. It will have to pressure these countries to provide basic political rights and due process. As the cold war should have taught us, cozying up to friendly authoritarians is a poor bet in the long term. America is still paying a price for its backing of the shah of Iran. In the Arab world today, the United States looks as if it is on the side of Louis XVI in 1789; come the revolution in Egypt or Saudi Arabia, American influence may be swept away.

The human rights movement is not in the business of preserving American power. But it should be concerned about stability, about moving strategically vital states like Egypt and Saudi Arabia from closed to open societies without delivering them up to religious fundamentalists. Nobody's rights in Egypt will be furthered if the state collapses into anarchy or fundamentalist absolutism. If the movement hopes to have a future, it has to advocate its objectives — freedom, participation, due process — in a way that addresses the necessity to create political stability. This doesn't mean suddenly going silent about arbitrary arrests and military courts. It means moving from denunciation alone to engagement, working with local activists, and with the parts of the government that will listen, moving these societies back from the precipice.

The movement aims at defending the rights of ordinary people. To do this, it has to help them construct strong civil societies and viable states. If it can't find new ways of achieving that goal, it will be remembered as a fashionable cause of the dim and distant 1990's.

Comments and Questions

1. Professor Bilder, writing in 1974, predicted that "international human rights considerations will not play a major role in U.S. foreign policy until government officials are persuaded that pursuit of these goals serves major national interests." Reviewing the "practical" reasons for supporting a human rights–oriented foreign policy, he concluded that "the problem of finding 'selfish' national interest reasons why governments such as the United States should be concerned with denials of human rights in other countries remains a basic one." Did President Carter or other key government officials in his administration ever identify and adequately explain those reasons? Were the explanations of the Clinton or Bush administrations any more enlightening or convincing? Review the justifications of the various administrations for "selfish" national interest reasons. What other reasons — "selfish" or otherwise — also might be advanced? Can a convincing argument be constructed to persuade the U.S. and other governments that they truly have a national interest in promoting and protecting human rights beyond their borders?

2. Bilder also observed that (as of 1974) human rights considerations were "relatively secondary factors" in the making of foreign policy decisions. Has that situation changed, and if so, to what extent, during the past three decades? Note that President Clinton, in his Milwaukee campaign speech, cautioned that "there may be times when other security needs or economic interests will diverge from our commitment to democracy and human rights. . . ." Does this caveat perhaps explain his decision to de-link trade and human rights insofar as China is concerned? Will a "waiver" of human rights principles in one instance not spark demands for similar "waivers" in other situations? If so, what should be the U.S. response? Is it possible to have a policy that will treat equally countries as diverse as Haiti and China?

3. The originator of the totalitarian/authoritarian distinction, former Secretary of State Kissinger, observed in 1977 that "[i]n recent decades no totalitarian regime has ever evolved into a democracy." The Introduction to the Department of State's Country Reports in 1983 noted that "the world has yet to witness the peaceful transformation of a single communist dictatorship into a democracy." Obviously, events in the former Soviet Union, Eastern Europe, and the Baltic states undercut the credibility of arguments based on the totalitarian/authoritarian distinction. Even if it once had some validity, is the distinction between totalitarian and authoritarian regimes now thoroughly discredited?

4. Did Jimmy Carter, Ronald Reagan, or George W. Bush make the following statement during his inaugural address: "Because we are free, we can never be indifferent to the fate of freedom elsewhere"? Which Secretary of State, Henry Kissinger or Cyrus Vance, said, "Human rights are the very essence of a meaningful life, and human dignity is the ultimate purpose of civil governments." See pages 1074, 1080. Have the differences in U.S. approaches to foreign policy over the past three decades reflected differences in ideology, rhetoric, domestic political pressure, implementation, or all of them?

C. *U.S. Foreign Policy, Human Rights, and Relations with China*

As the above readings demonstrate, human rights has been firmly established in U.S. foreign policy for more than three decades, although its importance relative to other concerns has varied from one administration to the next. Each administration government has had to consider how much weight to give to human rights compared to, e.g., national security, trade and investment, and cooperation on criminal matters, such as combating drug trafficking. In addition, Congress and the President must evaluate what type of measures may be most effective in pressing for improvements in human rights in other countries.

For as long as these issues have been debated, the case of China has been on the agenda. This section examines some of the tactics used by the United States to promote human rights in China, the Chinese government's response, and the debate over how best to deal with the most populous country on earth. The discussion focuses on public criticism, both through the annual State Department Country Reports and public diplomacy at the UN Human Rights Commission, and using trade and economic linkages as leverage.

1. The United States Evaluates the World: The State Department's Annual Reports on Human Rights

U.S. State Department, Country Reports on Human Rights Practices: China

2004, *http://www.state.gov/g/drl/rls/hrrpt/2004/41640.htm* (Feb.28, 2005)

The People's Republic of China (PRC) is an authoritarian state in which, as specified in its Constitution, the Chinese Communist Party (CCP or Party) is the paramount source of power. Party members hold almost all top government, police, and military positions. Ultimate authority rests with the 24-member political bureau (Politburo) of the CCP and its 9-member standing committee. Leaders made a top priority of maintaining stability and social order and were committed to perpetuating the rule of the CCP. Citizens lacked the freedom to express opposition to the Party-led political system and the right to change their national leaders or form of government. Socialism continued to provide the theoretical underpinning of national politics, but Marxist economic planning has given way to pragmatism, and economic decentralization has increased the authority of local officials. The Party's authority rested primarily on the Government's ability to maintain social stability; appeals to nationalism and patriotism; Party control of personnel, media, and the security apparatus; and continued improvement in the living standards of most of the country's 1.3 billion citizens. The Constitution provides for an independent judiciary; however, in practice, the Government and the CCP, at both the central and local levels, frequently interfered in the judicial process and directed verdicts in many cases. . . .

The Government's human rights record remained poor, and the Government continued to commit numerous and serious abuses. Citizens did not have the right to change their government, and many who openly expressed dissenting political views were harassed, detained, or imprisoned, particularly in a campaign late in the year against writers, religious activists, dissidents, and petitioners to the Central Government. Authorities were quick to suppress religious, political, and social groups that they perceived as threatening to government authority or national stability, especially before sensitive dates such as the 15th anniversary of the 1989 Tiananmen massacre and other significant political and religious occasions. However, the Constitution was amended to mention human rights for the first time.

Abuses included instances of extrajudicial killings; torture and mistreatment of prisoners, leading to numerous deaths in custody; coerced confessions; arbitrary arrest and detention; and incommunicado detention. The judiciary was not independent, and the lack of due process remained a serious problem. The lack of due process was particularly egregious in death penalty cases, and the accused was often denied a meaningful appeal. Executions often took place on the day of conviction or on the denial of an appeal. In Xinjiang, trials and executions of Uighurs charged with separatism continued. Government pressure continued to make it difficult for lawyers to represent criminal defendants. The authorities routinely violated legal protections in the cases of political dissidents and religious figures. They generally attached higher priority to suppressing political opposition and maintaining public order than to enforcing legal norms or protecting individual rights. According to 2003 government statistics, more than 250,000 persons were serving sentences in "reeducation-through-labor" camps and other forms of administrative detention not subject to judicial review. Other experts reported that more than 310,000 persons were serving sentences in these camps in 2003.

Throughout the year, the Government prosecuted individuals for subversion and leaking state secrets as a means to harass and intimidate, while others were detained for relaying facts about Chinese human rights issues to those outside the country. . . .

The number of individuals serving sentences for the now-repealed crime of counterrevolution was estimated at 500 to 600; many of these persons were imprisoned for the nonviolent expression of their political views. Nongovernmental organizations (NGOs) estimated that as many as 250 persons remained in prison for political activities connected to the 1989 Tiananmen demonstrations. . . .

The Government used the international war on terror as a pretext for cracking down harshly on suspected Uighur separatists expressing peaceful political dissent and on independent Muslim religious leaders. The human rights situation in the Tibet Autonomous Region (TAR) and in some Tibetan regions outside the TAR also remained poor (see Tibet Addendum).

The Government maintained tight restrictions on freedom of speech and of the press, and a wave of detentions late in the year signaled a new campaign targeting prominent writers and political commentators. The Government regulated the establishment and management of publications, controlled broadcast and other electronic media, censored some foreign television broadcasts, and jammed some radio signals from abroad. During the year, publications were closed and otherwise disciplined for publishing material deemed objectionable by the Government, and journalists, authors, academics, Internet writers, and researchers were harassed, detained, and arrested by the authorities. Although the scope of permissible private speech has continued to expand in recent years, the Government continued and intensified efforts to monitor and control use of the Internet and other wireless technology, including cellular phones, pagers, and instant messaging devices. During the year, the Government blocked many websites, began monitoring text messages sent by mobile phones, and pressured Internet companies to censor objectionable content. NGOs reported that 43 journalists were imprisoned at year's end.

The Government severely restricted freedom of assembly and association and infringed on individuals' rights to privacy. The authorities harassed and abused many who raised public grievances, including petitioners to the Central Government. The Government outlawed public commemoration of the 1989 Tiananmen massacre. Thousands of individuals protesting forced evictions and workplace and health issues were detained during the year. Petitioner issues were increasingly considered suspect by the Government, and petitioner leader Ye Guozhu was arrested in August while seeking permission to hold a 10,000-person rally against forced eviction.

While the number of religious believers in the country continued to grow, the Government's record on respect for religious freedom remained poor, and repression of members of unregistered religious groups increased in some parts of the country. Members of unregistered Protestant and Catholic congregations, Muslim Uighurs, and Tibetan Buddhists, including those residing within the TAR [Tibet Autonomous Region] . . . experienced ongoing and, in some cases, increased official interference, harassment, and repression. Government officials increased vigilance against "foreign infiltration under the guise of religion." The Government detained and prosecuted a number of underground religious figures in both the Protestant and Catholic Church. . . .

The extent of religious freedom varied significantly from place to place. The Government continued to enforce regulations requiring all places of religious activity to register with the Government. Many provincial authorities required groups seeking to register to come under the supervision of official, "patriotic" religious organizations. Religious worship in many officially registered churches, temples, and mosques occurred without interference, but unregistered churches in some areas were destroyed, religious services were broken up, and church leaders and adherents were harassed, detained, or beaten. At year's end, scores of religious adherents remained in prison because of their religious activities. No visible progress was made in normalizing relations between the official Patriotic Catholic Church and Papal authorities, although both the Government and the Vatican stated that they were ready to resume negotiations aimed at establishing diplomatic relations. The Government continued its crackdown against the Falun Gong spiritual movement, and tens of thousands of practitioners remained incarcerated in prisons, extrajudicial reeducation-through-labor camps, and psychiatric facilities. Several hundred Falun Gong adherents reportedly have died in detention due to torture, abuse, and neglect since the crackdown on Falun Gong began in 1999.

Freedom of movement continued to be restricted. However, the Government continued to relax its residence-based registration requirements. The Government denied the U.N. High Commissioner for Refugees (UNHCR) permission to operate along its border with North Korea and deported several thousand North Koreans, many of whom faced persecution and some of whom may have been executed upon their return, as provided in North Korean law. Abuse and detention of North Koreans in the country was also reported.

The Government did not permit independent domestic NGOs to monitor human rights conditions. However, in September, the U.N. Working Group on Arbitrary Detention visited Beijing, Sichuan, and the TAR and toured 10 detention facilities. Although the Government extended invitations to the U.N. Special Rapporteur for Torture and the U.N. Special Rapporteur for Religious Intolerance, those visits did not occur by year's end. The Government also extended an invitation to the leaders of the U.S. Commission on International Religious Freedom, but the visit did not occur due to restrictive conditions that the Government placed on the visit. In December, the Government postponed a planned seminar by the Organization for Economic Cooperation on Socially Responsible Investment, which resulted in the cancellation of a visit by the OECD's Trade Union Advisory Council to discuss labor issues.

Violence against women, including imposition of a coercive birth limitation policy that resulted in instances of forced abortion and forced sterilization, continued to be a problem, as did prostitution. Discrimination against women, persons with disabilities, and minorities persisted. Trafficking in persons continued to be a serious problem.

Labor demonstrations, particularly those protesting nonpayment of back wages, continued. Workplace safety remained a serious problem, particularly in the mining industry. The Government continued to deny internationally recognized worker rights, including freedom of association. Forced labor in prison facilities remained a serious problem.

Significant legal reforms continued during the year, including a Constitutional amendment specifically to include protection of citizens' human rights and legally obtained private property for the first time. In July, the Government enacted the Administrative Procedures Law, which prohibits government agencies from violating citizens' rights or seizing property without clear legal authority. A new infectious disease law was enacted prohibiting discrimination against people with HIV/AIDS and Hepatitis B, and employment discrimination against those with HIV/AIDS and Hepatitis B was outlawed. Treatment of some migrant workers was improved in many major cities through the passage of laws intended to guarantee migrant children access to public education and to protect migrant workers' rights to receive their salary on a regular basis. The Government enacted reforms related to interrogation of detainees, fighting corruption, procedures for requisitioning land, confiscation of personal property, extending social security, regulating religion, and providing legal aid. At year's end, it remained unclear how widely these reforms would be implemented and what effect they would have.

The State Department report on China continues for over 100 pages, providing detailed allegations about summary executions, disappearances, arbitrary detention, maltreatment of detainees, torture, political use of psychiatric institutions, violations of freedom of speech, assembly and religion, violations of workers' rights and trafficking in women and children. For an NGO report reaching similar conclusions, see Human Rights Watch, *World Report 2005* at 263. The government of China did not welcome either report, as the following two readings make clear.

China Lashes Out at U.S. Human Rights Report

China Daily, March 2, 2005

China on Tuesday condemned a US State Department report criticizing Beijing's human rights record, saying the review was a blow to relations between the two countries.

"We are very dissatisfied with this report and we protest this report," Chinese Foreign Ministry spokesman Liu Jianchao said. "The United States should stop using double standards on human rights and stop interfering in the internal politics of China under the pretext of human rights."

He added: "This kind of report will do nothing good for the improvement of bilateral relations. It will do no good to improve mutual confidence in each other."

The report, released Monday in Washington, said China continued to commit "numerous and serious abuses."

The United States is likely to seek censure of China next month at the annual meeting of the U.N. Human Rights Commission in Geneva, a routine move by Washington, although none of its proposals have been approved.

Liu defended China's record, saying that the protection of human rights had been written into the country's constitution last year.

"In the past years, China has made important progress in human rights, in political and legal areas," Liu said. "We are working to improve the human rights situation in China in more fields to build a society that is harmonious and united."

The Xinhua News Agency said the State Council, China's cabinet, will release its own assessment of the United States' human rights record on Thursday in a report that is "based on plenty of facts."

It will show "the bad records of the United States concerning the invasions into other countries and the mistreatment of foreign inmates, as well as the bad records in the aspects of life, freedom and personal security of U.S. citizens."

Liu urged dialogue between the United States and China to "narrow their differences."

Information Office of the State Council of the People's Republic of China, The Human Rights Record of the United States in 2004

Xinhua News Agency (Mar. 3, 2005), *http://www.fas.org/irp/news/2005/03/prc-humanrights.html*

In 2004 the atrocity of US troops abusing Iraqi POWs exposed the dark side of human rights performance of the United States. The scandal shocked the humanity and was condemned by the international community. It is quite ironic that on Feb. 28 of this year, the State Department of the United States once again posed as "the world human rights police" and released its Country Reports on Human Rights Practices for 2004. As in previous years, the reports pointed fingers at human rights situation in more than 190 countries and regions (including China) but kept silent on the US misdeeds in this field. Therefore, the world people have to probe the human rights record behind the Statue of Liberty in the United States.

I. On Life, Liberty and Security of Person

American society is characterized with rampant violent crimes, severe infringement of people's rights by law enforcement departments and lack of guarantee for people's rights to life, liberty and security of person.

Violent crimes pose a serious threat to people's lives. According to a report released by the Department of Justice of the United States on Nov. 29, 2004, in 2003 residents aged 12 and above in the United States experienced about 24 million victimizations, and there occurred 1,381,259 murders, robberies and other violent crimes, averaging 475 cases per 100,000 people. Among them there were 16,503 homicides, up 1.7 percent over 2002, or nearly six cases in every 100,000 residents, and one of every 44 Americans aged above 12 was victimized....

The United States has the biggest number of gun owners and gun violence has affected lots of innocent lives....

Police violence and infringement of human rights by law enforcement agencies also constitute a serious problem. At present, 5,000 law enforcement agencies in the United States use TASER — a kind of electric shock gun, which sends out 50,000 volts of impulse voltage after hitting the target. Since 1999, more than 80 people died from TASER shootings, 60 percent of which occurred between November 2003 and November 2004. A survey found that in the 17 years from 1985 to 2002, Los Angeles recorded more than 100 times increase in police shooting at automobile drivers, killing at least 25 and injuring more than 30 of them. Of these cases, 90 percent were due to misjudgment. (The Los Angeles Times, Feb. 29, 2004.)...

The New York Times reported on Apr. 19, 2004 a comprehensive study of 328 criminal cases over the last 15 years in which the convicted person was exonerated suggests that there are thousands of innocent people in prison today. The study identified 199 murder exoneration, 73 of them in capital cases. In more than half of the cases, the defendants had been in prison for more than 10 years.

The United States characterizes itself as "a paradise for free people," but the ratio of its citizens deprived of freedom has remained among the highest in the world. Statistics released by the Federal Bureau of Investigation last November showed that the nation made an estimated 13.6 million arrests in 2003. . . .

According to statistics from the Department of Justice, the number of inmates in the United States jumped from 320,000 in 1980 to 2 million in 2000, a hike by six times. From 1995 to 2003, the number of inmates grew at an annual rate of 3.5 percent in the country, where one out of every 142 people is behind bars. . . .

Most prisons in the United States are overcrowded, but still cannot meet the demand. The country has spent an average of 7 billion US dollars a year building new jails and prisons in the past 10 years. California has seen only one college but 21 new prisons built since 1984. Jails have become one of the huge and most lucrative industries, with a combined staff of more than 530,000 and being the second largest employer in the United States only after the General Motors. Private prisons are more and more common. . . . Abuse of prisoners and violence occur frequently in US jails and prisons, which are under disorderly management. The *Los Angeles Times* reported on Aug. 15 last year that over 40 state prison systems were once under some form of court order, for brutality, crowding, poor food and lack of medical care. . . .

Sexual harassment and encroachment are common in jails in the United States. *The New York Times* reported last October that at least 13 percent of inmates in the country are sexually assaulted in prison (*Ex-Inmate's Suit Offers View Into Sexual Slavery in Prisons*, The New York Times, Oct. 12, 2004). In jails of seven central and western US states, 21 percent of the inmates suffer sexual abuse at least once after being put in prison. The ratio is higher among women inmates, with nearly one fourth of them sexually assaulted by jail guards.

II. On Political Rights and Freedom

The United States claims to be "a paragon of democracy," but American democracy is manipulated by the rich and malpractices are common. Elections in the United States are in fact a contest of money. The presidential and Congressional elections last year cost nearly 4 billion US dollars, some 1 billion US dollars or one third more than that spent in the 2000 elections. The 2004 presidential election has been listed as the most expensive campaign in the country's history (see *http://www.opensecrets.org/overview*), with the cost jumping to 1.7 billion US dollars from 1 billion US dollars in 2000. To win the election, the Democratic Party and Republican Party had to try their utmost to raise funds. . . .

The US election system has quite a few flaws. The newly adopted Help America Vote Act of 2004 requires voters to offer a series of documents such as a stable residence or identification in registering, which in reality disenfranchises thousands of homeless people. The United States is the only country in the world that rules out ex-inmates' right to vote, which disenfranchises 5 million ex-inmates and 13 percent male black people (see Milenio, Mexico, Oct. 22 2004).

The 2004 US presidential election reported many problems, including counting errors, machine malfunctions, registration confusion, legal uncertainty, and lack of respect for voters. . . .

In the meantime, fabrications of disputable pictures and statements were put in the agenda of political maneuvers. Campaign advertisement and political debates were full of distorted facts, false information and lies. According to statistics of the Annenberg Public Policy Center of University of Pennsylvania, campaign advertisement for the 2004 US presidential election had a large proportion of false information that was enough to mislead voters, far beyond 50 percent in 1996. In the Republican camp, at least 75 percent contained untrue information and personal attacks. . . .

The US freedom of the press is filled with hypocrisy. Power and intimidation hang over the halo of press freedom. The *New York Times* published a commentary on March 30, 2004, saying that the US government's reliance on slandering had reached an unprecedented level in contemporary American political history, and the government prepared to abuse power at any moment to threaten potential critics. . . .

On Sept. 27, the Association of American University Presses, Association of American Publishers and other organizations jointly lodged a complaint to the district court of Manhattan, New York, charging the Office of Foreign Assets Control under the Department of the Treasury with deliberately preventing literary works of Iranian, Cuban and Sudanese writers from entering the United States and turning the economic sanctions against the three countries into a "censorship system" to stop free dissemination of information and ideology. (see *Xinhua* story, Sept. 30, 2004). In another case, eight reporters, including Jim Taricani of the TV station in Providence, Rhode Island with the National Broadcasting Company (NBC), Judith Miller of *The New York Times*, and Matthew Cooper of *Time* magazine, were declared guilty for they declined to disclose the confidential sources of news. The *New York Times* pointed out on Nov. 10, 2004 that through these cases, it was found out that press freedom suffered rampant infringement. . . .

III. On Economic, Social and Cultural Rights

The United States refuses to ratify the International Covenant on Economic, Social and Cultural rights and took negative attitude to the economic, social and cultural rights of the laborers. Poverty, hunger and homelessness have haunted the world richest country.

The population of people living in poverty has been on a steady rise. According to a report by *The Sun* on July, 6, 2004, from 1970 to 2000 (adjusted for inflation), the bottom 90 percent's average income stagnated while the top 10 percent experienced an average yearly income increase of nearly 90 percent. Upper-middle- and upper-class families that constitute the top 10 percent of the income distribution are prospering while many among the remaining 90 percent struggle to maintain their standard of living. Worsening income disparities have formed two Americas. (*Two Americas*, The Baltimore Sun, July 6, 2004.) According to a report of the *Wall Street Journal* on June 15, 2004, a study on the fall of 2003 by Arthur Kennickell of the Board of Governor of the Federal Reserve System showed that the nation's wealthiest 1 percent owned 53 percent of all the stocks held by families or individuals, and 64 percent of the bonds. They control more than a third of the nation's wealth. (*US Led a Resurgence Last Year Among Millionaires World-Wide*, The Wall Street Journal, June 15, 2004.) In Washington D.C., the top 20 percent of the city's households have 31 times the average income of the 20 percent at the bottom. (*D.C. Gap in Wealth Growing*, The Washington Post, July 22, 2004.) . . .

The homeless population continues to rise nationwide. . . .

Racial discrimination has been deeply rooted in the United States, permeating into every aspects of society. The colored people are generally poor, with living condition much worse than the white. According to a report of *The Guardian* of Britain on Oct. 9, 2004, the average net assets of a white family is 88,000 US dollars in 2002, 11 times of a family of Latin American ancestry, or nearly 15 times of a family of African ancestry. . . . The death rate of illness, accident and murder among the black people is twice that of the white.

The rate of being victim of murders for the black people is five times that of the white. The rate of being affected by AIDS for the black people is ten times that of the whites while the rate of being diagnosed by diabetes for the black people is twice that of the whites. (*The State Of Black America 2004*, Issued by National Urban League on March 24, 2004, *http://www.nuL.org/pdf/sobaexec.pdf*.)

. . . People of minority ethnic groups are biased against in employment and occupation. The Equal Employment Opportunity Commission of the United States received 29,000 complaints in 2003 of racial bias in the workplace (*Racism in the 21st Century*, published in USA Today May 5, 2004 issue.) Statistics provided by the United States Department of Labor also suggest that by November 2004, the unemployment rate for black and white people is 10.8 percent and 4.7 percent respectively (*http://bls.gov/news.release/pdf/empsit.pdf*). In New York City, one of every two black men between 16 and 64 was not working by 2003 (see *Nearly Half of Black Men Found Jobless*, published by *The New York Times* on Feb. 28 2004). Black people not only have fewer job opportunities, but also earn less than white people. Even with the same job, a black man only earns 70 percent of that for a white man. Regions such as California, where immigrants make up a larger proportion of the local population, are almost like traps of death. Mexican Laborers who have come to work in the United States have a mortality as high as 80 percent. . . .

Apartheid runs rampant at schools of the United States. On May 17, 1954, Chief Justice Earl Warren of the Supreme Court announced the court's decision over a case known as *Brown v. Board of Education* that the doctrine of "separate but equal" had no place in US public schools. Fifty years later, white children and black children in the United States still lead largely separate lives. One in eight southern black students attends a school that is 99 percent black. About a third attend schools that are at least 90 percent minority. In the Northeast, by contrast, more than half of blacks attend such schools (*Schools and Lives Are Still Separate*, The Washington Post, May 17, 2004)....

Racial prejudice has made social conflicts to become acute, causing a rise in hate crimes.... In a related development, because of the "lingering atmosphere of fear" stemming from the Sept. 11 attacks and fallout from the Iraq War, there were 1,019 anti-Muslim incidents in the United States in 2003, representing a 69 percent increase. There were 221 incidents in 2003 of anti-Muslim bias in California, tripled a year ago (Los Angeles Times, May 3).

Racial prejudice is ubiquitous in judicial fields. The proportion for persons of colored races being sentenced or being imprisoned is notably higher than whites. In accordance with a report published in November 2004 by the US Department of Justice, colored races accounted for over 70 percent of inmates in the United States. And 29 percent of black people have the experience of being in jail once. Black people make up 12.3 percent of the population in the United States, but by the end of 2003, out of 1.4 million prisoners who are serving jail terms above one year at the federal or state prisons, 44 percent were blacks,...

After the Sept. 11 incident, the United States openly restricts the rights of citizens under the cloak of homeland security, and uses diverse means including wire tapping of phone conversations and secret investigations, checks on all secret files, and monitoring transfers of fund and cash flows to supervise activities of its citizens, in which, people of ethnic minority groups, foreigners and immigrants become main victims....

[The report continues with chapters detailing concerns about the rights of women and children and the treatment of foreign nationals. It concludes as follows.]

It is the common goal and obligation for all countries in the world to promote and safeguard human rights. No country in the world can claim itself as perfect and has no room for improvement in the human rights area. And no country should exclude itself from the international human rights development process, or view itself as the incarnation of human rights which can reign over other countries and give orders to the others. Even the United States shall be no exception. Despite tons of problems in its own human rights, the United States continues to stick to its belligerent stance, wantonly trample on the sovereignty of other countries, and constantly stage tragedies of human rights infringement in the world.

Instead of indulging itself in publishing the "human rights country report" to censure other countries unreasonably, the United States should reflect on its erroneous behavior on human rights and take its own human rights problems seriously. The double standards of the United States on human rights and its exercise of hegemonism and power politics under the pretext of promoting human rights will certainly put itself in an isolated and passive position and beget opposition from all just members of the international community.

2. Multilateral Diplomacy at the UN Human Rights Commission

As noted in the U.S. country report, China has extended limited cooperation to UN human rights mechanisms. The UN Working Group on Arbitrary

Detentions visited China in 1997 and 2004. It urged China to bring national laws into compliance with international human rights standards and reported that the state refused its requests to meet with prisoners in Tibet's Drapchi prison, who were severely injured during and after the 1997 visit. See: Working Group on Arbitrary Detention: Report of Mission to China, UN Doc. E/CN.4/2005/add.4, 29 Dec. 2004, p. 7. The UN special rapporteur on torture succeeded in scheduling a visit to China, between November 21 and December 2, 2005. An earlier mission, set for June 2004 was postponed indefinitely two weeks before it was to occur, China being unwilling to agree to the standard UN terms for such a visit, which include unannounced visits to prisons and confidential interviews with prisoners (the U.S. also rejected these terms in 2005 with respect to detainees held at the Guantanamo base in Cuba). Following his two-week visit in 2005, during which he visited detention centers in various parts of China, the special rapporteur on torture announced that torture remains widespread in the country. He also accused some officials of obstructing his fact-finding mission. China denounced the report several days later, saying that the rapporteur did not spend enough time in the country to draw accurate conclusions. Audra Ang, "China denies U.N. report alleging torture," *The Boston Globe*, Dec. 6, 2005.

The U.S. has in recent years sponsored a resolution at the annual sessions of the UN Human Rights Commission in Geneva, seeking to censure Beijing for its rights record. Each year, China has garnered enough support to avoid having the U.S.-sponsored resolution discussed or brought to a vote, in part by utilizing its growing economic leverage to threaten states with loss of business contracts if they vote for resolutions critical of China. These threats were quite explicit with regard to Denmark and the Netherlands in 1997. While these and other states continued to align themselves with the United States in efforts to censure China, other European states (such as France, Germany, Italy, and Greece) refused to support the United States in the Commission beginning in 1997.

In 2001, Washington decided not to bring a resolution targeting China, citing leadership changes and "some limited but significant progress." At the same time it conceded that "China's human rights record remains poor." State Department Country Report on Human Rights Practices, "China" (2001), *http://www.state.gov/g/drl/rls/hrrpt/2001/eap/8289.htm*. The U.S. also did not sponsor a China resolution in 2002, because, for the first time in history of the United Nations, the United States was not elected as a member of the Commission.

At the 2004 annual Commission meeting, China again blocked consideration of a resolution condemning its human rights record by calling for a "no-action" motion. In 2004, as it had in the past, China suspended its dialogue with the United States in retaliation for the American sponsorship of the resolution. During talks in Beijing in October and November, both countries agreed to discuss resuming regular dialogues.

China has not been the only object of U.S. attention at the UN Human Rights Commission. For many years, the United States has proposed resolutions seeking to condemn Cuba for systematic human rights violations. Prior to the 2005 session of the Commission, Cuba submitted a *Note verbale* describing U.S. diplomatic efforts to have such a resolution adopted. In reading the text, consider whether it describes the appropriate use of U.S. diplomacy or whether Cuba has legitimate grounds for complaint.

Note verbale dated 14 March 2005 from the Permanent Mission of Cuba to the United Nations Office at Geneva addressed to the Office of the High Commissioner for Human Rights

UN Doc. E/CN.4/2005/G/26 (Mar. 24, 2005)

The Permanent Mission of Cuba to the United Nations Office and International Organizations based in Switzerland presents its compliments to the Office of the United Nations High Commissioner for Human Rights and the secretariat of the Commission on Human Rights, and has the honour to attach herewith, in English, French and Spanish, a document entitled "Cuba and human rights" (part 2), which deals with the manipulation of the proceedings of the Commission on Human Rights by the United States Government as an instrument of its policy of hostility and aggression against Cuba. . . .

In 1985 and 1986 the first failed attempts to have Cuba condemned over its human rights record were made in the Third Commission of the United Nations General Assembly.

The first attempt to achieve something similar in the Commission on Human Rights took place in 1987 when the United States proposed a draft resolution that was unsuccessful when a no-action motion was passed.

In 1988 the United States proposed another draft resolution aimed at singling Cuba out for criticism. This was also unsuccessful because of the positive reception given to the Cuban initiative to invite a mission made up of the Commission's president and five member state representatives to visit Cuba.

Neither was the United States able to achieve its objective of having Cuba condemned by the Commission in 1989. Several amendments proposed by US diplomats to the draft resolution submitted to the Commission were defeated. The text adopted simply took note of the report drawn up by the mission that visited Cuba and invited the Cuban government to work on implementing its recommendations.

On consolidating itself as the only superpower, after the Soviet Union disintegrated and socialism in Eastern Europe disappeared, in 1990 the United States managed, for the first time, to have a draft resolution condemning Cuba passed in the Commission on Human Rights.

Cuba refused to countenance any kind of cooperation with such an abomination, which was malformed from its very conception, motivated by illegitimate interests and the result of brutal pressure and blackmail.

The Cuban people's principled position, its dignified steadfastness in the face of lies and slander gradually won the respect and support of Commission members and when 1998 arrived, the draft anti-Cuban resolution proposed by the United States was clearly defeated by a vote of 16 in favour and 19 against.

After this unexpected defeat, the United States government buckled down to the task of creating a new image for its anti-Cuban manoeuvring in the CHR. Using its traditional methods, it convinced the government of the day in the Czech Republic, a country which at the time needed the United States' support for its application to join NATO, to become the public face of the draft resolution against Cuba in the Commission. Taking on such a degrading task presented no difficulty to the team of opportunists headed by former President Havel; over the years they had learned to obediently carry out Washington's orders and enjoy its money.

Armed with this new design and applying its usual pressure and blackmail to the fullest, the United States managed to get the anti-Cuban resolution passed from 1999 to 2001 but always with a tiny majority of between one and three votes.

By the end of 2001 it was obvious that this way of working was entering a crisis. The superpower realized that it needed to "spruce up" the image of its anti-Cuban exercise, something that became a strategic necessity after its humiliating exclusion from membership in the Commission as a result of elections by secret ballot held in the Social and Economic Commission.

So Bush administration top officials stepped up their efforts to have one or two Latin American countries propose the anti-Cuban resolution in the Commission's 58th session in 2002.

The intensity of the pressure exercised by top US officials and the increasing vulnerability and dependence of several Latin American governments — which had very low levels of popular support — on the US helped them to achieve their aim. So President Jorge Batlle of Uruguay was the marionette and gave a public performance of the anti-Cuban script that reflected nothing but the opinions of the Miami terrorist mafia and was written, down to the commas and full stops, in Washington. . . .

All the anti-Cuban text forced through the Commission's 58th period of sessions in 2002 did — those who touted it unsuccessfully attempted to present it as a "new" product with "constructive" approach — was to re-establish an unfair monitoring mechanism of a non-existent human rights "situation" in Cuba. The worst thing about this case was the decision, which exacerbated the anti-Cuban manipulation conceived by Washington in order to satisfy its lust for domination, to involve none other than the United Nations High Commissioner for Human Rights in this dirty business. . . .

Mrs. Poblete, assistant to the anti-Cuban congressperson Ileana Ros-Lehtinen, went to Geneva at the beginning of January 2003 and had separate meetings with some Latin American diplomatic representatives to explore what the[ir] feelings were on the anti-Cuban manoeuvre orchestrated by the United States, to gauge in which specific areas and subjects each one was vulnerable and to propose concrete recommendations to boost the effectiveness of the blackmail and conditions which would be worked out later by both the US congress and administration.

At the end of that same month, Undersecretary of State for Global Affairs Paula Dobriansky went to several Latin American countries where she met with presidents and foreign ministers, her goal being to coerce them into giving a commitment to propose the anti-Cuban motion at the 59th Commission on Human Rights.

Similarly, US ambassadors in various capital cities, as is traditional, undertook important tasks in support of the anti-Cuban manoeuvre. They stepped up their anti-Cuban misinformation and manipulative propaganda campaigns, distributing brochures cooked up by the State Department full of "updated" lies and distorted "facts." In addition, with varying degrees of subtlety and transparency — depending on how dependent the government in question is on the United States — they demanded support for what the superpower calls its priorities in the Commission on Human Rights and reminded them of the bounties that could stem from a good bilateral relation with the hegemonic power. . . .

To ensure it obtained the votes needed to push its anti-Cuban resolution through the Commission, the Bush administration paid no heed to legal or ethical constraints. Promise of financial aid and other benefits for those who delivered their vote rang out from Washington. Nevertheless, the most common practice was not offering something new; what predominated were direct or veiled threats to block loans and grants from international financial institutions which the United States controls, such as the International Monetary Fund, the World Bank and the Inter-American Development Bank, to withdraw bilateral trade and immigration concessions and even to make the United States' treatment of political matters of vital importance to the countries being blackmailed depend on how they voted. . . .

Reality once again dealt Washington a hard blow in the Commission's 60th session [in 2004]. The American authorship of the anti-Cuban resolution was obvious, as never before: A meeting was held in State Department headquarters on 24 March at which Marc Grossman, undersecretary for political affairs, told diplomats from several countries who had been invited that Honduras would be the "chief sponsor" of the anti-Cuban resolution at the 60th CHR. Grossman's assistants immediately distributed the English text of the resolution and only then was the Honduran ambassador allowed to speak. . . .

The anti-Cuban resolution was passed by the ridiculous margin of one vote, the votes being 22 in favour and 21 against and 10 abstentions. Such a result was a Pyrrhic victory for the Superpower whose henchmen had applied the strongest most brutal pressure on governments of developing countries. As a corroboration of the growing weakness and bad reputation of the anti-Cuban manoeuvring in Geneva, the resolution received more votes against than ever before and had 2 votes in favor less than in 2003. . . . [In 2005, a resolution on Cuba was adopted by a vote of 21 to 17, with 15 abstentions. Comm'n H.R. Res. 2005/12 (Apr. 14, 2005).]

If the way the United States behaved in Geneva were really motivated by a desire to protect human rights in Latin America, it would not force its spurious and unjustified anti-Cuban resolution down the Commission's throat. On the contrary, it would submit for the Commission's consideration two draft resolutions against those Latin American governments that co-sponsor and support the anti-Cuban resolution.

And the foregoing is not mere rhetoric. This thesis is based on the reports that the State Department drafts every year on the human rights situation in every country in the world with, of course, the exception of the United States. The State Department's report contains concrete facts and value judgments on the governments that co-sponsor their anti-Cuban manoeuverings, which far surpass the seriousness of the false allegations about Cuba. . . .

Nearly six decades after the Universal Declaration on Human Rights was adopted and twelve years after the World Conference on Human Rights was held in Vienna, the United Nations machinery demonstrates — time and time again — that it is incapable of promoting and protecting all human rights for everyone, on the basis of respect for and adherence to the principles of universality, impartiality, objectivity and non-discrimination.

The work of the Commission on Human Rights is bogged down by the political manipulation of a small group of powerful nations, most particularly by that of the world hegemonic superpower. This handful of rich countries regards the Commission as its own private property and makes ill use of it, as an instrument to jeopardize the interests of underdeveloped countries, which represent the immense majority of UN members, and to impose certain, supposedly universal norms and the pensee unique upon them. . . .

The Commission on Human Rights must be transformed into an instrument for all countries that protects all human rights. The Commission on Human Rights belongs to all peoples and not just to some. . . .

3. Linkages and Conditionality: Using U.S. Economic and Political Power

President Clinton made strong statements about China during his 1992 campaign. He labeled his predecessor's decision in favor of trade with China "yet another sad chapter in this administration's history of putting America on the wrong side of human rights and democracy." *Clinton Criticizes Bush Decision to Renew China's Most Favored Nation [MFN] Status*, U.S. Newswire, June 3, 1992, available in LEXIS, News Library, Wire File. Several months later, he criticized the perceived failings of the Bush Administration, especially its lack of response to the Tiananmen Square massacre. Consider the following passage from a speech in October 1992.

Remarks by Gov. William Clinton, A *Vision for Democracy*

Pabst Theater, Milwaukee, Wis., Oct. 1, 1992

. . . [T]here is no more striking example of President Bush's indifference to democracy than his policy toward China. None of us will ever forget the images of millions of Chinese people demonstrating peacefully for democracy; the solitary young man staring down a tank; or the students raising a model of our Statue of Liberty in Tiananmen Square. Neither will we ever forget the horror of seeing hundreds of innocent people mowed down for their belief in freedom.

But instead of allying himself with the democratic movement in China, George Bush sent secret emissaries to raise a toast with those who crushed it.

The stakes in China's future are very high. For the course taken by that great nation will help shape the future of Asia and the world. Three years after the Tiananmen Square tragedy, the tremors of change continue to shake China. We do not want China to fall apart or descend into chaos. Rather, we should use our relationship and influence to work with the Chinese for a peaceful transition to democracy and the spread of free markets.

But today, we must ask ourselves, what has President Bush's China policy really achieved? The Chinese leadership still sells missiles and nuclear technology to Middle Eastern dictators who threaten us and our friends. They still arrest and hold in prison leaders of the pro-democracy movement. They restrict American access to their markets, while our trade deficit with China will reach $15 billion this year. The Chinese now have the second biggest trade surplus of any nation in the world. Yet, just a few days ago, President Bush vetoed legislation passed with bipartisan Congressional majorities that would place conditions on most-favored nation trade status for China's state-owned enterprises. And just today, the Senate failed by a vote of 59-40 to override that veto.

I do not want to isolate China. But I believe our nation has a higher purpose than to coddle dictators and stand aside from the global movement toward democracy. For the greatest strength America can count on in today's world is not our personal relations with foreign dignitaries. Individual leaders come and go — even in the United States, I hope. Rather, it is the powerful appeal of our democratic values and our enduring political institutions to people around the world that make us special.

This does not mean embarking on a reckless crusade. Every ideal, including the promotion of democracy, must be tempered with prudence and common sense. We know that ballot boxes alone do not solve every world problem, and that some countries and cultures are many steps away from democratic institutions. We know there may be times when other security needs or economic interests will diverge from our commitment to democracy and human rights. . . .

Today, however, the danger that we will get carried away with ideals does not loom large. That has not been our problem in the last four years. The real danger in this time of sweeping change is that, under President Bush, we will cling to tired and outdated notions that do not work and cannot inspire.

Yet even before his inauguration the President-Elect started shifting ground. On December 14, 1992, he announced that he favored retaining China's MFN trade status (which essentially allows China's access to U.S. markets on the same terms as all other countries), although he would condition it upon progress in human rights and other areas. *President-Elect Clinton Supports Renewing MFN Trade Status for China*, 9 Intl. Trade Rep. (BNA) 2124 (1992). Once in office, moreover, the President issued an Executive Order unconditionally extending MFN until July 3, 1994, but conditioning subsequent extensions upon China's fulfillment of, inter alia, several human rights criteria. Exec. Order No. 12,850, 3 C.F.R. S606 (1994). As the end of the year approached, he came full circle and then some, using language strikingly similar to that employed by President Bush when he justified his unconditional extension of MFN to China in 1990 (see President's News Conference (May 24, 1990), 1990-I George Bush Pub. Papers 707 (1991)).

President's News Conference (May 26, 1994)

30 Weekly Comp. Pres. Doc. 1166, 1166-1169 (May 30, 1994)

The President. Good afternoon. Today I would like to announce a series of important decisions regarding United States policy toward China.

Our relationship with China is important to all Americans. We have significant interests in what happens there and what happens between us. China has an atomic arsenal and a vote and a veto in the U.N. Security Council. It is a major factor in Asian and global security. We share important interests, such as in a nuclear-free Korean Peninsula and in sustaining the global environment. China is also the world's fastest growing economy. Over $8 billion of United States exports to China last year supported over 150,000 American jobs.

I have received Secretary Christopher's letter recommending, as required by last year's Executive order, reporting to me on the conditions in that Executive order. He has reached a conclusion with which I agree, that the Chinese did not achieve overall significant progress in all the areas outlined in the Executive order relating to human rights, even though clearly there was progress made in important areas, including the resolution of all emigration cases, the establishment of a memorandum of understanding with regard to how prison labor issues would be resolved, the adherence to the Universal Declaration of Human Rights and other issues.

Nevertheless, serious human rights abuses continue in China, including the arrest and detention of those who peacefully voice their opinions and the repression of Tibet's religious and cultural traditions.

The question for us now is, given the fact that there has been some progress but that not all the requirements of the Executive order were met, how can we best advance the cause of human rights and the other profound interests the United States has in our relationship with China?

I have decided that the United States should renew most-favored-nation trading status toward China. This decision, I believe, offers us the best opportunity to lay the basis for long-term sustainable progress in human rights and for the advancement of our other interests with China. Extending MFN will avoid isolating China and instead will permit us to engage the Chinese with not only economic contacts but with cultural, educational, and other contacts and with a continuing aggressive effort in human rights, an approach that I believe will make it more likely that China will play a responsible role, both at home and abroad.

I am moving, therefore, to delink human rights from the annual extension of most-favored-nation trading status for China. That linkage has been constructive during the past year. But I believe, based on our aggressive contacts with the Chinese in the past several months, that we have reached the end of the usefulness of that policy and it is time to take a new path toward the achievement of our constant objectives. We need to place our relationship into a larger and more productive framework.

In view of the continuing human rights abuses, I am extending the sanctions imposed by the United States as a result of the events in Tiananmen Square, and I am also banning the import of munitions, principally guns and ammunition from China. I am also pursuing a new and vigorous American program to support those in China working to advance the cause of human rights and democracy. This program will include increased broadcasts for Radio Free Asia and the Voice of America, increased support for nongovernmental organizations working on human rights in China, and the development with American business leaders of a voluntary set of principles for business activity in China.

I don't want to be misunderstood about this: China continues to commit very serious human rights abuses. Even as we engage the Chinese on military, political, and economic issues, we intend to stay engaged with those in China who suffer from human rights abuses. The United States must remain a champion of their liberties. . . .

To those who argue that in view of China's human rights abuses we should revoke MFN status, let me ask you the same question that I have asked myself over and over these last few weeks as I have studied this issue and consulted people of both parties who have had experience with China over many decades.

Will we do more to advance the cause of human rights if China is isolated or if our nations are engaged in a growing web of political and economic cooperation and contacts? I am persuaded that the best path for advancing freedom in China is for the United States to intensify and broaden its engagement with that nation. . . .

Q. Mr. President, most of the conditions, the aspects of this problem were prevalent last year when you made very strong threats of a cutoff of human rights.

Aren't you really bowing to big business and backing off of human rights in terms of the world perception?

The President. No. No, I don't think so. And if you've seen the statements of recent days by many others — Senator Bradley and many other Members of the Senate, other members of the American political community who have also evolved in their view, I think most people believe, number one, that conditions have changed.

I think it's very important to say that under the terms of this agreement some progress has been made. Some important political dissidents have been released. We've gotten information on Tibetan prisoners for the first time. We have a process now with operable deadlines for looking into these disputes over prison labor matters. We have at least an adherence, an explicit adherence by the Chinese to the Universal Declaration of Human Rights. We have an ongoing set of negotiations now on how to deal with the jamming we've suffered on our Voice of America broadcast. So there have been some changes.

And interestingly enough, many of the most vocal human rights advocates have argued that — not that we should lift MFN status but that instead we should have some intermediate sanctions which cover a bigger section of the economy. But things have changed to the point, both in terms of what has gone on in China and in terms of the other strategic issues — the situation in Korea, for example, I think everyone would admit is somewhat different than it was a year ago — that I believe, that everybody believes we should do something differently. . . .

Q. Mr. President, how do you answer those who say you are — using your own words now — coddling tyrants? And with the leverage of linkage now moved away, what incentive is there for China to improve human rights?

The President. Well, let me turn it on its head, first of all. China is a very great and important nation. What gave rise to this MFN in the first place, this issue? Why did anyone believe human rights should be tied to MFN in China as opposed to other nations in the world? The MFN law basically is tied to emigration, and we have — I haven't said that, I don't think, today — we have successfully resolved all outstanding emigration cases with the Chinese. Why was it extended to involve human rights here? Because of the frustration in the Congress that the previous administration had reestablished relationships too quickly after Tiananmen Square, and there seemed to be no other aggressive human rights strategy.

The United States has pursued the cause of human rights around the world in many, many ways without tying it to MFN with those countries. I have had, for example, several conversations on this subject with one of our Nation's most dedicated human rights advocates, President Carter, who strongly believes that the decision I have taken today is the right one and more likely to produce human rights progress. Because, let me answer your question precisely, every nation, every great nation makes some decisions and perhaps most decisions based on what is in the interest of the nation at that moment in time internally. But no nation likes to feel that every decision it makes for the good, to do something that's right, that makes progress, is being made not because it's the right thing to do but only because of external pressure from someone else. . . .

Q. On the first question, aren't you coddling tyrants just as you accuse —

The President. No, because I do believe what happened — what has happened since then? Has there been any progress? There's been so much progress that even the people who have supported these strong resolutions, the legislation in the past, are now arguing for a different course: I'm not the only person arguing that the time has come to take a different path. It's that they will say, well, I should have done something else. But virtually everyone says the time has come to move out of the framework now.

We obviously have something going on in this relationship now. We obviously have a broader and deeper relationship, and we obviously are going to see some changes here. So I think everybody acknowledges that there is some dynamism in this relationship now which warrants a change. The question is what tactical path should we take. And I expect that many people who criticize my decision will say, "Well, he should have put stiffer tariffs on something or another or should have had a bigger section of the economy affected or gone after the military enterprises or something like that." But I think nearly everybody recognizes that there has been some real change in this and that we have the chance to move it to a different and better plane. And I think what I'm doing is the right thing to do.

President Clinton's decision to delink trade and human rights in the case of China was, in most respects, a replay of the decisions of earlier administrations. One might argue that the desire to protect U.S. jobs and increase corporate profits prevailed over human rights concerns, and China skillfully persuaded U.S. business and congressional interests to bring pressure to bear upon the President involved. See, e.g., Ken Brown, *China Human Rights Tactic Spreads*, N.Y. Times, Aug. 1, 1994, at D1 ("Nearly 800 big American companies wrote to President Clinton supporting China, a tactic crucial to China's success in the trade decision."). Moreover, as countries like Indonesia and India have seen, their own quickly growing markets are a key to muting U.S. criticism of their human rights records.

> After years of trying unsuccessfully to quiet criticism of human-rights records, Asian nations have found powerful allies: American businesses eager to invest in their growing markets and the Clinton Administration, with its emphasis on economic interests in the post-cold-war foreign policy.
>
> The Clinton Administration's spring decision to continue China's favorable trade status gave some of the largest and fastest growing countries new confidence that their influence is now strong enough to have an effect on American policy. And from India and Indonesia to smaller nations like Singapore, Vietnam, Thailand and Malaysia, they are showing it.
>
> "It seems to me the message is loud and clear: if American business gets strongly involved in a country, human rights takes second place or even less than that," Ashutosh Varshney, an India expert at Harvard, said of the China decision.

Id. at D2.

Moreover, in the case of China, it would appear that "the Chinese leadership has showed little good will, at least in the short term, in return for the political risks Mr. Clinton took in separating rights from China's trade status." Tyler, *Abuses of Rights Persist in China Despite U.S. Pleas*, N.Y. Times, Aug. 29, 1994, at A1, col. 6 (reporting that China has refused to permit ICRC inspection of its prisons to check reports of torture, political detention, and other abuses and has continued or increased the arrests of religious, labor, and democracy advocates). Nor apparently were the Chinese pressured greatly to improve their human rights record. When Secretary of Commerce Ron Brown made a much-publicized, week-long trip to Beijing to promote trade ties with China, he "barely mentioned human rights issues at his public appearances and did not publicly address the 12-hour detention of leading dissident Wang Dan just before his weekend arrival here." Steven Mufson, *U.S., China Act to Boost Trade Ties*, Wash. Post, Aug. 30, 1994, at A1. Suggestions about what the United States might do to recover a portion of its human rights credibility vis-á-vis China and similarly situated countries may be found in the following editorial.

Editorial, *Speak Louder on Rights in China*

N.Y Times, Aug. 29, 1994, at A14

Commerce Secretary Ron Brown, now in China with an entourage of U.S. executives, is being spared the personal humiliations showered on his Cabinet colleague, Warren Christopher, last March. Those spring tantrums achieved their goal of convincing the Clinton Administration to drop all human rights conditions for China's tariff privileges. Though Mr. Brown yesterday promised to raise human rights concerns with his hosts, he has made it clear that commerce is his priority.

Beijing is showing its appreciation by upgrading the Commerce Secretary's protocol status to "Presidential envoy." But on matters of substance, China has given the Administration little to show for its human rights retreat.

Mr. Brown arrived amid reports that Qin Yongmin, who protested against China hosting the 2000 Olympic Games, has been beaten and mutilated in a prison labor camp. Wang Dan, a student leader in the Tiananmen Square movement, was briefly detained Saturday after weeks of surveillance. Wei Jingsheng, China's leading democracy activist, who was harassed during Mr. Christopher's visit, soon after disappeared into the labyrinth of China's penal system and has not been heard from since.

As for Mr. Clinton's original human rights conditions, progress went into reverse the day the President changed his policy. As The *Times's* Patrick Tyler reports, China has continued to round up democracy, labor and religious activists, including some it had previously released, like Mr. Wei. It has broken off talks with the Voice of America over jamming of its broadcasts and dropped discussions with the Red Cross about humanitarian visits to prisons. China has also toughened its terms for talking to Washington about proliferation issues.

This tough-minded behavior should come as no surprise. While Beijing always reacts badly to public pressure, it never concedes anything when it believes there is no penalty for refusing.

How can the United States now recover its human rights credibility? One way would be for Mr. Brown to persuade American businessmen to adopt a voluntary code of conduct, which would assure minimal labor standards, restrict business cooperation with political surveillance activities and prohibit dealing with suppliers that use prison labor.

Another would be to begin loosely linking progress on particular U.S. grievances to relevant aspects of the official U.S.-China relationship. For example, progress on Voice of America broadcasts could be linked to the frequency of ceremonial visits by high U.S. officials, progress on proliferation to military cooperation and progress on prison labor exports to Chinese membership in the World Trade Organization. Perhaps other links could be found that would make Beijing more eager to permit Red Cross visits and release prominent dissidents.

These loose linkages need not insist on perfect performance, merely good-faith efforts measurable by results. Meanwhile, none of the new links should be interpreted to preclude actions that directly serve obvious American interests, such as holding high-level talks on North Korea.

If Mr. Clinton is at all serious about defending human rights in China, Cabinet officers like Mr. Brown need to use their private meetings to convince Chinese leaders that the quality of their relations with the United States will in part depend on how they treat their own people.

Despite criticisms from NGOs and the press, President George W. Bush has continued the policy of engagement with China, downplaying human rights in favor of other bilateral issues of trade, investment, and national security. That policy is set forth and discussed in the readings that follow.

Director of the State Department's Policy Planning Staff Richard N. Haass, *China and the Future of U.S.-China Relations*

Remarks to the National Committee on U.S.-China Relations, Dec. 5, 2002, *http://www.state.gov/s/p/rem/15687/htm* (emphasis in original)

. . . For thirty years, American strategists have debated how to "bring China into the international system." Well, today, to a considerable extent, China **is** "in." But we have yet to make permanent China's full integration in shaping and maintaining an international order in which all can live in peace, prosperity, and freedom. . . .

Today, we have an opportunity to fashion a different kind of relationship — one appropriate to a new era, one built on the basis of what we are *for.*

This transition should have begun in the late 1980s, when the Soviet hold on Central and Eastern Europe began to crumble. But efforts to rethink our relations were short-circuited by the Chinese government's suppression of demonstrators near Tiananmen Square. The United States could not stand idly by when the Chinese leadership used deadly force against peaceful demonstrators in the streets of Beijing. China's actions and the necessary American response precluded a new consensus from forming in the United States around a post–Cold War stance toward China. . . .

A historic opportunity now stands before us — to finally transform this relationship created at a unique moment in the Cold War. This transformation will require that we speak candidly about our differences; that we work hard to make certain these differences do not prevent us from cooperating where we share interests; and, most importantly, that we take tangible actions to build a more cooperative U.S.-China relationship. Talk — or so-called "engagement" for its own sake — is not enough. . . .

Our shared interests are many — from promoting trade and investment; to reducing tensions in regions in crisis; to fighting poverty and disease, environmental degradation and proliferation. But it is insufficient merely to **have** shared interests. What matters is whether these shared interests are translated into common — or at least complementary — policies....

Chinese Power....

It has become a cliché to speak about "the rise of Chinese power" — as if the complex historical process by which 1.3 billion people take their place in the international system can be captured by a simple turn of phrase. Yet there is no denying that China now plays a larger role in the region and the world than ever before. The interaction between China's citizens and those of other countries is more intense. China's manufactured exports — and, increasingly, its citizens' demands for imports — bulk larger in the global economy. China's military is acquiring unprecedented new capabilities....

...Many argue that China is likely to become the world's second-largest economy by 2030. Its hefty foreign exchange reserves should provide a cushion in any future financial crisis. One has to expect, therefore, that China's military power and political reach will increase commensurately....

Th[e] open and welcoming American response to China's rise reflects, above all, the U.S. need for partners to deal with new and emerging challenges. The very nature of the threats arrayed against us is changing day-by-day. Americans learned dramatically on September 11, 2001 that American primacy does not mean American invulnerability. Even a country with unprecedented global power and influence cannot insulate itself from every threat or hazard, particularly in a world shaped by globalization.

Globalization itself is a dynamic, evolving process that creates new vulnerabilities along with new opportunities. It ties us to others for trading goods and knowledge. But it also is a conduit for the spread of terrorism, weapons of mass destruction, disease, crime, drugs, financial contagion, global climate change, and trafficking in human beings.

Such problems, inevitably, demand collective responses. Without partners, the United States cannot easily or efficiently tackle problems that transcend America's borders. Al-Qaeda operates in more than sixty countries. HIV/AIDS and tuberculosis do not stop at Immigration and Customs. Industrial emissions from one country do not respect borders. To be sure, there will undoubtedly be occasions when unilateral action is warranted or necessary. Yet joint efforts need to be the norm, not the exception, if we are to successfully address the transnational challenges that define this era.

For this reason, the U.S. approach to China seeks to capture the opportunities presented by the absence of great power conflict. President Bush himself put this best in his speech at West Point last June: "We have our best chance since the rise of the nation-state in the 17th century to build a world where the great powers compete in peace instead of preparing for war." The 20th century was marked by struggles among great powers. But there is no reason why the 21st century should bear the same stamp. We can turn our efforts from containment and confrontation to consultation and cooperation. We can move and in fact are moving from a defensive balance of power to a pooling of power to meet the challenges and seize the opportunities of the new century.

The emerging reality of the Bush Administration's foreign policy aims at capturing these opportunities. It is best described as a process of "integration," in which the United States seeks to include other countries, organizations, and peoples in arrangements that will sustain a world consistent with the interests and values we and our partners share — values such as rule of law; opposition to terrorism and to the proliferation of weapons of mass destruction; limits on the power of the state; religious tolerance; private property rights; commitment to market principles; equal justice; and respect for women.

These interests and values guide U.S. policy toward China, just as they guide America's broader national security strategy. For the United States, integration of new partners can help us to deal with both traditional and transnational security threats. And these are not just threats to America. They threaten China, and other nations and peoples as well.

The biggest test of integration is China. The international community will be far better off if China is integrated into this system of shared interests and values, rather than languishing — or, worse yet, contesting it from the outside. U.S. policy is guided by the principle that we can be more successful in confronting pressing security, economic, and human challenges by working with partners rather than working alone — and by a belief that China has the potential to become one of our most important partners. . . .

In that vein, let me also highlight four pivotal areas that will provide a measure of our capacity to further expand our relationship.

The first is nonproliferation. China is now a member of nearly all key nonproliferation agreements. It has taken positive and welcome steps in recent months to promulgate export control regimes for missile-related technology and equipment, as well as for dual-use chemical and biological agents. This suggests that China's leaders are thinking more seriously about the need to halt the spread of weapons of mass destruction.

The second is Korea, where the entire international community now confronts a North Korean regime that has violated its own commitments to the Nonproliferation Treaty, the Agreed Framework, its IAEA safeguards agreement, and the Joint South-North Denuclearization declaration. China has supported the Agreed Framework; yet North Korea has said that it considers that Framework "nullified." China is a State Party to the Nonproliferation Treaty; yet North Korea — also a member — has clearly violated its NPT commitments with its covert uranium enrichment effort.

The United States and China have a unique opportunity to work with Japan, the Republic of Korea, Russia, and others in insisting that North Korea uphold its commitments and dismantle its program. President Jiang's public statement at the Crawford summit that "the Korean Peninsula should be nuclear-free" was an important and extremely positive step in building an international coalition. China's unique relationship with North Korea gives it the opportunity to continue playing an especially pivotal role — using all of the various tools at its disposal to help convince North Korea of what needs to be done, while demonstrating to Pyongyang that there will be costs to continued non-compliance.

The third area is Taiwan, especially China's rhetoric and actions about the use of military force. The United States well understands China's position on Taiwan, just as China understands ours. U.S. policy remains consistent and will not change. The United States is committed to its "one China" policy, as well as to longstanding obligations under the Taiwan Relations Act. We do not support Taiwan independence. We have an abiding interest, above all else, in the peaceful resolution of cross-Strait differences. China should share this interest....

Fourth, the United States will be looking to the underlying principles that guide China's foreign policy. Five years ago, we appeared to hold divergent views of international relations. China argued that sovereignty must be treated as inviolable, even as many countries in addition to the United States began to argue that sovereignty could no longer shield those, such as Slobodan Milosevic, who flout international norms or mercilessly abuse the rights of their citizens. China defended the principle of non-intervention — just as Americans and others began to think in new, creative directions about legitimacy and sovereignty.The world is changing in ways that require us all to reexamine our approaches to foreign policy.

The horrors of Rwanda — and the collective failure to adequately respond to them — underscore that sovereignty cannot shield those who commit genocide. Likewise, after September 11th, virtually everyone agreed that it was legitimate for the United States to intervene in Afghanistan and to target the Taliban, even though the Taliban had enabled — not executed — the attacks on the World Trade Center and the Pentagon. Sovereignty cannot be allowed to provide protection for governments that harbor, aid, or abet terrorists.

Now, we are confronting the challenge posed by Saddam Hussein. Sad to say, it is unlikely to be the only such challenge in a world that includes outlaw regimes who desire weapons of mass destruction and who have a history of terrorism and aggression. President Bush has said that "new threats require new thinking." We very much hope that China, too, is prepared to think anew.

CHINA'S DOMESTIC CHALLENGE....

China is a much-changed and changing place. Yet the gap between economic pluralism and a still-shuttered political system remains too great. Stability and continued economic success require that this gap be closed by steady progress toward democratization. China's leaders must open their society in ways that restore citizens' faith that they have a real voice in their political future.

Already, Chinese citizens are showing their frustration. This country with only one official labor union has seen waves of strikes and worker unrest. A country whose ruling party came to power in a peasant revolution now confronts rural protests. A government with extraordinary police powers has failed to beat back crime simply by meting out harsh punishments in the absence of social justice. Citizens are angry about corruption. China's leaders need to take the next step. Only by allowing the Chinese people to think, assemble, and worship freely can China unleash the talents of its people to realize their full potential, and thus China's potential. As in so many of the diverse societies that have guaranteed individual human rights and brought citizens into the political process — the Republic of Korea in East Asia,

Brazil in Latin America, Botswana in Africa — China's leaders eventually must realize that good governance, a vibrant civil society, and — ultimately — democracy are prerequisites for sustained stability and prosperity.

There is as well a foreign policy rationale for a more open China. A U.S.-China relationship based solely on common interests will, inevitably, be more brittle and more narrow than one that combines shared interests with shared values. It is no accident that our closest relationships — our true partnerships — are with fellow democracies. Societies that are like-minded are more likely to see the world similarly.

The United States wants to work with China toward this end of greater political participation and openness. We know that political change is a complex and multidimensional process. But one initial step, at least, is good governance. The focus of the State Department's Rule of Law program is moving beyond traditional commercial rule of law to address civil society reforms, as well as criminal and civil law reforms and human rights initiatives. Later this month, we will hold the second round of U.S.-China Human Rights Dialogue. We are talking more and more about these issues in an effort to turn what has been a source of tension in our relations into an accomplishment.

George Kourous and Tom Barry, *U.S. China Policy: Trade, Aid, and Human Rights*

Vol. 1, No. 5 Foreign Policy in Focus (Nov. 1996) (references omitted), ***http://www.fpip.org/briefs/vol1/china_body/html***

. . . Since the initial warming of U.S.-China relations in the early 1970s, policymakers have had difficulty balancing conflicting U.S. policy concerns in the Peoples' Republic of China (PRC). From Nixon to Clinton, presidents have had to reconcile security and human rights concerns with the corporate desire for expanded economic relations between the two countries.

. . . U.S. traders and investors are eager to expand their economic participation in the country the Commerce Department describes as the world's largest emerging market. In 1995 U.S. firms had investments in 3,474 different projects in China, many of which concern export-oriented production using low-paid, oppressed Chinese labor that is denied the right to form independent labor unions. After Hong Kong, the U.S. is the second largest source of contracted foreign direct investment for China; China is the second largest host country in the world, following the U.S., for foreign direct investment (see *In Focus: Foreign Investment in the U.S.*).

Although China's market is immense and expanding, at least in the short and medium terms it is likely that China will continue to enjoy large trade surpluses with the U.S. Trends indicate that the U.S. trade deficit with China may soon surpass the deficit with Japan. Most U.S. transnational corporations (TNCs), many of whom are investing directly in China, support current U.S. trade policy. Yet other elements of the U.S. business community that are affected adversely by Chinese exports, in particular small domestic businesses, have joined with human rights critics to oppose the annual renewal of China's MFN status.

PROBLEMS WITH CURRENT U.S. POLICY

...Under pressure to integrate human rights concerns more closely into overall U.S.-China policy, Washington has adopted a number of sanctions, including restrictions on bilateral and multilateral aid. Rather than conditioning trade relations on human rights improvements, the Clinton administration has argued that increased economic integration of China into the world market is the preferable and more effective way of advancing human rights.

Yet Chinese human rights practices, including respect for political and labor rights, continue to fall well below internationally accepted standards. Neither the existing U.S. sanctions nor the policy of comprehensive engagement has resulted in human rights improvements....

The U.S. government has not used its extensive influence at the World Bank to escalate international pressure on China to improve its human rights practices. In the case of neighboring Myanmar (Burma), where U.S. economic interests are comparatively insignificant, the United States endorses a ban on all World Bank lending. In China, however, where human rights violations are no less severe, Washington has not obstructed the rapid rise of bank lending. Occasionally, the U.S. casts a "no" vote on an infrastructure project in accordance with its commitment to support only basic needs projects. More often, the U.S. simply abstains, thereby allowing projects to proceed.

Furthering the inconsistency, the U.S. has actively opposed the rise in China funding by the Asian Development Bank, in which it is the second largest shareholder. Corporate interest in China trade and investment help explain the U.S. government's reluctance to support a ban on multilateral lending to China. U.S. corporations are the top suppliers for World Bank projects in China.

After its 1994 delinkage of human rights issues from China's MFN status, the Clinton administration announced the creation of a special human rights program that included promises of increased Radio Free Asia broadcasts to China, new support for NGOs working in China, and the formulation of a corporate code of conduct for companies doing business in China. The program, which has only been partially implemented, exerts little pressure on China and should not be regarded as an effective substitute for a tougher U.S. stance on human rights violations. The voluntary and unspecific character of the code of corporate conduct that the Commerce Department formulated is typical of U.S. unwillingness to endanger trade and investment in China. In the end, rather than making the code more China-specific, Commerce announced that the code was a loose and nonbinding list of suggestions for TNCs.

Trade and investment concerns have knocked U.S.-China policy out of balance. Despite expressions of concern for human rights conditions, the U.S. government has allowed narrow economic interests, particularly those of corporate investors, to guide its China policy. Although the U.S. government has let it be known that human rights improvements would be welcome, it has been unwilling to jeopardize U.S. economic relations by adopting stricter human rights conditionality on aid and trade.

TOWARD A NEW FOREIGN POLICY...

The Lawyers Committee for Human Rights offers four general principles that should guide U.S. policy toward human rights and would be helpful in establishing a new U.S.-China policy:

1. U.S. national interests are served by giving human rights a higher priority in the U.S. foreign policy process.
2. U.S. human rights policy should be based on internationally recognized laws and norms.
3. The credibility of any human rights policy stems from its uniform application.
4. Cooperative, international approaches to human rights problems are preferable to strictly unilateral actions. . . .

Specifically, we recommend the following actions

— The U.S. should not single out China, but instead condition all its bilateral and multilateral trade and investment programs on respect for internationally recognized labor and human rights.

— China's application for WTO membership underscores the need for international agreements that link trade privileges with respect for basic human rights. Just as environmental protection and trade need to be linked, so do trade and internationally recognized labor and human rights. As a global leader, the U.S. should use its influence to urge that human rights conditions be included in international trade and investment agreements such as GATT.

— Section 701 of the Foreign Financial Assistance Act, which mandates the U.S. government to advance international human rights through its voting power in international financial institutions, should be enforced. Until there are significant human rights improvements, the U.S. should oppose all multilateral lending (except for basic humanitarian aid) to all human rights violators.

— Washington should make its bilateral aid policy more consistent by blocking all further Eximbank lending and by ending all nonhumanitarian programs that benefit China.

— The U.S. should make greater use of its senior level contacts with the Chinese government to raise pressing human rights concerns.

— The U.S. should encourage other nations to take a firmer stance toward human rights violations in China and increase its own diplomatic efforts to raise these issues in such international forums as the Human Rights Commission and the International Labor Organization.

William H. Overholt, *Be Tougher on Burma Than China*

Asian Wall Street Journal, July 4, 2003,
http://www.rand.org/commentary/070403AWSJ.html

In Burma and China, United States foreign policy is confronted with a crucial question: do trade and investment with dictatorships strengthen their hold on power and lead to greater repression, or encourage moderation and greater human rights?

U.S. Secretary of State Colin Powell's denunciation of Burma's house arrest of opposition leader Aung San Suu Kyi is evidence of the tough line Washington has taken against that dictatorship. And Unocal Corp.'s trial in

Los Angeles on allegations that the oil company should be held responsible for human rights abuses that occurred during construction of its pipeline in Burma will certainly make U.S. companies think twice before doing business there.

Yet at the same time as the U.S. is imposing sanctions on Burma, it pursues a policy of open trade with China. This inconsistency is criticized from both sides. Business groups advocate engagement with both China and Burma, while human rights groups advocate trade restrictions against both.

But a closer look at both countries reveals enormous differences that justify pursuing two different policies.

In China, foreign investments have been numerous and widely dispersed. For instance, several years ago there were 80,000 Hong Kong-invested companies in Guangdong Province alone. These companies have created innumerable jobs that are outside government control and have distributed money, information and other resources widely in a country where all these were previously under tight government control. The companies have generated pressure groups that successfully advocated greater social openness, and have improved the welfare of workers.

Notwithstanding some widely publicized abuses, the typical Western company in China pays wages that are two or more times the local standard and has environmental and behavior standards that were virtually unknown prior to China's opening to the outside world in the 1980s. Before the opening up, there were virtually no independent sources of information. Now the average Chinese family has more than one television, with significant access to international news. While the government has had some successes at Internet censorship, educated Chinese can find out just about anything over the Web.

This is the kind of influence the U.S. wants. While China's government remains dictatorial and repressive of religious, labor, and other freedoms, the improvement compared with the era before reform is dramatic.

The last time I lectured at Peking University, a student stood up and said his class had been assigned to read both my book, "The Rise of China," and Gordon Chang's book, "The Coming Collapse of China." He asked whether Mr. Chang was correct in arguing that fast economic reform combined with an absence of political reform would eventually bring down the government. I told him the answer lay in the fact that he was assigned Mr. Chang's book and was allowed to ask such a question. Before China's opening up, even whispering such thoughts to a friend would have risked jail. That is why facilitating China's open-door policy is good for American values.

In the case of Burma, foreign investment has been focused on a few large deals, primarily with oil companies. Virtually all the benefits have gone directly to a few senior leaders of the ruling regime. There has been no broad exposure of the population to the global information flow, no widespread distribution of resources that are outside government control. The regime has become more repressive, not less.

In China, the bulk of foreign investment has been closely associated with advances in human well-being and the worst human-rights abuses have occurred in other areas, such as government repression of the Falun Gong. In Burma, the most egregious human-rights abuses have been directly connected with efforts to make particular Western companies profitable.

Many minority upland people in Burma, largely Christians in contrast to the lowland Buddhists who control the government, have been abducted and forced to work, often without food, until they die while building roads and other infrastructure for the oil companies. The companies involved say this is beyond their control and characterize it as government security policy, but undeniably large numbers of people have been killed for the specific purpose of making these investments profitable. Conversely, these projects have been used by the government as an excuse for annihilating many tribal people.

Consequently, the U.S. doesn't contradict itself when it implements different policies toward China and Burma. It is simply pursuing the same values in two quite different situations.

Many business groups and human rights groups will denounce this conclusion. Human rights groups will say that investment in any country run by a repressive dictatorship supports that dictatorship and should be banned in China as well as Burma. The problem with this argument is that, although as late as 1980 both South Korea and Taiwan were more repressive than China is today, the same kind of opening and development in Taiwan and South Korea freed the minds of people in those countries, created a middle-class society, and ultimately created social pressures for democratization.

Business groups will assert that Burma is just beginning to open and the benefits will appear later. That argument has weight, but not enough. Foreign investments in Burma are propping up one of the world's most brutal regimes, creating industries served by deliberately starved slave labor, and supporting the worst human-rights abuses outside Africa. That combination is just morally unacceptable.

Comments and Questions

1. The Chinese report on human rights in the United States received considerable publicity in 2004. As noted in various problems throughout the book, inter-state complaints to human rights bodies have been extremely rare. Does the Chinese publication, issued in reaction to the U.S. State Department's Country Report, suggest why a government might be reluctant to bring accusations of human rights violations against another government? Does the possibility of formal complaints by another state make human rights more, rather than less, political? Would it be better for the United States to accept the right of an individual to petition to the Committee Against Torture, the Human Rights Committee, and/or the Committee on the Elimination of Racial Discrimination?

2. Do the facts set out in China's report on human rights in the United States demonstrate human rights violations or socio-economic problems? Recall the discussion of fact-finding and measurement in Chapter 12; does the fact that a minority group is statistically disadvantaged in some way necessarily lead to the conclusion that a government is failing to live up to its human rights obligations? What degree of equality and fairness is required by international human rights law?

3. Most of the sources for China's report on U.S. human rights are taken from the U.S. media. Does this suggest an openness that is likely to promote human rights in the United States, or does it reinforce criticism that the United States has refused to address these concerns, even though they are widely known?

4. Engagement has been the relatively constant touchstone of U.S. policy toward China, while isolation has been the consistent factor in U.S. policy toward Cuba. Is this inconsistent, or are there distinctions between the two countries that justify differences in treatment? Does the existence of a strong anti-Castro exile community in Florida explain the difference?

5. On the debate over China policy see Zbigniew Brzezinski, *Living with China*, 59 Nat'l Interest 5-21 (2000); Roberta Cohen, *People's Republic of China: The Human Rights Exception*, 9 Hum. Rts Q. 447 (1987); Robert F. Drinan and Teresa T. Kuo, *The 1991 Battle for Human Rights in China*, 14 Hum. Rts Q. 21 (1992); Rosemary Foot, *Rights Beyond Borders: The Global Community and the Struggle over Rights in China* (2000); Chas. W. Freeman Jr., *Sino-American Relations: Back to Basics*, 104 For. Policy 3 (Fall 1996); Merle Goldman, "Monitoring Human Rights in China," in *Implementing U.S. Human Rights Policy* 115-45 (Debra Liang-Fenton ed., 2004); Ana Kent, *Waiting for Rights: China's Human Rights and China's Constitutions, 1949-1989*, 13 Hum. Rts. Q. 170 (1991); id., *China, the United Nations and Human Rights: The Limits of Compliance* (1999); David M. Lampton, *China: Think Again*, 120 For. Policy 13 (Spring 1998); Morton Abramowitz, *China: Can We Have a Policy?*, Carnegie Endowment for International Peace (1997); James Mann, *About Face: A History of America's Curious Relationship with China, from Nixon to Clinton* (1999); Andrew J. Nathan, "Influencing Human Rights in China," in *Beyond MFN: Trade with China and American Interests* (James R. Lilley and Wendell L/ Willkie II, eds.,1994); Arieh Neier, *The New Double Standard*, 105 For. Policy (Winter 1996/7) 91; Randall Peerenboom, *Assessing Human Rights in China: Why the Double Standard?*, 38 Cornell Int'l L. J. 71 (2005); Denny Roy, *Human Rights as a National Security Threat: The Case of the PRC*, 32 Issues and Studies 65 (1996); U.S. Congress, House Select Committee on U.S. National Security and Military/Commercial Concerns with the People's Republic of China, *U.S. National Security and Military/Commercial Concerns with the People's Republic of China* (3 vols. 1999) (popularly known as "The Cox Report").

II. Human Rights Policies of Other States

As noted at the beginning, this chapter has focused on the United States for reasons of convenience, history, and readily available debates and documentation. However, it should not be thought that other countries around the globe do not take human rights concerns into account in forging and applying their own foreign policies. Here we offer two examples: the European Union and Japan.

A. *The European Union*

The European Union provides an example of efforts to develop and apply a foreign policy that gives prominence to human rights issues. As described in Chapter 8, human rights emerged gradually in the policies of the European

Union, first through the jurisprudence of the European Court of Justice and then through texts adopted by the political bodies. Among the latter, the European Council (which is part of the European Union and should not be confused with the separate, 46-member Council of Europe) has issued declarations on respect for human rights which, according to the Declaration on Human Rights adopted on June 28-29, 1991, form an essential part of the EU's international relations and a cornerstone of European cooperation.

In 1991, the Council and the representatives of the Member States adopted a resolution on human rights, democracy, and development which laid down the guidelines, procedures, and priorities for improving the consistency and coherence of development initiatives undertaken with non-member states. As a result of these guidelines; the EC (now EU) began including a human rights clause in its bilateral trade and co-operation agreements with third countries from the early 1990s. Since adoption of a Council decision in May 1995, the human rights clause has been included in all subsequently negotiated bilateral agreements of a general nature. More than 20 such agreements have been signed, in addition to the more than 30 agreements negotiated before May 1995.

As European states have become more closely integrated within the European Union, some common foreign policies, including ones concerning human rights, have been articulated in the basic texts. The 1993 Treaty on European Union (TEU) considers as one of the objectives of the Common Foreign and Security Policy the development and consolidation of "democracy and the rule of law, and respect for human rights and fundamental freedoms." A new title in the treaty on development cooperation includes a second direct reference to human rights and democratization: "Community policy in this area shall contribute to the general objective of developing and consolidating democracy and the rule of law and to that of respecting human rights and fundamental freedoms."

The Treaty of Amsterdam, which entered into force in 1999, furthered these developments by inserting a new article 6 in the TEU, reaffirming that the European Union "is founded on the principles of liberty, democracy, respect for human rights and fundamental freedoms, and the rule of law, principles which are common to the Member States." Member States violating these principles in a "serious and persistent" way could have their rights under the Union Treaty suspended. The EU's action in the field of external relations is also guided by the rights and principles contained in the EU Charter of Fundamental Rights, proclaimed at the Nice Summit in December 2000 and now part of the draft European Constitution.

Since 1995, the EU Commission has issued a series of communications to the Council and the European Parliament that set out strategies aimed at enhancing the consistency and effectiveness of the human rights and democratization policy. The May 2001 communication, on the EU's Role in Promoting Human Rights & Democratization in Third Countries, concentrates mainly on developing a coherent strategy for EU foreign aid. According to the text, the EU has always favored an approach based on partnership and co-operation, rather than sanctions and other negative measures. The aim is to work both with governments and civil society to achieve sustainable change.

European Union, Guidelines on Human Rights Dialogues

Council of the European Union (Dec. 13, 2001), ***www.europa.eu.int/pol/rts/index***

2. Current Situation

The European Union is engaged in human rights dialogues with a number of countries. Those dialogues are in themselves an instrument of the Union's external policy. That instrument is one of a range of measures which the EU may use to implement its policy on human rights, and constitutes an essential part of the European Union's overall strategy aimed at promoting sustainable development, peace and stability. However, there are at present no rules to determine at what point it should be applied. It should also be said that there is room for greater consistency in the EU's current approach towards dialogues, which at present employs several different types: . . .

2.2. At present there is only one regular, institutionalised dialogue devoted solely to human rights between the European Union and a third country, namely that with China. This is a highly structured dialogue held at the level of senior human rights officials. At one time the European Union also maintained a human rights dialogue with the Islamic Republic of Iran. This type of dialogue, focusing solely on human rights, has so far only been used with countries with which the European Community had no agreement and/or where the agreement contained no "human rights" clause. The fact that such dialogue exists does not preclude discussion of the human rights issue at any level of the political dialogue;

2.3. *Ad hoc* dialogues extending to Common Foreign and Security Policy–related topics such as that of human rights. For instance, the EU currently maintains dialogues with Cuba and Sudan at the level of heads of mission;

2.4. Dialogues in the context of special relations with certain third countries, on the basis of broadly converging views. With the United States, Canada and the associated countries these take the form of six-monthly meetings of experts, with the Troika representing the EU, before the Commission on Human Rights and the annual United Nations General Assembly. The main objective of these dialogues is to discuss issues of common interest and the possibilities for cooperation within multilateral human rights bodies. . . .

Political dialogues with the African-Caribbean-Pacific countries under the Cotonou Agreement have their own detailed arrangements and procedures as laid down in Article 8 of the Agreement. . . .

3. Basic Principles

3.1. The European Union undertakes to intensify the process of integrating human rights and democratisation objectives ("mainstreaming") into all aspects of its external policies. Accordingly, the EU will ensure that the issue of human rights, democracy and the rule of law will be included in all future meetings and discussions with third countries and at all levels, whether ministerial talks, joint committee meetings or formal dialogues led by the Presidency of the Council, the Troika, heads of mission or the Commission. It will further ensure that the issue of human rights, democracy and the rule of law is included in programming discussions and in country strategy papers.

3.2. However, in order to examine human rights issues in greater depth, the European Union may decide to initiate a human rights-specific dialogue with a particular third country. . . .

4. Objectives of Human Rights Dialogues

The objectives of human rights dialogues will vary from one country to another and will be defined on a case-by-case basis. These objectives may include:

(a) discussing questions of mutual interest and enhancing cooperation on human rights *inter alia*, in multinational fora such as the United Nations;

(b) registering the concern felt by the EU at the human rights situation in the country concerned, information gathering and endeavouring to improve the human rights situation in that country.

Moreover, human rights dialogues can identify at an early stage problems likely to lead to conflict in the future.

5. Issues Covered in Human Rights Dialogues

The issues to be discussed during human rights dialogues will be determined on a case-by-case basis. However, the European Union is committed to dealing with those priority issues which should be included on the agenda for every dialogue. These include the signing, ratification and implementation of international human rights instruments, cooperation with international human rights procedures and mechanisms, combating the death penalty, combating torture, combating all forms of discrimination, children's rights, women's rights, freedom of expression, the role of civil society, international cooperation in the field of justice, promotion of the processes of democratisation and good governance, and the prevention of conflict. The dialogues aimed at enhancing human rights cooperation could also include — according to the circumstances — some of the priority issues referred to above (in particular the implementation of the main international human rights instruments ratified by the other party), as well as preparing and following up the work of the Commission on Human Rights in Geneva, of the Third Committee of the UN General Assembly in New York and of international and/or regional conferences.

6. Procedure For the Initiation of Human Rights Dialogues

6.1. Any decision to initiate a human rights dialogue will first require an assessment of the human rights situation in the country concerned. . . .

6.2. Any decision to initiate a human rights dialogue will first require the defining of the practical aims which the Union seeks to achieve by initiating dialogue with the country concerned, as well as an assessment of the added value to be gained from such dialogue. The European Union will also, on a case-by-case basis, establish criteria for measuring the progress achieved in relation to the benchmarks and also criteria for a possible exit strategy.

6.3. Exploratory talks will be held before a human rights dialogue with the country concerned is initiated. The aim of those talks will be twofold: first to define the objectives to be pursued by any country accepting or requesting a human rights dialogue with the EU and to determine possible ways of increasing that country's commitment towards international human rights instruments, international human rights procedures and mechanisms and the promotion and protection of human rights and democratization in general; and subsequently to update the information in the reports following the preliminary assessment. . . .

7. Practical Arrangements for Human Rights Dialogues

Flexibility and pragmatism are the keywords in the context of the practical arrangements for human rights dialogues, which should thus be determined on a case-by-case basis, by joint agreement with the country concerned. The arrangements will cover aspects such as where and how often the dialogue is to be held and the level of representation required.

To ensure that the discussions are as fruitful as possible, the dialogues should, as far as feasible, be held at the level of government representatives responsible for human rights. For the sake of continuity, the European Union should be represented by the Troika [representatives of the states that hold the immediate past, current, and next presidency of the EU, which rotates on a regular basis] — at the level either of representatives from the capitals or of Heads of Mission.

The European Union will ensure that dialogue meetings are regularly held in the country concerned. This approach has the advantage of giving the EU delegation a better opportunity to gauge for itself the situation on the spot and, subject to the agreement of the country's authorities, to contact the people and institutions in which it is interested. Traditionally, dialogues whose primary purpose is to discuss issues of mutual interest and to strengthen human rights cooperation are held in Brussels. That tradition should preferably be maintained.

As far as possible, the European Union will ask the authorities of countries involved in the human rights dialogue to include in their delegations representatives of the various institutions and Ministries responsible for human rights matters, such as the Justice and Interior Ministries, the police, prison administration etc. Likewise, civil society could become involved under the most suitable arrangement in the preliminary assessment of the human rights situation, in the conduct of the dialogue itself (particularly by organising meetings with civil society at local level in parallel with the formal dialogue), and in following up and assessing the dialogue. The European Union could thus signify its support for defenders of human rights in countries with which it maintains exchanges of this kind.

The EU will as far as possible give the human rights dialogues a degree of genuine transparency vis-à-vis civil society.

8. Consistency between Member States' bilateral dialogues and EU Dialogues

Information exchange is essential if maximum consistency between Member States' bilateral dialogues and EU dialogues is to be ensured. . . .

9. Consistency Between Human Rights Dialogues and EU Resolutions to the UNGA and the CHR

Human rights dialogues and Resolutions submitted by the European Union to the UNGA or the CHR on the human rights situations in certain countries are two entirely separate forms of action. Accordingly, the fact that there is a human rights dialogue between the EU and a third country will not prevent the EU either from submitting a Resolution on the human rights situation in that country or from providing support for an initiative by the third country. Nor will the fact that there is a human rights dialogue between the EU and a third country prevent the European Union from denouncing breaches of human rights in that country, inter alia in the appropriate international fora, or from raising the matter in meetings with the third countries concerned at every level.

10. Assessing Human Rights Dialogues

All human rights dialogues will be assessed on a regular basis, preferably every year. . . .

Civil society will be involved in this assessment exercise. The task will involve assessing the situation in relation to the objectives which the Union set itself before initiating the dialogue, and will examine how much added value has been provided by the dialogue. The examination will look particularly closely at the progress made on the priority areas of the dialogue. If progress has indeed been made, the assessment should, if possible, analyse how far the European Union's activities have contributed to that progress. If no progress has been made, the European Union should either adjust its aims, or consider whether or not to continue the human rights dialogue with the country concerned. Indeed, a dialogue assessment must allow for the possibility of a decision to terminate the exercise if the requirements given in these guidelines are no longer met, or the conditions under which the dialogue is conducted are unsatisfactory, or if the outcome is not up to the EU's expectations. Likewise, a decision may be taken to suspend a dialogue which has proved successful and has therefore become redundant. Such matters will be dealt with by the Working Party on Human Rights (COHOM) as a matter of priority.

As for dialogues aimed at strengthening human rights cooperation, particularly those held within international and regional bodies, the assessment will focus on those areas in which cooperation could be further improved. . . .

B. *Japan*

Yozo Yokota and Chiyuki Aoi, *Japan's Foreign Policy towards Human Rights: Uncertain Changes*

In Human Rights and Comparative Foreign Policy 115-45 (David P. Forsythe, ed., 2000) (references omitted)

Japan's foreign policy towards human rights was almost non-existent until the 1980s. Japan avoided taking political risks in its external relations as a matter of general principle, as exemplified by its single-minded pursuit of economic self-interest. Human rights, being seen by Tokyo as highly political and greatly complicating foreign relations, were not allowed to interfere with central concerns such as the economy — and national security. This posture resulted in contradictions with its pro-Western diplomatic allies in multilateral forums. Such a passive stance in human rights diplomacy is, however, gradually giving way — albeit slowly — to a more active one that gives some importance to human rights. This shift is still uncertain. It ranges from support for the abstract principles of universal human rights, and thus opposition to special Asian values, to a new foreign aid policy that sometimes includes considerations of democratization and human rights in the recipient countries....

II. Domestic Factors....

As with any other state, Japan's foreign policy can be considered as an outgrowth of its domestic political and social dynamics, interacting with the international environment.

One important domestic determinant of the Japanese approach to human rights abroad is the legacy of its behaviour in the 1930s and 1940s. After 1945, Japan, unlike some of its Western counterparts, did not feel itself to be in a position to promote international human rights standards. This was mostly owing to the recognition of its own serious and systematic violations of human rights committed before and during the Second World War, particularly in neighbouring Asian countries. Japan thus felt itself to be in a position to learn, rather than preach, about human rights, which it acknowledged as an imported concept from the West. Such reserve fitted well with an emerging preference for quiet diplomacy and a low-profile and non-confrontational approach, or equidistance stance, to international relations in general. Thus Japan's "lessons of history" fitted with its emerging national style in foreign policy. Both history and diplomatic style led to a desire to avoid the subject of human rights in the international arena.

Other important factors also supported this orientation. For much of the time between renewed independence (1952) and the 1980s, Japan was ruled by the Liberal Democratic Party (LDP), which reflected primarily business interests and emphasized a foreign policy of economic self-interest. The destruction caused by the Second World War naturally led to a central emphasis on economic growth and recovery. This emphasis was generally endorsed by the United States, first Japan's occupier and then its principal security and trading partner.

These LDP conservative governments built up a strong bureaucratic system that was itself devoted to traditional concerns in foreign policy such as economic interest and national security (traditionally understood). It should be stressed that dependence on bureaucracy in foreign policy-making and its implementation was particularly notable in the field of foreign economic aid, the single most visible foreign policy area for Japan. In Official Development Aid (ODA) policy, 19 agencies including the Ministry of Foreign Affairs (MOFA), the Ministry of Finance (MOF), and the Ministry of Construction hold their own ODA budget. In particular, with regard to highly technical multilateral economic assistance, the Ministry of Finance has traditionally exercised the strongest authority over aid policy. MOF and other economic bureaucracies, particularly the Ministry of

International Trade and Industry (MITI), have never considered human rights as within their routine competence.

For its part, MOFA lacked a unit specialized in human rights issues until 1984, when the Human Rights and Refugee Division was created in what was then the United Nations Policy Bureau. The creation of this division was clearly an important improvement, particularly given that only a few officers had been assigned to human rights issues prior to its creation. With its initial size of 10 persons, however, it was difficult for such a small division to do much more than just meet various human rights reporting obligations under various treaties, and deal with a growing number of Indo-Chinese refugees in the 1980s, and other related issues. . . .

During this period domestic human rights issues were indeed debated. But, ironically, this domestic debate served to reinforce passivity on human rights abroad. Because the domestic debates revealed ideological differences and great complexity, conservative governments found added reason to remain mostly silent on international human rights. Domestic debates covered such subjects as dowa issues (group of persons historically considered to belong to a lower caste, thus subject to serious discrimination), labour rights, the treatment of Koreans residing in Japan, and indigenous Ainu people. Less politicized human rights issues — freedom of expression, religion, and the press, children's rights, women's rights, and rights of the mentally handicapped — remained strictly domestic issues. Parts of the all-powerful bureaucracy that focused on domestic issues might take up such questions, but the Foreign Ministry and other related offices were indifferent.

However, some of these human rights issues that were debated in Japan began to be raised in various UN forums, usually triggered by a number of non-governmental organizations, which often put the government in a defensive position. For example, the International Labour Organization took up the issue of labour rights in national corporations in Japan during the late 1950s to 1960s at the request of the labour unions (Sohyo). ILO investigations, although leading to some progressive changes in Japan, certainly did not encourage conservative governments to take a leadership position on other human rights issues at the United Nations.

III. Indications of Change?

Since the mid-1980s, Japan's institutions have become more prepared to deal with human rights concerns more systematically — at least relative to the past. Japan's more active participation in international human rights forums contributed to this change. The size of the Human Rights and Refugee Division was expanded to more than 20 by the 1990s. The Foreign Policy Bureau was created in 1993, supervising the United Nations Policy Division, the Human Rights and Refugee Division, and other divisions. A more integrated foreign policy resulted, with more attention to human rights.

In the early 1990s, some signs of change in the conservative political alignment also emerged. Most notably, the shift in the political power alignment in the "reformist" era of 1993-1994 and the historic liberal — conservative coalition era of 1994–1996 gave a momentum to addressing issues that had not been dealt with under conservative one-party rule, including war reparation issues. In general, the historical consensus on foreign policy preferences among the conservative political forces, the bureaucracy, business, and the public became disrupted during these eras. The LDP's ties with the bureaucracy were weakened, and the public, discontented with a number of corruption incidents involving public officials, had less confidence in the bureaucracy.

One notable example reflecting this changed political environment was the public attention given to the issue known as "comfort women," and the subsequent actions taken by the conservative — liberal coalition government on this issue. . . .

Such a political process was quite different from traditional foreign policy-making, which was heavily influenced by the bureaucracy and business. This was also a case where non-governmental organizations in the area of human rights were more active and influential in their demands on the government. Given the rapid changes in Japanese politics that brought the LDP back to power, however, one cannot make any firm conclusions about the political foundation of Japanese foreign policy-making, particularly in the area of human rights diplomacy.

Another case of important change may be in the area of foreign economic policy. The Ministry of Finance and the Ministry of Foreign Affairs seem to be cooperating more closely and giving more attention to human rights. This tentative evaluation stems from the adoption of the 1992 ODA Charter (as explained below), with its provisions on human rights and democracy, and from the expansion of Japan's aid to former Soviet Union republics and Eastern Europe, where transitions to market democracies have required new thinking at MOF and MOFA. One study suggests that Japanese involvement in the politicized East European development encouraged closer coordination between these ministries. Yet these collaborations appear at best ad hoc and selective. Thus, national domestic factors in Japanese foreign policy-making exhibit some sporadic changes in selected issue areas, necessitated by the changed domestic and international environment. There are both continuities and changes.

IV. Multilateral Policy. . . .

In official statements on the occasion of the World Conference on Human Rights in Vienna held in June 1993, Tokyo supported the universality and indivisibility of human rights, carefully distancing itself from those Asian states championing "Asian values." Japan also claimed that human rights should not be sacrificed to development, and reaffirmed the role of Official Development Assistance (ODA) in promoting the human rights of individuals. Likewise in the Asia Regional Preparatory Meeting for the World Conference on Human Rights, held in Bangkok in March 1993, Japan defended the universality and indivisibility of human rights. It contested the sections of the Bangkok Declaration that opposed linking aid to human rights. The Japanese delegation stated: "Japan firmly believes that human rights are universal values common to all mankind, and that the international community should remain committed to the principles set forth in the Universal Declaration of Human Rights . . . It is the duty of all States, whatever their cultural tradition, whatever their political or economic system, to protect and promote these values.". . . .

REGIONAL DEVELOPMENTS

There is no regional intergovernmental organization for human rights in Asia, unlike most other regions of the world. There has been a consistent tendency in the Asian region to detach human rights dialogues from political and economic processes, especially within the Association of South East Asian Nations (ASEAN). State sovereignty is a particularly sensitive issue in Asia. Most Asian governments have argued that there is a necessity to accommodate multiple types of political systems within the region's diplomatic and security frameworks. The complexity of the region's colonial experiences, ethnic compositions, and institutional history on which authorities are founded further adds to the sensitivity of the issue of sovereignty. . . .

Japan's main foreign policy interest in the region has traditionally been economic and, even though Japan has recently sought to assume some political role in the region, it has not been so active yet in promoting human rights. Its approach to human rights violations in the region has been pragmatic and country specific.

Three interrelated factors account for this pragmatism, in addition to the general sensitivity over sovereignty in the region. The first factor is the security concern. Japan has long considered it important to keep China politically stable and economically "modernizing." Hence, it has been hesitant to apply conditionality to its aid based upon China's human rights record. It believes that an isolated China is highly destabilizing given the territorial disputes surrounding China, and given the unstable political situation in the Korean peninsula and in Indo-China. In addition, it understands China as a polity that is not susceptible to outside pressures, thus negative human rights diplomacy — sanctions and other punitive inducements — would be counter-productive. Other countries, such as Indonesia, are both important exporters of natural resources vital to Japan's national security and economy as well as important markets for its investment and goods, as Japan reduces its dependence on the US market. These economic factors are closely linked to Japan's security concerns.

The second factor behind Japan's pragmatic approach to human rights in Asia is its identity as a mediator between East and West. From the mid-1950s, Japan sought to identify closely with Asian countries as well as to cooperate with the free democratic nations as the foundation of its foreign policy. Further, it is seeking a more active role in Asia through multilateral political and economic forums such as the Asian Development Bank, the ASEAN Regional Forum, and the Asia-Pacific Economic Cooperation network. Such a dual role, however, has been difficult to play in human rights diplomacy. Japan has often found itself in the awkward position of having to balance Asian and Western preferences. One such example was the Tiananmen Square incident, where Japan's intermediary efforts evoked considerable suspicion and criticism among the Western nations. More recently, at the Bangkok meeting preceding the World Conference on Human Rights, Japan, having supported the universality of human rights, was subject to considerable criticism by some Asian representatives including China.

The third element behind the Japanese reluctance to play Western-style human rights diplomacy in Asia is its colonial and military history, as we noted earlier. Owing to its historical relations with its Asian neighbours, Japan has not been in a position to speak strongly for human rights. Even though Japan has vigorously pursued its goal of establishing friendly relations and a leadership role in Asia, its true intentions have often been viewed with suspicion by its neighbours. . . .

At the time of the admission of Myanmar (Burma) to ASEAN, a major event concerning ASEAN, Japan quietly observed the event, signalling its approval of the ASEAN argument for constructive engagement, in contrast with some Western governments which were more critical of Myanmar's admission. With regard to the coup in Cambodia in July 1997, when the then Second Prime Minister, Hun Sen, expelled the First Prime Minister, in violation of the Paris Peace Agreement and the prior election results, Japan also took a position largely in line with the ASEAN approach to Cambodia. Unlike some Western states, Japan did not officially freeze its Official Development Aid to Cambodia, though much of its implementation in effect ceased after the event. Japan also supported the ASEAN decision to postpone Cambodia's entry to ASEAN and continued dialogues with the Cambodian government, expressing its view that peace in that country was indispensable and that human rights must be respected. Japan then provided both financial contributions and personnel to supervise the general election held in 1998.

In this regard, it is noteworthy that the Japanese government has supported the idea of establishing a regional human rights mechanism. In the UN General Assembly as well as in the UN Commission on Human Rights, it has sponsored resolutions that state that any region without regional arrangements for human rights protection should promote discussions towards establishing one. Since 1995 the Japanese government has also held an international symposium for human rights experts from the region, with a view to promoting further discussions concerning the possibility for a regional mechanism for human rights in the Asia and Pacific region. Such an effort may be seen as Tokyo's cautious but increasingly active stance in the field of human rights.

INTERNATIONAL FINANCIAL INSTITUTIONS. . . .

The Asian Development Bank (ADB) is the only notable multilateral financial institution initiated and shaped by Japan, albeit under the general US tolerance particular to the era around the time the Bank was created and developed. Since the establishment of the ADB in 1966, Japan has been one of the two largest shareholders of the Bank, co-equal with the United States. All ADB presidents have been Japanese, mostly seconded from the Ministry of Finance. Since the mid-1980s, as Japan became particularly keen to increase its influence in the Bank to suit its general diplomatic agenda, its financial presence became stronger in the Bank. In 1996, Japan's contribution to the Asian Development Fund (ADF), a soft-loan arm of the Bank, stood at US$9,351.70 million out of total contributed resources of US$18,203.26 million. The US contribution was only US$2,287.91 million. Japan's contribution to the Technical Assistance Special Fund in 1996 amounted to about 56 per cent of the total supplied. Between 1988 and 1996, Japan contributed US$633.9 million to the Special Fund. Thus Japan's potential leverage in ADB is great, should it choose to link human rights conditions to such financial contributions.

In line with most international financial institutions, however, the ADB has followed strictly "non-political" objectives, with particular emphasis on developing infrastructure and industries in the region. The ADB has been particularly reluctant to link human rights with its operational objectives in any way. This reluctance can partly be attributed to the sensitivity of the Bank's shareholders, which include Asian states that particularly disfavour human rights diplomacy....

The general reluctance in the ADB to implement political conditionality based upon human rights records can be overcome in the case of exceptionally severe human rights violations, under the pressure of some key shareholders such as the United States. One such case was China, where after the Tiananmen Square incident in 1989 Japan followed the United States and other Western donors in suspending ADB loans to China. World Bank loans were also frozen after the event. In general, however, Japan played an intermediary role between China and major Western donors in the post-Tiananmen ADB process. This was consistent with Japan's intermediary role in getting China to join the ADB in 1986. After Tiananmen, having supported an early partial freeze on ADB loans to China, Japan then successfully lobbied in November 1990 for an approval of a US$50 million agricultural loan and a US$480,000 technical assistance (TA) grant to China. In April 1991, at the ADB Board of Directors' meeting, Japan pressed for a full resumption of loans to China. These actions inside the ADB coincided with Japanese actions outside the Bank. The ADB, nevertheless, was not the only agency to resume loans to China. The World Bank also decided partially to resume loans to China in February 1990, a move that indicated waning US interest in continued sanctions against China through multilateral banks as well as through private transactions....

Since the 1990s Japan's traditional development philosophy has been in some disarray, mainly because of the new thinking about development stemming from the East European situation. There had been a tendency among the economic ministries in Tokyo to argue that there is an Asian model of development, which favours political stability and an active and large governmental role, and that this model is more suitable to developing countries. Preference for this Asian or non-Western model of development persisted in the Japanese economic bureaucracy, despite rhetoric from other parts of the state rejecting Asian values and endorsing universal human rights. Japan's continuing support for this model can be compared to Western liberal models of development integrating liberalization, democratization, and other human rights simultaneously.

As Japan started to provide economic aid to Eastern Europe, where democratization was an official objective of the transition from communism that was supposedly as important as the introduction of a market economy, it found itself supporting both development models — the liberal one in Eastern Europe and the illiberal one in the non-Western world. This was not necessarily irrational, but it was not fully consistent with the new rhetoric, as at Vienna in 1993, in favour of universal human rights....

UNITED NATIONS....

Since the Tiananmen incident, Japan has joined other Western states in the UN Commission on Human Rights to sponsor draft resolutions critical of

China's human rights record. The draft resolutions, initiated by the United States and European states such as Denmark and the Netherlands, nevertheless were never adopted owing to Chinese blocking actions supported by much of the global South. The attempt to pass a critical resolution gradually lost impetus even among Western states after 1995, however, mainly owing to shifts in the policies of the larger European states to favour access to the Chinese market. Japan was among the defectors in 1997, together with France, Germany, Greece, Italy, and Spain, and did not co-sponsor the draft resolution on China, even though it voted against the Chinese blocking, or no-action, motion. The loss of Western cohesion on the issue was one factor that encouraged Japan to prioritize the improvement of its bilateral relations with China, which had deteriorated in 1996-1997 over events that heightened Japan's security concerns in East Asia.

V. Bilateral Policy

Linkage to Trade/Aid

It was in the middle of the 1970s that some aid agencies such as the World Bank began to question the wisdom of extending financial assistance to countries that were under authoritarian rule and characterized by corruption. They were pushed into this new orientation by certain Western states such as the Netherlands and the Scandinavians. They focused on countries such as Chile under Pinochet and the Philippines under Marcos, and on some African states. For Japan, however, which was becoming one of the leading donor countries, this policy of linking foreign aid to the human rights record of a recipient country was not yet a reality. This is confirmed by the fact that annual reports of the Japanese government on foreign aid in the 1970s made no reference to the human rights situations of the recipient countries. As noted above, the main concerns of the Japanese aid agencies at that time were economy and security.

Again as noted earlier, in the 1980s Japan began to pay more attention to the human rights record and to the condition of the human environment when extending assistance to a developing country. The issue became acute for Japan, as we have noted, when the Burmese/Myanmar military took power in 1988, and also when the Chinese authorities used violence at Tiananmen in 1989. There were strong pressures within and outside of Japan, both public and private, to criticize such repressive acts by the military and to stop extending foreign aid to these governments. In the wake of these events, the Japanese government adopted the Official Development Assistance Charter in June 1992, in which the government regulates how military spending, human rights, and democratization relate to ODA. The core of the ODA Charter reads as follows:

Taking into account comprehensively each recipient country's requests, its socio-economic conditions, and Japan's bilateral relations with the recipient country, Japan's ODA will be provided in accordance with the principles of the United Nations Charter (especially sovereign equality and non-intervention in domestic matters), as well as the following four principles:

1. Environmental conservation and development should be pursued in tandem.
2. Any use of ODA for military purposes or for aggravation of international conflicts should be avoided.
3. Full attention should be paid to trends in recipient countries' military expenditures, their development and production of mass destruction weapons and missiles, their export and import of arms, etc., so as to maintain and strengthen international peace and stability and from the viewpoint that developing countries should place appropriate priorities in the allocation of their resources on their own economic and social development.
4. Full attention should be paid to efforts for promoting democratization and introduction of a market-oriented economy, and the situation regarding the securing of basic human rights and freedoms in the recipient country.

Although the ODA Charter is clearly a step forward in the direction of placing human rights as a central goal of the Japanese government's foreign policy, it is by no means an ideal document from the viewpoint of human rights. First of all, the human rights element is included as the fourth principle instead of the first or second. Certainly there is no wording to suggest that the consideration of human rights in the recipient country is the sine qua non of Japanese ODA. As long as "[f]ull attention" is paid to "the situation regarding the securing of basic human rights and freedoms in the recipient country," the aid may continue. Even more troubling, the application of the four principles is subjected to the maintenance of Japan's bilateral relations with the recipient country and the principle of "non-intervention in domestic matters." The wording of the Charter suggests a certain reserve on the part of the Japanese government in addressing human rights abroad. According to one observer, in "implementing these principles, however, Japan makes it a rule to closely observe trends in the specific situation in which each country is placed since the security environment surrounding each country and its cultural and social conditions vary. When there are problems in the eyes of the international community and the Japanese people, Japan will first confirm the case by checking with the country involved and, if necessary, express its concern. If the situation is not improved, Japan will review its aid policy toward that country." The policy toward Myanmar/Burma and China illustrates this sort of flexibility. Tokyo's willingness to act on human rights is heavily conditioned by other considerations, not least of which is pressure to act from the West. . . .

China has been one of the largest recipients of Japanese bilateral ODA. Since Japan normalized its diplomatic relations with China in 1972, Japan has sought to develop economic, cultural, and political ties with the country. . . . After dropping to become the fourth-largest recipient of bilateral aid in 1991 (largely owing to the Tiananmen incident), by 1995 China was again the largest recipient of bilateral ODA. . . .

The Tiananmen incident on 4 June 1989 illustrated that, under pressure from Western states, grave human rights violations in an aid recipient country can affect Japan's aid policy, despite the strategic importance of the country. After the incident, though with a delay, Japan followed Western countries on 20 June in freezing new economic assistance to China. It stopped processing new grants and loans, while promising to implement already agreed, on-going projects. Diplomatically, albeit in milder language and with a slower reaction, many of the Japanese policies in the months following the event did not differ much in substance from those of the Western states....

Tiananmen, however, affected Japanese aid to China only briefly, and Tokyo had already moved to normalize its relations with Beijing one year later. Even during the Paris Summit, Japan was trying to persuade other Western states not to pressure China into diplomatic isolation, referring to the importance of China in maintaining security in the region, which led to the adoption of a joint communique short of imposing new joint sanctions, while encouraging China to do its utmost to avoid international isolation....

Overall, the Tiananmen incident again illustrated the difficult balance Japan maintained between its role as a Western partner and that as an Eastern state. Although economic assistance was halted in line with the policy of other Western states, Japan, from security concerns, refrained from taking an overly critical stance verbally, and also from continuing with the cancellation of its ODA to China for any length of time. Concerns about avoiding criticism and isolation from other Western states had to be balanced against the danger of isolating China. In addition, as Prime Minister Uno himself remarked on 7 June, it was widely recognized that past Japanese involvement in China made it inappropriate for Japan to take sides. He observed as well that Japan's relations with China could not be understood in the same way as US relations with China were. There was thus persistent support for the principle of non-interference within the Japanese government and direct reference to human rights was often avoided, even though there was constant mention of humanitarian concerns.

In 1995, in protest against the nuclear tests that China had carried out, the Japanese government applied the principles of the ODA Charter, thereby withholding its grant aid — except for humanitarian and grassroots assistance. Despite this action, Japan was still the largest bilateral aid donor to China, providing more than US$1.38 billion in 1995....

The spirit of the ODA Charter has been most closely followed in the context of Eastern Europe. In 1990 Prime Minister Toshiaki Kaifu promised to provide a US$150 million loan through the IMF to Poland, technical cooperation of US$50 million, a five-year loan of US$500 million from the Export-Import Bank, and export credits to Poland and Hungary. Japan has expanded its aid to other East European countries where democratization is a key issue, even though the sums remain small in comparison with key Asian aid recipients. As regards African countries, Japan has suspended aid to Nigeria, the Sudan, and the Gambia, on the grounds of serious human rights violations, and reduced aid to Kenya and Malawi.

Such examples signify an inconsistent application of the 1992 ODA Charter, which would suggest uneven political support for the text itself. Although the ODA Charter is certainly a cornerstone of Japanese aid philosophy, inconsistency in its application as well as ambiguity in its content remain issues to be addressed in the future.

Japan, Ministry of Foreign Affairs, Human Rights Pamphlet

http://www.mofa.go.jp/policy/un/pamph2000

Japanese Cooperation

Japan has actively participated in the UN Commission on Human Rights as its member since 1982. Japan has increased its contribution to the Voluntary Fund for Advisory Services and Technical Assistance, considering cooperation in legal systems building and awareness-raising in human rights as important to improve human rights situations. Japanese experts have also contributed to these activities, as members of the sub-commission and committee in the human rights field. Japan has also concluded a number of human rights instruments.

Partnership for Democratic Development (PDD)

Japan supports institution building in various fields, such as in the legislative, administrative, and electoral systems in order to foster democratic development and protect and promote human rights in developing countries. Japan announced at the G8 Lyon Summit in June 1996 an initiative for "Partnership for Democratic Development (PDD)," which seeks to strengthen cooperative activities in the human rights field and for democratization. This initiative is based on the understanding that there exist many countries which have the political will to promote democracy and human rights but lack the appropriate systems, institutions and human resources.... In the bilateral context, Japan will continue to make efforts in institutional building through dispatching and receiving official experts, assisting democratic elections, and sending personnel for monitoring elections. Japan is also eager to cooperate directly with NGOs and the people of developing countries through such activities as supporting NGOs, inviting the press, and organizing symposia.

Contributions to the UN Funds on Human Rights

Japan's annual contribution to the UN Funds on human rights totaled about US$ 1 million. In addition, Japan has contributed US$ 700,000 and US$ 111,000 to the Human Rights Field Operations in Rwanda (HRFOR) and in the former Yugoslavia, respectively.

Official Development Assistance

Guided by the belief that human rights are universal, Japan has expressed its concern for human rights violations, calling on countries of concern to improve their human rights situations. Japan pays full attention to the human rights situations and efforts for promoting democratization as proclaimed in the ODA Charter. When any improvement in human rights situations or any trace of democratization is recognized, Japan helps these changes through aid. On the contrary, when the situation is clearly accusable, Japan reviews its ODA projects to the country concerned.

Statement by H.E. Ambassador Shigeru Endo, Delegation of Japan, on Agenda Item 9: Question of the Violation of Human Rights and Fundamental Freedoms in Any Part of the World

UN Comm'n H.R., full text at *www.mofa.go.jp/policy/un*, summary available in UN Doc. E/CN.4/2004/SR.21, para. 68-71 (Mar. 25, 2004)

Thank you, Mr. Chairman.

Mr. Chairman,

Japan firmly believes that human rights are universal. For over 50 years, the notion of universal human rights has been thoroughly discussed, refined, and adapted to reflect the current situation of countries and regions everywhere. No country today can deny the precepts of good governance, non-discrimination, the rule of law, and democracy. Japan would like to emphasize the vital role of the Commission on Human Rights, especially with Items 9 and 19, in achieving this purpose.

Unfortunately, regardless of the efforts of the CHR, grave human rights violations still exist. The responsibility for the protection and promotion of the human rights of a country's citizens primarily lies with the government of those citizens. At the same time, the international community must maintain interest in the situation.

Grave human rights violations, if any, require our voices to be heard. In doing so, we must not forget the face of the individuals who are the victims of these abuses. Human rights lie first and foremost with the individual — each human being living with his or her family, with love and respect. This Commission should always focus on the individual in our efforts.

Mr. Chairman,

The particular circumstances of a country's history, culture, religion, and tradition bring unique consequences that must be taken into account with the appropriate understanding. However, they must never be used as an excuse for rationalizing the suppression of human rights. There are different approaches to addressing human rights issues. The unique characteristics and details of each situation will manifest themselves in differences in the methods and the time it will take to come to effective solutions.

In order to reach these solutions, tolerance and dialogue, as well as mutual respect, should play key roles. Mere criticism and reproach are counterproductive. Only when we have a clear understanding of the complexities and subtleties of a country's situation can we find the most suitable approach. We believe that without that understanding, real improvement cannot be achieved.

Countries' efforts and accomplishments should be adequately reflected in our discussion. Some countries listen sincerely to the voice of the international community to improve their situation, while others choose to ignore it. As the Commission reacts to a country who abuses human rights, so should it respond to a country that is exerting efforts to improve human rights there.

We find the possible move of some countries' resolutions to Item 19 or removal from the agenda altogether to be an appropriate response when the situation of a country is sufficiently improved, serving as a source of encouragement and a tangible outcome to its efforts for improvement. We should not shy away from considering a strategy for arriving at a meaningful outcome for countries in question. Furthermore, the Commission cannot simply continue to add resolutions or hold resolutions forever merely because a country is not perfect. The review of existing resolutions should be conducted regularly. Japan believes that such efforts can further strengthen the efficiency and credibility of the CHR. They can serve as an incentive for countries to strengthen their efforts and follow the CHR's advice.

On the other hand, a country that adamantly takes no strides toward improvement deserves the reprobation of the international community. In these cases, through positive incentive, the CHR has a duty to at least make the path clearer for bringing such countries back into the international fold.

Mr. Chairman,

I would now like to draw your attention to one such example. Last year, the CHR for the first time adopted a resolution on the situation of human rights in the Democratic People's Republic of Korea. The resolution specifically calls upon the DPRK to respond to questions concerning the abduction of foreign nationals, and the Government of Japan has also been striving to resolve the issue. These abductions are a grave and flagrant violation of human dignity, human rights and fundamental freedoms. Japan regrets that the DPRK has not been cooperating positively with the relevant international human rights institutions, and that the issue remains unresolved. Japan once again urges North Korea to rectify immediately the current inhumane situation in which the abduction returnees have been separated from their families who still remain in North Korea, and to conduct a full fact-finding investigation on the other victims, for resolving the abduction issue as soon as possible. In this regard, Japan also calls upon North Korea to cooperate fully — without restriction — with the Working Group on Enforced or Involuntary Disappearances and the OHCHR.

Mr. Chairman,

There is still much work to be done. Japan believes that a proper combination of criticism, encouragement, and cooperation is the key to a constructive outcome. I believe that this is the tone all of us would like to see in this Commission.

Thank you, Mr. Chairman.

Comments and Questions

1. Do you agree with the EU approach that links human rights issues with development cooperation or assistance? What are the arguments for and against such a position?

2. A number of countries devote consistent attention to human rights as part of their foreign policy. For example, the United Kingdom has published a Human Rights Annual Report since 1998, which is also available on the Foreign and Commonwealth Office website, *http://www.fco.gov.uk*; the 2005 report addressed human rights in 20 "major countries of concern." The Netherlands identifies as

the first of its eight "main goals" of foreign policy "[t]o strengthen the international legal order and respect for human rights" and has had a human rights ambassador since 1999. See generally Forsythe, supra page 1149.

III. Final Comments and Questions

1. The observation is often made that human rights in international relations simply means the "North" criticizing the "South" for the latter's deficiencies. Is there any truth to that observation? If so, what should be the response — for the North to stop talking about human rights or for the South to begin? Note that debates about colonialism and apartheid, obviously led by developing countries, were often couched in human rights terms; why are most developing countries so silent now? Cf. remarks by the UN special rapporteur on the right to adequate housing, Miloon Kothari, who, referring to a "clean up" campaign by the government of Zimbabwe that left over half a million people homeless, called "the silence of major governments in Africa . . . shocking." *Africa slated over Zim demolitions*, The Star (South Africa), Aug. 8, 2005. He also called on "other leading developing nations outside Africa," such as Brazil and India, to condemn the demolitions. Id.

4. As the title of Ambassador Schifter's article indicates, supra page 1100, U.S. human rights policy, in principle if not always in content, has been institutionalized during the past several decades. However, the costs of such a policy and its necessarily slow and episodic payoffs may cause future administrations, as well as the body politic, to lose interest in such concerns. Consider the following extract from a perceptive article by Vogelgesang, who correctly anticipated the demise of the Carter Administration.

> The "hell of good intentions" described by Stanley Hoffman is often due to the time it takes to achieve them. Americans are notoriously impatient with long-term crusades. Just as most turned against the Vietnam War because they were tired and saw no "light at the end of the tunnel," so might they turn on the policy envisaged as the moral antidote to the war. If stress on human rights provides few quick fixes, as seems likely, or costs too much, as seem possible, it could boomerang by 1980. Human rights might then, for that and other reasons, lose one of its most influential spokesmen.

Sandy Vogelgesang, *What Price Principle?* U.S. Policy on Human Rights, 56 Foreign Aff. 819, 829-830 (1978).

If you were a political adviser to the next president, how would you recommend that he or she articulate and justify the importance of human rights concerns to the U.S. electorate over the short run? Do the break-up of the Soviet Union, the liberation of Eastern Europe and the Baltic states, and the end of the apartheid regime in South Africa not provide arguments for maintaining an active U.S. human rights policy? How would you analyze the relationship, if any, between an assertive human rights policy and the post-2001 focus on combatting terrorism?

5. The totalitarian/authoritarian distinction that held sway during most of the Reagan Administration was seen by many observers as establishing a double

standard in applying diplomatic and other pressures to states violating basic human rights. Even before its adoption, however, arguments were heard that the United States was inconsistent in judging the human rights records of other states, heavily pressuring certain African countries (e.g., Uganda) or Latin American countries (e.g., Paraguay), but ignoring or soft-pedaling the records of certain communist states (e.g., China) with which it hoped to have better relations and various right-wing allies (e.g., Indonesia) with which it maintained military ties. Can this inconsistency, implicitly permitted under sections 502B and 116b of the Foreign Assistance Act of 1961 and other such legislation (see page 1073 supra), be justified? Consider the following comments by Vogelgesang:

> Concentration on consistency . . . misses the point. There can and should be consistent determination to take human rights into serious account for U.S. foreign policy. Yet stress on human rights must at all times be weighed against other factors. A rigid rubric for human rights can obscure the importance of other goals, some of which may have overarching global significance.

Vogelgesang, supra page 1162, at 828. Do you agree with the author? Is she attempting to find consistency in inconsistency or is she simply reflecting what the EU referred to over a decade later as "[f]lexibility and pragmatism"? Would the second President Bush agree (or disagree) with her conclusion?

6. The other charge of double standards, which is made explicit in the Chinese report on U.S. human rights problems, is that the United States employs different standards to judge its own conduct vis-à-vis that of other countries. See, e.g., Julie Mertus, *Bait and Switch: Human Rights and U.S. Foreign Policy* (2004). But is self-reporting by the United States (or any other country) the answer? Is that not the purpose of the UN reporting systems discussed in Chapter 7, pages xxx? Should the European Union prepare a report on human rights in the United States?

7. Has the debate changed over the past century? Consider the counsel contained in President Teddy Roosevelt's Message to Congress in 1904 ((1904) Foreign Relations of the United States XLII (1905)):

> Ordinarily it is very much wiser and more useful for us to concern ourselves with striving for our own moral and material betterment here at home than to concern ourselves with trying to better the conditions of things in other nations. We have plenty of sins of our own to war against, and under ordinary circumstances we can do more for the general uplifting of humanity by striving with heart and soul to put a stop to civic corruption, to brutal lawlessness and violent race prejudices here at home than by passing resolutions about wrongdoing elsewhere. Nevertheless there are occasional crimes committed on so vast a scale and of such peculiar horror as to make us doubt whether it is not our manifest duty to endeavor at least to show our disapproval of the deed and our sympathy with those who have suffered by it.

Would Roosevelt agree with Amartya Sen, supra page xxx, that "[a] foreigner does not need the permission of a repressive government to try to help a person whose liberties are being violated"?

8. The use of unilateral sanctions to promote human rights is discussed more fully in Chapter 10, page 818. Given the nature of the U.S. free enterprise system and its commitment to worldwide free trade, however, can any human rights

policy that utilizes economic pressure be successful if it is concerned only (as are Sections 502B and 116b) with the public sector? To take one example, did not the Chilean junta laugh all the way to the bank — perhaps literally — when, after Congress placed a $27.5 million ceiling on economic aid to Chile in 1975, Chile was able to turn immediately to private U.S. banks to satisfy its pressing financial needs? If the United States genuinely wishes to put pressure upon other countries to improve their human rights records, should U.S. corporations with branches or subsidiaries there not be required, at the very least, to adhere to a strict code of conduct in their dealings with foreign governments and their own workers? See generally the discussion of corporate responsibility for human rights in Chapter 5, page 373.

9. Every U.S. president has resisted attempts by Congress to dictate foreign policy, whether on human rights or other issues. Given the ways in which the Executive Branch in the past has circumvented international human rights legislation, what modifications might be made to general legislation such as Sections 116b and 502B of the Foreign Assistance Act to provide a better and less easily evaded statutory framework? Would such changes unduly limit an administration's flexibility, if a new administration in fact turned out to be genuinely committed to a vigorous but also pragmatic human rights policy?

10. This chapter looks primarily at unilateral human rights policy, but a great deal of human rights diplomacy is conducted in multilateral settings. As noted above, the European Union provides an important institutional setting for human rights discussions by European countries; the same might be said for the Organization of American States and the African Union. Even the Association of Southeast Asian Nations (ASEAN), historically more committed to the principle of non-interference in domestic affairs than to human rights, has become uncomfortable with the long-standing human rights violations by the repressive regime in Myanmar (Burma). Quiet diplomacy (along with public criticism from Europe) no doubt contributed to Myanmar's July 2005 decision to defer assuming the rotating presidency of ASEAN, as it was scheduled to do in 2006. Is multilateral human rights diplomacy always preferable to bilateral initiatives?

11. Yokoto and Aoi point to Japan's actions before and during World War II as one factor causing restraint in its human rights foreign policy. How important is this in Japan and elsewhere? Can a formerly repressive state become a strong proponent and leader in promoting human rights? The authors also note the absence of a regional human rights system in Asia. Why do you think none has emerged until now? How would you assess the prospects for an Asian human rights system in the future?

12. Michael Ignatieff argues that the human rights movement "has to help [ordinary people]... construct strong civil societies and viable states. If it can't find new ways of achieving that goal, it will be remembered as a fashionable cause of the dim and distant 1990's." Is constructing viable states an appropriate goal for a human rights lawyer? For a human rights "activist"? For the U.S. (or any other) government? Bearing in mind the discussion of armed intervention in Chapter 10, what are the limits, if any, on the kind of "help" that should be provided?

Index

D

M

N

O

P

T